NEW TESTAMENT LESSON MAKER

NAVPRESS
BRINGING TRUTH TO LIFE
NavPress Publishing Group
P.O. Box 35001, Colorado Springs, Colorado 80935

CONTENTS

How to Use This Book 5
Matthew 9
Mark 67
Luke 107
John 158
Acts 188
Romans 223
1 Corinthians 238
2 Corinthians 252
Galatians 261
Ephesians 268
Philippians 273
Colossians 277
1 Thessalonians 281
2 Thessalonians 284
1 Timothy 287
2 Timothy 291
Titus 293
Philemon 295
Hebrews 296
James 306
1 Peter 312
2 Peter 317
1 John 319
2 John 324
3 John 324
Jude 325
Revelation 326
List of Topics 347
Topical Index 351

The Navigators is an international Christian organization. Jesus Christ gave His followers the Great Commission to go and make disciples (Matthew 28:19). The aim of The Navigators is to help fulfill that commission by multiplying laborers for Christ in every nation.

NavPress is the publishing ministry of The Navigators. NavPress publications are tools to help Christians grow. Although publications alone cannot make disciples or change lives, they can help believers learn biblical discipleship, and apply what they learn to their lives and ministries.

Library of Congress Catalog Card Number:
92-81117
ISBN 08910-96884

Cover illustration:

Printed in the United States of America

HOW TO USE THIS BOOK

LessonMaker is a compilation of over 18,000 Bible study questions on the entire New Testament. It is a resource to equip any small-group Bible study leader to create a study that fits his or her group.

The section headings of the *New International Version* of the Bible were used to divide the New Testament into 695 passages. For each passage, *LessonMaker* includes twenty to thirty questions divided into these four categories:

"Open It" questions ask about common human experience or personal experience. They are designed to help a Bible study group begin thinking personally about the topic of the study.

"Explore It" questions ask about the content of the text.

"Get It" questions invite the group members to consider how the text applies to people in general.

"Apply It" questions ask each group member to nail down a specific plan for applying the passage to his or her life.

INSTANT STUDIES

If you, the study group leader, lack the time to construct a custom-made study of a passage, you can obtain a ready-made study by simply selecting those questions marked by a bullet (■). This instant study will always include Open It, Explore It, Get It, and Apply It questions.

DESIGNING YOUR OWN STUDY

Alternatively, you can construct your own study using any of the questions listed for a passage, as well as adapting them to better suit your group. To build a traditional study around one passage of the Bible:

1. Select the passage you want to study.
2. Select at least one question from each section—Open It, Explore It, Get It, and Apply It.

Choose enough questions to fit the amount of time you have. Plan to spend at least 75 percent of your time on Get It and Apply It questions. These usually require much more time to consider and discuss than Explore It questions.

A good mix of questions includes:

- ■ One Open It question (five to ten minutes).
- ■ One or two Explore It questions (five minutes). Use more if the members of your group are completely unfamiliar with the passage.
- ■ One to four Get It questions (ten to twenty minutes). These should build on the observations made in Explore It.
- ■ One or two Apply It questions (ten to twenty minutes). Allow time for each person to adapt his or her answers.

Tip: Don't be afraid to control the amount of time your group spends on each type of question. Many groups are used to analyzing the text for a long time and discussing application for only two or three minutes. By choosing more Get It and Apply It questions for a study, you'll increase the chances that the members of your group will come away with life-changing insights and a sense of accomplishments.

WRITING YOUR OWN QUESTIONS

Writing "Open It" Questions

Open It questions warm up the group and introduce the topic by asking about *personal experience* or *common human experience*. They usually relate in some way to the topic, but their main purpose is to create rapport, so they should not give away the punch line. They help everyone get on common ground.

Good Open It questions:

- Are questions that people would want to answer or would enjoy answering.
- Are answerable by anyone; everyone in your group should be able to answer them easily.
- Ask people to give their opinion, viewpoint, or thoughts.
- Do not require embarrassing self-disclosure.
- Do not depend on recall of past events that some people might not remember.
- Do not depend on unique knowledge.

Here are some examples:

Common human experience:
What's appealing about revenge?
To what sources do people often look for guidance?

Personal experience:
How do you hope people will remember you after you're gone?
What role did prayer play in your family's life when you were growing up?

✻ ✻ ✻

Tip: Different groups need different degrees of transition. Consider having two Open It questions handy for your meeting, one light and one more directly related to the topic you're going to study. If you sense that your group needs extra time to gel, you'll be prepared with a neutral opener.

Writing "Explore It" Questions

Explore It questions get the group to observe the passage. They help the participants identify what it says.

Good Explore It questions:

- Ask *who, what, when, where, how,* and sometimes *why*.
- Ask about the people in the text (they, them), rather than about people today (we, us).
- In expository passages (such as Paul's letters), ask what the writer says.
- In narrative passages (such as Old Testament or Gospel stories), ask what happened.
- Get people to think (require answers of more than one word, for example).

Here are some examples:

Who was Apollos?
What was Jesus' audience like?

When does Jesus say it's good to confront others with their faults?
Where does sin eventually lead if not dealt with?
How did the disciples react to Jesus' instructions?
Why did Jesus suggest modifying this law?

❋ ❋ ❋

Tip: People who have studied the Bible often before may find it tedious to answer many Explore It questions. If you are leading a group of people who are relatively familiar with Bible study, keep the number of Explore It questions to four or less.

Writing "Get It" Questions

Get It questions help the group participants answer this question: "So what?" They ask *why* the biblical event was significant or what area of life the text speaks to. In short, they ask what the writer *means*. By relating the text to *common human experience*, they identify how the passage is relevant to their own lives today.

Good Get It questions:

- Ask what the passage means to us, how it's relevant to our everyday lives.
- Ask about life today (we, us, you).
- Are personalized.

Here are some examples:

Why do you think Christ told the healed man to "show but not tell"?
What do you think it means to be Christ's "ambassadors"?
What is Paul's basic point in this passage?
What does it mean for us to "be perfect"?
What's difficult about giving secretly?
How might a person in your job have opportunity to be diligent?
How does this affect your use of free time as a single person?

❋ ❋ ❋

Tip: Sometimes the relevance of a Bible passage is not obvious. If you know some general facts about your group members, you can modify Get It questions to focus on specific categories of life that everyone recognizes—such as family life, work, leisure time, neighborhood, relaxation, current problems or needs, and parenting.

Writing "Apply It" Questions

Apply It questions help the group members answer this question: "Now what?" They help participants see how they can act on the principle they discovered in the passage. In short, Apply It questions lead to a plan of action.

Good Apply It questions:

- Ask about *you*.
- Address the short term: what the next step is, or what people can do this week.
- Ask about concrete action.
- Are personalized.
- Lead to a course of action that people can actually see themselves doing.

Here are some examples:

What can you do this week as a homemaker, professional, or parent to set an example for others?
What steps could you take to ensure that your giving is not done merely for show?
What can you do this week to insulate your marriage against affairs (or to keep from being drawn into a sexual entanglement)?
Whom could you encourage this week with a personal story of something God has done for you?

❊ ❊ ❊

Tip: The goal of Apply It questions is to help people see what they can do, not to force a commitment for which they're not ready. Be sensitive to group members who don't know if or how they will apply a given passage.

STUDYING A PARTICULAR TOPIC

Perhaps, instead of working through a book of the Bible, your group wants to spend a few weeks looking at a variety of passages that address the topic of money. In that case, you could look up *money* in the topical index that begins on page 351. There you would find a list of all the New Testament passages that discuss money. You can find a list of the topics available to you beginning on page 347.

To build a topical study around several verses from different parts of the Bible, follow these steps:

1. Select a topic from the list on page 347.
2. Find that topic in the index.
3. Select the Bible passage(s) you want to study. Decide which of these you want to do:
   - Examine *one passage* deeply and thoroughly.
   - Look more quickly at a *variety of passages*.
4. Find the question list for the first passage you want to study in the main body of this book.
5. If you are looking at a variety of passages, choose one or two questions that relate directly to your topic. If you choose an Explore It question, choose a Get It question to match.
6. Find the question list for the next passage you want to study.
7. Choose one or two questions that relate to your topic.
8. Continue choosing questions from the lists for all the passages you want to study.
9. When you finish selecting questions, you may have too many. Look over your study and eliminate questions that overlap.

❊ ❊ ❊

Tip: If you have the computer software for the *WordSearch* Bible concordance, you can use it instead of the index to find passages that address your topic.

THE *LESSONMAKER* SOFTWARE

This *LessonMaker* book is based on a *LessonMaker* software program, also available from NavPress. That program includes all of the questions, as well as the topical index. The program enables you to copy selected questions into a workspace in any order and with any additions or modifications you'd like, and then to print out your completed study. The program also includes outlines and introductions for each book of the New Testament. Using *WORDSearch*, our concordance program, you can print out the text of a biblical passage along with your selected questions.

Matthew 1:1-17
The Genealogy of Jesus

TOPICS
Family, Heritage, History, Jesus Christ, Messiah, Names, Sovereignty

OPEN IT
■ Why do you think genealogical research is such a growing and popular hobby?
✻ If you have ever researched your family tree, what can you tell the group about your heritage or about any especially interesting or famous ancestors?

EXPLORE IT
■ Whose genealogy is Matthew tracing? (1:1)
■ What prominent ancestors of Christ are mentioned? (1:1)
✻ Who is listed first in the various sections? (1:2, 6, 12)
✻ What significant women were ancestors of David? (1:5-6, 16)
✻ Who is the only person in the record who is listed with his title? (1:6)
✻ How does Solomon figure into the genealogy? (1:6)
✻ The genealogical record is divided into what three periods? (1:17)
✻ What span of time does the genealogical record cover? (1:17)
■ What important event and three people are used as a basis for marking the generations? (1:17)
✻ How many generations are cited in all? (1:17)

GET IT
✻ Why do you think the Bible includes long genealogical lists like this?
✻ Why do you think Matthew traces Christ's ancestors back only to Abraham and not all the way back to Adam?
✻ If God works sovereignly and graciously even when we sin and make poor choices (1:6), why should we make the effort to live righteously?
✻ Why do you think God waited so many generations to send Christ?
■ How do ancestors and family histories affect who we are?
✻ How might this passage encourage those who suffer from a dubious family history?
■ What can you do to minimize your family's past mistakes and maximize your family's potential in the future?
✻ How important is family heritage to you?

APPLY IT
■ What actions do you need to take (or choices do you need to make) this week so that your descendants look back on your life as something to live up to and not something to live down?
✻ How can you encourage a friend who is struggling in relationships with parents and/or children?

Matthew 1:18-25
The Birth of Jesus Christ

TOPICS
Abortion, Adoption, Angels, Commitment, Courage, Embarrassment, Gossip, Holy Spirit, Miracles, Names, Obedience, Trust

OPEN IT
✻ What are the tabloid headlines this week?
■ Why is our society so drawn to gossip and scandal?
✻ How do people typically react when facing embarrassing situations?

EXPLORE IT
■ What happened to Mary while she and Joseph were engaged? (1:18)
✻ What do you think Joseph initially thought upon hearing this news about his bride-to-be? (1:18-19)
■ What positive character qualities did Joseph possess? (1:19)
✻ How did Joseph plan to handle this delicate situation? (1:19)
✻ How was Joseph's ancestry significant? (1:20)
■ Why did Joseph change his plans to divorce Mary? (1:20)
✻ If Joseph wasn't the actual father of Christ, who was? (1:18, 20)
✻ What did the angel command Joseph to name the child and why? (1:21)
✻ What significant mission in life would Mary's child have? (1:21)
✻ Why is Mary's virginal conception of Christ significant? (1:22-23)
✻ What does Immanuel mean? (1:23)
✻ How did Joseph respond to the angelic message? (1:24)

GET IT
■ How might you have responded in Mary's situation?
✻ What would have been your reaction had you been in Joseph's situation?
✻ How do you think a typical church might have handled Mary's pre-marriage pregnancy?
✻ How do you imagine the "grapevine" treated the Mary-Joseph situation?
✻ How does it feel to be the victim of unsubstantiated rumors and gossip?
✻ How does it feel to know that you are innocent and yet have people attacking your character and whispering behind your back?
■ How does our desire for approval or acceptance keep us from doing the right thing?

APPLY IT
✻ What difficult, hard-to-swallow command of God do you need to obey today?
■ How will you respond the next time someone begins to tell you a juicy bit of gossip?

Matthew 2:1-12
The Visit of the Magi

TOPICS
Deceit, Ego, Gifts, Guidance, Motives, Prophecy, Sacrifice, Worship

OPEN IT
❊ Why do we give gifts at Christmas?
■ If you could give any gift to anyone, what would you give, to whom, and why?
❊ What prompts people to make great sacrifices for others?

EXPLORE IT
❊ Where was Jesus born? (2:1)
❊ During whose reign was Jesus born? (2:1)
■ Who came to visit the young Jesus? (2:1)
❊ What external and internal factors prompted the Magi to search for Jesus? (2:2)
❊ What title did the Magi give to Jesus? (2:2)
❊ How did King Herod react to the visit of the Magi? (2:3-4)
■ Why was a powerful king disturbed by the presence of a helpless baby? (2:3-6)
❊ Why is it significant that Christ was born in Bethlehem? (2:5-6)
❊ What were King Herod's instructions to the Magi? (2:8)
❊ How were the Magi led to Christ? (2:9-10)
■ What was the Magi's reaction when they realized they had found the Christ? (2:10)
❊ Where was Jesus when the Magi found Him? (2:11)
❊ How did the Magi react upon seeing Jesus? (2:11)
❊ What gifts did the Magi bring to Jesus? (2:11)
❊ Why didn't the Magi report back to Herod as he had requested? (2:12)

GET IT
❊ How would you define worship?
■ What sort of activities does worship involve?
■ What are some various "presents" we might give to Christ?
❊ How does it feel to have a rival—to feel as though you are being overlooked or replaced?
❊ How can a competitive, prideful, or insecure spirit alter a person's behavior?
❊ Why are many people reluctant to donate money to religious causes?
❊ What are some specific ways Christians can serve as "stars" and lead others to Christ?

APPLY IT
❊ What starlike, shining deed can you do today to point a non-Christian friend to Christ?
❊ What sacrifice do you need to make for Christ this week?
■ What gift of time, effort, or money would demonstrate your love for Jesus this week?

Matthew 2:13-18
The Escape to Egypt

TOPICS
Anger, Ego, Escape, Government, Guidance, Jealousy, Mourning, Murder, Obedience, Prophecy

OPEN IT
■ What are the pros and cons of fierce competition and rivalry?
❊ Why does the death of a child seem especially tragic?
❊ What was your most frightening brush with death?

EXPLORE IT
❊ What happened after the Magi left the home of Mary, Joseph, and Jesus? (2:13)
❊ How did God communicate with Joseph? (2:13)
■ Where did the angel tell Joseph to go? Why? (2:13)
❊ How long was Joseph to keep his family in hiding? (2:13)
■ Why was it necessary for Joseph to take his family and flee? (2:13)
❊ How did Joseph respond to the warning he received? (2:13)
❊ What event allowed Joseph to depart from Egypt with his family? (2:15)
❊ Why was the "escape to Egypt" significant in the life of Christ? (2:15)
❊ What was King Herod's emotional state when he realized the Magi had tricked him? (2:16)
■ What orders did King Herod give in an attempt to eliminate his competition? (2:16)
❊ Who prophesied the horrible episode of infanticide in Bethlehem? When? (2:17)
❊ What was the response to Herod's mass execution of children? (2:18)

GET IT
❊ How might our lives be different if Herod's death plot against Christ had succeeded?
❊ What happens when people try to thwart God's plan?
❊ Why is it important to listen to God?
❊ Why is it important to obey God immediately?
❊ What are some wise ways to handle anger?
■ What is it about competition that makes us feel so threatened?
■ What is the best response to "rivals" or "opponents"?
❊ How can Christians serve those who are the victims of senseless violence?

APPLY IT
■ In what area of your life do you need to trust God more instead of being driven by competition?
❊ What action could you take today to minister to someone who is in mourning?

Matthew 2:19-23
The Return to Nazareth

TOPICS
Family, Fear, God's Will, Guidance, Listening, Moving, Obedience, Prophecy, Security, Sovereignty

OPEN IT
✻ To what sources do people often look for guidance?
■ What do you like most and least about your hometown?
✻ Why is it so difficult to move to another place?

EXPLORE IT
✻ What happened when Herod died? (2:19)
✻ In what manner did God communicate with Joseph? (2:19)
■ Where were Joseph, Mary, and Jesus at the time? (2:19)
■ What did the angel tell Joseph to do? (2:20)
■ What was the reason behind the angel's command? (2:20)
✻ How did Joseph respond to the angel's instructions? (2:21)
✻ Who was reigning in Herod's place when Joseph, Mary, and Jesus left Egypt? (2:22)
✻ Why was it significant to Joseph that Archelaus was ruling in Judah? (2:22)
✻ What was Joseph's emotional response when he heard about Archelaus? (2:22)
✻ What did Joseph do when he heard the news of Archelaus's reign? (2:22)
✻ To what town did Joseph, Mary, and Jesus go? Why? (2:23)
✻ Why was it significant that Jesus' family settled in Nazareth? (2:23)

GET IT
✻ What modern-day forces threaten the institution of the family?
■ How has your hometown influenced who you are?
■ Why might God lead you to live in a certain area?
✻ How is your present location affecting your children?
✻ How can families reduce the stress and upheaval caused by a move or relocation?
✻ Which would you choose: a high-paying job in a big city that required long hours, or a lower-paying job in a smaller town that enabled you to spend more time with your family? Why?

APPLY IT
■ What specific act of kindness can you do this week for a new family in your neighborhood?
✻ As you look back over your life and see how God has guided you, how can you show your appreciation?

Matthew 3:1-12
John the Baptist Prepares the Way

TOPICS
Confession, Holiness, Holy Spirit, Hypocrisy, Jesus Christ, Judgment, Repentance, Zeal

OPEN IT
✻ What phrases, words, or images spring to mind when you hear the term "preacher"?
■ What preacher has influenced you most?
✻ Why are people uncomfortable with "fire and brimstone"- type preaching?

EXPLORE IT
✻ What famous preacher is described in this passage? (3:1)
✻ Where was John the Baptist's "sanctuary" or "pulpit"? (3:1)
■ What was John's message? (3:2)
✻ Why was John's ministry significant? (3:3)
✻ What did John look like? (3:4)
✻ What kind of unusual diet did John follow? (3:4)
■ How did people receive John's message? (3:5)
✻ Besides strong preaching, what went on at John's "desert revival meetings"? (3:6)
✻ Where did John perform his baptisms? Who came? (3:5-6)
✻ What kinds of religious leaders came to listen to John? (3:7)
■ What harsh name did John call the religious leaders? Why? (3:7-10)
✻ What was John's message to the local "men of the cloth"? (3:7-10)
✻ What was the purpose of John's water baptism? (3:11)
✻ How did John compare himself to the one who would come after him? (3:11)
✻ How did John describe the type of baptism Jesus would bring? (3:11)
✻ With what images did John describe Jesus? (3:12)

GET IT
✻ Why is it that coming from a religious family doesn't guarantee spiritual security?
■ What does it mean to repent?
✻ Why do you think John lived such an eccentric life?
✻ Why was John the Baptist so harsh with the religious leaders of his day?
■ What is the significance of the images "winnowing fork," "gathering His wheat," and "burning up the chaff"?
✻ What was John trying to communicate by using the word "fire" three times in this passage?
✻ What is the difference between God's discipline and God's punishment?
✻ What kind of "fruit" or character do repentant people produce?

APPLY IT
✻ What could you do this week to encourage your pastor or preacher?
■ What first step could you take toward obeying God better today?
✻ What particular sin(s) do you need to repent of today?

Matthew 3:13-17
The Baptism of Jesus

TOPICS
God, Heaven, Holy Spirit, Humility, Jesus Christ, Obedience

OPEN IT
❋ What are some initiation rites or affiliation procedures that organizations make new members go through?
❋ Why are transfers of power in some governments fragile?
■ How would you feel if the world's leading, most renowned expert in your field publicly solicited your help?

EXPLORE IT
❋ Where did Jesus come from? Why? (3:13)
❋ Why did Jesus leave Galilee and travel to the Jordan River? (3:13)
■ How did John react to Jesus' request? (3:14)
❋ What exactly did John say to Jesus? (3:14)
■ How did Jesus respond to John's reluctance? (3:15)
■ Why was it important for John to comply with Jesus' request? (3:15)
❋ What change took place in heaven after the baptism of Jesus? (3:16)
❋ How did the Spirit of God play a role in the baptism of Jesus? (3:16)
❋ What was the Spirit's appearance? (3:16)
❋ What kind of voice was heard at the baptism of Jesus? (3:17)
❋ What was the relationship between Jesus and the Father? (3:17)
❋ What did God the Father say about Jesus? (3:17)

GET IT
■ Why do you think John felt awkward about baptizing Jesus?
❋ In what ways are many Christians concerned about "proper" behavior and striving for righteousness?
❋ What does this passage show about God's triune nature?
❋ What do we tell the world by being baptized?
❋ If God spoke in an audible voice about you today, what might He say?
❋ What pleases God?
■ How are you able to please God?

APPLY IT
■ What could you do today for Christ out of obedience and respect for Him?
❋ What needs to change this week in order for you to see the Spirit of God work in and through your life?

Matthew 4:1-11
The Temptation of Jesus

TOPICS
Angels, Bible, Deceit, Holy Spirit, Jesus Christ, Obedience, Satan, Temptation, Victory

OPEN IT
■ What are some common food cravings?
❋ Why are some temptations harder to resist than others?
❋ Why do different people struggle with different types of temptations?

EXPLORE IT
❋ Who led Jesus into the wilderness? Why? (4:1)
❋ Where was Jesus led? By whom? (4:1)
❋ For what purpose was Jesus led into the desert? (4:1)
❋ What made Jesus weak at this time? (4:2)
❋ What three names are given to Jesus' adversary in the desert? (4:3, 5, 10)
❋ What was the first temptation presented to Jesus? (4:3)
■ How did Jesus respond to the first temptation? (4:4)
❋ Where did the devil take Jesus for the second temptation? (4:5)
❋ What tempting offer was made to Christ at the highest point of the temple? (4:6)
■ How did Jesus answer the second temptation? (4:7)
❋ To what final destination did Satan take Christ? (4:8)
❋ What did the devil show Jesus from a very high mountain? (4:8)
❋ What did the devil promise Jesus in exchange for worship? (4:9)
■ How did Jesus react to the third temptation? (4:10)
❋ What happened after Jesus had resisted Satan three times? (4:11)
❋ Who came and ministered to Jesus when all was said and done? (4:11)

GET IT
❋ How would you define temptation?
❋ Besides physical appetite, what are some other sins of the flesh?
❋ What would have been appealing to Christ about the devil's second temptation?
❋ What would have been appealing to Christ about the offer of all the kingdoms of the world?
❋ How can memorizing Scripture help us combat temptation?
■ What role does the Word of God play in resisting temptation?
❋ What happens when a Christian consistently resists temptation?
❋ What situations make us especially vulnerable to temptation?
❋ In what ways can we make temptation more difficult to resist?
■ What can we do to make temptation more manageable?
❋ What temptations are inevitable for most people?
❋ What temptations are inevitable for you?

APPLY IT
❋ In what specific area of your life is temptation the strongest these days?
■ What steps can you take this week to resist the temptations you are facing now?

Matthew 4:12-17
Jesus Begins to Preach

TOPICS
Darkness, Evangelism, Heaven, Light, Mission, Moving, Persecution, Prophecy, Repentance

OPEN IT
❊ What is the best sermon you have ever heard preached?
❊ If you could stand up and preach one sermon to your church, what would you like to say?
■ What do you remember about your first job?

EXPLORE IT
❊ What happened to John the Baptist? (4:12)
❊ What did Jesus do when He heard the news about John? (4:12)
❊ Where in Galilee had Jesus been living? (4:13)
❊ What is revealed here about the geography of Jesus' new home? (4:13)
❊ Where in Galilee did Jesus relocate? (4:13-14) Why?
■ What happened where Jesus relocated? (4:13-16)
■ Why was Christ's move significant? (4:14)
❊ Who foretold that Jesus would live in Capernaum? (4:14)
❊ In what spiritual state were the inhabitants of this region before Jesus moved there? (4:16)
❊ How is Jesus' arrival in Capernaum described? (4:16)
■ What did Jesus do in His new hometown? (4:17)
❊ What was Christ's message from that time on? (4:17)

GET IT
❊ How do you react when you hear that Christians in other countries are being persecuted for their faith?
❊ Why do you think so many of God's people become bold (instead of fearful) during times of persecution?
❊ What would you do if you learned your pastor was in jail for preaching?
❊ In what ways have you been ridiculed or hassled for your belief in Christ?
❊ How would you respond if you sensed God was leading you to pack up your family and move to an unevangelized area to be a missionary?
■ In what ways are your neighbors like the people of Zebulun and Naphtali?
■ How can you help your neighbors come to see the light of Christ?

APPLY IT
■ To what places and people do you need to go this week as a light for Christ?
❊ In what way can you encourage a missionary today, this week, or this month?

Matthew 4:18-22
The Calling of the First Disciples

TOPICS
Commitment, Evangelism, Excuses, Giving Up, Leadership, Obedience, Submission, Witnessing

OPEN IT
❊ If you could pass on some skill or knowledge to an apprentice, what would you want to pass on?
■ What kind of leader do you prefer to follow?
❊ What are some examples of well-functioning teams?

EXPLORE IT
❊ Where did these particular events take place? (4:18)
❊ Who did Jesus see as He walked by? (4:18)
❊ What nickname did one of Jesus' new disciples have? (4:18)
■ What were Simon and Andrew doing when Jesus approached them? (4:18)
❊ What did these brothers do for a living? (4:18)
■ What exactly did Jesus say to Simon and Andrew? (4:19)
❊ What was Simon and Andrew's response to Jesus' words? (4:20)
❊ How long did Simon and Andrew deliberate over Jesus' offer? (4:20)
❊ Whom did Jesus see next? (4:21)
❊ Who was Zebedee? (4:21)
❊ In what activity were James and John involved? (4:21)
■ What did Jesus do when He saw the two brothers, James and John? (4:21)
❊ How did James and John react to Jesus' challenge? (4:22)

GET IT
❊ What does it mean to be a "fisher of men"?
❊ How risky was it for Peter, Andrew, James, and John to drop everything (jobs and families) to go with Jesus?
❊ What thoughts do you think were racing through their minds as they headed off down the beach with Jesus?
❊ How do you think you might have responded had you been fishing with these men and heard Jesus direct this challenge to you?
❊ What are some reasons people make career changes?
❊ How do you think Jesus calls people into the ministry today?
❊ What do you think Jesus saw in these men?
❊ Why did Jesus handpick blue-collar fishermen to be the leaders of the Christian church?
❊ For what would you be willing to leave your family and go far away?
■ What possessions, goals, dreams, or relationships are keeping you from following Jesus wholeheartedly today?
❊ What does it mean for us to follow Jesus?
■ What does it mean for you to follow Jesus?

APPLY IT
■ In what area of your life will you follow Jesus more consciously this week?
❊ What can you do or stop doing today in order to become a more expert "fisher of men"?

Matthew 4:23-25

Jesus Heals the Sick

TOPICS
Good News, Handicapped, Health, Jesus Christ, Kingdom of God/Heaven, Pain, Sickness, Sorrow

OPEN IT
❊ How do you feel about doctors and hospitals?
■ If you could find the cure to any one disease, what illness would it be and why?

EXPLORE IT
❊ Where did the incidents in this passage take place? (4:23)
■ What did Jesus do at the synagogues of this region? (4:23)
❊ What did Jesus preach about? (4:23)
❊ What activities was Jesus involved in during this ministry tour? (4:23)
❊ How would you describe the publicity surrounding Jesus' ministry in Galilee? (4:24)
■ How did the masses react to the news of what Jesus was doing? (4:24)
❊ What kind of physically and spiritually ill people sought out Jesus? (4:24)
■ What did Jesus do for the suffering individuals who came to Him? (4:24)
❊ Jesus' audience grew to include people from what surrounding regions and cities? (4:25)
❊ How are the crowds described? (4:25)
❊ What did the people do after hearing Jesus and experiencing His healing touch? (4:25)

GET IT
■ What assorted reactions do people have to life-threatening illnesses?
❊ Which is worse in your opinion and why: to be physically ill, or to be spiritually sick?
■ How might God use sickness, pain, or difficulty to bring about good in a person's life?
❊ In times of sickness, why do we often pray or seek spiritual help only as a last resort?
❊ Why do people want to be healed of their illnesses?
❊ Why is it significant that Jesus was able to heal all the ailments people brought to Him?

APPLY IT
■ What can you do today to encourage someone who is ill?
❊ What realistic step can you take this week to share the good news of Christ with a non-Christian friend?

Matthew 5:1-12

The Beatitudes

TOPICS
Blessing, Character, Comfortable, Endurance, Enemies, Greatness, Heaven, Humility, Mercy, Mourning, Persecution, Purity, Rewards, Righteousness

OPEN IT
■ What are some ways people typically try to find happiness or fulfillment in life?
❊ What person (living or dead) do you respect most? Why?

EXPLORE IT
❊ What was the setting for this sermon? (5:1)
❊ Who was Jesus addressing? (5:1-2)
❊ According to Jesus, what is the reward for those who are poor in spirit? (5:3)
❊ Why are those who mourn blessed? (5:4)
❊ What is the reward for those who are meek? (5:5)
❊ What can those who hunger and thirst for righteousness expect? (5:6)
❊ What does God promise to those who are merciful? (5:7)
❊ According to this passage, who will see God? (5:8)
❊ Why are peacemakers blessed? (5:9)
■ What does the future hold for those who are persecuted because of righteousness? (5:10)
■ What unexpected command is given to Christians who are insulted, hassled, and lied about? (5:11-12)
■ What people in history have endured nasty persecution? (5:12)

GET IT
❊ How does it pay in the present to walk with God?
❊ What do you think it means to be poor in spirit?
❊ What does it mean to be meek?
❊ How would a person behave if he or she were hungering and thirsting after righteousness?
❊ What are some examples of showing mercy?
❊ How does society's list of admirable virtues compare and contrast with these kingdom virtues?
❊ How (if at all) does the promise of future blessing affect us in the present?
■ Which of these promises means the most to you today? Why?
■ What is the most common type of persecution that you face?
❊ What peacemaking responses work well at diffusing hostility?

APPLY IT
❊ What realistic steps can you take this week to make you hungrier and thirstier for righteousness?
■ What can you do this week to encourage a friend who is under fire due to his or her stand for the Lord?

Matthew 5:13-16
Salt and Light

TOPICS
Abortion, Culture, Darkness, Evil, Immorality, Influence, Involvement, Light, Morality, Reputation, Righteousness

OPEN IT
■ What is your favorite spice?
❊ What is it about darkness that frightens people?
❊ Why do people commit crimes and evil acts under cover of darkness?
❊ What are the top five moral problems our country is facing?

EXPLORE IT
❊ To what valuable substance did Jesus compare His disciples? (5:13)
❊ What is an essential characteristic of salt? (5:13)
❊ How did Jesus imply that a Christian's positive influence can wane or disappear? (5:13)
❊ What happens to salt that loses its flavor? (5:13)
❊ To what did Jesus compare His followers? (5:14)
■ How are we like light? (5:14)
❊ What are improper and proper uses for a lamp? (5:15)
❊ What use of a lamp teaches us about living? How? (5:15)
■ According to Jesus, how exactly are Christians to be like lamps? (5:16)
❊ What kind of behavior should other people see Christians exhibiting? (5:16)
■ If believers live as they are supposed to live, how will others respond toward God? (5:16)

GET IT
❊ What did Jesus mean when He called His followers salt?
❊ What sort of effect does salt have on food?
❊ How do salty things affect us?
❊ How can a Christian lose his or her saltiness?
❊ What does it mean to "let your light shine"?
❊ How might a believer hide his or her light?
❊ What is the effect of bright light in a dark place?
❊ What does light reveal?
■ What specific behaviors mark the lifestyle of a salty, shining Christian?
■ In light of your gifts, abilities, and interests, what specific problem in our world can you counteract as a representative of Christ?

APPLY IT
■ What phone calls or letters would you be willing to make or write this week in order to be salt and light in a decaying, dark world?
❊ To whom in your neighborhood, family, or workplace can you be salt and light this week?
❊ How can you be salt and light to the people God has placed in your life?

Matthew 5:17-20
The Fulfillment of the Law

TOPICS
Authority, Bible, Consistency, Criticism, Freedom, Heaven, Law, Legalism, Obedience, Rationalizing, Teaching

OPEN IT
■ What is the worst rule or law you've ever been aware of?
❊ When in your life did you feel closest to God?

EXPLORE IT
❊ What rumor was apparently being spread about Jesus and His view of the Old Testament? (5:17)
■ What did Jesus say was His goal with regard to the Law and the Prophets? (5:17)
❊ How much of the Law did Jesus say would be fulfilled or accomplished? (5:18)
❊ According to Jesus, what cataclysmic event would have to happen before God's Word could be invalidated in even a tiny way? (5:18)
❊ What two things result in one being called least in the kingdom of heaven? (5:19)
❊ What happens if a person lives a good life and breaks only minor commandments of God? (5:19)
■ What warning was given to those who would encourage others to disregard the Word of God? (5:19)
■ Who is considered great in the kingdom of heaven? (5:19)
❊ To what groups of religious leaders did Jesus make reference? (5:20)
❊ What degree of righteousness is necessary for entrance into the kingdom of heaven? (5:20)

GET IT
❊ How trustworthy are the words of Scripture?
❊ Why did Jesus talk about the righteousness of the Pharisees in this context?
❊ In discussing sin, why did Jesus make a point of saying, "one of the least of these commandments"?
■ What are some ways we occasionally encourage each other to bend or break God's rules?
❊ What level of reverence and submission do you think most people have toward the Bible?
■ What does it mean to "practice" the commandments of God?
❊ What are some ways to teach others about the righteousness of God?
❊ What good can we do to be acceptable to God?
❊ Why is it difficult for us to practice what we preach?
❊ What ideals are most difficult for you to uphold?

APPLY IT
❊ When and how this week can you consult the Bible for guidance on how to live?
❊ What should you do in the near future about someone who tends to "drag you down"?
■ What command of God will you commit to memory this week?

Matthew 5:21-26
Murder

TOPICS
Anger, Bitterness, Conflict, Enemies, Forgiveness, Hatred, Hell, Judgment, Murder, Punishment, Quarrels, Reconciliation

OPEN IT
■ When do you tend to get angry?
❊ Why do people murder each other over trivial matters—a parking space, a cigarette lighter, a crude remark?
❊ If you were given full governmental authority and resources, how would you go about reducing the amount of violent crime in this country?

EXPLORE IT
❊ What age-old prohibition was Jesus addressing in this context? (5:21)
❊ What was the penalty for violators of this law? (5:21)
❊ How did Jesus explain the meaning of the law against murder? (5:22)
❊ According to Jesus, what kind of name-calling made one answerable to the Sanhedrin? (5:22)
❊ What kind of angry name-calling puts one in eternal danger? (5:22)
❊ How did Jesus describe hell? (5:23)
■ What sort of realization did Jesus say should interrupt our worship? (5:23)
❊ If a person becomes aware of a relational problem, how quickly should he or she act? (5:24)
■ What should be a believer's goal in strained or shattered relationships? (5:24)
■ When is it best to settle disputes? (5:25)
❊ Where is it best to settle disputes? (5:25)
❊ What bad consequences can occur if a dispute escalates into a full-blown court battle? (5:25-26)

GET IT
■ Why did Jesus zero in on the emotions behind our violent actions?
❊ What modern-day equivalents to "Raca" do we level at others?
❊ What attitudes and emotions tend to lead to name-calling?
❊ Which of our religious activities would be closely akin to "offering your gifts at the altar"?
❊ According to Jesus, how do problems in our relationships with others affect our relationship with God?
■ Why is it necessary to get things right with people before we come to worship God?
❊ Why is it preferable for Christians to quietly resolve their differences rather than battle over them publicly?
❊ How might Christians be encouraged to reconcile with each other before coming to a Communion service?

APPLY IT
■ What relational conflict do you need to straighten out today?
❊ How can you help yourself remember this week to keep your anger under control?

Matthew 5:27-30
Adultery

TOPICS
Adultery, Commitment, Hardheartedness, Husbands, Immorality, Loyalty, Lust, Purity, Thinking, Vows, Wives

OPEN IT
❊ How is marriage commonly portrayed in the media?
■ What evidence have you seen that sexual standards have declined over the last ten years?
❊ What are some danger signs that a marriage is in trouble?

EXPLORE IT
❊ What commandment was Jesus interpreting? (5:27)
❊ How did Jesus explain the meaning of adultery? (5:28)
■ How does adultery start? (5:28)
■ When does looking at someone become inappropriate? (5:28)
❊ What did Jesus suggest we do with a sinning eye? Why? (5:29)
❊ Why did Jesus make this radical statement about eyes? (5:29)
❊ Where does sin ultimately lead if it is not dealt with? (5:29-30)
❊ What did Jesus recommend for a sinning hand? Why? (5:30)
❊ What was the rationale behind this graphic comment about hands? (5:30)
■ Why are our moral choices important? (5:30)

GET IT
❊ Why is adultery common in our society?
❊ Why are people willing to commit adultery?
❊ Why are people willing to harbor lust in their hearts?
❊ What are the devastating effects of adultery?
■ What does it mean to gouge out a habit for lust or to cut off a sinful practice?
❊ How does pornography feed the problem of adultery?
❊ What is wrong with the argument, "It's okay to look as long as you don't touch"?
❊ How might you respond to the popular claim that sexual fantasies are healthy and should be encouraged?
❊ What would you say to a friend in a bad marriage who was contemplating an affair?
❊ What does it mean to dress modestly?
■ What changes do you need to make in your reading or viewing habits to avoid temptations to lust?

APPLY IT
❊ What three steps can you take this week to insulate your marriage against affairs?
■ In what situations is it important for you to dress modestly this week?

Matthew 5:31-32

Divorce

TOPICS

Adultery, Commitment, Divorce, Faithfulness, Marriage, Remarriage, Unfaithfulness

OPEN IT

■ What commitments do adults commonly make?
❊ What commitments do adults sometimes break?
❊ What causes people to break their commitments?

EXPLORE IT

■ Why did Jesus need to say this about marriage and divorce? (5:31-32)
■ What is the best way to think about marriage and divorce? (5:31-32)
❊ Who is guilty of adultery? (5:31-32)
❊ What does God want us to do when we feel tempted to divorce a partner? (5:31-32)
❊ According to Jesus, what is the only acceptable reason for divorce? (5:32)
❊ When can a person divorce his or her partner? (5:32)
❊ When can a person not divorce his or her partner? (5:32)
❊ How can adultery affect a marriage commitment? (5:32)
❊ Why did Jesus give an exception to His "no divorce" command? (5:32)
■ What conditions are placed on divorce? (5:32)
❊ In what way does a person who divorces a partner "cause" the other to commit adultery? (5:32)

GET IT

❊ In what way can adultery damage a marriage?
■ Why is it important to try to hold a marriage together?
❊ In what ways can divorce hurt people?
❊ Why do people get divorced?
❊ Why do people commit adultery?
❊ What enables people to stay faithful to their partners?
❊ What can people do to strengthen their marriage?
■ In what ways can people show respect for marriage?
❊ What causes people to get divorced?
❊ For what reasons do people get divorced?
❊ On what or whom can a Christian depend to help him or her solve marriage problems?
❊ What can a person do when his or her marriage is in trouble?

APPLY IT

■ What can you do this week to strengthen your marriage or the marriage of a friend?
❊ How can you show respect for marriage this week?
❊ What can you do today or tomorrow to lessen the likelihood of ever getting divorced?

Matthew 5:33-37

Oaths

TOPICS

Character, Conversation, Faithfulness, Follow-through, Integrity, Swearing, Truth, Vows, Words

OPEN IT

■ What professions (for example, ministers, insurance agents, lawyers, car salesmen, and politicians) are often distrusted for what they say?
❊ How do you determine if someone is telling the truth?

EXPLORE IT

❊ What ancient teaching did Jesus bring up? (5:33)
❊ What oaths did Jesus' audience consider especially important to keep? (5:33)
■ How did Jesus update the ancient proverb about oaths? (5:34)
❊ What exceptions did Jesus permit in vow making? (5:34)
❊ Why was it inappropriate to swear by heaven? (5:34)
❊ Why was it inappropriate to swear by earth? (5:35)
❊ According to Jesus, why shouldn't people swear by Jerusalem? (5:35)
❊ Why not swear by one's own head? (5:36)
■ How should believers respond to questions? (5:37)
■ What's wrong with swearing oaths? (5:37)

GET IT

❊ How much does swearing on a Bible guarantee that a legal witness will tell the truth?
❊ Why do we swear?
■ In what situations do people typically swear?
❊ What are some ways that our society takes the name of God lightly or frivolously?
❊ What statements of assurance ("Trust me," "Would I lie to you?" "I really mean it this time," etc.) do you hear most often?
❊ How does lying in the name of God affect the reputation of God?
■ How should we respond when people try to get us to make promises or extra assurances?
❊ What does it imply when people don't take you at your word?

APPLY IT

■ What steps can you take this week to become known as a person who keeps his or her word?
❊ What unfulfilled promise have you made in the last week that you need to carry out today?

Matthew 5:38-42
An Eye for an Eye

TOPICS
Bitterness, Enemies, Gentleness, Humility, Oppressed, Persecution, Revenge, Strength, Unfairness

OPEN IT
❊ Why are movies about vengeance or vigilante justice so popular?
■ What is appealing about revenge?

EXPLORE IT
■ To what familiar saying was Jesus referring in this context? (5:38)
❊ What did the ancients require if a person put out someone else's eye? (5:38)
❊ What was the judgment for knocking out another's tooth? (5:38)
■ How did Jesus say we should respond to people who do us evil? (5:39)
■ What should we do to protect our rights and possessions? (5:39)
❊ What should be the Christian's response to physical violence? (5:39)
❊ What should a person do if someone else sues him or her? (5:40)
❊ What should a person do if someone else forces him or her to "go one mile"? (5:41)
❊ How should followers of Christ deal with those who ask them for things? (5:42)
❊ What is the proper response to a request to borrow something? (5:42)

GET IT
❊ What are the drawbacks to an "eye for eye" mentality?
■ Where do we draw the line between our rights and our responsibility to be forgiving and patient?
❊ What is the rationale behind Jesus' idea that love overcomes evil?
■ How can doing good change a bad situation?
❊ How should we respond to violent attacks?
❊ When are we responsible to stop an evil person from committing violent acts?
❊ What advice would you give to the little kid who is constantly being bullied at school?
❊ What do you think would happen if Christians followed these principles to the letter?
❊ What items would you find difficult to loan out or give away?
❊ In what ways have you been seeking vengeance or an opportunity to pay someone back for a wrong done to you?
❊ What grudge or personal vendetta do you need to lay aside?

APPLY IT
❊ What prayer will help you forgive some wrong you've had difficulty letting go of?
■ What act of kindness or reconciliation could you perform by next weekend to help "bury the hatchet"?

Matthew 5:43-48
Love for Enemies

TOPICS
Bitterness, Enemies, God, Hatred, Neighbor, Oppressed, Perfect, Persecution, Prayer, Righteousness

OPEN IT
❊ What TV character is most despicable to you? Why?
■ What underlying emotions and attitudes create cliques or cause divisions between groups of people?
❊ What character quality more than any other says to the world, "This person is a Christian"?

EXPLORE IT
❊ What ancient rule of life did Jesus challenge here? (5:43)
■ How did Jesus say we ought to treat our enemies? (5:44)
❊ What did Jesus say we ought to do for those who persecute us? (5:44)
❊ Why did Jesus suggest modifying this universally accepted law? (5:45)
■ How does God treat evil and good people in the same way? (5:45)
❊ How does God treat righteous and unrighteous people equally? (5:45)
❊ What type of people did Jesus cite as loving those who love them? (5:46)
❊ What does God think of us when we love those who love us? (5:46)
❊ Why is friendliness to friends and relatives not considered exceptional behavior? (5:47)
❊ What kinds of people are mentioned as greeting only their brothers? (5:47)
❊ What exceptional standard did Christ give us? (5:48)
■ Who has set an example for us? How? (5:48)

GET IT
■ If our Holy God is able to exhibit grace and mercy to everyone, why is it difficult for us to be like Him?
❊ What does it mean for us to be perfect?
❊ How is it possible for us to love our enemies?
■ What would have to happen in your heart in order for you to be able to pray for an enemy?
❊ What might praying for your enemy change?
❊ In what ways does a loving spirit demonstrate that we are God's people?

APPLY IT
❊ What are some specific ways you can show love today to someone whom you dislike?
■ For which of your "enemies" will you pray every day this week?

Matthew 6:1-4
Giving to the Needy

TOPICS
Ego, Generosity, Hypocrisy, Money, Motives, Poor, Pride, Rewards, Tithing

OPEN IT
■ What would you do if you discovered that a long-lost relative had left you a million dollars?
❇ Who are the needy people in our world?
❇ What is your favorite charity?
❇ How do you feel when a wealthy individual gives a large sum of money with the stipulation that a building be named after him or her?

EXPLORE IT
❇ What kind of acts was Jesus discussing? (6:1)
■ What specific motives did Jesus warn against? (6:1)
❇ What happens to the person who operates with impure motives? (6:1)
❇ Who can judge whether a person's actions are pure? (6:1)
❇ How did some individuals in Jesus' day publicize their generosity? (6:2)
❇ What name did Jesus give to insincere individuals? Why? (6:2)
❇ Where did people advertise their "acts of righteousness"? (6:2)
❇ What deep-seated desire prompted some people to give? (6:2)
❇ What future reward can showy givers expect? (6:2)
■ What style of giving did Jesus command us to adopt? (6:3-4)
❇ Who notices when we give according to Jesus' guidelines? (6:4)
■ What happens to those who give as Jesus told us to give? (6:4)

GET IT
❇ What motivates people to give money to churches or Christian ministries?
❇ Why are many people more apt to give money to an organization than to a needy individual?
❇ Why do most Christian organizations have their highest income at the end of the year?
❇ How much are your giving habits affected by the knowledge that charitable contributions are tax-deductible?
■ What are some specific ways Christians could be more secretive in their giving?
❇ Why do we value the recognition people give us?
■ What is difficult about giving secretly?
❇ How do some churches encourage showy giving?
❇ Why is it difficult for us to do a good deed and keep quiet about it?

APPLY IT
❇ What anonymous gift can you give today?
■ What steps could you take to ensure that your giving is not done for show?

Matthew 6:5-15
Prayer

TOPICS
Bitterness, Depend, Ego, Forgiveness, God, Humility, Hypocrisy, Motives, Prayer, Self-righteousness

OPEN IT
❇ What images or thoughts spring to mind when you hear the word "prayer"?
■ What role did prayer play in your family's life when you were growing up?

EXPLORE IT
❇ According to Jesus, what wrong motivation prompts some individuals to pray? (6:5)
■ What name did Jesus call people who pray for show? Why? (6:5)
❇ Where do hypocrites prefer to do their praying? (6:5)
❇ What type of reward will religious showmanship bring? (6:5)
■ How did Jesus command His followers to pray? (6:6)
❇ Where did Jesus suggest we talk to God? (6:6)
■ What type of reward will humility in prayer bring? (6:6)
❇ What did Jesus have to say about repetitive or long, windy prayers? (6:7)
❇ What insights or facts about God are revealed in this passage? (6:6, 8, 9)
❇ To whom did Jesus tell us to pray? (6:9)
❇ What should be our attitude toward God? (6:9)
❇ What should be our attitude toward God's kingdom and will? (6:10)
❇ What should be our attitude toward life's necessities? (6:11)
❇ What should be our attitude toward those who have wronged us? (6:12)
❇ What should be our attitude toward temptation? (6:13)
❇ Why is it crucial for us to forgive those who wrong us? (6:14-15)

GET IT
❇ What common or overused phrases do you hear frequently repeated in people's prayers?
❇ If God knows what we need before we ask, why should we pray?
■ If Jesus commands us to pray in secret, what is the value of public prayer?
❇ Why do many Christians feel uncomfortable praying out loud?
■ When you pray in front of a group, how can you concentrate fully on what you are saying to God rather than how your prayers sound to others?
❇ Why do we often use special language or words for talking to God?
❇ What sins or offenses by others do we find especially difficult to forgive?

APPLY IT
■ What changes do you need to make in your prayer life?
❇ What strained relationship will you seek to repair this week by forgiving an offense?

Matthew 6:16-18
Fasting

TOPICS
Commitment, Dedication, Discipline, Giving Up, Humility, Hypocrisy, Motives, Preparation, Spiritual Disciplines

OPEN IT
■ What is your all-time favorite meal?
❊ What is the hungriest you have ever been in your life?

EXPLORE IT
❊ What mood did certain individuals in Jesus' day assume when they fasted? (6:16)
■ What facial expressions did some people wear? Why? (6:16)
❊ Why did some people take on gloomy expressions when they fasted? (6:16)
■ What harsh name did Jesus give to people who made a public show of their fasting? Why? (6:16)
❊ According to Jesus, what rewards await people who show off their fasting? (6:16)
❊ What repeated phrase in this passage suggests that fasting is not an option? (6:16, 17)
❊ How should a person conceal the fact of his or her fasting? (6:17)
■ Who should know about an individual's fasts? Why? (6:18)
❊ Who alone can see what people do in secret? How? (6:18)
❊ Why are believers to be secretive about fasting? (6:18)

GET IT
❊ What is the modern day equivalent of putting "oil on your head"?
❊ How do God's rewards differ from the recognition we receive from others?
❊ What are some good reasons for fasting?
❊ Why do you believe this spiritual discipline is seldom discussed in Christian circles?
❊ What spiritual benefits might we receive from fasting?
■ Why is it tempting to show others that you are fasting?
■ What is the advantage of keeping your spiritual disciplines secret?
❊ For what need in your own life or in the life of a loved one would you be willing to skip a meal in order to devote yourself to prayer?

APPLY IT
❊ For what reason could you fast this week?
■ What steps can you take to devote your spiritual disciplines to God alone?
❊ What specific steps could you take this week in order to gain a better understanding of fasting?

Matthew 6:19-24
Treasures in Heaven

TOPICS
Darkness, Desires, Earth, Generosity, Heaven, Money, Perspective, Priorities, Resources, Rewards, Submission, Wealth

OPEN IT
■ If you were stranded on a desert island and could have only three possessions with you, what would you choose and why?
❊ What valuable possessions do you have that cannot be replaced?
❊ What are some things you'd never give up, no matter how much money you were offered for them?

EXPLORE IT
■ Where did Jesus urge His followers not to "store up treasures"? Why? (6:19)
❊ Why did Jesus discourage stockpiling things? (6:19)
❊ What can happen to a person's material possessions? (6:19)
■ Where did Jesus encourage us to invest our wealth? Why? (6:20)
❊ Why is heaven a better place to "bank" than earth? (6:20)
❊ What does the location of a person's treasure say about that person? (6:21)
❊ What is described as the "lamp of the body"? How is this so? (6:22)
❊ What is the result of "good eyes"? (6:22)
❊ When will people's lives be full of darkness? (6:23)
■ What did Jesus say about serving two masters? (6:24)
❊ Why did Jesus say we cannot serve two masters? (6:24)
❊ What two masters did Jesus mention in this context? Why? (6:24)

GET IT
❊ How have you felt whenever you have lost a valued possession?
■ How can we "store up . . . treasures in heaven"?
❊ How can we determine where our treasure is (and thus where our hearts are)?
❊ What sort of things do you think about most?
❊ Where does your mind naturally gravitate to in those moments just before you go to bed?
❊ How clear is your spiritual vision right now?
❊ What masters most often fight for your allegiance?
❊ In what ways do you serve money?
■ In what ways can you master your money?

APPLY IT
■ How could you make an investment in eternity today?
❊ What committed Christian friends could help you evaluate your use of money in the next month?

Matthew 6:25-34
Do Not Worry

TOPICS
Contentment, Creation, Faithfulness, Future, God, Materialism, Needs, Peace, Prayer, Trust, Worry

OPEN IT
■ What are your top three worries?
❊ What is your favorite kind of food?
❊ How would you describe your tastes in fashion?

EXPLORE IT
❊ What three worries did Jesus discourage among His followers? Why? (6:25)
❊ Why is food a trivial matter? (6:26)
❊ According to Jesus, how do clothes stack up as a subject of great concern? (6:26)
■ What creatures did Jesus use to illustrate God's reliability as a provider? Why? (6:26)
❊ Why are God's creatures consistently "fed and clothed"? (6:26)
■ Why should we take great comfort from the way the animal and plant kingdoms operate? (6:26)
❊ What benefits does worry bring? (6:27)
❊ What fact from nature did Jesus use to illustrate the folly of worrying over clothes? (6:28)
❊ How did Solomon's wardrobe measure up to the beauty of nature? (6:29)
■ What comfort can followers of Christ find in the beauty of nature? (6:30)
❊ Who is consumed by concern over food, water, and clothing? (6:32)
❊ What priorities should we have in life? (6:33)
❊ What does God do for His children when they keep the right perspective, refuse to worry, and trust Him? (6:33)
❊ Why is it silly to fret over the future? (6:34)

GET IT
❊ Why do some of us worry about clothes more than others?
❊ How do you think God feels about our society's preoccupation with food?
■ If God is really in control of the universe, why do we worry so much about so many things?
❊ How do you think worry is affecting you emotionally, physically, and spiritually?
❊ How would you answer someone who interprets this passage to mean that God promises to give His children everything their hearts desire?
❊ In light of this passage, what would be some good principles on food and clothing for us to follow?
❊ What is the difference between planning for the future and worrying about the future?
❊ What worries do you struggle to keep under control?
■ What can help you entrust your worries to God?

APPLY IT
■ What worry will you entrust to God today?
❊ What steps can you take today to change your priorities from worldly ones to kingdom ones?

Matthew 7:1-6
Judging Others

TOPICS
Church, Criticism, Faults, Hypocrisy, Judgment, Mercy, Opinions, Pride, Relationships, Wisdom, Words

OPEN IT
■ What are your pet peeves (at work, home, or in your community)?
❊ What kinds of things do people criticize you for most commonly?
❊ How do you tend to respond when someone calls you on the carpet or corrects you?
❊ What would your friends say is your biggest fault?

EXPLORE IT
❊ What happens to those who are judgmental or critical? (7:1)
❊ In what way will we be judged? (7:2)
■ By what measure will we be judged? (7:2)
❊ What kind of faults do we notice in others? (7:3)
❊ How did Jesus illustrate the foolishness of the way we find fault with others? (7:3)
❊ What figure of speech did Jesus use to illustrate how blind we are to the shortcomings in our own lives? (7:4)
■ What did Jesus call those who ignore their own imperfections and focus on the flaws of others? Why? (7:5)
❊ When is it good to confront others with their faults? (7:5)
■ Why is it necessary to deal with one's own sins first? (7:5)
❊ What are we not to do with sacred things? Why? (7:6)
❊ What may happen if we disregard Jesus' warning? (7:6)

GET IT
■ When, if ever, should we criticize or judge someone else?
❊ What sacred or valuable things should we withhold from people who have no concern for God?
❊ Why is it that the traits of others that irritate us most are often the very faults that are present in our own lives?
❊ What happened the last time you criticized someone else or judged another's actions?
❊ What causes us to become critical, judgmental people?
■ How can we become more merciful and nonjudgmental?
❊ What faults block your spiritual vision?

APPLY IT
■ How can you begin this week to get in the habit of examining your own life before you start criticizing others?
❊ What fault of your own can you focus attention on this week?

Matthew 7:7-12
Ask, Seek, Knock

TOPICS
Children, Endurance, Evil, Generosity, Gifts, God, Goodness, Humanness, Kindness, Law, Persistence, Prayer, Promises

OPEN IT
■ What sort of letters did you write to Santa Claus as a kid?
❇ What is the best answer to prayer you ever received?
❇ If you could make up one rule that everyone in the world had to live by, what would it be and why?

EXPLORE IT
❇ What did Jesus say will happen if we bring our requests to Him? (7:7)
❇ What happens when we seek in Christ's name? (7:7)
■ According to Jesus, what is the result for those who "knock" on God's door? (7:7)
❇ How do loving parents respond to a child's request for bread? (7:9)
❇ How do loving parents respond to a child's request for fish? (7:10)
■ What is true about the character of even the best human parent? (7:11)
■ How can we be encouraged by the sight of godless parents doing good things for their children? (7:11)
❇ What is the likelihood of God giving His praying children what they need? (7:11)
❇ How are we to treat others? (7:12)
❇ In what specific situations are we to follow the Golden Rule? (7:12)
❇ Why is the command to treat others as you want to be treated so significant? (7:12)

GET IT
■ What do you tend to pray about?
■ For what are you reluctant to pray?
❇ How do you react when your child comes to you with a legitimate need?
❇ What motivates you to want to provide for your children?
❇ In spite of their imperfection, how would you rate your parents as providers?
❇ If earthly parents generally attempt to care for their children, what can you conclude about God?
❇ How would the world be different if we all lived by the Golden Rule?
❇ When is it hardest for you to treat others with kindness and respect?

APPLY IT
■ What request will you bring to God every day this week?
❇ To what relationship do you most need to apply the Golden Rule this week?

Matthew 7:13-14
The Narrow and Wide Gates

TOPICS
Eternal Life, Evangelism, Grace, Guidance, Heaven, Hell, Lost, Pride, Rebellion, Unbelievers, Witnessing

OPEN IT
■ Why are most people apt to believe in heaven but quick to dismiss the reality of hell?
❇ If you were setting the standards for who gets into heaven, what requirements would you establish?
❇ What do you think heaven will be like?

EXPLORE IT
■ What command did Jesus give His followers in this passage? (7:13)
❇ What exactly are we called to enter? Why? (7:13)
❇ How did Jesus describe the gate to the kingdom of God? Why? (7:13)
■ In what way did Jesus describe the gate that leads to destruction? (7:13)
❇ What was said about the road that leads to destruction? (7:13)
❇ How many people are said to travel the path to destruction? (7:13)
❇ What kind of gate leads to life? (7:14)
❇ The small gate is attached to what kind of road? (7:14)
❇ Where does the narrow road lead? (7:14)
■ How many people find and follow the narrow road? Why? (7:14)

GET IT
❇ What is encouraging about Christ's words?
❇ What broad roads did you travel before you met Christ?
❇ How did you find Christ?
❇ What was your entry through the narrow gate like?
■ What wide gates and broad roads are some of your acquaintances following?
❇ How should we fit or not fit into the world?
❇ How might you respond to the charge that Christians are narrow-minded and arrogant?
■ In what sense is it narrow-minded to believe in Christ?
❇ Why do many people prefer the broad way that leads to destruction?
❇ Why is it difficult to stay on the narrow road?

APPLY IT
❇ What can you do this week to point someone toward the small gate?
❇ How can you show God your appreciation for His mercy and grace in leading you to the path of eternal life?
■ What action can you take this week to help you stay on the narrow path?

Matthew 7:15-23

A Tree and Its Fruit

TOPICS

Deceit, Discernment, Evil, Fruit, Heaven, Hypocrisy, Rejection, Religion, Unbelievers

OPEN IT

■ What do you know about vegetable gardening?
❇ What kind of inner alarm (if any) alerts you to fact that a person is a phony?
❇ What is your favorite fruit?

EXPLORE IT

❇ Against whom did Jesus warn us? Why? (7:15)
❇ What do false prophets look like on the outside? (7:15)
❇ What are false prophets like inwardly? (7:15)
❇ How did Christ say we could recognize false prophets? (7:16, 20)
■ What does nature reveal about a tree and its fruit? (7:16)
❇ What kind of fruit do good trees bear? Why? (7:17-18)
❇ What type of produce grows on bad trees? Why? (7:17-18)
■ What happens to trees that fail to produce good fruit? (7:18)
■ Who will enter the kingdom of heaven? (7:21)
❇ How will some people try to talk their way into heaven? (7:22)
❇ What credentials or accomplishments will some people claim? (7:22)
❇ How will Jesus respond to these impostors? (7:23)
❇ What is necessary for entry into heaven? (7:23)

GET IT

❇ Why do we continue to sin if we have Christ in our heart and the Holy Spirit in our lives?
■ What does this passage tell us about the importance of doing good works?
❇ How do good works and salvation fit together?
■ How can people be "religious" yet not follow Christ?
❇ What kind of good works have you been producing lately?
❇ What evidence in your life points to your relationship with Jesus?

APPLY IT

❇ What spiritual disciplines can you use to cultivate your soul this week?
■ In what area of your life can you place more emphasis on doing good works each day this week?

Matthew 7:24-29

The Wise and Foolish Builders

TOPICS

Attitude, Disobedience, Effort, Foundation, Hardheartedness, Obedience, Quality, Responsibility, Security, Stubbornness

OPEN IT

❇ What is the secret to building great sand castles?
❇ What is it like to ride out a violent thunderstorm, hurricane, or tornado?
■ How do you feel when you offer sound advice and it is rejected?

EXPLORE IT

❇ Who did Jesus say is wise? (7:24)
❇ Besides hearing the words of Christ, what else must a person do in order to be considered wise? (7:24)
❇ Jesus compared wise living to building a house on what kind of foundation? (7:24)
■ What sets fools apart from wise people? (7:24, 26)
❇ In Jesus' analogy, what strong forces of nature pounded on the wise person's house? (7:25)
❇ What was the effect of the wind and rain on the house? (7:25)
❇ Why wasn't the house part of a "disaster area"? (7:25)
■ What kind of people did Jesus talk about in contrast to the wise person? (7:26)
■ What individuals are like a man who builds a house on sand? (7:26)
❇ According to Jesus, foolish living is like building a house on what kind of foundation? (7:26)
❇ In Jesus' analogy, what happened when the wind and water crashed against the fool's house? (7:27)
❇ How did the crowd respond to Jesus' teaching? (7:28)
❇ Why did the crowd react with amazement to Jesus' teaching? (7:29)

GET IT

■ Why is it difficult to apply God's truth to our lives?
■ How does obedience to God bring security to our lives?
❇ What foundation are you building your life on?
❇ How can you build your life on Christ?
❇ What are some sandy foundations you have seen people base their lives on?
❇ How do you feel when you see people (friends or family members) ignoring God and making bad decisions?
❇ What is the most amazing thing to you about all that Jesus ever said?

APPLY IT

❇ What can you do today to encourage someone to listen to the voice of Jesus and obey what he or she hears?
■ What neglected command of Christ will you begin obeying this week?

Matthew 8:1-4

The Man With Leprosy

TOPICS

Alone, Attitude, Compassion, Healing, Help, Hopelessness, Humility, Love, Miracles, Sensitivity, Shame, Sickness, Sovereignty

OPEN IT

❇ How do you think you would react if you were disabled in an automobile accident?
■ Why are people afraid of AIDS?
❇ What illnesses are people often afraid of?

EXPLORE IT
❊ Where did Jesus go after He finished the Sermon on the Mount? (8:1)
■ What happened when Jesus came down from the mountain? (8:1)
❊ What was Jesus' audience like? (8:1)
❊ What was distinctive about the man who came and blocked Jesus' path? (8:2)
❊ What did the kneeling man say to Christ? (8:2)
■ What daring deed did Christ do for the man with leprosy? (8:3)
❊ What compassionate words did Christ say? (8:3)
❊ What happened when Christ finished speaking? (8:3)
❊ How long did this healing process take? (8:3)
❊ What strange instructions did Jesus give the man whom He healed? (8:4)
■ For what reasons did Jesus want the man to show his healed body to the priests? (8:4)

GET IT
❊ If you had an incurable disease, where would you turn for support?
■ How does this story about Christ encourage you?
■ How does the example of Christ challenge you?
❊ Why do you think Christ told the healed man to "show but not tell"?
❊ How is Christ's healing of this man with leprosy similar to the manner in which He forgives us?
❊ What is the benefit of personal testimony about God's deeds?
❊ Who are often treated like modern-day lepers?
❊ How can we follow Christ's example in our behavior toward modern-day lepers?
❊ What sort of attitude must we have when we come to God for help?
❊ What story of God's acts on your behalf could you use as a testimony to others?

APPLY IT
■ What sick or suffering person can you visit or talk to this week?
❊ Whom could you encourage this week with a testimony of something God has done for you?

Matthew 8:5-13
The Faith of the Centurion

TOPICS
Authority, Confidence, Faith, Healing, Humility, Initiative, Instructions, Kingdom of God/Heaven, Miracles, Trust, Unbelievers

OPEN IT
❊ Who is the most amazing person you've ever met?
■ For whom would you not hesitate to give blood or otherwise help recover from a severe illness?
❊ What did your mother do for you when you got sick as a child?

EXPLORE IT
❊ Where did the incident described in this passage take place? (8:5)
■ Who approached Jesus and asked for help? (8:5)
❊ What did the centurion tell Jesus? (8:6)
❊ What did Jesus promise the soldier? (8:7)
❊ What humble, surprising suggestion did the man make? (8:8)
❊ What rationale did the centurion have for making his request? (8:9)
❊ What effect did the soldier's words have on Jesus? (8:10)
❊ According to Jesus, how many Israelites had as much faith as the centurion? (8:10)
❊ What insight did Jesus give about the guest list of the kingdom of heaven? (8:11)
❊ What eternal destiny did Jesus suggest awaited many in His audience? (8:12)
■ What instructions did Jesus give the centurion? (8:13)
■ What happened to the centurion's servant? (8:13)

GET IT
■ How should you respond when friends or relatives have needs?
■ How does Jesus' ready willingness to help the centurion's servant encourage you?
❊ What keeps you from having the faith that God can do anything?
❊ How can we have greater faith in God?
❊ Why are we so often filled with doubt?
❊ What assurance do you have that you will be at the great heavenly feast Jesus mentioned in this passage?

APPLY IT
■ For what person who is sick or in trouble can you intercede today?
❊ What can you do every day this week to build your faith in God?
❊ For what promise of Jesus will you trust God and expect Him to work this week?

Matthew 8:14-17
Jesus Heals Many

TOPICS
Compassion, Demons, Despair, Family, Healing, Hospitality, Occult, Sensitivity, Serving, Thankfulness, Victory

OPEN IT
■ What kind of a patient are you (squeamish, brave, stoic, etc.)?
❊ For what disease do you wish there were a cure right now?
❊ What is the most amazing story of physical healing you have ever heard?

EXPLORE IT
❊ What kind of a building was Jesus in when the incidents of this passage took place? (8:14)
❊ Who owned the building? (8:14)

✻ Who was bedridden and sick with a fever? (8:14)
✻ What does the identity of the sick woman reveal about Peter's personal life? (8:14)
✻ What did Jesus do to the sick woman? (8:15)
✻ What happened when Jesus touched the woman's hand? (8:15)
✻ What did the woman immediately begin to do? (8:15)
■ What kinds of people were brought to Jesus that evening? (8:16)
■ What did Jesus do for the people who were brought to Him? (8:16)
■ What procedure or technique did Jesus use to help the people who were brought to Him? (8:16)
✻ How were these events significant in Jewish history? (8:17)

GET IT
✻ How patient are you with sick family members?
✻ How would you handle living with an ill in-law?
✻ How do we typically show appreciation for all the ways God has blessed our lives?
✻ How would you rate yourself as a servant?
■ What are some ways we can assist those who are ill?
■ What ill or suffering people do you know?
✻ How can you help those with needs?

APPLY IT
■ What will you do for someone who is sick or hurting this month?
✻ Who in your family can you touch today with the love of Christ?
✻ In what ways can you help a hurting family member this week?

Matthew 8:18-22
The Cost of Following Jesus

TOPICS
Abandon, Barriers, Commitment, Compromise, Expectations, Family, Invitation, Popularity, Procrastination, Rationalizing, Temptation, Zeal

OPEN IT
■ What excuses do people give for neglecting common responsibilities?
✻ What are the pros and cons of travelling all the time—always living out of a suitcase?
✻ Why do only a few people follow Christ for a lifetime?

EXPLORE IT
✻ What observation prompted Jesus to cross to the other side of the lake? (8:18)
✻ What orders did Jesus give? (8:18)
✻ What did the teacher of the law call Jesus? (8:19)
✻ What did the teacher of the law claim he would do? (8:19)
■ Who approached Jesus? (8:19-20)
✻ What did Jesus tell the teacher of the law he would have to do without? (8:20)
■ What animals did Jesus say were more secure than He? Why? (8:20)
✻ Who offered to follow Jesus? (8:21)
✻ What did one of Jesus' disciples request? (8:21)
■ What command did Jesus give to the disciple that offered to follow Him under certain conditions? (8:22)
✻ How did Jesus handle the disciple's request? (8:22)

GET IT
✻ Why do we value popularity?
✻ What are some places you would not want to go under any conditions?
✻ Why do we value home ownership?
✻ What are the pros and cons of putting down roots and getting settled into a community?
■ In what ways might a family (parents, siblings, or children) get in the way of following Jesus?
■ In what ways can our love for Christ cost us?

APPLY IT
✻ How can you model commitment to Christ for your children this week?
■ What can you do this week to encourage a Christian who has made sacrifices to follow Christ?

Matthew 8:23-27
Jesus Calms the Storm

TOPICS
Believe, Faith, Fear, God's Will, Help, Jesus Christ, Learning, Miracles, Nature, Security, Sovereignty, Trust

OPEN IT
■ What is your scariest "bad weather story"?
✻ When was the last time you were speechless?
✻ Why is it difficult for parents to watch their children go through hard times?
✻ What kind of a sleeper are you?

EXPLORE IT
✻ What did Jesus do with His disciples? (8:23)
✻ Who accompanied Jesus in the boat? (8:23)
■ What surprise did the boaters encounter in this scene? (8:24)
✻ How severe was the weather? (8:24)
✻ What was Jesus doing during the storm? (8:24)
✻ What did the disciples do? (8:25)
✻ What did the disciples say? (8:25)
■ How did Jesus reply to the disciples' expression of fear? (8:26)
✻ What did Jesus do when the disciples expressed fear? (8:26)
✻ What was nature's response to the command of Jesus? (8:26)
■ How did the disciples react to this astonishing sequence of events? (8:27)
✻ What excellent question did the disciples raise? (8:27)

GET IT
✻ Why do you think most people—even nonreligious folks—turn to God when things really fall apart?
■ What nerve-wracking situations have you faced lately?
✻ How do you typically react when circumstances get

out of control?
❇ Why is it necessary for us to go through scary times in life?
■ Why do we panic about the storms swirling around us when the God of the universe lives inside us?
❇ How does it make you feel to remember that you have a Savior who is greater than anything this world can throw at you?
❇ What amazing acts has God done for you?

APPLY IT
❇ How can you strengthen your faith in God today?
■ This week, what specific ways can you demonstrate your belief that Jesus will see you through the storms in your life?
❇ For what amazing acts do you need to thank God today?

Matthew 8:28-34
The Healing of Two Demon-possessed Men

TOPICS
Blindness, Compassion, Demons, Evidence, Hardheartedness, Healing, Miracles, Occult, Oppressed, Priorities, Rejection, Satan, Unbelievers

OPEN IT
❇ What is your favorite farm animal?
❇ What effect (if any) do you think violent horror movies have on people?
■ Why are Satan and the occult increasingly popular topics among young people?

EXPLORE IT
❇ Where did Jesus and the disciples come ashore? (8:28)
❇ Who met Christ and His men? (8:28)
❇ What was the spiritual state of the two individuals Jesus met? (8:28)
❇ Where did the strangers live? (8:28)
❇ What kind of behavior did the Gadarene men exhibit? (8:28)
■ What did the two Gadarene men shout at Jesus? (8:29)
❇ What was nearby? (8:30)
❇ Who spoke to Jesus about the nearby herd of pigs? Why? (8:30)
❇ What request was made of Jesus? Why? (8:31)
❇ How did Jesus respond to the request that He cast the demons into the herd of pigs? (8:32)
■ What happened as soon as Jesus spoke? (8:32)
❇ How did news of this event reach town? (8:33)
■ How did the townspeople react to what happened? (8:34)

GET IT
❇ How do you think you'd react if you encountered a demon-possessed person?
■ How does Christ's power over Satan encourage and comfort you?
❇ What do you think this passage says about the relative worth of a human soul compared to the value of an animal?
❇ Why do so many people want nothing to do with Christ?
❇ In what areas of your life is Jesus working?
❇ What areas of your life do you want Jesus to leave alone?
❇ If Jesus is powerful enough to drive out demons, why don't we see much evidence of His power in our lives?
■ How can we show confidence in Christ's power?

APPLY IT
■ What individuals in your town are in the grip of Satan and need your prayers today and every day this week?
❇ Into what specific area(s) of your life do you need to invite Jesus to work today?

Matthew 9:1-8
Jesus Heals a Paralytic

TOPICS
Authority, Blindness, Faith, Forgiveness, Friendship, Healing, Hypocrisy, Miracles, Power, Praise, Questions, Religion, Worship

OPEN IT
❇ What qualities do you look for in a friend?
❇ Why do most people take their physical health for granted?
■ What people did God use to bring you to Jesus?

EXPLORE IT
❇ What means of transportation did Jesus use to get to His own town? (9:1)
❇ What was Jesus' destination? (9:1)
■ Upon His arrival, whom did Jesus encounter? (9:2)
❇ What attribute did the men exhibit in coming to Christ? (9:2)
❇ What unexpected comment did Jesus make to the disabled person among them? (9:2)
❇ Who observed the exchange between the paralytic and Jesus? (9:3)
■ What did the teachers of the Law think about Jesus' declaration? (9:3)
❇ What supernatural ability did Jesus use? (9:4)
■ What did Jesus say about the teachers' opinions? (9:4-6)
❇ What was Jesus' argument for His authority to forgive sins? (9:5-6)
❇ What did Jesus do to prove His authority to forgive sins? (9:6)
❇ What happened to the paralytic? (9:7)
❇ What did the paralytic do? (9:7)
❇ What was the crowd's reaction to this event? (9:8)

GET IT
❇ How can we see a person's faith?
❇ What do you think it would be like to be a paraplegic or quadriplegic?
❇ How does it make you feel to realize that Jesus knows your every thought?

■ What experiences led up to you meeting Christ and having your sins forgiven?
❊ What emotions did you feel when you realized your sins were forgiven?
■ How do you typically react when someone else becomes a Christian?

APPLY IT
❊ What can you do for a hurting friend this week?
■ How can you show your appreciation to God today for His saving work in your life?

Matthew 9:9-13
The Calling of Matthew

TOPICS
Ambassadors, Backslide, Compassion, Darkness, Discernment, Effort, Evangelism, Foolishness, Good News, Involvement, Limitations, Lost, Obedience, Obligation, Purpose, Risk, Unbelievers, Witnessing

OPEN IT
❊ If you were starting your own business, what qualities would you look for in prospective employees?
■ What past misdeeds would disqualify someone from: your job? elected office? the Supreme Court? the ministry?
❊ What qualities make for a great leader?

EXPLORE IT
❊ Who did Jesus see sitting at a tax collector's booth? (9:9)
❊ What was Matthew's job? (9:9)
❊ What did Jesus tell Matthew to do? (9:9)
❊ How did Matthew respond to Jesus' statement? (9:9)
❊ Where did Jesus and Matthew go? Why? (9:10)
■ What kind of people joined Jesus and His new follower for dinner? (9:10)
❊ What did the Pharisees think of Jesus' attendance at Matthew's social function? (9:11)
❊ Who reported the Pharisees' comments to Jesus? (9:12)
❊ What was Jesus' response to the Pharisees? (9:12)
■ What did Jesus tell His listeners they needed to learn? (9:13)
■ What did Jesus say He had come to earth to do? (9:13)

GET IT
❊ What, in your opinion, are some respectable jobs, and what are some questionable careers for believers to pursue?
❊ How do you think you might react if several gang members or street people attended your church this Sunday?
❊ What do you think people would say if you associated with a "wild crowd" in order to be a witness for Christ?
❊ Why should we not follow this example of Christ if we are weak in our faith?
■ What dangers do we face when we befriend non-Christians?
■ What will happen if we never reach out to those outside the church?
❊ What surprises you about Jesus' actions in this passage?
❊ What individuals need your encouragement and support as they seek to minister to those who don't know Christ?

APPLY IT
■ How can you cultivate a relationship with a non-Christian friend this week?
❊ What can you do to remind yourself to view others as they can be, instead of seeing only their faults?

Matthew 9:14-17
Jesus Questioned About Fasting

TOPICS
Celebration, Change, Fasting, Freedom, Grace, Jesus Christ, Judging Others, Law, Legalism, Mourning, New Covenant, Simplicity, Traditions

OPEN IT
❊ What makes a party successful?
■ What are some traditions or customs from the past that you feel we ought to revive?
❊ Why do we feel uncomfortable with change?

EXPLORE IT
❊ Who approached Jesus after the dinner party at Matthew's house? (9:14)
❊ What topic were John's disciples interested in discussing with Christ? (9:14)
■ What did John's disciples want to know? (9:14)
■ How did Jesus explain the fact that His disciples did not fast? (9:15)
❊ What imagery did Jesus use as an illustration? (9:15)
❊ To what did Jesus compare Himself? (9:15)
❊ What did Jesus suggest would happen? (9:15)
❊ What sewing illustration did Jesus use? (9:16)
■ Using an illustration from the world of wine making, Jesus talked about the need to do what? (9:17)
❊ What did Jesus say would happen if new wine was poured into old wineskins? (9:17)

GET IT
■ Why is it that wonderful spiritual traditions can turn into dull, lifeless rituals?
❊ What are some reasons you might consider fasting?
❊ In what ways are you guilty of being legalistic?
❊ What legalistic habits or practices do you need to get rid of?
❊ How can we Christians do a better job of demonstrating the joy of Christ to the world?
■ Why is it wrong for us to measure our performance as Christians by a list of dos and don'ts?
❊ How would you explain this passage to a friend?

APPLY IT
■ Throughout this week, how can you embrace God's grace and acceptance in Christ?
❊ What specific steps can you take today to experience the joy that comes from appreciating Christ's saving work?

Matthew 9:18-26
A Dead Girl and a Sick Woman

TOPICS
Death, Doubt, Faith, Healing, Hope, Miracles, Patience, Resurrection, Trust, Unbelievers, Waiting

OPEN IT
❇ What epitaph would you like on your tombstone?
■ What punishment should be meted out to those who prey on weak or defenseless individuals?
❇ What do you think about people who claim to have died and then come back to life?

EXPLORE IT
❇ Who approached Jesus? (9:18)
❇ What did the man do? (9:18)
❇ With what startling situation and request did the man present Jesus? (9:18)
❇ How did Jesus react? (9:19)
❇ Who accompanied Jesus? (9:19)
■ While Jesus and the others made their way to the man's house, who touched Jesus' cloak? (9:20)
❇ From what kind of ailment did the woman suffer? (9:20)
■ What was the woman's reasoning for touching Jesus' cloak? (9:21)
❇ What happened as the woman made contact with Jesus? (9:22)
❇ What did Jesus do for the woman? (9:22)
■ Why was the woman healed? (9:22)
❇ Upon arriving at the ruler's house, what did Jesus say to the crowd? (9:24)
❇ What was the crowd's response to Jesus' unexpected statement? (9:24)
❇ What did Christ do after He put the crowd outside? (9:25)
❇ What happened after Christ left? (9:26)

GET IT
❇ What personal encouragement and comfort do you find in Christ's ability to heal the sick and raise the dead?
■ How is your faith challenged by the people in this story?
❇ What are some ways we "laugh at Jesus" in our beliefs and behavior?
❇ How do you think a twelve-year illness would affect your faith in God?
❇ What does this passage teach you about Jesus' sensitivity to the needs to a lonely, hurting individual?
■ What impossible situation are you facing?
❇ How can we follow Jesus' example?

APPLY IT
■ How can you trust God today to work in the impossible situation you are facing?
❇ What act of kindness can you show this week to someone who is ill or grieving?

Matthew 9:27-34
Jesus Heals the Blind and Mute

TOPICS
Awe, Blasphemy, Demons, Disobedience, Faith, Healing, Jealousy, Miracles, Opposition, Persistence, Rejection, Unbelievers, Worship

OPEN IT
■ Which of your senses would be the hardest to do without?
❇ On what recent occasion were you so excited about something that you could not resist telling everyone?

EXPLORE IT
❇ Who was following Jesus? (9:27)
❇ What were the men calling Jesus? (9:27)
❇ What were the men asking Christ to do? (9:27)
■ What question did Jesus ask the men who were following Him? (9:28)
■ How did the men respond to Jesus' question? (9:28)
■ What did Jesus do to grant the men's request? (9:29)
❇ What did Jesus say to the men? (9:30)
❇ What was the effect of Jesus' actions on the men? (9:30)
❇ What stern warning did Jesus give the men? (9:30)
❇ How well did the men heed Jesus' command? (9:31)
❇ Who was brought to Jesus for healing after the two blind men were healed? (9:32)
❇ What happened to the demon-possessed man? (9:33)
❇ What was the reaction of the onlookers when the demon was driven out? (9:33)
❇ How did the Pharisees explain what happened? (9:34)

GET IT
❇ How would you have handled the command not to tell anyone that you had been miraculously healed of blindness?
■ How can we be more persistent in asking God to help us or bless us?
❇ How can you be involved in spreading the news of Christ around the region in which you live?
❇ What commands of God are difficult for you to obey?
❇ Of what ailments would you like God to heal you?
■ In what area of your life do you need to have more faith in God?

APPLY IT
■ What is the first step you need to take in obeying one command that you have found difficult to obey?
❇ How might you demonstrate the love of Christ this week to someone who is disabled?

Matthew 9:35-38
The Workers Are Few

TOPICS
Ambassadors, Compassion, Evangelism, Healing, Lost, Miracles, Mission, Prayer, Priorities, Timing, Witnessing, World

OPEN IT
❊ In what situations do you tend to feel compassion?
❊ What missionaries do you know personally?
■ What do you pray about on a regular basis?

EXPLORE IT
❊ Where did Jesus go? To do what? (9:35)
❊ Where did Jesus teach? (9:35)
❊ What did Jesus preach about? (9:35)
❊ What kinds of disease and sickness did Jesus heal? (9:35)
■ What emotion did Jesus feel when He saw the crowds of people around Him? (9:36)
❊ Why did Jesus feel as He did? (9:36)
■ What helpless animals were the people compared to? (9:36)
❊ In what terms did Jesus describe the situation He and His disciples were observing? (9:37)
❊ How did Jesus describe the number of people helping others come to Him? (9:37)
❊ Who did Jesus tell His disciples to discuss the lack of workers with? (9:37)
■ For whom did Jesus tell His disciples to pray? (9:37)

GET IT
❊ For what nonChristians do you feel compassion?
❊ How would you describe the spiritual and moral state of the majority of the people in your town or on your campus?
■ Who are the nonChristians in your life?
■ What can you do to help people see their need for Christ?
❊ What skills, gifts, abilities, or talents can you use to help others come to Christ?
❊ What barriers stand in the way of people you know listening to the gospel?
❊ What can you do to overcome your friends' and neighbors' objections or reservations about following Jesus?

APPLY IT
■ For what nonChristians will you pray regularly from now on?
❊ What missionaries can you pray for this week?
❊ How can you make a difference today in the life of someone who is "harassed and helpless"?

Matthew 10:1-42
Jesus Sends Out the Twelve

TOPICS
Ambassadors, Approval, Challenge, Commitment, Confidence, Convictions, Danger, Depend, Discouragement, Endurance, Enemies, Faithfulness, Fear, Fruit, God's Will, Gospel, Holy Spirit, Instructions, Last Days, Persecution, Persistence, Problems, Purpose, Rejection, Results, Rewards, Risk, Sacrifice, Serving, Stress, Suffering, Unbelievers, Victory, Witnessing

OPEN IT
■ How might a parent feel sending his or her child off to school for the first time?
❊ What activity or responsibility absolutely terrifies you?
❊ Why do you think certain people are antagonistic to the gospel?

EXPLORE IT
❊ What kind of authority did Jesus give His twelve disciples? (10:1)
❊ What were the names of the twelve men with Jesus? (10:2-4)
❊ To what audience did Jesus command these men to go? (10:5-6)
❊ What last-minute ministry instructions did Jesus give His disciples? (10:7-10)
❊ What sort of accommodations were the disciples to seek in their travels? (10:11-13)
❊ How were the disciples supposed to respond to those who rejected them? (10:14-15)
❊ To what kind of animal did Jesus compare His disciples? (10:16)
■ What warnings of danger or hardship did Christ give His disciples? (10:17-23)
■ Why did Jesus predict trouble for the disciples? (10:24-25)
■ What kinds of things did Jesus say to bolster His disciples' courage? (10:26-31)
❊ Why did Christ tell His disciples that it was important for them to take a stand for Him? (10:32-33)
❊ What surprising comments did Jesus make about the goal of His ministry? (10:34-36)
❊ What radical requirements did Christ make of those who would follow Him? (10:37-38)
❊ What did Jesus promise those who obeyed Him fully? (10:39-42)

GET IT
■ Where specifically do you think Jesus wants you to minister?
❊ What things act as security blankets in your life and keep you from stepping out in faith?
❊ How can you be shrewd and innocent in your dealings with nonChristians?
■ How do you react when someone makes jokes about your faith or when people treat you harshly?
❊ How has Jesus created division in your family?
❊ In what ways have you been putting human relationships before your relationship with Christ?
❊ What do you think it means to lose your life for Christ's sake?

APPLY IT
❊ In what specific situations do you need to rely more on the Holy Spirit to give you the right words to say?
■ What promises from this chapter can you meditate on this week to make you a more effective minister for Christ?
❊ What are three or four concrete ways you can be more bold in standing up for Christ this week?

Matthew 11:1-19
Jesus and John the Baptist

TOPICS
Assumptions, Beliefs, Circumstances, Confusion, Doubt, Feelings, Greatness, Hope, Kingdom of God/Heaven, Maturity, Miracles, Surprises, Trust, World, Zeal

OPEN IT
■ What causes people to second-guess themselves?
❇ Other than Jesus Christ, who, in your opinion, was the greatest person who ever lived? Why?
❇ Of everything you know about Christ, what surprises you most?

EXPLORE IT
❇ What did Jesus do while His disciples were out on their mission trip? (11:1)
■ What message or question did John the Baptist send to Christ from prison? (11:2-3)
■ What instructions did Jesus give to John's messenger? (11:4)
■ What kind of proof did Jesus offer to establish His claim to be the Messiah? (11:5)
❇ What things did Jesus say John the Baptist was not? (11:7)
❇ How did Jesus identify John? (11:9-10)
❇ What high compliment did Jesus pay John? (11:11)
❇ Why was John's life and ministry significant? (11:10)
❇ What did Jesus claim about the kingdom of heaven? (11:12)
❇ Whose prophetic role did Jesus say John was fulfilling? (11:14)
❇ How did Jesus compare His generation to children? (11:16-17)
❇ What criticism did John the Baptist receive? Why? (11:18)
❇ What frequent charge was leveled at Jesus? Why? (11:19)

GET IT
❇ If you faithfully lived for God and were thrown in jail, how do you think you might react?
■ Based on this passage, how do you think Jesus reacts when we have moments of weakness and doubts about our faith?
■ How do you personally handle doubts when they come?
❇ Why do you believe that Jesus is God's Son and the Savior of the world?
❇ What have you seen and heard about Jesus that you could tell others?
❇ If Jesus were physically here today and began talking about you at a press conference, what kinds of remarks would he make?
❇ In what ways is the work of God advancing in your life or in your circle of influence?

APPLY IT
❇ What words of comfort could you share this week with a Christian who happens to be dealing with doubt?
■ What specific actions can you take today to strengthen a weak area of faith?
❇ What immature attitude or action do you need to change today in order to develop more fully in your faith?

Matthew 11:20-24
Woe on Unrepentant Cities

TOPICS
Denial, Judgment, Miracles, Pride, Punishment, Rebellion, Rejection, Repentance, Sin, Unbelievers

OPEN IT
❇ What are the pros and cons of living in a big city?
■ What city would you most like to visit? Why?
❇ What is your favorite city in the world? Why?
❇ How effective do you feel large evangelistic crusades are?

EXPLORE IT
❇ After His praise of John, what did Jesus begin to do? (11:20)
❇ Who was Jesus condemning? (11:20)
■ Why was Jesus denouncing the cities in which He performed most of His miracles? (11:20)
❇ What two cities did Jesus condemn first? Why? (11:21)
■ How did Jesus say Korazin and Bethsaida were different from Tyre and Sidon? (11:21)
❇ What did Jesus say would happen on the day of judgment? (11:22)
❇ What city did Jesus single out for comparison with Sodom? (11:23)
❇ What did Jesus predict for Capernaum? (11:23)
❇ Why did Capernaum have a bleak future? (11:23)
■ To what ancient, evil city did Jesus compare Capernaum? Why? (11:23-24)
❇ What city did Jesus say would face the sterner judgment than Sodom? Why? (11:24)

GET IT
■ How do you think God views our country's evil bent—especially in light of all the ways He has blessed us?
❇ As people who have experienced the goodness of God, how should we be living?
❇ In what ways are you treating the mercies of God or his blessings in your life as no big deal?
❇ Why is it dangerous for us to know the truth about God and yet continue to sin?
■ What would Jesus say if He came and preached in our city today?
❇ Why do you think we sometimes become indifferent toward God?

APPLY IT
❇ What specific sin do you need to repent of today?
■ What are three things you could do this week to be a brighter light for Christ in your city or town?
❇ In light of the certain judgment of God, what step could you take this week to reach a lost neighbor or friend?

Matthew 11:25-30

Rest for the Weary

TOPICS

Balance, Burdens, Commitment, Effort, Foolishness, God, Growth, Help, Humility, Legalism, Listening, Obedience, Partnerships, Rest, Submission, Wisdom

OPEN IT

■ If you had one week of vacation in which to recharge your physical and emotional batteries, where would you go to rest, relax, and get rejuvenated?
❊ What sorts of activities absolutely drain the life out of you?
❊ Why are many Christians frazzled and burned out?

EXPLORE IT

❊ After pronouncing woe on several unrepentant cities, what did Jesus do? (11:25)
❊ When did Jesus pray? (11:25)
❊ How did Jesus address God? (11:25)
❊ Why did Jesus say He was praising God? (11:25)
❊ What did Jesus say God had entrusted or committed to Him? (11:27)
❊ Who alone did Jesus say knew Him? (11:27)
❊ Besides himself, who did Jesus say could know God? (11:27)
❊ Who claimed to reveal God to the world? (11:27)
❊ What general invitation did Christ make at this time? (11:28)
■ What kind of people was Jesus addressing? (11:28)
■ What promise did Jesus make to those who would accept His offer? (11:28)
❊ What farming imagery did Jesus use to encourage people to come to Him? (11:29)
❊ How did Jesus describe Himself? (11:29)
■ How is walking with Christ described? (11:30)

GET IT

❊ In your eyes, what about Christ seems so obvious that everyone ought to be able to see it?
❊ Why do you think God hides certain truths from "the wise"?
■ In what ways do you feel weary and burdened right now?
❊ What aspects of the Christian life do you find especially taxing or burdensome?
■ What is it like to experience the promised "rest" of Christ?
❊ How would you describe your walk with Christ right now?

APPLY IT

❊ What are two specific ways you can work with Christ tomorrow instead of going in your own direction?
❊ Besides praying, what are some ways you can get to know your Father in heaven more intimately this week?
■ What burdens will you entrust to Christ today?

Matthew 12:1-14

Lord of the Sabbath

TOPICS

Bitterness, Blindness, Complaining, Criticism, Envy, Hatred, Healing, Hypocrisy, Judging Others, Legalism, Mercy, Rejection, Religion, Sacrifice, Stubbornness

OPEN IT

■ What do you like to do on your day off?
❊ What are some ways laws or rules are twisted to hurt the very people they were designed to help?
❊ What makes certain people in authority behave insensitively or rudely to the very people they ought to be serving?

EXPLORE IT

❊ Where were Jesus and His disciples when they were eating? (12:1)
❊ What difference did the day of the week make? (12:1)
❊ What activity were the disciples involved in? (12:1)
■ How did the Pharisees react when they saw the disciples eating? (12:2)
❊ What biblical precedent did Jesus cite to justify the actions of His followers? (12:3-4)
❊ What, according to Jesus, did the law say about priests and the temple and the Sabbath? (12:5)
❊ Over what honored religious symbol did Jesus claim superiority? (12:6)
■ What did Jesus accuse the Pharisees of failing to understand? (12:7)
■ What did Jesus claim about Himself? (12:8)
❊ Where did Jesus go after clashing with the Pharisees? (12:9)
❊ What miracle did Jesus perform in the synagogue? (12:10, 13)
❊ How did Jesus justify His actions? (12:11-12)
❊ What was the response of the Pharisees? (12:14)

GET IT

❊ What kinds of lawful behavior are Christians often quick to condemn in others?
■ What are some ways we trample over the feelings of others in our quest to be righteous?
■ How do you need to be more compassionate and merciful in your relationships with others?
❊ How do you use God to justify wrong attitudes such as snobbery, jealousy, prejudice, or selfishness?
❊ Why are we unwilling to bend rules for others but quick to rationalize when the rules adversely affect us?
❊ How do you think you would react if an undesirable person (a homeless person or drunk, for example) staggered into your church on Sunday and interrupted your worship service?
❊ What are some man-made symbols or traditions (like the Pharisee's views on the Law, the temple, and the Sabbath) that we value more than people?

APPLY IT

❊ In what specific ways can you show mercy and compassion to a hurting person today?
■ What legalistic rules that keep you from loving people do you need to ignore?

❊ Without being showy, how can you demonstrate today to a nonChristian friend the freedom that you have in Christ?

Matthew 12:15-21
God's Chosen Servant

TOPICS
Enemies, Expectations, Healing, Holy Spirit, Humility, Intimidation, Justice, Messiah, Ministry, Miracles, Prophecy, Rejection, Serving, Victory

OPEN IT
■ What kind of person (character, skills, knowledge) would make for a great national leader?
❊ How would you define justice?
❊ In what ways is our society unjust?
❊ Why do we often get disappointed?

EXPLORE IT
❊ How did Jesus respond to the hostility of the Pharisees? (12:15)
❊ Who accompanied Jesus? (12:15)
❊ What did Jesus do for the people who followed Him? (12:15)
❊ What did Jesus instruct the people He helped to do? (12:16)
❊ Who had foretold this event? (12:17)
■ In the prophetic passage quoted here, how did God identify the Messiah? (12:18)
❊ What message did the prophecy say Christ would preach? (12:18)
❊ How was the personality of Christ described by Isaiah? (12:19)
❊ How did Isaiah predict people would respond to this coming servant of God? (12:19)
■ According to Isaiah, what type of ministry would the Messiah have? (12:20)
■ According to the prophet Isaiah, how would the nations ultimately respond to Christ? (12:21)

GET IT
❊ If you were in charge of scripting the first and second comings of Christ, how would you have arranged them differently?
■ If God were to describe your life and influence right now, what might he say?
❊ What changes, events, and experiences in your life do you attribute to the supernatural work of the Holy Spirit?
❊ In what ways do you seek to bring justice or fairness to your relationships?
❊ How demanding are you?
■ What is the danger in our being quiet, humble, and submissive?

APPLY IT
❊ What are three practical ways you can serve God this week?
■ What specific areas of your life do you need to surrender to the control of the Holy Spirit today?
❊ Over the next few days, how can you bring God's justice and love to someone who is oppressed?

Matthew 12:22-37
Jesus and Beelzebub

TOPICS
Bitterness, Blasphemy, Demons, Denial, Enemies, Evil, Fruit, Hatred, Healing, Holy Spirit, Insults, Jealousy, Judging Others, Legalism, Messiah, Opposition, Rejection, Satan, Sickness, Stubbornness, Unbelievers, Words

OPEN IT
❊ Why are people prone to criticize those who are popular or successful?
■ Why do you think our mouth frequently gets us in trouble?
❊ How would you be affected if someone followed you around and taped all your conversations?
❊ How much demonic activity do you think goes on today?

EXPLORE IT
❊ What kind of man did Jesus heal? (12:22)
❊ How did the onlookers respond? (12:23)
❊ What kind of reaction did the Pharisees have to the miracle Christ did? (12:24)
❊ How did Jesus show the Pharisee's argument to be illogical? (12:25-26)
❊ What did Jesus say to show the significance of His ability to drive out demons? (12:28)
❊ What rationale did Jesus give for casting out demons? (12:29)
❊ What criteria did Jesus give for determining who supported and opposed Him? (12:30)
❊ What did Jesus discuss with the Pharisees? (12:31-32)
■ What did Jesus say a tree's "fruit" reveals? (12:33)
❊ What harsh name did Jesus call the Pharisees? Why? (12:34)
■ What did Jesus claim a person's words reveal? (12:34-35)
■ What will every single person do on the day of judgment? (12:36-37)

GET IT
❊ What is it that convinced you that Jesus is the Son of God and the Savior of the world?
■ How does it make you feel to know that Jesus knows every thought you have?
❊ What are some ways you see Satan at work in the world today?
❊ How do you see the kingdom of God overcoming the evil one?
❊ What evidence could others cite that you are in fact a follower of Jesus Christ?
■ What sins of the tongue are you currently struggling with that indicate a deeper problem in your heart?

APPLY IT
❊ When and how can you best bring your unconfessed sins to God?
■ What are some specific steps you can take this week to avoid sinning in your speech?
❊ What can you begin doing today to develop a pure heart so that your life produces good fruit?

Matthew 12:38-45
The Sign of Jonah

TOPICS
Arguments, Believers, Blindness, Demons, Denial, Evidence, Foolishness, Hardheartedness, Holy Spirit, Rationalizing, Rejection, Stubbornness, Unbelievers, Wisdom

OPEN IT
❊ What are some common uses for signs?
■ Why do some people say they want to see proof that God exists before they will believe in Him?
❊ In your opinion, what is the strongest evidence for God?

EXPLORE IT
❊ Who approached Jesus and demanded a sign? (12:38)
■ What did a hostile group of people ask Jesus to do? (12:38)
■ What kind of people did Jesus say asked for additional miraculous signs? (12:39)
❊ How did Jesus respond to the request for a sign? (12:39)
■ To what proof from history did Jesus point? (12:39-40)
❊ How did Jesus compare Himself to Jonah? (12:40)
❊ Who did Jesus say would one day stand and judge His generation? Why? (12:41)
❊ Why will the "men of Nineveh" be in a position to judge? (12:41)
❊ To what example from history did Jesus point as evidence for His identity? (12:42)
❊ How did "the Queen of the South" respond to Solomon? (12:42)
❊ How did Jesus compare Himself to Solomon? (12:43)
❊ What example did Jesus use to show the importance of ridding one's life of evil attitudes and filling one's life with love for God? (12:43-45)
❊ What did Jesus warn would happen to those who refused to open themselves up to the Lord? (12:45)

GET IT
■ What acts of God do you feel would strengthen your faith?
■ What evidence of God is there in your life that could point others to Christ?
❊ What areas of your life need cleansing?
❊ What specific areas of your life need the filling of the Holy Spirit?
❊ Why is it sometimes hard to believe in God without hard evidence?
❊ What are some subtle ways Satan gains a foothold in the lives of Christians?
❊ Why do you think certain "religious" people are sometimes skeptical about God?

APPLY IT
■ How can you demonstrate the reality of God in your life today?
❊ In what areas of your life do you need the Spirit of God to fill you this week?
❊ In what area has God already revealed to you that you need to obey Him more faithfully?

Matthew 12:46-50
Jesus' Mother and Brothers

TOPICS
Affections, Body, Conflict, Family, Feelings, God's Will, Home, Involvement, Obedience, Pressure, Priorities, Purpose, Unity

OPEN IT
■ What is your fondest family memory?
❊ If you had to belong to a family other than your own, what family would you choose to join? Why?
❊ What is ideal Christian fellowship or community to you?

EXPLORE IT
❊ What was Christ doing when His mother and brothers came to speak to Him? (12:46)
❊ Who was in the crowd? (12:38-46)
■ Who came to find Jesus? Why? (12:46)
❊ Why did Jesus' family want to see Him? (12:46)
❊ How did Jesus find out about His visitors? (12:47)
■ What two rhetorical questions did Jesus pose when He heard about His family's arrival? (12:48)
❊ How did Jesus answer His own questions? (12:49)
❊ What makes a person a member of Jesus' family? (12:50)
■ Who can become a member of Jesus' family? (12:50)
❊ How did Jesus refer to God? (12:50)

GET IT
❊ In what ways (if any) are you closer to certain Christian friends than you are to your own family members?
■ What circumstances led you to want to become a member of God's family?
■ What special bonds does the family of God have that earthly families do not?
❊ What are the dangers if we neglect our families?
❊ What are the risks if we become obsessed with our families?
❊ How are we sometimes guilty of neglecting our blood relatives?
❊ In what ways is it possible to idolize the family?

APPLY IT
■ What could you do today to strengthen the bonds you have with another Christian brother or sister?
❊ To what family member could you communicate your love and concern this week?
❊ What steps can you take this week to ensure that your family ties do not hinder God's will for you?

Matthew 13:1-23
The Parable of the Sower

TOPICS
Bible, Blessing, Compromise, Evangelism, Evidence, Fruit, Growth, Heart, Impulsiveness, Joy, Listening, New Life, Productivity, Prophecy, Timing, Witnessing, World

OPEN IT
■ When was the last time you "tuned out" a speaker?
❊ What are some spiritual clichs or religious catch-phrases that people often use?
❊ What misconceptions do non-Christians have about Christianity?

EXPLORE IT
❊ Where was Jesus when the crowds came? (13:1-2)
❊ Why did Jesus get on a boat to speak? (13:2)
❊ What kind of stories did Jesus use to teach the crowds? (13:3)
❊ The first story that Jesus told His audience was about what? (13:3)
❊ Into what various places did the seed fall? (13:4-5)
❊ Which seed ended up sprouting and bearing fruit? Why? (13:8)
❊ To whom did Jesus direct His story about the four soils? (13:9)
❊ How did the disciples respond to the Parable of the Four Soils? (13:10)
❊ How did Jesus defend His use of parables? (13:11-13)
❊ Why was the majority's inability or unwillingness to understand Christ's message significant? (13:14-15)
❊ Why did Jesus say the disciples were blessed? (13:16-17)
■ Whom did Jesus liken to seed along the path? Why? (13:19)
■ According to Christ, who is like the seed sown on rocky soil? Why? (13:20-21)
■ What kind of people were compared to seed sown among the thorns? Why? (13:22)
❊ Of whom is the fruitful seed a picture? How? (13:23)

GET IT
❊ How do stories and illustrations help us to understand more clearly the message of the Bible?
❊ How involved are you in "sowing the seed" of God's Word?
❊ What kind of soil would you say you are at this point in your life?
■ What are some thorns that tend to choke out your Christian faith?
■ What circumstances have a tendency to scorch your faith and cause it to wither?
❊ How long did it take for you to understand the gospel of Christ?
❊ How could you listen more faithfully and intently to the voice of God?

APPLY IT
■ What one action could you do this week to improve the way you listen to God's Word?
❊ How could you become a more effective sower of God's Word over the next month?
❊ How can you show gratitude to God today for opening your eyes to the truth of the gospel?

Matthew 13:24-30
The Parable of the Weeds

TOPICS
Appearance, Danger, Enemies, Fruit, Hell, Image, Judging Others, Judgment, Kingdom of God/Heaven, Life-style, Lost, Majority, People, Punishment, Satan, Unbelievers

OPEN IT
❊ What kind of gardening have you done?
❊ What is your least favorite type of yard work? Why?
■ Why do people dislike weeds?

EXPLORE IT
❊ What did Jesus use to communicate His point? (13:24)
❊ What was Jesus talking about in this passage? (13:24)
❊ To what did Jesus compare His topic? (13:24)
❊ In the Parable of the Weeds, what happened while the farmer slept? (13:25)
❊ What appeared in the farmer's field besides the wheat he had planted? (13:26)
❊ How did the owner's servants react when they found weeds in the field? (13:27)
❊ How did the owner reply to his servants? (13:28)
■ What did the servants volunteer to do for the owner of the field? (13:28)
■ On what grounds did the owner turn down the servant's suggestion? (13:29)
■ What plan of action did the owner choose? (13:30)

GET IT
❊ How would you respond if you tried to get a Bible study going and a group of non-Christians showed up to give you a hard time?
❊ What are some ways Christians blend in with non-Christians?
❊ What do you think about Christians who try to isolate themselves completely from non-Christians?
❊ What opportunities do you have by living among all different kinds of people?
■ In what ways does Satan try to mess up God's plan and your part in that plan?
❊ What dangers lie in trying to label people as either "weeds" or "wheat" (non-Christians or Christians)?
❊ Whose responsibility is it to label the weeds and deal with them?
■ Under what circumstances are you to live for Christ?

APPLY IT
■ In what ways do you need to alter your lifestyle (either attitude or action) today in order to be more like wheat and less like a weed?
❊ Whom do you need to judge and label less today?
❊ For what nonChristian coworkers, neighbors, and friends will you pray this week?

Matthew 13:31-35

The Parables of the Mustard Seed and the Yeast

TOPICS
Expectations, Growth, Influence, Kingdom of God/Heaven, Power, Prophecy, Quality, Results, Simplicity, Success, Surprises

OPEN IT
■ What small or seemingly insignificant possession is worth a great deal to you? Why?
❇ What are some big or important events that start out very small?
❇ What ingredients make for great storytelling?
❇ What is one fairytale you remember from childhood that you still enjoy today?

EXPLORE IT
❇ What did Jesus tell the crowd? (13:31)
❇ In the Parable of the Mustard Seed, what did the man do with the seed? (13:31)
■ To what kind of seed did Christ compare the kingdom of heaven? Why? (13:31-32)
■ How does the mustard seed compare to others in size? (13:32)
■ What is a mustard seed like when it is fully grown? (13:32)
❇ Besides bearing fruit, how is a mustard plant useful? (13:32)
❇ In the Parable of the Yeast, to what did Christ liken the kingdom of heaven? (13:33)
❇ How does yeast work? (13:33)
❇ In addition to parables, how else did Jesus get His point across to the crowd? (13:34)
❇ Why was Jesus' use of parables significant? (13:35)

GET IT
❇ In what small or seemingly insignificant ways has God worked in your life?
■ How can a Christian be a positive presence among his or her nonChristian friends and relatives?
❇ What are some ways God might use a person to spread the gospel in a place where there is little Christian influence?
❇ What are some little things we can do to make a big impact for Christ?
■ What does this passage say to those who don't feel talented, gifted, or brilliant?
❇ In what ways has your Christian life grown to bless others (like the mustard seed becoming a big tree)?

APPLY IT
■ What is one way you could quietly help the gospel permeate your family, workplace, or circle of friends?
❇ What illustrations, examples, or stories can you share with someone today to help him or her understand your faith in Christ?
❇ What prayer can you begin praying this week to cause the gospel to spread?

Matthew 13:36-43

The Parable of the Weeds Explained

TOPICS
Angels, Enemies, Future, Grief, Hell, Jesus Christ, Judgment, Kingdom of God/Heaven, Listening, Lost, Majority, Mourning, Punishment, Righteousness, Satan, Sin, Unbelievers, World

OPEN IT
❇ What school subject or subjects did you find difficult? Why?
■ What are your beliefs about the future of the world?
❇ Why are many people eager to believe in heaven but reluctant to believe in hell?

EXPLORE IT
❇ Where did Jesus go upon leaving His audience? (13:36)
❇ Who came to Jesus for further discussion? Why? (13:36)
❇ What specific story did Jesus' audience want explained to them? (13:36)
■ In the Parable of the Weeds, whom did the sower represent? How? (13:37)
■ What did the field represent? In what way? (13:38)
■ What groups of people are illustrated by good seed and weeds? (13:38)
❇ Who does the enemy who sowed the bad seed represent? (13:39)
❇ What future event is symbolized by the harvest? (13:39)
❇ Whom do the harvesters represent? (13:39)
❇ The burning of the weeds symbolizes what future event? (13:40-42)
❇ What will happen to those who are thrown "into the fiery furnace"? (13:42)
❇ What is the future for the righteous? (13:43)

GET IT
❇ How do you study the Bible in order to understand better what Christ has said?
❇ If we seldom pick up the Bible or spend time praying, what do our actions say about us?
■ If you had to guess, what would you estimate to be the ratio of "wheat" to "weeds" in your office, town, neighborhood, or school?
■ How do these kinds of passages (threats of judgment for unbelievers) make you feel?
❇ In which category (wheat or weed) would your associates place you? Why?
❇ What does this passage say to you about the prospect of the world getting better and better?

APPLY IT
■ In what ways can you "shine like the sun" in your contacts with unbelievers?
❇ What passage of Scripture do you need to ask God about and study this week?
❇ How could you minister to someone today with a quote or insight from the Bible?

Matthew 13:44-46

The Parables of the Hidden Treasure and the Pearl

TOPICS
Celebration, Commitment, Dedication, Desires, Joy, Kingdom of God/Heaven, Perspective, Priorities, Satisfaction, Value, Wealth

OPEN IT
■ What two or three expensive items do you wish you could afford?
❊ What are some good ways to determine what our priorities really are?
❊ What is the difference between value and price?
❊ How is the value of something determined?

EXPLORE IT
■ What is like treasure hidden in a field? How? (13:44)
❊ What is the kingdom of heaven like? Why? (13:44)
❊ Where was treasure hidden? (13:44)
❊ What happened when the man uncovered the hidden treasure? (13:44)
■ How did the man feel when he discovered the treasure? (13:44)
❊ How badly did the man want the treasure? (13:44)
❊ To what did Christ compare the kingdom of heaven? Why? (13:45)
❊ What did the man in the parable find? (13:46)
❊ How valuable was the pearl? (13:47)
■ How did the man who found the pearl react to its discovery? (13:47)

GET IT
■ If the gospel is true and heaven is our destiny, why are we often "ho-hum" about Christ and the Christian life?
■ How can we recover the joy and excitement that we had when we first met Christ?
❊ What sacrifices are you willing to make in order to fully embrace Christ and His kingdom?
❊ When, if ever, has your faith cost you something?
❊ What relationships, possessions, or personal ambitions are you reluctant to give up for Christ?
❊ What would you say to a someone who says that you can be a good Christian without completely "selling all" to follow Christ?
❊ Other than buried treasure or a precious pearl, what illustrations could you use to explain to a friend the value of knowing Christ?

APPLY IT
❊ What items do you need to "sell off" this week in order to follow Christ and His kingdom?
❊ With what person will you try to share the wealth you have in Christ today or tomorrow?
■ What first step will you take today to recover the joy of knowing Christ?

Matthew 13:47-52

The Parable of the Net

TOPICS
Angels, Evil, Future, Grief, Hell, Judgment, Kingdom of God/Heaven, Mourning, Punishment, Righteousness, Surprises, Unbelievers

OPEN IT
■ What is your favorite "fish story"?
❊ When someone says the word "angel," what kind of images come to mind?
❊ What one question would you like to ask God about heaven?

EXPLORE IT
■ To what did Jesus compare the kingdom of heaven? (13:47)
■ How was the net used, and what was the result? (13:47)
❊ In the Parable of the Net, what did the fishermen do with the full net? (13:48)
❊ What happened to the good fish? (13:48)
❊ What happened to the bad fish? (13:48)
■ Why did Jesus use this analogy? (13:49)
❊ What group did the fishermen in the story represent? (13:49)
❊ Jesus interpreted His parable to say that wicked people can expect what kind of eternal destiny? (13:50)
❊ What question did Jesus ask His disciples when He finished teaching? (13:51)
❊ How did the disciples answer Jesus' question? (13:51)
❊ To what did Jesus compare those in His audience who knew about the Old Testament law and the kingdom of heaven to come? (13:52)

GET IT
❊ What do you think it would have been like to hear Jesus teach about heaven?
❊ Since Jesus is in the fishing business, what can you do to help Him catch men and women?
❊ Why are we often reluctant to talk about hell?
❊ What could you say to a friend who expressed doubts about hell?
■ How would it alter the way we live if we kept in mind the fact that God will judge us?
■ How can we live more often with the wonder of heaven in mind?
❊ What new insight into God's kingdom do you have as a result of studying this passage?

APPLY IT
❊ What reminders can you use today to help you pray for nonChristian friends and relatives?
❊ In what way can you remind yourself of heaven this week?
■ How can you show your gratitude to God today for making you a "good fish"?

Matthew 13:53-58
A Prophet Without Honor

TOPICS
Acceptance, Accusation, Change, Conversation, Criticism, Doubt, Faithfulness, Family, Forgiveness, Habits, History, Honor, Image, New Life, Perseverance, Reputation, Surprises

OPEN IT
■ What do you like best and least about your hometown?
❊ What would your family say you were like as a little kid?
❊ How would your high school or college friends react if they heard you were in a serious Bible study?
❊ What former classmate has surprised you since you graduated from high school? Why?

EXPLORE IT
❊ What did Jesus do when He finished telling His parables? (13:53)
❊ Where did Jesus go? (13:54)
■ What did Jesus do in His hometown? (13:54)
❊ Where exactly did Jesus preach? (13:54)
❊ What was the public response to Jesus' message? (13:54)
❊ What kinds of questions were the folks in Nazareth asking? (13:55)
❊ What family ties did the townspeople of Nazareth recognize Jesus as having? (13:55)
■ How did the people feel about "one of their own" saying wise things and doing amazing miracles? (13:57)
❊ How did Jesus explain their reaction to Him? (13:57)
■ What did Jesus not do in Nazareth—at least in any great amount? Why? (13:58)
❊ What caused Jesus to refrain from doing miracles in Nazareth? (13:58)

GET IT
❊ How would you react if a guy from your neighborhood started doing miracles and claiming to be God?
❊ What are some ways we limit the work of Christ by our unbelief?
❊ Why are we more often impressed by people we don't know than by people we do know?
❊ Why do we have a tendency to downplay the accomplishments of people we are close to?
■ How did your family react when you placed your trust in Christ?
■ In what ways do you struggle to live down your past?

APPLY IT
❊ What are three things you need to trust Christ for in the coming week?
❊ How can you strengthen your faith in Jesus during this time so that He can work in and through you?
■ What family members or old friends will you commit to visit or call in the next month to tell them about the change Christ is making in you?

Matthew 14:1-12
John the Baptist Beheaded

TOPICS
Adultery, Bitterness, Consequences, Correction, Danger, Deceit, Discipline, Embarrassment, Foolishness, Impulsiveness, Injustice, Motives, Obedience, Peer Pressure, Pride, Responsibility, Sin, Stubbornness, Toleration

OPEN IT
❊ What, in your opinion, would be the preferred way to die?
■ What do you remember from your junior high and high school dances?
❊ What makes peer pressure difficult to resist?
❊ How does peer pressure become more sophisticated as we get older?

EXPLORE IT
❊ What powerful political figure heard about all the things Christ was doing? (14:1)
❊ What explanation did Herod have for the miracles Christ was doing? (14:2)
❊ What had Herod done to John the Baptist? (14:3)
■ Why did Herod put John in prison? (14:3)
❊ For what reason had John been rebuking Herod? (14:4)
❊ How did Herod react to John's reprimand? (14:5)
■ Why didn't Herod act on his wishes? (14:5)
❊ What happened on Herod's birthday? (14:6-7)
❊ What promise did Herod make to the daughter of Herodias? (14:7)
❊ Who was behind the plot to murder John? (14:8)
❊ How did Herod feel when he realized he'd been tricked? (14:9)
■ Why did Herod carry out the execution of John? (14:9)
❊ What happened in the aftermath of John's execution? (14:12)

GET IT
■ What situations make you most susceptible to peer pressure?
❊ In what ways do you promise more than you can (or should) deliver?
❊ Why do people hate to be corrected?
❊ What grandiose promises have you made and later regretted?
■ What should you do if you make a promise that pressures you to compromise or to do the wrong thing?
❊ What does a person's reaction to correction tell you about him or her?
❊ In what ways have you sensed danger or risk just by living for Christ?
❊ What impulsive words have later come back to haunt you?
❊ How would you react if your pastor or a spiritual mentor was brutally murdered?
❊ What correction have you recently received from an older and more mature Christian?

APPLY IT
■ What can you do to strengthen yourself against peer pressure this week?

❊ What reminder can help you refrain from making foolish promises in coming weeks?
❊ What can you do this week to respond to some correction you recently received?

Matthew 14:13-21
Jesus Feeds the Five Thousand

TOPICS
Compassion, Confidence, Delegation, Gifts, Help, Learning, Limitations, Ministry, Miracles, Quiet, Selfishness, Thankfulness, Trust

OPEN IT
■ What is your favorite restaurant in all the world? Why?
❊ What food do you never seem to tire of?
❊ Where do you go when you want to be alone?

EXPLORE IT
❊ How did Jesus respond to the death of John the Baptist? (14:13)
❊ Who came looking for Jesus? Why? (14:13)
❊ Who met Jesus at the shore? (14:14)
❊ What did Jesus do for the people that came to see Him? (14:14)
❊ What happened when it started getting dark? (14:15)
■ What did the disciples want Jesus to tell the crowds? Why? (14:15)
■ How did Jesus respond to the disciples' suggestion? (14:16)
❊ What did Jesus tell the disciples to do for the crowds? (14:16)
❊ How did the disciples react to Jesus' unusual request? (14:17)
❊ After having the crowd sit on the grass, what did Jesus do? (14:19)
❊ How much food did Jesus begin with? (14:19)
❊ How was the food distributed? (14:19)
❊ How much food was available to each person? (14:20)
❊ How much food was left over? (14:20)
■ How large a crowd was fed? (14:21)

GET IT
❊ Why is it important for us to spend regular time alone with God?
❊ What thoughts typically run through your mind when you see a big crowd of people?
❊ Why is it harder to be kind at certain times than at others?
❊ Why should we pray before meals?
❊ What is it about food that breaks down barriers between people and gives us opportunities to talk with them?
■ How would you have felt in the disciples' shoes?
■ What does this passage tell you about God?

APPLY IT
■ What gift, ability, or resource (no matter how insignificant) will you give to God today so that he can bless it and multiply it?
❊ To what quiet place will you go this week for a couple of hours to get away from your busyness, review your priorities, and let God renew your spirit?
❊ How can you minister to someone in need today?

Matthew 14:22-36
Jesus Walks on the Water

TOPICS
Believe, Challenge, Courage, Depend, Faith, Fear, Healing, Help, Miracles, Perspective, Protection, Security, Strength, Trust, Victory

OPEN IT
■ What is the most frightening experience you've ever had?
❊ What is the most worshipful experience you have ever had?
❊ Of all of Christ's miracles, which one would you most like to have witnessed? Why?

EXPLORE IT
❊ After feeding the crowd of five thousand people, what instructions did Jesus give His disciples? (14:22)
❊ Where did Jesus go after He dismissed the crowd? Why? (14:23)
❊ What did Jesus do on the mountain? (14:23)
❊ Where were the disciples when evening came? (14:24)
■ What conditions were the disciples encountering? (14:24)
■ What miracle did Christ perform? (14:25)
■ How did the disciples react to what they saw? (14:26)
❊ How did Jesus try to calm the disciples' fears? (14:27)
❊ What did Peter ask Jesus to do? (14:28)
❊ How did Jesus respond to Peter's request? (14:29)
❊ What happened to Peter as he made his way toward Jesus? (14:29-30)
❊ What did Jesus do and say when Peter got in trouble? (14:31)
❊ What was the consensus reaction to this amazing sequence of events? (14:33)
❊ What happened when Jesus and His disciples arrived at their destination? (14:35-36)

GET IT
❊ Why do you think Jesus spent time alone praying?
❊ How is your devotional life right now?
❊ What causes you to doubt and waver in your faith?
■ What situations cause you the most fear in life?
❊ How would you rate your faith on a scale from one to five (one being weak, five being strong)? Why?
❊ What events or experiences have led you to trust in Jesus?
■ What does this passage teach you to do?

APPLY IT
❊ What specific step could you take this week to improve your devotional life?
■ In what practical way can you demonstrate faith as you go through the coming week?
❊ What step of trust do you need to take today?
❊ What will help you remember to keep your eyes on Jesus and off your fears?

Matthew 15:1-20
Clean and Unclean

TOPICS
Appearance, Deceit, Disobedience, Hypocrisy, Interpretation, Law, Legalism, New Covenant, Pride, Purity, Rebellion, Religion, Self-righteousness, Stubbornness, Teaching, Thinking, Traditions, Worship

OPEN IT
■ What traditions have special meaning to you?
✻ Why do people value tradition?
✻ If you had to rank the five worst sins, what would your list include?

EXPLORE IT
✻ Who came from Jerusalem to see Christ? Why? (15:1)
✻ What complaint did the Pharisees and teachers of the law level against Jesus? (15:2)
✻ What did the Pharisees and teachers of the law value more than the Word of God? (15:2)
✻ What did Jesus cite as examples of the Pharisees' disobedience? (15:4)
✻ How did the Pharisees get around the requirements of the Law? (15:5)
■ What was wrong with the Pharisees? (15:7-9)
✻ What Scripture did Jesus apply to the Pharisees? (15:8-9)
■ How did Jesus shift the emphasis away from external issues like unclean and clean foods? (15:10-11)
✻ How did the Pharisees like Jesus' statements? (15:12)
✻ What advice did Jesus give to followers of the Pharisees? (15:14)
✻ Why did Jesus explain His statements to His disciples? (15:15)
■ How did Jesus redefine "unclean"? (15:17-20)

GET IT
■ How is it possible for us to be "religious" and yet be far from God?
✻ In what ways are we sometimes like the Pharisees?
■ What are some ways we "go through the motions" of the Christian life?
✻ Why do we sometimes use loopholes or rationalizations to avoid doing the right thing?
✻ What matters more: how people behave or their motives and attitudes?
✻ In what way do Christians get bogged down in unnecessary rules?
✻ What advice would you give a Christian friend who is far away from God?
✻ In what ways have you allowed man-made rules to obscure the spirit of the law (and the work of the Holy Spirit in your life)?

APPLY IT
✻ What is one step can you take to develop a pure heart this week?
✻ How can you nurture your love for God through your actions at work and at home over the next few days?
■ This week, what could help you keep your focus on Christ rather than mere outward conformity to rules?

Matthew 15:21-28
The Faith of the Canaanite Woman

TOPICS
Answers, Believe, Caring, Compassion, Delay, Demons, Determination, Faith, Healing, Help, Insensitivity, Perseverance, Persistence, Results, Testing, Victory

OPEN IT
■ What is it like to be on the outside of a group looking in?
✻ What behavior on the part of others absolutely drives you up the wall?
✻ What is your greatest success (in the sense of pursuing a goal for a long time and finally reaching it through persistence and determination)?
✻ What is the most desperate feeling and/or situation you have ever experienced?

EXPLORE IT
✻ To where did Jesus withdraw? When? (15:21)
✻ Who approached Jesus when He reached Gentile territory? (15:22)
✻ What frantic request did the Canaanite woman make of Jesus? (15:22)
✻ What was Jesus' response to the Canaanite woman's request? (15:23)
✻ What did the disciples urge Jesus to do? (15:23)
✻ How did Jesus answer His disciples? (15:24)
✻ How did the discussion between Christ and His disciples deter the woman in need of help? (15:25)
■ What reason did Jesus give for being reluctant to help the woman? (15:26)
■ What quick and insightful reply did the woman make to Christ? (15:27)
■ How did Jesus praise the woman? (15:28)
✻ What happened in the end? (15:28)

GET IT
✻ In what ways do you tend to be insensitive to those who are different?
✻ Why do you think Christ responded to this woman as He did?
✻ What kinds of lessons do we learn from waiting?
■ How does our persistence in prayer show God's character?
■ How persistent are you in your prayers to God?
✻ What would Jesus say about your faith today?

APPLY IT
■ What long-term, unanswered prayer request do you need to continue bringing before God on a regular basis?
✻ What encouraging principle from this passage can you share today with a Christian brother or sister?
✻ What individual in need of help do you need to assist today?

Matthew 15:29-39
Jesus Feeds the Four Thousand

TOPICS
Compassion, Delegation, Healing, Instructions, Miracles, Obedience, Praise, Resources, Serving, Submission, Worship

OPEN IT
✻ At what kind of restaurants do you like to eat?
✻ What is your favorite food?
■ What recent news regarding hunger or poverty have you heard?

EXPLORE IT
✻ When Jesus left the region of Tyre and Sidon, where did He go? (15:29)
✻ At what specific place did Jesus set up His "doctor's office"? (15:29)
✻ How many people came to Jesus? Why? (15:30)
✻ What are some of the diseases and ailments that Jesus cured? (15:30)
✻ How did the healings affect all those who watched? (15:31)
■ What note of concern did Jesus share with His disciples after He healed the people? (15:32)
✻ How did the disciples respond to Jesus' desire? (15:33)
■ Where did Jesus turn to feed the crowd? (15:34)
✻ How did the disciples' resources at that moment compare with the food at their disposal the last time they fed a hungry crowd (see Matthew 14:13-21)? (15:34)
✻ What instructions did Jesus give the crowd? (15:35)
✻ What procedures did Jesus follow in feeding this large crowd? (15:36)
■ How much food was left over? (15:37)
✻ How many people participated in this all-you-can-eat meal? (15:38)
✻ Where did Jesus then go? (15:39)

GET IT
✻ Why do you think the disciples failed to remember the previous instance of Christ feeding a large crowd?
✻ How do you think you would have responded if you had been with Jesus on this occasion?
✻ How can we remember God's past actions?
■ What feelings do you have toward the less fortunate?
■ Why do you think God works through us when he could get things done better and faster by doing miracles?
✻ How can we develop love for Christ so we avoid taking His blessings for granted?
✻ What small thing or resource can you offer to God?
✻ What experience from the past reminds you of God's work in your life?

APPLY IT
✻ What can you do today to feed someone spiritually?
■ How does God want you to meet the physical needs of someone in your life?
✻ For what specific blessings do you need to express your gratitude to God today?

Matthew 16:1-4
The Demand for a Sign

TOPICS
Answers, Attitude, Barriers, Discernment, Disobedience, Ego, Expectations, Humility, Knowledge, Learning, Pride, Rationalizing, Respect, Satisfaction, Understanding, Wisdom

OPEN IT
■ What are some examples of signs?
✻ What is your favorite season of the year? Why?
✻ What positive signs give you reason to be optimistic about the days ahead?
✻ What negative signs tell you that the world is getting worse?

EXPLORE IT
■ Who approached Jesus? (16:1)
✻ What were the people who approached Jesus really doing? (16:1)
■ What request did the people make of Jesus? (16:1)
✻ Jesus answered the Pharisees and Sadducees by talking about what? (16:2)
✻ What did a red sky at night mean in this context? (16:2)
✻ What did a red sunrise indicate in this context? (16:3)
■ Why did Jesus chastise the Pharisees and Sadducees? (16:3-4)
✻ What kind of generation did Jesus say looks for a sign? (16:4)
✻ What single sign did Jesus offer? (16:4)
✻ What did Jesus do after speaking with the Pharisees and Sadducees? (16:4)

GET IT
✻ What signs do we already have of Jesus' power?
✻ Why do you think these religious leaders sought a miraculous sign?
✻ What are some ways we try to put God to the test?
■ What demands or performance requirements do we sometimes place on God?
✻ Why would many of your nonChristian friends still not believe in Jesus even if they saw Him do a miracle?
✻ How would you answer someone who said, "I'll believe in God when I see Him do a miracle right before my eyes"?
■ What signs or proofs of God's power does our generation already have?

APPLY IT
■ What are some ways you could use nature or the Bible to share the truth of Christ with a friend?
✻ In what way can you show your faith in Christ this week?
✻ What has God done in your life that you can use as a sign to others?

Matthew 16:5-12
The Yeast of the Pharisees and Sadducees

TOPICS
Beliefs, Blindness, Danger, Deceit, Discernment, Evil, Faith, Heresy, Ignorance, Influence, Listening, Purity, Separation, Truth, Understanding

OPEN IT
❊ What dates or events do you have a hard time remembering?
■ How has a simple case of misunderstanding recently created problems for you?
❊ What philosophies or widely believed ideas do you feel are dangerous?

EXPLORE IT
❊ Where were Jesus and His disciples traveling? (16:5)
❊ What did the disciples forget to pack? (16:5)
❊ What warning did Jesus issue to His followers? (16:6)
■ Whom did Jesus mention in His warning? (16:6)
■ How did the disciples misunderstand Jesus' comments? (16:7)
❊ What did Jesus say the disciples lacked? (16:8)
❊ What did Jesus' disciples fail to understand? (16:9)
❊ What did Jesus' disciples forget? (16:9)
❊ What recent incidents did Jesus cite to make His point? (16:9-10)
❊ How did Jesus clarify His remarks about yeast? (16:11)
■ What was Jesus encouraging His disciples to avoid? Why? (16:11-12)
❊ What happened when Jesus explained His words? (16:12)

GET IT
■ What truths about God do you have a hard time understanding?
❊ What spiritual lessons and truths do you have a tendency to forget?
❊ How can one wrong idea get us into trouble?
❊ What are some ways we get so caught up in the mundane details of life that we miss the bigger-than-life lessons God wants to teach us?
❊ What forgotten experiences or neglected truths do you need to reflect upon more?
■ How can we judge whether the spiritual teaching we receive is healthy or dangerous?

APPLY IT
■ What can you do today to become more sensitive to what God is trying to teach you through His Word?
❊ What nonjudgmental and nonthreatening step can you take this week to warn a friend who is being led astray by unsound teaching?
❊ What small evil do you need to root out of your life this week before it spreads and causes much trouble?

Matthew 16:13-20
Peter's Confession of Christ

TOPICS
Assumptions, Beliefs, Blindness, Church, Confusion, Discernment, Ignorance, Insight, Jesus Christ, Knowledge, Leadership, Messiah, Opinions, Trust, Words

OPEN IT
■ If you could ask any person any question, whom would you ask, and what would you want to know?
❊ In what ways do you consider yourself blessed?
❊ How would you describe an ideal church?

EXPLORE IT
❊ In what region did the events of this passage take place? (16:13)
❊ What broad, impersonal question did Jesus ask His disciples? (16:13)
❊ What different answers did Christ get to His question? (16:14)
■ What pointed personal question did Christ ask His followers? (16:15)
❊ Who spoke up in answer to Christ's question? (16:16)
■ What answer did Peter give? (16:16)
❊ Why was Peter blessed? (16:17)
■ In what way is coming to faith and understanding the gospel a supernatural event? (16:17)
❊ What kind of leadership role did Jesus predict for Peter? (16:18)
❊ What did Jesus promise about the Church? (16:18)
❊ What authority did Jesus promise to Peter? (16:19)
❊ Against what did Jesus warn His disciples at the conclusion of this discussion? (16:20)

GET IT
■ What are some common views of Jesus among our generation?
❊ Who do you say Jesus is?
❊ What happened the first time you spoke publicly about your faith in Christ?
■ What difference does it make what we believe about Jesus?
❊ What forces try to hinder God's work today?
❊ Why should churches not be discouraged in their efforts to carry out God's work?

APPLY IT
❊ What part in the building of Christ's Church do you have now?
■ What can you do or say to help a friend overcome an erroneous idea about Jesus this week?
❊ What are three ways you could make a public statement of your faith in Christ?

Matthew 16:21-28
Jesus Predicts His Death

TOPICS

Affections, Angels, Basics of the Faith, Commitment, Courage, Dedication, Devotion, Enemies, God's Will, Jesus Christ, Kingdom of God/Heaven, Last Days, Loyalty, Opposition, Perspective, Priorities, Resurrection, Sacrifice, Second Coming, Sin, Submission, Victory

OPEN IT

■ What are some ways people try to "find themselves"?
❊ What is the most surprised you have ever been?
❊ What is the best reward you've ever received?

EXPLORE IT

❊ What did Christ begin telling His disciples would eventually happen to Him? (16:21)
❊ How did Christ say He would suffer? (16:21)
❊ Who did Christ say would oppose Him and make Him suffer? (16:21)
❊ What did Christ say would happen after He was killed? (16:21)
❊ How did Peter react to the news that Jesus would suffer and die? (16:22)
❊ How did Jesus characterize Peter's objections? (16:23)
■ What is required of the one who would follow Jesus? (16:24)
■ What two ways can a person lose his or her life? (16:25)
■ A person's soul is more valuable than what? How? (16:26)
❊ What did Jesus say would happen after His death and resurrection? (16:27)
❊ What will happen after Christ returns? (16:27)
❊ What did Jesus promise His disciples? (16:28)

GET IT

❊ How would you live differently if you knew exactly when and how you were going to die?
❊ How does it make you feel to realize that Jesus willingly died for your sins?
❊ If a person's soul is worth more than the whole world, how ought that affect the way we spend our time?
❊ What would change in your life if you denied yourself for Christ's sake?
■ What does it mean to you to "take up your cross" and follow Jesus?
■ In what situations do you find it difficult to follow Christ?
❊ How should eternal rewards motivate us to live for Christ?

APPLY IT

❊ What do you need to do this week to center your thoughts on the things of God?
❊ What is one way you can deny yourself today for Christ's sake?
■ What change in your weekly schedule could you make to better reflect what God considers important?

Matthew 17:1-13
The Transfiguration

TOPICS

Appearance, Devotion, Experience, Glory, God, Heaven, Holiness, Jesus Christ, Kingdom of God/Heaven, Listening, Power, Words, Worship

OPEN IT

■ What is the most spectacular event you have ever witnessed?
❊ What is the most embarrassing thing you've ever done or said?
❊ If you received an all-expense-paid trip for four to Europe, who would you take with you?

EXPLORE IT

❊ How much time elapsed between Christ's prediction of his death and the Transfiguration? (17:1)
❊ Which three disciples were with Christ on the mountain? (17:1)
■ Where did Christ and his three disciples go? (17:1)
■ What happened to Christ on the mountain? (17:2)
❊ Who else appeared and began talking to Jesus? (17:3)
❊ What did Peter volunteer to do? (17:4)
❊ What do you think prompted Peter to say he would build shelters? (17:4)
❊ What happened while Peter was speaking? (17:5)
■ How did the disciples react when God spoke out of the cloud? (17:6)
❊ Who calmed down the disciples? (17:7)
❊ What did Jesus say to the disciples as they departed? (17:9)
❊ What question did the disciples ask Jesus? (17:10)
❊ How did Jesus answer the disciples? (17:11-12)
❊ What did the disciples learn about John the Baptist? (17:13)

GET IT

❊ How would you have reacted if you had been with Christ for the Transfiguration?
❊ What does this passage tell you about the relationship between Jesus and God the Father?
■ What memories or insights do you think Peter, James, and John took home with them from this incident?
■ In what way is it difficult for us to worship God?
❊ How might seeing Christ in all His glory prompt us to obey Him more completely?
❊ In what ways does God reveal Himself to us today?

APPLY IT

❊ How can you make an effort to listen to Jesus this week?
❊ What could you do today to give Christ the glory He deserves?
■ What could you do over the next three months to become more adept and more faithful in worshiping God?

Matthew 17:14-23

The Healing of a Boy With a Demon

TOPICS

Abilities, Atonement, Authority, Death, Demons, Faith, Fasting, Grief, Healing, Miracles, Power, Prayer, Resurrection, Sin, Spiritual Disciplines, Trust

OPEN IT

■ How does it feel to have a problem you can't solve?
❇ Where is the line between being obsessed with death and never coming to grips with your mortality?
❇ Why do some people seem to have greater faith than others?

EXPLORE IT

❇ When Jesus returned with Peter, James, and John from the scene of the Transfiguration, what did he find? (17:14)
❇ Who approached Jesus? How? (17:14)
❇ What did the man who approached Jesus say? (17:15)
■ How did the man describe his child's situation? (17:15)
■ Who had already been unable to help the man's son? (17:16)
■ What reply did Jesus give when the man said Jesus' disciples had been unable to help? (17:17)
❇ How did Jesus resolve the problem presented to Him? (17:17-18)
❇ What question did the disciples ask Jesus? When? (17:19)
❇ How did Jesus answer his disciples' question? (17:20)
❇ What did Jesus say is the answer to the impossible? (17:20)
❇ What spiritual disciplines did Jesus recommend for confronting serious obstacles? (17:21)
❇ What sober subject did Jesus again bring up when the disciples came together in Galilee? (17:22-23)

GET IT

❇ How do you imagine the nine disciples felt as they attempted to cast the demon out of this man's boy?
❇ How do you think the disciples felt later when Jesus rebuked them?
■ Why do you think Jesus was upset by His disciples' lack of faith?
❇ What do you see as the purpose for fasting?
■ In what areas of your life do you find it difficult to believe and trust in God?
❇ If we truly believe in heaven and that we'll see our fellow Christians again in eternity, why do we grieve when a Christian dies?

APPLY IT

■ What impossible task can you assault with your faith this week?
❇ What spiritual discipline will you practice this week?
❇ How can you help someone who is hurting today?

Matthew 17:24-27

The Temple Tax

TOPICS

Citizenship, Government, Influence, Integrity, Miracles, Obedience, Obligation, Reputation, Responsibility, Submission

OPEN IT

■ How would you go about reforming the tax laws in this country?
❇ Why is it tempting to cheat on our taxes?
❇ How involved should Christians be in government?

EXPLORE IT

❇ When did Jesus and His disciples speak with the tax collectors? (17:24)
❇ Whom did Jesus and His disciples encounter upon their arrival in Capernaum? (17:24)
❇ What question did the tax collectors ask Peter? (17:24)
■ How did Peter respond to the tax collectors' questions? (17:25)
❇ Who spoke to Peter first when Peter entered the house? Why? (17:25)
❇ What tax question did Jesus ask Peter? (17:25)
❇ How did Peter answer Jesus? (17:26)
■ What did Jesus say about the obligation to pay taxes? (17:26)
■ Why did Jesus agree to pay the temple tax? (17:27)
❇ What unusual directions did Jesus give Peter for coming up with the money to pay the temple tax? (17:27)

GET IT

❇ In what ways do Christians not fit in or belong in our culture?
■ Why should we pay taxes?
❇ How do God's laws and human laws fit together?
❇ In what ways (if any) are Christians "above the law"?
❇ How do nonChristians react when Christians act as if they don't have to comply with worldly laws?
■ What are the pros and cons of churches being exempt from taxes?
❇ How is it possible for us to both serve Christ and obey the government?

APPLY IT

❇ How does your behavior need to change this week so you can better represent Christ as his ambassador in the world?
■ What changes do you need to make the next time you do your taxes to make sure you pay all that you owe?
❇ What areas of your life do you need to place under the control of the Holy Spirit today?

Matthew 18:1-9
The Greatest in the Kingdom of Heaven

TOPICS
Children, Evil, Example, Greatness, Humility, Influence, Purity, Responsibility, Simplicity, Sin, World

OPEN IT
❋ Who is the greatest person you know?
❋ Why is our culture so competitive—obsessed with the best and the greatest?
❋ What is your favorite childhood memory?
■ What do you miss most about being a little kid?
❋ What advice would you give to a thousand third graders?

EXPLORE IT
■ What question did the disciples ask Jesus? (18:1)
■ What did Christ do to illustrate His answer to the disciples' question? (18:2)
❋ What did Jesus say one had to be like in order to enter the kingdom of heaven? (18:3)
❋ How did Jesus finally answer the question that had been put to Him? (18:4)
■ What quality makes for true greatness? (18:4)
❋ Why did Jesus say a person's treatment of children was significant? (18:5)
❋ What advice did Jesus give to those who would cause a young follower of Christ to sin? (18:6)
❋ What "woes" did Jesus pronounce in this situation? (18:7)
❋ What comment did Jesus make that suggests the inevitability of sin in this world? (18:7)
❋ What radical figures of speech did Christ use to show the severity of sin? How? (18:8-9)
❋ What are the consequences of sin? (18:8-9)

GET IT
■ What is it about children that Christ wants us to emulate?
❋ What charming qualities do children possess?
❋ How does age and maturity cause us to lose our innocence and sense of humility?
❋ What danger is there for us if we influence children in a negative way?
❋ In what ways are you still like a child (in a good sense)?
■ What prevents us from being more like childlike in our faith?
❋ In what ways can you be more childlike?

APPLY IT
■ What can you do today to humble yourself?
❋ To what children in your life will you demonstrate the love and acceptance of Christ this week?
❋ What habits or actions do you need to abolish this week because of their negative influence on children?

Matthew 18:10-14
The Parable of the Lost Sheep

TOPICS
Angels, Celebration, Effort, Eternal Life, Evangelism, God's Will, Grace, Help, Initiative, Kindness, Patience, Reconciliation, Restoration

OPEN IT
❋ How does it feel to be lost and have no idea where you are?
■ To what lengths would you go to recover: a lost piece of jewelry? a missing pocketbook or wallet? an important misplaced document? a winning lottery ticket? your missing child?
❋ What do you believe about angels?

EXPLORE IT
❋ How does God protect children? (18:10)
❋ Who is especially important to God? Why? (18:10)
❋ What command about children did Jesus give the disciples? (18:10)
❋ What kind of guardians did Jesus suggest children have? (18:10)
❋ To whom do angels have constant access? (18:10)
❋ What kind of pastoral imagery did Jesus use to illustrate His point about the value of a soul? (18:12)
■ How did Jesus say the owner of one hundred sheep would react if just one of his sheep wandered off? (18:12)
■ According to Jesus, how would the owner of a lost sheep react upon finding his lost sheep? (18:13)
■ How did Jesus compare sheep to the way God views lost children? (18:14)
❋ How did Jesus describe God? Why? (18:14)

GET IT
❋ How would you convince a skeptic that children have guardian angels?
■ Why is it important for us to teach our children about God from the time they are very little?
❋ Why do you think children are more receptive than adults to spiritual truth?
■ How does it change your image of God to see Him described as a caring shepherd who searches frantically for one lost individual?
❋ How does it change your image of God to see Him described as a compassionate Father who doesn't want to see even one person lost?
❋ What does God's concern for each and every individual say to you about the way you treat certain people?
❋ How do you feel knowing that God is more concerned about finding a lost person than punishing him or her?

APPLY IT
❋ What "lost sheep" can you search for and try to round up this week by demonstrating the love and acceptance of Christ?
❋ To whom do you need to show more sensitivity and attentiveness this week?
■ How can you become a better role model for a young person today?

Matthew 18:15-20

A Brother Who Sins Against You

TOPICS

Accusation, Authority, Church, Compassion, Consequences, Correction, Disagreements, Friendship, Humility, Instructions, Judging Others, Mercy, Pain, Prayer, Quarrels, Reconciliation, Stubbornness, Unity

OPEN IT

■ What are some typical approaches people adopt in conflicts or disagreements?
❇ What is the greatest "miracle answer to prayer" you've ever experienced?
❇ What societal forces work to divide families, friendships, and churches?
❇ What is it like to be in the middle of a church split?

EXPLORE IT

❇ What situation was Jesus addressing in this context? (18:15)
■ What did Jesus set forth as the first step in resolving conflict? (18:15)
❇ What positive consequences can result from resolving conflict? (18:15)
■ What should we do if a person will not listen to correction and does not want to work things out? (18:16)
❇ What Old Testament principle is in view here? (18:16)
❇ What did Jesus say to do if a person doing wrong won't listen to correction? (18:17)
■ What extreme measures should be used if a wrongdoer turns a deaf ear to all pleas to reconcile? (18:17)
❇ How can Christians and/or churches be certain they have authority to exercise discipline? (18:18)
❇ What assurance did Jesus give His disciples about answered prayer? (18:19)
❇ What special promise did Jesus make to groups that gather in His name? (18:20)

GET IT

■ Why is it best to resolve conflicts in private?
❇ What attitudes can eliminate or help reduce friction in disagreements?
❇ How can a third party help resolve a conflict?
■ When should we air our grievances in public?
❇ How can gossip cause our conflicts to escalate?
❇ How can your church play a role in difficult or very serious quarrels?
❇ If Christ is with us always (Matthew 28:20), in what unique way is He with us when we gather in His name?
❇ Why is praying in a group a good idea?

APPLY IT

❇ What biblical principles can you practice today so as to avoid conflicts with others?
■ To what relationships or in what specific ways do you need to apply today's passage?
❇ What seemingly hopeless situation will you begin praying for today?

Matthew 18:21-35

The Parable of the Unmerciful Servant

TOPICS

Application, Attitude, Bitterness, Confession, Courage, Feelings, Forgiveness, Grace, Mercy, Obedience, Obligation, Procrastination, Rationalizing, Reconciliation, Risk, Wisdom

OPEN IT

■ What makes forgiveness difficult?
❇ What acts of mercy have you seen or heard about recently?
❇ What are some situations others have faced that you would find difficult to forgive?

EXPLORE IT

❇ What question did Peter ask Jesus? (18:21)
❇ What surprising answer did Jesus give Peter? (18:22)
❇ How did Jesus illustrate His answer to Peter's question? (18:23)
❇ To what did Jesus compare the kingdom of heaven? (18:23)
❇ In the Parable of the Unmerciful Servant, what did the king want to do? (18:23)
❇ How was the king prepared to get the large amount of money owed him by a particular servant? (18:24-25)
❇ What did the indebted servant do? (18:26)
❇ How did the king graciously respond to the indebted servant's desperate plea? (18:27)
❇ What did the servant go and do after his debt was cancelled? (18:28)
❇ How did the second servant respond to the demand for payment? (18:29)
❇ What effect did the second servant's pleas have on the first servant? (18:30)
■ Who watched with dismay as the first servant refused to have mercy on the second? Why? (18:31)
❇ How did the onlookers respond when they saw the first servant throw the second in jail? (18:31)
■ How did the king react to the news he heard? (18:32-34)
■ How did Jesus apply this parable to His followers? (18:35)

GET IT

❇ How likely are we to forgive someone once, twice, or even three times?
❇ How likely are people to forgive someone beyond three times?
❇ How are we to interpret Jesus' answer, "seventy-seven times"?
❇ Why is an unforgiving spirit so deadly?
■ In what ways has God shown mercy in forgiving our sins?
■ If God is so willing to forgive us, why are we sometimes unwilling to forgive others?
❇ How do we sometimes forgive with strings attached?
❇ What should we do if we don't feel like forgiving others?
❇ How is it possible for us to forget the wrongs others have done to us?

APPLY IT
❊ What individual(s) do you need to "release from their debts" today?
■ What are some practical ways you can show mercy today to someone who has wronged you?

Matthew 19:1-12
Divorce

TOPICS
Blessing, Celebration, Compromise, Conflict, Culture, Ego, Example, Forgiveness, God's Will, Hardheartedness, Marriage, Obligation, Protection, Purity, Unity, World

OPEN IT
■ Whose marriage do you most admire? Why?
❊ What ingredients make for a happy marriage?
❊ What factors tend to undermine a marriage and make a couple more susceptible to divorce?

EXPLORE IT
❊ Where did Jesus go after telling the Parable of the Unmerciful Servant? (19:1)
❊ Who accompanied Jesus? (19:2)
❊ Who approached Jesus with the motive of testing Him? (19:3)
❊ What trick question did the Pharisees ask Jesus? (19:3)
■ How did Jesus respond to the Pharisees' question? (19:4-6)
❊ What did Jesus quote? Why? (19:4-5)
❊ What did Jesus say is God's ideal for marriage? (19:6)
❊ What follow-up question did Jesus' enemies ask? (19:7)
■ How did Jesus respond to the second question about divorce? (19:8)
❊ Jesus allowed for divorce under what condition? (19:9)
■ What did the disciples think about Jesus' view of marriage and divorce? (19:10)
❊ What did Jesus teach about those who never marry? (19:11-12)

GET IT
❊ What are the most devastating consequences of divorce?
■ Which would be worse: to be unhappily married or never to be married?
❊ What is the ideal even in a marriage that was stained by adultery?
❊ How does the previous passage (Matthew 18:21-35) have application in this one?
■ What do you think churches can and should do to build stronger marriages and to reduce the divorce rate among their members?
❊ In what ways is singleness a great advantage?
❊ How would you feel if you never married?

APPLY IT
■ What habits can you develop, beginning today, that will make you a better marriage partner?
❊ How can you communicate to your children the sanctity and sacredness of the marriage relationship?
❊ What specific service can you (and will you) render to God in the coming year because of the freedom your singleness permits?

Matthew 19:13-15
The Little Children and Jesus

TOPICS
Blessing, Children, Complaining, Correction, Criticism, Eternal Life, Insight, Kingdom of God/Heaven, Ministry, Perspective, Plans, Schedule, Understanding

OPEN IT
❊ What are some ways people abuse positions of authority?
❊ Where do we draw the line between being productive and being rushed, or between being dedicated and being driven?
❊ What are the most exciting and the most frightening aspects of parenthood?
■ What would you do differently if you could live your childhood over again?

EXPLORE IT
❊ What people were being brought to Jesus? Why? (19:13)
■ Why were children being brought to Jesus? (19:13)
❊ To whom did some parents bring their children? Why? (19:13)
❊ How did the disciples react to the fact that children were being brought to Jesus? (19:13)
❊ On whom did the disciples vent their displeasure? (19:13)
■ How did Jesus correct the disciples? (19:14)
❊ Why did Jesus command the disciples to allow the children to come to Him? (19:14)
❊ According to Jesus, what kind of people will possess the kingdom of heaven? (19:14)
■ What did Jesus do for the little children? (19:15)
❊ What did Jesus do after He spent time with the children? (19:15)

GET IT
■ Why do you think the disciples got irritated about the children being brought to Jesus?
❊ What are some ways you get so caught up in your schedule or "to do" list that you are insensitive or even rude to the people around you?
❊ What is the purpose behind the church practice of "baby dedication"?
❊ What are some ways we might hinder children from coming to Christ?
■ What did Jesus mean by saying that "the kingdom of heaven belongs to such as these"?
❊ What are the advantages to trusting in Christ at an early age?
❊ How early can a child truly comprehend the gospel?

APPLY IT
❊ What are some specific ways you could bless a child today?
■ How can you become more childlike in your faith over the next month?

Matthew 19:16-30

The Rich Young Man

TOPICS

Confusion, Ego, Eternal Life, Generosity, Judgment, Law, Legalism, Materialism, Miracles, Perfect, Perspective, Possessions, Questions, Rewards, Righteousness, Wealth

OPEN IT

■ What would you do (buy, spend, give, save) if you suddenly received a million dollars?
❇ Which is more dangerous and why: being very rich or being very poor?
❇ What does a individual's checkbook reveal about him or her?

EXPLORE IT

❇ What question was asked of Jesus at the beginning of this story? (19:16)
❇ How did Jesus respond to the man's question? (19:17-19)
❇ What astonishing claim did the young man make? (19:20)
❇ What further assignment did Jesus give the man who came to Him? (19:21)
❇ How did the man react to Jesus' demands? (19:22)
■ What amazing statement did Jesus make to His disciples about riches and the kingdom of God? (19:23-24)
■ How did the disciples respond when they heard how hard it is for a rich person to enter the kingdom of heaven? (19:25)
❇ How did Christ explain His statement about rich people and heaven? (19:25)
❇ When he applied the truth about riches to the disciples, Peter asked what question? (19:27)
❇ What insights into the future did Christ give in His promise? (19:28)
■ What did Jesus promise the twelve disciples? (19:28-29)
❇ What further promise did Jesus make to Christians through the ages who make sacrifices for Him? (19:29)
❇ How are spiritual values different from worldly values? (19:30)

GET IT

❇ Why do many poor people have a great love for God and many rich people have no interest in God?
❇ Why do many poor people long to be rich?
❇ What would you say to the person who claims, "See, this passage teaches that eternal life is something we receive in exchange for the good things we do"?
❇ What point do you think Jesus was making with this rich man?
❇ Why can't moral, decent, good people make it to heaven on their own merit?
■ Why is it that we often do not become more generous as our wealth increases?
■ If we truly believe that God will one day reward His children in heaven, why are we reluctant to make sacrifices for God?

APPLY IT

■ What sacrifice are you willing to make for Christ this week, in the knowledge that you will be rewarded in heaven?
❇ What promise from this passage do you want to claim (or even memorize) today?
❇ How can you decrease your spending over the next month in order to increase the amount of money you can give to the work of God?

Matthew 20:1-16

The Parable of the Workers in the Vineyard

TOPICS

Appreciation, Benefits, Blessing, Character, Complaining, Contentment, Criticism, Employment, Generosity, Good News, Justice, Kingdom of God/Heaven, Perspective, Resentment, Salvation, Thankfulness, Unfairness

OPEN IT

❇ What do you think of deathbed or death-row conversions?
❇ What is the most generous thing anyone has ever done for you?
■ Who is the best employer you ever had? Why?

EXPLORE IT

❇ To what situation did Jesus compare the kingdom of heaven? (20:1)
❇ Who was the central character in this parable? (20:1)
❇ What did the landowner go out and do? (20:1)
❇ What wages were agreed upon by the landowner and his hired hands? (20:2)
❇ In the parable, what happened at about 9:00 a.m.? (20:3)
❇ What wage was agreed upon between the landowner and his workers? (20:4)
❇ How many additional times did the landowner go out and hire workers? (20:5-6)
❇ What explanation did the last group of workers give when asked why they were standing around doing nothing? (20:7)
❇ What happened to the last group of workers? (20:7)
❇ What did the landowner tell his foreman at the end of the day? (20:8)
❇ What wages did the workers hired at the eleventh hour receive? (20:9)
■ What did the landowner pay to the men who worked all day? (20:10)
■ How did the workers respond to the landowner's system of payment? (20:11-12)
■ What rationale did the landowner give for his actions? (20:13-15)

GET IT

❇ In what ways does God's grace seem unfair?
❇ How do our cultural values resist the idea of grace?
❇ Why is it dangerous to compare your own situation with someone else's?
❇ How would you answer the argument that God isn't fair in the way He forgives?
❇ How does it make you feel to know that heaven will include ex-murderers, former child molesters, and people who put their trust in Christ only minutes before death?
■ What would happen if God gave each of us what we deserve?

■ How can focusing on God's grace in our lives keep us from becoming jealous of others?

APPLY IT

❊ What can you do today to help someone who needs God's grace begin to understand the love of God?
■ In what way can you say thank you to God every day this week for his amazing grace in your life?
❊ In what way could you help a new Christian get oriented to life in the Master's kingdom sometime in the next month?

Matthew 20:17-19

Jesus Again Predicts His Death

TOPICS

Barriers, Danger, Death, Determination, Enemies, Evil, Future, Giving Up, Mission, Murder, Opposition, Preparation, Rejection, Resurrection, Sacrifice, Suffering, Victory

OPEN IT

❊ What funeral/burial arrangements do you want for yourself?
❊ Why are some people unshakable in their pursuit of goals, while others are easily deterred?
■ When do you feel safe enough to confide in a person?

EXPLORE IT

■ Who was traveling with Jesus at this time? (20:17)
■ Where was Christ going when He spoke of His death for the third time? Why? (20:17-18)
❊ How can you tell that the disciples weren't sure what lay ahead? (20:17-18)
❊ What title did Jesus use to refer to Himself? (20:18)
❊ To whom did Jesus say He would be betrayed? (20:18)
■ What did Jesus say the chief priests and teachers of the law would ultimately do? (20:18)
❊ Who did Jesus say would kill Him? (20:19)
❊ What pain and shame did Jesus predict for Himself before the actual crucifixion? (20:19)
❊ What did Jesus say would happen three days after His death? (20:19)
❊ When would Jesus be raised from the dead? (20:19)

GET IT

❊ How would you respond to someone who talked about their own death several times?
■ Why is the death of Christ significant to us?
■ Why is Christ's death significant to you?
❊ If Christ knew suffering and death awaited him in Jerusalem, why was He determined to go there?
❊ What goals in life are you committed to pursuing no matter what?
❊ Why would people who saw Christ's deeds and heard His words still reject Him?
❊ About what other future events has God given us some warning or glimpse?

APPLY IT

❊ What can you do this week to come to a greater appreciation for the death of Christ?
■ What can you do to say thank you to Christ for suffering for you?

Matthew 20:20-28

A Mother's Request

TOPICS

Ambition, Anger, Atonement, Authority, Divisions, Ego, Fairness, God, Honor, Jealousy, Kingdom of God/Heaven, Leadership, Motives, Position, Pride, Privilege, Rewards, Serving

OPEN IT

❊ What is it inside us that recoils at the idea of serving others?
❊ Why do some parents try so hard to plan and run their children's lives?
■ What are the pluses and minuses of ambition?

EXPLORE IT

■ Who came to Jesus? Why? (20:20)
❊ What favor did James and John's mother ask Jesus (20:21)
❊ How did Jesus respond to the request that James and John get special treatment? (20:22)
■ What curious question did Jesus ask James and John? (20:22)
❊ How did James and John answer Jesus' cryptic question? (20:22)
❊ What did Jesus promise James and John? (20:23)
❊ What did Jesus refuse to promise James and John? (20:23)
❊ According to Jesus, who will decide the positions of honor and authority in the kingdom of God? (20:23)
■ What was the reaction of the other disciples to this whole dialogue? (20:24)
❊ Whose leadership style did Jesus condemn? (20:25)
❊ How did Jesus define leadership? (20:26-27)
❊ What did Jesus say was His mission in life? (20:28)

GET IT

■ When does honorable ambition become dishonorable?
■ Who among the people in your church do you think will receive the greatest rewards in heaven?
❊ How does our culture follow the "Gentile pattern of leadership?"
❊ How can jealousy and pride destroy the unity of a group of people?
❊ On what basis should honors, awards, rewards be given?
❊ What do you think about people who use connections to try to get favors?
❊ In what ways might you have to suffer for the sake of Christ?
❊ What opportunities do you have to serve others as Christ taught?
❊ In what ways do you need to back off and let your children lead their own lives and make their own decisions?

APPLY IT

■ What three acts can you do today in service to others?
❊ What is one specific way you could build unity among your circle of Christian friends this week?

Matthew 20:29-34
Two Blind Men Receive Sight

TOPICS
Call, Compassion, Embarrassment, Handicapped, Healing, Messiah, Miracles, Peer Pressure, Persistence, Prayer, Reputation, Submission, Zeal

OPEN IT
❊ Which is more humiliating: being with someone who makes a scene, or losing control yourself and causing a scene?
■ What one miracle do you wish God would do for you?
❊ What makes some people quiet and others loud?

EXPLORE IT
❊ Where did the incident in this passage take place? (20:29)
❊ Who was with Jesus? When? (20:29)
❊ Who was following Jesus? When? (20:29)
❊ Who happened to be sitting by the roadside when Jesus passed by? (20:30)
■ What did the people sitting by the roadside do when they heard Jesus was nearby? (20:30)
■ What was the crowd's reaction to the scene that developed? (20:31)
■ How did the crowd's words affect the two blind men? (20:31)
❊ What did Jesus do in the midst of all the commotion? (20:32)
❊ What did Jesus ask the two blind men? (20:32)
❊ What request did the blind men make of Jesus? (20:33)
❊ Why did Jesus grant the request made of Him? (20:34)
❊ How did the men who were healed show their gratitude? (20:34)

GET IT
❊ Why would people discourage two blind men from seeking help from God?
❊ In what ways does the fear of embarrassment prevent us from following Christ?
❊ In what ways are we spiritually blind?
■ In what ways have people tried to discourage you from seeking Jesus or praying in a certain way?
■ How does it test our faith to hear others doubt God?
❊ To what area of your life does this passage apply most clearly?
❊ How would you define compassion?
❊ How are you doing in the area of showing compassion?
❊ What means has God given you for showing compassion in concrete gestures of kindness?
❊ After all that Christ has done for us, in what ways can we show our gratitude?

APPLY IT
❊ What person in your life needs your compassion today?
❊ How can you show love and kindness to a hurting individual?
■ What step of trust in God do you need to take today regardless of how foolish others might think it to be?

Matthew 21:1-11
The Triumphal Entry

TOPICS
Acceptance, Approval, Celebration, Glory, Messiah, Obedience, Peer Pressure, People, Praise, Prophecy, Worship

OPEN IT
■ What do you like best and least about parades?
❊ How would you define worship?
❊ Why do many Christians cheer like crazy at sporting events on Saturday and sheepishly sing praise songs to the Lord the next morning?

EXPLORE IT
❊ To where was Jesus traveling? With whom? (21:1)
❊ Through what village were Jesus and His disciples passing? (21:1)
❊ How were the disciples instructed to answer anyone who might object to their actions? (21:2)
❊ Jesus sent two of His disciples to find and return with what? Why? (21:2-3)
❊ Why was this incident significant? (21:4-5)
❊ How did the two disciples respond to Jesus' instructions? (21:6)
❊ When the men returned with the donkey and colt, what did Jesus do? (21:7)
■ What did the gathered crowd place on the road? Why? (21:8)
❊ What size crowd participated in welcoming Jesus? (21:8)
■ What did the crowds shout as Jesus entered Jerusalem? (21:9)
■ How did this "parade" affect those living in Jerusalem? (21:10)
❊ What did the crowd accompanying Jesus say about Him to those in the city? (21:11)

GET IT
❊ If you had lived in Jerusalem during that time, do you think you would have been a follower of Christ or one of the people who looked skeptically at all His activities?
❊ How much do you think "the crowds" today understand Jesus' purpose and mission?
■ In what ways do we simplistically "cheer" Jesus?
❊ Why did Jesus request a donkey instead of a big white stallion or a chariot?
❊ How would you answer if a friend asked, "Who is Jesus?"
❊ How might we be able to change our city or campus or country if we honored Christ as king over all?
■ How should worship play a role in your daily life?

APPLY IT
❊ How can you honor Jesus as king this week?
■ What special gift (time, money, possessions, effort, etc.) of worship can you present to Jesus today?
❊ What does the Lord "need" from you (see Matthew 21:3) today to accomplish His plan in your life?

Matthew 21:12-17
Jesus at the Temple

TOPICS
Accusation, Authority, Conflict, Ego, Evil, Handicapped, Hardheartedness, Hypocrisy, Jealousy, Messiah, Miracles, Popularity, Praise, Pride, Religion, Traditions, Zeal

OPEN IT
■ Why does the church have a reputation for being "money hungry"?
❊ What convictions of yours are so strong that you sometimes feel you'd like to do something radical to express your views?
❊ What gets you really angry?
❊ When do you tend to lose your temper?

EXPLORE IT
■ After entering Jerusalem, where did Jesus go? What happened there? (21:12)
❊ What did Jesus do in the temple area? (21:12)
❊ What sort of goods were being sold in the temple courts? (21:12)
■ What did Jesus quote to those in the temple? (21:13)
■ Jesus accused the merchants of turning the temple into what? Why? (21:13)
❊ What kinds of handicaps and infirmities did Jesus heal while at the temple? (21:14)
❊ What were the children in the temple area shouting? (21:15)
❊ How did the chief priests and teachers of the law feel when they heard the children shout praise to Jesus? (21:15)
❊ What did the religious leaders ask Jesus? (21:16)
❊ How did Jesus answer the religious leaders? (21:16)
❊ What did Jesus do when He left the temple? (21:17)

GET IT
■ How do you think God would like to alter some of the practices churches and ministries use to raise money?
■ How do you think God would like to alter some of the ways you use money?
❊ What is the most appropriate way for churches to fund their activities?
❊ Why is it easy to become jealous when others get recognized, praised, or rewarded?
❊ Why do people often honor their money above God?
❊ In what situations is your behavior altered or stymied by what others might think?
❊ Why do children sometimes have the ability to see more clearly than adults?
❊ In what areas do you have the prerogative to stand up for the righteousness and holiness of God?

APPLY IT
■ What change in your giving do you need to make this month?
❊ What hymn of praise would help you praise and worship God this week?
❊ What impure habits or practices are taking place in your temple (i.e., your body) that you need to drive out this week?

Matthew 21:18-22
The Fig Tree Withers

TOPICS
Appearance, Confusion, Deceit, Dishonesty, Faith, Fruit, Hypocrisy, Integrity, Lying, Miracles, Power, Prayer, Sin

OPEN IT
❊ What is the worst case of false advertising you've ever seen?
❊ Why do you think there are so many religious hypocrites?
■ When in your life were you the most disappointed?

EXPLORE IT
❊ Where was Jesus going? When? (21:18)
❊ What was Jesus feeling? When? (21:18)
■ What caught Jesus' attention? Why? (21:19)
❊ What did Jesus discover when he made a closer inspection of the fig tree? (21:19)
❊ What did Jesus do to the fig tree? (21:19)
❊ What happened immediately after Jesus cursed the fig tree? (21:19)
❊ How did the withered fig tree incident affect the disciples? (21:20)
■ What did the disciples ask Jesus? (21:20)
❊ What did Jesus cite as the necessary ingredient to doing "impossible" things? (21:21)
❊ What even more amazing feat than causing a fig tree to wither did Jesus claim was possible? (21:21)
■ What attitude did Jesus encourage us to have in prayer? (21:22)

GET IT
❊ How is religious legalism like a barren fig tree?
❊ What types of "fruit" should appear in our lives as we grow as Christians?
❊ What fruit has your life borne in the last couple of months?
❊ What are some ways Christians can look good to others from a distance and yet still be fruitless?
■ Why is the invitation to pray at the end of this passage not a blank check to ask for anything?
■ What requirements must our prayers meet?
❊ In what ways might you be giving others a false idea of what the Christian life is all about?

APPLY IT
■ What prayer of faith do you need to begin praying on a regular basis this week?
❊ What change in your life today would enable you to become more fruitful?

Matthew 21:23-27
The Authority of Jesus Questioned

TOPICS
Authority, Challenge, Conversation, Danger, Hardheartedness, Hypocrisy, Jealousy, Knowledge, Motives, Questions, Reputation, Resentment, Testing, Unbelievers, Wisdom

OPEN IT
❄ What comes to mind when you hear the word "authority"?
■ Why are people so resistant to authority?
❄ What do you like or dislike about debates (either presidential debates or TV shows where guests bat around a controversial topic)?

EXPLORE IT
❄ Where was Jesus when the incidents of this passage occurred? (21:23)
❄ What was Jesus doing when He was interrupted? (21:23)
■ Who interrupted Jesus? Why? (21:23)
❄ What questions did the chief priests and the elders ask Jesus? (21:23)
■ What deal did Jesus make with his accuser? (21:24)
❄ Jesus' question dealt with what subject? (21:24)
❄ What were the only two possible answers the religious leaders could give? (21:25-26)
❄ What was the drawback to claiming that John's ministry was divinely inspired? (21:25)
❄ What was the risk of claiming that John had no divine authority? (21:26)
■ How did the religious leaders finally respond to Jesus? (21:27)
❄ What reply did Jesus give to the chief priests and elders? (21:27)

GET IT
❄ What do you think is behind many people's "confrontations" with Jesus?
❄ Why do we feel threatened when someone challenges our beliefs or actions as Christians?
❄ How do we typically feel when our motives are exposed as selfish?
■ How can religious traditions, rules, and habits sometimes blind us to the truth?
❄ What are some ways we outright defy what Jesus has said?
■ In what ways do we try to rationalize our way out of submitting to Christ's authority?
❄ How does pride keep us from acknowledging our mistakes?

APPLY IT
■ In what area of your life do you need to submit to Jesus' authority today?
❄ How can you humble yourself before God today?

Matthew 21:28-32
The Parable of the Two Sons

TOPICS
Believe, Blessing, Change, Children, Eternal Life, Humility, Impulsiveness, Lying, Obedience, Perspective, Procrastination, Repentance, Sincerity, Stubbornness, Trust, Words

OPEN IT
❄ As you recall all the TV families you've ever seen, which character would make the best child? Why?
■ What is the best illustration you've ever seen of the old saying, "Actions speak louder than words"?
❄ In what ways can knowledge be dangerous?

EXPLORE IT
■ Who are the main characters in this parable? (21:28)
❄ In the Parable of the Two Sons, what did the man say to his first son? (21:28)
❄ How did the first son respond to his father's words? (21:29)
■ What happened to the first son later? (21:29)
❄ What did the man say to his second son? (21:30)
❄ How did the second son respond to his father's words? (21:30)
■ What did the second son actually do? (21:30)
❄ What question did Jesus ask His audience at the end of the parable? (21:31)
❄ Who did Jesus claim would be in heaven before the religious leaders in His audience? (21:31)
❄ According to Jesus, who came to show the Jews the way of righteousness? (21:32)
❄ How did the religious leaders respond to John's message? (21:32)

GET IT
❄ If the Jewish religious leaders were trained in the Law and familiar with the Old Testament, why did they oppose Jesus?
■ Why doesn't religious knowledge or information guarantee that we'll be godly?
❄ If Jesus really is the King of kings and Lord of lords, why do we often drag our feet doing what He has told us to do?
❄ What does it mean to repent?
❄ If, as Jesus claimed, many "unrighteous" people will enter the kingdom of God, and many "righteous" people won't, what does that say to you about God's system of justice?
■ When is it too late to do the right thing?

APPLY IT
❄ What step can you take this week toward correcting a mistake?
■ What command of Christ that you have been neglecting do you need to obey today?
❄ What promise that you made to Christ can you keep today?

Matthew 21:33-46
The Parable of the Tenants

TOPICS
Attitude, Blessing, Deceit, Enemies, Evil, Hardheartedness, Hatred, Intimidation, Kingdom of God/Heaven, Murder, Popularity, Prophecy, Punishment, Rejection, Sin, Submission, Unbelievers

OPEN IT
■ In what way does each of these hurt: being told an uncomfortable truth, and being lied to?
❄ What was your favorite bedtime story as a child?
❄ What attitudes in others make you want to be mean instead of nice?

EXPLORE IT
❋ How did the landowner in this parable prepare his vineyard? (21:33)
❋ What did the landowner do at harvest time? (21:34)
❋ How did the tenants of the vineyard treat the landowner's servants? (21:35)
❋ What did the landowner do after his servants were attacked? (21:36)
❋ How did the landowner's alternative plan work? (21:36)
■ What solution did the landowner finally decide on? (21:37)
■ How did the tenants react to the landowner's choice? (21:38-39)
■ What end did Jesus predict for the wicked tenants of the parable? (21:40-41)
❋ What did Jesus quote to the religious leaders? (21:42)
❋ How did Jesus personalize or apply this parable and Scripture to the nation of Israel? (21:43-44)
❋ What did the religious leaders realize when they heard Jesus' parable? (21:45)
❋ What did the chief priests and elders try to do? (21:46)
❋ Why didn't the chief priests and elders carry out their plan at that moment? (21:46)

GET IT
❋ What does the vineyard in this parable represent?
■ Who do the tenants of the parable symbolize?
■ Who are the servants and the son representative of?
❋ How would you feel if you were extremely kind and giving to someone for a long time and that person repeatedly scorned your kindness?
❋ Why does Christ's kindness often fail to impress people?
❋ Does God's Word soften your heart like wax or harden your heart like clay?
❋ What are some ways we react when God's Word convicts us or tells us to take demanding, difficult, or risky steps?
❋ In what area of your life do you tend to resist God's authority?

APPLY IT
❋ What is one practical step you can take to submit to God and obey His Word this week?
■ Today or tomorrow, how can you show God your appreciation for His goodness toward you?

Matthew 22:1-14
The Parable of the Wedding Banquet

TOPICS
Ambassadors, Apathy, Attitude, Celebration, Evil, Excuses, Grace, Hardheartedness, Hell, Indifference, Kingdom of God/Heaven, Marriage, Murder, Opposition, Punishment, Rejection, Sorrow, Unbelievers

OPEN IT
■ What do you like or dislike about weddings?
❋ What tips might you give to someone planning a big wedding?
❋ What is your funniest wedding story?
❋ How do you tend to react when long-awaited plans fail to materialize?

EXPLORE IT
❋ What preparations were being made in this parable? (22:2)
❋ What did the king send his servants to do? (22:3)
■ How did people respond to the king's invitation? (22:3)
❋ Upon hearing that no one would come to the wedding, what did the king do? (22:4)
■ How did the invited guests react to the king's second appeal? (22:5)
❋ To what shocking acts did some of the people who were invited resort? (22:6)
❋ How did the king deal with the lawbreakers? (22:7)
❋ The king went to a "Plan B" that included what changes? (22:8-9)
❋ How did the king's alternative plan work out? (22:10)
❋ What did the king say when he spotted an improperly dressed wedding guest? (22:11)
❋ What did the king order his servants to do with the man who was improperly dressed? (22:11-13)
■ Why did the king throw out the unwelcome wedding guest? (22:13-14)

GET IT
❋ What keeps people from accepting Jesus' offer of eternal life?
❋ The wedding clothes in the parable that were needed for admittance to the banquet are meant to symbolize what quality that is necessary for entry into the kingdom of heaven?
❋ What events led to your acceptance of Jesus' offer of forgiveness and heaven?
❋ For what reason are there impostors in the church?
❋ Why would a non-Christian want to be around Christians?
❋ How does God demonstrate His patience to unbelievers?
■ What will happen to those who either reject Christ or try to enter His kingdom on their own terms?
■ In what area(s) of your life have you been putting off a response to what God has asked you to do?

APPLY IT
■ What response should you give to God this week?
❋ To what individuals this week can you extend Jesus' offer of forgiveness and eternal life?

Matthew 22:15-22
Paying Taxes to Caesar

TOPICS
Accusation, Challenge, Composure, Dishonesty, Embarrassment, Flattery, Frustration, Government, Hardheartedness, Hypocrisy, Insight, Integrity, Motives, Obligation, Questions, Rejection, Responsibility, Testing, Unbelievers, Wisdom

OPEN IT
❋ What could governments do to make their citizens less opposed to paying taxes?

❊ What qualities mark a person of integrity?
■ What individuals would you like to see pictured on our money?

EXPLORE IT
❊ What group sought to trap Jesus? How? (22:15)
❊ What two groups were sent to Jesus? Why? (22:16)
❊ How did the Pharisees address Jesus? (22:16)
❊ How did the Pharisees describe Jesus' character? (22:16)
❊ How did the Pharisees describe Jesus' manner of teaching? (22:16)
❊ After all the flattery, what question did the Pharisees' disciples and the Herodians finally ask Jesus? (22:17)
❊ How did Jesus respond to all the false adulation He received in this incident? (22:18)
■ What did Jesus say to the men who questioned Him? (22:18)
❊ What object did Jesus use to illustrate His answer? How? (22:19-20)
■ How did Jesus answer the question without getting Himself in political hot water? (22:21)
■ How did Jesus' opponents respond to His words? (22:22)

GET IT
❊ In what situations are you guilty of flattery or brownnosing?
❊ Why do we resort to flattery?
❊ How does it make you feel to realize that Jesus can see right into your heart and tell when your motives are insincere?
■ What do you think Jesus called us to do when He said, "Give to Caesar what is Caesar's, and give to God what is God's"?
■ How can you be careful and wise in what you say to unbelievers?
❊ What responsibilities do you have to the government?

APPLY IT
■ What neglected civic responsibilities do you need to begin fulfilling today?
❊ What might be the first step in better living up to your obligations as a citizen of God's kingdom?

Matthew 22:23-33
Marriage at the Resurrection

TOPICS
Angels, Assumptions, Beliefs, Bible, Blindness, Children, Confusion, Death, Eternal Life, Future, God, Heaven, Ignorance, Law, Motives, Power, Resurrection, Testing, Traditions, Zeal

OPEN IT
❊ What topics often spark arguments among people?
■ What ideals do many people have about marriage?
❊ What are some secrets to a long and healthy marriage?

EXPLORE IT
■ What group confronted or opposed Jesus? How? (22:23)
■ What distinctive belief did the Sadducees hold? (22:23)
❊ To what authority did the Sadducees appeal in asking their question? (22:24)
❊ To what kind of law did the Sadducees defer? (22:24)
❊ What rare, unlikely scenario did the Sadducees describe for Jesus? (22:25-27)
❊ What question did the Sadducees finally put to Jesus? (22:28)
■ What two important facts did Jesus charge the Sadducees with not knowing? (22:29)
❊ What did Jesus say about the institution of marriage in eternity? (22:30)
❊ What did Jesus say about angels and marriage? (22:30)
❊ How did Jesus prove that people will be raised from the dead? (22:31-32)
❊ How did the crowd react to this exchange? (22:33)

GET IT
❊ What makes you think the Sadducees were not really interested in knowing the truth?
❊ What do you think their purpose was in confronting Jesus?
❊ How does it make you feel to realize that marriage as we know it will not exist in eternity?
❊ In what ways do all these groups questioning Jesus remind you of today's talk-show circuit?
❊ How well do you know the Scriptures and the power of God?
■ In what ways can our doctrinal beliefs blind us to the truth?
❊ How do you typically respond when you are attacked because of your faith?
■ What questions asked by unbelievers do you have the most difficult time answering?

APPLY IT
■ What area of Bible doctrine will you read about and study this week?
❊ To whom do you need to apologize for arguing about your faith or for browbeating with the Bible?
❊ What needs to change in your life today to reflect the fact that you serve a living God?

Matthew 22:34-40
The Greatest Commandment

TOPICS
Answers, Attitude, Blindness, Challenge, Commitment, Devotion, Hardheartedness, Hypocrisy, Law, Legalism, Listening, Love, Motives, Rationalizing, Rejection, Sin, Stubbornness, Unbelievers

OPEN IT
❊ What is the best advice your mother or father ever gave you?
❊ If you could give a four-sentence speech on worldwide television, what would you say in order to have the greatest possible impact?
■ If you had to summarize this past week, how would you describe it?

EXPLORE IT
❋ Who heard that the Sadducees had been embarrassed by Jesus? How did they respond? (22:34)
❋ What did the Pharisees do? Why? (22:34)
❋ What sort of person was selected to address Jesus? (22:35)
❋ What was the Pharisee's purpose in asking Jesus a question? (22:35)
■ What specific question did the man ask Jesus? (22:36)
■ How did Jesus answer the Pharisee's question? (22:37)
❋ What kind of love did Jesus describe? (22:37)
■ What important footnote did Jesus add to His answer? (22:39)
❋ What kind of love for one's neighbor did Jesus require? (22:39)
❋ How important did Jesus say these two principles were? (22:40)

GET IT
❋ How do you feel when people ask you a question that you're pretty sure they already know the answer to?
❋ In what ways do we sometimes try to sidestep our responsibility to obey God?
❋ How do you think some of the Pharisees who opposed Christ feel now—knowing that they were face to face with the Truth and they rejected Him?
❋ How do we measure the magnitude of our love for Jesus?
■ What does it mean to "love your neighbor as yourself"?
❋ How often do you argue just for the sake of arguing?
❋ Why do you think we like to debate what the Bible means, yet often resist changing our lives based on what it says?
■ How can we keep our focus on what really matters?
❋ What does God want you to do more than anything else in your job, family, church, and neighborhood?

APPLY IT
❋ What can you do today to love Christ with all your heart, soul, and mind?
■ What loving act will you plan to do soon for a neighbor in need?

Matthew 22:41-46
Whose Son Is the Christ?

TOPICS
Answers, Blindness, Conversation, Embarrassment, Enemies, Giving Up, Hardheartedness, Holy Spirit, Law, Legalism, Messiah, Opposition, Questions, Rejection

OPEN IT
❋ What is the most ingenious trick or prank you have ever played on anyone?
■ If you could ask anyone any question at all, what would you want to know?
❋ What is satisfying about "stumping the expert" or seeing a pro make a mistake?

EXPLORE IT
❋ In what setting did this conversation take place? (22:41)
■ What religious group had gathered? Why? (22:41)
❋ Who did the interrogation of Jesus? When? (22:41)
■ What questions did Jesus ask? (22:42)
❋ What important fact did the Pharisees admit about Christ? (22:42)
■ How did Jesus enlighten the Pharisees? (22:43-44)
❋ According to Jesus, under what special condition did David write? (22:43)
❋ What was important about the way David referred to Christ? (22:43-44)
❋ What final question did Jesus use to make His point? (22:45)
❋ What happened after Jesus silenced the Pharisees? (22:46)

GET IT
■ What objections to Jesus' identity do people raise today?
■ What are good ways to respond to people who doubt Jesus' identity?
❋ How would you answer a friend who says, "Prove to me that Jesus is God"?
❋ In telling people about Christ today, what are some of the more important details to include?
❋ Why is the question, "Who is Jesus?" far more significant than any other issue?
❋ To what issues do you tend to get sidetracked when you try to witness for Christ?
❋ What emotions or thoughts prompt people to stop talking about their relationship with God?

APPLY IT
❋ What area(s) of your life do you need to surrender to the lordship of Christ today?
■ What can you do (or stop doing) this week to become more effective in introducing your non-Christian friends to Christ?

Matthew 23:1-39
Seven Woes

TOPICS
Appearance, Barriers, Blindness, Confusion, Criticism, Danger, Dishonesty, Hardheartedness, Hypocrisy, Intimidation, Legalism, Opposition, Priorities, Punishment, Rejection, Sin, Stubbornness, Tithing, Traditions, Unbelievers

OPEN IT
■ What topic(s) or situations really get you upset?
❋ What is the worst name or label that someone could pin on you?
❋ Why do some people object to "organized religion"?

EXPLORE IT
❋ To whom was Jesus speaking? (23:1)
❋ About whom was Jesus speaking? (23:2)
■ Of what did Jesus accuse the religious leaders? (23:3)
❋ What motivation did Jesus say governed the behavior of the Pharisees? (23:5-7)
■ What eternal destiny did Jesus pronounce on religious hypocrites? (23:13)

❊ What are some of the names Jesus used to describe the respected, powerful, national leaders of Israel—the Pharisees? (23:13, 15-16, 27, 33)
❊ What did Jesus say about the Pharisees' evangelism? (23:15)
❊ What kind of picky manmade traditions did Jesus accuse the religious leaders of following blindly? (23:16-22)
■ What evidence of twisted priorities among the religious elite did Jesus give? (23:23-26)
❊ What analogies did Jesus use to show that Israel's religious leaders were more interested in external credentials than internal character? (23:25-28)
❊ How did Jesus argue that the Pharisees had failed to learn the lessons of Israel's history? (23:29-36)
❊ Because of her awful leadership, how did Jesus lament over Jerusalem? (23:37)

GET IT
■ How can a spiritual leader affect his or her followers?
❊ What kinds of nitpicky rules and regulations tend to blind us to more serious sins?
❊ In what ways do people sometimes fake the Christian life?
■ What are some of the dangers of having a "checklist" of dos and don'ts that go beyond God's written Word?
❊ What temptations are faced by those in positions of spiritual authority?
❊ Which feeling best describes how you view non-Christians: sadness or anger?
❊ In what area(s) have you been failing to practice what you preach?
❊ How would you reach out to someone who has become embittered by religious hypocrites or empty religion?

APPLY IT
❊ What attitudes or "matters of the heart" do you need to confess to God today so that your inside looks as good as your outside?
❊ What could you do to help a young Christian grow stronger this week?
■ What older, more mature Christian can you spend time with this week to seek advice and wisdom?

Matthew 24:1-35
Signs of the End of the Age

TOPICS
Angels, Awe, Backslide, Believers, Blasphemy, Confusion, Courage, Culture, Danger, Darkness, Death, Deceit, Earth, Endurance, Eternal Life, Evangelism, Evil, Experience, Faithfulness, Future, Good News, Hatred, Heaven, Hell, Idolatry, Insecurity, Instructions, Jesus Christ, Kingdom of God/Heaven, Last Days, Majority, Miracles, Mourning, Nature, Occult, Pain, Persecution, Perseverance, Prophecy, Punishment, Rebellion, Religion, Rewards, Satan, Second Coming, Sovereignty, Victory, World, Worship

OPEN IT
❊ What is the most beautiful building or structure you've ever seen?
❊ What is the popular press saying about the immediate and long-range future of planet Earth?
❊ Why are people interested in the future?
■ Why do many people consult psychics, palm readers, horoscopes, and other so-called sources of guidance?

EXPLORE IT
❊ When did the disciples approach Jesus with their question? (24:1)
❊ What topic of conversation did the disciples raise with Jesus? When? (24:1)
❊ What prophetic statement did Jesus make in reference to the temple? (24:2)
❊ As Jesus was sitting on the Mount of Olives, what questions did the disciples pose? (24:3)
❊ What wide-scale calamities did Jesus predict would occur near the end of the world? (24:6-8)
❊ What various events did Jesus say would happen to believers in the end times? (24:9-13)
❊ What did Jesus say about the moral state of the world in the end? (24:12)
❊ To what extent will the gospel be preached in the last days? (24:14)
❊ According to Jesus, what will the final days on earth be like? (24:15-22)
■ What important warning about spiritual deception did Jesus issue? (24:23-26)
■ How will true believers recognize Jesus' return? (24:27-30)
■ What heavenly signs and aberrations will accompany the return of Christ? (24:29)
❊ What part did Jesus say the angels of God would play in His return? (24:31)

GET IT
❊ What are some ways the world tries to desecrate or profane the holy things of God?
❊ How does talk of the end times motivate us to live a holy life?
❊ In what ways can we become sidetracked by discussion of the end times?
■ How is it helpful that Jesus didn't give us a specific time or date for His return?
■ What are some current examples of false prophets deceiving people?
❊ What signs do you see that we may be close to the beginning of the end?
❊ How could you use this passage to talk to a nonbeliever about Jesus Christ?
❊ In what specific ways does this passage encourage you to pray?

APPLY IT
❊ For what Christians around the world who are suffering because of their faith can you pray?
■ What step can you take this week to guard yourself from false teaching?
❊ What is one thing you can do in the next month to spread the gospel to your part of God's world?

Matthew 24:36-51

The Day and Hour Unknown

TOPICS

Blindness, Celebration, Delay, Eternal Life, Expectations, Hell, Hypocrisy, Ignorance, Judgment, Last Days, Mercy, Preparation, Second Coming, Sin, Surprises, Waiting

OPEN IT

■ What is the most surprised you've ever been in your life?
❊ What are some ways people show their unbelief in God?
❊ With what mysteries are people intrigued today?

EXPLORE IT

❊ Who knows when the end times will come? (24:36)
❊ When did Jesus say these end time events would occur? (24:36)
❊ Who did Jesus say knows the day and hour of the end? (24:36)
❊ To what did Jesus compare the end of the world? (24:37)
❊ How will most people react when the end comes? (24:38-41)
❊ What illustrations did Jesus use to show the suddenness of His return? (24:40-41)
❊ What warning did Jesus give His disciples? (24:42)
■ To what did Jesus liken His coming? Why? (24:43-44)
■ What qualities did Jesus say His servants will need to be ready for His coming? (24:45-47)
■ What did Jesus warn would happen to those who doubt His coming? (24:48-51)

GET IT

❊ What would you do if you hired a house sitter/caretaker to watch your home and children, left for a week-long vacation, and then returned a day early only to find that your caretaker had neglected your kids, destroyed your property, and ignored all your other instructions?
❊ What does it mean for us to be watchful?
❊ How can you tell when you are being watchful?
❊ What difference does it make whether we believe in the imminent return of Christ?
❊ Even if we claim to believe in Christ, what are some ways we live as though we were atheists?
❊ How might a nonChristian look at your life and accuse you of not believing in the imminent return of Jesus Christ?
■ How would you react if you knew a thief would try to burglarize your home or apartment tonight?
■ How can we have a sense of expectation about the return of Christ?
❊ How do you know that hell is a horrible place?

APPLY IT

■ How can you use your time today to honor the Lord's imminent return?
❊ What steps can you take today to be a better steward of the gifts and information God has entrusted to you?

Matthew 25:1-13

The Parable of the Ten Virgins

TOPICS

Celebration, Delay, Eternal Life, Expectations, Future, Hell, Judgment, Last Days, Marriage, Mercy, Preparation, Second Coming, Sin, Surprises, Waiting

OPEN IT

❊ What is the most elaborate or important social function you have ever been invited to?
❊ When was a time you were late to an important event, and why were you delayed?
■ How do you react when you are made to wait?

EXPLORE IT

❊ To what did Jesus compare the kingdom of heaven in this parable? (25:1)
❊ How were the ten women described? (25:1-2)
❊ Why were some of the virgins described as "foolish"? (25:3)
❊ What made some of the virgins "wise"? (25:4)
❊ What happened to the bridegroom? (25:5)
❊ What happened at midnight? (25:6-7)
❊ What did the foolish virgins ask of the others? (25:8)
■ How did the wise virgins respond when asked to help the ones who weren't prepared? (25:9)
❊ When did the bridegroom arrive and the wedding banquet begin? (25:10)
❊ What did the foolish virgins discover and do when they returned? (25:11)
■ How did the bridegroom respond when some virgins wanted to come to the wedding late? (25:12)
■ With what warning did Jesus conclude this parable? Why? (25:13)

GET IT

■ In what ways do you tend to count on more mature Christians or try to ride their coattails?
■ What responsibility does each Christian have before God?
❊ Why is continual preparation for Christ's return better than "last minute cramming"?
❊ Why do we tend to think (and act like) we have all the time in the world to get ready for Christ's return?
❊ What does this passage say about the need for individual readiness?
❊ What are the possible consequences of putting off thinking about Christ and spiritual growth until later?

APPLY IT

■ What spiritual preparation do you need to make today in order to "keep watch"?
❊ How can you change your attitude this week in order to reflect your belief in the imminent return of Christ?
❊ What Christian should you lovingly warn about the imminent return of Christ?

Matthew 25:14-30

The Parable of the Talents

TOPICS

Accomplishments, Accountability, Approval, Discernment, Effectiveness, Excuses, Generosity, Ignorance, Judgment, Laziness, Management, Opportunities, Possessions, Productivity, Resources, Rewards, Serving, Success

OPEN IT

❊ What are some typical images people have of God?
❊ What are your five best traits or greatest attributes?
■ What would you do for God if you knew you could not fail at it?

EXPLORE IT

❊ To what did Jesus liken the kingdom of God in this parable? (25:14)
❊ What did the man in the parable give to his servants? (25:15)
❊ What did the servant who received five talents do with his money? (25:16)
❊ What kind of return on his investment did the servant with two talents get? (25:17)
❊ What did the third servant do with the one talent his master gave him? (25:18)
■ How did the master react to the report of the first servant? (25:20-21)
■ What was the response to the report of the second servant? (25:22-23)
❊ What excuse did the third servant give for not investing his talent? (25:24-25)
■ How did the master respond to the third servant's explanation? (25:26-27)
❊ What orders did the master give about the third servant's one talent? (25:28-29)
❊ What judgment was handed down to the "wicked, lazy" servant? (25:30)

GET IT

■ With what talents or resources has God entrusted you?
❊ What gifts or talents has God given your church?
❊ Besides money or material possessions, what are some resources God has placed in our care?
❊ What thoughts or attitudes cause us to be lazy in carrying out our Christian responsibilities?
❊ What are the risks of investing our gifts for God's service?
❊ What are the rewards of investing our gifts for God's service?
■ In what ways can you be a "good and faithful" servant?
❊ Where are you able to invest your gifts?
❊ What people can benefit most from the gifts and abilities you have?
❊ What discourages you from investing your talents?
❊ What encourages you to serve God with your talents?
❊ How would you grade yourself in your Christian stewardship over the last year?

APPLY IT

■ What resource do you need to commit to Christ's use at this time in your life?
❊ How can you invest your talents in serving God this week?
❊ What reminder can you use to hold yourself accountable for the way you manage your God-given resources?

Matthew 25:31-46

The Sheep and the Goats

TOPICS

Angels, Blessing, Consequences, Demons, Eternal Life, Heaven, Hell, Judgment, Mercy, Messiah, Punishment, Righteousness, Satan, Second Coming, Self-righteousness, Separation

OPEN IT

❊ What are some ways we label or categorize others?
❊ Why is the belief in heaven and hell waning, while the belief in reincarnation becomes more popular?
■ What are some common examples of separating clean from dirty, fresh from spoiled, or good from bad?

EXPLORE IT

❊ How did Jesus describe His second coming? (25:31)
❊ Where will all the nations be at Christ's return? (25:32)
❊ According to Jesus, how will the people of the earth be divided? (25:32-33)
❊ How will Jesus divide humanity? (25:33)
■ What will Jesus say to those on His right? (25:34-36)
❊ Why will the group on Jesus' right be blessed? (25:35)
■ How will the "sheep" respond to Jesus' words on that day? (25:37-39)
■ What criterion will Christ use to judge people? (25:40)
❊ What will Jesus say to the "goats" on His left? (25:41)
❊ Why will the goats be judged? (25:42)
❊ What will cause the goats to be judged? (25:42-43)
❊ What defense will those on Christ's left use to justify themselves? (25:44)
❊ What will hell be like? (25:46)

GET IT

■ How do people usually determine whether they will be nice to somebody?
■ How would your behavior change if you treated each person in your life as if he or she were Jesus?
❊ In what way does this parable motivate you to tell your friends about Christ?
❊ How would you counter the idea that this passage teaches salvation by good works?
❊ What change does true faith make in a person's life?
❊ In what specific ways has your faith in Christ changed you?
❊ Who are the needy people around you?
❊ What resources do you have available to you for serving the needs of others?

APPLY IT

■ What act of kindness or mercy toward the needy can you do today?
❊ In what practical, realistic way can you begin today to treat each person you meet as though he or she were Jesus Himself?
❊ Without being overbearing or pushy, how can you serve your nonChristian friends this week?

Matthew 26:1-5
The Plot Against Jesus

TOPICS
Conversation, Death, Determination, Enemies, Fear, Future, Hardheartedness, Hatred, Motives, Murder, Opposition, Plans, Rejection, Resentment, Revenge, Sin, Sovereignty

OPEN IT
❊ What famous assassinations can you recall?
■ What is your theory about the assassination of John F. Kennedy?
❊ Why do "good people" get caught up in bad situations?

EXPLORE IT
❊ To whom was Jesus talking? When? (26:1)
❊ How close was the Feast of the Passover? (26:2)
❊ What did Jesus say would happen at the Feast of the Passover? (26:2)
❊ Who presided over the gathering of chief priests and elders? (26:3)
❊ Where did the chief priests and elders assemble? Why? (26:3-4)
■ What group got together in secret? Why? (26:3-4)
❊ What did the chief priests and elders gather to do? (26:4)
❊ What was the chief priests' and elders' ultimate desire concerning Jesus? (26:4)
■ Whom did the religious leaders plan to arrest? Why? (26:4-5)
■ When did the religious leaders not want to carry out their plan? (26:5)
❊ Why were the religious leaders reluctant to act during the feast? (26:5)

GET IT
■ Why would devout religious leaders plot to murder someone like Jesus?
❊ Historically, what other evil deeds have been done in God's name?
❊ How can we avoid justifying evil acts with the belief that we are serving God?
■ When might a Christian be tempted to take matters into his or her own hands instead of trusting God?
❊ What kinds of opposition do Christians face today?
❊ How should we respond to opposition to our faith?
❊ In what ways do these incidents tell us that God is sovereignly in control of all events?
❊ How can we show our trust in God when events turn against us?

APPLY IT
■ What uncertain situation will you entrust to God today?
❊ What can you do today to show your thankfulness for Christ's voluntary sacrifice?

Matthew 26:6-13
Jesus Anointed at Bethany

TOPICS
Actions, Devotion, Embarrassment, Example, Faith, Generosity, Kindness, Love, Praise, Preparation, Rationalizing, Sacrifice, Worship

OPEN IT
■ What is the most colossal waste of money you have ever witnessed?
❊ What is the most valuable possession you own?
❊ In what situations might it be wiser to be extravagant than frugal?

EXPLORE IT
❊ In what kind of place was Jesus when this scene opened? (26:6)
❊ Where was Jesus staying? (26:6)
❊ The woman who came to see Christ had what with her? Why? (26:7)
■ What did the woman do with her perfume? (26:7)
■ How did the disciples react to the sacrifice they witnessed? (26:8)
❊ What did the disciples claim would have been a better use for the perfume? (26:9)
■ How did Jesus respond to the disciples' indignation and muttering? (26:10)
❊ What did Jesus call the woman's act? Why? (26:10-11)
❊ Why did Jesus say the woman did the right thing? (26:11)
❊ How did Jesus describe this anointing? (26:12)
❊ What recognition did Jesus promise for the woman? (26:13)

GET IT
❊ What evidence is there that among Jesus' followers, only Mary understood that Jesus would soon be dead?
❊ How might Jesus' statement about the poor (26:11) be used as a justification to do nothing to help them?
❊ For what reasons do you think the disciples criticized Mary?
❊ When are we most likely to bad-mouth the efforts of other believers?
❊ What frequently happens when Christians become concerned about pleasing everyone around them?
■ What prompts us to sacrifice our time and goods for God?
❊ How can we increase our love for Jesus so that we will be willing to sacrifice for Him?
❊ What are the dangers in making a generous public gift?
■ What attitudes would make you more generous?

APPLY IT
■ What act of costly service can you give to Christ this week?
❊ What attitudes that keep you from being more generous do you need to renounce and repent of today?
❊ How can you begin to view the good works of others in a positive light rather than in a critical fashion?

Matthew 26:14-16
Judas Agrees to Betray Jesus

TOPICS
Abandon, Character, Convictions, Deceit, Friendship, Hatred, Lost, Plans, Rebellion, Rejection, Separation, Sin, Timing

OPEN IT
❇ What does it mean to be committed to something or someone?
❇ What images does the word "betrayal" bring to mind?
■ What does it take to build a lasting friendship?

EXPLORE IT
❇ Who is the central character in this passage? (26:14)
❇ To what elite group did Judas belong? (26:14)
❇ How did the meeting between Judas and the priests get started? (26:14)
■ With what group did Judas meet? Why? (26:14-15)
❇ What offer did Judas make to the chief priests? (26:15)
❇ How did Judas refer to Jesus? (26:15)
❇ How did the chief priests show they were interested in Judas's offer? (26:15)
■ What did Judas get for betraying Jesus? (26:15)
❇ What did Judas do once he struck a deal with the chief priests? (26:16)
■ How did Judas spend his last days with Jesus? (26:16)

GET IT
❇ What motives or feelings would prompt someone to betray a man like Jesus?
❇ In what ways does our behavior betray whether we truly love and serve Jesus?
❇ If Jesus knew everything, why do you think He picked as one of His disciples a man who would eventually betray Him?
❇ How does it make you feel to realize that Judas apparently was at one time a very devoted follower of Jesus?
❇ In what ways are we vulnerable to the temptations that snagged Judas?
❇ For what temporary thrills or situations have you "sold out" Jesus at one time or another?
■ How can we avoid making Judas's mistake?
■ In what ways can you rely on more mature Christians keep you accountable so that you do not drift in your commitment to Jesus?

APPLY IT
❇ To whom can you turn this week for accountability in your walk with God?
■ In what area of life this week can you make your deeds more closely match your stated loyalty to Jesus?

Matthew 26:17-30
The Lord's Supper

TOPICS
Atonement, Celebration, Covenant, Despair, Example, Feelings, Future, Habits, Important, Instructions, Love, New Covenant, Preparation, Sacrifice, Traditions, Victory, Worship

OPEN IT
❇ In what ways does sharing a meal bind people together?
❇ What names, dates, or events do you have a hard time remembering?
❇ If you were dying, what would you want for a last meal?
■ How do you hope people will remember you after you are gone?

EXPLORE IT
❇ What was going on during the time of the incidents described in this passage? (26:17)
❇ What question did the disciples ask Jesus? (26:17)
❇ What instructions did Jesus give His followers? (26:18)
❇ What was the response of the disciples to Jesus' instructions? (26:19)
❇ What did Jesus and His disciples do that evening? (26:20)
❇ What shocking statement did Jesus utter during His meal with the disciples? (26:21)
❇ How did the disciples react to Jesus' announcement? (26:22)
❇ How did Jesus identify the one who would betray Him? (26:23)
❇ What sobering statement did Jesus make about His betrayer? (26:24)
❇ How did Judas respond to the words of Christ? (26:25)
■ What did Jesus say about the bread on the table? (26:26)
■ What remarks did Jesus make about the wine they were drinking? (26:27-28)
■ When did Jesus say He would eat with His disciples again? (26:29)
❇ What did the group do after they finished eating? (26:30)

GET IT
❇ In what ways might Christ be uncomfortable to eat a meal in your home?
❇ When we respond to Christ's commands, do you think we tend to fulfill them completely, or only so far as we feel like it?
❇ How does it make you feel to realize that Christ's body was battered and broken because of your sin?
■ How do you feel when you remember that Jesus shed His blood on the cross for you?
❇ What do you imagine it would have been like to have been one of the participants at that first Lord's Supper, to have heard those men sing a hymn, to have looked Christ in the eyes?

❊ Why do you think Judas asked if he was the one who would betray Jesus?
■ What does Communion or the Eucharist mean to you personally?

APPLY IT
■ What do you want to change about the way you participate in the Lord's Supper the next time it is celebrated at church?
❊ What do you need to do today (or stop doing) to be a fully obedient servant of Jesus Christ?
❊ How can you encourage a friend this week with the message of this passage?

Matthew 26:31-35
Jesus Predicts Peter's Denial

TOPICS
Abandon, Commitment, Courage, Danger, Determination, Embarrassment, Endurance, Failure, Foolishness, Impulsiveness, Loyalty, Peer Pressure, Persecution, Promises, Rejection, Vows, Weaknesses, Words

OPEN IT
■ Why is it dangerous to begin a sentence with the words, "I would never . . ."?
❊ Why is it possible for a mature believer in Christ to sin?
❊ What do you think about the expression, "Talk is cheap"?

EXPLORE IT
■ What prediction about His followers did Jesus make on the Mount of Olives? (26:31)
❊ To what did Jesus compare Himself and His disciples? (26:31)
❊ What was significant about Jesus' statement and His situation? (26:31)
❊ What did Christ predict about Himself? (26:32)
❊ Where did Jesus say He would go? When? (26:32)
■ How did Peter respond to Jesus' statement that all the disciples would abandon Him? (26:33)
❊ What prediction did Jesus make about Peter? (26:34)
❊ What did Peter have to say when Jesus said Peter would disown Him? (26:35)
■ How did the rest of the disciples react to these depressing comments by Christ? (26:35)

GET IT
❊ How committed do you think the disciples were to Jesus?
❊ How is the commitment of many Christians today much like that of the eleven disciples with Jesus in the garden?
■ What is admirable about a promise never to abandon Christ?
■ What is foolish about a vow never to abandon Christ?
❊ What situations might tempt you to be quiet or low-key about your relationship with Jesus Christ?
❊ If wide-scale persecution of Christians broke out in this country, as it has in so many others, how do you think many Christians would respond? Why?
❊ What do you learn about God from the fact that Jesus did not yell at His disciples or disown them even though He knew they would abandon Him?
❊ Why is human willpower inadequate to keep us from sinning?
❊ What vow have you made to God that you need to fulfill?

APPLY IT
❊ In what particular situation(s) this week do you need to make it clear—for the first time—that you are a follower of Jesus Christ?
❊ How can you encourage a Christian brother or sister who has recently denied Christ and is feeling discouraged?
■ What first step in fulfilling your vow to God do you need to take this week?

Matthew 26:36-46
Gethsemane

TOPICS
Backslide, Carelessness, Comfortable, Compromise, Danger, Desires, Endurance, Friendship, God's Will, Help, Inadequacy, Intentions, Loyalty, Perseverance, Prayer, Selfishness, Sleep

OPEN IT
■ In what particular situations is it hardest for you to stay awake?
❊ How do you react emotionally and physically when you are facing extreme stress?
❊ What friends do you turn to when your world is turned upside down?

EXPLORE IT
❊ Who was Jesus with? When? (26:36)
■ Where did Jesus and His companions go together? Why? (26:36)
❊ What did Jesus tell the disciples? (26:36)
❊ With which disciples did Jesus choose to pray? (26:37)
❊ What was Jesus' state of mind at the time? (26:37)
❊ What kind of pain did Jesus confess to His friends? (26:38)
❊ When Jesus went on a bit further and fell to the ground, what did He do? (26:39)
❊ What scene greeted Jesus when He returned from praying? (26:40)
❊ What kind of warning did Jesus give Peter? (26:40-41)
❊ What did Jesus do after speaking with Peter? (26:42)
❊ What were the disciples doing while Jesus was praying the second time? (26:43)
■ How did Jesus react when He found His disciples sleeping a second time? (26:44)
■ When Jesus finished praying, what did He say to His disciples? (26:45)
❊ What event happened after Jesus prayed? (26:46)

GET IT
■ Why would it have been very advantageous for the disciples to have stayed awake and prayed?
❊ What clues from the passage suggest that Christ was

grieving about what lay ahead for Him?
■ What is amazing about Christ's attitude?
❊ What kind of help would friends get from you if they called you in the middle of the night?
❊ What generally wins out as you face decisions in life—your feelings or your commitments?
❊ What is the most agonizing situation you have ever faced?
❊ How might a faithful prayer life keep you strong in the faith?
❊ What are the barriers to your prayers?
❊ How can you improve your prayer life?

APPLY IT
❊ What changes do you need to make in your schedule this week so that you become more regular in prayer?
■ How can you be a better friend today to someone who is going through a difficult situation?
❊ In what area of your life do you need to say to God, "Your will be done"?

Matthew 26:47-56
Jesus Arrested

TOPICS
Challenge, Danger, Darkness, Enemies, Evil, Failure, Friendship, God's Will, Impulsiveness, Jesus Christ, Motives, Prophecy, Protection, Rejection, Sacrifice, Sin, Sovereignty

OPEN IT
❊ What is the fastest you have ever run in your life?
■ What is one time your beliefs or convictions were tested?
❊ What types of situations tend to make your heart sink?
❊ What prompts some people to rescue others in trouble, while others are interested only in helping themselves?

EXPLORE IT
❊ What happened just as Jesus finished praying in the garden of Gethsemane? (26:47)
❊ Who accompanied Judas? (26:47)
❊ What kind of crowd accompanied Judas? (26:47)
❊ How did Judas greet Jesus? (26:49)
❊ What was significant about the signal Judas used to point out Jesus? (26:48)
❊ What command did Jesus give Judas? (26:50)
❊ What did the men in the crowd do when Jesus spoke? (26:50)
■ What did one of Jesus' disciples do in an attempt to protect his master? (26:51)
❊ What did Jesus tell the disciple who attacked? (26:52)
❊ What truthful "boast" did Jesus make? (26:53)
■ Why didn't Jesus take advantage of His disciple's brave attack? (26:54)
❊ What did Jesus say to the crowd? (26:55)
■ What happened when it became obvious that Jesus would be arrested? (26:56)

GET IT
❊ What do you think the disciples were feeling as they saw the armed mob approaching?
❊ Why do you think this mob came at night to arrest Jesus?
❊ What is especially awful about the way Judas betrayed Jesus?
❊ What do you think would have been your reaction had you been in the garden that night?
❊ Whose trust have you violated recently?
■ When are we tempted to take matters into our own hands out of "devotion" to God?
❊ How has your faith been tested recently?
■ How can we stand firm when our faith is tested?
❊ How do you tend to react in frightening situations?

APPLY IT
■ What can you do today to ensure that you will stand strong the next time your faith is tested?
❊ In what specific situations this week do you need to trust God instead of resorting to human wisdom and tactics?

Matthew 26:57-68
Before the Sanhedrin

TOPICS
Accusation, Blasphemy, Challenge, Deceit, Enemies, Evil, Hatred, Humiliation, Insults, Jesus Christ, Lying, Messiah, Rejection, Second Coming, Suffering

OPEN IT
■ What is the most famous "miscarriage of justice" you have ever witnessed or heard about?
❊ When in your life have you ended up suffering because you tried to help someone else?
❊ In what ways are lies and gossip damaging?

EXPLORE IT
■ After being arrested, where was Jesus taken? (26:57)
❊ Who was assembled where Jesus was taken? Why? (26:57, 59)
❊ Who had followed Jesus at a distance? Where was he? (26:58)
❊ What did Peter do in an attempt to observe the proceedings against Jesus? (26:58)
❊ What were the chief priests and Sanhedrin hoping to find? (26:59)
■ Who came forward to testify at this "trial"? (26:60)
■ What did one witness claim to have heard Jesus say? (26:61)
❊ When the high priest first began questioning Jesus, how did Jesus respond? (26:62-63)
❊ What question did the high priest finally ask Jesus about His identity? (26:63)
❊ How did Jesus answer the high priest? (26:64)
❊ What prophetic statement did Jesus make in His defense? (26:64)
❊ How did Jesus' claim affect the high priest? (26:65-66)
❊ What emotional and physical abuse did Christ endure at the hands of these spiritual leaders? (26:67-68)

GET IT
■ How is it possible for an innocent person to be accused and convicted of a crime?

■ When have you been harmed by false accusers spreading malicious lies?
❊ How can we respond when attacked for no just reason?
❊ What is it like to be ganged up on?
❊ Why do you think Christ didn't argue with his accusers and make some sort of defense?
❊ In what situations are we tempted to water down or soft-pedal the truth?
❊ What is it that sometimes causes groups of people to become vicious and cruel?
❊ What do you think about Jesus' claim to be the Son of God?

APPLY IT
❊ In what group situations might you be able to act as a calming and peacemaking voice this week?
■ In what situation this week do you need to tell the truth, even if it may cost you?
❊ To what friend(s) in trouble can you show support by your physical presence?

Matthew 26:69-75
Peter Disowns Jesus

TOPICS
Accusation, Backslide, Compromise, Conversation, Denial, Depression, Embarrassment, Fear, Forsake, Grief, Loyalty, Peer Pressure, Pressure, Risk, Sorrow, Swearing, Trust, Words

OPEN IT
■ What does loyalty mean to you?
❊ What are some of your greatest fears?
❊ What examples could you cite to prove the old adage, "There is strength in numbers"?

EXPLORE IT
❊ Where was Peter? (26:69)
■ Who approached Peter? Why? (26:69)
❊ What did the servant girl say to Peter? Why? (26:69)
■ How did Peter respond to the servant girl's question? (26:70)
❊ What did Peter do after his exchange with the servant girl? (26:71)
❊ When another girl approached Peter, what did she say? (26:71)
❊ How did Peter handle the second girl's claim? (26:72)
❊ Why did a third group of folks insist that Peter had to be a follower of Christ? (26:73)
❊ What extreme reaction did Peter have to the allegation that he was a follower of Jesus? (26:74)
■ What happened when Peter denied knowing Christ? (26:74-75)
❊ What memory did the cock's crow trigger in Peter's mind? (26:75)
❊ How did Peter react when he realized what he had done? (26:75)

GET IT
❊ What do you think Peter was hoping to accomplish by hanging around the trial of Jesus?
❊ What happened through a couple of young girls to scare Peter into silence?
❊ How would you have felt in Peter's place?
■ When do you find you are most tempted to downplay or even deny your Christian beliefs?
■ When has your faith in Jesus cost you something?
❊ Why do some Christians seem to be able to stand up for Christ with no problem, while others stumble often?
❊ If you were accused of being a close follower of Jesus Christ and were put on trial, would witnesses be able to come forward to present evidence against you?
❊ How can close friendships with committed believers keep you from falling away from Christ?

APPLY IT
■ To what person should you demonstrate your loyalty this week? How?
❊ Whom might you be able to engage in a conversation about Jesus Christ this week?
❊ In what settings do you need to acknowledge Christ more consistently by your actions (or nonactions)?

Matthew 27:1-10
Judas Hangs Himself

TOPICS
Actions, Change, Despair, Feelings, Jesus Christ, Messiah, Pain, Prophecy, Religion, Repentance, Shame, Sin, Sorrow, Soul

OPEN IT
❊ Over what kinds of situations or mistakes do people decide to kill themselves?
■ What are some ways people try to deal with guilt?
❊ Who is the most compassionate and caring friend you know?
❊ What are inappropriate sources of income for churches and ministries?

EXPLORE IT
❊ When did the religious leaders decide to put Jesus to death? (27:1)
❊ What did the religious leaders do with Christ? (27:2)
❊ Where did the religious leaders take Jesus? (27:2)
❊ Why was it significant that Jesus was taken to Pilate? (27:2)
■ How did Judas feel when he saw that Jesus had been condemned to die? (27:3)
■ What action did Judas take in an attempt to undo his crime? (27:3)
❊ What did Judas say to the religious leaders? (27:4)
■ How did the religious leaders act when they heard Judas express second thoughts? (27:4)
❊ What did Judas do when the leaders rejected his offer to return the money? (27:5)
❊ What did the leaders do with the bounty they had paid Judas? (27:6-8)
❊ Why was Judas's suicide significant? (27:9-10)

GET IT
❊ Why do you think the chief priests were so insensitive to Judas's remorse?
❊ In what situations do we sometimes offer token compassion or ignore altogether those who are hurting?

■ What would you say to someone who was feeling extremely guilty and depressed?
■ How can we avoid (or break out of) a downward spiral of sin, guilt, depression, more sin, greater guilt, deeper depression, etc.?
❊ How does sin, if allowed to go unchecked, cause us to lose all sense of rightness and kindness?
❊ What practical steps can we take when confronted with wrongdoing?

APPLY IT
■ What big decision do you need to pray about this week so that you do not end up making a choice you will later regret?
❊ What can you do today or tomorrow to encourage a friend who is feeling especially low because of a bad or sinful choice?

Matthew 27:11-26
Jesus Before Pilate

TOPICS
Accusation, Answers, Authority, Blindness, Conscience, Death, Evil, Favoritism, Foolishness, God's Will, Government, Hardheartedness, Intimidation, Jesus Christ, Pressure, Rebellion, Rejection, Silence, Sin, Unbelievers, World

OPEN IT
■ What is the most ingenious or creative excuse you have heard someone give in an attempt to avoid responsibility?
❊ What is your opinion of politicians?
❊ What governmental customs or laws do you like best and least?
❊ How much stock do you put in dreams?

EXPLORE IT
❊ What title and position did Pilate have? (27:11)
❊ What question did Pilate ask Jesus? (27:11)
❊ How did Jesus answer the Roman authority? (27:11)
❊ How did Jesus answer the Jews when they made accusations against Him? (27:12)
❊ What did Pilate think of Christ's silence? (27:13-14)
❊ What custom did the governor follow at this particular time of year? (27:15)
❊ Who was in prison at the time? (27:16)
❊ What choice did Pilate put before the crowd? (27:17-18)
❊ What message did Pilate's wife send him? (27:19)
❊ How did the religious leaders influence the crowd? (27:20)
❊ What choice did the crowd make? (27:21)
■ What did the crowd ask Pilate to do to Christ? (27:22)
■ How did Pilate attempt to evade any responsibility in the condemnation of Jesus? (27:24)
❊ What ironic statement did the crowd make about Jesus' blood? (27:25)
■ What happened to the two prisoners—Barabbas and Jesus? (27:26)

GET IT
❊ How would you rate Pilate's performance?
❊ Why is it difficult not to defend yourself when people are saying mean and untrue things about you?
❊ What attitudes, emotions, or perspective must a person have in order to stay calm while being attacked?
❊ In what way is not defending an innocent person the same as condemning him or her?
❊ When might you be called upon to defend someone who is innocent?
❊ What risks are there in defending an innocent person?
❊ In what relationships do you need to trust more in the power and sufficiency of Christ?
❊ In what situations do you need to quit arguing and defending yourself?
■ What decisions have you been putting off for fear of the responsibility?
■ What helps you face your responsibilities?

APPLY IT
❊ How can you prepare yourself for the next time you have an opportunity to defend an innocent person?
■ What decision do you need to make today and then take responsibility for?

Matthew 27:27-31
The Soldiers Mock Jesus

TOPICS
Accusation, Authority, Blasphemy, Blindness, Evil, Government, Hardheartedness, Hatred, Intimidation, Jesus Christ, Pain, Persecution, Rejection, Sin, Unbelievers, World

OPEN IT
■ What effect do you think violence in the media has on our society?
❊ Which is worse, physical or emotional pain? Why?
❊ What are the most common ways Christians are mocked?

EXPLORE IT
■ Who took charge of the flogging and crucifixion of Jesus? (27:26-27)
❊ How many people were involved in torturing Jesus? (27:27)
■ Where did the guards take Jesus? Why? (27:27-28)
■ Once they had Jesus inside, what did the guards do? (27:27-31)
❊ What did the guards make Jesus wear? (27:28-29)
❊ What did the soldiers put on Jesus' head? Why? (27:29)
❊ In what way did these soldiers mock Jesus? (27:29)
❊ With what did the soldiers ridicule Christ? (27:29)
❊ What types of emotional and physical abuse did the guards inflict on Christ? (27:30)
❊ After mocking Jesus, what did the soldiers do? (27:31)

GET IT
❊ Why did Christ put up with torture when He could have destroyed all His attackers?
❊ What do you think the soldiers were thinking as they mocked, taunted, and assaulted Jesus?
❊ What would you do if you came upon a group of friends who were abusing (either verbally or physically)

some helpless individual?
❋ What can we do to curb the abusive mentality of others?
❋ Why do people pick on helpless individuals?
❋ In what ways does evil become easier to justify when many people are doing it?
■ What evils have become legitimized by consensus in our society today?
■ What can Christians do to resist the tendency for evil to spread once it becomes common?
❋ What sorts of opposition should we expect to face when resisting popular evils?

APPLY IT
❋ Whom can you encourage this week who has been facing persecution?
❋ What can you do or say to speak out against an evil that is being accepted as normal?
■ In what way can you be a peacemaker this week at home, at work, or among your neighbors?

Matthew 27:32-44
The Crucifixion

TOPICS
Atonement, Bitterness, Blasphemy, Blindness, Criticism, Death, Endurance, Foolishness, Hatred, Humiliation, Jesus Christ, Pain, Rejection, Sacrifice, Sin, Strength, Unbelievers

OPEN IT
❋ What do you think would be the most horrible way to die?
❋ Where do you stand in the ongoing debate over capital punishment?
❋ How accurate is the old saying, "Sticks and stones may break my bones, but words can never hurt me"?
■ What is the weakest and most exhausted you've ever been?

EXPLORE IT
❋ When did these events take place? (27:32)
❋ Whom did Jesus and his executioners meet as they were making their way to the site of the crucifixion? (27:32)
❋ What was Simon forced to do? For whom? (27:32)
❋ Where did the group take Jesus? (27:33)
❋ What is the meaning of "Golgotha"? (27:33)
❋ What was offered to Jesus? (27:34)
❋ After nailing Jesus to the cross, what did the soldiers do? (27:35-36)
❋ What did the soldiers place above Jesus' head? (27:37)
❋ Who was executed that day? (27:38)
■ What did onlookers shout at Jesus? (27:39-40)
■ What was the behavior of the religious leaders like as they watched Jesus die? (27:41-43)
■ How did the robbers act toward Jesus? (27:44)

GET IT
❋ In a passage where many people are anonymous, why do you think Simon of Cyrene is mentioned by name?
■ Why does it hurt to be mocked and laughed at and scorned?
❋ In what way were the soldiers showing mercy by offering Jesus wine?
❋ What are some ways we attempt to numb ourselves to the reality of the harsh world around us?
■ How does it make you feel to realize that Jesus underwent horrible abuse for you?
❋ How is it possible to love the very people who are the most cruel and vicious to us?
❋ When are you sometimes insulted?
❋ When is it worth undergoing unjustified abuse?

APPLY IT
❋ What "cross" (burden, problem, difficulty, grief) can you unselfishly agree to bear for someone else today?
■ In what way can you show your gratitude to Jesus today in light of all He suffered for you?
❋ What steps can you take this week to help you overlook insults and verbal taunts?

Matthew 27:45-56
The Death of Jesus

TOPICS
Atonement, Believe, Blindness, Darkness, Death, Devotion, God, Grief, Hopelessness, Loneliness, Mediator, Miracles, Mourning, Pain, Questions, Sacrifice, Separation, Unbelievers

OPEN IT
■ What is it like to be separated from someone you love?
❋ When in your life did you ever feel abandoned?

EXPLORE IT
❋ What happened from the sixth to the ninth hour (from 12 noon until 3 p.m.)? (27:45)
■ What did Jesus cry out at the ninth hour? Why? (27:46)
■ What did Jesus' last words mean? (27:46)
❋ What did some of the bystanders think Christ had yelled? (27:47)
❋ What did one man in particular try to do for Jesus? (27:48)
❋ How did the rest in the crowd respond to the gesture of kindness toward Jesus? (27:49)
❋ What happened the next time Jesus cried out in a loud voice? (27:50)
❋ What supernatural event took place inside the temple when Jesus died? (27:51)
❋ How were things in Jerusalem at that time? (27:51)
❋ How did the death of Jesus affect activity in some of the area's cemeteries? (27:52-53)
■ How did a Roman centurion react to the way Jesus died? (27:54)
❋ Who else was in the crowd watching the crucifixion? (27:55)
❋ Who in the crowd was most prominent at Jesus' death? (27:56)

GET IT
■ What did it mean that the sky turned black as Jesus hung on the cross?
❋ How would you explain to an inquiring friend the significance of the veil in the temple tearing in two as Jesus died?

❊ Why does it often take drastic measures or life-threatening upheavals to bring people to their senses and persuade them to follow Christ?
❊ What situations or events did God use to convince you that Jesus is the Son of God?
❊ Why are the women followers of Jesus mentioned, and not the male disciples?
■ What did Jesus accomplish for you with His death?

APPLY IT
■ What steps can you take this week to allow the profound truth of this passage to sink in?
❊ In the near future, with whom can you share the good news of Christ's payment for sin on the cross?

Matthew 27:57-61
The Burial of Jesus

TOPICS
Actions, Commitment, Courage, Danger, Fear, Generosity, Integrity, Ministry, Peer Pressure, Reputation, Strength, Witnessing

OPEN IT
❊ What do you think about fair-weather friends who depart at the first sign of trouble?
❊ What would your coworkers say if they found out that you were in this Bible study?
■ Where do you want to be buried? Why?

EXPLORE IT
❊ Who came to the execution site? When? (27:57)
❊ What was true about Joseph of Arimathea? (27:57)
❊ What did Joseph think about Jesus and His message? (27:57)
■ What kind of help did Jesus receive at His death? (27:57-58)
❊ How did Joseph ask for the body of Jesus? (27:58)
❊ How did Pilate respond to Joseph's request? (27:58)
■ What did Joseph do with Jesus' body? (27:59-60)
❊ Where did Joseph put Jesus' body? (27:60)
❊ How did Joseph seal the tomb? (27:60)
■ Who watched Joseph bury Jesus? (27:61)

GET IT
❊ Where were Jesus' disciples when all these events were going on?
❊ As a respected Jewish religious leader (see Mark 15:42-43 and John 19:38), what risk was Joseph taking in coming forward to bury Jesus?
■ In what ways are you a secret disciple of Christ, afraid to publicly follow him?
❊ How might your reputation suffer if you let it be known that your top desire in life is to love and serve Jesus Christ?
❊ When, if ever, is it inappropriate to use your power and position to support Christ and his work?
■ What brand-new possessions would you be willing to part with for the sake of Christ?

APPLY IT
■ What gift (of time, money, effort, possession, etc.) can you give this week out of love and devotion to God?
❊ In what setting today, tomorrow, or over the next week do you need to let it be known—maybe for the very first time—that you are a follower of Jesus Christ?

Matthew 27:62-66
The Guard at the Tomb

TOPICS
Authority, Bitterness, Blindness, Deceit, Determination, Effectiveness, Expectations, Hatred, Insecurity, Lost, Opposition, Plans, Power, Protection, Strength, Waiting

OPEN IT
■ If you could have five personal bodyguards (any people on earth) whom would you choose and then where would you go?
❊ Where do you feel the safest or most secure and why?
❊ When in your life have you been "taken for a ride?"

EXPLORE IT
❊ When did the chief priests go to Pilate? (27:62)
■ Who went to Pilate the day after Christ was buried? Why? (27:62-63)
❊ What words of Jesus did the chief priests remember and report to Pilate? (27:63)
❊ What did the religious leaders call Jesus? (27:63)
❊ What did the religious leaders want Pilate to do? (27:64)
■ For how long did the religious leaders want help from Pilate? Why? (27:64)
❊ What were the Jewish leaders afraid would happen if Pilate refused their request? (27:64)
❊ What were the chief priests afraid would happen if Jesus' body disappeared? (27:64)
❊ What command did Pilate give? (27:65)
■ What did the religious leaders do to secure the tomb where Jesus was buried? (27:65-66)

GET IT
❊ Knowing the attitudes and the actions of the Jews, what is ironic about them calling Jesus a "deceiver" guilty of "deception"?
❊ What manmade precautions are giving you a false sense of security that everything in your life is under control?
❊ In what ways do we trust in our own plans instead of in God?
■ In what areas of life are we prone to try to cover up the truth?
■ Why are we sometimes afraid to admit the truth?
❊ What claim or promise of Christ do you need to take more seriously?

APPLY IT
■ What truth do you need to face today?
❊ What foolish, fleshly attempts to control God and your own life do you need to repent of today?

Matthew 28:1-10

The Resurrection

TOPICS

Angels, Basics of the Faith, Believe, Celebration, Evangelism, Feelings, Gentleness, Good News, Gospel, Jesus Christ, Miracles, Power, Praise, Prophecy, Resurrection, Salvation, Success, Victory, Witnessing, Worship

OPEN IT

■ In your opinion, what is the most significant event in history?
❇ If you could go back in time and witness any historical event, which one would you choose? Why?
❇ What is the most awesome display of power you have ever seen?

EXPLORE IT

❇ When did the events of this passage occur? (28:1)
❇ Who went to Jesus' tomb? (28:1)
❇ What significant events took place that morning? (28:2)
❇ Where did the angel go, and what did he do? (28:2)
❇ What did the angel look like? (28:3)
❇ What effect did the angel have on the guards at the tomb of Jesus? (28:4)
■ What amazing news did the angel announce to the women at the tomb? (28:5-6)
❇ What invitation did the angel give the women? (28:6)
■ What command did the angel give Mary Magdalene and "the other Mary"? (28:7)
❇ How did the women feel as they left the tomb? (28:8)
■ What kind of meeting took place as the women were going to tell the disciples about Jesus? (28:9)
❇ How did the women respond when Jesus met them? (28:9)
❇ What words of challenge and comfort did the women receive? (28:10)

GET IT

❇ If you can mentally place yourself at the tomb of Christ on that first "Easter morning," what emotions would you be feeling?
■ Why is the Resurrection important to us as Christians?
■ What attitude should we have in light of the fact of Jesus' resurrection?
❇ How might you answer a skeptic who argued that Jesus didn't really rise from the dead?
❇ Why should we be interested and motivated to tell others about this amazing historical fact?
❇ How does Jesus' warm, loving attitude—even toward the disciples who deserted him—give you comfort?

APPLY IT

■ When and where could you spend a few minutes meditating on the truth of this passage over the next week?
❇ In what practical and realistic ways can you become more effective this week in spreading the good news about Christ?

Matthew 28:11-15

The Guards' Report

TOPICS

Answers, Blindness, Deceit, Details, Embarrassment, Excuses, Government, Interpretation, Lying, Motives, Plans, Rejection, Religion, Words

OPEN IT

■ How much of what goes on in the world (in government, in business, on the street, in families) is hidden or covered up?
❇ When you hear two wildly different versions of the same event, how do you determine which one is true?
❇ What bit of news or information do you remember more than any other?
❇ As a child, what elaborate cover-ups did you devise in order to hide your misbehavior?

EXPLORE IT

❇ While the women were going out to spread the good news, what did the guards from the tomb do? (28:11)
❇ What groups met to discuss the "emergency" of Jesus' missing body? (28:12)
❇ What did the meeting of religious leaders produce? (28:12)
■ What did the chief priests give the soldiers? Why? (28:12-13)
❇ Whom did the chief priests bribe? Why? (28:12-13)
❇ Whom did the chief priests and elders use? Why? (28:12-13)
❇ What did the religious leaders tell the soldiers to say? (28:13)
■ How did the religious leaders reassure the guards that they would not get in trouble with the Roman government? (28:14)
❇ What did the soldiers think about the plot? (28:15)
■ To what degree was the story made up by Jesus' enemies spread and believed? (28:15)

GET IT

❇ How do you think the soldiers felt as they made their way back to headquarters?
❇ To what do you account the Jewish leaders' stubborn unwillingness to acknowledge the Resurrection?
❇ If you had been living at the time, how might you have "poked holes" in the "official account" of the Resurrection?
❇ What are some other manmade explanations for the Resurrection?
■ How does money or the promise of wealth alter our ability to think clearly and reason purely?
■ Why are we willing to go to great lengths to cover up unpleasant truths?
❇ In what area(s) of your life have you been covering up the truth and living a lie?

APPLY IT

❇ What can you do this week to prepare for discussions with those who don't believe Jesus rose from the dead?
■ What first step do you need to take today to live with more integrity, no matter how much it costs you?

Matthew 28:16-20

The Great Commission

TOPICS
Authority, Believe, Call, Challenge, Evangelism, God's Will, Good News, Gospel, Help, Jesus Christ, Ministry, Plans, Purpose, Salvation, Witnessing, Worship

OPEN IT
■ What is the most exciting news you have received in the last month?
❇ What images spring to mind when you hear the words "missionary" or "evangelism"?
❇ What is the loneliest time you have ever experienced?

EXPLORE IT
❇ Who went to Galilee? When? (28:16)
❇ Where did the disciples gather? Why? (28:16)
❇ Why did the disciples assemble on the specific mountain they chose? (28:16)
❇ Who appeared to the disciples? When? (28:16-17)
❇ What responses did Jesus' appearance elicit? (28:17)
❇ What did Jesus say about Himself? (28:18)
❇ Where did Jesus tell His disciples to go? (28:19)
■ What did Jesus tell His disciples to make? (28:19)
■ What activities were the disciples to be involved in? (28:19-20)
■ With what words of comfort did Jesus leave His disciples? (28:20)

GET IT
❇ What insight into the triune nature of God do you find in this passage?
❇ Why do you think some of the disciples doubted when they saw Christ?
❇ What causes Christians to doubt God today?
❇ How do you think you might have reacted to the appearance of the risen Christ?
❇ What does it mean to us that Jesus has "all authority"?
❇ Over what does Jesus have all authority?
❇ Over whom does Jesus have all authority?
■ What does it mean to "make disciples"?
■ What role do you have in making disciples?
❇ How can knowing that Jesus is always with us make a difference in our daily lives?
❇ What specific teaching of Christ do you need to obey more consistently?

APPLY IT
❇ What older and wiser Christian can you approach in the next couple of days to ask for help in spiritual learning, training, and growing?
■ What step can you take this week in the process of making disciples?

Mark 1:1-8

John the Baptist Prepares the Way

TOPICS
Gospel, Humility, Preparation, Prophecy, Repentance, Witnessing

OPEN IT
■ How would you prepare for a home visit from your boss or another important person?
❇ Why is it important to prepare for the coming of an influential person?
❇ What attitudes do most ordinary people have about "very important persons"?

EXPLORE IT
❇ What do Mark's first words tell us about his gospel? (1:1)
❇ Who was John the Baptist? (1:2-3)
■ Who sent the messenger? Why? (1:2-3)
❇ How was Isaiah's prophecy fulfilled? (1:4)
■ What were the two aspects of John's ministry? (1:4)
❇ What reasons to be baptized did John give the people? (1:4)
❇ What had to happen before John could baptize a person? (1:5)
❇ When John said, "After me will come one more powerful than I," to whom was he referring? (1:7)
❇ What was John's attitude toward Jesus? (1:7)
■ What was the theme of John's message? (1:7-8)
❇ How did Jesus' baptism differ from John's? (1:8)

GET IT
❇ What is your reaction to the fact that Isaiah's prophecy was fulfilled?
❇ In what ways can we allow the Holy Spirit to work through us?
❇ How can Jesus' gift of the Holy Spirit make a difference in our lives?
■ What does the message of Jesus offer to people?
❇ What usually prevents us from being Christ's witnesses?
❇ How can a person's witness reflect humility and respect for Jesus?
❇ How can we ensure that our lives focus attention on Christ, and not on ourselves?
■ In what ways can you prepare others for Christ?

APPLY IT
■ What step could you take this week toward becoming a better witness for Christ?
❇ With whom can you share God's promise of forgiveness of sins? How?
❇ How can you encourage other Christians to be witnesses for Christ?

Mark 1:9-13

The Baptism and Temptation of Jesus

TOPICS

Affirmation, Angels, Approval, Heaven, Holy Spirit, Jesus Christ, Satan, Temptation, Testing

OPEN IT

❇ How do people typically show approval of others?
❇ When was a time you were affirmed by others?
❇ What is one form of recognition you received growing up, whether at school, at home, or from friends?
■ What does the word "temptation" bring to mind?

EXPLORE IT

❇ Who baptized Jesus? Why? (1:9)
❇ Why was this event significant? (1:9)
❇ What does Jesus' baptism tell us about His character? (1:10)
❇ What happened after Jesus was baptized? (1:10)
❇ How were the three persons of the Trinity present in this event? (1:10-11)
❇ To whom was the voice from heaven speaking? (1:11)
❇ What did the voice from heaven say about Jesus? (1:11)
■ What happened right after Jesus' baptism? (1:12)
❇ Who sent Jesus into the desert for forty days? Why? (1:12-13)
■ What happened to Jesus in the desert? (1:13)
❇ Under what conditions was Jesus tempted? (1:13)
■ What role did angels play in this event? (1:13)

GET IT

❇ How should we respond to Jesus' example of baptism?
❇ In what ways can we imitate Jesus' attitude of humility and submission?
❇ What implications does Jesus' experience of temptation have for the temptations we face?
❇ What difference does it make to you that the Holy Spirit allows you to be tempted?
❇ What might God be trying to teach you through tempting situations?
❇ How does it affect you to know that Satan is a force behind temptation?
■ What temptations are difficult for you to resist?
■ How can we depend more on the power of God to help us resist temptation?

APPLY IT

■ What concrete steps can you take this week to resist temptation?
❇ How can you remind yourself that Jesus understands the temptations you experience, and that He can help you resist them?

Mark 1:14-20

The Calling of the First Disciples

TOPICS

Believe, Family, Follow, Giving Up, Good News, Gospel, Invitation, Obedience, Sacrifice

OPEN IT

■ What kind of invitations do you enjoy receiving? Why?
❇ For what kinds of relationships are people willing to sacrifice their own needs?
❇ When are you most willing to set aside your own needs for another person's needs?

EXPLORE IT

❇ Why did Jesus go to Galilee? (1:14)
❇ What did Jesus do in Galilee? (1:14)
❇ How were the two parts of Jesus' message connected? (1:15)
■ How did Jesus want people to respond to the fact that the kingdom of God was near? (1:15)
■ What did Jesus tell the people they must do besides believe His good news? (1:15)
❇ Whom did Jesus call to be His followers? (1:16, 19)
■ How did Jesus get people to follow Him? (1:17)
❇ What does it mean to be "fishers of men"? (1:17)
❇ How did Simon and Andrew respond to Jesus' call? (1:17)
❇ What sacrifice did James and John make to follow Jesus? (1:20)

GET IT

■ What does Christ expect us to give up to follow Him?
❇ What are you willing to give up in order to follow Christ?
❇ What does it mean for a person to sacrifice personal achievements, friends, or even family for the sake of Christ?
❇ What does Jesus ask all of us to do?
■ What can you learn from the disciples' response to Jesus' call?
❇ How can you obey Christ's commands more faithfully?
❇ What prevents you from following Jesus wholeheartedly?
❇ What action is necessary to eliminate these hindrances from your life with Christ?

APPLY IT

❇ What specific attitude or action should you give up now as an act of following Christ?
■ How can you follow Jesus this week?

Mark 1:21-28

Jesus Drives Out an Evil Spirit

TOPICS

Demons, Healing, Miracles, Serving, Sickness

OPEN IT

❇ What makes a person a good teacher?

■ What are some examples of power and authority?
✻ What words describe people who have authority?
✻ Why do we often feel small around people of power and authority?

EXPLORE IT
✻ What do Jesus' actions tell us about his beliefs regarding the Sabbath? (1:21)
■ Why were the people amazed at Jesus' teaching? (1:22)
✻ What kinds of teachers were the people accustomed to that caused them to be amazed by Jesus' teaching? (1:22)
✻ Why did the man in the synagogue cry out to Jesus? (1:23-24)
✻ What did the evil spirit say to Jesus? (1:24)
■ What do the evil spirit's words tell us about Christ? (1:24)
✻ How did Jesus respond to the man possessed by the evil spirit? (1:25-26)
✻ How did the evil spirit respond to Jesus' command to leave the man? (1:26)
✻ What occurred in the synagogue after Jesus cast out the demon? (1:27)
✻ Why did the people describe Jesus' teaching as "new"? (1:27)
✻ Why were the people so excited about Jesus? (1:27)
■ Why did the news about Jesus spread so quickly over the region? (1:27-28)

GET IT
✻ How does Jesus' teaching differ from the teaching we are used to today?
✻ Why should we share the news of Jesus' power and authority with other people?
■ What does this story tell us about evil spirits and Jesus' power?
✻ According to Jesus, how should Christians respond to people controlled by sin?
✻ What authority does Jesus have over other areas of life?
✻ What makes us fearful of claiming Jesus' power over Satan's footholds in our lives?
✻ What is wrong with doubting Jesus' power?
✻ How can we show confidence in Christ's power over illness?
✻ How can we allow Jesus' power and authority to work in our lives?
✻ What specific areas of your life need the transforming power of Jesus?
■ What area of your life do you need to place under Jesus' power and authority?

APPLY IT
■ What is one way you can show submission to Christ's authority in your life throughout this week?
✻ What personal need or problem will you ask Jesus, through prayer, to heal this week?
✻ What could you do this week for someone who is sick or discouraged?

Mark 1:29-34

Jesus Heals Many

TOPICS
Authority, Demons, Healing, Miracles, Power, Teaching

OPEN IT
✻ Why is it sometimes difficult to help people who are sick?
■ What happens to your attitude when you get sick with a bad cold or the flu?

EXPLORE IT
■ What did Jesus do with His companions after teaching in the synagogue? (1:29)
✻ What problem did Jesus encounter in this situation? (1:30)
✻ Why did the men tell Jesus about Simon's mother-in-law? (1:30)
■ How did Jesus respond to the problem He was faced with? (1:31)
✻ Why did Jesus use personal contact to heal the woman of her fever? (1:31)
✻ What was the woman's immediate response to Jesus healing her? (1:31)
✻ What do the actions of the woman tell us about her? (1:31)
✻ When did the crowds of people come to Jesus? (1:32)
✻ How might Jesus have felt at this time, considering He had spent the day at the synagogue teaching and healing? (1:32)
✻ What attracted people to Jesus in this setting? (1:32)
■ What was Jesus' response to the crowds of sick and demon-possessed people? (1:34)
✻ Why did Jesus not allow the demons to speak? (1:34)

GET IT
✻ How do you feel about serving your family at home after a long, hard day?
■ What does this story tell us our attitude should be toward helping people?
✻ Why should we follow the disciples' example of bringing our problems to Jesus?
✻ What can we expect Jesus' response will be to our problems?
✻ Why is personal contact important in serving the needs of people?
✻ Following the example of the woman in the story, what should we do when others serve or help us?
■ What excuses do we use to neglect serving other people?
✻ What difference should it make in our lives that Jesus has the power to heal the sick and deliver the demon-possessed?

APPLY IT
✻ What specific area of your life do you need to turn over to Jesus for His healing touch?
■ What concrete step can you take to serve or help someone else this week?

Mark 1:35-39
Jesus Prays in a Solitary Place

TOPICS
Alone, Demons, Ministry, Prayer, Preparation, Purpose, Sacrifice, Solitude

OPEN IT
■ What do you like or dislike about being alone?
❇ What does our society think of loners?
❇ What is most difficult to you about praying?

EXPLORE IT
❇ What did Jesus do? When? (1:35)
❇ How did Jesus begin this particular day? (1:35)
❇ When did Jesus go out to pray? (1:35)
■ Where did Jesus go, and why did He go there? (1:35)
❇ What did Jesus consider important? (1:35-39)
❇ What did Simon and his companions do when Jesus went to pray alone? (1:36-37)
■ Why wasn't Jesus able to pray alone? (1:37)
■ What did Jesus plan to do after He was finished praying? (1:38)
❇ What attitude did Jesus have toward the people who demanded His time? (1:38)
❇ Which of Jesus' tasks did He consider most important: preaching, healing, or casting out demons? (1:38)
❇ What motivated Jesus to go to the nearby village? (1:38)

GET IT
❇ In light of this passage, how do you think Jesus knew His life purpose so clearly?
❇ Why do you think Jesus had to spend so much time in prayer if He was the Son of God?
■ How should we follow Christ's example of praying?
❇ What is the benefit of getting up before dawn to spend time with the Lord in prayer?
■ What area of need does Jesus' example of prayer reveal to you?
❇ What should be your response to other believers who are committed to prayer?
❇ How do you think you would have responded if you had been the one to find Jesus praying?
❇ What can you learn about your own responsibility to serve from Jesus' attitude toward the people who demanded His time?
❇ How can you order the parts of your life to reflect the priorities Jesus had?
❇ What one area of your spiritual life do you think the Lord wants you to develop or concentrate on the most right now?
❇ What role do you think solitude should have in the Christian life?

APPLY IT
❇ Following Jesus' example, what can you do this week to spend more quality time with the Lord in prayer?
■ When and where can you pray on a regular basis this week?
❇ What can you do to increase your consistency in prayer over the next month?

Mark 1:40-45
A Man With Leprosy

TOPICS
Compassion, Disobedience, Faith, Healing, Sacrifice, Sickness

OPEN IT
■ What childhood memories do you have of a peer being ridiculed or rejected?
❇ Who are some of the "untouchables" in our society?
❇ What are some illnesses that people often fear getting?

EXPLORE IT
■ What do the man's words to Jesus tell us about his attitude or spiritual condition? (1:40)
❇ What evidence do we see that the sick man in this story was desperate? (1:40)
■ Why did Jesus heal the man who came to Him? (1:41)
❇ How did Jesus heal the leper in this story? (1:41)
❇ What do Jesus' specific actions in this episode tell us about His character? (1:41)
■ What happened to the leper? (1:42)
❇ What specific instructions did Jesus give to the leper after He had healed him? (1:44)
❇ Why did Jesus want the leper to go to a priest? (1:44)
❇ Why did Jesus urge the leper to tell no one he was cured? (1:45)
❇ How did the leper respond to all that had happened to him? (1:45)
❇ What was the result of the leper's actions? (1:45)

GET IT
■ Who are the outcasts or untouchables in today's world?
■ In what ways can Christians serve or help people who have great need?
❇ When has the Lord ever healed you either physically or emotionally?
❇ How have you responded to the Lord's healing in your life?
❇ How would you react if you saw another person miraculously healed by the Lord?
❇ Looking at the leper's example, what attitude do you think is crucial to receive healing from the Lord?
❇ Why do you think God sometimes heals people miraculously yet at other times chooses not to?
❇ What does this passage tell you about Christ and His attitude toward our pain and suffering?
❇ When have you ever done the opposite of what you knew Jesus would have wanted you to do?
❇ How can disobedience cost us?
❇ What is one area of your life in which you need physical, emotional, or spiritual healing from God?

APPLY IT
■ To what person in your church or community could you reach out this week? How?
❇ What concrete action can you take this week to trust Jesus with your areas of need?

Mark 2:1-12
Jesus Heals a Paralytic

TOPICS
Authority, Blasphemy, Faith, Forgiveness, Friendship, God, Healing, Miracles, Sickness, Sin

OPEN IT
❇ What would you think of a person who claimed to be something he or she was not?
■ What do you think would be most difficult about being paralyzed?

EXPLORE IT
❇ Where did the events of this story take place? (2:1-2)
❇ What exactly was Jesus doing when the events of this story took place? (2:2)
■ What dilemma did the paralytic man and his friends face? (2:2-4)
❇ What do the details of the story tell you about the paralytic man, his friends, and Jesus' reputation? (2:3-4)
❇ How did the paralytic man's friends solve the dilemma that they faced? (2:4)
❇ How did the paralytic man's friends get Jesus' attention? (2:4-5)
❇ How did Jesus evaluate the faith of the paralytic man and his friends? (2:5)
■ What motivated Jesus to respond to the paralytic man's plight? (2:5)
❇ Why did the Pharisees accuse Jesus of blasphemy? (2:6-7)
❇ How did Jesus respond to the thoughts of the Pharisees? (2:8-9)
❇ How did Jesus show that He had authority to forgive sins? (2:9)
❇ What did Jesus mean by "Son of Man"? (2:10)
■ Why did Jesus heal the paralytic man? (2:10-12)
❇ Until now, Jesus had been preaching but not performing miracles; why did He heal this particular man? (2:10-12)

GET IT
❇ Why do you think Jesus chose to forgive the man's sins before healing him physically?
❇ Which is it easier for us to do—forgive others or care for them when they're sick?
❇ How is God's viewpoint different from ours regarding the forgiveness of sins?
■ What connection is there between a person's faith and God's working in his or her life?
❇ What does God require or not require to forgive us of our sins?
❇ How would you compare Jesus' response in this story to the Pharisees' attitudes?
❇ What does this story tell you is the difference between true spirituality and counterfeit spirituality?
❇ What is one paralysis in your life from which you want Jesus to release you?
■ What problems, needs, or weaknesses in your life are there that God can use?

APPLY IT
■ What specific steps can you take this week to show faith in Christ?
❇ What broken area of your life will you ask God to heal?
❇ Following the example of the paralytic man's friends, how could you go out of your way to help another believer who is experiencing pain or suffering?

Mark 2:13-17
The Calling of Levi

TOPICS
Call, Evangelism, Follow, Judging Others, Legalism, Ministry

OPEN IT
■ What feelings or attitudes do most people have about the Internal Revenue Service?
❇ When do you remember playing "follow the leader" as a kid?
❇ Who are some controversial leaders that you know of? Why are they controversial?

EXPLORE IT
❇ In what setting did the events of this story take place? (2:13)
■ What was Levi's status among his neighbors? (2:14)
❇ What did Jesus want when He spoke to Levi? (2:14)
❇ What was Levi's response to Jesus' words? (2:14)
❇ What did Levi stand to lose by leaving his work to follow Jesus? (2:14)
■ Why is it significant that Jesus went to Levi's house for dinner? (2:14-15)
❇ Who were the other dinner guests at Levi's house when Jesus had dinner with him? (2:15)
❇ How did the Pharisees respond to Jesus' actions? (2:16)
❇ What was Jesus' response to the Pharisees? (2:17)
■ What was it about Jesus' life-style and attitude that made the Pharisees so uncomfortable? (2:15-17)

GET IT
■ Why do you think Jesus chose to ask Levi to be one of His followers?
❇ Who would be the equivalent of a tax collector in our society?
❇ What do you think Jesus' disciples thought when He went to Levi's house?
❇ What do you think bystanders and other strangers thought of Jesus at this point?
❇ Why do you think that people of ill repute were so attracted to Jesus?
❇ How do churches tend to treat people like tax collectors?
❇ Judging from this passage, how does God want to relate to us?
❇ How should we view ourselves if we decide to respond to Christ's call?
■ How should we treat the outcasts of our society?

❄ How do you personally need to respond to Jesus' call on your life?
❄ What can you learn from Levi's example in this story?
❄ What does this passage teach you about the best way to tell others about Christ?
❄ When have you ever acted the same way that the Pharisees did in this story?
❄ How can you follow Jesus' example of associating with people of low reputation?

APPLY IT
■ In what specific way can you honor or recognize a person of "lower status" this week?
❄ What can you do to listen to Christ as He calls you?

Mark 2:18-22
Jesus Questioned About Fasting

TOPICS
Celebration, Fasting, Legalism, Obedience, Questions, Spiritual Disciplines

OPEN IT
❄ What do you like most and least about weddings?
■ What is the longest amount of time you ever went without food? When?
❄ If Jesus came to evaluate your church, how do you think He might want to change it?

EXPLORE IT
■ What dilemma puzzled the people who came to Jesus? (2:18)
❄ Why did the people come to Jesus? (2:18)
❄ What did John's disciples and the Pharisees have in common? (2:18)
❄ Looking at Jesus and the Pharisees in this story, how were their attitudes different? (2:18-22)
❄ How did Jesus respond to the question that was put to Him? (2:19)
❄ To whom was Jesus referring to when He spoke of the "guests" and the "bridegroom"? (2:19)
❄ Why did Jesus suddenly start speaking about a wedding feast? (2:19-20)
■ How did Jesus' story of the wedding feast answer the people's question about why His disciples did not fast? (2:19-20)
■ Why did Jesus tell two short stories? (2:21-22)
❄ What do the old garment and the old wineskins stand for? (2:21-22)
❄ What do the patch of the unshrunk cloth and the new wine stand for? (2:21-22)
❄ What are "new wineskins," and why are they needed? (2:22)

GET IT
■ How were Jesus' and the Pharisees' views of piety different?
❄ Why do you think Jesus used a wedding feast to illustrate following Him?
❄ What new insights into what it means to be a Christian does this story give you?
❄ What does this passage teach you about the role fasting should play in your own spiritual life?
■ How do you need to change your attitudes or actions regarding the spiritual disciplines such as fasting and praying?
❄ When has your attitude ever been similar to that of the Pharisees in this story?
❄ How can we guard against mere rule-keeping when it comes to spiritual disciplines such as fasting?
❄ What difference could the message of this passage make in the procedures and beliefs of your local church?

APPLY IT
■ What steps can you take this week to practice a spiritual discipline (fasting, prayer, Bible study, meditation, solitude, simplicity, etc.)?
❄ Where and how could you learn more about fasting and prayer over the next few weeks?

Mark 2:23–3:6
Lord of the Sabbath

TOPICS
Healing, Hypocrisy, Judging Others, Law, Legalism, Obedience, Rest

OPEN IT
■ How do you prefer to use your weekends?
❄ What do you understand to be the difference between "the letter of the law" and "the spirit of the law"?

EXPLORE IT
❄ What is the setting of the story, and why is it significant? (2:23)
■ What did the disciples do that outraged the Pharisees? (2:24)
❄ Why did the Pharisees confront Jesus about the actions of His disciples? (2:24)
■ What was Jesus' response to the Pharisees' charges? (2:25-27)
■ According to Jesus, why were both David and Jesus' disciples justified in breaking the Sabbath? (2:25-27)
❄ Why did Jesus say He was "Lord even of the Sabbath"? (2:28)
❄ What happened after the confrontation between Jesus and the Pharisees? (3:1)
❄ Why were some of the Pharisees watching Jesus so closely? (3:2)
❄ What was notable about the way Jesus performed this miracle? (3:3)
❄ To whom did Jesus address a provocative question about "the Sabbath"? (3:4)
❄ What was it about the Pharisees that so distressed Jesus? (3:5)
❄ What significance do you see in the fact that the Pharisees were willing to plot with their enemies, the Herodians, to kill Jesus? (3:6)
❄ What do Jesus' actions in this story tell you about His concerns? (2:23-3:6)

GET IT
❄ Why do you think Jesus healed the man publicly?

❇ How was Jesus' spirituality different from that of the Pharisees?
❇ Where have you seen rules-only spirituality in the church today?
❇ In what areas do you think your church might be following the "letter of the law" rather than the "spirit of the law"?
❇ How should we respond to suggestions that it only matters how closely we keep the letter of the law?
■ When have you ever experienced a time when the requirements of your Christian faith seemed to conflict with a human need?
■ What should we do when a requirement of the faith seems to conflict with a human need?
❇ In what areas of your faith do you tend to be too beholden to rules or traditions?
❇ What are your responsibilities on the Sabbath?
❇ What is Jesus' attitude toward the Sabbath?
❇ In what ways can we copy Jesus' example in how He used the Sabbath?
❇ What difference does it make that "the Sabbath was made for man"?

APPLY IT
■ In what settings are you able to "do good and save life"? How?
❇ What can you do this week to reflect God's design for the Sabbath?
❇ What can you use as a reminder to guard against a concern only for the letter of the law?

Mark 3:7-12
Crowds Follow Jesus

TOPICS
Demons, Follow, God, Healing, Ministry, Miracles, Sickness

OPEN IT
❇ What is a story of miraculous healing that you have heard?
■ What is it like to be lost in a huge crowd (such as in a store, airport, or stadium)?
❇ How is it possible to feel lost or lonely in a massive crowd of people?

EXPLORE IT
❇ What is the setting of this story? (3:7)
■ Why did Jesus want to leave? (3:7)
❇ Why did such large crowds follow Jesus? (3:7-8)
❇ Where did the crowds come from? (3:7-8)
❇ What was unusual about the crowds that came to see Jesus? (3:7-8)
■ Why were the crowds so interested in following Jesus? (3:7-12)
❇ What do the details of this story tell us about Jesus' popularity? (3:7-12)
■ What do the details of this story tell us about Jesus' priorities? (3:7-12)
❇ What did Jesus tell His disciples to get? Why? (3:9)
❇ What had been happening among the crowd that day? (3:10)
❇ How were the crowds approaching Jesus with their needs? (3:10)
❇ How did the evil spirits respond to Jesus when they saw Him? Why? (3:11)
❇ What warning did Jesus issue? (3:12)

GET IT
❇ For what reasons do you follow Jesus?
❇ How can you personally be involved in letting other people know what it is like to follow Jesus?
❇ What do you learn from this passage about Jesus' attitude toward His ministry?
■ What area of your life (physical, emotional, or spiritual) needs to be healed by Jesus?
❇ What difference should it make in our lives that even evil spirits fall down and recognize Jesus for who He really is?
❇ What can we learn from this passage about resisting the devil?
■ How would it make a difference in your spiritual life if you had more confidence in Christ's power and authority?
❇ How can we show confidence in Christ's power and authority?
❇ What attitude or tendency hinders you from following Jesus?

APPLY IT
❇ What physical, emotional, or other hurt will you ask God to heal?
■ What need can you bring to Jesus? How could you do so?
❇ What concrete action can you take this week in imitation of Jesus' priority of helping people?

Mark 3:13-19
The Appointing of the Twelve Apostles

TOPICS
Authority, Call, Choices, Demons, Evangelism, Follow, Leadership, Ministry, Teamwork, Witnessing

OPEN IT
■ By what criteria do you choose your friends?
❇ What qualities do you think are important in a friend?
❇ What qualities do you think are important for a person who is a leader in the church?

EXPLORE IT
■ What is the setting of this story? (3:13)
❇ How did the apostles respond to Jesus' call? (3:13)
❇ Why did Jesus choose His disciples? (3:14)
❇ What did Jesus want His apostles to do with their time? (3:14-15)
■ What did Jesus expect of the men He designated apostles? (3:14-15)
❇ Who would send out the apostles and give them authority to drive out demons? (3:14-15)
❇ What sort of declaration was Jesus making to His enemies by choosing and commissioning the Twelve? (3:14-15)

❄ What did Jesus do with some of His followers and not others? (3:16-19)
❄ What unusual men did Jesus choose? (3:16-19)
■ What was unusual about some of the men Jesus chose? (3:16-19)

GET IT
❄ What criteria do you think Jesus used to choose His apostles?
❄ Why do you think Jesus wanted the apostles to spend time with Him?
❄ What can we learn from Jesus' example of choosing apostles to be with Him and to help Him?
❄ What does the fact that Jesus chose as apostles both Simon the Zealot, a political extremist, and Matthew the tax collector, a traitor to the occupying government, tell us about the kingdom of God?
❄ How has the call of Jesus Christ in your life changed your attitude toward people with whom you previously would not have associated?
❄ Why do you think Jesus assigned new names to some of the apostles and not to all of them?
❄ What do you think the men themselves thought about their opportunity to be a disciple of Christ's?
❄ What attitudes or actions do you feel still need to be changed in your life to more fully obey Christ's call to follow Him?
■ What difference does it make to you that Jesus chose imperfect people to share in His ministry?
❄ What specific role do you think God has given you to fill in this world?
❄ How can we determine how best to serve God with our particular gifts and abilities?
❄ What do you think the leadership of your church could learn from the way Jesus chose His twelve followers?
❄ How can you personally become more involved in teaching and helping others serve Jesus?
■ From what other more mature believers can you learn?

APPLY IT
■ What would be your first step toward learning from a more mature believer in your church?
❄ In what ways can you depend on others to carry the weight of God's work at this time in your life?
❄ What specific steps can you take this week to help one other person use in God's service a skill that God has given him or her?

Mark 3:20-30
Jesus and Beelzebub

TOPICS
Blasphemy, Church, Demons, Divisions, Forgiveness, Holy Spirit, Sacrifice, Satan, Sin, Unity

OPEN IT
■ In your experience, when has faithfulness to a cause or person led to conflict with others?
❄ In what situations or settings can unity be important?

EXPLORE IT
❄ What was the problem at the onset of this story? (3:20)
❄ Who tried to solve Jesus' dilemma? Why? (3:21)
■ What did Jesus' family think of Him? (3:21)
❄ Where had Jesus' detractors come from? (3:21-22)
■ Besides Jesus' own family, who else found fault with Him? (3:22)?
❄ How did the teachers of the law try to explain Jesus' behavior? (3:22)
■ How did Jesus refute His opponents' accusation that He was possessed by the devil? (3:23-27)
❄ What does Jesus' speech about a "kingdom divided" tell us about the kingdom of God? (3:24-26)
❄ Who was the "strong man" of whom Jesus spoke? (3:27)
❄ Who was the "robber"? (3:27)
❄ What was the "blasphemy of the Holy Spirit" of which Jesus spoke? (3:29-30)
❄ Why is blasphemy of the Holy Spirit uniquely worthy of divine judgment? (3:29-30)

GET IT
❄ Why do you think Jesus' family thought He was "out of his mind"?
❄ In light of this passage, what do we fight against?
❄ Why do you think Jesus chose to speak to His audience in parables?
❄ What difference does it make in your life to know that Jesus has authority over all the evil powers of this world?
❄ What is the true significance of Jesus' ministry of casting out demons?
■ Why is unity among Christians so important?
❄ In what ways can we strengthen the unity of the church?
■ In what ways can you strengthen your local fellowship or church?
❄ What can a believer do to guard against disunity in the church?
❄ What can we do to avoid committing the "unforgivable sin"?
❄ When, if ever, have you been thought of as "out of your mind" by other people because of your efforts to live a Christian life?
❄ How should Christians respond to conflict with other people, both nonChristians and believers, in light of Jesus' example?
❄ What has following Jesus cost you?

APPLY IT
❄ What can you do over the next few days to restore a relationship that strains your unity with other Christians?
■ What is one step you can take this week to strengthen the unity of your local church?

Mark 3:31-35
Jesus' Mother and Brothers

TOPICS
Family, God's Will, Loyalty, Obedience, Parents, Relationships, Sacrifice

OPEN IT

■ What is one of your favorite childhood memories of your mother?
❇ With whom do you feel a kindred spirit? Why?
❇ What did you and your siblings fight about when you were in grade school?

EXPLORE IT

❇ What was the setting of this story? (3:31-32)
■ Who wanted to see Jesus? Why? (3:31-32)
❇ Why did Jesus' mother and brothers go to a particular house? (3:31-32)
❇ How did Jesus' family summon Him? (3:31-32)
❇ Who told Jesus of His family's request? (3:32)
■ What rhetorical question did Jesus ask? Why? (3:33)
■ How did Jesus respond to His mother's and brothers' request? (3:33-34)
❇ Who did Jesus designate as His "family"? (3:34)
❇ What unique name is given to "whoever does God's will"? (3:35)
❇ When did Jesus' mother and brothers get to see Him? (3:33-35)

GET IT

❇ How do you think Jesus' mother and brothers responded to His actions in this story?
❇ What feelings do you think Jesus had toward His family?
❇ How do you interpret Jesus' actions toward His family?
❇ What does this account tell you about Jesus' priorities?
■ In what way does doing God's will make a person Christ's brother or sister?
❇ How has your commitment to Christ affected your relationship with your family?
■ Why is it important for us to place even our families under the rule and place of Christ?
❇ In light of this passage, how should Christians relate to one another?
❇ How should you relate to members of your family who are not Christians?
❇ When has your commitment to Christ caused conflict in your family?
❇ How do you think God wants you to respond to conflict situations in your family?
❇ How can a person be sure to be included in the family of God?
❇ What do Jesus' actions in this episode tell you about what your priorities in life should be?

APPLY IT

■ What could you do or say to help your family understand your faith in Christ?
❇ In what areas of your work should your behavior reflect a greater kinship with Christ? How?
❇ What can you do each day to cultivate a kindred spirit with Christ?

Mark 4:1-20

The Parable of the Sower

TOPICS

Desires, Gospel, Kingdom of God/Heaven, Perseverance, Spiritual Growth, Teaching, Wealth, Witnessing, Worry

OPEN IT

❇ What illustration would you use to explain your job?
❇ What three words would you use to describe your spiritual life?
■ What do you do to keep your house plants alive?

EXPLORE IT

❇ Where does this story take place? (4:1)
❇ How did Jesus start to teach the crowds? (4:2)
❇ When did Jesus use parables instead of saying directly what He meant? (4:2)
■ What are the four scenes described in this parable? (4:3-10)
❇ How did those closest to Jesus respond to the parable He told? (4:10)
❇ In what way did Jesus limit His explanation of the parable? (4:11-12)
❇ What problem did this exchange bring up? (4:13)
■ To what was Jesus referring when He said, "The farmer sows the word"? (4:14)
❇ What did Jesus want us to understand about God from this parable? (4:14-20)
■ What are some obstacles that prevent people from accepting the gospel or hanging on to their faith? (4:15-19)
❇ What happens to those who hear the truth about Christ and accept it? (4:20)

GET IT

❇ Why do you think Jesus considered Isaiah's words relevant to His preaching about the kingdom of God?
❇ Knowing that most of the men in the crowd were farmers and Jesus used an illustration from farming, why did many in the audience not understand His message?
❇ Why do you think Jesus explained the "secret" only to his disciples and not to the crowds in general?
❇ When and where do we need to listen carefully?
❇ To what area of your life does this parable speak?
❇ What kind of soil do you think represents you?
❇ How will you respond to the coming of the kingdom of God?
❇ What can you do—and not do—to make the message "take root" when you teach or tell others about Christ?
❇ How does Satan "take away the word" before it has a chance to take root?
■ What troubles or persecutions cause believers to fall away?
❇ What do you think your church can do to help people be better hearers?
❇ What can we do to make sure the messages of God's Word take root and grow in us?
■ How can you make sure that the worries of life, the deceitfulness of wealth, and the other desires of the world will not choke the life out of your Christian walk?

❊ What is the first step in obeying what we already know to be God's will?
❊ What can you do to increase your fruit as a Christian?

APPLY IT
❊ What is one step you can take to guard against the desires of the world that threaten your devotion to Christ?
■ In what area of your life do you need to start listening to God?
❊ What is one biblical truth that you want to cultivate in your life each day this week?

Mark 4:21-25
A Lamp on a Stand

TOPICS
Accountability, Fairness, Listening, Obedience, Responsibility, Truth

OPEN IT
❊ What kinds of lights do you have in your home?
■ What is one thing you feel you can do well?
❊ How do most of your coworkers measure wealth?

EXPLORE IT
❊ With what observation did Jesus open His illustration? (4:21)
❊ What did Jesus say would be ridiculous? Why? (4:21)
❊ Who or what does the lamp in this parable represent? (4:21)
❊ What did Jesus mean by saying, "whatever is hidden is meant to be disclosed"? (4:22)
❊ What will happen to what is secret and hidden? (4:22)
❊ Who did Jesus want this message to reach? (4:23)
■ Why did Jesus warn us to "consider carefully" what we hear? (4:24)
❊ How did Jesus end His parable? (4:24-25)
❊ Who will be given more? Why? (4:24-25)
❊ Who will have things taken from them? Why? (4:24-25)
■ What will happen to those who use or put into practice what God has measured out to them? (4:24-25)
■ What will happen to those who neglect or misuse the truth God has already revealed to them? (4:24-25)

GET IT
❊ What is the meaning of this parable?
❊ When have you ever tried to hide or conceal what you know God "meant to be brought out into the open"?
❊ When Jesus said that those who have be given more, what exactly did He mean?
❊ How would you rewrite this parable to fit our modern-day culture, yet get the same message across?
❊ How do you think the people listening to Jesus' teaching responded to this parable?
❊ How can we consider more carefully what we hear?
❊ How would you describe the "measure" that has been given to you?
■ What responsibility do you have before God in light of the truth or knowledge God has already revealed to you?
■ In what ways do you think God expects more or less of you than others?
❊ In light of this passage, how can Christians expect to grow spiritually?
❊ Why do you think some believers remain immature Christians for a long time?
❊ What does this passage teach us about being examples?
❊ What does this passage teach us about telling others about Christ?

APPLY IT
■ What is one specific word of Jesus (a promise, truth, or command) that you can consciously remind yourself of throughout this next week?
❊ What is involved in fulfilling the areas of responsibility you have?

Mark 4:26-29
The Parable of the Growing Seed

TOPICS
Gospel, Growth, Kingdom of God/Heaven, Power, Productivity

OPEN IT
❊ What short phrase or clich would you use to describe this country?
❊ What experiences have you had with growing plants from seeds?
■ What does it take for plants to grow, and where do you get the things you need?

EXPLORE IT
❊ What did Jesus want the people to understand about the kingdom of God? (4:26)
❊ What role did the man in the parable play? (4:26-27)
■ What do the man and the seed in the parable represent? (4:26-29)
❊ What does this parable reveal about Jesus' concerns? (4:26-29)
❊ How did the seed in the parable sprout and grow? (4:27)
❊ What was the growth process like for the seed? (4:28)
❊ How did the seed grow? (4:28)
■ How did the man get the seed to grow? (4:28)
❊ At what point did the man get involved in the plant's growth after he planted it? (4:29)
■ To what does the phrase "the harvest is come" refer? (4:29)

GET IT
❊ Why do you think Jesus told parables to explain the kingdom of God to the crowds of people?
❊ The Jews of Jesus' day expected God's kingdom to come physically and politically. How does this compare with the description Jesus gave in this parable?
❊ What encouragement can believers glean from this parable regarding their own spiritual growth?
■ How does this parable help you better understand what the kingdom of God is like?

❇ How does it make you feel to know that the message of Christ contains a mysterious power in itself?
■ How does the message of this parable help believers evangelize and teach?
❇ What should our response be to the fact that one day "the harvest will come"?
❇ What have you learned about your own spiritual walk with the Lord from this parable?
❇ What can you do in your life, and in the lives of others, to create conditions where the Word of God will grow?

APPLY IT
■ What specific steps can you take to rely on the power of the Holy Spirit to change others when you tell them about Christ?
❇ What is one way you can spread God's Word this week to help God's kingdom grow?

Mark 4:30-34
The Parable of the Mustard Seed

TOPICS
Example, Greatness, Growth, Kingdom of God/Heaven, Productivity, Teaching, Understanding

OPEN IT
❇ If Jesus Christ had been sent to earth during our generation, how do you think He would have chosen to tell us His message?
■ What are some examples of something small that grows into something big?

EXPLORE IT
❇ What did Jesus use to explain the kingdom of God? (4:30)
❇ In what ways is this parable different from the previous one Jesus told? (4:30-31)
■ How is the kingdom of God like a mustard seed? (4:32)
❇ What is the kingdom of God like? (4:31)
❇ What does the mustard seed represent in this parable? (4:31)
❇ What do you think this parable meant to Jesus' original audience? (4:31)
❇ How could the beginning of the kingdom of God be compared to such a small, insignificant seed? (4:31)
■ What promise is given in this parable? (4:31-32)
■ Why did Jesus use the smallest seed known to the Galilean farmers in His audience as the example in this parable? (4:31-32)
❇ How did Jesus teach the crowds? (4:33-34)
❇ How did Jesus teach His disciples? (4:33-34)
❇ How did Jesus' approach to teaching the crowds differ from the way He taught His disciples? (4:33-34)
❇ What did Jesus do for His disciples to ensure that they learned from His parables? (4:34)
❇ How did Jesus make sure His disciples understood His teaching? (4:34)

GET IT
❇ How might this parable have encouraged Christians being persecuted by the Roman state?
❇ Why do you think Jesus spoke only in parables to the crowds at this point in His ministry?
■ What does this parable tell us about trying to persuade others to believe in Christ?
❇ How can you apply the principle of this parable to your situation in life right now?
❇ In what ways does this parable encourage you to persist in your faith?
❇ Why do you think God chose to introduce His kingdom through a controversial man with a handful of obscure followers?
❇ To what extent do you think you should model your style of evangelism after Jesus' example?
■ What does this parable teach you about sharing the message of Christ with your nonChristian friends?
❇ What difference can it make in your everyday life that Jesus' kingdom will prevail over the sin and corruption of this world?

APPLY IT
■ How can you get involved this week in spreading the Good News and participating in the growth of the kingdom of God?
❇ What word or message from the Bible can you share with someone else? How?
❇ Who is one person with whom you could share the promise of the kingdom of God?

Mark 4:35-41
Jesus Calms the Storm

TOPICS
Doubt, Faith, Fear, Miracles, Nature, Obedience, Power, Trust

OPEN IT
❇ What do you usually feel like doing after a long, hard day of work?
❇ When was the last time you felt out of control?
■ How do you tend to handle stress—thrive, panic, seek out distractions, procrastinate, etc.?

EXPLORE IT
❇ When did the events of this story take place? (4:35)
■ Where did Jesus and His disciples go? How? (4:35-36)
❇ Why did the disciples take Jesus along "just as He was"? (4:36)
❇ What emergency situation arose? (4:37)
■ Why were the disciples surprised with Jesus? (4:37-38)
❇ What was Jesus doing during a violent storm? (4:38)
❇ How was Jesus coping with the storm that threatened Him and His men? (4:38)
❇ What is significant about the disciples questioning Jesus saying, "Don't you care if we drown"? (4:38)
❇ How would you compare Jesus' behavior during this crisis with that of His disciples? (4:38)
❇ How did Jesus solve the dilemma He and His disciples were facing? (4:39)
■ Why did Jesus rebuke His disciples? (4:40)
❇ What was the answer to the rhetorical question that the disciples asked? (4:41)
❇ What did the disciples learn about Jesus from this event? (4:39-41)

GET IT

❋ How do you think Jesus felt after long days of teaching the people, responding to His opponents, and healing the sick?
❋ Where do you think Jesus found the strength to maintain such an exhausting level of ministry?
❋ When have you ever felt as the disciples did—distressed at events out of control?
❋ What have been some of the "storms" in your personal life?
■ What "storms" or difficulties are you going through right now?
❋ How has God helped you handle your fears and frustrations during difficult times?
❋ In what specific ways has God shown His care and love for you?
❋ What difference does it make to you that Jesus has authority over all the powers and forces of our world?
❋ In what area of your life is your faith lacking?
■ How can you trust more completely in the power and authority of Jesus?
❋ What miraculous work would you like Jesus to do in your life? How could you ask Him?
❋ In what specific area of your life do you need more faith in God?

APPLY IT

■ How can you trust God this upcoming week with situations that get out of control or seem hopeless?
❋ What do you want to remember the next time your life seems out of control?
❋ When could you pray regularly this week for the needs in your life?

Mark 5:1-20

The Healing of a Demon-possessed Man

TOPICS

Demons, Doubt, Fear, Healing, Miracles, Power, Witnessing

OPEN IT

❋ When was the last time you had such wonderful news that you could not wait to tell someone about it?
❋ What do people today think of the devil and demons?
■ What makes people resistant to talking about God or religion?

EXPLORE IT

❋ Where did the events of this story take place? (5:1)
❋ To what Gentile (non-Jewish) area did Jesus and His disciples go? (5:1) How?
❋ Who went out to meet Jesus? (5:2)
❋ What was the man's life like before he met Jesus? (5:3-5)
❋ How had the townspeople coped with the demon-possessed man Jesus met? (5:4)
■ Why was the man Jesus met chained up? (5:4-5)
❋ How did the demon-possessed man react to Jesus? (5:6-7)
❋ Why were the demons so terrified of Jesus? (5:7)
❋ How did Jesus treat the man He met? (5:8-20)
■ What did Jesus do to help the demon-possessed man? (5:8-20)
❋ What do Jesus' actions tell us about His character? (5:8-20)
❋ What did the demons beg of Jesus? (5:10)
❋ What happened when the demons asked to go into the pigs? (5:11-13)
❋ How did news of this event spread? (5:14-16)
❋ What was the man's life like after Jesus ordered the demons out of him? (5:15-20)
❋ What did the Gerasene people think of Jesus' gracious action on the man's behalf? (5:17)
❋ Where did the man whom Jesus had helped want to go? (5:18)
■ What request did Jesus deny? (5:18-19) Why?
❋ How did the man respond to Jesus' instructions? (5:19-20)

GET IT

❋ The Gerasene people opposed Jesus even though He helped them; why do people sometimes oppose Christians today?
❋ What are some ways that Satan tries to keep Christians from sharing the message of Christ with others?
❋ Over what areas of our lives does Jesus have power and authority?
❋ What are some concrete ways we can turn over control of our lives to Christ?
❋ What does God want to deliver us from?
❋ If you had been in the same situation as the Gerasene people, how would you have reacted to Jesus' healing of the demon-possessed man?
■ When and where do you tend to receive opposition to talking about God or religion?
■ What can we do to overcome resistance to the message of Christ?
❋ What sometimes causes us to oppose what God wants?
❋ What does Jesus' treatment of the man in this story tell us about his care for people?
❋ How does the man's actions after Jesus delivered him from demon-possession serve as an example to us?
❋ When has the Lord delivered you from a sickness or difficulty in your life? How did you react?
❋ How can we show gratitude to God for what He has given us?
❋ With whom do you think you should share the Good News of Jesus?

APPLY IT

■ What can you do this week to bring the message of Christ to a friend or coworker?
❋ What is one area of your life that you can ask God to heal?
❋ How can you say thank you to God for the way He has worked in your life?

Mark 5:21-43

A Dead Girl and a Sick Woman

TOPICS
Believe, Death, Faith, Fear, Healing, Miracles, Sickness, Suffering

OPEN IT
■ How did your mother take care of you when you were sick?
❇ When has the Lord ever healed you or someone you knew?
❇ What are some common fears people have?

EXPLORE IT
■ Who was Jairus, and why did he want to see Jesus? (5:22-23)
❇ Who wanted to see Jesus? Why? (5:22-23)
❇ What was Jairus' attitude toward Jesus? (5:23)
❇ How would you compare the faith of Jairus with the faith of the woman in the story? (5:23, 28)
❇ What did Jesus do for Jairus? (5:24)
❇ What was the plight of the woman in this story? (5:25-26)
❇ How was the bleeding woman healed? (5:25-29)
❇ Why did the woman touch Jesus' clothing? (5:27-28)
❇ What happened when the woman touched Jesus' cloak? (5:29)
❇ What was Jesus' immediate response to the woman's action? (5:30-32)
❇ Why did Jesus suddenly stop walking? (5:30-32)
❇ Why could the disciples not understand Jesus' action? (5:31)
❇ Why did the woman fall down? (5:33)
❇ What was the woman afraid of? (5:33)
❇ How did Jesus' reply give the woman comfort and reassurance? (5:34)
❇ What happened while Jesus was still speaking to the woman? (5:35)
■ Whom did Jesus tell not to be afraid and to "just believe"? Why? (5:35-36)
❇ Who were the only people who went with Jesus to Jairus' home? Why? (5:37-38)
❇ What did Jesus mean when He said, "The child is not dead but asleep"? (5:39)
❇ How did people react when Jesus expressed confidence that the dead girl would be all right? (5:40)
■ Who witnessed the girl being raised from the dead by Jesus? (5:40-42)
❇ What were Jesus' final instructions? (5:43)

GET IT
❇ What connection is there between a person's faith and whether God heals him or her of a sickness?
❇ How does Jesus' treatment of the sick woman and Jairus offer comfort to us today?
❇ Why do you think the bleeding woman was afraid to admit she was the one who had touched Jesus?
❇ When have you ever felt afraid of God, like the woman who touched Jesus?
❇ In what way is it good for a person to be afraid of God?
❇ In what way do we need to feel that God is approachable?
■ In what situations do you need God's help?
❇ What does this passage tell us about Jesus' character?
❇ In what situation in your life do you need to heed Jesus' words "Don't be afraid, just believe"?
❇ Why do you think Jesus urged people not to spread the news of the girl's healing?
❇ How do you hope God will work in the situations that cause you fear?
■ What attitude or action do you need to change in your own life in light of the fact that Jesus is willing to respond miraculously to our needs?

APPLY IT
❇ What is one fear that you can ask the Lord to help you face this week?
■ With what concrete action can you show your faith in the Lord this week?

Mark 6:1-6

A Prophet Without Honor

TOPICS
Doubt, Faith, Family, Home, Honor, Miracles, Rejection, Unbelievers

OPEN IT
❇ Do you think it's easier to talk about your faith with a stranger, a family member, or a close friend? Why?
❇ What does the clich "Familiarity breeds contempt" mean?
■ What is one piece of advice your parents gave you that you ignored growing up?

EXPLORE IT
❇ Who went to his hometown? With whom? (6:1)
❇ What did Jesus do when He returned to His hometown? (6:2)
❇ Why were the people of Nazareth amazed by Jesus? (6:2)
■ Why did the people of Nazareth react negatively to Jesus' visit? (6:2-3)
❇ Why did the people of Nazareth talk among themselves about Jesus' family background? (6:3)
■ What did Jesus say to the people who scoffed at Him? (6:4)
❇ What did Jesus do in Nazareth? (6:5)
■ What prevented Jesus from doing no more than a few miracles in Nazareth? (6:5-6)
❇ At what was Jesus amazed? Why? (6:6)
❇ How did the response to Jesus in Nazareth compare to the response in the other regions Jesus had visited? (6:6)

GET IT
❇ How have your family or close friends responded to your faith?
❇ What does this story tell us is one cost of following Christ?
❇ What can we learn from this story about the cost of following Christ?

❊ What can we do to prevent ourselves from having the same lack of faith that the people in Nazareth had?
❊ In what ways do you think we prevent Jesus from working miraculously in our own lives?
❊ In what area of your life would you like the Lord to give you more faith?
❊ How could your local church step out in faith, believing that the Lord rewards those who trust Him?
■ What prevents us from listening to the people we know well?
■ How can we make ourselves more open to the insights of parents, siblings, or others who are close to us?

APPLY IT
❊ In what way could you share the message of Christ with a family member or friend this week?
❊ With what specific step could you turn over one area of your life to the Lord as an act of faith in Him?
■ In what matter could you seek the counsel of a family member or close friend? When?

Mark 6:7-13
Jesus Sends Out the Twelve

TOPICS
Authority, Demons, Faith, Healing, Ministry, Money, Repentance, Sacrifice, Teamwork

OPEN IT
■ In what ways have you ever had to depend on others for some of your needs?
❊ What does society tell us about depending on others?
❊ When have you been able to give support to another person who was having problems?

EXPLORE IT
■ What task did Jesus give the disciples? (6:7)
❊ What do Jesus' actions tell us about His attitude toward His men? (6:7)
❊ How did Jesus send out the disciples? (6:7)
■ How did Jesus equip the disciples for their job? (6:7-11)
❊ What specific instructions did Jesus give the Twelve? (6:8-11)
■ How did Jesus want His men to travel? (6:8-11)
❊ Who was to provide the food and money for the disciples? (6:8)
❊ What was the central focus of the mission of the Twelve? (6:7, 13)
❊ What were the disciples to do if anyone would not welcome them? Why? (6:11)
❊ What did Jesus mean by saying, "as a testimony against them"? (6:11)
❊ What does this episode tell us about why Jesus came to earth? (6:12-13)

GET IT
❊ How do you think the disciples felt about Jesus sending them on their assigned task?
❊ Why do you think Jesus told His men to pack lightly?
❊ How can you know whether God is directing you to do a specific task?
❊ How do you feel when you receive a challenging opportunity like the one Jesus gave the disciples?
■ How has God equipped you for serving Him?
■ How can you apply Jesus' advice to your Christian witness at work?
❊ How should you react to people who do not respond to the message of Christ?
❊ What does this passage teach about our responsibility to those who minister full-time?
❊ In what ways have you fallen short of what Jesus teaches in this passage?
❊ What can you do to ensure your life is reflecting the same message that Jesus taught when He was on the earth?
❊ How can you equip yourself for Christian service?

APPLY IT
❊ What can you do this week to show support for someone who ministers full-time?
■ To whom can you take the message of Christ this week? How?

Mark 6:14-29
John the Baptist Beheaded

TOPICS
Doubt, Holiness, Lust, Murder, Persecution, Power, Sacrifice, Sin

OPEN IT
■ Who do your friends and acquaintances think Jesus is?
❊ What do most people believe about miracles and the supernatural?
❊ In what sense do you think it is or is not harder to believe in miracles today than it was in New Testament times?

EXPLORE IT
❊ How did Herod hear about Jesus' miracles? (6:14)
❊ What were people saying about Jesus? Why? (6:14-16)
■ What do Herod's actions throughout this episode say about the way sin operates in a person's life? (6:14-29)
❊ What was it about Jesus that kept most people from believing that He was the Messiah? (6:14-16)
❊ What did Herod think of Jesus? (6:16)
■ Why had Herod arrested and imprisoned John the Baptist? (6:17-18)
❊ What had John told Herod that caused Herodias to hold a grudge against John? (6:18-19)
❊ How was John's condemnation of Herod's adulterous marriage related to the central message of John's preaching? (6:18)
❊ Why did Herod fear and protect John? (6:20)
❊ What did Mark mean when he wrote "finally the opportune time came"? (6:21)
■ What happened at the party described in this passage? (6:21-28)
❊ What caused Herod to offer Herodias's daughter almost anything she wanted? (6:22-23)
❊ Why did Herod make a foolish promise? (6:22-23)
❊ What resulted from Herod's foolish promise? (6:24-25)

❇ How did Herod respond to the girl's request? (6:26-28)
❇ What became of John? (6:29)

GET IT
❇ What false ideas about Jesus do people entertain today?
❇ How should we as Christians respond to others who malign the name of Christ?
❇ When has it been difficult for you to confront someone about sin, as it was for John to confront Herod?
❇ What responsibility do Christians have to confront nonbelievers with their sin and to tell them of the remedy that Christ offers?
■ What can we learn from Herod's negative example about preventing sin from "snowballing" or getting out of control?
■ How do you think Christians can keep one another accountable?
❇ How can you guard against holding a grudge against another person?
❇ Herod knew John to be a righteous and holy man; how do you think people view you?
❇ How can we guard against making foolish promises?
❇ What do you need to change in your life to have a stronger witness for Christ?

APPLY IT
❇ Whom do you need to confront sometime soon? How can you?
■ What concrete action can you take to prevent a certain area of sin in your personal life from controlling you? When?

Mark 6:30-44
Jesus Feeds the Five Thousand

TOPICS
Compassion, Doubt, Faith, Miracles, Quiet, Rest, Teaching, Thankfulness

OPEN IT
❇ What was a time when you had to do something that you thought was impossible? What happened?
■ What is your idea of a feast?

EXPLORE IT
❇ What did the apostles do upon returning from their trip? (6:30)
❇ Why did Jesus want to go away with the disciples to a quiet place? (6:31-32)
❇ What prevented Jesus and His disciples from getting some rest and relaxation? (6:33)
❇ How did Jesus respond to the crowds of people waiting to see Him? (6:34)
❇ What does Jesus' reaction to the crowds tell you about His character and mission? (6:34)
❇ What problem did the disciples notice? (6:35-36)
■ What problem did the disciples bring to Jesus? Why? (6:35-36)
❇ What solution did the disciples suggest to the problem they faced? (6:36)
■ What did Jesus think of the disciples' suggestion? (6:37)
■ What did the disciples think of Jesus' solution? (6:37)
❇ What does the disciples' reaction to Jesus tell us about them? (6:37)
❇ What unique plan did Jesus come up with? (6:38-41)
❇ How much food did Jesus provide (6:42-44)
❇ What did Jesus' disciples do with the leftovers? (6:43)
❇ How many people did this event directly affect? (6:44)

GET IT
■ What do you think Jesus wanted to teach His disciples through this miracle?
■ What do you think Jesus' disciples learned through this experience?
❇ Why do you think Jesus provided much more than enough food for the people, then had the surplus carefully collected?
❇ Why do you think God tells us to do things that seem to be impossible?
❇ What do you think Jesus wants to teach you through this miracle?
❇ When have you felt it necessary to take some time to be alone with the Lord?
❇ When is it good to take time out to rest? Why?
❇ What can we learn and apply to our own lives from Jesus' attitude toward helping people?
❇ How can we expand our expectations of what God can do through us?
❇ What is one "impossible situation" that you are now facing?
❇ In what way can we show faith in God in the "impossible situations" of our everyday lives?
❇ For what person in your life do you need to have compassion?
❇ How do you think you should react when God tells you to do something that you are sure is beyond your ability?
❇ What does this story teach us about being caretakers of what God has given us?
❇ What is one possession or ability that you need to give to the Lord so that He can use it for His glory?
❇ In what area of your life do you need to have more faith in God?

APPLY IT
❇ In what specific way can you show compassion to another person this next week?
❇ How can you show your willingness to give what you have back to God?
■ What can you do this week to increase your confidence in God?

Mark 6:45-56
Jesus Walks on the Water

TOPICS
Courage, Faith, Fear, Healing, Miracles, Nature, Prayer, Sickness

OPEN IT
❇ When is the last time you remember being in a terrible storm?
■ What is one lesson you had to learn the hard way?

EXPLORE IT
❊ When did Jesus make His disciples go on ahead of Him (6:45)
❊ How did Jesus and the disciples get separated? (6:45-47)
❊ What did Jesus do while He was alone? (6:46)
❊ What problem were the disciples having? (6:48)
❊ How did Jesus respond to the disciples' needs? (6:48)
❊ How did the disciples react when they saw Jesus walk on the water? (6:49)
■ When did the disciples cry out? Why? (6:49-50)
❊ What difference did it make that the disciples' hearts were hardened? (6:49-52)
■ Why were the disciples "completely amazed"? (6:51-52)
❊ What is significant about the wind dying down? (6:51)
■ What had the disciples failed to understand? (6:52)
❊ Where did Jesus and His disciples finally land? (6:53)
❊ What did Jesus do after He and the disciples had crossed over the lake? (6:54-56)
❊ How did the crowds respond to Jesus when He came to their villages? (6:56)
❊ What difference did it make that the crowds welcomed Jesus? (6:56)
❊ What does the fact that "all who touched Jesus were healed" tell us about the people's attitude? (6:56)

GET IT
❊ Why do you think Jesus, who was the Son of God, spent time in prayer?
❊ Why do you think Jesus chose to walk on the water to get to the disciples' boat?
❊ How do you think you would have reacted if you had been with the disciples that night?
■ What did the disciples have to learn the hard way?
❊ When has God done something for you that was completely amazing to you? What was it?
❊ How did you respond the last time you sensed God's work in your life?
❊ Why do you think we are sometimes so surprised by God's goodness to us?
❊ How can we follow Jesus' example of prayer?
❊ How should you follow Jesus' example in this story of taking time out for prayer?
❊ When have you been terrified, as the disciples were in this story?
❊ How can Christ calm our fears or help us when we are afraid?
❊ What difference does it make that Jesus has the power to control the forces of nature?
❊ What does this story tell us about Jesus?
■ What does this story tell us about human nature?
❊ What can we learn from Jesus' commitment to help people and teach them?
❊ In light of this story, how can you increase your faith in Jesus?

APPLY IT
❊ How can you discipline yourself this week to spend time in undistracted prayer each day?
❊ What specific fear or anxiety do you need to turn over to the Lord and entrust to Him?
■ How can you make yourself sensitive to the lessons God wants to teach you this week?

Mark 7:1-23
Clean and Unclean

TOPICS
Attitude, Evil, Heart, Honor, Hypocrisy, Integrity, Parents, Rules, Teaching

OPEN IT
❊ What are some of the traditions in your church?
❊ When did you first learn to wash your hands before eating?
■ What are some of your favorite traditions?

EXPLORE IT
❊ Who was gathered around Jesus? (7:1)
❊ What did the Pharisees and teachers of the law notice? (7:1-2)
❊ How were the practices of Jesus' disciples different from those of the Pharisees and the teachers of the law? (7:2-4)
■ What were the Pharisees and teachers of the law concerned about? Why? (7:2-5)
❊ Why were the Pharisees and teachers of the law concerned about what Jesus' disciples were doing? (7:3-4)
❊ What did the Pharisees ask Jesus? (7:5)
❊ How did Jesus avoid answering the Pharisees' question directly? (7:6)
■ What were the Pharisees doing wrong? (7:6-8)
❊ Of what did Jesus accuse the Pharisees? (7:6-13)
❊ How were the Pharisees being hypocritical in this instance? (7:9)
❊ What example did Jesus give to prove His accusations against the Pharisees? (7:10-12)
❊ How did Jesus use the Law of Moses? (7:10-19)
■ How did Jesus place tradition in proper perspective? (7:10-19)
❊ How did the Pharisees' use of "unclean" differ from Jesus'? (7:14-23)
❊ How did Jesus explain the parable to His disciples? (7:18-23)
❊ What actually makes a person "unclean"? (7:20-23)

GET IT
■ What's wrong with "holding on to the traditions of men"?
■ What did Jesus want His audience to do?
❊ In what ways are Christians today hypocritical?
❊ What church traditions either can or do stand in the way of non-believers becoming interested in Christianity?
❊ What traditions do you hold on to that can go against the commands of God?
❊ What can we do to place tradition—especially religious traditions—in proper perspective?
❊ In what ways do you think it is possible to worship the Lord in vain?
❊ From the list of "unclean" things that come from within a person's heart (greed, deceit, envy, etc.), which attitude or action do you need to work on eliminating from your life?
❊ How can we be sure we are "clean" in God's sight?

❊ What can we do to work toward being clean in God's sight?
❊ What practices in your local church do you think might be distracting people's attention from the central concerns of the faith?
❊ How can you guard against practicing the type of tradition-bound, external religion that Jesus condemned?

APPLY IT
■ What can you do to honor the commands of God above your traditions?
❊ What is one practice that you can eliminate or modify to help you focus on the teaching of Jesus?
❊ What is one step you can take to guard against hypocrisy?

Mark 7:24-30
The Faith of a Syrophoenician Woman

TOPICS
Courage, Demons, Faith, Gospel, Humility, Priorities, Rationalizing

OPEN IT
■ When was a time when you felt like an outsider?
❊ Why do you think some Christians lose or give up their faith in God?

EXPLORE IT
❊ What did Jesus try to keep secret? How? (7:24)
❊ Why did a certain woman want to see Jesus? (7:25)
❊ What did the woman do when she saw Jesus? Why? (7:25)
■ Who came to see Jesus? Why? (7:25-26)
❊ What was this woman's background? (7:26)
❊ What did the woman in the story want from Jesus? (7:26)
❊ How did Jesus respond to this woman? (7:27)
❊ To whom was Jesus referring when He spoke of children? (7:27)
❊ What did this woman call Jesus? (7:28)
❊ How did the woman appeal Jesus' decision not to help her? (7:28)
❊ What made the woman so persistent? (7:28)
■ Why was Jesus impressed with the woman? (7:28-29)
■ What happened to the woman and her daughter? (7:30)

GET IT
■ What was exemplary about the woman who came to see Jesus?
❊ Why do you think Mark included this episode in his Gospel?
❊ Why would you or wouldn't you have gone to see Jesus if you had been in the same situation as this woman?
❊ What have you "begged" Jesus to do for you in the past? How did He answer?
❊ How would you compare your level of faith with that of the woman in this story?
❊ In what ways has Jesus rewarded you for your faith?
❊ What difference does it make in your life that Jesus has the power and authority over all the evil forces of the world?
■ What about the woman's attitude can we apply to our prayer life?
❊ No two of Jesus' healings were exactly alike; how should our witness for Christ be tailored to each situation and person?
❊ How can you be personal and sensitive in the way you meet the needs of those around you?

APPLY IT
❊ What is one area of your life that you will commit to the Lord in faith today?
■ What concrete step can you take to show your faith in the Lord and your dependence on His power?

Mark 7:31-37
The Healing of a Deaf and Mute Man

TOPICS
Faith, Healing, Instructions, Mercy, Miracles, Thankfulness, Witnessing

OPEN IT
■ What do you think it would be like to be deaf or unable to speak?
❊ What attitudes does our society have toward disabled people?
❊ How do most ordinary folks treat people who have disabilities?

EXPLORE IT
❊ Where did the events of this story take place? (7:31)
■ Who was brought to Jesus? Why? (7:32)
❊ What attitude did the people have toward Jesus? (7:32)
❊ What did Jesus do for the man who was deaf and could hardly speak? (7:33-36)
❊ What method did Jesus use to heal the man who came to Him? (7:33-36)
■ What did Jesus do so that the man would know it was Jesus who helped him? (7:33-36)
❊ What happened to the deaf man? (7:35)
❊ How was the deaf man's life changed because of Jesus? (7:35-37)
■ What command of Jesus got the opposite effect He intended? (7:36)
❊ How did the people react to Jesus and His miraculous power? (7:36-37)
❊ What difference did this miracle make in the lives of the people who witnessed it? (7:36-37)
❊ Why couldn't the people stop talking about Jesus? (7:37)

GET IT
❊ Whom do you know who has experienced the healing of Jesus in his or her life?
❊ How do people respond to Jesus' miraculous work in their lives?
❊ What can you learn from the people's attitude toward Jesus in this story?
❊ In what area of your life do you need God's healing power?

❊ How can you increase your faith in God?
■ How has God helped you in a way that met your personal, unique needs, as He did for the man in this story?
■ How can we tailor the way we reach out to each person?
❊ What difference does it make in your everyday life that Jesus has all power and authority over the world?
❊ Whom could you tell about the goodness of God in your life?

APPLY IT
❊ What is one area of your life that you can commit to the Lord and trust Him to work through?
❊ What can you do this next week to show your thanks to God for His work in your life?
❊ How can you trust God with your needs?
■ What can you do to reach out to someone in need this week?

Mark 8:1-13
Jesus Feeds the Four Thousand

TOPICS
Abundance, Doubt, Faith, Ministry, Miracles, Needs, Questions, Teaching, Thankfulness

OPEN IT
❊ When was a time someone showed compassion to you?
❊ Why is it sometimes difficult to accept help or sympathy from others?
■ How does it make you feel to receive support or help from others?

EXPLORE IT
■ Why did Jesus call the disciples to Him? (8:1-3)
❊ How did Jesus feel toward the crowd of people that had gathered? (8:2)
❊ How long had the crowd in this story been gathered? Why? (8:2)
❊ Why couldn't Jesus just send the people to their homes for food? (8:3)
❊ What did Jesus' disciples think of the crowd's dilemma? (8:4)
■ How did Jesus involve His disciples in this problem? (8:5-8)
❊ What did Jesus do with the seven loaves and few small fish that the disciples had found? (8:6)
■ How much food went uneaten? (8:8)
❊ What did Jesus do after He had fed the crowd? (8:9-10)
❊ Who came to see Jesus? Why? (8:11)
❊ How did the Pharisees plan to "test" Jesus? (8:11)
❊ Why did Jesus "sigh deeply"? (8:12)
❊ What announcement did Jesus make to the generation of His day? (8:12)
❊ What did Jesus think of His visitors? (8:12-13)

GET IT
■ What can we learn from Jesus' attitude and actions toward the crowds that followed Him?
■ How can you become a more compassionate person?
❊ When have you consciously trusted the Lord for food or another essential of life?
❊ What did it feel like to have to trust the Lord to supply your basic needs?
❊ In what ways has God provided for the needs of you and your family?
❊ How does God's work in the past encourage you to trust Him with your future?
❊ How can you show your thankfulness to God for the way He takes care of you?
❊ When was a time you tried to test the Lord as the Pharisees did? What happened?
❊ What kinds of people today have the same attitude the Pharisees did?
❊ Why do people demand signs from God?
❊ Why does God refuse to give us signs or proof of His existence and presence?

APPLY IT
■ To whom can you show compassion? How and when?
❊ In what one area of your life will you ask God to work miraculously this week?
❊ How can you trust God this week to supply your needs?
❊ For what difficult problem will you depend on God? How?

Mark 8:14-21
The Yeast of the Pharisees and Herod

TOPICS
Criticism, Evil, Forget, Heart, Miracles, Remembering

OPEN IT
❊ When was a time you misunderstood what someone said or did? What resulted?
❊ What is one negative example from which you have learned?
■ In what ways do many adults grow hardened as they get older?

EXPLORE IT
❊ What had the disciples forgotten on their trip? (8:14)
❊ When did Jesus start talking about the Pharisees? (8:15)
■ What did Jesus warn His disciples against? (8:15)
❊ How did the disciples misunderstand Jesus' warning? (8:16)
❊ What was Christ's explanation for why the disciples could not understand what He meant? (8:17-18)
■ Why couldn't the disciples understand what Jesus said? (8:17-18)
❊ What would have enabled the disciples to understand Jesus better? (8:17-18)
■ Why was Jesus amazed at His disciples? (8:17-21)
❊ Why did Jesus remind the disciples about the miracles of feeding the crowds? (8:19)
❊ How did Jesus try to get through to His disciples? (8:18-20)
❊ Of what miracles did Jesus remind the disciples? Why? (8:19-20)

GET IT
❇ What did Jesus want His disciples to learn from the Pharisees and Herod?
❇ When have you ever misunderstood what the Bible said about a certain topic or idea?
■ What passages or ideas from the Bible have you struggled to understand?
■ How can we guard against misinterpreting or ignoring the Scriptures?
❇ When has your heart been "hardened" to God's message?
❇ When has your heart been "hardened" to the voice of the Holy Spirit?
❇ How can you be more sensitive to God's will for you?
❇ If Jesus had been speaking directly to us, what negative example might He have warned us to learn from?
❇ If Jesus had been speaking to you personally, what negative example might He have warned you to watch out for?
❇ How can you separate yourself from the corruption of the world and yet still be an effective witness for Christ?

APPLY IT
❇ What miracles of Christ's, negative examples, or object lessons can you use as reminders of Christ's proper place in your life?
■ What is one step you can take to soften your heart toward God this week?
❇ What is one specific command of Christ's that you want to apply to your life this week?
❇ What can you do to steer clear of the evil and corruption in your workplace, community, or home life?

Mark 8:22-26
The Healing of a Blind Man at Bethsaida

TOPICS
Blindness, Guidance, Healing, Prayer, Restoration, Separation

OPEN IT
■ When have you experienced a time when God answered a prayer only partially?
❇ Why do you think God would not answer prayer as we hope?
❇ How do you respond when God answers your prayers completely?

EXPLORE IT
❇ Where did the events of this story take place? (8:22)
■ What did the people do about the blind man's condition? (8:22)
❇ Where did Jesus perform this miracle? (8:23)
❇ How did Jesus get the blind man out of the village? (8:23)
■ How did Jesus heal the blind man? (8:23-25)
❇ How did Jesus treat the blind man differently from the many other people He had healed? (8:23-26)
❇ What do we learn about Jesus' character from the way He treated the blind man? (8:23-26)
❇ What is unique about this healing compared to every other healing Mark recorded in his Gospel? (8:23-26)
❇ What did the blind man see after the first touch from Jesus? (8:24)
❇ What occurred after Jesus touched the blind man a second time? (8:25)
■ What did Jesus urge the man to do after he was healed? (8:26)

GET IT
❇ Why do you think Jesus returned to Bethsaida?
❇ Why do you think the people begged Jesus to heal the blind man?
❇ What connection do you think there is between this gradual healing and the disciples' slowness to understand who Jesus was?
❇ Why do you think Jesus healed people in so many unique ways?
❇ What difference does it make to you that God views us all as unique individuals and treats us according to our own needs?
❇ How should Jesus' actions and attitudes in this story affect the way you represent Christ to others?
❇ When has your "sight" been clouded by circumstances in your life?
❇ How has God opened your eyes in a difficult situation?
■ Whom do you know who has been changed by Jesus but now needs a "second touch" in his or her life?
■ How could you help a person you know who needs a "second touch" from Jesus?
❇ What have you learned from this passage about Jesus' attitude toward people?
❇ How can you show thanks to the Lord for His personal interest in you as an individual?

APPLY IT
■ What can you do this week for someone in need?
❇ What is one area of your life in which you can pray for God's healing?
❇ How do you want to respond the next time the Lord answers prayer in an unexpected way?

Mark 8:27-30
Peter's Confession of Christ

TOPICS
Beliefs, Choices, Confession, Convictions, Faith, Jesus Christ, Peer Pressure

OPEN IT
❇ Where do you tend to experience the pressure of a larger group?
■ When have you ever succumbed to group pressure when you knew you should not have?

EXPLORE IT
❋ Where did this episode take place? (8:27)
■ What did Jesus ask His disciples? (8:27)
■ What did people theorize about Jesus? (8:27-28)
❋ How did the disciples respond to Jesus' question? (8:28)
❋ How had people connected Jesus with Elijah, John the Baptist, and other prophets? (8:28)
❋ How did Jesus make this discussion personal? (8:29)
■ How did the disciples answer Jesus' question? (8:29)
❋ Whom did Peter say Jesus was? (8:29)
❋ Who spoke for the whole group of disciples? (8:29)
❋ What was Peter's declaration of faith? (8:29)
❋ What warning did Jesus give His disciples? (8:30)

GET IT
❋ Why do you think Jesus asked about His identity at this particular point?
❋ Why would people think that Jesus was John the Baptist, Elijah, or one of the other prophets?
❋ Why do you think Jesus asked the two questions in the order He did?
❋ Why would Jesus warn the disciples not to tell anyone that He was the Messiah?
■ Who do you say Jesus is?
❋ How do your beliefs go against the flow of the majority in our world?
❋ What is it like to stand up against the views of the crowd?
❋ How does the knowledge that one day everyone will know that Christ is Lord affect your attitude about the pressure you feel from the world?
■ Why is it important for a Christian not to hide his or her faith in Christ?
❋ How can we stand up for what is right in the face of pressure from others to compromise?
❋ What can we learn from Peter's example?
❋ How do your beliefs in Jesus Christ affect your everyday life?

APPLY IT
■ How can you state your faith in Christ's Lordship?
❋ Whom should you tell this week about your faith in Christ?
❋ What specific area of your life do you need to submit to the Lordship of Christ? How?

Mark 8:31–9:1
Jesus Predicts His Death

TOPICS
Denial, Disagreements, Eternal Life, Gospel, Preparation, Rewards, Sacrifice, Second Coming, Suffering, Temptation

OPEN IT
■ In what ways has your life been different from what you expected?
❋ How do unrealistic expectations block people from following Christ?

EXPLORE
❋ Who referred to Himself as the "Son of Man"? (8:31)
❋ What did Jesus teach the disciples? (8:31)
❋ How did Jesus speak about what would happen to Him? (8:32)
❋ Why did Peter rebuke Jesus? (8:32)
❋ How was what Jesus predicted different from what Peter expected? (8:32)
❋ What surprised Peter? (8:32)
■ Who rebuked whom? (8:32-33) Why?
❋ What did Jesus say to Peter in response to his rebuke? (8:33)
❋ Why did Jesus rebuke Peter? (8:33)
❋ Why did Jesus speak harshly with Peter? (8:33)
■ In what way did Peter have in mind the "things of man" as opposed to the "things of God"? (8:33)
❋ What was wrong with Peter's thinking? (8:33)
❋ What did Jesus do after rebuking Peter? (8:34)
■ What did Jesus want His disciples to do? (8:34-35)
❋ Why did Jesus say, "If anyone would come after me, he must deny himself and take up his cross and follow me"? (8:34-38)
❋ How did Jesus refer to the people to whom He was speaking? (8:38)
❋ How will Jesus come back to earth? (8:38)
❋ What promise was given to Jesus' audience? (9:1)

GET IT
❋ When have you ever doubted the words of Jesus?
❋ In what ways has Christ rebuked you in the past?
■ Why does Christ ask us to "deny yourself, take up your cross, and follow" Him?
❋ What does it mean to deny yourself?
❋ What does it mean to take up your cross?
❋ What does it mean to follow Christ?
❋ In what way can a person both save his life and lose it at the same time?
❋ What did Jesus mean when He said, "Some who are standing here will not taste death before they see the kingdom of God come with power"? (9:1)
❋ How do you usually respond to the Lord's correction or discipline in your life?
■ How can we make sure we "have in mind the things of God"?
❋ What do you think Christ wants you to give up for the sake of the gospel?
❋ What does it mean to be ashamed of Christ?
❋ In what ways does Satan tempt us to do the opposite of what Christ wants for us?

APPLY IT
■ What attitude or practice do you need to change in obedience to Christ?
❋ What specific steps can you take to listen closely to Christ this week?

Mark 9:2-13
The Transfiguration

TOPICS
Holiness, Obedience, Prophecy, Representatives, Witnessing, Worship

OPEN IT
❊ When were you last speechless?
■ How do people react when they watch fireworks? Why?

EXPLORE IT
❊ Where did Jesus take Peter, James, and John? (9:2)
❊ Whom did Jesus take with Him to the mountain? (9:2)
■ What happened to Jesus on the mountain? (9:3)
❊ Who appeared with Jesus in the transfiguration? (9:4)
❊ What was significant about the people who appeared to Jesus? (9:4)
❊ How did Peter respond to the transfiguration of Jesus? (9:5)
❊ Why did Peter want to put up three shelters? (9:5)
❊ Why were the disciples frightened when they saw Jesus? (9:6)
❊ How did God appear to Jesus and the others? (9:7)
■ What did God say to the disciples? (9:7)
■ What did God want the disciples to do? (9:7)
❊ What did the disciples see after the cloud vanished? (9:7-8)
❊ What orders did Jesus give the disciples? (9:9)
❊ How did Peter, James, and John respond to Jesus' order? (9:10)
❊ What caught the "elite three" off guard and became the topic of discussion as they headed down the mountain? (9:10)
❊ Why did the disciples ask Jesus about Elijah? (9:11)
❊ About whom was Jesus speaking when He said, "Elijah has come"? (9:12-13)

GET IT
❊ Why do you think Jesus chose only three of His disciples to witness His transfiguration?
❊ How do you think this account would encourage an audience of Christians being harassed and threatened?
❊ What encouragement does this passage give you?
■ How do you think you would have reacted if Jesus had chosen you to witness His transfiguration?
❊ When has a spiritual experience caused you to be speechless or frightened?
■ What is implied by God's command that we listen to Jesus?
❊ What can we learn from this account about the relationship between God the Father and His Son, Jesus Christ?

APPLY IT
❊ What specific word or command of Jesus can you obey more carefully this week? How?
■ What can you do over the next week to become more sensitive to God's voice (whether from His Word or His Spirit)?

Mark 9:14-32
The Healing of a Boy With an Evil Spirit

TOPICS
Believe, Demons, Discipline, Doubt, Faith, Healing, Prayer, Unbelievers

OPEN IT
■ When was the last time you felt inadequate to do a job you had to do?
❊ In what situation have you done something that you thought was impossible?

EXPLORE IT
❊ What was the setting of the events in this story? (9:14)
❊ How did the people react when they saw Jesus? (9:15)
❊ What did Jesus ask the crowd and the teachers of the law? (9:16)
❊ What were the people arguing about? (9:17)
❊ What had the evil spirit done to the boy it possessed? (9:17-18)
■ Why were the disciples unable to cast the demon out of the boy? (9:19)
■ How did Jesus feel at this point? (9:19)
❊ What was the evil spirit's response to Jesus? (9:20)
❊ What was the boy's life like before Jesus healed him? (9:21-22)
■ How were prayer and faith related in this situation? (9:22-23)
❊ What problem did the father need to overcome? (9:24)
❊ When did Jesus cast the demon out? (9:25-26)
❊ How did Jesus treat the demon-possessed boy? (9:24-27)
❊ What necessary step had the disciples failed to take in this situation? (9:28-29)
❊ Why did Jesus want to avoid the crowds of people? (9:30-31)
❊ What news did Jesus repeat privately to the disciples? (9:31)
❊ What frightened the disciples? (9:31-32)

GET IT
❊ How do you think Jesus felt about His disciples in this situation?
❊ How should we pray when we feel inadequate?
❊ In what ways do you think we are an "unbelieving generation" like the people of Jesus' day?
❊ What difference does it make that "everything is possible for him who believes"?
❊ In what area of your life do you struggle with doubt?
❊ What can we learn from the father's example in this story?
❊ How has God helped you overcome your unbelief in the past?
■ In what areas of life do you think we fail to see success because we do not pray?
■ How can you become more dedicated to prayer?

APPLY IT
■ About what in your life will you pray every day this week? When?
❊ What concrete action can you take today to show a commitment to prayer?

Mark 9:33-37
Who Is the Greatest?

TOPICS
Arguments, Greatness, Humility, Pride, Sacrifice, Serving, Status

OPEN IT
❊ What makes a person look prestigious or "respectable" in our society?
■ Whom do you consider to be a great person? Why?

EXPLORE IT
❊ What did Jesus ask the disciples when they got to Capernaum? (9:33)
❊ Why did the disciples suddenly stop talking? (9:33-34)
■ How did Jesus get His disciples' attention? (9:33-34)
❊ What does the disciples' argument tell you about their understanding of who Jesus was and why He had come? (9:33-34)
❊ Why were the disciples embarrassed to answer Jesus' question? (9:34)
■ How did Jesus explain what it means to be great? (9:35)
❊ What kind of person tries to be a servant? (9:35)
■ How did Jesus illustrate His point? (9:36)
❊ What did Jesus say about children? (9:37)
❊ How is it possible to welcome God? (9:37)

GET IT
■ What does it mean to be a servant of all?
❊ What does it mean to welcome someone in Jesus' name?
❊ What does it mean to be great in God's eyes?
❊ How can a person become great in God's eyes?
❊ Why do you think Jesus used a child to illustrate His point?
❊ How can you welcome someone in Jesus' name?
❊ What sorts of issues cause ill will among Christians today?
❊ How do we strive to be the "greatest"?
■ How can you become a "servant of all" in your everyday actions and attitudes?
❊ What does this passage tell us about Jesus' attitude toward children and other weaker members of society?
❊ How should we treat people of "lower status"?
❊ What attitude change do you want to make in light of the principles you discovered in this passage?

APPLY IT
■ What is one concrete way you can serve another person this week?
❊ In what specific situation can you consciously choose to be a servant for Christ's sake sometime this next week?

Mark 9:38-41
Whoever Is Not Against Us Is for Us

TOPICS
Arguments, Believers, Demons, Divisions, Jealousy, Judging Others, Ministry, Miracles, Pride, Rewards, Unity

OPEN IT
■ What do people argue about in your family?
❊ What happens to a team of workers when members become jealous and use power plays against each other?
❊ What do you think are the advantages and disadvantages of church denominations?

EXPLORE IT
❊ Who told Jesus about the dilemma facing the disciples? (9:38)
❊ How did John refer to Jesus and how was that significant? (9:38)
■ What issue concerned the disciples? (9:38)
❊ Why did the disciples try to stop a man from driving out demons? (9:38)
■ What attitudes did the disciples have in this situation? (9:38)
■ How did Jesus respond to the disciples' question? (9:40)
❊ Why did Jesus not mind others, who were not part of His group of disciples, performing miracles in His name? (9:40)
❊ What attitude did Jesus want the disciples to have? (9:41)
❊ How will God treat those who do good in Christ's name? (9:41)
❊ What principle was Jesus trying to teach the disciples? (9:39-41)

GET IT
❊ What jealousies and power struggles do you see in the church today?
■ Over what issues do we tend to be divided as believers?
■ How does Christ want us to respond to others who minister in His name, even if they do not come from the same group or background as we do?
❊ How do you think God views the various denominations and separate societies that the Christian church has divided into?
❊ How can we become more unified as a body of believers?
❊ How can you ensure that you are serving in the name of Christ and not allowing wrong motives to steal any of the glory that belongs to Christ?
❊ What ministry do you think God might be leading you to get involved in?
❊ What do you think we could do as churches and denominations to lay aside our differences and put up a united front to the world?
❊ What can churches do to support those who are not against them?

APPLY IT

❄ What step can you take this week to help another person in Christ's name?

■ What can you do to support someone who does good and is "not against you"?

Mark 9:42-50

Causing to Sin

TOPICS

Accountability, Believers, Example, Hell, Judgment, Kingdom of God/Heaven, Peace, Sin, Temptation

OPEN IT

■ What are your favorite seasonings?

❄ What is pleasant and unpleasant about salt?

❄ What do you believe are the marks of maturity?

EXPLORE IT

❄ To whom did Jesus refer when He spoke of "little ones"? (9:42)

❄ What behavior did Jesus condemn? (9:42)

❄ What figure of speech did Jesus use to show how serious His point was? (9:42-47)

■ What was Jesus' attitude toward sin? (9:43-47)

❄ What does this passage teach about the kingdom of God? (9:43-47)

■ Why did Jesus use extreme examples in this context? (9:43-48)

❄ How did Jesus use figurative language to get His message across? (9:43-48)

❄ How did Jesus describe hell? (9:48-49)

❄ What did Jesus mean when He said, "Everyone will be salted with fire"? (9:49)

■ When Jesus talked about "salt," what exactly was He referring to? (9:50)

❄ Why is "saltiness" necessary in a Christian's life? (9:50)

❄ With what final instruction did Jesus conclude? (9:50)

❄ How do Jesus' final words relate to the rest of the passage? (9:50)

GET IT

❄ Who are the "little ones" in our society?

❄ What do our hands, feet, and eyes represent?

❄ How can a person's hand, foot, or eye cause him or her to sin?

■ How do you think a Christian can cause others to sin?

■ In what ways is causing another person to sin worse than sinning yourself?

❄ What should be our attitude toward sin?

❄ How do you plan to apply to your life the principles Jesus taught about avoiding sin?

❄ What specific steps can a Christian take to avoid sin?

❄ What could a church do as a group to apply these principles?

❄ How can this passage motivate us to share our faith with unbelievers?

❄ What do you need to do to add some "salt" to your witness?

❄ What can we do to create peace among believers?

APPLY IT

■ What concrete action can you take this week to avoid a sin that you have struggled with in the recent past?

❄ What can you do this week to make your witness for Christ clearer to the unbelievers around you?

Mark 10:1-12

Divorce

TOPICS

Adultery, Creation, Law, Marriage, New Covenant, Separation, Teaching

OPEN IT

■ What do you think makes a marriage strong and lasting?

❄ How do the people you work with view people with struggling or failed marriages?

EXPLORE IT

❄ Where did this episode take place? (10:1)

❄ What does this passage say about Christ's attitude toward His ministry? (10:1)

■ Why did the Pharisees go to see Jesus? (10:2)

❄ How did the Pharisees try to trick Jesus? (10:2)

❄ How did Jesus respond to the Pharisee's question? (10:3)

❄ Why do you think Jesus brought Moses into this discussion? (10:3)

❄ What did Moses allow in the area of divorce? (10:4)

■ How did Jesus explain Moses' instructions? (10:5)

❄ What do we learn about the Pharisees from Jesus' explanation of Moses' words? (10:5)

❄ How did Jesus explain the relationship between the Law and the will of God? (10:5-9)

❄ How did Jesus lend authority to His words? (10:6-9)

■ What was God's original plan for marriage before sin entered the picture? (10:6-9)

❄ What is the meaning of "they are no longer two, but one"? (10:8)

❄ What overriding principle did Jesus want us to follow? (10:9)

❄ Why did this topic come up a second time that day? (10:10)

❄ What specific instructions did Jesus give regarding divorce? (10:11-12)

❄ How did Jesus protect women with His instructions? (10:11-12)

GET IT

❄ How do you think the Pharisees expected to trick Jesus?

❄ What do we learn about human nature from Jesus' answer to the Pharisees' question?

❄ Why do you think Jesus referred back to the "beginning of creation" in this debate?

❄ How could a person separate "what God has joined together"?

❄ Why do you think the disciples asked Jesus about their question privately?

❄ How should we view people with struggling or failed marriages?

■ How can the church help people with struggling or failed marriages?

❄ How can the church help its members strengthen and even save their marriages?

❋ Why do you think so many marriages fail?
■ What can you do to strengthen your own marriage or encourage a couple who is experiencing difficulty in this area?
❋ What attitude should we have toward marriage?
❋ How should a Christian's understanding of marriage differ from that of the popular image?
❋ How can a strong Christian marriage be an effective witness to unbelievers?

APPLY IT
❋ What is one specific step you can take this week to show respect for the sanctity of marriage?
■ For what couple can you pray every day this week?

Mark 10:13-16
The Little Children and Jesus

TOPICS
Assumptions, Blessing, Children, Humility, Inadequacy, Kingdom of God/Heaven, Salvation

OPEN IT
■ What's the best thing about being a child?
❋ How should children be treated differently from adults?
❋ In what ways do children think differently from adults?

EXPLORE IT
❋ Why were people bringing their children to Jesus? (10:13)
❋ How did the disciples react to this situation? (10:13)
■ How was Jesus different from the disciples? (10:13-16)
❋ What about Jesus surprised the disciples in this situation? (10:13-16)
❋ How did Jesus respond to the disciples sending the children away? (10:14)
❋ What do Jesus' actions tell us about His attitude toward children? (10:14)
■ What did Jesus want His disciples to do? (10:14)
❋ Why did Jesus want the children to come to Him? (10:14)
❋ What unique connection do children have to the kingdom of God? (10:14)
❋ What can we learn from children about the kingdom of God? (10:15)
❋ How did Jesus want people to respond to Him? (10:15)
■ How did Jesus treat the children He met? (10:16)

GET IT
❋ What does it mean that "the kingdom of God belongs to such as" little children?
❋ What does it mean to receive the kingdom of God like a little child?
■ What about the behavior of children does God want us to copy?
■ How can we have the same attitude toward God that children had toward Jesus?
❋ How should we treat children?
❋ How do you think your church needs to change the way it treats children?
❋ How can we receive the kingdom of God "like a little child"?
❋ What does Jesus' display of emotion in this account tell you about Him?
❋ In what specific ways do you need to change your attitude toward God?

APPLY IT
❋ What concrete steps can you take this week to imitate Christ's love and compassion for children?
■ In what concrete way can you depend on God in your day-to-day affairs?

Mark 10:17-31
The Rich Young Man

TOPICS
Basics of the Faith, Eternal Life, Gospel, Heaven, Impossible, Obedience, Possessions, Rejection, Rewards, Sacrifice, Salvation, Wealth

OPEN IT
■ What are the advantages and disadvantages of being wealthy?
❋ Why do you think most people want to be rich?

EXPLORE IT
❋ What was the attitude of the wealthy man as he came to Jesus? (10:17)
■ What did the man want Jesus to explain to him? (10:17)
❋ Why did Jesus say to the man, "No one is good, except God alone"? (10:18)
■ How did Jesus explain the way to inherit eternal life? (10:19-21)
❋ How did the rich man respond to Jesus? (10:20)
❋ What does the rich man's answer to Jesus tell us about his spiritual state? (10:20)
❋ What attitude did Jesus have toward the rich man? (10:21)
❋ What was difficult about the instruction that Jesus give the young man? (10:21-22)
❋ In what way would selling all of his earthly possessions give the wealthy man "treasure in heaven"? (10:21)
■ Why could the man not obey Christ's instructions? (10:22)
❋ What did Jesus mean when He said, "It is easier for a camel to go through the eye of the needle than for a rich man to enter the kingdom of God"? (10:24-25)
❋ When the disciples were astonished and dismayed at Jesus' words, how did He encourage them? (10:26-27)
❋ How did Peter respond to this situation? (10:28)
❋ With what promise did Jesus conclude His teaching in this passage? (10:29-31)

GET IT
❋ Why do you think Jesus demanded such a tall order from this man?
■ In what way can money stop us from doing what God wants?
❋ How can wealth interfere with a person's Christian faith?
❋ What have you ever sacrificed for the sake of following Christ?

❇ What interferes with your walk with the Lord?
■ How do you think God wants you to use the material wealth He has given you?
❇ How can we prevent ourselves from allowing wealth to interfere with our Christianity?
❇ What can you learn about Jesus from His actions in this story?
❇ What can we learn through the negative example of the rich young man in this episode?
❇ What makes it difficult for a rich person to be saved?
❇ What makes it difficult for anyone, rich or poor, to enter the kingdom of God?
❇ What can you give to the poor? How?
■ What practical steps can we take to insure that we place value on eternal things and not merely on material things?

APPLY IT
■ What can you sell or give away in the near future to reflect a concern for God's kingdom over things?
❇ What is one distraction you can set aside from your routine this week to help you concentrate on more on devotion to Christ?

Mark 10:32-34

Jesus Again Predicts His Death

TOPICS
Death, Emotions, Fear, Leadership, Promises, Prophecy, Resurrection, Suffering

OPEN IT
❇ Why do we avoid talking about death in everyday conversation?
■ What attitudes do people in our society have about dying?
❇ When have you had to deal with the death of someone close to you?

EXPLORE IT
❇ Where does this story take place? (10:32)
❇ What emotions were displayed by the disciples? (10:32)
■ Why was there such a range of strong emotions on this trip? (10:32)
■ What important news did Jesus tell the Twelve once again about what would happen to Him? (10:32-33)
❇ What did Jesus say about the "Son of Man"? (10:33)
❇ How did Jesus refer to Himself? (10:33)
❇ When Jesus predicted His death and resurrection this third time, what else did He say would happen? (10:33-34)
■ How did Jesus say He would die? (10:33-34)
❇ How would Jesus be treated at the time of His death? (10:33-34)
❇ Who was going to torture and kill Jesus? (10:33-34)

GET IT
❇ Why do you think Jesus was "leading the way"?
❇ Why do you think Jesus told His disciples that He would be mocked and tortured?
❇ How do you think the disciples responded to what Jesus told them?
❇ What prevented some followers of Jesus from understanding that He was predicting His death and resurrection?
❇ What do Jesus' actions in this account tell us about the relationship He wants to have with us?
❇ What does this passage tell us about Jesus?
❇ What can we learn from the disciples in this event?
■ When has God ever led you down a road which you felt uncomfortable or frightened about?
❇ How have you experienced God's leading in times of uncertainty?
■ How can you trust God more fully to lead you through difficult circumstances in the future?
❇ What difference does it make to you that Jesus correctly predicted everything that happened to Him?
❇ Why did Christ willingly go to Jerusalem when He knew the pain and humiliation He would experience there?

APPLY IT
■ What is one difficult situation that you need Jesus to lead you through this upcoming week?
❇ How can you place your trust in Christ each day rather than in your own abilities?

Mark 10:35-45

The Request of James and John

TOPICS
Authority, Greed, Heaven, Jealousy, Power, Sacrifice, Serving, Status, Suffering

OPEN IT
❇ What issues do people often argue about?
■ In what way does society pressure us to seek status and power?

EXPLORE IT
❇ What was the relationship between James, John, and Jesus? (10:35)
❇ With what attitude did James and John confront Jesus? (10:35)
■ What did James and John want from Jesus? (10:37)
❇ What did James and John's request reflect about their character? (10:37)
■ How did Jesus answer James and John's request? (10:38-40)
❇ What were the "baptism" and "cup" of which Jesus spoke? (10:38-39)
❇ What figure of speech did Jesus use in speaking with James and John? (10:38-39)
■ How did Jesus explain to James and John the impossibility of granting what they had requested? (10:39-40)
❇ Who will grant the seats to Christ's right and left in glory? (10:40)
■ How did the other disciples react to James and John's request? (10:41)
❇ What did Jesus warn all His disciples about? (10:42-43)
❇ What value did Jesus place on serving? (10:42-45)
❇ What value did Jesus place on status? (10:42-45)

❇ How did Jesus advise the disciples regarding greatness? (10:43-44)
❇ What did Jesus mean when He said He "did not come to be served, but to serve"? (10:45)

GET IT
❇ Why was Jesus unwilling to do what James and John asked for?
❇ Why were the other disciples angry at James and John?
❇ What sort of unreasonable requests do we sometimes make of God? Why do we?
❇ In what way does God protect us from our foolish requests?
■ In what ways do we vie for power and authority?
❇ How does Jesus want us to handle power and authority?
❇ How do Jesus' words to James and John change your attitude about power and authority?
❇ How can you adopt Christ's example as your own?
■ How can you become a servant of others?
❇ How do you need to change your attitude or actions in light of Jesus' words about serving?
❇ Jesus, the Son of God, left us a perfect example of humility and service to others. What does this imply for us?
❇ How should you respond to Jesus' giving His life as a ransom for you?

APPLY IT
■ What specific act of service could you do this week for someone else?
❇ What steps can you take to guard yourself against an attitude of selfishness or greed?

Mark 10:46-52
Blind Bartimaeus Receives His Sight

TOPICS
Blindness, Faith, Healing, Miracles, Persistence, Prayer

OPEN IT
■ When has persistence paid off for you?
❇ In what circumstances might it not be good to be persistent?

EXPLORE IT
❇ Where did the events of this story take place? (10:46)
❇ Where was the blind man sitting when Jesus passed by? (10:46)
❇ What was significant about the way the blind man addressed Jesus? (10:47-48)
■ Why did the people rebuke the blind man? (10:48)
■ How did the blind man respond to the criticism from the crowd? (10:48)
❇ What do the blind man's actions tell you about his character and his attitude toward Jesus? (10:48)
■ How did the crowds of people treat Bartimaeus after they found out Jesus had called for him? (10:49)
❇ How did Bartimaeus react when Jesus called him? (10:50)
❇ How did Jesus help Bartimaeus? (10:51)
❇ How did Bartimaeus respond to Jesus' question? (10:51)
❇ How did the blind man's actions reveal to Jesus that he had faith? (10:52)
❇ What did Bartimaeus do after Jesus had healed him? (10:52)

GET IT
❇ What do you think motivated the blind man to call out for Jesus?
❇ Why do you think Jesus singled out Bartimaeus for healing among the many needy people He must have encountered along the way?
■ When have you persistently prayed for one particular request? What happened?
❇ What role does persistence play in prayer?
■ What does it mean to be persistent in prayer?
❇ What specifically can you learn from Bartimaeus's example?
❇ What connection is there between a person's faith and whether God answers their prayer?
❇ What does this passage tell you about Jesus' attitude toward hurting people?
❇ How does Jesus' actions in this account encourage you to get more involved in helping others?

APPLY IT
■ What is one request that you will commit yourself to pray for regularly this week?
❇ How is it possible for a Christian to increase their faith?

Mark 11:1-11
The Triumphal Entry

TOPICS
Blessing, Humility, Instructions, Jesus Christ, Obedience, Praise

OPEN IT
❇ What is enjoyable about watching parades?
❇ What would you like or dislike about actually participating in a big parade?
■ What kinds of events or occasions do we celebrate with parades?

EXPLORE IT
❇ Where did the events of this story take place? (11:1)
❇ What did Jesus tell His disciples to do? (11:2)
■ What did Jesus ask the disciples to do? (11:2-3)
■ How did the disciples' experience match with what Jesus said? (11:4-7)
❇ What did the people in the village do when the disciples asked to take their colt? (11:6)
❇ What did Jesus do with the colt? (11:7)
❇ How did Jesus enter Jerusalem? (11:7-11)
■ Why did the people spread cloaks and branches on the road for Jesus? (11:8-10)
❇ What was the atmosphere of the crowd when Jesus rode into Jerusalem? (11:8-10)
❇ What did the people shout when Jesus entered the city? (11:9)
❇ What does the reaction of the crowd tell us about how they interpreted Jesus' entry into Jerusalem? (11:9-10)

❇ Why do you think Jesus went to the temple first but then went out to Bethany with His disciples? (11:11)
❇ Why didn't Jesus stay in Jerusalem? (11:11)

GET IT
■ What do you think the disciples thought about what Jesus asked them to do?
❇ Why do you think the people in the village let the disciples take their colt?
❇ What did Jesus communicate to the crowds by riding a donkey into Jerusalem?
❇ Why do you think Jesus went to the temple first but then went out to Bethany with His disciples?
■ When has God told you to do something that you thought was unusual or difficult to justify?
❇ How should we imitate the disciples' example?
❇ Why do you think God does not always reveal His intentions or long-range plans for us when we find ourselves in difficult circumstances?
❇ What should we do when we do not understand what God is trying to accomplish in us and through us?
❇ What can we learn from the attitudes of the people who followed Jesus into Jerusalem?
❇ How can we express our praise to the Lord?

APPLY IT
❇ What could you do this week to celebrate what Jesus has done for you?
■ How should you react the next time a situation arises that you don't understand?

Mark 11:12-19
Jesus Clears the Temple

TOPICS
Anger, Dishonesty, Emotions, Fruit, Money, Prayer, Worship

OPEN IT
■ If you could change one thing about your church, what would it be?
❇ How well do you think your church fulfills its purpose?
❇ Over what are you most likely to lose your temper?

EXPLORE IT
❇ Where did the events of this story take place? (11:12)
❇ Where did Jesus go? Why? (11:12-13)
■ Why did the fig tree have no fruit? (11:13)
■ What did Jesus do to the fig tree? Why? (11:13-14)
❇ How did this event differ from every other miracle Jesus performed? (11:13-14)
■ What do both the cursing of the fig tree and the cleansing of the temple tell us about Jesus' attitude toward the people of Israel? (11:13-17)
❇ What happened when Jesus entered the temple area in Jerusalem? (11:15-18)
❇ Whose authority was Jesus challenging when He drove the money changers from the temple area? (11:17)
❇ What was Jesus saying about His own authority? (11:17)
❇ Why was Jesus so upset about the "marketplace" atmosphere in the temple? (11:17)
❇ How did the crowds and the religious leaders react to Jesus' actions in the temple? (11:18)

GET IT
❇ Why do you think Jesus cursed the fig tree?
❇ How do you think the disciples reacted to hearing Jesus curse a fig tree?
■ The fig tree had leaves but no fruit; what is one area of your life that looks good, but isn't producing what God wants?
■ How can you grow and become more productive in one of your weak areas?
❇ What difference does it make to you that Jesus showed anger?
❇ What practices in the church today do you think hinder nonChristians from coming to Christ?
❇ Where is God's temple today?
❇ How should we treat God's temple?
❇ How do you need to change your attitudes or actions when worshiping?

APPLY IT
■ What specific steps can you take this next week to concentrate on a weak area of your spiritual life, aiming to bear fruit for the Lord?
❇ How can you show respect for God's temple?

Mark 11:20-26
The Withered Fig Tree

TOPICS
Answers, Doubt, Faith, Forgiveness, Prayer, Relationships, Resentment

OPEN IT
❇ Why do people hold grudges?
■ Why is it easy to hold grudges?
❇ How do you think holding a grudge would affect your relationship with your best friend?

EXPLORE IT
❇ What happened when the disciples saw the fig tree withered along the road? (11:20)
❇ How did Peter react to what he saw? (11:21)
■ How did Jesus use a seemingly insignificant event as an opportunity to teach the disciples? (11:22)
■ On what do answers to prayer depend? (11:22-25)
❇ What truth did Jesus illustrate with the withered fig tree? (11:23-24)
❇ What elements did Jesus single out of this object lesson regarding a strong prayer life? (11:23-25)
❇ What promise did Jesus offer about receiving answers to prayers? (11:24)
❇ How can a person be sure God has forgiven his or her sins? (11:24)
❇ What can stand in the way of God's forgiveness? (11:25)
■ How can holding a grudge affect the way God answers prayer? (11:25)
❇ How is some unanswered prayer accounted for? (11:25)

GET IT
❇ Why does Jesus tie God's forgiveness of us with our forgiveness of others?
❇ What does this passage say about the relationship between faith and forgiveness?

❊ What should we be willing to do to resolve conflicts between us and others?
■ Why is it necessary to forgive others for what they have done?
■ When is it difficult for you to forgive others?
❊ What will happen if you refuse to forgive others?
❊ In what ways has this passage challenged you to reexamine your faith and your prayer life?
❊ When have you experienced frustrations or doubts in your prayer life?
❊ How can God be both sovereign and bound to grant every prayer request we lay before Him?
❊ For what other reasons besides grudges do our prayers go unanswered?

APPLY IT
❊ What is one specific request that you want to commit yourself to pray for regularly this week?
■ What can you do today to let go of a grudge or feeling of offense?

Mark 11:27-33
The Authority of Jesus Questioned

TOPICS
Authority, Conflict, Doubt, Fear, Heaven, Power, Questions

OPEN IT
■ Who are some authorities or experts who influence public opinion (such as media, politicians, religious leaders, etc.)?
❊ What are some examples of authority?
❊ In what ways should a Christian's values differ from those of "the experts"?

EXPLORE IT
❊ Where did the events of this story take place? (11:27)
■ Who confronted Jesus? Why? (11:27-28)
❊ What were "these things" to which the religious leaders referred? (11:28)
❊ How did the religious leaders challenge Jesus' authority? (11:28)
❊ What do Jesus' actions tell you about His attitude toward the religious leaders of His day? (11:28-33)
■ How did Jesus answer the challenge put to Him? (11:29-33)
❊ What condition did Jesus place on answering the challenge put to Him? (11:29)
❊ How did Jesus challenge his accusers to stand up for the truth? (11:30-32)
❊ How did Jesus expose his accusers' true motives? (11:30-32)
❊ Why was Jesus' question so difficult for the religious leaders to answer? (11:29-32)
❊ How did the religious leaders respond to Jesus' question? (11:33)
■ How did Jesus silence His critics? (11:33)

GET IT
❊ What were the priorities of the chief priests, teachers of the law, and elders who confronted Jesus?
❊ What do you think prompted the religious leaders to question Jesus about His authority?
❊ Why do you think Jesus decided not to answer the religious leaders directly, but instead posed another question in response?
❊ By whose authority did Jesus clear the temple?
❊ Why do you think Jesus did not want to reveal to the religious leaders the source of His authority?
■ In what ways do human authorities challenge God's authority?
■ How can we ensure that we follow God's authority rather than the "authorities" who challenge His Word?
❊ When have you ever questioned God's authority in your life?
❊ What does this passage tell us about Jesus' attitude toward people who reject His authority?
❊ What could you learn Jesus' example in this episode about dealing with people who try to trick or discredit Christians?
❊ When is it most difficult to submit to God's authority?
❊ How can we find the strength to rely completely on God's authoritative Word rather than trust in our own abilities?
❊ What does God do for us when we completely turn over to Him the areas of our lives that we have tried to manage on our own?

APPLY IT
■ What specific steps can you take this week to obey God's authority in one area of your life?
❊ How should you respond the next time someone challenges you for doing what God has told you to do?

Mark 12:1-12
The Parable of the Tenants

TOPICS
Criticism, Dishonesty, Greed, Mediator, Murder, Possessions, Prophecy, Punishment

OPEN IT
■ When have you ever been cheated out of something that was rightfully yours?
❊ What was your reaction to a time when you were cheated?

EXPLORE IT
❊ How did Jesus get across His point in this situation? (12:1)
❊ To whom was Jesus speaking? (12:1)
❊ Why did the man in the parable plant a vineyard? (12:1)
❊ What happened to the man's vineyard while he was away on a journey? (12:1)
■ Whom do the farmer, servants, and son in the parable represent? (12:1-6)
■ Why did the owner of the vineyard send so many servants to the tenants looking after the vineyard? (12:2-5)
❊ Who was the last person the owner sent to his vineyard? (12:6)
❊ How did the tenants want to cheat the son? (12:7)
■ How did the tenants treat the owner's son? Why? (12:7-8)

❊ What would be the response of the vineyard owner when he discovered how the tenants treated his son? (12:9)
❊ What is the significance in Jesus saying that He will fulfill Psalm 118:22-23? (12:10-11)
❊ How did the religious leaders respond to the parable Jesus told? (12:12)

GET IT
❊ What is the meaning of this parable?
❊ Who are God's messengers?
❊ How has God delivered His message to us today?
■ In what ways is it possible to mistreat the messengers or message God has sent us?
❊ How does God want us to treat His message?
❊ When have you ever been mistreated because of your faith in Christ?
■ How can we show respect for the message God has given us?
❊ How does Jesus' example encourage you to respond when you are faced with difficult circumstances?
❊ How can you be a better steward of the spiritual responsibility God has given you?
❊ What can we expect the Lord to do if we try to rob Him of what is rightfully His?
❊ How does this passage encourage you to use your gifts and abilities for the Lord's glory?

APPLY IT
❊ What is one area of your life that you are holding back from the Lord for fear that He may ask too much of you?
❊ What step can you take this week to commit yourself completely to the Lord?
■ What can you do every day this week out of respect for God's Word?

Mark 12:13-17
Paying Taxes to Caesar

TOPICS
Authority, Deceit, Government, Hypocrisy, Money, Peer Pressure, Truth

OPEN IT
■ What does it mean to you to be patriotic?
❊ What feelings do you have about your home country?
❊ What do you believe is fair or unfair about having to pay taxes?

EXPLORE IT
❊ Who sent the Pharisees and Herodians to Jesus? (12:13)
❊ Who made a special trip to see Jesus? Why? (12:13)
❊ What were the Pharisees and Herodians trying to accomplish with their visit to Jesus? (12:13)
■ How did the religious leaders try to trick Jesus? (12:13-15)
❊ How did the religious leaders flatter Jesus? (12:14)
❊ How did Jesus respond to the Pharisees and Herodians? (12:15)
❊ In what way were the religious leaders guilty of hypocrisy? (12:15)
■ What did Jesus ask the religious leaders to bring Him? Why? (12:15-17)
■ What did Jesus mean when He said, "Give to Caesar what is Caesar's and to God what is God's"? (12:17)
❊ How did the religious leaders react to Jesus' words? (12:17)
❊ How successful were the religious leaders in trapping Jesus? (12:17)

GET IT
❊ Why do you think the religious leaders complimented Jesus on His integrity and commitment to the truth before they asked their trick question?
❊ Why do you think the religious leaders were so amazed at Jesus?
❊ What does this passage reveal about Jesus' attitude toward hypocritical behavior?
❊ In what way do we flatter people?
❊ What is good or bad about flattery?
❊ What does it take to speak the truth and avoid using flattery with people?
❊ What does this story teach about being patriotic to your country?
❊ What should we do when a civil law goes against God's law?
❊ Who do you know who has felt a clash between a civil law and God's law? What happened?
❊ What did Jesus want the Pharisees and Herodians to do?
■ What values was Jesus communicating with His answer to the Pharisees' question?
■ What belongs to God that we should give back to Him?
❊ What do you think you have held back from the Lord (such as an ability, a possession, or block of time)?
❊ What is one thing or area of your life that you have withheld from the Lord but want to give back to Him?
❊ Which is more difficult for you, letting go of what won't last or giving your life to God? Why?
❊ Who do you know who is not swayed by others?
❊ What can you do to become more like Christ?

APPLY IT
■ What is a prayer you can use to give to God what belongs to Him?
❊ In what ways can you stand up for the truth in your place of work this week?

Mark 12:18-27
Marriage at the Resurrection

TOPICS
Angels, Death, Disagreements, Faith, Life, Marriage, Power, Questions, Resurrection

OPEN IT
■ What misconceptions do people often have about God?
❊ How could a person's misunderstanding of God's character influence his or her attitude toward Christianity?
❊ What is one thing you have learned about God that you did not understand when you were a child?

EXPLORE IT
■ Who were the Sadducees, and what did they want from Jesus? (12:18)
❊ What unique belief did the Sadducees have? (12:18)

❇ How did the Sadducees address Jesus? (12:19)
❇ What instruction of Moses did the Sadducees cite to support their theology about the Resurrection? (12:19)
❇ What complicated scenario did the Sadducees develop to get Jesus' opinion about the Resurrection? (12:20-23)
❇ What was the basic principle underlying the Sadducees' question? (12:23)
❇ How did Jesus respond to the Sadducees' question? (12:24-27)
■ In what way were the Sadducees "in error"? (12:24-27)
■ What was wrong with the Sadducees' viewpoint? (12:24-27)
❇ How will life in heaven differ from life on earth? (12:25)
❇ What did God say to Moses "in the account of the bush"? (12:26)
❇ How is God's description of His own character relevant to this discussion with the Sadducees? (12:26)
❇ How did Jesus lend authority to His response to the Sadducees? (12:26)
❇ What did Jesus mean when He referred to God as "not the God of the dead, but of the living"? (12:27)
❇ How did Jesus show the Sadducees that the dead are raised? (12:26-27)

GET IT
❇ Why did Jesus refer to the book of Moses in His response to the Sadducees?
❇ How do you think the Sadducees reacted to Jesus' stern rebuke in this passage?
■ In what ways do you think Christians today misinterpret what the Scriptures actually say?
■ How can we guard against reading into Scripture what we want it to say?
❇ What specifically can you do to prevent yourself from being as "badly mistaken" about what Jesus taught as the Sadducees were?
❇ Over what issues do religious leaders disagree today?
❇ How can we know who is right when we hear conflicting opinions about God or theology?
❇ Do you think you "know the Scriptures" and "the power of God" in your life, and if not, what can you do to mature in these areas of your Christian walk?
❇ What can you learn from the Sadducees' negative example in this episode?
❇ What difference does it make to you that God "is not the God of the dead, but of the living"?
❇ How could you benefit from the insight of another believer?

APPLY IT
■ What concrete action would you be willing to take this next week to get to know the Scriptures better?
❇ How could you make a conscious effort to learn from those who are more informed about the Scriptures and wiser than you?
❇ How can you learn more about the Scriptures this week?

Mark 12:28-34
The Greatest Commandment

TOPICS
Commitment, Devotion, God, Kingdom of God/Heaven, Love, Neighbor, Priorities, Sacrifice

OPEN IT
■ What do you remember about your very first next-door neighbor?
❇ What responsibility do you feel toward your neighbors?
❇ In what ways do you think Christians should treat their neighbors differently from the way nonChristians do?

EXPLORE IT
❇ Why did the teacher of the law come over to speak to Jesus? (12:28)
■ What significant question did the teacher of the law pose to Jesus? (12:28)
■ How did Jesus respond to the man's question? (12:29-31)
❇ How did Jesus use Scripture in answering the question put to Him? (12:29-31)
❇ What did Jesus say was the second most important commandment? (12:31)
❇ How did the teacher of the law respond to Jesus' answer? (12:32)
■ How did the man speaking with Jesus show that he understood God's heart? (12:32-34)
❇ What does God value more highly than sacrifices and offerings? (12:33)
❇ How did Jesus evaluate the teacher's response to Him? (12:34)
❇ What did Jesus mean when He said to the teacher, "You are not far from the kingdom of God"? (12-34)
❇ How did the surrounding crowd react to this conversation? (12:34)

GET IT
❇ What do you think motivated the teacher of the law to question Jesus?
❇ Why do you think Jesus quoted Scripture to answer the question instead of replying with His own words?
❇ How familiar do you think this passage Jesus quoted was to the teacher of the law?
❇ Why do you think the teacher added a note about offerings and sacrifices to what Jesus had said?
❇ Why do you think other people were too scared to ask Jesus questions after this conversation?
❇ What does Jesus' treatment of this teacher of the law tell you about His own character and view of people?
■ What do "offerings and sacrifices" have to do with the greatest commandment?
■ What does it mean to love God with all your heart, soul, mind, and strength?
❇ What do you think it means to "love your neighbor as yourself"?
❇ How can we practice the greatest commandment in everyday life?
❇ What modern-day religious practices would be like the burnt offerings and sacrifices to which the teacher of the law referred?
❇ Why is wholehearted love for the Lord more important

than outward actions that Christians practice today?
❊ How does a person's love for God manifest itself in everyday life?

APPLY IT
❊ What specific steps can you take this week to deepen your relationship with the Lord and demonstrate your love for Him?
■ Who is one neighbor to whom you can show your love in a practical way this next week? How?

Mark 12:35-40
Whose Son Is the Christ?

TOPICS
Authority, Holy Spirit, Honor, Jesus Christ, Pride, Punishment, Self-centeredness, Self-righteousness, Status, Teaching

OPEN IT
❊ How would you describe a good teacher?
❊ What good teachers (whether school teachers, Sunday School teachers, pastors, parents, or others) have influenced you? How?
■ If you wanted to be noticed for being an especially good worker at your job, how would you go about doing it?

EXPLORE IT
❊ Where was Jesus teaching? (12:35)
❊ What question did Jesus ask of His audience? (12:35)
❊ What was significant about the passage Jesus quoted? (12:36)
❊ In what way was the Holy Spirit involved in this account? (12:36)
❊ What did Jesus point out from one of David's psalms? (12:36-37)
❊ To whom was David referring in the Scripture Jesus quoted? (12:36)
❊ What point was Jesus making by quoting David's words? (12:36)
❊ How did the crowd respond to Jesus' teaching? (12:37)
❊ How are the two parts of Jesus' teaching in this passage related? (12:35-40)
❊ About whom did Jesus warn the crowds? (12:38)
■ Why did Jesus condemn the teachers of the law? (12:38-39)
■ What did the teachers of the law betray about themselves through their actions? (12:38-39)
❊ How did the teachers of the law "devour widows' houses"? (12:40)
❊ For what did Jesus condemn the teachers of the law? (12:40)
■ What did Jesus say would happen to the teachers of the law? (12:40)

GET IT
❊ What difference does it make to you to know that the biblical writers were "speaking by the Holy Spirit" when they wrote the Scriptures?
❊ What can you learn about the power and authority of the Messiah from Jesus' teaching in this passage?
■ What do Christians do that is like the actions of the teachers of the law described in this passage (such as walking around in flowing robes, being greeted in the marketplace, having the most important seats at the synagogues and places of honor at banquets)?
❊ How do we let pride and self-seeking attitudes interfere with our Christian witness?
❊ What is one specific way that you have let pride into your life?
■ What can we do to avoid being showy about our faith?
❊ Who are the less fortunate people in our society who are vulnerable to exploitation, as were the widows in New Testament times?
❊ What can churches do to guard against taking advantage of vulnerable people
❊ What specifically has the Lord convicted you of through Jesus' teaching in this passage?

APPLY IT
■ What step can you take this week to pray, go to church, and do other spiritual devotions only out of a desire to please God?
❊ What small act of kindness could you show to a less fortunate believer in your church this week?

Mark 12:41-44
The Widow's Offering

TOPICS
Attitude, Generosity, Gifts, Giving Up, Money, Motives, Poor, Sacrifice, Tithing, Wealth

OPEN IT
❊ In what ways are outward appearances misleading?
❊ When was the last time you found out the true identity of an impostor or person who pretended to be something he or she was not?
■ What does it mean to be poor?

EXPLORE IT
❊ Where did the events of this story take place? (12:41)
❊ Where did Jesus sit? (12:41)
❊ What did Jesus see from where He sat near the temple? (12:41)
❊ What did the "rich people" do at the temple treasury? (12:41)
❊ What do the "rich people's" actions tell us about their motivation for giving? (12:41)
■ What did the "poor widow" give to the treasury? (12:42)
■ Why did Jesus call His disciples when He saw the widow put in her offering? (12:43)
■ How did Jesus compare the actions of the wealthy people to the actions of the poor woman? (12:43-44)
❊ Why did the large amounts of money given by the rich people not impress Jesus? (12:44)
❊ Why was the widow's gift so significant in Jesus' eyes? (12:44)

GET IT
❊ Why do you think Jesus purposely sat near the temple treasury?
❊ What central principle did Jesus focus on in this story?

■ How does God evaluate a person's giving?
❇ What place does a person's motivation and attitude have in their giving to the Lord, according to Jesus' teaching in this passage?
❇ How does Jesus evaluate your giving?
■ In what ways can we give to God?
❇ Why do you think God wants us to give sacrificially?
❇ What has been your attitude toward giving your money to the Lord?
❇ When have you ever simply given out of your wealth instead of giving sacrificially to the Lord?
❇ How do you need to change your attitude about giving?
❇ What else does God want from us besides our material wealth?
❇ What attitude should we have about giving of ourselves to the Lord?

APPLY IT
❇ What specific steps are you willing to take this week to give sacrificially to the Lord, of either your material wealth or your abilities and time?
■ How can you ensure that your attitude and motivation is right when you give to the Lord this week?

Mark 13:1-31
Signs of the End of the Age

TOPICS
Family, Future, Gospel, Holy Spirit, Last Days, Persecution, Perseverance, Prophecy, Second Coming, War, Worry

OPEN IT
❇ What have you read or been taught about the second coming of Christ?
■ Where do you see yourself ten years from now?
❇ What do you find confusing or difficult to understand about what the Bible says about the future?

EXPLORE IT
❇ How did Jesus use the conversation of His disciples as an opportunity to teach? (13:1-2)
❇ What did Jesus mean when He said the temple stones will be "thrown down"? (13:2)
■ What did Jesus' disciples ask Him privately on the Mount of Olives? (13:3-4)
■ How did Jesus respond to His disciples' question? (13:5-8)
❇ What was Jesus' main reason for telling His disciples what signs would precede the end of the age? (13:5)
❇ How do we know Jesus was talking about a time still to come and not merely the fall of Jerusalem that took place in 70 A.D.? (13:6-30)
❇ Why did Jesus tell His disciples not to be alarmed when they would hear of wars? (13:7)
❇ What must happen before Christ returns? (13:10)
❇ How did Jesus tell His followers to act when they were arrested for their faith? (13:11)
❇ What did Jesus tell His followers to do to be assured of eternal life? (13:12-13)
❇ Where will "the elect" be during the "days of distress"? (12:19-20)
■ What will be the greatest temptation during the "days of distress"? (13:21-23)
❇ What do Christ's words "if that were possible" mean? (13:22)
❇ What events will happen right before the second coming of Christ? (13:24-25)
❇ What will Christ's return be like? (13:26-27)
❇ What did Jesus want us to learn from the blossoming of a fig tree? (13:28-29)
❇ What did Jesus say we could count on happening? (13:29-30)

GET IT
❇ Why do you think Jesus told His disciples not to worry about what to say whenever they were arrested for their faith?
❇ Why do you think Jesus has told us "everything ahead of time" about His return and the end times?
■ What signs from this passage do you think have already been fulfilled?
❇ What can we do to make Christ's return closer?
❇ How can we be involved in spreading the gospel to all nations?
❇ How can a person be sure he or she is saved and will inherit eternal life?
❇ How can we be on our guard against false Christs and false prophets who perform signs and miracles to deceive us?
❇ How does the promise of the Holy Spirit's active presence encourage you to follow Christ through difficult times?
■ What can we do to avoid being deceived by false teachings about God or spiritual matters?

APPLY IT
■ What can you read or do this week to strengthen your hold on the truth about Christ?
❇ What concrete action can you take to become more actively involved in telling others about Christ?

Mark 13:32-37
The Day and Hour Unknown

TOPICS
Angels, Ignorance, Jesus Christ, Knowledge, Perseverance, Tasks, Waiting

OPEN IT
❇ What is it like to wait for a guest that has not told you exactly when he or she will arrive?
■ Why is it so difficult to wait patiently for an exciting event (such as an upcoming party, vacation, or Christmas)?
❇ How would you act differently if the exact time of an exciting upcoming event was unknown to you?

EXPLORE IT
❇ To what "day" was Christ referring? (13:32)
❇ Why didn't Christ tell us the exact time when He would return to earth? (13:32)
❇ In what way did Jesus live by faith and obedience to the Father? (13:32)

■ What will Jesus' return be like? How? (13:34)
❊ What example did Jesus use to explain what His return to earth will be like? (13:34)
❊ Who are the servants to which Christ referred? (13:34)
■ What should the "servants" do to occupy their time while they wait for the owner's return? (13:34)
❊ Who is the "owner of the house" in Jesus' story? (13:34-35)
❊ What conclusion did Jesus draw from the fact that the day of His return is secret? (13:35)
❊ What might happen if the "owner of the house" returned suddenly and the servants were not watching carefully? (13:36)
■ What did Jesus want us to do? (13:37)

GET IT
❊ Why do you think Jesus felt that being on guard was such an important point to emphasize to His disciples?
❊ How does this passage emphasize the fact that even Jesus had to live by faith and obedience to the Father?
❊ How can we follow Christ's example of living in complete faith and obedience to the Father?
❊ How does Jesus' teaching in this passage relate to the previous section?
❊ What task do you think God has given you until His return?
❊ How do you think the disciples would have responded if Jesus had told them He would not return for at least another 2,000 years?
❊ How might a detailed outline of future events be a hindrance, instead of a help, to our faith in God?
❊ In light of Jesus' words, how should we respond to those who try to set dates for the second coming of Christ?
❊ How should we occupy our time as we wait for Christ to return?
■ What tends to distract us from living for Christ?
■ In what way do we need to be on guard until Christ returns?
❊ Against what do we need to watch out?
❊ What practical effect should the warnings of Jesus regarding His return have in your life?

APPLY IT
■ How can you "keep watch" in your day-to-day activities at work?
❊ What distractions might you be able to set aside from your life? How?
❊ What is one pursuit you want to add to your routine in light of this passage?

Mark 14:1-11

Jesus Anointed at Bethany

TOPICS
Beauty, Criticism, Devotion, Giving Up, Gospel, Judging Others, Love, Money, Poor, Preparation, Sacrifice

OPEN IT
■ When have you ever been criticized for doing something good?
❊ What do you think motivates parents to sacrifice for their children?
❊ What is one sacrifice you made for someone else?

EXPLORE IT
❊ When and where did the events of this story take place? (14:1-3)
❊ Why did the Jewish leaders not want to arrest Jesus during the Feast of Unleavened Bread? (14:2)
❊ What attitude did many of the common people have toward Jesus? (14:2)
■ What amazing thing did a woman do while Jesus was visiting Bethany? (14:3) Where?
■ What reaction did the woman's actions get? Why? (14:4-5)
❊ What caused some people with Jesus to become indignant? (14:4-5)
❊ What does this incident tell us about some people's understanding of who Jesus was and why He had come? (14:4-6)
■ Whom did Jesus rebuke? Why? (14:6)
❊ How did Jesus evaluate the behavior of the woman who poured out the perfume? (14:6)
❊ What did Jesus predict? (14:9)
❊ What did Judas do? (14:10-11)
❊ How did Judas betray Jesus? (14:10-11)
❊ How did the chief priests react to Judas's visit? Why? (14:10-11)

GET IT
■ Why do you think the woman sacrificed so much perfume?
❊ How would you have reacted if you had witnessed the woman pouring out a full year's wages' worth of perfume on someone's head?
❊ In what way can a person betray Jesus?
❊ What do you think might motivate a person to give up on Jesus, as Judas did?
❊ When are Christians tempted to give up on their faith?
❊ For what reasons do people reject Christ?
■ What can we learn about values from the woman in this story?
❊ How can we demonstrate our devotion to Christ?
❊ How should we deal with the criticism and scorn of unbelievers?
❊ How should you respond when others rebuke or harshly criticize your actions?
❊ How does Jesus want us to treat the poor?
❊ What tends to distract you from being fully devoted to Christ?
❊ What kinds of sacrifices can a person make for God?
❊ What sacrifice do you think God wants you to make for the sake of the gospel?

APPLY IT
■ What is one way you can show your devotion to Christ above all other things, people, or ambitions in your life? When?
❊ What is one step you could take this week toward helping the poor in a practical way?

Mark 14:12-26
The Lord's Supper

TOPICS
Deceit, Emotions, Judgment, Kingdom of God/Heaven, Lord's Supper, Preparation, Prophecy, Remembering, Sacrifice

OPEN IT
■ What is one ceremony or observance that is important to you?
❇ How does your church celebrate the Lord's Supper?

EXPLORE IT
❇ When did the events of this story take place? (14:12)
❇ What did Jesus' disciples ask Him? (14:12)
❇ How did Jesus make the arrangements for the Passover meal? (14:13)
❇ Whom did Jesus send to make the arrangements for the Passover meal? (14:13)
❇ What specific instructions did Jesus give the disciples He sent out? (14:13-15)
❇ How did Jesus' predictions compare to what the disciples actually found when they got into the city? (14:16)
❇ What was the reaction of the disciples to Jesus' prediction of His betrayal? (14:19)
❇ How did Jesus specify who would betray Him? (14:20-21)
■ The central emphasis of the Passover meal was traditionally the sacrificial lamb; where did Jesus place His emphasis? (14:22-24)
■ What important announcement did Jesus make? (14:25)
■ How did Jesus and the disciples conclude their Passover meal? (14:26)

GET IT
❇ Why do you think Jesus made arrangements for the Passover meal in such a secretive manner?
❇ Why do you think Jesus told His disciples that one of them would betray Him?
❇ How does the fulfillment of Jesus' predictions in this account encourage you to trust Him?
❇ When have you had opportunity to trust God with your future?
❇ Why do you think God seldom chooses to reveal the future to us?
❇ What does the account of Judas' betrayal of Jesus tell us about God's sovereignty?
❇ What does the account of Judas' betrayal of Jesus tell us about our accountability to God?
❇ What causes Christians to betray or reject Christ after following Him for a while?
■ What can we learn about the practice of Communion through this passage?
■ Why is Communion or the Lord's Supper important?
❇ How does God want us to use the Lord's Supper?
❇ How does the old covenant God made with Israel compare or differ to the new covenant He has made through the blood of Jesus Christ?
❇ What difference should it make in your everyday life that Jesus sacrificed His body and blood for your eternal salvation?

APPLY IT
■ What are two or three steps you can take to prepare for the next time you celebrate the Lord's Supper?
❇ What do you want to remember the next time you take the Lord's Supper?
❇ How can you say thank you to Jesus each day this week for the suffering He endured for you?
❇ How can you trust Christ with the circumstances you do not yet understand?

Mark 14:27-31
Jesus Predicts Peter's Denial

TOPICS
Death, Denial, Determination, Faith, Fear, Forsake, Prophecy, Rejection

OPEN IT
❇ What is one fact about the future you wish you knew?
❇ What is one part of your past you wish you could do over?
■ What is one institution, person, or organization to which you have felt loyal over the years? Why?

EXPLORE IT
■ What did Jesus reveal to His disciples? (14:27)
❇ How would Jesus' prediction fulfill Scripture? (14:27)
❇ What did Jesus quote? (14:27) Why?
❇ To what "shepherd" and "sheep" did Jesus refer? Why? (14:27)
❇ What information did Jesus give the disciples? (14:28)
■ How did Peter respond to Christ's words? (14:29)
❇ What was Peter's state of mind when Jesus predicted that the disciples would betray Him? (14:29)
■ What did Jesus say about Peter's loyalty? (14:30)
❇ What was the reaction when Jesus said that Peter would disown Him? (14:31)
❇ What did Peter claim? (14:31)
❇ What do the disciples' reactions tell us about them? (14:31)

GET IT
❇ What does the verse that Jesus quoted mean: "I will strike the shepherd, and the sheep will be scattered"?
❇ Why do you think Jesus sometimes chose to reveal to His disciples what would happen in the future and at other times left them in the dark?
❇ Why do you think Jesus told Peter that he was not as faithful a friend as he assumed?
❇ What is the benefit in knowing we are vulnerable to failure?
❇ Why do you think Peter boasted of his loyalty to Christ?
❇ In what ways do Christians declare their loyalty to Christ?
❇ Why do some Christians fall away from following Christ?
■ What specific area of your life most tests your loyalty to Christ?
❇ What can we do to strengthen our commitment to Christ?
■ What exactly can we do to stay committed to Jesus in the face of testing or suffering?
❇ What role does accountability play in helping Christians remain loyal to Christ?

❊ How should you react if another believer falls away from his or her faith?
❊ What difference does it make that all of Jesus' predictions about the future came true?
❊ What can we learn from this passage about Jesus' character and attitude?

APPLY IT
❊ In what way can you show your dependence on God for the strength to follow Christ?
■ What can you do over the next week to renew and strengthen your faith in Christ?

Mark 14:32-42
Gethsemane

TOPICS
Depression, Despair, Giving Up, Pain, Prayer, Solitude, Sorrow

OPEN IT
■ How have your friends helped you through difficult times in your life?
❊ What is it like to have a friend let you down when you really need support?
❊ Who has been a faithful friend to you during difficult times in your life?

EXPLORE IT
❊ Where did the events of this story take place? (14:32)
❊ What did Jesus tell the disciples to do? (14:32)
❊ Who did Jesus take with him to pray? (14:33)
■ What emotions was Jesus feeling? (14:33-34)
❊ What do Jesus' actions at this time tell us about His character? (14:33-34)
❊ Why was Jesus so distressed and troubled? (14:33-34)
❊ What did Jesus do in response to His deep sorrow? (14:35-36)
❊ What "hour" did Jesus pray to "pass from Him"? (14:35-36)
❊ What does Jesus' prayer tell us about His relationship to God the Father? (14:36)
■ What distressed Jesus when He returned to His disciples? (14:37)
❊ What did Jesus find when He returned to the disciples who were keeping watch? (14:37)
❊ How did Jesus instruct the disciples to prevent themselves from falling into temptation? (14:38)
■ Why did the disciples have so much trouble praying with Jesus? (14:38)
❊ How did Jesus explain the difference between the spirit and the body? (14:38)
❊ What caused the disciples to be speechless when Christ returned to them the second time? (14:40)
❊ When did Jesus stop praying? (14:41-42)
❊ What caused Jesus to stop praying? (14:41-42)

EXPLORE IT
❊ Why do you think Jesus chose three disciples to pray with Him?
❊ What does the fact that God did not grant Jesus' request teach us about prayer?
❊ If Mark's readers were Roman Christians undergoing persecution, what would this section of his Gospel say to them?
❊ How does this passage encourage you to react when you feel distressed or troubled?
❊ What about Christ's humanity can we learn from this event in His life?
❊ What difference does it make that Jesus experienced such despair and pain firsthand?
❊ What can we learn about prayer from Jesus' example?
❊ When do you need to pray?
■ Why didn't the disciples watch and pray with Jesus as He asked them to?
❊ What was the difference between the disciples' intentions and their actions?
■ What stops us from helping people in need?
❊ What human weaknesses make it hard for us to do what God wants?
❊ How should you pray when you must face a difficult or painful task?
❊ How can we trust God with our extremely difficult circumstances?
❊ What does it mean to "watch and pray"?
❊ How can we prevent ourselves from falling into temptation?

APPLY IT
❊ Who is someone you can ask to help you overcome a weakness?
❊ What needs of others will you commit yourself to pray for during this next week?
■ How can you support a friend or relative facing a difficult task this week?

Mark 14:43-52
Jesus Arrested

TOPICS
Armor, Fear, Friendship, Hypocrisy, Persecution, Rebellion

OPEN IT
❊ When have you ever been blamed for something you did not do?
■ What is one friendship you once had that went sour?
❊ What does it feel like to be wrongly accused?

EXPLORE IT
❊ Who was Judas? (14:43-44)
❊ Who accompanied Judas to Gethsemane? Why? (14:43-44)
❊ How did the religious leaders treat Jesus? (14:43-46)
❊ Why did the religious leaders bring a large, armed force to arrest Jesus? (14:43-48)
❊ What signal had Judas prearranged with the armed leaders to identify Jesus? (14:44)
❊ How did Judas greet Jesus? Why? (14:44-45)
❊ In what way were Judas's actions contradictory? (14:44-45)
❊ How did one of Jesus' disciples (we know from John 18:10 that it was Peter) react to the arrest of Jesus? (14:47)

■ How did Jesus respond to the sight of the armed men? (14:48-49)
❇ How was Jesus' response to this situation different from that of His followers? (14:48-50)
❇ What had to happen? (14:49)
■ Who fled the scene? When? (14:50-52)
■ What is significant about the fact that all of Jesus' followers deserted Him? (14:50-52)

GET IT
❇ What do we know about Judas from this passage?
❇ What kind of person was Judas?
❇ In what way was Judas hypocritical?
❇ In what way is Judas a negative example to all of us?
❇ In what ways are we like Judas in the way we treat Jesus?
❇ What do Peter's actions tell us about his character and understanding of Jesus?
❇ How do you think Jesus must have felt about the fact that His disciples deserted him?
■ Why did Jesus' disciples desert Him?
❇ When are you most tempted to compromise your commitment to Christ?
■ How can we prepare for times when our dedication to Christ is tested?
❇ How can we guard against saying one thing and doing another?
❇ How does Jesus' perseverance in this situation encourage you to endure your difficult circumstances?
❇ What can we learn about Jesus' character from His actions?
❇ When have you ever felt that all of your friends deserted you?
❇ What difference does it make to you that Jesus was deserted by all of His friends?
❇ How can you lean on Jesus when you go through very distressing and frightening experiences?

APPLY IT
■ What can you do now to prepare for times when your dedication to Christ is tested at work, at home, or around neighbors?
❇ What friend can you support through a difficult situation? How?

Mark 14:53-65
Before the Sanhedrin

TOPICS
Blasphemy, Confession, Death, Evidence, Fear, Messiah, Persecution, Punishment, Silence, Testing, Witnessing

OPEN IT
■ When was the last time you were misunderstood or misinterpreted?
❇ What do you think is good or bad about capital punishment?

EXPLORE IT
❇ Before whom did Jesus have to stand trial? (14:53)
❇ Who followed Jesus as He was being led away? How? (14:54)
■ What did the men of the Sanhedrin want to do to Jesus? Why? (14:55)
❇ Why did the Sanhedrin have such a difficult time convicting Jesus? (14:55-59)
■ What testimony did some witnesses bring against Jesus? (14:57-58)
❇ How did the high priest try to get Jesus to answer the questions put to Him? (14:60)
■ What was Jesus' response to all the accusations against Him? (14:61)
❇ How did Jesus use silence during all the testimony against Him? (14:61)
❇ What did the high priest finally do in an attempt to speed up the trial? (14:61)
❇ When did Jesus choose to speak? (14:62)
❇ What did Jesus tell the Sanhedrin? (14:62)
❇ Why did the high priest respond with such shock to Jesus' testimony? (14:63-64)
❇ What did the Sanhedrin consider blasphemy? (14:64)
❇ To what punishment did the Sanhedrin sentence Jesus? Why? (14:64)
❇ How did the people in the courtroom abuse Jesus after He was sentenced to death? (14:65)

GET IT
❇ Why do you think Peter followed Jesus "at a distance"?
❇ What emotions do you think Peter felt as he was following Jesus?
❇ When have you ever felt that circumstances got beyond your control?
❇ What should we do when circumstances are beyond our control?
■ How do you think Jesus felt during His trial? Why?
❇ Why do you think Jesus chose to remain silent throughout the initial testimony against Him?
❇ What can we learn about dealing with stress and fear from Jesus' example?
■ What can we learn about dealing with false accusations from Jesus' example?
❇ What difference does it make to you that Jesus will one day return?
❇ What do we learn about Jesus from this trial?
❇ How can we live our lives blamelessly as Jesus did?

APPLY IT
■ How do you want to react the next time you are falsely accused or tricked?
❇ What specific steps can you take this week to entrust your circumstances to God?

Mark 14:66-72
Peter Disowns Jesus

TOPICS
Deceit, Dishonesty, Embarrassment, Fear, Jesus Christ, Rejection, Relationships, Sorrow, Witnessing

OPEN IT
❇ What subjects do most people try to avoid in polite company? Why?
■ What is one fact about you that most people don't know?

EXPLORE IT
❊ Where did the events of this story take place? (14:66)
❊ What was Peter doing at this critical time? (14:66)
❊ How do we know Peter was concerned for Jesus? (14:66)
❊ What was the servant girl's opinion of Jesus? (14:66-69)
■ How did Peter's denial of Christ happen? (14:66-72)
❊ Who confronted Peter about his association with the Jesus? (14:67)
❊ How did Peter respond to the servant girl's questioning? (14:68, 70)
❊ Why did Peter move "out into the entryway"? (14:68)
❊ Who else besides the servant girl confronted Peter? Why? (14:70)
■ Who in the courtyard was curious and insistent about finding out who Jesus' followers were? (14:66-70)
❊ How did Peter respond to the third question about whether he was a follower of Christ? (14:71)
❊ Why did Peter cry? (14:72)
❊ What reminded Peter of Jesus' words to Him earlier? (14:72)
■ How did Peter react when he realized what he had done? (14:72)

GET IT
❊ What does this story tell us about Peter?
❊ Why do you think Peter denied knowing Christ?
❊ What does this story tell us about human nature?
❊ What does this story tell you about you?
❊ What different kinds of reactions have you received when you have told others about your faith in Christ?
❊ Why are Christians sometimes afraid to identify themselves as believers in Christ?
❊ Why are Christians sometimes afraid to tell non-Christian friends about Christ?
■ In what sorts of situations are you sometimes uncomfortable or fearful about identifying with Christ or Christianity?
❊ What can we learn about the cost of being a disciple of Christ's from this passage?
❊ How do other people's attitudes toward Christ affect your willingness to talk about your Christian faith?
■ How can you affirm your faith in Christ in situations where others may be indifferent or hostile to it?

APPLY IT
■ In what situation or context will you consciously identify with Christ publicly this week? How?
❊ What person do you need to tell of your faith in Christ? When can you?

Mark 15:1-15

Jesus Before Pilate

TOPICS
Compromise, Envy, Injustice, Judgment, Leadership, Peer Pressure, Reputation

OPEN IT
❊ In what situations have you felt the power of a group?
❊ When have you ever been influenced by the opinions of a group?
■ What sort of reputation did you have in high school?

EXPLORE IT
❊ When did the members of the Sanhedrin decide what to do with Jesus? (15:1)
❊ What did all the religious leaders decide to do with Jesus? (15:1)
❊ What did the Sanhedrin do with Jesus after deciding He was guilty? (15:1)
❊ What did Pilate question Jesus about? (15:2)
❊ How did Jesus respond to the Sanhedrin and Pilate? (15:2)
■ What prompted Pilate to goad Jesus about defending Himself? (15:3-4)
❊ What amazed Pilate? (15:3-5)
■ How did Jesus react to the accusations raised against Him by the chief priests? (15:5)
❊ What did Pilate think of Jesus? (15:5)
❊ Who was Barabbas and what role did he play in this situation? (15:6-8)
❊ What did the crowd ask Pilate to do for them? (15:8, 13)
❊ Why did Pilate try to have Jesus released instead of Barabbas? How? (15:9-10)
❊ Why did Pilate's attempt to release Jesus fail? (15:11-15)
❊ What reason did the crowd give Pilate to crucify Jesus? (15:14)
❊ How did the crowd influence Pilate's decision? (15:15)
■ What finally happened to Jesus? Why? (15:15)

GET IT
❊ Of those involved in trying and sentencing Jesus, who do you think bore the greater responsibility, the religious leaders or Pilate? Why?
❊ Why do you think the Sanhedrin handed Jesus over to Pilate?
❊ How did Jesus' enemies use lies and false accusations against Him?
❊ How did Jesus' enemies manipulate public opinion against Him?
❊ Why was Pilate amazed by Jesus' behavior?
❊ Why do you think Pilate did what the crowd wanted?
❊ When have you ever done something because the crowd pressured you to?
❊ Why is group pressure so powerful?
❊ What is difficult about standing up to the crowd?
❊ Where do you often feel pressured by others to go against your Christian beliefs?
❊ How can we remember to respond properly when pressured by the crowd?
❊ Why didn't Jesus defend Himself?
■ When is it unimportant to defend ourselves or our actions?
❊ What is difficult about being unpopular or disliked by a group?
❊ Why is it so difficult to trust God with our reputation?
■ In what way can you entrust your reputation to God?

APPLY IT
■ What reminder can you use this week to entrust your reputation to God each day?
❊ What is one step you can take this week to strengthen your conviction against pressure from coworkers, friends, or family?

Mark 15:16-20

The Soldiers Mock Jesus

TOPICS

Criticism, Endurance, Humiliation, Pain, Persecution, Sacrifice, Suffering

OPEN IT

❊ How have your friends encouraged you during difficult times in your life?

■ What kids do you remember being mocked or put down when you were in grade school?

❊ What do you think it would be like to go through a painful experience without the support of your friends or family?

EXPLORE IT

❊ Where did the soldiers take Jesus after His trial with Pilate? (15:16)

❊ Who was present there in the palace? (15:16)

❊ Once Jesus had been tried, convicted, and sentenced, who mocked and struck Him? (15:16-20)

❊ What kind of suffering did Jesus undergo even before being crucified? (15:16-20)

■ What did the soldiers do to Jesus? (15:17-20)

❊ Why did the soldiers put a purple robe and a crown on Jesus? (15:17)

■ What did the soldiers say in mockery of Jesus? (15:18)

■ Why did the soldiers fall on their knees before Jesus? (15:19)

❊ How did the soldiers hurt Jesus? (15:17-20)

❊ What do the soldiers' actions tell us about their understanding of who Jesus really was? (15:17-20)

GET IT

❊ What do you think the soldiers had heard about Jesus?

❊ How do you think the soldiers' actions affected Jesus emotionally?

■ What difference does it make that Jesus endured harsh ridicule and pain for our sake?

❊ When have you been ridiculed for being a Christian?

❊ How does it feel to be mocked by others?

■ How should we respond when others mock our faith?

❊ How can we show our appreciation to Jesus for enduring such humiliation for us?

❊ What can we learn from Jesus about how to deal with pain and suffering?

❊ Why does God allow us to suffer?

❊ For what Christians who are suffering for their faith can you pray?

APPLY IT

■ What should be your response if you are criticized for your faith this next week?

❊ What could you say or do to encourage another believer who is suffering for his or her faith?

Mark 15:21-32

The Crucifixion

TOPICS

Atonement, Endurance, Giving Up, Insults, Jesus Christ, Pain, Sacrifice, Salvation, Suffering, Temptation

OPEN IT

❊ What is one of your favorite symbols? Why?

■ What do people mean when they say that someone "did not die in vain"?

❊ When you see a cross in or on a church building, what usually comes to mind?

EXPLORE IT

❊ Who was Simon of Cyrene? (15:21)

❊ What role did Simon of Cyrene play in Jesus' life? (15:21)

■ Why did Jesus not carry the cross Himself? (15:21)

❊ What did the soldiers offer Jesus once they reached the place where He would be crucified? (15:23)

❊ What offer of help did Jesus refuse? (15:23)

❊ What did the soldiers do with Jesus' clothes? (15:24)

❊ What was significant about the notice that was placed on the cross above Jesus? (15:26)

❊ Who was crucified with Jesus? (15:27)

■ How did the people insult Jesus when He was on the cross? (15:29-30)

❊ What did the teachers of the law say about Jesus while He was dying? How? (15:31-32)

■ What challenge did Jesus ignore? (15:31-32)

GET IT

❊ Why do you think Jesus refused to accept a drink that could deaden His pain?

■ What kind of suffering did Jesus endure for us?

❊ What emotions do you think Jesus felt as He was led away and crucified?

❊ Simon's encounter with Jesus was very unusual; how did you first "encounter Christ"?

❊ When have you ever experienced apparently "random" events in your life, that upon later reflection showed God's sovereign will being worked out in you?

❊ How can you thank the Lord for the hidden ways He works in your life?

❊ Jesus was closely identified with criminals during His death; what significance does this have to you?

❊ How would your life be different if Jesus had taken up the challenge of the religious leaders and come down off the cross?

❊ What emotions do you feel when you think about the crucifixion of Christ?

❊ Why is this tragic story about Christ called "good news"?

❊ What has Christ's accomplished for you?

❊ What did Jesus do for every person with His death on the cross?

■ What did Jesus do for you with His death on the cross?

APPLY IT

■ What is one way you can say thank you to Jesus for paying for your sins?

❊ With what one person can you share the good news of Christ's sacrifice? How?

Mark 15:33-41
The Death of Jesus

TOPICS
Believe, Death, Forsake, Jesus Christ, Loneliness, Miracles, Reconciliation, Sacrifice, Suffering

OPEN IT
■ At what time in your life have you feel most lonely?
❋ What is your first recollection of dealing with the death of a pet or grandparent?

EXPLORE IT
❋ What unusual occurrence took place as Jesus was dying? (15:33)
■ What did Jesus say "at the ninth hour"? (15:34)
❋ What do Jesus' words at the ninth hour reveal about how He was feeling right before He died? (15:34)
■ What did Jesus mean when He said that God had "forsaken" Him? (15:34)
■ How did the bystanders misunderstand what Jesus was going through? (15:35)
❋ What offer of help did Jesus receive? (15:36)
❋ What does the fact that Jesus twice cried out in a loud voice tell us about the way He died? (15:34, 37)
❋ What happened right after Jesus' death? (15:38)
❋ How did the centurion react to Jesus' crucifixion and death? (15:39)
❋ What caused the centurion to believe in Jesus? (15:39)
❋ Who watched Christ's crucifixion from a distance? Why? (15:40-41)

GET IT
❋ What do you think motivated one man to offer Jesus a drink of wine vinegar?
❋ What does it mean that the curtain of the temple tore?
❋ What did the tearing of the temple curtain symbolize?
❋ What difference does Jesus' death make in your life?
❋ What did Jesus' words on the cross mean?
■ What kind of isolation did Jesus experience in His death on the cross?
❋ How can we draw encouragement from the loneliness Jesus endured?
■ In what way can following Christ or doing what God wants be a lonely experience?
❋ How does it make you feel to know that Christ endured such intense suffering for your salvation?
❋ What significance is there for you in the fact that a Roman soldier recognized the great truth that even the religious leaders could not see?
❋ How has your study of this passage changed your perception of Jesus?
❋ In what way is every person indebted to Christ?

APPLY IT
❋ What can you do as a reminder of what Christ did for you?
■ When might you have to face loneliness as a part of following Christ this week?

Mark 15:42-47
The Burial of Jesus

TOPICS
Body, Courage, Humanness, Kingdom of God/Heaven, Love, Respect, Risk, Status

OPEN IT
❋ How might you comfort a person grieving over the death of a loved one?
❋ What is most comforting to you when you are feeling upset?
■ Who is the most courageous person you know?

EXPLORE IT
❋ When did the events described in this passage take place? (15:42)
■ Who was Joseph? (15:43)
❋ What kind of person took it upon himself to bury Jesus' body? (15:43)
❋ What was significant about the fact that Joseph asked for Jesus' body? (15:43)
❋ What kind of man was Joseph of Arimathea? (15:43)
❋ What was courageous about what Joseph did? (15:43)
■ What risks did Joseph take in approaching Pilate? (15:43)
■ What do Joseph's actions tell us about his own understanding of Jesus? (15:43-46)
❋ What took Pilate by surprise? (15:44)
❋ How did Pilate respond to Joseph's request? (15:45)
❋ What did Joseph do to Jesus' body? (15:46)
❋ Who witnessed Jesus' burial? (15:47)

GET IT
❋ Why do you think Pilate was surprised to hear that Jesus had died?
❋ Why do you think Mark mentioned that two women saw where Jesus was buried?
❋ What was exemplary about Joseph?
❋ What was courageous about what Joseph did?
■ What did Joseph risk in burying Jesus' body?
❋ What do you risk in being a follower of Christ?
■ In what situations might doing the right thing require courage?
❋ How did Joseph's position and status conflict with his actions?
❋ In what way does being a Christian go against what people expect of you?
❋ How can we follow Joseph's example?

APPLY IT
■ What step of courage can you take in serving God this week?
❋ What person or reminder can help you draw courage to do what God wants?

Mark 15:42-47
The Burial of Jesus

TOPICS
Body, Courage, Humanness, Kingdom of God/Heaven, Love, Respect, Risk, Status

OPEN IT
❈ How might you comfort a person grieving over the death of a loved one?
❈ What is most comforting to you when you are feeling upset?
■ Who is the most courageous person you know?

EXPLORE IT
❈ When did the events described in this passage take place? (15:42)
■ Who was Joseph? (15:43)
❈ What kind of person took it upon himself to bury Jesus' body? (15:43)
❈ What was significant about the fact that Joseph asked for Jesus' body? (15:43)
❈ What kind of man was Joseph of Arimathea? (15:43)
❈ What was courageous about what Joseph did? (15:43)
■ What risks did Joseph take in approaching Pilate? (15:43)
■ What do Joseph's actions tell us about his own understanding of Jesus? (15:43-46)
❈ What took Pilate by surprise? (15:44)
❈ How did Pilate respond to Joseph's request? (15:45)
❈ What did Joseph do to Jesus' body? (15:46)
❈ Who witnessed Jesus' burial? (15:47)

GET IT
❈ Why do you think Pilate was surprised to hear that Jesus had died?
❈ Why do you think Mark mentioned that two women saw where Jesus was buried?
❈ What was exemplary about Joseph?
❈ What was courageous about what Joseph did?
■ What did Joseph risk in burying Jesus' body?
❈ What do you risk in being a follower of Christ?
■ In what situations might doing the right thing require courage?
❈ How did Joseph's position and status conflict with his actions?
❈ In what way does being a Christian go against what people expect of you?
❈ How can we follow Joseph's example?

APPLY IT
■ What step of courage can you take in serving God this week?
❈ What person or reminder can help you draw courage to do what God wants?

Mark 16:1-20
The Resurrection

TOPICS
Believe, Criticism, Doubt, Faith, Fear, Gospel, Heaven, Joy, Life, Miracles, Resurrection, Witnessing

OPEN IT
❈ What is the most extraordinary event you have ever witnessed?
❈ What does the saying mean, "Truth is stranger than fiction"?
■ What is one piece of news you heard today?
❈ From whom do you like to hear regularly?

EXPLORE IT
❈ Why did the women go to Jesus' tomb? (16:1)
❈ What question was at the back of the women's minds as they traveled to the tomb? (16:2)
■ What did the women see when they got to the tomb? (16:4)
❈ Who was the "young man" in the tomb? (16:5)
❈ How did the women react to the man dressed in white? (16:6, 8)
■ What did the angel tell the women to do? (16:6-7)
❈ To whom did the angel want the women to tell his message? (16:7)
■ Why did the women flee from the tomb and not tell anyone what they had witnessed? (16:8)
❈ To whom did the resurrected Jesus appear first? (16:9)
❈ How did Jesus' disciples respond each time someone told them that He had risen from the dead? (16:11-12)
❈ Why did Jesus rebuke the disciples when He first saw them? (16:14)
❈ What instructions did Jesus give to His followers? (16:15-18)
❈ What happened to Jesus after He was taken up into heaven? (16:19)
❈ What did the disciples do after Jesus had left earth to return to heaven? (16:20)

GET IT
❈ Why do you think the resurrected Jesus appeared first to Mary Magdalene?
❈ What would you have thought and felt if you had entered Jesus' empty tomb?
❈ What can we learn from this passage about the importance of baptism?
❈ What is at stake when a person first hears about Christ?
❈ What difference has the ascended Lord made in your life this past year?
❈ In what ways has your view of Jesus Christ changed as a result of studying this part of Mark's Gospel?
■ What is the responsibility of every Christian in fulfilling Christ's command to tell others about Him?
■ What do you see as your personal role in helping spread the news about Christ?
❈ How does the Lord "confirm His word" through Christians today?

❊ What causes us to have a lack of faith in God or a "stubborn refusal to believe"?
❊ What does it mean to have faith in God?
❊ How do you celebrate Easter?

APPLY IT
❊ What is one concrete step of faith you can take this week in your life at work, among your family, or in your personal life?
■ What can you do this week to obey Christ's command to "preach the good news to all creation"?
❊ How can you honor the resurrected Christ next Easter?

Luke 1:1-4
Introduction

TOPICS
Anwers, Assurance, Authority, Believe, Bible, Christianity, Confidence, Evidence, Instructions, Learning, Reliability

OPEN IT
❊ How would a biographer prepare for writing about someone's life?
■ What period in history do you wish you could visit? Why?
❊ How would you prepare to serve as a character witness in court for your best friend?

EXPLORE IT
❊ What clues about the relationship between Luke and Theophilus can be found in this introduction? (1:1-3)
❊ How had Luke received his evidence for the "things fulfilled among us"? (1:2)
■ On what kind of people did Luke rely for his information? (1:2)
❊ How did Luke rely on eyewitnesses in writing his Gospel? (1:2)
❊ Who were the "servants of the word"? (1:2)
■ What credentials did Luke use to back up the trustworthiness of what he wrote? (1:3)
❊ How did Luke describe his approach to historical research? (1:3)
❊ What reasons did Luke give for deciding to write his Gospel? (1:3-4)
■ What did Luke hope would be the result of this Gospel in the life of Theophilus? (1:4)
❊ What does the phrase "know the certainty of the things you have been taught" mean? (1:4)

GET IT
❊ What characteristics of the time in which Luke lived might make him a better observer, listener, and witness than people today are?
❊ On what evidence would you rely to be certain of the things you were taught?
■ In what ways can we identify with Theophilus?
■ Why is Luke's assurance of accuracy important?
❊ If you got a personal letter tomorrow that began just like this introduction, with your name in the place of Theophilus, how would you treat the letter?
❊ Are you a person who needs to be taught or a person who needs to be more certain of what you have already been taught?
❊ Why would an accurate account of Jesus' life be a powerful evangelistic tool?

APPLY IT
❊ How do you personally plan to approach this study of the Gospel of Luke?
❊ What question about the life of Christ would you like answered by a study of this Gospel?
■ What difference would you like there to be in your relationship with Christ as a result of reading Luke?

Luke 1:5-25

The Birth of John the Baptist Foretold

TOPICS

Age, Angels, Answers, Children, Consistency, Family, Greatness, Impossible, Miracles, Parents, Patience, Prayer, Promises, Purpose, Surprises, Value

OPEN IT

❊ What significant events happened the year you were born?
■ What experiences of complete surprise have you recently had?
❊ At this point in your life, what do you consider your most important responsibilities?

EXPLORE IT

❊ Who were Zechariah and Elizabeth? (1:5-7)
❊ What characteristics did Zechariah and Elizabeth have in common? (1:5-7)
❊ How well did Zechariah and Elizabeth handle the frustration of childlessness? (1:6, 13, 25)
❊ How were Zechariah and Elizabeth "upright in the sight of God"? (1:6)
❊ For what duty was Zechariah chosen by lot? (1:8-10)
■ What experience gripped Zechariah with fear? (1:11-12)
❊ What facts can we note about angels from the information in this passage? (1:11-12, 19)
❊ What promises did Gabriel make concerning the child who would be born to this elderly couple? (1:13-17)
❊ What instructions did Gabriel give Zechariah about his and Elizabeth's role as parents? (1:14-16)
❊ How did Gabriel describe the main purpose of John's life? (1:16-17)
❊ What conclusions can we draw about Zechariah from his answer to the angel's announcement? (1:18)
■ Why was Zechariah rendered unable to speak until the day of the prophecy's fulfillment? (1:19-20)
■ How did Elizabeth react to Zechariah's news? (1:25)
❊ How many miracles are referred to in this passage? (1:9, 11, 20, 24)

GET IT

❊ What can we learn from Zechariah and Elizabeth that would help us handle long-term disappointments?
■ How did God demonstrate in the lives of these two people that He is sovereign?
❊ Why were Zechariah and Elizabeth entrusted with the knowledge of God's purpose for the life of their son?
■ When have you doubted the reality of God's wonderful provision for you?
❊ What do you think Zechariah or Elizabeth felt during those extraordinary days?
❊ What could God do in a person's life today that would have as big an impact as the angel's visit to Zechariah?
❊ In what way is the birth of a child a sign of God's blessing?
❊ In what ways does God want to use us today?
❊ On a scale of one to ten (one being low, ten being high), how would you rate your level of expectation that God could do something amazing through your life?

APPLY IT

■ What long-term frustration can you identify in your life that needs to be entrusted to God?
❊ How can you strengthen your realization that God is in control of the events of your life?

Luke 1:26-38

The Birth of Jesus Foretold

TOPICS

Angels, Attitude, Faith, Greatness, Holy Spirit, Honor, Humility, Impossible, Jesus Christ, Miracles, Obedience, Serving, Trust

OPEN IT

❊ When was an occasion when you received an unexpected honor?
■ How do you tend to react when you receive unexpected good news?

EXPLORE IT

❊ Who greeted Mary? Why? (1:26-28)
❊ How did Mary learn of her role in Jesus' birth? (1:26-28)
❊ How did Mary feel when the angel appeared to her? (1:29-30)
■ How did Gabriel describe the child that would be born to Mary? (1:31-33)
❊ What title would Jesus have? (1:32)
❊ What Old Testament personalities were part of Jesus' royal line? (1:32-33)
❊ Why wasn't Mary struck dumb by the angel as Zechariah was? (1:34)
■ How did Mary's response to the angel differ from Zechariah's? (1:34, 38)
❊ Why did Gabriel mention Elizabeth's pregnancy to Mary? (1:36-37)
❊ What kind of attitude was apparent in Mary's response to the angel's visit? (1:38)
■ What did Mary's final statement to Gabriel show about her relationship with God? (1:38)

GET IT

■ What do Mary's responses to Gabriel tell us about the kind of people through whom God works?
❊ In what different ways do people respond to the story of Christ's birth?
❊ What difference does it make whether or not a person believes that the child born to Mary was really the Son of God?
■ How has the fact that "with God, nothing is impossible" taken root in your life?
❊ In what ways would you say Mary's responses to Gabriel summarize what our relationship with God ought to be like?

APPLY IT

■ What "impossibilities" in your life do you want to thank God for this week?
❊ What can you do to maintain a servant's attitude as you live from day to day?
❊ In what ways can you develop the kind of humble spirit that Mary had?

Luke 1:39-45
Mary Visits Elizabeth

TOPICS
Advice, Affirmation, Age, Appreciation, Blessing, Children, Culture, Encouragement, Holy Spirit, Honor, Joy, Maturity, Relationships, Respect, Wisdom

OPEN IT
❊ What was the first trip you can remember taking by yourself?
■ What relative do you look forward to visiting the most?
❊ What benefits have you derived from personal relationships with older people?

EXPLORE IT
❊ To where did Mary hurry? (1:39)
■ What two remarkable things happened as soon as Mary called her greeting to Elizabeth? (1:41)
❊ What was the significance of the baby leaping at the sound of Mary's voice? (1:41, 44)
❊ How did Elizabeth respond to the baby's leaping inside her? (1:42-45)
❊ In what way was Mary blessed? (1:42)
■ Why did Elizabeth describe herself as "favored"? (1:43)
❊ In what significant way did Elizabeth address Mary? (1:43)
❊ Why did Elizabeth's baby leap in her womb? (1:44)
■ Who was blessed? (1:45)
❊ What general spiritual principle did Elizabeth express? (1:45)

GET IT
❊ In what ways could we describe both Mary and Elizabeth as "blessed" women?
❊ How did Elizabeth indicate that she knew what her and Mary's pregnancies meant?
❊ How would you describe the mood in Zechariah's home during the time Mary visited?
■ Judging from Elizabeth's experience, what is it like to be filled with the Holy Spirit?
❊ How does it feel to be genuinely complimented by someone older than you?
■ What significance do you think it had for Mary that Elizabeth knew the importance Mary's baby?

APPLY IT
■ What older Christian could you contact or visit this week to express appreciation for the help they have been to you?
❊ What work of God do you want to celebrate or praise God for?

Luke 1:46-56
Mary's Song

TOPICS
Appreciation, Assurance, Attitude, Awe, Benefits, Blessing, Confidence, Devotion, Enthusiasm, Faith, God, Humility, Joy, Justice, Mercy, Poor, Praise, Promises, Reliability, Sovereignty, Worship

OPEN IT
❊ What songs are you most likely to be caught singing in the shower?
❊ Which church hymns are your favorites? Why?
■ If you had the skill and opportunity, how would you tell the world about a life-changing experience: write a poem, sing a song, publish a novel, or make a movie? Why?

EXPLORE IT
❊ What were the two parts of Mary's song? (1:46-55)
■ What attributes of God are extolled in the first part of Mary's song? (1:46-49)
❊ What different titles for God did Mary mention in her song? (1:46-47, 49)
❊ What specific actions did Mary say God had done for her? (1:46-49)
■ How did Mary describe herself in her song? (1:47-48)
❊ What reasons did Mary give for believing that all generations would call her "blessed"? (1:48)
❊ What characteristics of God did Mary sing about in the second part of her hymn? (1:50-56)
■ According to Mary's song, what kinds of people are given special treatment by God? (1:50-55)
❊ What happens to people who fear God? (1:50)
❊ What happens to the proud? (1:51)
❊ To whom was God merciful? (1:54-55)

GET IT
■ What words best describe Mary's attitude?
■ What reasons can we give for calling Mary a woman blessed by God?
❊ What evidence do we have today that God is still keeping His promises?
❊ How can we illustrate God's "bringing down rulers and lifting up the humble" today?
❊ What different methods have you used to tell others your experiences with God?
❊ What actions of God which Mary mentioned have you observed or experienced?
❊ How does God show mercy to us today?

APPLY IT
■ In what way can you glorify the Lord and rejoice in your Savior this week?
❊ What person close to you still needs to hear you express your faith?

Luke 1:57-66
The Birth of John the Baptist

TOPICS
Answers, Appreciation, Awe, Celebration, Children, Choices, Culture, Curiosity, Delay, Desires, Expectations, Family, Joy, Obedience, Parents, Persistence, Promises, Silence, Traditions

OPEN IT
■ What is the significance, meaning, or story behind your name?
❊ How do parents often choose names for their children?

❊ If you lost your speech for a year, what would be your first words when you were finally able to talk again?

EXPLORE IT
❊ What two groups celebrated the birth of Zechariah and Elizabeth's baby? (1:58)
❊ Why did the relatives and neighbors think that God had shown Elizabeth great mercy? (1:58)
❊ When did Elizabeth's relatives come to visit her child? Why? (1:59)
■ What was the relatives' response when Elizabeth told them the child wouldn't be called Zechariah? (1:61)
❊ Why did the relatives have to make signs to Zechariah about what he wanted to call the child? (1:62)
■ Why was Zechariah's voice restored? (1:63-64)
■ How did Zechariah react when his voice was restored? (1:64)
❊ What was effect of all these events on the people in the region in which Zechariah and Elizabeth lived? (1:65-66)
❊ What was special about Elizabeth's child? (1:66)
❊ What was the question on everybody's lips who heard about the birth of John? (1:66)

GET IT
❊ In what ways do Zechariah and Elizabeth serve as models to us?
❊ In what ways should we you held to the course God determines for us over the counsel of friends or relatives?
■ How significant is it for us to celebrate with others?
■ How do you tend to react when someone you know has cause to celebrate?
❊ In what ways has God's favor on you caused people to talk?
❊ What qualities of Zechariah do you want to build in your own life?

APPLY IT
■ With what person can you celebrate a happy or joyous event this week? How?
❊ What can you do to remind yourself that the Lord's hand is with you each day?

Luke 1:67-80
Zechariah's Song

TOPICS
Appreciation, Benefits, Covenant, Expectations, Heritage, History, Mercy, Messiah, Mission, Praise, Promises, Prophecy, Salvation, Tasks

OPEN IT
❊ What is it like to be around someone whose first child has just been born?
■ What are the most important things parents ought to tell their children while they are growing up?
❊ What compliment will you never forget?

EXPLORE IT
❊ What are the parts of Zechariah's song? (1:68-79)
❊ Who is described in the first part of Zechariah's song? (1:68-75)
❊ Who is the subject of the second part of Zechariah's song? (1:76-79)
❊ Who was the source of inspiration for Zechariah's song? (1:67)
❊ How does Zechariah speak about God in his song? (1:68-75)
■ For whom and from what was the salvation that Zechariah described? (1:69-71, 77)
❊ How did Zechariah describe the "covenant" with God? (1:72)
❊ What two results did Zechariah say were guaranteed by God's oath? (1:74)
■ What title did Zechariah say would be given to his son? (1:76)
■ For whom was John supposed to prepare a way? How? (1:76)
❊ How did Zechariah predict his son's purpose in life? (1:76-77)
❊ What basic facts did Luke include about John's childhood? (1:80)

GET IT
❊ What are the themes in Zechariah's song?
❊ What does it mean to be strong in spirit?
❊ In what way do we need to have the knowledge of salvation through the forgiveness of our sins?
■ How important is it for children to hear from their parents what God's place ought to be in their lives?
■ What can parents learn from Zechariah about passing on faith to their children?
❊ How might you describe God's ongoing work in the world today?

APPLY IT
■ What idea from Zechariah's song would you most like to communicate to your family this week?
❊ What would it take for you to be more like Zechariah in your faithfulness to God?

Luke 2:1-7
The Birth of Jesus

TOPICS
Celebration, Children, Circumstances, Citizenship, Government, History, Jesus Christ, Parents, Prophecy, Schedule, Simplicity, Timing

OPEN IT
❊ What feelings do you get when you have to fill out income tax forms?
❊ What nationalities or cultures make up the ancestry of your family?
■ When you think about uncomfortable travel, what personal experiences do you recall?

EXPLORE IT
❊ Who decreed that a census be taken of the entire Roman world? (2:1)
❊ What historical facts did Luke provide that allow us to approximate the date of Christ's birth? (2:1-2)
❊ What did the Roman census require of everyone? (2:3)
■ What was the purpose of Joseph and Mary's trip to Bethlehem? (2:1-4)

❊ What reason did Luke give for Joseph having to travel to Bethlehem for the census? (2:4)
❊ What did Luke say about Bethlehem which indicates it was a famous place? (2:4)
❊ What was Joseph and Mary's marital status at the time of Jesus' birth? (2:5)
■ Why was travel especially difficult for Mary? (2:5)
❊ What details about the birth of Jesus do we know or can we infer from Luke's description? (2:5-7)
■ What were the conditions in Bethlehem the night Jesus was born? (2:7)

GET IT
❊ How well have Christmas carols captured the significance of the birth Luke described?
■ How are people like the town of Bethlehem on the night of Christ's birth?
❊ What can we learn about responding to unexpected difficulties from the examples of Mary and Joseph?
■ In what ways did God manage the events of history to get Joseph and Mary where He wanted them at the appropriate time?
❊ In what way was Christ's birth a simple event?
❊ How do you celebrate Christ's birth?

APPLY IT
❊ In what ways can you praise God for Jesus' arrival into the world this week?
❊ What is one aspect of Christmas that you want to emphasize more next Christmas?
■ How can you honor Jesus with your Christmas celebrations?

Luke 2:8-20
The Shepherds and the Angels

TOPICS
Actions, Ambassadors, Angels, Awe, Follow-through, Good News, Instructions, Messiah, Obedience, Praise, Witnessing

OPEN IT
■ What is the most unique birth announcement you've ever seen?
❊ What do you imagine angels look like?
❊ If you could sleep out under the stars anywhere in the world, where would you put down your pillow?

EXPLORE IT
❊ At what time and place did the angels appear to the shepherds? (2:8)
❊ How many angels did the shepherds see at first? (2:9)
❊ How did the shepherds react when they saw the angel? (2:9)
❊ To whom did the angel address his good news? (2:10)
■ What message did the angel tell the shepherds? (2:10, 12)
❊ Who did the angel say the newborn child really was? (2:11)
■ By what symbol or sign were the shepherds supposed to identify the Christ child? (2:12)
❊ How many angels did the shepherds hear praising God? (2:13)
■ What was the immediate reaction of the shepherds after the angels left? (2:15)
❊ After finding the Christ child, what did the shepherds do? (2:17-20)
❊ What kind of reactions did the shepherds get when they told others what had happened that night? (2:18)
❊ How did Mary respond to the shepherds' visit? (2:19)

GET IT
❊ If you had been with the shepherds on the night Christ was born, what would you have done after the angels left?
❊ In what ways did the shepherds obey God that night?
■ What should be our response when we discover what God wants us to do?
❊ What does it mean that Mary "treasured up all these things and pondered them in her heart"?
❊ Of what significance is it that the shepherds went back to their flocks?
■ What is the responsibility of those who "discover" the good news about Jesus?
❊ Who needs to be told about the birth and life of Christ?

APPLY IT
❊ In what ways can you renew your enthusiasm for the message of Jesus' birth?
■ How can you glorify and praise God with other Christians this week?

Luke 2:21-40
Jesus Presented in the Temple

TOPICS
Actions, Affirmation, Age, Celebration, Devotion, Expectations, Faithfulness, Holy Spirit, Praise, Prophecy, Wisdom

OPEN IT
■ What ceremony, ritual, or tradition in your church do you enjoy the most?
❊ Who is one of your most interesting elderly friends?
❊ What wisdom have you gained from your grandparents or elderly relatives?

EXPLORE IT
■ Why did Mary and Joseph take Jesus to the temple? When? (2:22-23)
❊ How old was Jesus the first time Mary and Joseph took Him to the temple? (2:22-23)
❊ Who was Simeon? (2:25-27)
❊ How did Luke describe the man named Simeon? (2:25-32)
❊ What did Simeon do with the Christ child? (2:28-32)
■ What special significance did Christ's arrival have for Simeon? (2:26-29)
❊ How did Simeon's prophecy point out that Christ would be the Savior for the world? (2:32)
❊ What did Joseph and Mary do after they heard what Simeon had to say? (2:33)

❊ To whom did Simeon address his second statement about Jesus? (2:34-35)
❊ What did Simeon say to Mary? (2:34-35)
❊ Who was Anna? (2:36-38)
❊ How did Luke describe the woman named Anna? (2:36-38)
■ What was Anna's response to finding Mary, Joseph, and the Christ child in the temple? (2:38)
❊ What were Jesus' childhood years like? (2:40)
❊ How did Luke summarize Jesus' childhood years? (2:40)
❊ What character qualities were apparent in Jesus during His childhood? (2:40)

GET IT
■ In what ways can we see God working behind the scenes in the events of Christ's childhood?
❊ What of Simeon's prophecy is still true today?
❊ What did Simeon's warning to Mary mean?
■ In what ways are Simeon and Anna examples to us?
❊ Using Christ's childhood as an example, what character qualities should parents seek to develop in their children?
❊ In what different ways did Anna and Simeon each receive the Christ child?
❊ What roles can other Christians have in our life of faith?
❊ How important is it to introduce our children to faith in God as early and consistently as possible?
❊ If you could step back in time and stand next to Simeon, what would you want to say about the Christ child?

APPLY IT
■ How could you express your thanks to God this week for becoming a human being to provide a way of salvation?
❊ What action could you take this week to show your desire to be faithful to God?

Luke 2:41-52
The Boy Jesus at the Temple

TOPICS
Children, Church, Example, Family, Growth, Habits, Learning, Maturity, Obedience, Parents, Questions, Training, Youth

OPEN IT
■ When have you accidentally left someone behind during a trip or activity?
❊ If you had to get lost, would you rather it be in a city or a wilderness? Why?
❊ What do you find most characteristic of young adolescents?

EXPLORE IT
❊ Why did Jesus' parents go to Jerusalem every year? (2:41)
■ How did Jesus get left behind in Jerusalem? (2:43-44)
■ Why did three days pass before Mary and Joseph found Jesus? (2:46)
❊ What was Jesus doing during the three days that He was on His own? (2:46)
❊ What were the effects of Jesus' questions and answers on the teachers in Jerusalem? (2:46-47)
■ How did Mary respond when she and Joseph finally found Jesus? (2:48)
❊ What was Jesus' response to His parents' frantic arrival? (2:49)
❊ How did Jesus answer His parents' concern for Him? (2:49)
❊ After replying to His parents, what did Jesus do? (2:51)
❊ What do we learn about Mary through this incident? (2:41, 48, 50-51)
❊ What happened to Jesus as He grew? (2:52)

GET IT
❊ What would you have wanted to ask Jesus had you been around during those three days in the temple?
■ What kind of pattern or model were Mary and Joseph setting for Jesus by their family traditions?
❊ How often do children carry on the habits and beliefs that really are significant to their parents?
❊ What happens when parents try to pass on to their children beliefs or habits which they do not have themselves?
■ How does this story illustrate the tension Jesus may have felt between obedience to His Father and obedience to His earthly parents?
❊ In what way should we strive to grow in wisdom and stature and in favor with God and others?
❊ How did Jesus demonstrate His uniqueness as the Son of God?

APPLY IT
■ Of the four ways in which Jesus grew (in wisdom, in stature, in favor with God, in favor with man), which one needs the most work in your life?
❊ What difference might it make to you this week if you prepared for church as if it were a visit to your Father's house?

Luke 3:1-20
John the Baptist Prepares the Way

TOPICS
Accountability, Actions, Appearance, Authority, Choices, Curiosity, Employment, Humility, Obedience, Repentance, Serving, Work

OPEN IT
❊ When have you participated in a meaningful outdoor worship service?
❊ If you could make a certain style of clothes or hair popular again, which would it be?
■ What well-known public person would you most readily describe as a great speaker?

EXPLORE IT
❊ What different rulers did Luke mention in giving a historical setting to John the Baptist's ministry? (3:1-2)
■ What was John's basic message? (3:3)
❊ Where did John the Baptist carry out his ministry? (3:3)

❊ What Old Testament prophecy was fulfilled by John the Baptist? (3:4)
❊ How sensitive was John's welcome of the crowds who came to hear him? (3:7-8)
❊ What responses did John expect from his listeners? Why? (3:8-9)
■ What attitude did John warn the people not to have? Why? (3:8-9)
❊ How did people react to John's message? (3:10)
❊ What advice did John give those in the crowd who wanted to respond to his message? (3:11)
❊ What practical examples of repentance did John use to help people who asked for direction? (3:11-14)
❊ In what way was John becoming famous? (3:15)
■ What title were the people beginning to give John? (3:15)
❊ What was John's response to those who thought he might be the Messiah? (3:16)
❊ How did John explain his phrase, "Produce fruit in keeping with righteousness"? (3:8, 11-14)
❊ How did John describe Jesus? (3:16-18)
❊ What finally got John thrown into prison? (3:19-20)

GET IT
❊ What is repentance?
❊ When John explained repentance to people, how did it relate to the work they did in life?
■ When we are confronted with a call to repent, why do we tend to accept or reject the invitation strongly?
❊ What connection is there between repentance and forgiveness?
❊ In what ways could John the Baptist's directions to his listeners help someone today who reaches the point of repentance?
❊ How did John apply the principle that while God is at work changing people, He often does not change their work or their place in life?
■ In what ways does John's life teach us about humility?
❊ How should your relationship with God make your work habits differ from those around you?

APPLY IT
■ In what areas of your life do you need to show the fruits of repentance this week?
❊ At work this week, what action can you take because of agreement with God's priorities?

Luke 3:21-38

The Baptism and Genealogy of Jesus

TOPICS
Affirmation, Call, God, Holy Spirit, Life, Ministry, Prayer, Submission

OPEN IT
❊ From what period of history would you most like to meet one of your ancestors?
❊ What mental image comes to mind when you hear the word "baptism"?
■ Of all the things a person could hear God say to them, what would be one of the most meaningful?

EXPLORE IT
❊ Who baptized Jesus? (3:21)
■ How were Jesus, the dove, and the voice all related in Jesus' baptism? (3:21-22)
❊ To whom did the voice from heaven speak during Jesus' baptism? (3:22)
■ What did the voice from heaven actually say about Jesus? (3:22)
■ What was Jesus doing when the Holy Spirit descended on Him? (3:22)
❊ When did Jesus start His ministry? (3:23)
❊ How old was Jesus when He started His ministry? (3:23)
❊ Whose ancestors did Luke list? Why? (3:23)
❊ In what way could Joseph's ancestors be called Jesus' genealogy, even though Joseph was not Jesus' father? (3:23)
❊ Which of the names in the genealogy are the most famous? (3:23-38)
❊ How far back in time did Luke trace the genealogy of Jesus? (3:23-38)

GET IT
❊ What about Luke's description of Jesus' baptism leads us to think of God in terms of three persons—the Trinity?
❊ Since Jesus was sinless, what made His baptism necessary?
❊ How does Jesus' baptism demonstrate His willingness to identify with our human condition?
❊ What does it mean that God publicly claimed Jesus as His Son?
■ In what ways were the events during Jesus' baptism a commissioning ceremony for Him?
■ What does it mean for someone to call his or her way of life a ministry?
❊ How are repentance, baptism, forgiveness, prayer, the Holy Spirit's presence, and God's blessing all important in the life of a Christian?

APPLY IT
■ In what kinds of ways can you be a minister of God to others this week?
❊ To whom can you express support for his or her public ministry this week?

Luke 4:1-13

The Temptation of Jesus

TOPICS
Alone, Answers, Application, Bible, Character, Choices, Convictions, Desires, Evil, Isolation, Jesus Christ, Power, Satan, Suffering, Temptation, Testing, Worship

OPEN IT
■ In what ways have you experienced being very hungry or thirsty?
❊ If you were stranded with only one canteen of water in the desert, in the jungle, or on a deserted island, what would you do? Why?
❊ Why do people laugh when they hear someone say, "I can resist anything except temptation"?

EXPLORE IT

❇ How did Jesus end up alone in the desert? (4:1)
❇ For how long was Jesus tempted by the devil? (4:2)
■ After forty days of fasting and facing temptations, how did Jesus feel? (4:2)
❇ How did the devil challenge Jesus to prove He was the Son of God? (4:3, 9-10)
■ How did Jesus reply when the devil urged Him to turn a stone into bread? (4:4)
■ Where did Jesus get the answers He gave the devil? (4:4, 8, 12)
❇ For his second temptation where did the devil take Jesus and what did he show Him? (4:5)
❇ By what right did the devil claim to be able to offer Jesus the kingdoms of the world? (4:6)
❇ What did the devil offer Jesus in exchange for His worship? (4:6-7)
❇ What was Jesus' reply to the devil's offer of power and authority? (4:8)
❇ Where did the devil take Jesus in Jerusalem? (4:9)
❇ What did the devil dare Jesus to prove by jumping off the temple roof? (4:9-11)
❇ Why wasn't the devil successful in enticing Jesus to jump off the temple? (4:12)
❇ What did the devil do after Jesus' third resistance to his temptations? (4:13)

GET IT

❇ How did Jesus and the devil use the Bible differently?
❇ In what areas of life can we expect to be tempted?
■ What physical needs or desires make us vulnerable to temptation?
❇ How might we be tempted to worship the devil in exchange for power or position?
❇ In what situations are you sometimes tempted to put the Lord to the test?
❇ What did Jesus use repeatedly in resisting the devil's temptations?
❇ How did Jesus resist temptation?
■ How can a person become skillful at using the Bible as Jesus did?
❇ Since the Bible can be misused, how can we learn to use the Bible the right way?
❇ What did Jesus prove in the way he resisted the devil's temptations?
❇ What is the difference between testing God and claiming His promises?

APPLY IT

■ How can you prepare for tempting situations at work?
❇ What frequent temptation can you fight this week by memorizing Scripture?
❇ What passage of Scripture would be most helpful to memorize this week?

Luke 4:14-30

Jesus Rejected at Nazareth

TOPICS

Acceptance, Achievements, Anger, Bible, Church, Example, Expectations, Hardheartedness, Home, Miracles, Opposition, People, Prophecy, Rejection, Shame, Truth, Worship

OPEN IT

■ What are some of the best things that happen when a person comes back home after being away at school or in the service?
❇ What special place in you life do you dream about visiting again?
❇ What does the old saying mean, "You can never go home again"?

EXPLORE IT

❇ What was Jesus' reputation at this point in His life? (4:14-15)
❇ Where was Jesus teaching? (4:15)
■ What was Jesus' hometown? (4:16)
❇ What did Jesus customarily do on the Sabbath? (4:16)
❇ What happened once Jesus entered the synagogue? (4:16-30)
❇ What did Jesus do when He was handed the scroll of the prophet Isaiah? (4:17-20)
❇ How familiar was Jesus with Isaiah's words? (4:17-20)
❇ What five activities show that the Spirit of the Lord is on a person? (4:18-19)
■ How did the audience respond to Jesus' reading? (4:20)
❇ How did Jesus apply the passage He read from Isaiah? (4:21)
❇ What difficulty were the people having in accepting Jesus' words? (4:22)
■ What were the main points of Jesus' words to the people in His hometown? (4:23-27)
❇ Why were the people angry with what Jesus said? (4:23-29)
❇ How did the people express their anger at Jesus' message? (4:28-30)

GET IT

❇ How did Jesus' experience in His hometown illustrate the fickleness of a crowd?
❇ In what different ways can we see the Spirit of God on Jesus throughout these events?
❇ How did Jesus demonstrate the importance of worship?
❇ During this incident, in what ways did Jesus demonstrate the importance of knowing the Scriptures?
■ What kind of reception should we expect when we speak the truth?
❇ How did Jesus' message illustrate the fact that God does not favor one culture over another?
❇ What did Jesus know firsthand about rejection?
■ To what extent will people go to avoid hearing the truth about themselves?
❇ Why do we sometimes try to avoid facing the truth about ourselves?

APPLY IT
■ In what way could you renew your commitment to worship with other Christians?
❊ How could you improve your present habit of Bible reading?

Luke 4:31-37
Jesus Drives Out an Evil Spirit

TOPICS
Authority, Awe, Demons, Evil, Healing, Miracles, Power, Restoration, Teaching

OPEN IT
❊ In your own experience, exactly how fast does news travel?
■ What is your most compelling personal reason for believing in the existence of evil?
❊ What teachers have you known or heard whose speaking style made an unforgettable impression on you?

EXPLORE IT
❊ Where was Capernaum? (4:31)
❊ What was Jesus doing in the synagogue? (4:31)
❊ Why were people amazed at Jesus? (4:32)
■ In what setting did Jesus drive out the demon from the man in Capernaum? (4:33)
❊ How did the demon-possessed man react to Jesus' presence? (4:33-34)
❊ With what expressions did the demon-possessed man identify Jesus? (4:34)
■ How did Jesus respond to the evil spirit's presence? (4:35)
❊ To whom did Jesus speak when the man cried out against him? (4:35)
❊ What happened to the man who was demon-possessed? (4:35)
■ How was Jesus' reputation affected by the healing of the demon-possessed man? (4:36)
❊ How did Jesus demonstrate the power of His teaching and actions? (4:32, 35-36)

GET IT
■ What does it mean for a message to have authority?
❊ What did Jesus usually do when He arrived in a new town?
❊ How important is it that Jesus regularly taught in the synagogues everywhere He went?
❊ What significance is there in the fact that an evil spirit was able to pick Jesus out of a crowd as someone to be feared?
■ What does this incident tell us about good and evil?
❊ What comfort or confidence can we gain from Jesus' power to expel the evil spirit from the man?
❊ What is Jesus' attitude toward evil?
❊ How would you describe your present confidence in the power of God?

APPLY IT
■ What area of worldly or evil influence in your life needs to experience the power of Jesus more directly?
❊ In what way can you meet with Christ personally this week?

Luke 4:38-44
Jesus Heals Many

TOPICS
Actions, Compassion, Demons, Healing, Kingdom of God/Heaven, Miracles, People, Purpose, Sickness, Solitude, Teaching

OPEN IT
■ What is the most ill you have ever been?
❊ When have you found yourself overwhelmed with the needs of a person or group of people?

EXPLORE IT
❊ Why did Jesus heal Simon's mother-in-law? (4:38)
❊ What problem was Simon's mother-in-law experiencing? (4:38)
❊ Whom did Jesus meet in Simon's home and what did he do for her? (4:38-39)
■ How did Jesus heal Simon's mother-in-law's fever? (4:39)
❊ How did Luke describe the evening of this particular day? (4:40-41)
■ What kinds of healing did Jesus perform that day? (4:40-41)
❊ What did the demons shout about Jesus as they were expelled? (4:41)
■ Beside exorcising them, how did Jesus treat the demons? (4:41)
❊ How did Jesus begin the next day? (4:42)
❊ When the crowd found Jesus the next day, what did they try to convince Him to do? (4:42)
❊ How did Jesus respond to the people's wish that He stay in Capernaum? (4:43)
❊ What did Jesus say was His mission? (4:43)
❊ What did Jesus say He was trying to communicate to people? (4:43)

GET IT
■ In what ways did Jesus demonstrate compassion in the way He treated people?
■ What did Jesus accomplish by healing so many people?
❊ What experiences have you had with the unexpected healing of people in response to prayer?
❊ How did Jesus balance the constant exposure to the needs of others in his life?
❊ What is the benefit of solitude?
❊ How important is it to have regular times of solitude?
❊ What can a person accomplish in solitude that can't be accomplished with other people around?
❊ What kind of demands did people place on Jesus?
❊ What kind of demands do people place on you?
❊ How did Jesus present Himself as someone worth following?

APPLY IT
■ In what ways can you thank God this week for healing your life or the life of someone you know?
❊ When can you take time for solitude this week?

Luke 5:1-11

The Calling of the First Disciples

TOPICS

Awe, Call, Commitment, Decisions, Evangelism, Failure, Faithfulness, Ministry, Miracles, Mission, Obedience, Persistence, Submission, Surprises, Tasks, Timing, Trust, Witnessing

OPEN IT

❇ What is your favorite "fish story"?
❇ What qualities does your favorite leader possess?
■ When have you participated in a project at which everyone worked very hard, only to experience failure?

EXPLORE IT

❇ In what setting did Jesus find Himself? (5:1)
❇ Why were the people crowding around Jesus? (5:1)
❇ What were the owners of the boats doing nearby? (5:2)
❇ What did Jesus use to create a little space between Himself and the crowd? (5:2-3)
❇ Whose boat did Jesus choose for His podium? (5:3)
❇ What did Jesus suggest to Simon following His message? (5:4)
■ How did Simon reply to Jesus' instructions to cast their nets again? (5:4-5)
❇ What happened when Simon lowered his nets into the water? (5:6)
❇ When Simon saw their nets were tearing from the weight of fish in them, what did he do? (5:7)
■ How did Simon react when he realized Jesus had just done a miracle for them? (5:8-9)
❇ Who were Simon's partners? (5:10)
■ How did Jesus speak to the men's fears? (5:10)
❇ How did Simon and the others respond to Jesus' invitation? (5:11)

GET IT

■ How did Jesus test Simon?
❇ In what way did Jesus test Simon's faith?
❇ What does God expect us to do when obeying Him does not yield any immediate benefit?
❇ In what way is Simon's reaction to Jesus' miracle an example for us to follow?
■ What do we have to "leave behind" in order to follow Christ today?
❇ How does a person go about being a fisher of men?

APPLY IT

■ What areas in your own life can you identify as places where God is requiring long-term obedience from you, in spite of failures?
❇ What do you need to leave behind today in following Christ?

Luke 5:12-16

The Man With Leprosy

TOPICS

Acceptance, Actions, Alone, Attitude, Believe, Compassion, Expectations, Mercy, Needs, Prayer, Restoration, Sacrifice, Sickness, Solitude, Thankfulness

OPEN IT

❇ If you could see one obvious miracle performed before your eyes, what would you want to see?
■ When was a time you were treated as an outcast or reject by other kids when you were growing up?
❇ When have you helped someone that no one else was willing to help?

EXPLORE IT

■ What did the leprous man do when he saw Jesus? (5:12)
❇ How did the man present his request for help to Jesus? (5:12)
■ In what way did the man's words to Jesus show belief in Christ? (5:12)
❇ What did Jesus say to the sick man? (5:13)
■ How did Jesus treat the sick man? (5:13)
❇ Did Jesus respond to the man's request? (5:13)
❇ What was the result of Jesus' first words to the man? (5:13)
❇ What were Jesus' orders to the man after he had been healed? (5:14)
❇ To whom was the healed man supposed to show himself? Why? (5:14)
❇ Why was the man to report to the priest? (5:14)
❇ Besides showing the priest that he was healed, what else did Jesus tell the man to do? (5:14)
❇ In spite of Jesus' request that the man not tell anyone, what resulted from this healing? (5:15)
❇ What was Jesus' response to His popularity? (5:16)

GET IT

❇ How did the sick man regard Jesus?
❇ In what ways do the words and actions of the sick man provide a pattern for the way we ought to approach Christ with our needs?
■ Being affected with a disease that made him an outcast, what must it have been like for the man to have been touched by Jesus?
❇ What are some of the ways in which Jesus still manages to touch people who are sick and in need today?
■ How important is it for us to imitate the private life of Jesus?
❇ How well do your present prayer habits match the man's willingness to approach Jesus?

APPLY IT

■ What person or people in your life could most benefit from a caring touch from you in Christ's name?
❇ What times in the next week can you set aside to listen to God and tell Him your needs?

Luke 5:17-26

Jesus Heals a Paralytic

TOPICS

Authority, Barriers, Believers, Commitment, Determination, Effort, Faith, Forgiveness, Healing, Mercy, Miracles, Sickness, Teamwork, Thinking

OPEN IT

❇ When was a time you went out of your way to help a friend?
❇ In what ways have you seen that "a friend in need is a friend indeed"?
■ Whom would you describe as having a great deal of faith in God?

EXPLORE IT

❇ How did Luke describe the crowd that was listening to Jesus? (5:17)
❇ Who came to see Jesus, and why did they come? (5:18)
❇ Why were the men initially unable to bring their paralyzed friend to Jesus? (5:19)
■ What did the team of men do when they could not find a way through the crowded house? (5:19)
❇ What did Jesus acknowledge as the paralytic man was lowered through the roof? (5:20)
❇ What were Jesus' first words to the paralytic man? (5:20)
❇ Why did the Pharisees and teachers think that Jesus' words to the paralytic man were blasphemous? (5:21)
■ What did Jesus show by responding to what the Pharisees were thinking? (5:22)
❇ What challenging question did Jesus pose to the Pharisees? (5:23)
❇ How did Jesus answer His own question? (5:24)
❇ What did Jesus prove by healing the paralytic man? (5:24)
■ How did the paralytic man respond to Jesus' invitation to "get up, take your mat and go home"? (5:25)
❇ What was the response of the crowd to what happened that day? (5:26)

GET IT

■ In what ways did the paralytic and his friends demonstrate faith in Christ?
❇ Why is it easier to say, "Your sins are forgiven" than to say to a paralyzed person, "You are healed"?
❇ In what ways is sin a paralysis?
■ How is forgiveness a kind of healing?
❇ From whom do we need forgiveness?
❇ What was Jesus proving about Himself whenever He healed diseases and forgave sinners?
❇ How does this incident illustrate the conditions under which forgiveness is given?

APPLY IT

■ Who is one friend you could help by a gesture of faith today?
❇ At what time each day this week can you place the needs of your friends before Christ?

Luke 5:27-32

The Calling of Levi

TOPICS

Acceptance, Actions, Call, Change, Decisions, Follow, Invitation, Mission, Repentance, Reputation, Unbelievers

OPEN IT

❇ How do you feel about the Internal Revenue Service?
■ What jobs do you think present the greatest temptation to do wrong? Why?
❇ What is the most important consideration in finding and enjoying a career?

EXPLORE IT

■ What was Levi's profession? (5:27)
❇ What did Jesus say to Levi? (5:27)
■ What actions did Levi take upon hearing Jesus' invitation to follow Him? (5:28)
❇ What did Levi leave behind when he followed Jesus? (5:28)
■ What was Levi's first action as a new follower of Jesus? (5:29)
❇ Whom did Levi invite to his "new career party"? (5:29)
❇ In accepting Levi's hospitality, what was Jesus accused of doing? (5:30)
❇ What groups made a point of condemning Christ's choice of companions? (5:30)
❇ How did the Pharisees and others express their disapproval of Jesus' presence at Levi's banquet? (5:30)
❇ What was the point of the Pharisees' question to Jesus' disciples? (5:30)
❇ To what occupation did Jesus liken His ministry? (5:31)
❇ Why did Jesus come? (5:32)
❇ What reason did Jesus give for His coming? (5:32)

GET IT

❇ What did Jesus mean by saying that He came to call sinners to repentance and not to call the righteous?
■ What reasons could Jesus have had for calling Levi, a deserter to the Roman government, to follow Him?
❇ Why do you think Levi followed Jesus without knowing much about Him?
❇ How can we follow Christ today?
■ What do people find most difficult to leave behind when they follow Jesus?
❇ Why was Jesus comfortable at a party attended almost entirely by people whom others had rejected?
❇ Who are "the righteous" that don't need Jesus?

APPLY IT

■ How can you reach out in the days ahead to one person whom others neglect or ignore?
❇ What can you do to follow Christ's example more consciously this week?

Luke 5:33-39
Jesus Questioned About Fasting

TOPICS
Actions, Change, Criticism, Differences, Fasting, Habits, Legalism, Peer Pressure, Religion, Rules, Traditions

OPEN IT
✻ What person do you know who is not receptive to new ideas or ways of doing things?
■ In what areas of your life do you often resist change?
✻ What is one memorable wedding celebration you recall?

EXPLORE IT
✻ Who asked Jesus about fasting? (5:33)
✻ With what other groups were Jesus' disciples compared? By whom? (5:33)
✻ What were Jesus' disciples failing to do, according to those questioning Jesus? (5:33)
✻ How did Jesus identify Himself in His answer to the Pharisees? (5:34)
✻ What did Jesus say would cause His disciples to fast? (5:34)
✻ What was the point of Jesus' illustration about new and old garments? (5:36)
✻ What happens when a patch meant for an old garment is taken from a new garment? (5:36)
■ How did Jesus' two illustrations address the challenge that had been put Jesus? (5:36-39)
■ Which did Jesus say was better, the old or the new? (5:36-39)
✻ What was the point of Jesus' illustration about new and old wineskins? (5:37)
✻ What happens when new wine is poured into old wineskins? (5:37-38)
■ Why doesn't someone want new wine after drinking old wine? (5:39)

GET IT
✻ What are some of the most common religious habits that people compare?
✻ What kinds of dangers are created when people compare their religious customs and habits with those of other people?
■ In what way does following Christ require us to replace old habits with new ones?
■ Why do we resist the changes God asks of us?
✻ How can a person decide when differences between groups are unimportant and when they are crucial?

APPLY IT
✻ How can you show respect for the way other Christians honor God?
■ What can you do this week to become more open to changing as God directs?

Luke 6:1-11
Lord of the Sabbath

TOPICS
Accusation, Church, Compassion, Habits, Hardheartedness, Healing, Hypocrisy, Legalism, Needs, Traditions

OPEN IT
✻ What was Sunday like around your house when you were growing up?
■ What is your idea of a truly restful day?
✻ What does the word "Sabbath" mean to you?

EXPLORE IT
✻ What were the disciples doing that irritated the Pharisees? (6:1-2)
■ What were the disciples accused of doing when they picked the grain? (6:2)
✻ How did Jesus respond to the Pharisees' accusation? (6:3-5)
■ What historical example did Jesus use to justify what His disciples were doing on the Sabbath? (6:3-5)
✻ What claim did Jesus make about Himself? (6:5)
✻ What did Jesus' identity as Lord of the Sabbath have to do with the disciples eating grain on the Sabbath? (6:5)
✻ In what setting did Jesus heal the man with a shriveled hand? (6:6-8)
✻ Why were the teachers of the law watching Jesus closely? (6:7)
✻ Why were the Pharisees and teachers angry at Jesus? (6:7, 11)
✻ What difference did it make that Jesus was being watched? (6:7-10)
■ How did Jesus heal the man's hand? (6:9-10)
✻ What did Jesus ask the crowd? (6:9-10) Why?
✻ How did the Pharisees and teachers respond to the miracle Jesus did? (6:11)

GET IT
✻ How did Luke use these two Sabbath incidents to illustrate the tension that was growing between Jesus and the religious leaders?
✻ What harmful "religious" tendencies was Jesus resisting by His actions and words during these incidents?
■ Why did Jesus heal on the Sabbath?
✻ In these incidents, whose actions were really "Sabbath-keeping"?
■ Why is it important for us to take time off from work to rest?
■ How well were the Pharisees honoring the Sabbath while they discussed plans to retaliate against Jesus?
✻ When is it easiest apply a spiritual discipline unthinkingly?
✻ How can we guard against misapplying spiritual disciplines?

APPLY IT
■ What could you do to make next Sunday a day of service to God?
✻ What spiritual disciplines (such as fasting, prayer, Bible study, or church activities) should you reexamine this week?

Luke 6:12-16
The Twelve Apostles

TOPICS
Alone, Call, Choices, Decisions, Invitation, Prayer, Spiritual Disciplines

OPEN IT
❊ How competitive was your high school or college when it came to academics?
■ In neighborhood or school games, when were you usually chosen?

EXPLORE IT
❊ What did Jesus do before choosing the twelve apostles? (6:12)
❊ How much time did Jesus spend in prayer before He chose His apostles? (6:12)
■ What details did Luke give us about Jesus' prayer vigil? (6:12)
■ From what larger group did Jesus name His twelve apostles? (6:13)
❊ For which apostles are we given more information than simply their names? (6:14-16)
❊ How many apostles shared the same first names? (6:14-16)
■ What personal facts can you recall about some of the apostles? (6:14-16)
❊ What significance is there in the order of the apostles' names? (6:14-16)
❊ How many of the apostles had already been introduced by Luke earlier in his Gospel? (6:14-16)
❊ What does the description of Judas Iscariot actually say about him? (6:16)

GET IT
■ What significance can be drawn from the fact that Jesus singled out some of His disciples to be apostles?
❊ What is the difference between disciples and apostles?
■ Why do you think Jesus prayed before choosing the apostles?
❊ What purposes could Jesus have had in spending the night in prayer?
❊ What kinds decisions or events might cause someone to spend extended time in prayer?
❊ What could spending extended time in prayer accomplish that could not be accomplished in a shorter time of prayer?
❊ Why are extended times of prayer important?

APPLY IT
■ What do you want to keep in mind from this passage to help you in making choices in the future?
❊ When in the near future could you pray about God's plan for your life?

Luke 6:17-26
Blessings and Woes

TOPICS
Basics of the Faith, Believers, Blessing, Challenge, Comparisons, Consequences, Encouragement, Future, Insults, Joy, Opposition, Persecution, Poor, Suffering, Wealth

OPEN IT
■ What is the largest crowd that you have ever been a part of?
❊ What significant worship experiences have you had in a large group?
❊ Who is your favorite public speaker?

EXPLORE IT
❊ What different groups made up the crowd to which Jesus gave this sermon? (6:17)
■ What effect did Jesus' presence have on the crowd? (6:18-19)
■ Why did the crowd gather? (6:18-19)
❊ Besides Jesus' message, what else was going on that day? (6:18-19)
❊ To whom did Jesus specifically direct His message? (6:20)
❊ What four groups did Jesus single out for receiving a blessing? (6:20-22)
❊ How did the promised blessings vary to fit the character of each group? (6:20-22)
❊ What blessings did Jesus promise then and which ones did He promise for the future? (6:20-23)
■ What response to hardship did Jesus encourage His disciples to have? (6:23)
❊ Who were the disciples to think of as examples during times of suffering? (6:23)
❊ What times and places did Jesus give for the blessings He promised? (6:23)
❊ What four groups did Jesus single out for woes? (6:24-26)
❊ How did the woes vary to fit each group? (6:24-26)

GET IT
■ What contemporary groups resemble the ones Jesus spoke to in this sermon?
❊ For what different reasons are people interested in Jesus Christ in our times?
❊ To what conditions other than material poverty could Jesus have been referring when He said, "Blessed are you who are poor"?
■ What effect do you think Jesus' words had on the crowd?
❊ If you had been a rich and famous person in Jesus' day, how would you have reacted to His sermon?
❊ In what specific areas of life do Jesus' promised blessings and woes touch you?
❊ In what way are these words of Jesus comforting?
❊ In what way are these words of Jesus challenging?

APPLY IT
❊ What is one way you can store up rewards in heaven this week?

❊ In what way can you nurture the qualities that Jesus described as blessed?
■ Whom can you encourage with Jesus' words this week?

Luke 6:27-36
Love for Enemies

TOPICS
Actions, Blessing, Choices, Differences, Direction, Enemies, Forgiveness, Instructions, Insults, Love, Mercy, Opposition, Relationships, Revenge, Unfairness

OPEN IT
❊ Why do people often call revenge "sweet"?
❊ If you took a public opinion poll on the meaning of the Golden Rule, what would you expect to hear?
■ Who have been some of your enemies through the years?

EXPLORE IT
❊ How many positive responses to mistreatment did Jesus command? (6:27-31)
■ What different kinds of mistreatment did Jesus refer to in His commands? (6:28-30)
❊ Which statement best summarizes what Jesus said about responding to enemies? (6:31)
❊ How did Jesus explain the difference between His followers and those He called "sinners"? (6:32-34)
■ About what three positive actions did Jesus ask, "What credit is that to you?" (6:32-34)
❊ What was Jesus' basic argument in backing up His command to love others unconditionally? (6:32-35)
■ What results will those who practice loving their enemies obtain? (6:35)
❊ What title did Jesus give to those who love their enemies? (6:35)
❊ Who are we imitating when we love our enemies? (6:36)

GET IT
❊ According to this passage, what are the observable differences between "sinners" and "saints"?
■ What does it mean to "bless those who curse you"?
❊ Why was Jesus so critical of conditional love?
❊ Why is treating others as you wish to be treated called the Golden Rule?
❊ Which of Jesus' commands do you think goes most against human nature?
❊ What does it take for a person to live the way Jesus described here?
❊ When is forgiveness most difficult to give?
❊ How did Jesus in this sermon say His followers were to be distinctly different from the ordinary pattern?
■ What is realistic or unrealistic about the kind of love Jesus wants us to show?

APPLY IT
❊ To what enemy in your life can you show a gesture of love?
■ How can you remember to do good to someone who is unkind to you this week?

Luke 6:37-42
Judging Others

TOPICS
Acceptance, Accusation, Benefits, Consequences, Criticism, Forgiveness, Gifts, Help, Judging Others, Learning, Promises, Relationships, Teaching

OPEN IT
❊ From what teacher or wise person have you learned the most so far?
■ How does the expression "What goes around, comes around" apply in personal relationships?
❊ When have you criticized someone for an action that you also were guilty of?

EXPLORE IT
❊ What specific promises did Jesus make? (6:37-38)
❊ How much did Jesus want His disciples to give? Why? (6:38)
■ What does God give to those who give? (6:38)
❊ How did Jesus summarize the importance of extending grace, mercy, and help to others? (6:38)
❊ What will God give to each person? (6:38)
■ What reason did Jesus give for discouraging the blind from attempting to lead others who were also blind? (6:39)
❊ How do a student and his or her teacher relate? (6:40)
■ What is the main point of the parable of the plank and the sawdust? (6:41-42)
❊ What is a person who fails to see his or her own shortcomings? (6:42)
❊ What is required of a person before he or she can teach or instruct someone else? (6:42)

GET IT
❊ What does it mean to give "a good measure, pressed down, shaken together and running over"?
❊ When is it easy to judge others?
❊ Why is it important not to judge or condemn others?
❊ What do judging, condemning, forgiving, and giving have in common?
■ To what kind of giving did Jesus refer when He said, "Give, and it will be given to you"?
■ What kind of blindness did Jesus have in mind when He spoke of the blind leading the blind?
❊ How is a well-trained student like his teacher?
❊ What bothersome circumstances could Jesus have had in mind as He told the parable of the sawdust and plank?
❊ What shortcomings in ourselves do we tend to overlook?
❊ Who is most qualified to point out shortcomings in others?

APPLY IT
■ In what relationship in your life do you want to show more grace, mercy, and giving? How?
❊ In what ways can you be a more diligent student of your heavenly Teacher this week?

Luke 6:43-45
A Tree and Its Fruit

TOPICS
Application, Change, Character, Consistency, Evil, Expectations, Fruit, Goodness, Heart

OPEN IT
❇ What experiences have you had with growing and harvesting fruit?
❇ If you could own a fruit orchard, what kinds of fruit would you prefer to grow?
■ How have you been fooled by someone whose words were contrary to his or her actions?

EXPLORE IT
❇ What determines the quality of a fruit? (6:43)
■ What specific statements did Jesus make about fruit before applying the same truths to people? (6:43-44)
❇ In what different but related ways is the word "good" used in these verses? (6:43, 45)
❇ What do the tree and fruit symbolize in these words of Jesus? (6:43, 45)
❇ What did Jesus say about what people expected when collecting fruit? (6:44)
❇ What do "thornbushes" and "briers" represent? (6:44)
■ What did Jesus describe as the source of good and evil things? (6:45)
❇ How did Jesus describe the role of the human heart? (6:45)
■ How do people ultimately know about the state of our hearts? (6:45)
❇ What did Jesus mean by His final statement, "For out of the overflow of his heart his mouth speaks"? (6:45)

GET IT
❇ How can a person change his or her heart?
■ What is it about a person that actually has to change in order for good behavior to be produced?
■ When was the last time someone helped you examine how your life reflects or doesn't reflect the presence of Christ?
❇ What role has Christ played in your life in determining what kind of fruit you produce?
❇ How would you describe the things you have been storing up in your heart lately?

APPLY IT
❇ How can you cultivate the love for God that is in your heart?
■ What mature believer could you talk with this week to help you store up good things in your heart?

Luke 6:46-49
The Wise and Foolish Builders

TOPICS
Accomplishments, Actions, Believers, Benefits, Comparisons, Consequences, Differences, Foundation, Life, Listening, Obedience, Security, Stress, Suffering, Wisdom, Words

OPEN IT
❇ What do you think is the single most important decision when it comes to building a house?
■ If you could build a house anywhere in the world, where would you want to build it?
❇ Who you do know who has lost their home through a natural disaster?

EXPLORE IT
❇ What inconsistency did Jesus call to His followers' attention? (6:46)
■ What three things did Jesus say the wise person did that are similar to building well? (6:47)
❇ To whom does the wise person go? (6:47)
❇ What did Jesus say His two house building examples were meant to illustrate? (6:47, 49)
❇ How would you characterize the wise and foolish person's relationship to Jesus? (6:47, 49)
❇ How many differences can you find between the two people Jesus described in His story? (6:47-49)
■ What characteristics does the well-built house have? (6:48)
❇ What event did Jesus describe as happening to both houses? (6:48-49)
❇ How are the final results different for the wise and foolish builders? (6:48-49)
■ What does the foolish person do right and wrong in relation to Christ's words? (6:49)

GET IT
❇ Why was Jesus concerned that people would not do what He said?
❇ What could the various parts of Christ's story (the house, the rock, the sand, the foundation, the storm) represent in a person's life?
■ What specific actions was Jesus challenging His disciples to take?
❇ What specific action was Jesus challenging the crowd to avoid?
❇ What kind of life does Jesus want His followers to have?
❇ What common experiences do we all have whether we obey Jesus or not?
❇ How has knowing Jesus Christ made a difference during the storms in your life?
■ At what point in the building process is your life now?

APPLY IT
■ What can you do to be ready for the next storm that hits your life?
❇ Which of Jesus' words in this passage do you need to heed this week?

Luke 7:1-10
The Faith of the Centurion

TOPICS
Affirmation, Answers, Appreciation, Attitude, Authority, Character, Confidence, Delegation, Faith, Healing, Humility, Leadership, Prayer, Representatives, Reputation, Trust

OPEN IT

❇ When you hear the word "authority," who first comes to mind?

■ When have you been amazed by someone else's faith?

❇ From whom have you learned the greatest part of your understanding of faith?

EXPLORE IT

❇ In what town did Jesus heal the centurion's servant? (7:1-2)

❇ What did the centurion ask Jesus to do? (7:3)

❇ Whom did the centurion send to present his request to Jesus? (7:3)

❇ What reason did the elders give Jesus to honor their request on behalf of the centurion? (7:3)

❇ What kind of reputation did the centurion have among the people of Capernaum? (7:3)

■ What different character qualities were demonstrated by the centurion? (7:3-8)

■ What message did the centurion send when he discovered Jesus was actually coming to his house? (7:6-8)

❇ What was the centurion's perception of Jesus? (7:6-7)

❇ How did the centurion understand the concept of authority? (7:6-8)

❇ If your knowledge were limited to this passage, what would you know about centurions? (7:8)

■ How did Jesus react to the centurion's words? (7:9)

❇ To whom did Jesus remark on the uniqueness of the centurion's faith? (7:9)

❇ What happened to the centurion's servant? (7:10)

GET IT

■ What characteristics of the centurion's attitude and request would be helpful to remember when we ask God for help?

❇ What do people usually mean when they refer to Jesus Christ as Lord?

■ Why is it difficult for us to be as dependent on God as the centurion was?

❇ The centurion presented his request to Jesus through friends; how much is this like asking friends to pray for us?

❇ Why is it important to be encouraged about the quality of our faith, even as Jesus affirmed the faith of the centurion?

❇ What are some of the ways in which Jesus is Lord of your life?

❇ What happens when we depend on God?

APPLY IT

■ How could you affirm the faith of someone who has been an example to you?

❇ How can you strengthen your friendships with other Christians this week?

Luke 7:11-17

Jesus Raises a Widow's Son

TOPICS

Awe, Compassion, Faith, Healing, Miracles, Praise, Resurrection

OPEN IT

■ What different reactions do people have to the death of a friend?

❇ How does our culture generally treat the elderly?

❇ What do most people think about miracles today?

EXPLORE IT

❇ Who went with Jesus to Nain? (7:11)

❇ What pairs of opposites can you find in the passage? (7:11-17)

■ What can we learn about mourning in Jesus' day? (7:12)

❇ What kind of person died? (7:12, 14)

■ What was Jesus' reaction to the people He encountered? (7:13-15)

❇ What commands did Jesus give? (7:13-14)

■ How did the mother and her son react to Jesus? (7:14-15)

❇ How did the crowd react to Jesus? (7:16)

❇ Who did the people think Jesus was? (7:16)

❇ What was the result of the miracle? (7:17)

GET IT

❇ How do you respond to another person's grief?

❇ What can we learn from the example of the crowd from the town through their words and actions?

■ What picture of Jesus do you take from this passage?

■ How much do you expect God to work miracles in your life?

❇ In what ways can you spread the news about Jesus?

APPLY IT

■ What people in pain might you reach out to this week?

❇ How can you nurture your expectancy about Jesus' power?

❇ With whom can you share your expectation of what God can do today?

Luke 7:18-35

Jesus and John the Baptist

TOPICS

Expectations, Faith, Healing, Legalism, Messiah, Prophecy, Waiting

OPEN IT

❇ What do you do while you're waiting in a line?

■ What's the longest length of time you've waited for an answer from God?

❇ In your opinion, what causes most people to doubt?

EXPLORE IT

❇ How did John react to the reports about Jesus? (7:18-19)

■ For what two questions did John want answers? (7:19)

❇ What was Jesus doing when John's disciples arrived? (7:21)

■ How did Jesus answer the visitors' questions? (7:21-22)

❇ According to Jesus, what was John's role? (7:24-27)

❇ How did Jesus describe greatness? (7:28)

❇ Why did the people react in different ways to the words of Jesus? (7:29-30)

■ What did the people's reactions say about their relationship with God? (7:29-30)

❇ To what did Jesus compare the people of His day? (7:31-32)

❊ How did people characterize John the Baptist? (7:33)
❊ How did the description of John the Baptist compare with their characterization of Jesus? (7:34)
❊ What did Jesus conclude about the people of His day? (7:35)

GET IT
❊ In what ways can you relate to John the Baptist in this passage?
■ Why didn't Jesus condemn John's doubts?
❊ How is it possible, in the words of verse 23, to "fall away on account of" Jesus?
❊ Why do the appearances of God's servants affect how they are received?
❊ How can a person be more aware of the message than of the messenger?
❊ What is your response to Jesus' claim that the least in God's kingdom is greater than John the Baptist?
■ How can a person cultivate the wisdom and expectant response described by Jesus?

APPLY IT
■ What can you do this week to be on guard against faltering faith?
❊ Of what messengers of Jesus do you need to be more wary today?
❊ What opportunities might you have in the next few days to express your beliefs, as well as your doubts?

Luke 7:36-50
Jesus Anointed by a Sinful Woman

TOPICS
Forgiveness, Hospitality, Judging Others, Love, Salvation, Sin, Thankfulness

OPEN IT
❊ In what ways have you been thanked recently?
■ What limits do most people place on hospitality?
❊ In our culture, what sorts of behavior are considered the most shocking?

EXPLORE IT
❊ Who invited Jesus to dinner? (7:36)
❊ What did one woman do when she heard where Jesus was to dine? (7:37-38)
■ What did the Pharisee say about what the woman did? (7:39)
❊ How did Jesus respond to Simon the Pharisee's harsh thoughts? (7:40-43)
❊ What did Jesus know about the woman's motivation? (7:41-42)
■ What did Jesus think of Simon's hospitality? (7:44-46)
❊ What contrasting treatment did Jesus mention? (7:44-46)
❊ What was the result of the woman's kindness? (7:47-48)
■ How did the other guests react to Jesus' forgiveness of the woman? (7:49)
❊ What did Jesus say to the disapproving guests? (7:50)
❊ Why, according to Jesus, was the woman saved? (7:50)
❊ What was Jesus' double blessing on the woman? (7:50)

GET IT
❊ With what character in the story do you most identify?
❊ Which of the woman's actions do you find most compelling?
■ When have you ever felt like Simon or the other guests when confronted with a person of questionable morals?
❊ What did Jesus receive from people who had sinned?
❊ What were the limits of Jesus' compassion in this story?
■ What are the limits of Jesus' compassion toward us?
❊ Why was it necessary for the guests to ask about Jesus' identity?
❊ If you were the woman described in this story, how would the words and touch of Jesus make you feel?

APPLY IT
❊ What can you do to foster your own thankfulness to God this week?
■ What people do you want to view more with Jesus' eyes?

Luke 8:1-15
The Parable of the Sower

TOPICS
Good News, Growth, Perseverance, Satan, Testing, Worry

OPEN IT
❊ If you were a plant, what would you be?
❊ What are some things that distinguish one kind of plant from another?
■ In what areas of your life have you had to persevere?

EXPLORE IT
❊ Where did Jesus bring His message? (8:1)
❊ What women do we meet in this passage? (8:2-3)
❊ What facts about the women who followed Jesus do we learn? (8:2-3)
❊ What did the various "supporting characters" do in this story? (8:1-4)
❊ What method did Jesus choose to use in communicating His message? (8:4)
■ What happened to each group of seeds? (8:5-8)
❊ How did Jesus conclude His parable? (8:8)
❊ How much of the parable did the people understand? (8:9-10)
❊ How much of the parable did the disciples understand? (8:9-10)
❊ What did the seed represent? (8:11)
❊ What was the seed on the path like? (8:12)
■ Why couldn't those who received the word with joy stay faithful? (8:13)
❊ What choked those who were represented by the seed among the thorns? (8:14)
■ How did the seed scattered on good soil fare? (8:15)

GET IT
❊ Why do you think Luke took the time to mention the women in Jesus' following?
❊ What obstacles have prevented acquaintances of yours from receiving the Word?
■ Why is perseverance necessary for all who receive the Word?
■ What kind of soil do you most resemble right now?

❇ Which of life's worries has choked your growth as a Christian recently?
❇ What can we do to improve our receptivity to the Word of God?

APPLY IT
■ What will most help you be responsive to God in your study of the Bible?
❇ With whom can you share the truth about what Jesus means to you, that your faith may bear fruit?

Luke 8:16-18
A Lamp on a Stand

TOPICS
Abundance, Hiding, Listening, Openness, Witnessing

OPEN IT
■ What are the features of your favorite kind of lamp?
❇ What kinds of things do people try to hide?

EXPLORE IT
■ In what places would it be absurd to put a lamp? (8:16)
❇ According to Jesus, what is not done with a lamp? (8:16)
■ What is done with a lamp? (8:16)
❇ What contrasts do we see in this passage? (8:16-18)
❇ Why would someone put a light on a stand? (8:16)
❇ How much can ultimately be hidden? (8:17)
❇ What will happen to those things that are hidden? (8:17)
❇ What are we to consider carefully? (8:18)
❇ What did Jesus say our response should be to what we hear? (8:18)
■ What did Jesus say about what God entrusts to us? (8:18)

GET IT
■ What does the lamp stand for?
■ What sorts of things would God have us bring "out into the open"?
❇ How good a listener do you think you are, in the sense of this passage?
❇ What have you been given by God?
❇ When have you tried to hide your Christian identity from other people?

APPLY IT
■ What are some symbols you can use to show others your Christian identity?
❇ What step can you take to be a better listener to this and other parables?

Luke 8:19-21
Jesus' Mother and Brothers

TOPICS
Bible, Family, Listening, Obedience

OPEN IT
■ What is it like to be kept from seeing someone you know?
❇ How does it feel when someone you know acts as if your relationship is unimportant?

EXPLORE IT
■ Who came to see Jesus? (8:19)
■ What kept Jesus' family from seeing Him? (8:19)
❇ How can we infer that Jesus' family was anxious to see Him? (8:19-20)
❇ Where did Jesus' mother and brothers wait for Him? (8:20)
❇ How did Jesus hear of His family's arrival? (8:20)
❇ How did Jesus respond to His family's desire to see Him? (8:21)
■ What did Jesus consider more important than family? (8:21)
❇ With what is "hearing" closely associated? (8:21)
❇ How did Jesus identify those who heard God's Word and put in into practice?
❇ What two things constituted family ties to Jesus? (8:21)

GET IT
■ In what way was Jesus hard on His mother and brothers?
❇ In what ways can we feel too comfortable about our relationship with Jesus?
■ In what ways do we put family ahead of the needs of other people?
❇ When have you heard God's Word but failed to put it into practice?
❇ In what areas do you need to put God's word into practice more diligently?

APPLY IT
❇ What practical change in your daily routine would help you listen to God's Word better?
■ With whom can you share your concerns about putting Scripture into practice so that he or she can pray for you?

Luke 8:22-25
Jesus Calms a Storm

TOPICS
Danger, Doubt, Faith, Fear, Obedience

OPEN IT
■ What is it like to fear for your physical safety?
❇ How do you react to someone else's utter calm when all you feel is panic?

EXPLORE IT
❇ Whom did Jesus ask to accompany Him? (8:22)
❇ Where did Jesus and His disciples go? How? (8:22)
❇ What happened after Jesus and His disciples set sail? (8:23)
■ How did Jesus react to the growing storm? (8:23)
■ What did the disciples think of the turn of events? (8:24)
❇ How and how quickly did the situation change? (8:24)
❇ After the storm was calmed, what did Jesus ask the disciples? (8:25)
■ What emotions overwhelmed the disciples? (8:25)
❇ What did the disciples realize about Jesus' identity? (8:25)
❇ What did the disciples see of Jesus' manner? (8:25)

GET IT
✻ What is faith?
■ If you had been in the boat that day, would you have been more like Jesus or like the disciples? Why?
✻ Would you have been reassured or angered by Jesus' calmness?
■ If Jesus asked you, "Where is your faith?" how would you respond?
✻ Why do you suppose the disciples asked each other who Jesus was, rather than asking Jesus?
✻ How should the knowledge of Jesus' supreme authority affect our faith?

APPLY IT
✻ What can you do today to build up your faith in Jesus for the next time you feel overwhelmed?
■ In what way can you show your assurance in God's ability to rescue His people?

Luke 8:26-39

The Healing of a Demon-possessed Man

TOPICS
Demons, Evil, Grace, Miracles, New Life, Thankfulness

OPEN IT
■ What situations or people do you consider hopeless?
✻ What people do others try to avoid when they encounter them on the street?

EXPLORE IT
✻ Where did Jesus and His disciples go? By what means? (8:26)
✻ What was the first thing to greet Jesus and His disciples upon their arrival? (8:27)
■ What had the demon-possessed man's life been like until he met Jesus? (8:27, 29)
■ How did the demon-possessed man react to Jesus? (8:28)
✻ Of what was the man afraid? (8:28)
✻ Why was the man called Legion? (8:30)
✻ What did the demons choose over life in the Abyss? (8:31-32)
✻ What resulted from the demons' choice? (8:33)
✻ How did those tending the pigs react to what happened? (8:34)
✻ Who else heard what happened, and what did they find at the region of the Gerasenes? (8:35)
■ What emotion gripped all but the man who had been possessed by demons? (8:34-37)
✻ What did the man want to do? (8:38)
✻ Why did Jesus say no to the man's request to go with Him? (8:38-39)
✻ What was the result of the man's obedience? (8:39)

GET IT
■ If you had been one of the disciples, what would have been your first reaction to the demon-possessed man?
✻ What does this story say about Jesus' concern for an individual's life?
✻ To what extent do you believe demons are active today?
✻ Why do the words "fear" and "afraid" come up so much?
■ In what ways do people today ask Jesus to leave them alone?
✻ What would have happened if Jesus had given in to the man's request to go with Him?
✻ What situations or forces have at times left you not in your right mind?

APPLY IT
■ What can you do this week to be more aware of Jesus' ability to help you with your most serious problems?
✻ Whom can you tell today how much God has done for you?

Luke 8:40-56

A Dead Girl and a Sick Woman

TOPICS
Beliefs, Death, Fear, Healing, Kindness, Miracles, New Life, Power, Resurrection

OPEN IT
✻ What do your coworkers think about miraculous healing?
✻ How much have television evangelists and disreputable faith healers harmed people's opinions of Jesus?
■ How far would you go to bring physical healing to someone you love?

EXPLORE IT
✻ What kind of reception did Jesus get when He returned? (8:40)
✻ Who was Jairus? (8:41-42)
■ What did Jairus want Jesus to do? (8:41-42)
✻ What role do crowds play in this passage? (8:40, 42, 45, 47, 52-53)
■ What do we know about the sick woman? (8:43-44)
✻ How did Jesus know that someone had been healed? (8:45-46)
✻ What was the woman's reaction to being discovered? (8:47)
✻ To what did Jesus attribute the woman's healing? (8:48)
✻ What happened to Jairus's daughter while Jesus was traveling? (8:49)
■ What commands did Jesus give before the girl was given new life? (8:50, 52, 54)
✻ How did Luke describe the sequence of events inside Jairus's house? (8:53-56)
✻ What did Jesus tell the girl's parents? (8:55-56)

GET IT
✻ What is similar about the two healings?
✻ What is different about the two healings?
■ What emotional effect can long-term pain have on someone?
✻ How must Jesus' words have sounded to the woman?
✻ In what ways do you imagine the woman's life changed from that day on?
✻ How did Jesus' manner and words stand in sharp contrast to the mood outside and inside Jairus's house?
■ How did Jesus show His care for the whole person in both situations?
✻ What can we learn from the boldness of both the woman and Jairus?

APPLY IT
■ For what people with long-term pain or other physical problems can you start to pray regularly?
❊ How should you be bold in the way you approach God?

Luke 9:1-9
Jesus Sends Out the Twelve

TOPICS
Discipline, Evangelism, Gospel, Healing, Mission, Obedience, Poor

OPEN IT
❊ How much preparation and packing do you usually do before a trip?
■ How willing are most people to "pull up stakes" and move to unfamiliar surroundings?
❊ How much are the people you know willing to believe in miracles?

EXPLORE IT
■ What happened after Jesus had called the twelve disciples together? (9:1-2)
❊ What authority was granted to the Twelve? (9:1-2)
■ How did Jesus instruct the Twelve to proceed? (9:3-5)
❊ What were the disciples to do if a town would not welcome them? (9:6)
■ What was the disciples' response to Jesus' instructions? (9:6)
❊ Who became aware of Jesus and the Twelve? (9:7)
❊ What did Herod think of Jesus' healing and preaching? (9:7)
❊ What were the various explanations of Jesus? (9:7-8)
❊ What resurrection images did Luke mention? (9:7-8)
❊ What basic question did Herod have about Jesus? (9:9)
❊ What did Herod want to do? Why? (9:9)

GET IT
❊ How foreign to your thinking do Jesus' instructions to the Twelve seem?
❊ How strange might Jesus' instructions have seemed to the Twelve?
■ Why do you suppose Jesus sent the Twelve out so with so few provisions?
■ What sort of callings do we receive from God?
❊ Who is preaching and healing under Jesus' authority in our day?
❊ What do people in power usually think of Jesus? Why?
❊ What callings from God are you aware of in your life?

APPLY IT
■ How can you prepare yourself this week for the future God has in mind for you?
❊ How can you better take advantage of God's power and authority in your life?

Luke 9:10-17
Jesus Feeds the Five Thousand

TOPICS
Faith, Healing, Kingdom of God/Heaven, Miracles, Responsibility

OPEN IT
❊ In what situations do you really want to be alone?
■ How do people react when given an overwhelming responsibility?

EXPLORE IT
❊ From where had the apostles returned? (9:10)
❊ What was the first thing the disciples did? (9:10)
❊ What did Jesus decide to do after the apostles had returned? (9:10)
❊ How did Jesus' plans change? (9:11)
■ What did the apostles want to do with the crowd? (9:12)
❊ What did Jesus propose to do with the crowd? (9:13)
■ What were the choices for feeding the crowds? (9:13)
❊ In what order of events did Jesus go about feeding the people? (9:16)
❊ How did the disciples help Jesus? (9:16)
■ What were the results Jesus' miracle? (9:17)

GET IT
■ If you had been an apostle, how would you have reacted to the crowd's overwhelming need?
❊ What is surprising (and not surprising) to you about Jesus' response to the people's hunger?
❊ What can we learn about Jesus' rapport with people from this account?
❊ What can we learn about the abundance of God's provision from this passage?
❊ What can we assume about the apostles' attitudes at the end of the story?
■ With what projects can your church or community group be involved to help people in need?

APPLY IT
■ What people in need living in your community can you take steps to help this month?
❊ What can you do to increase your faith in God's miraculous powers?

Luke 9:18-27
Peter's Confession of Christ

TOPICS
Beliefs, Confession, Kingdom of God/Heaven, Prophecy, Sacrifice, Shame, Suffering, Witnessing

OPEN IT
❊ What are some of the roles you fill at home, work, and in your community?
■ When have you made a sacrifice for the sake of someone else?
❊ In what do you take the most pride? Why?

EXPLORE IT
❊ What was Jesus doing when He was alone with His disciples? (9:18)
❊ What was Jesus' series of questions? (9:18, 20)
❊ Who did the crowd think Jesus was? (9:19)
❊ Who spoke up when Jesus brought up the question of His identity? (9:20)
❊ What was Jesus' reaction to the statement by Peter? (9:21)
❊ What kind of future did Jesus predict for Himself? (9:22)
❊ How often is our allegiance to Christ demanded? (9:23)
■ What are the conditions for discipleship with Jesus? (9:23)
■ What kind of commitment does discipleship require? (9:24-25)
❊ What did Jesus say would happen to anyone who is ashamed of Him and His words? (9:26)
■ With what prediction did Jesus conclude His admonition to the disciples? (9:27)

GET IT
❊ How would you answer Jesus today if He asked, "Who do crowds say I am?"
❊ In what situations would you be uncomfortable stating plainly that Jesus is the Christ of God?
❊ Why do you suppose that Jesus strictly warned His disciples not to tell anyone about His heavenly identity?
❊ In what ways do we behave as if we are not to tell anybody who Jesus is?
■ What celebrities recently seem to have "gained the whole world" yet lost or forfeited their very selves?
■ In what ways can you lose your life for Jesus?
❊ What might it feel like to have the Son of Man ashamed of us?

APPLY IT
❊ What situations this week might call for you to speak out about Jesus' identity?
❊ How can you pray this week to help you talk about Jesus with others?
■ With whom can you pray this week for the purpose of denying yourself and following Jesus?

Luke 9:28-36
The Transfiguration

TOPICS
Faith, Fear, Glory, Listening, Prayer, Prophecy

OPEN IT
■ What special events in your life do wish could have lasted forever?
❊ When you're deeply involved in something, what does it take to get you to listen to something else?

EXPLORE IT
❊ Who went with Jesus up a mountain? (9:28)
❊ Why did Jesus and His disciples go up the mountain? (9:28)
■ What happened to Jesus while He was praying? (9:29)
❊ Who suddenly appeared, and what did they do? (9:30-31)
❊ How did Moses and Elijah describe Jesus' departure? (9:31)
❊ How were Peter, John, and James feeling at this point? (9:32)
❊ What did Peter and his companions see? (9:32)
■ How did Peter react to the amazing scene? (9:33)
❊ Why were the disciples suddenly afraid? (9:34)
❊ What did the voice from the cloud say about Jesus? (9:35)
❊ What happened to Moses and Elijah? (9:36)
■ How did the disciples handle their experience? (9:36)

GET IT
❊ If you had been with Peter, James, and John, how might you have felt?
❊ What does "bring to fulfillment" (9:31) imply about Jesus' departure?
■ In describing Peter's suggestion about the shelters, why did Luke say, "He did not know what he was saying"?
❊ What would have happened if it were possible to stay on the mountain with Moses and Elijah?
❊ What does the timing of the voice from the cloud say to you?
❊ What might God want to say to us about Jesus today?
■ Why do you think the disciples told no one what they had seen that day?

APPLY IT
❊ What book or passage of the Bible could you read to help you better understand your relationship to Jesus?
❊ What can you do in your private devotions to help you listen to God's Son?
■ With what person or people could you share what you have learned from this passage?

Luke 9:37-45
The Healing of a Boy With an Evil Spirit

TOPICS
Believe, Children, Demons, Evil, Fear, Healing, Listening, Miracles, Parents, Unbelievers

OPEN IT
❊ What is it like to feel that you're not in control of your body?
❊ What do people today think about demon possession?
■ What are typical first reactions to things we don't understand?

EXPLORE IT
❊ What did Jesus and His disciples encounter when they came down from the mountain? (9:37)
❊ Why did the man ask Jesus to look at his son? (9:38)
❊ What had been happening to the boy? (9:39)
■ What had the father tried to no avail? (9:40)
■ To what did Jesus attribute the disciples' failure to heal the boy? (9:41)
❊ What happened to the boy while he was being brought to Jesus? (9:42)
❊ What three things did Jesus do? (9:42)
❊ What was the crowd's reactions to what they saw? (9:43)
❊ How did Jesus respond to the people's admiration? (9:43-44)

❊ What did Jesus predict about Himself? (9:44)
■ How much did the disciples understand of what Jesus told them? (9:45)
❊ What was the disciples' overriding emotion at the time? (9:45)

GET IT
❊ What must life have been like for the father and son Jesus met?
■ What is the connection in this story between belief and healing?
❊ What is the connection between belief and healing in our lives today?
❊ How would you contrast the people's belief in God's working through the disciples and through Jesus?
❊ What similarities to this story do you see in the way people approach belief today?
❊ Why would Jesus speak to His disciples about being betrayed instead of preaching to the crowd about the miracle they had just seen?
■ What could have kept understanding hidden from the disciples?
❊ What clouds our understanding of Jesus?
❊ What can we do when we are confused or uncertain about God?

APPLY IT
❊ What area of unbelief do you want to talk with God about this week?
■ For those aspects of Jesus that you still don't understand, what is one step you can take to learn more?

Luke 9:46-50
Who Will Be the Greatest?

TOPICS
Ambition, Arguments, Children, Demons, Envy, Favoritism, Greatness, Humility, Self-righteousness, Teamwork

OPEN IT
■ What does greatness mean to you?
❊ What do you like and dislike most about children?

EXPLORE IT
❊ How did an argument start among the disciples? (9:46)
■ About what did the disciples argue? (9:46)
❊ How did Jesus find out what was happening? (9:47)
■ What did Jesus use to reply to the disciples' ambition? (9:47)
❊ What connections between the child and God did Jesus make? (9:48)
■ What reason did Jesus give for connecting children with God? (9:48)
❊ How did John change the subject? (9:49)
❊ Why had the disciples tried to stop the man? (9:49)
❊ What did Jesus think of the disciples' gallantry? (9:50)
❊ What reason did Jesus give for not stopping the man who was driving out demons? (9:50)

GET IT
■ What effect must the example of a child have had on the disciples?
❊ What opportunities do we have to welcome children (and thereby welcome Jesus and God the Father)?
■ What different ambitions and motivations can we see in churches and other religious organizations today?
❊ What reaction was John probably expecting to his efforts to stop the man from driving out demons?
❊ What kind of teamwork might Jesus be looking for today among His followers?
❊ How can we be more cooperative with each other?

APPLY IT
■ What is one step you can take to subject your ambitions to the ambitions of Jesus?
❊ How can you foster a spirit of teamwork in your church or religious group in the weeks ahead?

Luke 9:51-56
Samaritan Opposition

TOPICS
Goals, Opposition, Rejection

OPEN IT
❊ What kinds of things happen when a big project, such as a political campaign or a special event, nears its completion?
❊ What are some examples of prejudice that you have seen?
■ When something or someone for whom you've worked very hard is rejected, how do you typically react?

EXPLORE IT
❊ What significant event was looming on the horizon? (9:51)
❊ Where was Jesus going? (9:51)
❊ In what manner did Jesus set out for His journey? (9:51)
❊ What preparations did Jesus make? Why? (9:51-52)
❊ What were the messengers supposed to do? (9:52)
■ Why didn't the Samaritans welcome Jesus? (9:53)
❊ Where did Jesus and His disciples go? Why? (9:53-56)
❊ What did James and John think of Samaritan hospitality? (9:54)
■ What did James and John want to bring down on the Samaritans? Why? (9:54)
■ What did Jesus think of His disciples' suggestion? (9:55)
❊ What did Jesus do about the Samaritans' rejection? (9:56)

GET IT
❊ What possible connection might there have been between welcoming Jesus and His going to Jerusalem?
■ How do you handle it when someone rejects you because of prejudice or for petty reasons?
■ If you had been a disciple, what would you have suggested been done to the villagers?
❊ When have you resolutely faced up to a situation that you knew was going to be difficult or even dangerous?
❊ In what ways do we get sidetracked by retaliation?

APPLY IT
❊ What steps can you take over the next few days to keep your God-inspired goals in mind?
■ What do you want to remember the next time you feel a desire to retaliate or get even?

Luke 9:57-62

The Cost of Following Jesus

TOPICS

Devotion, Faithfulness, Follow, Home, Kingdom of God/Heaven, Loyalty, Relationships

OPEN IT

❊ About what sorts of things do you get enthusiastic?
■ When working on a group project, what excuses do people use to postpone or avoid fulfilling their obligations?

EXPLORE IT

❊ Where were Jesus and His disciples when this story began? (9:57)
❊ To what lengths did the first man say he would follow Jesus? (9:57)
❊ What was Jesus' reply to the first man's statement of devotion? (9:58)
❊ In what way were foxes and birds of the air more secure than Jesus? (9:58)
■ What did the second man want to do before following Jesus? (9:59)
❊ What was the second man to do instead of burying his father? (9:60)
❊ How did Jesus respond to the obligations of family life? (9:60, 62)
■ What did the third person want to do before following Jesus? (9:61)
■ Who is not fit for the kingdom of God? (9:62)
❊ What imagery did Jesus evoke to examine the person's loyalties? (9:62)

GET IT

■ Given Jesus' replies to the three would-be followers, what do you suppose their conflicting loyalties were?
❊ What did Jesus want the three men to do?
❊ With which of these men do you most easily identify?
❊ Why did Jesus encourage the one man to place such little value on family responsibilities?
❊ What loyalties conflict with our allegiance to God?
■ From this account, how would you summarize the costs of following Jesus?
❊ What are the costs of following Jesus?
❊ Why are there costs in following Jesus?

APPLY IT

■ What would help you this week to remember your loyalty to Christ?
❊ With whom in your circle of family or friends can you reaffirm your desire to follow Jesus?

Luke 10:1-24

Jesus Sends Out the Seventy-two

TOPICS

Children, Demons, Evangelism, Joy, Kingdom of God/Heaven, Mission

OPEN IT

❊ How would you treat the representatives of a famous person?
■ What difficult project have you worked on recently?
❊ How do you feel when you complete a difficult task?

EXPLORE IT

❊ In what manner were the seventy-two followers sent out? (10:1)
❊ According to Jesus, why were His followers to pray for more workers? (10:2)
❊ To what did Jesus liken His followers? (10:3)
❊ What instructions did Jesus give the seventy-two concerning their departure? (10:4)
■ What were Jesus' followers to do about accommodations? (10:5-8)
❊ What were the seventy-two sent out to do? (10:9)
■ To what could unbelieving towns look forward? (10:10-15)
❊ What did the disciples report upon their return? (10:17)
■ What authority did Jesus give His disciples? (10:18-19)
❊ Why were the seventy-two to rejoice? (10:20)
❊ What was the Father's pleasure? (10:21-22)
❊ Who was envious of the disciples? Why? (10:23-24)

GET IT

❊ What was life like for the seventy-two disciples?
❊ Which of the jobs done by the seventy-two do we see in action today?
■ What instructions has Jesus given you?
■ When have you been rejected as a representative of Christ?
❊ What are the trappings of being "wise and learned"?
❊ What are the benefits of being like "little children"?
❊ What can we see and hear about God that the disciples, prophets, and kings could not?

APPLY IT

❊ This week, how can you observe children to help you understand more of God's revelation?
■ When can you set aside time to pray regularly to learn your place among those whom God has sent out?
❊ Whom else can you encourage in your church or fellowship group to join you in prayer and service?

Luke 10:25-37

The Parable of the Good Samaritan

TOPICS

Eternal Life, Kindness, Law, Love, Mercy, Neighbor, Testing

OPEN IT

❊ What are the greatest inconveniences in your life?
■ When has someone gone out of his or her way to help you?
❊ What do you think motivates most people to do good?

EXPLORE IT

❊ What did the legal expert ask Jesus? (10:25)
❊ Why did the legal expert ask a question about eternal life? (10:25)

❊ How did Jesus turn the question back on the legal expert? (10:26)
❊ How did the legal expert summarize the demands of the Law? (10:27)
❊ What did the expert ask about loving one's neighbor? (10:29)
❊ What did the legal expert want to do? (10:29)
❊ How did Jesus reply to the question, "Who is my neighbor"? (10:30-35)
■ What did the priest and the Levite do to help the man who was robbed and beaten? (10:31-32)
■ What was the Samaritan's response to what he saw? (10:33-35)
❊ Why did the Samaritan help the beaten man? (10:33)
❊ What relationship did Jesus use to characterize the Samaritan's behavior? (10:36)
■ How did the legal expert define the neighbor in the parable? (10:37)
❊ What did Jesus command the expert to do in response to the parable? (10:37)

GET IT
❊ What different motivations do people have for asking questions about God and of God?
❊ How effective is this parable in communicating love for one's neighbor?
■ What natural inclinations make it easier for you to act like the priest and the Levite than like the Samaritan?
■ How practical was the Samaritan's approach to the man in need?
❊ How does it feel when someone has mercy on you?
❊ In what ways can we as individuals and as groups of Christians be more like the Samaritan?

APPLY IT
■ What step can you take to help meet someone else's physical needs?
❊ What people who have helped you in times of need do you want to thank this week?

Luke 10:38-42
At the Home of Martha and Mary

TOPICS
Choices, Family, Hospitality, Jealousy, Listening, Preparation

OPEN IT
■ What is your home like shortly before guests arrive?
❊ What do you enjoy about formal or informal dinners? Why?
❊ What is involved in clean-up at your house?

EXPLORE IT
❊ What did Martha do for Jesus and His disciples? (10:38)
❊ Who was Mary? (10:39)
❊ Where was Mary while Jesus was talking? (10:39)
■ What did Mary do while Martha attended to household preparations? (10:39-40)
❊ How much could Martha concentrate on Jesus' words while preparing for her guests? (10:40)
❊ Of what did Martha accuse Jesus? (10:40)
■ Of what did Martha accuse her sister? (10:40)
❊ What did Martha want Jesus to do? (10:40)
❊ How did Jesus try to calm down Martha? (10:41)
■ What did Jesus think of the sisters' choices? (10:41-42)

GET IT
❊ How would you describe the "Marys" (male and female) that you know?
❊ To what extent do you resemble the hurried, frantic personality of Martha?
■ If you had been Martha in this situation, how would you have reacted to your sister's choice?
❊ What did Jesus mean when He said that "only one thing is needed"?
■ Why did Jesus favor Mary's choice?
❊ In what way do you identify with Mary's choice in your relationship to Jesus?

APPLY IT
❊ What events or opportunities are coming up in which you can focus on being a student of Christ?
■ What steps can you take this week to help a friend with domestic tasks so that he or she can have more time to pray or read the Bible?

Luke 11:1-13
Jesus' Teaching on Prayer

TOPICS
Children, Friendship, Generosity, Holy Spirit, Needs, Persistence, Prayer

OPEN IT
❊ What are children like when they want a certain toy?
■ How do you react to someone's relentless requests for something?

EXPLORE IT
❊ What was Jesus doing when one of His disciples approached Him? (11:1)
■ What was the disciple's request? (11:1)
❊ Who had taught his disciples to pray? (11:1)
❊ What topics did Jesus' prayer cover? (11:2-4)
❊ With what is God's forgiveness of us linked? (11:4)
■ Why did the person in need go to the friend at midnight? (11:5-8)
❊ Whom does the friend in the house represent? (11:5-8)
■ Why did the friend eventually grant the man's request? (11:8)
❊ What cause-and-effect connection did Jesus use to follow up on the parable? (11:9-10)
❊ How do most parents respond to their children's requests? (11:11-12)
❊ Why do parents grant their children's requests? (11:13)
❊ How is God the Father like and unlike human fathers? (11:13)
❊ What does God give to us? (11:13)

GET IT
❊ Why did the disciples need to be taught how to pray?
❊ Why do we need to learn how to pray?
❊ What opinions have you heard on how God responds to our prayers?

■ How can we ask, seek, and knock when we approach our heavenly Father?
■ What kinds of things do we—individually and collectively—usually ask for?
❇ How might this passage change your expectations of prayer?

APPLY IT
■ Whom can you call today or tomorrow and offer to pray on his or her behalf?
❇ When can you plan for an extended period of prayer in the next few months?

Luke 11:14-28
Jesus and Beelzebub

TOPICS
Blessing, Demons, Evil, Family, Judging Others, Kingdom of God/Heaven, Satan, Testing

OPEN IT
❇ In what groups or situations have you seen a great deal of chaos?
■ How do you feel when good works are attributed to bad motives?

EXPLORE IT
❇ What sort of demon did Jesus drive out? (11:14)
■ By whose power did some think Jesus could drive out demons? (11:15)
❇ What did some people say about Jesus' work? (11:16)
■ How did Jesus react to criticism? (11:17-20)
❇ How was the question of Jesus' authority turned back on those who questioned Him? (11:19-20)
❇ In Jesus' illustration, what does an attacker take in addition to a person's possessions? (11:21-22)
■ If a person is not with Jesus, what is his status? (11:23)
❇ Where does an evil spirit go when it is exorcised from a person? (11:24)
❇ What happens to a person if an evil spirit is cast out of him or her and replaced with nothing? (11:25-26)
❇ What is the final condition of the person who does not replace evil with good? (11:26)
❇ What did a woman from the crowd call out? (11:27)
❇ Who is blessed, according to one of the people in the crowd? (11:27)
❇ To whom was the woman in the crowd referring? (11:27)
❇ Who is blessed, according to Jesus? (11:28)

GET IT
❇ How do we see the various attitudes toward Jesus and His followers demonstrated today?
■ Why was it impossible for Jesus to be working under Satan's power?
❇ What might Jesus think of those who don't let their religion affect their lives beyond "religious activities"?
■ When evil leaves our lives, what must replace it?
❇ How surprising to you is Jesus' reply to the woman in the crowd?
❇ How might one have expected Jesus to answer the woman's blessing?
❇ What does it mean to be blessed?

APPLY IT
■ What action can you take today to fill a void in your life with something good and holy?
❇ What can you do this week to improve your responsiveness to the Word of God?

Luke 11:29-32
The Sign of Jonah

TOPICS
Comparisons, Example, Judgment, Miracles, Repentance, Wisdom

OPEN IT
■ What do you think characterizes your generation?
❇ What do people mean by the phrase, "It's a sign of the times"?

EXPLORE IT
❇ What had happened to Jesus' following as this story opens? (11:29)
■ What did Jesus think of the generation in which He lived? (11:29)
■ What did Jesus' generation want? (11:30)
❇ Who was to be a sign to Jesus' generation? (11:30)
❇ With what group of people was Jesus' generation compared? (11:30)
■ What made the Queen of the South fit for judging the people of Jesus' generation? (11:31)
❇ How did Jesus use Solomon's reputation to describe Himself? (11:31)
❇ Who was to condemn Jesus' generation? (11:31-32)
❇ What had the men of Nineveh done? (11:32)
❇ How did Jesus use Jonah's reputation to describe Himself? (11:32)

GET IT
❇ How do you think Jesus was feeling at this point?
❇ Why did Jesus use the examples of the Queen of the South and the Ninevites?
❇ For what signs from God have you looked?
■ What would Jesus say about your diligence in seeking wisdom and willingness to repent?
■ In what ways would Jesus consider your generation a wicked one?
❇ What does God want us to do about living in a "wicked generation"?

APPLY IT
■ What can you do to be sensitive to the signs God has already given you in the Bible?
❇ Whom can you ask to join you this week in praying for wisdom and repentance?

Luke 11:33-36
The Lamp of the Body

TOPICS
Body, Darkness, Light, Morality, Witnessing

OPEN IT
❇ How do you react to a power failure, especially at night?
❇ How does your favorite lamp in your home make you feel?
■ How good or bad is your eyesight?

EXPLORE IT
❇ What is not done with a lamp? (11:33)
❇ What is done with a lamp? (11:33)
❇ Who benefits from the proper handling of a lamp? (11:33)
❇ To what did Jesus compare the human eye? (11:34)
❇ What is the "lamp of your body"? (11:34)
■ What happens when the eyes are good? (11:34)
■ What happens when the eyes are bad? (11:34)
❇ What did Jesus counsel His listeners to do? (11:35)
■ What is the result of having the whole body full of light? (11:36)
❇ To what did Jesus compare having a whole body full of light? (11:36)

GET IT
❇ What kinds of lamps are there, and what are their purposes?
■ Why did Jesus choose the illustration of light and darkness?
❇ What does it feel like to be "full of light"?
❇ What does it feel like to be "full of darkness"?
■ What kinds of things can you do to make your life a lamp to yourself and to others?
❇ What things, people, or situations tend to fill you with darkness?

APPLY IT
■ To whom can you be a lamp this week, sharing what Jesus means to you? How?
❇ What is one step you need to take to keep old habits or tempting situations from darkening your life?

Luke 11:37-54
Six Woes

TOPICS
Criticism, Enemies, Hardheartedness, Hypocrisy, Judging Others, Justice, Law, Opposition, Prophecy

OPEN IT
■ How important are appearances in our culture?
❇ In what way do many people show that they care more about how they look to others than about what they're really like inside?

EXPLORE IT
❇ What did the Pharisee do when Jesus finished speaking? (11:37)
■ What surprised Jesus' host? (11:38)
■ According to Jesus, what did the Pharisee emphasize and overlook? (11:39-40)
❇ How could the Pharisees have made everything clean for themselves? (11:41)
■ What did the Pharisees neglect in favor of tithing herbs? (11:42)
❇ Why did Jesus say "woe" six times? (11:42-52)
❇ Who else besides the Pharisees was offended by Jesus' strong words? (11:45)
❇ What did the Pharisees' forefathers do? (11:47)
❇ Why were Jesus' listeners held responsible for the prophets' fates? (11:48-51)
❇ To what did Jesus liken knowledge? (11:52)
❇ What did the Pharisees and teachers of the law do when Jesus left? (11:53)
❇ What motivated the Pharisees and teachers of the law to ask questions? (11:54)

GET IT
❇ How would you describe the Pharisees?
■ Who today imitates the Pharisees' attitudes and actions?
❇ Who today tries to change other people on the outside without helping them change on the inside?
❇ In what ways do Christians try to change the way people act outwardly rather than how they respond to God?
❇ What trade-offs do we make in emphasizing appearance over substance?
❇ Of what "woes" might Jesus warn us?
❇ In what way do we hinder others from coming to God?
■ How can we be sure that we are emphasizing justice and the love of God instead of our own lists of things others ought to do?
❇ Why was it fair for Jesus to condemn His contemporaries for their forefathers' sins?
❇ To whom else might Jesus want you to give "the key of knowledge"?
❇ How can we be sure that we are asking questions to gain knowledge rather than to catch someone in his or her words?

APPLY IT
❇ What person can you ask to spend some time this week helping you weed out hypocrisy?
■ Whom can you encourage to learn from God's Word this week? How?

Luke 12:1-12
Warnings and Encouragements

TOPICS
Authority, Blasphemy, Caring, Darkness, Encouragement, Holy Spirit, Hypocrisy, Light

OPEN IT
■ What individuals or groups are most feared in our society?
❇ In what situations have you had to stand before someone with considerable authority over you?

EXPLORE IT
❊ What was the crowd like? (12:1)
❊ Against what did Jesus warn His disciples? (12:1)
❊ What contrasts did Jesus use to prepare the disciples for the future? (12:2-3)
■ What did Jesus say His disciples should and should not fear? (12:4-5)
❊ What proofs of God's care did Jesus offer to His disciples? (12:6-7)
■ How was the disciples' loyalty to Jesus linked to Jesus' loyalty to them? (12:8-9)
❊ What was to happen to those who speak against the Son of Man? (12:10)
❊ What sin could not be forgiven? (12:10)
■ How much were the disciples to prepare for their encounters with religious and political authorities? (12:11)
❊ How were the disciples to know what to say? (12:12)

GET IT
❊ How might Jesus' words about the troubles to come have made His disciples feel?
■ How does the possibility of persecution make you feel?
❊ What does the imagery about the sparrows and hairs say to us?
❊ Why are we important to God?
■ What situations tempt people not to acknowledge Jesus before others?
❊ What is it about blaspheming against the Holy Spirit that makes it unforgivable?
❊ Before what sorts of religious and political authorities are believers brought today?
❊ Of what benefit is it to rehearse what you will say in difficult circumstances?

APPLY IT
❊ How can you remind yourself of your importance to God every day this week?
❊ How can you pray for those who suffer for their relationship with God?
■ What step can you take this week to prepare for persecution?

Luke 12:13-21
The Parable of the Rich Fool

TOPICS
Abundance, Complacency, Foolishness, Judgment, Possessions, Preparation

OPEN IT
❊ Over what did you and your siblings fight when you were growing up?
■ How did your family regard possessions while you were growing up?
❊ What measures of a person does our society value?

EXPLORE IT
❊ What did the person in the crowd want Jesus to do? (12:13)
■ Against what did Jesus warn the crowd? Why? (12:13-15)
❊ How did Jesus respond to the request from the crowd? (12:14)
❊ From what did Jesus distinguish a person's life? (12:15)
❊ What teaching device did Jesus use? (12:16)
❊ What was the rich man's dilemma in the parable? (12:16-17)
❊ What did the man decide to do about his bumper crop? (12:18)
■ How did the rich man view his possessions and good fortune? (12:19)
❊ How did God intervene in the rich man's life? (12:20)
■ What would become of the man's abundance? (12:20)
❊ What kinds of abundance did Jesus mention? (12:21)
❊ To whom did Jesus apply His teaching about greed? (12:21)

GET IT
❊ What signs of greed can show up in a person's life?
❊ On what basis would you like your life to be judged?
❊ With what parts of the parable can you identify?
■ What parts of the parable make you uncomfortable?
❊ In what ways do we act as if we will live for many, many years?
❊ Why is it difficult for us to accept the fact that our life and things are temporary?
■ How is it possible to be rich toward God?

APPLY IT
■ What is one step you can take this week to become less dependent on your possessions?
❊ With which of your possessions do you want to be more generous? How can you?

Luke 12:22-34
Do Not Worry

TOPICS
Body, Fear, Kingdom of God/Heaven, Possessions, Priorities, Worry

OPEN IT
■ About what do people you know tend to worry?
❊ What do most people want for their children?

EXPLORE IT
❊ Why did Jesus start talking about worry? (12:22)
■ About what are we not to worry? (12:22)
❊ What is more important than food or clothes? (12:23)
■ What are we to learn from birds? (12:24)
■ What does worrying accomplish? (12:25-26)
❊ What do flowers teach us? (12:27-28)
❊ What does worry about clothes indicate about us? (12:28)
❊ On what basis are we not to worry? (12:30)
❊ What does God want us to seek? (12:31)
❊ How did Jesus continue with the Father-child analogy? (12:32)
❊ What are we to do with our possessions? (12:33)
❊ Where can treasure be found? (12:33)
❊ What goes with treasure in heaven? (12:34)

GET IT
❊ Why do we worry about food and clothes?
■ What situations bring out the worrier in you?
❊ What has worrying done for you?
❊ How do the images of God's provision for birds and nature affect you?
■ When have you seen the truth that God knows your needs and meets them?
❊ How can a person seek God's kingdom?
❊ What is the connection between seeking God's kingdom and the Father giving us the kingdom?
❊ How can we store up treasure in heaven?
❊ How big is your treasure in heaven?

APPLY IT
■ When can you pray today to hand over your worries to God?
❊ What step can you take this week to share your earthly treasures with others?
❊ What can you do to encourage your church to help meet the needs of homeless people?

Luke 12:35-48
Watchfulness

TOPICS
Patience, Preparation, Second Coming, Waiting

OPEN IT
❊ What sort of preparations have you been involved in making?
■ What is it like to wait for someone without knowing when he or she is coming?

EXPLORE IT
❊ What did Jesus tell His disciples to do? (12:35)
❊ According to Jesus, what are the two traits of the one who is ready? (12:35)
■ What did the men in the story do when their master returned? (12:36)
❊ What happened to the servants who were watching properly? (12:37)
■ How long should the servants have been willing to wait? (12:38)
■ When do important things often happen? (12:39-40)
❊ What did Peter ask Jesus? (12:41)
❊ How did Jesus reply to Peter's question? (12:42)
❊ What distinguished the faithful and wise manager? (12:42-44)
❊ How did some servants handle responsibilities in their masters' absence? (12:45)
❊ What happened to the foolish servants? (12:46)
❊ What was to be the fate of the servants who knew what to do but wouldn't do it? (12:47)
❊ What happened to the servants who acted out of ignorance? (12:48)
❊ What is expected of those who have been given and entrusted with much? (12:48)

GET IT
❊ How are "watching" and "waiting" used throughout this passage?
❊ What does watchfulness involve?
❊ For what are we to be watchful?
❊ Why is watchfulness not a passive activity?
❊ What does this passage say about Jesus' return?
■ How should we act while waiting for Jesus to return?
❊ What do we learn of God's fairness here?
❊ What has God given us?
❊ What has God given you?
❊ How much have we, individually and collectively, been given and entrusted with?
❊ What responsibilities or duties may be demanded of us?
❊ How should we use what God has given us?
■ What can you do for God in your areas of responsibility?
❊ How can we use wisely what God gives each of us?

APPLY IT
❊ What is one area of need in your church or among other Christians that you can serve?
❊ How can you get ready for Christ's return?
■ What steps can you take toward fulfilling your God-given responsibilities this week?

Luke 12:49-53
Not Peace but Division

TOPICS
Children, Conflict, Disagreements, Divisions, Family, Peace, War

OPEN IT
❊ What in your view makes it hard for families to fit the image of perfect domestic harmony?
❊ What do families typically fight about?
■ What causes family members to turn against each other?

EXPLORE IT
■ What did Jesus come to bring? (12:49)
❊ For what did Jesus wish? (12:49)
❊ For what was Jesus waiting? (12:50)
❊ How did Jesus feel about the baptism He would undergo? (12:50)
❊ Until when would Jesus be distressed about His baptism? (12:50)
■ What, evidently, did most people think Jesus was bringing? (12:51)
❊ In what way did Jesus indicate that division would affect everyone until He returned? (12:51)
❊ What did Jesus bring? (12:51)
■ Where would the division that Jesus brings be noticed? (12:52-53)
❊ What relationships would suffer division because of Christ? (12:52-53)

GET IT
❊ Why did Jesus wish that the "fire . . . were already kindled"?
❊ What did Jesus mean by baptism?
■ In what way did Jesus bring division?

❊ How common is the view that Jesus came to bring peace on earth?
❊ How is division the opposite of peace?
❊ How would you describe a divided family?
❊ Over what issues are any of your relatives divided?
■ Over what issues should we be willing to divide?

APPLY IT
■ What can you do to prepare for clashes over your beliefs?
❊ From what other Christian can you draw encouragement and strength in standing for Jesus? How?

Luke 12:54-59
Interpreting the Times

TOPICS
Arguments, Hypocrisy, Interpretation, Judgment, Reconciliation

OPEN IT
■ What various interpretations have been offered to explain the dramatic world events of the last few years?
❊ How have you seen arguments get out of control?

EXPLORE IT
❊ To whom was Jesus talking? (12:54)
❊ What did a cloud in the west mean to Jesus' audience? (12:54)
❊ What did the south wind indicate to Jesus' audience? (12:55)
■ What name did Jesus call the crowd? (12:56)
■ What didn't the crowd know how to interpret? (12:56)
❊ About what was Jesus exasperated? (12:56)
■ What did Jesus want His audience to do? (12:57)
❊ Where did Jesus recommend the people patch up differences with others? (12:58)
❊ What could be the consequences if people did not settle their differences? (12:58-59)
❊ When would a person thrown in jail be able to get out? (12:59)

GET IT
■ What accounted for the crowd's inability to interpret the signs of Jesus' time?
❊ How does God communicate with us today?
❊ To what "signs" does God want us to pay attention?
■ When has God given you a sign that you should do something?
❊ When have you had a dispute with another person that had to be settled by a third party?
❊ Why does Jesus want us to judge for ourselves what is right?
❊ How is the "out of court" settlement better than a judge's decision?

APPLY IT
■ What spiritual discipline can you work on to help you listen to God's Word?
❊ What relationship can you work to reconcile this week?

Luke 13:1-9
Repent or Perish

TOPICS
Fruit, Repentance, Sacrifice, Suffering

OPEN IT
■ What connection do many people make between how bad they are and how much they suffer?
❊ When was a time you felt that God was letting you suffer because you had sinned?
❊ What have been some of your frustrating experiences with gardening?

EXPLORE IT
■ What did Jesus hear about a group of Galileans? (13:1)
■ What explanation for the tragedy did Jesus propose? (13:2)
❊ How did Jesus reply to His own question? (13:3)
❊ What was the story involving the tower of Siloam? (13:4)
■ What were Jesus' listeners to learn from the two stories? (13:3-5)
❊ In the parable, what did the man seek from his fig tree? (13:6)
❊ Where was the fig tree? (13:6)
❊ What did the man say to the person who took care of the vineyard? (13:7)
❊ Why did the man want the fig tree chopped down? (13:7)
❊ What did the vineyard tender suggest? (13:8-9)

GET IT
❊ What does it mean to "bear fruit"?
■ Why do we often assume that people suffer because they are uniquely bad?
❊ What people or groups of people do we sometimes blame for their suffering?
❊ What's wrong with saying that people suffer because of how sinful they are?
■ What can we do to keep from judging people by their circumstances?
❊ What did Jesus mean by His warning, "But unless you repent, you too will all perish"?
❊ Why did Jesus tell the fig tree parable after discussing the two tragic incidents?
❊ Whom do the fig tree, the man, and the vineyard tender represent?
❊ What second chances have you been given?
❊ What can we learn from this parable?
❊ What does God want us to do?

APPLY IT
❊ What godly characteristic do you want to focus your attention on this week? How?
■ How can you show acceptance to one or two people who have been falsely judged as unrighteous for their circumstances?
❊ What can you do to comfort, help, or encourage someone who is suffering this week?
❊ What step of repentance would communicate to God your gratitude for second chances?

Luke 13:10-17
A Crippled Woman Healed on the Sabbath

TOPICS
Demons, Healing, Hypocrisy, Judging Others, Miracles, Opposition, Praise, Satan

OPEN IT
❊ When has someone criticized you for doing something good?
■ What rules about Sunday have you heard?

EXPLORE IT
❊ When was Jesus teaching in one of the synagogues? (13:10)
■ Whom did Jesus see in the synagogue? (13:11)
❊ What did Jesus do when He saw the crippled woman? (13:12)
❊ What led to the crippled woman's healing? (13:12-13)
❊ How did the woman respond to what Jesus had done? (13:13)
■ Why was the synagogue ruler indignant? (13:14)
❊ What rule did the synagogue ruler announce to the crowd? (13:14)
❊ What did Jesus think of the religious leaders? (13:15)
■ What example did Jesus give to justify His healing of the woman? (13:15-16)
❊ What had caused the woman's malady? (13:16)
❊ How did different people react to what had happened? (13:17)

GET IT
■ How did the Jewish leader view the Sabbath?
❊ What must it have taken for the crippled woman to go to the synagogue?
❊ What do you think the crippled woman expected?
❊ What do you think Jesus' touch meant to the woman He healed?
■ What restrictions do we foolishly put on God's work?
❊ What good deeds do we sometimes restrict because of traditions or rules about Sunday?
❊ What opportunities to free others from physical or emotional pain do you know about?

APPLY IT
■ When can you evaluate your use of Sundays to make sure you allow for doing good?
❊ What self-imposed rule or tradition do you need to modify to allow for God's work?
❊ How can you help or comfort a person in pain this week?

Luke 13:18-21
The Parables of the Mustard Seed and the Yeast

TOPICS
Beliefs, Believe, Faith, Growth, Kingdom of God/Heaven

OPEN IT
■ What is it like to plant something and watch it grow?
❊ What happened the last time you goofed up following a recipe?

EXPLORE IT
❊ To what did Jesus liken the kingdom of God? (13:18-20)
■ How did the mustard seed start out? (13:19)
❊ Where was the mustard seed planted? (13:19)
■ What transformation did the mustard seed make? (13:19)
■ From what can we infer that the tree became a substantial plant? (13:19)
❊ What creatures came to live in the mustard tree's branches? (13:19)
❊ What contrast would Jesus' listeners have noticed in the first parable? (13:19)
❊ What did the woman add to the flour? (13:21)
❊ What did the woman do with the yeast? (13:21)
❊ What did the yeast do once added to the dough? (13:21)

GET IT
❊ What do a mustard seed and yeast have in common?
❊ What does the mustard seed represent?
❊ What does the yeast and dough represent?
■ What makes a mustard seed a good illustration of God's kingdom?
❊ What makes yeast a good illustration of God's kingdom?
❊ In what way does each Christian make a small contribution to God's kingdom?
■ What do these two parables tell us about God's kingdom?

APPLY IT
■ What contribution to God's kingdom can you make this week?
❊ What can you do in the next day or two to nurture your faith?

Luke 13:22-30
The Narrow Door

TOPICS
Believe, Faith, Kingdom of God/Heaven, Salvation, Teaching

OPEN IT
■ In what areas of life do you tend to procrastinate?
❊ How does it feel to miss a good opportunity?
❊ What is it like when an important person whom you know acts as if you are a stranger?

EXPLORE IT
❊ What was Jesus doing on His way to Jerusalem? (13:22)
❊ What did someone ask Jesus? (13:23)
■ According to Jesus, what is worth every effort to accomplish? (13:24)
■ What happens once the door is shut? (13:25)
❊ How will the owner of the house respond to those who want to go in after the door is shut? (13:25)
❊ How will those left outside try to appeal to the owner? (13:26)
■ How successful will attempts to enter the house be after the door is shut? (13:27)

❇ What will those who cannot enter hear? (13:28)
❇ What will those who cannot enter see? (13:28)
❇ What will take place in the kingdom of God? (13:29)
❇ How will the usual order be turned around? (13:30)

GET IT
❇ Why did someone ask how many would be saved?
■ What does the narrow door represent?
■ In what sense is the way to God narrow?
❇ How does a person "enter through the narrow door"?
❇ Who is the "owner of the house," and why will he refuse entry to people?
❇ When will it be too late for people to come to God?
❇ Why do people put off coming to God?
❇ When are you tempted to put off responding to God's commands?
❇ What do you think the feast in the kingdom of God will be like?
❇ What was Jesus saying about human relationships when He said that the first will be last?
❇ In what way is the first last and the last first?
❇ How would the owner of the house respond to you?
❇ Who is someone you want to introduce to Jesus before the door of opportunity closes?

APPLY IT
❇ What can you do this week toward introducing someone to Jesus? How?
■ What can you do to keep your beliefs and responses to God faithful to His Word?

Luke 13:31-35
Jesus' Sorrow for Jerusalem

TOPICS
Blessing, Caring, Compassion, Murder, Prophecy, Sorrow

OPEN IT
■ What sort of goals do you make on a well-planned day?
❇ What are some hopes or expectations you have for a close relative (such as a child, a spouse, or a sibling)?
❇ With what images of Jesus are most people familiar?

EXPLORE IT
■ Who came to Jesus? Why? (13:31)
■ How was Jesus in danger? (13:31)
❇ What did Jesus call Herod? (13:32)
❇ What message did Jesus have for Herod? (13:32)
■ What were Jesus' goals? (13:32-33)
❇ Why did Jesus have to go to Jerusalem? (13:33)
❇ What had Jerusalem done to deserve Jesus' condemnation? (13:34)
❇ To what did Jesus compare His concern for Jerusalem? (13:34)
❇ How did Jesus want to show His compassion for Jerusalem? (13:34)
❇ What sad words did Jesus have for Jerusalem? (13:35)
❇ When would Jerusalem see Jesus again? (13:35)

GET IT
■ What prompted the Pharisees to warn Jesus of Herod's intentions?
■ How was Jesus driven by His mission?
❇ What does this passage tell us about God?
❇ How does God show His care for us?
❇ What is meaningful to you about the image of God as a mother hen?
❇ What can we learn from Jesus' clear sense of Himself and His future?

APPLY IT
■ What step can you take this week to get a clearer sense of God's goals for you?
❇ What is one small way this week you can show compassion for your unbelieving friends?

Luke 14:1-14
Jesus at a Pharisee's House

TOPICS
Handicapped, Healing, Honor, Humility, Invitation, Judging Others, Law, Miracles, Poor, Resurrection, Righteousness, Self-righteousness

OPEN IT
■ When have you attended a very formal dinner?
❇ How does it feel to give a gift to someone who doesn't expect it?

EXPLORE IT
❇ Where did Jesus go to eat? (14:1)
❇ Who else was present at the meal besides Jesus? (14:2-3)
❇ Who asked the first question? (14:3)
❇ What was the Pharisees' and legal experts' reply to Jesus' question? (14:4)
❇ What happened to the man with dropsy? (14:4)
❇ Under what circumstance did the religious and legal experts allow work on the Sabbath? (14:5-6)
❇ Why did Jesus tell a parable? (14:6-7)
■ How did most people seat themselves at a wedding feast? (14:8)
❇ What did Jesus command? (14:10)
❇ How did Jesus communicate the value of humility? (14:11)
■ Whom was the host not to invite to a luncheon or dinner? (14:12)
❇ Whom did Jesus want people to invite to dinner? (14:13)
■ In what way would the host be repaid? (14:14)

GET IT
■ How was the meal at the Pharisee's a setup to trap Jesus?
❇ What caused the religious and legal experts to be speechless?
■ What does the wedding feast in the parable represent?
❇ How important is position and title in your circles? Why?
❇ What benefits could you realize by consistently making humble choices?
❇ Why is it a blessing to invite those who cannot repay?

APPLY IT

■ What steps can you take to lessen the importance of position, title, or other status symbols in your life?
❊ What is something special you can do this week for someone who is unable to repay you in kind?

Luke 14:15-24
The Parable of the Great Banquet

TOPICS

Anger, Excuses, Handicapped, Invitation, Kingdom of God/Heaven, Preparation, Serving

OPEN IT

■ What kinds of excuses do you most resent others using?
❊ How does it feel when you plan a big event and it is poorly attended?

EXPLORE IT

❊ What was one person prompted to say when Jesus spoke of repayment for kindness to others? (14:15)
❊ How did Jesus use to reply to the blessing He heard? (14:16)
❊ What did the man in the parable do? (14:16)
❊ How did the man let his guests know that the time for the banquet had arrived? (14:17)
❊ How did the guests respond to the invitation? (14:18)
■ What excuses did people make? (14:18-20)
■ How did the master find out about the excuses? (14:21)
❊ What was the master's reaction to the excuses people made? (14:21)
❊ Whom did the master invite to the banquet to replace the original invitees? (14:21)
❊ What happened when all the other people came to the master's banquet? (14:22)
❊ How did the master ensure that the banquet hall would be full? (14:23)
■ What was to become of the original guests? (14:24)

GET IT

❊ Why was the master justified in his anger at the guests who made excuses?
■ What was wrong with the guests' excuses?
❊ How did the character of the banquet change, given the "new" guest list?
■ How is the kingdom of God like this banquet?
❊ In what ways do you identify with the different guests?
❊ How does our responsibility to God correspond to the servant's role?

APPLY IT

❊ What is one way you can thank God this week for inviting you into His presence?
■ Whom can you invite to the kingdom banquet? How?

Luke 14:25-35
The Cost of Being a Disciple

TOPICS

Affections, Discipline, Family, Foundation, Listening, Risk

OPEN IT

■ How have you counted the costs recently before tackling a project at home or at work?
❊ How much do people take into account the potential reaction of others when planning something?
❊ In what way can a project fail before it starts?

EXPLORE IT

❊ Who was traveling with Jesus? (14:25)
❊ What natural affections did Jesus denounce in favor of following Him? (14:26)
❊ What does it take to be Jesus' disciple? (14:27)
❊ What should a person consider before building a tower? (14:28)
■ What consequences result from not counting the cost before building? (14:29-30)
■ How did a king determine his odds in a war? (14:31)
❊ What would be the logical step if a king discovered his manpower was insufficient? (14:32)
❊ When would a king send a delegation to another king? (14:32)
■ How did Jesus use the examples of building a tower and preparing for war? (14:33)
❊ What can be done with salt that has lost its saltiness? (14:34-35)
❊ What phrase did Jesus use to compel the crowd to consider His words? (14:35)

GET IT

❊ What does it mean to "hate" your parents, wife, children, siblings, and your own life?
■ How might the crowds have reacted to Jesus' terms of discipleship?
❊ How do most people react to Jesus' terms of discipleship?
❊ How possible do these conditions of discipleship seem to you now?
■ What costs do we need to count in responding to Jesus?
❊ What costs of following Jesus seem especially high to you?
❊ Why is it worth paying the price to follow Jesus?
❊ What are the properties of salt?
❊ How are we like salt?
❊ What is a person like who has lost his or her "saltiness"?

APPLY IT

■ What relationships or other loyalties do you need to pray about to strengthen your loyalty to Jesus?
❊ In what area of your life can you have a deliberate effect for Christ this week? How?

Luke 15:1-7
The Parable of the Lost Sheep

TOPICS

Hypocrisy, Reconciliation, Repentance, Restoration, Sin

OPEN IT

❊ What comes to mind when you hear the word, "sinner"?
■ As a child, when was a time you got lost from your family or a group?

EXPLORE IT
❇ Who had gathered to hear Jesus? (15:1)
❇ What were the Pharisees and teachers of the law doing? (15:2)
❇ Why were the Pharisees and teachers of the law grumbling? (15:2)
❇ What did Jesus do instead of directly rebuking the religious leaders? (15:3)
■ What does a conscientious shepherd do when one of the flock is lost? (15:4)
❇ How does a shepherd bring a lost sheep home? (15:5)
■ What happens when a shepherd returns to his home and flock after finding a lost sheep? (15:6)
■ How does heaven react when a sinner repents? (15:7)
❇ What causes God to rejoice most? (15:7)
❇ What kind of people do not need to repent? (15:7)

GET IT
❇ Why did the religious leaders miss the point of what Jesus' ministry was about?
■ Why did Jesus choose a parable about sheep to make His point?
❇ How might the one sheep have gotten lost?
■ In what ways do we go astray?
❇ How does the picture of "rejoicing in heaven" over repentance make you feel?
❇ In what situations are you most tempted to stray from God?

APPLY IT
■ What can you do this week to help a fellow believer who may be straying from God's ways?
❇ What practical step can you take to avoid tempting situations?

Luke 15:8-10
The Parable of the Lost Coin

TOPICS
Caring, Joy, Repentance, Sin

OPEN IT
❇ What things of value have you lost or misplaced recently?
■ What emotions do you feel when you find a valuable item that was lost?

EXPLORE IT
❇ In the parable, what did the woman possess? (15:8)
■ How do we know that the woman lost something valuable? (15:8)
❇ What steps did the woman take to find her lost coin? (15:8)
■ What did the woman do when she finally found the lost coin? (15:9)
❇ Whom did the woman call together to share the news? (15:9)
■ What emotions are obvious from the woman's statement to her friends? (15:9)
❇ What did the woman say to her friends? (15:9)
❇ Where is there rejoicing? (15:10)
❇ What causes angels to rejoice before God? (15:10)
❇ How many repenting sinners does it take to cause heavenly rejoicing? (15:10)

GET IT
■ What value did the woman place on each coin?
❇ Whom do the friends and neighbors represent?
❇ Why did the woman look so hard for the lost coin?
❇ What can we learn about God from this parable?
❇ What does God consider important?
❇ What is a "sinner who repents"?
❇ Why does God care so much about repentant sinners?
■ How is a repentant sinner like a found coin?
❇ In what ways does God's value of people differ from ours?

APPLY IT
❇ When can you thank God this week for His patience and persistence in restoring you to Him? How?
■ With whom do you want to share the news of God's persistent love? How can you?

Luke 15:11-32
The Parable of the Lost Son

TOPICS
Bitterness, Celebration, Compassion, Family, Forgiveness, Greed, Jealousy, Judging Others, Love, Salvation, Wealth

OPEN IT
■ In what way did you and your siblings compete with each other?
❇ How do you feel when other people get rewards greater than they deserve?
❇ How do you normally react when you feel you have been treated unfairly?

EXPLORE IT
❇ What did the younger son ask his father to do? (15:12-13)
❇ What did the younger son do after arriving in the distant country? (15:13)
❇ How did the younger son live once he was out on his own? (15:13-20)
❇ Why did the younger son have to hire himself out for work? (15:14-15)
❇ What made the younger son decide to return home? (15:17-19)
■ How did the father respond to the younger son's return home? (15:20)
■ Why did the father call for a celebration? (15:22-24)
❇ What was wrong with the older brother's reaction to his brother's return? (15:25-32)
❇ How did the older son respond to his brother's return and the celebration afterward? (15:28)
■ What complaints did the older brother bring to his father? (15:29-30)
❇ Why did the father want the older brother to be happy? (15:31-32)

GET IT
❇ What does the forgiving love of the father in this story represent?

❇ How have you been like the prodigal son in this story?
❇ When have you been like the older brother?
❇ From whom do we tend to withhold mercy?
❇ What people do you tend to think don't deserve God's mercy?
❇ How have you personally experienced the forgiving love of the Father?
■ What causes us to harbor resentment when mercy is shown to someone else?
❇ What should we do when a vile person wants to be forgiven?
❇ How should we react when a person comes to know Christ?
■ How can you show compassion for those who have not believed in Christ?
❇ What could you do to thank God for His amazing love for you?
❇ What responsibility do you have to your unbelieving friends?
❇ What does this parable reveal to you about the Lord's love?

APPLY IT
❇ How can you guard yourself against feeling resentment when God shows mercy to people you think don't deserve it?
❇ How can you show acceptance to someone who doesn't seem to deserve it? When?
■ To what "undeserving" person can you extend God's love and forgiveness this week? How?

Luke 16:1-15
The Parable of the Shrewd Manager

TOPICS
Devotion, Dishonesty, Eternal Life, God, Heart, Loyalty, Money, Resources, Serving, Wealth

OPEN IT
■ How is a shrewd businessperson viewed in our society today?
❇ In what ways does our culture pressure us to love money?
❇ How can the love of money hurt a person?

EXPLORE IT
❇ How did the rich man respond to the manager who was "wasting his possessions"? (16:1-2)
❇ Why was the manager scared to lose his job? (16:3)
■ What plan did the manager devise to secure his future? (16:4-7)
■ How did the rich master react to the dishonest dealings of the manager? (16:8)
❇ Who are the "people of light" to whom Jesus referred? (16:8)
■ How does Jesus want us to use money? (16:9)
❇ What main principle should govern the way we use our resources? (16:10-12)
❇ Why is it impossible to serve two masters? (16:13)
❇ Why were the Pharisees upset with Jesus' teaching? (16:14)
❇ How did the Pharisees "justify" themselves? (16:15)
❇ How does God judge people? (16:15)
❇ What does God think of the things that we typically value? (16:15)

GET IT
❇ What did Jesus mean when He said, "Use worldly wealth to gain friends for yourselves"?
■ Why is it so difficult to keep a proper perspective on money?
■ How do you think God wants you to change the way you handle your resources?
❇ How can we be sure that we will be "welcomed into eternal dwellings"?
❇ How can you become more trustworthy in handling the money and things that God has given you?
❇ How do you need to change your attitude toward your wealth?
❇ What can you do to demonstrate your devotion to the Lord?

APPLY IT
■ What can you do during this next week to become a better steward of the resources God has given you?
❇ During the next few weeks, what is one way you can use money to serve others and show them the love of God?
❇ During the next few weeks, what is one way you can live more simply?

Luke 16:16-18
Additional Teachings

TOPICS
Adultery, Good News, Kingdom of God/Heaven, Law, Prophecy, Teaching

OPEN IT
■ What attitudes does our culture have toward divorce?
❇ How does our society view adultery?
❇ What messages does the media communicate to us about the issues of adultery and divorce?

EXPLORE IT
❇ What two eras did John the Baptist's ministry divide? (16:16)
❇ What changed after the ministry of John the Baptist? (16:16)
❇ What was being preached? (16:16)
❇ Who was "forcing his way" into the kingdom of God? (16:16)
❇ What is easier than for the least stroke of a pen to drop out of the Law? (16:17)
❇ Why did Jesus emphasize the importance of the Law? (16:17)
■ What relation does the section on divorce have to the previous verses about the Law? (16:18)
■ What two conditions constitute adultery? (16:18)
■ How does Jesus view divorce? (16:18)
❇ How has Jesus' life changed the importance of the Law? (16:16-18)

GET IT

❊ What responsibility do you have to obey God's Law?
❊ What difference does it make that Jesus' ministry was a perfect fulfillment of the Law and the Prophets?
❊ How are people's responses to the good news different today than in Jesus' time?
■ What should be our attitude toward divorce?
■ How do you think Jesus would want you to treat Christians who are divorced?
❊ In what ways has our obedience to the commands of Christ resembled the hypocrisy of the Pharisees?
❊ What attitude should we have toward God's Law today?
❊ If you have been hypocritical in your strict adherence to the letter of the law, what can you do to increase your commitment to the spirit of the law?

APPLY IT

❊ What can you do this week to renew your obedience to the commands of Jesus in your everyday life?
■ What could you do to help a person who is experiencing marriage difficulties?

Luke 16:19-31
The Rich Man and Lazarus

TOPICS

Angels, Death, Eternal Life, Heaven, Hell, Judgment, Punishment, Suffering, Wealth

OPEN IT

■ What do you imagine heaven and hell will be like?
❊ What do your friends and coworkers imagine heaven and hell will be like?

EXPLORE IT

❊ How did Jesus describe the rich man in the story? (16:19)
❊ What does the story tell us about Lazarus? (16:20)
❊ What role did angels play in this story? (16:22)
❊ Where did the angels take Lazarus? (16:22)
❊ What difference did the rich man's wealth make in his eternal destiny? (16:22-23)
■ What does this parable reveal about heaven and hell? (16:22-31)
■ What did the rich man see from his place in hell? (16:23)
❊ How did Abraham respond to the request of the rich man? (16:25)
■ What was the other reason why Lazarus could not help the rich man? (16:26)
❊ Why did the rich man want Lazarus to go to his father's house on earth? (16:27-28)
❊ Why did Abraham say that Moses and the Prophets should be enough for the rich man's brothers? (16:29, 31)
❊ What did the rich man think was necessary to convince his brothers to believe? (16:30)

GET IT

❊ If Christians believe in the reality of hell, what do you think stops them from sharing their faith with others?
❊ What do you think prevents people from accepting the gospel of Jesus Christ?
❊ How does this story affect your understanding of the afterlife?
❊ What have you learned from this parable about the eternal value of material possessions?
■ What things do you think have eternal value?
■ What could you do to be less concerned with earthly things and more devoted to things that have eternal significance?
❊ How would this Scripture passage encourage Christians who are sick, poor, or disadvantaged?
❊ How can we gain confidence in our eternal security?
❊ Why does God not always provide miracles to help people believe in Him?
❊ How has this parable changed your attitude toward witnessing to unbelievers?

APPLY IT

❊ In the next few days, how can you demonstrate your thankfulness to the Lord for His provision of eternal life?
■ How many people like Lazarus do you know who could benefit from your compassion today?

Luke 17:1-10
Sin, Faith, Duty

TOPICS

Dedication, Faith, Forgiveness, Humility, Repentance, Serving, Sin, Temptation

OPEN IT

❊ How do you feel after you have done something good for another person?
❊ What expectations do we usually have when we help someone?
■ What makes it difficult to forgive a person who has wronged you?

EXPLORE IT

❊ What did Jesus say about people who tempt others to sin? (17:1)
❊ Who are the "little ones" Jesus cares so much about? (17:2)
■ What advice did Jesus give His disciples about how to react when others sin against them? (17:3-4)
❊ According to Jesus, how often were His disciples to forgive those who sinned? (17:4)
■ What principle of forgiveness was Jesus promoting? (17:4)
❊ What did the disciples ask Jesus to do? (17:5)
■ Why did the disciples think more faith would help them forgive in the way that Jesus instructed? (17:5)
❊ How much faith is needed to do great things? (17:6)
❊ Why was Jesus' example of the mustard seed so startling? (17:6)
❊ Why did Jesus tell the story of the servant and the master? (17:7-9)
❊ In the parable, who do the master and the servant represent? (17:7-9)
❊ What attitude should we have in working for the Lord? (17:10)

GET IT

❇ How can we guard against tempting others to sin?
❇ What should you do if you discover that you have encouraged another believer to sin?
■ When have you found it difficult to forgive someone?
■ What can you do to increase your faith so that you will be able to forgive in the way Christ requires?
❇ What is our "duty" as Christians?
❇ Why is a spirit of humility important for a Christian's witness?
❇ What attitudes and actions indicate a spirit of humility?

APPLY IT

❇ What relationship can you work toward healing this week? How?
■ To what person do you need to demonstrate forgiveness?
❇ What "duty" would the Lord urge you to fulfill this next week?

Luke 17:11-19

Ten Healed of Leprosy

TOPICS

Criticism, Faith, Healing, Miracles, Praise, Thankfulness

OPEN IT

❇ For what are you most thankful?
■ How would you react if you were suddenly healed from a disease or sickness?

EXPLORE IT

❇ Where did the events of this story take place? (17:11)
❇ Who met Jesus as He entered the village? (17:12)
■ What did the ten men want from Jesus? (17:13)
❇ How did the men refer to Jesus? (17:13)
❇ How did Jesus respond to the ten men? (17:14)
■ What happened to the men as they went to show themselves to the priest? (17:14)
❇ What did one of the ten do that the others did not? (17:15)
■ How did one man express his thankfulness to Jesus? (17:15-16)
❇ What difference did it make that the man who thanked Jesus was a Samaritan? (17:16,18)
❇ How did Jesus respond to the one man who returned? (17:17-19)
❇ What did Jesus tell the man about his faith? (17:19)

GET IT

❇ What does this story say about the importance of thanking Jesus?
❇ What difference does faith make in your life?
■ How does Jesus want you to respond the work He performs in your life?
❇ What prevents us from praising the Lord for His blessings?
❇ When have you ever failed to thank the Lord for something He did for you?
❇ When is it difficult to say thank you to God?
❇ How can you remind yourself to thank God throughout each day?
❇ Why does God desire our praise?
■ What should we do when we need physical or spiritual healing from the Lord?
❇ Why is faith necessary for spiritual healing?

APPLY IT

■ About what will you praise the Lord more faithfully this week that you have neglected to notice in the past?
❇ Who is one person you could tell today about the great things God has done for you?

Luke 17:20-37

The Coming of the Kingdom of God

TOPICS

Jesus Christ, Kingdom of God/Heaven, Life, Prophecy, Second Coming, Suffering

OPEN IT

■ What would you do if you were told you only had a few months left to live?
❇ Why does the topic of death often make us feel uneasy?

EXPLORE IT

❇ Who prompted Jesus to begin to talk about the kingdom of God? (17:20)
❇ What prompted Jesus to say, "The kingdom of God does not come with your careful observation"? (17:20-21)
❇ Where is the kingdom of God? (17:21)
❇ What did Jesus tell His disciples they would long to see? (17:22)
■ How did Jesus describe what the days of the Son of Man will be like? (17:24-30)
❇ What do the days of Noah and Lot have in common with the days of the Son of Man? (17:26-29)
■ What warning did Jesus give to those present on the day of the Son of Man? (17:31)
■ What will happen to the person who attempts to keep his life? (17:33)
❇ What "phenomenon" will affect people on the day of the Son of Man? (17:34-35)
❇ What would gather where there is a dead body? (17:37)

GET IT

■ How would you describe your readiness for Christ's second coming?
❇ For what reason did Jesus warn, "Remember Lot's wife"?
❇ What should we remember about Lot's wife?
❇ How can you follow Jesus' instruction to "Remember Lot's wife"?
■ What can you do to guard yourself against clinging too closely to your earthly life?
❇ How does Jesus want us to view our earthly lives?
❇ Practically speaking, how could Jesus' teaching about losing your life make a difference in your daily routine?

APPLY IT

■ What people could you pray for this week who are still trying to keep their own life?
❇ This week, what is one way you can loosen your attachment to this life?
❇ How can you reaffirm your commitment to follow Jesus whatever the cost?

Luke 18:1-8

The Parable of the Persistent Widow

TOPICS

Faith, Faithfulness, Justice, Perseverance, Prayer

OPEN IT

❊ In what circumstances is persistence beneficial?

■ When was a time your persistence paid off?

EXPLORE IT

❊ What was Jesus' purpose in telling His disciples this parable? (18:1)

❊ How did Jesus describe the judge in the story? (18:2)

❊ Why was the woman in the story especially helpless? (18:3)

■ What did the woman need from the judge? (18:3)

■ Why did the judge finally give in to the woman's request? (18:4-5)

❊ Why should we take note of how the unjust judge responded to persistence? (18:6)

■ How will God's actions differ from those of the unjust judge? (18:7)

❊ What can Christians expect from God? (18:7)

❊ What promise does this parable offer to Christians? (18:8)

❊ What did Jesus ask about? (18:8)

❊ To what kind of faith did Jesus refer at the end of this passage? (18:8)

GET IT

■ Why do people stop praying?

■ What does it mean to be persistent in our prayers?

❊ How should we respond when we do not see our prayers answered?

❊ How can we be sure we are praying for things that are within the will of God?

❊ What can Christians do to increase their trust in God's desire to answer prayer?

❊ What does this parable teach you about what your prayer life should be like?

❊ How do your prayer habits need to change?

❊ What justice do you need to see administered in your life or the lives of others?

❊ How can you guard against the temptation to give up praying when you do not see immediate results?

APPLY IT

❊ What changes in your daily routine can you make that will enable you to pray more persistently?

■ For what need or concern will you commit to praying persistently?

❊ What fellow believer could you ask to hold you accountable for praying more persistently?

Luke 18:9-14

The Parable of the Pharisee and the Tax Collector

TOPICS

Confidence, Fasting, Forgiveness, Humility, Mercy, Prayer, Pride, Righteousness

OPEN IT

■ How does it feel to be in the presence of someone markedly better than you at what you do best?

❊ What feelings or attitudes do you have toward proud people?

❊ How does our society regard the quality of humility?

EXPLORE IT

❊ To whom did Jesus tell this parable? (18:9)

❊ Why did Jesus tell this parable? (18:9)

❊ Who were the two men described in the story? (18:10)

❊ What did the Pharisee do? (18:11)

■ What motivated the Pharisee to pray? (18:11)

❊ How did the Pharisee pray? (18:11-12)

❊ Why was the Pharisee confident in his own righteousness? (18:11-12)

❊ Why did the tax collector stand at a distance? (18:13)

❊ What does the tax collector's posture reveal about his own attitude? (18:13)

❊ What prompted the tax collector to pray? (18:13)

❊ How did the tax collector pray? (18:13)

■ What difference did it make how these men prayed? (18:14)

❊ What does it mean that one man was justified and the other wasn't? (18:14)

❊ What principle did Jesus stress? (18:14)

GET IT

❊ What reputations did Pharisees and tax collectors have in Bible times?

❊ What kind of people were Pharisees and tax collectors?

❊ Who would be examples of "Pharisees" and "tax collectors" in our society today?

❊ How do we judge people according to outward appearances?

❊ How important are outward appearances in our culture today?

■ How do you approach God in your prayers?

❊ What does this parable teach us about our prayer habits?

❊ What enables us to be confident before God?

❊ In whose righteousness should we have confidence?

❊ In what circumstance have you wrongly exalted yourself?

■ Why does God honor the prayers of a humble person?

APPLY IT

■ What specific steps can you take this week to cultivate a spirit of humility?

❊ In what area of your life do you want to combat a tendency to exalt yourself instead of Christ?

Luke 18:15-17
The Little Children and Jesus

TOPICS
Children, Disagreements, Jesus Christ, Kingdom of God/Heaven

OPEN IT
■ When you were a child, who made you feel most accepted? How?
❊ What does it feel like to be rejected by others?
❊ In general, how does our society treat children?

EXPLORE IT
❊ Why were people bringing babies to Jesus? (18:15)
■ How did the disciples respond to what the parents were doing? (18:15)
❊ What was it about Jesus that motivated parents to bring their children to Him? (18:15-16)
❊ Why did the disciples rebuke those who were bringing their babies to Jesus? (18:15)
❊ How did Jesus react to His disciples' attitudes? (18:16)
■ How did Jesus treat the children? (18:16)
❊ What did Jesus say about the children? (18:16)
■ Why should we receive the kingdom of God like a child? (18:17)
❊ What will happen to those who do not receive the kingdom "like a little child"? (18:17)

GET IT
❊ What can we learn from this passage about the character of Jesus?
❊ How can you imitate the qualities Jesus showed in this story?
❊ What can we learn from the negative example of the disciples?
■ What childlike qualities do we need to enter the kingdom of God?
❊ What can you do to cultivate your trust and dependence on the Lord?
❊ What does this passage reveal about how we need to change?
■ What hinders us from having the childlike qualities that God wants us to have?
❊ How can you combat the tendency to depend on yourself rather than God?

APPLY IT
■ What is one childlike quality that you want to cultivate this next week? How?
❊ What is one way you can show love and compassion toward children?

Luke 18:18-30
The Rich Ruler

TOPICS
Eternal Life, Family, Greed, Home, Kingdom of God/Heaven, Law, Money, Wealth

OPEN IT
■ What is the best example of "materialism" that you can think of?
❊ In what ways would your life change if you lost all you had, including your job?
❊ What do you think of "the American dream"?

EXPLORE IT
❊ What did the ruler ask Jesus? (18:18)
❊ What does the wording of the ruler's question reveal about his attitude? (18:18)
❊ How did Jesus respond to the ruler's question? (18:19)
❊ Of what did Jesus remind the ruler? (18:20)
❊ What does the ruler's response to Jesus reveal about his character? (18:21)
■ What did the ruler lack? (18:22)
❊ Why did Jesus advise this man to sell all he had, especially when He did not require this of others? (18:22)
■ How did the ruler respond to Jesus' instructions? (18:23)
❊ How did the man's wealth interfere with his eternal salvation? (18:23)
■ What was the rich man's problem? (18:24-25)
❊ How did Jesus' listeners respond to Jesus' harsh words? (18:26)
❊ What did Jesus reveal about how a person can inherit eternal life? (18:27)
❊ What did Jesus teach about sacrifice? (18:29-30)

GET IT
❊ What prevents people today from following Christ?
❊ Why did Jesus tell the rich man that "no one is good—except God alone"?
❊ How did the rich man's money hurt him?
❊ How can money interfere with our commitments?
■ How do you need to change your attitude toward money or your financial practices?
■ What specific sacrifice do you think Jesus would ask of you if you asked Him, "What must I do to inherit eternal life?"
❊ How might a person leave "home or wife or brothers or parents or children for the sake of the kingdom of God"?
❊ What person you know has left "home or wife or brothers or parents or children for the sake of the kingdom of God"? How?
❊ What rewards could someone who left home for the kingdom of God expect?
❊ What difference does it make to you to know that you will receive great eternal rewards for the sacrifices you make for Christ during this lifetime?

APPLY IT
■ What is one sacrifice God is calling you to make?
❊ How can you remind yourself of the benefits of following Christ each day?

Luke 18:31-34
Jesus Again Predicts His Death

TOPICS
Death, Future, Ignorance, Jesus Christ, Prophecy, Resurrection, Sacrifice, Suffering, Understanding

OPEN IT
❇ What expectations do you have of your friends?
❇ What sacrifices would you be willing to make for a friend?
■ When have you ever had to suffer for a friend?

EXPLORE IT
❇ To whom was Jesus speaking? (18:31)
■ Where were the disciples and Jesus planning to go? (18:31)
❇ To whom was Jesus referring when He spoke of the "Son of Man"? (18:31)
❇ What did Jesus reveal to the disciples about the future? (18:31-32)
❇ Why did Jesus take the Twelve aside from the crowds to tell them about certain events? (18:31)
❇ How did Jesus describe what would happen? (18:32)
■ To whom would the "Son of Man" be handed over? (18:32)
❇ How would the Gentiles treat the "Son of Man"? (18:32)
■ What did Jesus predict would happen after the "Son of Man" was killed by the Gentiles? (18:33)
❇ Why did Jesus reveal details of the future to His disciples? (18:31-33)
❇ How did the disciples respond to Jesus' prediction of the future? (18:34)
❇ What prevented the disciples from understanding what Jesus explained to them? (18:34)

GET IT
❇ What can we learn from this passage about the character of Christ?
❇ What does this passage reveal about the relationship between Jesus and His disciples?
❇ How important is it to you to know that Jesus predicted everything that would happen to Him?
■ How does it make you feel to know that Jesus was willing to suffer a great deal just for you?
■ How should you respond to Jesus' willingness to sacrifice for you?
❇ Why do we sometimes not understand the clear voice of God?
❇ What prevents us from listening to the Lord?
❇ What could we do to become more sensitive to the leading of God in our lives?

APPLY IT
■ In what way could you imitate in your personal relationships the Lord's willingness to suffer for you?
❇ What do you need to do in the next few days to be more sensitive to the Lord's instructions?

Luke 18:35-43
A Blind Beggar Receives His Sight

TOPICS
Blindness, Faith, Healing, Jesus Christ, Mercy, Miracles, Persistence, Praise

OPEN IT
❇ Why do you think peer pressure is so powerful?
❇ What does it feel like to be criticized by other people?
■ In what circumstances does the criticism of others not matter to you?

EXPLORE IT
❇ Where did this event take place? (18:35)
❇ What was the man by the roadside doing? (18:35)
❇ How did the blind man know that something unusual was happening? (18:36)
❇ How did the blind man know who Jesus was? (18:37-38)
❇ How did the blind man respond to the situation? (18:38)
■ How did the crowd respond to the blind man's actions? (18:39)
■ What did the blind man do in response to the criticism of the crowd? (18:39)
❇ How did Jesus respond to the blind man? (18:40)
❇ If Jesus could see that the man was blind, why did He ask the man what he wanted? (18:41)
❇ Why did Jesus heal the blind man? (18:42)
❇ What role did the blind man's faith play in his healing? (18:42)
■ How did the blind man and the crowds respond to the miracle Jesus performed? (18:43)

GET IT
❇ What can we learn from this passage about persistence in prayer?
■ What can we learn from the blind man in this account?
❇ How is faith involved in Jesus' miracles?
❇ In what settings do you experience group pressure?
❇ How should you respond to group pressure?
■ In what situations should you not be concerned about the criticism of others?
❇ In what way do we all need healing from the Lord?
❇ Why do you think God heals some people and not others?
❇ How should you respond to the Lord's healing touch in your life or in the life of another believer?

APPLY IT
❇ For what do you want to praise God today?
■ What can you do this week to respond more appropriately to the criticism of others?
❇ What steps can you take to be persistent in your prayers this week?

Luke 19:1-10
Zacchaeus the Tax Collector

TOPICS
Dishonesty, Gossip, Judging Others, Repentance, Salvation, Wealth

OPEN IT
❇ How has gossip affected you in the past?
❇ Why do people pay attention to tabloids?
❇ Why do you think people pay attention to gossip and rumors?
■ Who are the despised and disrespected people in our society today?

EXPLORE IT
❄ Where did the events of this story take place? (19:1)
■ How did Luke describe Zacchaeus? (19:2)
❄ What problem did Zacchaeus have? (19:3)
❄ How did Zacchaeus solve his problem? (19:4)
❄ What did Jesus say to Zacchaeus? (19:5)
❄ How did Zacchaeus respond to Jesus' request? (19:6)
❄ What do Zacchaeus' actions reveal about his character? (19:6, 8)
■ Why did the crowds begin to mutter and gossip among themselves? (19:7)
❄ What reputation did Zacchaeus have in Jericho? (19:7)
❄ What changes did Zacchaeus make in his life in response to Jesus' interest in him? (19:8)
■ How had salvation come to Zacchaeus' house? (19:9)
❄ How is the concluding verse of this passage significant? (19:10)

GET IT
❄ How does a person's reputation affect our opinion of them?
■ If we want to share our faith with someone, how much attention should we pay to their status and reputation?
❄ What's wrong with gossiping?
❄ What responsibility do we have to help people of bad reputation?
❄ What do the actions of Zacchaeus reveal about the power of God to change hearts?
■ How can we guard against the temptation to judge others?

APPLY IT
❄ In what settings will you most need to guard yourself from the temptation to gossip this week?
■ With what person of bad reputation or low status could you share your company and God's love?

Luke 19:11-27
The Parable of the Ten Minas

TOPICS
Accountability, Expectations, Judgment, Kingdom of God/Heaven, Leadership, Money, Punishment, Resources, Responsibility, Rewards, Serving

OPEN IT
❄ What does the word "stewardship" bring to mind?
❄ How would you describe a responsible person?
❄ Who is the most responsible person you know?
■ In what areas of your own life would you say you are the most responsible?

EXPLORE IT
❄ For what reason did Jesus choose to tell this parable? (19:11)
❄ What false expectations did Jesus' followers have? (19:11)
❄ In the parable, why did the man of noble birth go to a distant country? (19:12)
❄ Who do the king, the servants, and the subjects represent in this parable? (19:12-27)
❄ For what reason did the man call together ten of his servants? (19:13)
■ What did the man want his servants to do with the money he gave them? (19:13)
❄ How did the people of the distant country react to their new king? (19:14)
❄ Why did the man later send for his servants? (19:15)
■ What did the first two servants do with the money the king entrusted to them? (19:16-18)
❄ How did the king respond to the first two servants? (19:17-19)
❄ What did the third servant think of the king? (19:20-21)
❄ How did the third servant's feelings for his king affect his actions? (19:20-21)
❄ How did the king treat the third servant? (19:22-24)
■ What principle summarizes the parable? (19:26)
❄ Why did the king punish so severely those who did not want him to be king? (19:27)

GET IT
❄ What does this parable teach us about stewardship?
■ What responsibilities and gifts has Jesus given you?
❄ What can you do to develop and use the abilities God has already given you?
❄ How do you need to change your attitude toward your talents?
■ What can we learn from this parable about neglecting to obey the truth that we already know?
❄ Why is it dangerous to neglect the truth we know about God?
❄ How can you be a better steward of what God has already given you?
❄ What can you expect from the Lord if you use your resources for His glory?

APPLY IT
■ What can you do to remind yourself of the responsibilities that God has entrusted to you?
❄ How can you use your spiritual gifts and abilities for the Lord in the next few days?

Luke 19:28-44
The Triumphal Entry

TOPICS
Compassion, Criticism, Joy, Miracles, Praise, Prophecy

OPEN IT
❄ When have you seen a famous person?
❄ Whom do you look up to the most? Why?
■ How do people commonly show admiration for famous people?

EXPLORE IT
❄ Where did the events of this story take place? (19:28-29)
❄ Where did Jesus send two of His disciples? (19:30)
❄ What specific instructions did Jesus give two of His disciples? (19:30-31)
❄ What happened to the disciples who went ahead into the village? (19:32-34)
❄ Why did Jesus choose to ride into the city on a colt? (19:35)
■ How did people react to Jesus' entrance into the city? (19:36-37)

❊ Why did all of the disciples begin to praise God? (19:37)
■ In what way were the words of the disciples' praises significant? (19:38)
❊ Why were the Pharisees in the crowd upset? (19:39)
■ How did Jesus respond to the Pharisees' rebuke? (19:40)
❊ How did Jesus react when He saw the city of Jerusalem? (19:41)
❊ In what way did the people of Jerusalem miss a golden opportunity? (19:44)

GET IT
■ What does this passage teach us about Jesus' regard for celebrity status?
❊ What can we learn from the example of the disciples in this account?
■ What has the Lord done for you recently that causes you to praise Him?
❊ When do we tend to neglect to praise the Lord as He deserves?
❊ What can we learn from Jesus' words about and feelings toward Jerusalem in this passage?
❊ What responsibility do we have toward non-Christians?

APPLY IT
❊ How can you imitate Christ's compassion for unsaved people this week?
■ How can you voice your praise to the Lord today for all that He has done for you?

Luke 19:45-48
Jesus at the Temple

TOPICS
Anger, Church, Dishonesty, Judgment, Popularity, Prayer

OPEN IT
■ When was a time you felt justified in being angry?
❊ What makes you really angry?

EXPLORE IT
❊ Where did the events of this story take place? (19:45)
■ What did Jesus do in the temple area? (19:45)
❊ Who was plotting to kill Jesus? (19:45-47)
❊ What attitude did Jesus have toward the merchants in the temple area? (19:46)
❊ Why did Jesus quote Scripture? (19:46)
■ What did Jesus accuse the merchants of doing? (19:46)
❊ How had the temple area been misused? (19:46)
■ What was the real purpose of the temple? (19:46)
❊ Why did the religious leaders want to kill Jesus? (19:47)
❊ Why were the religious leaders unable to carry out their plot? (19:48)
❊ How did the people respond to Jesus' teaching in the temple? (19:48)

GET IT
■ What can we learn about God from this passage?
❊ In what way is a church like the temple of Jesus' day?
❊ In what way can a church be made a "den of robbers"?
■ How can we guard against misusing the church for our own purposes?
❊ What made people hang on Jesus' words?
❊ What ungodly practices make you angry?
❊ How should we respond to abuses of God's Word or His church?
❊ When might anger lead someone to sin?

APPLY IT
■ What can you do to prepare for a worshipful experience in church next week?
❊ In what ways would your daily prayer life be helped by "hanging on the words" of Jesus this week?

Luke 20:1-8
The Authority of Jesus Questioned

TOPICS
Authority, Deceit, Hypocrisy, Jesus Christ, Questions, Wisdom

OPEN IT
❊ How do you react to other people's hypocrisy?
■ When has someone questioned authority that you rightfully possessed?

EXPLORE IT
❊ Where did the events of this story take place? (20:1)
❊ What was Jesus doing in the temple courts? (20:1)
❊ Who approached Jesus while He was preaching in the temple? (20:1)
■ What question did the religious leaders ask Jesus? (20:2)
❊ How was Jesus put to the test? (20:2)
■ In what way were the actions of the religious leaders hypocritical? (20:2-7)
❊ Why did Jesus answer the religious leaders' question with another question? (20:3)
❊ What was it about Jesus' question that stumped the religious leaders? (20:5-6)
❊ How did the crowds' beliefs affect the religious leaders' willingness to answer Jesus' question? (20:6)
■ How did the leaders respond to Jesus' question? (20:7)
❊ In what way did Jesus demonstrate His wisdom? (20:8)

GET IT
❊ What motivated the religious leaders to ask their question?
■ By whose authority was Jesus able to teach, preach, and perform miracles?
❊ Why didn't Jesus answer the religious leaders' question?
❊ What is wrong with the advice, "Do what I say, not what I do"?
❊ How can we guard against hypocrisy?
❊ When has fear of others kept you from speaking honestly about Christ?
■ When have you questioned God's authority in a particular area in your life?
❊ What traits did the religious leaders possess that followers of Jesus should not possess?

APPLY IT
❊ In what settings do you need to put forth extra effort to be completely honest and forthright in all your dealings with people?
■ In the next few days, how can you rely on Jesus' authority and wisdom?

Luke 20:9-19

The Parable of the Tenants

TOPICS

Criticism, Enemies, Hardheartedness, Jesus Christ, Mediator, Peer Pressure, Prophecy, Punishment, Unfairness

OPEN IT

■ Why do you think stories often communicate better than lectures?
❇ How has peer pressure ever affected your actions?

EXPLORE IT

■ Why did Jesus choose to tell the people a parable in this situation? (20:9, 19)
❇ What are the main points of the parable Jesus told? (20:9-16)
❇ Whom does the man who planted the vineyard represent? (20:9)
❇ Whom do the servants the owner sent to the vineyard represent? (20:10-12)
❇ How were the servants treated? (20:10-12)
❇ Whom do the tenants in the story represent? (20:10, 19)
❇ Why did the owner send his son to the vineyard? (20:13)
❇ What is the inheritance to which the tenants referred? (20:14)
❇ How will the owner of the vineyard respond to the terrible actions of the tenants? (20:16)
■ How did the people listening to Jesus respond to the parable? (20:16)
❇ What is the meaning of the Scripture that Jesus quoted? (20:17-18)
■ How did the religious leaders react to Jesus' teaching? (20:19)
❇ How did the mood of the people affect the actions of the religious leaders? (20:19)

GET IT

❇ In what ways can the threat of criticism affect our decisions?
■ What does this parable tell us about the fate that awaits those who reject Jesus as the Messiah?
❇ How does this passage motivate you to share your faith with unbelievers?
❇ Who are the servants of Christ?
■ In what ways have people not treated the servants of Christ properly?
❇ How does God want us to treat those who serve Him and spread the message of Christ?
❇ What will God do to people who mistreat His servants?
❇ How can we avoid letting the crowd make our decisions for us?

APPLY IT

■ What people could you reach this week with the news of God's mercy? How?
❇ Over the next few days, what can you do to support or encourage a person devoted to telling others about Christ?

Luke 20:20-26

Paying Taxes to Caesar

TOPICS

Deceit, Dishonesty, Government, Hypocrisy, Jesus Christ, Money, Questions, Silence, Truth, Wisdom

OPEN IT

❇ What is the general attitude in our country toward government?
■ When was the last time someone tried to deceive you?
❇ What do your friends and coworkers think about having to pay taxes?

EXPLORE IT

❇ Who sent the spies? (20:19-20)
■ Why did the religious leaders send spies? (20:20)
❇ Why did the religious leaders want to hand Jesus over to the governor? (20:20)
❇ What did the spies do to trap Jesus? (20:21)
❇ How did the spies demonstrate hypocrisy? (20:21)
■ In what way was the question the spies asked a trick question? (20:22)
❇ What did Jesus think of the spies? (20:23)
■ How did Jesus respond to the spies' question? (20:24)
❇ How was Jesus' response a show of His wisdom? (20:24-25)
❇ Why were the spies astonished by Jesus' answer? (20:26)

GET IT

❇ How might you have responded to the spies' question?
■ When have you been asked difficult or misleading questions by people hostile to Christianity?
❇ How did the spies use flattery?
❇ Why do we like to be flattered?
❇ Why do we flatter others?
❇ In what way do we need to guard against flattery?
■ What does this passage reveal about Jesus' wisdom?
❇ What belongs to the government that we should give to it?
❇ How would you define your responsibility to the government?
❇ When should a Christian go against the demands of the government?
❇ What responsibility do you think we have to obey the laws of the government?
❇ Jesus taught us to "give to God what is God's"; what importance does this statement have for you?
❇ What belongs to God that we should give to Him?
❇ What have you held back from the Lord that you are now willing to commit to Him?

APPLY IT

■ What preparations can you make for the tough questions that you will encounter as a follower of Christ?
❇ In what situations this week do you want to make a conscious effort to avoid flattery?
❇ What obligations to the government do you need to fulfill?
❇ How can you obey more fully this week Christ's command to "give to God what is God's"?

Luke 20:27-40

The Resurrection and Marriage

TOPICS
Angels, Children, Death, Life, Marriage, Questions, Resurrection, Wisdom

OPEN IT
❊ What do you imagine happens to us after death?
❊ Why do you think there is so much confusion and controversy about the afterlife in our world today?
■ How have your beliefs in the afterlife changed over the years?

EXPLORE IT
❊ How did Luke describe the Sadducees? (20:27)
❊ Why did the Sadducees approach Jesus? (20:27)
■ What was the main point of the lengthy story the Sadducees told Jesus? (20:28-33)
❊ What controversial question did the Sadducees want Jesus to answer? (20:33)
❊ How did Jesus respond to the Sadducees' question? (20:34-35)
❊ What is the "age" to which Jesus referred? (20:35)
❊ Who is "considered worthy"? (20:35)
■ In the age to come, what did Jesus promise to those who take part in the resurrection of the dead? (20:36)
❊ Who is like the angels? (20:36)
❊ For what reason did Jesus refer to Moses? (20:37)
❊ How did Jesus describe God? (20:37-38)
■ Why did Jesus describe God as "the God of the living"? (20:38)
❊ Why did people stop asking Jesus questions? (20:40)

GET IT
❊ How can we guard against misinterpreting Scripture, as the Sadducees did in Jesus' day?
❊ In what ways can academic or speculative questions hinder our seeking after God?
❊ Why should we believe in the resurrection of the dead?
■ What makes belief in the resurrection an important Christian belief?
❊ How should we respond to the death of a loved one who was a Christian?
❊ Why do you think there will be no marriage in heaven?
■ How should the promise of eternal life affect your everyday actions?

APPLY IT
■ Whom can you encourage with the truth of the resurrection? How?
❊ What younger or less knowledgeable Christian could you instruct this week? How?
❊ What can you do this week to prepare for people's tough religious questions?

Luke 20:41-47

Whose Son Is the Christ?

TOPICS
Advice, Doctrine, Jesus Christ, Judgment, Pride, Punishment

OPEN IT
■ What importance do the people with whom you work place on status and power?
❊ What are people willing to do to gain recognition and respect?
❊ What are some of the trappings of high status?

EXPLORE IT
❊ What dilemma did Jesus set before His listeners? (20:41)
❊ What was Jesus revealing to His listeners about His own identity? (20:41-44)
❊ For what reason does Jesus quote the words of David to His listeners? (20:42-43)
❊ How does David refer to the Christ? (20:44)
❊ Why could Jesus' opponents not answer His question? (20:44)
❊ What did the teachers of the law seek? (20:45-46)
❊ About what did Jesus warn His disciples? (20:45-47)
■ Of what were the teachers of the law guilty? (20:46-47)
❊ What point was Jesus trying to make about such religious behavior? (20:46-47)
❊ How did Jesus criticize the teachers of the Law? (20:47)
■ What did Jesus mean when He said, "They devour widows' houses"? (20:47)
■ How did Jesus say proud people would be treated for their actions? (20:47)

GET IT
❊ For whose sake did Jesus pose the difficult question regarding the Son of David?
❊ Why is pride such a dangerous sin?
■ How do proud Christians hinder the work of God?
❊ How can you prevent yourself from doing things for show?
❊ Why do we seek out positions of honor and importance?
■ Why are positions of honor and importance so difficult to give up?
❊ How is seeking the honor and respect of people related to the exploitation of the poor and defenseless?

APPLY IT
■ In what areas of your life do you need to battle a pride that prevents you from drawing closer to God?
❊ In what ways could you be an advocate this week for those who are mistreated by powerful persons?

Luke 21:1-4

The Widow's Offering

TOPICS
Gifts, Money, Poor, Possessions, Sacrifice, Tithing, Wealth

OPEN IT
❊ To what charities or special causes do you like giving?
■ When have you given sacrificially to a special cause?

EXPLORE IT
❊ What did Jesus notice? (21:1)
❊ What were the rich people doing? (21:1)
■ How did Luke describe the woman Jesus saw? (21:2)
❊ What did the woman do that Jesus noticed? (21:2)
❊ How were the motives of the rich different from those of the woman? (21:1-2)
❊ How did Jesus use this situation as an opportunity to teach His followers? (21:3)
■ How did the woman "put in more than all the others" when her gift was much smaller than the gifts of the rich? (21:3)
❊ What was lacking in the gifts the rich people gave? (21:4)
❊ What had the poor widow actually sacrificed? (21:4)
■ What principle of giving did Jesus communicate? (21:4)

GET IT
❊ How important is a person's attitude toward giving?
❊ What is wrong with judging people by their outward appearances?
■ How does God judge our gifts?
■ Why do you think the widow gave all that she had to live on?
❊ Why did Jesus draw attention to a seemingly unremarkable event?
❊ Why is giving out of our wealth a relatively easy thing to do?
❊ In what ways do you need to give sacrificially?

APPLY IT
■ What sacrifice of money could you make in God's service?
❊ What besides money can you give sacrificially to others this week? How?

Luke 21:5-38

Signs of the End of the Age

TOPICS
Death, Expectations, Last Days, Persecution, Prayer, Prophecy, Punishment, Second Coming, War, Wisdom, Worry

OPEN IT
❊ What do you think of people who make predictions about the future?
■ What do you already know about your future?

EXPLORE IT
❊ What did the disciples say about the temple that prompted a prophecy from Jesus? (21:5)
❊ How did the disciples respond to Jesus' prediction concerning the temple? (21:7)
❊ What did Jesus say could deceive Christians in the last days? (21:8)
■ What signs of the end of the age did Jesus tell us to expect? (21:9-13)
❊ Why did Jesus advise His followers not to worry about what will happen to them? (21:14)
■ What promises did Jesus give to His disciples? (21:18-19)
❊ What will be the result of "standing firm" in the last days? (21:19)
❊ Why will the "time of punishment" be necessary? (21:22)
❊ What signs will usher in the end of the age? (21:23-26)
■ What should be the response of Christians to the many signs of the end? (21:28)
❊ For what purpose did Jesus tell the parable of the fig tree? (21:29-31)
❊ What final advice did Jesus give? (21:34-36)

GET IT
❊ How can a Christian avoid being deceived by the events Jesus describes?
■ Why did Jesus reveal to us these prophecies about the last days?
❊ What distinguishes Jesus' view of the future from the predictions of modern-day seers and astrologers?
❊ Why would the wisdom Jesus provides be so necessary during persecution?
❊ Which of the signs that Jesus detailed do you believe have been fulfilled or are being fulfilled today?
■ What does this passage teach us about the trustworthiness of Jesus' promises?
❊ Why should we not allow our hearts to be weighed down with the anxieties of life?

APPLY IT
❊ What Christian can you meet with this week to pray for preparedness for the times to come?
■ What can you do now to get ready for Christ's return?
❊ Who is one unbeliever you can tell about the saving grace of the gospel? How?

Luke 22:1-6

Judas Agrees to Betray Jesus

TOPICS
Bargaining, Deceit, Dishonesty, Forsake, Greed, Hypocrisy, Money, Opposition

OPEN IT
❊ What are the necessary elements of a friendship?
■ In your experience, what destroys friendships?
❊ The last time you had to mend a broken friendship, how did you do it?

EXPLORE IT
❊ What event were the people anticipating? (22:1)
❊ Why was this event important? (22:1)
❊ What was the plan of the chief priests and teachers of the law? (22:2)
❊ Why were the religious leaders afraid of the people? (22:2)

■ What motivated Judas to approach the religious leaders who wanted to get rid of Jesus? (22:3)
❊ In what way is Satan's role in this story significant? (22:3)
■ What did Judas and the religious leaders discuss? (22:4)
❊ How did the leaders respond to Judas's willingness to betray Jesus? (22:4)
■ What did Judas get in return for betraying Jesus? (22:5-6)
❊ How was Judas's plan deceitful? (22:6)
❊ Why was it important for Judas to hand Jesus over "when no crowd was present"? (22:6)

GET IT
❊ What does this passage teach us about human weakness?
■ How did greed influence Judas's decisions?
❊ When has greed or materialism negatively influenced your decisions?
❊ How can we guard against greed?
❊ What can we learn from the hypocritical actions of Judas?
■ How have your own selfish desires interfered with your relationship with others and your relationship with Jesus?
❊ What can you do to be a more faithful, loyal friend?
❊ In what areas of life are you most vulnerable to temptation?
❊ How can you protect yourself from the temptations of Satan?

APPLY IT
❊ What evidence of selfishness and greed do you see in your own life that could be remedied with the Lord's help?
■ How could you demonstrate today your own faithfulness and loyalty to a friend?

Luke 22:7-38
The Last Supper

TOPICS
Disagreements, Faith, Fellowship, Jesus Christ, Kingdom of God/Heaven, Lord's Supper, Prophecy, Remembering, Sacrifice, Serving, Suffering, Thankfulness

OPEN IT
■ In what ways do you observe or celebrate past important events in your life?
❊ What do you think it is important to remember about the past?
❊ Why is it important to remember the past?

EXPLORE IT
❊ What was significant about the day of Unleavened Bread? (22:7)
❊ What instructions did Jesus give to Peter and John? (22:8-13)
■ Why did Jesus eagerly desire to eat the Passover with His disciples? (22:15-16)
❊ What did Jesus mean when He said, "I will not eat it again until it finds fulfillment in the kingdom of God"? (22:16)
■ What did Jesus instruct His disciples to do in remembrance of Him? (22:17-20)
■ What did the cup represent? (22:20)
❊ Why did a dispute arise among the disciples? (22:23-24)
❊ What principle did Jesus promote in response to the disciples' disagreement? (22:25-27)
❊ What did Jesus tell Simon about his future? (22:31-32)
❊ How did Simon respond to Jesus' prediction? (22:33)
❊ How did Jesus warn His disciples of the difficult time ahead? (22:35-37)
❊ In what way did the disciples take Jesus' instructions too literally? (22:38)

GET IT
❊ What joyful moments have you experienced in a Communion fellowship?
■ Why is Communion important for Christians to observe?
■ Why do you believe Jesus chose the elements of bread and wine to represent His body and the new covenant?
❊ Why is it so tempting to seek greatness and recognition?
❊ How can we follow Christ's example of servanthood?
❊ What opportunities for service has the Lord already provided for you?
❊ What responsibility do we have to pray for the perseverance of other Christians?

APPLY IT
■ How will you prepare for Communion next time so that you will appreciate more the provision Jesus made for you?
❊ How can you serve others this week with an attitude of humility?

Luke 22:39-46
Jesus Prays on the Mount of Olives

TOPICS
Angels, Expectations, Habits, Prayer, Sorrow, Submission, Temptation

OPEN IT
❊ How have your friends helped you through difficult times in your life?
■ When have you agreed to do something that you didn't look forward to doing?

EXPLORE IT
❊ What does this passage reveal about Jesus' habits? (22:39)
❊ For what purpose did Jesus go to the Mount of Olives? (22:39)
❊ What instructions did Jesus give to His disciples? (22:40)
❊ Why did Jesus withdraw from His followers? (22:41)
■ What does Jesus' prayer reveal about His own character and His relationship with the Father? (22:42)

❇ What did Jesus want to avoid if possible? (22:42)
❇ What was Jesus referring to when He said, "Take this cup from me"? (22:42)
■ How was Jesus strengthened at this difficult time? (22:43)
❇ How did Jesus confront His own anguish and dread? (22:44)
■ What does this passage tell us about Jesus' physical and emotional condition shortly before His death? (22:44)
❇ What did Jesus find when He returned to the disciples? (22:45)
❇ Why were the disciples so exhausted? (22:45)
❇ For what reason did Jesus advise His disciples to pray? (22:46)

GET IT
❇ What can we learn from Jesus' example of dealing with difficult circumstances in life?
■ How do you think God wants you to respond to painful, even overwhelming, events in your life?
■ What role should prayer play in times of trouble?
❇ What can we learn from the disciplines Jesus developed while He was on earth?
❇ How can you guard against falling into temptation?
❇ What does Jesus teach us through His own example of submission to the Father?
❇ For what situation in your life right now do you need to say to God, "Not my will, but yours be done"?

APPLY IT
❇ In the next few weeks, what might you do to develop better habits of prayer and spiritual discipline?
■ What particular area of your own life do you want to consciously submit to the Father's will?

Luke 22:47-53
Jesus Arrested

TOPICS
Conflict, Darkness, Deceit, Enemies, Evil, Healing, Hypocrisy, Testing

OPEN IT
■ How does it feel to be let down by a friend?
❇ What would you describe as a low point in your life?
❇ What polite insincerities do people often use?

EXPLORE IT
❇ Who was leading the crowd that approached Jesus? (22:47-48) Why?
❇ Why did Judas approach Jesus? (22:47-48)
❇ What actions of Judas were hypocritical and insincere? (22:47-48)
❇ How did Jesus respond to Judas's greeting? (22:48)
❇ Why did Jesus reveal His identity to His opponents? (22:48)
■ How did Jesus' followers respond to Jesus' arrest? (22:49)
❇ What motivated one of Jesus' followers to attack one of the servants? (22:50)
❇ How did Jesus react when one of His disciples tried to protect Him? (22:50-51)
■ How did Jesus show compassion even to His captors? (22:51)
■ What emotions did Jesus show during this difficult time? (22:51-53)
❇ What did Jesus say to the religious leaders who had come for Him? (22:52-53)
❇ What did Jesus mean when He said, "This is your hour—when darkness reigns"? (22:53)
❇ In what way did Jesus submit to the Father's will in this situation? (22:53)

GET IT
❇ In what way is Judas a negative example to all of us?
❇ When are you most tempted to be insincere in your actions or words?
❇ What is the best way to keep yourself from turning away from your faith during difficult times?
❇ What does Jesus teach you through His own demonstration of obedience to the Father's will?
❇ In what areas of your life are you struggling to trust fully in God's will and plan?
❇ What does submission to God's will entail?
❇ In what ways are you tempted to rely on yourself when faced with danger, as the disciples were?
■ What principles for dealing with difficult and stressful circumstances do you see in Jesus' example?
■ How can you respond when you face stressful and difficult circumstances?
❇ How do you think God wants you to treat your enemies?

APPLY IT
❇ In what situations do you want to be more sincere and forthright?
❇ In what areas of your life do you need to rely more consistently on the strength of the Lord?
■ In what way could you prepare yourself now for future uncertainties?

Luke 22:54-62
Peter Disowns Jesus

TOPICS
Denial, Embarrassment, Forsake, Friendship, Peer Pressure, Repentance, Sorrow, Testing, Weaknesses

OPEN IT
❇ How does peer pressure affect our decisions?
■ In what circumstances have you felt pressured into going along with the opinions of your friends?
❇ When do you feel uncomfortable succumbing to group pressure?

EXPLORE IT
❇ Where did the events of this story take place? (22:54)
❇ What had happened to Jesus? (22:54)
■ For what reason did Peter follow Jesus "at a distance"? (22:54)
■ What do the actions of Peter in this story reveal about his personal character? (22:54-62)

❇ Of what did the servant girl accuse Peter? (22:56)
❇ How did Peter respond to the servant girl? (22:57)
❇ How many times was Peter accused of knowing Jesus? (22:56-59)
❇ How did Peter respond to the second two accusations put to him? (22:58-60)
❇ Why did the third person suspect Peter was a follower of Jesus? (22:59)
❇ What happened when Peter denied Jesus the third time? (22:60-61)
❇ What caused Peter to remember Jesus' earlier prediction? (22:60-61)
❇ What did Jesus do the third time Peter denied knowing Him? (22:61)
■ Why was Peter so upset and bitter about his actions? (22:61-62)
❇ How did Peter respond to the realization that he had denied his Lord? (22:62)

GET IT
❇ What would make Peter deny that he knew Jesus, when earlier he said he was willing to die for Him?
■ When have you ever done something because of peer pressure, then later regretted it?
❇ In what circumstances are other people able to influence us to act in ways we know we should not?
❇ How was Peter's denial of Christ different from Judas's betrayal of Jesus?
■ What can we do to stand against the pressure of others to do things we know are wrong?
❇ How should we respond when we fail to obey Christ?
❇ What can we learn about repentance from Peter's example in this story?
❇ How would you define true repentance?
❇ What methods does God use to make us aware of ways we need to change?
❇ In what ways has the Lord made you aware of a sin in your life?
❇ How should we respond to the convicting voice of God?

APPLY IT
■ What could you do this week to strengthen your stand for Christ in the face of pressure from others?
❇ In the future, how could you encourage another believer who has done something wrong but shows a willingness to repent?

Luke 22:63-65
The Guards Mock Jesus

TOPICS
Insults, Persecution, Prophecy, Shame, Suffering, Toleration

OPEN IT
❇ What emotions do most people have when insulted by others?
❇ How do we guard ourselves against criticism from other people?
■ What bullies do you remember from grade school?

EXPLORE IT
❇ In light of what had happened before this point, what was Jesus probably feeling? (22:63)
❇ Who had control of this situation? (22:63)
❇ How was Jesus treated by His guards? (22:63-64)
■ In what way did the guards mock Jesus? (22:63-64)
❇ Why was Jesus blindfolded? (22:64)
❇ What prompted the guards to mock Jesus as they did? (22:64)
❇ How did news of Jesus' reputation influence the guards' actions? (22:64)
■ What was the guards' purpose in demanding that Jesus prophesy for them? (22:64)
❇ What was so demeaning about the guards' treatment of Jesus? (22:64)
■ What did Luke imply about Jesus' actions by not mentioning any details about how He responded to the guards? (22:63-65)
❇ In what way are the details of Christ's humiliation significant to the overall story? (22:63-65)

GET IT
❇ How are the details of Jesus' mockery relevant to us today?
❇ What does this passage tell us about Jesus' character and His response to persecution?
■ How does Jesus want us to react to criticism, insults, or scorn?
❇ In what way could you benefit by suffering for your faith?
❇ What steps could you take to prepare yourself for being persecuted for your faith?
❇ Why do you think God spares some believers from persecution but not others?
■ How could you show your support for other Christians who suffer persecution for the sake of Christ?

APPLY IT
■ How could you encourage a Christian who is in some way suffering for his or her faith? When?
❇ How can you look past the criticism or scorn people use against you for your beliefs?
❇ What is one way you can say thank you to Jesus for enduring humiliation for your sake?

Luke 22:66–23:25
Jesus Before Pilate and Herod

TOPICS
Accusation, Answers, Blasphemy, Evidence, God, Injustice, Jesus Christ, Persecution, Pressure, Punishment, Rationalizing, Testing, Unfairness, Witnessing

OPEN IT
❇ What constitutes a fair trial in our legal system today?
❇ What are some common ways people try to bend the rules?
■ Why might a person try to influence the process of justice deceitfully?

EXPLORE IT
❇ When did the events of this story take place? (22:66)

❋ Who was first to question Jesus? (22:66)
❋ How did Jesus respond to the question about His identity? (22:67-70)
❋ Where was Jesus taken? (23:1)
■ Of what was Jesus accused? (23:2)
❋ How did Jesus respond to Pilate's question about His identity? (23:3)
■ Of what did Pilate find Jesus guilty? (23:4)
❋ How was Jesus treated throughout His trial? (23:5, 9-11)
❋ For what reason did Pilate send Jesus to Herod? (23:5-7)
❋ Why was Herod pleased to see Jesus? (23:8-9)
❋ How did Pilate explain what he decided to do with Jesus? (23:13-16)
❋ How did the crowds respond to Pilate's ruling? (23:18)
■ In what way did popular pressure influence Pilate's decisions? (23:20-25)
❋ What finally happened to Jesus at the conclusion of His trial? (23:25)

GET IT
❋ Why were the people, priests, and rulers so determined to put Jesus to death?
■ What can we learn from studying Jesus' response to His accusers?
❋ In what ways do you feel you have been mistreated because of your faith in Jesus Christ?
■ How should Christians respond to unfair treatment?
❋ How does Jesus' response to Pilate and Herod demonstrate for us how we should endure unjust use of authority?
❋ What difference does it make that Jesus underwent humiliation and unfair treatment?

APPLY IT
❋ In what way can you renew your resolve to serve Jesus, no matter what the cost?
■ What do you want to remember the next time you receive unfair treatment or criticism?

Luke 23:26-43
The Crucifixion

TOPICS
Despair, Forgiveness, Future, God's Will, Insults, Kingdom of God/Heaven, Mourning, Prophecy, Salvation, Submission

OPEN IT
❋ When have you had to endure teasing or abuse?
■ How were you dependent on your parents when you were young?

EXPLORE IT
❋ Why did the soldiers seize Simon of Cyrene? (23:26)
❋ What do the soldiers' actions reveal about Jesus' condition? (23:26)
❋ Why did such a large crowd gather? (23:27)
❋ How did many of the women respond to Jesus' impending death? (23:27)
❋ How did Jesus treat the women mourning for Him? (23:28-31)
❋ Why did Jesus tell the women to weep for themselves? (23:28-31)
❋ What did Jesus mean when He said, "If men do these things when the tree is green, what will happen when it is dry"? (23:31)
❋ What do Jesus' words on the cross reveal about His character? (23:34)
❋ How was Jesus treated by others while He was hanging on the cross? (23:35-39)
■ What did the first criminal demand of Jesus? (23:39)
■ What request did the second criminal on the cross make of Jesus? (23:42)
■ How did Jesus respond to the criminal's plea? (23:43)

GET IT
❋ What can you learn from the actions of the repentant criminal?
❋ Why didn't both criminals plead for mercy from Jesus?
❋ What prevents many people from turning to Jesus?
❋ What do Jesus' words to the repentant criminal reveal about conversion?
■ In what way are we all like the criminals on the cross?
■ For what do we need to approach Jesus?
❋ For what are we dependent on God?
❋ How does Jesus' response to His approaching death set an example for all Christians?
❋ What does this passage teach you about forgiveness?
❋ How should we imitate Christ's example of forgiveness?
❋ Why did Jesus choose not to save Himself from His suffering on the cross?
❋ Toward what people do you need to follow Christ's example of forgiveness?

APPLY IT
❋ With what prayer could you say thank you to Jesus this week for His gift of salvation?
■ How can you place a new area of your life in Christ's hands?

Luke 23:44-49
Jesus' Death

TOPICS
Darkness, Death, Mourning, Praise, Righteousness, Sorrow

OPEN IT
❋ What experiences have caused you to be amazed?
❋ What is the most you've ever sacrificed for someone else?
■ Who are some people you considered unapproachable at one point or another in your life? Why?

EXPLORE IT
❋ When did the events of this story take place? (23:44)
❋ What unusual natural occurrence took place and what did it signify? (23:44-45)
■ What happened to the curtain in the temple? (23:45)

■ What did the tearing of the temple curtain signify? (23:45)
❊ Why did Jesus call out from the cross? (23:46)
❊ What was significant about Jesus' words on the cross? (23:46)
❊ What occurred after Jesus called out to the Father? (23:46)
■ How did the centurion in charge of the crucifixion react to Jesus' death? (23:47)
❊ What motivated the centurion to praise God? (23:47)
❊ Why did the centurion call Jesus a righteous man, and in what way was this declaration significant? (23:47)
❊ How did the witnesses to Christ's crucifixion react to His death? (23:48)
❊ Why did those people who knew Jesus watch from a distance? (23:49)

GET IT
❊ Why did Jesus need to die on the cross?
❊ What difference did Christ's death make in our relationship with God the Father?
■ How did Christ open the path between us and God?
❊ What does it mean to approach God?
■ How are we able to approach God?
❊ What do Jesus' actions teach us about submission to God's will?
❊ Why was the centurion's reaction to Jesus' death so remarkable?
❊ What does this passage teach us about how we should respond to death?
❊ From what has Jesus' death on the cross saved you?

APPLY IT
■ In what ways can you approach God each day this week, to honor the path to the Father He opened for you?
❊ With what younger Christian can you share today your thankfulness for Christ's great sacrifice?

Luke 23:50-56
Jesus' Burial

TOPICS
Body, Devotion, Faith, Kingdom of God/Heaven, Loyalty, Obedience, Respect

OPEN IT
❊ What Christians have you known who have served God faithfully without fanfare?
❊ How much of a risk-taker are you?
■ What's the biggest risk you've ever taken?

EXPLORE IT
❊ Who was Joseph? (23:50)
■ How did Luke describe Joseph's character? (23:50)
❊ How did Joseph feel about Jesus' trial and punishment? (23:51)
❊ What did Luke mean by describing Joseph as a man who was "waiting for the kingdom of God"? (23:51)
❊ What kind of man was Joseph? (23:51)
❊ What did Joseph ask of Pilate? (23:52)
■ Why was it courageous for Joseph to approach Pilate for Jesus' body? (23:52)
■ How did Joseph prepare Jesus' body? (23:53)
❊ Who followed Joseph? (23:55)
❊ What do the actions of the women reveal about their faith? (23:55-56)
❊ Why did the women not take their prepared spices and perfumes directly to Jesus' tomb? (23:56)

GET IT
❊ How can we be known as people who are "waiting for the kingdom of God"?
■ What was courageous about what Joseph did?
❊ What sort of risks did Joseph take?
■ What can we learn from Joseph's example?
❊ What risks are involved in serving Christ today?
❊ What risks are involved in serving Christ in your situation?
❊ In what ways can we show our respect for Jesus Christ today?
❊ When is it difficult to demonstrate openly our loyalty to Jesus?
❊ What should we do if we feel nervous about sharing our faith because of the threat of criticism from others?
❊ Why do you think Luke mentioned that the women saw the tomb and the burial of Christ's body?
❊ What example do the women in this story set for us?
❊ What do the women in the story teach us about obedience?

APPLY IT
■ What risks might you have to take in serving Christ this week?
❊ What spiritual disciplines can you work on that will help you become a "good and upright" person?

Luke 24:1-12
The Resurrection

TOPICS
Angels, Believe, Evangelism, Fear, Good News, Jesus Christ, Miracles, Remembering, Resurrection, Witnessing

OPEN IT
❊ How do you react to good news from home?
■ When was a time you told a true story that other people found hard to believe?

EXPLORE IT
❊ Why did the women go to Jesus' tomb? (24:1)
❊ What did the women find once they arrived at the tomb? (24:2)
■ What happened while the women were wondering what had happened to Jesus' body? (24:4)
❊ Who were the two men who appeared to the women? (24:4)
❊ How did the women respond to the angels? (24:5)
❊ What did the angels tell the women about Jesus? (24:5-7)
❊ Of what words of Jesus were the women reminded? (24:7)
■ What did the women do after the men had told them

that Jesus had risen from the dead as He had predicted? (24:9)
❊ How did the apostles react to the women's testimony? (24:11)
❊ Why did the apostles not believe the women? (24:11)
❊ In what way were Peter's actions different from the other apostles? (24:12)
■ How did Peter respond to the sight of the empty tomb? (24:12)

GET IT
❊ Why is Jesus' resurrection central to the Christian faith?
❊ If the gospel is such good news, why are Christians sometimes reluctant to tell others about Christ?
❊ What would be different if Jesus had not risen from the dead?
■ Why did the disciples express disbelief even though Jesus had told them clearly that He would rise from the dead?
❊ What does this passage teach us about witnessing and evangelism?
❊ What does this account teach you about the people to whom God reveals His good news?
❊ How does this story encourage you to share your faith with others?
■ What should you do if others reject you or your testimony when you share your faith?
❊ Why do people sometimes not believe the truth of the gospel?
❊ What responsibility do we have to witness to others, even if they continue to reject the gospel?

APPLY IT
■ How can you reaffirm your faith in God's promises this week?
❊ How can you prepare yourself for your next encounter with someone who criticizes you or does not accept your testimony?

Luke 24:13-35
On the Road to Emmaus

TOPICS
Angels, Believe, Confusion, Expectations, Foolishness, Hardheartedness, Ignorance, Jesus Christ, Prophecy, Witnessing

OPEN IT
■ When have you ever suddenly understood a truth that had earlier confused you?
❊ What is it like to have an event turn out differently than you had expected?

EXPLORE IT
❊ Who was going to Emmaus? (24:13)
❊ What were the two men discussing along the way? (24:14)
❊ Who appeared to the men on the way to Emmaus? (24:15)
❊ What did Jesus ask the two men? (24:17)
❊ What emotions did the two men display? (24:17)
❊ Why did Cleopas think that Jesus must have been a visitor to Jerusalem? (24:18)
■ How did the two men describe Jesus and what had happened? (24:19-24)
❊ How had the events of the last few days crushed the expectations of the two men talking with Jesus? (24:21)
■ Why did Jesus explain the Scriptures to the men? (24:25-27)
❊ When did the men finally recognize Jesus? (24:31)
■ What did the men recall after they reflected on their conversation with Jesus? (24:32)
❊ How did these men respond to their encounter with Jesus? (24:33-35)

GET IT
■ How are your expectations of the Christian life sometimes changed by life's trials?
❊ What did you think your life would be like after you became a Christian?
❊ When have you been guilty of unbelief?
❊ Why are we so often "slow of heart to believe"?
❊ What do you think prevents people from believing in Jesus?
■ What great truths has God taught you that you failed to understand at first?
❊ In what ways has God clearly spoken to you?
❊ What can you learn about witnessing from the example of the two men in this account?

APPLY IT
❊ What could you do this week to make yourself more sensitive to the Lord's leading in your life?
■ What could you do in the future to prevent yourself from failing to recognize God's voice?

Luke 24:36-49
Jesus Appears to the Disciples

TOPICS
Believe, Doubt, Fear, Holy Spirit, Instructions, Joy, Promises, Prophecy, Resurrection, Understanding, Witnessing

OPEN IT
❊ When have you ever been really surprised?
❊ What do you like or dislike about surprises?
■ With what subjects did you have the most difficulty in school? Why?
❊ When have you ever been entrusted with a significant responsibility?

EXPLORE IT
❊ How did Jesus approach the disciples? (24:36)
■ Why were the disciples frightened? (24:37)
❊ How did Jesus try to calm and reassure the disciples? (24:38-39)
❊ What evidence did Jesus give to prove He was not a ghost? (24:39)
■ How did the disciples react to the evidence and convincing words of Jesus? (24:41)
❊ What did the disciples' actions reveal about their

understanding of what Jesus had told them earlier about His death and resurrection? (24:41)
❇ What emotions did the disciples display? (24:41)
❇ What was significant about Jesus' eating a piece of fish? (24:43)
■ When did the disciples finally understand the Scriptures? (24:44-45)
❇ How were the disciples finally able to understand the prophecies about Christ in Scripture? (24:44-45)
❇ What did Jesus explain would be the result of His resurrection? (24:47)
❇ What instructions did Jesus give to His disciples? (24:48)
❇ What was Jesus going to send the apostles? (24:48)
❇ What was the "power from on high" to which Jesus referred? (24:48)

GET IT
❇ Why did Jesus consider it important to teach the disciples from the Old Testament?
■ What does this passage teach us about God's role in our understanding of the gospel?
❇ According to this passage, how can we expect to understand the Scriptures?
■ What causes us to disbelieve the Scriptures?
❇ What proof did you need to be convinced of the truth of the gospel?
❇ In what ways have you experienced the power Jesus promised us?
❇ What responsibility do we have to share our faith with others?

APPLY IT
❇ How can you become a more regular student of the Scriptures?
■ What could you do this week to settle the doubts about salvation that your non-Christian friends have?

Luke 24:50-53
The Ascension

TOPICS
Believers, Blessing, Heaven, Jesus Christ, Joy, Praise, Worship

OPEN IT
❇ Why do engaged couples often seek their parents' blessing?
■ Whose "blessing" would you value above all? Why?
❇ In what ways do you feel you have been blessed?

EXPLORE IT
❇ Where did Jesus lead His disciples? (24:50)
❇ What did Jesus do for His disciples? (24:50)
■ Why did Jesus bless His disciples at this point? (24:50)
❇ What happened while Jesus was blessing His disciples? (24:51)
❇ How did the disciples know that Jesus was taken up into heaven? (24:51)
❇ How was this time with Jesus significant for the disciples? (24:51)
■ What was the response of the disciples to Jesus' ascension into heaven? (24:52)
❇ Why were the disciples so joyful? (24:52)
■ What is significant about the fact that Jesus' followers worshipped Him? (24:52)
❇ Why did the disciples return to Jerusalem? (24:52)
❇ What did Jesus' followers do after He left them? (24:52-53)

GET IT
❇ What do you find inspiring about the actions of Jesus' followers in this account?
■ How can we experience joy in Christ?
❇ Why is Jesus worthy of our worship?
❇ Why is it appropriate and important for Christians to praise and worship Jesus?
■ What blessings from the Lord have you experienced recently?
❇ What does this passage teach us about the mission of the church?

APPLY IT
❇ How can you worship and praise the Lord today?
❇ How can you honor Jesus for all He came and did for you?
■ When could you set aside time this week to think about the many blessings the Lord has given you?

John 1:1-19
The Word Became Flesh

TOPICS
Believe, Believers, Creation, Darkness, Glory, Grace, Jesus Christ, Law, Spiritual Rebirth

OPEN IT
❇ What are some of the slang expressions you used growing up?
■ In what ways are words different from visual images?

EXPLORE IT
❇ Who is the Word? (1:1)
■ What is the relationship between the Word and God? (1:1-2)
❇ What was the Word's role in creation? (1:3)
❇ How is the "life" the light of men? (1:4)
❇ What was John's role in relation to the light? (1:6)
❇ How did the light give light to every person? (1:9)
❇ Why didn't the world recognize the light? (1:10)
■ What is the benefit of receiving or believing in the Word? (1:12)
■ How and why did the Word make His dwelling among us? (1:14)
❇ Whose glory did the Word reveal? (1:14)
❇ What did God give us through Moses? (1:17)
❇ What did God give us through Jesus? (1:18)
❇ Why is it significant that no one has seen God but "God the One and Only"? (1:18)

GET IT
❇ Why did the Word become flesh and live among us?
■ How does a person receive the Word?
❇ What happens when we receive or believe in the Word?
❇ In what way can you receive or welcome Christ into your life?
■ What insights can you gain from seeing Jesus as God's Word?
❇ How should being a child of God affect our lives?
❇ In what way is John an example for us to follow?
❇ How did Jesus reveal God's glory to us?

APPLY IT
❇ What do you need to do to be certain of your relationship with God?
■ What will you do this week to better enjoy your status as a child of God?
❇ How should the reality that God became a man affect your life today?

John 1:19-28
John the Baptist Denies Being the Christ

TOPICS
Attitude, Believers, Humility, Integrity, Jesus Christ, Messiah, Witnessing

OPEN IT
❇ Why do people enjoy boasting about themselves and their accomplishments?
❇ Why is it hard to be humble?
■ What are the characteristics of a humble person?

EXPLORE IT
❇ What did the Jews want to know? (1:19)
❇ Who did the Jews think John was? (1:20-21)
■ What did John say about who he was? (1:20-22)
❇ In what way was John a "voice of one calling in the desert"? (1:23)
❇ What does the phrase "make straight the way for the Lord" mean? (1:23)
■ How did John "make straight the way for the Lord"? (1:23)
❇ Why did the Pharisees care that John was baptizing people? (1:24)
❇ What did John say he was not worthy to do? (1:27)
■ Whom did John say was coming after him? (12:27)
❇ Where did these events take place? (1:28)

GET IT
■ In what ways can you honor Christ with your accomplishments?
❇ How can we point others to Christ?
❇ In what situations is it difficult for you to be humble?
■ If you had been John how would you have felt about your role?
❇ In what ways is your life like John's?
❇ What special or unique means has God given you to share His Word?

APPLY IT
❇ In what way can you be a voice for Jesus?
■ What are some areas in which you struggle to be humble at this time in your life?
❇ In what specific ways can you point others to Christ this week?

John 1:29-34
Jesus the Lamb of God

TOPICS
Forgiveness, History, Holy Spirit, Jesus Christ, Messiah, Names, Security, Sin, World

OPEN IT
❇ What function do initiation rites serve in a club or society?
■ What can you infer about someone from his or her title (such as doctor, professor, or prince)?

EXPLORE IT
■ Why did John call Jesus the Lamb of God? (1:29)
❇ What are the sins of the world? (1:29)
❇ What does Jesus do with the sins of the world? (1:29)
■ What did John mean that Jesus surpassed him because He was before him? (1:30)
❇ How was Jesus before John? (1:30)
❇ Why did John say he didn't know who Jesus was? (1:31)
❇ What reason did John give for baptizing Jesus? (1:31)
❇ Why did John come to baptize people? (1:31)
❇ What creature represented the Spirit of God? (1:32)

❇ Why did the Spirit come down upon Jesus? (1:33)
❇ With what did John baptize? (1:31, 33)
❇ With what will Jesus baptize? (1:33)
■ What title did John ascribe to the person he baptized? (1:34)

GET IT
❇ What sin of yours has Jesus taken away?
■ How do we receive the forgiveness that Christ bought for us?
❇ In what way do you share Jesus' identity as a child of God?
❇ What role does the Holy Spirit play in your life?
■ How does Jesus baptize us?

APPLY IT
■ How can you honor Jesus' Sonship with your life this week?
❇ What steps can you take to appreciate better who Jesus is?
❇ In what way can you reveal Christ to others this week?

John 1:35-42
Jesus' First Disciples

TOPICS
Follow, Humility, Jesus Christ, Messiah, Names, Priorities, Witnessing

OPEN IT
❇ What gets you excited or enthusiastic?
■ How would you feel if a good friend abandoned your friendship in favor of someone else?
❇ What nicknames have you had over the years?

EXPLORE IT
❇ Who besides Jesus had disciples? (1:35)
❇ What did John say when he saw Jesus? (1:36)
❇ How did John identify Jesus for his disciples? (1:37)
■ What did John's disciples do when John identified Jesus? (1:37)
❇ What did Jesus ask John's disciples? (1:38)
❇ What did John's disciples call Jesus? (1:38)
❇ What did John's disciples ask Jesus? (1:38)
■ What was the first thing Andrew did after he had followed Jesus? (1:40)
❇ Who was Andrew's brother? (1:40)
■ What did Andrew tell his brother about Jesus? (1:41)
❇ What nickname did Jesus give to Simon? (1:42)
❇ What words did the author interpret for us? (1:37, 41, 42)

GET IT
■ What does it mean to follow Jesus?
❇ What hinders us from following Jesus?
■ What must we leave to follow Jesus?
❇ To what friends and relatives could you introduce Jesus?
❇ How can we spend time with Jesus to get to know Him better?

APPLY IT
❇ Whom do you want to introduce to Jesus this week?
❇ How could you introduce Christ to a friend or relative?
■ What change in your daily routine would enable you to follow Jesus better?

John 1:43-51
Jesus Calls Philip and Nathanael

TOPICS
Angels, Believe, Follow, God, Goodness, Heaven, Jesus Christ, Names, Surprises

OPEN IT
❇ How do people feel when they find something that's been missing for a for long time?
❇ What famous people would you like to meet? Why?
■ About what things are people today skeptical?

EXPLORE IT
❇ How did Jesus and Philip meet? (1:43)
❇ What did Jesus say to Philip? (1:43)
■ How did Philip respond to Jesus' invitation? (1:44-46)
❇ What did Philip do after he followed Jesus? (1:45)
❇ What did Philip tell Nathanael about Jesus? (1:45)
■ Why was Nathanael skeptical that Philip had found the Messiah? (1:46)
❇ How did Nathanael respond to the fact that Jesus was from Nazareth? (1:46)
❇ What did Jesus say when he saw Nathanael? (1:47)
■ What convinced Nathanael that Jesus was the Son of God? (1:47-50)
❇ What was Nathanael's response to Jesus' greeting? (1:48)
❇ Why was Nathanael surprised? (1:48)
❇ Why did Nathanael call Jesus the Son of God and the King of Israel? (1:48-49)
❇ What were the greater things to which Jesus referred? (1:50)
❇ What did Jesus tell Nathanael he would see? (1:51)
❇ Who is the Son of Man? (1:51)

GET IT
❇ What about Christ stirs skepticism today?
■ What stereotypes about Christ prevent people from trusting Him today?
❇ What convinced you that Jesus was the Son of God?
■ What makes Jesus qualified to rule our lives?
❇ How is Jesus the King of your life?
❇ What do you have in common with Jesus?
❇ How can Jesus' identity as the Son of God inspire your confidence in Him?

APPLY IT
❇ How will you show your trust in the God who knows all about you this week?
■ How would you share your faith with a skeptical person this week?
❇ In what way will you recognize Jesus as the ruler of your life today?

John 2:1-11
Jesus Changes Water to Wine

TOPICS
Assurance, Change, Confidence, Faith, Glory, Jesus Christ, Miracles, New Life, Spiritual Rebirth

OPEN IT
❊ Why are people interested in miraculous or supernatural events?
■ What makes an event miraculous or supernatural?
❊ What supernatural or miraculous events have you witnessed?

EXPLORE IT
❊ Where did the wedding take place? (2:1)
❊ Who was at the wedding? (2:1-2)
❊ What did Jesus' mother say to Him? (2:3)
■ What was Jesus' response to His mother? (2:4)
❊ How did Jesus' mother respond to His reply? (2:5)
❊ What were the water jars used for? (2:6)
❊ What did Jesus tell the servants to do? (2:7)
❊ To whom did the servants take the water? (2:8)
❊ What happened to the water? (2:9)
■ What was the banquet master's response? (2:10)
■ Why did Jesus perform this miracle? (2:11)
❊ How did Jesus' disciples respond to this miracle? (2:11)

GET IT
❊ How have you had faith in Jesus' power this week?
■ What is something you would like Jesus to change in your life?
■ What recent miracle has Jesus done in your life?
❊ How does Jesus reveal His glory to us today?
❊ In what ways has Jesus transformed you into a new person?
❊ How has Jesus given you a new life?
❊ What things has Jesus done that have caused you to have faith in Him?

APPLY IT
■ What is one specific habit or characteristic you will ask God to change in your life this week?
❊ How will you enjoy today the new life Jesus has given you?

John 2:12-25
Jesus Clears the Temple

TOPICS
Attitude, Authority, Believe, Church, Compromise, Faith, Hypocrisy, Jesus Christ, Miracles, Money, Resurrection, Zeal

OPEN IT
❊ How do you feel after a much-needed bath or shower?
■ Why do we put off necessary cleaning (such as the bedroom, car, or garage)?

EXPLORE IT
❊ With whom did Jesus go to Capernaum? (2:12)
❊ What time was it when Jesus went to Jerusalem? (2:13)
■ What did Jesus find in the temple courts? (2:14)
❊ What did Jesus do in the temple courts? (2:15)
■ How did Jesus respond to those who were selling doves? (2:16)
■ What did Jesus' disciples remember? (2:17)
❊ What did the Jews demand from Jesus? (2:18)
❊ How did Jesus respond to the demand from the Jews? (2:19)
❊ What temple did the Jews think Jesus was talking about? (2:20)
❊ What temple was Jesus talking about? (2:21)
❊ When did the disciples remember what Jesus had said? (2:22)
❊ How did the people respond to Jesus' miracles? (2:23)
❊ What was Jesus' response to those who believed in Him? (2:24-25)

GET IT
■ How has Jesus cleansed our lives?
❊ What does Jesus still need to clear out of our lives?
❊ What do we demand from Jesus?
■ How do we attempt to use the church to our own advantage?
❊ In what ways do people accuse the church or believers of being corrupt or hypocritical?
❊ What sign has Jesus given us to believe in?
❊ Why is it sometimes hard to recognize how God is working in our lives?

APPLY IT
■ What will you ask Jesus to clear out of your life this week?
❊ What demanding attitude do you need to change today?

John 3:1-21
Jesus Teaches Nicodemus

TOPICS
Assurance, Basics of the Faith, Believe, Darkness, Eternal Life, Faith, Gifts, God, Gospel, Heaven, Humility, Jesus Christ, Kingdom of God/Heaven, Love, New Life, Salvation, Unbelievers, Understanding, World

OPEN IT
■ When have you felt like you wanted to start life all over again?
❊ Why do people like to get new things (such as clothes, cars, or gadgets)?
❊ What is the best gift you have ever received?

EXPLORE IT
❊ To what group did Nicodemus belong? (3:1)
❊ At what time did Nicodemus visit Jesus? (3:2)
❊ Why did Nicodemus believe Jesus was from God? (3:2)
❊ What is the qualification for seeing the kingdom of God? (3:3)
❊ What did Nicodemus think Jesus meant when He said that a person must be born again? (3:4)
■ What is required to enter the kingdom of God? (3:5-6)
❊ How did Jesus compare the wind to the Spirit? (3:8)
❊ Why should Nicodemus have understood what Jesus said? (3:10)

❋ About what category of things did Jesus say He was talking? (3:12)
❋ Whom did Jesus say had gone to heaven? (3:13)
❋ How did Jesus compare Moses' snake with the Son of man? (3:14)
■ What is the result of believing in the Son of Man? (3:15, 18)
❋ How did God demonstrate His love for the world? (3:16)
■ Why did God send His Son into the world? (3:17)
❋ How does the person who lives by truth respond to the light? (3:19-21)

GET IT
❋ When would you say you were born again?
■ How would you describe what it means to be born again to someone?
❋ What were some of the circumstances that led you to Jesus?
❋ What were some of the things that caused you to believe that Jesus was the Son of God?
❋ Why are spiritual truths often hard to understand?
❋ What are a few spiritual truths that you struggle to understand?
■ How does God's gift of His Son affect our lives?
❋ How can a person live by the light?

APPLY IT
❋ How will you change your daily routine to better appreciate and enjoy God's gift of His Son?
■ For what specific spiritual truths will you seek answers this week?

John 3:22-36
John the Baptist's Testimony About Jesus

TOPICS
Assurance, Believe, Character, Earth, Eternal Life, Example, Faith, Gifts, God, Gospel, Heaven, Jealousy, Jesus Christ, Joy, Popularity, Rejection, Unbelievers

OPEN IT
❋ How would you feel if a friend received more recognition than you for something you both did?
■ What makes someone's testimony about an event seem either credible or incredible?

EXPLORE IT
❋ What did Jesus do with His disciples in the Judean countryside? (3:22)
❋ What was John doing at Aenon? (3:23)
❋ What eventually happened to John? (3:24)
❋ What took place between John's disciples and some Jews? (3:25)
❋ What news did John receive? (3:26)
❋ What did John say a person can receive? (3:27)
■ Who did John say he was, as well as who he wasn't? (3:28)
❋ How did John describe his feelings about Jesus becoming more important than him? (3:29)
❋ What did John say about his future status? (3:30)
■ What did John say about Jesus' future status? (3:30)
❋ Who is above all? (3:31)
❋ What did Jesus come to say? (3:32)
■ What did the people do who accepted Jesus' testimony? (3:33)
❋ What did the person whom God sent do? (3:34)
❋ What has the Father done for the Son? (3:35)
❋ What is the result of either believing or rejecting the Son?(3:36)

GET IT
❋ In what way do people only receive what is given to them from God?
■ Why is it sometimes hard to give God credit?
❋ How are we like John?
❋ What are some areas in which you struggle with being humble?
■ How can we certify that God is truthful in our lives ?
❋ How would you describe your relationship with Jesus?
❋ How does a person reject the Son?
❋ What are the consequences of rejecting the Son?

APPLY IT
■ How can you give Jesus the place of prominence He deserves in your life today?
❋ What can you do this week to show that God is truthful in your life?
❋ In what area of your life will you ask God to help you to be more humble?

John 4:1-26
Jesus Talks With a Samaritan Woman

TOPICS
Evangelism, Gifts, God, Good News, Immorality, Jesus Christ, Judging Others, Marriage, Messiah, Morality, New Life, Prejudice, Salvation, Satisfaction, Spiritual Rebirth, Status, Traditions, Witnessing, Worship

OPEN IT
■ How do people satisfy their hungers and thirsts in life?
❋ Why are the messages in TV commercials so appealing and persuasive?
❋ In what ways are people you know prejudiced?

EXPLORE IT
❋ What had the Pharisees heard about Jesus? (4:1)
❋ What did Jesus do when he heard what the Pharisees were saying about Him? (4:3)
❋ Through what place did Jesus have to travel? (4:4-5)
■ Why did Jesus sit down by Jacob's well? (4:6)
❋ What did Jesus say to the Samaritan woman? (4:7)
❋ Where were Jesus' disciples? (4:8)
❋ Why was the Samaritan woman surprised that Jesus spoke to her? (4:9)
❋ How did Jesus answer the Samaritan woman's question? (4:10)
❋ What did the Samaritan woman think Jesus was talking about? (4:11-12,15)
■ What did Jesus say would be the result of drinking the water He offered? (4:13-14)
❋ Whom did Jesus tell the Samaritan woman to go and get? (4:15)
❋ How did Jesus respond to the Samaritan woman's

answer to His request? (4:17-18)
❇ How did the Samaritan woman respond to Jesus' statements about her situation? (4:19-20)
■ How did Jesus say people would worship God? (4:21-23)
❇ What kind of worshipers does God seek? (4:23)
❇ What did Jesus say about God? (4:24)
❇ Who did Jesus say He was? (4:25-26)

GET IT
❇ What groups of people do you feel uncomfortable being around? Why?
❇ How might a person feel put off by another's background, nationality, or race?
❇ How can prejudice affect a Christian's witness?
■ How have you responded to Jesus' invitation to receive His living water?
❇ How is Jesus' gift of salvation different from what the world offers?
■ How is the world's need for salvation and eternal life like thirst?
❇ In what other ways besides thirst might you describe eternal life?
❇ How can we can worship God in spirit and in truth?

APPLY IT
■ How can you encourage others to quench their spiritual thirst this week?
❇ What are some prejudices you will ask God to help you overcome?

John 4:27-38
The Disciples Rejoin Jesus

TOPICS
Discipline, Eternal Life, Evangelism, Jesus Christ, Judging Others, Messiah, Prejudice, Tasks, Witnessing, Work

OPEN IT
■ What must a farmer do in order to enjoy an abundant harvest?
❇ When have you ever been so consumed with a task that you forgot to eat?

EXPLORE IT
❇ How did the disciples respond when they saw Jesus talking to the Samaritan woman? (4:27)
❇ What did the Samaritan woman do after she had spoken to Jesus? (4:28)
❇ What did the Samaritan woman tell the townspeople? (4:29)
❇ How did the townspeople respond to what the Samaritan woman said? (4:30)
❇ What did the disciples urge Jesus to do? (4:31)
■ What did Jesus tell the disciples? (4:32)
❇ How did the disciples respond to what Jesus told them about food? (4:33)
■ What did Jesus say was His food? (4:34)
❇ What did Jesus say about the fields? (4:35)
■ What kind of crop did Jesus say "the reaper" was harvesting? (4:36)
❇ What did Jesus send the disciples to do? (4:38)

GET IT
❇ What barriers keep us from talking to other people about Christ?
❇ How does spending time talking to Jesus affect your life?
■ What tasks in life tend to consume your attention?
❇ What are some of the sayings of Jesus that surprise you?
❇ In what way has God surprised you by what He's done in your life?
❇ What unique work has God given you to do?
■ How would you describe today the fields Jesus described to His disciples?
❇ What role can you play in the reaping and harvesting of lives for Christ?

APPLY IT
❇ What obstacle will you ask God to remove so you can help bring someone to Christ?
■ In what way can you be involved in reaping and harvesting for God's kingdom today?

John 4:39-42
Many Samaritans Believe

TOPICS
Beliefs, Believe, Convictions, Evangelism, Evidence, Faith, Jesus Christ, Knowledge, Salvation, Witnessing

OPEN IT
❇ What people have had the biggest influence on your life?
■ What are some things that we have believed based on someone else's testimony?
❇ What are some things that we can trust in because of our own personal experience?

EXPLORE IT
■ What impact did the Samaritan woman's testimony have on the townspeople? (4:39)
❇ What did the woman tell the Samaritan people Jesus told her? (4:39)
❇ What did the Samaritans urge Jesus to do? (4:40)
❇ What did Jesus do in response to the Samaritan's request? (4:40)
■ What did Jesus rely on to convince more people to believe in Him? (4:41)
❇ What impact did Jesus' words have on the Samaritan people? (4:41)
❇ Why did the Samaritan people originally believe in Jesus? (4:42)
❇ What new basis did the Samaritans have for their belief in Jesus? (4:42)
❇ What difference did hearing Jesus for themselves make to the Samaritans? (4:42)
■ What did the Samaritan people believe about Jesus? (4:42)

GET IT
❇ What impact does your testimony have on other people?
■ What impact have other people's testimonies had on your life?

❇ Who do most people think Jesus is and what is the basis for their belief?
❇ Who do you think Jesus is? Why?
■ What led you to believe in Jesus?
❇ What people were influential in leading you to believe in Jesus?
❇ How has believing in Jesus changed your life?

APPLY IT
❇ Whom can you tell about Jesus? When?
■ In what ways could you be a better testimony for Jesus today?
❇ What can you do to help clear up other people's misconceptions about who Jesus is?

John 4:43-54
Jesus Heals the Official's Son

TOPICS
Attitude, Believe, Convictions, Courage, Determination, Faith, Healing, Jesus Christ, Miracles, Motives, Sickness, Trust

OPEN IT
■ What are some things that people believe in that they either haven't seen or can't see?
❇ What celebrity you would gladly welcome as a guest in your home? Why?

EXPLORE IT
❇ Where did Jesus go after He left Samaria? (4:43)
❇ What did Jesus say about prophets? (4:44)
❇ Why did the Galileans welcome Jesus? (4:45)
❇ What had Jesus done in Cana? (4:46)
❇ What did the royal official ask Jesus to do? (4:47)
■ What did Jesus say about miraculous signs? (4:48)
❇ How did the royal official respond to Jesus' comment about miraculous signs? (4:49)
■ What did Jesus say in response to the royal official's renewed request? (4:50)
❇ What was the royal official's response to what Jesus said? (4:50)
❇ When did the royal official's son get better? (4:51-53)
■ What impact did Jesus' healing have on the royal official's household? (4:53)
❇ How many miracles had Jesus performed? (4:54)

GET IT
❇ For what reasons are people are interested in Jesus today?
❇ In what ways are we typically more interested in what Jesus can do for us than what we can do for Jesus?
❇ What miracles have you asked Jesus to do in your life?
■ When do we usually find ourselves asking God to help us?
❇ Why is it sometimes hard to take Jesus at His word?
❇ What are some things God has told us in His Word that are hard for you to believe?
❇ How have you exercised believing—sight unseen—faith in Jesus?
❇ What miraculous signs are people looking for today?
❇ In what ways are we demanding of God in our relationship with Him?
■ What impact would a miraculous event have in your life?
❇ What are some miracles has God worked in your life?

APPLY IT
■ What is something specific you can thank God for doing in your life?
❇ How do you need to trust in God this week to handle a situation you can't control or work out on your own?

John 5:1-15
The Healing at the Pool

TOPICS
Attitude, Church, Depend, Healing, Jesus Christ, Law, Legalism, Miracles, New Life, Religion, Sin, Trust

OPEN IT
■ Why might someone prefer rules and regulations to freedom?
❇ In what way are relationships more important than rules and regulations?

EXPLORE IT
❇ For what event did Jesus go to Jerusalem? (5:1)
❇ Who came to the pool near the Sheep Gate in Jerusalem? (5:2-3)
❇ How long had the one invalid man been at the pool? (5:5)
■ What did Jesus ask the invalid man? (5:6)
❇ How did the invalid man respond to Jesus' question? (5:7)
❇ What did Jesus command the invalid man to do? (5:8)
❇ What happened to the invalid man after Jesus spoke to him? (5:9)
❇ On what day of the week did this miracle take place? (5:9)
■ What did the Jews say to the healed man? Why? (5:10)
❇ How did the healed man respond to the Jews' question? (5:11)
❇ What did the Jews ask the healed man? (5:12)
❇ Why didn't the man know who healed him? (5:13)
■ What did Jesus tell the man he had healed on their second encounter? (5:14)
❇ What did the healed man do after he spoke with Jesus a second time? (5:15)

GET IT
❇ In what way do you think life is unfair?
❇ When have you felt as if life has dealt you a bad hand?
❇ When have you felt that God was waiting too long to do something you'd trusted Him to do?
❇ When do we tend to get impatient with God's timing in our lives?
❇ On what in life, other than God, do we sometimes depend?
❇ Why do we attempt to take matters into our own hands, rather than trust God to work them out?
■ When has someone tried to squelch your freedom in Christ with religious rules or regulations?
■ Why do some people care more about keeping certain

"religious" rules than they do about developing a meaningful relationship with Jesus?
❇ What rules tend to interfere with your enjoyment of your relationship with Christ?
❇ In what way has Jesus made you well?

APPLY IT
❇ What is something you need to trust God with today?
❇ Who is someone you can encourage to enjoy his or her relationship with Christ this week?
■ What "religious" rule that hinders your relationship with Christ will you make secondary to that relationship this week?

John 5:16-30
Life Through the Son

TOPICS
Assurance, Believe, Enemies, Eternal Life, Faith, God, Jesus Christ, Judgment, New Life, Parents, Persecution, Salvation, Security

OPEN IT
❇ What different groups of people have suffered persecution throughout history?
■ What are some of the positive aspects of your relationship with your parents?

EXPLORE IT
❇ Why did the Jews persecute Jesus? (5:16)
❇ Whose work did Jesus do? (5:17)
❇ Why did certain Jews want to kill Jesus? (5:18)
■ What did Jesus say that the Son could do? (5:19)
❇ What did Jesus tell the Jews that He would show them? (5:20)
❇ What did Jesus say He was able to do? (5:21)
❇ To whom did God entrust all judgment? (5:22)
■ Why did God entrust judgment to Christ? (5:23)
❇ How did Jesus say a person can gain eternal life? (5:24)
❇ What time did Jesus say had already come? (5:25)
■ What did Jesus say the Father has in Himself that He has granted to the Son? (5:26)
❇ What time did Jesus say was coming? (5:28-29)
❇ Whom did Jesus say He desires to please? (5:30)

GET IT
❇ In what way does the world persecute Christians today?
❇ How have you been persecuted as a believer?
❇ When have you experienced pressure not to practice or share your faith in Christ?
❇ Why does the world persecute Christians?
■ How can we honor the Son and the Father with our lives?
❇ How can we know for sure that we have eternal life?
■ Why should we feel secure in our relationship with God?
❇ How should we prepare ourselves for Jesus' judgment?
❇ In what way are we like Jesus with respect to our relationship with God the Father?
❇ In what way is Jesus an example for us to follow?

APPLY IT
■ What steps can you take this week to enjoy more fully your relationship with your Heavenly Father?
❇ What can you do today to bring honor to God?
❇ How will you allow Jesus' example in this passage of Scripture to influence your life this week?

John 5:31-47
Testimonies About Jesus

TOPICS
Assurance, Authority, Believe, Bible, Church, Eternal Life, God, Jesus Christ, Legalism, Life, Light, Popularity, Praise

OPEN IT
❇ What motivates people to want to be famous, rich, successful, or powerful?
■ What makes someone's testimony valid or invalid?
❇ How can the details sometimes prevent us from seeing the big picture?

EXPLORE IT
■ Whose testimony did Jesus say was valid? (5:31-32)
❇ What did Jesus say John did? (5:33)
❇ Why did Jesus mention John's testimony? (5:34)
❇ What did Jesus say John was? (5:35)
■ What did Jesus say testified to the fact that the Father had sent Him? (5:36)
❇ Who else did Jesus say testified about Him? (5:37)
■ Why did the Jews study the Scriptures? (5:39)
❇ What was the result of all the Jews' study of the Scriptures? (5:40)
❇ What did Jesus' audience not have in their hearts? (5:42)
❇ Whose praise did the Jews neglect to seek? (5:43-44)
❇ Who was the Jews' accuser? (5:45)
❇ About whom did Moses write? (5:46)
❇ What effect should Moses' writings have had on the Jews? (5:46-47)

GET IT
■ How is your life like a lamp pointing others to Jesus?
❇ Why do you believe in Jesus?
❇ On what authority can we rest our belief in Jesus?
■ How could someone study the Scriptures and still not believe in Jesus?
❇ From whom do you seek praise and recognition?
❇ In what do you find your significance and security in life?
❇ In what way might the church sometimes prevent people from seeing and believing in Jesus?
❇ What should we do to gain the praise of God?

APPLY IT
■ Starting today, how can you seek greater recognition for God's ways?
❇ How can you make your study of Scripture more Christ-centered this week?
❇ What step can you take to become a brighter lamp pointing to Jesus?

John 6:1-15
Jesus Feeds the Five Thousand

TOPICS
Appreciation, Expectations, Faith, Jesus Christ, Miracles, Motives, Needs, Testing, Thankfulness

OPEN IT
■ What is the most difficult situation in which you have ever found yourself?
❊ In what exciting events have you recently participated? What made them exciting?

EXPLORE IT
❊ Where did Jesus go? (6:1)
❊ Why did the crowd of people follow Jesus? (6:2)
❊ Where did Jesus and His disciples go? (6:3)
❊ What Jewish feast was near? (6:4)
■ What question did Jesus ask Philip? (6:5)
❊ Why did Jesus ask Philip a question? (6:6)
❊ How did Philip respond to Jesus' question? (6:7)
❊ Who was Andrew? (6:8)
❊ What role did Andrew play in feeding the five thousand? (6:8-9)
❊ What solution did Andrew propose to Jesus' question? (6:8-9)
■ What miracle did Jesus perform? (6:10-11)
❊ How much bread was left over? (6:12-13)
■ How did the crowd of people respond to Jesus' miracle? (6:14)
❊ What did the crowd of people intend to do? (6:15)
❊ What was Jesus' reaction to the crowd's intention? (6:15)

GET IT
❊ For what reasons do people follow Jesus today?
❊ What makes you want to follow Jesus?
❊ What is your typical reaction to situations that seem to present no readily available solution?
■ With what situations in life do you have a difficult time trusting God?
❊ What does God provide for us on a daily basis?
❊ In what ways do people attempt to use Jesus or His name inappropriately?
❊ What misconceptions have you had about Jesus or His role in your life?
■ How and when has God miraculously provided for your needs?
❊ How can we trust God with our needs?

APPLY IT
❊ What things do you need to thank God for providing?
■ What tough situation do you need to trust God to work out in your life this week?

John 6:16-24
Jesus Walks on the Water

TOPICS
Circumstances, Fear, Insecurity, Jesus Christ, Miracles, Nature, People, Power, Sovereignty

OPEN IT
■ What is the most frightening situation you have ever experienced?
❊ What is something you feared as a child?
❊ What is something you have diligently pursued in life?

EXPLORE IT
❊ Where did Jesus' disciples go? (6:16)
❊ Who hadn't joined the disciples yet? (6:17)
❊ What happened to the water? (6:18)
■ What miraculous feat did Jesus perform? (6:19)
■ How did the disciples react to what they saw? (6:19)
❊ What did Jesus do to calm His disciples' fear? (6:20)
■ What miraculous event took place once Jesus entered the boat? (6:21)
❊ Where was the crowd? (6:22)
❊ What did the crowd realize? (6:22)
❊ What did the crowd do when they realized that neither Jesus nor His disciples were there? (6:24)

GET IT
❊ When and why have you ever been afraid for your life or personal safety?
■ When do you feel alone and in need of God's presence?
❊ When do you tend to leave Jesus behind and out of the picture in your life?
■ What fears has Jesus calmed in your life?
❊ Under what circumstances are you often unwilling to allow Jesus to enter your problems or troubling situations?
❊ What circumstances or events have caused you to search for Jesus?

APPLY IT
■ How will you depend on God the next time a threatening situation confronts you?
❊ What specific fears do you need to ask God to calm in your life?

John 6:25-59
Jesus the Bread of Life

TOPICS
Acceptance, Assurance, Attitude, Believe, Depend, Eternal Life, Faith, God, Gospel, Heaven, Insecurity, Jesus Christ, Lord's Supper, Love, New Life, Promises, Salvation, Security, Self-esteem, Value

OPEN IT
❊ What kind of bread do you like most?
■ How do people attempt to satisfy their need to feel secure and significant in life?
❊ What needs do you spend the majority of your time trying to satisfy?

EXPLORE IT
■ Why did the crowd seek Jesus? (6:26)
❊ What did Jesus say the Son of Man would give to these people? (6:27)
❊ What did Jesus say was the work of God? (6:28-29)
❊ What did the crowd ask Jesus to do? (6:30-31)

❇ Who did Jesus say was the true bread of life? (6:32-33)
■ What did Jesus say would be the result of coming to Him? (6:35)
❇ What did Jesus say He would never do to those who came to Him? (6:37)
❇ Why did Jesus come down from heaven? (6:38)
❇ What did Jesus say is the Father's will? (6:39-40)
❇ Why did the Jews begin to grumble? (6:41-42)
❇ Who did Jesus say could come to Him? (6:43-44)
❇ What did Jesus say would be the result of believing? (6:47)
■ What contrast does Jesus make between manna and the bread of life? (6:48-51, 58)
❇ What did Jesus say about His flesh and His blood? (6:53-57)

GET IT
■ What things do we seek from Jesus?
❇ In what ways do you have a demanding attitude toward God?
❇ When and why did you come to Jesus?
■ In what way has Jesus satisfied your hunger and thirst for acceptance and meaning in life?
❇ In what ways do you still feel empty?
❇ What situations cause you to feel insecure?
❇ When do you feel secure in your relationship with God? Why?
❇ How has the Christian life turned out to be different from what you expected?
❇ In what way is Jesus an example for us to follow?

APPLY IT
■ What can you do today to rely on God, rather than on things or people, to satisfy your needs?
❇ What demanding attitudes do you need to ask God to help you change?

John 6:60-71
Many Disciples Desert Jesus

TOPICS
Abandon, Believe, Confusion, Decisions, Doubt, Eternal Life, Hardheartedness, Jesus Christ, People, Questions, Rejection, Satan, Security, Understanding

OPEN IT
■ What is something that you enthusiastically started but were later tempted to quit?
❇ For what causes have people willingly suffered and even died?

EXPLORE IT
■ How did many of Jesus' disciples respond to His teaching? (6:60)
❇ What did Jesus ask the grumbling disciples? (6:31)
❇ What kind of words did Jesus speak to His audience? (6:63)
■ What did Jesus know? (6:64)
❇ Who did Jesus say could come to Him? (6:65)
❇ What did many of Jesus' disciples do after Jesus spoke these words? (6:66)
❇ What question did Jesus ask His twelve disciples? (6:67)
■ What was Peter's reply to Jesus' question? (6:68-69)
❇ What did Jesus say about His disciples? (6:70)
❇ Whom did Jesus call a devil? (6:71)

GET IT
■ What teachings of Jesus have you found difficult to understand or accept?
❇ What makes some of Jesus' teachings difficult to understand and follow?
❇ What might cause someone to stop following Jesus?
❇ When have you ever felt like turning away from following Jesus?
■ What has kept you from turning away from Christ?
❇ What makes you believe that Jesus is the Son of God?

APPLY IT
■ What difficult teaching of Jesus will you ask God to help you understand and apply to your life?
❇ What struggling Christian could use your encouragement this week as he or she continues to follow Jesus?

John 7:1-13
Jesus Goes to the Feast of Tabernacles

TOPICS
Believe, Compromise, Doubt, Evil, Faith, Family, Fear, Friendship, God's Will, Jesus Christ, Mission, Timing, Truth, Unbelievers, World

OPEN IT
❇ Who are some of today's most controversial personalities?
■ What dynamic figure from history do you admire? Why?

EXPLORE IT
❇ Why did Jesus stay away from Judea? (7:1)
❇ What feast was near? (7:2)
■ What did Jesus' brothers tell Him to do? (7:3-4)
❇ Why did Jesus' brothers tell Him to do this? (7:5)
❇ How did Jesus respond to His brothers' words? (7:6-8)
■ Why did Jesus say the world hated Him? (7:7)
❇ What did Jesus do when His brothers had left? (7:9)
❇ What were the Jews doing at the feast? (7:11)
■ What were people at the feast saying about Jesus? (7:12)
❇ Why didn't the people speak publicly about Jesus? (7:13)

GET IT
❇ What sort of things are people today saying about Jesus?
❇ How would you feel if either a family member or friend doubted you or your abilities?
■ How have you been punished or put down for speaking the truth?
❇ How would you feel if you knew that someone hated you?
❇ What would you do if you knew that someone hated you?
■ In what different ways do people react to unwelcome truth?
❇ When have you been afraid to openly share your beliefs about Jesus?
❇ In what way is the world today evil?

APPLY IT

❊ How will you encourage either a family member or friend today?

■ In what area of your life do you need to ask God to help you boldly speak the truth?

John 7:14-24

Jesus Teaches at the Feast

TOPICS

Appearance, Assumptions, Demons, Hypocrisy, Jesus Christ, Judging Others, Law, Legalism, Traditions, Truth, Unbelievers

OPEN IT

❊ When have you gotten so caught up with rules and regulations that you missed entirely the joy of living?

■ When have you judged someone or something on appearance alone only to find out later that you were wrong?

EXPLORE IT

❊ What did Jesus do halfway through the Feast? (7:14)

❊ How did the Jews respond to Jesus' teaching? (7:15)

❊ From where did Jesus' teaching come? (7:16)

■ How did Jesus say someone could discover whether or not His teaching came from God? (7:17)

❊ What quality did Jesus say a person of truth possesses? (7:18)

❊ What questions did Jesus ask the Jews? (7:19)

■ What did the crowd accuse Jesus of being? (7:20)

❊ Why did Jesus say the Jews were astonished? (7:21)

❊ Why did Jesus comment on circumcision? (7:22-23)

❊ What evidence did Jesus use to show that the Jews also believed in doing good on the Sabbath? (7:22-23)

❊ How did Jesus compare His healing with circumcision? (7:23)

■ What did Jesus instruct His audience to do? (7:24)

GET IT

■ How do people today respond to the teaching of Jesus?

❊ What gives you the confidence to believe that what Jesus taught is true?

❊ How can we become men and women of truth?

■ What rules do we force on others while overlooking our own violations?

❊ What are the important issues in today's society about which the Church should be concerned?

❊ Why do we tend to judge things and people based solely on appearances?

APPLY IT

❊ What hypocritical standard do you need to change in your life this week?

■ How can you put aside a prejudice in order to get to know a person you have misjudged?

John 7:25-44

Is Jesus the Christ?

TOPICS

Believe, Divisions, Doubt, Faith, God, Jesus Christ, Messiah, Miracles, Rejection, Religion, Satisfaction, Security, Society, Unbelievers, World

OPEN IT

❊ In what do people today put their faith?

■ What ideas tend to cause division among the people you know?

EXPLORE IT

■ What questions did the people begin asking about Jesus? (7:25-26)

❊ Why was it significant that people knew where Jesus was from? (7:27)

❊ What did Jesus cry out in the temple court? (7:28-29)

❊ What did the people try to do? (7:30)

❊ Why were the people unsuccessful in trying to seize Jesus? (7:30)

■ What reason did some of the people give for putting their faith in Jesus? (7:31)

❊ What did the Pharisees do when they heard the crowd talking about Jesus? (7:32)

❊ How long did Jesus say He would be with His audience? (7:33)

❊ What did Jesus say the people would be unable to do? (7:34)

❊ How did the Jews respond to what Jesus said? (7:35-36)

❊ What invitation did Jesus offer on the last day of the Feast? (7:37)

❊ What result did Jesus promise for those who believed in Him? (7:38)

❊ Why hadn't the Spirit been given yet? (7:39)

■ What conclusions did the people come to about Jesus? (7:40-41)

❊ Why did the people get confused over Jesus' identity? (7:41-42)

❊ What affect did Jesus have on these people? (7:43)

❊ What did some of the people want to do? (7:44)

GET IT

❊ What has the world as a whole concluded about Jesus?

❊ What can you tell about a person from his or her hometown?

❊ How has your background shaped you into the person you are today?

❊ When do you feel most refreshed in your relationship with Christ?

■ How has Jesus caused division among groups of people with whom you are associated?

❊ How has Jesus satisfied your thirsts and longings in life?

■ In what way do we attempt to satisfy our thirsts and longings in life outside of Christ?

APPLY IT

■ What specific thirst or longing do you need to trust Christ to satisfy this week?

❊ How can you refresh your relationship with God today?

John 7:45-52
Unbelief of the Jewish Leaders

TOPICS
Acceptance, Authority, Influence, Jesus Christ, Leadership, Motives, Peer Pressure, Prejudice, Society, Status, Unbelievers, World

OPEN IT
❊ Why do people join groups, clubs, and associations?
■ To what groups do you belong? Which is your favorite?

EXPLORE IT
❊ What explanation did the temple guards give for not bringing Jesus to the chief priests and Pharisees? (7:45-46)
■ How can we infer that the temple guard recognized Jesus' authority? (7:46)
❊ Of what did the Pharisees accuse the temple guards? (7:47)
❊ What groups of people had not believed in Jesus? (7:48)
❊ Why did the Pharisees claim there was a curse on the mob of people who believed in Jesus? (7:49)
■ To what group did Nicodemus belong? (7:50)
❊ What question did Nicodemus ask? (7:51)
❊ What question was Nicodemus asked? (7:52)
■ What claim did the Pharisees make about Galilee? (7:52)

GET IT
■ To what groups in your church do you belong?
❊ How might your membership in certain groups influence your opinions or beliefs?
❊ What religious groups have power and authority in today's society?
■ How might today's religious leaders react to Jesus if He came back today?
❊ Why do we tend to judge others before we actually get to know them?
❊ How do we sometimes abuse spiritual authority?

APPLY IT
■ What groups that further the cause of Christ can you support? How?
❊ How can you glorify God in the places of authority you hold?

John 7:53–8:11
A Woman Caught in Adultery

TOPICS
Accusation, Adultery, Failure, Faults, Forgiveness, Hypocrisy, Immorality, Jesus Christ, Judging Others, Legalism, Punishment, Self-righteousness, Sin

OPEN IT
■ What sins do most people think they are incapable of committing?
❊ What activities or behavior do you consider to be immoral?
❊ What do you think is the biggest challenge to marriages today?

EXPLORE IT
❊ Where did Jesus go? (8:1)
❊ What did Jesus sit down to do in the temple courts? (8:2)
❊ Whom did the Pharisees bring before Jesus? (8:3-4)
■ What did the Law of Moses say should happen to the woman caught in adultery? (8:5)
❊ Why did the Pharisees bring the woman before Jesus? (8:6)
❊ How did Jesus answer the Pharisees' question? (8:6-8)
■ Why did Jesus issue a challenge to the Pharisees? (8:7)
❊ How did the Pharisees respond to Jesus' challenge? (8:9)
❊ What did Jesus ask the woman? (8:10)
■ What did Jesus tell the woman to do? (8:11)

GET IT
■ Which sins do we tend to categorize as "big" sins (those that are worse than all others)?
❊ Why do we rush to point out other people's sin?
❊ Which sins do you think God classifies as "big" sins?
❊ How do we treat people who have fallen into one of the so-called "big" sins?
■ How should we treat people who have sinned?
❊ About what do you tend to be self-righteous?
❊ What should we do when we've sinned?

APPLY IT
❊ How can you challenge a friend or family member caught in sin to sin no more?
❊ Away from what bad habit or tendency do you need to take the first step today?
■ What self-righteous attitude will you ask God to change in your prayers this week?

John 8:12-30
The Validity of Jesus' Testimony

TOPICS
Authority, Believe, Darkness, Eternal Life, Faith, God, Jesus Christ, Judgment, Knowledge, Leadership, Light, People, World

OPEN IT
❊ What kind of credentials are valued most by the people you work with?
■ When was a time you were able to verify someone else's testimony?

EXPLORE IT
❊ Who did Jesus say that He was? (8:12)
❊ What did Jesus say would be the result of following Him? (8:12)
❊ How did the Pharisees challenge Jesus? (8:13)
■ Why did Jesus say His own testimony was valid? (8:14)
❊ Why did Jesus say His decisions were right? (8:15-16)
■ What two witnesses did Jesus claim testified on His behalf? (8:17-18)

❊ Why did Jesus say that the Pharisees didn't know His Father? (8:19)
❊ Why didn't anyone seize Jesus? (8:20)
❊ How did the Jews respond to Jesus' words? (8:21-22)
❊ What did Jesus say would be the consequence of not believing in Him? (8:23-24)
❊ What question did the Jews ask Jesus? (8:25)
❊ How did Jesus answer the Jews' question? (8:25-26)
■ At what point did Jesus say that the people would know who He was? (8:27-28)
❊ Whom did Jesus say He pleased? (8:29)
❊ How did the people respond to Jesus' words? (8:30)

GET IT
❊ How do you know God the Father?
❊ In what way is Jesus a "light"?
❊ How is Jesus the light in your world?
❊ How were you in darkness before you believed in Jesus?
■ Why is Jesus' testimony credible to you?
❊ Why are people today confused about Jesus' identity?
❊ How is Jesus' relationship with God an example for our relationship with God?
❊ In what way has God been reliable in your life?
■ What would people say about the validity of your testimony?

APPLY IT
❊ How can you seek to please God with what you do today?
■ In what way can you testify on behalf of Jesus this week?

John 8:31-41
The Children of Abraham

TOPICS
Believe, Children, Freedom, God, Jesus Christ, New Life, Salvation, Sin, Slavery, Unbelievers, Understanding, Words

OPEN IT
■ To what sort of things do people today become enslaved?
❊ What does it mean to you to be free? What doesn't it mean?

EXPLORE IT
❊ What did Jesus say to the Jews who had believed in Him? (8:31)
■ What did Jesus say the truth would do for those who knew it? (8:32)
❊ How did the Jews respond to Jesus' statement about freedom? (8:33)
■ Who did Jesus say is a slave to sin? (8:34)
❊ How does Jesus distinguish a slave from a son? (8:35)
■ What is the result of being freed by the Son? (8:36)
❊ What did Jesus say the Jews were ready to do? (8:37)
❊ Who did the Jews say was their father? (8:39)
❊ In what way were the Jews mistaken about Abraham? (8:39)
❊ What did Abraham not do? (8:40)
❊ What claim did Jesus' accusers make? (8:41)

GET IT
❊ How are you like your mother or father?
❊ To what sin are you a slave?
■ From what sin have you been set free?
■ How does truth set someone free?
❊ How has the Son set you free?
❊ In what way are we like God our Father?
❊ When do we act like illegitimate children?

APPLY IT
■ How can you better enjoy your freedom in the Son?
❊ From what enslaving sin will you ask God to set you free?
❊ What action will you take in order to act more like a child of God?

John 8:42-47
The Children of the Devil

TOPICS
Believe, Children, God, Heresy, Jesus Christ, Love, Parents, Satan, Sin, Truth, Understanding, Words

OPEN IT
❊ What languages other than English have you learned or would you like to learn?
■ What makes mastering a second language so difficult?

EXPLORE IT
❊ What did Jesus say the Jews would do if God were their Father? (8:42)
❊ Who sent Jesus? (8:42)
■ Why did Jesus say that His language was unclear to His audience? (8:43)
❊ What shocking fact did Jesus reveal about His audience? (8:44)
❊ What did Jesus say was not in the devil? (8:44)
■ What is the devil's native language? (8:44)
❊ Of what did Jesus say the devil was the father? (8:44)
❊ Why did Jesus' audience not did believe Him? (8:45)
❊ What did Jesus ask His audience to prove? (8:46)
■ What did Jesus say that the person who belonged to God heard? (8:47)
❊ What reason did Jesus give for these people's lack of hearing? (8:47)

GET IT
❊ In what way are you like your parents?
❊ What points to the fact that you belong to God?
❊ How does a person show love for Jesus?
■ What truths do you have a difficult time accepting?
❊ How is our love for God reflected in our love for Christ?
■ What does your speech reveal about you?
❊ What is your native language: truth, lies, or another language?
❊ How can we learn a new language?

APPLY IT
❊ What truth that is difficult for you to face will you ask God to help you confront today?
❊ What change in your speech can you make this week to reflect your status as a child of God?

John 8:48-59

The Claims of Jesus About Himself

TOPICS

Accusation, Authority, Believe, Death, Demons, Glory, God, Hardheartedness, Heresy, Jesus Christ, Motives, Truth, Unbelievers, Understanding, Words

OPEN IT

❇ Over what area of your life do you feel you have the least amount of control?
■ How would you respond if you were falsely accused of doing something you hadn't done?

EXPLORE IT

■ Of what did the Jews accuse Jesus? (8:48)
❇ How did Jesus respond to the accusation against Him? (8:49)
❇ What did Jesus say He wasn't seeking? (8:50)
❇ What did Jesus say would be the result of keeping His word? (8:51)
❇ How did the Jews respond to Jesus' claim? (8:52)
❇ What question did the Jews ask Jesus? (8:53)
❇ Who glorifies Jesus? (8:54)
■ Whom did Jesus claim to know? (8:55)
❇ What made Abraham rejoice? (8:56)
■ Why were the Jews so astonished by what Jesus said? (8:57)
❇ Before whom did Jesus claim He had existed? (8:58)
❇ What did the Jews attempt to do to Jesus? (8:58-59) Why?

GET IT

❇ How do you usually respond to things you don't understand or can't explain?
❇ How do you respond to situations that you can't control?
■ How do you respond when your authority is being challenged?
❇ To what authorities in life do you appeal for truth?
❇ Whose glory do you seek?
■ How can you honor God with your life?
❇ How does a person keep Jesus' word?
❇ How well do you keep Jesus' word?
❇ How do you know that you know God?

APPLY IT

❇ What is one way that you can honor God with your life today?
■ How can you seek God's glory rather than your own in your work this week?
❇ What do you need to do in order to keep Jesus' word?

John 9:1-12

Jesus Heals a Man Born Blind

TOPICS

Abilities, Circumstances, Glory, God, Healing, Jesus Christ, Light, Miracles, New Life, Parents, Sin, World

OPEN IT

❇ What goes through your mind when you see a disabled person?
■ In what way would being blind change your life?

EXPLORE IT

❇ How long had the man Jesus saw been blind? (9:1)
■ What question did Jesus' disciples ask Him about the blind man's condition? (9:2)
■ Why had this man had been born blind? (9:3)
❇ What did Jesus say that they should be doing as long as it is day? (9:4)
❇ What did Jesus claim to be? (9:5)
❇ What did Jesus put on the blind man's eyes? (9:6)
❇ What happened to the blind man? (9:7)
❇ How did the blind man's neighbors respond to his new condition? (9:9)
❇ What question did the blind man's neighbors ask him? (9:10)
■ How did the blind man answer his neighbors' question? (9:11)
❇ What did the man's neighbors want to know? (9:12)

GET IT

❇ How do our sins affect us physically or emotionally?
❇ How do our sins affect others?
❇ With what condition were you born so that God might be glorified?
❇ Through what disability or weakness can you glorify God?
❇ What work has God given you to do while you still have time?
■ In what way has God healed you?
■ In what ways are we spiritually blind?
❇ From what "blindness" has God healed you?
❇ How did your family and friends respond when you put your faith in Christ?

APPLY IT

■ Through what shortcoming in your life will you ask God to glorify Himself today?
❇ For what healing in your life will you praise God today?

John 9:13-34

The Pharisees Investigate the Healing

TOPICS

Believe, Challenge, Church, Comfortable, Complacency, God, Hardheartedness, Healing, Heresy, Hypocrisy, Jesus Christ, Leadership, Miracles, Parents, Sin, Status, Traditions, Unbelievers

OPEN IT

■ Who do you know who has challenged "the establishment" or "the system"?
❇ About what do you tend to get complacent?

EXPLORE IT

❇ To whom was the blind man taken? (9:13)
❇ On what day did Jesus heal the blind man? (9:14)
❇ What did the Pharisees ask the blind man? (9:15)

❊ Over what were the Pharisees divided? (9:16)
❊ Who did the blind man think Jesus was? (9:17)
❊ Why did the Pharisees send for the blind man's parents? (9:18)
■ How did the blind man's parents answer the Pharisees' questions? (9:19-21)
❊ What did the blind man's parents fear? (9:22-23)
❊ What did the Pharisees ask the blind man to do? (9:24)
■ How did the blind man respond to the Pharisees? (9:25)
❊ What question did the blind man ask the Pharisees? (9:27)
❊ Whose disciples did the Pharisees claim to be? (9:28)
❊ What did the blind man say was remarkable? (9:29-30)
❊ What did the blind man say nobody had ever done? (9:31-32)
■ What convinced the blind man that Jesus was from God? (9:33)
❊ What did the Pharisees do to the man who was born blind? (9:34)

GET IT
❊ What divides Christian leaders today?
❊ How would you react to a miraculous healing?
❊ Why do you believe Jesus is from God?
❊ When have your parents disappointed you?
❊ How do you respond when your authority is challenged?
■ What authority have you ever challenged?
❊ How do people respond when the status quo is disturbed?
■ In what way has Jesus upset the status quo in your life?
❊ When have you allowed fear to control your behavior?
❊ In what way are Christians today complacent?
❊ In what way has Jesus opened your once-blind eyes?

APPLY IT
❊ What area of your life about which you have become complacent do you need to allow Jesus to revitalize? How?
❊ What program in your church about which people have become complacent can you help revitalize?
■ How would you challenge someone this week who disputed the authority of God?

John 9:35-41
Spiritual Blindness

TOPICS
Acceptance, Believe, Faith, Jesus Christ, Judgment, Religion, Sin, World, Worship

OPEN IT
❊ What is one cause or person for which you would risk being disowned by your family and all your friends?
■ What person outside your family has had the biggest impact on your life?

EXPLORE IT
❊ What had Jesus heard? (9:35)
■ What did Jesus ask the man who had been blind? (9:35)
❊ Why did the blind man ask Jesus to identity the Son of Man? (9:36)
■ Who did Jesus claim to be? (9:37)
■ What did the blind man do when Jesus told him who He was? (9:38)
❊ According to Jesus, why had He come into the world? (9:39)
❊ What people expressed shock at what Jesus said? (9:40)
❊ What did the Pharisees ask Jesus? (9:40)
❊ What did Jesus mean by saying "but now that you claim you can see, your guilt remains"? (9:41)
❊ Why did Jesus say that the Pharisees' guilt would remain? (9:41)

GET IT
❊ When have you felt unaccepted by other believers?
■ In what circumstances do you usually worship Jesus?
■ In what way are people today spiritually blind?
❊ How has Jesus healed you of your spiritual blindness?
❊ How has Jesus' healing of your spiritual blindness changed your life?

APPLY IT
❊ For what do you need to worship Jesus and God today?
■ For what person who is spiritually blind will you pray that God would open his or her eyes?

John 10:1-21
The Shepherd and His Flock

TOPICS
Eternal Life, Follow, God, Jesus Christ, Life, Listening, Love, New Life, Obedience, Relationships, Sacrifice, Salvation

OPEN IT
■ What person or group did you and your friends "follow" when you were a teenager?
❊ What qualities do the best friends possess?

EXPLORE IT
❊ Who did Jesus say was a thief and a robber? (10:1)
❊ What kind of relationship do sheep have with their shepherd? (10:2-4)
■ Why won't sheep follow a stranger? (10:5)
❊ What effect did Jesus' words have on His audience? (10:6)
❊ What did Jesus say He was? (10:7)
❊ To whom did Jesus say the sheep did not listen? (10:8)
❊ What did Jesus say would be the result of entering through Him? (10:9)
■ How did Jesus contrast His coming with the coming of a thief? (10:10)
❊ Whom did Jesus claim to be? (10:11)
❊ Why did Jesus say the hired hand would abandon his sheep? (10:12-13)
❊ What type of a relationship did Jesus say He had with His sheep? (10:14)
■ What did Jesus say He did for His sheep? (10:15)
❊ What did Jesus say He had? (10:16)

❋ Why did Jesus say the Father loved Him? (10:17-18)
❋ What effect did Jesus' words have on the Jews who heard Him speak? (10:19-21)

GET IT
❋ In what way is Jesus like a gate?
❋ How has Jesus been a gate in your life?
■ In what way is Jesus like a shepherd?
❋ How are we like sheep?
❋ In what way is Jesus your shepherd?
❋ How would you describe your relationship with Jesus?
■ How can we better hear the voice of Jesus?
❋ What tempts people to follow a stranger? Why?
❋ How has Jesus made your life full?

APPLY IT
❋ How can you develop a more intimate relationship with Jesus this week?
■ How can you be more attentive to the voice of Jesus?

John 10:22-42
The Unbelief of the Jews

TOPICS
Assurance, Believe, Blasphemy, Doubt, Eternal Life, God, Hardheartedness, Jesus Christ, Messiah, Miracles, Rejection, Relationships, Sin, Unbelievers

OPEN IT
❋ What truths are hard for you to accept? Why?
■ How did your family typically handle conflict when you were growing up?

EXPLORE IT
■ What question did the Jews ask Jesus? (10:22-24)
❋ How did Jesus answer the Jews' question? (10:25-26)
❋ What did Jesus say His sheep did? (10:27)
❋ What did Jesus say He gave to His sheep? (10:28)
❋ What did Jesus say that no one could do to His sheep? (10:28-29)
❋ With whom did Jesus claim to be one? (10:30)
■ How did the Jews respond to Jesus' claim? (10:31)
❋ Why did the Jews want to kill Jesus? (10:33) How?
❋ How did Jesus respond to the Jews' accusation of blasphemy? (10:34-36)
❋ Under what circumstance did Jesus say that the Jews should believe in Him? (10:37)
■ Why did Jesus say that the Jews should believe in His miracles? (10:38)
❋ What did the Jews try to do to Jesus? (10:39)
❋ Where did Jesus go after He escaped from the Jews? (10:40)
❋ Why did the people across the Jordan believe in Jesus? (10:41-42)

GET IT
❋ Why do people today fail to realize that Jesus is God?
❋ In what way are you Jesus' sheep?
❋ What makes you feel secure in your relationship with your friends?
■ What makes you feel secure in your relationship with God?
❋ How secure is your relationship with God?
■ Why does Jesus' claim to be God cause people to oppose Him?
❋ Who today would find Jesus' claim to be God offensive?
❋ In what way is Jesus' relationship with God significant for your relationship with God?
❋ Why should people believe in Jesus?

APPLY IT
❋ How will you demonstrate your thankfulness to God today for your secure relationship with Him?
■ What steps will you take to follow your Shepherd closely this week?

John 11:1-16
The Death of Lazarus

TOPICS
Believe, Challenge, Circumstances, Darkness, Death, Glory, God, God's Will, Jesus Christ, Light, Mission, Mourning, Sickness, Sin

OPEN IT
❋ What polite phases do we use to describe death?
■ When has someone you've known died unexpectedly?

EXPLORE IT
❋ What was wrong with Lazarus? (11:1)
❋ To whom was Lazarus related? (11:2)
❋ How did Jesus get word about Lazarus? (11:3)
■ Why did Jesus say Lazarus was sick? (11:4)
❋ What did Jesus do when He heard about Lazarus? (11:6)
❋ Why did Jesus' disciples respond negatively to Jesus' plan to return to Judea? (11:7-8)
❋ How did Jesus answer His disciples' hesitancy about returning to Judea? (11:9-10)
❋ What did Jesus say had happened to Lazarus? (11:11)
■ How did the disciples misunderstand Jesus? (11:12)
❋ What did Jesus mean when he used the word "sleeping"? (11:13-14)
■ Why did Jesus say that He was glad He wasn't with Lazarus? (11:15)
❋ What melancholic suggestion did Thomas make? (11:16)

GET IT
❋ How would you respond if you heard that a good friend was very sick?
■ When have you thought you had a better plan for your life than the one God was working out?
❋ In what way has God used sickness in your life or the life of another to bring someone to Himself?
❋ Why would God choose to use sickness to bring someone to Himself?
❋ What shortcoming or disability in your life has God chosen to use to draw others to Himself?
■ How would you respond differently from the way Jesus did if you heard that a good friend had died?
❋ When have you felt that you had to perform a task

regardless of the obstacles in your path?
❊ What gave you the confidence to pursue a hard task that others strongly opposed?
❊ When have you felt misunderstood by your friends or family?

APPLY IT
❊ To what unfulfilled task that God has given you will you recommit yourself today?
■ What shortcomings or weaknesses in your life will you give to God in prayer, that He may use them to bring glory to Himself?

John 11:17-37
Jesus Comforts the Sisters

TOPICS
Anger, Believe, Circumstances, Comfortable, Confidence, Death, Delay, Discouragement, Eternal Life, Example, Faith, God, Jesus Christ, Ministry, Mourning, Resurrection, Salvation, Sorrow

OPEN IT
■ What is one of your greatest disappointments in life?
❊ In what different ways do people respond when a loved one dies?

EXPLORE IT
❊ What did Jesus find when He arrived at Bethany? (11:17)
❊ What did Mary and Martha do when they heard that Jesus was coming? (11:20)
■ What did Martha say to Jesus about His having come after Lazarus had died? (11:21-22)
❊ What did Jesus tell Martha Lazarus would do? (11:23)
❊ How did Martha misunderstand Jesus? (11:24)
❊ What did Martha and the others learn about Jesus' identity? (11:25)
■ What did Jesus say would happen to those who believed in Him? (11:26)
❊ What belief did Martha express to Jesus? (11:27)
❊ What did Martha tell Mary? (11:28)
❊ What did Mary do after Martha told her Jesus was asking for her? (11:29)
❊ Where did the Jews think Mary was going? (11:30-31)
❊ How did Mary respond when she saw Jesus? (11:32)
❊ What did Mary say to Jesus when He finally arrived? (11:32)
■ How did Jesus respond to Mary and the others' weeping? (11:33-35)
❊ What question did some people have about what Jesus could have done? (11:37)

GET IT
❊ When has God's response to your situation in life seemed untimely?
❊ In what way do we sometimes second-guess God?
■ When do we tend to second-guess God?
❊ How and when has God disappointed you?
❊ Why are we sometimes disappointed by God?
■ How should we respond to disappointment?
❊ When has God given you comfort in the middle of a sad time of life?
❊ In what way is Jesus' response to Lazarus's death a model for us to follow?

APPLY IT
■ What attitude of disappointment do you need to confess to God and change to trust in His sovereign control?
❊ How can you be a comfort to a struggling or hurting believer this week?

John 11:38-44
Jesus Raises Lazarus From the Dead

TOPICS
Believe, Death, Doubt, Glory, God, God's Will, Jesus Christ, Miracles, Mourning, New Life, Resurrection, Sorrow

OPEN IT
❊ What do the people you know fear most in life?
■ What sort of miracle would be the most spectacular to witness?

EXPLORE IT
❊ How did Jesus feel when He went to Lazarus's tomb? (11:38)
❊ In what type of tomb was Lazarus buried? (11:38)
■ What did Jesus tell the others to do? (11:39)
❊ How did Martha respond to Jesus' request? (11:39)
■ How did Jesus show Martha the importance of her belief? (11:40)
❊ What did Jesus do before He called to Lazarus? (11:41-42)
❊ What did Jesus say to the Father? (11:41-42) Why?
■ How did Jesus raise Lazarus from the dead? (11:43-44)
❊ What did Lazarus do when Jesus called to him? (11:44)
❊ What did Jesus tell the people to do? (11:44)

GET IT
❊ When have you been deeply moved?
❊ Under what circumstances have you doubted the power of God?
■ When have you had faith in God's ability to work out an impossible situation?
■ What is one miracle God has done in your life?
❊ How does God show His glory to us?
❊ In what way has God shown His glory to you?
❊ In what way has God "raised you from the dead"?
❊ If you had been there when Jesus raised Lazarus from the dead, how do you think you might have responded?

APPLY IT
■ What specific situation do you need to trust God to work out in your life?
❊ For what "miracle" do you want to thank God today?
❊ What can you do today so that others might believe in Jesus?

John 11:45-57
The Plot to Kill Jesus

TOPICS
Ambition, Believe, Christianity, Church, Deceit, Hypocrisy, Jesus Christ, Leadership, Ministry, Miracles, Motives, Power, Prophecy, Religion, Self-centeredness, Self-righteousness, Unbelievers

OPEN IT
❇ Without naming names, who is the most dishonest and self-serving person you've ever known?
■ What examples of selfishness do you see in a typical day?
❇ How do you deal with problem people in your life?

EXPLORE IT
❇ How did many of the Jews who had come to visit Mary respond to Jesus' miracle? (11:45)
❇ Who was told about Jesus' miracle? (11:46)
■ What did the Sanhedrin fear? (11:47-48)
❇ What did Caiaphas say about Jesus? (11:49-50)
■ How did Caiaphas prophesy? (11:51-52)
❇ What did the Jewish leaders of the Sanhedrin plot to do? (11:53)
❇ How did Jesus respond to the Sanhedrin's plot? (11:54)
❇ Why did many people go to Jerusalem? (11:55)
❇ For whom did the people in Jerusalem look? (11:56)
■ What orders had the chief priests and Pharisees given to the people? (11:57)

GET IT
■ What motive other than ministry might people have for engaging in Christian service?
❇ What personal ambitions might subvert the goal of serving God and others in Christian organizations?
❇ When have you intentionally or unintentionally used the church to pursue your own agenda?
■ Why is it so difficult to have pure and selfless motives in life?
❇ How do you respond when your goals and your motives conflict with one another?
❇ How might Christianity be challenged or threatened by Jesus if He were to come back today?

APPLY IT
❇ How would you tell a self-centered person the gospel message?
■ What self-centered motive will you ask God to help you change?

John 12:1-11
Jesus Anointed at Bethany

TOPICS
Devotion, Dishonesty, Faith, Honor, Hypocrisy, Jesus Christ, Loyalty, Money, Plans, Poor, Possessions, Preparation, Value, Worship

OPEN IT
■ When have you indulged another person with an expensive gift?
❇ How do you deal with the tension of helping people in need while enjoying your wealth and possessions?

EXPLORE IT
❇ When did Jesus arrive in Bethany? (12:1)
■ What was done in honor of Jesus in Bethany? (12:2)
❇ What did Mary do to Jesus? (12:3)
■ How did Judas respond to Mary's act? (12:4-5)
❇ What motivated Judas's response to Mary's act? (12:6)
■ Why did Jesus say that Mary had anointed Him with perfume? (12:7)
❇ What did Jesus say about the poor? (12:8)
❇ Why did the large crowd come to Mary and Martha's home? (12:9)
❇ What did the chief priests plan to do? (12:10)
❇ What motive did the chief priests have? (12:11)

GET IT
❇ How do you worship Jesus with your resources?
■ What concern should we have for the poor among us?
❇ In what way can we help those less fortunate than ourselves?
❇ Why are there poor people?
■ How do we selfishly use God's resources for our own pleasure?
❇ When have we masked our own selfishness with the appearance of concern for others?

APPLY IT
■ How can you worship and honor God with your resources today?
❇ How can you help someone less fortunate than yourself this week?
❇ What impure motives do you need to confess to God and ask Him to purify?

John 12:12-19
The Triumphal Entry

TOPICS
Enthusiasm, Evangelism, Expectations, Glory, Good News, Honor, Jesus Christ, Miracles, Praise, Prophecy, Worship

OPEN IT
■ How do people usually react when they meet a celebrity? Why?
❇ Who are today's religious celebrities?

EXPLORE IT
❇ What had the crowd heard about Jesus? (12:12)
■ How did the crowd greet Jesus when He arrived in Jerusalem? (12:13)
❇ What title did the crowd ascribe to Jesus? (12:13)
❇ What prophetic event took place? (12:14-15)
❇ What had been written about this event? (12:15)
❇ When did Jesus' disciples realize the significance of these events? (12:16)
■ What did the crowd that was with Jesus do when He raised Lazarus? (12:17)
■ Why did many of the people go out to meet Jesus? (12:18)
❇ How did the Pharisees react to this event? (12:19)

GET IT
■ What did you hear about Jesus that led you to seek Him?
❊ How should Jesus be the ruler in our lives?
❊ When are you reluctant to allow Jesus to take His rightful place as king in your life?
❊ What area of your life is difficult for you to surrender to Christ's authority?
❊ How should we honor and worship Jesus as King?
■ How should we spread the word about Jesus?

APPLY IT
❊ What specific area of your life do you need to submit more consistently to the authority of Jesus? How?
❊ With whom do you need to share the good news about Jesus Christ? How can you?
■ How will you honor and worship Jesus with your life today?

John 12:20-36
Jesus Predicts His Death

TOPICS
Commitment, Darkness, Death, Discipline, Faith, Follow, Glory, God, Heaven, Honor, Jesus Christ, Judgment, Life, Life-style, Light, Satan, Self-centeredness, Selfishness

OPEN IT
■ Who or what in life encourages you to be self-centered?
❊ When have you set aside your own needs temporarily to meet the needs of other people?

EXPLORE IT
❊ What did the group of Greeks ask Philip? (12:20-22)
❊ What did Jesus say had come? (12:23)
❊ What did Jesus say about a kernel of wheat? (12:24)
■ What did Jesus say about loving and hating life? (12:25)
❊ What did Jesus say about the person who wants to serve Him? (12:26)
❊ How did Jesus feel? (12:27)
❊ What was Jesus' attitude? (12:27)
■ Why didn't Jesus ask the Father to save Him? (12:27)
❊ What did Jesus ask the Father to do? (12:28)
❊ How did the crowd react to God's voice? (12:29)
❊ What time did Jesus say it was? (12:31)
■ What did Jesus say would happen when He was lifted up? (12:32)
❊ How did the crowd respond to Jesus' words? (12:34)
❊ In what way was Jesus' audience running out of time? (12:35)
❊ What did Jesus tell the crowd to do? (12:36)

GET IT
■ How do we love our own lives?
❊ How does Jesus want us to hate our lives?
❊ When and why is it difficult for you to serve and follow Jesus?
■ What does it mean for us to "walk in the light"?
❊ What tempts you to wander in the darkness rather than walk in the light?
❊ What example has Jesus set for us to follow?
❊ How can a group of people all have the same experience but interpret it differently?

APPLY IT
■ What is one change you can make in your life to become more attentive to the needs of others over your own?
❊ To whom can you be helpful today? How?

John 12:37-50
The Jews Continue in Their Unbelief

TOPICS
Acceptance, Believe, Complacency, Darkness, Eternal Life, Faith, Fear, Follow, God, Hardheartedness, Jesus Christ, Judgment, Life, Light, Love, Miracles, Peer Pressure, Prophecy, Rejection, Salvation, Unbelievers, Words

OPEN IT
■ Why do people seek fame and the acceptance of others?
❊ Aside from God's, whose love and acceptance have you tried to get?

EXPLORE IT
❊ What effect did Jesus' miracles have on the unbelieving Jews? (12:37)
❊ What was significant about the response of the Jews to Jesus' ministry? (12:38)
■ Why couldn't the Jews of Jesus' day believe in Him? (12:39-40)
❊ What did Isaiah say about the Jews of Jesus' day? (12:41)
■ Why didn't the leaders who did believe in Jesus admit their faith? (12:42-43)
❊ What is true about any person who believes in Christ? (12:44-45)
❊ Why did Jesus come into the world? (12:46)
❊ What did Jesus say about the person who hears His words, but does not keep them? (12:47)
■ What did Jesus say would condemn the person who did not accept His words? (12:48)
❊ What kind of teaching did Jesus give us? (12:49)
❊ Why are Jesus' words important? (12:50)

GET IT
❊ How can people see the work of Jesus in others' lives and still not believe in Him?
■ What blinds us to spiritual truth?
❊ When and why have you been afraid to admit your faith in Jesus?
■ What consequences might a Christian face for publicly admitting faith in Jesus?
❊ Why do we want to pursue the praise and acceptance of other people rather than the praise and acceptance of God?
❊ Out of what kind of darkness has Jesus taken you?
❊ How can we accept and keep the words of Jesus?

APPLY IT
■ To whom do you need to admit your faith in Jesus, regardless of the consequences? When can you?
❊ In what personal circumstance do you want to seek God's acceptance over the praise and acceptance of others?

John 13:1-17
Jesus Washes His Disciples' Feet

TOPICS
Ambition, Attitude, Example, Forgiveness, Glory, Greatness, Help, Honor, Humility, Jesus Christ, Life-style, Love, Ministry, Motives, Pride, Self-centeredness, Serving

OPEN IT
■ What is your idea of great customer service?
❊ In what way does our society instill in us the desire to be served?
❊ What do your neighbors consider to be signs of high position or status?

EXPLORE IT
❊ What did Jesus know it was time to do? (13:1)
❊ What had the devil prompted Judas to do? (13:2)
❊ What did Jesus know that the Father had done? (13:3)
❊ What did Jesus do when He got up from His meal with the disciples? (13:4-5)
❊ Why did Peter express shock? (13:6)
❊ How did Jesus respond to Peter's amazement? (13:7)
■ What did Peter declare he would never allow? (13:8)
❊ Why was it important for Jesus to wash the disciples' feet? (13:8)
❊ What did Peter want Jesus to do? (13:9)
❊ Why did Peter need only his feet washed? (13:10)
❊ Why did Jesus qualify His statements? (13:11)
■ What did Jesus tell His disciples they should do? (13:12-15)
■ What is the difference between servants and masters? (13:16)
❊ How did Jesus say that His disciples would be blessed? (13:17)

GET IT
❊ When and why do you find it difficult to allow others to serve you?
■ When and why is it difficult for you to serve others?
❊ How has Jesus cleansed us?
■ In what way does Jesus wash our feet today?
❊ In what way are we to wash the feet of others?
❊ What example did Jesus set for us to follow?
❊ In what areas do you struggle with being humble?
❊ What makes being humble so difficult?
❊ When and why do you feel in competition with other believers?

APPLY IT
❊ Who is someone you can serve today? How?
■ Whose service do you need to accept the next time he or she offers?
❊ What proud attitude do you still exhibit that could benefit from Jesus' example?

John 13:18-30
Jesus Predicts His Betrayal

TOPICS
Acceptance, Affections, Character, Choices, Evil, Fellowship, Friendship, Hardheartedness, Hypocrisy, Jesus Christ, Life-style, Love, Motives, Relationships, Satan

OPEN IT
❊ What persons in history or literature are known as traitors?
■ Why is trust important to a friendship?

EXPLORE IT
❊ What did Jesus say about the person who shared His bread? (13:18)
❊ Why did Jesus tell His disciples He would be betrayed? (13:19)
❊ What did Jesus say about His disciples? (13:20)
■ Why was Jesus troubled? (13:21)
❊ How did Jesus' disciples respond when He said one of them would betray Him? (13:22)
❊ What did Peter do? (13:23-24)
■ How did Jesus answer the beloved disciple's question? (13:26)
❊ What happened to Judas when he took the bread? (13:27)
❊ What did Jesus say to Judas? (13:27)
■ What did the other disciples think Jesus was telling Judas to do? (13:28-29)
❊ What did Judas do? (13:30)

GET IT
❊ Why is it hard to maintain an intimate and growing relationship with another person?
■ How would it feel to be betrayed by a close friend?
❊ Whom do you know who has been hurt by betrayal?
■ What can you do to build trust in all your friendships?
❊ How do we betray Jesus with our words or by our life-style?
❊ Why and how are we tempted to betray Jesus?
❊ What are the consequences of betraying Jesus?

APPLY IT
❊ What behavior that betrays your relationship with Jesus will you ask God to help you change?
■ What is the first step you can take toward building trust in one personal relationship this week?

John 13:31-38
Jesus Predicts Peter's Denial

TOPICS
Basics of the Faith, Character, Choices, Denial, Follow, Glory, God, Jesus Christ, Life, Life-style, Love, Loyalty, Sacrifice

OPEN IT
❊ What can you learn about a person from they way he or she dresses?

❋ How do people reveal their convictions through their lifestyle?
■ What does it mean to love someone?

EXPLORE IT
❋ What did Jesus say when Judas had gone? (13:31)
❋ What did God do through Jesus? (13:32)
❋ How much longer did Jesus say He would be with His disciples? (13:33)
❋ Why was Jesus saying farewell? (13:33)
❋ What was Jesus giving to His disciples? (13:34)
■ What did Jesus command His disciples to do? (13:34)
■ How did Jesus say people would know His disciples? (13:35)
❋ What question did Peter ask Jesus? (13:36)
❋ What did Jesus tell Peter? (13:36)
■ What did Peter pledge to do? (13:37)
❋ What blunt statement did Jesus make about Peter? (13:38)

GET IT
❋ How is God glorified by our behavior?
■ What does it mean for you to love people as Jesus has loved them?
❋ What kind of love was Jesus talking about?
■ How is love a sign that someone is a disciple of Christ?
❋ How do we deny Christ with our words or lifestyle?
❋ When and why are we tempted to deny Jesus?
❋ How does our denying Christ affect our relationship with Him as well as our relationships with other Christians?

APPLY IT
■ Who is someone you need to love as Christ has loved you? How?
❋ What can you do to stay loyal to Christ this week with either your words or your lifestyle?
❋ How can you show Christ's love to others at your place of work, at home, or in your neighborhood?
❋ What steps can you take to become more loving to others?

John 14:1-4
Jesus Comforts His Disciples

TOPICS
Assurance, Confidence, Eternal Life, Feelings, God, Heart, Home, Hope, Jesus Christ, Security, Trust, Worry

OPEN IT
❋ What is it about your home that makes it feel like home to you?
■ In what way do you sometimes feel that this world is not your home?
❋ Who or what is most comforting to you when you are upset?

EXPLORE IT
■ How didn't Jesus want His disciples to respond to His departure? (14:1)
❋ How did Jesus want His disciples to respond to His departure? (14:1)
❋ In what did Jesus want His disciples to trust? (14:1)
❋ Where did Jesus say He was going? (14:2)
❋ What assurance did Jesus give His disciples that what He said was true? (14:2)
■ What is in God's house? (14:2)
❋ What did Jesus say He was going to do in His Father's house? (14:2)
■ What did Jesus tell His disciples that He would do for them? (14:3)
❋ What promise did Jesus make? (14:3)
❋ What did Jesus' disciples know? (14:4)

GET IT
❋ What troubles your heart?
❋ How do you usually handle worries that trouble you?
❋ Why is it sometimes hard to trust God with our problems?
■ How does it make you feel to know that Jesus is preparing a place for you in His Father's house?
❋ In what way is Jesus preparing you to be with Him?
■ How are you preparing to be with Jesus?

APPLY IT
❋ What troubles do you need to entrust to God today?
■ What can you do today to prepare yourself for an eternity with Jesus?

John 14:5-14
Jesus the Way to the Father

TOPICS
Answers, Basics of the Faith, Beliefs, Believe, Evidence, Faith, Fellowship, Glory, God, God's Will, Gospel, Jesus Christ, Knowledge, Life, Mediator, Miracles, Name, Truth, Words

OPEN IT
❋ What are some widely accepted "truths" that you believe to be false?
■ In what ways do you resemble your parents?

EXPLORE IT
❋ What did Thomas ask Jesus? (14:5)
■ What did Jesus tell Thomas that He was? (14:6)
❋ Whom did Jesus say that His disciples would know if they really knew Him? (14:7)
❋ Whom did Philip ask Jesus to show them? (14:8)
■ What did Jesus ask Philip in response to Philip's request to be shown the Father? (14:9)
❋ How did Jesus characterize His relationship with the Father? (14:10-11)
■ What evidence did Jesus use to prove that He is in the Father and the Father is in Him? (14:11)
❋ What did Jesus say that those who had faith in Him would do? (14:12)
❋ Why did Jesus say that anyone who had faith would do greater things? (14:12)
❋ Why did Jesus say that He would do whatever His believers asked in His name? (14:13)
❋ What did Jesus say that He would do for His followers? (14:14)

GET IT

■ In what way is faith in Jesus Christ exclusive or narrow?
✻ In what way is Christianity an exclusive belief system?
■ How is Jesus the way, the truth, and the life in your life?
✻ How are we related to Jesus Christ and God the Father?
✻ What does it mean to know someone?
✻ What does it mean to know Jesus and God?
✻ What "greater things" are we doing today?
✻ What can we ask Jesus to do?
✻ What should our motivation be when we make requests of Jesus?
✻ How can we bring glory to the Father?

APPLY IT

✻ What can you do this week to deepen your relationship with Christ?
✻ What can you do today to bring glory to God?
■ Whom do you need to tell about the way Jesus offers to a relationship with God?

John 14:15-31

Jesus Promises the Holy Spirit

TOPICS

Assurance, Encouragement, Faithfulness, Fellowship, Help, Holy Spirit, Jesus Christ, Knowledge, Learning, Love, Obedience, Peace, Relationships, Security, Words, Work, World, Worry

OPEN IT

■ What people, things, or experiences in life bring you comfort and peace of mind?
✻ How do the people you love (whether close friends, spouse, or family members) know that you love them?
✻ What relationship in life brings you the most satisfaction? Why?

EXPLORE IT

✻ What did Jesus say His disciples would do if they loved Him? (14:15)
■ What did Jesus say He would ask God to give His disciples? (14:16)
✻ Why could the world not accept the Spirit of Truth? (14:17)
✻ What did Jesus promise the disciples? (14:18)
✻ Why did Jesus tell His disciples that they would live? (14:19)
✻ How is Jesus related to the Father and to His disciples? (14:20)
✻ What is the result of obeying Jesus' commands and loving Him? (14:21-23)
■ What did Jesus say the Counselor would do? (14:25-26)
✻ What did Jesus leave with His disciples? (14:27)
■ Why were the disciples to be glad that Jesus was leaving them? (14:28)
✻ Why did Jesus tell His disciples about the future? (14:29)
✻ Why did Jesus say He wouldn't speak much longer? (14:30)
✻ What did Jesus intend to show the world? (14:31)

GET IT

✻ How can we show Jesus that we love Him?
✻ What are the commands of Jesus that we should obey?
■ How are we taught by the Holy Spirit?
✻ When have you been comforted by the Holy Spirit?
■ What is the peace that Jesus has given us?
✻ How can we experience the peace Jesus has given us?
✻ What concerns trouble you or cause you to fear?
✻ How should we deal with the fear in our lives?
✻ What example has Jesus set for us in His relationship with God?

APPLY IT

✻ In what specific way can you show Jesus that you love Him today?
■ What can you do today to experience and enjoy the peace Jesus has give you?
✻ What troubling problem or fear do you need to turn over to God?

John 15:1-17

The Vine and the Branches

TOPICS

Failure, Faithfulness, Fellowship, Friendship, Fruit, Glory, God, Jesus Christ, Joy, Love, Relationships, Rewards, Work

OPEN IT

✻ What are the marks of a true friendship?
■ What do you do to maintain your friendships?

EXPLORE IT

✻ How are Jesus and the Father related? (15:1)
✻ What is Jesus and who is the Father? (15:1)
✻ How does the gardener tend to the branches that bear fruit and the branches that do not? (15:2)
✻ What did Jesus say the branches must do in order to bear fruit? (15:4)
✻ Who are the branches? (15:5)
✻ What did Jesus say would happen to the branches that did not remain in Him? (15:6)
✻ What privilege was given to the branches that remained in the vine? (15:7)
✻ What would be demonstrated by the disciples' bearing much fruit? (15:8)
■ What did Jesus urge His disciples to do? (15:9)
✻ How were Jesus' disciples to remain in His love? (15:10)
✻ Why did Jesus talk with His disciples about vines and branches? (15:11)
✻ What command did Jesus give His disciples? (15:12)
■ What is the greatest manifestation of love? (15:13)
✻ Who did Jesus say were His friends? (15:14)
■ Why did Jesus call His disciples friends? (15:15)
✻ Why did Jesus choose His disciples? (15:16)
✻ What was Jesus' command? (15:17)

GET IT

✻ How are we to remain in Jesus? Why?
✻ What does it mean to bear fruit as a Christian?
✻ How are we to bear fruit?

■ When is it difficult to develop and maintain a personal relationship with Jesus?
❊ In what way has God been removing "dead" or useless pieces from your character?
❊ In what way is your joy complete?
❊ When do you struggle with loving others the way Jesus has loved you?
■ What kind of a friend are you to Jesus?
❊ Why is it hard to be Jesus' friend?

APPLY IT
❊ What steps can you take to develop a more intimate relationship with Christ?
■ How can you be a better friend to Jesus beginning today?

John 15:18–16:4
The World Hates the Disciples

TOPICS
Christianity, God, Guilt, Hatred, Holy Spirit, Jesus Christ, Love, Miracles, Obedience, Persecution, Sin, Truth, Unbelievers, Witnessing, World

OPEN IT
■ What are some things that you hate or dislike?
❊ Why are some nonChristians antagonistic toward Christianity?
❊ What causes people to hate each other?

EXPLORE IT
■ What did Jesus want His disciples to keep in mind? (15:18)
❊ Who does the world love? (15:19)
❊ Why does the world hate Jesus' disciples? (15:19)
❊ What did Jesus want His disciples to remember? (15:20)
❊ What difference does it make that the world does not know God? (15:21)
❊ Why do the people of the world have no excuse for their sin? (15:22)
❊ What is the significance of hating Jesus? (15:23)
❊ What has made the world fully accountable for its sin? (15:24)
■ What did the world's hatred fulfill? (15:25)
❊ What would the Counselor do when He came? (15:26)
❊ Why did Jesus say that His disciples must testify about Him? (15:27)
❊ For what reason did Jesus tell the disciples these things? (16:1,4)
■ What was going to happen to the disciples for following Christ? (16:2-3)

GET IT
❊ What is "the world"?
■ If you were one of Jesus' twelve disciples, how would you have responded to His warning about the world's hatred?
■ How does the world today hate the followers of Jesus?
❊ When have you experienced the hatred of the world?
❊ How does the world today display its hatred for Jesus and God?
❊ How has God chosen you out of the world?
❊ How and when do you still feel a part of the world?
❊ Who is "the Counselor"?
❊ How does the Holy Spirit testify about Jesus to the world?
❊ How are you a testimony for Jesus?

APPLY IT
❊ How can you be a testimony for Jesus today? To whom?
■ How should you adjust your expectations of being accepted by nonChristians?

John 16:5-16
The Work of the Holy Spirit

TOPICS
Believers, Convictions, Doctrine, God, Guidance, Guilt, Holy Spirit, Jesus Christ, Judgment, Knowledge, Righteousness, Sin, Teaching, Truth, Unbelievers, Wisdom, World

OPEN IT
❊ How did you feel the last time you were separated from a friend by a move?
■ In what way can a conscience be both good and frustrating?

EXPLORE IT
❊ Where did Jesus tell His disciples He was going? (16:5)
❊ What hadn't the disciples asked Jesus? (16:5)
❊ How did Jesus' disciples feel about His leaving? (16:6)
❊ Why was it for His disciples' benefit that Jesus was leaving? (16:7)
■ What would the Counselor do for the world? (16:8)
❊ What would the Counselor do for the world when He came? (16:8-11)
■ What did Jesus say about the prince of this world? (16:11)
■ What would the Spirit of truth do for Jesus' disciples when He came? (16:12-14)
❊ In what way would the Spirit bring Jesus glory? (16:14-15)
❊ When would the disciples see Jesus? (16:16)

GET IT
❊ Why do most people feel guilty when they commit a sin?
❊ If you had been one of Jesus' disciples, how would you have felt about His leaving?
❊ How is the Holy Spirit convicting the world of sin, righteousness, and judgment?
❊ Of what sins is the world guilty?
■ What role do Christians and the church play in prodding the conscience of the world?
■ How does the Holy Spirit teach believers?
❊ About what truth is the Holy Spirit presently teaching you?
❊ How has the Holy Spirit used you to bring glory to Jesus Christ?

APPLY IT
■ How can you seek the Holy Spirit's guidance in reaching people who are dead in their sins?
❊ About what spiritual truths will you ask the Holy Spirit to teach you?

John 16:17-33
The Disciples' Grief Will Turn to Joy

TOPICS
Assurance, Believe, Encouragement, God, Grief, Hope, Jesus Christ, Joy, Love, Mourning, Pain, Peace, Prayer, Questions, Truth, Understanding, Words, World

OPEN IT
❇ When might you use a figure of speech to explain something? Why?
❇ What painful experiences in your life have resulted in joy?
■ When have you enthusiastically anticipated someone's return or arrival?

EXPLORE IT
❇ How did the disciples react to Jesus' "in a little while" statement? (16:17-18)
■ What did Jesus tell His disciples would happen to them? (16:19-20)
❇ To what did Jesus compare His disciples' response to His departure and return? (16:21-22)
❇ What did Jesus tell His disciples they would do when they saw Him again? (16:23)
❇ What hadn't the disciples done up until this point? (16:24)
❇ What kind of language did Jesus use to speak to His disciples? (16:25)
❇ Why did the Father love the disciples? (16:26-27)
■ From where did Jesus come and to where was He going? (16:28)
❇ Why did the disciples say that they believed Jesus had come from God? (16:29-30)
❇ What did Jesus predict the disciples would do? (16:31-32)
❇ What did Jesus want for His disciples? (16:33)
■ Why did Jesus tell the disciples to take heart? (16:33)

GET IT
❇ How would you have responded to Jesus' words had you been there with His disciples?
■ What grief or sorrow in your life has God turned to joy?
❇ For what can we ask the Father?
❇ How has God made your joy complete?
■ How does the knowledge of Jesus' return make you joyful?
❇ What figures of speech have helped you better understand spiritual truths?
❇ What relationship do we have with the Father today?
❇ What trouble do we have in the world as followers of Christ?
❇ How does the fact that Jesus has overcome the world encourage you?

APPLY IT
■ In the midst of trouble, what encouraging truth from this passage will you rely on?
❇ Because of your restored relationship with the Father, what can you ask Him to give to you in Jesus' name?
❇ What grief or sorrow do you need to entrust to God?

John 17:1-5
Jesus Prays for Himself

TOPICS
Authority, Depend, Eternal Life, Fellowship, Glory, God, Honor, Jesus Christ, Knowledge, People, Prayer, Work

OPEN IT
■ How do people try to bring recognition to themselves?
❇ What sort of a relationship do you have with your parents?
❇ How would you describe "eternal life" to someone?

EXPLORE IT
❇ What did Jesus do when He had finished speaking to His disciples? (17:1)
❇ What did Jesus announce to the Father? (17:1)
■ Why did Jesus want the Father to glorify the Son? (17:1)
■ For what purpose did God grant Jesus authority over all people? (17:2)
❇ Whom were those given eternal life to know? (17:3)
❇ What is eternal life? (17:3)
❇ What had Jesus done by completing the work the Father had given him? (17:4)
■ How did Jesus bring God glory on earth? (17:4)
❇ How did Jesus ask to be glorified? (17:5)
❇ With what glory did Jesus ask the Father to glorify Him? (17:5)

GET IT
❇ When do we turn to God in prayer?
❇ About what sort of things do we usually pray?
■ What example with regard to prayer did Jesus give us?
❇ How can we experience the eternal life of which Jesus spoke?
❇ What does it mean to know God?
■ How can we bring glory to God?

APPLY IT
❇ What do you need to do to prepare for the joy of eternal life?
■ What can you do today to bring God glory?

John 17:6-19
Jesus Prays for His Disciples

TOPICS
Glory, God, Hatred, Jesus Christ, Joy, Knowledge, Lifestyle, Obedience, Prayer, Protection, Satan, World

OPEN IT
❇ What do you like and dislike about living in this country?
❇ What do you think is most challenging for a Christian living in today's society?
■ In what way might you say the world is a dangerous place for a Christian to live in?

EXPLORE IT
❇ What did Jesus tell the Father He had done? (17:6)
❇ What did Jesus say His disciples knew? (17:7-8)

■ Why did Jesus pray for His disciples? (17:9)
❄ What did Jesus ask His Father to do for His disciples? (17:11)
❄ What did Jesus pray His disciples would become? (17:11)
❄ Who did Jesus say was lost? (17:12)
❄ Why did Jesus say these things while He was still in the world? (17:13)
■ Why did the world hate Jesus' disciples? (17:14)
❄ What was Jesus' prayer concerning His disciples? (17:15)
■ What relationship did Jesus' disciples have with the world ? (17:16)
❄ How would Jesus' disciples be set aside for God's use? (17:17)
❄ Where did Jesus send His disciples? (17:18)
❄ Why did Jesus set Himself apart for God's use? (17:19)

GET IT
■ As believers, what is our relationship to the world?
❄ What does your lifestyle indicate about your relationship to the world?
■ Why is it so easy for us to become closely involved in the world?
❄ Why do you think believers are still in the world?
❄ When and from what has God protected you?
❄ Where would you say you were in the process of being set apart for God's use?
❄ How does God's truth sanctify us or make us holy?

APPLY IT
■ What change in your lifestyle do you need to make to distinguish your identity from that of the world?
❄ What can you do today to set yourself apart to God's use?

John 17:20-26
Jesus Prays for All Believers

TOPICS
Believers, Creation, Divisions, Doctrine, Example, Fellowship, Glory, God, Jesus Christ, Love, People, Prayer, Unity, World

OPEN IT
■ When have you longed for unity in your family, church, or community?
❄ With what things or traditions do you identify?
❄ Why are religious beliefs divisive?

EXPLORE IT
❄ For whom did Jesus pray? (17:20)
■ Why did Jesus want all believers to be one? (17:21)
❄ What had Jesus given the disciples? (17:22)
❄ How did Jesus want believers to be unified? (17:22)
■ What did Jesus want the world to know? (17:23)
❄ Why had the Father given glory to Jesus? (17:24)
❄ What did Jesus want for those the Father had given Him? (17:24)
❄ When did the Father love the Son? (17:24)
❄ What did Jesus say that the world did and did not know? (17:25)
■ Why was Jesus going to continue to make the Father known? (17:26)

GET IT
❄ In what way are all Christians one?
■ How are Christians today divided? Why?
❄ Why is unity so difficult for Christians to achieve?
❄ What does the world today know about the Father?
■ How is the Father's relationship with the Son an example for us to follow in our relationships with other Christians?
❄ What relationship do you have with the Father and the Son?

APPLY IT
■ What can you do to promote unity among fellow Christians?
❄ How can you be a testimony of God's love to the world?
❄ What is one thing you can do this week to strengthen your bond with other Christians?

John 18:1-11
Jesus Arrested

TOPICS
Awe, Character, Denial, Doubt, Enemies, Fear, Friendship, God's Will, Hardheartedness, Intentions, Jesus Christ, Life-style, Opposition, Protection

OPEN IT
■ Why might a person betray a cause he or she had actively participated in?
❄ When have you ever felt betrayed by a person or a cause that you believed in?

EXPLORE IT
❄ Where did Jesus and His disciples go when Jesus had finished praying? (18:1)
■ How did Judas know about the place where Jesus and His disciples had gone? (18:2)
❄ Whom did Judas guide into the grove? (18:3)
❄ What question did Jesus ask Judas and the others with him? (18:4)
❄ How did Jesus identify Himself? (18:5)
■ How did people react when Jesus identified Himself? (18:6-7)
■ What did Jesus tell the soldiers and officials to do? (18:8)
❄ Why did Jesus tell the soldiers to release His disciples? (18:9)
❄ How did Peter respond to the threat to Jesus? (18:10)
❄ How did Jesus correct Peter? (18:11)

GET IT
❄ If you had been with Jesus the night He was arrested, how do you think you would you have responded?
■ How have you been betrayed by a friend?
❄ How would you respond if someone betrayed your best friend?
❄ In what way are you like Peter?
■ How is Jesus' response to His betrayal an example for us to follow?
❄ How do we betray Jesus with our words and conduct?

APPLY IT
■ What do you want to remember about Christ the next time someone lets you down?
❋ What aspect of your lifestyle should you change so that you don't betray Jesus with either your words or deeds?

John 18:12-14
Jesus Taken to Annas

TOPICS
Atonement, Authority, Hardheartedness, Humiliation, Jesus Christ, Persecution, Unbelievers

OPEN IT
❋ About which modern leaders might it be said that they sacrificed their life for their duty?
■ Who are today's recognized religious authorities?

EXPLORE IT
❋ What authorities participated in Jesus' arrest? (18:12)
❋ Who arrested Jesus? (18:12)
❋ What did the soldiers and Jewish officials do to Jesus? (18:12)
❋ How was Jesus treated by His captors? (18:12-13)
■ To whom was Jesus taken first? (18:13)
❋ What was Annas' relationship to Caiaphas? (18:13)
■ What duty was Caiaphas fulfilling that year? (18:13)
■ About what had Caiaphas advised the Jews? (18:14)
❋ Why did Caiaphas think it good that one man die for the people? (18:14)
❋ What was ironic about Caiaphas' remarks about Jesus? (18:14)

GET IT
❋ How do you think Jesus felt when He was arrested?
❋ When have you ever felt humiliated for being a Christian?
■ How would you feel if you were falsely arrested? What would you do?
❋ What religious authorities do you respect?
■ If Jesus were arrested today, to what religious authority might He be taken?

APPLY IT
❋ Following Jesus' example, how will you respond when you are wrongly mistreated?
■ How should you pray for the religious authorities in your church or denomination this week?

John 18:15-18
Peter's First Denial

TOPICS
Denial, Disobedience, Doubt, Enemies, Forsake, Hypocrisy, Jesus Christ, Loyalty, Privilege

OPEN IT
❋ Who is someone you would say is "well connected with the right people"?
■ Who is someone you would describe as being loyal?
❋ When was a time you got caught lying as a child?

EXPLORE IT
❋ Who followed Jesus? (18:15)
❋ How did Peter's companion get into the high priest's courtyard? (18:15)
❋ How did the unnamed disciple manage to follow Jesus into the courtyard? (18:15)
❋ Why did Peter have to wait outside? (18:16)
❋ Where did Peter have to wait? (18:16)
■ How did Peter get into the courtyard? (18:16)
❋ What did the girl at the door of the courtyard ask Peter? (18:17)
■ How did Peter reply to the question about his association with Jesus? (18:17)
❋ Why was Peter standing around with the servants and officials? (18:18)
■ With whom did Peter warm himself inside the courtyard? (18:18)

GET IT
❋ What inside connections do you have in the church?
❋ How do you use your inside connections in the church and elsewhere?
❋ What potentially dangerous situations has your faith gotten you into?
■ Under what circumstances might you be tempted to deny knowing Jesus?
❋ When and why have you denied knowing Jesus by either your words or your lifestyle?
■ With what enemies of Christ do we sometimes associate?

APPLY IT
❋ How can you use your inside connections to benefit others this week?
■ What can you do to affirm your relationship with Jesus Christ before others?
❋ In what areas of your life do you want to express your loyalty to Jesus more openly?

John 18:19-24
The High Priest Questions Jesus

TOPICS
Authority, Challenge, Church, Consequences, Convictions, Courage, Discipline, Disobedience, Enemies, Hardheartedness, Hatred, Injustice, Jesus Christ, Persecution, Punishment, Self-righteousness, Unbelievers

OPEN IT
■ Who is someone who has been harassed for speaking the truth?
❋ When do you think it would be necessary to challenge an established authority?

EXPLORE IT
❋ About what did the high priest question Jesus? (18:19)
❋ Who questioned Jesus about His teaching? (18:19)
❋ In what way did Jesus say that He had always spoken? (18:20)
❋ Where did Jesus say that He had always spoken? (18:20)
❋ Why did Jesus advise the high priest to ask those who heard Him? (18:21)

■ To whom did Jesus tell the high priest he should ask his questions? (18:21)
■ Why did one of the officials strike Jesus? (18:22)
■ What did Jesus say in response to being hit? (18:23)
❊ To whom did Annas send Jesus? (18:24)
❊ How was Jesus sent to Caiaphas? (18:24)

GET IT
❊ What thoughts do you think were running through Jesus' mind while He was being interrogated?
■ When have you felt as if you were being interrogated because of your faith?
❊ Who are the respected authorities in the church today?
❊ When have you found it necessary to challenge a respected authority or belief?
❊ What effect do you think Jesus' reply had on the official who hit him?
■ What would the people with whom you talk on a regular basis say about your "teachings"?
❊ When have you been punished or disciplined for speaking the truth?

APPLY IT
■ What is one truth you need to speak today regardless of the consequences?
❊ What can you change about your speech in order to be a more open and consistent follower of Jesus?

John 18:25-27
Peter's Second and Third Denials

TOPICS
Backslide, Christianity, Circumstances, Commitment, Compromise, Denial, Enemies, Failure, Jesus Christ, Life-style, Peer Pressure, Persecution, Self-centeredness, Temptation

OPEN IT
■ Why are people sometimes tempted to compromise their beliefs, principles, or standards?
❊ When have you told a lie that you caused you pain later?

EXPLORE IT
❊ What was Peter doing? (18:25)
❊ What question was Peter asked as he tried to keep warm? (18:25)
■ How did Peter respond to the question about his association with Jesus? (18:25)
■ Who challenged Peter's statement? (18:25)
❊ What did the people around the fire believe to be true about Peter? (18:25-26)
❊ To whom was one of the high priest's servants related? (18:26)
❊ Where had the high priest's servant seen Peter? (18:26)
❊ What did the high priest's servant ask Peter? (18:26)
❊ How did Peter respond to the question asked by the high priest's servant? (18:26-27)
■ What happened the moment Peter denied knowing Christ a third time? (18:27)

GET IT
❊ What thoughts do you think were running through Peter's mind?
■ Had you been in Peter's shoes, what reasons might you have had for denying that you were a disciple of Christ?
❊ When have you found yourself in a situation that was hostile to Jesus Christ?
❊ What self-protective reasons might tempt us to deny that we are followers of Christ?
■ When and where is it hardest for you to openly acknowledge your relationship with Christ?

APPLY IT
■ Under what circumstances do you need to determine to live openly as a follower of Christ?
❊ What pressure should you ask God to help you resist?
❊ What self-centered attitude will you ask God to help you change?

John 18:28-40
Jesus Before Pilate

TOPICS
Acceptance, Ambition, Consequences, Fear, Jesus Christ, Justice, Kingdom of God/Heaven, Law, Legalism, Obedience, Opposition, Peer Pressure, Position, Priorities, Rationalizing, Rules, Status, Truth

OPEN IT
■ How might a politician rationalize his or her bending of the rules in order to please a group of concerned citizens?
❊ When have you been tempted to do what works rather than what's right?

EXPLORE IT
❊ Why didn't the Jews who lead Jesus to the Roman governor enter the palace? (18:28)
❊ How did the Jews introduce Jesus to governor Pilate? (18:28-30)
■ What did Pilate want the Jews to do with Jesus? (18:31)
❊ How was prophecy fulfilled by this event? (18:32)
❊ What question did Pilate ask Jesus? (18:33)
❊ What question did Jesus ask Pilate in reply? (18:34)
❊ What did Jesus tell Pilate about His kingdom? (18:36)
■ How did Jesus affirm Pilate? (18:37)
❊ What last question did Pilate have for Jesus? (18:38)
■ What choice did Pilate present to the Jews? (18:38-39)
❊ What choice did the Jews make? (18:40)

GET IT
❊ Why is it easier to observe religious traditions than to love other people?
■ When have you felt betrayed or used by people hiding behind religious motives?
■ When, like Jesus, have you been willing to stand your ground regardless of the consequences?
❊ When, like Pilate, have you been willing to sacrifice your principles in order to do something self-serving?
❊ How would you answer the question, "What is truth?"?
❊ How is Jesus the king in your life?

APPLY IT
■ In what settings might you need to stand up for the truth this week regardless of the consequences?
✻ What is one way you can rearrange your priorities this week in honor of God as king over you?

John 19:1-16
Jesus Sentenced to be Crucified

TOPICS
Beliefs, Character, Circumstances, Convictions, Fear, Hardheartedness, Hypocrisy, Jesus Christ, Peer Pressure, Power, Self-centeredness, Status, Truth

OPEN IT
■ What pressure tactics do special interest groups use on politicians?
✻ In what ways do people sometimes compromise what's important in order to advance their career or status?

EXPLORE IT
✻ What did Pilate and the soldiers do to Jesus? (19:1-3)
✻ To what conclusion had Pilate come concerning Jesus? (19:4-5)
✻ How did the Jews react when Pilate presented Jesus to them? (19:6)
✻ What did Pilate want the Jews to do with Jesus? (19:6)
■ Why did the Jews insist that Jesus had to die? (19:7)
✻ How did Pilate respond to the Jews' demands? (19:8-9)
✻ What authority did Pilate claim to have? (19:10)
✻ What authority did Pilate really have? (19:11)
✻ What did Pilate try to do for Jesus? (19:12)
■ How did the Jews pressure Pilate to give in to their demand to crucify Jesus? (19:12)
■ How did Pilate respond to the Jews' pressure tactics? (19:13-16)
✻ Whom did the crowd claim as their king? (19:15)

GET IT
✻ What would you have done had you been in Pilate's situation?
■ What position or possession might you be tempted to preserve at the expense of doing the right thing?
■ When and why might we allow the pressures of the moment to compromise our beliefs or standards?
✻ Who or what are the "kings" that people worship today?
✻ What person or thing often competes with God for rule of your life?

APPLY IT
✻ How can you make Jesus the king of your life?
■ What pressure to compromise your principles will you determine to resist this week?
✻ How can you use your status or position of power to do right and help others?

John 19:17-27
The Crucifixion

TOPICS
Atonement, Believers, Caring, Enemies, Family, Humiliation, Jesus Christ, Love, Sacrifice, Suffering, Unbelievers

OPEN IT
■ What sort of sacrifices did your parents make for you?
✻ What to you is the most humiliating situation you can imagine?

EXPLORE IT
✻ To where was Jesus forced to take His own cross? (19:17)
■ What did the soldiers do to Jesus? (19:18)
✻ Who was crucified with Jesus? (19:18)
✻ What notice did Pilate have fastened to Jesus' cross? (19:19)
■ How did the chief priests want Pilate to change the sign over Jesus' head? (19:21)
✻ What did Pilate tell the chief priests? (19:22)
■ What happened to Jesus' clothes? (19:23-24)
✻ Why were Jesus' clothes divided among the soldiers? (19:24)
✻ Who stood near the cross of Jesus? (19:25)
✻ What did Jesus say to His mother and the disciple with her? (19:26-27)

GET IT
✻ Why do you think Pilate had the notice placed on the cross?
■ If you had been a member of Jesus' family or one of His disciples, how do you think you would have reacted to His crucifixion?
✻ How was Jesus humiliated?
✻ What sort of humiliation did Jesus suffer?
■ What humiliation have you suffered for being a Christian?
✻ How can we sacrifice our wants and desires so that others might benefit?
✻ In what way has God's family become your family?
✻ To what degree are we responsible for caring for the needs of other believers?

APPLY IT
■ What want or desire can you sacrifice so that someone else might benefit? How?
✻ How can you care for another Christian's needs this week?

John 19:28-37
The Death of Jesus

TOPICS
Atonement, Beliefs, Believe, Bible, Body, Death, Faith, Jesus Christ, Prophecy, Sacrifice

OPEN IT
✻ What is one important event you have witnessed?

❇ What is your idea of "expensive"?
■ What is one project of yours that is still unfinished?

EXPLORE IT
■ What did Jesus know during His last moments on the cross? (19:28)
❇ What did Jesus ask for during His last minutes of life? (19:28)
❇ What was Jesus given to drink? (19:29)
■ What did Jesus do once He had received the drink? (19:30)
❇ Why didn't the Jews want the bodies of those crucified left on the cross? (19:31)
❇ What did the soldiers do to the men who had been crucified with Jesus? (19:32)
❇ What did the soldiers discover when they came to Jesus? (19:33)
❇ What did the soldiers do to Jesus? (19:34)
❇ Why did John record the details of Jesus' death? (19:35)
■ What was fulfilled by the circumstances of Jesus' death? (19:36-37)

GET IT
❇ How important are the historical eyewitness accounts of Jesus' life, death, and resurrection to your faith in Him?
■ What did Jesus mean when He said, "It is finished"?
❇ How does this account of Jesus' crucifixion make you feel?
❇ What does Jesus' death mean to us?
■ What is significant about Jesus' death on the cross?
❇ What price did Jesus pay for our sins?
❇ How was Jesus able to endure the suffering of the Cross?
❇ What significance does the fulfillment of Scripture in the Gospels have for your belief in Jesus today?
❇ Whose testimony persuaded you to believe in Jesus?
❇ How has your testimony influenced others to believe in Jesus?

APPLY IT
■ How can you thank Jesus today for His sacrifice on the cross?
❇ How can you use the testimony of Christ's crucifixion in telling others about Christ?

John 19:38-42
The Burial of Jesus

TOPICS
Believe, Christianity, Courage, Death, Faith, Fear, Jesus Christ, Loyalty, Peer Pressure, Sorrow, Traditions

OPEN IT
❇ What is one misdeed or truth that you kept secret when you were growing up?
■ What is one fact about you that most of your friends don't know?
❇ In what way do some Christians try to keep their faith hidden or secret? Why?

EXPLORE IT
❇ How did Joseph ask Pilate for Jesus' body? (19:38)
❇ Who went to get Jesus' body? (19:38)
■ Why did Joseph go to see Pilate? (19:38)
■ Why was Joseph a secret disciple? (19:38)
■ What was significant about the person who went with Joseph to take away Jesus' body? (19:39)
❇ How did Joseph and Nicodemus prepare Jesus' body for burial? (19:40)
❇ Where was the tomb in which Jesus was buried? (19:41)
❇ In what kind of tomb was Jesus buried? (19:41)
❇ Why did Joseph and Nicodemus put Jesus in the particular tomb they chose? (19:42)
❇ What holiday affected the preparations for Jesus' burial? (19:42) How?
❇ How did the "Day of Preparation" affect the way in which Jesus was buried? (19:42)

GET IT
■ When and why have you been a secret disciple of Jesus?
❇ When have you recently revealed your faith in Christ either by your words or actions?
■ When have you taken a stand that you were previously afraid to take?
❇ When have you been willing to go out of your way to serve Jesus?
❇ When are you most tempted to do only what is convenient?

APPLY IT
■ To whom do you want to reveal openly that you are a disciple of Jesus?
❇ How can you serve Christ this week regardless of the inconvenience you expect it to involve?

John 20:1-9
The Empty Tomb

TOPICS
Basics of the Faith, Believe, Death, Doctrine, Doubt, Expectations, Fear, Jesus Christ, Prophecy, Resurrection, Running, Sorrow, Surprises, Understanding

OPEN IT
❇ What is one dark moment of your life that ended happily?
■ Why do people visit the grave sites of close friends and family members?
❇ About what sort of news would you get excited right now?

EXPLORE IT
■ What did Mary Magdalene discover when she went to Jesus' tomb? (20:1)
❇ What did Mary Magdalene tell Peter? (20:2) When?
❇ Who responded to the news Mary brought? (20:3)
■ How did Peter respond to what Mary told him? (20:3)
❇ Who examined Jesus' tomb? (20:4-5)
❇ What did John discover when he arrived at the tomb? (20:4-5)

❊ What did Peter discover when he arrived at the tomb? (20:6-7)
❊ What did John do after he looked in the tomb? (20:8)
■ How did John respond to what he found in the tomb? (20:8)
❊ What did Peter and John not understand even after they visited Jesus' empty tomb? (20:9)

GET IT
❊ Why do you think Mary went to the tomb?
■ If you had been either Mary, Peter, or John, what thoughts would have run through your mind when you discovered the empty tomb?
❊ When have you made an exciting unexpected discovery?
❊ How do you usually respond to life's unexpected events?
■ What motivates us to share our surprises (both pleasant and unpleasant) with other people?
❊ When has a positive happening in your life appeared at first to be a confusing, unfortunate, or tragic event?

APPLY IT
❊ What truths of the gospel do you want to investigate more closely over the next few weeks? How can you?
■ Whom do you need to tell about the empty tomb of Christ? How?
❊ How can you celebrate the resurrection of Christ next Easter?

John 20:10-18
Jesus Appears to Mary Magdalene

TOPICS
Affections, Angels, Death, Devotion, Discouragement, Emotions, Encouragement, God, Jesus Christ, Joy, Love, Relationships, Resurrection, Surprises

OPEN IT
❊ How has someone recently surprised you with what he or she did or said?
■ What is the most exciting news you've heard this week?

EXPLORE IT
❊ What did Mary and the disciples do after seeing that Jesus' body was gone? (20:10-11)
❊ What did Mary see where Jesus' body had been? (20:12)
■ What did the angels ask Mary? (20:13)
❊ How did Mary answer the angels' question? (20:13)
❊ Who tried to comfort Mary? (20:14-15)
❊ What question did Jesus ask Mary? (20:15)
❊ How did Mary respond to Jesus' question? (20:15)
■ What happened when Mary realized who was talking to her? (20:16)
❊ Why did Jesus tell Mary not to hold on to Him? (20:17)
■ What did Jesus tell Mary to tell His brothers? (20:17)
❊ What did Mary do? (20:18)

GET IT
❊ How would you respond if you met someone you had presumed to be dead?
❊ What would you do if you saw an angel?
❊ Over what loss have you recently shed tears?
❊ How do you think Mary felt when she realized she was talking to Jesus?
❊ When is it tempting to hold on to something good rather than share it with others?
■ If you had been one of the disciples who had heard Mary's exciting news, how do you think you would have reacted?
■ When have you been exceptionally thrilled about your relationship with Christ?
❊ How can you demonstrate your devotion to Jesus?

APPLY IT
❊ Who is someone you want to tell about the news of Jesus' resurrection? How can you?
■ How can you celebrate your relationship with the living Christ this week?

John 20:19-23
Jesus Appears to His Disciples

TOPICS
Evidence, Fear, Forgiveness, God, Holy Spirit, Jesus Christ, Joy, Peace, Resurrection, Sin

OPEN IT
❊ Where is it dangerous to openly follow Christ today?
❊ What hideaways did you have when you were growing up?
■ What friend or relative that you haven't seen for a while would you be overjoyed to see again?

EXPLORE IT
❊ What day of the week was it when the disciples were together? (20:19)
❊ Why did the disciples have the doors locked? (20:19)
❊ Who surprised the disciples in their hideaway? (20:19)
■ What did Jesus say to the disciples? (20:19) When?
❊ What did Jesus show His disciples? (20:20) Why?
■ How did the disciples respond to seeing Jesus? (20:20)
❊ What greeting did Jesus repeat? (20:21)
❊ What did Jesus tell His disciples about their future? (20:21)
❊ Why did Jesus breathe on His disciples? (20:22)
❊ What did Jesus tell the disciples to receive? (20:22)
■ What did Jesus tell His disciples about forgiving sins? (20:23)

GET IT
❊ When have you been afraid to follow Jesus openly?
■ If you had been in that room with the disciples, how might you have reacted when Jesus appeared?
■ When have you been overjoyed to see someone?
❊ To whom has Jesus sent us?
❊ To whom has Jesus sent you?
❊ Why is it important for us to forgive others?
❊ When is it most difficult for you to forgive?
❊ What can we do to become forgiving of others?

APPLY IT
❊ Whom do you need to forgive?
❊ Whose forgiveness do you need to seek? How can you?
■ With whom do you want to share your joy in Christ?

John 20:24-31
Jesus Appears to Thomas

TOPICS
Believe, Bible, Christianity, Confession, Doubt, Eternal Life, Evidence, God, Jesus Christ, Life, Miracles, Peace, Resurrection, Salvation

OPEN IT
❇ Why do people write books?
■ What book (besides the Bible) have you enjoyed most?
❇ When have you doubted a story from a reliable source?

EXPLORE IT
❇ What disciple was not with the others when Jesus appeared to them? (20:24)
❇ What had the other disciples told Thomas? (20:24)
■ What did Thomas say he needed in order to believe that Jesus was raised? (20:25)
❇ How did Jesus restore Thomas's faith? (20:26)
■ What did Jesus say to Thomas? (20:27)
❇ What did Thomas say in response to Jesus' words? (20:28)
■ What did Jesus say about seeing and believing? (20:29)
❇ What did John leave out of his Gospel? (20:30)
❇ Why was the book of John written? (20:31)
❇ What results from believing that Jesus is the Son of God? (20:31)

GET IT
❇ When have you had doubts about your faith in Christ?
❇ How should we deal with our doubts about Christianity?
■ Why is it difficult to believe in Christ?
❇ In what ways do we need to trust Christ?
❇ On what evidence do you rely for your belief that Jesus rose from the dead?
■ What sort of evidence for the truth of Christianity has John given us?

APPLY IT
❇ What doubts concerning your faith in Christ do you want to discuss with a knowledgeable believer?
❇ How can you use the Gospel of John to tell others about Jesus?

John 21:1-14
Jesus and the Miraculous Catch of Fish

TOPICS
Abundance, Devotion, Fellowship, Jesus Christ, Miracles, Needs

OPEN IT
❇ What are some of your hobbies or favorite pastimes?
❇ Why do people enjoy eating together?
❇ What kind of foods do you like to prepare when you have people over for dinner?
■ With whom have you recently shared a meal?

EXPLORE IT
❇ When did Jesus appear to His disciples? (21:1)
❇ What familiar activity did several of Jesus' disciples do together? (21:2-3)
❇ Who had gone out to fish? (21:2-3)
❇ How successful had Peter and the others been at fishing that night? (21:3)
❇ What did Jesus ask His disciples? (21:5)
❇ What did Jesus tell His disciples to do? (21:6)
■ What happened when the disciples did what Jesus had told them to do? (21:6)
❇ What did Peter do when he realized that it was the Lord who was talking? (21:7)
■ What did Jesus ask His disciples to do once they were on shore? (21:8-10)
❇ Why didn't the disciples ask Jesus who He was? (21:12)
■ What did Jesus do with the bread and fish? (21:13)
❇ How many times had Jesus appeared to His disciples? (21:14)

GET IT
❇ Why do you think several of Jesus' disciples went fishing?
❇ How has God brought you together with other Christians?
■ When have you been so glad to see someone that you just had to run out to meet that person?
❇ Why is it hard for us to see God working in our lives?
❇ Through what ordinary events in life have you encountered Jesus?
❇ When has God miraculously and abundantly provided for your needs?
■ When do you experience fellowship with Jesus?

APPLY IT
■ What steps can you take to have fellowship with God today?
❇ For what specific need that God has met in your life will you thank Him today?

John 21:15-25
Jesus Reinstates Peter

TOPICS
Caring, Death, Glory, God, Jesus Christ, Love, Serving, Witnessing

OPEN IT
■ Who are some people who have died for their beliefs?
❇ When did you ever have to restore a broken relationship?
❇ When have you taken care of another person?

EXPLORE IT
❇ What did Jesus ask Peter three times? (21:15-17)
❇ What did Jesus tell Peter to do? (21:15-17)
❇ How did Peter feel after Jesus had asked him the same question three times? (21:17)
❇ What did Jesus predict about Peter's future? (21:18-19)
❇ What command did Jesus give to Peter? (21:19)
■ What concern did Peter raise? (21:20-21)

■ What did Jesus want Peter to concern himself with? (21:22)
❇ How did Jesus want Peter to serve Him? (21:22)
❇ What rumor spread as the result of Jesus' talk with Peter? (21:23)
■ How did John serve Christ after Jesus left earth? (21:24)
❇ What did John do with the testimony he had concerning Jesus? (21:24)
❇ How many of Jesus' deeds did John leave out of his Gospel? (21:25)

GET IT
❇ How should we demonstrate our love for Jesus?
❇ Who are Jesus' sheep?
❇ How are we to serve and care for other Christians?
■ How do we each serve God in a unique way?
■ How can you bring glory to God through your life and the unique opportunities God has given you?
❇ What might cause us to be more concerned about someone else's relationship with Christ than our own?

APPLY IT
■ How can you focus your attention solely on your service to God this week?
❇ How can you serve or care for a fellow Christian?

Acts 1:1-11
Jesus Taken Up Into Heaven

TOPICS
Angels, Evidence, Heaven, Holy Spirit, Instructions, Jesus Christ, Witnessing

OPEN IT
■ If you could take a trip somewhere far away, where would you go?
❇ What kind of reading material would you take along on a lengthy trip away from home?

EXPLORE IT
❇ To what "former book" was Luke referring? (1:1)
❇ Who was Theophilus? (1:1)
❇ What did Luke write about? (1:1-2)
❇ After His resurrection, how did Jesus spend His time with the apostles? (1:3-5)
❇ What specific commands did Jesus give the apostles? (1:4)
❇ What gift did Jesus promise to the apostles? (1:4-5)
❇ What did the apostles misunderstand? (1:6)
❇ How did Jesus answer the apostles' question? (1:7-8)
■ What task did Jesus assign the apostles? (1:8)
❇ Who would help the apostles get their job done? (1:8)
❇ How would the apostles be able to carry out the task Jesus gave them? (1:8)
❇ After speaking to the apostles, where did Jesus go? (1:9-11)
❇ How did the apostles react to Jesus' departure? (1:10)
■ Who were the figures in white? (1:10)
■ How did the men in white encourage the apostles? (1:11)
❇ How will Jesus' return be like His ascension? (1:11)

GET IT
❇ After His resurrection, Jesus spent some forty days with His disciples; how do you think they felt about this time with Him?
❇ What Christian leader do you value spending time with? Why?
■ What is the importance of Jesus' final promise and command to you?
❇ When is a time you wanted to move on from a location, job, or difficult relationship but were held back by God's leading?
❇ How do we know when the Holy Spirit is at work in our lives?
■ What specific means (abilities, opportunities, relationships) has God given you to carry out the task of being His witness?
❇ When you talk to a nonbelieving friend about Christ, what proofs of Jesus' existence can you offer?
❇ How should the prospect of Christ's return affect the way you live your Christian life?

APPLY IT
❇ When can you include reading the book of Luke in your Bible study this month?
■ What steps can you take to be actively involved in telling others about Christ?
❇ How can you invite the Holy Spirit to guide you throughout this week?

Acts 1:12-26
Matthias Chosen to Replace Judas

TOPICS
Authority, Church, Consequences, Deceit, Leadership, Prayer, Teamwork

OPEN IT
■ When you were growing up, how did you and your friends choose teams for games of kickball, tag, or other such games?
❄ If you had to serve on a church committee, which one would you choose? Why?
❄ When you work together with other people, what kind of role suits you best?
❄ When working with others as part of a team, do you prefer to give orders or follow orders? Why?

EXPLORE IT
❄ Where did the ascension of Jesus take place? (1:12)
❄ How did the apostles show that they were following Jesus' orders? (1:12-13)
❄ How many apostles were still following Christ after His death and resurrection? (1:13)
❄ Who was present at the meeting of eleven apostles? (1:14)
❄ What did the group of eleven apostles do when they got together? (1:14)
❄ Who took the leadership among the early Christians? (1:15)
■ How did Peter take leadership of the early Christians after Jesus' ascension? (1:15-17)
❄ How did Peter show high regard for the Scriptures? (1:16-17)
❄ How did Judas betray both Jesus and the other disciples? (1:16-17)
❄ What happened as a result of Judas' treachery? (1:18-20)
■ What did Peter propose to do about the vacancy left by Judas? (1:21-22)
❄ Who was named to replace Judas? (1:23)
❄ What did the apostles do to select the right candidate to succeed Judas? (1:24-26)
■ How did the apostles choose Judas' successor? (1:24-26)
❄ Who was selected to be the twelfth apostle? (1:26)

GET IT
❄ Recalling that Peter denied Jesus earlier, how do you think the disciples felt about Peter's leadership?
❄ When have you felt uncomfortable submitting to someone's leadership?
■ How do you make important decisions in your family?
■ Why is prayer important in our decision-making process?
❄ What approach does your church follow in making important decisions?
❄ How can you support and encourage your church leaders?
❄ In what way do you need to be more involved or less involved in church ministries?

APPLY IT
■ What is one way you can include God in all important decisions you make?
❄ What can you do in the next few days to show support for your pastor?
❄ How can you improve your prayer life?

Acts 2:1-13
The Holy Spirit Comes at Pentecost

TOPICS
Awe, Believers, Church, Holy Spirit, People, Unbelievers, Witnessing

OPEN IT
❄ What everyday expressions can you say in another language? How did you learn them?
■ If you could speak another language fluently, which one would you choose? Why?

EXPLORE IT
❄ What was celebrated on the day of Pentecost? (2:1)
❄ What group of people was gathered together? (2:1)
❄ Where did a violent wind come from? (2:2)
❄ What did the followers of Christ hear and see? (2:2-3)
❄ What was the importance of the wind and fire? (2:2-4)
■ When the Holy Spirit filled the believers, what did they do? (2:4)
❄ Who was staying in Jerusalem? (2:5)
■ How did the God-fearing Jews visiting Jerusalem react when they heard Christians speaking their languages? (2:6-11)
❄ What languages were the Jews from Galilee speaking? (2:9-11)
❄ What was the topic of conversation among the crowds? (2:11)
■ Besides being amazed, how did the crowd react to the unusual happening they witnessed? (2:12-13)

GET IT
❄ If you saw the coming of the Holy Spirit at Pentecost, how do you think you would have responded? Why?
❄ Why is the coming of the Spirit associated with wind, fire, and different languages?
■ What does it mean to be filled with the Holy Spirit?
❄ How does God use us to witness to others?
❄ When has God enabled you to do something that you didn't think you could do?
❄ How could your church benefit from greater sensitivity to the Holy Spirit?
❄ What areas of unbelief must you deal with in order to become more open to the movement of God in your life?
■ How can we cultivate sensitivity to the Holy Spirit?

APPLY IT
■ How can you be more open to seeing, hearing, and feeling the presence of the Holy Spirit in your prayer and Bible reading?
❄ What can you do each day to invite the Holy Spirit to use you?
❄ What steps can you take this week to be better prepared for God's use?

Acts 2:14-41
Peter Addresses the Crowd

TOPICS
Basics of the Faith, Believers, Church, Evangelism, Gospel, Holy Spirit, Jesus Christ, Messiah, Miracles, People, Power, Prophecy, Repentance, Salvation, Witnessing

OPEN IT
❇ If you had to give a twenty-minute speech in front of a large crowd, what topic would you speak on?
❇ How would you prefer to give a speech—well prepared ahead of time, or impromptu? Why?
■ How would you feel just before getting up to speak to a large group of people?

EXPLORE IT
❇ When Peter stood up to speak, who stood up with him? (2:14)
❇ Whom did Peter address and what command did he give them? (2:14)
❇ What was Peter's defense? (2:15)
❇ What were the believers experiencing? (2:16-21)
❇ Why did Peter quote from Joel 2? (2:17-21)
■ What did Peter say about Jesus of Nazareth? (2:22-24)
❇ How was God in control of Jesus' life, death, and resurrection? (2:22-24)
■ How did Peter explain Christ's work as Messiah? (2:25-35)
❇ What testimony of the apostles did Peter give? (2:32)
❇ Who sent the Holy Spirit? (2:32-33)
■ How did the hearers respond to Peter's words? (2:37)
❇ What did Peter tell his audience to do? (2:38-40)
❇ What happened to those who accepted Peter's message? (2:41)
❇ What effect did Peter's sermon have? (2:41)
❇ How many were added to the fellowship of believers that day? (2:41)

GET IT
❇ Whose preaching challenges you most? Why?
❇ What is your favorite quote from a famous preacher?
❇ How did you become a Christian?
■ How were you challenged to become a believer?
■ How can you challenge others to follow Christ?
❇ How have you been changed by the presence of the Holy Spirit in your life?
❇ What is the significance of baptism to you?
❇ In what ways do you need to be more like Peter?

APPLY IT
❇ What could you say to help someone else see God's perspective on an issue of personal concern?
■ How can you prepare your friends and neighbors for the news that Christ can change their lives?

Acts 2:42-47
The Fellowship of the Believers

TOPICS
Believers, Church, Devotion, Fellowship, Generosity, Growth, Joy, Life-style, Lord's Supper, Miracles, Needs, People, Praise, Salvation

OPEN IT
❇ What possessions do you have that you enjoy sharing with others?
❇ Which of your belongings would you not want to share with anyone else? Why?
❇ How would you describe your life-style: Self-centered, family-centered, or others-centered?

EXPLORE IT
❇ What were the activities of the early church? (2:42)
❇ How did the new believers approach what they did? (2:42)
❇ What unusual deeds did the apostles do? (2:43)
❇ How did people respond to what was going on? (2:43)
❇ What life-style did the early believers adopt? (2:44-45)
❇ Why might the early Christians have had "everything in common"? (2:44)
❇ How were the goods distributed among the early believers? (2:45)
❇ How often did the believers meet? (2:46)
❇ Where did the early believers meet? (2:46)
❇ How did the early Christians meet together? (2:46-47)
❇ What did the Christians do when they met together in homes? (2:46-47)
❇ What was the spirit of the believers in all they did? (2:46-47)
❇ What was the growth of the early church like? (2:47)

GET IT
❇ What were the early believers actually doing when they "broke bread"?
❇ How do the activities of the early church compare with the activities of your church?
❇ How do you think your church should be more like the early church?
❇ In what ways should your church be different from the early church? Why?
❇ The early church was joyful, victorious, and full of praise. How would you describe the spirit of your church?
❇ When do you most enjoy spending time with other believers?
❇ Would you describe your church as self-centered or others-centered?
❇ How is the celebration of Communion meaningful to you?
❇ What "miracles" have you witnessed in your church fellowship?
❇ In what ways do you see your church growing?

APPLY IT
❇ What can you do to help your church be more like the early church?
❇ How can your daily prayers help bring about spiritual renewal in your church fellowship?

Acts 3:1-10

Peter Heals the Crippled Beggar

TOPICS

Actions, Authority, Emotions, Handicapped, Healing, Help, Instructions, Jesus Christ, Miracles, Money, Needs, People, Poor, Praise

OPEN IT

❊ If a stranger were to ask you for a handout, what would you most likely do? Why?
❊ How do you feel toward people who are poor, homeless, or obviously needy?
■ What do you remember about a time when you were very sick or hurt?

EXPLORE IT

❊ Where were Peter and John going? (3:1) When?
❊ Why were the apostles going to the temple? (3:1)
❊ Who was carried to the temple gate every day? (3:2)
❊ How long had the beggar been crippled? (3:2)
■ Why did the crippled man spend every day at the gate called Beautiful? (3:2)
■ What did the beggar do when he saw Peter and John approaching? (3:3)
❊ How did the two apostles first respond to the crippled man? (3:4)
■ What did Peter say to the beggar? (3:4-6)
❊ In what ways did the crippled man respond to Peter's words? (3:5,7-8)
❊ After he was healed, where did the beggar go? (3:8)
❊ What did Peter and John do after the miraculous healing? (3:8)
❊ What happened when the man responded to his miraculous healing? (3:8-10) Why?
❊ How did the people feel about what had happened to the crippled beggar? (3:9-10)

GET IT

❊ If God were to do a miracle of healing among the people in your church, how do you think most people would respond? Why?
❊ When do you meet for prayer at your church?
❊ When was the last time God answered a prayer of yours in a delightful way?
❊ How did you respond the last time God answered a prayer?
■ What specific attitudes toward the weak and needy need to change before God can effectively use a person to help them?
❊ Besides providing financial aid, what can Christians do to help those who are poor or needy?
❊ How can your congregation be helpful to people with disabilities?
❊ How can your congregation be sensitive to the needs of those who are physically disabled?
■ What do you have to offer to others who are disabled or in need?
❊ When have you witnessed God's miraculous healing power at work?
❊ How do you need to change so that God can work through you in a powerful way?

APPLY IT

■ How can you be prepared to help a person in need this week?
❊ What crippled area of your life needs Jesus' healing touch?

Acts 3:11-26

Peter Speaks to the Onlookers

TOPICS

Accusation, Authority, Blessing, Challenge, Change, Faith, Good News, Healing, Ignorance, Jesus Christ, Persecution, Prophecy, Punishment, Renewal, Sin, Witnessing

OPEN IT

❊ If you had to be a journalist, lawyer, or preacher, which occupation would you choose? Why?
■ What is good and bad about confronting another person?
❊ How effective are you at describing and explaining a sequence of events to someone else?

EXPLORE IT

❊ Why did a beggar hold on to Peter and John? (3:11)
❊ Where were the people in the crowd assembled? (3:11) Why?
❊ What did Peter do in response to the gathered crowd? (3:12)
❊ How did Peter address the group? (3:12)
❊ What disclaimer was implied in Peter's opening words? (3:12)
❊ To whom did Peter attribute the power for healing the beggar? (3:13-15)
■ How did Peter set the scene to speak out against the actions of those who crucified Jesus? (3:13-15)
❊ Why was the healing of the man best understood against this profile of Jesus? (3:13-16)
❊ What is the significance of Jesus' name in the healing of the lame man? (3:16)
❊ According to Peter, why did certain Jews mistreat Jesus? (3:17)
❊ How did the Jews' ignorance further the plan of God? (3:18)
■ What did Peter tell his audience to do in order to be forgiven of their sins? (3:19)
❊ What results would follow if Peter's audience responded to his words? (3:19-21)
❊ How did Moses and the prophets predict the coming of Jesus? (3:22-23)
■ How did Peter offer hope to his audience in spite of his warnings? (3:24-26)

GET IT

❊ When have you felt convicted by strong preaching?
❊ By what means does your church encourage others to come to Christ?
■ What does it mean—and not mean—to be bold in encouraging others to believe in Christ?
❊ What can you do to be active in telling others about Christ?
■ What can we learn from Peter's example about confronting others with God's message?

❊ How can a knowledge of the Old Testament build our faith in Christ?
❊ What can we learn from Peter's approach to explaining the truth?
❊ What does it mean to repent and turn to God?
❊ Why do we need to turn to God?
❊ What areas of your life do you need to turn over to God at this time in your life?

APPLY IT
❊ What plan of study can you start to increase your knowledge of God's messages in the Old Testament?
■ How can you be bold in encouraging others to come to Christ?
❊ How might you examine your life this week for areas God may want to change?

Acts 4:1-22
Peter and John Before the Sanhedrin

TOPICS
Authority, Believers, Consequences, Good News, Healing, Holy Spirit, Jesus Christ, Judgment, Kindness, Law, Names, People, Persecution, Prophecy, Salvation, Sin, Witnessing

OPEN IT
❊ How do you tend to respond to criticism?
■ When you are misunderstood, what do you usually do to clear things up?
❊ If you had to defend yourself in a court of law, how well do you think you would hold up under cross-examination?

EXPLORE IT
❊ Why did the religious officials approach Peter and John? (4:1-2) When?
❊ What did the officials do to the apostles? (4:3)
❊ In spite of opposition, how did the early church fare? (4:4)
❊ After a night in jail, whom did Peter and John face the next day? (4:5-7)
❊ To what event did the Jewish leaders refer when they questioned the apostles? (4:7)
❊ What empowered Peter to speak? (4:8)
❊ How did Peter answer the council's question? (4:8-10)
❊ How did Peter's reference to Psalm 118:22 relate to the resurrected Lord? (4:11)
❊ How did Peter's remarks about salvation relate to the healed man, the audience, and the Old Testament passage reference to Christ in Psalm 118:22? (4:10-12)
■ How did the authorities respond to Peter and John? (4:13-14)
■ After the Sanhedrin consulted together, what action did they take against the apostles? (4:15-17)
■ What was the apostles' reply to the judgment handed down by the council? (4:18-20)
❊ Why was the Sanhedrin powerless to take action against Peter and John? (4:21)
❊ How old was the man who had been healed? (4:22)
❊ What was amazing about the healing that caused this controversy? (4:22)

GET IT
❊ In our society, when should Christian leaders stand up to political and religious groups?
❊ In our society, when should a Christian stand up for his or her faith in Christ?
❊ What is the most difficult situation you've faced because of your faith in Christ?
■ What are some of the risks in telling others about Christ?
■ How can we prepare ourselves for the costs we may have to pay for following Christ?
❊ How would you handle being put in jail because you took an unpopular stand for Christ?
❊ How do you think you might affect unbelievers around you by your Christian testimony?
❊ How many new Christians have joined your church fellowship this past year?
❊ How can you be prepared to stand up for Christ when your beliefs are challenged?

APPLY IT
❊ For which public leaders will you pray today that God would call them to repentance and salvation?
■ In what way could you strengthen your sense of courage about being a Christian in your place of work, neighborhood, or family?
❊ To whom might you be able to tell the Good News this week? How?

Acts 4:23-31
The Believers' Prayer

TOPICS
Authority, Believers, Bible, Gospel, Holy Spirit, Jesus Christ, Leadership, Ministry, Miracles, Persecution, Perseverance, Power, Prayer

OPEN IT
■ After going through a stressful experience, what do you do to unwind?
❊ When have you felt most supported and encouraged by your church family?
❊ When you pray, what are some favorite expressions that you like to use?

EXPLORE IT
■ Where did Peter and John go after they were released by the Sanhedrin? (4:23)
■ How did the believers respond to the apostles' report? (4:24)
❊ In the prayer, how did the believers express their view of the persecution they faced? (4:24-26)
❊ How did the believers use the Psalms in their prayer? (4:25-26)
❊ How was God's hand in all that was plotted and done against Jesus? (4:27-28)
❊ How would God orchestrate the destruction and defeat of Jesus' enemies? (4:28-30)
■ What did the Christians ask God to do? (4:29-30)
❊ How would the believers be enabled to carry out God's work? (4:30)
❊ What was the effect of the believers' prayer? (4:31)

❋ What did the Christians experience and do after they finished praying? (4:31)

GET IT

■ Where do you go for help in times of trouble?
❋ How could your church benefit from handling crises the way the early church did?
❋ When we pray, why is it helpful to recall the way God has acted in the past?
❋ How does it build our faith to quote Scripture in our prayers?
❋ How does it build our faith to remember past works of God on behalf of His people?
❋ When was the last time you were amazed by the power of prayer?
■ How can your faith in God be expressed through the prayers you pray?
❋ If your church were more sensitive to the Holy Spirit, what changes might take place?

APPLY IT

■ What changes can you make in your personal prayer life today?
❋ When can you pray for the leaders and ministries of your church?
❋ How might you participate in times of prayer with other Christians over the next month?

Acts 4:32-37

The Believers Share Their Possessions

TOPICS

Believers, Church, Encouragement, Fellowship, Generosity, Jesus Christ, Life-style, Possessions, Power, Resurrection, Teamwork, Toleration, Witnessing

OPEN IT

■ If you had a successful yard sale, what would you do with the profits?
❋ When have you worked with others to raise money for a worthy cause?
❋ What possessions would you be willing to part with to help a friend in need?

EXPLORE IT

■ What attitude did the believers have toward one another? (4:32)
❋ How did the Christians show their unity? (4:32)
❋ How effective was the apostles' witness? (4:33)
❋ What godly quality enhanced the unity and service of the early Christians? (4:33)
❋ How was the command of Deuteronomy 15:4 exemplified by the members of the early church? (4:34-35)
■ What did some better-off Christians do from time to time? (4:34-35)
❋ Why were there no needy persons among the members of the early church? (4:34)
❋ Who dealt with the common fund of the church? (4:35)
❋ How did the early wealthy believers disburse the money they got from selling their lands or houses? (4:35)
❋ Who was Joseph? (4:36)
❋ Who was Barnabas? (4:36)
■ What was exemplary about Barnabas? (4:36-37)
❋ How was Barnabas' generosity singled out? (4:36-37)
❋ What did Barnabas do? (4:37)

GET IT

■ What is difficult about sharing the things we have?
❋ How do the members of your church care for each other's physical needs?
❋ How can you be generous toward your Christian family?
❋ In what ways can you help your Christian leaders meet practical needs of people in the community?
■ How can we copy Barnabas's example?
❋ Where does generosity need to become more evident in the life of your church?
❋ Which member of your congregation stands out as a true "Barnabas" in your view?

APPLY IT

❋ What is one change you can make to improve your relationships with others in your church?
■ What can you do to show Christian generosity to someone in need this week?

Acts 5:1-11

Ananias and Sapphira

TOPICS

Accusation, Church, Consequences, Death, Deceit, Discipline, Fear, God, Holy Spirit, Insight, Money, Punishment, Satan, Sin

OPEN IT

■ When was a time you kept a gift that you had planned to give away?
❋ If you found out that you had been deceived by someone you trusted, what would you do?
❋ How do you know when someone is lying to you?

EXPLORE IT

❋ What did Ananias and Sapphira sell? (5:1)
❋ How did Ananias and Sapphira's transaction compare with Barnabas's? (5:1-2)
■ What did Ananias and Sapphira do with the proceeds from the sale of their property? (5:1-2)
❋ How did Peter recognize when he was being lied to? (5:3-4)
❋ To whom did Ananias lie? (5:3-4)
■ What was Ananias's sin? (5:3-4)
■ What was the consequence of Ananias's sin? (5:5)
❋ After listening to Peter's words, what happened to Ananias? (5:5)
❋ How did people respond to Ananias's death? (5:5)
❋ What was done with Ananias's body? (5:6)
❋ How long after Ananias's death did Sapphira come before Peter? (5:7)
❋ How did Peter test Sapphira? (5:7-8)
❋ How did Sapphira respond to Peter? (5:8)
❋ What rhetorical question did Peter ask Sapphira? (5:9)
❋ What devastating announcement did Peter make to Sapphira? (5:9)
❋ How did Sapphira's end compare with that of her husband? (5:10)

❇ How did the early church respond to these events? (5:11)

GET IT

❇ If there was deception in your church community, how would your church leaders handle it?
❇ In what ways do we sometimes try to gain undue credit or recognition?
❇ How could Ananias and Sapphira have acted differently?
❇ When have you regretted your dealings with other Christians?
❇ How do your Christian leaders deal with sin in the church?
❇ How do you handle your own sin?
❇ When have you been afraid of the Lord?
❇ In what way is it appropriate to be afraid of God?
■ What do we tend to hold back from the Lord?
❇ Why do we sometimes hold back in our giving to God?
■ What can we do to trust God to take care of us?
❇ How can you help yourself be honest with God and with other Christians?

APPLY IT

❇ When can you set aside time this week to evaluate your motives for giving?
■ What act of sacrificial giving can you do this week? How?

Acts 5:12-16

The Apostles Heal Many

TOPICS

Believers, Demons, Faith, Fear, Healing, Miracles, People, Reputation, Sickness

OPEN IT

❇ When you're sick, what kind of patient do you tend to be (cranky, nervous, upbeat, distracted, etc.)?
❇ If you were ill in the hospital, whose visit would probably be most comforting to you?
❇ If you were a physician, what part of the job would you like best?
■ How did your mother take care of you when you were sick as a child?

EXPLORE IT

■ What kind of work did the apostles do among the people? (5:12)
❇ Where did the believers meet? (5:12)
❇ Even though the Christians were highly thought of, why were some people afraid to join them? (5:13)
■ Why did the people seek physical healing from the apostles? (5:13-15)
❇ Despite the fear which kept many people away, what happened to the Christian church during this time? (5:14)
❇ How did some people reveal both superstition and confidence in the apostles? (5:13-16)
❇ Why did some people feel that even Peter's shadow might help them? (5:14-15)
❇ Where did the people who gathered around the apostles come from? (5:16)
❇ Besides the sick, who else was brought to the apostles for healing? (5:16)
■ What happened to all those who came to be made well? (5:16)

GET IT

❇ How would you describe the reputation of the church in your community?
❇ In what ways does your church help or serve those who are ill?
❇ If you were ill, how might your church be able to help you?
■ When is it helpful or comforting to visit a sick person in the hospital or at home?
■ How can we reach out to those who are sick or ill?
❇ If the sick were brought to your church for healing, what would your church leaders do?
❇ How do you think your church could learn from the example of the early Christians in the way they took care of the physical and mental needs of people?

APPLY IT

❇ For whom can you pray today that God would heal his or her pain?
■ What are some of the ways you can serve those who are sick in your church?
❇ What practical help can you provide this week for a church member who is ill?

Acts 5:17-42

The Apostles Persecuted

TOPICS

Angels, God, Good News, Holy Spirit, Jealousy, Jesus Christ, Joy, Leadership, Miracles, Obedience, People, Persecution, Perseverance, Punishment

OPEN IT

❇ What was the most fearful experience you ever had?
❇ When was the last time you felt intimidated by an individual or group of people?
■ What bullies do you remember from grade school?

EXPLORE IT

❇ Why were the religious leaders opposed to the apostles? (5:17)
❇ What happened when the Christians were put in jail? (5:18-19)
❇ What did the angel tell the apostles to do? (5:20)
❇ When did the apostles start teaching? (5:21)
❇ What did the elders of Israel discover after they met together? (5:21-24)
❇ How were the apostles brought before the Sanhedrin? (5:25-27)
❇ How had the apostles disobeyed the council? (5:28)
❇ Why did the high priest avoid mentioning the name of Jesus? (5:28)
❇ What reason did the apostles give for their disobedience? (5:29)
■ What made the Jewish elders furious? (5:29-32)
■ Who intervened on behalf of Peter and the others? (5:34-39) How?
❇ How did Gamaliel intervene? (5:34-39)
❇ What advice did Gamaliel offer the council? (5:38-39)
❇ What effect did Gamaliel's speech have? (5:40)

■ How did the elders deal with the apostles? (5:40)
❇ What did the apostles do after they left the Sanhedrin? (5:41-42)

GET IT
❇ What might make someone jealous of a church leader?
❇ If the government told you that you could not pray, show your Bible, or talk about God in public, what would you do?
❇ Would you describe your church as courageous, timid, or somewhere in between? Why?
■ What forms of opposition do Christians experience today?
■ For what principles should a Christian stand at all costs?
❇ If Peter were your pastor, what do you think your church would be like?
❇ If you had to go through the sufferings of the apostles, how would you cope?
❇ How is it possible to have joy in the middle of a difficult circumstance?
❇ What should we copy from the character and example of Peter?
❇ How can you become more like Peter in your witness for Christ?
❇ How can we experience God more fully, so that you are set free to rejoice no matter what sufferings you experience?

APPLY IT
■ What do you want to remember the next time you are challenged or hurt for your faith in Christ?
❇ In what situations can you serve as a witness for Christ this week? How?

Acts 6:1-7
The Choosing of the Seven

TOPICS
Bible, Church, Complaining, Growth, Holy Spirit, Leadership, Ministry, Neglect, Prayer, Responsibility

OPEN IT
❇ When working as part of a team, do you prefer to “do the work” or to lead and coordinate others?
■ If you could spend next Saturday morning doing anything you like, what would you do?
❇ If you had to spend next Saturday morning leading a Bible study, praying with other Christians, or serving breakfast to a group of widows, which activity would you choose? Why?

EXPLORE IT
■ What complaint did the Grecian Jews make? (6:1)
■ What did the apostles—the Twelve—do in response to criticism? (6:2-4)
❇ Why did the Twelve choose prayer and teaching over caring for the poor? (6:2-4)
❇ What did the Twelve tell the other believers to do? (6:3)
■ How did the group respond to the apostles’ proposal? (6:5)
❇ Who was selected to serve the widows? (6:5)
❇ Who chose the seven candidates? (6:5)
❇ How were the men given authority to do their task? (6:6)
❇ What was the effect of the appointment of certain people to serve the widows? (6:7)
❇ How did the church fare after the apostles delegated the serving of food to others? (6:7)

GET IT
❇ In what ways do the people of your church differ from one another?
❇ What different ethnic or cultural groups are there in your church?
❇ How can differences among believers cause friction?
❇ What benefits and challenges arise from having different kinds of people in your church?
■ How should we deal with tensions between differences among church members?
❇ What qualities must Christian leaders have to resolve differences between believers?
❇ How could your church ensure that no one group of people is neglected?
❇ What do we tend to complain most about?
❇ What complaints arise in your church most often?
■ How can we learn to channel our complaints into solutions?
❇ In what ways can you use your gifts and skills in your church?

APPLY IT
❇ How can you help free your church leaders to focus on their mission of prayer, evangelism, and teaching?
■ What could you do this week to help resolve a conflict between believers?

Acts 6:8-15
Stephen Seized

TOPICS
Accusation, Blasphemy, Conflict, Grace, Holy Spirit, Jesus Christ, Law, Miracles, Opposition, People, Power, Traditions, Wisdom

OPEN IT
❇ Who, in your view, is one of the most outstanding leaders in the world today?
❇ Among your coworkers and neighbors, what do you think people consider you—controversial, moderate, liberal, or conservative? Why?
■ When was a time you were falsely accused? What happened?

EXPLORE IT
■ Who was Stephen? (6:8)
❇ What kind of person was Stephen? (6:8)
❇ Besides caring for the needs of the widows, what did Stephen do among the people? (6:8)
❇ Who opposed Stephen? (6:9)
❇ Why couldn’t Stephen’s opponents get the better of him? (6:10)
■ What kind of charges did Stephen’s enemies make against him? (6:11)
❇ How did the people react to the charges against Stephen? (6:12)

■ How did the false witnesses misrepresent Stephen? (6:13-14)
❊ Why did certain people consider Stephen dangerous? (6:13-14)
❊ When those in the Sanhedrin looked at Stephen, what did they see? (6:15)
❊ What did the expression on Stephen's face show about his relationship to God? (6:15)

GET IT
■ What does it mean to be "full of God's grace and power"?
❊ If Stephen were alive today, how might other religious groups oppose him?
❊ What qualities of Stephen would you like to see in your own life?
❊ What theological issues do people argue about in your church?
❊ What are some good ways to handle disagreements about doctrine?
❊ What religious traditions do Christians sometimes value or cling to over biblical truth?
❊ What character qualities help a person face conflict or opposition?
■ What should we do when we are falsely accused?
❊ In what ways do we need the Holy Spirit's filling so our gifts can be used effectively?

APPLY IT
❊ How can you be open to God's use this week?
■ What can you do to copy Stephen's example whenever you are falsely accused in some way?
❊ What do you want to remember the next time you are falsely accused?

Acts 7:1-53
Stephen's Speech to the Sanhedrin

TOPICS
Accusation, Covenant, Disobedience, God, History, Holy Spirit, Law, Messiah, People, Punishment, Rejection

OPEN IT
■ What is one time of your life you wish you could do over? Why?
❊ What is the longest speech or talk you've ever given?
❊ In what ways are you just like your parents?
❊ In what ways are you different from your parents?
❊ If you had to defend in court your views on something you cared about, how do you think people would respond to what you had to say?

EXPLORE IT
❊ What did the high priest ask Stephen? (7:1)
■ Why did Stephen make this speech? (7:1-2)
❊ What was Stephen's initial response to the leaders? (7:2)
❊ In his speech to the court, Stephen showed that there was progress and change in God's plan for His people; how was Abraham an example of this change? (7:2-8)
■ As he wove the history of the Jews, how did Stephen show a pattern of opposition to God and His plan for them? (7:2-4, 9, 23-29)
❊ How did God bless His people outside the land of Israel? (7:2-5, 7-10, 29-34)
❊ How was the move to Egypt a great change for Jacob's descendants? (7:9-16)
❊ How did deliverance under Moses mark progress for God's people? (7:17-43)
❊ Where was the law of Moses given to God's people? (7:38)
❊ From the tabernacle to the temple, the place of God's presence changed and progressed; how did Stephen show this? (7:44-50)
❊ How did Stephen show that the temple is not God's true dwelling place? (7:47-50)
❊ What did Stephen say in direct attack on his audience? (7:51-53)
■ How did Stephen compare the attitude of those in the Sanhedrin with that of God's people down through the centuries? (7:51-53)
❊ Of what did Stephen accuse his hearers? (7:51-53)
❊ According to Stephen, in what ways did the people resist the Holy Spirit? (7:52-53)

GET IT
❊ In reviewing your life, how would you like to rewrite history?
❊ What rituals or traditions hinder change and spiritual progress among believers?
■ Which "spiritual ancestors" from the Bible do you admire most?
■ How can we learn from those who have gone before us?
❊ In what ways should we be like Stephen?
❊ How can a group of believers be a "stiff-necked people"?
❊ What stiff-necked attitudes prevent us from seeing what God wants us to see?
❊ What kind of opposition to God's message is there today?
❊ What kind of opposition or pressure on your faith have you felt from friends, coworkers, or unbelieving family members?
❊ How can we deal with opposition to God's message?

APPLY IT
■ From what older, more mature believer can you learn? How?
❊ What can you do this week to know Jesus more fully?
❊ How can you uncover the attitudes that hinder the work of the Holy Spirit in your life?
❊ What can you do this week to learn from the example of other believers in the Old Testament?

Acts 7:54-8:1
The Stoning of Stephen

TOPICS
Anger, Church, Death, Glory, God, Heaven, Holy Spirit, Jesus Christ, Persecution, Prayer

OPEN IT
❊ When have you felt uncomfortable in a large crowd of people?

■ How do you respond to reports of violence in the news?
❊ How do you tend to deal with anger?

EXPLORE IT
❊ How did the hearers react to Stephen's accusations? (7:54) Why?
■ Why did the Jewish leaders respond to Stephen as they did? (7:54)
❊ Faced with the fury of his persecutors, why wasn't Stephen afraid? (7:55)
❊ How did Stephen's heavenly vision prepare him for what was to follow? (7:55)
❊ How did God prepare Stephen for his death? (7:55)
❊ What did Stephen say that enraged his adversaries? (7:56)
■ Why was Stephen put to death? (7:56-60)
❊ Why did Stephen's enemies yell and cover their ears? (7:57)
❊ How was Stephen taken out of town? (7:57-58)
❊ Where was Stephen stoned to death? (7:58)
❊ Why did people lay their clothing at Saul's feet? (7:58)
❊ What were Stephen's two last requests before he died? (7:59-60)
❊ How did Stephen die? (7:60)
❊ Who approved of Stephen's death? (8:1)
■ What change in the church did Stephen's death bring about? (8:1)
❊ Who left and who stayed in Jerusalem? (8:1)

GET IT
❊ Why do Christians sometimes get angry at preachers?
❊ When your conscience is pricked, how do you tend to react?
❊ If your congregation decided the pastor was a heretic, how would they remove him from office?
■ Faced with the violent mob, Stephen seemed fearless; how was he able to face this danger?
■ What would make it possible for you to be calm and sure in the middle of extreme danger?
❊ When should we call on the Lord for help?
❊ How can you be more forgiving of others?
❊ What hardships has your church faced recently?
❊ How does God "scatter" the church to carry His message to others?
❊ How has God "scattered" your church?

APPLY IT
❊ In what hostile setting could you be a witness for Christ this week? How?
■ How can Stephen's example help you be prepared to handle rejection?
❊ Which former member of your congregation now living elsewhere can you encourage this week? How?

Acts 8:2-3
The Church Persecuted and Scattered

TOPICS
Church, Courage, Death, Persecution, Zeal

OPEN IT
❊ What would you like people to remember most about you after your death?
❊ If you could write your own obituary, what would you say about yourself?
❊ What is the most important accomplishment of your life so far?
■ When is a time you remember being rejected by childhood peers?

EXPLORE IT
❊ Who buried Stephen? (8:2)
❊ How did the early believers react to Stephen's martyrdom? (8:2)
❊ How did Stephen's sympathizers show that they disapproved of the Sanhedrin's condemnation of him? (8:2)
■ How did Stephen's mourners show courage at his burial? (8:2)
❊ How did the godly men mourn for Stephen? (8:2)
■ What was happening to the church at this time? (8:2-3)
■ Who began to attack the church? (8:3) How?
❊ Who took a leading role in attacking the early church? (8:3)
❊ During this period of opposition, what did Saul do? (8:3)
❊ How were Saul's actions cruel? (8:3)
❊ How did the martyrdom of Stephen and the persecution of the church show that Israel had rejected the Messiah? (8:3)

GET IT
❊ Why was it dangerous for people in the church to give Stephen a proper burial?
❊ Though there was much sadness at Stephen's funeral, why was there also cause for celebration?
❊ Why can we experience joy along with grief at a Christian's funeral?
❊ How can you show courage in difficult circumstances, just as the "godly men" did in burying Stephen?
■ In what ways are Christians under attack today?
■ How can you respond whenever others attack or reject you for your Christian identity, views, or life-style?
❊ How is our Christian experience very different from that of the early church?
❊ How can you live each day as if it were your last?
❊ How do you need to be more courageous in your identity as a Christian?

APPLY IT
■ What will most remind you to respond with courage when you are attacked or rejected for your faith in Christ?
❊ In what setting (at work, at home, in your neighborhood, etc.) can you show courage in identifying with Christ this week? How?

Acts 8:4-8
Philip in Samaria

TOPICS
Bible, Joy, Miracles, Witnessing

OPEN IT
■ If you could give all your effort to a single occupation and be among the best in the world at it, what occupation would you choose?
❊ What one talent or gift would you really like to have?

❇ When was the last time you had a celebration of some kind?

EXPLORE IT
❇ What were the Christians doing who had been scattered throughout Judea and Samaria? (8:4)
❇ What happened to the word of God? (8:4)
❇ Why was the scattering of Christians a step forward for the church? (8:4-8)
■ Who was Philip? (8:5)
❇ Where did Philip go? (8:5)
■ What did Philip do in Samaria? (8:5)
■ What did the crowds do in response to Philip's teaching and miracles? (8:6)
❇ What miraculous signs did Philip perform? (8:7)
❇ How did Philip's work draw attention to his message? (8:6-7)
❇ Why did the people rejoice? (8:8)

GET IT
■ How is your church, through its mission work, scattered throughout the world?
■ How can you help spread the gospel in your community?
❇ What is a miracle?
❇ What signs and miracles have you witnessed in your church?
❇ What makes your congregation joyful?
❇ How can you help people who are sick or troubled?

APPLY IT
■ What can you do this week to support or encourage a missionary?
❇ What is one way you can support your church's ministry?
❇ For whom can you pray for healing?

Acts 8:9-25
Simon the Sorcerer

TOPICS
Awe, Follow, Good News, Holy Spirit, Jesus Christ, Kingdom of God/Heaven, Leadership, Money, Prejudice, Sin, Witnessing

OPEN IT
❇ In what situations would you describe yourself as quiet or outgoing?
❇ If you were a magician, whom would you have most fun entertaining?
■ What people of different ethnic groups do you know?

EXPLORE IT
❇ What was Simon's line of work? (8:9)
❇ What did Simon talk about? (8:9)
❇ How did the Samaritans react to Simon's sorcery? (8:9-11)
❇ When Philip preached about Christ, what did the people do? (8:12)
❇ What did Simon do when he heard the gospel? (8:13)
■ Why did Peter and John leave Jerusalem and go to Samaria? (8:14)
■ What did Peter and John do when they arrived in Samaria? (8:15-17)
❇ What did Simon want to buy from Peter and John? (8:18-19)
❇ How did Peter answer Simon's request? (8:20-23)
❇ Why did Peter use strong language with Simon? (8:20)
❇ How did Peter imply that Simon was not a Christian? (8:21-23)
❇ What was Simon's attitude in response to Peter? (8:24)
■ How did Peter and John's trip to Samaria influence their trip to Jerusalem? (8:25)

GET IT
❇ How are some religious leaders today like Simon?
❇ How are some religious leaders today like Peter and John?
❇ When is it most tempting to brag?
❇ What are some of the trappings of money?
❇ In what way do some people try to "buy" God's favor?
❇ What does it mean for your heart to be right before God?
❇ Why is it important for us to have our heart right before God?
❇ Most Samaritans and Jews didn't get along; why then did early Jewish Christians tell Samaritans about Christ?
■ What ethnic or religious prejudices do you have a hard time shaking?
■ What can help us change our prejudices against people groups?
❇ Why did you become a Christian?
❇ What motivates you to grow in your relationship with Christ?

APPLY IT
■ What can you do this week to get to know someone who is from a different ethnic group or culture?
❇ Whom can you invite from another culture to visit your church? When?
❇ How can you invite the Holy Spirit to help you grow in faith in the coming days?

Acts 8:26-40
Philip and the Ethiopian

TOPICS
Angels, Bible, Evangelism, Holy Spirit, Important, Instructions, Jesus Christ, Joy, Justice

OPEN IT
❇ If you could travel overseas, to which country would you like to go?
■ What reading material do you find difficult to understand?
❇ Who is one of the best teachers you ever had?

EXPLORE IT
❇ What did the angel tell Philip to do? (8:26)
■ Whom did Philip meet on the desert road? (8:27)
❇ What was the eunuch's position? (8:27)
❇ Why was the eunuch on his way to Jerusalem to worship? (8:27)

❄ What was the eunuch doing while he sat in the chariot? (8:28)
■ What was the eunuch's problem? (8:28-34)
❄ What did the Holy Spirit tell Philip to do? (8:29)
❄ What did Philip ask the eunuch? (8:30)
❄ How did the eunuch respond to Philip? (8:31)
❄ What was the eunuch reading? (8:32-33)
■ How did Philip present the good news about Jesus? (8:35)
❄ What did the eunuch do after he believed in Jesus? (8:36-38)
❄ What happened to Philip after he baptized the eunuch? (8:39)
❄ How did believing in Christ affect the eunuch? (8:39)
❄ What was the eunuch's attitude as he went on his way? (8:39)
❄ Where did Philip go to preach? (8:40)

GET IT
❄ How does the Holy Spirit lead us?
❄ When has the Holy Spirit led you to speak to someone?
❄ In what ways can your church reach out beyond its neighborhood to others?
■ How does God use us to take the message of Christ to others?
❄ What passages of Scripture are difficult for you to understand?
❄ Why are some parts of the Bible difficult to understand?
❄ Where can we get help understanding the Bible better?
❄ When was the last time you explained the Scriptures to someone else?
❄ To whom could you turn for help in understanding the Bible better?
■ How can you be involved in telling others about Christ or in helping others do so?
❄ What fears prevent us from telling others about Christ?
❄ What barriers prevent us from helping others understand the message of Christ?

APPLY IT
❄ What can you do to be sensitive to the Holy Spirit's leading each day?
■ What is one thing you can do this week to overcome fear in witnessing?
❄ In your Bible study this week, how can you prepare yourself for opportunities to share what you learn?

Acts 9:1-19
Saul's Conversion

TOPICS
Blindness, Christianity, Church, Fasting, Holy Spirit, Jesus Christ, Obedience, Prayer, Restoration, Salvation

OPEN IT
❄ How would you describe the most intimidating person you know?
■ If you could have a surprise visit from someone, whom would you want to visit you?
❄ What was the most unusual experience that ever happened to you when you were growing up?

EXPLORE IT
❄ What was Saul doing against the Lord's disciples? (9:1-2)
❄ What was "the Way"? (9:2)
❄ What happened to Saul as he approached Damascus? (9:3-6)
❄ Whom did Saul meet? (9:3-6)
❄ In persecuting the church, who was Paul really attacking? (9:5)
❄ What did the resurrected Lord Jesus order Saul to do? (9:6)
❄ What did Saul's traveling companions experience when Saul met the risen Christ? (9:7)
❄ How did Saul get to Damascus after his meeting with the Lord? (9:8)
❄ Who was Ananias? (9:10)
■ What did the Lord instruct Ananias to do? (9:10-12)
■ Why was Ananias reluctant to do as the Lord asked? (9:13-14)
■ How did God persuade Ananias that it was all right to go to Saul? (9:15-16)
❄ To what service had Saul been called? (9:15-16)
❄ How did Ananias do the Lord's bidding? (9-17)
❄ What did Saul do when his vision returned? (9:18-19)

GET IT
❄ What was your conversion experience like?
❄ To what ministry has God called you?
❄ In what ways do we sometimes hold back from doing what God wants?
❄ Why do we sometimes resist what God asks of us?
❄ What happens when we resist doing what God wants?
❄ If you were temporarily disabled, how might it benefit your spiritual life?
❄ How can fasting help us focus on spiritual needs?
❄ What are some of the many ways a person can play a part in leading someone to Christ?
❄ What are some ways we can welcome new believers into the body of Christ?
■ What do older, more mature Christians have to offer younger, less mature Christians?
■ How can you be a guide and help to younger Christians in your church?
❄ How can you lean on another Christian to help you uncover God's will for your life? Who is this person?

APPLY IT
❄ How can you challenge a friend or neighbor with the message of salvation this week?
■ What is one thing you could do this week to help a younger Christian grow in his or her faith?
❄ From what more mature Christian can you seek advice or counsel this week?

Acts 9:20-31
Saul in Damascus and Jerusalem

TOPICS
Change, Church, Holy Spirit, Jesus Christ, Peace, Persecution, Power, Witnessing

OPEN IT
❋ If you could make one significant change in your life this year, what would it be?
■ If you were constantly harassed on your job, what would you most likely do about it?

EXPLORE IT
❋ After spending some days with the Christians in Damascus, what did Saul do? (9:20-21)
❋ What was the focus of Saul's message? (9:20)
❋ How did people react to their former enemy? (9:21)
❋ Why were the Jews living in Damascus baffled by Saul? (9:22)
■ What did the Jews plan for Saul? (9:23) Why?
■ How did Saul outwit his enemies? (9:24-25)
❋ Who mistrusted Saul in Jerusalem? (9:26)
❋ Who welcomed Saul in Jerusalem? (9:27)
❋ How did Barnabas help the apostles accept Saul? (9:27)
■ What did Saul do while he was with the apostles? (9:28-29)
❋ How did Saul follow in Stephen's footsteps? (9:29)
❋ As a result of the threat on his life, where was Saul taken by his friends? (9:30)
❋ What was the state of the young church at this time? (9:31)

GET IT
■ Why do unbelievers sometimes oppose those who tell others about Christ?
❋ What is the difference between opposition to our faith and opposition to our personality?
❋ How have you changed because of knowing Jesus?
❋ Why did the disciples in Jerusalem fear Saul?
❋ Why did Saul have a significant testimony to others?
■ In what ways can a new Christian have a unique witness to friends and associates?
❋ What fellow Christian has served as an inspirational example to you?
❋ How could a person like Barnabas help heal wounds in a church group?
❋ If your life were threatened, whom could you count on to protect you?
❋ What particular group of people would you feel most comfortable telling about Christ?
❋ How does the state of your church compare with that of the early church?

APPLY IT
■ This week, how can you prepare for discussions about God with your coworkers or nonChristian friends?
❋ What can you do to welcome people to your church?
❋ Who could you welcome into your place of work, church, or community this week? How?

Acts 9:32-43
Aeneas and Dorcas

TOPICS
Believers, Death, Goodness, Healing, Instructions, Jesus Christ, Miracles, Poor, Prayer, Witnessing

OPEN IT
■ What are some of your most treasured memories of a late friend, relative, or coworker?
❋ What would you find easy or hard about helping inner-city poor people find jobs?
❋ What would you find easy or hard about helping paraplegics learn to live with their disabilities?

EXPLORE IT
❋ Where did Peter's mission work take him? (9:32)
❋ Whom did Peter visit in Lydda? (9:33)
❋ How was Peter able to cure Aeneas? (9:34)
❋ What effect did the healing of Aeneas have on the residents of Lydda and Sharon? (9:35)
❋ What did Tabitha (Dorcas) do in Joppa? (9:36)
■ What happened to Dorcas? (9:37)
❋ Where was Joppa in relation to Lydda? (9:38)
❋ Why was Peter summoned by the disciples to Joppa? (9:38)
❋ Where was Peter taken when he arrived in Joppa? (9:39)
❋ How was the miracle of raising the woman to life performed? (9:40)
■ What did Peter do when he was alone with the dead woman? (9:40-41)
❋ After Peter helped Tabitha to her feet, what did he do next? (9:41)
■ How did the miracle of raising Tabitha further the kingdom of God? (9:42)
❋ With whom did Peter stay in Joppa? (9:43)

GET IT
❋ Why are the signs and wonders of the early church largely absent from the Christian community today?
■ Why do some Christians suffer and die, while others are healed of their sickness?
❋ In what ways would you like to follow the example of Dorcas?
❋ When you die, what group of people besides your family will miss you most?
❋ If Peter were visiting your church, whom would you ask him to help?

APPLY IT
❋ What areas of your life need God's healing today?
❋ How can you help a needy person this week?
■ What can you do to help a widow who needs assistance?

Acts 10:1-8
Cornelius Calls for Peter

TOPICS
Angels, Generosity, Gifts, God, Instructions, Leadership, Poor, Prayer

OPEN IT

■ What would be appealing or unappealing to you about a career in the armed forces?
❊ If you were in military service, where would you like to be stationed?
❊ As an army officer, what would you like or not like about commanding a company of soldiers?

EXPLORE IT

❊ Who was Cornelius? (10:1)
❊ Where did Cornelius live? (10:1)
❊ What did Cornelius do for a living? (10:1)
❊ How did the Roman officer and his family relate to God? (10:2)
❊ How did Cornelius help those in need? (10:2)
❊ What did Cornelius experience one afternoon? (10:3)
❊ How did Cornelius respond to the angel? (10:4)
■ How did the angel affirm the centurion's life-style? (10:4)
■ What did the angel command Cornelius to do? (10:5-6)
■ When the angel left, what did Cornelius do? (10:7-8)
❊ Who did Cornelius send to Joppa? (10:7-8)

GET IT

■ What neighbors and friends remind you of Cornelius?
❊ Why is it that many kind, "God-fearing" people do not have a personal relationship with Christ?
■ How do you need to be more like Cornelius?
❊ How do you know when God is speaking to you?
❊ When do you act on what God tells you to do?
❊ How can you be more open to God taking command of your life?

APPLY IT

■ This week, what can you do to imitate the centurion's God-fearing life-style?
❊ What can you give to someone who is in need?

Acts 10:9-23

Peter's Vision

TOPICS

Acceptance, Culture, Heaven, Holy Spirit, Hospitality, Instructions, Prayer, Respect

OPEN IT

■ At an ethnic food festival, would you try a variety of international dishes or immediately seek out the hot dog stand? Why?
❊ If you lived overseas, what about your life-style would you try to maintain, and how would you try to fit in with the nationals?

EXPLORE IT

❊ Where was Peter when the centurion's men approached Joppa? (10:9)
❊ What was Peter doing? (10:9)
❊ How did Peter feel? (10:10)
■ What did Peter experience while food was being prepared for him? (10:10-16)
❊ What did Peter see in a vision? (10:11-12)
❊ What did the voice instruct Peter to do? (10:13)
❊ Why did Peter protest against the command to eat? (10:14)
❊ How were Peter's objections silenced? (10:15)
❊ Why was this incident repeated three times? (10:16)
■ What happened while Peter was wondering about the vision? (10:17-20)
■ How was Peter prepared for the messengers? (10:19-20)
❊ What did Peter say to the messengers? (10:21)
❊ What did the messengers tell Peter? (10:22)
❊ How did Peter respond to the messengers' request? (10:23)

GET IT

❊ How do you think Peter felt when he was told to kill and eat unclean food?
■ What are some reasons we reject or avoid certain people?
❊ Peter's dream was unexpected; how does God deal with us in surprising ways?
❊ How does God give us clear directions through other Christians?
❊ How did Peter's hospitality to the messengers show that he was beginning to put into practice what he had learned in the vision?
❊ How should your church treat visitors who are different from the rest of the congregation?
■ How can you show acceptance of those who don't "fit in"?

APPLY IT

■ What new relationships can you ask God to bring into your life this week?
❊ How can you become more open-minded toward others?
❊ Starting today, how can you help another Christian move beyond his or her cultural limits?

Acts 10:24-48

Peter at Cornelius' House

TOPICS

Acceptance, Forgiveness, God, Good News, Holy Spirit, Jesus Christ, People, Power, Praise, Prayer, Prejudice, Resurrection, Witnessing

OPEN IT

❊ If you could have been born and raised in another culture, which one would you like to have been raised in? Why?
■ If a family from another country moved in next door, how might you welcome them to the neighborhood?
❊ When was the first time you faced prejudice?

EXPLORE IT

❊ Who was with Peter when he arrived in Caesarea? (10:23-24)
❊ How had Cornelius prepared for Peter's visit? (10:24-25)
❊ How did Peter refuse the centurion's homage? (10:25-26)
❊ Who was inside the centurion's house? (10:27)
❊ What did Peter say to show that he had learned what God had wanted him to learn? (10:28-29)

❇ What did Peter ask? (10:29)
❇ How did Cornelius respond? (10:30-33)
■ In what way was Peter's understanding of God changed by his vision? (10:34-35)
■ What was Peter's message to the group? (10:34-43)
❇ How was Peter's message interrupted? (10:44-46)
■ Why did Peter suddenly stop talking? (10:44-46)
❇ What happened to the non-Jewish believers to show the Jewish believers that God accepted them? (10:44-46)
❇ How did the circumcised believers react to what happened? (10:45-46)
❇ How did Peter sum up what had happened? (10:47-48)
❇ What did Peter command? (10:48)
❇ In what ways was fellowship between believing Jews and believing non-Jews improved during Peter's stay in Caesarea? (10:48)

GET IT
■ How do cultural and religious barriers hinder growth in our faith?
■ If you had a vision like Peter's, what deep-seated prejudices would you be called on to get rid of?
❇ How would Cornelius and his group fare at your church?
❇ Why might someone visiting your church for the first time feel unwelcome?
❇ What could you and others do to make people of all kinds feel welcome in your church?
❇ What cultural and religious barriers hinder growth in your church?
❇ How is your pastor like Peter?
❇ How could your pastor benefit from an encounter with Cornelius and Peter?
❇ How can your church be open to the power of the Holy Spirit in a new way?
❇ If someone asked you to tell them about your faith, what would you say?

APPLY IT
■ What is the first step you could take to show respect for a racial or cultural group that is different from you?
❇ How can you be an effective witness for Christ this week among people who are different from you?

Acts 11:1-18
Peter Explains His Actions

TOPICS
Angels, Believers, Bible, Church, Criticism, God, Holy Spirit, Jesus Christ, Praise, Prayer, Prejudice, Repentance, Salvation

OPEN IT
❇ What dream stands out in your memory?
❇ What favorite story do you like retelling?
■ What is one family tradition you want to keep at all costs?

EXPLORE IT
❇ What did the apostles and Christians in Judea hear? (11:1)
❇ When Peter went to Jerusalem, who criticized him? (11:2)
❇ Who were the "circumcised believers"? (11:2)
❇ What did the circumcised Christians say? (11:3)
■ Why did the circumcised believers imply that it was wrong for Peter to eat with Gentiles? (11:3)
■ How did Peter explain his actions? (11:4-17)
❇ What did Peter include in his brief explanation? (11:4-17)
❇ What additional information did Peter provide concerning the angel's message to Cornelius? (11:14)
■ How did Peter dispel the idea that the Gentiles were second-class citizens? (11:15-17)
❇ On what did Peter's defense rest? (11:17)
❇ How did Peter's argument prove convincing? (11:18)
❇ How did Peter's step of including non-Jews affect the church? (11:18)

GET IT
❇ Why do you think Peter told the whole story behind his actions?
❇ How was the criticism against Peter helpful to the church?
❇ When might it be helpful to be openly critical about church matters?
■ In what ways do we need to be less like the "circumcised believers" in our approach to others?
❇ Whom do you find "unacceptable"?
■ How can you be more accepting of those who don't match your values or life-style?
❇ What principle of accepting others do you want to copy from Peter's example?

APPLY IT
❇ When might you need to take a stand for what is right in your place of work, family, or church this week?
■ How can you open your heart and mind to others whom you tend to dislike?

Acts 11:19-30
The Church in Antioch

TOPICS
Believe, Believers, Christianity, Church, Encouragement, Faith, Gifts, Good News, Grace, Help, Holy Spirit, Jesus Christ, Ministry, Persecution, Prophecy

OPEN IT
❇ What do you like or dislike about traveling?
❇ When you have too much to do, whom do you call on for help?
❇ If those who know you best were discussing your character, what do you think they would say was one of your strengths?

EXPLORE IT
❇ What was one of the results of Stephen's martyrdom? (11:19)
❇ To whom was the news about Christ being told? (11:19)
❇ Who spoke to the Greeks in Antioch about the Lord Jesus? (11:20)
❇ What caused the news about Christ to take hold among many who heard it? (11:21)

❇ What resulted from the ministry of the Christians? (11:21)
❇ How did the church at Jerusalem respond to the increase in numbers of new believers? (11:22)
❇ How did Barnabas encourage the Christians at Antioch? (11:23)
❇ What was exemplary about Barnabas? (11:24)
❇ What happened to the work in Antioch? (11:24)
❇ Why did Barnabas go to Tarsus to look for Saul? (25-26)
❇ Where were the disciples first called Christians? (11:26)
❇ Who was Agabus? (11:27)
❇ What did Agabus predict? (11:28)
❇ What did the Christians do for the believers in Judea? (11:29-30) Why?
❇ To whom did Saul and Barnabas give the gift collected in Antioch? (11:29-30)

GET IT
❇ How was Stephen's martyrdom good for the church?
❇ How can good sometimes come out of tragedies?
❇ Why is someone like Barnabas a real asset to a church?
❇ If you were more like Barnabas, how might people respond to you differently from the way they do now?
❇ Which label are you most comfortable with: disciple, saint, believer, or Christian? Why?
❇ Following the example of the early church, how should we help other Christians who face economic hardship?

APPLY IT
❇ How can you do good for someone who needs your help this week?
■ What can you do to enlarge the circle of people to whom you reach out?

Acts 12:1-19
Peter's Miraculous Escape From Prison

TOPICS
Angels, Assurance, Church, Instructions, Joy, Persecution, Prayer

OPEN IT
❇ If you had to write a short story, what is one thing you would do to make it interesting to the reader?
■ What is one dream you remember as having been very vivid?
❇ If you told someone about an exciting dream you had, how would you make it come alive to the listener?

EXPLORE IT
❇ Why was King Herod so cold-hearted toward the church? (12:1-3)
❇ Whom did King Herod arrest? (12:1, 3-4)
❇ Whom did the king have put to death? (12:2)
❇ What did Herod do with Peter? (12:3-4) Why?
■ What did the king plan to do with Peter after the Passover? (12:3-4) Why?
❇ What did the church do while Peter was in prison? (12:5)
❇ While in jail, why didn't Peter seem to fear for his life? (12:6)
■ What happened on the night before Peter's trial? (12:6-11)
❇ Who enabled Peter to escape? (12:7-10)
❇ How did Peter escape from prison? (12:7-10)
■ When did Peter know that what he had experienced was real? (12:11)
❇ Where did Peter go once he realized what had happened? (12:12)
❇ What happened when Peter appeared at Mary's door? (12:13-16)
❇ Once inside the house, what did Peter say? (12:17)
❇ How did the soldiers react when they discovered Peter was gone? (12:18)
❇ What did Herod do? (12:19)

GET IT
❇ When have you seen a person try to take advantage of Christians, as Herod did?
■ How do you tend to react in trying circumstances?
❇ How can a church use prayer when faced with a crisis?
■ What can we learn from the way Peter handled his situation?
❇ How can you help and encourage Christians who serve in difficult situations?
❇ What can you do to make your prayers for others a part of their ministry?

APPLY IT
■ What do you want to remember the next time you suffer for your faith?
❇ For what missionary can you pray throughout this week?
❇ To what other family can you show hospitality this week? How?

Acts 12:20-25
Herod's Death

TOPICS
Angels, Bible, Death, Flattery, God, Growth, Mission, Partnerships, Peace, Pride, Quarrels

OPEN IT
■ If you were a celebrity, what would you like most and least about your status?
❇ If your job gave you tremendous power over others, in what ways could it bring out the worst in you?

EXPLORE IT
❇ What was Herod's relationship with the cities of Tyre and Sidon? (12:20)
❇ Why did the people of Tyre and Sidon want to make peace with Herod? (12:20)
❇ Whom did the people appoint to make peace with the king? (12:20)
■ On the day of the public assembly, what did Herod do? (12:21)
■ What did the people say to honor king Herod? (12:22)
■ How did God judge Herod? (12:23)
❇ How did the work of God continue, in spite of persecution and opposition? (12:24)
❇ What did Saul and Barnabas set out to do? (12:25)
❇ When the apostles completed their mission in Jerusalem, where did they go? (12:25)

✻ Whom did the apostles take with them to Antioch? (12:25)

GET IT

✻ How could a season of hardship benefit your church?
■ How does the example of Herod serve as a warning to us today?
✻ In what ways do pride and position affect the way we treat others?
■ How can we guard against pride and conceit?
✻ What should we do when others credit us with great deeds?
✻ For what ministries in your church are you thankful?
✻ Why is it helpful to work with a partner in doing Christian ministry?

APPLY IT

✻ How can you be more honest in your relationships with Christian brothers and sisters?
✻ What church leader can you pray for today?
■ What can you do today as a discipline of humility?

Acts 13:1-3
Barnabas and Saul Sent Off

TOPICS

Fasting, Holy Spirit, Jesus Christ, Leadership, Mission, Prayer, Worship

OPEN IT

■ What send-off or farewell stands out in your memory?
✻ If you were going away on a long trip, what kind of send-off would you prefer?
✻ If you and a coworker of your choice were transferred to jobs overseas, whom would you want to go along with you?

EXPLORE IT

■ Who made up the leadership of the church at Antioch? (13:1)
✻ What was the leadership like at the church in Antioch? (13:1)
✻ What was the background of the church leaders at Antioch? (13:1)
✻ How did the church at Antioch become so cosmopolitan? (13:1)
✻ Despite their various backgrounds, how did the leaders of the church at Antioch function? (13:2)
✻ While they were worshiping and fasting, what did the Holy Spirit say to the men? (13:2)
✻ What did God want the church to do with Barnabas and Saul? (13:2)
✻ Why did the Holy Spirit tell the leaders to "set apart" Barnabas and Saul? (13:2)
■ What were Barnabas and Saul called to do? (13:2)
✻ What preceded the departure of the missionaries? (13:3)
■ Why did the church leaders lay hands on Barnabas and Saul? (13:3)
✻ Where did the missionaries go? (13:3)

GET IT

✻ What variety of people attend your church?
✻ How diverse is your church leadership?
■ Why should churches pray over and lay hands on missionaries and other ministers?
■ When should church leaders lay hands on members of the congregation?
✻ How important is worship to the life of a church?
✻ How can your church best serve missions?
✻ What can you do to serve missions and missionaries?
✻ What is the purpose of fasting?
✻ Why should Christians fast?
✻ When might a church want to fast as a congregation?
✻ How can you show support for the leadership of your church?

APPLY IT

■ What time can you commit to prayer each day for the staff of your church?
✻ When can you find time this week to write a letter of encouragement to a missionary?

Acts 13:4-12
On Cyprus

TOPICS

Believe, Bible, Evangelism, Faith, Holy Spirit, Jesus Christ, Opposition, Satan, Teaching

OPEN IT

✻ When was the last time you were taken in by a particularly good sales pitch?
✻ When you were in grade school, what tricks did you play on others?
■ Who helped you get settled into your first full-time job? How?

EXPLORE IT

■ Who directed Barnabas and Saul on their journey? (13:4)
✻ Where did Barnabas and Saul go? (13:4-5)
■ What did the missionaries do in Salamis? (13:5)
■ Who helped Barnabas and Saul? (13:5)
✻ Whom did Barnabas and Saul meet at Paphos? (13:6-7)
✻ Why did the proconsul send for Barnabas and Saul? (13:7)
✻ What did Bar-Jesus (Elymas) do? (13:8)
✻ How did Saul (also called Paul) respond to Elymas? (13:9-11)
✻ Why did Elymas oppose the word of God? (13:10)
✻ What was the judgment against the sorcerer? (13:11)
✻ When Sergius Paulus saw the miracle, what did he do? (13:12)

GET IT

✻ How often do missionaries speak at your church?
■ When missionaries visit your church, how can you benefit from their teaching and experience?
■ How can we be helpful to missionaries and other Christian workers?
✻ What are some ways that people oppose the gospel?
✻ How is Paul's aggressive approach to dealing with sin a helpful example for us to follow?
✻ Given your background, training, and interests, to what group of people are you best suited to share the news about Christ?

APPLY IT
■ How can you be helpful to a missionary or Christian worker in your church this week?
✻ In what situation do you need the Holy Spirit's guidance this week?

Acts 14:1-7
In Iconium

TOPICS
Believe, Divisions, Effectiveness, Good News, Jesus Christ, Miracles, People, Persecution

OPEN IT
✻ What makes a person successful in your line of work?
✻ When do you feel best about your work?
■ What are some issues that often cause disagreement among people?

EXPLORE IT
✻ At Iconium, where did Paul and Barnabas go? (14:1)
✻ Where did the apostles begin telling others about Christ? (14:1)
✻ Who became believers at Iconium? (14:1) Why?
■ How did unbelievers oppose what Paul and Barnabas were doing? (14:2)
■ How did the apostles respond to the opposition? (14:3)
✻ What did the Lord enable Paul and Barnabas to do? (14:3) Why?
■ How was the city divided? (14:4)
✻ What did certain people plot against the apostles? (14:5)
✻ When Paul and Barnabas discovered the plot against them, what did they do? (14:6)
✻ Despite the setback Paul and Barnabas suffered, what did they do in Lystra and Derbe? (14:6-7)

GET IT
✻ When faced with conflict and opposition, how did the apostles pull together?
✻ Which pastoral task do you think your minister enjoys most?
✻ When does your pastor speak most effectively?
■ What happens to the church when a congregation divides its loyalties among leaders?
■ How can you and others in your church support your ministerial staff?
✻ What should you do when people oppose you for being a Christian?
✻ When is it best to run from persecution or leave a situation that threatens your faith?
✻ Why is important for us to pray daily for the missionaries we support?

APPLY IT
✻ When you face conflict this week, how can you rely on the Lord for help?
■ How can you support those whom God has called to lead your church?
✻ For what missionary will you pray every day this week?

Acts 14:8-20
In Lystra and Derbe

TOPICS
Blasphemy, Faith, God, Good News, Handicapped, Healing, Idolatry, Instructions, People, Persecution, Witnessing

OPEN IT
✻ If you suddenly could have the ability to do something you had never done before, what skill would you like to have?
■ What would you do if you received an expensive gift that you didn't think you deserved?
✻ When has someone unexpectedly turned against you?

EXPLORE IT
✻ What did Paul do for the crippled man in Lystra? (14:8-10)
■ How did the crowd respond to what Paul had done? (14:11-13)
✻ Why were the apostles horrified when they discovered what was happening? (14:14)
■ Why did Paul and Barnabas tear their clothes? (14:14)
■ What was the apostles' message to the crowd? (14:15-17)
✻ How did Paul tailor his message to the audience? (14:15-17)
✻ In spite of the apostles' message, why was it difficult to restrain the crowd? (14:18)
✻ Who came from Antioch and Iconium to poison the minds of the people against the missionaries? (14:19)
✻ What did the crowd do to Paul? (14:19)
✻ Who helped Paul? (14:20)
✻ When did Paul return to Lystra? (14:20)
✻ After Paul and Barnabas left Lystra, where did they go? (14:20)

GET IT
✻ Paul knew when someone needed to be healed and what people needed to hear; why was he so perceptive?
✻ How can you be sensitive to the needs of others?
■ When have you received credit or recognition you didn't deserve?
■ Why is it important to give glory to God?
✻ The early missionaries had a demanding schedule and dangerous life-style; how might you have coped with the pressures they faced?
✻ When are you typically in the company of people who are very different from you?
✻ In talking about Christ with nonChristians, what can you do to speak their language?
✻ Paul paid an enormous price for his testimony; what risks are there for you in living for Christ?

APPLY IT
✻ How can you challenge yourself to serve the Lord completely each day?
■ What can you do to direct people's attention to Christ and away from you?
✻ Where can you go to witness to an unbeliever this week?

Acts 14:21-28

The Return to Antioch in Syria

TOPICS
Church, Encouragement, Faith, Fasting, Good News, Jesus Christ, Kingdom of God/Heaven, Prayer, Strength, Suffering, Trust

OPEN IT
■ What kind of vacation most appeals to you (trips to other cities, backwoods hiking, visits to the beach, etc.)?
❊ How busy is your daily schedule?
❊ What do you do to relax?

EXPLORE IT
■ What did Paul and Barnabas do in Derbe? (14:21)
❊ What was the result of the apostles' evangelism? (14:21)
■ Why did Paul and Barnabas retrace their steps to Antioch? (14:22)
❊ What kind of warnings did the missionaries give the young converts? (14:22)
❊ How did the apostles establish leadership in the young churches? (14:23)
■ What encouragement and help did the apostles give the new Christians? (14:22-23)
❊ Where did the return journey to Antioch take the apostles? (14:24-26)
❊ On their way to Antioch, where did the apostles preach? (14:25)
❊ When they returned to Antioch, what did Paul and Barnabas do? (14:27)
❊ Why was it important that Paul and Barnabas report on their activity to the church at Antioch? (14:26)
❊ How long did the apostles remain in Antioch? (14:28)

GET IT
❊ Why would you return to a church or community that had made you feel unwelcome before?
❊ What does the apostles' ability to withstand rejection say about their faith and leadership?
❊ What would your pastor do if faced with persecution?
■ How does your church disciple new Christians?
❊ In your church, how does a person become a leader?
❊ How should missionaries be accountable to the church?
❊ How has your church been blessed by the work of missionaries?
■ How can you help younger Christians get established in the faith?

APPLY IT
❊ In what ways can you benefit from the teaching of your church elders this week?
■ What younger Christian can you encourage this week? How?
❊ What can you do this week to become a stronger Christian?

Acts 15:1-21

The Council at Jerusalem

TOPICS
Believers, Bible, Church, Doctrine, God, Grace, Holy Spirit, Judging Others, Judgment, Prophecy, Questions, Teaching

OPEN IT
❊ When faced with a problem, do you want someone else to solve it, or do you like to figure out for yourself what you should do? Why?
■ What is most challenging to you about enforcing rules?
❊ When you think your opinion is right, how do you tend to express your view?

EXPLORE IT
■ Who came to Antioch? (15:1) Why?
❊ What were the men from Judea teaching the Christians? (15:1)
❊ On what did the men of Judea base their theology? (15:1)
❊ How did Paul and Barnabas respond to the teaching problem at Antioch? (15:2)
■ How did the apostles determine to resolve the problem in Antioch? (15:2)
❊ What were the apostles' experiences on their way to Jerusalem? (15:3)
❊ When Paul and Barnabas arrived in Jerusalem, how did the church receive them? (15:4)
❊ What did the believing Pharisees say? (15:5)
❊ How did the church leaders respond to the Pharisees? (15:6)
❊ What did Peter say to the party of the Pharisees? (15:7-11)
❊ What did Paul and Barnabas add to Peter's testimony? (15:12)
■ How did James summarize his views? (15:13-21)
❊ How did James deal with the circumcision question from a biblical standpoint? (15:15-18)
❊ What practical judgment did James make? (15:19-21)
❊ What did James mean by his concluding statement? (15:21)

GET IT
■ What was wise about using a council to deal with the thorny issue of how non-Jews could be saved?
❊ How was the problem of this council larger than the issue of circumcision?
■ When dealing with difficult issues, what do we need to include in the decision-making process?
❊ Why were Paul, Barnabas, Peter, and James the right men to resolve the conflict?
❊ How could your church follow the council's approach in dealing with issues that trouble the church?
❊ What areas of your faith create conflict within you?
❊ What beliefs or practices do Christians add to the gospel?
❊ How can we remind ourselves to require of new believers only what God requires?

APPLY IT

■ Where can you get help resolving an issue you are unsure about?

❊ This week, what change in your schedule can you make to allow enough time for studying God's Word?

Acts 15:22-35

The Council's Letter to Gentile Believers

TOPICS

Advice, Believers, Blessing, Church, Encouragement, Jesus Christ, Leadership, Obligation, Peace

OPEN IT

■ How often do you write letters to friends?

❊ What was the most important letter you ever received?

❊ When was the last time you received a letter from your pastor?

EXPLORE IT

❊ Who went to Antioch with Paul and Barnabas? (15:22)

❊ Why did the men go to Antioch? (15:23)

❊ In whose name was the letter to Gentile believers sent? (15:23)

❊ To whom was the letter addressed? (15:23)

■ What was the letter to Gentile believers about? (15:24-29)

❊ What was the tone of the letter? (15:24-29)

❊ How did the letter confirm the findings of the council? (15:24-29)

❊ How was the letter delivered? (15:30)

■ How did the Christians in Antioch respond to the message from Jerusalem? (15:31)

❊ How did Judas and Silas help the Christians in Antioch? (15:32)

■ When Judas and Silas left for Jerusalem, what kind of send-off were they given? (15:33)

❊ What did Paul and Barnabas do in Antioch? (15:35)

GET IT

■ What is the best way to solve disagreements among Christians?

■ How would you handle a difficult problem with another Christian?

❊ What are the lines of division in your church?

❊ If Paul were to pastor your church for awhile, what thorny problems might he address?

❊ If you were to design a model for unity among believers of different ethnic backgrounds, what would it look like?

❊ Why should Christians work toward unity within diversity?

APPLY IT

■ What difficult relationship should you improve this week for the sake of Christ? How?

❊ When can you spend time with other Christians who are ethnically different from you?

Acts 15:36-41

Disagreement Between Paul and Barnabas

TOPICS

Church, Disagreements, Jesus Christ, Partnerships, Strength

OPEN IT

■ When you have a sharp disagreement with a friend, how do you usually handle it?

❊ When have you held a grudge against someone?

EXPLORE IT

❊ What did Paul suggest to Barnabas? (15:36)

■ What did Barnabas want to do? (15:37)

❊ Why might Barnabas have wanted to take John Mark with him? (15:37)

■ Why didn't Paul want Mark to accompany the apostles on their trip? (15:38)

❊ Whom did Barnabas take with him when he went to Cyprus? (15:39)

■ What did the apostles do about their difference of opinion? (15:39-40)

❊ How did both men reach a solution? (15:39-40)

❊ Whom did Paul select as a traveling companion in ministry? (15:40)

❊ As a result of the separation between Barnabas and Paul, how many missionary expeditions set out? (15:39-40)

❊ What did Paul and Silas do on their journey? (15:41)

GET IT

■ Why do you think Paul and Barnabas's difference of opinion turned into such a deep division?

❊ How do you think differences in personality affected the disagreement between Paul and Barnabas?

❊ When you disagree with someone, why is it important to try to see the issue from the other person's point of view?

❊ How do you think the apostles' conflict affected their ministry afterward?

■ When should you give up your rights, your position, or your point of view for the sake of peace with another person?

❊ How can God use the strengths and weaknesses of your personality to get His work done?

APPLY IT

■ What step can you take toward resolving an old disagreement with another Christian? When?

❊ Where can you channel your anger or hurt feelings when they become a problem? How?

Acts 16:1-5

Timothy Joins Paul and Silas

TOPICS

Believers, Church, Culture, Decisions, Faith, Leadership, Mission, Reputation, Strength

OPEN IT
■ As far as you know, what nationalities are included in your family tree?
❄ What family traditions from the "old country" do you treasure?
❄ What ethnic values do you want to pass on to future generations of your family?

EXPLORE IT
■ Who visited Derbe and then Lystra? (16:1)
❄ Where was Timothy from? (16:1)
■ What was Timothy's parentage? (16:1)
❄ What was Timothy's reputation? (16:2)
❄ What reputation did Timothy have among Christians? (16:2)
❄ Why did Paul want to take Timothy along on the journey? (16:2-3)
■ What did Timothy have to do in order to minister with Paul? (16:3)
❄ Why did Paul have Timothy circumcised? (16:3)
❄ How is it safe to assume that Timothy was being treated as a Jew rather than a Gentile? (16:3-4)
❄ What did Paul and his companions do as they traveled from town to town? (16:4)
❄ What was the effect of the missionaries' visit? (16:5)

GET IT
❄ How could Timothy's mixed background help him in ministering to both Jews and Gentiles?
■ How did Timothy's heritage create a problem?
❄ What type of pastor could best serve a multiethnic congregation?
■ How might a multiethnic background be both an advantage and a disadvantage?
❄ How does God use us in spite of our imperfections and weaknesses?

APPLY IT
■ How do you need to open your heart and home to Christians who are ethnically different from you?
❄ What missionaries can you support in prayer this week?

Acts 16:6-10
Paul's Vision of the Man of Macedonia

TOPICS
Bible, God, Gospel, Guidance, Holy Spirit, Jesus Christ, Teamwork

OPEN IT
❄ When was the last time you were disappointed?
❄ How persistent are you in trying to get things to go your way?
■ If you arranged a long vacation and you were suddenly required to cancel it for business, what would you do?

EXPLORE IT
❄ Where did the journey westward from Iconium take Paul and his companions? (16:6)
❄ Who directed the missionaries away from Asia? (16:6)
❄ How were the travelers hindered from entering Bithynia? (16:7)
■ How did God guide the missionaries in their travels? (16:6-7)
❄ After leaving Mysia, where did the travelers go next? (16:8)
❄ When did Paul experience the vision? (16:9)
❄ What did Paul see in his vision? (16:9)
❄ How did Paul and his companions interpret this vision? (16:10)
■ What did the missionaries do after they understood what God wanted them to do? (16:10)
■ When did Paul and his companions respond to God's instructions? (16:10)
❄ How did the narrator of the story participate in Paul's travels? (16:10)

GET IT
■ How do you think Paul, Silas, and Timothy recognized the Holy Spirit's directions as they traveled around Asia Minor?
■ How can we be receptive to the Holy Spirit's guidance?
❄ What do you do when the Holy Spirit thwarts your plans?
❄ Why do you think God has sometimes spoken to His people through visions and dreams?
❄ How does God usually speak to His children?
❄ How does God speak to you?
❄ What does the example of Paul and his companions teach us about obedience to God?
❄ With whom has God led you to share the gospel?

APPLY IT
❄ How can you listen more closely to the Holy Spirit's direction in your life?
■ What is one thing you can do to make yourself responsive to God and His will?

Acts 16:11-15
Lydia's Conversion in Philippi

TOPICS
Believers, Evangelism, God, Heart, Hospitality, Jesus Christ, Listening

OPEN IT
❄ If you had to make a living in sales, what would you most like to sell?
■ What is your idea of hospitality?

EXPLORE IT
❄ How did Paul and his companions travel from Troas to Philippi? (16:11-12)
❄ Where did the travelers stop on their way from Troas to Philippi? (16:11-12)
❄ How did Luke describe Philippi? (16:12)
❄ Where did Paul and his friends go to pray on the Sabbath? (16:13)
❄ Why was there no synagogue at Philippi? (16:13)
❄ Whom did the travelers find at the place of prayer? (16:13)
❄ Who was Lydia? (16:14)
■ How did Lydia respond to Paul's words? (16:14)

❇ Who opened Lydia's heart? (16:14)
■ After Lydia became a believer, what did she and her household do? (16:15)
■ What did Lydia offer Paul and his group after her baptism? (16:15)

GET IT
❇ How did Paul establish his mission as soon as he and his group arrived in Philippi?
■ Why should we extend hospitality to others?
❇ How can we have fellowship with other Christians when we are away from home?
❇ What responsibility do you feel to witness to others wherever you happen to be?
■ In what ways is Lydia's example one we should follow?
❇ How should we treat Bible teachers?
❇ How can you extend hospitality to a missionary?

APPLY IT
❇ In what area of your life do you need to be more open to the Lord's teaching this week?
■ How can you share your home and possessions with those called to the ministry?
❇ Following Lydia's example, how can you take the initiative in helping someone else today?

Acts 16:16-40
Paul and Silas in Prison

TOPICS
Authority, Caring, Church, Demons, Encouragement, God, Good News, Healing, Holy Spirit, Jesus Christ, Justice, Praise, Prayer, Prejudice, Salvation

OPEN IT
■ How would you respond if your neighbor told you she had psychic powers and could tell you about your future?
❇ If you were caring for someone with a mental disorder, what would you find most difficult about your work?

EXPLORE IT
❇ Where were Paul and his companions going when they met the slave girl? (16:16)
■ What was distinctive about the slave girl that Paul and his companions met? (16:16)
❇ How did Luke describe the slave girl? (16:16)
❇ How was the girl exploited? (16:16)
■ How did the demon-possessed girl damage Paul's ministry? (16:17-18)
❇ How did Paul gain victory over the slave girl's demonic condition? (16:18)
■ Why were the owners of the slave girl angry with Paul and Silas? (16:19)
❇ What did the girl's owners do with Paul and Silas? (16:19-20) Why?
❇ What happened to Paul and Silas after several accusations were made against them? (16:20-24)
❇ What happened while Paul and Silas were praying and singing hymns? (16:25-26)
❇ Why did the jailer turn to God? (16:27-30)
❇ What were the results of the talk Paul and Silas had with the jailer? (16:31-34)
❇ Why did the magistrates change their mind about Paul and Silas? (16:35-36)
❇ Why did Paul respond the way he did to the officers? (16:37)
❇ What did Paul and Silas do after their release from prison? (16:40)

GET IT
❇ Why were Paul and Silas so poorly treated?
❇ How might Paul have been helping the cause of the Philippian church when he asserted his rights as a Roman citizen?
■ Why is it often difficult for a Christian leader to deal with someone involved in occult practices?
■ In our society, what are some ways people are in bondage to evil?
❇ In what ways are some Christians victims of racism?
❇ Although severely tested and persecuted, Paul and Silas held on to their faith and their joy; how do you think you would hold up under such extraordinary pressure? Why?
❇ What can a Christian do to be prepared for persecution?
❇ When in your experience has the Lord provided a happy ending to a bad turn of events?
❇ When should Christians stand up for justice?
❇ When should Christians give up their legal rights for the sake of Christ?
❇ What can we learn from Paul and Silas to help us cope with difficult times ahead?

APPLY IT
■ What can you pray about this week to put a check on evil in your place of work, neighborhood, or community?
❇ What songs and prayers of praise can you offer God today?
❇ How can you encourage someone else in his or her Christian walk this week?

Acts 17:1-9
In Thessalonica

TOPICS
Bible, Church, Gospel, Jealousy, Jesus Christ, Persecution, Resurrection, Suffering

OPEN IT
■ When is a time you remember being jealous of someone else?
❇ When was the last time you missed church on Sunday?
❇ If you were involved in a Bible study group, would you prefer to be the leader or one of the participants? Why?

EXPLORE IT
❇ Why did Paul and his companions stop at Thessalonica? (17:1)
■ What did Paul and his companions do in Thessalonica? (17:1-3)
❇ What was Paul's mission in the synagogue? (17:2-3)
❇ What resulted from Paul's teaching? (17:4)
❇ Why were some Jews jealous? (17:5)
■ How did the Jews act against Paul and Silas? (17:5) Why?

■ How did the plan of the Jews misfire? (17:6)
❊ What did the crowd do to Jason and some other Christians? (17:6-7)
❊ What were the accusations against the Christians? (17:6-7)
❊ How was Jason implicated in the charges? (17:7)
❊ How did the crowd and city officials react to the accusations? (17:8)
❊ Why were the Christians required to post bond? (17:9)
❊ What did the city officials do with the believers? (17:9)

GET IT
■ Why were the Jews jealous of Paul and Silas?
❊ What was Paul's evangelistic style?
❊ How does your minister present the gospel?
❊ In what settings are you most effective as a witness for Christ?
❊ How can you share your faith with others?
❊ As a missionary, would you be more effective telling others about Christ, or teaching them how to live a Christian life? Why?
❊ How can rejection, abuse, and other kinds of opposition affect a believer's stand for Christ?
■ How should we cope with opposition to the message of Christ?
❊ How should Christian brothers and sisters support one another in their work for Christ?

APPLY IT
❊ When can you spend more time studying the Scriptures with other Christians?
■ In what setting can you be a verbal witness for Christ this week? How?

Acts 17:10-15
In Berea

TOPICS
Believe, Believers, Bible, Character, Church, Conflict, God, Gospel, People

OPEN IT
■ What do you typically look over closely before buying?
❊ How open are you to new ideas?
❊ If someone offered you a free college course of study, what subject would you study?

EXPLORE IT
❊ When did Paul and Silas leave Thessalonica? (17:10)
❊ Why did Paul and Silas leave at night? (17:10)
❊ What town did the missionaries visit? (17:10)
■ On arriving in Berea, where did Paul and Silas go? (17:10)
❊ How were the Bereans different from the Thessalonians? (17:11)
■ How did the Bereans interact with Paul's message? (17:11)
■ How did the people respond to the gospel? (17:12)
❊ Who responded to the gospel? (17:12)
❊ What did the Jewish unbelievers from Thessalonica do? (17:13)
❊ Why did Paul leave Berea? (17:14)
❊ Why did Silas and Timothy remain in Berea? (17:14)
❊ Who went with Paul to Athens? (17:15)
❊ What instructions did Paul leave for Silas and Timothy? (17:15)

GET IT
❊ How interested is your congregation in Bible study?
❊ If your church offered daily Bible studies, why might people go or not go to them?
■ What does it mean to welcome the message of Christ?
■ Why is it important to think about what we are taught?
❊ How should all Christians interact with what they are taught about the Bible?
❊ When might a Christian viewpoint stir up controversy?

APPLY IT
■ How can you make time to study the Bible every day this week?
❊ How can you help younger Christians grow in their faith?

Acts 17:16-34
In Athens

TOPICS
Arguments, Believe, Church, Creation, God, Idolatry, Ignorance, Image, Judgment, People, Religion, Resurrection

OPEN IT
■ When do you tend to be skeptical of the news?
❊ How many famous statues and sculptures can you name?
❊ Would you describe yourself as more theoretical than practical, or more practical than theoretical? Why?
❊ What kinds of discussions do you enjoy?

EXPLORE IT
❊ What distressed Paul about Athens? (17:16)
❊ Where did Paul present his message to the diverse listeners? (17:17)
❊ How did the philosophers react to Paul's ideas? (17:18)
❊ Why did the Council of the Areopagus want to hear what Paul had to say? (17:19-21)
❊ How did Paul address the intellectual pagans? (17:22-23)
❊ Why did the Athenians have an altar dedicated to an "unknown god"? (17:23)
■ How did Paul use his knowledge of the Athenians' "unknown god" to present the true God? (17:23)
■ How did Paul describe God to his hearers? (17:24-25)
❊ Why was Paul's lesson in biblical history a blow to Athenian pride? (17:26)
❊ Why did God reveal Himself in creation and history? (17:27-28)
❊ How did Paul use Greek poetry to tell others about Christ? (17:28)
❊ How did Paul prove that God was not an idol? (17:29)

❊ What were Paul's concluding remarks? (17:30-31)
■ How did the Greeks respond to Paul? (17:32-34)
❊ Who among Paul's hearers became believers? (17:34)

GET IT
❊ What made Paul well-suited to presenting the gospel to the Athenians?
■ How did Paul tailor his message to the Athenians?
❊ What can we learn from Paul's example here?
■ How should we be flexible in our approach to evangelism?
❊ How should we react when others don't take us or what we say seriously?
❊ What did Paul emphasize about God that was different from what the Stoics and Epicureans believed?
❊ What incorrect views of God are held in our society?
❊ How would you judge Paul's ministry in Athens—as a success or failure? Why?
❊ How can you deal with attitudes of pride and arrogance that surface in you from time to time?

APPLY IT
❊ What will help you persevere in your witness when no one seems to care or listen?
■ What is one thing you can do to make the message of Christ understandable to your non-Christian friends and coworkers?

Acts 18:1-17
In Corinth

TOPICS
Believe, Bible, Church, Encouragement, God, Hardheartedness, Judgment, Law, Prejudice, Witnessing, Work

OPEN IT
❊ What makes you most impatient?
❊ How do you express your feelings when you are frustrated?
■ When you are disheartened, what usually encourages you?

EXPLORE IT
❊ Where did Paul go after leaving Athens? (18:1)
❊ With what Jewish couple did Paul meet? (18:2)
❊ What did Paul have in common with Aquila and Priscilla? (18:3)
❊ What did Paul do every Sabbath in Corinth? (18:4)
■ What did Paul spend his time doing when Silas and Timothy arrived? (18:5)
❊ Why was Paul able to stop tentmaking when his friends arrived from Macedonia? (18:5)
■ When the Jews opposed Paul, how did he react? (18:6)
❊ In Corinth, why did Paul turn to the Gentiles? (18:6-7)
❊ Who believed in the Lord? (18:8)
■ What prompted Paul's vision of the Lord? (18:9-11)
❊ Why was Paul brought to court? (18:12-13)
❊ What crucial decision did Gallio make? (18:14-16)
❊ Why did the crowd attack Sosthenes? (18:17)
❊ Why didn't Gallio intervene in the attack against Sosthenes? (18:17)

GET IT
❊ Why would Paul have welcomed an encouraging word from the Lord?
❊ In what ways does your church support full-time missionaries?
❊ What difference would it make if missionaries weren't given financial support?
❊ What similarities do you see in the pattern of Jewish opposition to the gospel?
❊ How should we respond when people reject the gospel?
❊ What Christian issues create conflict in our legal system today?
❊ How do Christians take for granted their freedom to practice their faith?
■ What encouraging encounters and experiences did Paul have while in Corinth?
❊ What means has God given you to be an encouragement to others?
❊ How has God brought encouragement to you recently?

APPLY IT
■ What missionary family can you encourage this week? How?
❊ What new member of your congregation can you pray for this week?
❊ How can you encourage a Christian friend today?

Acts 18:18-28
Priscilla, Aquila and Apollos

TOPICS
Believe, Bible, Church, Encouragement, God, Grace, Help, Jesus Christ, Learning, Teaching, Teamwork, Vows, Witnessing

OPEN IT
■ What do you like best about getting letters?
❊ If you were to go on a long trip overseas, what kind of preparations would you need to make to get ready?
❊ After a lengthy trip abroad, what would be best about returning home?

EXPLORE IT
❊ After Paul's extended stay in Corinth, where did he go next? (18:18)
❊ What did Paul do before he sailed for Syria? (18:18) Why?
❊ What did Paul do at Ephesus? (18:19)
❊ Whom did Paul leave behind in Ephesus? (18:19)
❊ What promise did Paul make to the Jews? (18:19-21)
❊ After greeting the church at Caesarea, what places did Paul visit? (18:22-23)
■ Who was Apollos? (18:24)
■ How did Apollos put his gifts and knowledge to good use? (18:24-26)
❊ How did Apollos serve God with his skills and abilities? (18:24-26)
❊ How did Priscilla and Aquila help Apollos become a more effective missionary? (18:26)
■ How did Apollos serve God in Achaia? (18:27-28)
❊ How did God use Apollos in Achaia? (18:27-28)

❊ What approach did Apollos use in defending the Christian faith? (18:28)

GET IT
❊ Why might Paul have made a vow?
❊ What kind of vows have you made?
❊ Why was it OK, theologically and culturally speaking, for Paul to make a vow to the Lord?
❊ Why is it that Christians today do not often make solemn promises to God?
❊ How was Paul's trip to Ephesus encouraging for him?
❊ What might Priscilla and Aquila do to help your church staff?
■ What methods did Apollos use to encourage and teach other Christians?
■ What means has God given us for communicating encouragement to one another?
❊ How effective would Apollos be in your church evangelism ministry?

APPLY IT
❊ Who can you help grow in the faith this week? How?
■ How can you encourage another Christian through a letter or card?

Acts 19:1-22
Paul in Ephesus

TOPICS
Believe, Christianity, Church, Demons, Fear, Holy Spirit, Jesus Christ, Kingdom of God/Heaven, Miracles, Money, Occult, Opposition, Partnerships, People, Prophecy

OPEN IT
❊ What is your idea of an adventure?
❊ If you knew that traveling to a remote place would enrich your life, what kinds of hardships would you be willing to endure for the trip?
■ Why do you think some people read horoscopes or consult palm readers?

EXPLORE IT
❊ While Apollos ministered at Corinth, where did Paul go? (19:1)
❊ What did Paul ask the disciples at Ephesus? (19:2)
❊ How did the group respond to Paul? (19:2)
❊ What was the significance of John's baptism? (19:3-4)
❊ Why were the disciples rebaptized? (19:5)
❊ How did the Spirit come on the disciples? (19:6)
❊ Who received the Holy Spirit? (19:7)
❊ How long did Paul speak at the synagogue before confronting trouble? (19:8)
❊ Why did Paul stop speaking at the synagogue? (19:9)
❊ From his new base of operations, how long did Paul spend spreading the word of the Lord? (19:10)
■ What extraordinary events happened during this time? (19:11-16)
■ Why did people both fear and praise Jesus? (19:17)
❊ How did faith in Christ change the Ephesians? (19:18-19)
■ What practices did the Ephesians give up? (19:18-19)
❊ What happened to the spread of Christianity? (19:20)
❊ After Ephesus, what was on Paul's itinerary? (19:21-22)

GET IT
❊ How long did it take you to become a Christian?
❊ Who helped you understand God's plan of salvation?
❊ When did you realize that the Holy Spirit was at work in your life?
❊ How was Paul able to deal with people involved in occult practices?
■ What occult practices are popular today?
❊ Why is it important for us to avoid occult practices?
❊ What battles might Paul fight if he were a missionary to your community?
■ Why did those who practiced magic burn their books publicly?
❊ What is the value of public confession?
❊ When should we confess our sins publicly?
❊ What do you need to confess and burn in order to be used by God?

APPLY IT
❊ To whom do you want to confess a sin or desire in order to serve God more faithfully?
❊ Whom can you invite to church to hear the message of salvation?
■ What is one practical way you can oppose Satan's efforts among the people you know?

Acts 19:23-41
The Riot in Ephesus

TOPICS
Arguments, Christianity, Confusion, Craftsmanship, Idolatry, Leadership, Money, Motives, People, Prejudice, Worship

OPEN IT
❊ Would you more likely go for a creative job with a low salary, or boring work that paid twice as much? Why?
■ If you were given a lot of money to spend at the mall, what would you buy?
❊ If you were caught in a crowd, would you like to be at a fun fair, a rally, or in a large department store?

EXPLORE IT
❊ To whom does "the Way" refer? (19:23)
■ Who was the ringleader against Paul and the Christians? (19:24)
■ On what basis did Artemis make a case against those of the Way? (19:25-27)
❊ To what group did the silversmith present his case? (19:24-25)
■ Why did the silversmith's talk create such an uproar? (19:27-29)
❊ Whom did the mob seize? (19:29)
❊ Where did the angry crowd take the two men? (19:29)
❊ Why did Paul want to appear before the crowd? (19:30)
❊ Why wouldn't the Christians and some officials let Paul appear before the crowd? (19:30-31)
❊ What was the mood of the mob? (19:32)
❊ Why wouldn't the people listen to Alexander? (19:33-34)
❊ How did the city clerk bring order to the crowd in the Ephesian theater? (19:35-40)

❋ What reasons did the city clerk give for dispersing the mob? (19:35-41)

GET IT
❋ What underlying motive did the silversmith have for his protest?
❋ How do Christians sometimes compromise the kingdom of God for money?
❋ How can a person make idols out of work, money, or success?
■ In what ways can money become more important to us than it should?
❋ In a time of economic recession, why might Christians be tempted to act like the Ephesian mob?
❋ How did Demetrius and the city clerk use reasoned arguments to support their twisted versions of the truth?
■ How can we show our trust in God as provider?
❋ How must we be on guard against speakers who defy the gospel in subtle ways?
❋ What price did Paul and his friends pay for doing what was right?
❋ What types of work should Christians stay away from?

APPLY IT
■ What is one way you can trust God with your money this week?
❋ How can you honor the Lord without all the religious and cultural trappings that Christians have placed on Him?

Acts 20:1-6
Through Macedonia and Greece

TOPICS
Celebration, Encouragement, Fellowship, Money, Partnerships, Plans

OPEN IT
■ If you kept a diary or journal, what kinds of details would you tend to include?
❋ What might someone learn about you from reading your diary?
❋ What do you do or take with you to make long road trips more bearable?

EXPLORE IT
■ Why did Paul travel so much? (20:1-6)
❋ What did Paul do after the uproar in Ephesus was over? (20:1)
❋ Where did Paul go after he left Ephesus? (20:1)
■ What did Paul do while he was in Macedonia? (20:2)
❋ Where did Paul stay for three months? (20:2-3)
❋ How was Paul's plan to sail for Syria frustrated? (20:3)
❋ Where did Paul go in order to avoid his enemies? (20:3)
❋ Who was appointed to go with Paul? (20:4)
■ Who were Paul's traveling companions on his journey? (20:4-5)
❋ What was Paul's group's rendezvous point? (20:5)
❋ At what point did the author of Acts rejoin Paul and his party? (20:5-6)
❋ Where did Paul's group celebrate the Feast of Unleavened Bread? (20:6)
❋ How long did it take to make the trip from Philippi to Troas? (20:6)

GET IT
❋ How could Paul teach and encourage Christians when his own life was in danger?
❋ When you experience trouble, how does it affect your Christian witness?
❋ What made Paul effective in dealing with his enemies?
❋ Why was it important to collect money from the Gentile churches to help the church in Jerusalem?
❋ How much of a church's budget should be set aside to help the poor?
■ How can you be involved in ministry with other Christians?
■ How could keeping a daily journal of your experiences help you keep track of your walk with the Lord?

APPLY IT
❋ What amount of money can you give on a regular basis to help the poor?
❋ What can you do this week to encourage someone else?
■ Where and when could you write down your thoughts as you reflect on God's Word each day this week?

Acts 20:7-12
Eutychus Raised From the Dead at Troas

TOPICS
Believers, Death, Encouragement, Healing, Lord's Supper, Youth

OPEN IT
❋ What was the longest talk you ever listened to?
■ When was the last time you had difficulty staying awake?
❋ What would you do if someone sitting next to you fell asleep during a worship service?

EXPLORE IT
❋ When did the Christians meet to break bread? (20:7)
❋ At what time of day did the church probably meet? (20:7-8)
❋ Who was sitting in a window? (20:9)
■ What made it hard for Eutychus to stay awake? (20:8-9)
■ What happened when Eutychus fell sound asleep? (20:9)
❋ What was the boy's condition when he was picked up? (20:9)
■ What did Paul say to the group when he embraced Eutychus? (20:10)
❋ How did Paul care for the young man? (20:10)
❋ After the interruption to the meeting, what did Paul do? (20:11)
❋ After the meal, what did Paul do? (20:11)
❋ Why were the people comforted when they took young Eutychus home? (20:12)

GET IT

❊ What does it mean for Christians to "break bread"?
❊ Why do you think Paul talk on and on to the Ephesian Christians?
■ If your worship service lasted longer than usual, what complaints would the pastor probably get?
❊ How often do you celebrate Communion at your church?
■ When do you tend to be inattentive or sleepy during a church service?
❊ How did Eutychus, whose name means "fortunate," prove true to his name?

APPLY IT

■ What are some steps you can take to be alert and thoughtful in church each Sunday?
❊ How can you keep from being inattentive or careless during prayer and quiet times?

Acts 20:13-38

Paul's Farewell to the Ephesian Elders

TOPICS

Believers, Church, God, God's Will, Grace, Grief, Holy Spirit, Kingdom of God/Heaven, Leadership, Mission, Pastors, Prayer, Serving, Testing, Work

OPEN IT

❊ Who is one person you have trained or taught a skill in the last few years?
❊ What is one of the hardest things about leaving home?
■ If you knew that this would be your last day with your loved ones, what would you want to say to them?
❊ How do you usually say good-bye?

EXPLORE IT

❊ What did Paul do when the rest of his party sailed for Assos? (20:13)
❊ After meeting at Assos, where did the journey take Paul and his companions? (20:14-15)
❊ Why did the group bypass Ephesus? (20:16)
❊ At Miletus, for whom did Paul send? (20:17)
❊ What was the gist of Paul's talk to the Ephesian elders? (20:18-35)
■ What did Paul say in review of his ministry in Ephesus? (20:18-21)
❊ How did the apostle describe the present situation? (20:22-27)
❊ Why did Paul expect trouble in Jerusalem? (20:22-23)
❊ How did Paul describe his life and mission? (20:24)
■ What made Paul "innocent of the blood of all men"? (20:26-27)
■ What were the future responsibilities of the Ephesian elders? (20:28-35)
❊ How did the elders display their deep love for Paul? (20:36-38)
❊ How did Paul and the elders say their good-byes? (20:36-38)
❊ What saddened the group most? (20:38)

GET IT

❊ What kind of send-off does your church give someone on his or her way to the mission field?
❊ When your church loses a member, how do people tend to grieve over the loss?
■ How does Paul's life and work challenge you?
❊ How is your pastor's work in the church like Paul's ministry among the Ephesians?
❊ How did the Holy Spirit help Paul?
❊ How does the Holy Spirit lead and guide us?
■ Why do mature Christians need to "be on guard" and "watch over" younger believers in their congregation?
❊ How would you describe your work for God's kingdom?
❊ What does it mean to commit someone else to God?
❊ Why did Paul support himself financially?
❊ How can we stay blameless in the way we support ourselves and our church's work?

APPLY IT

❊ How can you give to others this week?
❊ How can you draw guidance and comfort from the Holy Spirit today?
■ Who is one other believer for whom you can be a "shepherd" or guide this week? How?

Acts 21:1-16

On to Jerusalem

TOPICS

Advice, Believers, God's Will, Holy Spirit, Jesus Christ, Prayer, Prophecy

OPEN IT

❊ What do you tend to worry about?
❊ Do you tend to avoid conflict, resolve it as soon as possible, or go looking for it?
■ When was a time you rejected the advice or counsel of virtually everyone who cared about you?

EXPLORE IT

❊ How did Paul and his companions leave their friends at Miletus? (21:1)
❊ Between Cos and Tyre, what stops did the party make? (21:1-3)
■ At Tyre, what did the Christians advise Paul to do? (21:4)
❊ What warning did Paul ignore? (21:5-6) Why?
■ Why did Paul ignore the believers' warning? (21:5-6)
❊ How was the departure scene at Tyre meaningful? (21:5-6)
❊ What did the group do on their one-day stop in Ptolemais? (21:7)
❊ Who was Paul's host in Caesarea? (21:8)
❊ What role did Philip have in the early church? (21:8)
❊ What gift did Philip's four daughters have? (21:9)
❊ Who was Agabus? (21:10)
❊ Where did Agabus come from? (21:10)
❊ How did Agabus dramatize what would happen to Paul in Jerusalem? (21:11)
❊ After the people heard the prophecy about Paul, how did they respond? (21:12)
■ What did Paul say to the Christians at Caesarea? (21:13-14)

❊ When they realized that Paul would not be dissuaded, what did the believers say to him? (21:14)
❊ What did Paul and his companions do on the final stage of their journey? (21:15-16)

GET IT
■ How do you think Paul felt about going to Jerusalem?
■ Why did Paul ignore all the warnings against going to Jerusalem?
❊ When might doing God's will involve pain, suffering, or risk?
❊ How can we build our courage when we are afraid to do what God wants?
❊ What support does your church make available to Christians (perhaps missionaries) in dangerous or difficult settings?
❊ If you had been one of Paul's traveling companions, how would you have advised him?

APPLY IT
❊ How can you support a Christian brother or sister on the mission field?
■ What decision do you stand by even though some others don't approve of your choice?
❊ What fears or misgivings can you hand over to the Holy Spirit?

Acts 21:17-26
Paul's Arrival at Jerusalem

TOPICS
Believers, Church, Law, Leadership, Obedience, Praise, Rules, Vows, Zeal

OPEN IT
■ What are some ways your life-style or way of life is different from that of your parents?
❊ If most people in your community shaved their head because it was the fashion, how long (if ever) would it take you to follow suit?

EXPLORE IT
❊ How were Paul and his companions received in Jerusalem? (21:17)
❊ After a day in Jerusalem, with whom did the missionaries meet? (21:18)
■ What did Paul report? (21:18-19) To whom?
❊ How did the leaders of the Jerusalem church respond to Paul's report? (21:20)
■ What concern did the church leaders voice? (21:20)
❊ What false report had gone out concerning Paul? (21:21)
■ What did the leaders of the church suggest that Paul do? (21:22-24) Why?
❊ Why did the leaders suggest that Paul join in the purification rites of four men and pay for their expenses? (21:22-24)
❊ What decision of the Jerusalem Council was repeated? (21:25)
❊ Why did the leaders bring up the Jerusalem decree? (21:25)
❊ What did Paul and the young men do the next day? (21:26)

GET IT
❊ What was at the heart of the controversy between the Jews and the Gentiles?
❊ What causes divisions among Christians?
❊ What divisions do we see in the Christian church today?
❊ Why did Paul support the Jewish leaders?
❊ What rules or traditions should you support for the sake of peace?
■ What is the difference between compromising God's will and doing something in order to avoid offending someone?
■ How can we decide when we should stand up for our beliefs and when we should give in for the sake of others?
❊ When are Christians often tempted to make a rule or tradition as important as God's written Word?

APPLY IT
❊ How can you live more by God's grace and less by self-imposed dos and don'ts?
■ In what situations will you need to adjust your behavior for the sake of others? How?

Acts 21:27-36
Paul Arrested

TOPICS
Assumptions, Confusion, Culture, Enemies, People, Persecution

OPEN IT
■ How does it make you feel when someone is treated unfairly?
❊ If you were challenged to take part in a peaceful demonstration for a good cause, what would you do?

EXPLORE IT
❊ What happened when Paul went to the temple? (21:27)
■ Who stirred up the crowd and seized Paul? (21:27-29) Why?
❊ What did the Jews from Ephesus say? (21:28)
❊ What were the false charges against Paul? (21:28-29)
❊ How did the city respond to the furor over Paul? (21:30)
❊ What did the people do to Paul? (21:30-31)
■ Why were the temple gates shut? (21:30-31)
❊ How did the commander of the Roman troops and his men intervene while Paul was under attack? (21:31-32)
■ How did the commander and his soldiers save Paul's life? (21:32)
❊ What did the commander do to Paul? (21:33)
❊ How was Paul arrested? (21:33)
❊ When the Roman commander asked what Paul had done, why couldn't he get at the truth? (21:33-34)
❊ Why was Paul taken to the barracks? (21:34)
❊ Why was Paul carried away by the soldiers? (21:35-36)

GET IT
■ Why were the Jews from Asia so angry at Paul?
❊ What groups in our society infuriate each other?
❊ Why are people so protective of their ethnic heritage?

❇ How can Christians help bridge ethnic and racial barriers?
❇ Why was there so much animosity between Jews and Christians at the time of Paul's arrest?
■ What groups are particularly anti-Christian today?
❇ What are some ways we can and should defend the truth about our faith?
❇ Why do crowds of people often behave in unpredictable and unreasonable ways?

APPLY IT
■ What "false reports" about Christianity can you help dispel? How?
❇ How can you be a peacemaker this week at work, at home, or in your neighborhood?

Acts 21:37–22:21
Paul Speaks to the Crowd

TOPICS
Blindness, Christianity, God, Instructions, Jesus Christ, Light, People, Persecution, Salvation, Sin, Witnessing, Zeal

OPEN IT
❇ What personal accomplishment has been most satisfying to you?
■ What do you have in common with a friend, a coworker, or a neighbor?
❇ If you told your life story to a group of friends, what would surprise them most?

EXPLORE IT
■ What did Paul ask as he was about to be taken away? (21:37)
❇ Why was the tribune surprised that Paul could speak Greek? (21:38)
❇ In establishing his background, what did Paul say? (21:39)
❇ What did Paul request? (21:39)
■ What language did the apostle use in speaking to the crowd? (21:40)
■ How did Paul address his audience? (22:1)
❇ What made the crowd quiet down? (22:2)
❇ What did Paul say about his rearing and training? (22:3)
❇ What was Paul like before his conversion? (22:4-5)
❇ How was Paul converted to Christ? (22:6-9)
❇ How did Paul learn about the nature of his future ministry? (22:10-16)
❇ Who was Ananias? (22:12)
❇ Why did Paul leave Jerusalem? (22:17-18)
❇ What did Paul's reply to the Lord show? (22:19-20)
❇ What did the Lord tell Paul to do? (22:21)

GET IT
❇ Why do you think Paul told his own story instead of preaching a sermon?
❇ When is it useful to share your personal experiences with others?
■ How did Paul show respect to his audience?
■ Why is it important to be kind toward and respectful of others?
❇ How can we show respect to the people around us?
❇ What gave Paul credibility to his audience?
❇ How can a Christian gain credibility with non-Christians?
❇ What are some things you can do to build credibility with your friends and coworkers?
❇ How did Paul rebel against the Lord?
❇ When have you rebelled against the Lord?
❇ How has the Lord's activity in your life surprised you recently?
❇ To what kind of service has God called you?
❇ How does God direct us?
❇ How might you have to endure hardship for the sake of Christ?
❇ How can your nationality be helpful in sharing the message of Christ with others?

APPLY IT
■ What words, gestures, or practices can you use to show respect in how you speak to others?
❇ With whom can you share your personal story of faith this week?

Acts 22:22-29
Paul the Roman Citizen

TOPICS
Anger, Citizenship, Fear, Law, Protection, Punishment

OPEN IT
■ How do you tend to react under pressure?
❇ What might make you consider giving up your citizenship?
❇ If you could become a citizen of another country, which country would you choose?
❇ What rights does your citizenship give you that people of other countries don't have?

EXPLORE IT
■ How did Paul anger the crowd? (22:22)
■ How did the mob express their intense anger? (22:23)
■ Why did the commander order that Paul be taken away and beaten? (22:24)
❇ Why was the commander confused by what was going on? (22:24)
❇ To what fact did Paul call the centurion's attention? (22:25)
❇ What was reported to the commander? (22:26)
❇ What did the commander ask Paul? (22:27)
❇ Why did the commander tell Paul that his citizenship had been bought? (22:28)
❇ How did Paul cap the commander's comment? (22:28)
❇ Why did the commander become alarmed? (22:29)

GET IT
❇ What was hard for the Jews to accept?
■ What was wrong with the Jewish unwillingness to lead Gentiles to God?
■ What people do we tend to exclude from the message of God's grace?
❇ How do we sometimes compromise the Christian faith by clinging to cultural or racial biases?

❊ Why was Paul's Roman citizenship an asset?
❊ How did Paul show good judgment in the middle of an extremely stressful situation?
❊ What about you gives you unique opportunities to talk with others about Christ?
❊ In what ways can we show respect to others even when they treat us disrespectfully?

APPLY IT
■ For whose salvation will you pray each day this week?
❊ What do you want to remember the next time you have to deal with a difficult person?

Acts 22:30–23:11
Before the Sanhedrin

TOPICS
Accusation, Angels, Conflict, Confusion, Conscience, Courage, God, Jesus Christ, Law, Persecution, Resurrection, Witnessing

OPEN IT
❊ When was the last time you had to deal with an overbearing person?
❊ When you've just about had it, how do you express your anger?
■ When was the last time you said something that caused misunderstanding or conflict?

EXPLORE IT
❊ Why did the commander order the Sanhedrin to assemble? (22:30)
■ What bold claims did Paul make? (23:1)
■ What order did Ananias give? (23:2)
■ What did Paul say in reaction to the high priest's illegal command? (23:3)
❊ How did those standing nearby challenge Paul? (23:4)
❊ Why did Paul respond the way he did to the challenge? (23:5)
❊ How did Paul disrupt the proceedings? (23:6-9)
❊ How did Paul divide his enemies? (23:6-9)
❊ Why did the Pharisees side with Paul? (23:9)
❊ Why was Paul in extreme danger? (23:10)
❊ Where was Paul taken? (23:10)
❊ How was Paul comforted and encouraged? (23:11) When?
❊ How did the Lord confirm Paul's plans to go to Rome? (23:11)

GET IT
■ Why did the high priest react so strongly to Paul's statement about fulfilling his duty to God?
❊ When do we tend to get ourselves in trouble with our words?
❊ How can our words get us in trouble?
■ In what situations do you need to be careful with what you say?
❊ What is every Christian's duty to God?
❊ What is your duty to God?
❊ Why was it shrewd for Paul to get the Pharisees and Sadducees to fight among themselves?
❊ How do the members of your congregation handle disagreements in church business meetings?
❊ Why would Paul have needed the Lord's support and comfort?
❊ When do you often need the Lord's support?
❊ When you feel attacked or discouraged, how can you draw encouragement from the Lord?

APPLY IT
❊ How can you prepare for the next difficult step in your spiritual journey?
❊ In what trying situations will you need to show patience and perseverance this week?
■ What reminder can you use to help you be wise with your words this week?

Acts 23:12-22
The Plot to Kill Paul

TOPICS
Death, Deceit, Leadership, Plans

OPEN IT
❊ If your job was to watch others closely and secretly, how well would you do?
■ What kinds of secrets did kids like to keep when you were growing up?
❊ How well do you keep secrets?

EXPLORE IT
❊ Why did the Jews form a conspiracy? (23:12)
■ Who took an oath? Why? (23:12)
❊ How many men were involved in the plot against Paul? (23:13)
❊ How were the chief priests and elders accomplices in the plot against Paul? (23:14-15)
❊ What did the plotters want the Jewish elders to do? (23:15)
■ When Paul's nephew heard about the plot, what did he do? (23:16)
■ How was the young man able to go before the commander? (23:17-18)
❊ What did the commander ask Paul's nephew? (23:19)
❊ What did the young man tell the commander? (23:20-21)
❊ How did the commander respond to the informant? (23:22)

GET IT
❊ Why would the conspirators risk their own lives to kill Paul?
❊ What groups are fervently anti-Christian today?
❊ When have Christians been overzealous in rejecting others?
❊ What does their complicity in the plot tell you about the chief priests and elders?
❊ When have Christian leaders in your community compromised their faith and position?
❊ How did Paul's nephew demonstrate courage and honesty?
❊ How did Paul's family help him?

❇ When might helping someone require courage or sacrifice today?
■ When might exposing a wrong require courage or sacrifice today?
❇ What kind of person exposed the plot against Paul?
❇ How did God use a young person in this situation?
■ When is it right for you to play the role of informant in correcting a wrong?
❇ Why is it important to stand up for the truth?

APPLY IT
■ In what setting this week will you need to be prepared to stand up for the truth?
❇ How can you prepare to face hardships this week?
❇ How can you rely on the Holy Spirit to protect you from the attacks of others?
❇ What kind of practical support can you give someone facing difficulty right now?

Acts 23:23-35
Paul Transferred to Caesarea

TOPICS
Accusation, Citizenship, Instructions, Law, Leadership, Protection

OPEN IT
❇ If you could select only one form of protection for your home, what kind would you want?
■ What safety precautions do you take when you go out at night?
❇ When or where do you feel most safe and protected?

EXPLORE IT
❇ Why was Paul sent to Caesarea? (23:23)
❇ Why was the apostle escorted from Jerusalem at night? (23:23)
■ What orders did the commander give to get Paul away from danger? (23:23-24)
❇ How did the commander protect Paul? (23:23-24)
❇ To whom did the tribune write a letter? (23:26)
■ Who wrote a letter to whom? Why? (23:25-30)
❇ Why did Claudius Lysias send a letter along with Paul? (23:25-30)
❇ What did the tribune say in his letter to Governor Felix? (23:25-30)
❇ In his letter, how did the commander bend the truth? (23:27)
❇ What important fact did Claudius omit from the record? (23:25-30)
❇ What important declaration did the commander make concerning Paul? (23:29)
❇ Where did the soldiers take Paul the first night? (23:31)
❇ Who escorted Paul the rest of the journey? (23:32)
■ When the cavalry and Paul arrived, what did the governor do? (23:33-35)
❇ After Felix learned that Paul was from Cilicia, what did the governor determine to do? (23:34-35)

GET IT
❇ What kind of reputation did Paul have?
❇ Why did the commander provide such elaborate protection for Paul?
❇ What did Paul's citizenship have to do with the just treatment he received?
❇ Why is it that the legal system protects some people but not all?
❇ How do you think the conspirators felt once they discovered that Paul was gone from Jerusalem?
❇ How protected would you feel in a court of law?
❇ What is your attitude toward civil authority?
■ How did God protect Paul?
■ What "human means" does God use to protect His people?
❇ How can we show support for the government's civil authority?
❇ What injustices in our legal system should Christians challenge? How?

APPLY IT
■ As a Christian, what is one way you can protect the rights of the poor and weak?
❇ How can you show your support for the government's civil authority?

Acts 24:1-27
The Trial Before Felix

TOPICS
Accusation, Christianity, Conscience, Faith, Flattery, God, Hope, Jesus Christ, Law, Leadership, Names, Resurrection, Rules

OPEN IT
■ What do you admire most about your favorite political figure?
❇ Why do you think most people do not trust or like public officials?
❇ If you were sued or taken to court, why might you hire a lawyer rather than defend yourself?

EXPLORE IT
❇ Why did the religious leaders hire Tertullus? (24:1)
■ Who went to Caesarea? (24:1-8) Why?
❇ Why did Tertullus flatter Felix? (24:2-4)
❇ What three accusations did Tertullus make against Paul? (24:5-8)
❇ Who supported Tertullus in his accusations? (24:9)
❇ Speaking in his own defense, how was Paul's introduction different from the lawyer's? (24:10)
❇ What points did Paul make in his defense before the governor? (24:11-16)
❇ What was Paul's objective in visiting Jerusalem? (24:17)
❇ What did Paul say about the charges brought against him? (24:11-18)
❇ How did the apostle show that Tertullus did not have any legitimate charges against him? (24:18-21)
■ What did Felix do about Paul's case? (24:22-23)
❇ How did the governor provide Paul with limited freedom? (24:23)
❇ How did Paul's speaking affect Felix? (24:24-25)
❇ What motivated Felix to send for Paul? (24:26)

■ Why did Paul languish in prison for over two years? (24:26-27)
❇ Before leaving his position as governor, what did Felix do to placate the Jews? (24:27)

GET IT
❇ Why would Felix, known as a mean-spirited and selfish leader, show restraint in dealing with Paul?
■ How was Paul "caught in the system"?
❇ How did Tertullus show contempt in dealing with the early believers?
❇ With what terms do people deride Christianity today?
❇ Paul was obviously misread by the Jewish religious leaders; how are some Christian leaders misunderstood and maligned by other religious leaders today?
❇ How might you be misunderstood by others when your faith in Christ shows in how you live or act?
❇ How can we use misunderstanding as an opportunity to explain our faith?
❇ Why do you think Felix rejected Christ even though he showed interest in Paul's teaching?
❇ For what reasons do people reject Christ today?
❇ In what way is the gospel difficult to accept?
❇ When in the past have you had to wait for justice?
❇ In what areas of your life do you need to wait for the Lord's timing?

APPLY IT
❇ How do you want to be ready for the next time you are misunderstood?
❇ For what public officials can you pray this week?
❇ How can you show patience with the changes you are still waiting for?

Acts 25:1-12
The Trial Before Festus

TOPICS
Accusation, Fairness, Favoritism, Law, Leadership, Right

OPEN IT
❇ How did you and your siblings settle most of your disputes while you were growing up?
■ When was the last time someone did a favor for you? What was it?

EXPLORE IT
❇ How did the procurator's visit to Jerusalem show that he wanted to rule justly? (25:1)
❇ Who appeared before Festus in Jerusalem? (25:2)
■ What did the Jewish leaders want? (25:2)
■ Why did the leaders want Paul transferred from Caesarea to Jerusalem? (25:3)
■ How did Festus reply to the request to transfer Paul? (25:4-5)
❇ How did the scene of previous trials repeat itself when Paul was brought before Festus? (25:6-7)
❇ What did Paul say to the court? (25:8)
❇ Why did Festus ask Paul if he was willing to go to Jerusalem? (25:9)
❇ Why did Paul want nothing to do with standing trial in Jerusalem? (25:10-11)
❇ Why did Festus send Paul's case to Caesar? (25:11-12)

GET IT
■ Why was opposition to Paul by the Jewish leaders still strong, even though Paul had been under house arrest for two years?
❇ Why do we tend to hold on to past grievances?
❇ What should we do with old grudges? How?
■ In what way did Paul's enemies try to manipulate circumstances to serve their own ends?
❇ What made Festus appear to be a fair ruler?
❇ In what way was Paul mistreated?
❇ When have you felt mistreated?
❇ What does Paul's example of self-defense have to teach us?
❇ Why did Paul appeal to Caesar?
❇ Why was Paul able to be confident in his appeal to a higher court?
❇ How did Paul's innocence help him in this situation?
❇ When have you been called on to defend yourself?
❇ What was Paul's style in communicating to the court?
❇ How do you express yourself when you are on the defensive?
❇ How did Paul hold to his civil rights?

APPLY IT
❇ What or whom should you avoid to protect your spiritual well-being?
❇ What rights of yours should you stand up for this week? How?
■ What person or situation can you place in God's hands this week as a discipline against turning events to your own ends?

Acts 25:13-22
Festus Consults King Agrippa

TOPICS
Accusation, Advice, Law, Leadership

OPEN IT
❇ When you want sound advice, to whom do you often turn?
■ When you don't feel up to a job you've been asked to do, what do you often feel inside?

EXPLORE IT
❇ Why did King Agrippa and his sister visit Festus? (25:13)
■ What motivated Festus to bring up Paul's case to King Agrippa? (25:14-21)
❇ Why would Agrippa's insight and advice be helpful to Festus? (25:14-21)
❇ How did Festus tell the story from a Roman point of view? (25:14-21)
❇ How did Festus handle this long-standing case? (25:17)
■ In reviewing the case with Agrippa, what did Festus say was the main charge against Paul? (25:17-19)
❇ Why was Festus, in a sense, paralyzed by Paul's case? (25:19)

❊ Why did Festus feel incapable of handling Paul's case? (25:19-20)
❊ Why had Paul wanted to remain in Roman custody? (25:21)
■ How did Agrippa respond to the governor's story? (25:22)

GET IT
❊ Why was Paul's case difficult for Festus?
❊ How were Roman legal proceedings different from the way the Jews approached the law?
❊ Why didn't Festus release Paul when there were no clear charges against him?
❊ If you were Paul's lawyer, what would you say to Festus to clear up his misunderstandings about the case?
❊ How did God use Paul's arrest and imprisonment?
■ In what way did Paul's arrest help him spread the news about Christ?
■ Why might God allow us to suffer for no apparent reason?

APPLY IT
■ In what difficult situation do you want to remember that God is sovereignly in control?
❊ Over the next few weeks, how can you gather practical wisdom from your Bible study?

Acts 25:23–26:32
Paul Before Agrippa

TOPICS
Accusation, Advice, Beliefs, Fairness, God, Jesus Christ, Opposition, People, Persecution, Position, Power, Religion, Serving, Witnessing

OPEN IT
■ What is one story from your past that you enjoy telling?
❊ What sorts of ceremonial events have you attended?
❊ If you could spend an evening with any president, prime minister, or other national leader, whom would you choose?

EXPLORE IT
❊ How did Agrippa and Bernice use the occasion of their meeting with Paul to display their position and power? (25:23)
❊ Who commanded Paul to be brought in? (25:23)
❊ How was this meeting a fulfillment of the prophecy in Luke 21:12? (25:23)
❊ How did Festus open the proceedings? (25:24-26)
❊ In opening the proceedings, what did Festus say to his royal guests? (25:24-26)
❊ Why did Festus bring Paul before this group? (25:26-27)
❊ How had Festus become tangled in a difficulty of his own making? (25:25-27)
❊ How did Paul begin his address to Agrippa? (26:1-3)
❊ What did Paul say about his early years in Judaism? (26:4-8)
❊ What was Paul's obsession before his conversion? (26:9-11)
■ How did Paul describe his conversion and new life? (26:12-18)
❊ How did Paul fulfill his commission? (26:19-23)
■ How did Paul deal with Festus and Agrippa during his speech? (26:24-29)
■ How did Paul conclude his defense? (26:29)
❊ What did Agrippa—a man well-trained in Judaism—conclude about Paul? (26:31-32)

GET IT
❊ How are some Christians like Agrippa and Bernice?
❊ How did Festus use Paul to placate the Jews?
❊ How did Agrippa's background and experience help Festus deal with Paul?
❊ When you need the right kind of help, how do you go about getting it?
❊ Why do you think Festus brought Paul's case before Agrippa and Bernice?
❊ What was Paul's primary goal in his speech?
■ How did Paul tailor his message to the audience and situation he faced?
❊ How did Paul take advantage of his wretched, unjust situation?
❊ What should be our objective when we tell others about the way we came to believe?
■ How can we use stories of our own experience to share the message of Christ?
❊ How do you think you would have reacted to Paul's testimony if you had been in the audience?

APPLY IT
❊ Why is it important to pray for your political leaders?
■ What story of God's working in your life can you rehearse for sharing with others?
❊ This week, how can you support a minister of the gospel who is in trying circumstances?

Acts 27:1-12
Paul Sails for Rome

TOPICS
Advice, Danger, Kindness, People

OPEN IT
❊ If you had a chance to visit Turkey, Greece, or Italy, which country would you choose? Why?
■ What stops would you want to make on a Mediterranean cruise?
❊ On a journey overseas, would you feel safer going by airplane or ship to your destination?

EXPLORE IT
❊ Who accompanied Paul to Italy? (27:1)
❊ Why did Luke use the term "we"? (27:1)
❊ Who was in charge of the group? (27:1)
❊ When Paul and Luke boarded ship, who joined them? (27:2)
❊ How did Paul's friends support him along the way? (27:3)
❊ Why was it difficult for Paul's ship to sail? (27:4)
❊ Where did the group change ships? (27:5-6)
❊ On the second ship, where did the journey take Paul

and the others? (27:7-8)
❇ Why was sailing difficult after the Day of Atonement? (27:9)
■ Why did Paul have the opportunity to offer advice? (27:9-10)
■ How were Paul's warnings ignored? (27:11)
■ Why did the crew decide to sail on? (27:12)

GET IT
❇ Who helped make Paul's difficult journey easier?
❇ Why was Paul's advice ignored even though he had traveled by sea many times?
❇ How would you have liked sharing in Paul's sea adventures?
❇ When do you count on the support of Christian friends?
■ How do you feel when your wise counsel is bypassed?
■ What can a person do to make his or her counsel likely to be heard?

APPLY IT
❇ How can you prepare yourself to handle difficult circumstances this week?
❇ How could relying on Christian friends help you cope with a tough situation?
■ To whom should you offer sound advice this week? When?

Acts 27:13-26
The Storm

TOPICS
Courage, Encouragement, Endurance, Faith, Fear, Giving Up, God, Hopelessness

OPEN IT
❇ What was the most frightening experience you ever had?
■ If a severe storm was approaching your area, what might you do to get ready for it?
❇ How well do you function in a crisis?

EXPLORE IT
❇ How was the ship's crew deceived by "a gentle south wind"? (27:13)
■ How was the ship forced away from safety? (27:14-15)
■ What did the Northeaster do to the ship? (27:15)
❇ How did Cauda provide a break from the storm? (27:16)
■ What efforts did the men on board make to battle the storm? (27:16-19)
❇ At what point did those on board ship give up hope? (27:20)
❇ When did Paul speak to the others? (27:21)
❇ How did Paul reprimand the crew? (27:21)
❇ What message from God did Paul give the crew? (27:22-26)
❇ How did Paul prepare the crew for bad news? (27:22-26)
❇ What did Paul say to encourage everyone on board in spite of the hardships ahead? (27:22-26)

GET IT
■ Once they lost control of the ship and their situation, how do you think the men on board felt?
■ What do you do when circumstances get beyond your control?
❇ How could Paul offer an upbeat message when life on board seemed hopeless?
❇ If you had been on board with Paul, what kind of Christian witness would you have had to offer during the storm?
❇ What does this account tell us about God?
❇ What does this story tell us about times when our lives are in danger?
❇ How can you be joyful in spite of your circumstances?

APPLY IT
❇ When can you encourage someone this week? How?
■ How can you remember—each day this week—to trust in God's sovereign control of your life?

Acts 27:27-44
The Shipwreck

TOPICS
Encouragement, Escape, God, Leadership, Plans, Stress, Thankfulness

OPEN IT
❇ If you had to be stuck on an island somewhere, what island would you choose? Why?
■ What are some responsibilities that adults often try to escape?
❇ If you were on a ship that was sinking fast, what one treasured item would you take with you on the lifeboat?

EXPLORE IT
❇ How long was the ship at the mercy of the storm? (27:27)
❇ How did the sailors sense that they were approaching land? (27:27-28)
❇ Why did the sailors drop four anchors? (27:29)
■ Who tried to escape? (27:30)
■ How did Paul thwart the sailors' plan to escape? (27:31-32)
❇ How did the group resolve their problems of tension and hunger? (27:33, 36)
❇ Why did Paul urge those on board to eat? (27:33-34)
❇ What did Paul do to give public testimony to his faith? (27:35)
❇ How many people were on board the ship? (27:37)
❇ What did the men do after they ate? (27:38)
❇ What did the crew decide to do when daylight came? (27:39-40)
❇ What unexpectedly happened to the ship? (27:41)
■ Why did the centurion save the lives of the prisoners? (27:42-43)
❇ How did Paul's predictions prove to be true? (27:44)

GET IT
❇ How did the sailors show that they knew how to weather a storm?
❇ How can we prepare to handle bad times?

■ Why did the sailors try to jump ship?
❇ If you had been on board, why would you or wouldn't you have been tempted to leave the ship along with the sailors?
■ How can we know when to get out of a bad situation and when to face it?
❇ How did Paul take charge of the situation on board?
❇ What qualities in Paul do you admire?
❇ Why did the soldiers plan to kill the prisoners?
❇ In what ways do you look out for your interests before considering the needs of others?
❇ How was God at work in the details of the shipwreck?
❇ How can we benefit from frustrations and problems?

APPLY IT
❇ To what "storms" that you are now facing do you need to respond with faith in God?
■ What do you need to request from God to endure the rough passages of life?
❇ How can you provide encouragement and practical help to someone who is in the middle of a personal storm?

Acts 28:1-10
Ashore on Malta

TOPICS
Assumptions, Healing, Help, Kindness, Leadership, Miracles, Prayer, Sickness

OPEN IT
❇ How might you show hospitality to a new family in the neighborhood?
■ If you moved to a new neighborhood, how would you want the neighbors to welcome you?

EXPLORE IT
❇ Where were the people shipwrecked? (28:1)
❇ How did the islanders treat Paul and the others? (28:2)
❇ What did the islanders do to welcome the victims of the shipwreck? (28:2)
❇ What happened to Paul when he was building the fire? (28:3)
❇ Seeing that Paul was bitten by the snake, what did the islanders conclude? (28:4)
❇ When Paul was unaffected by the snake's bite, how did the people of Malta show their superstition? (28:5-6)
❇ What was distinctive about the home Paul and the others were near? (28:7)
❇ What was Publius's title? (28:7)
❇ What did the governor do for Paul and his companions? (28:7)
■ How did Paul help Publius's father? (28:8)
■ What happened when word of a healing spread? (28:9)
■ What was the effect of what Paul did for Publius's father? (28:10)

GET IT
❇ Why did the islanders show unusual kindness to the victims of the shipwreck?
❇ Even in this terrible mishap, how did God provide for Paul and the crew?
❇ When you are in a predicament, whom do you trust to get you out of it? How?
■ What was the nature of Paul's ministry on the island?
■ What effect did Paul's acts of service have on the islanders?
❇ How can you help those who are ill?

APPLY IT
■ What act of service or help can you do for people in your neighborhood this week?
❇ What act of kindness can you do for a sick friend, church member, or coworker today?

Acts 28:11-16
Arrival at Rome

TOPICS
Church, Encouragement, Fellowship, God, Thankfulness

OPEN IT
❇ If you could have your way, where would you spend next winter?
■ After a three-month stay overseas, whom would you most look forward to seeing on your return home?
❇ When was the last time you were on a boat?

EXPLORE IT
❇ For how long did the crew stay on Malta? (28:11) Why?
❇ When Paul and the others finally set sail, what kind of ship did they use? (28:11)
❇ What was the first stop for Paul and the others along their continued journey to Rome? How long did the stop last? (28:12)
❇ How long did the group stay at Syracuse? (28:12)
❇ What port along the Italian coastline marked the next stop? (28:13)
❇ When the group arrived at Puteoli, what did they do? (28:13-14)
■ After the week-long visit with Christians, what was the next destination for Paul and his group? (28:14)
■ What did the Christians at Rome do when they heard of Paul's coming? (28:15)
■ How did Paul feel when he saw his Christian brothers? (28:15)
❇ Because Paul was a trusted prisoner, what was he allowed to do in Rome? (28:16)

GET IT
❇ The mariners believed that the ship's figurehead would bring them good luck; on what things do Christians tend to rely?
❇ Why would Paul have been encouraged to find Christians at Puteoli?
❇ How does the evangelistic work of your church encourage you?
■ How do you think the Christians of Rome felt when they first saw Paul?
■ What fellow Christian has come to mean a lot to you?
❇ How do you greet your pastor when he returns after being away for a while?
❇ How were Paul's living conditions in Rome quite different from his housing in Jerusalem?

APPLY IT
✻ For what can you thank God today?
✻ How can you affirm a diligent Christian servant this week?

Acts 28:17-31
Paul Preaches at Rome Under Guard

TOPICS
Believe, Christianity, Convictions, God, Hardheartedness, Holy Spirit, Jesus Christ, Kingdom of God/Heaven, Law, Leadership, Prophecy, Salvation

OPEN IT
■ What are some ways in which you have grown callous over the years?
✻ If you had a career in sales, what do you think you could sell with heartfelt conviction? Why?

EXPLORE IT
✻ With whom did Paul first speak in Rome? (28:17)
✻ In his presentation to the Jewish leaders, what significant points did Paul make? (28:17-20)
✻ What did Paul mean by "the hope of Israel"? (28:20)
✻ What kind of response did Paul get from the leaders? (28:21-22)
✻ How did the Jewish leaders in Rome show increasing interest in the apostle and his message? (28:23-24)
✻ What did Paul do all day long while meeting with the Jewish leaders? (28:23)
■ How did the Jews in Rome respond to Paul's teaching? (28:24-25)
✻ To whom did Paul ascribe Isaiah's words? (28:25)
■ How did Paul apply the words of Isaiah to his audience? (28:26-27)
■ What prediction did Paul make about the future? (28:28)
✻ Though the Jews had turned away from Christ, what group had God promised to tell of His salvation? (28:28)
✻ What did Paul do for two years in Rome? (28:30-31)

GET IT
✻ Why do you think Paul's teaching was hard for some followers of Judaism to accept?
✻ Why do you think the attitude of the Jewish leaders in Rome was less hostile than that of the Jews in Jerusalem?
✻ What made Paul and the gospel he represented less of a threat to unbelievers than in the past?
✻ Why do many people dismiss the message of salvation in Christ?
✻ In what way do we become hardened to God?
■ When have you observed hardheartedness in your own life?
■ When do you need to guard against hardheartedness?

APPLY IT
✻ How can you go beyond the boundaries of your neighborhood in telling others about the Lord?
■ What is one way you can maintain sensitivity to the Holy Spirit each day this week?

Romans 1:1-7
Introduction

TOPICS
Affirmation, Ambassadors, Call, Witnessing

OPEN IT
✻ What are some of the normal ways people begin a letter or a phone call?
✻ When have you been startled by the opening paragraph of a letter?
■ If you were writing the initial letter to a pen pal, how would you introduce yourself?

EXPLORE IT
■ How did Paul introduce and identify himself to the Romans? (1:1)
✻ What special calling on his life did Paul feel? (1:1)
✻ In what ways has God revealed His gospel to people? (1:2-4)
✻ Who is the focus of God's gospel? (1:2-4)
✻ What credentials does Jesus have to confirm His claim as Son of God? (1:3-4)
■ What did Paul and others receive as a calling for their lives? (1:5)
✻ Who were the new group of people being exposed to the gospel message? (1:5)
✻ What were the Gentiles and all people being called to believe? (1:5)
✻ How did Paul describe the people who were receiving this letter? (1:6)
✻ To whom was this letter written? (1:7)
■ What kind of greeting did Paul send to his audience? (1:7)

GET IT
■ In what way do you feel God has placed a special calling on your life?
✻ What purpose for living has God given you?
■ What words do you use to describe yourself to others as a follower of Jesus Christ?
✻ How did you feel when you realized God's gospel was meaningful to you?
✻ What do most people today believe about God's plan for the world?
✻ What do most people today believe about God's plan for their personal salvation?
✻ How have your beliefs about Jesus Christ changed during the various stages of your life?
✻ In what ways would remembering in prayer each day God's calling on and plan for your life affect your daily walk with Christ?

APPLY IT
✻ With whom could you share God's unfolding plan of salvation for the whole world?
✻ How would you explain God's plan of salvation to a friend?
■ To what friend could you explain God's love and your response to His plan of salvation? How?

Romans 1:8-17
Paul's Longing to Visit Rome

TOPICS
Caring, Confidence, Good News, Salvation, Witnessing

OPEN IT
❇ How do you stay in touch with friends or family members who live in another city?
■ What trips to see friends or family members would you like take in the future?
❇ How do people feel when circumstances force them to cancel a long-anticipated trip?

EXPLORE IT
❇ For what was the church at Rome well-known? (1:8)
❇ How did Paul describe his commitment to God? (1:9)
■ What kind of concern did Paul have for his audience? (1:9-10)
■ What happened to Paul's plans to visit the church in Rome? (1:10-13)
❇ What did Paul want to give the Romans when he visited? (1:11-12)
■ Who would benefit from Paul's visit? (1:12)
❇ To whom had God called Paul to communicate the gospel? (1:14-15)
❇ How did Paul feel about what others thought about him and his message? (1:16)
❇ To whom does God grant salvation? (1:16)
❇ How does a person become righteous? (1:17)
❇ What does a person's faith accomplish? (1:17)

GET IT
■ What are some of the positive reports you would want other people to hear about your faith in God?
■ How does remembering someone in prayer help him or her?
❇ In what ways are we helped when we help someone else?
❇ When have you learned something from someone whom you initially believed had nothing to teach you?
❇ How does Paul's attitude about sharing the gospel compare with the prevailing attitude in your church?
❇ For what reasons do Christians sometimes feel ashamed of the gospel?
❇ How do people attempt to find salvation outside of faith in Christ alone?
❇ For what reasons are you confident that the gospel is true?

APPLY IT
■ What can you do this week to help a person for whom you are concerned?
❇ With whom can you be more honest and forthright about the gospel message you believe?
❇ For what "unreachable" person will you begin praying this week?

Romans 1:18-32
God's Wrath Against Mankind

TOPICS
Evil, Hardheartedness, Homosexuality, Immorality, Self-centeredness, Separation, Sex, Sin, Stubbornness, Thankfulness, Truth, Unbelievers, World

OPEN IT
■ If God were to deliver a "state of the world" speech for all of us to hear, what do you think He would say?
❇ How do people today distinguish between right and wrong?
❇ Why do a high percentage of people today say they believe in God?

EXPLORE IT
■ What is God's response to the people who ignore and disobey Him? (1:18)
❇ How does God reveal Himself to people? (1:19-20)
■ What makes all people accountable to God? (1:20)
❇ What is the primary problem people have in their relationship with God? (1:21)
❇ What happens to the hearts and minds of people who reject God? (1:21-22)
❇ When people deny God, what do they often put in His place? (1:21-23)
■ How does God respond to people who ignore and deny Him? (1:24, 26)
❇ How are attitudes toward sexuality affected when a person denies God? (1:24, 26-27)
❇ What lie do people naturally believe by denying the truth? (1:25)
❇ When thoughts of God are pushed out, what evil attitudes and actions replace them? (1:28-31)
❇ Instead of fearing God, what attitude do people naturally have toward Him? (1:32)

GET IT
❇ What is the real barrier between us and God?
■ How can God hold us responsible for breaking His laws?
❇ How do people today suppress the truth about God?
❇ In what ways is our thinking futile and our mind darkened?
■ What examples can you list of how we worship created things rather than the Creator?
❇ How common in our world are the specific sins listed in the passage?
❇ What is God's attitude toward promiscuous heterosexual activity and homosexuality?
❇ How can God be so angry with us and still love us?
❇ How does God want us to respond to Him?

APPLY IT
❇ In what ways can you lessen your dependence on the things you are tempted to "worship" and serve more than God?
❇ How can you glorify God and give thanks to Him this week?
■ Who among your friends is caught in this trap of rejecting God and needs your prayers of intercession this week?

Romans 2:1-16
God's Righteous Judgment

TOPICS
Judging Others, Judgment, Repentance, Witnessing

OPEN IT
❇ How does a critical review of a movie or concert affect your decision about attending it?
■ On what basis do people often judge other people?
❇ What does it take to judge disputes fairly?

EXPLORE IT
❇ When we judge others, what do we do to ourselves? (2:1)
■ If God is judging others for their sins, what will He do to us? (2:2-3)
❇ For what reason is God kind, tolerant, and patient? (2:4)
❇ What keeps us from acknowledging and repenting of our sins? (2:4-5)
❇ What is God's reaction to our stubbornness? (2:5-6)
■ On what basis will God render His judgments? (2:5-8)
❇ What are the qualities of those who gain eternal life? (2:7)
❇ What characteristics do condemned people display? (2:8)
❇ How can Jews expect to be treated by God? (2:9-11)
❇ How can Gentiles expect to be treated by God? (2:9-11)
■ How will those who know God's law be treated compared to those who never heard God's law? (2:12-15)
❇ How will God judge people? (2:12-16)
❇ When will the Law judge people? (2:16)

GET IT
❇ In what circumstances do you find yourself passing judgment on other people?
■ When have you ever judged someone else and realized you were guilty of the same offense?
❇ When has God's patience, tolerance, and kindness brought you to repentance?
■ How should your anticipation of a coming judgment day affect your daily behavior?
❇ How much exposure have you had to God's law during your life?
❇ How you have responded to your exposure to God's law?
❇ How will God deal with people who have never heard His law?

APPLY IT
❇ What do you need to do today to get ready for judgment day?
■ Whom have you judged in a manner not pleasing to God? How can you seek forgiveness?
❇ Who in your life is not ready for their day of judgment before God and needs your prayers this week?

Romans 2:17-29
The Jews and the Law

TOPICS
Approval, Beliefs, Character, Consistency, Hypocrisy, Self-righteousness

OPEN IT
❇ What advertisements do you have trouble believing?
❇ How would you judge the character of a person who wanted to date your only daughter?
■ What are some "wrong" reasons a person might have for going to church?

EXPLORE IT
❇ What special relationship did the Jews have with God? (2:17-18)
❇ How did Jews describe themselves in relation to Gentiles? (2:19-20)
■ Of what did Paul accuse the Jews? (2:21-24)
❇ Why would the Gentiles blaspheme God's name because of the Jews? (2:21-24)
❇ What was the purpose of circumcision? (2:25-26)
❇ What is more important to God than being physically circumcised? (2:26-27)
■ How did Paul redefine what it means to be a Jew? (2:28-29)
❇ What is more important than physical circumcision? (2:29)
■ What is more important than knowing God's written law? (2:29)
❇ Whose approval does a true Jew seek? (2:29)

GET IT
■ How could a person be very religious and yet be lacking a real relationship with God?
❇ What are the most important qualities of an effective teacher?
❇ How do our actions show others what we genuinely believe?
❇ How does hypocrisy in a religious person affect people who observe that person?
❇ How could a person be outwardly a Christian and inwardly something else?
❇ What is more important than keeping outward standards of Christian behavior?
■ What makes a person a true Christian?
❇ How much does peer pressure from friends and coworkers influence our beliefs and behavior as Christians?

APPLY IT
❇ How can you begin to change some inconsistent behaviors and attitudes in your Christian life this week?
■ In which of your present situations should you be more concerned about pleasing God than pleasing other people?

Romans 3:1-8
God's Faithfulness

TOPICS
Confession, Judgment, Justice, Law, Self-righteousness, Sin, Unfairness

OPEN IT
■ What could you learn about the character of a person by watching the behavior of his or her children?
❊ How do you determine if a person is telling the truth?

EXPLORE IT
❊ What is the advantage of being a Jew? (3:1-2)
❊ How did God show favor toward the Jews? (3:1-2)
❊ With what have Jews been entrusted? (3:2)
■ How does failure to be true to God reflect on the character of God? (3:3-4)
❊ When we realize our own sinfulness, what do we learn about the character of God? (3:5)
❊ What brings out God's righteousness more clearly? (3:5)
■ What was Paul's response to the charge that God is unjust in judging us? (3:5)
❊ What was Paul's human argument about the fairness of God's judgment of us? (3:5-8)
■ How is God's character affected by the level of our sinfulness? (3:7)
❊ What false statement or teaching was being attributed to Paul? (3:8)
❊ Who did Paul say deserves condemnation? (3:8)

GET IT
❊ How can good come out of evil?
❊ What danger results from defining our goodness in relative terms—such as comparing ourselves to notorious villains like Adolf Hitler or Charles Manson?
■ What religious activities are we tempted to rely on as the basis of our justification before God?
❊ How do you react when you see a well-known Christian leader exposed for sinful activities?
❊ How is your faith in God affected by the public sins of Christian leaders?
❊ In what practical ways can our lives be changed by the belief that God's promises will never change?
❊ In what ways do we minimize the effects of sin or of disobeying God's law?
■ What excuses do we use to explain away continuing sinful behavior in our lives?
❊ What would Paul's reaction be to the statement, "You can't appreciate the good until you have experienced the bad"?

APPLY IT
❊ What sins in your life do you need to confess to God and repent of this week?
■ What step or action can you take this week to keep you from taking God's grace for granted?
❊ Which of God's promises do you want to keep in your thoughts this week?

Romans 3:9-20
No One Is Righteous

TOPICS
Accountability, Basics of the Faith, Deceit, Disobedience, Excuses, Favoritism, God, Judgment, Law, Rebellion, Righteousness, Salvation, Sin

OPEN IT
■ In what ways are all people the same?
❊ How would baby-sitting a two-year-old for a week influence your opinion about the goodness or badness of humans in general?

EXPLORE IT
❊ How did Paul compare himself to others? (3:9)
■ How are Jews and Gentiles alike? (3:9)
❊ Who is righteous? (3:10)
❊ What is our natural tendency toward God? (3:11)
❊ What is the result of turning away from God? (3:12)
■ What is human nature? (3:12)
❊ How do our conversations and speech reflect our sinful nature? (3:13-14)
■ What are the characteristics of people who stand condemned before God? (3:13-18)
❊ What does God's law show us about ourselves? (3:19)
❊ What is the purpose of having God's law? (3:19-20)
❊ What reward does a person receive for observing the Law? (3:20)

GET IT
❊ How do you feel when the Bible describes you as standing guilty before God?
❊ How can Christianity be described as "good news" when it teaches that all people are guilty before God?
■ What reasons would you give for describing people as either basically good or basically evil?
■ How would you explain this passage to a person who believes that he or she is good and not guilty of any serious sins?
❊ How will God judge His chosen people, the Jews?
❊ How can we sin with our mouth?
❊ For what are we accountable to God?
❊ What misinformation about God's judgment have you believed at one point in your life?

APPLY IT
■ What "laws" do you need to put aside in your life in favor of the true righteousness God offers?
❊ With what believer could you meet and spend time in prayer and confession? When?

Romans 3:21-31
Righteousness Through Faith

TOPICS
Atonement, Faith, Jesus Christ, Justice, Law, Righteousness

OPEN IT
■ What hero do you remember who always seemed to arrive at just the right moment to save the day?

❊ If you had a message of good news for someone, how would you deliver it?
❊ When have you escaped a penalty you were sure you were going to have to pay?

EXPLORE IT
❊ What new righteousness has been made known? (3:21)
❊ What previous indication was there about the existence of the new righteousness? (3:21)
❊ What is the source of our righteousness? (3:22)
■ How does a person obtain righteousness? (3:22)
❊ What heritage do you share with every person who has ever lived? (3:23)
❊ What justifies us in God's sight? (3:24)
■ What is the cost or price of justification with God? (3:24)
❊ What did God do to provide a means of justification and forgiveness for every person? (3:25)
■ How does providing Christ Jesus as a sacrifice demonstrate the justice of God? (3:25-26)
❊ On what basis can a person brag about his or her righteousness? (3:27)
❊ What justifies a person in God's sight? (3:28)
❊ How will Jews and Gentiles be judged by God? (3:29-30)
❊ What is the relationship between having faith and observing the Law? (3:29-31)

GET IT
■ What makes it difficult for many of us to believe that we can gain God's forgiveness by faith in Christ alone?
❊ What makes Christianity good news in our world?
❊ What makes Christianity good news for you personally?
■ Why would God offer His righteousness free to every person?
❊ What do we need to do to be declared righteous in God's sight?
❊ What does it mean to believe and put your faith in Jesus Christ?
❊ Why do some people object to the idea that God has offered forgiveness to every person, even the worst sinners?
❊ How should our boasting and bragging about our relationship to God be different when we realize it is by faith alone?
❊ What role, besides judge, is God playing in our lives?

APPLY IT
❊ When could you meet with another person to share the good news of God's redemptive plan?
■ In what areas are you still boasting about your own abilities? How can you submit those areas to God's control?

Romans 4:1-25

Abraham Justified by Faith

TOPICS
Covenant, Faith, New Covenant, Promises, Righteousness, Sin

OPEN IT
❊ What are some of the many religious acts and practices people perform in an attempt to please God?
■ How much faith do you put in the promises people make to you?

EXPLORE IT
❊ What was the main characteristic of Abraham's relationship with God? (4:1-3)
❊ How was Abraham righteous before God? (4:3)
❊ How did David describe what God does to make a person righteous? (4:6-8)
❊ What was the relationship between Abraham's righteousness and his circumcision? (4:9-11)
❊ What was the purpose of circumcision in Abraham's life? (4:11)
❊ On what basis can both the circumcised and the uncircumcised claim Abraham as their father? (4:11-12)
■ On what basis did Abraham receive the promise of inheriting the world? (4:13)
■ Why would God's promise be worthless if a person had to keep the Law perfectly to receive it? (4:14-15)
❊ What does the Law bring to those who live by it? (4:15)
❊ What was God's promise to Abraham? (4:18)
❊ What facts might have convinced Abraham that God's promise of a son was impossible? (4:19)
❊ How was Abraham able to resist the temptation to doubt God's promise? (4:20)
■ What did Abraham believe about God that convinced him God could keep His promise? (4:20-21)
❊ How does Abraham's righteousness by faith apply to us? (4:23-24)
❊ Who has God provided as a worthy object of our faith? (4:24-25)

GET IT
❊ What is righteousness?
❊ What is true faith?
❊ Why is it impossible to be saved by following God's laws?
❊ What customs and religious habits can give people a false sense of righteousness?
❊ What causes many people to think that works are more important than faith for pleasing God?
■ What is fair or unfair about the fact that all people, including very wicked people, can inherit God's promises by putting their faith in God?
❊ In what ways do people act as if they must earn God's love?
❊ What must a person do to have his or her sins completely forgiven?
■ What promise are you waiting for God to fulfill in your life?
❊ How does God's relationship with Abraham help you understand His workings in your life?

APPLY IT
❊ How can you pray this week to reaffirm your faith in God and not in works?
■ What promise of God do you need to trust in this week?

Romans 5:1-11
Peace and Joy

TOPICS
Endurance, Enemies, God, Hope, Joy, Love, Peace

OPEN IT
✻ What circumstances can turn two people into enemies?
■ How do most people treat their enemies?
✻ What results can difficult circumstances have in a person's life?

EXPLORE IT
✻ What is the basis for our justification with God? (5:1)
✻ What is our relationship with God if we have been justified by faith? (5:1)
✻ How does Jesus Christ change a person's standing with God? (5:2)
✻ For what reasons can a Christian rejoice? (5:2-3)
✻ What good things can result from suffering? (5:3-5)
✻ Why does hope not disappoint us? (5:5)
✻ How has God demonstrated His love for us? (5:6-8)
✻ What comparisons can be made between people giving their lives for others and Christ's death for all people? (5:7-8)
■ What was our relationship to God when Christ came to die for us? (5:8)
✻ What aspect of Christ's death justifies a person in God's sight? (5:9)
■ How did God act to remove the barrier between Himself and all people? (5:9-10)
✻ If God has demonstrated His love to us through Jesus' death, what can we anticipate concerning our future relationship with God? (5:10)
■ For what reasons can a Christian rejoice? (5:11)

GET IT
✻ How is peace with God different from peace of mind?
■ What does it mean to be justified?
■ How were we formerly God's enemies?
✻ What are the benefits of being justified with God?
✻ What is the connection between suffering and hope?
✻ How should Christian hope affect a person's attitude toward his or her current circumstances or goals?
✻ What is hope?
✻ What keeps us from being full of joy and hope in the middle of difficult circumstances?
✻ In what ways does suffering produce endurance?
✻ How can suffering produce positive rather than negative results?
✻ How did Jesus' death affect our security in God's love?

APPLY IT
✻ In what difficult circumstances do you need to stop grumbling and stay focused on joy in Christ?
■ Who in your life needs to hear that through Jesus Christ they are no longer enemies with God?

Romans 5:12-21
Death Through Adam, Life Through Christ

TOPICS
Death, God, Grace, Jesus Christ, Law, Life, Sin

OPEN IT
✻ What advantages and experiences have you had that many others in the world have not?
■ In what ways can the decisions of a few leaders change the lives of millions of people?
✻ What experiences have you had with death?

EXPLORE IT
✻ What did Adam introduce into the world and pass on to his descendants? (5:12)
✻ What is the root cause of death? (5:12)
✻ How did the coming of God's law affect the presence of sin in the world? (5:13)
✻ How did the coming of God's law affect our understanding of what sin is? (5:13)
■ What came into the world through Jesus Christ? (5:15)
✻ What is God's solution to the inevitable problem of sin and death? (5:16-17)
■ In what ways are the acts of Jesus and Adam similar? (5:18-19)
✻ What is the relationship between the amount of sin and grace in the world? (5:20)
✻ What effect did God's righteous law have on rebellious people? (5:20)
✻ What does sin in this world produce? (5:21)
■ What does grace given by God to this world produce? (5:21)

GET IT
✻ In what ways are all people the same?
✻ What fears or anticipation do you have about death?
✻ What effect did Christ's death on the cross have on your life?
✻ At what point in your life did you realize you were guilty of sin?
✻ At what point in your life did you realize God's love for you?
■ How can God justly judge us for Adam's sin?
✻ How can a person have his or her sins forgiven by God?
■ What makes Jesus' action more powerful than Adam's?
✻ How can knowing you are forgiven and righteous before God through Jesus Christ affect your attitudes and actions?

APPLY IT
✻ In what ways can you thank God today for the grace He has bestowed on you?
■ What can you do this week for unsaved friends still suffering from the consequences of sin?

Romans 6:1-14
Dead to Sin, Alive in Christ

TOPICS
Change, Consequences, God, Holiness, Jesus Christ, Life-style, New Life, Salvation, Sin, Slavery

OPEN IT
❇ What would most people like to change about their lives?
❇ What is one thing you'd like to change about your life?
■ What motivates people to make major changes in their lives?

EXPLORE IT
❇ Why should a forgiven, justified person make a strong effort not to sin? (6:1-2)
❇ For what reason would a person not want to live in sin any longer? (6:2)
❇ What does baptism symbolize about our relationship to Christ? (6:2-4)
■ What makes it possible for a person to live a new life? (6:4)
❇ Before a person is united to Christ, to what is he or she a slave? (6:6)
❇ How does being united with Christ through His death change our relationship to sin? (6:7)
❇ After Christ died and was raised, why did neither sin nor death have any power over Him? (6:7, 9-10)
■ How will uniting with Christ in His death change the future of our lives? (6:8-10)
■ In a person's new relationship with God, what is his or her relationship to sin supposed to be? (6:11-12)
❇ What change in attitude and action toward God happens in a person who follows Christ? (6:11-13)
❇ Under whose control does a Christian live? (6:14)
❇ How does being under grace change a person? (6:14)

GET IT
❇ What does this passage tell us about God and Christ?
❇ What does this passage tell us about all people and their relationship to God?
❇ What kind of changes does God want to make in our lives when we become Christians?
■ Why should a Christian stop sinning even though he or she knows God has forgiven and will forgive those sins?
■ How does God help a person discard old habits and tendencies?
❇ How does God give a person a new self?
❇ What are the symptoms of a person in slavery to sin?
❇ How would you describe the character of someone who is alive to God in Christ?
❇ What does it mean to live a new life for God?
❇ In what practical sense is sin no longer the master of a Christian even though he or she might still commit specific sins?
❇ In what ways is a Christian truly free?

APPLY IT
❇ How can you actively resist the tendency to sin in your everyday life?
■ How can you offer yourself as an instrument of righteousness to God and to others this week?

Romans 6:15-23
Slaves to Righteousness

TOPICS
Change, Consequences, Eternal Life, Life-style, New Life, Righteousness, Sin, Slavery

OPEN IT
■ What bad habits can control and damage a person's life?
❇ If you had to forfeit your personal freedom to become a slave, whom would you want to be your master?

EXPLORE IT
❇ Why shouldn't a Christian continue to sin willingly? (6:15-18)
❇ Who or what determines the things that dominate or control a person? (6:16)
■ How does sin dominate a person's life? (6:16-18)
■ What results follow from being a slave to obedience to God? (6:16, 19, 22)
■ What is the result of being a slave to sin? (6:16, 21, 23)
❇ With what attitude do believers obey their new master, righteousness? (6:17)
❇ What change has happened to people who have put their trust in Christ? (6:17-18)
❇ What is the result of being a slave to righteousness? (6:19, 22)
❇ What are the wages of sin? (6:23)
❇ What is the gift of God? (6:23)

GET IT
❇ What attitude should a Christian have toward sin?
❇ What causes a person to be a slave to sin?
■ What benefits and pleasures do people think they gain from sinful, selfish living?
❇ Before knowing Christ, when did you feel regret for the selfish things you had done?
❇ How does sin destroy a person's life?
■ What are the benefits and pleasures of righteous living?
❇ Why can't a person be his or her own master, enslaved to neither God nor sin?
❇ In what ways is our relationship to God not like slavery?
❇ To what degree is each person responsible for his or her sinful or righteous living?

APPLY IT
■ How can you show your wholehearted obedience to God this week?
❇ In what areas of your life do you need God's help to loosen the grip of certain sins?

Romans 7:1-6
An Illustration From Marriage

TOPICS
Change, Growth, Holy Spirit, Law, Marriage, New Life

OPEN IT
❇ What were some of the basic rules of behavior you were taught as a child?

■ How do your present values differ from the ones you were taught as a child?

EXPLORE IT

✻ What illustration did Paul use to explain a Christian's relationship to the written law? (7:1-3)
✻ Who does the husband represent in Paul's illustration? (7:2-3)
✻ Who does the married woman represent in Paul's illustration? (7:2-3)
■ To what did Paul compare the death of a woman's husband? (7:2-5) Why?
✻ What is the purpose or goal of a Christian's new life? (7:4)
✻ What changes a person's relationship to the Law? (7:4-6)
■ What are the primary differences between the old life under the Law and the new life in the way of the Spirit? (7:4-6)
✻ What controls a person before he or she becomes a Christian? (7:5)
■ How is a person released from being bound by the Law? (7:6)
✻ How does the Christian's new life compare with the old life? (7:6)

GET IT

✻ What role should God's written law play in a Christian's life?
✻ What keeps a Christian from sinning if the penalties of the Law have been forgiven by God?
✻ How can strict adherence to God's law affect a Christian negatively?
■ What does it mean to be a new person in Christ?
✻ How can the Spirit help us please God in a way that following the Law couldn't?
✻ How do a person's attitudes and outlook on life change when he or she comes to Christ?
✻ How can knowing that God loves you unconditionally change your behavior?
■ What is the difference between keeping religious laws and following the Spirit of Christ?

APPLY IT

■ What old ideas about pleasing God through religious activity do you need to discard this week?
✻ What can you do this week to build your living relationship with Christ instead of merely following the rules?

Romans 7:7-25
Struggling With Sin

TOPICS

Conflict, Death, Discouragement, Law, Sin, Weaknesses

OPEN IT

✻ As a child, how did you respond to the commands given to you by your parents?
✻ How do you tend to respond to authority?
■ What sort of bad habits are hardest to break?

EXPLORE IT

✻ What is the purpose of the Law? (7:7-8)
✻ What bad effect does knowing the Law have on a person? (7:7-8)
✻ When a person has no knowledge of the Law, what becomes of sin? (7:9)
■ How does knowing the Law bring the possibility of death to a person? (7:9-11)
✻ How does the Law put a person to death? (7:11)
✻ What are the characteristics of the Law and the commandment? (7:12)
✻ How does the awareness of the Law produce death in a person? (7:13)
■ What did Paul share about his own attempts to follow the Law? (7:14-16)
■ What did Paul blame for his continuing failure to do good? (7:17-20)
✻ How did Paul describe his own struggle to do what was right? (7:21-23)
✻ How did Paul describe himself and his situation? (7:24)
✻ To whom did Paul turn for rescue from his agonizing situation? (7:24)
✻ What division did Paul acknowledge in his own mind and nature? (7:24)

GET IT

✻ What are some of the various ways people respond to God's law?
✻ How can reading and understanding God's law be discouraging to a person?
✻ How can a Christian continue to commit sins even though God is his or her master?
■ How have you experienced a struggle with sin similar to what Paul describes?
■ What hope do we have of deliverance from sin here on earth?
✻ How can we take hold of the power of Christ to overcome sin?
✻ What should we do when we become discouraged and confused in our Christian lives?
✻ How can knowing that God has achieved the ultimate victory over sin affect your prayers, thoughts, and attitudes?

APPLY IT

■ How can you remind yourself each day this week of God's victory over sin?
✻ What recent struggle with sin do you need to hand over to God today?

Romans 8:1-17
Life Through the Spirit

TOPICS

Desires, Holy Spirit, Law, Sin, Spiritual Rebirth, Weaknesses

OPEN IT

■ If you were released from a three-year captivity as a hostage, what would you do during your first week of freedom?
✻ What impact can a good father or a bad father have on a person's life?

EXPLORE IT
❊ What is the status of a person who trusts in Jesus Christ? (8:1)
■ How is a person set free from the law of sin and death? (8:2)
❊ What did God do that the Law was powerless to do? (8:3-5)
❊ What is the difference between those who live according to their sinful nature and those who live according to the Spirit? (8:5-8)
■ How can a person know if he or she is controlled by the sinful nature or by the Spirit? (8:9)
❊ What promise is given to people living in the Spirit? (8:11)
❊ What kind of obligation do Christians have? (8:12-14)
❊ What happens to the person who lives according to the sinful nature? (8:13)
■ By what means can a person find life? (8:13)
❊ What is true of people who are led by God's Spirit? (8:14)
❊ What kind of spirit do God's children have? (8:15)
❊ What are the benefits of being a child of God? (8:15-17)

GET IT
❊ What feelings of condemnation and rejection may Christians feel?
■ In what ways does knowing Christ set us free?
❊ How does living for Christ change the desires of our heart?
❊ What have you seen the Spirit of God do in a person's life?
■ What does unchecked sin and selfishness produce in a person's life?
❊ How does seeing and experiencing God as a loving Father change your understanding of what it means to live as a Christian?
❊ What benefits does God give to His children?

APPLY IT
❊ What area of your life do you need to turn over to God's mighty power? How will you?
■ What changes have you been resisting in your life that you are now willing to allow your loving heavenly Father to complete?

Romans 8:18-27
Future Glory

TOPICS
Future, Hope, Prayer, Suffering, Waiting, Weaknesses

OPEN IT
■ What type of sacrifices do people commonly make for the sake of a future reward?
❊ What makes it hard for some people to pray?

EXPLORE IT
■ How did Paul describe the difference between his present and his future? (8:18)
❊ What is the world waiting to see? (8:19)
❊ For what reason has the world been forced to wait? (8:20-21)
❊ To what human experience did Paul compare his waiting? (8:22-23)
❊ For what are the children of God waiting? (8:23)
■ What is and is not genuine hope? (8:24-25)
❊ What causes us to wait patiently? (8:25)
❊ How does the Spirit help us in our weakness? (8:26)
❊ For whom does the Spirit intercede? (8:27)
❊ What is the relationship between God and the Spirit? (8:27)

GET IT
❊ What are some of the sufferings a Christian can experience?
■ What does God promise to us that can make any suffering bearable?
❊ How does suffering affect our relationship with God?
❊ What hinders us from being what God intends us to be?
❊ In what ways do Christians live in glorious freedom?
❊ What frustrations do Christians feel as they wait for Christ to return?
❊ What counsel would you give a Christian who has grown weary of waiting for Christ's return?
■ What is real hope?
❊ In what circumstances do Christians find it hard to pray?
❊ What do we learn about God's love for us when we realize that the Holy Spirit helps us even when we cannot pray?

APPLY IT
■ In what circumstances of your life do you need to wait patiently for God to act?
❊ For what can you ask the Spirit's help this week?

Romans 8:28-39
More Than Conquerors

TOPICS
Angels, Demons, Love, Persecution, Purpose, Security, Victory, Zeal

OPEN IT
■ How do you explain why bad things happen to nice people?
❊ What causes people to lose their faith in God?

EXPLORE IT
■ How does God work in all the situations and events of a person's life? (8:28)
❊ For whom does God promise to work all things for good? (8:28)
❊ Who is our ultimate example? (8:29)
❊ How does God seek to change His people? (8:29)
❊ What does God want each person to become? (8:29)
❊ What has God done to make people what He wants them to be? (8:30)
❊ What made Paul confident that God takes care of His people? (8:31-32)
■ Why should we feel confident that God is not against us or condemning us? (8:31-34)
❊ Where is Jesus Christ right now? (8:34)
■ What possible tragedies or hardships are unable to separate us from the love of Christ? (8:35-39)

❋ What kind of persecutions have God's people often faced? (8:36)
❋ How are God's people to respond to persecutions and tragedies? (8:37)
❋ What gives God's people the ability to respond in triumph to persecution? (8:37)

GET IT
❋ How can God produce good results out of bad situations?
❋ What is God's intention and plan for each Christian?
❋ In what practical ways can each of us be like Christ?
❋ How can we be sure God really loves us?
❋ What can Christians expect God to do for them?
❋ How important should the opinions of others be to a Christian?
■ How can a person be sure that bad times aren't a signal of God's displeasure with him or her?
■ What gives Christians confidence as they go through hard times?
❋ In what situations do you need God's conquering power?
❋ How have you experienced God's never-ending love in your life?

APPLY IT
■ How can you commit your difficult circumstances to God this week?
❋ How can you show trust in God to work out your circumstances for good?

Romans 9:1-29
God's Sovereign Choice

TOPICS
Blessing, Burdens, Justice, Opportunities, Rejection, Sovereignty

OPEN IT
❋ When have you felt that you were judged unfairly in a contest?
■ How do you react when someone brags that God is on his or her side?

EXPLORE IT
❋ What strong emotion was Paul feeling? (9:2)
❋ What situation made Paul feel sad and anguished? (9:2-3)
❋ How far was Paul willing to go for his fellow Jews? (9:3)
❋ What gifts and opportunities had God given to the Jewish people? (9:4-5)
❋ How did Paul explain the difference between Jews who believe and Jews who do not believe? (9:6-8)
❋ Whom did God bless as the parents of the nation of Israel? (9:7-9)
■ What did Paul say to people who claim to be children of God merely because they are descendants of Abraham? (9:8-9)
❋ Who were the children of Isaac and Rebekah? (9:10-13)
❋ What decision did God make about Jacob and Esau before they were born? (9:12-13)
■ How did Paul defend the accusation that God is unjust in His treatment of people? (9:14-15)
■ What determines how God bestows favor on people? (9:16)
❋ What examples from history did Paul use to demonstrate God's choice of blessing? (9:17-18)
❋ What right do we have to question God? (9:19-21)
❋ Why does God show great patience with us even though we deserve His wrath? (9:22-24)
❋ What did the prophets Isaiah and Hosea tell us about God's patience and justice? (9:25-29)

GET IT
❋ What burdens do you carry for friends or relatives who do not know Christ?
■ How could a person come from a very religious background and still not have a personal faith in God?
❋ In what ways do people depend on a religious heritage for their salvation?
❋ What's wrong with depending on a religious background or heritage for favor with God?
❋ What sacrifices would you be willing to make to give others a chance to know Christ?
❋ Why do we tend to question God's actions toward us or anyone else?
❋ According to this passage, why are Jewish people often resistant to the message of peace with God through Jesus Christ?
❋ What does this passage teach us about God's character?
❋ What implications does Paul's burden for Israel have for our lives today?
■ On what basis does God choose people to inherit His promises?
❋ How have you experienced God's mercy and patience in your life?

APPLY IT
■ What sacrifices or efforts can you make this week to help a friend come to faith in Christ?
❋ When can you take time this week to thank God for His acts of mercy and love to you?

Romans 9:30–10:21
Israel's Unbelief

TOPICS
Desires, Jesus Christ, Law, Righteousness, Salvation, Self-righteousness, Unbelievers, Zeal

OPEN IT
■ When have you known someone who refused to listen to any advice or instruction?
❋ How carefully do you follow the instruction sheet in a ready-to-assemble product?

EXPLORE IT
❋ By what means have the Gentiles (non-Jews) obtained righteousness? (9:30)
■ What kept Israel from obtaining righteousness? (9:31-32)
❋ Over what has Israel stumbled? (9:33)
❋ What was Paul's greatest desire? (10:1)
❋ What positive trait did Paul recognize in the Israelites? (10:2)

❇ What had the Israelites done instead of submitting to God's righteousness? (10:3-4)
❇ What is the relationship between Christ and the Law in a person's pursuit of righteousness? (10:4)
❇ How did Moses describe righteousness that comes by the Law? (10:5)
❇ How does righteousness produced by faith come about? (10:6-9)
❇ What were the simple instructions Paul gave regarding personal salvation? (10:9-10)
❇ What promise is given to anyone who puts his or her faith in Christ? (10:11)
■ What distinctions did Paul note in the way that Jews and Gentiles obtain their salvation? (10:12-13)
❇ What does it take to get the message of God to someone? (10:14-15)
❇ How have the Israelites responded to hearing the message of God? (10:16-18)
■ How did Paul answer the argument that the Jews have not had adequate opportunity to hear God's message? (10:18-21)
❇ How had the response of the Gentiles to the message of God differed from the response of the Jews? (10:18-21)

GET IT
❇ What makes it hard for Jews to believe Jesus Christ is the Messiah?
❇ What hinders non-Jews from believing Jesus Christ is the Lord and Savior of the world?
■ How can a person have great zeal for God or religious activities and yet be misguided?
❇ What are the similarities and differences between a sports fanatic and a committed Christian?
❇ How legitimate are claims by people who profess ignorance about Jesus' identity as Savior?
■ What groups of people in our society resemble the unbelieving Jews of Paul's time?
❇ Why is it essential to believe that God raised Jesus from the dead?
❇ Why is both believing with the heart and confessing with the mouth important for salvation?

APPLY IT
■ When could you spend extended time in prayer to bring before God those groups or peoples who have shown little interest in the gospel?
❇ Who in your circle of friends and family needs to hear about God's plan of salvation? When?

Romans 11:1-10
The Remnant of Israel

TOPICS
Christianity, God, Hardheartedness, Lost, Rejection, Stubbornness

OPEN IT
❇ How would you turn down an invitation to an event that your boss wanted you to attend?
■ What might a person do to get another person to love him or her?
❇ When in your experience has a large project been saved by the efforts of a few people?

EXPLORE IT
❇ What was Paul's background? (11:1)
❇ How did Paul answer those who believed that God had rejected the Jews? (11:1-6)
■ How did God answer Elijah's call to destroy Israel? (11:2-4)
■ What has God chosen by grace? (11:5)
❇ What caused God's remnant of people to survive? (11:5)
❇ How did Paul describe the people in Israel who please God? (11:5-6)
❇ Who are the elect? (11:7)
❇ What had Israel done to try to obtain righteousness in God's sight? (11:7-9)
■ What prevented Israel from responding to God as the elect had responded? (11:7-9)
❇ What results from God's decision to harden people's hearts? (11:9-10)

GET IT
❇ What commitment has God shown to the Jews?
■ What characteristics separated the remnant of Israel from the rest of Israel?
❇ What causes God's people to turn away from Him?
❇ What causes people reared in Christian families and church activities to turn away from God?
■ In what ways do you see a remnant at work in your community?
❇ By what means other than grace do people try to please God?
❇ How is it possible to seek intently for God by doing good deeds, and yet miss Him?
❇ What hardens a person's heart against God?
❇ What can God do to change the hearts of people who have turned away from Him?

APPLY IT
❇ What can you do this week to avoid the influences in your life that could harden your heart against God?
■ What can you do this week to encourage a Christian who feels outnumbered or overwhelmed?

Romans 11:11-24
Ingrafted Branches

TOPICS
Attitude, Faith, Grace, Humility, Repentance, Salvation, Spiritual Rebirth

OPEN IT
❇ What is your favorite fruit? Why?
■ What success have you had with gardening?

EXPLORE IT
❇ What hope do the Jews ever have of recovering their relationship with God? (11:11)
❇ How have Gentiles been helped by the Jews' rejection of God's salvation plan? (11:11-12)
❇ What will be an even greater result than just the response of the Gentiles to God's plan? (11:12)
❇ How did Paul hope his own Jewish people would respond when they saw him ministering to the Gentiles? (11:13-14)

✻ What did Paul imagine the response of the Jews to God could bring to the world? (11:15)
■ What long illustration did Paul use to describe the situation of the Jews and Gentiles? (11:16-24)
■ To what did Paul liken the Gentiles? (11:17)
✻ Why do we need to be careful not to boast that God has reached out to us? (11:18)
✻ To whom does God show severity and kindness? (11:22)
■ What is promised to Jews who do not persist in unbelief? (11:23)

GET IT
■ What lessons can we draw from Paul's analogy of the olive tree?
✻ How would the repentance of Israel affect the world?
✻ What is significant about the fact that the Jews have stumbled but not fallen?
✻ How could the kind of envy Paul described help lead a person to Christ?
✻ For what reasons could a Gentile be tempted to feel superior to a Jew?
■ What attitude should we have toward the fact that God has chosen to reach out to us?
✻ How could a person miss salvation by trusting in family background or heritage?

APPLY IT
■ What can you do this week to acknowledge that you depend on God's kindness?
✻ What can you do this week to share Christ with a friend who is separated from God?

Romans 11:25-32
All Israel Will Be Saved

TOPICS
Covenant, Disobedience, God, Hardheartedness, Mercy, Salvation, Sin

OPEN IT
✻ What would it take to get you to knowingly break an important promise you made?
■ How can a bad situation bring good results?

EXPLORE IT
✻ To what mystery did Paul refer? (11:25)
✻ How had Israel responded to the message Paul preached? (11:25)
■ When would Israel's period of hardening end? (11:25)
✻ What will eventually happen to Israel? (11:26)
■ What promise has God made to Israel? (11:26-27)
✻ In what two contrasting ways were the Jews described by Paul? (11:28-29)
✻ What did Paul say about God's promises? (11:29)
■ What has been the good result of the disobedience and unbelief of the Jews? (11:30)
✻ How is God responding to the unbelief of the Jews? (11:31)
✻ For what reason has God allowed all people to be disobedient? (11:32)

GET IT
✻ What makes God's plan of salvation a mystery?
■ What does this passage reveal about God's character?
✻ How will "all Israel" be saved?
■ How does our commitment to God affect His dependability and trustworthiness?
✻ When has God shown you mercy despite your disobedience?
✻ What promises of God can help us deal with the difficult circumstances of our lives?

APPLY IT
■ Which of God's promises do you need to focus on and memorize this week?
✻ What can you do this week to show God's unique love to someone who has turned away from Him?

Romans 11:33-36
Doxology

TOPICS
God, Knowledge, Praise, Wisdom, Worship

OPEN IT
✻ What was your idea of God when you were a child?
■ How has your idea of God changed as you have grown up?
✻ When are you most inclined to praise God?

EXPLORE IT
✻ How did Paul describe God's judgments? (11:33)
✻ What is beyond our understanding? (11:33)
■ How did Paul describe the mind of God? (11:33-34)
✻ What force or power is higher or wiser than God? (11:33-34)
✻ How did Paul describe God? (11:33-36)
✻ Why did Paul praise God? (11:33-36)
■ What does God owe? (11:35)
■ What is God's place in the universe? (11:36)
✻ What is from God, through God, and to God? (11:36)
✻ How did Paul summarize his doxology? (11:36)

GET IT
✻ Why do you think Paul concluded his discussion of Israel's salvation with this doxology?
✻ How do skeptics and agnostics try to explain God?
■ In what ways do we underestimate God?
✻ What limits all human explanations of God?
■ What reasons do we have to worship God?
✻ How can God's wisdom help us?
✻ How does God hold you and your life together?

APPLY IT
■ How can you worship and praise God with enthusiasm and devotion this week?
✻ What is one way you can reflect God's character to others through your personal life?

Romans 12:1-8
Living Sacrifices

TOPICS
Body, Commitment, Gifts, God's Will, Humility, Mind, Sacrifice, Self-esteem, Thinking, Worship

OPEN IT
■ What skills or qualities are necessary to play a team sport well?
✻ What influences have significantly shaped your life?

EXPLORE IT
✻ How do people properly worship God? (12:1)
✻ What is the most reasonable response to God's great mercy? (12:1-2)
■ How is the Christian to be different from unbelieving people? (12:2)
✻ How should the mind of a Christian be changed? (12:2)
✻ What must happen in order for a person to discern and agree with the will of God? (12:2)
✻ How should Christians think about themselves? (12:3)
✻ What facts should keep a person from feeling superior or inferior to other Christians? (12:3-6)
■ What did Paul use the human body to illustrate? (12:4-5)
✻ What makes Christians different from one another? (12:4-6)
✻ In what way are all Christians alike? (12:4-6)
✻ What are the gifts of God? (12:6-8)
■ How should each person use his or her gifts? (12:6-8)

GET IT
✻ What right does God have to ask us for a full-life commitment to Him?
■ What makes offering our bodies as living sacrifices an act of worship?
✻ To what worldly lifestyles or values do we typically conform?
✻ What are the patterns of the world that tempt us to conform?
✻ How can a Christian renew his or her mind?
✻ How does understanding God's love raise our self-esteem?
✻ How does understanding God's love reduce our selfishness and conceit?
✻ How do people united in Christ act toward each other?
■ How can the gifts God bestows on Christians help others in the church or community?
✻ What gifts from God do you see in others?
✻ What gifts from God do you see in your life?

APPLY IT
✻ What is one step you can take this week toward eliminating habits that merely conform to the world's pattern?
■ How can you put a spiritual gift to work for others this week?

Romans 12:9-21
Love

TOPICS
Conflict, Enemies, Forgiveness, Life, Love, Revenge

OPEN IT
✻ What might a friend do to you that you would have trouble forgiving?
■ What advice would you give to someone who wanted some practical wisdom on how to get along with others?

EXPLORE IT
✻ What should we hate? (12:9)
✻ What is genuine love like? (12:9, 13, 18-21)
✻ What attitudes should we strive to have? (12:9-16)
■ What down-to-earth advice did Paul give? (12:9-21)
■ In what ways ought we to treat others as more important than ourselves? (12:10, 13, 16, 20)
✻ What instructions does God want us to observe in our relationships? (12:10, 13-21)
✻ How is a Christian to treat enemies? (12:14, 17-21)
■ With whom does God want us to live at peace? (12:18)
✻ Why should we not take revenge? (12:19)
✻ What is the purpose of showing kindness to an enemy? (12:20)

GET IT
✻ What can we do to learn to hate evil?
✻ How can one hate evil yet not hate the evildoer?
■ How can a Christian learn to love others as God loves them?
✻ In what ways is Christian love more than emotion?
✻ What does it mean to honor one another?
✻ Why should we be joyful when we are suffering?
✻ Why is it wrong to repay evil with evil?
■ How does doing good to an enemy overcome evil?

APPLY IT
■ In what ways can you honor someone above yourself? Who?
✻ Whom do you need to love and bless this week even though he or she hurts you?

Romans 13:1-7
Submission to the Authorities

TOPICS
Authority, God's Will, Government, Law, Submission

OPEN IT
✻ What irritates you most about our government?
■ How do you feel when you have to prepare your income tax forms?

EXPLORE IT
✻ How is the establishment of any government related to God? (13:1)
✻ How is a Christian to respond to the laws and leadership of government? (13:1-7)
■ What attitude is a Christian showing toward God when he or she rebels against the government? (13:2)

❊ What consequences will those who rebel against the government bring upon themselves? (13:2)
■ What should a Christian do to maintain a good relationship with the government? (13:3-4)
❊ For what reason are government officials in power? (13:4)
❊ What motivation does the Christian have to submit to the government? (13:5)
❊ What are governmental authorities? (13:6)
■ How should a Christian respond to the tax laws and requirements of the government? (13:6-7)
❊ In addition to tax revenues, what does a Christian owe to his or her government? (13:7)

GET IT
❊ How would God want us to act if government leaders were openly persecuting Christians?
❊ How do evil, cruel rulers serve God's plan and do good for God's people?
■ Under what circumstances should Christians disobey the clear commands of government authorities?
■ What is the Christian's responsibility for maintaining a good government?
❊ What positive support should Christians give to government leaders?

APPLY IT
❊ To which government official could you write or talk to this week and express your concerns?
■ How and when could you set aside time to pray for national, state, and local public officials?

Romans 13:8-14
Love, for the Day Is Near

TOPICS
Holiness, Last Days, Law, Love, Purity, Sin

OPEN IT
■ What sort of actions communicate love to you?
❊ What are some of the evil activities tolerated and even promoted by our society?

EXPLORE IT
■ In what area of life is a Christian to maintain a continuing debt? (13:8)
❊ What is the sign that a Christian has fulfilled the Law? (13:8)
■ What one command sums up all the other commands? (13:9)
❊ What act and attitude is the fulfillment of the Law? (13:10)
❊ What "hour" had arrived for the Roman Christians? (13:11)
❊ How did Paul encourage his audience to live godly lives? (13:11-12)
❊ What specific behaviors does God forbid? (13:12-13)
❊ What kind of behavior contrasts with what God wants of us? (13:13)
❊ With what are Christians to clothe themselves? (13:14)
■ What should a Christian be thinking about each day? (13:14)

GET IT
■ What does it mean that love is the fulfillment of the Law?
❊ What specific acts of love can Christians show to friends, family, neighbors, and strangers?
❊ What are the signs that the present age is nearly over?
❊ How would you live if you knew the world would end in six months?
❊ What deeds of darkness practiced in our world today sometimes attract and seduce Christians?
❊ In what practical ways can a person clothe him or herself with Jesus Christ instead of pursuing evil desires?
■ What personal relationship do you want to improve by earnestly loving that person as yourself?

APPLY IT
■ What specific gesture of love or kindness can you use to build a relationship this week?
❊ When can you take time this week to identify habits or tendencies in your life that hinder your relationship with the Lord?

Romans 14:1–15:13
The Weak and the Strong

TOPICS
Acceptance, Freedom, Help, Love, Sin, Unity

OPEN IT
❊ What do you do when a homeless person asks you for money?
■ When have you refused to eat something that was put before you?

EXPLORE IT
❊ How should a fellow believer who is weak in the faith be treated? (14:1)
■ What reasons did Paul give for not judging people on disputable matters? (14:1-12)
❊ What issues did Paul believe were not worth fighting over? (13:2, 5)
■ What should be the primary motivation for a person's decision to eat meat or celebrate a sacred day? (13:6-8)
❊ What will each person do when standing before God's judgment seat? (14:12)
❊ What should we do instead of judging fellow Christians? (14:13)
❊ What was Paul's personal belief about unclean foods? (14:14)
❊ What consideration should a Christian give to the opinions of fellow believers on controversial matters? (14:14-15)
❊ When should a Christian defer to another Christian's beliefs? (14:15-16)
❊ What is the true focus of the kingdom of God? (14:17-18)
■ What is a Christian's responsibility for building peace among the other believers? (14:19-21)
❊ How should concern for other believers affect our personal choices? (14:21)
❊ What is the responsibility of a strong Christian toward others? (15:1-2)

❊ What is the purpose of Scripture? (15:4)
❊ What does God want to give each believer to guide his or her Christian life? (15:5-6)
❊ By what standards should a person accept others? (15:7)
❊ For what reason was Jesus sent to the Jews? (15:8-12)
❊ With what does God want to fill us? (15:13)

GET IT
■ What lifestyle rules and issues do Christians argue about today?
❊ What responsibility do you have to be a good example for others?
❊ What practice would you be willing to give up if it proved to be a bad influence on others?
■ When Scripture is not explicit on an issue, how should a person decide what is right and wrong?
❊ What are some areas of life that we should examine carefully for practices that cause others to sin?
❊ How can Christians share a spirit of unity despite having different views on certain practices?
❊ How would you distinguish between an activity that is merely permissible and one that is clearly immoral?
❊ How can a strong Christian use his or her strength to help other Christians?

APPLY IT
❊ What area of your life can you review this week for practices that may cause difficulty for Christian friends or associates?
■ What can you do this week to spread peace and mutual edification among Christians?

Romans 15:14-22
Paul, the Minister to the Gentiles

TOPICS
Ambition, Evangelism, Humility, Mission, Pride, Serving, Witnessing

OPEN IT
❊ What foreign culture interests you most? Why?
■ What factors influence a person's calling or vocation in life?

EXPLORE IT
❊ How did Paul describe the Christians at Rome? (15:14)
❊ How did Paul understand his own mission? (15:14-16)
■ Why did Paul preach to the Gentiles? (15:16)
❊ What was Paul's "priestly duty"? (15:16)
❊ What was the focus of Paul's life? (15:17-18)
■ What was the only thing that Paul was willing to speak of? (15:18-19)
❊ To what did Paul credit his success in evangelism? (15:18-19)
■ What was Paul's ambition? (15:20)
❊ Why did Paul preach the gospel where Christ was not known? (15:20)
❊ What had hindered Paul from coming to see the people in the church at Rome? (15:22)

GET IT
❊ What various tasks does God give to people like us to serve Him?
■ What has God given you to use in serving Him?
❊ For what do you want to be known?
❊ When is being proud of your work for God a sin?
■ How can you tell if your work for God is motivated by selfish pride or selfless devotion to God?
❊ What groups of people have not heard the gospel message?
❊ What sections of your community have not had enough opportunities to hear the gospel message?

APPLY IT
■ At this point in your life, what could you do to determine whether your vocation is in line with God's desires for your life?
❊ How can God best use you as a witness, both this week and in the future?

Romans 15:23-33
Paul's Plan to Visit Rome

TOPICS
Ambition, Generosity, Gifts, Help, Mission, Plans, Serving

OPEN IT
❊ How do you react when your travel plans are delayed or canceled?
■ If a friend had $10,000 to donate to charity and asked you for advice, what worthy causes would you recommend?

EXPLORE IT
❊ Where was Paul planning to travel? (15:23-24) Why?
❊ Why was Paul planning to visit Rome? (15:23-25)
■ How did Paul want the Roman Christians to help him? (15:24, 30-32)
❊ What was Paul's immediate destination? (15:25)
■ What was Paul taking to Jerusalem? (15:26)
❊ What had the Jews done for the Gentiles? (15:27)
■ How did Paul explain why Gentiles should give financial assistance to Jews in Jerusalem? (15:27)
❊ What would Paul bring with him when he visited Rome? (15:29)
❊ For what did Paul ask the people to pray? (15:30-32)
❊ With what benediction did Paul close his request? (15:33)

GET IT
❊ What is your greatest ambition?
❊ How does your greatest ambition compare with Paul's?
❊ How can our plans to serve God be hindered?
❊ How should we react when our plans to serve God are hindered?
■ How can we help fellow believers and missionaries?
❊ What benefits are realized by helping a missionary?
■ How should we show sensitivity when giving someone a gift?

APPLY IT
■ What sacrifice can you make this week to help another believer who is struggling with a burden?

❋ How could you help and show appreciation to the person who helped you come to faith in Christ?

Romans 16:1-27
Personal Greetings

TOPICS
Appreciation, Friendship, God, Praise, Serving

OPEN IT
■ What do you do to thank people who help you with a project?
❋ How valuable is a letter of thanks and appreciation?

EXPLORE IT
❋ What did Paul ask the Roman church to do for Phoebe? (16:1-2)
■ Why did Paul praise Priscilla and Aquila? (16:3-4)
❋ What risks did Priscilla and Aquila take? (16:3-4)
❋ What special distinction did Epenetus hold? (16:5)
❋ For what did Paul commend Mary? (16:6)
❋ What experiences did Andronicus and Junias share with Paul? (16:7)
❋ What qualities did Paul recognize in Apelles? (16:10)
❋ Why did Paul praise Tryphena, Tryphosa, and Persis? (16:12)
❋ What greeting did Paul suggest the church share? (16:16)
❋ What kinds of divisions should the church not allow? (16:17)
❋ How should the church deal with a person who causes divisions? (16:17)
❋ What should we do about people who cause division among Christians? (16:17-18)
■ What encouragement did Paul give the people in their struggle with evil in the world? (16:19-20)
❋ Who actually wrote down this letter for Paul? (16:22)
❋ With whom had Paul been living? (16:23)
■ What did Paul say about God? (16:25-27)
❋ What did Paul say about the gospel? (16:25-27)

GET IT
■ What is a meaningful compliment a Christian could give to another believer?
❋ For what would you like to be remembered?
❋ What opportunities does a Christian have to serve?
■ In what areas of life should Christians take risks for God, as Priscilla and Aquila did?
❋ What does our level of generosity reveal about our understanding of God?
❋ What causes division in churches and between Christians today?
❋ How can we avoid dividing churches unnecessarily?
❋ How does focusing on the greatness of God increase our ambition to serve Him?

APPLY IT
❋ In what specific ways could you be generous to other Christians in need?
■ To what fellow workers in the Lord's service do you want to express your appreciation? How?

1 Corinthians 1:1-9
Thanksgiving

TOPICS
Endurance, Faithfulness, Fellowship, Grace, Growth, Holiness, Spiritual Gifts, Thankfulness, Waiting

OPEN IT
❋ What are you most thankful for today?
■ When was a time you were especially thankful for someone else? Why?

EXPLORE IT
❋ How did Paul describe himself? (1:1)
❋ What themes did Paul repeat several times? (1:1-9)
❋ What specific truths did Paul affirm? (1:1-9)
❋ What kind of people were the Corinthian Christians? (1:2)
❋ What words of affirmation did Paul have for his readers? (1:2-3)
■ For what traits of the Corinthians did Paul thank God? (1:4-9)
❋ In what ways had the Corinthian Christians been "enriched"? Why? (1:5-6)
■ What did the Corinthian Christians have? (1:7)
❋ What spiritual gifts did the Corinthians have? (1:7)
❋ Why did the Corinthians not lack for any spiritual gift? (1:7)
❋ For what period of time were the Corinthians' spiritual gifts given? (1:7)
❋ For what were the Corinthians waiting? (1:7)
❋ How would the Corinthians be able to live as God called them? (1:8-9)
❋ What words of encouragement did Paul include in his opening? (1:8-9)
❋ How are Christians able to live as God has called them? (1:8-9)
■ To what has God called all Christians? (1:9)

GET IT
❋ For what can you thank God?
❋ For what should we thank God?
❋ Who is someone for whose faith you are thankful?
❋ What does it mean that God has given us grace?
❋ How is a person enriched by trusting in Christ?
❋ What spiritual gifts has God given you?
❋ How can your gifts be used in service to Jesus as we wait for His return?
❋ In what ways does God keep a believer strong to the end?
❋ What does it mean that God is faithful?
■ In what ways is God faithful to you?
■ How can we say thank you to God for His faithfulness?
❋ For what specific reasons do you want to thank God?

APPLY IT
❋ How can you use your spiritual gift at least once this next week?
❋ What Christian do you want to affirm?
❋ In what part of your daily routine this week can you take time out to thank God?
■ How can you remind yourself to say thank you to God at least once each day this week?

1 Corinthians 1:10-17
Divisions in the Church

TOPICS
Arguments, Church, Disagreements, Divisions, Follow, Gospel, Power, Quarrels, Unity

OPEN IT
❊ Over what matters do families often argue?
❊ When was a time you hurt someone because you were forced to take sides?
■ When was a time you helped two people settle a dispute?

EXPLORE IT
❊ On what basis did Paul appeal to the Corinthian believers? (1:10)
■ Why did Paul ask the Corinthians to agree with one another? (1:10)
❊ What kind of action did the Corinthian church need to take? (1:10-17)
■ What specific problem were the Corinthian Christians having? (1:11-12)
❊ How was Paul a part of the Corinthians' problems? (1:13-17)
❊ How did baptism cause division in the Corinthian church? (1:13-17)
❊ What can result from preaching the gospel with "words of human wisdom"? (1:17)
❊ What did Christ enable Paul to do? (1:17)
❊ What danger is there in dividing a church? (1:17)
■ What danger was Paul trying to avoid? (1:17)
❊ What's wrong with preaching the gospel with "words of human wisdom"? (1:17)

GET IT
❊ How did Paul show his concern for the Corinthians?
❊ What difference does local church unity make?
❊ What does it mean for Christians to be "perfectly united in mind and thought"?
❊ Why is it important for Christians to be united?
❊ How should we respond to arguments among Christians today?
❊ What church divisions have you known or heard about?
❊ What has been the outcome in church splits of which you are aware?
❊ How can division among Christians empty Christ's message of its power?
❊ What witness does a unified church give to a lost world?
❊ What social and cultural forces present the greatest threat to the unity of Christ's church today?
■ How can Christians avoid becoming distracted by petty disagreements?
■ What can your church do to build unity and guard against division?
❊ What practices can help us be more united with other Christians?

APPLY IT
■ What is the first step you could take to heal a damaged relationship with another Christian?
❊ How could you help your church leaders build the unity of your congregation?

1 Corinthians 1:18–2:5
Christ the Wisdom and Power of God

TOPICS
Call, Fear, Foolishness, God, God's Will, Gospel, Greatness, Holy Spirit, Ignorance, Knowledge, Learning, Power, Strength, Weaknesses, Wisdom, World

OPEN IT
■ In what way might your life-style seem foolish to some of your friends or relatives?
❊ In what ways did you depend on your parents' wisdom when you were a child?

EXPLORE IT
❊ To whom is the message of the Cross foolishness? (1:18)
❊ To whom is the message of the Cross powerful? (1:18)
❊ How can people hear the message of Christ differently? (1:18)
❊ What does God's message mean to the person being saved? (1:18)
❊ How does the message of the Cross contrast with what most people consider wise? (1:18-19)
❊ How does God get His message across? (1:19-31)
■ How does God's wisdom contrast with the world's wisdom? (1:20)
❊ How did the demands of the Jews and Greeks contrast with the Corinthians' hope? (1:22-23)
❊ How do God's attributes compare with ours? (1:25-26)
❊ What were the Corinthians like before they were called? (1:26-27)
❊ How does God use the foolish and weak things of the world? (1:27)
■ Why does God express His power and wisdom through "foolish," "weak," and "lowly" means? (1:28-29)
❊ What has Jesus Christ become for us? (1:30)
❊ What kind of boasting is good? (1:31)
■ How did Paul's regard for the world's wisdom affect his preaching and testimony? (2:1-5)
❊ Why was it good that Paul came to Corinth in weakness and fear? (2:3-5)
❊ On what should our faith rest? (2:5)

GET IT
❊ Why do Christians and nonChristians value the message of Christ so differently?
■ What are some examples of the world's wisdom?
❊ What common difficulties do people mention when trying to understand the gospel of Christ?
❊ What are some doctrines of the Christian faith that are difficult for nonChristians to understand?
❊ When have you heard nonChristians balk at the message of Christ?
❊ How has God made foolish the wisdom of the world?
❊ In what ways do God's commands seem like foolishness to the nonChristians you know?
❊ What difference should it make in your life to know that God chooses the weak and lowly people of the world to do His work?
■ What unbelievers have you known who wanted miraculous signs or airtight philosophical proofs before believing in Christ?

❇ Why do you think people demand signs, or proof, of God?
❇ What's wrong with demanding signs, or proof, from God?
❇ How can you share the truth of the gospel with people who demand signs, or proof, of God?
❇ How is it encouraging to know that Paul was weak and fearful?
❇ What does it mean to preach with a "demonstration of the Spirit's power"?
❇ How can we make sure that our faith rests on God's power and not our own wisdom?
❇ Whom could you encourage with the knowledge that God's weakness is stronger than our strength?
❇ What kinds of wisdom do you depend on that could be changed by the light of God's Word?

APPLY IT
❇ To what area of your life now could you apply God's "foolishness"? How?
❇ From whom can you learn more of God's wisdom? How and when?
■ How could you seek out God's wisdom and power this week? Where?
❇ What can you do this week to witness for Christ in only God's wisdom and not your own craftiness?

1 Corinthians 2:6-16
Wisdom From the Spirit

TOPICS
Discernment, Foolishness, Holy Spirit, Ignorance, Judgment, Mind, Spiritual Growth, Thinking, Wisdom

OPEN IT
❇ To what sources do people most often look for wisdom?
❇ What is it like to know a secret and keep it from your friends?
❇ For what reasons do we keep secrets from other people?
■ In what ways could you learn about a secret that was hidden from you?

EXPLORE IT
❇ What kinds of wisdom are there? (2:6)
❇ In what way does the world's wisdom fall short? (2:6)
❇ Where does the world's wisdom lead? (2:6)
■ How does God's wisdom differ from the wisdom of this age? (2:6-16)
■ What is God's secret wisdom that only the mature will attain? (2:7)
❇ How was Jesus' crucifixion related to the world's lack of understanding God's wisdom? (2:8)
❇ Why do people often fail to see God's purpose for them? (2:9)
❇ Why is it possible to understand God's wisdom only if His Spirit reveals it? (2:9-16)
■ What characteristics will the wisdom that the Spirit teaches us have? (2:13)
❇ How are spiritual and unspiritual people different? (2:15-16)
❇ Who can make "judgments about all things"? Why? (2:15-16)

GET IT
❇ In what way are the "rulers of this age" coming to nothing?
■ When in the past has the Spirit enabled you to understand God's wisdom and gifts?
❇ Why did God keep His wisdom a secret?
❇ In what ways should your actions conform to the teaching of the Spirit who lives in you?
❇ How should you respond to the Spirit's revelation about what God has prepared for you?
■ What does it mean to have the mind of Christ?
❇ How can you know if you have the mind of Christ?
❇ What benefit is there in praying for spiritual discernment?

APPLY IT
■ What spiritual disciplines (prayer, Bible study, meditation on Scripture, etc.) could you practice this week to make you sensitive to the Holy Spirit?
❇ How might you approach a person you know who believes strongly in the wisdom of the world?

1 Corinthians 3:1-23
On Divisions in the Church

TOPICS
Church, Divisions, Foundation, Growth, Holy Spirit, Quarrels, Testing, Wisdom, World

OPEN IT
❇ How have you changed since you were a child?
❇ Why is laying a strong foundation important in building a house?
■ What foundational truths did you learn in school?

EXPLORE IT
❇ Why did Paul call the Corinthians "mere infants"? (3:1-3)
❇ What were the Corinthians like? (3:3-5)
❇ What traits did the Corinthians have that made them worldly? (3:3-5)
❇ How did Paul want his readers to view both Apollos and himself? Why? (3:5-7)
❇ What is each Christian worker's purpose in ministering to others? (3:8)
❇ How is the person who plants like the person who waters? (3:8-9)
❇ Who were the "fellow workers" who worked together on the Corinthian "field" or "building"? (3:9)
■ What made Paul and Apollos equals under God? (3:9)
❇ What is the foundation of the church? (3:11)
■ What is like either gold, silver, costly stones, wood, hay, or straw? How? (3:12-14)
■ What happens to the person who builds in others' lives? (3:13-15)
❇ What important fact had the Corinthians failed to appreciate? (3:16)
❇ Why should we abandon the world's idea of wisdom? (3:19)
❇ Why were the Corinthians to stop boasting about the individual leaders they followed? (3:21-23)

GET IT
❇ What is our role in God's work?

❇ What does it mean to plant and water God's Word in others?
❇ How do we plant and water God's Word in others?
❇ What is your particular role in God's work?
❇ In what ways are you able to plant and water God's Word in others?
❇ What opportunities do you have to plant and water God's Word in others?
❇ How is Christian teaching and discipleship like building a building?
■ How can a person's efforts in teaching or discipleship be like gold, silver, costly stones, wood, hay, or straw?
❇ In what ways can Christians be influenced by the wisdom of the world?
❇ What does it mean that a Christian is God's temple?
❇ How should our attitudes and actions be influenced by the fact that we are the temple of the Holy Spirit?
❇ What are some implications of the fact that God's Spirit lives in every Christian?
❇ How could a person destroy God's temple?
❇ How are Christians who are involved in discipleship similar to builders?
■ In what ways should all Christians point others to Christ alone?
❇ What responsibility do Christians not involved in formal leadership have for building up God's church?
❇ What can you do to help build up the church in some way?

APPLY IT
■ What is one way you can point another person to Christ this week?
❇ In whose life do you want to build God's Word? How can you start?
❇ What need could you meet in your church over the next month to build up other Christians?

1 Corinthians 4:1-21
Apostles of Christ

TOPICS
Conscience, Discipline, Example, Faithfulness, Judgment, Kingdom of God/Heaven, Motives, Persecution, Pride

OPEN IT
■ What kinds of things do people usually brag about?
❇ Why would a person boast about a gift he or she had received?
❇ Who is someone you look up to and try to be like? In what way?

EXPLORE IT
■ How did Paul want the Corinthians to regard Christian leaders? (4:1)
❇ What does this passage teach about the life of an apostle? (4:1-5, 8-16)
■ What attitudes should Christian leaders have? (4:2-4)
❇ Whom did Paul take pains to avoid judging? Why? (4:3-5)
❇ Why should we judge "nothing before the appointed time"? (4:5)
❇ How were the Corinthians going beyond the teaching of Scripture in their behavior and attitudes? (4:6)
■ Why did Paul warn the Corinthians about pride?(4:7-13)
❇ In what way had Paul become a father to the Corinthians? (4:15)
❇ Why did Paul send Timothy to the Corinthians? (4:17)
❇ How is the kingdom of God a "matter of power"? (4:20)

GET IT
❇ How does God want Christians to treat church leaders?
❇ What qualities should Christian leaders have?
❇ What did Paul mean when he said that he did not even judge himself?
❇ Why should we not judge our own service to God or even that of other people?
❇ How can we be faithful to the trust that God has given us?
❇ How closely do you think our lives should conform to Paul's own experience?
❇ How should we respond to Paul's instruction to imitate him?
■ What exemplary qualities about Paul should we imitate? How?
❇ What about Paul's character do you want to copy?
❇ What more mature Christian do you want to be like? How?
■ What problems do Christians create when they divide into factions and elevate some leaders over others?
❇ How can a church's unity be threatened by personal disputes?
❇ How can you allow the power of the kingdom to be more active in your life?

APPLY IT
■ What is one way you could imitate the example or wisdom of a more mature Christian you know?
❇ How can you remember to avoid a judgmental spirit toward others this week?

1 Corinthians 5:1-13
Expel the Immoral Brother!

TOPICS
Church, Discipline, Greed, Idolatry, Immorality, Judgment, Pride, Sacrifice, Salvation, Sin

OPEN IT
■ For what kinds of things were you disciplined as a child?
❇ When was a time you had to stop associating with a friend because of his or her bad influence on you?

EXPLORE IT
■ Why did the Corinthians tolerate immorality in their church? (5:2)
❇ What disciplinary action should the Corinthians have taken? (5:2)
❇ Under what conditions was the Corinthian church to expel their immoral member? Why? (5:4-5)
■ Why was it necessary for the Corinthian church to expel a man from their congregation? (5:5-6)
❇ To what boasting did Paul refer? (5:6)
❇ What should Christians be like? How? (5:7)
❇ Why was it necessary to expel an immoral Christian from his or her church? (5:7-13)

✻ To what festival did Paul refer? Why? (5:7-8)
✻ How should we "keep the Festival"? (5:8)
✻ What kind of distinction do we need to make in dealing with immoral people? (5:9-13)
✻ For what reasons were the Corinthians to expel a professing Christian? (5:11)
■ Why is it unnecessary for Christians to judge non-Christians? (5:12-13)

GET IT
✻ At what point would you stop associating with a person who continued to do wrong?
✻ From what harm could a church protect itself by expelling an immoral member?
✻ What are the pain and problems created by sexual immorality?
■ How should any church react to gross sin practiced by a stubborn member?
✻ What is difficult and complicated about disciplining a sinning Christian?
✻ To what extent should people cleanse their lives of sin before joining a church? Why?
✻ What does it mean to "hand someone over to Satan"?
✻ How should we treat Christians who are greedy, slanderers, or swindlers?
■ What warnings should careless Christians take to heart?
✻ How can we expel immoral Christians from our churches and at the same time have Jesus' love for sinners?

APPLY IT
✻ What should you do the next time you learn of a Christian friend who is unwilling to turn away from a particular sin?
■ What habits can you cultivate to prevent yourself from becoming callous to the sins of other people?

1 Corinthians 6:1-11
Lawsuits Among Believers

TOPICS
Angels, Believers, Disagreements, Immorality, Judgment, Kingdom of God/Heaven, Sin, Unbelievers

OPEN IT
✻ For what reasons do people take each other to court?
■ How does a court of law solve and not solve problems between people?
✻ What do you think is the best way to settle disputes between strangers?

EXPLORE IT
■ Why was Paul disturbed by the practice of Christians bringing their disputes before nonChristians? (6:1-6)
✻ Who will judge the world? (6:2)
✻ By what authority will Christians judge angels? (6:3)
■ Who is qualified to serve as a judge for disputes among Christians? (6:4)
■ What did the Corinthians need to do when they were wronged by other Christians? (6:7)
✻ How were the Corinthian Christians settling disputes with each other? (6:7-8)
✻ What did the fact that the Corinthians were suing each other prove about them? (6:7-10)
✻ How were the Corinthians deceived in their beliefs? (6:9)
✻ Who will not inherit the kingdom of God? (6:9-10)
✻ What were some of the Corinthians before they were saved? (6:11)
✻ What had changed the Corinthians' standing before God? (6:11)

GET IT
■ What should we do whenever we are wronged by other Christians?
✻ How do people in your church settle disputes?
✻ What could you do differently when settling disputes to better reflect God's priorities?
✻ Why is it better to be wronged than to take a fellow Christian to court?
✻ What would God say to Christians today who sue one another?
■ What should you do if you feel you have been wronged by another Christian?
✻ What should a Christian do if the person he or she accuses is unwilling to submit to the judgment of other believers?
✻ What does it mean that God sanctifies His people?
✻ What does it mean that God justifies His people?
✻ What difference does it make that we have been sanctified and justified by the Spirit of God?
✻ How should the knowledge of Jesus' redemptive work motivate you to abandon sin in your life?

APPLY IT
■ What do you want to remember the next time you are wronged by another Christian?
✻ What particular action or attitude can help you forgive others when you are wronged?

1 Corinthians 6:12-20
Sexual Immorality

TOPICS
Adultery, Body, Desires, Holy Spirit, Immorality, Lust, Marriage, Maturity, Morality, Sex, Sin, Singleness, Slavery, Temptation, Weaknesses

OPEN IT
✻ In what ways do Americans typically mistreat their bodies?
■ In your opinion, what are the biggest challenges to sexual purity in our society?

EXPLORE IT
✻ What did Paul mean by saying, "I will not be mastered by anything"? (6:12)
✻ Why should we abstain from sex outside of marriage? (6:12-20)
✻ What value does God place on our bodies? (6:12-20)
✻ What will God destroy? Why? (6:13)
■ For what are our bodies meant? (6:13)
✻ What promise is given to Christians because God raised Jesus from the dead? (6:14)
✻ What makes our bodies special? (6:15)
✻ What's wrong with sex outside of marriage? (6:15-16)
✻ Why is it not possible to be one with both Christ and a prostitute? (6:15-17)

■ What does it mean to be one with Christ in spirit? (6:17)
■ How is sexual immorality different from other sins? (6:18)
❊ How are Christians' bodies unique? (6:19-20)

GET IT
❊ How can we distinguish between what is merely permissible and what is beneficial?
❊ How should we treat our bodies if they are actually temples of the Holy Spirit?
❊ How do advertising and other media encourage wrong attitudes about our bodies?
❊ How do friends, coworkers, and other peers encourage wrong attitudes about our bodies?
❊ How does sexually uniting with someone outside of marriage affect a person?
■ In what specific ways is it possible for you to honor God with your body?
❊ What can a person do to master natural human desires that can lead to sin?
■ What can you do to master areas of your life that could cause you to sin against your body?
❊ How can we avoid compromises that lead to sexual sin?

APPLY IT
■ In what way can you remind yourself this week that you were bought at a price and are God's temple?
❊ In what settings or situations should you take precautions against sexual immorality? How?

1 Corinthians 7:1-40
Marriage

TOPICS
Body, Freedom, Immorality, Marriage, Ministry, Morality, Prayer, Sex, Sin, Singleness, Slavery, Temptation, Unbelievers

OPEN IT
■ What couple have you met recently that displays the ingredients of a good marriage?
❊ What to you is good and bad about remaining single?

EXPLORE IT
❊ What guiding principles about marriage does God want us to know? (7:1-40)
❊ Why should "each man . . . have his own wife"? (7:2)
❊ What obligations does a Christian wife have toward her husband? (7:3)
❊ To whom does a Christian's body belong if he or she is married? (7:4)
❊ Under what circumstances may married partners deprive each other's sexual needs? (7:5)
❊ Why is it important for husbands and wives not to deprive each other's sexual needs? (7:5)
❊ What instruction did Paul give to the unmarried and widowed? (7:8-9)
■ To what has God called us? (7:15)
■ What is more important than whether a person is married or single? (7:17-19)
❊ What is more important than whether a person is a slave or free? (7:20-24)
❊ What is one advantage in remaining single? (7:28)
❊ Why did Paul think it best to remain single? (7:28)
■ What perspective can help us serve God well whether married or single? (7:29-31)
❊ What advantage do unmarried people have in ministry? (7:32-35)

GET IT
■ In what sense is it good not to marry?
❊ In what ways might singleness keep us free from concern?
❊ What are the advantages of being married?
■ What opportunities do married people have that single people do not?
❊ What unique concerns do married people have that single people do not?
❊ What part of God's instruction on marriage do you find encouraging?
❊ What circumstance in your life would benefit from God's perspective on marriage and singleness?
❊ How should the fact that the time is short affect our priorities and actions?
❊ What does it mean to live as if not engrossed in the things of the world?
❊ What does it look like when a married person is engrossed in the things of the world?
❊ What does it look like when a single person is engrossed in the things of the world?
❊ How should our lifestyle be detached from the concerns of the world?

APPLY IT
❊ What is one step you can take this week to free yourself from concern about a mortgage, a job, a project, or some other earthly matter?
■ How can you use your unique experiences as a married or single person in service to God?

1 Corinthians 8:1-13
Food Sacrificed to Idols

TOPICS
Believers, Example, Freedom, Idolatry, Knowledge, Love, Sin, Temptation, Unity

OPEN IT
■ When have you refused to participate in an event that everyone else seemed to be enjoying?
❊ When have you experienced conflicts with people who wanted to do something you considered bad or improper (such as social drinking or gambling)?

EXPLORE IT
❊ What was troubling the Corinthians? (8:1)
❊ What's the problem with knowledge? (8:1-2)
❊ What mistaken assumption does a person who thinks he knows something make? (8:2)
❊ Why is it more important to be known by God than to know about God? (8:2-3)
■ How did Paul counsel the Corinthians to regard food sacrificed to idols? (8:4-13)

✻ What importance does God attach to idols? (8:5-6)
✻ Why were the Corinthian Christians continuing to struggle over the matter of idols? (8:7-8)
■ How could the exercise of a believer's freedom hurt a weaker Christian? (8:9)
■ What overriding principle should govern our freedom? (8:9-13)
✻ How can a Christian destroy someone? (8:11)
✻ How did Paul limit his freedom out of sensitivity to the weaker Christians of his day? (8:13)

GET IT
✻ In what way can knowledge puff up a person?
✻ How can we build up others in a loving way?
✻ How can a person be sure of the fact that he or she is known by God?
■ What are some customs in our society that weaker Christians often need to avoid?
■ How should we limit our freedom out of sensitivity to weaker Christians?
✻ What should you do if you know your actions would cause another Christian to violate his or her conscience?
✻ How can we make our behavior accountable to other Christians?
✻ What specific things could you do to protect a new Christian's faith in God?

APPLY IT
■ What is one attitude or action in your life that you need to limit at this point? How?
✻ What nurture could you give to a new Christian this week to help him or her grow stronger in the faith?

1 Corinthians 9:1-27
The Rights of an Apostle

TOPICS
Believers, Discipline, Example, Judgment, Law, Perseverance, Rewards, Right, Sacrifice, Salvation, Serving

OPEN IT
■ What training is necessary for a person in your chosen profession?
✻ What emotions do athletes usually feel on the day of a big event?
✻ How can you be disqualified from a game or race?

EXPLORE IT
✻ What proofs did Paul use to show that he was a genuine apostle? (9:1-2)
■ What rights did Paul waive to be an apostle? (9:3-6, 12)
✻ What case could Paul make for asserting his rights as an apostle? (9:7-11, 13-14)
✻ What are the rights of those who preach the gospel? (9:12)
✻ Why was Paul willing to set aside his rights? (9:12)
✻ Why didn't Paul take full advantage of his rights? (9:12-18)
✻ What has the Lord commanded for those who preach the gospel? (9:14)
✻ How did Paul preach? Why? (9:16-17)
✻ What motivated Paul to preach as he did? (9:16-17)
■ What reward is there in preaching the gospel? (9:18)
✻ Why did Paul make himself a slave to everyone? (9:19)
✻ To what extent did Paul go to save people? (9:20-23)
■ Why is it necessary to live with purpose and discipline? (9:25-27)
✻ Why did Paul lead a disciplined life? (9:27)

GET IT
■ What are some of your rights and freedoms as a Christian?
■ Under what circumstances should we take advantage of our rights, and when should we willingly waive them?
✻ How can we show our love to unbelievers while refusing to participate in activity that is sinful?
✻ Why is it helpful to adjust our actions for the people around us?
✻ How does insisting on our rights hinder the gospel of Christ?
✻ What right have you given up because it may have caused others to stumble?
✻ What actions could disqualify a person from being rewarded by God for serving Him?
✻ What should you do to be assured of finishing your life well?
✻ How can neglecting spiritual disciplines (such as prayer, Bible study, and worship) disqualify a Christian from having an influence on unbelievers?

APPLY IT
■ What specific rights could you waive for Christ's sake? How?
✻ When can you make time for prayer, Bible study, and worship this week to help you train for telling others about Christ?

1 Corinthians 10:1-13
Warnings From Israel's History

TOPICS
Complaining, Example, Faithfulness, History, Idolatry, Ignorance, Immorality, Temptation, Testing

OPEN IT
■ What lessons can we learn from history?
✻ What is one event in your own extended family history that has influenced your life?

EXPLORE IT
✻ Why did Paul refer to Israel's history? (10:1)
■ How do the Israelites serve as examples to us? (10:1-6)
✻ How were the ancient Israelites baptized? (10:2)
✻ What was the Israelites' spiritual food and drink? (10:3)
✻ Who was the "rock" that accompanied the Israelites in the wilderness? (10:4)
✻ How was the Israelites' rock in the wilderness significant? (10:4)
✻ How did God feel about the Israelites in the wilderness? (10:5)
✻ Why did God record the experiences of the Israelites? (10:6, 11)

■ What evil actions cost many of the Israelites their lives? (10:7-10)
■ Why should we care what happened to the ancient Israelites? (10:11)
❊ What warning did Paul give the Corinthians? Why? (10:12)
❊ Why is it important that all the temptations Christians face are common to everyone? (10:13)
❊ How is God faithful? (10:13)
❊ How does God help us when we are tempted? (10:13)

GET IT
❊ What have you learned about God from this history of Israel?
❊ What have you learned about yourself from this history of Israel?
❊ What does it mean that the Israelites were "baptized into Moses"?
❊ What warning should we recall when tempted to participate in idolatry, sexual immorality, testing the Lord, or grumbling?
❊ When have you avoided doing something wrong because you recalled God's commands?
■ How does God help us escape temptation?
❊ What difference should it make in your daily life that God will not let you be tempted beyond what you can bear?
■ How can a person escape when faced with temptation?

APPLY IT
❊ What escape route has God provided for a specific temptation you face?
■ What promise or warning do you want to remember to help you stand up under temptation this week?

1 Corinthians 10:14-22
Idol Feasts and the Lord's Supper

TOPICS
Demons, History, Idolatry, Jealousy, Lord's Supper, Sacrifice, Thankfulness, Unity

OPEN IT
■ What kind of meals hold special significance for you? Why?
❊ What does the Lord's Supper mean to you?

EXPLORE IT
■ What importance did Paul assign to Communion? (10:14-17)
❊ What is the cup of thanksgiving? (10:16)
■ How can a Christian participate in the body of Christ? (10:16)
❊ How can a diverse group of Christians remain unified? (10:17)
❊ Why did Paul refer to Israel's history? (10:18)
❊ What did Paul mean when he wrote, "Those who eat the sacrifices participate in the altar"? (10:18-22)
❊ What was Paul's purpose in discussing idol feasts? (10:18-22)
❊ What should the Corinthians have known about sacrifices made to idols? (10:19-20)
■ Why should we work hard to celebrate the Lord's Supper only out of devotion to Christ? (10:20-21)
❊ How can a Christian provoke the Lord to jealousy? (10:22)

GET IT
❊ What are today's idols?
❊ What besides God do people worship today?
❊ What kinds of activities today are like the pagan temple parties in Corinth?
❊ How do these words affect your attitude toward the Lord's Supper?
❊ What can we learn here about the Lord's Supper?
■ Why is the Lord's Supper important?
■ How can you renew your reverence for the Lord when you celebrate Communion?
❊ What kinds of behavior provoke the Lord to jealousy?
❊ Why is it important to know that the Lord is a jealous God?

APPLY IT
■ What do you want to remember the next time you take Communion?
❊ What can you do to prepare for the next time you celebrate the Lord's Supper?
❊ How can you encourage others to honor only the Lord when celebrating the Lord's Supper?
❊ What idols do you need to avoid in your place of work or in your community? How?

1 Corinthians 10:23–11:1
The Believer's Freedom

TOPICS
Believers, Conscience, Example, Freedom, Glory, Sacrifice, Salvation, Thankfulness, Unbelievers

OPEN IT
❊ When was a time you were talked into participating in an activity that you later regretted?
■ When have you enjoyed doing something that benefited someone else?

EXPLORE IT
❊ What are we free to do? How? (10:23)
■ What qualifications go with the adage, "Everything is permissible"? (10:23-24)
❊ What is the guiding principle on our freedom? (10:24)
❊ How did Paul resolve the dilemma of whether to eat meat that had been sacrificed to idols? (10:25-26)
■ What stipulations did Paul place on eating meat served in an unbeliever's home? (10:27-30)
❊ What were the Corinthian Christians to do if meat being served to them had been sacrificed to idols? (10:28-29)
❊ Under what conditions were the Corinthians not to eat meat offered in sacrifice? (10:28-29)
❊ In what areas of life can we glorify God? (10:31)
■ What overriding value governs why we do what we do? (10:33)
❊ Whose good should we seek? (10:33)
❊ Whose example should all Christians follow? (11:1)

GET IT

❇ What does it mean for a person's freedom to be judged by another person's conscience?
■ What principles can we learn here about making difficult ethical decisions?
■ What do Christians today sometimes avoid buying or doing for conscience's sake?
❇ When is it good for a Christian to avoid buying or doing something because other believers are bothered by its association with sin or evil?
❇ How does Christian use of freedom contrast with our society's idea of freedom?
❇ What does it mean to eat and drink for the glory of God?
❇ How might you avoid a situation that would cause another believer to stumble?
❇ What is one way you can follow the example of someone who is following Christ?
❇ What can you learn from a fellow Christian who is following Christ?
❇ How may seeking the good of other people lead to their salvation?

APPLY IT

❇ What is one setting in which you can seek the good of other Christians over your own rights this week? How?
■ Which of your buying or spending habits should you change because of its associations? How?
❇ How could you remember to do every task or activity this week for God's glory?

1 Corinthians 11:2-16

Propriety in Worship

TOPICS

Angels, Appearance, Authority, Fellowship, Image, Worship

OPEN IT

❇ How have women's roles changed since you were a kid?
■ When has challenging authority caused you to hurt yourself or others?

EXPLORE IT

❇ For what did Paul praise the Corinthian church? (11:2)
■ What public worship practices did Paul rebuke? (11:2-16)
■ Who is the head of women, men, and Christ? (11:3)
❇ Why were women to have a sign of authority on their head? (11:3-11)
❇ Why does it dishonor a man's head to pray or prophesy with his head covered? (11:3-4, 7)
❇ Why does it dishonor a woman's head to pray or prophesy with her head uncovered? (11:3, 5-10)
❇ How seriously did Paul regard the woman who did not cover her head? (10:6)
❇ How are women and men different? (11:7-8)
■ What relationship do men and women have to each other? (11:11-12)
❇ How did Paul try to head off criticism about these instructions? (11:16)

GET IT

■ What matters most to God about worship in the church?
■ What excesses in worship does God want us to avoid?
❇ How is man the image and glory of God?
❇ How should women today respond to the command to cover their heads in public worship?
❇ In what ways were these instructions a response to problems unique to the Corinthian church?
❇ In what ways could this passage be misinterpreted or misapplied?

APPLY IT

■ What can you do personally to promote a proper spirit of worship in your church?
❇ What can you do next Sunday to insure a proper attitude in your worship?

1 Corinthians 11:17-34

The Lord's Supper

TOPICS

Discipline, Disobedience, Divisions, Honor, Judgment, Lord's Supper, Remembering, Respect, Sin, Witnessing

OPEN IT

■ For what kinds of occasions does your church sponsor meals?
❇ How does your church observe the Lord's Supper?

EXPLORE IT

❇ Why did Paul have no praise for the Corinthians here? (11:17)
❇ Why are there differences among believers? (11:19)
■ What severe problem did Paul address in this passage? (11:20-22)
❇ What essential truths about the Lord's Supper and Jesus' redemptive work are presented in this passage? (11:23-26)
❇ Why should Christians celebrate Communion? (11:24)
❇ What is accomplished by eating the bread and drinking the wine of the Lord's Supper? (11:26)
■ What role does Communion play in the task of evangelism? (11:26)
❇ What is the result of partaking of the Lord's Supper in an unworthy manner? (11:27)
■ What should a person do before partaking of the Lord's Supper? (11:28)
❇ What did the illness and death suffered by the Corinthians reveal about God's attitude toward Communion? (11:30)
❇ Why does the Lord discipline His children? (11:32)
❇ What additional advice did Paul give to Christians preparing for Communion? (11:33-34)

GET IT

❇ How important is the Lord's Supper in your life?
❇ Why is the Lord's Supper important?
❇ How should a person prepare for Communion?
❇ When is the best time for you to examine yourself before Communion?
■ What additional wisdom have you gained from these instructions on Communion?

❊ How have you prepared yourself for Communion in the past?
❊ How is Communion practiced in your church?
■ Why is a spirit of reverence important when partaking of the Lord's Supper?
❊ Why should we be grateful for the Lord's discipline?
❊ How have you seen the Lord's discipline benefit you?
❊ When was a time you benefited from the Lord's discipline?
❊ What practice in your local fellowship may need to be reexamined in light of this Scripture?

APPLY IT
■ How do you want to prepare for the next time you take Communion?
❊ What advice would you give to a new Christian who wants to participate in Communion?

1 Corinthians 12:1-11
Spiritual Gifts

TOPICS
Faith, Healing, Holy Spirit, Idolatry, Ignorance, Knowledge, Prophecy, Serving, Spiritual Gifts, Wisdom

OPEN IT
■ What is one unique talent or ability you have (whether useful or pointless)?
❊ How did you find out what your greatest interests were?

EXPLORE IT
■ Why did Paul give the Corinthians advice about spiritual gifts? (12:1)
❊ What was the condition of the Corinthians when they were pagans? (12:2)
❊ Why can someone speaking by the Spirit of God not say, "Jesus be cursed"? (12:3)
❊ What is the only way a person can say, "Jesus is Lord"? (12:3)
■ What common element exists in the diversity of gifts, service, and working? (12:4-6)
❊ Who works through the various gifts Christians have? (12:4-6)
❊ Who is given the manifestation of the Spirit? (12:7)
❊ For whose good is the manifestation of the Spirit given? (12:7)
■ What spiritual gifts did Paul describe? (12:8-10)
❊ Who determines how the gifts are distributed? (12:11)

GET IT
❊ How are we ignorant about spiritual gifts today?
■ What spiritual gifts have you seen used in your local church?
❊ What happens when Christians do not use their gifts?
■ What person you know would be encouraged by the knowledge that God gives a spiritual gift to every Christian?
❊ What is your spiritual gift?
❊ If you do not know what your spiritual gift is, what can you do to find out?
❊ How can you use your spiritual gift for the good of the people in your church?
❊ What spiritual gifts have you seen in the lives of other Christians?
❊ What can you learn from other Christians who faithfully use their spiritual gifts?
❊ What Christian discouraged by failure can you challenge to use the gifts God has given him or her?

APPLY IT
■ How can you use your spiritual gift this week for the benefit of others in your church?
❊ What observation could you share with another Christian to help him or her identify or use a spiritual gift?

1 Corinthians 12:12-31
One Body, Many Parts

TOPICS
Holy Spirit, Honor, Humility, Spiritual Gifts, Suffering, Unity

OPEN IT
❊ When have you felt insignificant in an organization?
■ What functions in the church do you feel are most important? Why?

EXPLORE IT
❊ In what way are Christians like a human body? (12:12-13)
❊ Why should outward appearances or status not matter to us? (12:13)
❊ What unifies all Christians? (12:13)
❊ What makes Christians unified and dependent on one another? (12:13)
■ What lessons are there in seeing the church as a human body? (12:14-17)
❊ Who arranged the parts of the body of Christ? (12:18)
❊ Why shouldn't all Christians perform the same function? (12:19)
❊ Why should members of the body of Christ not say to each other, "I don't need you"? (12:21-22)
■ Why should the less honorable parts be treated with special attention? (12:23)
❊ How has God combined the members of the body of Christ? (12:24-26)
❊ Who is part of the body of Christ? (12:27)
❊ What functions are necessary in the body? (12:28-29)
■ Who appoints members of the body to their positions? Why is this significant? (12:28-29)
❊ What are the greater gifts? (12:31)

GET IT
❊ How might you compare your place in the body of Christ to a part of the human body?
❊ How well do you interact with other members in the body of Christ?
❊ When have you felt like an important or insignificant part of the body?
❊ What part do you serve in the body of Christ?
■ How are you able to help other Christians?
❊ What has God appointed you to be in the body of Christ?
❊ Why do people often assume that certain duties in the church are more important?

❊ How can you honor the contributions of others in your church?
■ How can you treat the "weaker" members of your fellowship as indispensable?
❊ What can you do to suffer with those in the church who suffer and rejoice with those who are honored?
❊ What should we do when there is division among Christians in a local church?
❊ What do you think are your personal responsibilities in the body of Christ?
❊ What difference should it make in your life that you have been given the Holy Spirit?
❊ How can you show a desire for the greater gifts?

APPLY IT
■ What is one way you can show concern and love for another member of your church?
❊ What would be the best way to use your unique abilities in the body of Christ this year?

1 Corinthians 13:1-13
Love

TOPICS
Friendship, Humility, Kindness, Kingdom of God/Heaven, Knowledge, Love, Patience, Perseverance, Relationships, Trust

OPEN IT
❊ What to you is an unmistakable demonstration of love?
■ Who is the most loving person you know? Why do you think so?
❊ What qualities do you associate with love?

EXPLORE IT
❊ What makes speaking in tongues, faith, generosity, and even martyrdom worthless? (13:1-3)
❊ How could a person use spiritual gifts in a useless manner? (13:1-3)
■ What do we gain if we don't have love? (13:3)
❊ Why is love important? (13:3)
■ What qualities does love have? (13:4-8)
❊ Why will prophecy, tongues, and knowledge pass away? (13:8-9)
❊ How will we be different when we see Christ? (13:10-12)
❊ What is our spiritual imperfection like? (13:11)
❊ How do adults and children act and reason differently? (13:11)
❊ How will our knowledge of God change when we see Christ? (13:12)
■ What is the greatest of all gifts? (13:13)

GET IT
❊ Why do you think Paul wrote about love to the Corinthians?
❊ Why might it be easy to use a spiritual gift without love?
❊ How can a person demonstrate love?
❊ How should Christians demonstrate love for each other?
■ In what practical ways can you show a love that never fails?
❊ How did Jesus exemplify love?
❊ Why won't prophecy, knowledge, and tongues be necessary when Jesus returns?
■ When have you received the love described in this passage?
❊ What is difficult about loving?
❊ What expectations do you have, knowing you will see Jesus face to face one day?

APPLY IT
❊ What will help you to remember to use your gifts in a loving way?
■ How could you show love to a difficult person this week?

1 Corinthians 14:1-25
Gifts of Prophecy and Tongues

TOPICS
Motives, Praise, Prophecy, Spiritual Gifts, Unbelievers, Understanding, Worship

OPEN IT
❊ When have you been confused by a lack of clear instructions?
■ What are some traditions or practices in your family that would seem strange to someone outside your family?

EXPLORE IT
❊ What did God want the Corinthians to follow? (14:1)
❊ What did God want the Corinthians to desire? (14:1)
■ Why were the Corinthians to desire the gift of prophecy more than the gift of tongues? (14:1-5)
❊ In what circumstance is speaking in tongues as good as prophesying? (14:5)
❊ What must be combined with the gift of tongues to make it useful to others? (14:6)
❊ Why did Paul use the example of musical instruments in talking about prophecy? (14:7-8)
❊ In which gifts did Paul encourage the Corinthians to excel? (14:12)
■ How should speaking in tongues be like praying and singing? (14:14-16)
❊ Why is it crucial that a message in tongues be interpreted? (14:16-17)
❊ What priority does God give to speaking in tongues? (14:19)
❊ Why did Paul quote from Isaiah in instructing the Corinthians on tongues? (14:21)
❊ How does the quotation from Isaiah 28:11-12 clarify the purpose of the spiritual gift of tongues? (14:21-22)
❊ What is the problem with speaking in tongues in church? (14:23)
■ Why is it beneficial for unbelievers to hear prophesying in the church? (14:24-25)

GET IT
❊ How would you summarize God's priorities concerning the spiritual gifts of prophecy and tongues?
■ What practices can every local church use to ensure that spiritual gifts are used to build up people?
❊ What can we do to value spiritual gifts as God does?
❊ For what reasons should we desire spiritual gifts?

■ How can you guard against desiring spiritual gifts for the wrong motives?
❊ What more can your church or fellowship do to attract unbelievers?
❊ In what ways does your church attract unbelievers?

APPLY IT
■ How could you use one spiritual gift this week to help another Christian?
❊ What personal action could you take this week to make your worship services more welcoming to visitors?

1 Corinthians 14:26-40
Orderly Worship

TOPICS
Church, Conflict, Divisions, Law, Peace, Prayer, Quiet, Submission, Worship

OPEN IT
■ What is it like to attend a disorderly meeting or gathering?
❊ Why is it important to be organized when you have a task to accomplish?

EXPLORE IT
■ What contributions were the Corinthians to make when coming together? (14:26)
❊ How can Christians be involved in worship services? (14:26)
■ What kind of order were the Corinthians to observe when speaking in tongues? (14:27-28)
❊ How did Paul advise the Corinthians regarding prophesying in church? (14:29-32)
❊ How is the gift of prophecy beneficial to the church? (14:31)
❊ What makes order essential to worship? (14:33)
❊ Why were women not allowed to speak in the Corinthian church? (14:34)
❊ How were women to act during worship in the Corinthian church? (14:34-35)
❊ What were Corinthian women to do if they wanted to ask something in church? (14:35)
❊ What gave Paul the authority to teach the Corinthians? (14:37)
■ What was Paul's conclusion regarding corporate worship? (14:40)

GET IT
■ How might a church exhibit disorder in its worship?
❊ What can Christians do to prepare for worship services?
❊ How can you improve your preparation for church services?
❊ When have you neglected to participate properly in worship?
❊ How could you participate in worship so as to strengthen the church?
■ How can you use your spiritual gift in a fitting and orderly manner?

APPLY IT
■ What part of your Saturday can you use to help you prepare for the worship service you attend?
❊ How could you encourage fitting and orderly worship in your church each week?

1 Corinthians 15:1-11
The Resurrection of Christ

TOPICS
Gospel, Grace, Jesus Christ, Resurrection, Salvation

OPEN IT
■ How do people pass on their beliefs and traditions to others?
❊ What do you think is important to pass on from one generation to the next?
❊ What do you want others to remember about you?

EXPLORE IT
❊ How can a Christian avoid believing the gospel in vain? (15:1-2)
❊ Why is it important to "hold firmly to the word"? (15:2)
■ Why did Paul pass on what he had received? (15:3)
❊ How did Christ's life fulfill the Scriptures? (15:3)
❊ What are the key points of the gospel? (15:3-8)
❊ To whom did Christ appear after His resurrection? (15:5-8)
■ Why did Paul emphasize the facts of Christ's resurrection? (15:5-8)
❊ Why did Paul describe himself as one "abnormally born"? (15:8)
❊ Why did Paul feel unworthy to be called an apostle? (15:9)
■ For what reason was Paul able to call himself an apostle? (15:10)
❊ On what did Paul's apostleship rest? (15:10)

GET IT
❊ How would you describe, in your own words, the importance of the gospel to your life?
❊ What has God's grace accomplished in you?
❊ In what one area of your life have you been stubborn about allowing God's grace to work?
❊ What does it mean for you to hold firmly to the gospel?
■ What are the implications of the fact that the truth of the gospel is of first importance to God?
❊ What difference does it make that Christ's death and resurrection fulfilled Old Testament prophecy?
■ How does Christ appear or make Himself known to us today?

APPLY IT
■ What evidence could you use to persuade others this week about the truth of the gospel?
❊ How could you rely on God's grace in your efforts to tell your friends about Christ?

1 Corinthians 15:12-34
The Resurrection of the Dead

TOPICS
Death, Disagreements, Faith, Hope, Resurrection, Witnessing

OPEN IT
❊ What are some beliefs about life after death that others have shared with you?
■ What do people you know believe about the afterlife?
❊ What does the promise of eternal life mean to you?

EXPLORE IT
■ What were some Corinthians saying that troubled Paul? (15:12)
❊ How was the gospel of Christ's death and resurrection relevant to the dispute in Corinth? (15:12-13)
■ If Christ had not in fact been raised, what would be true of Christianity and Christians? (15:14-19)
❊ What condition would make a Christian's faith futile? (15:17-18)
❊ Why is faith in Christ useless and pitiable if Jesus has not been raised? (15:19)
❊ In what way did Christ's resurrection lead the way for us? (15:20)
❊ How does the resurrection of the dead come? (15:21)
❊ What is "the end"? (15:24-25)
❊ When and why will "the end" come? (15:24-25)
❊ What will be the last enemy destroyed? (15:26)
■ What will happen when Christ asserts His authority over all? (15:28)
❊ What would be true if the dead were not raised? (15:32)
❊ What was shameful about the Corinthians? (15:34)

GET IT
❊ When have you ever doubted any of the truths of the gospel?
❊ What can you do when you doubt what the Bible teaches?
■ What hope does Jesus' resurrection provide for your daily life?
❊ When is it best to reason logically with people who doubt the gospel?
■ How can you be more effective in sharing the message of salvation with others?
❊ When have you ever associated with bad company that could have corrupted your character?
❊ Why is it important to avoid people who want to distract you from your commitment to the gospel?
❊ What kind of discipline enables a person to face problems?

APPLY IT
❊ How would you counsel a Christian who was falling in with the wrong crowd?
■ How can you incorporate the truth of Christ's resurrection into your witness to others?

1 Corinthians 15:35-58
The Resurrection Body

TOPICS
Body, Death, Differences, Earth, Heaven, Last Days, Power, Questions, Resurrection, Victory, Weaknesses

OPEN IT
■ What feelings have you experienced when a friend or relative passed away?
❊ Why do you think some people feel angry at God when they lose a loved one?

EXPLORE IT
■ Why did Paul discuss the resurrection body? (15:35)
❊ What analogy did Paul use to explain the body's death and resurrection? (15:36-38)
❊ How did Paul explain the resurrection body? (15:39-41)
■ How does the body on earth differ from the body in heaven? (15:42-44)
❊ What example did Paul use to explain natural and spiritual bodies? (15:45-49)
❊ Why can't flesh and blood inherit the kingdom of God? (15:50)
❊ What mystery did Paul reveal? (15:51)
❊ How will all Christians be changed? When? (15:51-52)
❊ Why must all physical bodies be changed, even those that have not died? (15:50, 53)
■ What will happen after the dead are resurrected? (15:54-55)
❊ How has God given Christians the victory over death? (15:56-57)
❊ What difference does it make that we will be resurrected? (15:58)

GET IT
❊ How should Christians regard death?
■ How could this passage encourage a person who has lost a loved one who was a believer?
❊ How should we regard the future?
❊ What difference does it make that death has been defeated by Christ?
❊ How can a Christian grieve for someone's death while still holding on to the hope of resurrection?
■ How should Christ's resurrection and the hope of your own bodily transformation affect your priorities?
❊ In what area of your Christian life has it been a struggle to stand firm?
❊ What encouragement can we take from the fact that the work we do for the Lord is not in vain?
❊ In what specific ways do you need to be committed to the work of the Lord?

APPLY IT
■ In what ways could you show this week your thankfulness to Christ for His victory over death and sin?
❊ In the future, what hope could you share with a person who experiences the loss of a loved one?

1 Corinthians 16:1-4

The Collection for God's People

TOPICS

Church, Generosity, Giving Up, Money, Possessions, Sacrifice, Tithing

OPEN IT

■ Who has been generous to you over the years?
❊ What do you think of organizations that depend on donations?

EXPLORE IT

❊ For whom was the collection that Paul requested? (16:1)
❊ Whose example was the Corinthian church to follow? (16:1)
■ Who was to contribute to the collection? (16:2)
■ How were the Corinthians to know how much money to give? (16:2)
❊ When were the Corinthians to set aside money for their gifts? (16:2)
■ Why did Paul give such specific instructions to the Corinthians? (16:2)
❊ What specific instructions did Paul give the Corinthians regarding the collection? (16:2-3)
❊ What did Paul plan to do during his visit to the Corinthian church? (16:3)
❊ Who was to deliver the gift to Jerusalem? (16:3)
❊ Why would letters of introduction be important for those delivering the gift? (16:4)

GET IT

❊ What can we learn from the giving practices of the early church?
❊ What attitudes or actions of the early Christians do you think you should imitate?
❊ What characteristics of the early church should your church imitate?
❊ Which of Paul's instructions on giving were meant exclusively for the Corinthian church?
❊ What principles should govern our giving to the work of the Lord?
■ How should we decide how much to set aside for the church?
❊ What kind of discernment should we show in our giving?
❊ In what ways can church leaders be kept accountable to use the money given to the church?
■ How do you think you can be a better steward of the resources God has given you?

APPLY IT

■ How can you improve your attitude or practices in supporting God's work financially?
❊ What considerations should you keep in mind when planning your giving?

1 Corinthians 16:5-24

Personal Requests

TOPICS

Acceptance, Courage, Love, Ministry, Responsibility, Teamwork, Work

OPEN IT

❊ How much contact do you have with people in other countries?
■ Whom would you greet in a letter addressed to all your out-of-town friends?

EXPLORE IT

❊ What were Paul's plans after going through Macedonia? (16:5-6)
❊ What did Paul expect from the Corinthians during his visit with them? (16:6)
❊ Why was Paul informing the Corinthian church about his plans? (16:6-9)
■ What opportunity awaited Paul in Ephesus? (16:9)
❊ What words did Paul share about Timothy's visit? (16:10-11)
❊ What did Paul's words reveal about Timothy? (16:10-11)
❊ What were Paul's specific instructions on how to live? (16:13)
❊ What service had the household of Stephanas provided? (16:15)
■ How were the Corinthians to treat those who labored for God? (16:16)
■ Why did Paul think some men deserve recognition? (16:18)
❊ How did Paul authenticate his letter? (16:21)
❊ What closing thoughts did Paul leave with the Corinthians? (16:22-24)

GET IT

❊ What can we learn from the circumstances of the Corinthian church?
■ If Paul were writing a letter to your church, what would he affirm and what would he challenge?
❊ How should we treat church leaders?
❊ How can we actually do everything in love?
❊ About what should you be on guard in your Christian walk?
❊ What does it mean to be submissive to believers who are involved in the work of the Lord?
❊ For what reasons should churches from all parts of the world try to work together?
■ How do you think God wants you to support ministers of the gospel?

APPLY IT

■ How can you show your support to a believer who lives in another part of the world?
❊ How can you help the ministry of your local church?

2 Corinthians 1:1-11
The God of All Comfort

TOPICS
Compassion, Despair, Endurance, Hope, Prayer, Rest, Sacrifice, Suffering, Testing

OPEN IT
■ How do you normally react to hardship or suffering?
❊ Why do people sometimes blame God for difficult circumstances?

EXPLORE IT
❊ How did Paul describe God? (1:3)
❊ Why do you think Paul began his letter by praising God? (1:3)
❊ What does God do when we are troubled? (1:4)
■ How does God involve Himself in our troubles? (1:4-5)
❊ What did Paul's distress produce for the Corinthians? (1:6)
❊ In what way is patient endurance produced in Christians? (1:6)
❊ Why did Paul tell the Corinthians about the hardships he had endured? (1:8)
■ Why did Paul despair? (1:8)
❊ How did Paul's confidence in God enable him to rise above his despair? (1:8-10)
❊ For what reason did Paul endure suffering? (1:9)
■ How did the Corinthians help Paul through his hardships? (1:11)
❊ What was the gracious favor Paul anticipated? (1:11)

GET IT
❊ How does God want us to help one another in difficult circumstances?
❊ Who do you know who is experiencing hardship?
■ How can you help other Christians who are suffering?
❊ When have you ever suffered for the gospel?
■ How have other Christians helped you through difficult circumstances?
❊ How can you rely more on God instead of yourself in times of hardship?
❊ What can we do to learn patience and endurance from our hardships?

APPLY IT
■ How could you remind yourself to pray this week for Christians who are suffering hardship for their faith?
❊ What can you do this week to show love and concern for a Christian brother or sister who is suffering?

2 Corinthians 1:12–2:4
Paul's Change of Plans

TOPICS
Change, Confidence, Criticism, Faith, Love, Plans, Promises, Sincerity

OPEN IT
❊ How do you feel when someone postpones or cancels a social engagement that you were looking forward to?
■ How do you go about letting friends know that you cannot keep your appointment with them?

EXPLORE IT
■ How did Paul support his claim that he had been sincere with the Corinthians? (1:12)
❊ What accusation from the Corinthians was Paul most likely responding to? (1:12-14)
❊ Why did Paul say that the Corinthians could boast of him just as he would boast of them? (1:14)
❊ Why had Paul planned to visit the Corinthian church? (1:15)
■ Why did Paul change his travel plans? (1:15-16)
❊ How did Paul's opponents at Corinth use his change of plans against him? (1:17)
❊ What is the chief feature of God's promises? (1:18-22)
❊ How did Paul explain how reliable his words were? (1:18-23)
❊ What did Paul emphasize to strengthen his self-defense? (1:22)
❊ How does God's Spirit act as a deposit? (1:22)
❊ What is guaranteed to come? (1:22)
■ Why did Paul decide not to return to Corinth? (1:23)
❊ What was Paul's main purpose in working with the Corinthian church? (1:24)
❊ What were Paul's visits to Corinth like? (2:1)
❊ Why did Paul write about his distress and anguish? (2:4)

GET IT
■ In light of Paul's experience, how should you seek to discern God's will for your daily plans?
❊ When might it be necessary to question the actions of a Christian leader?
❊ When is it wrong to accuse another believer?
❊ When have you ever made plans without consulting God?
❊ How can we ensure that our lives send out a sincere and consistent message of commitment to Christ?
❊ What difference does it make that God puts His Spirit in every Christian's heart?
❊ Why do you think Paul's visits to Corinth were painful?
❊ In what circumstances might it be necessary to make a "painful visit" to another believer?
■ How can we demonstrate love for other Christians?

APPLY IT
■ How can you remind yourself to listen to the Holy Spirit's guidance and direction in your daily life?
❊ What is one interpersonal conflict that you need to try to work out this week?

2 Corinthians 2:5-11
Forgiveness for the Sinner

TOPICS
Forgiveness, Grief, Love, Punishment, Restoration, Satan, Sin, Sorrow

OPEN IT
■ When is it most difficult to forgive someone?
❊ How could a friendship be ruined by an unforgiving spirit?
❊ What is it like to experience God's forgiveness?

EXPLORE IT

❄ What situation is Paul responding to in this passage? (2:5)
❄ What did Paul mean when he said that the sinner in the Corinthian church had hurt all of the Corinthians? (2:5)
■ How did the Corinthians finally respond to the person who hurt Paul? (2:6)
❄ What was the man's reaction to the Corinthian's discipline? (2:7)
■ What advice did Paul give the Corinthians regarding the man who had sinned? (2:7-8)
❄ How were the Corinthians to reaffirm their love for the man they disciplined? (2:8)
❄ Why did Paul write to the Corinthians? (2:9)
■ Why was it important that the Corinthians forgive the man whom they disciplined? (2:10-11)
❄ In what way can Satan outwit us? (2:10-11)
❄ What danger did Paul want to avoid? (2:11)
❄ What were the Corinthian Christians not naive about? (2:11)

GET IT

❄ When was a time you learned of a church disciplining a member?
❄ What results ideally follow from church discipline?
❄ What is the difference between discipline and punishment?
■ Why do you think many churches neglect to discipline wayward members?
❄ In what ways are Christians aware of Satan's schemes?
■ How does Satan take advantage of our refusal to forgive each other?
❄ For whose benefit should we forgive others?
❄ What does Paul's example tell us about the role older Christians should play in the lives of younger believers?
❄ When have you ever grieved a fellow Christian?
❄ What should you do if you feel wronged by another person?

APPLY IT

■ What is the first step you should take this week to forgive and reaffirm your love for someone who has sinned against you?
❄ How do you plan to seek forgiveness the next time you wrong someone?

2 Corinthians 2:12–3:6

Ministers of the New Covenant

TOPICS

Example, Gospel, Holy Spirit, Knowledge, Ministry, New Covenant, Sincerity, Witnessing

OPEN IT

❄ What does the phrase "the letter of the law" mean to you?
■ What mentor or friend of yours lives by the "spirit of the law"?

EXPLORE IT

❄ Why was Paul willing to leave Troas, despite the opportunities there? (2:12-13)
■ Why was Paul thankful to the Lord? (2:14)
❄ How can knowledge of Christ be a fragrance? (2:14)
❄ By what method did Paul expect the gospel to be spread? (2:14)
❄ In what way are Christians the aroma of Christ? (2:15)
❄ Which two groups of people are affected by how Christians live? (2:15)
❄ In what way are Christians the smell of death to some and the fragrance of life to others? (2:16)
❄ How did some people of Paul's day misuse the Word of God? (2:17)
❄ Who might have needed letters of recommendation? Why? (3:1)
■ In what sense were the Corinthians a record of Paul's values and concerns? (3:2-3)
❄ In what sense were the Corinthians a record of God's values and concerns? (3:2-3)
■ Where did Paul get his competence? (3:5-6)
❄ What's the difference between the letter and the Spirit? (3:6)

GET IT

❄ What causes Christians to be legalistic about their faith?
❄ What can we learn from Paul's pastoral concern for the Corinthians?
■ What qualities do you think are essential to a good pastor?
❄ When has the Lord opened a door of ministry for you? How did you respond?
❄ In what ways are you an aroma of Christ among others?
■ How could you better represent Christ to the unbelievers you know?
❄ How do some Christians peddle the Word of God for profit?
❄ In what ways has God made you competent?

APPLY IT

■ When could you talk with your pastor to learn of your church's concerns and thus be able to pray for these needs more effectively?
❄ What about Christ do you want people to "read" in you this week?

2 Corinthians 3:7-18

The Glory of the New Covenant

TOPICS

Covenant, Freedom, Glory, Holy Spirit, Hope, Ministry, New Covenant

OPEN IT

■ What glorious sights have you seen in nature?
❄ In what circumstances do people in our society wear veils or coverings?

EXPLORE IT

❄ What ministry brought death? (3:7)
■ Why could the Israelites not look at Moses' face? (3:7)
❄ What faded away? (3:7, 11)
■ What is the difference between the old covenant and the new covenant? (3:11)

❊ What hope did Paul have? (3:12)
❊ Why was Paul bold? (3:12)
❊ Why did Moses cover his face with a veil? (3:13)
❊ Why do people fail to understand their need for salvation? (3:14)
❊ What must people do to have the veil that covers their hearts taken away? (3:16)
❊ What does the Spirit of the Lord offer believers? (3:17)
❊ How is it possible for us to reflect the Lord's glory? (3:18)
■ How does the glory of the new covenant differ from that of the old covenant? (3:18)

GET IT
❊ How has this passage added to your understanding of God and salvation?
■ How can the knowledge of the hope you have in Jesus Christ increase your boldness?
❊ What are some common misconceptions people have about the Holy Spirit's role in the Christian's life?
❊ How have you experienced the Spirit's freedom in your personal life?
■ In what ways do you see the Lord's glory reflected in your life?
❊ In what ways do you struggle to allow the Holy Spirit to control your life?
❊ With whom could you share the message of the new covenant?

APPLY IT
■ For what people do you want to pray this week, that the veil over their understanding will be removed?
❊ How can you turn to the Lord each day?

2 Corinthians 4:1-18
Treasures in Jars of Clay

TOPICS
Death, Deceit, Endurance, Gospel, Knowledge, Ministry, Power, Renewal, Satan

OPEN IT
❊ What are some things or people in which you have a lot of faith?
■ For what reasons do you most often get discouraged?
❊ What areas of life are difficult to entrust completely to God?

EXPLORE IT
■ Why did Paul tell the Corinthians not to lose heart? (4:1)
❊ What did Paul believe would result from telling the plain truth? (4:2)
❊ How did Paul respond to his opponents' accusations? (4:2)
❊ Why did Paul's opponents not understand his ministry? (4:3-4)
❊ Who is the god of this age? (4:4)
❊ What has the god of this age done? (4:4)
❊ Whom did Paul preach? Why? (4:5-6)
❊ What kind of jars contained Paul's treasure? (4:7)
■ How did Paul contrast his own weakness with God's power? (4:8-9)
❊ What did Paul call his sufferings? (4:10)
❊ What value did Paul see in his sufferings? (4:10-12)
❊ What motivated Paul to preach the gospel in spite of hardship? (4:13-14)
■ How did Paul encourage the Corinthians to carry on despite difficulty? (4:16-18)

GET IT
❊ How would you define faith?
❊ What elements of the Christian faith that we cannot see are central to our life with Christ?
❊ What does it mean for us to renew our faith?
❊ In what ways do some religious people distort the Word of God?
❊ When have you been discouraged or perplexed in your Christian life?
■ What makes it difficult for us to fix our attention and hope on God?
■ How can God help us through difficult times?
❊ When have you felt inner peace in spite of trying circumstances?

APPLY IT
■ What do you want to remember the next time you feel discouraged?
❊ How could you encourage another Christian who is confused or bogged down by the cares of life?

2 Corinthians 5:1-10
Our Heavenly Dwelling

TOPICS
Confidence, Death, Earth, Eternal Life, Faith, Heaven, Holy Spirit, Judgment

OPEN IT
❊ What do you imagine heaven will be like?
■ What common clichs do you frequently hear when people talk about heaven?

EXPLORE IT
❊ To what kind of tent did Paul refer? Why? (5:1)
❊ To what can Christians look forward? (5:1)
❊ How could Paul feel confident in the face of ill health and death? (5:1-10)
■ Why did Paul long for heaven? (5:2-3)
❊ For what purpose has God made us? (5:4-5)
❊ How does the Spirit guarantee what is to come? (5:5)
■ What is true as long as we are alive on this earth? (5:6)
❊ How is the Christian life lived? (5:7)
❊ What future realities motivated Paul to please the Lord in all he said and did? (5:8-10)
■ What should be the believer's goal? (5:9)
❊ Who will be judged by Christ? (5:10)
❊ Why must we all appear before the judgment seat of Christ? (5:10)
❊ What will people receive at the judgment seat of Christ? (5:10)

GET IT
❊ What's wrong with highly valuing beauty and youth?
❊ How can Christ be glorified through the weaknesses of men and women?

❊ What does it mean to live by faith and not by sight?
■ How often do you long for the heavenly body promised to believers at the resurrection?
❊ What comfort or satisfaction can we derive from knowing that the Holy Spirit guarantees our future in heaven?
❊ How does this passage give us hope for believers who have passed away?
■ How should we regard death?

APPLY IT
■ In what small way can you detach yourself from worldly things?
❊ How can you prepare yourself today to face the judgment seat of Christ?

2 Corinthians 5:11–6:2
The Ministry of Reconciliation

TOPICS
Ambassadors, Forgiveness, Grace, Love, Ministry, New Life, Reconciliation

OPEN IT
■ When have you seen someone change in a significant way?
❊ What about you is most difficult for your acquaintances to understand or accept?

EXPLORE IT
❊ Why did Paul try to persuade others to follow Christ? (5:11)
❊ Why was Paul concerned about justifying his ministry to the Christians at Corinth? (5:12)
❊ How were Paul's opponents building themselves up at his expense? (5:12)
❊ What motivated Paul? (5:14)
■ Why did Christ die for everyone? (5:15)
❊ How did Paul change the way he looked at people? (5:16)
❊ What is true about every person in Christ? (5:17)
❊ What happened when God sent His Son to earth? (5:18)
❊ What does God do with our sins when we are reconciled to Him? (5:19)
■ How is a Christian an ambassador? (5:20)
❊ Why did Paul try to persuade the Corinthians to respond to God's Word? (6:1)
■ Why should we listen carefully to the message about Christ? (6:1-2)

GET IT
❊ How do Christians sometimes take pride in ministries that give them attention and popularity?
❊ How is it possible for us to be motivated both by the fear of the Lord and Christ's love?
❊ Why was it necessary for Christ to die in order for us to be reconciled to God?
❊ In what ways do people today receive the grace of God in vain?
❊ In what ways are all Christians new creations?
❊ For what other Christians are you concerned?
❊ How can you encourage your Christian friends to listen to God's Word?
❊ How did God make His reconciliation with you?
❊ How can you personally be involved in the ministry of reconciliation?
■ What difference does it make that Christians are counted as Christ's ambassadors?
■ Where is your ministry of reconciliation?
❊ To whom are you an ambassador?

APPLY IT
■ What is one way you can represent Christ to your friends and coworkers this week?
❊ What Christian friend can you encourage to listen to God's Word? How?

2 Corinthians 6:3-13
Paul's Hardships

TOPICS
Affections, Ministry, Patience, Persecution, Perseverance, Serving, Witnessing

OPEN IT
❊ What do you consider to be distinctive about members of your family?
■ What images does the word "hardships" bring to mind?

EXPLORE IT
❊ What is the connection between the credibility of Christianity and the people who call themselves Christians? (6:3)
❊ Whose authority did Paul claim? (6:4)
❊ What does this passage say about Paul's attitude toward the ministry of sharing the gospel? (6:4)
❊ What does this passage say about the cost of being Christ's disciple? (6:4-10)
■ What price did Paul pay for following Christ? (6:4-10)
■ What kind of weapons did Paul use? (6:7)
❊ How did the accusations against Paul differ from the reality Paul experienced as an ambassador for Christ? (6:9-10)
■ In what way was Paul poor yet rich? (6:10)
❊ To what lengths did Paul go to show his love for the Corinthians? (6:11-13)

GET IT
❊ How do you think Paul was able to keep an attitude of sincere love for people when so many opposed him?
❊ What do you think caused the Corinthians to withhold their full loyalty from Paul?
❊ What can we learn from Paul's relationship with the Corinthians that can help us deal with friends who frustrate us?
❊ How can you guard against causing other Christians to stumble in their faith?
■ When have you ever suffered for the sake of the gospel?
❊ How does God use hardships to strengthen our relationship with Him?
❊ What can you learn from Paul's example that will help you endure suffering for the sake of the gospel?
■ How can you rely on the spiritual weapons of the Holy Spirit more in your everyday life?

❊ How do Paul's words put a new perspective on wealth and poverty?

APPLY IT
❊ Of the virtues purity, understanding, patience, and kindness, which do you want to ask God to help you practice this week?
■ What can you do this week to help another Christian persevere through hard times?

2 Corinthians 6:14–7:1
Do Not Be Yoked with Unbelievers

TOPICS
Fellowship, Friendship, Holiness, Marriage, Partnerships, Purity, Relationships, Separation, Unbelievers, Unity

OPEN IT
❊ How do you choose your friends?
■ What sort of partnerships have you been involved in over the years?
❊ How would you describe the perfect companion?

EXPLORE IT
❊ Who were the "unbelievers" Paul described? (6:14)
■ Why is it wrong and dangerous for Christians to be bound together with unbelievers? (6:14-16)
❊ How did Paul balance encouragement with warnings in this passage? (6:14-7:1)
❊ In what way are Christians unique? (6:16)
■ Why is it important for Christians to be separate from non-Christian influences? (6:16-18)
❊ What did Paul warn Christians not to do? (6:16-18)
❊ On what condition does the Lord receive people? (6:17)
❊ What does God call His people? (6:18)
❊ How did Paul sum up his quotation of Isaiah 52:11? (7:1)
■ From what did the Corinthians need to purify themselves? (7:1)
❊ Why should we strive to perfect holiness in our lives? (7:1)

GET IT
❊ Why do you think this passage is so often applied to marriage?
❊ In what other areas of life besides marriage do Christians need to be separate from non-Christians?
❊ How seriously does your church take God's command about the relationship Christians should have with unbelievers?
❊ What difference does it make that each believer is a temple of the living God?
❊ How do you need to purify yourself from things that have contaminated your life?
❊ How should Christians balance their involvement with non-Christians?
■ In what kinds of relationships can a Christian become bound too tightly to unbelievers?
❊ When have you witnessed the consequences produced when a believer was obliged to an unbeliever?
■ What can a Christian do if he or she is beholden to an unbeliever too much?
❊ How can you keep your relationships with non-Christians without tightly binding yourself to them?

APPLY IT
■ In what relationships do you need to maintain your freedom to follow Christian convictions?
❊ What can you do this week to show your reverence for God?

2 Corinthians 7:2-16
Paul's Joy

TOPICS
Confidence, Conflict, Devotion, Encouragement, Joy, Obedience, Repentance, Salvation, Sorrow

OPEN IT
❊ When has a friend ever disappointed you?
■ What is it like to have a loyal and faithful friend?
❊ When was a time you had to confront a friend?

EXPLORE IT
❊ Why did Paul not condemn the Corinthians? (7:2-3)
❊ Why did Paul have to defend himself again to the Corinthians? (7:2-4)
■ Why did Paul have such great confidence in the Corinthian Christians? (7:4)
❊ How could Paul be joyful in such difficult circumstances? (7:4)
❊ What was Paul's experience in Macedonia? (7:5)
❊ What was the nature of the trouble Paul was facing? (7:5)
■ How did God comfort Paul? (7:6-7)
❊ What was the cause of the sorrow felt by the Corinthians? (7:8)
❊ Why did Paul change his feelings about sending his "tearful letter"? (7:8-9)
❊ What qualities were produced by the Corinthians' godly sorrow? (7:11)
❊ How did the Corinthians prove themselves to be innocent? (7:11)
❊ For what reason did Paul write this letter to the church at Corinth? (7:12)
■ What did Titus do to encourage Paul? (7:13-16)
❊ Why did Paul have confidence in the Corinthian Christians? (7:16)

GET IT
■ What can we learn from the relationship between Paul and Titus?
❊ What could your church learn from the relationship between Titus and the Corinthian church?
❊ What relationship is there between adversity and spiritual growth?
■ When have you ever been confronted by a friend regarding a spiritual matter?
❊ How should we respond when someone points out a wrong in our lives?
❊ How do Paul's warnings and encouraging words in this passage motivate you to behave in a godly manner?
❊ What can we learn from this passage about dealing with Christians who have fallen away from the faith?
❊ What should we do when a Christian friend turns away from Christ?
❊ Why is it not enough just to feel sorry for your sins?

APPLY IT
❊ What do you need to do this week to turn sorrow for sin into godly living?
■ What specific step can you take this week to build up another believer who is discouraged?

2 Corinthians 8:1-15
Generosity Encouraged

TOPICS
Desires, Encouragement, Equality, Generosity, Giving Up, Money, Poor, Sacrifice, Serving

OPEN IT
❊ How do you feel when your pastor preaches about tithing?
■ What is your idea of generosity?
❊ What example of generosity have you seen recently?

EXPLORE IT
❊ What had God given to the Macedonian Christians? (8:1)
■ Out of what circumstances did the Macedonian Christians give? (8:2)
❊ What attitude did the Macedonians have in their giving? (8:3-4)
■ What three things did the Macedonian Christians do that impressed Paul? (8:3-5)
❊ What surprised Paul about the Macedonians' giving? (8:5)
❊ What was it that Titus had begun to do? (8:6)
❊ In what area did Paul want the Corinthians to excel? (8:7)
❊ Why did Paul avoid commanding the Corinthians to give? (8:8)
❊ What example did Christ set for us? (8:9)
❊ Why did Paul use the actions of the Macedonian Christians to motivate the Corinthians to give? (8:11)
■ What is it about a gift to the Lord that makes it acceptable? (8:12)
❊ What end does God want our charitable giving to achieve? (8:13)
❊ What Old Testament example guides our giving? How? (8:15)

GET IT
❊ What can we learn from Titus' example?
❊ How do you feel about the methods Paul used to motivate the Corinthians to participate in the collection?
❊ How have your views on giving changed over the years?
■ How can joy lead to generosity, even when a person lives in poverty?
❊ How does Christ's example motivate you to give?
❊ How can the fact that Christ became poor on your behalf, and was later exalted by God, motivate you to follow His example?
❊ How can the example of the Macedonian church challenge those who have little money to give?
❊ What prevents people from giving a fair portion of their money to the Lord for His work?
❊ How crucial do you think it is for Christians to give their money to the church?
■ How are you challenged by Paul's discussion of generosity?
❊ How can you find out how much God wants you to give and what ministries He wants you to support?

APPLY IT
■ What step can you take this week to review and improve your financial support of the Lord's work?
❊ In what ways besides giving money can you be generous to others in the name of Christ this week?

2 Corinthians 8:16–9:5
Titus Sent to Corinth

TOPICS
Criticism, Example, Generosity, Gifts, Giving Up, Money, Preparation, Sacrifice, Tithing

OPEN IT
■ When is it most difficult to try to please everybody?
❊ What good qualities do you see in the lives of your own church leaders?

EXPLORE IT
❊ Why did Paul and Titus share the same concern for the Christians at Corinth? (8:16)
❊ Why was Titus traveling to Corinth? (8:17)
■ Why did Paul send two other Christians along with Titus to Corinth? (8:18-23; 9:3-5)
■ How did Paul instruct the Corinthian church to treat Titus and his fellow worker? (8:23-24)
❊ Why did Paul explain there was no need for him to write the Corinthians? (9:1)
❊ How did Paul motivate the Macedonians to join in the collection for the Christians of Jerusalem? (9:2-3)
❊ How would Paul's boasting have been hollow? (9:3)
■ Why did Paul send Titus to collect the gift from the Corinthian church? (9:3-5)
❊ What attitude did Paul want the Corinthians to have regarding their gift? (9:5)

GET IT
❊ What motivates you to give to your church or Christian ministries?
■ What should be a Christian's attitude regarding sacrificial giving to the church?
❊ Why did Paul take pains to do what was right in the eyes of others?
❊ Why did Paul want to avoid criticism in how the gift was administered?
❊ In what ways should we try to avoid criticism with the way we carry out our Christian responsibilities?
❊ When is it appropriate to increase your giving?
■ What can you do to guard against a grudging attitude when you offer your resources to the Lord?
❊ What was exemplary about the people who worked with Paul (Titus and the others)?
❊ What was exemplary about the Corinthians?
❊ What should be our attitude toward those who are full-time Christian workers?
❊ How can you imitate the qualities of the Christian workers?

APPLY IT

■ What step can you take this week to foster a willing attitude in your giving?

❇ What is one setting in which you can strive to avoid criticism for the way you live your Christian life? How?

2 Corinthians 9:6-15

Sowing Generously

TOPICS

Generosity, Gifts, Giving Up, Grace, Praise, Serving, Thankfulness

OPEN IT

❇ What images come to your mind when you hear about a "cheerful giver"?

■ Who is the most generous person you know? Why do you think so?

EXPLORE IT

❇ Why did Paul begin this passage with a discussion of farming? (9:6)

■ How should we give? Why? (9:7)

■ What promise does God give to believers who do give generously? (9:8)

❇ For what reason did Paul quote Scripture here? (9:9)

❇ What does God provide? (9:10)

■ What results from the generosity of Christians? (9:11)

❇ What was the most important benefit that would arise from the collection for the Jerusalem church? (9:12-14)

❇ What did God give the Corinthians? (9:14)

❇ For what kind of gift did Paul praise God in his letter? (9:15)

GET IT

❇ Why does God love a cheerful giver over someone who grudgingly gives large sums of money?

❇ What does this passage tell us about motivating people?

❇ What does this passage tell us about accountability?

■ What does this passage tell us about the relationship between Christian faith and giving?

■ What could a reluctant giver do to become a more cheerful giver?

❇ Why does giving in a grudging manner make any difference if the need is met?

❇ How should you react when other Christians give generously to you or your family?

❇ What principles of accountability should govern Christian giving?

APPLY IT

■ What could you do this week to encourage a Christian friend to be a cheerful giver?

❇ What is one way you can set an example of giving?

❇ How can you remind yourself of God's generosity the next time you are tempted to hold back from giving cheerfully?

2 Corinthians 10:1-18

Paul's Defense of His Ministry

TOPICS

Armor, Confidence, Gentleness, Obedience, Power, Pride, War, Work, World

OPEN IT

❇ What is it like to have people talk about you behind your back?

■ When have you ever had to defend your actions to another person?

EXPLORE IT

❇ What was the source of Paul's authority and influence over others? (10:1)

■ Of what did Paul's opponents accuse him? (10:2)

❇ How did the spiritual warfare that Paul fought, and the spiritual weapons that he used, differ from ordinary warfare and weapons? (10:3-4)

❇ What did Paul want to demolish? How? (10:4-6)

❇ What did Paul take captive? (10:5)

■ How were Paul's opponents generating their misguided ideas? (10:7)

❇ Why was Paul not ashamed of boasting about the Corinthians? (10:8)

❇ Why would Paul's opponents try to convince the Corinthians that Paul was unimpressive in person? (10:10)

❇ How did Paul respond to the accusations against him? (10:11)

■ Why was Paul justified in boasting, whereas his opponents were not? (10:13-16)

❇ What would enable Paul to expand the area in which he could preach the gospel? (10:16)

❇ In what did Paul's opponents pride themselves? (10:16)

❇ Why did Paul endorse boasting in the Lord, but condemn all other forms of boasting? (10:18)

GET IT

❇ In what way did Jesus exemplify meekness and gentleness?

❇ How do Paul's actions and attitudes influence your ideas about ministry?

■ Why do people often look only on the surface of things?

❇ How can looking only on the surface mislead us?

❇ What surface judgments do you tend to make?

❇ How does it feel when a person boasts or tries to take credit for work that someone else did?

❇ Why does God want us to boast about Him and not about ourselves?

❇ In what circumstances do you think it would be it be proper for a Christian to boast?

❇ What spiritual weapons are available to you?

❇ How can you better utilize the spiritual weapons that are available to you?

■ Why did Paul defend the truth?

❇ What can we learn from Paul's concerns?

APPLY IT

❇ What is one specific way you can show the meekness and gentleness of Christ in one of your important relationships?

■ In what area of life do you need to defend the truth? How?

2 Corinthians 11:1-15
Paul and the False Apostles

TOPICS
Deceit, Devotion, Gospel, Jealousy, Money, Purity, Satan, Toleration, Witnessing

OPEN IT
❇ When is it difficult to hold to your convictions?
❇ When was the first time you remember being jealous?
■ What widely followed practices might a person be criticized for not doing?

EXPLORE IT
❇ Why did Paul ask the Corinthians to put up with him? (11:1)
❇ Of whom was Paul jealous? Why? (11:2)
❇ Why was Paul jealous? (11:2)
❇ To what biblical event did Paul compare the Corinthians' risk of deception? (11:3)
❇ Why did Paul ask the Corinthians to put up with his boasting? (11:4)
■ Why was Paul sarcastic about the "super-apostles"? (11:5)
❇ What criticism did Paul's opponents voice against him? (11:6)
❇ How did Paul respond to his opponents' criticism? (11:6)
❇ Why did Paul "lower himself"? (11:7)
■ How did Paul make sure he was not a burden on the Corinthians? (11:7-9)
❇ Why did Paul accept support from the Macedonian Christians while in Corinth, yet refuse to accept money from the Corinthians themselves? (11:8-12)
■ How did Paul's behavior contrast with that of his opponents? (11:12)
❇ How did Paul's opponents try to deceive the Corinthians? (11:13-15)

GET IT
❇ What qualities do you think should characterize a minister of Christ?
❇ How does godly jealousy differ from worldly jealousy?
❇ Who is one person you are concerned may abandon Christ?
❇ Who are false prophets in our society?
■ How do modern-day false prophets try to deceive Christians?
❇ How should we respond to those people who claim a spiritual authority that they do not have?
■ What can you do to avoid being deceived in spiritual matters by the world?
❇ In what way should we follow Paul's example in matters of financial support and accountability?

APPLY IT
❇ What is one thing you can do this week to help your Christian friends stay loyal to Christ?
■ What is one step you can take this week to guard against the deceit of false prophets and evil pressures?

2 Corinthians 11:16-33
Paul Boasts About His Sufferings

TOPICS
Confidence, Foolishness, Persecution, Pressure, Sin, Status, Suffering, Weaknesses, Wisdom, World

OPEN IT
❇ What kind of boasting do you dislike hearing?
■ What are some of the playground boasts you remember hearing in grade school?
❇ What is the most dramatic testimony you have ever heard?

EXPLORE IT
❇ Why did Paul write, "Let no one take me for a fool"? (11:16)
❇ What sort of boasting characterizes a fool? (11:17)
❇ What kind of language did Paul use in this passage? (11:16-21)
❇ What did the Corinthians put up with too easily? (11:19-20)
❇ In what way did Paul act like a fool? (11:21)
■ What qualifications did Paul have to justify his boasting? (11:22-28)
❇ Why did Paul give so many examples of how he endured hardship for Christ? (11:22-28)
❇ How did Paul's boasting change after his insistence that he had worked much harder than his opponents? (11:23)
■ Why did Paul boast about his hardships? (11:24-26)
❇ What kind of pressure did Paul experience? (11:28)
❇ What was Paul's attitude toward Christians who were weak in their faith and led into sin? (11:29)
■ How did Paul qualify his boasting? (11:30)

GET IT
❇ How do you think Christian pastors today should handle rivalry and competition in the church?
❇ How do you feel when a fellow believer sins against you or a friend?
■ What does it mean to boast in the Lord?
❇ What should we boast about?
❇ What should we avoid boasting about?
■ What are the dangers of boasting?
❇ How can our boasting be glorifying to the Lord?
❇ Why did Paul criticize the practice of striving for status?
❇ What do you think are some of the pressures your pastor feels in leading your congregation?
❇ In what specific ways can you be supportive of your church leaders?
❇ How should you respond to suffering or hardship that you experience for the sake of Christ?
❇ How could you help Christians who are harassed for their faith?
❇ How can you guard against leading another believer into sin?

APPLY IT
❇ How could you encourage the leaders in your church who may be enduring hardship?
❇ In what ways could you work this week to reduce rivalry and conflict among Christians?

■ What boasts can you have handy for the next time you need to defend your credibility as a representative of Christ's message?

2 Corinthians 12:1-10
Paul's Vision and His Thorn

TOPICS
Body, Grace, Health, Heaven, Joy, Pain, Power, Pride, Weaknesses

OPEN IT
❊ How are powerful people treated in our society?
❊ Why are we typically afraid to disclose our weaknesses to each other?

EXPLORE IT
❊ Who was the man in Christ whom Paul described? (12:2)
❊ Why did Paul tell the Corinthians about his vision, despite his misgivings? (12:2-4)
❊ Why was Paul reluctant to speak about his vision? (12:3-6)
❊ What happened during the revelation Paul described? (12:4)
■ Why did Paul refrain from boasting? (12:6)
❊ For what reason might Paul have become conceited? (12:7)
❊ What prevented Paul from developing a proud spirit? (12:7)
❊ Why did Paul have a "thorn"? (12:7)
❊ Who was responsible for giving Paul a "thorn in the flesh"? (12:7)
■ What was Paul's response to his "thorn"? (12:8, 10)
■ What purpose can suffering serve? (12:9)

GET IT
■ What are some weaknesses or afflictions that you find difficult to live with?
❊ What can we learn from Paul's example about dealing with physical discomfort or hardship?
❊ How can you allow the Lord's power to take over where you are weak?
❊ How does the Christian perspective on power and weakness differ from that of the world?
❊ What weaknesses, handicaps, or problems in your life is God able to use?
❊ What does this passage teach us about the problem of evil and God's sovereign will?
❊ Why does God choose to heal some people of their sickness or disability and not others?
■ How should you respond if God chooses not to heal you?
❊ What difference should it make knowing God has promised you an all-sufficient grace?

APPLY IT
■ What weakness can you turn over to the Lord through prayer this week?
❊ In what area of your life do you want to rely more on God's strength and power, rather than your own?

2 Corinthians 12:11-21
Paul's Concern for the Corinthians

TOPICS
Burdens, Expectations, Fear, Humiliation, Humility, Love, Ministry, Miracles, Money, Sacrifice, Sin

OPEN IT
❊ In your experience, what issues cause the most disagreement among friends?
❊ Who is the best friend you ever had?
■ How can a gesture of goodwill be misunderstood or unappreciated?

EXPLORE IT
❊ How did Paul maintain humility while defending himself against his opponents at Corinth? (12:11)
❊ What tone did Paul use in this passage? (12:11-13)
❊ Why should the Corinthians have recognized the apostles? (12:12)
❊ What did Paul want from the Corinthians? (12:14)
■ To what did Paul liken his relationship with the Corinthians? (12:14)
❊ Why did Paul ask the Corinthians, "If I love you more, will you love me less?" (12:15)
■ How do we know that Paul had a deep affection for the Corinthians? (12:15-18)
❊ Why was Paul's conscience clear about the men he had sent to Corinth? (12:17-18)
■ What prompted Paul to write this letter? (12:20-21)
❊ In what ways did Paul fear that the Corinthians might cause him to be humbled before God? (12:21)

GET IT
❊ What role do you think signs, wonders, and miracles should play in Christian evangelism today?
❊ What is an example of an experience that taught you a lesson, but which you would not want to go through again?
❊ What misgivings might Paul have after visiting your church?
❊ How can you maintain a spirit of humility if you have to defend yourself against the accusations of others?
❊ What does Paul's relationship with the Corinthians reveal about the type of friendships God wants for you?
❊ Why might a local congregation become divided?
❊ How should we be accountable to one another? Why?

APPLY IT
❊ What simple act of concern can you show for the people in your church this week?
■ In the future, how can you follow Paul's example in healing divisions between Christians?

2 Corinthians 13:1-14
Final Warnings

TOPICS
Authority, Discipline, Example, Faith, Perfect, Power, Prayer, Sin, Testing, Truth, Unity, Weaknesses

OPEN IT
❄ How would you prepare for a visit from a friend you haven't seen in a long time?
■ What is one warning you're thankful you received?

EXPLORE IT
❄ Why did Paul return to Corinth a third time? (13:1-2)
❄ How do we know the Corinthians were doubting Paul's authority? (13:3)
❄ Why did Paul plan to be firm with the chronic sinners in Corinth? (13:3-4)
■ Why did Paul advise the Corinthians to examine themselves? (13:5)
❄ How could the Corinthians "fail the test"? (13:5)
■ What does this passage reveal about Paul's concern for the Corinthians' spiritual welfare and regard for his own reputation? (13:7)
❄ How could Paul be glad despite his problems? (13:9)
■ Why did Paul write to the church at Corinth? (13:10)
❄ For what purpose had God given authority to Paul? (13:10)
❄ What did Paul want the Corinthians to do? (13:11-14)
❄ What was Paul's appeal in the conclusion to his letter? (13:11-14)

GET IT
❄ When should we demand proof that a person's teaching about God is true?
❄ How has God demonstrated His power in your life?
❄ What difference does it make that God's power lives in you?
■ When is it helpful to examine yourself to see whether you are in the faith?
❄ How do you think a person could fail the test of faith?
■ What does it mean to submit to those in authority in the church?
❄ What should you do to mend the relationship whenever you are at odds with another Christian?
❄ What does it mean to aim for perfection?
❄ What goals should Christians set for themselves?

APPLY IT
■ In what way would it be helpful for you to test your faith? How could you?
❄ Who could help you test yourself this week to see whether you are in the faith?
❄ What realistic, measurable goal could you set for your own growth toward godliness this week?

Galatians 1:1-10

No Other Gospel

TOPICS
Angels, Anger, Approval, Church, Confusion, God, Gospel, Grace, Legalism, Peace

OPEN IT
■ What is your usual way of starting a letter?
❄ When you have something difficult to share with a loved one, how can jotting down your thoughts help?
❄ When you want to emphasize an important point to someone, how do you do it?

EXPLORE IT
❄ How did the author of the letter identify himself? (1:1)
■ How did Paul bring up two vital concerns in the beginning of his letter? (1:1, 4)
❄ Who joined Paul in sending the letter? (1:2)
❄ To whom was the letter sent? (1:2)
■ What traditional form of greeting did the apostle use in his letter? (1:3)
❄ How did Paul conclude his salutation? (1:4-5)
■ What attitude did Paul express? Why? (1:6-7)
❄ How were the Galatian Christians being thrown "into confusion"? (1:7)
❄ What hypothetical case did Paul present to show the purity of the gospel? (1:8-9)
❄ How did Paul emphasize the importance of representing the gospel accurately? (1:8-9)
❄ What accusation had been directed at Paul? (1:10)
❄ How did Paul affirm his purpose to please God? (1:10)

GET IT
■ The tone of Paul's letter is serious and abrupt; why did he write this way?
❄ Why was it important that Paul establish his credentials?
❄ Why do some Christians base their identity on things other than Christ?
■ How did Paul assert his authority in this letter?
❄ Why was it important for the Galatian churches to be reminded that salvation lay in the work of Christ, not in human works?
❄ How do Christians have a tendency to bypass God's grace in their daily experience?
❄ What was at stake in Paul's warning to the Galatians (1:8-9)?
❄ How do you need to examine the doctrine of salvation you pass on to others?

APPLY IT
❄ How can you prepare to respond the next time you hear a distorted message about Christ?
❄ As a servant of Christ, what are some ways you can best share the true gospel with the unbelievers you know?
■ What important letter to a struggling believer can you write today?

Galatians 1:11-24
Paul Called by God

TOPICS
Church, Evangelism, God, Gospel, Grace, Jesus Christ, Persecution, Praise, Religion, Traditions, Truth

OPEN IT
■ What personal accomplishment makes you feel proud?
❇ If you could teach yourself a new hobby, skill, or line of work, what would you choose?
❇ What kind of recognition do you want for the work you do?

EXPLORE IT
❇ What gospel did Paul preach? (1:11-12)
■ What did Paul try to establish by bringing up his personal history? (1:13-14)
❇ Before his conversion, what was Paul's approach to Judaism? (1:14)
❇ What three things did God do for Saul when he intervened in his life? (1:15-16)
❇ How did Paul emphasize that his conversion and calling were none of his own doing? (1:15-16)
■ What did Paul do after his conversion? (1:16-17)
❇ How did Paul form his theology? (1:16-17)
❇ How long did Paul wait before going to Jerusalem? (1:18)
❇ How much time did Paul spend with Peter? (1:18)
❇ While in Jerusalem, which other apostle did Paul meet? (1:19)
❇ Why did Paul want his readers to know how limited his relationship was to the apostles? (1:18-19)
❇ What did Paul say to confirm the truth of his testimony? (1:20)
❇ How was Paul's ministry clearly not under the authority or oversight of the Jerusalem church? (1:21-22)
■ What was reported to the Judean churches about Paul? (1:23-24)

GET IT
❇ Why did the Galatian church have misgivings about Paul and his message?
❇ Why was it important for Paul to establish the independent nature of his ministry?
❇ By what criteria did Paul establish his apostleship?
❇ What kind of support does your pastor receive from members of your congregation?
❇ What kind of support should a pastor receive from members of the congregation?
■ Paul had a clear and unique sense of his calling; how do you feel about God's imprint on your life?
❇ Paul knew what God wanted him to do with his life; to what line of service has God called you?
❇ Why did the Judean churches praise God when they heard the report about Paul?
■ What are your "before and after" conversion pictures like?
❇ How has God changed you so far?

APPLY IT
■ What change do you want to make in your life this week to reflect your walk by faith?
❇ What kind of prayer and Bible study this week would most help you in your witness to others?

Galatians 2:1-10
Paul Accepted by the Apostles

TOPICS
Approval, Doctrine, Gospel, Grace, Law, Leadership, Partnerships, Poor, Truth

OPEN IT
❇ What location do you enjoy visiting?
❇ If you could work in a new location among a particular group of people, where and whom would you select?
■ Whose opinion of your work is very important to you?

EXPLORE IT
❇ On a return trip to Jerusalem, whom did Paul take along? (2:1)
❇ Why did Paul go to Jerusalem? (2:2)
■ Why did Paul seize the opportunity to meet with the other apostles? (2:2)
❇ What was Paul's motive in bringing Titus along on the Jerusalem trip? (2:3-5)
■ What did the "false brothers" do? (2:4)
❇ How did Paul and his partners respond to the Judaizers? (2:5)
❇ How did the Jerusalem leaders respond to Paul's message? (2:6)
■ How did James, Peter, and John respond to Paul's mission? (2:7-9)
❇ What was the "right hand of fellowship"? (2:9)
❇ What was the only thing that the Jewish leaders requested of Paul? (2:10)

GET IT
■ Even though Paul asserted his independence from the apostles, how did he also show his solidarity with them?
■ Why was it important for Paul to have the apostles' approval?
❇ Why was it important for Paul to stand up for freedom from the Law?
❇ In what ways do some Christians try to impose rules on others?
❇ What does caring for the poor have to do with telling others about Christ?

APPLY IT
■ How can you express today your appreciation and respect for older Christians who have helped you in your spiritual walk?
❇ What can you do to help a poor person or family this week?

Galatians 2:11-21
Paul Opposes Peter

TOPICS
Compromise, Death, Doctrine, Faith, God, Gospel, Hypocrisy, Jesus Christ, Law, Life, Opposition, Righteousness

OPEN IT
■ If a colleague of yours were doing something wrong, how would you confront the person?
❇ How do you tend to take criticism?

EXPLORE IT
❇ When Peter visited Antioch, what did Paul do? (2:11)
■ Why did Paul rebuke Peter? (2:11-13)
❇ Why did Peter feel free to eat with Gentiles at one time? (2:12)
❇ Who pressured Peter to stop eating with Gentiles? (2:12) Why?
❇ How did Peter's behavior influence other Christians? (2:13)
■ What did Paul say in response to Peter's hypocritical behavior? (2:14)
❇ What did Paul say to those who were Jews by birth? (2:15)
■ How is a person justified before God? (2:16)
❇ How does a Christian avoid being a lawbreaker? (2:17-19)
❇ How is the new life characterized by faith and not works? (2:20)
❇ How does Christ live out His life through Christians? (2:20)
❇ How had Peter set aside God's grace? (2:21)
❇ If righteousness were possible by keeping the Law, why would the Cross have been absolutely useless? (2:21)

GET IT
❇ What hypocritical practices have you seen in churches you have visited?
■ Why is it easier for Christians to live by rules and traditions than by faith?
❇ If Paul hadn't spoken out against Peter's inconsistency, what could have happened among Hebrew and Gentile Christians?
❇ How did the matter of legalism provide Paul with the opportunity to spell out the doctrine of justification by faith?
■ How could addressing a problem in your congregation provide a real opportunity for spiritual growth?

APPLY IT
■ How do you plan to confront troubling behavior the next time you see it in your local fellowship?
❇ In the future, how can you show courage in resisting well-meaning Christians who want to impose their own rules on others?

Galatians 3:1-14
Faith or Observance of the Law

TOPICS
Believe, Bible, Blessing, Faith, Gospel, Holy Spirit, Jesus Christ, Law, Miracles, Questions, Righteousness, Suffering

OPEN IT
❇ When was the last time you were sarcastic to someone?
❇ If you were trying to convince a friend to believe in what you were saying, what tone of voice would you use?
■ If someone close to you displayed a lack of knowledge about a subject you knew well, what would you do about it?

EXPLORE IT
■ Why did Paul scold the Galatians? (3:1)
❇ What rhetorical question did Paul ask? (3:2)
❇ How did Paul expect the Galatians to answer his question? (3:2)
❇ Based on Paul's second question to the Christians, how did he think the Galatians felt the Law could help them? (3:3)
❇ Why did Paul ask the Galatians if their suffering had been for nothing? (3:4)
❇ On what basis did the Holy Spirit perform miracles? (3:5)
■ How did Paul's use of Abraham as an example of faith strike a blow to the champions of the Law? (3:6-8)
❇ How did Paul link the past with the present? (3:9)
❇ What is the curse of the law? (3:10)
❇ How does a person become justified before God? (3:11)
■ Why is combining faith and Law impossible? (3:11-12)
❇ How does Christ save people from the curse of the Law? (3:13)
❇ Why is Christ's redemptive work effective for both Jews and Gentiles? (3:14)

GET IT
■ When has your pastor corrected the congregation?
❇ What rules have become very important in your church?
❇ How much of your righteousness is self-righteous behavior?
❇ If you were to write a two-line summary of the doctrine of justification, what would you say?
■ In your view, what is the biggest difference between Law and faith?
❇ What is your relationship to Abraham?
❇ What has Christ done for you?

APPLY IT
❇ In what situation can you share the blessings of Christ with someone else this week?
■ How can you help new Christians get a clear understanding of their position in Christ?

Galatians 3:15-25
The Law and the Promise

TOPICS
Believe, Bible, Covenant, Faith, God, Jesus Christ, Law, Mediator, Promises, Righteousness, Sin

OPEN IT
■ Where do you keep important personal or family documents?
❉ If you lost all your legal papers, what would you do?
❉ What is the oldest legal document you possess?

EXPLORE IT
❉ What spiritual truth did Paul explain by using an everyday example? (3:15-16)
■ Through whom were the promises of Abraham fulfilled? (3:16)
❉ How long after the promises to Abraham was the Law given? (3:17)
❉ What was the relationship of the Law to the covenant? (3:17)
■ What was the promised inheritance? (3:18)
❉ What was the purpose of the Law? (3:19)
❉ How was the Law put into effect? (3:19)
❉ The Law required a mediator; how was the promise given to humanity without a mediator? (3:20)
■ Why did God give both the Law and promises? (3:21-22)
❉ How did the Law pave the way for the gospel? (3:22-23)
❉ What freedom did faith in Christ bring? (3:23-25)
❉ How did Christ's coming change the role of the Law? (3:24-25)

GET IT
❉ Why did Paul go to such lengths to explain Law and grace?
❉ When have you perceived God as a harsh disciplinarian?
❉ How much of your experience as a Christian is based on a set of rules?
❉ If you had lived in Old Testament times, how would you have benefited from living under the Law?
■ How does faith in Christ set us free from legalism?
■ How has faith in Christ set you free from legalism?
❉ How does God fulfill His promises in your life?

APPLY IT
■ How can you help an unbelieving friend understand that being a good, law-abiding person is not enough to get right with God?
❉ What life-changing promise of God do you want to hold on to this week?
❉ For what spiritual inheritance can you praise God today?

Galatians 3:26–4:7
Sons of God

TOPICS
Children, Faith, Family, God, Heart, Heritage, Holy Spirit, Jesus Christ, Law, Promises, Slavery

OPEN IT
❉ What would be the advantages of growing up in a multiethnic neighborhood?
■ If you could become part of another family, which family would you choose?

EXPLORE IT
■ What was the family status of the Galatian believers? (3:26)
❉ How are Christians joined to Christ? (3:27)
❉ What new garments did the Galatians put on? (3:27)
❉ How does God cut across cultural and human distinctions in the family of faith? (3:28)
■ How were the Galatians heirs of the promise to Abraham? (3:29)
❉ How are those who live under the Law immature? (4:1-2)
❉ Before the Galatians became Christians, how were they like slaves? (4:3)
❉ How did the coming of Jesus perfectly satisfy the requirements of the Law ? (4:4-5)
■ How did the believers benefit by becoming part of God's family? (4:5)
❉ Whom did God send into the lives of the Galatian Christians? (4:6)
❉ How did the Spirit move the believers to address God? (4:6)
❉ Since the Galatians were no longer slaves, what had they become? (4:7)

GET IT
❉ How would you describe your spiritual clothing?
❉ What is your favorite way to address God?
❉ If you were a Galatian Christian, how would you feel after learning of your position in God's family?
■ As a child of God, do you behave like a slave or more like an heir?
❉ In what ways do even Christians discriminate or value some types of people over others?
■ How do many churches hold on to cultural barriers even as they represent Christ?
❉ In what ways should churches work to break down barriers between groups?

APPLY IT
■ How can you take action to step beyond your cultural boundaries in befriending Christians who are different from you?
❉ How can you develop more intimacy with and trust in your heavenly Father during the coming days?

Galatians 4:8-20
Paul's Concern for the Galatians

TOPICS
Children, Choices, God, Gospel, Idolatry, Influence, Jesus Christ, Joy, Legalism, Rejection, Sickness, Slavery, Truth

OPEN IT
❉ How have you become estranged from a former friend?

■ In what ways have you switched alliances among your circle of friends during the past few years?
❊ Are you more or less joyful than you used to be? Why?

EXPLORE IT
❊ Before becoming Christians, to what were the Galatians enslaved? (4:8)
■ After they became believers, how did the Galatians turn back to their paganism? (4:9-10)
❊ Why did these Christians go back to observing the Mosaic calendar? (4:9-10)
❊ How did Paul express his concern for the Galatians? (4:11)
■ Why did Paul tell the Christians to follow his example? (4:12)
❊ What had been Paul's experience with the Galatian believers? (4:12-14)
❊ How had the Galatians esteemed Paul? (4:15)
❊ Why did the believers turn away from Paul? (4:16)
■ What motivated the Judaizers to turn the Galatians against Paul? (4:17)
❊ What did Paul say in defense of zealousness? (4:18)
❊ How did Paul express his attitude toward the Galatians? (4:19-20)
❊ How did Paul want his "dear children" to change? (4:19)
❊ Why did Paul want to be with the believers? (4:20)

GET IT
❊ What are some of the "weak and miserable principles" by which non-Christians live their lives?
■ After experiencing salvation, why do some Christians return to their former bad habits?
❊ What bad habits are hard for you to break?
❊ How have we allowed cultural practices to affect the way we celebrate Christmas and Easter?
❊ How does your pastor show concern for your spiritual growth?
■ When have you turned away from friends because you did not like what they had to say?
❊ How can we show concern for Christians who have turned away from the truth?

APPLY IT
❊ What is one step you can take, starting today, to increase the joy in your life?
■ What friendship can you mend this week for the sake of Christ?

Galatians 4:21-31
Hagar and Sarah

TOPICS
Believers, Bible, Children, Covenant, Freedom, Holy Spirit, Law, Slavery

OPEN IT
■ What is unique about being the firstborn child in a family?
❊ In your family, how were you and your siblings each treated differently?

EXPLORE IT
❊ Before the Galatians truly gave themselves over to the Law, what did Paul ask them to consider? (4:21)
❊ Why did Paul appeal to the example of Abraham? (4:22)
■ What was the difference in status between Abraham's two sons? (4:22)
❊ How were Abraham's sons conceived? (4:23)
❊ How did Hagar represent the covenant at Mount Sinai? (4:24)
❊ How did Paul refer to the birth of Abraham's sons? (4:24-27)
❊ In what way did Hagar typify first-century Jerusalem? (4:25)
❊ How was Sarah an example of the "Jerusalem that is above"? (4:26-27)
❊ How did Paul apply an ancient prophecy to Sarah's history? (4:27)
■ How were the Galatians like Isaac (the child of promise)? (4:28)
❊ How were the Judaizers like Ishmael (the child of slavery)? (4:29)
❊ Based on his illustration, how did Paul expect the Galatians to deal with the legalists? (4:28-30)
■ How did Paul compare Ishmael's persecution of Isaac to the legalists' opposition to the Christians? (4:29-30)
❊ How did Paul align himself with the Galatians and Sarah? (4:31)

GET IT
❊ Why was Paul's allegory helpful in explaining Law and grace?
❊ In your family, do you feel like a child of Hagar or a child of Sarah? Why?
■ In what ways do Christians try to impose extrabiblical standards on one another?
■ Which of your own rules or personal standards are you tempted to require of others?
❊ How does the new birth in Christ give us freedom?
❊ What do you have in common with Isaac?
❊ How should you treat people who try to impose their standards on you?

APPLY IT
❊ What can you do this week to encourage other Christians to enjoy their freedom in Christ?
■ What will help you avoid unfairly imposing your own standards on others?
❊ How can you start drawing on your inheritance in Christ today?

Galatians 5:1-15
Freedom in Christ

TOPICS
Burdens, Confusion, Disobedience, Freedom, Grace, Holy Spirit, Jesus Christ, Law, Love, Righteousness, Serving, Sin

OPEN IT
■ If you took up running, would you jog for enjoyment or train to compete in races? Why?
❊ Do you prefer group or individual sports? Why?

❇ Do you like games with challenging instructions and rules, or games with simple instructions and few rules? Why?

EXPLORE IT
■ What challenge did Paul set before the Galatians? (5:1)
❇ Why did Paul challenge the Christians to be resolute? (5:1)
❇ What warning did Paul issue to the Galatians? (5:2)
❇ How would turning to the Law obligate the Galatian Christians? (5:3)
❇ What consequence would seeking justification by Law bring? (5:4)
❇ How did Paul contrast legalists and true believers? (5:5)
❇ How did Paul sum up the significance of circumcision? (5:6)
❇ What really matters? (5:6)
■ How did Paul describe the Galatians' Christian experience? (5:7)
❇ How had false teaching affected the Galatian church? (5:8-9)
❇ Why was Paul optimistic about the Galatians? (5:10)
❇ How did the Cross mark the end of the Law? (5:11)
❇ What strong words did Paul have for the Judaizers? (5:12)
■ How were the Galatian Christians to use their freedom? (5:14)
❇ What were the Galatians called on to guard against? (5:15)

GET IT
■ What challenge does this passage set before your church?
❇ What are the side effects of trying to be saved by keeping the Law?
❇ What unnecessary rules and regulations do Christians tend to impose on one another?
❇ What difference will it make if you run the Christian race with your attention on Christ?
■ How do some Christians abuse their freedom in Christ?
❇ In what ways are you hindered from loving others?
❇ When have you been guilty of backbiting and gossip?
❇ Why should you serve the family of God in love?

APPLY IT
❇ Who is one neighbor to whom you can show a gesture of love this week?
■ As you run your race for Christ today, how can you free yourself of unnecessary rules and regulations that hinder your progress?
❇ Whom can you invite to join you in running a good race?

Galatians 5:16-26
Life by the Spirit

TOPICS
Believers, Conflict, Desires, Discipline, Fruit, Gentleness, Goodness, Holy Spirit, Jesus Christ, Joy, Kindness, Kingdom of God/Heaven, Law, Love, Patience, Peace, Sin

OPEN IT
■ If you could change one personality trait in yourself, what would you change?
❇ What do you really like about yourself?

EXPLORE IT
❇ What would happen if the Galatians lived by the power of the Holy Spirit? (5:16)
❇ What is the conflict between the sinful nature and the Spirit? (5:17)
❇ How were the Galatians affected by the conflict between the sinful nature and the Spirit? (5:17)
■ How could the Galatian Christians lead godly lives? (5:18)
❇ What is one obvious feature of human nature? (5:19)
❇ To what sexual sins are we prone? (5:19)
■ What religious sins does the sinful nature produce? (5:20)
❇ What societal evils come from our sinful nature? (5:20-21)
❇ In what sense is Paul's list of sins incomplete? (5:21)
❇ What warning is given to those who live sinful lives? (5:21)
■ What happens to a Christian who is under the control of the Holy Spirit? (5:22-23)
❇ What is the result of yielding to the Spirit? (5:22-23)
❇ How do the Christian graces affect all areas of the believer's life? (5:22-23)
❇ How is a Christian empowered to live by the Spirit? (5:24-25)
❇ What did Paul tell the Galatian Christians not to do? (5:26)

GET IT
❇ How much should we rely on the Holy Spirit for guidance and power in our lives?
❇ How is your response of faith necessary in order for the Holy Spirit to have victory in you?
■ Why do Christians tend to excuse the behavior of their old nature?
❇ What acts of the sinful nature tend to entangle you?
❇ What is the fruit of the Spirit?
❇ In what sense do love, joy, peace, patience, kindness, goodness, faithfulness, gentleness, and self-control grow in a person much the way fruit grows on a tree?
❇ How can a person cultivate the character qualities of the Holy Spirit in his or her life?
❇ What can a Christian do to promote the growth of godly character in his or her life?
■ How do you see the character of the Holy Spirit growing in your life?
❇ Who is kept out of the kingdom of God?
❇ How does the warning against living a sinful life apply to someone you know?
❇ In what ways do Christians need to guard against conceit and envy?

APPLY IT
■ What can you do this week to nurture the character of the Holy Spirit in your life?
❇ How can you and the Spirit get rid of the dead wood that stifles your growth?
❇ What do you want to do the next time you encounter conceit or envy in your church?

Galatians 6:1-10
Doing Good to All

TOPICS
Believers, Burdens, Encouragement, Eternal Life, Holy Spirit, Money, Pastors, Restoration, Rewards, Self-centeredness, Sin

OPEN IT
■ How easily do you share your time and skills with others?
❇ What's hardest about serving others?
❇ How do you feel when you aren't thanked for going out of your way to help someone?

EXPLORE IT
❇ What did Paul say about helping a Christian overtaken by sin? (6:1)
❇ What warning about sin do strong Christians need to heed? (6:1)
■ How should Christians support each other? (6:2)
❇ What is the law of Christ? (6:2)
■ What is the antidote to self-deception? (6:3-4)
❇ How is carrying one's own load different from bearing the burdens of others? (6:5)
❇ What is the responsibility of church members toward their teaching elders? (6:6)
❇ How did Paul warn against a lack of financial support for the Christian workers in the Galatian churches? (6:7-8)
❇ How did Paul encourage the Christians to endure in service? (6:9)
❇ What did Paul say about a Christian's social responsibility? (6:10)
■ What responsibility do believers have toward each other? (6:10)

GET IT
■ What is the best approach to helping a Christian brother or sister caught in sin?
❇ How is your view of yourself in line with God's?
■ What encourages you to keep going in Christian service even when you feel like giving up?
❇ How would you evaluate your history of tithing?
❇ How can you help meet the needs of others outside the church?

APPLY IT
■ How can you help a member of your church this week with a particular burden he or she has?
❇ This week, what can you do to support someone in missions in a way that will please the Spirit?

Galatians 6:11-18
Not Circumcision but a New Creation

TOPICS
Believers, Body, Grace, Jesus Christ, Law, Mercy, Peace, Persecution, World

OPEN IT
■ What family traditions are very important to you?
❇ How willing are you to try new things?

EXPLORE IT
❇ What kind of letters did Paul inscribe? (6:11)
■ Why did certain people want the Galatians circumcised? (6:12-13)
❇ How did the legalists practice hypocrisy? (6:13)
❇ Who was being hypocritical? How? (6:13)
■ What did the legalists boast about? (6:13)
❇ What was Paul's only boast? (6:14)
❇ How did Paul and the legalists view the cross of Christ differently? (6:14)
■ In terms of salvation, how significant were outward religious symbols? (6:14-15)
❇ What was the only thing that mattered? (6:14-15)
❇ What blessing did Paul pronounce on believing Galatians and on believing Jews? (6:16)
❇ What did Paul want ended? (6:17)
❇ How did Paul show that he belonged to Christ? (6:17)
❇ How would you describe the tone of Paul's benediction to the Galatians? (6:18)

GET IT
■ What motivates you to observe certain religious traditions in your church?
❇ How important is it to make a good impression outwardly?
❇ In what ways should we be "crucified" to the world?
■ How did Paul show his love for the Galatians?
❇ How do other Christians recognize your love for them?

APPLY IT
❇ What sacrifices are you willing to make for the cross of Christ this week?
■ How can you show to the world in the coming weeks that you are becoming a new creation?

Ephesians 1:1-14

Spiritual Blessings in Christ

TOPICS
Adoption, Believers, Blessing, Doctrine, Glory, God, God's Will, Gospel, Holiness, Holy Spirit, Jesus Christ, Praise, Purpose, Salvation

OPEN IT
✻ How often do you compliment others?
✻ How do you usually respond when someone compliments you?
■ What blessings have you received recently?

EXPLORE IT
✻ How was Paul made an apostle? (1:1)
✻ To whom was the letter addressed? (1:1)
✻ What greetings did Paul extend to the believers at Ephesus? (1:2)
■ How has God blessed believers? (1:3)
✻ When did God's work of election take place? (1:4)
✻ What is the purpose of God's election? (1:4)
✻ What did God determine beforehand for those who believe in Christ? (1:5)
✻ What is the goal of God's election? (1:6)
✻ What is redemption? (1:7)
■ What does the work of Christ do for the believer? (1:7)
✻ What has God given the believer? (1:8-10)
✻ When will everything be brought together? (1:10)
✻ How did God's plan include people of different cultures? (1:11-12)
■ What is the role of the Holy Spirit in the lives of those called to receive spiritual blessings in Christ? (1:13-14)

GET IT
✻ What are spiritual blessings?
■ In everyday language, how would you describe the spiritual blessings given to you?
✻ How do you picture the persons of the Trinity at work in your life?
✻ How should knowing that you were chosen to be in the family of God affect your involvement in evangelism?
✻ What has Christ done on our behalf?
✻ How have you benefited from the grace of God?
■ For what work of God on your behalf are you most thankful? Why?
✻ Why did God do this amazing work for us?

APPLY IT
■ How can you say thank-you to God this week for what He has done for you?
✻ What do you need to do differently to live for the praise of God's glory this week?
✻ In the days ahead, how can you share with other people those blessings God has given you?

Ephesians 1:15-23

Thanksgiving and Prayer

TOPICS
Authority, Body, Church, Creation, Faith, God, Heaven, Holy Spirit, Jesus Christ, Love, Power, Prayer, Thankfulness

OPEN IT
✻ How do you celebrate Thanksgiving Day?
■ For what do you thank God on a daily basis?
✻ How do you show that you are thankful for those around you?

EXPLORE IT
■ What motivated Paul to pray for the Ephesians? (1:15-16)
✻ What did Paul ask God to give to the Ephesian Christians? (1:17)
✻ What is the purpose of having wisdom and revelation? (1:17)
■ Why did Paul ask that the Ephesians' hearts would continue to be enlightened? (1:18)
✻ What kind of help is available to all Christians? (1:19-20)
✻ How is God's power at work in all creation? (1:21)
✻ How does God's power reach across time? (1:21)
■ What did God place under Christ's control? (1:22)
✻ What appointment did God give Christ? (1:22)
✻ What is the church's relationship to Christ? (1:22-23)

GET IT
■ How did Paul support the Ephesian Christians?
✻ How can you encourage growth in other Christians?
■ The Ephesians showed faith in Christ and love for one another; what qualities distinguish your Christian walk?
✻ How do you know that Christ's power is sufficient for your life?
✻ How does the knowledge of God's authority and control make you secure?
✻ When did you last express a prayer of thanks for other saints?

APPLY IT
✻ Since God's power is available to you, what do you need to do to take hold of it this week?
■ What people in need could you remember in your prayers this week?

Ephesians 2:1-10

Made Alive in Christ

TOPICS
Believers, Craftsmanship, Death, Faith, Gifts, God, Grace, Heaven, Jesus Christ, Life, Love, Mercy, Sin

OPEN IT
■ When have you shown mercy to a person who deserved to be punished?
✻ What is the best gift you've ever received?

EXPLORE IT
✻ Before conversion, what was the spiritual position of the Ephesians? (2:1)

■ What three characteristics mark the condition of a person without Christ? (2:2-3)
❋ How are both Jew and Gentile alike? (2:3)
■ Why did God make those who were dead alive with Christ? (2:4-5)
❋ What describes God's action in making us alive? (2:5)
❋ What position has God given Christians in Christ by His divine power? (2:6)
❋ What will God show in the future eternal state? (2:7)
❋ What is the means of salvation? (2:8)
❋ Where does salvation come from? (2:8)
■ Why can no one boast in his own salvation? (2:8-9)
❋ How is the believer God's work of art? (2:10)
❋ What is the purpose of God's workmanship? (2:10)

GET IT
❋ What were you like before you became a Christian?
■ Why was your position hopeless before becoming a Christian?
❋ When did you receive the gift of new life?
❋ How would you describe God's grace to you?
❋ Why hasn't anyone deserved God's grace, mercy, or riches?
■ How do you see God's creative workmanship operating in your life?

APPLY IT
■ With whom can you share the news of God's mercy? How?
❋ Empowered by the Holy Spirit, what good work for the kingdom of God can you do this week?

Ephesians 2:11-22
One in Christ

TOPICS
Church, Citizenship, God, Good News, Holy Spirit, Jesus Christ, Law, Peace, Reconciliation, Separation

OPEN IT
❋ When was a time you felt deprived?
■ What people have you known whose upbringing and family connections provided them with certain advantages?

EXPLORE IT
❋ What did Paul command the Ephesians to remember? (2:11)
❋ Why was being uncircumcised a desperate problem for the Gentiles? (2:11-12)
■ How did Christ's work on the cross transform the condition of the Gentiles? (2:13)
❋ Who brought peace to Jewish and Gentile believers? (2:14)
❋ Why did Christ end the hostility between Jews and Gentiles? (2:14-16)
❋ How did the enmity between Jews and Gentiles come to an end? (2:15-16)
❋ What is the result of believing the message of Christ? (2:17-18)
■ In Christ, how did the Gentiles achieve new spiritual and social status? (2:19)
❋ On what foundation were the Ephesian believers built? (2:20)
❋ How was Christ part of the foundation? (2:20)
❋ How was the church described as living and growing? (2:21)
■ How were the Ephesians becoming part of God's dwelling? (2:22)
❋ How did God live in the Ephesian Christians? (2:22)

GET IT
■ How does the gospel break down religious and social barriers?
❋ Why is it that many churches maintain a dividing wall that keeps out other social and ethnic groups?
■ How does your church treat foreigners and aliens?
❋ How should churches treat foreigners and aliens?
❋ If Paul were speaking to your congregation about reconciliation, would his words be ones of praise or disappointment?
❋ In Christ, what is every Christian's relationship to other Christians?
❋ What is your role in helping your congregation show unity in Christ?

APPLY IT
■ How can you show God's love to an "outsider" this week?
❋ To what groups or individuals can you extend the peace of Christ this week? How?

Ephesians 3:1-13
Paul the Preacher to the Gentiles

TOPICS
Church, God, Grace, Holy Spirit, Humility, Insight, Jesus Christ, Power, Purpose, Serving, Suffering

OPEN IT
❋ If you found buried treasure in your backyard, what would be your first course of action?
■ Do you like to figure things out for yourself or get help as soon as possible?
❋ How good are you at explaining things to others?

EXPLORE IT
❋ Why did Paul go to prison? (3:1)
❋ How familiar was Paul with the company of believers at Ephesus? (3:2)
❋ What would the Ephesians have heard about Paul? (3:2-3)
■ To what mystery did Paul refer? (3:2-3)
❋ How did Paul receive insight into the mystery of Christ? (3:4-5)
❋ Who revealed the mystery of Christ to Paul? (3:5)
❋ When was the mystery of Christ disclosed? (3:5)
■ How did Paul reveal the mystery of Christ? (3:6)
❋ How was Paul enabled to be a servant? (3:7)
❋ What was Paul's attitude to his call? (3:8)
❋ What was Paul called to disclose? (3:9)
❋ Through what medium was God's wisdom communicated? (3:10)
■ How did God accomplish His plan? (3:11)
❋ In light of God's work, how may believers approach Him? (3:11-12)

❊ Why were Paul's sufferings the glory of the Ephesians? (3:13)

GET IT

■ How do you think Gentile believers responded to Paul's explanation of "the mystery of Christ"?
❊ How should we all be involved in evangelism?
❊ How can you serve others who need salvation?
❊ What helps you to serve the Lord when it is inconvenient, awkward, or painful for you?
❊ What gives you confidence and freedom in approaching God?
■ How is sharing the gospel with someone like discovering priceless treasure?

APPLY IT

❊ In the days ahead, what can you do to help outsiders feel welcome in your church?
■ What can you do this week to help others understand the mystery of Christ's provision for sin?
❊ What can you do this week to develop a patient spirit so that you will not become discouraged by suffering?

Ephesians 3:14-21

A Prayer for the Ephesians

TOPICS

Church, Faith, Family, Glory, God, Heart, Holy Spirit, Jesus Christ, Love, Power, Prayer

OPEN IT

❊ What is your favorite posture for praying? Why?
■ How often do you pray for those you love?

EXPLORE IT

❊ When Paul prayed, what posture did he assume? (3:14)
❊ To whom is God the Father? (3:14-15)
■ What did Paul request of the Father? (3:16)
❊ Through whom would the Ephesians be empowered? (3:16)
■ How would Christ dwell in the believers' hearts? (3:17)
❊ Why did Paul want the Ephesians to be rooted and established in love? (3:17-19)
❊ What did Paul want the Ephesians to grasp? (3:18)
❊ What does the love of Christ surpass? (3:19)
■ How did Paul close his prayer? (3:20-21)
❊ How did Paul's doxology serve as a fitting conclusion to the doctrine he had presented in the first three chapters of this letter? (3:20-21)

GET IT

❊ How would you pray Paul's prayer in your own words?
■ If Paul were your prayer partner, how might he encourage you in your devotional life?
❊ What is your understanding of Christ's love for you?
❊ In what ways do you need to become firmly rooted in love?
❊ How have you allowed God to become too small in your life?
■ How does Paul's doxology encourage you?
❊ What is your favorite doxology? Why?
❊ How do you usually end your prayers?

APPLY IT

❊ How can you take a new and creative approach to your prayer life?
❊ What do you need to do to spread Christ's love to others this week?
■ How could you include Paul's doxology as a part of your personal devotion each day?

Ephesians 4:1-16

Unity in the Body of Christ

TOPICS

Body, Church, Faith, Gentleness, Gifts, God, Grace, Holy Spirit, Hope, Humility, Jesus Christ, Love, Pastors, Patience, Peace, Serving, Teaching, Unity, Work

OPEN IT

❊ What one quality would you like to develop in your character?
■ What keeps sports teams unified?
❊ What do you consider yourself good at doing?
❊ What skill or talent would you like to master?

EXPLORE IT

❊ What did Paul urge the Ephesians to do? (4:1)
❊ What three virtues foster unity among Christians? (4:2)
■ How should Christians conduct themselves toward each other? Why? (4:2-6)
■ What are the seven elements of Christian unity? (4:4-6)
❊ How is Christian unity related to the nature of God? (4:4-6)
■ How are we enabled to live at peace with each other? (4:7)
❊ Who gives grace to each believer? (4:7)
❊ How did Paul confirm God's giving of gifts? (4:8)
❊ What commentary did Paul make on the Old Testament passage he quoted? Why? (4:9-11)
❊ With what kind of people does God fill the church? (4:11)
❊ What is the purpose of spiritual gifts? (4:12-13)
❊ What results from gifted believers equipping the church? (4:14-16)

GET IT

❊ Why did Paul stress the theme of Christian unity to the Ephesians?
■ How do you get along with other Christians?
■ What is God's prescription for unity among believers?
❊ How does the Spirit help you maintain the "bond of peace" with others in your church?
❊ How have you benefited from the Christian leadership in your church?
❊ What is your responsibility to help others in the body of Christ?
❊ How unified is your church?

APPLY IT

■ How do you need to show humility, gentleness, and patience in dealing with a difficult relationship this week?
❊ What service can you offer another church member to help build up the body of Christ?
❊ To whom do you need to speak the truth lovingly this week?

Ephesians 4:17–5:21
Living as Children of Light

TOPICS
Anger, Believers, Children, Darkness, Forgiveness, God, Hardheartedness, Help, Holiness, Holy Spirit, Ignorance, Immorality, Jesus Christ, Kindness, Light, Love, Lust, Lying, Nature, Needs, Righteousness, Separation, Sin, Submission, Wisdom

OPEN IT
❊ Do you prefer wearing old, comfortable clothing or dressy outfits? Why?
❊ How do you feel when you wear a brand-new suit or outfit?
■ What do you do with your worn-out clothing?

EXPLORE IT
❊ In what way were Ephesian believers instructed not to live as Gentiles? (4:17-19)
❊ How did Paul contrast the Ephesian Christians with the Gentiles? (4:20-21)
■ In what way does God want Christians to change? (4:22-24)
❊ How should new Christians stop living? (4:22)
❊ How should new Christians begin living? (4:23-24)
❊ What should we keep in mind concerning lying, anger, and stealing? (4:25-28)
❊ How should believers speak to one another? (4:29)
❊ How can the Holy Spirit be hurt? (4:29-30)
❊ What five vices are believers to get rid of? (4:31)
❊ What positive commands did Paul give the Ephesians? (4:32)
■ How are Christians to imitate God? (5:1-2)
■ From what practices should Christians abstain? (5:3-6)
❊ Whom do we need to avoid? Why? (5:5-7)
❊ Why should Christians not become partners with non-Christians? (5:7-8)
❊ How does life in darkness contrast with life in the light? (5:9-20)
❊ How should Spirit-controlled believers relate to one another? (5:21)

GET IT
■ Since becoming a Christian, what old habits have you discarded?
❊ What aspects of your old nature do you still need to get rid of?
❊ How do you see the new nature taking hold in your life?
■ What evidence do you see that your life is controlled by the Holy Spirit?
❊ What fruit of the light do you see in your life?
❊ In what way should you be submissive to other Christians?
❊ How would you rate your spiritual wardrobe: basic? adequate? overflowing?
❊ What aspect of your Christian life do you want to practice more consistently?

APPLY IT
■ What would be the first step for you in changing an old pattern of behavior?
❊ What can you do this week to make your Christian living more consistent?
❊ How can you relate to others today in new, joyful ways?

Ephesians 5:22-33
Wives and Husbands

TOPICS
Bible, Body, Church, Family, Holiness, Jesus Christ, Love, Marriage, Respect, Submission, Unity

OPEN IT
❊ What husband-and-wife team do you greatly admire?
■ In your view, what one quality or ability sustains a marriage relationship?

EXPLORE IT
❊ What service should wives render to the Lord? (5:22)
❊ What is the relationship of the husband to the wife? (5:23)
❊ How is Christ's headship of the church an example to the husband? (5:23)
■ How is the relationship of the church to Christ an example to wives? (5:24)
❊ How are husbands commanded to love their wives? (5:25)
❊ How did Christ prepare a bride for Himself? (5:26-27)
■ How should husbands love their wives? (5:28-30)
❊ How is the bond between husband and wife greater than the bond between parent and child? (5:31)
■ How does the bond between Christ and the church illustrate the love of a husband for his wife? (5:32)
❊ In sum, what are the responsibilities of the husband and wife toward each other? (5:33)

GET IT
■ How should both husband and wife model themselves on Christ?
■ Why would unselfishness be an essential part of a Christian marriage?
❊ What should a Christian wife give her husband?
❊ How should a Christian husband care for his wife?
❊ How does a healthy Christian marriage relationship honor the Lord?
❊ What are some ways local churches can help Christian couples strengthen their marriages?

APPLY IT
■ What is something you can do to help a Christian couple strengthen their marriage?
❊ How can you treat your spouse with more respect and love this week?
❊ How can you express your thankfulness to Christ today for making you His bride?

Ephesians 6:1-4
Children and Parents

TOPICS
Children, Discipline, Discouragement, Honor, Instructions, Jesus Christ, Marriage, Parents, Promises, Training

OPEN IT
❊ What are some of the enjoyable aspects of being a parent?
❊ How do you treat children differently from the way your parents treated you?
■ If you could change one thing about your parents, what would you change?

EXPLORE IT
❊ Why is a child's obedience to his or her parents pleasing to the Lord? (6:1)
❊ Why should children obey parents? (6:1)
❊ How is obedience to parents part of a child's obligation to Christ? (6:1)
■ What does it mean to "honor your father and mother"? (6:2-3)
❊ What was promised to Israelite children who obeyed their parents? (6:2-3)
❊ How does God's commandment and promise to children hold true today? (6:2-3)
■ What does God want fathers not to do? (6:4)
❊ What does God want fathers to do? (6:4)
■ How should children be reared and nourished? (6:4)
❊ How is the Lord to be the center of parent-child relationships? (6:4)

GET IT
❊ Why should parents pay attention to their child's natural bent?
■ Why is it easier for children to obey fair and loving parents than unreasonable and demanding parents?
❊ How does rearing children in the "training and instruction of the Lord" provide guidelines for fathers?
■ How does honoring your parents bring you blessing?
❊ How do you feel about your ability to be a good parent?
❊ How can the Lord support you in your role as a parent?
❊ How can a parent avoid exasperating his or her children?

APPLY IT
■ What can you do to improve or strengthen your relationship with your parents?
❊ How can you avoid exasperating your children?
❊ How do you need to nurture healthy family relationships this week?

Ephesians 6:5-9
Slaves and Masters

TOPICS
Favoritism, Heart, Jesus Christ, Obedience, Respect, Rewards, Serving, Sincerity, Slavery, Work

OPEN IT
❊ Had you lived long ago and owned slaves, what kind of slave owner would you have been?
■ If you were a slave, what would be the worst part of being someone's property?

EXPLORE IT
■ Why did Paul tell slaves to obey their masters "with respect and fear"? (6:5)
❊ What did Paul tell slaves to do? (6:5-8)
❊ What responsibilities did slaves have to their masters? (6:5-8)
❊ How did Paul transform the work of the slave? (6:5-8)
■ How could slaves serve the Lord while working for their masters? (6:5-8)
■ How would slaves benefit from winning the favor of their masters? (6:6)
❊ With what attitude should the slave serve his master? (6:7)
❊ What reward for Christian service could the slave expect? (6:7-8)
❊ What directives did Paul give slave owners? (6:9)
❊ Why did Paul warn owners against abusing their slaves? (6:9)
❊ How does God view rank or social status? (6:9)

GET IT
■ Why did Paul call slaves to obey and not to revolt against the system of slavery?
❊ How were Paul's instructions helpful and protective to both slave and slave owner?
❊ How did Paul's words to slaves and masters relate to the teaching in the rest of his letter to the Ephesians?
❊ How do we enslave certain groups in our society?
❊ How does God want us to treat people who are subordinate to us?
❊ How does God want us to treat people who are over us?
■ How does God want us to treat all people with whom we work?
❊ When should Christians work for social justice?
❊ What importance do you attach to rank or social status?
❊ What importance should we attach to rank or social status?

APPLY IT
❊ How can you improve your attitude toward someone you work with?
■ How can you remember to serve all people wholeheartedly, as if you were serving the Lord?

Ephesians 6:10-24
The Armor of God

TOPICS
Armor, Bible, Blessing, Darkness, Encouragement, Evil, God, Holy Spirit, Power, Prayer, Satan, Strength

OPEN IT
❊ How do you protect your home from danger?
■ If you were a police officer, what extra precautions would you take to guard against danger?
❊ Do you tend to be the trusting type, or are you suspicious of other people? Why?

EXPLORE IT
❊ What did Paul say to exhort his audience? (6:10)
■ What did Paul tell the believers to put on? (6:11)
❊ Why do Christians need to put on God's armor? (6:11-12)
❊ What can Christians dressed in the full armor of God expect? (6:13)
❊ What mandate does God give all Christians? (6:14)

■ How should Christians be armed for battle? (6:14-17)
■ What last two pieces of armor did Paul tell all Christians to take up? (6:18)
❊ Why did Paul ask the Ephesians to pray for him? (6:19-20)
❊ Who took Paul's letter to the Christians at Ephesus? (6:21)
❊ How would Tychicus help the Ephesians? (6:21-22)
❊ With what kind of words did Paul bless his audience? (6:23)
❊ What did Paul say in benediction? (6:24)

GET IT
❊ Why do you think Paul used the detailed description of a Roman soldier's armor to explain spiritual warfare?
❊ How would you describe the armor of God in your own words?
❊ What is spiritual warfare?
■ How often are you engaged in spiritual warfare?
❊ In what way is the Christian life like a battle?
❊ Why is the Christian life like a battlefield?
■ What pieces of armor are you missing?
❊ How often do you pray in the Spirit?
❊ How often do you pray for other Christians?
❊ In what ways do you need peace, love, faith, and grace in your life right now?

APPLY IT
❊ How can you lean on the Holy Spirit's help in doing battle for the kingdom of God each day?
■ How can you encourage another Christian in his or her spiritual battles?

Philippians 1:1-11
Thanksgiving and Prayer

TOPICS
Believers, Blessing, Glory, God, Gospel, Grace, Jesus Christ, Partnerships, Peace, Praise, Prayer, Righteousness, Serving

OPEN IT
■ What's your usual way of saying hello to your friends?
❊ In your family, how important are greetings in affirming each other?

EXPLORE IT
❊ Who was the author of the letter to the Philippians? (1:1)
■ How did Paul identify himself and his coworker? (1:1)
❊ To whom did Paul address this letter? (1:1)
■ How did Paul greet the Philippians? (1:2)
❊ When Paul thought about the Philippians, what did he do? (1:3)
❊ How were the Philippians in partnership with Paul? (1:4-5)
■ What was Paul confident about? (1:6)
❊ How did Paul feel about the Philippian church? (1:7-8)
❊ What did Paul report that he prayed for? (1:9)
❊ What two results did Paul seek? (1:10-11)

GET IT
❊ How does your pastor greet church members?
❊ Why is it a good practice to begin a letter with a Christian blessing?
■ What godly encouragement can you offer other Christians?
■ Paul complimented the church at Philippi; what positive things can you say about your congregation?
❊ How is Paul's prayer for the Philippians a good prayer for you to copy?

APPLY IT
❊ What prayer of thanksgiving can you offer for your church today?
❊ How can you encourage someone in his or her Christian journey this week?
■ Which Christian brother or sister would be heartened to receive a letter from you this week?

Philippians 1:12-30
Paul's Chains Advance the Gospel

TOPICS
Believers, Circumstances, Courage, Death, Faith, Gospel, Holy Spirit, Jesus Christ, Joy, Life, Motives, Prayer, Reputation, Salvation, Suffering

OPEN IT
❊ How interested are you in the lives of famous people?
■ How often do you watch TV shows or read articles about celebrities?

EXPLORE IT
❊ How was Paul's ministry affected by his bondage? (1:12-14)
■ Why was Paul being talked about? (1:13)
❊ How did Paul's incarceration affect the testimony of others? (1:14)
❊ Why did some people preach Christ out of envy and rivalry? (1:15-17)
❊ Why did some people preach Christ in love? (1:15-16)
■ What made Paul rejoice? (1:18)
❊ Why did Paul expect to be delivered from his predicament? (1:19)
❊ How did Paul expect to be delivered? (1:19-20)
❊ What was Paul's main purpose in living? (1:21)
■ What were Paul's convictions about living and dying? (1:22-24)
❊ Why did Paul think he would remain alive? (1:24-26)
❊ What did Paul want the believers to do? (1:27-30)
❊ How did Paul tell the Philippians to face opposition? (1:27-30)
❊ How did Paul encourage the Christians at Philippi? (1:29)

GET IT
■ How did Paul's notoriety work to his advantage?
❊ How would you like the reputation of being a fearless Christian?
❊ To what degree do you share Paul's passion for the gospel?
❊ For what do you truly live?
❊ Whom do you know who is suffering for Christ right now?
❊ How is your church different from the Philippian church?
■ What's the toughest thing you've had to experience as a Christian?
❊ What are you willing to risk to have the reputation of being a fearless Christian?
❊ What about your life-style do you most want to change in your desire to live for Christ?

APPLY IT
❊ What step toward dedicating every area of your life to Christ can you take today?
■ What can you do today to encourage someone who is suffering because of his or her faith?

Philippians 2:1-11
Imitating Christ's Humility

TOPICS
Believers, Compassion, Confession, Death, Encouragement, Example, Fellowship, God, Holy Spirit, Humility, Jesus Christ, Joy, Love, Names, Obedience, People, Pride, Self-centeredness, Serving, Unity

OPEN IT
❊ When was the last time you had a squabble with a family member?
■ How much of a peacemaker are you?

EXPLORE IT
■ What four qualities mark unity with Christ? (2:1)
❊ How can Christians show their unity in Christ in practical ways? (2:2)
■ What did Paul say about self-centeredness? (2:3-4)
❊ What did Paul exhort believers to have? (2:5)
❊ What did Christ set aside when He became a man? (2:6-8)
❊ How did Jesus limit Himself? (2:6-8)
❊ How was Christ fully God and fully man at the same time? (2:6-8)
■ How is Christ the best example of humility and unselfishness for us? (2:6-8)
❊ Why did Christ take on the limitations of being human even though He was of the same nature as God? (2:7)
❊ How did God exalt Jesus? (2:9)
❊ How did Christ win sovereignty over all people and over everything? (2:10)
❊ What confession will every person make? (2:11)

GET IT
❊ How does your life show that you count on Christ?
❊ How do petty quarrels hold you back in your Christian walk?
■ How can Christ help you keep peace with others?
❊ What hinders unity in your church?
❊ What kind of disposition does Christ want us to have?
■ How does Christ's example of humility challenge our natural self-centeredness?

APPLY IT
■ What practical steps can you take this week to demonstrate humility in your relationships?
❊ For the sake of unity in Christ, what petty squabbles should you clear up right away? How?

Philippians 2:12-18
Shining as Stars

TOPICS
Arguments, Believers, Complaining, God, Jesus Christ, Joy, Obedience, People, Sacrifice, Salvation, Serving, Sin, Witnessing, Work

OPEN IT
❊ Would you prefer to explore the universe aboard a spacecraft or looking through a powerful telescope? Why?
❊ What do you most enjoy about the nighttime sky?
❊ What is the most frequent complaint you hear?
■ Who pointed the way for you in your first job?

EXPLORE IT
■ What did the Philippian Christians need to obey? (2:12)
❊ What were the Philippian believers to work out? (2:12-13)
❊ How would God help the Philippians obey Him? (2:12-13)
❊ What instructions did Paul give in relation to everyday Christian living? (2:14-16)
■ Why were the Philippians not shining "like stars" in their world? (2:14-16)

❇ Why did the Philippian assembly need to show a united front to unbelievers? (2:14-16)
❇ What would enable Paul to boast about the Philippians? (2:14-16)
❇ Whose honor was Paul concerned about? (2:16)
■ How did Paul view his own life? (2:17)
❇ How did Paul view the faith of the Philippian believers? (2:17)
❇ What did Paul want his friends at Philippi to experience? (2:18)

GET IT
❇ What does it mean "to work out your salvation with fear and trembling"?
❇ What do you tend to complain and argue about?
■ What godly qualities make Christians "shine like stars"?
■ How does shining for Christ encourage others to be drawn to Him?
❇ What Christian leader has personally invested in your growth as a follower of Christ?
❇ How can you help new believers "shine like stars" for God's kingdom?

APPLY IT
❇ In what situations this week do you need to make a conscious effort not to complain or argue?
■ Before whom do you want to shine in your place of work or neighborhood? In what ways can you do so?
❇ What sacrifices can you make for the sake of others today?

Philippians 2:19-30
Timothy and Epaphroditus

TOPICS
Church, Encouragement, God, Honor, Jesus Christ, Partnerships, Risk, Sacrifice, Sickness

OPEN IT
■ When was the last time you gave a character reference for a friend?
❇ If close friends were to talk about you behind your back, what would they say?

EXPLORE IT
❇ Why did Paul plan to send Timothy to the Philippians? (2:19)
■ What was Paul's opinion of Timothy? (2:20)
❇ What was Timothy's relationship with the church at Philippi? (2:20)
■ In Paul's view, why did Timothy stand out? (2:21-22)
❇ When would Paul send Timothy to the Philippians? (2:23)
❇ Why was Paul confident that he would revisit the believers at Philippi? (2:24)
❇ Who was Epaphroditus? (2:25)
❇ Why did the Philippians send Epaphroditus to Paul? (2:25)
❇ How did Epaphroditus feel about his friends in Philippi? (2:26)
❇ What happened to Epaphroditus? (2:26-27)
❇ How did God spare Paul tremendous sorrow? (2:27)
❇ How did Paul demonstrate his selflessness? (2:28)
■ How were the Philippians told to welcome home Epaphroditus? (2:29-30)
❇ Why were the Philippians told to honor their messenger? (2:30)

GET IT
■ Among your circle of Christian friends, for whom do you have the highest regard? Why?
❇ Why could Paul count on Timothy and Epaphroditus?
❇ What reputation do you have in your church?
■ In what ways have you proved to be a reliable servant of God?
❇ What risks are you willing to take on behalf of other Christians?
❇ In what ways can you be God's "courier" to others?

APPLY IT
■ How can you be a model of humility and service to other Christians this week?
❇ This week, how can you look out for the interests of the Lord rather than your own interests?

Philippians 3:1-11
No Confidence in the Flesh

TOPICS
Accomplishments, Believers, Faith, Heresy, Holy Spirit, Jesus Christ, Joy, Reputation, Resurrection, Righteousness, Suffering

OPEN IT
■ If you were to update your resume today, what recent accomplishment would you want to include?
❇ What do you feel are your most valuable skills and gifts?
❇ How do you feel when someone is better than you at something you do well?

EXPLORE IT
❇ What did Paul call on believers to do? (3:1)
❇ Why did Paul repeat essential truths to the Philippians? (3:1)
❇ What did Paul say about certain false teachers? (3:2)
❇ Whom did Paul identify as "true"? (3:3)
■ What autobiographical facts did Paul give? (3:4-6)
❇ In what sense was Paul not boasting, even though he was calling attention to his accomplishments? (3:7-9)
■ Why did Paul view his former accomplishments as "rubbish"? (3:8)
■ What was Paul's status in Christ? (3:9)
❇ What longings did Paul admit to the Philippians? (3:10-11)
❇ What hope did Paul express? (3:11)

GET IT
❇ What sort of things tend to draw you away from Christ?
■ What do you usually boast about?
❇ Why do we tend to base our worth as Christians on our performance?

■ Why should our identity and confidence be in the Lord?
❇ How is the Apostle Paul's commitment to Christ an example to you?

APPLY IT
■ What do you need to start counting as rubbish for the sake of Christ?
❇ When you face struggles this week, how can you remember to rejoice rather than complain?

Philippians 3:12–4:1
Pressing on Toward the Goal

TOPICS
Believers, Citizenship, Enemies, Example, Goals, God, Heaven, Jesus Christ, Maturity, Power, Shame

OPEN IT
■ How physically fit are you?
❇ If you lived in ancient times and participated in sports, would you prefer chariot racing or spear throwing? Why?
❇ How much time do you spend watching or participating in sports?

EXPLORE IT
❇ What was Paul's testimony? (3:12-14)
■ In what ways did Paul's spiritual life resemble the discipline of a runner? (3:12-14)
❇ What was Paul's view of the past? (3:13)
■ What was Paul's goal? (3:14)
❇ How did Paul call the Philippians to share his view? (3:15)
❇ What did Paul hope for the believers who disagreed with him? (3:15)
❇ What was Paul's plea to the Philippians? (3:16)
■ How did Paul want believers to imitate him? (3:17)
❇ How did Paul describe God's enemies? (3:18-19)
❇ Where did the Philippian Christians have their citizenship? (3:20)
❇ Whom did the Philippian believers eagerly await? (3:20)
❇ What characterizes citizens of heaven? (3:21)

GET IT
■ What kind of race are you running for Christ?
❇ What prize do you seek?
■ What kind of opposition do you face in your struggle to live as a Christian?
❇ How can you imitate Paul's life and example?
❇ How can Christ help you stay on track and reach the goal?

APPLY IT
■ What spiritual workout or training this week will help you run your Christian marathon?
❇ In what way can you renew your commitment to press on toward the goal of being like Christ?

Philippians 4:2-9
Exhortations

TOPICS
Believers, Example, Gentleness, God, Jesus Christ, Joy, Partnerships, Peace, Prayer, Thankfulness, Thinking, Value

OPEN IT
❇ How do you tend to respond when things don't go your way?
■ What does it take to live at peace with difficult family members or colleagues?

EXPLORE IT
❇ How did Paul feel toward the Philippian congregation? (4:1)
❇ What did Paul exhort the Philippian believers to do? (4:1)
■ Why did Paul plead with Euodia and Syntyche? (4:2)
❇ How had Euodia and Syntyche helped Paul in the past? (4:3)
❇ What was Paul's relationship with Clement? (4:3)
❇ How could Paul count on his "loyal yokefellow"? (4:3)
❇ What did Paul encourage his readers to do? (4:4)
■ How did Paul tell the Philippian Christians to treat others? (4:5)
❇ How should an awareness of Christ's imminent return affect a person's attitude? (4:5-7)
❇ What did Paul say about anxiety? (4:6-7)
❇ What were the Philippians to do instead of worrying? (4:6-7)
■ How can a believer enjoy the peace of God? (4:6-7)
❇ What are the qualities of wholesome thoughts? (4:8)
❇ What were the Philippians to put into practice? (4:9)
❇ How can believers enjoy the presence of the God of peace? (4:9)

GET IT
❇ How have disagreements between people affected your church?
■ When have you been involved in helping Christians resolve differences?
❇ How can you have a peaceful spirit?
■ If you were more thankful, joyful, and gentle, how might your family and friends be affected?
❇ What does it take for you to think worthy thoughts?
❇ What does it mean to live a righteous life-style?
❇ In what areas of your life do you need to follow Paul's example?

APPLY IT
❇ What can you do today to reduce your level of anxiety?
■ How can you be an effective peacemaker this week?

Philippians 4:10-23
Thanks for Their Gifts

TOPICS
Abundance, Church, Confidence, Contentment, Generosity, Gifts, God, Gospel, Grace, Jesus Christ, Joy, Poor, Sacrifice, Strength

OPEN IT
❉ What experiences bring you the most contentment?
■ When was a time you felt contentment in the middle of problems or uncertainty?

EXPLORE IT
❉ Why was Paul glad? (4:10-13)
■ What lesson had Paul learned about contentment? (4:10-13)
❉ Why could Paul handle any kind of circumstance? (4:13)
❉ What did the Philippians do about Paul's troubles? (4:14)
❉ How did Paul feel toward the Philippians believers? Why? (4:14)
■ How had the Philippians supported Paul in the past? (4:15-16)
❉ What did Paul not want? (4:17)
❉ What did Paul want for the Philippians? (4:17)
❉ What was Paul's current financial situation? (4:18)
❉ How did Paul respond to the Philippians' generosity? (4:18-19)
■ How would God reciprocate the believers' generosity? (4:19)
❉ To whom did Paul give thanks and praise? (4:20)
❉ Who sent final greetings to the Philippians? (4:21-22)
❉ To what did Paul give prominence in closing his letter? (4:23)

GET IT
■ How could Paul be so flexible in his approach to life's circumstances?
❉ How do you handle the unexpected?
❉ What can you learn from Paul about being content?
■ The Philippian Christians helped Paul when he needed it; how are you able to help others in trouble?
❉ What can you do to be ready for others when they need financial help?
❉ What can your church do to help missionaries with financial needs?
❉ How will God honor a giving spirit?
❉ How can the relationship between Paul and the Philippians help your church in its relationship to those involved in missions?

APPLY IT
❉ This week, what can you do to help a Christian who needs financial support?
❉ Whom do you know who needs a note of encouragement from you today?
■ What can you do to develop an attitude of contentment in all circumstances?

Colossians 1:1-14

Thanksgiving and Prayer

TOPICS
Church, Faith, Forgiveness, Fruit, God, Gospel, Grace, Heaven, Holy Spirit, Hope, Jesus Christ, Kingdom of God/Heaven, Knowledge, Love, Partnerships, Peace, Praise, Prayer, Sin, Strength, Thankfulness

OPEN IT
❉ How many cards and letters do you usually receive at Christmas?
❉ When was the last time you received a letter from a stranger?
■ When was the last time you received a letter that really cheered you up?

EXPLORE IT
❉ Who wrote the letter to the Colossians? (1:1)
❉ Who was with Paul when he wrote this letter? (1:1)
❉ How did Paul address the Colossian Christians? (1:2)
❉ How did Paul greet his audience? (1:2)
■ Why did Paul offer prayers of thanksgiving for the Colossians? (1:3-4)
❉ From what source did the believers' faith and love spring? (1:5)
❉ What did Paul stress about the gospel? (1:5-6)
❉ Who taught the gospel to the Colossians? (1:7)
❉ How did Paul describe Epaphras? (1:7)
❉ What did Epaphras tell Paul and Timothy about the Colossians? (1:7-8)
■ What was Paul's primary prayer for these Christians? (1:9)
■ What results did Paul want for the Colossians? (1:10)
❉ How could the church at Colosse have spiritual strength? (1:11-12)
❉ How does God enable believers to share in His inheritance? (1:12-14)

GET IT
❉ What do you find appealing about the way Paul started his letter to the Colossians?
■ Why did Paul praise a group of Christians he had never met?
❉ How are the results of faith, love, and hope evident in your life?
❉ How is the gospel bearing fruit in your church?
■ What can we learn about praying for others from Paul's prayers for the Colossians?
❉ If Paul were to write you a personal letter, what might he say to you?

APPLY IT
❉ What is one way you can improve your prayer this week?
❉ What missionaries can you pray for on a regular basis over the next month?
■ To whom can you write an encouraging letter sometime during the next week?

Colossians 1:15-23

The Supremacy of Christ

TOPICS
Believers, Church, Creation, Death, Doctrine, Enemies, Image, Reconciliation

OPEN IT
■ What person comes to mind when you think of greatness?
❋ Whom do you look up to? Why?
❋ What qualities stand out in a person you admire?

EXPLORE IT
❋ What is Christ's relationship to God? (1:15)
■ What is Christ's relationship to Creation? (1:15-17)
❋ How do "all things . . . hold together" under Christ? (1:16-17)
❋ What is Christ's relationship to the church? (1:18)
■ Why was the resurrection of Jesus significant? (1:18)
❋ How did Paul explain the deity of Christ? (1:19)
■ What did God achieve through the work of His Son? (1:20)
❋ How did Christ bring us to God? (1:21-22)
❋ Why was reconciliation necessary? (1:21-22)
❋ What is a Christian's position before God? (1:22)
❋ What is the role of faith in reconciliation with God? (1:23)
❋ What kind of faith did the Colossians have? (1:23)
❋ What was Paul's confident expectation? (1:23)

GET IT
■ Why did Paul take the time to describe the qualities of Christ?
■ What difference does our understanding about Christ make?
❋ How would you explain reconciliation (with God) to a nonChristian friend?
❋ What does the work of Christ on your behalf mean to you?
❋ In what way are we all under Christ's authority?
❋ In what way are you under Christ's authority?
❋ How firm is your faith?
❋ What can a person do if his or her faith is weak?

APPLY IT
■ When can you take time this week to meditate on this powerful, compelling description of Christ?
❋ What truths about Christ do you want to remember when you present the gospel to unbelieving friends?
❋ How can you strengthen your faith in Christ this week?

Colossians 1:24–2:5

Paul's Labor for the Church

TOPICS
Body, Church, Encouragement, Glory, God, Hope, Jesus Christ, Joy, Serving, Suffering, Teaching, Unity, Wisdom

OPEN IT
❋ When was the last time you had a good physical workout?
■ How do you feel after strenuous physical exercise?

EXPLORE IT
❋ Why did Paul rejoice? (1:24)
■ What did Paul do for the sake of the church? (1:24)
❋ What commission did God give Paul? (1:25)
❋ To what mystery did Paul refer? (1:26)
❋ To whom had God chosen to make known a mystery? (1:27)
❋ How did Paul help believers become spiritually mature? (1:28-29)
■ What kind of effort did Paul expend in preaching and teaching? (1:29)
❋ What did Paul want his audience to know? (2:1)
❋ What was Paul's stated purpose? (2:2-3)
❋ What is hidden in Christ? (2:3)
■ How would a commitment to the full knowledge of Christ protect the Colossians? (2:4)
❋ How was Paul unified with the church at Colosse? (2:4)
❋ What delighted Paul? (2:5)

GET IT
❋ Paul had never met the Colossian Christians; how could he have suffered for them?
❋ How is suffering an essential part of the Christian life?
■ Why did Paul work so hard for the Colossians?
❋ What results did Paul expect from his work for the sake of the gospel?
❋ What can you do for the church of Christ?
■ When have you become tired because of your work for the kingdom of God?
❋ What makes a church encouraged and united?
❋ What "fine-sounding arguments" draw some Christians away from the faith?
❋ What can we do to grow in our understanding of Christ?
❋ What can you do to grow in your understanding of Christ?

APPLY IT
■ What kind of "spiritual workout" would increase your stamina for the Christian journey ahead this week?
❋ How can you learn more about Christ this week?

Colossians 2:6-23

Freedom From Human Regulations Through Life With Christ

TOPICS
Angels, Authority, Body, Church, Death, Doctrine, Faith, Freedom, God, Jesus Christ, Judging Others, Legalism, Rules, Worship

OPEN IT
❋ What good advice have you never forgotten?
■ In what ways would you characterize yourself as permissive, and in what ways would you characterize yourself as strict?

EXPLORE IT
❇ How did Paul tell the Colossians to continue in Christ? (2:6-7)
❇ What false teaching was Paul concerned about? (2:8)
❇ What did Paul affirm about Christ? How? (2:9-10)
■ What did God give the Colossian believers? (2:10)
❇ Why do Gentile Christians have no need to conform to Jewish rules and regulations? (2:11-12)
❇ How did the Cross cancel the written code? (2:13-14)
❇ From what did Christ deliver us? How? (2:15-17)
■ How did Paul encourage the Colossians to practice their freedom in Christ? (2:16)
❇ How did Christ fulfill what the Old Testament foreshadowed? (2:17)
❇ Whom did Paul accuse of trying to rob believers of their spiritual rewards? (2:18)
■ What were the characteristics of the false teachers? (2:18-19)
❇ How did Paul challenge the legalism that had infected the church? (2:20-21)
❇ What are the failings of human commands and teachings? (2:20-23)

GET IT
■ What "additions" to faith in Christ have you encountered from teachers in your Christian community?
❇ How are you affected by popular religious rules floating around today?
❇ What does "fullness in Christ" mean to you?
■ Paul's advice kept the Colossians growing in their faith; what Christian leaders have helped you stay on track spiritually?
❇ How deep are the roots of your faith?

APPLY IT
■ This week, how can you best exercise the freedom you have in Christ?
❇ How can you help a Christian friend get rid of his or her false ideas about Christ?

Colossians 3:1-17
Rules for Holy Living

TOPICS
Actions, Believers, Death, Equality, Glory, God, Heart, Heaven, Holiness, Image, Jesus Christ, Knowledge, Love, Peace, Renewal, Security, Sin, Thankfulness

OPEN IT
❇ What's the nicest suit or outfit you have ever worn?
■ When you're finished with your old clothes, what do you often do with them?

EXPLORE IT
❇ Where did Paul tell the Colossians to turn their attention? (3:1)
❇ Where did Paul tell the believers to focus their concern? (3:2)
❇ What was the Colossians' security? (3:3)
■ Why should believers look forward to Christ's return? (3:4)
❇ What must die? (3:5)
❇ What evil activities does God seek to eliminate from our lives? (3:5)
❇ Why is God's wrath coming? (3:5-6)
■ What had the Colossians taken off? (3:7-9)
❇ What had the Colossians put on? (3:10)
❇ What distinctions are removed in Christ? (3:11)
❇ What virtues does God seek to plant in us? (3:12, 14)
■ How were the Colossian believers called to clothe themselves? (3:12-17)
❇ Why did Paul call on the believers to be peaceful and thankful? (3:15-16)
❇ What should we do? How? (3:17)
❇ What is one principle that ought to guide everything we do? (3:17)

GET IT
❇ If you consistently set your sights on Christ and heaven, how would your life be different?
■ What old, "earthly" clothing do you need to get rid of?
■ How does wearing "Christ's clothing" affect the way you live your daily life?
❇ What Christian virtues are you lacking?
❇ What spiritual process is involved in "putting off" and "putting on"?
❇ What is involved in replacing old habits with new ones?
❇ How should life in Christ affect the way you treat others?
❇ How are all your relationships to be built around Christ?
❇ Why do we need to be loving toward others?
❇ Why is a thankful spirit an important part of holy living?

APPLY IT
■ Which of God's goals for holy living do you need to apply to your life this week?
❇ How can you be more thankful and loving to those who are close to you?

Colossians 3:18–4:1
Rules for Christian Households

TOPICS
Believers, Children, Discouragement, Fairness, Family, Favoritism, Heaven, Jesus Christ, Justice, Love, Obedience, Pleasure, Rewards, Right, Sincerity, Slavery, Submission, Work

OPEN IT
■ If you were to make up a slogan that describes your family, what would it be?
❇ Generally speaking, how do you get along with others?

EXPLORE IT
❇ What should wives do? (3:18)
❇ What should husbands do? (3:19)
■ How should children respond to parents? (3:20)
■ Why does obedience to parents please the Lord? (3:20)
■ What do fathers need to be careful of? (3:21)
❇ How can children become discouraged? (3:21)
❇ What directives did Paul give slaves? (3:22-25)
❇ How were slaves called on to serve Christ? (3:23-24)

❊ How would God mete out full justice in the master-slave relationship? (3:25)
❊ What instructions did Paul give masters? (4:1)
❊ What insight did Paul give masters? (4:1)

GET IT
■ How do God's instructions to families help family members become mature Christians?
❊ Why should wives submit to their husbands?
❊ Why does God tell husbands not to be harsh with their wives?
■ Why should Christian parents rear their children in an atmosphere of encouragement?
❊ How can Christian parents rear their children in an atmosphere of encouragement?
❊ How can God's instructions to slaves apply today to Christian employees?
❊ Which of God's principles for Christian households challenge you to change?

APPLY IT
■ What is one way you can improve the way you treat each member of your family?
❊ How can you have an attitude of service toward others in your work?

Colossians 4:2-18
Further Instructions

TOPICS
Believers, Church, Circumstances, Conversation, Encouragement, Grace, Jesus Christ, Kingdom of God/Heaven, Maturity, Partnerships, Prayer, Serving, Thankfulness, Wisdom

OPEN IT
■ What's your favorite salty snack?
❊ If you had to eat all food without salt for a day or two, how would this affect your eating habits?

EXPLORE IT
■ What did Paul prescribe for all believers? (4:2)
❊ What request did Paul make of his readers? (4:3-4)
❊ What did Paul say about the Christian's public life? (4:5-6)
■ How should believers speak to others? (4:6)
❊ Who was Tychicus? (4:7)
❊ Why did Paul send Tychicus to Colosse? (4:7-8)
❊ Who was Onesimus? (4:9)
❊ Whose greetings to the Colossians did Paul include in his letter? (4:10-14)
❊ Which of Paul's partners in ministry were Jews? (4:10-11)
■ What did Epaphras do on behalf of his church at Colosse? (4:12-13)
❊ What relationship did Luke and Demas have to Paul? (4:14)
❊ To whom did Paul send greetings? (4:15)
❊ Where did Paul want his letter read? (4:16)
❊ What instruction did Paul send Archippus? (4:17)
❊ How did Paul conclude his letter? (4:18)

GET IT
❊ Why is prayer important?
❊ How much time do you devote to prayer each day?
❊ How did Paul set an example for mature interpersonal relationships?
■ In what ways is your conversation "seasoned with salt"?
❊ How well do you relate to unbelievers?
■ Paul demonstrated the value of teamwork in ministry; how well do you work with other Christians for the kingdom of God?
❊ Paul spoke highly of his Christian friends; what can you praise about your Christian friends?

APPLY IT
■ How can you season your speech with God's grace among nonChristians?
❊ How can you remember to speak well of family members and Christian friends this week?
❊ What personal relationship can you improve during the next few days? How?

1 Thessalonians 1:1-10
Thanksgiving for the Thessalonians' Faith

TOPICS
Change, Commitment, Devotion, Faith, Persecution, Suffering

OPEN IT
❇ Who in your opinion are the best role models for young people?
■ What would it take for someone to make a lasting impression on you?
❇ What causes a person to really change his or her attitudes and behavior?

EXPLORE IT
❇ Who wrote this letter? (1:1)
❇ To whom was this letter written? (1:1)
■ What did Paul remember about the Thessalonians? (1:2-3)
❇ What made Paul believe God had chosen the Thessalonian believers? (1:4-10)
❇ How had Paul presented the gospel to this audience? (1:5-6)
❇ How had the Thessalonians responded to the gospel message? (1:6-7)
■ For what kind of faith were the Thessalonians known? (1:6)
❇ Whom did the Thessalonians imitate? (1:6)
■ How had the Thessalonians' lives been a model for others? (1:7-10)
❇ What changes did the Thessalonians make in their lives when they heard the gospel? (1:9)
❇ What were the Thessalonians anticipating? (1:10)

GET IT
❇ How was the Thessalonians' hope visible for others to see?
■ What characteristics in a person would convince you that he or she was a genuine Christian chosen by God?
❇ What convinces people Christianity is true?
■ What is the difference between presenting the gospel with power and deep conviction, and presenting the gospel without it?
❇ How are the Thessalonians examples for our daily living?
❇ What persecution and suffering can Christians expect when they publicly declare their faith?
❇ In what ways do we need to imitate Jesus Christ and other Christians we know?
❇ In what visible ways have you been changed by turning away from sin and turning toward God?
❇ How can actively waiting for Jesus' return affect our daily attitudes and actions?

APPLY IT
■ How can you be more of a model to other believers this week?
❇ In what way can you present the gospel with power and conviction the next time you share it?

1 Thessalonians 2:1-16
Paul's Ministry in Thessalonica

TOPICS
Integrity, Motives, Persecution, Suffering, Teaching, Work

OPEN IT
■ How do you know when someone is using flattery to manipulate you?
❇ What are the signs of genuine love between a parent and a child?
❇ What qualities should a Christian leader have?

EXPLORE IT
❇ Under what conditions did Paul share the gospel with the Thessalonians? (2:2)
❇ What false charges had been made about Paul? (2:3-5)
■ How did Paul answer the charges against him? (2:3-5)
❇ How were other traveling religious teachers deceiving people? (2:5)
❇ How did Paul describe his relationship with the Thessalonians? (2:7)
■ What were Paul and his companions delighted to do? Why? (2:8)
■ What did Paul want the Thessalonians to remember about his time with them? (2:9)
❇ How did Paul describe his work with the Thessalonians? (2:10)
❇ In what way was Paul like a father to the Thessalonians? (2:11-12)
❇ How did the Thessalonians receive the Word of God? (2:13)
❇ How were the Thessalonians like the churches in Judea? (2:14)
❇ What kind of opposition had Paul faced? (2:15-16)
❇ What is God's response to people who oppose the preaching of His gospel? (2:16)

GET IT
■ How can we judge the success or failure of our work with people?
❇ What kind of opposition can we expect whenever we speak out for Jesus Christ?
❇ How do the opinions of others influence how we share our faith?
■ How can a desire for popularity (even among Christians) twist our desire and commitment to serve God?
❇ Why did Paul work so hard not to be a burden to the Thessalonians?
❇ What standards of behavior and care should Christians follow as they try to reach out to people?
❇ What's the difference between accepting a teaching as the Word of God and responding to it?

APPLY IT
❇ In what ways can you share your life with others in your efforts to share Christ with them?
■ What can you do this week to make sure that you are trying to please God and not other people?

1 Thessalonians 2:17–3:5

Paul's Longing to See the Thessalonians

TOPICS:
Encouragement, Future, Persecution, Rewards, Satan, Separation, Temptation

OPEN IT
❋ If you were accused of a crime you didn't commit, how would you respond?
■ How do you encourage a friend who is feeling down and hopeless?

EXPLORE IT
❋ How did Paul describe his departure and separation from the Thessalonians? (2:17)
❋ What stopped Paul from returning to Thessalonica? (2:18)
❋ What did Paul say would be his crown or reward at the second coming of the Lord? (2:19)
❋ Why did Paul consider the Thessalonians his glory and joy? (2:20)
■ Whom did the apostles send to Thessalonica to check up on the church? (3:2)
■ What was Timothy's mission? (3:2)
❋ What did Paul say about trials? (3:3)
❋ What concern did Paul have for the Thessalonian church? (3:3-5)
❋ What did Paul think might undercut the faith of the new believers at Thessalonica? (3:3-5)
■ Why did Paul send someone to check on the Thessalonians? (3:5)

GET IT
❋ How does Satan hinder or stop our efforts or plans?
■ How can investing your life in someone pay eternal dividends?
❋ What personal accomplishments will count for something when we stand in the presence of Christ?
■ What practical things can we do to strengthen and encourage others in their faith?
❋ How can opposition discourage and damage the faith of a young believer?
❋ How could you help a young believer whose faith has been damaged by opposition or discouragement?

APPLY IT
❋ This week, how could you resist the temptations that hinder your spiritual progress?
■ What younger believer can you help get established in the faith? How?

1 Thessalonians 3:6-13

Timothy's Encouraging Report

TOPICS
Encouragement, Faith, Love, Prayer, Second Coming

OPEN IT
❋ If you could make a surprise visit to a dear friend or relative, whom would you select?
■ How can you express love to someone when you can't see or talk to the person?

EXPLORE IT
❋ What news did Timothy bring to Paul from Thessalonica? (3:6-7)
■ How had Paul's work among the Thessalonians fared during his absence? (3:6-7)
❋ How were the Thessalonians an encouragement to Paul? (3:7-9)
❋ Why did Paul say, "for now we really live"? (3:8)
❋ For what did Paul pray concerning the Thessalonians? (3:10)
❋ How did Paul pray? (3:10)
■ When did Paul pray? For whom? (3:10)
❋ What was Paul hoping for? (3:11)
❋ What did Paul ask the Lord to do? (3:11-13)
■ What did Paul pray would grow and prosper among the Thessalonians? (3:11-13)
❋ How should we prepare for Christ's return to earth? (3:13)

GET IT
❋ How would you define and evaluate the depth of a person's faith?
❋ How would you define and evaluate the depth of a person's love?
■ How do you show your concern for Christians in distant places?
❋ What are the characteristics of someone who is standing firm in the Lord?
❋ In what ways should we imitate Paul's example when assigning credit for bringing someone to Christ?
❋ What place did the Thessalonians have in Paul's prayer life?
■ How does a person's love for others increase?
❋ How can a person have his or her heart strengthened?

APPLY IT
❋ What preparations can you make this week to get ready for Christ's return?
■ What changes do you need to make to focus your prayer on others?

1 Thessalonians 4:1-12

Living to Please God

TOPICS
Ambition, Faithfulness, Holiness, Immorality, Jobs, Marriage, Purity, Sex

OPEN IT
❋ How much do you think people are influenced by what they watch on television?
■ How is sex viewed by many of the people you know and work with?

EXPLORE IT
❋ What instruction had Paul given to the Thessalonians when he was with them? (4:1)
❋ What did Paul urge his audience to do? (4:1)
❋ By what authority did Paul give his instructions? (4:2)

❊ What are God's desires for our sexuality? (4:3-8)
■ How is the Christian's sexual conduct to be different from that of the non-Christian? (4:4-5)
■ How did Paul characterize the heathen? (4:5)
■ When a person ignores or rejects God's instructions on sexual behavior, what are they rejecting? (4:8)
❊ What command of God were the Thessalonians known for obeying? (4:9-10)
❊ What ambition were the Thessalonians to pursue? (4:11-12)
❊ What is the result of living a quiet, respected, and responsible life? (4:11-12)

GET IT
❊ How often do we need to be reminded about God's instructions for our lives?
❊ In what way can ambition for fame, success, or wealth hurt a believer?
❊ How does God want us to use our bodies?
■ How would you respond to someone who says it is possible to be a good Christian while also being sexually immoral?
❊ How do the media influence our attitudes about sex?
❊ How can we wrong a person through our sexual behavior?
❊ What is a holy life?
■ What would motivate you to live a life that is pure and holy?
❊ What influence on people and society can a hardworking, quiet person have?

APPLY IT
❊ In the future, how could you help a Christian caught in sexual sin?
■ What can you do to maintain your purity?
❊ When can you spend some time examining your ambitions in light of God's priorities for you?

1 Thessalonians 4:13–5:11
The Coming of the Lord

TOPICS
Assurance, Death, Future, Hope, Jesus Christ, Resurrection, Second Coming

OPEN IT
❊ How can the death of a loved one change a person's life?
■ What do you think happens to us when we die?
❊ How do you react when you hear predictions about the end of the world?

EXPLORE IT
❊ What concern was Paul addressing? (4:13-14)
❊ How is a Christian's grief over the loss of a loved one different from a non-Christian's grief? (4:13-14)
■ What was the source of Paul's teaching about what happens to those who die? (4:15)
■ What sequence of events will signal the Lord's return? (4:16-17)
❊ What effect did Paul believe this teaching about the Lord's return would have on his listeners? (4:18)
■ When will the Lord return? (5:1-2)
❊ How will the Lord return? (5:1-3)
❊ What contrast is there between believers and non-believers? (5:4-8)
❊ What should we do to get ready for the Lord's return? (5:6-8)
❊ What roles should faith, hope, and love play in our lives? (5:8)
❊ To what does God appoint believers? (5:9-10)
❊ For what reason can we be assured of our salvation? (5:9-10)
❊ How should a believer use this information to help others? (5:11)

GET IT
■ How should a Christian mourn the death of a fellow believer?
❊ Who has no hope when they die?
❊ What hope do Christians have in death?
❊ How can these words help a person who is grieving over loved ones who have died?
❊ Why is the date and time of Christ's second coming of such interest to many people?
■ What influence should the promise of Christ's second coming have on how a person lives day to day?
❊ How are faith and love like a breastplate?
❊ How is salvation like a helmet?
❊ How can talking about God's promises for our future encourage us in our daily lives?

APPLY IT
❊ What can you do to make sure you are ready for Christ's return each day?
■ What hope can you share with someone who is convinced that death is the end of our existence?

1 Thessalonians 5:12-28
Final Instructions

TOPICS
Advice, God's Will, Leadership, Prophecy, Quarrels, Respect, Revenge, Thankfulness

OPEN IT
■ What instructions would you give to someone taking care of your home while you were away on a long vacation?
❊ If you could ask God any three questions about how to live your life, what would you ask?

EXPLORE IT
❊ How does God want us to regard church elders? (5:12-13)
■ How does God want us to treat each other? (5:13-15)
■ What attitudes represent God's will for us? (5:16-18)
❊ How should we pray? (5:17)
❊ When should we give thanks? (5:18)
❊ What is God's will for us? (5:16-18)
❊ How should we show respect for the Holy Spirit's presence in us? (5:19-22)
❊ What does God want to happen inside us? (5:23)
❊ For what reason can we depend on God? (5:24)

■ What kind of affection did Paul have for the Thessalonian Christians? (5:26)
✻ Who was to hear the contents of this letter? (5:27)

GET IT
✻ How can you show respect for the elders of your church?
■ What can we do to live in peace with everyone in the church?
✻ How can the peace among people in the church be damaged?
✻ What situations tend to test your patience?
✻ What does it mean to pray continually?
✻ What happens when you pay back evil to a person who has done wrong to you?
✻ Why should we give thanks in all circumstances?
✻ What value is there in giving thanks in all circumstances?
■ How can you remain joyful when things go badly?
✻ How does prayer relate to a person's joy?
✻ How could a person put out the Spirit's fire?
✻ How can we tell if God is actually at work in us?
✻ How can we help or hinder God's work within us?

APPLY IT
■ Which of Paul's short, direct commands in this passage do you most need to remember this week?
✻ With whom do you need to make peace? How can you start?

2 Thessalonians 1:1-12
Thanksgiving and Prayer

TOPICS
Assurance, Benefits, Faith, Future, Heaven, Hell, Hope, Judgment, Last Days, Perseverance, Rewards, Second Coming

OPEN IT
■ What experiences can destroy a person's desire to live?
✻ What fictional or real-life person endured difficulties and trials on the way to eventual triumph?

EXPLORE IT
✻ To whom is this letter addressed? (1:1)
✻ Who wrote this letter? (1:1)
✻ Why did Paul thank God for the church at Thessalonica? (1:3)
✻ What was the reputation of the church at Thessalonica? (1:4)
■ What difficulties was the church at Thessalonica experiencing? (1:4)
■ What do persecution and trials prove about God's work in the church and the world? (1:5)
✻ How will God deal with unbelievers and believers alike? When? (1:6-7)
✻ When will God reward and punish people? (1:7)
✻ For what reason will God punish people? (1:8)
■ How did Paul describe the punishment of those who reject Christ? (1:9)
✻ What will believers experience when they see the Lord Jesus? (1:10)
✻ What was Paul's prayer for the church at Thessalonica? (1:11-12)

GET IT
✻ What can we do to keep our faith growing?
✻ What can we do to increase our love for others?
✻ How can a person go through trials and yet have their faith strengthened?
■ When we are going through difficulties, how do we know God hasn't forgotten us?
✻ What are some reasons we use to explain why we experience trials and hard times?
✻ How could trials and hard times be part of God's plan for us?
✻ How will our view of the trials during our life be different after Jesus returns?
✻ How does Paul's description of hell compare to your ideas about what hell is like?
✻ How do we discover God's purpose for our lives?
■ What lessons do you think God is trying to teach you through the trials and difficulties you have experienced recently?

APPLY IT
✻ How could your life glorify the name of the Lord Jesus this week?
■ In what trials and difficulties do you need patience and perseverance this week to see God's eventual good results?

2 Thessalonians 2:1-12
The Man of Lawlessness

TOPICS
Confusion, Evil, Future, Hell, Hopelessness, Judgment, Last Days, Lost, Miracles, Second Coming

OPEN IT
❊ What would make you think that the end of the world was near?
❊ If you were convinced the world would end in six months, what would you do until then?
■ What evidence do you see of evil forces active in the world today?

EXPLORE IT
❊ What subject was Paul addressing? (2:1)
❊ What reaction had Paul's previous letter caused among his readers? (2:2)
❊ What must happen before the day of the Lord comes? (2:3)
■ What kind of person will the man of lawlessness be? (2:4)
❊ What is delaying the coming of the man of lawlessness? (2:6)
■ What will happen to allow the man of lawlessness to be revealed? (2:7)
❊ What will happen when the man of lawlessness encounters the Lord Jesus? (2:8)
■ How will Satan's power be evident during the time of the man of lawlessness? (2:9-10)
❊ Why will people perish? (2:10-12)
❊ What will God do to allow those who delight in wickedness to persist in their ways? (2:11-12)

GET IT
❊ How should a Christian react to any predictions about Christ's return?
❊ How close do you think we are to the end times and the return of Christ? Why?
❊ What can a person do to get ready for Christ's return?
■ What gives Christians confidence as they face the end times and the forces of the anti-Christ?
■ What powers of lawlessness and rebellion are already present in our world?
❊ How can you decide if a miracle or a miracle worker is from God or from Satan?
❊ What will cause people to turn away from God during the end times?

APPLY IT
■ How can you strengthen your faith today so that you are ready to face any evil days that will come?
❊ What can you say to a loved one or friend this week that will lovingly draw them away from wickedness and unbelief?

2 Thessalonians 2:13-17
Stand Firm

TOPICS
God, God's Will, Maturity, Perseverance, Spiritual Growth

OPEN IT
❊ What causes many people to give up their plans for self-improvement (diet, exercise, etc.)?
❊ What causes some people to lose their religious faith as they grow older?
■ If God could give you an audible word of encouragement, what would help you most?

EXPLORE IT
❊ For what reasons did Paul encourage people to thank God? (2:13)
❊ How did Paul describe God's role in our salvation? (2:13)
❊ When did God choose the Thessalonian Christians for salvation? (2:13)
■ What forces work for our salvation? (2:13)
❊ Who calls people to salvation? (2:14)
❊ For what reason did God call us to salvation? (2:14)
■ What encouragement did Paul give to the church? (2:15)
❊ What media did Paul use to send instruction to the church at Thessalonica? (2:15)
❊ What impact did Paul want God to have on every believer in the church? (2:16)
■ What did Paul want God to encourage and strengthen in the Thessalonian believers? (2:17)

GET IT
❊ How does God work in our lives even before we put our trust in Him?
❊ How does God use other people to bring us to Him?
❊ How has God changed you since you became a Christian?
■ What does it mean to stand firm as a Christian?
❊ What teachings should a Christian hold on to as he or she lives for Christ?
■ How does God encourage us?
❊ What does God do to strengthen us?
❊ What weakens a person's relationship with God?
❊ What strengthens a person's relationship with God?

APPLY IT
❊ What can you do this week to remind yourself every day what God has done for you?
❊ In what area of your life would taking a firm stand for Christ benefit you this week?
■ When can you make time in your schedule this week to encourage another believer?

2 Thessalonians 3:1-5
Request for Prayer

TOPICS
Growth, Love, Maturity, Prayer, Salvation, Spiritual Growth

OPEN IT
❊ How frequently do you stay in touch with a friend who is many miles away?
■ What motivates most people to pray?

EXPLORE IT
❊ How had the gospel been received by the Thessalonians? (3:1)

❊ How did Paul want to see the gospel received? (3:1)
■ What prayer requests did Paul ask of the Thessalonians? (3:1-2)
❊ What did Paul want? (3:1-2)
❊ What type of people were threatening Paul? (3:2)
❊ How did Paul describe God? (3:3)
■ What will God do for people who are threatened by the evil one? (3:3)
❊ What confidence did Paul have in the Christians at Thessalonica? (3:4)
■ How did Paul remind his readers of the Lord's direction? (3:5)
❊ What did the Paul want his readers to remember about the Lord? (3:5)

GET IT
■ How does prayer change people or circumstances?
❊ How could prayer help spread the message of the Lord?
■ How does prayer protect us?
❊ How does our belief about God affect the way we pray?
❊ How can meditating on God's love change us?
❊ How can thinking about Christ's perseverance strengthen our own stand?

APPLY IT
❊ For what kind of growth in your Christian life can you pray this week?
■ For whom will you pray this week that their faith may be strengthened?

2 Thessalonians 3:6-18
Warning Against Idleness

TOPICS
Character, Consequences, Discipline, Employment, Example, Jobs, Laziness, Work

OPEN IT
■ How does a person learn good work habits?
❊ When have you been frustrated with a lazy person?
❊ What kind of help do you think should be given to people who do not work?

EXPLORE IT
❊ Whom should we avoid? (3:6)
❊ What example had Paul set when he was with the church at Thessalonica? (3:7-8)
■ What work habits did Paul display while he was in Thessalonica? (3:8)
■ Why did Paul work so hard and pay for his food? (3:8-9)
❊ What rule had Paul given about working and eating? (3:10)
❊ What reports had Paul heard about some of the believers in Thessalonica? (3:11)
❊ What had some people in Thessalonica become? (3:11)
■ What was Paul's command to the busybodies in Thessalonica? (3:12)
❊ What encouragement did Paul give to those he called "brothers"? (3:13)
❊ How were the Thessalonians to regard anyone who ignored Paul's instructions? (3:14-15)
❊ What should we do with people who do not obey these instructions? (3:14-15)
❊ What blessing did Paul invoke on the Thessalonian believers? (3:16)
❊ What did Paul do to make his final greeting special? (3:17)

GET IT
■ How can associating with idle, lazy people influence your work habits?
❊ What bad habits can you develop by associating with the wrong crowd of friends?
❊ Why should a Christian stay away from a person who has bad habits or doesn't follow Christ?
■ What example should a Christian set for others at a job or as a student?
❊ What disciplinary action should be taken toward a Christian who ignores the teachings of the Word of God?
❊ How should Christians respond to someone who doesn't work or support his or her family?

APPLY IT
■ What improvements in your work habits can you make this week?
❊ What can you do this week to be a good influence on your fellow workers or students?
❊ From what bad influences do you need to distance yourself? How?

1 Timothy 1:1-11
Warning Against False Teachers of the Law

TOPICS
Adultery, Basics of the Faith, Beliefs, Believers, Church, Devotion, Disobedience, Doctrine, Encouragement, Faith, God, Gospel, Heart, Jesus Christ, Law, Love, Lying, Motives, Obedience, Religion, Sin, Teaching, Truth

OPEN IT
❊ Which would you rather receive from a good friend: a letter, or a phone call? Why?
■ What are some laws that you benefit from directly?

EXPLORE IT
❊ Who wrote this letter? (1:1)
❊ To whom was this letter written? (1:2)
❊ Why did Paul want Timothy to stay in Ephesus? (1:3-4)
❊ What did Paul say about myths and genealogies? (1:4)
❊ What was the goal of the command Paul urged Timothy to enforce? (1:5)
❊ In what way had some believers been misguided? (1:6)
■ How did Paul assess those who wanted to be teachers of the law? (1:7)
■ When is the Law good? (1:8)
■ For whom was the Law made? (1:9-11)
❊ What did God entrust to Paul? (1:11)

GET IT
❊ When was the last time you wrote someone a letter of encouragement or received such a letter?
❊ With whom do you have a relationship of mutual discipleship?
❊ What false doctrines still plague many churches today?
❊ What sort of doctrines promote controversy in the church?
❊ What goals motivate the leaders you respect in your church?
❊ What goals motivate your service in the church?
■ In what way should we use God's law today?
❊ What impact does or should God's law have on your life?
■ How should we determine what is and isn't sound doctrine?
❊ With what unique task has God entrusted you?

APPLY IT
❊ Who is someone to whom you can write a letter of encouragement this week?
■ What steps can you take to make sure your motives are from a pure heart, a good conscience, and a sincere faith?

1 Timothy 1:12-20
The Lord's Grace to Paul

TOPICS
Atonement, Basics of the Faith, Beliefs, Believers, Blasphemy, Call, Consequences, Disobedience, Doctrine, Example, Failure, Faith, Glory, God, Gospel, Grace, Jesus Christ, Mercy, Obedience, Salvation, Serving, Sin

OPEN IT
■ Who are some people you know whose lives were dramatically changed at some point? How?
❊ What sort of people try your patience the most?

EXPLORE IT
❊ Why did Paul thank Jesus? (1:12)
❊ What did Paul say he once was? (1:13)
■ Why was Paul shown mercy? (1:13)
❊ What was poured out on Paul? (1:14)
❊ Why did Jesus come into the world? (1:15)
■ How was Paul "the worst"? (1:15)
❊ Why was Paul shown mercy? (1:16)
■ How does a person receive eternal life? (1:16)
❊ What qualities did Paul ascribe to God? (1:17)
❊ Why did Paul give Timothy his instructions? (1:18)
❊ What did Paul say some have done with their faith? (1:19)
❊ Why did Paul hand Hymenaeus and Alexander over to Satan? (1:20)

GET IT
❊ To what service has God appointed you?
■ How and when has God shown you mercy?
■ In what way has God used you as an example so that others might believe?
❊ How do God's attributes of being eternal, immortal, and invisible encourage you?
❊ In what way is God the King of your life?
❊ What does it mean to fight the good fight?
❊ What do you fight in your life as a Christian?
❊ How and why do people shipwreck their faith?
❊ What distractions draw Christians away from their proper course?

APPLY IT
❊ What steps can you take today to ensure that your faith is on the proper course and not in danger of being shipwrecked?
■ For what grace and mercy that God has shown you do you want to thank Him today?
❊ What events or experiences in your life can you use to encourage others to believe?

1 Timothy 2:1-15
Instructions on Worship

TOPICS
Appearance, Atonement, Authority, Basics of the Faith, Church, Dignity, Ego, Faith, God, Jesus Christ, Knowledge, Life-style, Mediator, Ministry, Peace, Prayer, Salvation, Sex, Sin, Society, Sovereignty, Submission, Teaching, Truth, Words, Work, World

OPEN IT
❊ What are some of the controversial issues today?
❊ What do you like or dislike about the worship of the church you attend?
■ How would you characterize the worship of the church you attend?
❊ What examples show that people in our society are obsessed with their physical appearance?

EXPLORE IT
■ What did Paul urge first of all? (2:1-2)
❊ What did Paul hope would be the result of the church's prayers? (2:2)
❊ What pleases God? (2:2-3)
❊ What does God want? (2:4)
❊ For whom is Jesus Christ a mediator? (2:5)
❊ For whom did Jesus give Himself? Why? (2:6)
❊ Why did Paul insist he was not lying? (2:7)
■ What did Paul want people everywhere to do? (2:8)
❊ How should women dress? (2:9-10)
❊ What instructions did Paul give women? (2:9-12)
❊ How did Paul instruct women to learn? (2:11)
■ What didn't Paul permit women to do? (2:11)
❊ What explanation did Paul give for not allowing women to teach or have authority over men? (2:12-14)
❊ In what way did Paul say that women would be saved? (2:15)

GET IT
❊ For what authorities or leaders should we pray?
■ What sort of prayers should we make on behalf of our leaders?
❊ If God wants all people to be saved, why then aren't all people saved?
❊ When have you ever served as a mediator between two people?
❊ In what way is Jesus a mediator between us and God?
❊ To what task would you say God has appointed you?
❊ What does it mean to dress modestly?
■ How does your church understand and apply Paul's restrictions on women?
❊ In what way might a woman be saved through childbearing?

APPLY IT
❊ For what national and international leaders can you pray this week?
■ How can you focus your attention on Christian service and worship of God over outward appearance?

1 Timothy 3:1-16

Overseers and Deacons

TOPICS
Abilities, Accountability, Administration, Ambition, Anger, Authority, Character, Children, Church, Drinking, Effectiveness, Ego, Family, Gentleness, Greed, Home, Hospitality, Impulsiveness, Initiative, Integrity, Leadership, Management, Marriage, Maturity, Money, Morality, Pastors, People, Power, Pride, Quarrels, Reputation, Respect, Responsibility, Teaching

OPEN IT
■ What were some of the qualifications you had to meet for your job?
❊ What important qualities should managers possess?

EXPLORE IT
❊ What did Paul say about the person who wants to be an overseer? (3:1)
■ What qualities must an overseer possess? (3:2-7)
❊ Why is good family management a qualification for being an overseer? (3:4-5)
■ Why shouldn't the overseer be a new convert? (3:6)
❊ Why must an overseer have a good reputation? (3:7)
■ What qualities must a deacon possess? (3:8-10, 12)
❊ What is required before someone can serve as a deacon? (3:10)
❊ What sort of a person must the wife of a deacon be? (3:11)
❊ What do those who serve well gain? (3:13)
❊ What benefit is there in serving well? (3:13)
❊ Why did Paul write these instructions? (3:14-15)
❊ What is said about Jesus in the hymn Paul quoted? (3:16)

GET IT
❊ What role do you desire in your church?
❊ To what noble tasks have you aspired?
■ Which of the character qualities needed by both overseers and deacons do you think is the most important for a church leader to possess?
■ If you applied the lists of qualifications for these positions to yourself, how would you measure up?
❊ What is the common ingredient in the lists of qualifications for leaders in the church?
❊ What hymn or praise chorus that you know centers on the person and work of Jesus Christ?

APPLY IT
■ What quality from the lists in 1 Timothy 3 do you want to improve in your life? How could you start?
❊ In what way can you serve in your church?
❊ What hymn or song could you include in your devotions this week?

1 Timothy 4:1-16

Instructions to Timothy

TOPICS
Abandon, Abilities, Believe, Bible, Conscience, Demons, Devotion, Doctrine, Example, Faith, Gifts, God, Holy Spirit, Hypocrisy, Jesus Christ, Last Days, Legalism, Life, Life-style, Love, Ministry, Reading, Salvation, Teaching

OPEN IT
❊ Why do you think there is such emphasis on physical fitness in our society?
■ What qualities do you look for in a pastor or minister?

EXPLORE IT
❊ What did the Spirit say some would do in the later time? (4:1)
❊ What did Paul say about the consciences of hypocritical liars? (4:2)

❇ What did the liars whom Paul attacked forbid people to do? (4:3)
❇ What is true about all that God created? (4:4)
❇ Why shouldn't anything received with thanksgiving be rejected? (4:4-5)
■ Under what circumstances would Timothy be a good minister? (4:6)
❇ What did Paul instruct Timothy do? (4:7)
❇ How did Paul contrast physical training with godliness? (4:8)
❇ What saying is trustworthy? (4:9-10)
❇ What should young people strive for? (4:12)
❇ What kind of an example did Paul want Timothy to set? (4:12)
■ To what was Timothy to devote himself? (4:13)
❇ What was Timothy not to neglect? (4:14)
■ What did Paul want others to see? (4:15)
❇ What could Timothy do to save himself and his hearers? (4:16)

GET IT
❇ For what reasons do people today abandon their faith?
❇ From what good things have people persuaded you to abstain?
■ How can we be good ministers of Jesus Christ?
❇ What does your use of time show about how much you value training for godliness?
❇ In what ways can you be an example to other believers?
❇ What importance does your church assign to the public reading of Scripture?
❇ What gift has God given to you that should not neglect?
■ How will watching your life and doctrine save you?

APPLY IT
■ What specific actions can you schedule into your daily routine to nurture your godliness?
❇ For what other Christians can you set an example in speech, lifestyle, love, faith, or purity? How?
❇ How can you keep watch over your life and doctrine this week?

1 Timothy 5:1–6:2

Advice About Widows, Elders and Slaves

TOPICS
Caring, Children, Church, Culture, Drinking, Family, Favoritism, God, Gossip, Help, Holiness, Husbands, Jesus Christ, Life-style, Marriage, Ministry, Neglect, Parents, Pastors, Resources, Satan, Serving, Singleness, Teaching, Temptation, World

OPEN IT
❇ What groups of people are treated with special favor in our society today?
■ Whose responsibility is it to care for the needy?
❇ How much money do you think a pastor should make? Why?
❇ What adjectives would you use to describe our society's morality?

EXPLORE IT
❇ How should believers treat older men, younger men, older women, and younger women? (5:1-2)
❇ To whom did Paul tell Timothy to give proper recognition? (5:3)
■ What should the children and grandchildren of a widow do? (5:4)
❇ What does the widow who is really in need and left alone do? (5:5)
❇ What is true about the widow who lives for pleasure? (5:6)
❇ Why did Paul tell Timothy to give these instructions? (5:7)
❇ Why is it important to provide for your family? (5:8)
■ When should the church go out of its way to care for widows? (5:9-10)
❇ Why shouldn't younger widows be put on the "list of widows"? (5:11)
❇ How do younger widows bring judgment upon themselves? (5:12)
❇ To what habits may younger widows fall prey? (5:13)
■ What was Paul's advice to younger widows? (5:14)
❇ What had some of the younger widows already done? (5:15)
❇ Why did Paul encourage Christian women to care for the widows in their families? (5:16)
❇ Of what is the elder who directs the affairs of the church worthy? (5:17)
❇ Why should elders be paid? (5:18)
❇ How should accusations against an elder be handled? (5:19)
❇ Why should those who sin be rebuked publicly? (5:20)
❇ How did Paul encourage Timothy to keep these instructions? (5:21)
❇ What did Paul encourage Timothy to do and not to do? (5:22)
❇ Why did Paul encourage Timothy to use a little wine? (5:23)
❇ What is the impact of a person's sins and good deeds? (5:24-25)
❇ Why should slaves consider their masters worthy of respect? (6:1)
❇ How should slaves treat masters who are believers? (6:2)

GET IT
❇ How should we treat fellow Christians?
■ What plan does your church have for caring for the needs of the widows in your church?
❇ What sort of people besides widows are tempted to misuse their idle time?
■ What does it mean to care properly for needy family members?
❇ Which of your family members need your active care?
❇ Are the pastors in your church properly provided for?
❇ How do you think a pastor's salary should be determined? Why?
❇ When and how have you learned from the mistakes of others?
❇ In what negative ways does favoritism affect how we treat others?
❇ How can we keep ourselves pure in a society that does not support God's ideals?
❇ In what way might our sins and good deeds precede us and follow us in life?

APPLY IT
❇ In what area of your life do you need to depend on God to help you keep yourself pure?

■ How can you assist your church in the care of widows or others in need?
❊ In what specific way do you need to treat older men, younger men, older women, or younger women?

1 Timothy 6:3-10
Love of Money

TOPICS
Attitude, Contentment, Desires, Doctrine, Evil, Faith, Foolishness, Greed, Jesus Christ, Love, Materialism, Money, Quarrels, Teaching, Temptation, Truth, Weaknesses, Words, World

OPEN IT
❊ What evidence do you see of a love for money among your friends or coworkers?
■ Why do you think most people are or aren't content with what they have?

EXPLORE IT
❊ What do false teachers ignore? (6:3)
❊ What harsh words did Paul have for those who teach false doctrines? (6:3-4)
❊ In what did the false teachers of Paul's day have an unhealthy interest? (6:4)
❊ What was the result of the false teachers' unhealthy interests? (6:4-5)
❊ What did the false teachers of Paul's day really want? (6:5)
■ What brings us great gain? (6:6)
❊ What do we bring into the world? (6:7)
❊ What will we take out of the world? (6:7)
■ With what should we be content? (6:8)
❊ What often happens to people who want to get rich? (6:9)
❊ What is a root of all kinds of evil? (6:10)
■ What price do some people eager for money pay? (6:10)

GET IT
❊ What controversial false doctrines have been an issue in your church?
■ How could someone think that godliness was a means to financial gain?
❊ How do people attempt to use the Christianity for their own profit?
■ Why is it hard to be content?
❊ What would it take to make you content right now?
❊ What get-rich-quick schemes (big or small) have you fallen for?
❊ On a scale of one to ten (ten being very important), how important is money to you?
❊ Why do you think that money is important or not very important?
❊ How can you guard against placing too much stock in your personal possessions?

APPLY IT
■ About what situation in life will you ask God to help you be more content each day this week?
❊ How can you help a fellow believer keep a proper perspective on money and possession?

1 Timothy 6:11-21
Paul's Charge to Timothy

TOPICS
Caring, Confession, Eternal Life, Faith, Gentleness, God, Heaven, Jesus Christ, Joy, Knowledge, Love, Money, Righteousness, Truth, Words

OPEN IT
■ What well-known people or historical figures are known to you as fighters?
❊ What sort of goals do people in your profession tend to pursue?
❊ What goals do TV commercials and print ads encourage us to pursue?

EXPLORE IT
■ What did Paul tell Timothy to pursue? (6:11)
■ What was Timothy urged to fight? (6:12)
❊ What did Paul tell Timothy to take hold of? (6:12)
❊ Before whom did Timothy make a confession? What kind? (6:12-13)
❊ When did Jesus make "the good confession"? (6:13)
■ How long was Timothy supposed to keep Paul's command? (6:14-15)
❊ When will Christ return? (6:14-15)
❊ What titles and attributes did Paul ascribe to God? (6:15-16)
❊ Why should those who are rich not be arrogant or put their hope in wealth? (6:17)
❊ What command is given to those who are rich? (6:18)
❊ Why would someone want to lay up treasure for themselves? (6:19)
❊ What was Timothy to guard? (6:20)
❊ What was Timothy to turn away from? (6:20)
❊ How had some wandered away from the truth? (6:20-21)

GET IT
■ In what way is the Christian life a fight?
❊ How are we to pursue righteousness, godliness, faith, love, endurance, and gentleness?
■ What does it mean to "fight the good fight"?
❊ Before whom have you made a confession of your faith?
❊ How do God's attributes influence your worship of Him?
❊ Why is it so easy for us to trust in our possessions, accomplishments, or abilities?
❊ In what ways do people place their treasure here on earth?
❊ How can a person lay up treasure in heaven?
❊ How is it possible for someone to wander away from the faith?
❊ What actions can you take that will store treasure in heaven for you?

APPLY IT
❊ In what way can you pursue righteousness, godliness, faith, love, endurance, or gentleness in your life this week?
■ How can you fight the good fight of faith each day?
❊ What preventive measure can you take each day to be sure that you don't wander from the faith?

2 Timothy 1:1–2:13

Encouragement to Be Faithful

TOPICS

Abandon, Backslide, Death, Discipline, Encouragement, Endurance, Example, Faith, Faithfulness, Forsake, Gifts, God, God's Will, Gospel, Grace, Growth, Heritage, Holy Spirit, Influence, Jesus Christ, Love, Neglect, Salvation, Sovereignty, Spiritual Growth, Witnessing

OPEN IT

■ What is characteristic of the people you enjoy being around?
❊ In what ways have your parents or grandparents significantly shaped your life?

EXPLORE IT

❊ What did Paul do night and day? (1:3)
❊ Why did Paul long to see Timothy? (1:4)
❊ Who were Lois and Eunice, and what did Paul say about them? (1:5)
❊ What was Timothy reminded to do? (1:6)
❊ What kind of spirit does God give to His people? (1:7)
❊ In what way did Timothy need courage? (1:8)
❊ Why has God called us to a holy life? (1:9)
❊ What did Christ do? (1:10)
❊ Of what was Paul appointed a herald, an apostle, and a teacher? (1:11)
❊ Why was Paul not ashamed of the gospel? (1:12)
■ What did Paul tell Timothy to do with his training? (1:13)
❊ What was Timothy to guard? (1:14)
❊ Where does the Holy Spirit live? (1:14)
❊ Who had deserted Paul? (1:16)
❊ What had Onesiphorus done for Paul? (1:16-17)
❊ What did Paul want the Lord to grant Onesiphorus? (1:18)
❊ What did Paul encourage Timothy to do with what he had been taught? (2:2)
■ How was Timothy to endure hardship? (2:3)
❊ How does a soldier limit himself? Why? (2:4)
■ What must an athlete do in order to win? (2:5)
❊ What should a hardworking farmer receive? Why? (2:6)
❊ What was Paul's gospel? (2:8)
❊ Why was Paul willing to endure anything? (2:10)
❊ How did Paul encourage Timothy? (2:11-13)
❊ What "trustworthy saying" did Paul leave with Timothy to encourage him? (2:11-13)

GET IT

❊ For whom do you pray on a regular basis?
■ What family member or friend has had the biggest role in your spiritual growth and development?
❊ What gift has God given you?
❊ How is the spirit of power, love, and self-discipline shown in your life?
❊ When have you ever felt ashamed about something that you believe?
❊ When and how have you suffered for the gospel?
❊ What or whose pattern of sound teaching are you following?
❊ When have you felt abandoned by a friend?
■ When have you been refreshed by another believer?
❊ What example do the soldier, athlete, and the farmer set for us?
❊ How should God's faithfulness affect our commitment to Christ?

APPLY IT

❊ How can you refresh another believer today?
❊ Who is someone for whom you can commit to pray on a regular basis?
■ What person who has had a substantial impact on your spiritual life will you take the time to thank personally this week?

2 Timothy 2:14-26

A Workman Approved by God

TOPICS

Approval, Arguments, Confession, Conversation, Demons, Desires, Disagreements, Embarrassment, Evil, Faith, Goals, God, Life-style, Lust, Obedience, Repentance, Satan, Truth, Words, Work

OPEN IT

❊ Whose approval did you seek most as a teenager?
❊ When was the last time you felt thoroughly embarrassed?
■ What was the last really stupid argument you had with someone?

EXPLORE IT

■ What results from quarreling about words? (2:14)
❊ How did Paul encourage Timothy to present himself before God? (2:15)
❊ Why should we avoid godless chatter? (2:16)
■ What had Hymenaeus and Philetus done? (2:17-18)
❊ What must everyone who confesses the name of the Lord do? (2:19)
❊ What sort of articles are found in a large house? (2:20)
❊ How could someone become an instrument used for noble purposes? (2:21)
❊ What was Timothy encouraged to flee? (2:22)
❊ What was Timothy encouraged to pursue? (2:22)
■ What produces quarrels? (2:23)
❊ What must the Lord's servant do and avoid? (2:24)
❊ How should we deal with those who oppose the Lord's servants? Why? (2:25)
❊ What did Paul hope would happen to those who opposed the Lord's servant? (2:25-26)

GET IT

■ About what sorts of things do we get into senseless arguments with other Christians?
❊ What does it mean to be approved by God?
■ How can we please God with our work?
❊ What circumstances make you feel ashamed or embarrassed?
❊ When are you tempted to engage in godless chatter or stupid arguments?
❊ What false doctrines have destroyed the faith of someone you know?
❊ How can we cleanse ourselves from insignificant pursuits?

❊ What evil desires of youth continually tempt us?
❊ How do we usually deal with people who oppose us?
❊ How should we deal with people who oppose us?
❊ In what way have people in society today been taken captive by the devil?

APPLY IT
❊ What can you do to present yourself as one approved to God?
■ How do you need to change in your daily speech to weed out senseless and godless chatter?
❊ What can you do to flee temptation?

2 Timothy 3:1-9
Godlessness in the Last Days

TOPICS
Ambition, Culture, Desires, Disobedience, Ego, Evil, Faith, God, Greed, Last Days, Learning, Morality, Parents, Pleasure, Power, Pride, Self-centeredness, Sin, Society, Truth, World

OPEN IT
■ What adjectives would you use to describe the world in which we live today?
❊ What goals drive the people with whom you work and live?

EXPLORE IT
❊ What did Paul call to our attention? (3:1)
■ What will people be like in the last days? (3:2)
❊ What will people in the last days lack? (3:3)
❊ What will people in the last days love instead of God? (3:4)
■ What kind of "godliness" will people have in the last days? (3:5)
❊ What should we do with the kind of people Paul described? (3:5)
❊ How do godless people exploit others? (3:6)
❊ What controls the kind of godless people Paul described? (3:6)
■ What are godless people always doing? (3:7)
❊ Why do certain people oppose the truth? (3:8)
❊ To what historical figures were these godless people compared? (3:8)
❊ Why will godless people not get very far? (3:9)

GET IT
❊ Why do you think we are or are not living in the last days?
❊ Why are there people like the ones Paul described?
❊ Why is it so tempting to be a lover of pleasure rather than a lover of God?
❊ How can someone have a form of godliness yet deny its power?
■ What relationship should we have with people who flaunt their ungodly behavior?
■ In what way does our society encourage people to let themselves be controlled by evil desires?
❊ In what way is the folly of ungodly people clear and apparent to everyone?
❊ What do you think it means that godless people have depraved minds?

APPLY IT
■ From what ungodly person or group do you need to encourage other believers to disassociate themselves?
❊ What specific sinful attitude or behavior will you ask God to help you overcome this week?

2 Timothy 3:10–4:8
Paul's Charge to Timothy

TOPICS
Basics of the Faith, Bible, Christianity, Commitment, Correction, Death, Doctrine, Encouragement, Evangelism, Faith, Follow-through, God, Inspiration, Instructions, Jesus Christ, Persecution, Reputation, Rewards, Righteousness, Second Coming, Teaching, Training, Words, Work

OPEN IT
■ If the story of your life were made into a movie, what would the title be?
❊ If you could be known for only one thing when you died, what would you want it to be?
❊ Who is someone whose reputation you admire?

EXPLORE IT
■ What did Timothy know about Paul? (3:10-11)
❊ From what did Paul say the Lord rescued him? (3:11)
❊ What will happen to everyone who wants to live a godly life? (3:12)
❊ What will evil men and impostors do? (3:13)
❊ What did Paul encourage Timothy to do? (3:14)
❊ How long had Timothy known the holy Scriptures? (3:15)
❊ What are the holy Scriptures able to do? (3:15)
❊ What is true of all Scripture? (3:16)
❊ For what is Scripture useful? (3:16)
❊ For what good work does the Scripture equip the person of God? (3:17)
❊ Who will Jesus Christ judge? (4:1)
■ What did Paul want Timothy to be prepared for? (4:2)
❊ What time did Paul say was coming? (4:3)
❊ What will people one day do with the truth? (4:4)
❊ What did Paul instruct Timothy to do? (4:5)
■ Why was Paul ready for his impending death? (4:6)
❊ What had Paul done? (4:7)
❊ What was in store for Paul? (4:8)
❊ To whom will God award a crown of righteousness? (4:8)

GET IT
❊ What sort of a reputation do you want to have?
■ What sort of a reputation do you have at work, at school, and in your neighborhood?
❊ When and how have you been persecuted for living a godly life?
❊ What does it mean that the Bible is God-breathed?
❊ In what sort of ways should we use the Bible?
■ How equipped are you to do every good work?
❊ What type of doctrines do people today like to hear?
❊ In what way are all Christians able to be evangelists?

APPLY IT
❊ How can you use the Bible in your own spiritual

growth this week?
■ What can you do this week toward discharging all your duties?

2 Timothy 4:9-22
Personal Remarks

TOPICS
Abandon, Caring, Compromise, Good News, Heaven, Help, Love, Ministry, Sickness, Strength, Witnessing, World

OPEN IT
❇ What person would you like to visit whom you haven't seen in a while?
■ When have you felt abandoned by your friends?
❇ For what cause would you being willing to suffer?

EXPLORE IT
❇ What did Paul want Timothy to do? (4:9)
■ What had Demas done? Why? (4:10)
❇ Who was with Paul? (4:11)
❇ Why did Paul want Timothy to bring Mark? (4:11)
❇ Whom did Paul send to Ephesus? (4:12)
❇ What did Paul want Timothy to bring with him? (4:13)
❇ Who was Alexander? (4:14)
❇ What did Paul say about Alexander? (4:14)
❇ How did Paul instruct Timothy to deal with Alexander? (4:15)
■ What happened at Paul's first defense? (4:16)
❇ In what way did the Lord deliver Paul? Why? (4:17)
■ Of what was Paul convinced? (4:18)
❇ Who was Timothy supposed to greet? (4:19)
❇ What did Paul say about Erastus and Trophimus? (4:20)
❇ When did Paul want Timothy to come? (4:21)

GET IT
❇ In what way are you tempted to love the world?
❇ Why is it sometimes more tempting to love the world than to love God?
❇ What about the world do we naturally tend to love?
■ What keeps some Christians from holding on to their faith?
❇ What people today strongly oppose the Christian message? Why?
■ When has the Lord delivered you from a hostile situation?

APPLY IT
❇ To what fellow Christian can you show support this week? How?
❇ How can you help a church leader with his or her ministry?
■ What comfort or encouragement can you provide to a person who is battling for the faith in a hostile setting?

Titus 1:1-16
Titus' Task on Crete

TOPICS
Children, Disobedience, Faithfulness, Holiness, Leadership, Maturity, Serving

OPEN IT
❇ What characteristics do you think are necessary in a good leader?
■ What leader has had the most influence on you? How?

EXPLORE IT
❇ How is Paul's description of himself at the beginning of this letter significant? (1:1)
❇ How did Paul describe the faith that he had? (1:1-2)
❇ In light of Paul's reference to Titus, what kind of relationship did these two believers have? (1:4)
❇ Why did Paul leave Titus in Crete? (1:5)
■ For what reason was it necessary to appoint elders in the towns? (1:5, 10)
■ What qualifications were necessary to be an elder in Titus's church? (1:6-9)
❇ Why is it necessary for an elder to be blameless? (1:7)
■ What is the result of holding firm to the "trustworthy message"? (1:9)
❇ How should believers respond to "rebellious people" in the church? (1:10-13)
❇ What were the rebellious people doing that Paul so strongly condemned? (1:11)
❇ What did Paul tell his audience to pay no attention to? (1:14)
❇ How is it possible to learn whether a person truly knows God? (1:16)

GET IT
❇ What does it mean that, "To the pure, all things are pure"?
❇ What does the relationship between Paul and Titus teach us about how we should treat other Christians?
■ Why is it necessary to appoint elders and leaders in the church?
■ Who are the overseers in your church?
❇ To what extent should we choose church elders according to the guidelines in this passage?
❇ How should the qualifications for a church leader be different from those for a leader outside of the church?
❇ Why do you think it is important for leaders' children to believe in the Lord and not be disobedient?
❇ What work in the church has God entrusted to you?
❇ What area of your character most needs your attention at this time in your life?
❇ How can you encourage others?
❇ What are rebellious people in the church like?
❇ How should we treat rebellious people in the church?
❇ What should our motivation be in correcting those who teach things they ought not to teach?
❇ What do your actions reveal about your relationship with God?

APPLY IT
❇ What can you do in the next few days to encourage another Christian in his or her faith?

■ How can you show support for your church leaders? When?
❋ What is one way you can support true doctrine and sound teaching in your church?

Titus 2:1-15
What Must Be Taught to Various Groups

TOPICS
Authority, Example, Holiness, Life-style, Righteousness, Teaching, Training

OPEN IT
❋ How do parents teach their children their values and beliefs?
■ What religious beliefs were you taught growing up? How?

EXPLORE IT
❋ What main theme begins this chapter? (2:1)
❋ What is important for older men to be taught? (2:2)
■ How can older and younger Christians help each other? (2:2-8)
❋ What must older women be taught? Why? (2:3-5)
❋ What responsibility do older women have? (2:4)
❋ What should younger women be taught? (2:4-5)
❋ Why is it important for Christians to live blameless lives? (2:5)
❋ What advice did Paul give to younger men? (2:6-8)
❋ Who should set an example for others? How? (2:7)
❋ What response did Paul hope for? (2:8)
❋ How did Paul instruct slaves? Why? (2:9-10)
❋ What does the grace of God bring? (2:11)
■ Why should all Christians, whether old or young, be taught? (2:11-14)
❋ What motivation do we have to live righteous lives? (2:12-13)
■ How did Paul emphasize the importance of teaching all Christians? (2:15)

GET IT
❋ What does a person's lifestyle reveal about his or her beliefs?
❋ What should a Christian's lifestyle be like?
■ What responsibility do Christians have to each other?
❋ What role should accountability play among Christians?
❋ What can we learn about work from Paul's instructions to slaves?
❋ How can you make the gospel of Christ attractive to unbelievers in the way you work?
❋ What motivates you to live a godly life?
■ From what older, more mature believer do you want to learn?
❋ How can you teach other Christians?
❋ What do you have to share with other Christians about what you have learned in your own Christian walk?
❋ How can you ensure that what you teach other Christians, even by your own life's example, is in accordance with sound doctrine?

APPLY IT
❋ Of all the advice Paul gives in this passage about how to live a holy life, what is one specific area that you will commit yourself to concentrate on this next week?
❋ How can you remind yourself each day that the way you work is a testimony to others?
■ What step can you take in the near future to learn from another more mature Christian?
❋ What step can you take in the near future to share what you have learned with a younger believer?

Titus 3:1-15
Doing What Is Good

TOPICS
Authority, Eternal Life, Holy Spirit, Humility, Mercy, Obedience, Quarrels, Salvation, Spiritual Rebirth

OPEN IT
■ What is the dirtiest job you ever had to do?
❋ When is it beneficial to argue about an issue?
❋ In your experience, how can an argument damage a friendship?

EXPLORE IT
❋ How does God want us to respond to authority? (3:1)
■ How does God want us to treat all people? (3:1-2)
❋ What are we like before we are saved? (3:3)
■ What changes when we believe in Christ? How? (3:3-7)
❋ What saved Paul from his foolishness? (3:4)
❋ Why does God save people? (3:4-5)
❋ What role does the Holy Spirit play in a person's salvation? (3:5)
❋ What is the result of being justified by faith? (3:7)
❋ What did Paul tell Titus to stress? Why? (3:8)
❋ Why is it important to avoid controversies and arguments? (3:9)
❋ How should we treat a person who divides friends? (3:10-11)
■ Why is it important for us to do what is good? (3:14)

GET IT
❋ In what ways do you need to subject yourself to rulers and authorities?
■ What does it mean to show true humility?
■ How can you show humility in all you do?
❋ What difference does it make that God saves us out of His great mercy, and not because of anything we do?
❋ What role does the Holy Spirit play in your life?
❋ What can you do to devote yourself to doing what is good?
❋ What can you do to guard yourself against getting involved in useless arguments?

APPLY IT
■ What is one way you can serve others in your home, place of work, or church this week?
❋ What can you do this next week to reconcile a damaged relationship?
❋ How can you say thank you to God in the next few days for His saving grace toward you?

Philemon 1-7
Thanksgiving and Prayer

TOPICS
Encouragement, Friendship, Prayer, Relationships, Slavery, Thankfulness, Words

OPEN IT
❋ Who has prayed for you in the past?
■ What role has someone's words of encouragement played in your life?
❋ How much of what is said to you each week at work and home is negative or positive?

EXPLORE IT
❋ Who wrote this letter? (v. 1)
❋ To whom was this letter written? (v. 1)
❋ What do we know about the church from this brief introduction? (v. 2)
❋ What two godly qualities did Paul desire for his readers? (v. 3)
■ What was always a part of Paul's prayers? (v. 4)
■ What had Paul heard about the readers of this letter? (v. 5)
■ How did Paul pray for his audience? (v. 6)
❋ What did Paul suggest that Philemon would gain by actively sharing his faith? (v. 6)
❋ What had Philemon done for Paul? (v. 7)
❋ What had Philemon done for the other Christians in the region? (v. 7)

GET IT
❋ When are the normal times in a day or week that you pray?
❋ What are the subjects or concerns you most often address in your prayers?
❋ What are the marks or ingredients of a good prayer?
■ When should we ever tell someone that we are praying for them?
❋ What is your reaction when someone says they are praying for you?
❋ How does it help a person to tell them you are praying for them?
■ How can compliments and encouragement influence someone's life?
❋ How does it help a person to pray for them?
❋ What is the difference between what a person should and should not pray for?

APPLY IT
❋ Who are several people for whom you need to pray this week?
■ Who in your life needs a word of compliment or encouragement at this time?
❋ Whom could you write or call this week to thank for the joy or encouragement they have given to you during your life?

Philemon 8-25
Paul's Plea for Onesimus

TOPICS
Change, Compassion, Forgiveness, Friendship, Reconciliation, Restitution, Slavery

OPEN IT
■ When you have to ask someone for a favor, how do you go about it?
❋ How would you welcome back into your home a family member who had run away?
❋ What does it take to reestablish trust with someone who has made a major mistake?

EXPLORE IT
❋ What type of attitude did Paul project toward Philemon? (vv. 8-9)
❋ How did Paul describe himself? (v. 9)
❋ Who is the subject of Paul's appeal to Philemon? (v. 10)
■ How did Paul describe his relationship with Onesimus? (vv. 10-11)
■ Why was Paul sending Onesimus back to Philemon? (vv. 12-16)
❋ What was Onesimus's former relationship to Philemon? (vv. 12-16)
❋ What was Paul's motivation for sending Onesimus back to Philemon when Paul could have used him as a helper? (vv. 12-14)
❋ What happened to Onesimus during the time he had been away from Philemon and with Paul? (vv. 15-16)
❋ How did Paul want Philemon to greet Onesimus when he returned? (v. 17)
❋ To what level was Paul willing to be involved in the reconciliation between Philemon and Onesimus? (vv. 18-19)
❋ Of what debt did Paul remind Philemon? (v. 19)
■ What response from Philemon did Paul anticipate? (vv. 20-21) Why?
❋ For what future event did Paul hope? (v. 22)

GET IT
❋ Why do you think this short letter related to a specific relationship problem is included in the Bible?
❋ Why do you think was it important to Paul that Onesimus return to his former master?
❋ What risks did Onesimus take by going back to Philemon?
❋ How should someone else's new commitment to Christ change our relationship with him or her?
❋ In what circumstances should Christians return to people they knew before their conversion to rectify past mistakes?
■ What role should we play in helping people be reconciled to others with whom they have had conflicts?
■ What do you think was Philemon's response when Onesimus returned to him? Why?

APPLY IT
❋ What broken relationship or promise from your earlier life are you willing to take steps to rectify this week?
■ What can you do this week to help other people settle their disputes or separation?
❋ Who needs your affirmation this week to help him or her more fully understand the changes God is working in his or her life?

Hebrews 1:1-14
The Son Superior to Angels

TOPICS
Angels, Basics of the Faith, Creation, Glory, Heaven, Jesus Christ, Prophecy, Worship

OPEN IT
■ What are some restaurants, vacation spots, books, movies, or other areas of interest, that you consider the best of their kind?
❋ What situations might tempt a Christian to turn his or her back on Christ?
❋ How do you think you might react if you saw an angel?

EXPLORE IT
❋ How did God speak to people in the past? (1:1)
❋ What was God's means for speaking to mankind in "these last days"? (1:2)
❋ What unique honors or activities did God the Father delegate to Jesus? (1:2)
❋ What works did Jesus do that only God could do? (1:2-3, 10)
■ Who is Jesus? (1:2-4)
❋ What does Jesus show us about the nature of God? (1:3)
❋ What astonishing feat is attributed to the word of Christ? (1:3)
❋ What was Jesus' primary ministry on earth? (1:3)
❋ What did Jesus do after completing His earthly ministry? (1:3)
❋ What does Christ's exalted status in heaven say about His similarity to angels? (1:4)
■ How is Jesus distinguished from God? (1:5)
❋ What is the relationship of Jesus and the angels? (1:6)
❋ To what extent do the angels honor the Son? (1:6)
❋ What are angels like? (1:7)
❋ What name or title applies to Jesus, the Son? (1:8)
■ What is Jesus' nature? (1:10-12)
❋ What will happen to the enemies of Christ? (1:12)
❋ What do angels do? (1:14)

GET IT
■ What difference does it make to you that Jesus is "heir of all things" and that the Father made the universe through Him?
❋ Why do you think the author of Hebrews made such a point of Christ's deity to these Hebrew Christians?
❋ What impact would you suspect these words had on Jewish Christians who were considering returning to Judaism?
■ What are some ways we can honor Christ?
❋ What difference does it make to you that Jesus sustains everything by His powerful word?
❋ When, if ever, have you sensed that angels were ministering to you or watching over you?
❋ What in your life tempts you to back away from your commitment to Christ?

APPLY IT
■ What steps can you take to remind yourself that Jesus is the Son of God and worth following?
❋ In what ways can you honor the Son of God as God in your worship this week?
❋ Who can you tell today about the unique person of Jesus Christ?

Hebrews 2:1-4
Warning to Pay Attention

TOPICS
Angels, Backslide, Carelessness, Disobedience, Good News, Gospel, Holy Spirit, Law, Legalism, Miracles, New Covenant, Persecution, Religion, Salvation, Traditions

OPEN IT
❋ What are some warnings you are glad you heeded?
■ What are some warnings you wish you had heeded?
❋ What trouble have you gotten into from not paying attention?
❋ How did you feel when you first followed Christ (or when you first realized your need for Christ)?

EXPLORE IT
■ What did the writer of Hebrews want his readers to pay attention to? (2:1)
■ What danger awaits Christians who carelessly forget the truth? (2:1)
❋ What happened to those who violated the "message spoken by angels" (that is, the Mosaic Law)? (2:2)
❋ Who played a major role in delivering the Mosaic Law? (2:2)
■ What are the consequences for those who pay no attention to the gospel? (2:3)
❋ Who revealed the message of "great salvation" to the world? How? (2:3)
❋ Who confirmed the salvation that Jesus announced? How? (2:3-4)
❋ What did God do to validate the gospel message? (2:4)
❋ How did God distribute gifts of the Holy Spirit? (2:4)
❋ What is the role of each member of the Trinity in delivering the gospel message? (2:3-4)

GET IT
❋ Why do you think the Hebrew Christians were in greater danger if they ignored "such a great salvation" than those who violated Old Testament law?
❋ How do we as modern Christians tend to "drift away" from God?
■ How do we as modern Christians fail to pay careful attention to what God tells us?
❋ What advice or counsel would you give to a Christian friend who was drifting spiritually?
❋ What kind of attitudes or actions would mark a Christian who is drifting?
■ How can we help ourselves pay closer attention to God's Word?
❋ Why do you think God is stricter on those who have been given more revelation than others?
❋ In what specific ways can you pay greater attention to God's Word?

APPLY IT
❋ What safeguards can you put in place this week to help you stay close to the Lord?

■ What are some ways you can nurture your attention span toward God this week?
❇ Who can you ask this week to help you resist the temptations to drift away from Christ?

Hebrews 2:5-18

Jesus Made Like His Brothers

TOPICS
Angels, Atonement, Creation, Freedom, Grace, Jesus Christ, Mercy, Reconciliation, Salvation, Satan, Suffering, Temptation

OPEN IT
❇ What does it mean to be free?
❇ How would you describe the ideal brother or sister?
❇ What qualities or accomplishments of one of your siblings make you most proud?
■ What is the most helpful act a brother or sister has ever done for you?

EXPLORE IT
❇ What is our God-given place on earth? (2:6-8)
❇ What is the relationship between Jesus Christ and the rest of the universe? (2:8)
■ What is Christ's present heavenly status? (2:9)
❇ What actions by Christ led to His current exalted position at the right hand of God? (2:9)
❇ What was unique about the death that Christ suffered? (2:9)
❇ What is God's ultimate goal for us? (2:10)
❇ What does Christ do to qualify a person for membership in the family of God? (2:11)
❇ What is the relationship between Christ and those who experience the salvation He gives? (2:11-12)
❇ What effect did the death of Christ have on Satan and his power? (2:14)
❇ What effect did the death of Christ have on those who were enslaved to the fear of death? (2:15)
■ In what ways is Christ like us? (2:14, 17)
■ What makes Christ especially qualified to help Christians when they are being tempted? (2:18)

GET IT
❇ In what ways are we "a little lower than the angels"?
■ What difference does it make that Christ "tasted death for everyone"?
■ What is the significance of the fact that no trial or temptation can come upon you that Christ does not perfectly understand?
❇ How do the temptations Christ suffered on earth affect the way He represents us before God as high priest?
❇ What counsel would you give to a Christian friend who was terrified of death?
❇ How can it help you on a daily basis to know that you have a "big brother" like Christ?
❇ What are the implications of the fact that Jesus' death and resurrection destroyed Satan and his power?
❇ What areas of your life do you need to entrust to your understanding, merciful, and powerful high priest/big brother?

APPLY IT
❇ Knowing that Christ understands your temptations, how can you respond differently today to the difficulties you face?
■ What Christian friend(s) can you encourage today with the message that Christ is our sympathetic high priest? How?

Hebrews 3:1-6

Jesus Greater Than Moses

TOPICS
Call, Faithfulness, Honor, Jesus Christ, Messiah, Obedience

OPEN IT
■ Who are (or were) some of the heroes of your generation?
❇ Who would you describe as a dedicated employee at your place of work?
❇ What assorted titles or designations describe who you are? (For example: postal clerk, husband, dad, baby brother, Sunday-school teacher, president of the Rotary Club, and coach of the little league football Eagles.)

EXPLORE IT
❇ How did the author of Hebrews address those reading his letter? (3:1)
❇ What blessing is promised to those who know Christ? (3:1)
❇ What command is given to those who want to be faithful followers of Jesus Christ? (3:1)
■ Who is Jesus? (3:1-2)
❇ How is Jesus like Moses? (3:2)
■ In what ways are Moses and Jesus similar? (3:2, 5-6)
■ Why is Jesus worthy of more honor than Moses? (3:3-6)
❇ What has Jesus done as God? (3:4)
❇ How are the people of God or the family of God described in this passage? (3:4-6)
❇ How do we demonstrate that we are members of God's household? (3:6)
❇ What qualities are necessary for us to be faithful children of God? (3:6)

GET IT
❇ How ought our identity affect the way we live in our daily lives?
❇ What do you think faithfulness looks like in the life of a Christian?
❇ Why is it important for us to fix our thoughts on Jesus, our apostle and high priest?
❇ What are some of the distractions that keep you from fixing your thoughts on Christ?
■ What great spiritual leaders do we look to today, much as the first century Jewish Christians looked to Moses?
■ In what ways is Christ greater than our greatest spiritual leaders and mentors?
❇ In what way are we God's house?
❇ How does biblical hope differ from ordinary hope?
❇ How would a healthy dose of spiritual courage change the way you live on a daily basis?
❇ What specific behaviors, habit patterns, or attitudes need to change so that you live up to your heavenly calling?

APPLY IT
❊ What can you do over the next twenty-four hours to fix your thoughts on Jesus?
■ What is one concrete way can you give to Jesus the honor that He deserves today?
❊ What Scriptural promise or biblical truth can you hold on to today to help you remain a faithful part of God's house?

Hebrews 3:7-19
Warning Against Unbelief

TOPICS
Anger, Deceit, Disobedience, Encouragement, Hardheartedness, Holy Spirit, Judgment, Punishment, Rest, Sin

OPEN IT
❊ How do you decide whether you take a particular warning seriously?
❊ What are the pros and cons of procrastination?
■ What is the most restful time or place you have ever experienced?
❊ Why do you think some people follow Christ for a little while and then turn away from Him?

EXPLORE IT
❊ Who is identified as the author of Psalm 95:7-11? (3:7)
❊ What warning (first issued by the psalmist) is repeated here by the author of Hebrews? (3:7-8)
■ How is Israel's period of wandering in the wilderness described in this passage? (3:8)
■ Why was God angry with the generation of Israelites who came out of Egyptian exile? (3:9)
❊ How did the Spirit of God describe the Israelites of the Exodus? (3:10)
❊ What were the consequences of the Israelites' stubborn disobedience? (3:11)
■ In light of the disobedience of the Israelites of the Exodus, what command was given to the Jewish Christians of the first century? (3:12)
❊ How are those described who turn away from the living God? (3:12)
❊ What is the connection between sin and unbelief? (3:12-13)
❊ How might a person show that he or she has "come to share in Christ"? (3:14)
❊ How long did the disobedient Israelites wander in the wilderness? (3:17)
❊ What happened to the generation of Israelites who rebelled against God in the wilderness? (3:17-18)

GET IT
❊ How do we "hear God's voice" in our daily lives?
■ What does it mean to harden one's heart?
❊ How does a person's heart become hard?
❊ What can we do to avoid hardening our hearts toward God?
❊ How might the encouragement of a fellow Christian affect you today?
❊ What are the consequences when Christians fail to encourage each other or hold each other accountable?
❊ What circumstances or situations in your life are currently fostering an attitude of unbelief toward God?
■ What can we learn from the Israelites of the Exodus?

APPLY IT
❊ What practical steps can you take this week to soften your heart toward God?
■ What routine can you set up and follow over the next month to help soften your heart toward God?
❊ Whom can you encourage today? How?

Hebrews 4:1-13
A Sabbath-Rest for the People of God

TOPICS
Anger, Deceit, Disobedience, Faith, Gospel, Hardheartedness, Judgment, Punishment, Rest, Sin

OPEN IT
❊ What is the most powerful sermon you have ever heard?
■ What situations or circumstances tend to make you feel restless?
❊ What different ideas have you heard (from friends, neighbors, or relatives) about how a person is made right with God?
❊ What is your favorite Bible verse or story? Why?

EXPLORE IT
❊ What important promise is the subject of this passage? (4:1)
■ How do we know that not everyone will experience God's rest (that is, His salvation)? (4:1-2)
■ Why didn't the Israelites of the Exodus enter God's rest? (4:2)
❊ What must a person do to experience God's rest? (4:3)
❊ How long has God been giving us a chance to enter His rest? (4:4)
❊ What was the consequence for the Israelites' disobedience? (4:5)
❊ Why did some who heard the promise of rest fail to enjoy that promise? (4:6)
❊ How did the author show that the rest God promised the Israelites involved more than mere physical rest in the land of Canaan? (4:8)
❊ What rest awaited God's people after Joshua and the Israelites had conquered Canaan? (4:8-9)
❊ Entering God's rest has what effect on our work? (4:10)
■ How should we seek to learn from the Israelites' negative example? (4:11)
❊ What is the Word of God? How? (4:12)
❊ What is unique about God? (4:13)
❊ What sort of future awaits all of us? (4:13)

GET IT
■ What does it mean to enter God's rest?
■ How is enjoying God's salvation a reality in your life?
❊ How does disobedience or unbelief keep us from enjoying God's rest?
❊ What prevents you from enjoying God's rest (or salvation)?
❊ What does God's rest have to do with one trying earn salvation with good works?

❇ How does the fact that God sees and knows everything about you (actions, words, thoughts, motives, feelings, and attitudes) motivate you to live a holy life?
❇ What has the Word of God revealed about your own thoughts and attitudes of the heart?

APPLY IT
■ What one area of your life do you need to turn over to God today?
❇ What steps can you take this week to learn from the negative examples of others?

Hebrews 4:14–5:10
Jesus the Great High Priest

TOPICS
Confidence, Faith, Grace, Obedience, Prayer, Sacrifice, Salvation, Submission, Temptation, Weaknesses

OPEN IT
■ To whom do you often turn when you feel discouraged? Why?
❇ How do you typically respond to folks who get in trouble—anger? impatience? sympathy? pity? encouragement? disgust?
❇ If Jesus walked in the room right now, how do you think you might feel?

EXPLORE IT
❇ To what important spiritual leader did the author of Hebrews compare Jesus? (4:14)
■ In what way is Jesus the ultimate high priest? (4:15)
❇ In what ways was Jesus tempted? (4:15)
❇ How is Jesus able to sympathize with us? (4:15)
❇ Because of Jesus' superior high priesthood, how can forgiven sinners approach God? (4:16)
■ How does Christ respond to those who approach Him in faith? (4:15-16) Why?
■ What is the role and primary duty of a high priest? (5:1)
❇ What makes a good high priest sympathetic to those he represents? (5:2)
❇ For whom did a high priest offer sacrifices? (5:3)
❇ Who chose Israel's high priests? (5:4)
❇ How is Jesus like Melchizedek? (5:6)
❇ In what priestly activities did Jesus engage while on earth? (5:7)
❇ What did Jesus' sufferings teach Him? (5:8)
❇ Who is described in this passage as the "source of eternal salvation"? (5:9)

GET IT
❇ How does it encourage you to have Jesus as your high priest?
❇ What is the difference between sinning and being tempted?
❇ How would the need for priests to offer sacrifices for their own sins have applied to Jesus Christ?
❇ How did suffering to the point of death give Jesus insights into obedience?
■ Why do you think suffering was part of God's will for Jesus as our high priest?
❇ How does the sympathy and understanding nature of Christ motivate you to turn to him when temptations arise?
❇ What does it mean for us to approach God?
■ How can we honor Christ as our high priest?
❇ What does it mean to you that Jesus has gone through the problems and temptations you face?
❇ For what specific area of your life do you need to approach Jesus and ask for mercy and grace?

APPLY IT
■ When will you pray each day this week, approaching God through Christ?
❇ What steps do you need to take this week to follow the obedient example of Jesus, who did God's will even when it resulted in personal suffering?

Hebrews 5:11–6:12
Warning Against Falling Away

TOPICS
Backslide, Denial, Holy Spirit, Judgment, Laziness, Maturity, Rejection, Repentance, Righteousness, Salvation, Spiritual Growth, Unbelievers

OPEN IT
■ What are some immature, childlike habits or actions that simply would not be tolerated if seen in an adult?
❇ What theological truth or biblical concept is most difficult for you to comprehend?
❇ What is the most disgraceful or damaging thing ever done in God's name?
❇ What hero did you emulate and imitate as a kid? Why?

EXPLORE IT
■ What was wrong with the group of Hebrew believers originally addressed in this passage? (5:11-14)
■ What are the marks of spiritual maturity? (5:11-14)
❇ Of what are infant or baby Christians ignorant? (5:13)
❇ What is the benefit of "solid food"? (5:14)
❇ What challenge did the author give to his readers? (6:1)
■ What fundamental or basic doctrines form the foundation of our faith? (6:1-2)
❇ In the end, what enables us to reach spiritual maturity? (6:3)
❇ What are maturing, committed Christians like? (6:7)
❇ What are those who fall away from the faith like? (6:8)
❇ What does it show when Christians help other Christians? (6:10)
❇ What danger did the author warn against? (6:12)

GET IT
❇ What is "solid food"?
❇ How would you describe your present level of spiritual maturity?
❇ What actions and attitudes would you expect to find in a mature Christian?
■ How have you grown since you first became a Christian?
❇ What decisions are you facing that call for extra discernment?
❇ Of what does your spiritual diet consist?
❇ How does it disgrace Christ when a person lapses back into his or her old way of life?

❊ In what way can a Christian become useless to God?
■ What can we do to move forward, or become more mature, in our relationship with Christ a little each day?
❊ How can you rely on the goodness of God's Word for discernment in the decisions you must make?

APPLY IT
■ In what concrete ways can you strengthen your hold on Christ this week?
❊ What changes can you make in your daily routine over the next three days to combat laziness and exercise discipline?

Hebrews 6:13-20
The Certainty of God's Promise

TOPICS
Assurance, Believe, Faith, God, Heaven, Hope, Jesus Christ, Mediator, Promises, Sincerity, Truth, Waiting

OPEN IT
❊ How good are you at keeping your promises?
■ What gives you a sense of security?
❊ What, if anything, are you willing to die for?
❊ What biblical truth gives you the most encouragement and hope?

EXPLORE IT
❊ Why did God "swear by himself"? (6:13)
■ What promise did God make to Abraham? (6:13-14)
❊ How did God guarantee His promise to Abraham? (6:13-14)
❊ What do we learn from this passage about God? (6:13, 17-18)
■ How did Abraham respond to God's promise, and what was the result? (6:15)
❊ What is the function of oaths? (6:16)
❊ How did God confirm His promise? (6:16-17)
■ Why did God confirm His promise with an oath? (6:16-18)
❊ How do we know God won't retract His promise? (6:18)
❊ What happens to those who find the hope that Christ offers? (6:18)
❊ How is the hope that Christ gives described in this passage? (6:19)
❊ Where is the believer's hope anchored? (6:19)
❊ How was Christ able to "enter the inner sanctuary behind the curtain"? (6:19-20)
❊ What did Christ do on our behalf? (6:20)

GET IT
■ How does Abraham's patience in waiting for God's promise encourage you?
❊ What does it mean to you personally that God gives every believer an eternal inheritance secure in heaven?
■ How does it help us to know that it is impossible for God to lie?
❊ How would you describe to a friend the hope that you have in Jesus Christ?
❊ What problems or troubles currently threaten your sense of security?
❊ What truths in this passage give you security in your relationship with God?
❊ What new insights does this passage give you about the character of God?
❊ In what area of your life do you need to follow Abraham's example of patience?

APPLY IT
❊ What step can you take over the coming week to put your sense of security in Christ?
■ To what promise of God do you need to cling at this time in your life?
❊ In what way can you express confidence in God's promises this week?

Hebrews 7:1-10
Melchizedek the Priest

TOPICS
Blessing, Comparisons, Greatness, Heritage, Jesus Christ, Mediator, Peace, Righteousness, Tithing

OPEN IT
❊ What does your name mean?
❊ Does the meaning of your name fit your personality?
■ What person from history do you most admire? Why?
❊ If you could have dinner with any three Bible characters, who would you choose? Why?

EXPLORE IT
■ Who was Melchizedek? (7:1)
❊ How was Melchizedek associated with Abraham? (7:1)
❊ What did Abraham give to Melchizedek? (7:2)
❊ What does the name Melchizedek mean? (7:2)
❊ What is significant about the title, "king of Salem"? (7:2)
■ What about the Genesis record of Melchizedek's life foreshadowed or anticipated the priesthood of Christ? (7:3)
■ How do we know that Melchizedek was "great"? (7:4)
❊ How did the Mosaic law ensure that the Levitical priests were provided for? (7:5)
❊ Why was it unusual for Melchizedek to receive a tithe from Abraham? (7:6)
❊ What did the ancient practice of one person blessing another say about the two parties involved? (7:7)
❊ How did the tithe collected by Melchizedek differ from the tithes collected by the Levites? (7:8)
❊ How did Levi—the yet-unborn collector of tithes—pay tithes to Melchizedek? (7:9-10)

GET IT
■ In what ways is Jesus like Melchizedek?
❊ What point is there in seeing that the historical Melchizedek was greater than Abraham and Levi?
■ What does it mean to you that Christ, like Melchizedek, is both a great king and priest?
❊ In what ways has Christ blessed you?
❊ Why is it important to tithe or give to God?
❊ What kind of behavior should the greatness of Christ elicit from us?
❊ What does it mean that Christ is a high priest forever?

APPLY IT

■ Because Jesus is great and worthy of our all, what gift of time, money, or energy will you give to Him this week?
❊ What insight from this passage can you meditate upon today to keep you from drifting away from Christ?
❊ In what way can you honor Christ this week?

Hebrews 7:11-28

Jesus Like Melchizedek

TOPICS

Atonement, Blessing, Comparisons, Eternal Life, Greatness, Heritage, Inadequacy, Mediator, Messiah, New Covenant, Perfect, Prayer

OPEN IT

■ When might a person want to be represented by a lawyer? Why?
❊ What is something that you have replaced or gotten rid of recently?
❊ What is one regular task or chore that you hate doing?
❊ How might you react if you found yourself alone in an elevator with the president or the prince of Wales?

EXPLORE IT

❊ Why did a new priest from the order of Melchizedek come along to replace the order of Aaron? (7:11)
❊ What does a new priesthood require? (7:12)
❊ What made Jesus unique as a member of His tribe? (7:13-14)
❊ From what tribe did Jesus Christ come? (7:13-14) How is this significant?
❊ What connection did Jesus' tribe have to the Jewish priesthood? (7:14)
■ On what basis did Christ become a priest? (7:15-16)
❊ Why is the new covenant superior to the old covenant of law? (7:18-19)
■ How is Jesus unique among the priests who represented Israel before God? (7:23-25)
❊ What does Jesus do for those who come to God through Him? How? (7:25)
■ What is Jesus, our high priest, like? (7:26-27)
❊ What did the Levitical priests have to do before they offered sacrifices for the sins of the people? (7:27)
❊ How did Jesus perform his function as high priest when he was on earth? (7:27)

GET IT

■ How does it make you feel to know that Jesus is praying for you at this very moment?
❊ What does this passage say to people who feel the need for a human priest?
❊ What role does the law of God play in making us right before God or giving us the power to live for God?
❊ What comfort can we find in Jesus' role as our high priest?
❊ What could you say to someone who says, "I don't see what Christ accomplished by dying on the cross"?
❊ How is the resurrection of Christ important?
■ In what way can Christ's priesthood give us confidence to draw near to God?

APPLY IT

❊ How can you make a special effort each day this next week to draw near to God?
❊ For whom will you pray every day this week?
■ How can you honor Christ as your high priest in your prayer throughout the coming week?

Hebrews 8:1-13

The High Priest of a New Covenant

TOPICS

Change, Comparisons, Forgiveness, Heaven, Inadequacy, Jesus Christ, Limitations, Mediator, Messiah, New Covenant, Sacrifice

OPEN IT

❊ What is involved in knowing someone?
❊ What is involved in having an intimate relationship with God?
■ What items in your home or office would you consider obsolete? Why?
❊ Why is it so difficult to forget the wrongs others do to us?

EXPLORE IT

❊ Where is Christ right now? (8:1)
❊ With what title is God described? (8:1)
❊ What is Christ doing presently in heaven? (8:2)
❊ What is the "job description" for a high priest? (8:3)
❊ How do earthly sanctuaries and tabernacles differ from the heavenly one in which Christ is currently serving? (8:2, 5-6)
❊ Why would Jesus not be a priest on earth? (8:4)
❊ What do the terms "copy," "shadow," and "pattern" indicate about the Levitical priesthood? (8:5)
■ In what ways is the new covenant superior to the old? (8:6)
■ Why did God decide to initiate a new covenant? (8:7-12)
❊ How did Israel handle their part in the old covenant? (8:9)
❊ How did God say the new covenant would be different from the old one? (8:10)
❊ What is God's response to sin under the new covenant? (8:12)
■ What became of the old covenant when the new was introduced? (8:13)

GET IT

❊ How does it make you feel to realize that under the new covenant, you can have an intimate relationship with God?
■ How motivated would you be to love and worship God if you had to depend solely on animal sacrifices offered by a stranger?
■ What do we learn about God from the fact that He set aside the old covenant in favor of the new?
❊ What three words best describe how you feel knowing that Jesus Christ is in the presence of God representing you before your Creator?
❊ How much do biblical principles and God's truths govern your thoughts and actions?

APPLY IT

❋ In what ways can you show your thanks to God today for the fact that He remembers your sins no more?
■ What can you do this week to get to know God better?
❋ How can you use the truths of this passage in coming days to help a friend who is struggling to earn God's approval?

Hebrews 9:1-10

Worship in the Earthly Tabernacle

TOPICS

Atonement, Comparisons, Forgiveness, Holy Spirit, Inadequacy, Jesus Christ, Limitations, Mediator, Messiah, New Covenant, Sacrifice

OPEN IT

❋ What is the most beautiful church, cathedral, or religious shrine you have visited?
■ If you could show three objects or artifacts that best tells the story of your own spiritual journey, what items would you show? Why?
❋ What religious customs do you observe that you really don't understand the meaning or purpose of?

EXPLORE IT

❋ What aspect of the old and new covenants is compared in this passage? (9:1)
❋ What was in the first room of the earthly tabernacle? (9:2)
❋ What was the first room called? (9:2)
❋ What was behind the second curtain in the tabernacle? (9:3)
❋ What two objects were in the room behind the second curtain? (9:4)
❋ What was inside in the ark of the covenant? (9:4)
❋ What was above the ark? (9:5)
❋ During the year, who typically ministered at the tabernacle, and in which part did this ministry take place? (9:6)
■ What three severe restrictions were placed upon entrance to the inner room of the temple? (9:7)
❋ For whom was blood offered on the Day of Atonement? (9:7)
■ What truth was the Holy Spirit teaching through the once-a-year offering for sin under the old covenant? (9:8)
■ What symbolic truth did the Mosaic tabernacle teach about sin? (9:9-10)

GET IT

❋ From Hebrews 9:1-5 and the background information in Exodus, what is your impression of the old covenant's "regulations for worship"?
■ What does the earthly tabernacle and sacrificial system tell us about Christ's once-for-all sacrifice for sin?
❋ What do you think went through the high priest's mind on the Day of Atonement as he prepared to enter the Holy of Holies?
❋ What is significant about the contents of the ark of the covenant?
❋ How can we alter our lives to reflect the fact that God dwells only in holy places?
❋ What arbitrary religious rules or traditions make it difficult for you to serve God?
■ How does Christ's sacrifice enable us to have a clear conscience?
❋ How can we be sure to approach God as the Holy God He is?

APPLY IT

■ What are some practical steps you can take when you feel touched by a guilty conscience?
❋ What do you want to remember the next time you approach God in worship?

Hebrews 9:11-28

The Blood of Christ

TOPICS

Atonement, Comparisons, Death, Forgiveness, Heaven, Holy Spirit, Inadequacy, Jesus Christ, Judgment, Limitations, Mediator, Messiah, New Covenant, Sacrifice

OPEN IT

❋ What are some ways people typically try to deal with their own mortality?
■ What images come to mind when you hear the phrases, "blood sacrifice," and, "cleansed with blood"?
❋ What do you imagine death being like?

EXPLORE IT

❋ How is the heavenly tabernacle in which Christ serves as high priest described? (9:11)
❋ By what means did Christ enter the Most Holy Place? (9:12)
❋ How many times did Christ enter the Most Holy Place? (9:12)
❋ What ritual cleansing ceremony did a high priest typically complete before he entered the Most Holy Place? (9:13)
❋ To what degree was a high priest considered clean? (9:13)
■ How was Christ's sacrifice on our behalf different from the usual sacrifice for sin on the Day of Atonement? (9:14)
■ What benefits do believers in Christ derive from the sacrifice Christ made on their behalf? (9:14)
❋ What is our promised eternal inheritance? (9:15)
■ What must happen in order for sins to be forgiven? (9:22)
❋ As a high priest, why did Christ enter heaven instead of an earthly manmade sanctuary? (9:24)
❋ How is Christ categorically different from every other high priest? (9:25-26)
❋ What fate awaits every person? (9:27)
❋ How will Christ's second coming differ from His first advent? (9:28)

GET IT

❋ In what ways was Christ an unblemished sacrifice?
❋ What does it mean that Christ fully and completely satisfied God's wrath over sin and can make us right with God?
❋ Why couldn't we receive our promised eternal inheritance apart from the death of Christ?

■ Why do you think the author kept emphasizing that Christ's sacrifice was "once for all"?
❊ How would it change the way we live if we kept in mind the fact that we all will be judged?
■ If Christ has done all these fantastic things for us, why are we so prone to stray from Him?
❊ What might motivate you to be more consistent in your commitment to Christ?
❊ How can the fact of your own mortality (that is, our lives on earth are temporary) motivate us to a holier life-style?

APPLY IT
■ In what concrete way can you show gratitude for Christ's sacrifice?
❊ With whom do you want to share the good news this week of a Savior who offers forgiveness, freedom from sin, and eternal life? How?

Hebrews 10:1-18
Christ's Sacrifice Once for All

TOPICS
Atonement, Comparisons, Forgiveness, Heaven, Holy Spirit, Inadequacy, Jesus Christ, Legalism, Limitations, Mediator, Messiah, New Covenant, Perfect, Sacrifice

OPEN IT
■ What is one thing you would buy at a very high price if paying that price meant you never had to pay for it again?
❊ What jobs would you consider unfulfilling, frustrating, or even futile?
❊ What are some ways people try to deal with bad habits?

EXPLORE IT
❊ How is the Law compared to the new covenant brought by Christ? (10:1)
■ In what way was the Law of Moses glaringly inadequate? (10:1-2)
❊ How did the author of Hebrews show that the Law was inadequate? (10:2)
❊ What function did the annual sacrifices serve? Why? (10:3-4)
❊ How successful were animal sacrifices under the old covenant? (10:4)
❊ Why wasn't God pleased with the sacrifices and offerings of the old covenant? (10:5-6)
❊ What was the attitude of Christ when He came into the world? (10:7)
❊ What evidence of the futility and emptiness of the old covenant did the author cite? (10:8)
■ If God neither desired nor was pleased with old covenant sacrifices, why did the Israelites make them? (10:8)
❊ What role does a believer play in earning God's approval? (10:9-14)
❊ What did Christ's single act of dying accomplish for those who would trust in Him? (10:14)
❊ How did the new covenant change the way God motivates His people to live for Him? (10:16)
■ What effect did the sacrifice of Christ have on the way God views our sins? (10:17)
❊ Why are additional sacrifices for sin unnecessary? (10:18)

GET IT
❊ What has Christ done for us?
❊ How would you contrast the shortcomings of the old covenant with the blessings of the new covenant?
❊ Why do Christians still feel guilt when God says He forgives and forgets their transgressions?
■ How does being cleansed of sin by Christ change us?
❊ What do you think prompted or motivated Jesus to make the sacrifice He made?
■ In what sense have we "been made holy" (10:10) while at the same time "are being made holy" (10:14)?
❊ What insights from this passage can we use to show that being saved from sin requires faith in Christ?

APPLY IT
❊ In what specific areas of your life today do you need to follow the example of Christ in saying, "I have come to do your will, O God"?
■ What can you do this week to show trust in Christ's provision for forgiveness?
❊ When could you speak with a friend or relative who would be encouraged by the truths of this passage?

Hebrews 10:19-39
A Call to Persevere

TOPICS
Atonement, Backslide, Encouragement, Forgiveness, Hope, Jesus Christ, Joy, Judgment, Love, Mediator, New Covenant, Persecution, Perseverance, Rewards, Salvation, Sincerity

OPEN IT
❊ When in your life did you "hang in there" the longest in the face of an extremely difficult situation?
❊ Who has encouraged you the most in the last six months?
■ How highly does your boss value perseverance in his or her employees?

EXPLORE IT
❊ Why did the author say that those under the new covenant could draw near to God? (10:19-22)
❊ What has Jesus done for those under the new covenant? (10:20)
❊ What privilege comes to those who are part of the "house of God"? (10:22)
❊ What must happen before a person can draw near to God? (10:22)
❊ What happens to the guilty conscience of those who put their faith in Christ? (10:22)
■ Why are Christians able to persevere in following Christ? (10:23)
❊ What kind of behavior should believers in Christ exhibit toward one another? (10:24-25)
❊ What will happen to God's enemies? (10:26-27)
❊ Why is rejecting Christ more serious than rejecting the old covenant? (10:28-29)

❇ What did the author consider "a dreadful thing"? (10:31)
■ How had the Hebrew Christians responded to persecution at first? (10:32-34)
■ What is promised to those who persevere? (10:35-39)

GET IT
❇ How does the complete forgiveness and help offered by Christ motivate you to draw near to God?
❇ When in your life have you felt the cleanest or most innocent? Why?
■ How could someone best spur you on "toward love and good deeds"?
❇ How do you personally feel about going to church or involvement in Christian groups?
■ How does the certainty of God's judgment challenge you?
❇ What is behind the ups and downs in your spiritual journey?

APPLY IT
■ What is one small project you could complete today to encourage a Christian friend to persevere in his or her faith?
❇ What can you do differently in your devotional times this week to "draw near to God"?
❇ Since we are called to live by faith (10:38), what is one bold step of trust in God you can take today?

Hebrews 11:1-40
By Faith

TOPICS
Believers, Circumstances, Danger, Endurance, Faith, Glory, Heroes, Obedience, Promises, Risk, Trust, Waiting

OPEN IT
❇ If you were able to listen to your own funeral eulogy (Tom Sawyer style), how would you like to hear yourself described?
■ When you were a child, what are some ways you showed trust in your parents?
❇ What do you consider the greatest example of faith you have ever seen? Why?

EXPLORE IT
❇ What is faith? (11:1)
❇ What does faith help us to comprehend about the creation of the world? (11:3)
❇ How did Abel demonstrate faith? (11:4)
❇ What was unusual about Enoch? (11:5)
■ What role does faith play in approaching and pleasing God? (11:6)
❇ What did Noah's faith prompt him to do? (11:7)
❇ How did faith affect Abraham's life? (11:8-12)
❇ How does faith change a person's focus and perspective? (11:13-16)
❇ What ultimate test of faith did God put Abraham through? (11:17-19)
❇ What hard choices did Moses make because of his faith? (11:24-28)
❇ What "secret" enabled Moses to persevere through rough times? (11:27)
■ What were some of the victories enjoyed by faithful Old Testament believers? (11:32-34)
❇ How does this passage disprove the notion that faith always leads to earthly blessing? (11:35-38)
■ What happened to a great many Old Testament saints who exercised faith in God? (11:39)

GET IT
❇ According to this passage, what is the only way we can please God with our lives?
■ What prompts committed followers of Christ to continue to exercise faith even when He never seems to "come through" for them?
■ Why do you think the author said that "the world was not worthy of" the heroes of faith mentioned in Hebrews 11?
❇ How do you think the individuals praised in Hebrews 11 were looked upon by those of their day?
❇ Why do you think God sometimes leaves us in the dark about His will?
❇ What are some examples from your life of both trusting God and doubting Him?
❇ Which characters named in this chapter would you most like and least like to trade places with? Why?
❇ In what concrete ways can we demonstrate the truth that we are "aliens and strangers" on earth? (11:13)

APPLY IT
❇ What is one way you can remind yourself to live as an alien and stranger at work and in your community?
■ With what do you need to trust God even though you can't see what the future holds? How can you show this trust?

Hebrews 12:1-3
God Disciplines His Sons

TOPICS
Barriers, Discipline, Encouragement, Fruit, Holiness, Jesus Christ, Peace, Perseverance, Perspective, Righteousness, Sin, Weaknesses

OPEN IT
❇ What is your favorite sporting event? Why?
❇ How were you disciplined or corrected as a child?
■ What do you think was good or bad about the way you were disciplined as a child?
❇ When did you endure difficult or arduous circumstances only because you knew you would later be rewarded?

EXPLORE IT
❇ What should motivate followers of Christ to live for Him? (12:1)
❇ What kind of athletic imagery did the writer of Hebrews use in this passage? (12:1)
❇ What warning is given to those who would run the race of the Christian life? (12:1)
❇ What should be the focus of those who would live for Christ? (12:2)
❇ How is Jesus described in this passage? (12:2)
❇ What is the benefit of remembering what Christ has done? (12:3)

■ What measures does the Lord sometimes take toward those who are His "sons"? Why? (12:5-6)
■ What do we learn about God from the fact that He disciplines us? (12:6-7)
■ What sobering truth can be inferred by those who never experience the discipline of God? (12:8)
❄ Why does God discipline His children? (12:9-10)
❄ In what sense does discipline have two sides? (12:11)

GET IT
❄ How well are you running the Christian race?
❄ What wrong attitudes or actions tend to stop your spiritual growth?
❄ What do you think it means to "fix our eyes" on Jesus (12:2)?
■ What are some specific ways God disciplines us?
❄ How can we tell when God is disciplining us?
■ What state might your life be in if God neglected to discipline you when you went astray?
❄ How has God's discipline made positive changes in your life?
❄ Why shouldn't we lose heart when the Lord rebukes or corrects us?

APPLY IT
❄ How can you focus your thinking on Christ this week?
❄ How could you call on your Christian friends this week to help you persevere as a Christian?
❄ What do you want to remember the next time God disciplines you?
❄ What step of obedience can you take beginning today to eliminate the need for God to discipline you?

Hebrews 12:14-29
Warning Against Refusing God

TOPICS
Angels, Bitterness, Celebration, Heaven, Holiness, Immorality, Jesus Christ, Judgment, Mediator, New Covenant, Peace, Unbelievers

OPEN IT
❄ What causes bitterness?
❄ How do you think you would react if your life were suddenly threatened by a severe earthquake, volcanic eruption, or avalanche?
■ What are some warnings that you have been grateful for? Why?

EXPLORE IT
❄ To what extent are Christians to try to resolve conflicts? Why? (12:14)
❄ In what way should believers pursue holiness? Why? (12:14)
■ Why is holiness important? (12:14)
❄ What wrong attitude should we watch out for? (12:15)
■ What kinds of things do Christians need to watch out for? Why? (12:15-17, 25-27)
❄ What did Esau do that is described as godless? (12:16)
❄ What did Esau's godless behavior cost him? (12:17)
❄ In what ways was the old covenant intimidating or frightening? (12:18-21)
❄ How is Mount Sinai described—the place where the old covenant was revealed? (12:18)
❄ How did the author describe the new covenant? (12:22-24)
❄ In what way were God's thunderous pronouncements from Sinai only a foreshadowing of what is to come? (12:26-27)
❄ Of what kind of kingdom are Christians a part? (12:28)
❄ How should God's promises and glorious kingdom affect believers? (12:28)
■ How should we worship God? Why? (12:28-29)

GET IT
❄ Why is it difficult to get along with some people?
❄ When we have conflicts with one another, why do we typically want the other person to make the first move toward reconciliation?
■ What roadblocks make it difficult for you to pursue holiness?
❄ How would you counsel a friend who was extremely bitter?
❄ What are some ways wrong values and impulsive actions might bring heartache and grief?
❄ What does it mean to live at peace with everyone?
❄ What is dangerous about bitterness?
❄ How is your view of God different as a result of studying this passage?
❄ For which of God's acts on your behalf are you most thankful?
■ What does it mean to worship God with reverence and awe?

APPLY IT
❄ What bitter or unforgiving attitudes do you need to confess today?
■ What practical steps can you take this week to avoid becoming bitter toward someone who has hurt you?
❄ What actions do you need to take today so that you can truly say you have made every effort to live in peace with everyone?

Hebrews 13:1-25
Concluding Exhortations

TOPICS
Angels, Atonement, Challenge, Confidence, Heaven, Holiness, Immorality, Jesus Christ, Judgment, Leadership, Love, Marriage, Materialism, Mediator, Money, New Covenant, Peace, Praise, Prayer, Unbelievers

OPEN IT
❄ What would you want to say to your loved ones if you could write them a last letter or make a final videotaped message?
❄ What images come to mind when you hear the word "authority"?
■ What is one change you'd like to make but don't think you can right now?
❄ How do you think angels are involved in human affairs?

EXPLORE IT
❇ What kind of love are Christians to demonstrate? (13:1)
❇ Why did the author encourage his readers to entertain strangers? (13:2)
❇ What kinds of people does God want Christians to try to help? (13:3)
❇ Why is sexual purity important? (13:4)
■ What attitude toward money ought Christians have? Why? (13:5)
■ What fact about God can foster a contented spirit? (13:5)
■ How can we learn to be content? (13:5)
❇ How should Christians view their spiritual leaders? (13:7, 17)
❇ What attribute or characteristic of Christ is highlighted here? (13:8)
❇ What illustrations did the author use to challenge his readers to resist the temptation to go back to Judaism? (13:9-14)
❇ What kind of sacrifices should we offer to God? (13:15-16)
❇ What are the benefits of obeying one's spiritual leaders? (13:17)
❇ What did the writer pray would happen to his readers? (13:20-21)

GET IT
■ Why do you think is it so difficult to be content?
❇ What is significant to you about the fact that Jesus never changes?
■ How can we draw contentment from God's unchanging nature?
❇ What Christian leaders do you look up to and consider worth imitating? Why?
❇ What does hospitality mean or entail?
❇ How are you able to extend hospitality to others?
❇ Why do you think praise of God is so important for us to practice?
❇ How would you counsel a friend who was struggling in the area of sexual purity?
❇ What are some practical steps we can take to avoid temptations to immorality?
❇ How do you think you should respond if a Christian leader corrected you in a personal matter?

APPLY IT
❇ What can you do to show love to a person who is in prison or being mistreated?
■ What one action could you take this week to practice contentment with what you have?
❇ What Christian friend or friends can you encourage to continue walking with Christ? How?

James 1:1-18
Trials and Temptations

TOPICS
Believe, Desires, Doubt, Evil, God, Prayer, Temptation, Wealth

OPEN IT
❇ Why would you agree or disagree with the statement, "Life is 10 percent what happens to you and 90 percent how you respond to what happens to you"?
■ How would you respond to someone who tells you that good can come from the trials which you are experiencing?
❇ What doubts about God and prayer does the average person usually experience?

EXPLORE IT
❇ Who wrote this letter? (1:1)
❇ To whom was this letter written? (1:1)
■ What attitude did James tell people to exhibit when they are facing trials? (1:2)
■ What is produced when our faith is tested? (1:3-4)
❇ What is God's response when we ask for wisdom? (1:5)
❇ What effect does doubt have on a person when he or she prays? (1:6-8)
❇ What will eventually happen to the wealth of a rich person? (1:10-11)
■ What reward awaits the person who perseveres under trial? (1:12)
❇ From where does temptation come? (1:13-15)
❇ How does sin start and end? (1:13-15)
❇ From where do all good and perfect gifts come? (1:16-17)
❇ How did James describe God's relationship with the people He created? (1:17-18)

GET IT
❇ What trials and difficulties have you experienced during your life?
❇ Why does God allow people to go through trials and difficulties?
■ What good has ever come out of a difficult situation in your life?
❇ How does a person's relationship with God change as he or she goes through trials and problems?
❇ When do you find it hardest to pray?
❇ With what doubts have you struggled concerning God and prayer?
❇ How can doubting affect a person's prayer life?
❇ How can a person who pursues wealth and riches be disappointed?
❇ In what way have material possessions disappointed you once you possessed them?
■ How would you explain to a ten-year-old why a person does something wrong or evil?
❇ Why do we often blame God for tempting us when we sin?
❇ What can a person do to stop an evil desire from becoming an actual evil act?

APPLY IT
■ What do you believe God is trying to teach you this week through the trials and situations you are experiencing?
❊ In what specific areas do you need to ask God for His wisdom this week?
❊ What temptations do you need God's help to resist this week?

James 1:19-27
Listening and Doing

TOPICS
Anger, Caring, Compassion, Evil, Forget, Hypocrisy, Law, Listening, Obedience, Religion, Words

OPEN IT
❊ Who do you admire as a religious or spiritual role model?
❊ How does it affect you when a person is caught doing what he or she tells others not to do?
■ When are you most likely to lose your temper?

EXPLORE IT
■ What instruction did James give about the relationship between speaking, listening, and anger? (1:19)
■ What is the relationship between anger and righteous living? (1:20)
■ What should a Christian clean out of his or her life? (1:21)
❊ What is the relationship between listening to God's word and doing it? (1:22)
❊ What analogy did James use to describe a person who does not do what the Bible says? (1:23-24)
❊ What promise did James give to the person who studies God's Word and practices it? (1:25)
❊ What does the Bible give to people? (1:25)
❊ How is a person's speech related to the credibility of his or her faith? (1:26)
❊ What did James describe as pure religion? (1:27)
❊ What is pure religion? (1:27)

GET IT
❊ What makes it hard for us to be good listeners?
■ How can being quick to speak and quick to anger get you into trouble?
■ How do displays of anger and temper affect the witness of a Christian?
❊ What attitudes and habits can inhibit our growth as disciples of Christ?
❊ What makes it hard for us to practice what we know to be good?
❊ How does our speech reflect our relationship with God?
❊ How have you experienced freedom by doing the Word of God?
❊ What can we do to help widows and orphans?
❊ In what ways can the world pollute us?
❊ How can we keep ourselves from being polluted by the world?

APPLY IT
■ In what situations this week will you need to curb your anger? How can you?
❊ What do you need to change in your actions this week to match your talk?
❊ Whom will you help this week in obedience to God's Word?

James 2:1-13
Favoritism Forbidden

TOPICS
Change, Differences, Equality, Favoritism, Judging Others, Poor, Prejudice, Status

OPEN IT
■ How much money would it take to make you consider yourself rich?
❊ For what reasons might a person think he or she is more important than another person?
❊ Where do you see prejudice being practiced?

EXPLORE IT
❊ What practical example did James use to illustrate how favoritism was practiced in the church? (2:1-4)
■ What has God promised to the poor of this world? (2:5)
■ What does the church do to the poor person when it shows favoritism toward the rich? (2:6)
■ What do rich people have a history of doing to people in the church? (2:6-7)
❊ What is the royal law found in Scripture? (2:8)
❊ What does practicing favoritism do to a person who is trying to keep the law? (2:9)
❊ What does a person have to do to be considered a lawbreaker? (2:10-11)
❊ By what standards should a person speak and act? (2:12)
❊ What promise is made to people who judge without mercy? (2:13)
❊ Why should we be merciful? (2:13)

GET IT
❊ In what ways have you been a victim of favoritism or prejudice?
❊ How have you shown favoritism or prejudice toward other people?
❊ Why do we often treat rich people as more important than poor people?
❊ How do we use physical appearance, job status, and athletic ability to show favoritism toward people?
■ How can we welcome poor people in our church?
❊ Why does God have a special concern for poor people?
■ In what practical ways can we show genuine love to people of different races, cultures, and economic standing?
❊ Why is favoritism or prejudice often overlooked as a sin?
❊ Why would God condemn us as lawbreakers if our sins are only "minor" ones, such as prejudice?

APPLY IT
❊ From whom can you ask forgiveness this week for showing prejudice toward him or her?
■ How can you change the way you look at wealth this week so that you value it as God does?

James 2:14-26
Faith and Deeds

TOPICS
Actions, Faith, God, Hypocrisy, Righteousness

OPEN IT
■ If you were 100 miles from home with no money, no credit cards, no friends, no transportation, and no place to stay, what would you do to survive and make it home?
❄ What is the difference between someone who talks about a problem and someone who does something about the problem?

EXPLORE IT
❄ What is the relationship between faith and deeds? (2:14)
❄ What illustration did James use to explain how real faith affects a person's deeds? (2:15-17)
❄ How did James describe faith that has no accompanying deeds? (2:17)
❄ What is wrong with having faith without deeds? (2:18-26)
❄ What do the demons believe about God? How does it affect them? (2:19)
■ What did Abraham do to show his faith? (2:21-23)
■ What made Abraham righteous? (2:23)
■ How is a person justified before God? (2:24)
❄ What did Rahab do? (2:25)
❄ How did Rahab show faith? (2:25)
❄ How are faith and deeds like the body and the spirit? (2:26)

GET IT
❄ How is being a Christian supposed to change the way we live?
❄ What can a Christian do to help the people around him or her?
❄ What is one way to tell if a person has a real, living faith?
■ What is difficult about applying what we hear in church to our everyday lives?
❄ What are some of the biblical commands which are hard for you to live out?
❄ If God has forgiven us and promised us eternal life, what motivation do we have to live in obedience to Him today?
❄ Which is easier for you—talking about your faith with others, or demonstrating love toward them?
■ In what areas of your life do you want to begin acting more like a Christian?

APPLY IT
■ What home, work, or neighborhood situations might you be able to show faith in God this week? How?
❄ How can you show greater faith in God by what you do this week?

James 3:1-12
Taming the Tongue

TOPICS
Change, Conversation, Teaching, Words

OPEN IT
■ If you could hear a tape recording of everything you said last week, what would you want to edit out?
❄ How do you react when you hear someone cursing and using abusive language?
❄ How can a person be hurt by the words of others?
❄ What can you learn about a person by listening to him or her speak?

EXPLORE IT
❄ What unique responsibility does a teacher bear? (3:1)
■ If a person were never at fault in what he or she said, what would that show about the person? (3:2)
■ What is significant about the way we talk? (3:2)
❄ What is the purpose of a bit in the mouth of a horse? (3:3)
❄ What is the purpose of the rudder of a ship? (3:4)
❄ What damage can a small spark cause to a great forest? (3:4)
❄ What similarity does a person's tongue have to a horse's bit, a ship's rudder, and a spark of fire? (3:5)
❄ How did James describe the tongue? (3:6-8)
❄ What damage do our tongues do to us? (3:6)
■ What is so difficult about taming the tongue? (3:7-8)
❄ Of what inconsistencies are we capable? (3:9-10)
❄ In what ways are we inconsistent? (3:9-10)
❄ What illustrations from nature did James use to condemn cursing? (3:11-12)
❄ What can a spring or a fruit tree teach us about speech? (3:11-12)

GET IT
❄ What motivates a person to teach others?
❄ How is a teacher in the church supposed to be different from the average member?
❄ Why will God judge teachers more strictly than other people?
■ What are the ways we sin with our speech?
❄ Why are sins of speech often overlooked as not serious?
❄ How is our speech influenced by others around us?
❄ What practical advice would you give someone who wanted to control his or her tongue better?
❄ What weaknesses in our lives does our speech often expose?
■ In what times or places can your tongue be used for good?
❄ How can you change your daily speech to reflect its importance in your life?

APPLY IT
❄ What do you need to remove from your speech habits this week to make your words more pleasing to God?
■ What positive words do your family and coworkers need to hear from your mouth this week?

James 3:13-18
Two Kinds of Wisdom

TOPICS
Ambition, Bitterness, Envy, Humility, Rewards, Wisdom

OPEN IT
❊ What occupations or jobs require lots of knowledge and training?
❊ What is the difference between knowledge and wisdom?
■ What kinds of jobs or occupations require wisdom or discernment?
❊ Where do people often go to get wisdom?

EXPLORE IT
■ How can a person demonstrate wisdom and understanding? (3:13)
❊ How can we tell when a person is wise? (3:13)
❊ What common attitudes do we need to avoid boasting about? (3:14)
■ What is wrong with the "wisdom" of a selfish and bitter person? (3:14-15)
❊ How is a person's character related to his or her ability to discern? (3:14-16)
❊ From where does the "wisdom" of a selfish and bitter person come? (3:15)
❊ To what do envy and selfish ambition lead? (3:16)
❊ What are the qualities of the wisdom that comes from heaven? (3:17)
■ How does a wise person act? (3:17-18)
❊ What happens when people "plant seeds of peace"? (3:18)

GET IT
❊ What is the best way to make a lasting positive impression on others?
❊ What is the difference between earthly wisdom and God's wisdom?
■ What life experiences increase our wisdom?
❊ What are the marks of humility in a person?
❊ What damage can bitter envy or selfish ambition do to a person?
■ How can we get or experience heavenly wisdom?
❊ What are practical ways we can sow seeds of peace during our life?
❊ What godly characteristics are present in our speech when we are pursuing God's wisdom?
❊ What kind of bitter envy or selfish ambition do you tend to hold in your heart?

APPLY IT
❊ What can you do this week to plant peace in a relationship or situation which has been troubling you?
■ What can you do this week to seek God's wisdom?

James 4:1-12
Submit Yourselves to God

TOPICS
Attitude, Commitment, Forgiveness, Grace, Humility, Pride, Quarrels, Repentance, Submission

OPEN IT
❊ If you could ask God for anything, what would it be?
■ What do families and friends commonly fight about?

EXPLORE IT
❊ What are the battles going on inside a person? (4:1-2)
■ What is the root cause of fights and quarrels between people? (4:1-3)
❊ Why don't people have what they want? (4:2)
❊ Why doesn't God give some people what they ask for? (4:3)
❊ What does friendship with the world do to our relationship with God? (4:4)
❊ Whom does God oppose and favor? (4:6)
■ When does God give us grace? (4:6)
■ How did James describe the way we should come to God? (4:7-10)
❊ How does the devil react when a person resists him? (4:7)
❊ What does God do to us when we have an attitude of humility before Him? (4:10)
❊ How are we to speak to one another? (4:11)
❊ When we speak against a fellow believer, what attitude are we having toward God and His law? (4:11-12)

GET IT
❊ What do most people think God wants from them?
❊ How has your belief about what God wants from you changed over the years?
❊ How does pride show up in our work? home? church? community?
❊ Why does God oppose people who are proud?
■ What is the difference between pride and a sense of accomplishment?
❊ How can a person tell when he or she has become proud?
■ How can we reduce or remove the pride from our lives?
❊ What do we want from God most of the time?
❊ Why do we hesitate to give our lives to God?

APPLY IT
❊ What sins of action and attitude do you need to confess to God today?
❊ What can you do this week to draw near to God?
❊ In what situations do you need to resist the devil this week?
■ What can you do this week to help you bring more humility into your life?

James 4:13-17
Boasting About Tomorrow

TOPICS
Ambition, Decisions, Future, Goals, Greed, Judgment, Materialism, Plans, Sin

OPEN IT
❊ To where in the world would you like to travel?
❊ If you could start your own business, what would it be?
■ If you knew you had just three months to live, what are some things you would want to do?

EXPLORE IT
❄ Whose attention did James want to get? (4:13)
■ What warning did James give to those who make plans for the future? (4:13-14)
❄ What could happen to destroy even the best laid plans? (4:14)
❄ To what did James compare our lives? (4:14)
■ What is the best way to plan ahead? (4:15)
■ What should we say when we are making plans? (4:15)
❄ What outlook toward the future does God want us to change? (4:16)
❄ What sinful attitudes often accompany the act of making plans? (4:16)
❄ How did James define sin? (4:17)
❄ How do we sin? (4:17)

GET IT
❄ What's wrong with planning out our lives?
■ What responsibility does God want us to take in planning our lives?
❄ What is the best use we can make of our lives?
■ How can we make plans for business or living which are pleasing to God?
❄ Given how long you think you could live, how can you plan for the future with humility and faith?
❄ What would you like to accomplish before you die?
❄ What accomplishment from your life do you want to present to God?
❄ How can you determine in your daily life what is sinful and what is pleasing to God?

APPLY IT
❄ What aspects of your life plans do you need to present to God in prayer this week?
■ What can you do this week to place your plans for the future in God's hands?
❄ In what part of your job or occupation do you need to do the good you know you ought to do this week?

James 5:1-6
Warning to Rich Oppressors

TOPICS
Compassion, Greed, Injustice, Judgment, Justice, Materialism, Money, Oppressed, Wealth

OPEN IT
■ How does it take to be considered rich in your community?
❄ If you won $1 million, what would you do with it?
❄ How does money change people?

EXPLORE IT
❄ Whom did James address in this passage? Why? (5:1)
❄ What warning did James give to rich people? (5:1-3)
❄ What misfortune lies ahead for the wealthy? (5:1-3)
■ Who should "weep and wail"? Why? (5:1-6)
❄ What will happen to all the possessions of the wealthy? (5:2-3)
❄ What attitude does God have toward hoarding wealth? (5:3)
❄ For what reasons will the rich be punished? (5:4-6)
❄ Who have been the victims of rich people? (5:4-6)
■ How have rich people hurt others? (5:4-6)
■ What do luxury and self-indulgence have to do with the trouble that lies ahead for rich people? (5:5)

GET IT
❄ How do money and riches affect our relationship with God?
❄ What does God think about people who are rich?
❄ What problems are solved by being rich?
❄ What problems are not solved by being rich?
❄ How does God want us to handle money?
■ What does it mean to live in "luxury and indulgence"?
❄ What common business and financial practices are different from God's standards?
❄ How should a Christian business owner or employer be different from others who do not follow Christ?
❄ How does a person's use of money reflect what is important to him or her?
■ How can we use money to reflect what is important to God?
❄ What material possessions would you find it difficult to give up to help someone else?
❄ What do you possess that money cannot buy?

APPLY IT
❄ What can you do with your money this week to demonstrate your love for God?
■ What changes can you make in your habitual use of money to please God?
❄ What plans for the future can you make to reflect God's concern for the poor?

James 5:7-12
Patience in Suffering

TOPICS
Attitude, Complaining, Discouragement, Endurance, Giving Up, Judgment, Patience, Perseverance, Suffering, Swearing

OPEN IT
■ What kinds of experiences try your patience?
❄ What good things in life are worth waiting for?
❄ How can you tell if a person is telling the truth or making a promise that he she will keep?

EXPLORE IT
❄ What do we need to do as we wait for the Lord's return to earth? (5:7)
❄ What illustration did James use to describe the kind of patience we need? (5:7)
❄ When will the Lord's coming occur? (5:8)
❄ Why should we be patient about Christ's return? (5:8)
■ Why should we avoid judging others or grumbling against them? (5:9)
■ What will happen to Christians who grumble against their fellow believers? (5:9)
■ What people serve as good examples to us? How? (5:10-11)
❄ In what ways does God help us when we must endure suffering? (5:11)

❈ What warning did James give concerning swearing? (5:12)
❈ What is the alternative to swearing? (5:12)

GET IT
■ How does God use others to build patience in our lives?
❈ What makes it hard to wait on God's timing?
❈ What kind of changes does God want to make in us over an extended period of time?
❈ How have you suffered as a Christian?
❈ What blessing or reward came to you for suffering as a Christian?
❈ How will God reward us if we are patient?
❈ What does it mean to stand firm as a Christian?
❈ What lessons from Job's experience can we apply to our lives?
■ For what kinds of reasons do Christians judge each other?
❈ What causes us to grumble against each other?
❈ What does God think about Christians fighting among themselves?
❈ What can a Christian do to be trusted with his word and promises?

APPLY IT
❈ With what situation or problem can you ask God for help and patience this week?
■ What steps will you take this week to avoid judging others in your home? workplace? church?
❈ What promise do you need to keep? How?

James 5:13-20
The Prayer of Faith

TOPICS
Answers, Backslide, Confession, Correction, Faith, Healing, Instructions, Perseverance, Prayer, Sickness

OPEN IT
❈ What are some of the most memorable moments of your life?
■ What are some situations in life when most people pray?

EXPLORE IT
❈ What should a person do when he or she is in trouble? Why? (5:13, 15)
❈ What should a person do when he or she is happy? Why? (5:13, 15)
❈ What should a person do when he or she is sick? Why? (5:14-15)
■ Why is prayer important? (5:15)
❈ What are the elders of the church to do for someone who is sick? Why? (5:14-15)
❈ How can prayer affect a person's health? (5:15)
❈ How can a person have his or her sins forgiven? (5:15)
❈ Why should we confess our sins to one another? (5:16)
■ What is the effect of a righteous person's prayers? (5:16)
■ Who is a good example of how God answers prayer? How? (5:17-18)
❈ What is a Christian's responsibility toward a fellow believer who has wandered away from the truth? (5:19)
❈ What is the benefit of helping a person get back into following the truth? (5:20)

GET IT
❈ How can we use prayer to help someone who is sick?
❈ When have you had the opportunity to pray specifically for someone or for a special need?
❈ How have you seen prayer bring changes in people or circumstances?
■ What hinders Christians from praying with confidence?
❈ What hinders Christians from confessing sins and praying for each other?
❈ If we confess our sins to God, why should anyone else have to know about it?
■ What circumstances beyond our control can we affect through prayer?
❈ What causes Christians to stumble and fall away from their faith?
❈ How could you help someone who has drifted away from his or her relationship with Christ?
❈ How have others helped you when you were drifting in your relationship with Christ?

APPLY IT
■ What situation or person will you pray for in faith this week?
❈ What personal needs can you ask others to pray for through the coming week? Whom will you ask?
❈ Who do you know who has been drifting away from the Lord and who needs an encouraging word from you this week?

1 Peter 1:1-12
Praise to God for a Living Hope

TOPICS
Assurance, Believe, Character, Circumstances, Doctrine, Endurance, Faith, God, God's Will, Holy Spirit, Hope, Interpretation, Jesus Christ, Joy, Knowledge, Last Days, Obedience, Power, Prophecy, Resurrection, Salvation, Sovereignty, Spiritual Growth, Suffering

OPEN IT
❉ What is something you once searched for very hard?
❉ Complete this sentence any way you'd like: I hope that. . . .
■ To what do people often turn in times of sorrow or suffering?

EXPLORE IT
❉ To whom did Peter address his letter? (1:1)
❉ How had Peter's readers been chosen? (1:2)
❉ For what had Peter's readers been chosen? (1:2)
❉ What had God given Peter and his readers? (1:3)
❉ Into what kind of an inheritance did Peter say his readers had been born? (1:4)
❉ By what are believers shielded? For how long? (1:5)
■ What did Peter tell his readers they may have to suffer? (1:6)
■ Why had trials come to Peter's audience? (1:7)
■ What benefit is there in suffering? (1:7)
❉ What had Peter's readers done even though they had not seen Jesus? (1:8)
❉ What did Peter say was the goal of their faith? (1:9)
❉ About what did the prophets speak and for what did they search? (1:10)
❉ What did the Spirit of Christ predict? (1:11)
❉ Whom did Peter say these prophets were serving? (1:12)
❉ What did the angels long to do? (1:12)

GET IT
❉ When do you feel as if you're a stranger in the world?
❉ When did God give you new birth?
■ What trials are you or have you suffered recently?
■ How have the trials you've been through strengthened and refined your faith?
❉ How have your trials prepared you for Christ's coming?
❉ What fills you with joy in life?
❉ What is the goal of your faith?
❉ When and for what have you searched for something intently?
❉ In what way have the prophets who wrote about Christ served us?
❉ When was the last time God used you to serve someone else?
❉ How could God use you to serve others in the near future?
❉ How do you need to adjust your attitude about the trials in your life?

APPLY IT
■ What can you do this week to welcome the present trials in your life?
❉ How will you rejoice in your salvation today?

1 Peter 1:13–2:3
Be Holy

TOPICS
Atonement, Basics of the Faith, Believe, Believers, Bible, Desires, Discipline, Evil, Faith, God, Growth, Holiness, Jesus Christ, Judgment, Life-style, Love, Obedience, Priorities, Sacrifice, Salvation, Sin, Truth, Words

OPEN IT
■ What standards or examples do many people use to determine how they should live?
❉ When was the last time you felt like a stranger?

EXPLORE IT
■ What bold challenge did Peter give his readers? (1:13)
■ What pressure must we resist conforming to? (1:14)
■ What does God challenge us to be? Why? (1:15-16)
❉ Why did Peter tell this believers to live as strangers "in reverent fear"? (1:17)
❉ With what are believers redeemed from their sins? (1:18-19)
❉ When was Christ chosen and revealed? Why? (1:20)
❉ What did these readers believe? (1:21)
❉ How had these Christians purified themselves? (1:22)
❉ What did Peter urge his readers to do? (1:22)
❉ How had these believers been born again? (1:23)
❉ What lasts forever? (1:25)
❉ Of what did Peter urge us to rid ourselves? (2:1)
❉ What should we crave? Why? (2:2)
❉ What have believers tasted? (2:3)

GET IT
❉ When are we tempted by evil desires? Why?
■ In practical terms, what does it mean to be holy?
■ Why is being holy difficult?
❉ In what situations do you tend to feel like a stranger?
❉ What does it mean to live like a stranger in this world?
❉ How can you love other believers?
❉ What truth should we obey in order to purify ourselves?
❉ How can our priorities reflect the fact that our lives are temporary while God's Word is eternal?
❉ What things in life do you crave?
❉ How do we satisfy our spiritual longings?

APPLY IT
❉ What sins (such as malice, deceit, hypocrisy, envy, slander, etc.) do you need to rid yourself of, starting today?
❉ How will you tangibly show love for another Christian this week?
■ What step can you take right away in order to live a more holy life?

1 Peter 2:4-12
The Living Stone and a Chosen People

TOPICS
Believers, Bible, Call, Church, Citizenship, Darkness, Desires, Glory, God, Heritage, Jesus Christ, Life-style, Light, Mercy, Obedience, People, Rejection, Sacrifice, Sin, Unbelievers

OPEN IT
❄ What is something that is very precious to you?
❄ When have you felt rejected?
■ What is your ethnic heritage and how has it influenced you?

EXPLORE IT
❄ How did God and people treat the living Stone (Christ) differently? (2:4)
■ In what way are we like living stones? (2:5)
❄ What will happen to those who trust in the "Cornerstone"? (2:6)
❄ How was Christ treated differently by believers and unbelievers? (2:7)
❄ In what way did the "Stone" (Christ) cause some people to stumble? (2:8)
■ What status did Peter ascribe to believers in Christ? (2:9)
■ How does our past compare with our present condition? (2:10)
❄ From what did Peter urge his readers to abstain? Why? (2:11)
❄ Why is it important for believers to live good lives? (2:12)

GET IT
❄ How is Christ still being rejected by people today? Why?
❄ How is Christ precious to you? Why?
❄ How could being disobedient to God cause someone else to stumble?
■ How does being chosen by God for a special task make you feel?
❄ What are the implications of believers being a chosen people, a royal priesthood, and a holy nation?
❄ In what way were you in darkness before you became a believer?
❄ When have you felt that you were at war with sinful desires?
❄ Why is it so hard to abstain from sinful desires?
❄ Why do we need encouragement to live good lives among nonChristians?
❄ What good deeds in your life do nonChristians see?
❄ How can we do good deeds so they are both a witness and a discrete act of service (that is, not merely for show)?
❄ What does it mean to live a good life?
■ To what people can your good deeds be a witness?

APPLY IT
❄ From what specific sinful desires will you ask God to help you abstain this week?
❄ What good deeds can you use as a witness to your neighbors?
■ How do you need to change your plans for the near future so that you will be an example to the unbelievers with whom you have regular contact?

1 Peter 2:13-25
Submission to Rulers and Masters

TOPICS
Atonement, Authority, Citizenship, Endurance, Enemies, Example, Fear, Freedom, God, God's Will, Government, Jesus Christ, Leadership, Life-style, Persecution, Righteousness, Sin, Suffering, Unfairness

OPEN IT
❄ Who are some people (famous or ordinary) who have suffered for something in which they believed?
❄ How do people in different countries view and treat their leaders differently?
■ What is your general attitude toward people in authority over you (bosses, parents, police, etc.)?

EXPLORE IT
❄ To whom did Peter urge his readers to submit themselves? Why? (2:13-14)
■ Why does God allow government? (2:14)
■ What effect does obedience to government have on many people? (2:15)
❄ What did Peter tell his readers not to do with their freedom? (2:16)
■ What role does respect play in our interactions with authority? (2:17)
❄ To whom did Peter encourage his readers to submit? Why? (2:18-19)
❄ What commendable act is unique among Christians? (2:19)
❄ How did Peter contrast just with unjust suffering? (2:20)
❄ To what were the readers of this letter called? (2:21)
❄ What did Christ leave us? Why? (2:21)
❄ What does Isaiah 53:9 say about Christ? (2:22)
❄ How did Christ deal with His suffering? (2:22-23)
❄ Why did Christ bear our sins? (2:24)
❄ What animal are we like? How? (2:25)

GET IT
■ To what authorities or masters should we submit ourselves today?
❄ Why is it so difficult to submit to people who have authority over us?
❄ How would you paraphrase God's will as Peter described it?
❄ When have you suffered under someone's harsh authority?
❄ When have you suffered unjustly for Christ's sake?
❄ What does it mean to fear God?
❄ How might we use our freedom to cover up evil?
❄ What example has Christ left for us to follow?
❄ What challenges does Christ's example give us?
❄ Why is it so hard to suffer in silence without retaliating?
❄ In what way are we like sheep?
❄ What does it mean to live for righteousness?
❄ Of what wounds has Christ healed us?
❄ What specific changes do you need to make in your lifestyle in order to live for righteousness?
■ How can you exercise your freedom in a way that honors God?

APPLY IT

■ To what authority (person or institution) will you ask God to help you submit today?
❇ In what situation can you follow Christ's example of suffering without retaliating?

1 Peter 3:1-7
Wives and Husbands

TOPICS

Appearance, Attitude, Beauty, Believe, Doctrine, God, Husbands, Marriage, Obedience, Partnerships, Purity, Self-esteem, Submission, Unbelievers, Wives

OPEN IT

■ What examples would you point to in our society to illustrate our obsession with outward appearance?
❇ How have the roles of a husband and wife changed in the last 20 years?
❇ What do you think is good and bad about the changes in male and female roles over the last 20 years?
❇ What do you remember most vividly about your parents' relationship?

EXPLORE IT

❇ What is the challenge of being a wife? (3:1)
❇ Why did Peter encourage wives to submit to their husbands? (3:1-2)
❇ What qualities can a believing wife use to witness to an unbelieving husband? (3:1-2)
■ What kinds of beauty can a woman have? (3:3-4)
■ What is the disadvantage of a woman's outward beauty? (3:3-6)
■ What is the advantage of inward a woman's inward beauty? (3:4-6)
❇ How can a godly woman make herself beautiful? (3:5)
❇ What example did Peter set forth for wives to follow? (3:6)
❇ What is the challenge of being a husband? (3:7)
❇ Why should husbands treat their wives with respect? (3:7)

GET IT

❇ How would you reply to the challenge that Peter's instructions are outdated and don't apply in today's world?
❇ How are the responsibilities of wives and husbands different?
■ Why is it easier to be beautiful on the outside rather than on the inside?
■ How can someone develop inner beauty as Peter described?
❇ What does it mean to be submissive to another person? What does it not mean?
❇ How are we heirs to the gracious gift of life?
❇ How might the way a man treats his wife hinder his prayers?
❇ Why is the husband-wife relationship so important?
❇ How do you need to change the way you treat your spouse?
❇ What are some steps every spouse can take to honor his or her partner?

APPLY IT

■ What specific steps will you take this week to develop your inner character?
❇ What can you do today to become a better spouse?

1 Peter 3:8-22
Suffering for Doing Good

TOPICS

Answers, Atonement, Beliefs, Believers, Caring, Compassion, Conscience, Doctrine, Evil, Faith, God, God's Will, Heaven, Holy Spirit, Hope, Humility, Jesus Christ, Resurrection, Righteousness, Sacrifice, Salvation, Sin, Suffering, Unbelievers, Words

OPEN IT

■ What childhood fight do you remember most vividly?
❇ On a scale of 1 to 10 (10 being nerves of steel), how good would you say you are at controlling your temper?

EXPLORE IT

■ What incredible challenge did Peter give his readers? (3:8-9)
■ Why did Peter instruct his readers to live at peace with everyone? (3:9)
■ What must a person do who wants to love life? (3:10-11)
❇ Who does God listen to? (3:12)
❇ How did Peter use a rhetorical question to explain his point? (3:13)
❇ What did Peter write about suffering for what is right? (3:14)
❇ What did Peter instruct his readers to be prepared for? (3:15)
❇ How were these readers to give the reason for their hope in Christ? (3:15)
❇ Why are believers to keep a clear conscience? (3:16)
❇ When is it all right to suffer, and when is it a waste? (3:17)
❇ What did Peter say about Christ's death? (3:18)
❇ Through whom and to whom did Christ preach? (3:19-20)
❇ What do the flood waters from which Noah and his family were saved say to us? (3:21)
❇ How are we saved? (3:21)
❇ Where did Christ go after His resurrection? (3:22)

GET IT

❇ When is it hard for Christians to live in harmony with each other? Why?
■ When are you tempted to return evil with evil and insult with insult? Why?
❇ Why do our words get us into so much trouble?
■ What concrete actions can we use to promote harmony?
❇ How could suffering for doing right be a blessing?
❇ How should we set Christ apart as Lord in our hearts?
❇ How prepared are you to explain your hope in Christ?
❇ What can you do to be better prepared for discussions about Christ with nonChristian friends?
❇ Why is it better to suffer for doing good rather than evil?

❊ How has Christ's death and resurrection changed your life?
❊ How does Christ's place of authority at God's right hand make you feel about your relationship with Him?

APPLY IT
❊ What can you do over the next few days to promote harmony between you and the believers you know?
■ What response could you use when you are mistreated or insulted?
❊ What step can you take this week to become more prepared to answer questions about your hope and faith in Christ?

1 Peter 4:1-11
Living for God

TOPICS
Attitude, Believers, Caring, Desires, Drinking, Faith, Gifts, God, Gospel, Hospitality, Jesus Christ, Judgment, Life-style, Love, Lust, Ministry, Serving, Sex, Sin, Suffering, Unbelievers

OPEN IT
■ In your opinion, what best distinguishes Christians from nonChristians?
❊ Imagine that the world is going to end in twenty-four hours and you have been granted one wish for anything you want. What would you wish for? Why?

EXPLORE IT
❊ What did Peter say about the person who has suffered? (4:1-2)
❊ What benefit can there be in suffering? (4:2)
❊ What did Peter's readers do in the past? (4:3)
■ What did the pagans think was strange? (4:4)
❊ To whom did Peter say the pagans would have to give account? (4:5)
❊ For what reason was the gospel preached? (4:6)
❊ What did Peter say was near? (4:7)
■ What did Peter instruct his readers to do since the end of all things was near? (4:7)
❊ What did Peter encourage his readers to do above all? (4:8)
❊ How did Peter encourage his audience to love each other? (4:8-9)
❊ How were Peter's readers to use their gifts? (4:10)
❊ How were these believers to speak and serve? (4:11)
■ What goal did Peter want his audience to reach with all they did? (4:11)

GET IT
■ What does it mean to be done with sin?
❊ With what human desires do we continue to struggle?
■ What about your lifestyle do unbelievers find strange?
❊ In what way is the end of all things near?
❊ How would knowing that the world was going to end this year change the way you think or act?
❊ How does love cover a multitude of sins?
❊ Why is it sometimes difficult to love other believers?
❊ To whom do you find it difficult to offer hospitality? Why?
❊ In what ways can you offer hospitality?
❊ What gift has God given you that you could use to serve others?

APPLY IT
❊ What human desires with which you continue to struggle will you ask God to help you overcome?
■ In what simple way this week can you let unbelievers see that you live by a unique set of priorities?
❊ To whom will you offer hospitality sometime this week?

1 Peter 4:12-19
Suffering for Being a Christian

TOPICS
Believers, Glory, God, Gospel, Insults, Jesus Christ, Joy, Judgment, Name, Persecution, Second Coming, Shame, Suffering, Unbelievers

OPEN IT
■ What is something for which you were wrongly punished when you were growing up?
❊ When was the last time you were greatly surprised by something that happened to you?

EXPLORE IT
❊ By what were Peter's readers not to be surprised? (4:12)
■ In what did Peter tell his readers to rejoice? (4:13)
❊ What would participating in Christ's suffering prepare these believers for? (4:13)
❊ Under what circumstance did Peter tell these believers they would be blessed? (4:14)
❊ How did Peter say these believers shouldn't suffer? (4:15)
■ What did Peter urge his readers to do if they suffered as Christians? (4:16)
❊ For what did Peter say it was time? (4:17)
❊ What question did Peter ask his readers? (4:17)
❊ What does the verse Peter quoted say about the righteous and the ungodly? (4:18)
■ What should those who suffer according to God's will do? (4:19)

GET IT
❊ What painful trials have you gone though as a believer?
■ How can participating in Christ's suffering prepare us for His second coming?
❊ When have you been insulted because of the name of Christ?
❊ How is suffering as a wrongdoer (such as a murder) significantly different from suffering as a Christian?
❊ When have you ever been ashamed of being a Christian? Why?
■ Why might it be God's will for someone to suffer?
❊ What sort of judgment do members of God's family face?

APPLY IT
■ In what difficult circumstance do you need to praise God this week?
❊ What steps do you need to take so that your suffering is not the result of your own wrongdoing?

1 Peter 5:1-14

To Elders and Young Men

TOPICS

Believers, Caring, Church, Example, Fellowship, Glory, God, Greed, Humility, Jesus Christ, Leadership, Money, Pride, Rewards, Satan, Serving, Submission, Suffering, Worry

OPEN IT

❋ What does the average person believe about the devil?
■ What people might consider you a leader or example?
❋ What motivates people to be leaders in the church?

EXPLORE IT

❋ To whom did Peter appeal? (5:1)
■ What did Peter instruct elders to do? (5:2)
❋ What instructions did Peter give concerning greed? (5:2)
■ How did Peter tell elders not to lead? (5:3)
■ How did Peter tell elders to lead? (5:3)
❋ What reward were elders going to receive when the Chief Shepherd appeared? (5:4)
❋ What were the young men encouraged to do? (5:5)
❋ Why were all the readers encouraged to clothe themselves with humility? (5:5)
❋ Why were these believers encouraged to humble themselves? (5:6)
❋ What did Peter tell his readers to do with their anxieties? (5:7)
❋ What did Peter say the devil was doing? (5:8)
❋ How were these believers instructed to respond the devil? (5:9)
❋ To what did Peter say these believers had been called? (5:10)
❋ What did Peter assure his readers God would do after they had suffered a little while? (5:10)
❋ What did Silas help Peter do? (5:12)
❋ Who sent greetings along with Peter? (5:13)
❋ How did Peter tell these believers to greet one another? (5:14)

GET IT

❋ What leadership style do the pastors and elders in your church have?
❋ What attitude do the young people in your church have toward the leaders of the church?
❋ What leadership positions have you held?
■ How can you be an example to the people in your family?
■ What changes do you need to make in the way you lead?
❋ How do you need to change your attitude toward those who are in positions of authority over you?
❋ Why do we sometimes find it difficult to be submissive to those in authority over us?
❋ Why might we be tempted to "lord it over" the people we are leading?
❋ Why is being humble so difficult?
❋ What worries tend to plague you?
❋ What does it mean to cast your anxieties on the Lord?
❋ How can we cast our anxieties on the Lord?
❋ What means does the devil use to "devour" people in our society?
❋ How should we resist the devil?
❋ When have you suffered as a believer?

APPLY IT

■ In what concrete way this week can you be a better example to the people who look to you for leadership?
❋ What worries will you cast upon God today?
❋ In what area will you ask God to help you to be more humble this week?

2 Peter 1:1-11

Making One's Calling and Election Sure

TOPICS

Assurance, Call, Character, Desires, Discipline, Eternal Life, Evil, Faith, God, Goodness, Heaven, Jesus Christ, Kindness, Knowledge, Love, Perseverance, Quality, Rewards, Sin, Sovereignty, Spiritual Growth, World

OPEN IT

■ What character qualities do you find most attractive in other people?
❋ What do people often do to "grow" intellectually, culturally, or in some similar way?
❋ If you could be better at one thing, what would you want to improve?

EXPLORE IT

❋ Who wrote 2 Peter? (1:1)
❋ To whom was 2 Peter written? (1:1)
❋ What did Peter say had been given to his audience? (1:3)
❋ How do God's people benefit from the promises God has given them? (1:4)
■ What did Peter urge his readers to add to their faith? (1:5-7)
❋ How did Peter encourage his audience? (1:5-7)
❋ What would be the result of possessing godly character in increasing measure? (1:8)
❋ What happens to the person who does not possess godly qualities? (1:9)
■ What did Peter want his audience to be eager to do? Why? (1:10-11)
■ What happens when we pursue the qualities Peter described? (1:11)

GET IT

❋ How equipped do you feel for life and godliness?
❋ What is the relationship between knowledge of God and Christ and spiritual growth?
❋ Which of the character qualities that Peter listed do you find the most difficult to practice?
■ Which of the qualities listed by Peter do you consider to be the most important to add to your faith? Why?
❋ What does it mean to be ineffective and unproductive?
■ How can the qualities Peter mentioned keep us from being ineffective and unproductive?
❋ Why is it easy to forget what God has done for us?
❋ How can someone make his or her calling and election sure?
❋ Which of the qualities listed do you want most to add to your faith?

APPLY IT

■ How will you add a godly quality to your faith today?
❋ What steps will you take in order to make your calling and election sure?
❋ What steps will you take this week to make your faith more effective and productive?

2 Peter 1:12-21

Prophecy of Scripture

TOPICS

Basics of the Faith, Bible, Death, Doctrine, Glory, God, Honor, Inspiration, Interpretation, Jesus Christ, Prophecy, Remembering, Truth

OPEN IT

■ If you knew you were about to die and had time to make only one phone call or write one letter, whom would you contact? Why?
❋ To what interesting event have you been an eyewitness?

EXPLORE IT

❋ In what did Peter say his readers were established? (1:12)
❋ What did Peter think it was right for him to do? (1:13)
❋ What did Peter know that he would soon do? (1:14)
❋ What did Peter want his audience to be able to do after he had died? (1:15)
❋ What did Peter say he and others had not followed? (1:16)
■ What gave Peter credibility? (1:16)
❋ What did God say about Jesus? (1:17)
❋ Who heard the voice of God? Where? (1:18)
■ What did Peter tell his readers that they should do? (1:19)
❋ What did Peter want his readers to understand? (1:20)
■ What makes prophecy special? (1:21)

GET IT

❋ About what do you need to be constantly reminded?
■ Why do we need to have our memory refreshed about biblical truths?
❋ Why is it easy for us to forget truths that are important to us?
❋ In what way are our bodies like tents?
❋ How important to your faith is it that Peter (and other New Testament writers) were eyewitnesses of the life of Christ?
❋ Why is it important to know that our faith is grounded in history?
■ How do you need to change your Bible study habits in light of Scripture's importance?
❋ How do you think the Bible was written?
❋ How should Peter's statements about the origin of Scripture impact our faith as well as our study of the Bible?
❋ Why is it important to know about the origin of the Bible?
❋ What is unique about Scripture?
❋ How can we be confident that the Bible is the Word of God?

APPLY IT

■ What portion of Scripture that you have neglected lately will you take the time to study this week?
❋ How can you read the Bible differently this week in light of its importance?

2 Peter 2:1-22
False Teachers and Their Destruction

TOPICS
Abandon, Angels, Backslide, Blasphemy, Choices, Complacency, Desires, Enemies, Faithfulness, Forsake, Freedom, God, Hardheartedness, Hell, Heresy, Jesus Christ, Judgment, Law, Lust, Morality, Punishment, Rebellion, Rejection, Repentance, Righteousness, Sin, Slavery, World

OPEN IT
❊ What is your favorite proverb or wise saying (for example, "Haste makes waste")?
■ What activities or pursuits are popular today?
❊ In what ways do people today abuse their freedom?

EXPLORE IT
❊ What did Peter warn his readers that false prophets would attempt to do? (2:1)
❊ What did Peter say would happen when people followed false prophets? (2:2)
❊ What did God do to the angels who had sinned? (2:4)
❊ Whom did Peter say God protected? (2:5)
❊ What did God use as an example of what will happen to the ungodly? (2:6)
■ What affect did living among immoral people have upon Lot? (2:7-8)
❊ How did Peter say the Lord would deal with the godly and the unrighteous? (2:9)
❊ What kind of people are unafraid to slander celestial beings? (2:10-15)
❊ How did God rebuke Balaam? (2:16)
❊ What did Peter say was reserved for people who rebel against God? (2:17)
■ How did the evil people of whom Peter wrote affect others? (2:18)
❊ What did such sinful men promise? (2:19)
❊ To what were sinful people slaves? (2:19)
■ How did Peter say a person could escape the corruption of the world? (2:20)
❊ In what way would it have been better for ungodly people to have never heard of God? Why? (2:21)
❊ What proverbs did Peter apply to the blatantly ungodly? (2:22)

GET IT
■ What affect does living and working among sinful people have upon you?
■ How do you deal with the influence of immoral or rebellious people around you?
❊ What false prophets attempt to influence the church today?
❊ Why is it important to know how God has dealt with unrighteous people in the past, including angels?
❊ When and why have you felt like Lot—distressed by the filthy lives of lawless people?
❊ Why and how could someone who has known Christ return to the unrighteousness from which he or she had been rescued?
❊ When are you tempted to return to some sinful activity or attitude? Why?
❊ What lustful desires entice people today?
❊ When and how does slavery sometimes appear to be a promise of freedom?
❊ To what sorts of desires can we become unknowingly enslaved?
❊ Why might it be important for us to know what Peter wrote about angels?
❊ What false teachings do you need to expose as untrue?

APPLY IT
❊ Beginning today, from what sinful desire will you ask God to help you escape?
❊ What steps will you take today to ensure that you don't allow your exercise of freedom to result in your enslavement to sin?
■ How will you deal with the effect of living in a sinful world today?

2 Peter 3:1-18
The Day of the Lord

TOPICS
Basics of the Faith, Bible, Creation, Doctrine, Earth, Encouragement, God, Growth, Heaven, Holiness, Hope, Inspiration, Jesus Christ, Judgment, Last Days, Lifestyle, Obedience, Patience, Promises, Repentance, Salvation, Spiritual Growth, Thinking, Unbelievers, World

OPEN IT
❊ When was the last time someone wrote you an encouraging letter?
■ With what sort of people do you find it hard to be patient?

EXPLORE IT
❊ Why did Peter write this letter as well as his first letter? (3:1)
❊ What did Peter want these believers (his audience) to recall? (3:2)
❊ What did Peter say would occur in the last days? (3:3)
❊ What will the "scoffers" say in the last days? (3:4)
❊ What will the "scoffers" deliberately forget? (3:5)
❊ How was the world once destroyed and how will it be destroyed in the future? (3:6-7)
■ What did Peter tell his readers not to forget? (3:8)
■ Why is the Lord patient? (3:9)
❊ How will the day of the Lord appear? (3:10)
❊ What reason did Peter give his readers for living holy and godly lives? (3:11-12)
❊ What will the day of God bring? (3:12)
❊ What reason did Peter give his readers to hope for the future? (3:13)
❊ What did Peter urge his readers to make every effort to do? Why? (3:14)
■ What does the Lord's patience mean? (3:15)
❊ What did Peter say about the apostle Paul's writings? (3:16)
❊ Why did Peter instruct his readers to be on their guard? (3:17)
❊ What final instruction did Peter leave with his readers? (3:18)

GET IT

❊ What stimulates you to wholesome thinking?
❊ What discourages you from engaging in wholesome thinking?
❊ About what biblical truths have you heard people scoff, and why were they scoffing?
❊ How does the fact that the earth will one day be destroyed affect your daily life?
❊ How should the reality that the earth will one day be destroyed affect the way we live our lives from day to day?
■ How have you personally benefited from God's patience?
❊ When have you thought that God was either not patient enough or too patient with you or someone else?
❊ Why is it easy to spend little time looking forward to the new heaven and new earth?
❊ How can we guard against falling into error in what we believe?
❊ How can we grow in the grace and knowledge of Christ?
■ How do you need to alter your lifestyle in light of the certain future destruction of the earth?

APPLY IT

❊ What specific step will you take this week to grow in Christ?
■ How can you change your routine to reflect your hope for Christ's return?
❊ What will you do this week to stimulate wholesome thinking?
❊ To whom can you write a letter of encouragement this week?

1 John 1:1-4
The Word of Life

TOPICS

Basics of the Faith, Doctrine, Eternal Life, Evidence, Faith, Fellowship, God, History, Jesus Christ, Joy, Life, Words

OPEN IT

■ What do you associate with the term "fellowship"?
❊ How do we know that the events we read about in history books really happened?

EXPLORE IT

❊ What was from the beginning? (1:1)
❊ What contact did the writer and this community of believers have with the Word of life? (1:1)
■ How did God reveal Himself to us? (1:2)
❊ What was being proclaimed by this community of believers? (1:2)
❊ Where had the eternal life been, and to whom had it appeared? (1:2)
❊ Why was the author and his fellow believers telling others about Christ? (1:3)
■ With whom did this community of believers have fellowship? (1:3)
■ Why was this letter written? (1:4)

GET IT

❊ Why do you think John stressed his and this community of believers' personal, physical, historical encounter with Jesus?
❊ How important are firsthand eyewitness testimonies, such as this writer's, to your belief in Jesus?
❊ What fellowship do you have with the Father and His Son Jesus Christ?
❊ What fellowship do you have with other believers?
❊ How is our fellowship with God related to our fellowship with other believers?
■ What blocks our fellowship with God and others?
■ In what ways can we enhance our fellowship?
❊ In what way is your joy complete?

APPLY IT

❊ What can you do to gain a better appreciation of the historical foundation of your faith in Christ?
■ What specific steps will you take this week in order to deepen your fellowship with other believers?

1 John 1:5-2:14
Walking in the Light

TOPICS

Atonement, Children, Confession, Darkness, Denial, Disobedience, Doctrine, Evil, Fellowship, Forgiveness, God, Guilt, Habits, Jesus Christ, Life, Light, Lying, Obedience, Pride, Reconciliation, Sacrifice, Satan, Sin, Truth

OPEN IT

■ Why might it be hard for someone to admit that he or she was wrong about something?

❄ About what do we tend to deceive ourselves?
❄ When and why might someone need an attorney?

EXPLORE IT
❄ What message did the writer hear and declare? (1:5)
■ What inconsistency did John address? (1:6)
❄ What result from "walking in the light"? (1:7)
■ How were some believers apparently deceiving themselves? (1:8)
❄ What is the result of confessing one's sins? (1:9)
❄ In what way can a person make God out to be a liar? (1:10)
■ Why did John write this letter? (2:1)
❄ For whom is Jesus an atoning sacrifice? (2:2)
❄ What test did John describe for knowing whether or not a person truly knows God? (2:3-6)
❄ What did John say he was giving to his readers? (2:7-8)
❄ How are claiming to be a Christian and loving one's fellow Christians related? (2:9-11)
❄ Why did John write to "the dear children"? (2:12-13)
❄ Why did John write to "the fathers"? (2:13-14)
❄ Why did John write to "the young men"? (2:13-14)

GET IT
❄ What do you think the terms "light" and "darkness" represent?
❄ In what way is God similar to light?
■ In what way do we "walk in darkness"?
■ How can we "walk in the light"?
❄ How does the promise of being purified from all sin make you feel?
❄ Why would someone claim that he or she was without sin?
❄ What role does the confession of sins play in your daily life?
❄ How important is fellowship with other believers to you?
❄ In what way is Jesus like our attorney?
❄ How can we get to know God better?
❄ What does the way in which we treat other believers reveal about us?
❄ What confidence does Jesus' atoning death give to us?
❄ What confidence should our relationship with the Father give us?
❄ What area of your life do you need to examine in order to see your sins more clearly?
❄ How do you need to change the way you relate to fellow believers in order to develop a deeper relationship with God?

APPLY IT
■ What steps will you take this week to walk in the light?
❄ What will you do to incorporate the confession of sins into your daily routine?

1 John 2:15-17
Do Not Love the World

TOPICS
Affections, Culture, Desires, Ego, Eternal Life, God, God's Will, Happiness, Joy, Life-style, Love, Lust, Needs, Obedience, Peer Pressure, Pride, Relationships, Satisfaction, Self-esteem, Sin, World

OPEN IT
■ What makes TV commercials and advertisements so appealing?
❄ What sort of promises do TV commercials and advertisements make?
❄ Which of these three most clearly motivates the people you know and live near: (1) the drive to meet their physical needs, (2) the drive to get things, or (3) the drive to succeed?

EXPLORE IT
■ What restrictions should we place on our affections? (2:15)
❄ What should believers not love? Why? (2:15)
❄ What is the result of loving the world? (2:15)
❄ Why did John tell us not to love the world? (2:15-17)
❄ What are the things of the world? (2:16)
❄ How did John categorize the things in the world? (2:16)
❄ From where do the things in the world come? (2:16)
❄ From where do the things in the world not come? (2:16)
■ What passes away? (2:17)
■ Who lives forever? (2:17)

GET IT
■ How do we love the world and the things in it?
❄ What things in the world are you tempted to love?
❄ What would you categorize as "the cravings of sinful man"?
❄ What would you categorize as "the lust of the eyes"?
❄ What would you categorize as "the boasting of what he has or does"?
■ Why are the things and values of the world so enticing to us?
❄ What worldly things or values do we substitute for God?
❄ What does it mean to do the will of God?
❄ How can we guard against adopting the values of the world?
❄ From what worldly thing or value do you need to turn in order to pursue your relationship with God?

APPLY IT
■ What specific steps will you take in order to find satisfaction in your relationship with God rather than in the things of the world?
❄ How will you do the will of God today?

1 John 2:18-27
Warning Against Antichrists

TOPICS
Believers, Christianity, Church, Denial, Doctrine, Eternal Life, Fellowship, Forsake, God, Heresy, Holy Spirit, Jesus Christ, Knowledge, Last Days, Rejection, Teaching, Truth, Unbelievers

OPEN IT
❇ Who are the enemies of the Church today?
❇ What do you think is the best defense against cults and other false spiritual teaching?
■ What affect do you think warning labels on cigarettes and alcohol have?

EXPLORE IT
❇ What time did John say it is? (2:18)
■ Who was coming and who had come at the time John wrote this? (2:18)
❇ What did John say about those who had left? (2:19)
❇ What did the readers of 1 John have? (2:20)
❇ What did the readers of 1 John know? (2:21)
❇ How is the antichrist identified? (2:22)
■ In what way is denying (or acknowledging) the Son related to having the Father? (2:23)
■ What did John encourage his readers to do? (2:24)
❇ What did the Father promise? (2:25)
❇ Why did the author write these things? (2:26)
❇ What was the relationship between the anointing these believers received and their need to be taught? (2:27)

GET IT
❇ What makes you think that we are living in the last hour today?
❇ What antichrists are among us today?
❇ What truths do we know about Christ?
❇ What have we been taught by the anointing of the Holy Spirit?
❇ How can we remain in or have fellowship with Jesus Christ?
■ What groups of people are trying to lead believers astray today?
■ How can we protect ourselves against false teachers and antichrists?

APPLY IT
❇ What will you do this week to deepen your fellowship with Jesus Christ?
■ What steps do you need to take to better prepare yourself against antichrists and their false doctrines?
❇ Who is someone you can encourage in their relationship with Christ this week?

1 John 2:28–3:10
Children of God

TOPICS
Basics of the Faith, Believers, Children, Disobedience, Doctrine, Fellowship, God, Habits, Jesus Christ, Life-style, Obedience, Satan, Second Coming, Sin, Unbelievers, World

OPEN IT
■ In what way(s) are you like your mother or father?
❇ What was one of benefit of being the child of your parents as you were growing up?
❇ How would most people define the term "sin"?

EXPLORE IT
❇ Why did John encourage his readers to continue in Christ? (2:28)
■ What is true about everyone who does what is right? (2:29)
❇ How has the Father lavished love upon believers? (3:1)
❇ Why doesn't the world know Christians? (3:1)
❇ What will happen to the children of God when they see Christ? (3:2)
❇ What kind of person purifies himself or herself? (3:3)
❇ What is sin? (3:4)
❇ Why did Christ appear? (3:5)
■ How is a person who lives in Christ unusual? (3:6)
❇ What does it mean to do what is right? (3:7)
❇ What did John say about the person who does what is sinful? (3:8)
❇ Why did the Son of God appear? (3:8)
■ Why can't the person who is born of God continue to sin? (3:9)
❇ How are children of God and children of the devil identified? (3:10)

GET IT
❇ What does it mean to continue in Christ?
❇ How are you preparing yourself for Christ's return?
❇ What is so great about being a child of God?
■ When have you felt that your nonChristian friends did not really know or understand you?
■ How do you reconcile the fact that Christians do sin with the statements that they cannot sin or keep on sinning?
❇ How can we know that we are children of God?
❇ How do you need to change your daily routine so that you may be confident and unashamed before Christ at His second coming?

APPLY IT
❇ What step will you take today to purify yourself?
■ What area of weakness will you ask God to strengthen this week?

1 John 3:11-24
Love One Another

TOPICS
Basics of the Faith, Believers, Caring, Children, Compassion, Death, Disobedience, Eternal Life, Evil, God, Hardheartedness, Hatred, Heart, Holy Spirit, Hypocrisy, Jesus Christ, Life, Life-style, Love, Murder, Obedience, Poor, Prayer, Satan, World

OPEN IT
■ Who is someone (in history or alive today) whose life is an example of what it means to love?
❇ Who is someone (in history or alive today) whose life is an example of what it means to hate?

EXPLORE IT
❇ What message had the readers of 1 John heard from the beginning? (3:11)
❇ Why did Cain murder his brother? (3:12)
❇ About what should believers not be surprised? (3:13)
❇ How can a person know that he or she has passed from death to life? (3:14)
❇ What is the result of hating one's brother? (3:15)

■ How do we know what love is? (3:16)
❄ What question did the author ask his readers? (3:17)
■ How should Christians love? (3:18)
❄ What is God greater than? (3:20)
❄ What is the result of not being condemned by one's heart? (3:21-22)
❄ What is God's command? (3:23)
■ What is the result of obeying God's command? (3:24)
❄ How do believers know that God lives in them? (3:24)

GET IT
❄ How does the world hate believers today?
❄ When have you experienced the hatred of the world?
❄ What does it mean to love one's brother?
■ When do you struggle with loving other Christians?
■ How do you demonstrate your love for fellow believers?
❄ Why do we struggle with loving other Christians with our material possessions?
❄ Why is it easier to love with words rather than actions?
❄ In what way does love result in life, and hate result in death?

APPLY IT
■ For what fellow Christian whom you have difficulty loving will you do something kind this week?
❄ How can you use your material possessions to love another believer this week?
❄ What specific step will you take this week to put your love for another Christian into action?

1 John 4:1-6
Test the Spirits

TOPICS
Basics of the Faith, Believers, Christianity, Confession, Demons, Denial, Doctrine, God, Holy Spirit, Jesus Christ, Satan, Testing, Unbelievers, Victory, World

OPEN IT
■ What standard would you use for testing a person's credentials to do your job?
❄ What makes something either "worldly" or "Christian"?

EXPLORE IT
■ What did John instruct his readers to do? (4:1)
❄ Who did John say had gone into the world? (4:1)
❄ How is the Spirit of God recognized? (4:2)
■ How can we distinguish truth from error in spiritual matters? (4:2-3)
❄ What spirit does not acknowledge that Jesus is from God? (4:3)
❄ Why did the writer say that believers had overcome the spirit of the antichrist? (4:4)
❄ Where is the spirit of the antichrist from? (4:5)
❄ From what viewpoint does the spirit of the antichrist speak? (4:5)
■ Who does and does not listen to those who are from God? (4:6)
❄ How are the Spirit of truth and the spirit of falsehood recognized? (4:6)

GET IT
❄ What spirits should we be testing today?
❄ What false prophets are in the world today?
■ What segments of our society would you say are influenced or controlled by the spirit of the antichrist?
❄ What is the significance of acknowledging that Jesus Christ has come in the flesh?
❄ In what way have you overcome the world?
❄ How does the truth that Christ is greater than the devil make you feel?
■ How can we reflect our confidence in Christ's supremacy over the devil?
❄ How would you distinguish between seeing from the world's viewpoint and seeing from God's viewpoint?

APPLY IT
■ What influences in your life (for example, books, movies, music, ideas, etc.) will you "put to the test" this week to see whether they are from God?
❄ What false prophets do you need to guard yourself against this week?

1 John 4:7-21
God's Love and Ours

TOPICS
Atonement, Believers, Caring, Fear, Fellowship, Friendship, God, Hatred, Holy Spirit, Jesus Christ, Judgment, Love, Lying, Perfect, Sacrifice, Sin, World

OPEN IT
❄ Which do you think is a more powerful motivator—love, fear, or hate? Why?
❄ What popular figure alive today or from history used hate to motivate people?
❄ When have you been motivated by love?

EXPLORE IT
❄ What were the readers of 1 John encouraged to do? (4:7)
■ What is the relationship between loving and knowing God? (4:7-8)
❄ How did God show His love? (4:9)
❄ Why did God send His Son? (4:9)
❄ What is love? (4:10)
❄ Why should Christians love one another? (4:11)
❄ What is the result of loving one another? (4:12)
■ How can believers know that they live in God and God lives in them? (4:13)
❄ What did John testify concerning? (4:14)
❄ What happens when we acknowledge that Jesus is the Son of God? (4:15)
❄ Why is love important? (4:16-17)
❄ How is love made complete? (4:17)
❄ What does perfect love do? Why? (4:18)
■ Why should we love? (4:19)
❄ What is the relationship between loving God and loving one's brother? (4:20-21)

GET IT
■ How can we demonstrate our love for God?
❄ What example has Jesus set for us to follow?
❄ How should God's love motivate you to love others?

❇ How do you know that God lives in you?
❇ What does it mean to live in God?
❇ Why is it be easier to love God than other Christians?
■ When you have difficulty loving other believers, what is it that makes it difficult?
■ How can we demonstrate our love for others?
❇ What are you afraid of?
❇ How can we overcome our fears?
❇ How does love drive out fear?

APPLY IT
❇ Who is someone that you have a difficult time getting along with that you need to ask God to help you love this week?
❇ What fear will you ask God to help you overcome?
■ What specific steps will you take this week to demonstrate your love for another believer?

1 John 5:1-12
Faith in the Son of God

TOPICS
Basics of the Faith, Believe, Believers, Children, Eternal Life, Faith, Fellowship, God, Holy Spirit, Jesus Christ, Life, Love, Obedience, Truth, Victory, Witnessing, World

OPEN IT
❇ What makes a person's testimony seem credible or incredible?
❇ How do you demonstrate love for your parents?
■ What do you find burdensome or a drag to do?

EXPLORE IT
❇ Who is born of God? (5:1)
❇ What can be said about the person who loves the Father? (5:1)
❇ How can a person know if he or she loves God's people? (5:2)
❇ What is love for God? (5:2)
■ What unique quality do God's commands have? Why is this true? (5:3-4)
■ Who overcomes the world? (5:4-5)
■ How can we overcome the world? (5:4-5)
❇ How did Jesus Christ come? (5:6)
❇ Why does the Spirit testify? (5:6)
❇ What three things are in agreement? (5:7-8)
❇ Why is God's testimony greater than man's testimony? (5:9)
❇ Who has made God out to be a liar? (5:10)
❇ What testimony has God given concerning His Son? (5:10-11)
❇ What do we have if we have Christ in us? (5:12)

GET IT
❇ What does it mean to be born of God?
❇ How can we know that we are born of God?
❇ How do you know that you are a child of God?
❇ What are the commands of God with which you struggle with obeying?
❇ In what way should we love the children of God?
■ When have you thought that God's commands were burdensome?
■ What does it mean to overcome the world?
❇ How have you overcome the world?
❇ What is your relationship to the Son?
❇ How can a person receive eternal life?

APPLY IT
■ How will you demonstrate your love for the Father today?
❇ What steps do you need to take in order to be certain you are a child of God?
❇ What will you do to celebrate your life in the Son today?

1 John 5:13-21
Concluding Remarks

TOPICS
Believe, Believers, Children, Confidence, Death, Disobedience, Eternal Life, Evil, God, God's Will, Jesus Christ, Life, Obedience, Prayer, Satan, Sin, Understanding

OPEN IT
■ What might make someone afraid to ask another person for something?
❇ What sort of things do people today pin their hopes on?

EXPLORE IT
❇ Why did John write this letter? (5:13)
❇ What confidence can believers have? (5:14-15)
■ About what type of sin did John say his readers should pray? (5:16)
❇ What is sin? (5:17)
❇ What does the person born of God stop doing? (5:18)
❇ What sort of protection do Christians enjoy? (5:18)
■ Under whose control is the whole world? (5:19)
■ What has the Son of God done, and what has He given? (5:20)
❇ Who is Jesus Christ? (5:20)
❇ What was the last instruction John left with his readers? (5:21)

GET IT
❇ How can we be confident that we have eternal life?
■ When is it hard for you to approach God with confidence?
❇ How can we know whether something is according to God's will?
❇ In what way can sin lead to death?
❇ To what sort of death might sin lead?
❇ In what way has sin led to death in your life?
❇ What type of sin does not lead to death?
❇ By what modern "idols" are you tempted?
■ About what issue do you need to approach God more confidently?

APPLY IT
❇ What specific step can you take this week to place more confidence in God and less in the idols of this world?
❇ For what fellow believer who has sinned will you pray today?
■ What matter will you bring before God this week?

2 John 1-13
From the Elder

TOPICS
Believers, Caring, Children, Deceit, Family, Fellowship, God, Jesus Christ, Love, Obedience, Peace, Rewards, Teaching, Truth, Work

OPEN IT
■ Who is someone to whom you have written recently?
❇ Why is starting something (an exercise program, for example) relatively easy, while continuing it is usually more difficult?

EXPLORE IT
❇ To whom was this letter addressed? (v. 1)
■ Who wrote this letter? Why? (vv. 1-2)
❇ What unique characteristic do Christians have? (v. 2)
❇ What did the elder say would be with him in truth and love? (v. 3)
■ What gave the elder great joy? (v. 4)
■ What command did the writer give to his readers? (v. 5)
❇ What is love? (v. 6)
❇ What did many false teachers of John's day deny? (v. 7)
❇ What did the elder encourage his readers to do? (v. 8)
❇ What is true about someone who does or does not continue in the teaching of Christ? (v. 9)
❇ Who was the reader of this letter not to welcome into his or her house? Why? (vv. 10-11)
❇ Why did John not want to write all that he had to say? (v. 12)
❇ Who shared in John's greeting? (v. 13)

GET IT
■ In what way does truth live in us?
❇ When has it given you joy to see another believer walking in the truth?
❇ How should we show our love for one another?
■ What does it mean to continue in the teaching of Christ?
❇ What does it mean not to welcome a person who does not share in the teaching of Christ?
❇ How would welcoming someone without correct teaching about Christ be sharing in his or her wickedness?
❇ How can we avoid false teachers without being cold or inhospitable?
❇ What sort of people should you deny a welcome into your home?

APPLY IT
❇ What specific steps will you take this week to demonstrate your love for other believers?
■ What can you do today to continue in the teaching of Christ?

3 John 1-14
From the Elder

TOPICS
Ambition, Attitude, Caring, Children, Church, Evil, Faithfulness, God, Gossip, Jesus Christ, Joy, Love, Popularity, Prayer, Reputation, Self-centeredness, Serving, Status, Truth

OPEN IT
❇ What gives you the greatest joy in life?
■ What sort of people in your church are well thought of?
❇ What famous people are presently the objects of malicious gossip in the tabloids?

EXPLORE IT
❇ To whom was this letter addressed? (v. 1)
❇ For what did "the elder" pray? (v. 2)
■ What gave the writer of 3 John great joy? (vv. 3-4)
❇ In what was the recipient of this letter faithful? (v. 5)
■ What information was circulating among the people in Gaius's church? (v. 6)
❇ Why were "the brothers" sent out? (v. 7)
❇ Why did the elder say that believers ought to show hospitality to Christians who serve God? (v. 8)
❇ What did Diotrephes love? (v. 9)
❇ What was Diotrephes doing? (vv. 9-10)
■ What did the elder encourage Gaius to do? (v. 11)
❇ What is true about people who do good and people who do evil? (v. 11)
❇ What was commendable about Demetrius? (v. 12)
❇ Why is 3 John so short? (vv. 13-14)
❇ What did the writer of 3 John hope to do? (v. 14)

GET IT
❇ What does it mean to love someone in the truth?
■ If other believers were to give a report about you, how would they describe your faithfulness?
❇ What about being a believer gives you joy?
❇ In what area of life do you struggle to be faithful?
❇ How can we show hospitality to other Christians?
❇ In what situations do we love to be first, like Diotrephes?
❇ What motivates people to gossip?
❇ In what areas of your life do you need to do better at "imitating good" rather than evil?
■ What can you do to improve your record of faithfulness?
❇ What kind of reputation do you have at your church?

APPLY IT
■ In what area of your life can you be more faithful this week?
❇ To whom can you show hospitality this week?
❇ In what way will you imitate good rather than evil today?

Jude 1-16
The Sin and Doom of Godless Men

TOPICS
Angels, Consequences, Grace, Hell, Homosexuality, Immorality, Judgment, Prophecy, Punishment, Salvation, Second Coming, Sin

OPEN IT
❊ Who was someone everyone tried to avoid in grade school? Why?
■ What is something you have learned or taken note of from history?

EXPLORE IT
❊ How did the author of this letter describe himself? (v. 1)
❊ Why was Jude initially eager to write this letter? (v. 3)
❊ What made Jude change the topic of his letter? (vv. 3-4)
■ What are "godless" people? (v. 4)
❊ Why did Jude describe certain people as "godless"? (v. 4)
❊ How do godless people misuse the grace of God? (v. 4)
■ Of what historical events did Jude remind his readers? Why? (vv. 5-7)
■ How do the stories about Israelites, angels, and Sodom and Gomorrah add to Jude's warning about godless people? (v. 8)
❊ What sins do godless people commit? (v. 8)
❊ In what ways are godless people like "unreasoning animals"? (v. 10)
❊ What destroys godless people? (v. 10)
❊ How are godless people like clouds, trees, waves, and stars? (vv. 12-13)
❊ What affect does Jude's figurative language have? (vv. 12-13)
❊ How does Enoch's prophecy add to the warning about godless people? (v. 14)

GET IT
❊ What affect does the repetition of the word "ungodly" in Jude's message have on you?
❊ How could the grace of God be changed into a license for immorality?
❊ How do we ever misuse the knowledge of God's grace for our own desires?
❊ In what ways is it necessary for us to contend for the faith?
■ How does it help us to recall past events (either from the Bible, church history, or our own lives)?
■ What past events are most instructive to you?
❊ How should our belief in eternal punishment motivate us?
❊ What difference should it make in your life that the Lord will return to judge and convict?
❊ How can we prevent ourselves from becoming self-absorbed as the people Jude warned against were?
❊ What responsibility do we have to protect our church congregations from godless people?
❊ In what ways do you need to guard yourself against the sins of grumbling, finding fault in others, boasting, and flattering others for your own advantage?

APPLY IT
■ How can you keep past events that teach you to live for God at the front of your thinking this week?
❊ What step can you take this week to guard against grumbling, faultfinding, boasting, or using flattery?
❊ In what specific ways do you need to contend for your faith this next week?
❊ What could you do in the near future to come to a better appreciation for God's grace?

Jude 17-25
A Call to Persevere

TOPICS
Divisions, Eternal Life, Faith, Fear, Holiness, Last Days, Mercy, Prayer

OPEN IT
❊ What is it like to anticipate an exciting, important event?
■ Who is the most difficult coworker or boss you've ever had to work with?

EXPLORE IT
❊ What did Jude urge his readers to do? (v. 17)
❊ What will it be like in the last times? (v. 18)
■ What are "scoffers" like? (vv. 18-19)
❊ How do those without the Spirit behave? (v. 19)
■ How can Christians stand against scoffers? (vv. 20-23)
❊ How did Jude advise Christians to pray? (v. 20)
❊ What were Jude's readers waiting for? (v. 21)
❊ How is Jesus' return described? (v. 21)
❊ How should we treat believers who doubt? (vv. 22-23)
❊ What did Jude tell his readers to do for those who await "the fire"? (v. 23)
❊ Who is able to keep believers from falling? (vv. 24-25)
■ How did Jude praise God? (vv. 24-25)
❊ How did Jude conclude this letter? (v. 25)

GET IT
■ Who are some "scoffers" you must work or associate with?
❊ How should you respond to the ungodly people you must work or associate with?
■ How should your life be different from the lives of the nonChristians around you?
❊ How can we show mercy to believers who doubt?
❊ What does it mean to "show mercy, mixed with fear"?
❊ How is it possible to build yourself up in the faith?
❊ What often causes division in churches today?
❊ How can you show mercy to believers who doubt?
❊ What difference does it make that Jesus is able to keep you from falling?
❊ How can you voice your praise to God?

APPLY IT
■ What do you want to remember the next time you must work with a difficult nonChristian?
❊ How can you show mercy to a believer you know who doubts his or her faith?
❊ What can you do to build up your faith this week?
❊ When and how can you voice your praise to God this week?

Revelation 1:1-3
Prologue

TOPICS
Angels, Doctrine, Future, Jesus Christ, Last Days, Listening, Obedience, Prophecy

OPEN IT
❊ What is the strangest dream you have ever had?
❊ How would you describe, in 25 words or less, what angels are and what they do?
■ What outlandish predictions about the future have you heard at one time or another?
❊ Why do you think people are often interested in studying the book of Revelation?

EXPLORE IT
❊ What did John call his writing? (1:1)
❊ What is this book about? (1:1)
❊ For whose benefit did God intend the book of Revelation? (1:1)
■ What did God want us to learn from the book of Revelation? (1:1)
❊ How did God deliver this revelation? (1:1)
❊ To whom did God deliver this revelation? (1:1)
❊ Why did God give us the book of Revelation? (1:1-3)
❊ How much of the revelation he received did John report? (1:2)
❊ What sources did John say was the basis of his revelation? (1:2)
■ What is promised to those who take the time to study this revelation? (1:3)
■ What did John urge his readers to do? Why? (1:3)
❊ How did John show urgency in what he wrote? (1:3)

GET IT
❊ How can we benefit from studying this book?
❊ What do you understand to be "revelation"?
❊ In what way does this "revelation of Jesus Christ" reveal Jesus to us?
❊ Why do you think this New Testament author referred to himself as a servant of Christ?
❊ What does it mean to "take to heart what is written"?
❊ What steps can we take to pay close attention to what we read in Revelation?
■ How does it make you feel to realize that God wants us to know what the future holds?
■ What are some ways God might bless us through a study of Revelation?

APPLY IT
■ What commitment can you make today that will help you get the most out of your study of Revelation?
❊ How can you alter your life-style this week so that you can more honestly say that you are a servant of Jesus Christ?
❊ For whom can you pray who needs to know the good news about our great Savior, Jesus Christ?

Revelation 1:4-8
Greetings and Doxology

TOPICS
Church, Grace, Holy Spirit, Jesus Christ, Love, Peace, Resurrection, Second Coming, Serving, Sovereignty

OPEN IT
❊ What do you remember about church from growing up?
❊ How did you feel the first time you realized that someone was in love with you?
■ With what typical phrases do you open and close your letters?
❊ What is the most moving worship experience you have ever been a part of? Why?

EXPLORE IT
❊ To whom did John write this letter? (1:4)
❊ How did John begin his letter? (1:4)
❊ What was unique or very Christian about the way John opened his letter? (1:4)
❊ How did John refer to God? (1:4)
❊ How did John greet his readers in Christ's name? (1:4)
❊ By what threefold description is Jesus presented? (1:5)
■ What is Jesus' attitude toward Christians? (1:5)
❊ What does Jesus do on behalf of Christians? (1:5)
❊ In what way does Jesus make all believers new? (1:6)
■ What is Jesus' purpose for the church? (1:6)
❊ How did John react when he recounted all the things that Jesus had done for Christians? (1:6)
■ What prophecy opens this book? (1:7)
❊ By what unique description does God explain Himself in this passage? (1:8)

GET IT
❊ What does grace mean to you?
❊ What does the peace of God look like in our lives?
❊ What does the description, "him who is, and who was and who is to come," tell us about God? (1:4)
❊ What does it mean that God is the "Alpha and Omega"?
■ How should we act in light of the fact that we have been freed from our sins?
❊ How might you explain to a friend the concept that God is "Almighty"?
■ What changes need to take place in your life to reflect the truth that Jesus may return at any moment?

APPLY IT
❊ With what priestly actions can you serve God this week?
❊ What is one way you can show your gratitude to Christ today for all that He has done for you?
■ What can you do now to prepare for Jesus' return?

Revelation 1:9-20
One Like a Son of Man

TOPICS
Angels, Church, Death, Endurance, Future, Hell, Last Days, Patience, Prophecy, Resurrection, Suffering

OPEN IT
❊ What do you think Jesus might have looked like as a man? Why?
❊ When was a situation in which you sensed the presence of God? How did it make you feel?
■ What is the most frightened you have ever been?

EXPLORE IT
❊ In what way was John a companion of his readers? (1:9)
❊ Where was John when he received his revelation of Jesus Christ? (1:9)
❊ Why was John where he was when he received this revelation? (1:9)
❊ What kind of voice did John hear in his vision? (1:10)
❊ What did God's voice command John to do? (1:11)
❊ When John turned around, what objects did he see? (1:12)
❊ Whom did John observe standing behind him? (1:13)
❊ How was the person "among the lampstands" dressed? (1:13)
❊ What was the appearance of the one "like a son of man"? (1:14-16)
❊ What was John's reaction to his supernatural visitor? (1:17)
❊ How did John react to seeing Christ in His glory? (1:17)
■ Why did Jesus comfort and reassure John? How? (1:17-18)
❊ What did Jesus say about himself as He comforted John? (1:17-18)
■ What did Jesus tell John to do? (1:19)
■ How did Jesus interpret the meaning of the seven stars and golden lampstands? (1:20)

GET IT
❊ What do you make out of John's reference to "the suffering . . . that [is] ours in Jesus"?
❊ In what ways do you suffer for your faith in Christ?
❊ Of the more than twenty titles for Christ in Revelation 1, which one means the most to you? Why?
■ What overall impression does this passage give you about Jesus Christ?
❊ What does it mean to you that Christ, in all His splendor and majesty, made the effort to calm John when he was frightened?
❊ How difficult do you think it was for John to describe what he was seeing?
■ How might you have felt in John's place?

APPLY IT
■ In what ways can you remind yourself today of the awesome nature and power of Christ?
❊ In what situations this week will you need to strive for "patient endurance"? How can you do so?
❊ With what friends or family members can you plan to share Christ?
❊ What are some specific questions you could ask to lead into a discussion about Christ?

Revelation 2:1-7
To the Church in Ephesus

TOPICS
Accomplishments, Affections, Angels, Approval, Backslide, Commitment, Correction, Faithfulness, Love, Perseverance, Reconciliation, Repentance

OPEN IT
❊ Why does love—even the most fervent and committed love—sometimes grow cold over time?
❊ What are some mementos or heirlooms you are especially attached to?
■ What is something you remember loving dearly as a child that you eventually outgrew?

EXPLORE IT
❊ Who was addressing John with this message? (2:1)
❊ What church was the subject of this letter from Jesus? (2:1)
❊ How did the speaker in this passage identify Himself? (2:1)
■ Jesus praised the church at Ephesus for what deeds? (2:2-3)
❊ What did Christ say about the Ephesian church's "staying power"? (2:3)
❊ With what in the Ephesian church was Christ unsatisfied? (2:4)
❊ What did Christ command the church at Ephesus to remember? (2:5)
■ How did the church at Ephesus need to change? (2:5)
❊ What warning was given to the church if it failed to obey Christ's words? (2:5)
■ What did the church at Ephesus have in its favor? (2:6)
❊ Who else did Jesus want to benefit from this message? (2:7)
❊ What final promise was made to "him who overcomes"? (2:7)

GET IT
❊ If Jesus were to write a letter to your church, what do you think He'd say?
❊ If Jesus were to write you a personal letter, for what would He commend you, and in what ways would He correct you?
❊ What do your actions say about who or what is most important in your life?
❊ What do you think Christ meant when He said, "You have forsaken your first love"?
❊ What does it mean to repent?
❊ What about our faith are we prone to "outgrow"?
❊ At what time in your life did you feel closest to God or the most dedicated to God?
❊ How would you assess the health of your relationship with Christ right now?
■ What can cause us to lose our love for God?
■ How can we keep our commitment to Christ from waning over time?
❊ Besides knowing all the right answers and doing all the right activities, what do we need for spiritual vitality?

APPLY IT

❇ In what concrete ways can you show today that Jesus Christ is your first love?
■ What is one step you can take this week to build the quality of perseverance in your faith?
❇ What can you do or say to encourage a Christian friend to remain loyal to Christ?

Revelation 2:8-11

To the Church in Smyrna

TOPICS

Accomplishments, Angels, Approval, Commitment, Death, Faithfulness, Fear, Persecution, Perseverance, Poor, Resurrection, Satan, Suffering, Wealth

OPEN IT

❇ What were some of your biggest fears as a child?
❇ How does talk of death and dying affect you?
❇ What are the most valuable things you own—those things that make you feel rich?
■ What is the most hurtful thing anyone has ever done to you because of something you stood for?

EXPLORE IT

❇ Who was addressing John? (2:8)
❇ What church was the subject of this letter from Jesus? (2:8)
❇ How did the speaker in this passage identify Himself? (2:8)
❇ What kind of contrast did Jesus draw? (2:9)
❇ What did Christ say about some so-called Jews in Smyrna? (2:9)
❇ What did Jesus say to comfort the Christians in Smyrna? (2:10)
■ What prophetic warning did Christ give to the church in Smyrna? (2:10)
❇ How long would the church in Smyrna suffer? (2:10)
■ What challenge did Christ give His audience? (2:10)
■ What reward was promised the Christians at Smyrna if they hung on? (2:10)
❇ Who else did Jesus say could benefit from the message to the church at Smyrna? (2:11)
❇ What final promise was made to "him who overcomes"? (2:11)

GET IT

❇ What is significant about the title Christ gave Himself ("the First and the Last, who died and came to life again")?
❇ How can a person in poverty be considered rich?
❇ In your view, which is worse—physical or verbal persecution? Why?
❇ If you had been in Smyrna about to suffer for your faith, how comforted would you feel with this revelation from Christ?
■ What kinds of persecution do Christians face today?
❇ What kinds of persecution do you think would most tempt you to deny Christ?
❇ What kinds of persecution have you faced for your faith?
■ How can the eternal promises of God give us courage and strength in the face of attacks on our stand for Christ?

APPLY IT

❇ What are some ways you can express your thanks to God today for the riches you enjoy?
■ What steps can you take today to build your courage against persecution?
❇ How can you show faithfulness to Christ in the week ahead?

Revelation 2:18-29

To the Church in Thyatira

TOPICS

Angels, Authority, Church, Compromise, Faith, Holy Spirit, Idolatry, Immorality, Love, Perseverance, Repentance, Satan, Serving, Sin, Stubbornness, Suffering, Toleration

OPEN IT

❇ What would be good or bad about having the ability to read others' minds? Why?
■ What are the three best habits you have?

EXPLORE IT

❇ Who was telling John to write down this vision? (2:18)
❇ What church was the subject of this letter from Jesus? (2:18)
❇ How did the speaker in this passage identify Himself? (2:18)
❇ How did Christ address the church at Thyatira? (2:18)
❇ What did Christ know about the church at Thyatira? (2:19)
❇ For what did Christ praise the church at Thyatira? (2:19)
❇ For what did Christ chastise the church at Thyatira? (2:20)
❇ How did Christ show patience? (2:21)
❇ What judgments did the Son of God pronounce on the one He called Jezebel? (2:22-23)
■ What challenge did Christ give to those who resisted Jezebel's teaching and sinful behavior? (2:24-25)
■ What two gifts were promised to "him who overcomes"? (2:26-28)
❇ How did Jesus refer to God? (2:28)
■ In addition to the church at Thyatira, who else was commanded to pay heed to this message? (2:29)

GET IT

❇ What are some things people make idols (gods) of today?
❇ What does it mean that Christ's eyes were "like blazing fire"?
■ What sins do we tend to tolerate in our own lives or in the lives of our Christian friends when we should not?
❇ What dangers do we face when we refuse to respond to God or repent of our sins?
❇ What value is there in choosing to remain ignorant of certain evil ideas and practices?
■ When we are misled by others, what can we do to correct our mistakes? How?
❇ When should we take responsibility for the errors of others in the church? How?
❇ What have you been tolerating in your life that you need to reject and change?

APPLY IT
❋ What can you do this week to grow and add to your service for Christ?
■ How can you include repentance and renewal in your devotional life this week?
❋ What specific steps can you take this week to monitor what you take into your thoughts?

Revelation 3:1-6
To the Church in Sardis

TOPICS
Angels, Church, Death, Faith, Holy Spirit, Obedience, Preparation, Repentance, Reputation, Second Coming, Sin, Sleep

OPEN IT
❋ What is the absolute dirtiest (we're talking mud and slime here) you've ever gotten? When and how did it happen?
❋ What is the difference between character and reputation?
❋ Which do you think is worse—wrongfully having a bad reputation, or wrongfully having a good reputation? Why?
■ When are you most prone to being lazy?

EXPLORE IT
❋ Who instructed John to write down this vision? (3:1)
❋ What church was the focus of this letter from Jesus? (3:1)
❋ How did the speaker identify Himself? (3:1)
❋ What did Christ know about the church at Sardis? (3:1)
❋ What was the reputation of the church at Sardis? (3:1)
❋ How did the church's true nature match its reputation? (3:1)
■ What did Christ think about the church at Sardis? (3:1-3)
❋ What was wrong with the church at Sardis? (3:2)
❋ What warnings did Christ issue to the church at Sardis? (3:2)
❋ What did Christ urge as the first step to restoration? (3:3)
❋ What consequences were promised to those who refused to wake up? (3:3)
■ How do we know that not all the Christians in Sardis were "asleep"? (3:4)
■ What blessings were promised to those who would "overcome"? (3:5)
❋ In addition to the church at Sardis, who else was commanded to pay heed to this message? (3:6)

GET IT
❋ How can a person know if his or her name is in the book of life?
❋ What do you think is your reputation among your coworkers? Neighbors? People at church?
❋ When in your life has your reputation been misleading? How?
❋ How can a church appear to be alive and thriving and yet be dead?
❋ In what way do we "soil our clothes"?
❋ What does it mean to be "dressed in white"?
❋ What advice would you give to a young Christian who asked, "How can I keep from sinning?"
■ Why isn't it enough just to know what God wants from us?
❋ What does it mean to "overcome" as a Christian?
■ In what specific areas of Christian devotion (Bible reading, evangelism, prayer, etc.) have you been lazy or sleepy over the last month?

APPLY IT
❋ What can you do today to enhance your reputation in the world and in heaven?
■ What can you do to improve your acts of Christian devotion (prayer, Bible reading, etc.)?
❋ What temptations that you know you'll be facing in the coming week do you need to prepare for in advance? How?

Revelation 3:7-13
To the Church in Philadelphia

TOPICS
Angels, Church, Endurance, Faithfulness, Holy Spirit, Obedience, Rewards, Strength, Suffering, Weaknesses

OPEN IT
■ What are some examples of progress we've seen in the last ten years?
❋ What is the weakest you've ever felt?
❋ What is a nickname you had (or wish you'd had) as a child?
❋ What groups would you cite as the biggest present-day enemies of the church?

EXPLORE IT
❋ Who spoke these words and instructed John to write them down? (3:7)
❋ What church was the focus of this letter from Jesus? (3:7)
❋ How did the speaker in this passage identify Himself? (3:7)
❋ What did Christ say about His power? (3:7)
❋ By what descriptions or names did Jesus call those who claimed to be Jews? (3:9)
❋ What humbling act did Jesus say He would force the enemies of the church of Philadelphia to perform? (3:9)
❋ What worldwide event was predicted by Christ? (3:10)
■ Why will the world experience an "hour of trial"? (3:10)
■ What was promised to the church at Philadelphia because of its patient endurance? (3:10)
■ How did Jesus instruct the believers in Philadelphia to prepare for His coming? (3:11)
❋ What did Jesus promise at the conclusion of this letter? (3:11-12)
❋ How did Jesus challenge us? (3:11-13)
❋ What promises were made to "him who overcomes" in Philadelphia? (3:12)
❋ In addition to the church at Philadelphia, who else was encouraged to heed this message? (3:13)

GET IT
■ What do you think about the idea that the world is getting better and better?
❋ What difference does it make to you that Christ is "holy and true"?

❋ How can we obey Christ and keep standing up for him even when we are physically exhausted?
❋ How might you persuade a friend that Christ is the ultimate power in the universe?
■ What can we do to prepare for Christ's return?
❋ Why can we rejoice even when we are persecuted by hostile anti-God forces?
❋ Who are some of the "pillars" of your church (faithful, godly members who give their full support)?
❋ Why are some Christians seemingly more able or better equipped to "endure patiently"?
❋ What advice would you give to a Christian friend who expressed physical exhaustion and a lack of spiritual strength?

APPLY IT
❋ How can you share what you have learned so far in Revelation with a nonChristian friend who is looking for spiritual answers?
■ How can you pray this week as a result of your study?
❋ In what areas of your life do you need to turn away from wrong attitudes?
❋ Where can you go for the encouragement you need to keep walking with Christ in a hostile world?

Revelation 3:14-22
To the Church in Laodicea

TOPICS
Angels, Apathy, Church, Complacency, Deceit, Discipline, Faithfulness, Holy Spirit, Invitation, Jesus Christ, Repentance, Wealth

OPEN IT
❋ What is the nastiest food or drink you ever tasted?
■ What are some foods or drinks that taste better cold or hot than at room temperature?
❋ If you could have dinner with anyone in the world, who would you pick? Why?

EXPLORE IT
❋ Who spoke these words and told John to write them down? (3:14)
❋ What church was the focus of this letter from Jesus? (3:14)
❋ By what unusual description did Jesus identify Himself? (3:14)
■ How did Jesus describe the church at Laodicea? (3:15)
■ What response did Jesus promise to the Laodicean church because of its behavior? (3:16)
■ In what ways was the Laodicean church deceived? (3:17)
❋ What counsel did "the ruler of God's creation" give to this church? (3:18)
❋ What did the Laodicean Christians need? Why? (3:18)
❋ What reason did Jesus give for His stern warnings? (3:19)
❋ What invitation was given to individual Christians in Laodicea? (3:20)
❋ What did Christ promise to do if accepted and embraced by the Laodiceans? (3:20)
❋ What promise was made to "him who overcomes" in Laodicea? (3:21)
❋ How did Christ conclude His message to this wayward church? (3:22)

GET IT
❋ What do we know about the Laodicean Christians from the fact that Jesus described Himself as being outside the door?
❋ What are some ways people in our society are deceived?
❋ What does it mean that Jesus "stands at the door and knocks"?
❋ How can a person "invite Jesus in" and eat with Him?
❋ What is a hot Christian, a cold Christian, or a lukewarm Christian?
■ What does a lukewarm Christian act like?
■ In what ways can a person be religious yet indifferent to what God wants?
❋ What should we do to be hot in our devotion to God?
❋ How much stock do we tend to put in our own resources (especially money and things)?
❋ What is the significance of the phrase, "He who has an ear to hear, let him hear . . ." at the end of each of the letters to the churches?
❋ What can we learn about the Lord's character based on His strong words to the Laodicean church?
❋ Which of the seven churches described in Revelation 2:1-3:22 are you most like? Why?
❋ What can we do to listen more closely to Christ?
❋ How can we pray to invite Christ into all areas of our lives?

APPLY IT
■ What steps can you take this week to keep from being indifferent to what God wants?
❋ How can you use the Word of God to help clear up your perspective on life?
❋ What possession or portion of money can you use to "buy gold" from Christ? How?
❋ Into what specific areas of your life do you want to invite Christ today?

Revelation 4:1-11
The Throne in Heaven

TOPICS
Creation, Future, Glory, Heaven, Holiness, Holy Spirit, Honor, Power

OPEN IT
❋ What do you most look forward to about heaven?
■ What is a place or experience that is difficult for you to describe to others?
❋ When and where was your most meaningful worship experience?

EXPLORE IT
❋ After receiving messages for the seven churches, what did John see? (4:1)
❋ What kind of voice did John hear? (4:1)
❋ What did the voice John heard say to him? (4:1)

❊ What incredible sights did John see? (4:2-11)
❊ How did John describe the one sitting on a throne? (4:3)
❊ How did John describe what he saw? (4:3)
❊ What encircled or surrounded the throne? (4:3-4)
❊ How were the twenty-four elders dressed? (4:4)
❊ What came from the throne? (4:5)
❊ What did John see in front of the throne? (4:5-6)
❊ What kind of creatures were "in the center, around the throne"? (4:6-7)
❊ How were the four living creatures around the throne similar? (4:8)
■ What attribute of God did the four living creatures praise again and again? (4:8)
■ How did the twenty-four elders worship the Lord God? (4:9-10)
■ Why did the elders say God was worthy of their worship? (4:11)

GET IT
❊ Why do you think God's throne figures prominently in the book of Revelation?
❊ What attitudes do you think are expressed by falling down before God?
■ What does it mean to worship God?
❊ What impressions does this passage give you of God the Father?
❊ How would you describe God to someone who had never read the Bible?
❊ Based on this chapter, what seems to be an important occupation in heaven?
❊ How would you answer someone who complained that "heaven will be boring . . . like one eternal church service"?
❊ What is the significance of the lightning and thunder that comes from God's throne?
■ What changes are you moved to make when you reflect on the holiness and majesty of God Almighty?

APPLY IT
❊ What reminders can you use this week to keep the reality and glory of God at the front of your mind?
■ How can you begin today to make praise and worship of God a more regular part of your life?

Revelation 5:1-14
The Scroll and the Lamb

TOPICS
Angels, Atonement, Jesus Christ, Power, Praise, Prayer, Sacrifice, Serving, Strength, Wealth, Wisdom, Worship

OPEN IT
■ What kind of books do you like to read? Why?
❊ What was the biggest and most electric crowd you were ever a part of?
❊ What foreign language were you first exposed to? When and how?

EXPLORE IT
❊ What was in the hand of the one sitting on the throne in heaven? (5:1)
■ What loud proclamation did a mighty angel make? (5:2)
❊ Who first came forward to open the scroll? (5:3)
■ What was John's reaction when the scroll could not be opened? (5:4)
❊ What did one of the twenty-four elders say to John? (5:5)
❊ Who was only one worthy to open the scroll and its seals? (5:5)
❊ What did the Lamb that John saw look like? (5:6)
❊ Where was the Lamb that John saw? (5:6)
❊ What did the Lamb do? (5:7)
❊ How did the creatures around the throne respond to the actions of the Lamb? (5:8-9)
■ For what was the Lamb praised and worshipped? (5:9-10)
❊ How many angels did John see? (5:11)
❊ What were the angels doing? (5:12)
❊ What were all the other living creatures doing and singing? (5:13)

GET IT
❊ Why do you think John was upset when nobody came forward to open the scroll?
❊ Why do you think the prayers of the saints appeared as "golden bowls full of incense"?
■ What did Christ do for us?
❊ What evidence do we have from this passage that God makes no distinction between races or ethnic groups?
❊ Why should we value people of all races equally and treat everyone with equal respect?
❊ Who in your sphere of influence needs to know about Christ?
❊ What is the benefit of bowing down to worship God?
■ How can we serve God as His priests?

APPLY IT
❊ How can you worship God in your private times of prayer this week?
■ How can you develop an attitude of praise and thanksgiving to God as you go throughout your day?

Revelation 6:1-17
The Seals

TOPICS
Death, Hell, Holiness, Jesus Christ, Judgment, Last Days, Peace, Truth

OPEN IT
❊ What do you picture the end of the world being like?
❊ What is one natural disaster (earthquake, tornado, etc.) that stands out in your memory?
❊ How do you react in really frightening situations?
■ Given the human power and authority, what would you do to try to bring about lasting peace and prosperity on earth?

EXPLORE IT
❊ What happens in the opening scenes of this passage? (6:1)
❊ What did John hear after Christ opened the first seal? (6:2)
❊ What was the nature and the appearance of the first horse and its rider? (6:2)

❊ What happened after the second seal was opened? (6:3)
❊ How are the second horse and its rider described? (6:4)
❊ What happened at the opening of the third seal? (6:5)
❊ How did the voice that John heard explain the meaning of the scales in the hand of the third rider? (6:6)
❊ What were the fourth horse and its rider like? (6:7-8)
❊ What did John see at the opening of the fifth seal? (6:9)
■ What question did the martyrs ask God? (6:10)
■ What answer was given the slain ones? (6:11)
❊ What happened at the opening of the sixth seal? (6:12-14)
■ How did the inhabitants of earth respond to the events unleashed by the breaking of the seals? (6:15-17)
❊ How will people try to escape from being judged by God? (6:15-17)

GET IT
■ How does reading this passage make you feel?
❊ What do you think each of the four horsemen represents?
❊ What do the judgments wrought by the horsemen have in common?
❊ When do you think the judgments (represented by the four horsemen) will take place?
❊ Why will God judge the earth?
❊ Why do people try to escape from God?
❊ Why do you think some people react so negatively to the message of Christ?
❊ How long do you think God will wait before judging the earth?
■ What does God want us to do as we wait for Him to judge the earth?
❊ How should we pray in light of the fact that God will judge all people?

APPLY IT
❊ How can you help a nonChristian friend or family member see his or her need for Christ?
■ How can you encourage a faithful Christian today who is being persecuted for following Christ?

Revelation 7:1-8
144,000 Sealed

TOPICS
Angels, Earth, Judgment, Last Days, Serving

OPEN IT
■ What forms of identification do you typically carry?
❊ How do you protect or mark items that you don't want to lose or have stolen?
❊ How might you prove ownership of your valued possessions?

EXPLORE IT
❊ Who did John see after the breaking of the first six seals? (7:1)
❊ Where were the four angels located? (7:1)
❊ What were the four angels at the four "corners of the earth" doing? Why? (7:1)
❊ What did John see coming from the east? (7:2)
■ What did the angel from the east have in his possession? (7:2)
❊ What power or authority did the four angels possess? (7:2)
❊ What did the angel from the east say to the other four angels? (7:3)
■ When were the angels given permission to "harm the land and the sea"? (7:3)
■ What people were marked? How? (7:4)
❊ How many individuals were sealed in John's vision? (7:4)
❊ How many individuals were sealed from each of the 12 tribes of Israel? (7:4-8)

GET IT
■ How has God marked or sealed His people?
❊ Whom does God protect?
❊ How will God protect His people during the coming judgment?
❊ In what ways does God protect His people now?
❊ Why is it important for us to know that God's servants will be sealed before God afflicts the land and the sea with the final judgments?
❊ Who are the 144,000 sealed servants?
❊ What are some ways angels are at work in the world today?
❊ What can we do to reflect the fact that we are servants of God who bear His mark (or seal) of ownership?
■ What mark of ownership is there in your life-style that shows God's possession of your life?

APPLY IT
❊ What mark of ownership do you need to place in your life today to show your obedience to God?
❊ What Bible-study tools could you get in the next couple of weeks that would help you gain a better understanding of Revelation and the rest of Scripture?
■ How do you need to alter your routine to reflect the fact that God owns every area of your life?

Revelation 7:9-17
The Great Multitude in White Robes

TOPICS
Angels, Atonement, Eternal Life, Glory, Heaven, Honor, Joy, Power, Praise, Purity, Salvation, Serving, Wisdom, Worship

OPEN IT
■ What are some things about earth you won't miss in heaven?
❊ When was the last time you saw or experienced racial prejudice?
❊ What is the hardest you ever cried in grade school?

EXPLORE IT
❊ What did John see after seeing the revelation of the 144,000 sealed servants of God? (7:9)
❊ Where did John see a great throng of people? (7:9)
❊ What were the people John saw wearing and holding? (7:9)
❊ What was the crowd before the throne saying? (7:10)
❊ What group was around the throne worshiping? (7:11)
❊ What were the angels, the elders, and the four creatures saying to God and about God? (7:12)

❇ Who spoke to John and what did this person say? (7:13)
❇ How did John respond to the elder's question? (7:14)
■ How did the elder explain the identity of those wearing the white robes? (7:14)
■ What is the main job of the believers who come out of the great tribulation? (7:15)
■ What blessings await those who are martyred in the great tribulation? (7:16-17)
❇ What is the involvement of the Lamb with those in white robes? (7:17)

GET IT
❇ Why is it important for us to know that the "robes" of the martyrs will be made white in the blood of the Lamb as they come out of the tribulation?
■ What does it mean to you that "a great multitude" will serve God day and night in His heavenly temple?
❇ What is the difference between singing a hymn and singing an ordinary song?
❇ How do we know that God does not favor people for their skin color or ethnic background?
❇ How can we thank God for salvation?
❇ On a scale of 1 to 10 (with 1 being "terrible" and 10 being "terrific"), how would you rate the quality and consistency of your personal praise life?
■ What new insights into the character of God does this passage give you?
❇ What is the significance of the fact that the angels and elders around the throne of God fall down and worship God?

APPLY IT
■ What step can you take this week to praise and thank God more consistently?
❇ What are some specific ways you and your family can encourage or support a missionary?
❇ How can you imitate God today in leading someone to Him or comforting a friend in grief?

Revelation 8:1-5
The Seventh Seal and the Golden Censer

TOPICS
Angels, Heaven, Listening, Praise, Prayer, Sacrifice, Serving, Silence, Worship

OPEN IT
■ In what ways can silence be good or helpful?
❇ In what way can silence make us uncomfortable?
❇ How would you describe heaven to a friend?

EXPLORE IT
❇ Who is the one here described as opening the seventh seal? (8:1)
■ What happened in heaven upon the opening of the seventh seal? (8:1)
❇ For how long was there silence in heaven during John's vision? (8:1)
❇ What did John see after the opening of the seventh seal? (8:2)
❇ What was given to the creatures seen by John? (8:2)
❇ What did John see another angel come and do? (8:3)
❇ What did the angel standing at the altar have in his possession? (8:3)
■ What was the angel at the altar assigned to do? (8:3)
■ What did John see going up before God? (8:4)
❇ With what did the angel fill the censer? (8:5)
❇ What did the angel eventually do with the censer? (8:5)
❇ What happened on the earth after the angel's actions? (8:5)

GET IT
■ What is dramatic about silence in heaven?
■ How can we make silence a part of our worship?
❇ What is a censer?
❇ How is it significant that incense accompanies the prayers of all God's people?
❇ What needs are you praying about these days?
❇ When the seventh seal is opened there is first silence, then prayer; how do you interpret the heavenly response to the saints' prayers?
❇ What does this passage teach us about prayer?
❇ Why do you think the angel hurled his censer to the earth?
❇ The angels in heaven have God-given tasks; what are your God-given tasks or areas of responsibility?

APPLY IT
■ When could you make time this week for silent meditation on God's word and on what God has done for you?
❇ How might you improve the way you pray?
❇ What God-given responsibility do you need to carry out today?

Revelation 8:6–9:21
The Trumpets

TOPICS
Angels, Blindness, Danger, Darkness, Death, Enemies, Environment, Evil, Heaven, Hopelessness, Judgment, Last Days, Pain, Rebellion, Stress, World

OPEN IT
❇ What do you think of when you think of a "trumpet blast"?
❇ What is most moving to you about wildfires, earthquakes, floods, hurricanes, and tornadoes?
■ Why do you think some people believe that everyone will go to heaven (that is, no one will be punished or sent to hell by God)?

EXPLORE IT
■ What did the seven angels who stand before God prepare to do? (8:6)
❇ What happened when the first angel sounded his trumpet? (8:7)
■ What were the trumpet blasts that John heard? (8:7-8, 10, 12; 9:1, 13-15)
❇ What was the result when the second angel sounded his trumpet? (8:8-9)
❇ What happened when the third angel blew his trumpet? (8:10-11)
❇ What events followed the fourth angel's trumpet blast? (8:12)

❋ What did John see an eagle do? (8:13)
❋ What did John see at the sounding of the fifth trumpet? (9:1)
❋ What creatures came out of the Abyss? (9:2-3)
❋ What special powers did the creatures from the Abyss have? (9:4-6)
❋ What did the creatures from the Abyss look like? (9:7-10)
❋ What events transpired when the sixth angel blew his trumpet? (9:13-19)
■ How were the few human survivors affected by these horrible plagues and catastrophes? (9:20-21)

GET IT
■ What significance is there to the plagues that will befall the world in the final days?
❋ Why do you think the survivors in the last days will still refuse to turn to God—especially after seeing the horrible judgment all around them?
❋ What does this passage tell us about God?
❋ Why do you think so many of the plagues described here stop short of complete devastation?
❋ What difference does it make to you that God chooses what these judgments will and will not mean?
❋ What is most frightening to you about these judgments? Why?
■ What difference does it make that we are making life more and more comfortable with better and better technology?
❋ How can you use what you've learned in Revelation as a tool in talking with nonChristian friends who are looking for spiritual answers?

APPLY IT
■ What changes can you make in your prayer life this week as a result of what you have studied today?
❋ In what areas of your life do you need to turn away from wrong attitudes and actions this week so that you can avoid the disciplining hand of God?

Revelation 10:1-11
The Angel and the Little Scroll

TOPICS
Angels, Creation, Delay, Encouragement, God's Will, Guidance, Instructions, Judgment, Obedience, Responsibility, Silence, Surprises, Witnessing

OPEN IT
❋ About what beloved hobbies or special interests of yours might someone remark, "He or she can't get enough of that"?
■ On a scale of 1 to 10 (with 1 being ghastly and 10 being great), how good are you at keeping secrets?
❋ What is something for which you have waited a long time?

EXPLORE IT
❋ After the first six trumpets of judgment, what did John see? (10:1)
❋ What did the mighty angel of John's vision look like? (10:1)
❋ What did the mighty angel have in his possession? (10:2)
❋ What did the mighty angel do? (10:2-3)
❋ What did John try to do about what he heard? (10:4)
❋ What command did John receive from heaven? (10:4)
❋ What did the mighty angel do after John sealed up what the seven thunders said? (10:5-6)
❋ What did the angel swear? (10:6)
❋ How did the angel describe God in his oath? (10:6)
❋ What announcement did the angel make? (10:6-7)
❋ What did the voice from heaven tell John to do? (10:8)
■ What did the angel tell John to do with the little scroll? (10:9)
❋ What unusual act was John asked to perform? (10:9)
❋ What warning did the angel give John? (10:9)
■ What happened when John ate the scroll? (10:10)
■ What is the last thing John was told at this time? (10:11)

GET IT
❋ What does it mean that the angel's voice sounded like thunder?
❋ Why is it significant that God sent His angel to announce that there would be no more delay in God's intervention?
❋ Why is it significant that the angel called God "him who lives for ever and ever"?
■ What do you think is symbolized by John's eating the scroll of God's words and finding it sweet in his mouth and sour in his stomach?
■ In what situations has God's word ever tasted sweet at first hearing but then sour as you "digested" it?
❋ What is the "mystery of God" that will be accomplished?
❋ When will the "mystery of God" be accomplished?
❋ What confidence or secret do you need to keep that you may be tempted to share?

APPLY IT
■ What step can you take this week to help you internalize what you have heard from God's word?
❋ How can you practice patience and trust today in an area of your life where God's working seems to have been delayed?
❋ Who in your life has God called you to speak His truth to this week?

Revelation 11:1-14
The Two Witnesses

TOPICS
Ambassadors, Angels, Celebration, Death, Enemies, Heaven, Judgment, Miracles, Persecution, Resurrection, Unbelievers, Witnessing, Worship

OPEN IT
❋ Why are people so turned off by "fire and brimstone" type preachers?
❋ What determines how you interpret a hard-to-understand Bible passage?
❋ What groups seem to you to be most opposed to the Christian message and to the spread of the gospel?
■ Why do you think so many people are gleeful to learn of the moral failures of prominent Christians?

EXPLORE IT
❊ What was John given? (11:1)
❊ What was John told to do with the object he had been given? (11:1)
❊ What was John told to count? (11:1)
❊ What part of the temple was John to exclude from his "fact-finding mission"? (11:2)
■ What important "end times" individuals are mentioned in this passage and what will be their mission? (11:3-6)
❊ What special protection will be given the ones called the "two olive trees and the two lampstands"? (11:4-5)
❊ What supernatural powers will the two witnesses possess? (11:6)
■ What will happen to the two witnesses when they have finished their God-ordained ministry? (11:7)
❊ How will the two witnesses die? (11:7)
■ What will take place in the three and a half days after the two witnesses die? (11:8-10)
❊ In John's vision, what happened three and half days after the two witnesses were killed by the beast? (11:11-12)
❊ What catastrophic events will follow the two witnesses? (11:13)

GET IT
❊ What do the events in this passage tell us about God?
■ What do the events in this passage tell us about the world?
■ What encouragement for Christians today does the story of the two witnesses offer?
❊ How do you explain the response of the people described in this passage?
❊ How do you think you might react if you saw two men dead for three and half days come back to life?
❊ How does it make you feel to know that God and His servants will ultimately triumph over the evil of the world?

APPLY IT
❊ How can you be a witness this week to those who don't know Christ?
■ What can you do to show your support this week for ministers, evangelists, and Christian leaders?
❊ What sins do you need to confess and renounce today in order that the Spirit of God might fill your life with His power?

Revelation 11:15-19

The Seventh Trumpet

TOPICS
Angels, Eternal Life, Heaven, Judgment, Rewards, Serving, Thankfulness, Victory, Worship

OPEN IT
❊ Who is one famous and one not-so-famous Christian that you think will receive great reward in heaven? Why?
■ What are you most thankful for?
❊ What about this world would you most like to see changed? Why?

EXPLORE IT
❊ What did John observe? (11:15)
❊ What did John hear? (11:15)
■ What did the voices say about the world? (11:15)
❊ What did the voices say about the reign of Christ? (11:15)
❊ What group of people in addition to John heard the heavenly voices? (11:16)
❊ Where were the twenty-four elders seated? (11:16)
❊ How did the twenty-four elders respond in the wake of the message of the heavenly voices? (11:16)
❊ How did the elders describe "the Lord God Almighty"? (11:17)
■ Why were the elders thankful to God? (11:17)
❊ How did the elders describe the nations of the world? (11:18)
❊ In the elders' prayer, what "time has come"? (11:18)
■ Who did the elders describe as deserving a reward? (11:18)
❊ Who did the elders describe as deserving destruction? (11:18)
❊ What happened in the heavenly temple of God after the prayer of the elders? (11:19)
❊ What spectacular phenomena accompanied the opening of the temple? (11:19)

GET IT
■ How is the promise that God will reign over the earth significant to you?
■ For what do we have to be thankful to God?
❊ What does the promise of both reward and judgment mean to you personally?
❊ What determines whether a Christian receives a big or a small heavenly reward?
❊ What does it say to us that even angels with awesome power and beauty and elders with great heavenly position worship God in total humility?
❊ What are some ways nations display anger toward God?
❊ What changes need to take place in your personal worship of God?

APPLY IT
❊ What is one specific act you could perform this week to advance the kingdom of God in your neighborhood, school, office, or home?
■ For what spiritual and material blessings will you spend some time today thanking God? How?

Revelation 12:1–13:1

The Woman and the Dragon

TOPICS
Accusation, Angels, Atonement, Conflict, Deceit, Earth, Heaven, Judgment, Power, Salvation, Satan, Victory, War

OPEN IT
■ How does it feel to be accused of something you didn't do?
❊ What is the clearest examples of the existence of Satan that you're aware of?

EXPLORE IT
❊ After the seventh trumpet, what "great and wondrous sign" did John observe in heaven? (12:1)

❇ How did John describe the woman in his vision? (12:2)
❇ What second sign did John see in heaven? (12:3)
❇ In what activities was the enormous red dragon involved? (12:4)
❇ What did John say about the child born to the woman? (12:5)
❇ What happened to the newborn child? (12:5)
❇ Where did the woman go right after giving birth? (12:6)
❇ What was taking place in heaven in John's vision? (12:7)
❇ What happened to the dragon and his angels? (12:8-9)
❇ By what names was the dragon known? (12:9)
❇ What did a voice from heaven announce? (12:10)
❇ How did the voice from heaven refer to Satan? (12:10)
■ According to the voice from heaven, how was Satan defeated? (12:11)
❇ What warning was sounded to the earth and sea? Why? (12:12)
■ What happened when the dragon tried to destroy the woman? (12:13-13:1)
■ When the dragon was unable to kill the woman, where did he redirect his destructive efforts? (12:17-13:1)

GET IT

❇ Of what events is the story of the woman a parable or parallel?
❇ What can we learn about Satan (his character, activities, and destiny) from this passage?
❇ What does it mean not to love your life so much as to shrink from death?
■ In what way does Satan try to oppose God today?
❇ In what ways is Satan limited? Why?
❇ What does it mean that Satan was "hurled to earth"?
❇ How, in your own words, would you describe Satan's earthly exploits after he has been cast from heaven?
❇ What do we learn about God from this passage?
❇ What does this passage tell us about God's people?
❇ When tempted by Satan, "the accuser of our brothers," how can we resist and fight back?
■ In what ways does Satan try to tempt and hurt us?
❇ How can we strengthen ourselves against Satan's attempts to weaken and tempt us?

APPLY IT

■ What can you do this week to strengthen your hold on the testimony of Jesus?
❇ What books, tapes, articles, or fellow believers could you use to help you grow in your commitment to Christ? How?
❇ How can you take the message of today's passage and encourage a fellow Christian who is struggling in his or her walk with Christ?

Revelation 13:2-10

The Beast out of the Sea

TOPICS

Authority, Blasphemy, Death, Deceit, Endurance, Faithfulness, Last Days, Persecution, Perseverance, Power, Satan, War, Worship

OPEN IT

■ What alternatives to God do some of your coworkers or friends have (such as New Age beliefs, Islam, atheism, etc.)?
❇ What names of living and/or dead individuals have you heard end times enthusiasts mention as being the "Antichrist"?

EXPLORE IT

❇ What kind of creature did John observe? (13:2)
❇ What did the beast look like that John saw? (13:2)
❇ What did the dragon (Satan) give the beast out of the sea? (13:2)
❇ What was unusual about one of the heads of the beast? (13:3)
❇ How did the world react and respond to the beast out of the sea? (13:3-4)
❇ How long did the beast have authority? (13:5)
❇ What kind of pronouncements did the beast make? (13:5-6)
❇ How did the beast use his authority? (13:7)
■ Who will worship the beast? (13:8)
■ What warning did John give to all who would listen? (13:9-10)
■ What do we need to do about this? (13:10)

GET IT

❇ In light of verses such as Psalm 24:1; Matthew 4:8-10; John 8:44, 12:31; and 2 Corinthians 4:4, who controls events on earth?
❇ What is significant about the way the beast is described?
❇ If you were facing death because of your Christian beliefs, how do you think you might respond?
❇ Why do you think people will worship the beast?
■ What difference does it make who we worship?
❇ What are some simple steps we can take to ensure that we give worship to God alone?
■ In what sense do we need to be closed-minded about faith in Christ?
❇ Why is it important that the beast will exercise authority for a period of only forty-two months?
❇ Why do you think God allows His people to undergo severe trials and the kinds of persecution that are described in this passage?
❇ What insights into spiritual warfare and blindness does this passage give you?
❇ What are some situations you are facing that call for patient endurance and faithfulness?

APPLY IT

❇ What can you do to prepare for those times this week when you will need patient endurance and faithfulness?
■ How can you worship God in your attitudes and actions today?

Revelation 13:11-18

The Beast out of the Earth

TOPICS

Authority, Death, Deceit, Enemies, Idolatry, Loyalty, Miracles, Opposition, Power, Pressure, Satan, Wisdom, Worship

OPEN IT
■ What is the most amazing trick you have ever seen a magician or an illusionist perform?
❊ What are the most incredible special effects you have ever seen in a movie?

EXPLORE IT
❊ What kind of creature did John observe? (13:11)
❊ How did John describe the beast he saw coming out of the earth? (13:11)
❊ Who did the second beast represent? (13:12)
❊ What did the second beast make the inhabitants of earth do? (13:12)
❊ What powerful signs did the second beast use? (13:13)
■ How did the second beast deceive everyone all over the world? (13:13-14)
❊ What evil act did the second beast require of everyone all over the world? (13:14)
■ How did the beast out of the earth use his Satanic power in relation to the image of the beast out of the sea? (13:15)
■ What happened to those who refused to worship the image of the beast out of the sea? (13:15)
❊ What did the beast out of the earth (also called the false prophet) force every living person to do? (13:16)
❊ What consequences awaited those who refused to take the mark of the beast? (13:17)
❊ What difference did it make whether a person took the mark of the beast? (13:17)
❊ What does the rise of the beast call us to? (13:18)
❊ How did John say one could "calculate the number of the beast"? (13:18)

GET IT
❊ What do you think is the significance of the fact that the beast's number is 666?
❊ How could Satan use economics (the ability to buy and sell) to control people and gain their allegiance?
■ What are some chief ways people are deceived or blinded by Satan today?
❊ How might you respond to someone who insisted that every miracle is from God?
❊ How do you interpret and explain the kind of mark that Satan will require people to put on their hands and foreheads?
❊ How would you react to a giant statue that could talk and move?
❊ How can we tell whether a miracle is from God or from Satan?
❊ What value is there in trying to determine the identity of the beast and the meaning of the symbols of the Book of Revelation?
■ What should we do to be wise about the schemes of Satan?

APPLY IT
❊ How can you shine the light of Christ in your part of our world?
❊ What steps can you take today to renew your commitment to Jesus Christ?
■ What actions could you take today to instruct or guide a young Christian?

Revelation 14:1-5
The Lamb and the 144,000

TOPICS
Ambassadors, Commitment, Dedication, Eternal Life, Fruit, Heaven, Integrity, Obedience, Purity, Righteousness, Worship

OPEN IT
❊ What are your favorite sounds in all the world?
❊ What five adjectives do you think your friends and family would use to describe you?
■ What is one song you would like to learn to sing by heart?

EXPLORE IT
■ Who did John see standing before him? (14:1)
❊ Where in this vision of John's was the central character standing? (14:1)
❊ Who was standing with the Lamb? (14:1)
❊ What was written on the foreheads of the 144,000? (14:1)
❊ What was the sound that John heard from heaven like? (14:2)
■ What did the 144,000 do as John looked on? (14:3)
❊ Who besides John heard the 144,000 singers? (14:3)
❊ Who was given the privilege of learning the song of the 144,000? (14:3)
❊ How is the purity of the 144,000 described? (14:4)
❊ How is the commitment and faithfulness of the 144,000 pictured? (14:4)
■ What is said here about the unique spiritual condition of the 144,000? (14:4-5)
❊ How is the integrity of the 144,000 described? (14:5)

GET IT
❊ What is significant about the sound from heaven described in this passage?
■ Why do you think only the 144,000 are able to learn the new song of praise?
❊ In your own words, how would you describe the redeemed 144,000?
❊ In what ways are you tempted to place your affections on the world of business, politics, social life, etc.?
■ What does it mean to "follow the Lamb wherever he goes"?
❊ What does it mean to be blameless?

APPLY IT
❊ What is one step can you take today to keep yourself pure and devoted to God?
■ What can you do to make yourself more open to follow the Lord wherever He leads you?

Revelation 14:6-13
The Three Angels

TOPICS
Angels, Blessing, Creation, Death, Earth, Endurance, Faithfulness, Fear, Glory, Gospel, Hell, Judgment, Obedience, Patience, Worship

OPEN IT
■ What do your coworkers believe about hell?
❊ If you could get on international television and deliver a 10-second message to the whole human race, what would you say?

EXPLORE IT
❊ What did John see? (14:6)
❊ What was an angel dispatched to do? (14:6)
■ What did the angel tell the inhabitants of earth to do? Why? (14:7)
❊ Why was it important that people heed the angel's message? (14:7)
❊ What pronouncement did the second angel make? (14:8)
❊ How was Babylon's sin described by the second angel? (14:9)
❊ What warning did the third angel give? (14:9-10)
■ What would be the consequence of taking the mark of the beast? (14:9-10)
❊ How is God's judgment on those who worship the beast pictured? (14:10)
❊ What words are used to portray God's anger over sin? (14:10)
❊ How is the future torment of the unbelieving described in this passage? (14:10-11)
■ What does the future hold for those who do not believe? (14:10-11)
❊ How should Christians respond to this sober warning? (14:12)
❊ What instructions did John receive from heaven? (14:13)
❊ In what sense are the dead blessed? (14:13)

GET IT
■ What temptations and trials make it difficult to live for Christ in this society?
❊ How is it significant that the angel proclaimed the eternal gospel to "every nation, tribe, language and people"?
■ What does it mean to fear God?
❊ In your own words, how would you describe God's hatred for sin?
❊ Why do we need "patient endurance" as followers of Christ?
❊ In what way is it a blessing to die as a believer in Christ?

APPLY IT
❊ In what concrete way could you encourage or support a missionary this week?
❊ In what way can you be a witness for Christ today?
■ How can you cultivate faithfulness to Jesus in all you do each day?

Revelation 14:14-20
The Harvest of the Earth

TOPICS
Angels, Anger, Consequences, Earth, Heaven, Judgment

OPEN IT
■ What do you think is the average person's view of heaven?
❊ Why do you think death is personified as the Grim Reaper?

EXPLORE IT
❊ What did John see? (14:14)
❊ How did John describe the person he saw? (14:14)
❊ What unusual instrument did the one "like a son of man" have in his possession? (14:14)
❊ What happened as John stared at the angel sitting on a cloud? (14:15)
■ What did the angel from the heavenly temple tell the other angel to do? Why? (14:15)
❊ Why did the one angel command the other to harvest the earth? (14:15)
❊ How did the one seated on the cloud respond to the angel's command? (14:16)
❊ How did John describe the next angel he saw? (14:17)
❊ What did John see "still another angel" do? (14:18)
■ What instructions did the angel give to the one with the "sharp sickle"? (14:18)
■ What happened to the grapes that were gathered by the reaping angel? (14:19-20)
❊ How much blood was produced by the crushing of the "grapes"? (14:20)

GET IT
❊ What does this passage tell us about angels?
■ What does this passage tell us about God?
❊ What does this passage tell us about people?
❊ How would you answer a nonChristian's charge that the Bible is too full of blood and judgment?
❊ How do you interpret this vision of John's?
❊ Why do you think God delays His judgment when the world is already filled with evil?
■ How do we know that God takes our sin seriously?
❊ How (if at all) would it change your view of God if God didn't punish sin?
❊ What would you tell a person about how he or she could escape judgment?
❊ Who do you think the grapes in this vision represent?
❊ What difference should the promise of judgment and wrath against evil make to the way we live?

APPLY IT
❊ For what unbelievers will you pray this week?
■ In what way can you express your gratitude to God for sparing you from His wrath?

Revelation 15:1-8
Seven Angels With Seven Plagues

TOPICS
Angels, Anger, Confidence, Fear, Glory, Greatness, Heaven, Holiness, Justice, Perseverance, Power, Purity, Righteousness, Satan, Worship

OPEN IT
❊ Of what difficult accomplishment are you most proud?
❊ When in your life have you felt the most spiritually clean or the closest to God?
■ What is your favorite hymn or worship song? Why?

EXPLORE IT
❊ What great sign did John see in heaven? (15:1)
❊ Why did John refer to the plagues he saw as the "seven last plagues"? (15:1)
■ How did John describe the part of heaven revealed to him? (15:2)
❊ Who did John see standing before him? (15:2)
❊ Who will be "victorious over the beast"? (15:2)
■ What were the saints in heaven doing? (15:2-3)
■ What attributes of God are praised in the "song of Moses"? (15:3-4)
❊ By what names was God called in the heavenly hymn heard by John? (15:3-4)
❊ What did John see opened in heaven? (15:5)
❊ What creatures came out of the temple? (15:6)
❊ How did John describe the heavenly beings he saw? (15:6)
❊ What was given to the seven angels? (15:7)
❊ What events took place in the heavenly temple after the angels were dispatched with their plagues? (15:8)

GET IT
❊ When and where have you most sensed the awesomeness and greatness of God?
❊ How would you answer someone who complained that heaven is "boring because people just sit on clouds and play harps for eternity"?
❊ When will believers be "victorious over the beast"?
■ What are some ways to praise or worship God?
❊ How can singing help us worship God?
■ How can we use singing in our worship of God?
❊ What evidence does this passage give us that God is just and fair?
❊ What does it mean that God is marvelous or glorious?
❊ Based on this passage, what new insights do you have about heaven?
❊ What do you most look forward to about heaven?
❊ What God-given provisions do we have in our battle against the devil?

APPLY IT
❊ What God-given provisions can you use today in your battle to be victorious over the devil?
■ What is one practical step you can take to include singing more in your worship of God?

Revelation 16:1-21
The Seven Bowls of God's Wrath

TOPICS
Angels, Anger, Blasphemy, Consequences, Darkness, Death, Demons, Earth, Heaven, Holiness, Judgment, Justice, Last Days, Pain, Repentance, Sickness

OPEN IT
■ What is the most pain you have ever experienced?
❊ Which do you think is worse—physical or emotional pain?
❊ What kinds of natural disasters would you least like to be in the middle of?
❊ What injustices in the world sometimes cause you to wonder if God is just?

EXPLORE IT
❊ What did John hear from the heavenly temple? (16:1)
■ What instructions did the loud voice give to the seven angels? (16:1)
❊ What happened when the first angel poured out his bowl? (16:2)
❊ What happened when the second angel emptied his bowl? (16:3)
❊ What happened in the wake of the third angel pouring out his bowl? (16:4)
■ What did the angel in charge of the waters say about the judgments being poured out? (16:5-7)
❊ Why were the judgments that John witnessed called just? (16:5-7)
❊ What kinds of judgment did the fourth bowl contain? (16:8-9)
❊ What effect did the judgment of the fourth bowl have? (16:9)
❊ What effect did the "raising of the thermostat" have on the earth's inhabitants? (16:9)
❊ What happened when the fifth angel poured out his bowl? (16:10-11)
❊ Where was the judgment of the sixth angel directed? Why? (16:12)
❊ What was the appearance of the three evil spirits after the judgment of bowl number six? (16:13-14)
❊ What did the three evil spirits do? (16:13-14)
■ What blessing was pronounced in the middle of this outpouring of judgment? (16:15)
❊ What happened to the kings of the East? (16:16)
❊ What were the results when the seventh angel poured out his bowl of judgment? (16:17-21)

GET IT
❊ How (if at all) do you think current events fit in with the judgments described in this passage?
❊ How is the first plague appropriate for those who have allowed the mark of the beast on their bodies?
❊ How do plagues two and three fit mankind's crimes?
■ What makes the judgments described here—horrible as they are—perfectly just?
■ How can we "keep our clothes white"?
❊ What makes a person blessed for "keeping his clothes white"?
❊ Why would people undergoing judgment still not turn to God in repentance and for salvation?

APPLY IT
❊ In what situations this week can you be fair and just?
■ What is one step you can take this week to fight spiritual laziness?
❊ How could you use the message of this passage to engage a nonChristian friend in a discussion about Christ?

Revelation 17:1-18
The Woman on the Beast

TOPICS
Ambassadors, Angels, Authority, Blasphemy, Faithfulness, Hell, Holy Spirit, Immorality, Judgment, Power, Sin, War, Wisdom

OPEN IT
■ What are some examples of champions or winners?
❋ If you life was being threatened and you could hire anyone in the world to be your personal bodyguard, who would you pick?
❋ What do you think of all the recent talk of a "new world order"?

EXPLORE IT
❋ What did one of the seven angels show John? (17:1)
❋ How did the angel describe the evil of the "great prostitute"? (17:2)
❋ What did John see when the angel carried him away? (17:3)
❋ How did John describe the woman he saw? (17:4-5)
❋ What could John tell about the woman he saw? (17:6)
❋ What amazed John? (17:6)
❋ How did the angel react to John's astonishment? (17:7)
❋ What did the angel explain to John? (17:7)
■ Why will people all over the world be astonished at the beast? (17:8)
❋ What do people need in light of the events that are coming? (17:9)
■ How did the angel explain the seven heads of the beast? (17:9-11)
❋ How did the angel explain the ten horns that covered the beast? (17:12)
■ What action will the ten kings take and what will be the result? (17:13-14)
❋ What was the significance of the waters that John saw the woman sitting on? (17:15)
❋ What is the relationship between the beast, the ten kings, and the prostitute? (17:16-18)

GET IT
❋ How significant do you think it is that ancient Babylon is being rebuilt in modern day Iraq?
❋ Why do you think idolatry (worship of false gods) is described as adultery in the Bible?
❋ In what way is the beast's "resurrection" a weak imitation of Christ's resurrection?
❋ What in your opinion is the best way to understand the symbolism in this passage—the prostitute, the seven heads or hills, and the ten kings?
❋ How would you describe the difference between knowledge and wisdom?
❋ Why is it so important for us to seek wisdom from God?
❋ What can we do to become wise?
❋ What is the significance of the way in which the prostitute is dressed?
❋ What does it mean that the beast and the ten horns will eventually turn against the prostitute?
■ What systems ("babylons") in the world today are hostile to God?
❋ How do you think you should respond differently to worldly events and situations after having studied this chapter?
❋ In what ways do you need to reaffirm your commitment, devotion, and loyalty to Jesus Christ this week?
■ What difference does it make that Jesus is the Lord of lords and King of kings?
❋ How should our behavior or lifestyle reflect the truth that Jesus is Lord of lords and King of kings?
❋ In what areas of your life do you need more of God's wisdom?

APPLY IT
■ What can you use to remind yourself each day this week of God's rule and superiority over all evil in the world?
❋ What can you do to learn from the wisdom of more mature Christians?

Revelation 18:1-24
The Fall of Babylon

TOPICS
Adultery, Angels, Authority, Consequences, Demons, Immorality, Judgment, Power, Sin, Wealth

OPEN IT
■ Why do you think many people enjoy seeing the rich, the great, and the famous toppled from their lofty pedestals?
❋ What is the most extreme or humiliating fall from power you have ever seen someone undergo?
❋ What place epitomizes evil to you?

EXPLORE IT
❋ What amazing sight did John see? (18:1)
❋ How did John describe the angel he saw coming down from heaven? (18:1)
❋ What pronouncement did the angel bring? (18:2)
❋ Why did the angel say that Babylon was being judged? (18:3)
❋ What did a voice from heaven urge? (18:4)
❋ What specific message of judgment did the angel bring concerning Babylon's sins? (18:5, 8)
■ How will the fall of Babylon affect rulers and merchants all over the earth? (18:9, 11, 15)
■ What will happen to Babylon's wealth? (18:10-19)
❋ Why will the merchants be upset? (18:11-13, 15)
■ Why will the sea captains and sailors be upset over the destruction of Babylon? (18:17-19)
❋ Why will Babylon be judged? (18:20)
❋ What instructions did the angel give for heaven and its inhabitants? (18:20)
❋ Near the end of his vision of Babylon's fall, what did a mighty angel do? (18:21)
❋ What did the mighty angel's action illustrate? (18:21)
❋ How will Babylon be judged? (18:22-23)
❋ What symbol of violence was found in Babylon? (18:24)

GET IT
❋ What is pride and why is it dangerous?
❋ How is your view of God expanded when you read that mere creatures (such as angels) have great authority and splendor?
❋ What do you think Babylon symbolizes or represents?
❋ What warning does the harlot's fate offer us today?
❋ Why do you think the kings, merchants, and sailors are singled out to mourn the great city's fall?
❋ What does the harlot's fate tell you about God? (18:4-8, 20)
■ In what ways can we become ensnared by wealth?
■ What can we do to avoid being slaves to money?

❇ What will be Babylon's most glaring sins?
❇ What worldly attitudes and actions hinder us from having an impact on the world around us?

APPLY IT
❇ What can you do to maintain a spirit of humility as you go about your day?
■ What is one step you can take today to put things and money in proper perspective?
❇ How can you comfort a suffering friend with the message that God sees every injustice and will one day right every wrong?

Revelation 19:1-10
Hallelujah!

TOPICS
Adultery, Angels, Consequences, Demons, Glory, Immorality, Judgment, Justice, Power, Praise, Prophecy, Purity, Salvation, Serving, Worship

OPEN IT
■ What is one of the most memorable weddings or banquets you have ever been to?
❇ Who is one Christian leader or authority that you respect? Why?
❇ What is one hymn, praise chorus, or spiritual song that summarizes how you feel about God?

EXPLORE IT
❇ What was the roar that John heard coming from heaven? (19:1)
❇ Why were the inhabitants of heaven praising God? (19:1-2)
❇ Who shouted? Why? (19:3)
❇ How did the creatures closest to God act? (19:4)
❇ What did the voice from the throne urge? (19:5)
■ Why did the great multitude urge everyone to be happy? How? (19:6-7)
■ In what ways did the bride get ready for the heavenly wedding? (19:7-8)
❇ What is the significance of the fine linen worn by the bride of Christ? (19:8)
■ Who is called "blessed"? (19:9)
❇ How did John respond to the angel who was his "writing instructor"? (19:10)
❇ What was the angel's instruction to John? (19:10)
❇ What did John learn about worship? (19:10)
❇ What did John learn about angels? (19:10)

GET IT
❇ How would you describe the mood in heaven when judgment is done and God prepares to unite believer with Him forever?
❇ What does "hallelujah" mean?
❇ Why do you think "hallelujah" is repeated again and again in heaven?
❇ What is the value in praising God?
❇ What are some of the ways we can praise God?
❇ What difference does it make to you that God's judgments are true and just?
■ What are some implications of the fact that Christ's relationship with the church is described as a marriage?
■ In what ways ought we to act as people "engaged" to Christ?
❇ To what extent are our "wedding garments" earned, and to what extent are they a gift?
❇ Who does God invite to the wedding supper of the Lamb? How?

APPLY IT
■ What is one way you could become a more worshipful person in how you participate in worship services at church?
❇ When, where, and how could you praise God this week?
❇ In what way can you honor Christ in your conversations with others?

Revelation 19:11-21
The Rider on the White Horse

TOPICS
Angels, Death, Enemies, Humiliation, Jesus Christ, Judgment, Last Days, Punishment, Rebellion, Sin, Victory, War

OPEN IT
❇ What is your opinion of (attitude toward, feelings for or against, indifference toward, etc.) horses?
❇ Who do you think is the greatest military leader of all time?
■ How do most people characterize Jesus?
❇ What, to you, is the value of faithfulness?

EXPLORE IT
❇ What did John see in heaven as this portion of his vision began to unfold? (19:11)
❇ What is the name of the individual John saw? (19:11)
■ What is the rider of the white horse like? (19:11-13)
❇ What does the rider of the white horse do? (19:11)
❇ How did John describe the appearance of the rider he saw? (19:12-13, 16)
■ Who followed the rider of the white horse? (19:14)
❇ What did John note about the rider's mouth? (19:15)
❇ What message did an angel deliver? How? (19:17-18)
❇ What will be the main course served to the birds at the great supper of God? (19:17-18)
❇ What battle took place? (19:19-21)
■ Who fought against the rider of the white horse, and what was the outcome? (19:19-21)
❇ Who gathered together? Why? (19:19)
❇ What happened to the beast and the false prophet? (19:20)
❇ What happened to the rest of the those who followed the beast? (19:21)

GET IT
❇ Who is the rider?
■ Why is Jesus depicted as a rider on a white horse?
❇ What impressions of the rider does this passage give you?
❇ How is Jesus described in this passage?
■ What do all the symbols in this passage tell us about Jesus?
❇ What does it mean to be faithful and true?

❇ In what area of your life do you want to build a reputation of being faithful and true?
❇ What is your impression of the battle described in this passage?
❇ How does this snapshot of Christ compare to the typical image most people have of Him?
❇ How do you interpret the place called "the fiery lake of burning sulfur"?
❇ What's the difference between the wedding supper of the Lamb and the great supper of God?
❇ What enables us to be "white and clean" in the sight of God?

APPLY IT
■ For what "confrontations" do you need to prepare this week? How?
❇ How can you develop faithfulness and integrity in your work or home life this week?

Revelation 20:1-6
The Thousand Years

TOPICS
Angels, Authority, Death, Deceit, Enemies, Hell, Jesus Christ, Judgment, Last Days, Punishment, Rebellion, Resurrection, Satan, Victory

OPEN IT
❇ Why do you think our society is growing more and more preoccupied with Satan and the occult?
■ What is your general attitude about politics?
❇ What makes people interested in the future?

EXPLORE IT
❇ What did John see an angel carrying? (20:1)
❇ Whom did the angel seize? (20:2)
❇ By what assorted names did John call the dragon? (20:2)
❇ What did the angel do to the dragon? (20:2)
❇ Where did the angel throw the dragon? (20:3)
❇ For how long was the dragon locked up? (20:3)
❇ What else did John see in his vision? (20:4)
■ Why had some believers died? (20:4)
❇ How had the "beheaded souls" defied the beast? (20:4)
❇ What happened to the martyrs as John watched? (20:4)
■ When would the rest of the dead be resurrected? (20:5)
■ In what way are the people raised in the first resurrection blessed? (20:6)

GET IT
❇ When do you think Christ's reign is—after He takes us to heaven, before He takes us to heaven, or now? Why?
❇ What do you think is the point of God binding Satan and then releasing Him?
❇ Who are the ones seated on thrones and given authority to judge?
❇ In what ways is Satan already bound?
❇ In what ways does Satan appear to be unbound?
■ In what ways do God's people already reign with Christ?
■ How can we show our allegiance to Christ the King over all the earth?
❇ Who notices when we give our allegiance to Christ?

APPLY IT
■ In what ways can you give testimony of God's word to the people you know?
❇ In what concrete ways this week can you resist Satan's attempts to rule in your life?

Revelation 20:7-10
Satan's Doom

TOPICS
Deceit, Enemies, Hell, Jesus Christ, Judgment, Last Days, Punishment, Rebellion, Satan, Victory, War

OPEN IT
■ In literature, movies, or television, who do you think is the all-time worst villain or bad guy?
❇ How likely do you think it is that there will be a nuclear war in your lifetime?

EXPLORE IT
❇ What will happen after the thousand year reign of Christ and His saints? (20:7)
❇ How is the Abyss described? (20:7)
■ What will Satan do right after his release from the Abyss? (20:7-8)
❇ Where will Satan go to find followers? (20:8)
❇ What is Satan's ultimate goal in gathering people at this point? (20:8)
❇ How did John describe those who will be deceived by Satan? (20:8)
■ In John's vision what battle plan did Satan follow in his war against God? (20:9)
❇ What is special about the place where the people of God gathered? (20:9)
■ How did God defeat the armies of Satan? (20:9-10)
❇ Where was Satan dispatched after his defeat? (20:10)
❇ What is Satan's, the beast's, and the false prophet's final destination? (20:10)
❇ What will Satan, the beast, and the false prophet experience in their final destination? (20:10)

GET IT
❇ How does this passage help explain the presence of evil in the universe?
❇ What insights into Satan's nature and character do we gain from this passage?
❇ Why do you think people are so willing to follow a doomed loser like Satan?
❇ Who or what are Gog and Magog?
❇ How are you encouraged by the way God acts on behalf of His people?
❇ Why do you think God is still waiting to judge Satan finally and completely?
❇ Why is it just and fair that Satan will be "tormented day and night for ever and ever"?
❇ How does knowing the end of history affect the way you feel and live in the present?
❇ In what way does Satan try to deceive us?
❇ How does Satan deceive us?
❇ In what areas of your life have you been most susceptible to Satan's deceptions?
❇ What can we do to keep from being deceived by Satan?

■ When are we prone to lose confidence in God's power and authority over Satan and evil?
■ How can we draw encouragement from the certainty of Satan's doom?

APPLY IT
❄ What do you want to remember the next time you are unsure of whether it is worth following Christ?
■ What is one simple way you can remind yourself of God's certain victory over evil?
❄ How can you make a dent today in the large following and the power that Satan possesses and enjoys?
❄ What step of faith do you need to take today in the face of a desperate situation that makes you feel surrounded by the enemy?

Revelation 20:11-15
The Dead Are Judged

TOPICS
Consequences, Death, Earth, Eternal Life, Heaven, Hell, Jesus Christ, Judgment, Last Days, Punishment, Resurrection

OPEN IT
❄ What is your favorite book? Why?
■ What is one time you remember getting in trouble as a child?

EXPLORE IT
❄ What particular vision begins this portion of John's revelation? (20:11)
❄ How will creation react to the "great white throne" judgment? (20:11)
❄ What will be the effect of God's presence on "Earth and sky" at the great white throne judgment? (20:11)
❄ Where will the final judgment of all people take place? (20:11-12)
■ Who will be involved in the final judgment? (20:12)
❄ What records will be used to judge everyone? (20:12)
❄ How does God keep track of what people do in this life? (20:12)
■ On what basis will people be judged at the end of time? (20:12-13)
❄ From what diverse places will the dead assemble for this judgment? (20:13)
❄ What will happen to death and Hades? (20:14)
❄ How did John describe the lake of fire? (20:14)
❄ What will hell be like? (20:14)
■ What will happen to those whose names are not found in the book of life? (20:15)
❄ Who will be thrown into the lake of fire? (20:15)

GET IT
❄ How does a person get his or her name recorded in the book of life?
❄ How is it significant that earth and sky fled from the presence of the one seated on the throne of judgment?
❄ What is the "lake of fire"?
❄ What does it mean that death and Hades "were thrown into the lake of fire"?
❄ What does it mean that "the lake of fire is the second death"?
❄ What is the only way we can escape the lake of fire?
❄ Who are the people whose names are not recorded in the book of life?
■ What is the value in knowing that we will be judged for the way we live?
❄ Why should the certainty of future judgment affect the way we live?
■ How should the certainty of future judgment affect the way we live?

APPLY IT
■ What can you do to remind yourself of the reality of a future judgment?
❄ What step do you need to take today to ensure that your name is written in the book of life?
❄ How can you help a friend or family member avoid a future in the lake of fire?

Revelation 21:1-27
The New Jerusalem

TOPICS
Angels, Death, Earth, Glory, Heaven, Hell, Holiness, Idolatry, Immorality, Jesus Christ, Joy, Light, Mourning, Purity, Unbelievers

OPEN IT
❄ What is the most beautiful place you have ever been?
■ What is one of the happiest or best memories you have?
❄ If you could change one thing about your city, what would you change?
❄ What is the most exotic gem or precious stone you have ever seen?

EXPLORE IT
❄ What did John see once all the judgments had taken place? (21:1)
❄ In his vision, what did John see coming down out of heaven from God? (21:2)
❄ What did the voice that John heard speaking from the throne of God announce? (21:3)
❄ What will life be like in heaven? (21:4)
■ How did the voice from heaven describe the new world to come? (21:4-5)
❄ What did the one on the throne promise to those who are thirsty? (21:6)
❄ What did the one on the throne promise to those who overcome? (21:7)
❄ What fate was assured for those who are evil? (21:8)
❄ What did an angel do with John? Why? (21:9-10)
■ What were some of the more spectacular features of the New Jerusalem that John saw? (21:10-21)
■ In what way will the New Jerusalem reflect God's glory and holiness? (21:21-27)
❄ What did John discover about the temple in the New Jerusalem? (21:22)
❄ What will be the New Jerusalem's source of light? (21:23-24)
❄ How did John describe the New Jerusalem in terms of safety or security? (21:25)
❄ How did John describe the heavenly city in terms of purity? (21:26-27)

GET IT

❇ What are the implications for us that this present earth will pass away?
❇ In what ways is the promise that God will dwell with us meaningful to you?
❇ What does it mean that God will wipe every tear from our eyes?
❇ What kind of thirst does God promise to fill in heaven?
■ Why do you think God revealed so many details about the measurements and appearance of the New Jerusalem?
❇ What does the Bible mean when, speaking about the New Jerusalem, it says, "the Lord God Almighty and the Lamb are its temple"?
❇ What is the Holy City?
❇ What is signified by the fact that the nations will bring their splendor to the Holy City?
❇ How should we act in light of the fact that the God of the universe wants to live in us?
■ How can we prepare ourselves for a place like the New Jerusalem?

APPLY IT

❇ What can you do to remind yourself to be faithful to Lord?
■ How can you remind yourself every day this week of God's promised future for His people?
❇ How can you bring comfort today to someone who is facing death or pain or some other kind of sadness?

Revelation 22:1-6
The River of Life

TOPICS

Angels, Beauty, Glory, Healing, Heaven, Holiness, Jesus Christ, Joy, Light, Purity

OPEN IT

■ What is your favorite fruit? What do you like about it?
❇ Of all the world's great cities that are situated on rivers, which one would you most like to visit? Why?
❇ What disease do you most wish there were a cure for?

EXPLORE IT

❇ What sight did John's heavenly "tour guide" show him? (22:1)
❇ How did John describe the appearance of the river of life? (22:1)
❇ How did John describe the location of the river of life? (22:2)
■ What was growing on each side of the river of life? (22:2)
■ When did the tree that John saw in the city bear fruit? (22:2)
■ Of what value are the leaves on the tree of life? (22:2)
❇ What will be missing from the new heavens and new earth? (22:3)
❇ What will God's people do in heaven? (22:3)
❇ What kind of relationship will God have with His people in heaven? (22:3-4)
❇ Where will the inhabitants of heaven get their light? (22:5)
❇ How long will God's people reign? (22:5)
❇ How did the angel assure John? (22:6)

GET IT

❇ What kind of service will God's people perform in heaven?
❇ What will life be like in heaven?
❇ What do you imagine it will be like to look into the face of the Lord?
❇ Why do you think it is difficult to imagine how wonderful heaven will be?
❇ In what ways does the new Jerusalem restore what God created in the Garden of Eden?
❇ How do you interpret the images "tree of life" and "river of life"?
❇ What is the significance of the water of life and tree of life being in heaven?
■ What does this passage tell us about God?
❇ In what way can a person "wear God's name on his or her forehead"?
❇ To what acts of service does God call us now?
❇ What difference does it make that God has told us what the future holds?
■ How can we honor God as creator and sustainer of life?

APPLY IT

■ How can you honor the life that God created?
❇ What act of service can you do for God this week? How?
❇ What act or deed can you do today as a "mark of ownership" placed on your life by God?

Revelation 22:7-21
Jesus Is Coming

TOPICS

Angels, Eternal Life, Glory, Grace, Heaven, Holiness, Jesus Christ, Prophecy, Sin, Worship

OPEN IT

❇ What nicknames did you or your friends have when you were growing up?
❇ What is your most memorable "returning home" experience?
■ What is one reward you remember getting?

EXPLORE IT

❇ What promise did Christ make? (22:7)
❇ What blessing did Christ promise us? (22:7)
❇ Who did Jesus say is a blessed person? (22:7)
❇ How did the revelations John saw affect him? (22:8)
❇ What command was given to John by his angelic assistant? (22:9)
❇ Why was John commanded not to seal up the prophecies of his book? (22:10)
❇ What additional instructions did the angel give? (22:11)
❇ When Jesus comes, what will He bring with Him? (22:12)
❇ How did Jesus describe Himself? (22:13, 16)
■ Who will be entitled to citizenship in the new Jerusalem? (22:14)
❇ Who will be barred from entering the heavenly city? (22:15)
❇ What is the consequence of living a life of disobedience to God, no matter what it involves? (22:15)
❇ What was Jesus' method for getting His message to us? (22:16)

■ What invitation is given by the Spirit and the bride? (22:17)
❇ What warning did John give? (22:18-19)
■ What do we know for sure about Christ's return? (22:20)
❇ How did John bless his readers? (22:21)

GET IT
❇ How might you react if you were to see an angel?
❇ In what ways do we put Christian leaders on pedestals or revere them too highly?
❇ How can we put believers we respect in proper perspective?
❇ How can a person "keep the words of the prophecy in this book"?
■ What do you think is the point of the angel telling everyone to continue doing what they are doing, whether good or bad?
❇ What does it mean to be thirsty for God?
❇ What does it mean to "wash your robes"?
■ What is involved in responding to God's invitation to come to Him?
❇ What does it mean that "the time is near" and that Christ is "coming soon"?
❇ What do we know about the timing of Christ's return?
❇ What does it mean to add to or take away from God's prophetic word?
❇ How might a person add to or take away from the words of Christ's revelation?
❇ How can we show respect for the revelation Jesus gave us in this book?
❇ How do the self-descriptions of Jesus here change the way you view Him?
❇ How might we bless others with the way we greet or say good-bye to them?

APPLY IT
❇ What are some concrete ways you can show respect for the messages in the Bible?
■ What can you "continue to do right" this week?
❇ What can you do to remind yourself not to put Christian leaders on pedestals or to make them the focus of your praise?
❇ How could you bless others this week with the way you greet or say good-bye to them?

LIST OF TOPICS

A
ABANDON 351
ABILITIES 351
ABORTION 351
ABUNDANCE 351
ACCEPTANCE 351
ACCOMPLISHMENTS 351
ACCOUNTABILITY 351
ACCUSATION 351
ACHIEVEMENTS 351
ACTIONS 351
ADMINISTRATION 351
ADOPTION 351
ADULTERY 351
ADVICE 352
AFFECTIONS 352
AFFIRMATION 352
AGE 352
ALONE 352
AMBASSADORS 352
AMBITION 352
ANGELS 352
ANGER 353
ANSWERS 353
APATHY 353
APPEARANCE 353
APPLICATION 353
APPRECIATION 353
APPROVAL 353
ARGUMENTS 353
ARMOR 353
ASSUMPTIONS 353
ASSURANCE 354
ATONEMENT 354
ATTITUDE 354
AUTHORITY 354
AWE 355

B
BACKSLIDE 355
BALANCE 355
BARGAINING 355
BARRIER 355
BASICS OF THE FAITH 355
BEAUTY 355
BELIEFS 355
BELIEVE 355
BELIEVERS 356
BENEFITS 356
BIBLE 357
BITTERNESS 357
BLASPHEMY 357
BLESSING 357
BLINDNESS 357
BODY 358
BURDENS 358

C
CALL 358
CARELESSNESS 358
CARING 358
CELEBRATION 358
CHALLENGE 358
CHANGE 358
CHARACTER 359
CHILDREN 359
CHOICES 359
CHRISTIANITY 359
CHURCH 359
CIRCUMSTANCES 360
CITIZENSHIP 360
COMFORTABLE 360
COMMITMENT 360
COMPARISONS 360
COMPASSION 361
COMPLACENCY 361
COMPLAINING 361
COMPOSURE 361
COMPROMISE 361
CONFESSION 361
CONFIDENCE 361
CONFLICT 361
CONFUSION 361
CONSCIENCE 362
CONSEQUENCES 362
CONSISTENCY 362
CONTENTMENT 362
CONVERSATION 362
CONVICTIONS 362
CORRECTION 362
COURAGE 362
COVENANT 362
CRAFTSMANSHIP 362
CREATION 362
CRITICISM 363
CULTURE 363
CURIOSITY 363

D
DANGER 363
DARKNESS 363
DEATH 363
DECEIT 364
DECISIONS 364
DEDICATION 364
DELAY 364
DELEGATION 364
DEMONS 364
DENIAL 365
DEPEND 365
DEPRESSION 365
DESIRES 365
DESPAIR 365
DETAILS 365
DETERMINATION 365
DEVOTION 365
DIFFERENCES 365
DIGNITY 365
DIRECTION 365
DISAGREEMENTS 365
DISCERNMENT 366
DISCIPLINE 366
DISCOURAGEMENT 366
DISHONESTY 366
DISOBEDIENCE 366
DIVISIONS 366
DIVORCE 366
DOCTRINE 366
DOUBT 367
DRINKING 367

E
EARTH 367
EFFECTIVENESS 367
EFFORT 367
EGO 367
EMBARRASSMENT 367
EMOTIONS 367
EMPLOYMENT 367
ENCOURAGEMENT 367
ENDURANCE 368
ENEMIES 368
ENTHUSIASM 368
ENVIRONMENT 368
ENVY 368
EQUALITY 368
ESCAPE 368
ETERNAL LIFE 368
EVANGELISM 369
EVIDENCE 369

EVIL 369
EXAMPLE 369
EXCUSES 370
EXPECTATIONS 370
EXPERIENCE 370

F
FAILURE 370
FAIRNESS 370
FAITH 370
FAITHFULNESS 371
FAMILY 371
FASTING 372
FAULTS 372
FAVORITISM 372
FEAR 372
FEELINGS 372
FELLOWSHIP 372
FLATTERY 373
FOLLOW 373
FOLLOW-THROUGH 373
FOOLISHNESS 373
FORGET 373
FORGIVENESS 373
FORSAKE 373
FOUNDATION 373
FREEDOM 373
FRIENDSHIP 373
FRUIT 374
FRUSTRATION 374
FUTURE 374

G
GENEROSITY 374
GENTLENESS 374
GIFTS 374
GIVING UP 374
GLORY 374
GOALS 375
GOD 375
GOD'S WILL 376
GOOD NEWS 376
GOODNESS 377
GOSPEL 377
GOSSIP 377
GOVERNMENT 377
GRACE 377
GREATNESS 378
GREED 378
GRIEF 378
GROWTH 378
GUIDANCE 378
GUILT 378

H
HABITS 378
HANDICAPPED 378
HAPPINESS 378
HARDHEARTEDNESS 378
HATRED 379
HEALING 379
HEALTH 379
HEART 379
HEAVEN 380
HELL 380
HELP 380
HERESY 380
HERITAGE 381
HEROES 381
HIDING 381
HISTORY 381
HOLINESS 381
HOLY SPIRIT 381
HOME 382
HOMOSEXUALITY 382
HONOR 382
HOPE 382
HOPELESSNESS 382
HOSPITALITY 382
HUMANNESS 382
HUMILIATION 382
HUMILITY 382
HUSBANDS 383
HYPOCRISY 383

I
IDOLATRY 383
IGNORANCE 383
IMAGE 384
IMMORALITY 384
IMPORTANT 384
IMPOSSIBLE 384
IMPULSIVENESS 384
INADEQUACY 384
INDIFFERENCE 384
INFLUENCE 384
INITIATIVE 384
INJUSTICE 384
INSECURITY 384
INSENSITIVITY 384
INSIGHT 384
INSPIRATION 384
INSTRUCTIONS 384
INSULTS 385
INTEGRITY 385
INTENTIONS 385
INTERPRETATION 385
INTIMIDATION 385
INVITATION 385
INVOLVEMENT 385
ISOLATION 385

J
JEALOUSY 385
JESUS CHRIST 385
JOBS 387
JOY 387
JUDGING OTHERS 388
JUDGMENT 388
JUSTICE 388

K
KINDNESS 389
KINGDOM OF GOD/ HEAVEN 389
KNOWLEDGE 389

L
LAST DAYS 389
LAW 390
LAZINESS 390
LEADERSHIP 390
LEARNING 390
LEGALISM 391
LIFE 391
LIFE-STYLE 391
LIGHT 391
LIMITATIONS 391
LISTENING 391
LONELINESS 392
LORD'S SUPPER 392
LOST 392
LOVE 392
LOYALTY 392
LUST 393
LYING 393

M
MAJORITY 393
MANAGEMENT 393
MARRIAGE 393
MATERIALISM 393
MATURITY 393
MEDIATOR 393
MERCY 393
MESSIAH 393
MIND 394
MINISTRY 394
MIRACLES 394
MISSION 395
MONEY 395
MORALITY 395
MOTIVES 395
MOURNING 396
MOVING 396
MURDER 396

N
NAME 396
NAMES 396
NATURE 396
NEEDS 396
NEGLECT 396
NEIGHBOR 396
NEW COVENANT 396
NEW LIFE 396

O
OBEDIENCE 396
OBLIGATION 397
OCCULT 397
OPENNESS 397
OPINIONS 397
OPPORTUNITIES 397
OPPOSITION 397
OPPRESSED 397

P
PAIN 398
PARENTS 398
PARTNERSHIPS 398
PASTORS 398
PATIENCE 398
PEACE 398
PEER PRESSURE 398
PEOPLE 398
PERFECT 399
PERSECUTION 399
PERSEVERANCE 399
PERSISTENCE 400
PERSPECTIVE 400
PLANS 400
PLEASURE 400
POOR 400
POPULARITY 400
POSITION 400
POSSESSIONS 400
POWER 400
PRAISE 401
PRAYER 401
PREJUDICE 402
PREPARATION 402
PRESSURE 402
PRIDE 402
PRIORITIES 402
PRIVILEGE 402
PROBLEMS 402
PROCRASTINATION 402
PRODUCTIVITY 402
PROMISES 402
PROPHECY 403
PROTECTION 403
PUNISHMENT 403
PURITY 403
PURPOSE 404

Q
QUALITY 404
QUARRELS 404
QUESTIONS 404
QUIET 404

R
RATIONALIZING 404
READING 404
REBELLION 404
RECONCILIATION 404
REJECTION 404
RELATIONSHIPS 405
RELIABILITY 405
RELIGION 405
REMARRIAGE 405
REMEMBERING 405
RENEWAL 405
REPENTANCE 405
REPRESENTATIVES 406
REPUTATION 406
RESENTMENT 406
RESOURCES 406
RESPECT 406
RESPONSIBILITY 406
REST 406
RESTITUTION 406
RESTORATION 406
RESULTS 406
RESURRECTION 406
REVENGE 407
REWARDS 407
RIGHT 407
RIGHTEOUSNESS 407
RISK 407
RULES 407
RUNNING 407

S
SACRIFICE 407
SALVATION 408
SATAN 408
SATISFACTION 409
SCHEDULE 409
SECOND COMING 409
SECURITY 409
SELF-CENTEREDNESS 409
SELF-ESTEEM 409
SELF-RIGHTEOUSNESS 409
SELFISHNESS 409
SENSITIVITY 409
SEPARATION 410
SERVING 410
SEX 410
SHAME 410
SICKNESS 410
SILENCE 410
SIMPLICITY 410
SIN 410
SINCERITY 411
SINGLENESS 411
SLAVERY 411
SLEEP 412
SOCIETY 412
SOLITUDE 412
SORROW 412
SOUL 412
SOVEREIGNTY 412
SPIRITUAL DISCIPLINES 412
SPIRITUAL GIFTS 412
SPIRITUAL GROWTH 412
SPIRITUAL REBIRTH 412
STATUS 412
STRENGTH 412
STRESS 412
STUBBORNNESS 413
SUBMISSION 413
SUCCESS 413
SUFFERING 413
SURPRISES 413
SWEARING 413

T
TASKS 413
TEACHING 413
TEAMWORK 414
TEMPTATION 414
TESTING 414
THANKFULNESS 414
THINKING 414
TIMING 414
TITHING 415
TOLERATION 415
TRADITIONS 415
TRAINING 415
TRUST 415
TRUTH 415

U
UNBELIEVERS 415
UNDERSTANDING 416
UNFAIRNESS 416
UNFAITHFULNESS 416
UNITY 416

V
VALUE 416
VICTORY 416
VOWS 417

W
WAITING 417
WAR 417
WEAKNESSES 417
WEALTH 417
WISDOM 417
WITNESSING 417
WIVES 418
WORDS 418
WORK 418
WORLD 418
WORRY 419
WORSHIP 419

Y
YOUTH 419

Z
ZEAL 419

TOPICAL INDEX

■ **ABANDON**
1 Timothy 4:1-16 - Instructions to Timothy
2 Peter 2:1-22 - False Teachers and Their Destruction
2 Timothy 1:1–2:13 - Encouragement to Be Faithful
2 Timothy 4:9-22 - Personal Remarks
John 6:60-71 - Many Disciples Desert Jesus
Matthew 8:18-22 - The Cost of Following Jesus
Matthew 26:14-16 - Judas Agrees to Betray Jesus
Matthew 26:31-35 - Jesus Predicts Peter's Denial

■ **ABILITIES**
1 Timothy 3:1-16 - Overseers and Deacons
1 Timothy 4:1-16 - Instructions to Timothy
John 9:1-12 - Jesus Heals a Man Born Blind
Matthew 17:14-23 - The Healing of a Boy With a Demon

■ **ABORTION**
Matthew 1:18-25 - The Birth of Jesus Christ
Matthew 5:13-16 - Salt and Light

■ **ABUNDANCE**
John 21:1-14 - Jesus and the Miraculous Catch of Fish
Luke 8:16-18 - A Lamp on a Stand
Luke 12:13-21 - The Parable of the Rich Fool
Mark 8:1-13 - Jesus Feeds the Four Thousand
Philippians 4:10-23 - Thanks for Their Gifts

■ **ACCEPTANCE**
1 Corinthians 16:5-24 - Personal Requests
Acts 10:9-23 - Peter's Vision
Acts 10:24-48 - Peter at Cornelius' House
John 6:25-59 - Jesus the Bread of Life
John 7:45-52 - Unbelief of the Jewish Leaders
John 9:35-41 - Spiritual Blindness
John 12:37-50 - The Jews Continue in Their Unbelief
John 13:18-30 - Jesus Predicts His Betrayal
John 18:28-40 - Jesus Before Pilate
Luke 4:14-30 - Jesus Rejected at Nazareth
Luke 5:12-16 - The Man With Leprosy
Luke 5:27-32 - The Calling of Levi
Luke 6:37-42 - Judging Others
Matthew 13:53-58 - A Prophet Without Honor
Matthew 21:1-11 - The Triumphal Entry
Romans 14:1-15:13 - The Weak and the Strong

■ **ACCOMPLISHMENTS**
Luke 6:46-49 - The Wise and Foolish Builders
Matthew 25:14-30 - The Parable of the Talents
Philippians 3:1-11 - No Confidence in the Flesh
Revelation 2:1-7 - To the Church in Ephesus
Revelation 2:8-11 - To the Church in Smyrna

■ **ACCOUNTABILITY**
1 Timothy 3:1-16 - Overseers and Deacons
Luke 3:1-20 - John the Baptist Prepares the Way
Luke 19:11-27 - The Parable of the Ten Minas
Mark 4:21-25 - A Lamp on a Stand
Mark 9:42-50 - Causing to Sin
Matthew 25:14-30 - The Parable of the Talents
Romans 3:9-20 - No One Is Righteous

■ **ACCUSATION**
Acts 3:11-26 - Peter Speaks to the Onlookers
Acts 5:1-11 - Ananias and Sapphira
Acts 6:8-15 - Stephen Seized
Acts 7:1-53 - Stephen's Speech to the Sanhedrin
Acts 22:30–23:11 - Before the Sanhedrin
Acts 23:23-35 - Paul Transferred to Caesarea
Acts 24:1-27 - The Trial Before Felix
Acts 25:1-12 - The Trial Before Festus
Acts 25:13-22 - Festus Consults King Agrippa
Acts 25:23–26:32 - Paul Before Agrippa
John 7:53-8:11 - A Woman Caught in Adultery
John 8:48-59 - The Claims of Jesus About Himself
Luke 6:1-11 - Lord of the Sabbath
Luke 6:37-42 - Judging Others
Luke 22:66–23:25 - Jesus Before Pilate and Herod
Matthew 13:53-58 - A Prophet Without Honor
Matthew 18:15-20 - A Brother Who Sins Against You
Matthew 21:12-17 - Jesus at the Temple
Matthew 22:15-22 - Paying Taxes to Caesar
Matthew 26:57-68 - Before the Sanhedrin
Matthew 26:69-75 - Peter Disowns Jesus
Matthew 27:11-26 - Jesus Before Pilate
Matthew 27:27-31 - The Soldiers Mock Jesus
Revelation 12:1–13:1 - The Woman and the Dragon

■ **ACHIEVEMENTS**
Luke 4:14-30 - Jesus Rejected at Nazareth

■ **ACTIONS**
Acts 3:1-10 - Peter Heals the Crippled Beggar
Colossians 3:1-17 - Rules for Holy Living
James 2:14-26 - Faith and Deeds
Luke 2:8-20 - The Shepherds and the Angels
Luke 2:21-40 - Jesus Presented in the Temple
Luke 3:1-20 - John the Baptist Prepares the Way
Luke 4:38-44 - Jesus Heals Many
Luke 5:12-16 - The Man With Leprosy
Luke 5:27-32 - The Calling of Levi
Luke 5:33-39 - Jesus Questioned About Fasting
Luke 6:27-36 - Love for Enemies
Luke 6:46-49 - The Wise and Foolish Builders
Matthew 26:6-13 - Jesus Anointed at Bethany
Matthew 27:1-10 - Judas Hangs Himself
Matthew 27:57-61 - The Burial of Jesus

■ **ADMINISTRATION**
1 Timothy 3:1-16 - Overseers and Deacons

■ **ADOPTION**
Ephesians 1:1-14 - Spiritual Blessings in Christ
Matthew 1:18-25 - The Birth of Jesus Christ

■ **ADULTERY**
1 Corinthians 6:12-20 - Sexual Immorality

1 Timothy 1:1-11 - Warning Against False Teachers of the Law
John 7:53-8:11 - A Woman Caught in Adultery
Luke 16:16-18 - Additional Teachings
Mark 10:1-12 - Divorce
Matthew 5:27-30 - Adultery
Matthew 5:31-32 - Divorce
Matthew 14:1-12 - John the Baptist Beheaded
Revelation 18:1-24 - The Fall of Babylon
Revelation 19:1-10 - Hallelujah!

■ **ADVICE**

1 Thessalonians 5:12-28 - Final Instructions
Acts 15:22-35 - The Council's Letter to Gentile Believers
Acts 21:1-16 - On to Jerusalem
Acts 25:13-22 - Festus Consults King Agrippa
Acts 25:23–26:32 - Paul Before Agrippa
Acts 27:1-12 - Paul Sails for Rome
Luke 1:39-45 - Mary Visits Elizabeth
Luke 20:41-47 - Whose Son Is the Christ?

■ **AFFECTIONS**

1 John 2:15-17 - Do Not Love the World
2 Corinthians 6:3-13 - Paul's Hardships
John 13:18-30 - Jesus Predicts His Betrayal
John 20:10-18 - Jesus Appears to Mary Magdalene
Luke 14:25-35 - The Cost of Being a Disciple
Matthew 12:46-50 - Jesus' Mother and Brothers
Matthew 16:21-28 - Jesus Predicts His Death
Revelation 2:1-7 - To the Church in Ephesus

■ **AFFIRMATION**

Luke 1:39-45 - Mary Visits Elizabeth
Luke 2:21-40 - Jesus Presented in the Temple
Luke 3:21-38 - The Baptism and Genealogy of Jesus
Luke 7:1-10 - The Faith of the Centurion
Mark 1:9-13 - The Baptism and Temptation of Jesus
Romans 1:1-7 - Introduction

■ **AGE**

Luke 1:5-25 - The Birth of John the Baptist Foretold
Luke 1:39-45 - Mary Visits Elizabeth
Luke 2:21-40 - Jesus Presented in the Temple

■ **ALONE**

Luke 4:1-13 - The Temptation of Jesus
Luke 5:12-16 - The Man With Leprosy
Luke 6:12-16 - The Twelve Apostles
Mark 1:35-39 - Jesus Prays in a Solitary Place
Matthew 8:1-4 - The Man With Leprosy

■ **AMBASSADORS**

2 Corinthians 5:11–6:2 - The Ministry of Reconciliation
Luke 2:8-20 - The Shepherds and the Angels
Matthew 9:9-13 - The Calling of Matthew
Matthew 9:35-38 - The Workers Are Few
Matthew 10:1-42 - Jesus Sends Out the Twelve
Matthew 22:1-14 - The Parable of the Wedding Banquet
Revelation 11:1-14 - The Two Witnesses
Revelation 14:1-5 - The Lamb and the 144,000
Revelation 17:1-18 - The Woman on the Beast
Romans 1:1-7 - Introduction

■ **AMBITION**

1 Thessalonians 4:1-12 - Living to Please God
1 Timothy 3:1-16 - Overseers and Deacons
2 Timothy 3:1-9 - Godlessness in the Last Days
3 John 1-14 - From the Elder
James 3:13-18 - Two Kinds of Wisdom
James 4:13-17 - Boasting About Tomorrow
John 11:45-57 - The Plot to Kill Jesus
John 13:1-17 - Jesus Washes His Disciples' Feet
John 18:28-40 - Jesus Before Pilate
Luke 9:46-50 - Who Will Be the Greatest?
Matthew 20:20-28 - A Mother's Request
Romans 15:14-22 - Paul, the Minister to the Gentiles
Romans 15:23-33 - Paul's Plan to Visit Rome

■ **ANGELS**

1 Corinthians 6:1-11 - Lawsuits Among Believers
1 Corinthians 11:2-16 - Propriety in Worship
2 Peter 2:1-22 - False Teachers and Their Destruction
Acts 1:1-11 - Jesus Taken Up Into Heaven
Acts 5:17-41 - The Apostles Persecuted
Acts 8:26-40 - Philip and the Ethiopian
Acts 10:1-8 - Cornelius Calls for Peter
Acts 11:1-18 - Peter Explains His Actions
Acts 12:1-19 - Peter's Miraculous Escape From Prison
Acts 12:20-25 - Herod's Death
Acts 22:30–23:11 - Before the Sanhedrin
Colossians 2:6-23 - Freedom From Human Regulations Through Life With Christ
Galatians 1:1-10 - No Other Gospel
Hebrews 1:1-14 - The Son Superior to Angels
Hebrews 2:1-4 - Warning to Pay Attention
Hebrews 2:5-18 - Jesus Made Like His Brothers
Hebrews 12:14-29 - Warning Against Refusing God
Hebrews 13:1-25 - Concluding Exhortations
John 1:43-51 - Jesus Calls Philip and Nathanael
John 20:10-18 - Jesus Appears to Mary Magdalene
Jude 1-16 - The Sin and Doom of Godless Men
Luke 1:5-25 - The Birth of John the Baptist Foretold
Luke 1:26-38 - The Birth of Jesus Foretold
Luke 2:8-20 - The Shepherds and the Angels
Luke 16:19-31 - The Rich Man and Lazarus
Luke 20:27-40 - The Resurrection and Marriage
Luke 22:39-46 - Jesus Prays on the Mount of Olives
Luke 24:1-12 - The Resurrection
Luke 24:13-35 - On the Road to Emmaus
Mark 1:9-13 - The Baptism and Temptation of Jesus
Mark 12:18-27 - Marriage at the Resurrection
Mark 13:32-37 - The Day and Hour Unknown
Matthew 1:18-25 - The Birth of Jesus Christ
Matthew 4:1-11 - The Temptation of Jesus
Matthew 13:36-43 - The Parable of the Weeds Explained
Matthew 13:47-52 - The Parable of the Net
Matthew 16:21-28 - Jesus Predicts His Death
Matthew 18:10-14 - The Parable of the Lost Sheep
Matthew 22:23-33 - Marriage at the Resurrection
Matthew 24:1-35 - Signs of the End of the Age
Matthew 25:31-46 - The Sheep and the Goats
Matthew 28:1-10 - The Resurrection
Revelation 1:1-3 - Prologue
Revelation 1:9-20 - One Like a Son of Man
Revelation 2:1-7 - To the Church in Ephesus
Revelation 2:8-11 - To the Church in Smyrna
Revelation 2:12-17 - To the Church in Pergamum
Revelation 2:18-29 - To the Church in Thyatira
Revelation 3:1-6 - To the Church in Sardis
Revelation 3:7-13 - To the Church in Philadelphia
Revelation 3:14-22 - To the Church in Laodicea

Revelation 5:1-14 - The Scroll and the Lamb
Revelation 7:1-8 - 144,000 Sealed
Revelation 7:9-17 - The Great Multitude in White Robes
Revelation 8:1-5 - The Seventh Seal and the Golden Censer
Revelation 8:6–9:21 - The Trumpets
Revelation 10:1-11 - The Angel and the Little Scroll
Revelation 11:1-14 - The Two Witnesses
Revelation 11:15-19 - The Seventh Trumpet
Revelation 12:1-13:1 - The Woman and the Dragon
Revelation 14:6-13 - The Three Angels
Revelation 14:14-20 - The Harvest of the Earth
Revelation 15:1-8 - Seven Angels With Seven Plagues
Revelation 16:1-21 - The Seven Bowls of God's Wrath
Revelation 17:1-18 - The Woman on the Beast
Revelation 18:1-24 - The Fall of Babylon
Revelation 19:1-10 - Hallelujah!
Revelation 19:11-21 - The Rider on the White Horse
Revelation 20:1-6 - The Thousand Years
Revelation 21:1-27 - The New Jerusalem
Revelation 22:1-6 - The River of Life
Revelation 22:7-21 - Jesus Is Coming
Romans 8:28-39 - More Than Conquerors

■ **ANGER**

1 Timothy 3:1-16 - Overseers and Deacons
Acts 7:54-8:1 - The Stoning of Stephen
Acts 22:22-29 - Paul the Roman Citizen
Ephesians 4:17–5:21 - Living as Children of Light
Galatians 1:1-10 - No Other Gospel
Hebrews 3:7-19 - Warning Against Unbelief
Hebrews 4:1-13 - A Sabbath-Rest for the People of God
James 1:19-27 - Listening and Doing
John 11:17-37 - Jesus Comforts the Sisters
Luke 4:14-30 - Jesus Rejected at Nazareth
Luke 14:15-24 - The Parable of the Great Banquet
Luke 19:45-48 - Jesus at the Temple
Mark 11:12-19 - Jesus Clears the Temple
Matthew 2:13-18 - The Escape to Egypt
Matthew 5:21-26 - Murder
Matthew 20:20-28 - A Mother's Request
Revelation 14:14-20 - The Harvest of the Earth
Revelation 15:1-8 - Seven Angels With Seven Plagues
Revelation 16:1-21 - The Seven Bowls of God's Wrath

■ **ANSWERS**

1 Peter 3:8-22 - Suffering for Doing Good
James 5:13-20 - The Prayer of Faith
John 14:5-14 - Jesus the Way to the Father
Luke 1:1-4 - Introduction
Luke 1:5-25 - The Birth of John the Baptist Foretold
Luke 1:57-66 - The Birth of John the Baptist
Luke 4:1-13 - The Temptation of Jesus
Luke 7:1-10 - The Faith of the Centurion
Luke 22:66–23:25 - Jesus Before Pilate and Herod
Mark 11:20-26 - The Withered Fig Tree
Matthew 15:21-28 - The Faith of the Canaanite Woman
Matthew 16:1-4 - The Demand for a Sign
Matthew 22:34-40 - The Greatest Commandment
Matthew 22:41-46 - Whose Son Is the Christ?
Matthew 27:11-26 - Jesus Before Pilate
Matthew 28:11-15 - The Guards' Report

■ **APATHY**

Matthew 22:1-14 - The Parable of the Wedding Banquet
Revelation 3:14-22 - To the Church in Laodicea

■ **APPEARANCE**

1 Corinthians 11:2-16 - Propriety in Worship
1 Peter 3:1-7 - Wives and Husbands
1 Timothy 2:1-15 - Instructions on Worship
John 7:14-24 - Jesus Teaches at the Feast
Luke 3:1-20 - John the Baptist Prepares the Way
Matthew 13:24-30 - The Parable of the Weeds
Matthew 15:1-20 - Clean and Unclean
Matthew 17:1-13 - The Transfiguration
Matthew 21:18-22 - The Fig Tree Withers
Matthew 23:1-39 - Seven Woes

■ **APPLICATION**

Luke 4:1-13 - The Temptation of Jesus
Luke 6:43-45 - A Tree and Its Fruit
Matthew 18:21-35 - The Parable of the Unmerciful Servant

■ **APPRECIATION**

John 6:1-15 - Jesus Feeds the Five Thousand
Luke 1:39-45 - Mary Visits Elizabeth
Luke 1:46-56 - Mary's Song
Luke 1:57-66 - The Birth of John the Baptist
Luke 1:67-80 - Zechariah's Song
Luke 7:1-10 - The Faith of the Centurion
Matthew 20:1-16 - The Parable of the Workers in the Vineyard
Romans 16:1-27 - Personal Greetings

■ **APPROVAL**

2 Timothy 2:14-26 - A Workman Approved by God
Galatians 1:1-10 - No Other Gospel
Galatians 2:1-10 - Paul Accepted by the Apostles
Mark 1:9-13 - The Baptism and Temptation of Jesus
Matthew 10:1-42 - Jesus Sends Out the Twelve
Matthew 21:1-11 - The Triumphal Entry
Matthew 25:14-30 - The Parable of the Talents
Revelation 2:1-7 - To the Church in Ephesus
Revelation 2:8-11 - To the Church in Smyrna
Romans 2:17-29 - The Jews and the Law

■ **ARGUMENTS**

1 Corinthians 1:10-17 - Divisions in the Church
2 Timothy 2:14-26 - A Workman Approved by God
Acts 17:16-34 - In Athens
Acts 19:23-41 - The Riot in Ephesus
Luke 9:46-50 - Who Will Be the Greatest?
Luke 12:54-59 - Interpreting the Times
Mark 9:33-37 - Who Is the Greatest?
Mark 9:38-41 - Whoever Is Not Against Us Is for Us
Matthew 12:38-45 - The Sign of Jonah
Philippians 2:12-18 - Shining as Stars

■ **ARMOR**

2 Corinthians 10:1-18 - Paul's Defense of His Ministry
Ephesians 6:10-24 - The Armor of God
Mark 14:43-52 - Jesus Arrested

■ **ASSUMPTIONS**

Acts 21:27-36 - Paul Arrested
Acts 28:1-10 - Ashore on Malta
John 7:14-24 - Jesus Teaches at the Feast
Mark 10:13-16 - The Little Children and Jesus
Matthew 11:1-19 - Jesus and John the Baptist
Matthew 16:13-20 - Peter's Confession of Christ
Matthew 22:23-33 - Marriage at the Resurrection

■ ASSURANCE

1 Peter 1:1-12 - Praise to God for a Living Hope
1 Thessalonians 4:13–5:11 - The Coming of the Lord
2 Peter 1:1-11 - Making One's Calling and Election Sure
2 Thessalonians 1:1-12 - Thanksgiving and Prayer
Acts 12:1-19 - Peter's Miraculous Escape From Prison
Hebrews 6:13-20 - The Certainty of God's Promise
John 2:1-11 - Jesus Changes Water to Wine
John 3:1-22 - Jesus Teaches Nicodemus
John 3:22-36 - John the Baptist's Testimony About Jesus
John 5:16-30 - Life Through the Son
John 5:31-47 - Testimonies About Jesus
John 6:25-59 - Jesus the Bread of Life
John 10:22-42 - The Unbelief of the Jews
John 14:1-4 - Jesus Comforts His Disciples
John 14:15-31 - Jesus Promises the Holy Spirit
John 16:17-33 - The Disciples' Grief Will Turn to Joy
Luke 1:1-4 - Introduction
Luke 1:46-56 - Mary's Song

■ ATONEMENT

1 John 1:5–2:14 - Walking in the Light
1 John 4:7-21 - God's Love and Ours
1 Peter 1:13–2:3 - Be Holy
1 Peter 2:13-25 - Submission to Rulers and Masters
1 Peter 3:8-22 - Suffering for Doing Good
1 Timothy 1:12-20 - The Lord's Grace to Paul
1 Timothy 2:1-15 - Instructions on Worship
Hebrews 2:5-18 - Jesus Made Like His Brothers
Hebrews 7:11-28 - Jesus Like Melchizedek
Hebrews 9:1-10 - Worship in the Earthly Tabernacle
Hebrews 9:11-28 - The Blood of Christ
Hebrews 10:1-18 - Christ's Sacrifice Once for All
Hebrews 10:19-39 - A Call to Persevere
Hebrews 13:1-25 - Concluding Exhortations
John 18:12-14 - Jesus Taken to Annas
John 19:17-27 - The Crucifixion
John 19:28-37 - The Death of Jesus
Mark 15:21-32 - The Crucifixion
Matthew 17:14-23 - The Healing of a Boy With a Demon
Matthew 20:20-28 - A Mother's Request
Matthew 26:17-30 - The Lord's Supper
Matthew 27:32-44 - The Crucifixion
Matthew 27:45-56 - The Death of Jesus
Revelation 5:1-14 - The Scroll and the Lamb
Revelation 7:9-17 - The Great Multitude in White Robes
Revelation 12:1–13:1 - The Woman and the Dragon
Romans 3:21-31 - Righteousness Through Faith

■ ATTITUDE

1 Peter 3:1-7 - Wives and Husbands
1 Peter 4:1-11 - Living for God
1 Timothy 6:3-10 - Love of Money
3 John 1-14 - From the Elder
James 4:1-12 - Submit Yourselves to God
James 5:7-12 - Patience in Suffering
John 1:19-28 - John the Baptist Denies Being the Christ
John 2:12-25 - Jesus Clears the Temple
John 4:43-54 - Jesus Heals the Official's Son
John 5:1-15 - The Healing at the Pool
John 6:25-59 - Jesus the Bread of Life
John 13:1-17 - Jesus Washes His Disciples' Feet
Luke 1:26-38 - The Birth of Jesus Foretold
Luke 1:46-56 - Mary's Song
Luke 5:12-16 - The Man With Leprosy
Luke 7:1-10 - The Faith of the Centurion
Mark 7:1-23 - Clean and Unclean
Mark 12:41-44 - The Widow's Offering
Matthew 7:24-29 - The Wise and Foolish Builders
Matthew 8:1-4 - The Man With Leprosy
Matthew 16:1-4 - The Demand for a Sign
Matthew 18:21-35 - The Parable of the Unmerciful Servant
Matthew 21:33-46 - The Parable of the Tenants
Matthew 22:1-14 - The Parable of the Wedding Banquet
Matthew 22:34-40 - The Greatest Commandment
Romans 11:11-24 - Ingrafted Branches

■ AUTHORITY

1 Corinthians 11:2-16 - Propriety in Worship
1 Peter 2:13-25 - Submission to Rulers and Masters
1 Timothy 2:1-15 - Instructions on Worship
1 Timothy 3:1-16 - Overseers and Deacons
2 Corinthians 13:1-14 - Final Warnings
Acts 1:12-26 - Matthias Chosen to Replace Judas
Acts 3:1-10 - Peter Heals the Crippled Beggar
Acts 3:11-26 - Peter Speaks to the Onlookers
Acts 4:1-22 - Peter and John Before the Sanhedrin
Acts 4:23-31 - The Believers' Prayer
Acts 16:16-40 - Paul and Silas in Prison
Colossians 2:6-23 - Freedom From Human Regulations Through Life With Christ
Ephesians 1:15-23 - Thanksgiving and Prayer
John 2:12-25 - Jesus Clears the Temple
John 5:31-47 - Testimonies About Jesus
John 7:45-52 - Unbelief of the Jewish Leaders
John 8:12-30 - The Validity of Jesus' Testimony
John 8:48-59 - The Claims of Jesus About Himself
John 17:1-5 - Jesus Prays for Himself
John 18:12-14 - Jesus Taken to Annas
John 18:19-24 - The High Priest Questions Jesus
Luke 1:1-4 - Introduction
Luke 3:1-20 - John the Baptist Prepares the Way
Luke 4:31-37 - Jesus Drives Out an Evil Spirit
Luke 5:17-26 - Jesus Heals a Paralytic
Luke 7:1-10 - The Faith of the Centurion
Luke 12:1-12 - Warnings and Encouragements
Luke 20:1-8 - The Authority of Jesus Questioned
Mark 1:29-34 - Jesus Heals Many
Mark 2:1-12 - Jesus Heals a Paralytic
Mark 3:13-19 - The Appointing of the Twelve Apostles
Mark 6:7-13 - Jesus Sends Out the Twelve
Mark 10:35-45 - The Request of James and John
Mark 11:27-33 - The Authority of Jesus Questioned
Mark 12:13-17 - Paying Taxes to Caesar
Mark 12:35-40 - Whose Son Is the Christ?
Matthew 5:17-20 - The Fulfillment of the Law
Matthew 8:5-13 - The Faith of the Centurion
Matthew 9:1-8 - Jesus Heals a Paralytic
Matthew 17:14-23 - The Healing of a Boy With a Demon
Matthew 18:15-20 - A Brother Who Sins Against You
Matthew 20:20-28 - A Mother's Request
Matthew 21:12-17 - Jesus at the Temple
Matthew 21:23-27 - The Authority of Jesus Questioned
Matthew 27:11-26 - Jesus Before Pilate
Matthew 27:27-31 - The Soldiers Mock Jesus
Matthew 27:62-66 - The Guard at the Tomb

Matthew 28:16-20 - The Great Commission
Revelation 2:18-29 - To the Church in Thyatira
Revelation 13:2-10 - The Beast out of the Sea
Revelation 13:11-18 - The Beast out of the Earth
Revelation 17:1-18 - The Woman on the Beast
Revelation 18:1-24 - The Fall of Babylon
Revelation 20:1-6 - The Thousand Years
Romans 13:1-7 - Submission to the Authorities
Titus 2:1-15 - What Must Be Taught to Various Groups
Titus 3:1-15 - Doing What Is Good

■ AWE

Acts 2:1-13 - The Holy Spirit Comes at Pentecost
Acts 8:9-25 - Simon the Sorcerer
John 18:1-11 - Jesus Arrested
Luke 1:46-56 - Mary's Song
Luke 1:57-66 - The Birth of John the Baptist
Luke 2:8-20 - The Shepherds and the Angels
Luke 4:31-37 - Jesus Drives Out an Evil Spirit
Luke 5:1-11 - The Calling of the First Disciples
Luke 7:11-17 - Jesus Raises a Widow's Son
Matthew 9:27-34 - Jesus Heals the Blind and Mute
Matthew 24:1-35 - Signs of the End of the Age

■ BACKSLIDE

2 Peter 2:1-22 - False Teachers and Their Destruction
2 Timothy 1:1–2:13 - Encouragement to Be Faithful
Hebrews 2:1-4 - Warning to Pay Attention
Hebrews 5:11–6:12 - Warning Against Falling Away
Hebrews 10:19-39 - A Call to Persevere
James 5:13-20 - The Prayer of Faith
John 18:25-27 - Peter's Second and Third Denials
Matthew 9:9-13 - The Calling of Matthew
Matthew 24:1-35 - Signs of the End of the Age
Matthew 26:36-46 - Gethsemane
Matthew 26:69-75 - Peter Disowns Jesus
Revelation 2:1-7 - To the Church in Ephesus

■ BALANCE

Matthew 11:25-30 - Rest for the Weary

■ BARGAINING

Luke 22:1-6 - Judas Agrees to Betray Jesus

■ BARRIER

Hebrews 12:1-3 - God Disciplines His Sons
Luke 5:17-26 - Jesus Heals a Paralytic
Matthew 8:18-22 - The Cost of Following Jesus
Matthew 16:1-4 - The Demand for a Sign
Matthew 20:17-19 - Jesus Again Predicts His Death
Matthew 23:1-39 - Seven Woes

■ BASICS OF THE FAITH

1 John 1:1-4 - The Word of Life
1 John 2:28–3:10 - Children of God
1 John 3:11-24 - Love One Another
1 John 4:1-6 - Test the Spirits
1 John 5:1-12 - Faith in the Son of God
1 Peter 1:13–2:3 - Be Holy
1 Timothy 1:1-11 - Warning Against False Teachers of the Law
1 Timothy 1:12-20 - The Lord's Grace to Paul
1 Timothy 2:1-15 - Instructions on Worship
2 Peter 1:12-21 - Prophecy of Scripture
2 Peter 3:1-18 - The Day of the Lord
2 Timothy 3:10–4:8 - Paul's Charge to Timothy
Acts 2:14-41 - Peter Addresses the Crowd
Hebrews 1:1-14 - The Son Superior to Angels
John 3:1-22 - Jesus Teaches Nicodemus
John 13:31-38 - Jesus Predicts Peter's Denial
John 14:5-14 - Jesus the Way to the Father
John 20:1-9 - The Empty Tomb
Luke 6:17-26 - Blessings and Woes
Mark 10:17-31 - The Rich Young Man
Matthew 16:21-28 - Jesus Predicts His Death
Matthew 28:1-10 - The Resurrection
Romans 3:9-20 - No One Is Righteous

■ BEAUTY

1 Peter 3:1-7 - Wives and Husbands
Mark 14:1-11 - Jesus Anointed at Bethany
Revelation 22:1-6 - The River of Life

■ BELIEFS

1 Peter 3:8-22 - Suffering for Doing Good
1 Timothy 1:1-11 - Warning Against False Teachers of the Law
1 Timothy 1:12-20 - The Lord's Grace to Paul
Acts 25:23–26:32 - Paul Before Agrippa
John 4:39-42 - Many Samaritans Believe
John 14:5-14 - Jesus the Way to the Father
John 19:1-16 - Jesus Sentenced to be Crucified
John 19:28-37 - The Death of Jesus
Luke 8:40-56 - A Dead Girl and a Sick Woman
Luke 9:18-27 - Peter's Confession of Christ
Luke 13:18-21 - The Parables of the Mustard Seed and the Yeast
Mark 8:27-30 - Peter's Confession of Christ
Matthew 11:1-19 - Jesus and John the Baptist
Matthew 16:5-12 - The Yeast of the Pharisees and Sadducees
Matthew 16:13-20 - Peter's Confession of Christ
Matthew 22:23-33 - Marriage at the Resurrection
Romans 2:17-29 - The Jews and the Law

■ BELIEVE

1 John 5:1-12 - Faith in the Son of God
1 John 5:13-21 - Concluding Remarks
1 Peter 1:1-12 - Praise to God for a Living Hope
1 Peter 1:13–2:3 - Be Holy
1 Peter 3:1-7 - Wives and Husbands
1 Timothy 4:1-16 - Instructions to Timothy
Acts 11:19-30 - The Church in Antioch
Acts 13:4-12 - On Cyprus
Acts 13:13-52 - In Pisidian Antioch
Acts 14:1-7 - In Iconium
Acts 17:10-15 - In Berea
Acts 17:16-34 - In Athens
Acts 18:1-17 - In Corinth
Acts 18:18-28 - Priscilla, Aquila and Apollos
Acts 19:1-22 - Paul in Ephesus
Acts 28:17-31 - Paul Preaches at Rome Under Guard
Galatians 3:1-14 - Faith or Observance of the Law
Galatians 3:15-25 - The Law and the Promise
Hebrews 6:13-20 - The Certainty of God's Promise
James 1:1-18 - Trials and Temptations
John 1:1-19 - The Word Became Flesh
John 1:43-51 - Jesus Calls Philip and Nathanael
John 2:12-25 - Jesus Clears the Temple
John 3:1-22 - Jesus Teaches Nicodemus
John 3:22-36 - John the Baptist's Testimony About Jesus
John 4:39-42 - Many Samaritans Believe

John 4:43-54 - Jesus Heals the Official's Son
John 5:16-30 - Life Through the Son
John 5:31-47 - Testimonies About Jesus
John 6:25-59 - Jesus the Bread of Life
John 6:60-71 - Many Disciples Desert Jesus
John 7:1-13 - Jesus Goes to the Feast of Tabernacles
John 7:25-44 - Is Jesus the Christ?
John 8:12-30 - The Validity of Jesus' Testimony
John 8:31-41 - The Children of Abraham
John 8:42-47 - The Children of the Devil
John 8:48-59 - The Claims of Jesus About Himself
John 9:13-34 - The Pharisees Investigate the Healing
John 9:35-41 - Spiritual Blindness
John 10:22-42 - The Unbelief of the Jews
John 11:1-16 - The Death of Lazarus
John 11:17-37 - Jesus Comforts the Sisters
John 11:38-44 - Jesus Raises Lazarus From the Dead
John 11:45-57 - The Plot to Kill Jesus
John 12:37-50 - The Jews Continue in Their Unbelief
John 14:5-14 - Jesus the Way to the Father
John 16:17-33 - The Disciples' Grief Will Turn to Joy
John 19:28-37 - The Death of Jesus
John 19:38-42 - The Burial of Jesus
John 20:1-9 - The Empty Tomb
John 20:24-31 - Jesus Appears to Thomas
Luke 1:1-4 - Introduction
Luke 5:12-16 - The Man With Leprosy
Luke 9:37-45 - The Healing of a Boy With an Evil Spirit
Luke 13:18-21 - The Parables of the Mustard Seed and the Yeast
Luke 13:22-30 - The Narrow Door
Luke 24:1-12 - The Resurrection
Luke 24:13-35 - On the Road to Emmaus
Luke 24:36-49 - Jesus Appears to the Disciples
Mark 1:14-20 - The Calling of the First Disciples
Mark 5:21-43 - A Dead Girl and a Sick Woman
Mark 9:14-32 - The Healing of a Boy With an Evil Spirit
Mark 15:33-41 - The Death of Jesus
Mark 16:1-20 - The Resurrection
Matthew 8:23-27 - Jesus Calms the Storm
Matthew 14:22-36 - Jesus Walks on the Water
Matthew 15:21-28 - The Faith of the Canaanite Woman
Matthew 21:28-32 - The Parable of the Two Sons
Matthew 27:45-56 - The Death of Jesus
Matthew 28:1-10 - The Resurrection
Matthew 28:16-20 - The Great Commission

■ BELIEVERS

1 Corinthians 6:1-11 - Lawsuits Among Believers
1 Corinthians 8:1-13 - Food Sacrificed to Idols
1 Corinthians 9:1-27 - The Rights of an Apostle
1 Corinthians 10:23–11:1 - The Believer's Freedom
1 John 2:18-27 - Warning Against Antichrists
1 John 2:28–3:10 - Children of God
1 John 3:11-24 - Love One Another
1 John 4:1-6 - Test the Spirits
1 John 4:7-21 - God's Love and Ours
1 John 5:1-12 - Faith in the Son of God
1 John 5:13-21 - Concluding Remarks
1 Peter 1:13–2:3 - Be Holy
1 Peter 2:4-12 - The Living Stone and a Chosen People
1 Peter 3:8-22 - Suffering for Doing Good
1 Peter 4:1-11 - Living for God
1 Peter 4:12-19 - Suffering for Being a Christian
1 Peter 5:1-14 - To Elders and Young Men
1 Timothy 1:1-11 - Warning Against False Teachers of the Law
1 Timothy 1:12-20 - The Lord's Grace to Paul
2 John 1-13 - From the Elder
Acts 2:1-13 - The Holy Spirit Comes at Pentecost
Acts 2:14-41 - Peter Addresses the Crowd
Acts 2:42-47 - The Fellowship of the Believers
Acts 4:1-22 - Peter and John Before the Sanhedrin
Acts 4:23-31 - The Believers' Prayer
Acts 4:32-37 - The Believers Share Their Possessions
Acts 5:12-16 - The Apostles Heal Many
Acts 9:32-43 - Aeneas and Dorcas
Acts 11:1-18 - Peter Explains His Actions
Acts 11:19-30 - The Church in Antioch
Acts 15:1-21 - The Council at Jerusalem
Acts 15:22-35 - The Council's Letter to Gentile Believers
Acts 16:1-5 - Timothy Joins Paul and Silas
Acts 16:11-15 - Lydia's Conversion in Philippi
Acts 17:10-15 - In Berea
Acts 20:7-12 - Eutychus Raised From the Dead at Troas
Acts 20:13-38 - Paul's Farewell to the Ephesian Elders
Acts 21:1-16 - On to Jerusalem
Acts 21:17-26 - Paul's Arrival at Jerusalem
Colossians 1:15-23 - The Supremacy of Christ
Colossians 3:1-17 - Rules for Holy Living
Colossians 3:18–4:1 - Rules for Christian Households
Colossians 4:2-18 - Further Instructions
Ephesians 1:1-14 - Spiritual Blessings in Christ
Ephesians 2:1-10 - Made Alive in Christ
Ephesians 4:17–5:21 - Living as Children of Light
Galatians 4:21-31 - Hagar and Sarah
Galatians 5:16-26 - Life by the Spirit
Galatians 6:1-10 - Doing Good to All
Galatians 6:11-18 - Not Circumcision but a New Creation
Hebrews 11:1-40 - By Faith
John 1:1-19 - The Word Became Flesh
John 1:19-28 - John the Baptist Denies Being the Christ
John 16:5-16 - The Work of the Holy Spirit
John 17:20-26 - Jesus Prays for All Believers
John 19:17-27 - The Crucifixion
Luke 5:17-26 - Jesus Heals a Paralytic
Luke 6:17-26 - Blessings and Woes
Luke 6:46-49 - The Wise and Foolish Builders
Luke 24:50-53 - The Ascension
Mark 9:38-41 - Whoever Is Not Against Us Is for Us
Mark 9:42-50 - Causing to Sin
Matthew 12:38-45 - The Sign of Jonah
Matthew 24:1-35 - Signs of the End of the Age
Philippians 1:1-11 - Thanksgiving and Prayer
Philippians 1:12-30 - Paul's Chains Advance the Gospel
Philippians 2:1-11 - Imitating Christ's Humility
Philippians 2:12-18 - Shining as Stars
Philippians 3:1-11 - No Confidence in the Flesh
Philippians 3:12-4:1 - Pressing on Toward the Goal
Philippians 4:2-9 - Exhortations

■ BENEFITS

2 Thessalonians 1:1-12 - Thanksgiving and Prayer
Luke 1:46-56 - Mary's Song

Luke 1:67-80 - Zechariah's Song
Luke 6:37-42 - Judging Others
Luke 6:46-49 - The Wise and Foolish Builders
Matthew 20:1-16 - The Parable of the Workers in the Vineyard

■ BIBLE

1 Peter 1:13–2:3 - Be Holy
1 Peter 2:4-12 - The Living Stone and a Chosen People
1 Timothy 4:1-16 - Instructions to Timothy
2 Peter 1:12-21 - Prophecy of Scripture
2 Peter 3:1-18 - The Day of the Lord
2 Timothy 3:10–4:8 - Paul's Charge to Timothy
Acts 4:23-31 - The Believers' Prayer
Acts 6:1-7 - The Choosing of the Seven
Acts 8:4-8 - Philip in Samaria
Acts 8:26-40 - Philip and the Ethiopian
Acts 11:1-18 - Peter Explains His Actions
Acts 12:20-25 - Herod's Death
Acts 13:4-12 - On Cyprus
Acts 13:13-52 - In Pisidian Antioch
Acts 15:1-21 - The Council at Jerusalem
Acts 16:6-10 - Paul's Vision of the Man of Macedonia
Acts 17:1-9 - In Thessalonica
Acts 17:10-15 - In Berea
Acts 18:1-17 - In Corinth
Acts 18:18-28 - Priscilla, Aquila and Apollos
Ephesians 5:22-33 - Wives and Husbands
Ephesians 6:10-24 - The Armor of God
Galatians 3:1-14 - Faith or Observance of the Law
Galatians 3:15-25 - The Law and the Promise
Galatians 4:21-31 - Hagar and Sarah
John 5:31-47 - Testimonies About Jesus
John 19:28-37 - The Death of Jesus
John 20:24-31 - Jesus Appears to Thomas
Luke 1:1-4 - Introduction
Luke 4:1-13 - The Temptation of Jesus
Luke 4:14-30 - Jesus Rejected at Nazareth
Luke 8:19-21 - Jesus' Mother and Brothers
Matthew 4:1-11 - The Temptation of Jesus
Matthew 5:17-20 - The Fulfillment of the Law
Matthew 13:1-23 - The Parable of the Sower
Matthew 22:23-33 - Marriage at the Resurrection

■ BITTERNESS

Hebrews 12:14-29 - Warning Against Refusing God
James 3:13-18 - Two Kinds of Wisdom
Luke 15:11-32 - The Parable of the Lost Son
Matthew 5:21-26 - Murder
Matthew 5:38-42 - An Eye for an Eye
Matthew 5:43-48 - Love for Enemies
Matthew 6:5-15 - Prayer
Matthew 12:1-14 - Lord of the Sabbath
Matthew 12:22-37 - Jesus and Beelzebub
Matthew 14:1-12 - John the Baptist Beheaded
Matthew 18:21-35 - The Parable of the Unmerciful Servant
Matthew 27:32-44 - The Crucifixion
Matthew 27:62-66 - The Guard at the Tomb

■ BLASPHEMY

1 Timothy 1:12-20 - The Lord's Grace to Paul
2 Peter 2:1-22 - False Teachers and Their Destruction
Acts 6:8-15 - Stephen Seized
Acts 14:8-20 - In Lystra and Derbe
John 10:22-42 - The Unbelief of the Jews
Luke 12:1-12 - Warnings and Encouragements
Luke 22:66–23:25 - Jesus Before Pilate and Herod
Mark 2:1-12 - Jesus Heals a Paralytic
Mark 3:20-30 - Jesus and Beelzebub
Mark 14:53-65 - Before the Sanhedrin
Matthew 9:27-34 - Jesus Heals the Blind and Mute
Matthew 12:22-37 - Jesus and Beelzebub
Matthew 24:1-35 - Signs of the End of the Age
Matthew 26:57-68 - Before the Sanhedrin
Matthew 27:27-31 - The Soldiers Mock Jesus
Matthew 27:32-44 - The Crucifixion
Revelation 13:2-10 - The Beast out of the Sea
Revelation 16:1-21 - The Seven Bowls of God's Wrath
Revelation 17:1-18 - The Woman on the Beast

■ BLESSING

Acts 3:11-26 - Peter Speaks to the Onlookers
Acts 15:22-35 - The Council's Letter to Gentile Believers
Ephesians 1:1-14 - Spiritual Blessings in Christ
Ephesians 6:10-24 - The Armor of God
Galatians 3:1-14 - Faith or Observance of the Law
Hebrews 7:1-10 - Melchizedek the Priest
Hebrews 7:11-28 - Jesus Like Melchizedek
Luke 1:39-45 - Mary Visits Elizabeth
Luke 1:46-56 - Mary's Song
Luke 6:17-26 - Blessings and Woes
Luke 6:27-36 - Love for Enemies
Luke 11:14-28 - Jesus and Beelzebub
Luke 13:31-35 - Jesus' Sorrow for Jerusalem
Luke 24:50-53 - The Ascension
Mark 10:13-16 - The Little Children and Jesus
Mark 11:1-11 - The Triumphal Entry
Matthew 5:1-12 - The Beatitudes
Matthew 13:1-23 - The Parable of the Sower
Matthew 19:1-12 - Divorce
Matthew 19:13-15 - The Little Children and Jesus
Matthew 20:1-16 - The Parable of the Workers in the Vineyard
Matthew 21:28-32 - The Parable of the Two Sons
Matthew 21:33-46 - The Parable of the Tenants
Matthew 25:31-46 - The Sheep and the Goats
Philippians 1:1-11 - Thanksgiving and Prayer
Revelation 14:6-13 - The Three Angels
Romans 9:1-29 - God's Sovereign Choice

■ BLINDNESS

Acts 9:1-19 - Saul's Conversion
Acts 21:37–22:21 - Paul Speaks to the Crowd
Luke 18:35-43 - A Blind Beggar Receives His Sight
Mark 8:22-26 - The Healing of a Blind Man at Bethsaida
Mark 10:46-52 - Blind Bartimaeus Receives His Sight
Matthew 8:28-34 - The Healing of Two Demon-possessed Men
Matthew 9:1-8 - Jesus Heals a Paralytic
Matthew 12:1-14 - Lord of the Sabbath
Matthew 12:38-45 - The Sign of Jonah
Matthew 16:5-12 - The Yeast of the Pharisees and Sadducees
Matthew 16:13-20 - Peter's Confession of Christ
Matthew 22:23-33 - Marriage at the Resurrection
Matthew 22:34-40 - The Greatest Commandment
Matthew 22:41-46 - Whose Son Is the Christ?

Matthew 23:1-39 - Seven Woes
Matthew 24:36-51 - The Day and Hour Unknown
Matthew 27:11-26 - Jesus Before Pilate
Matthew 27:27-31 - The Soldiers Mock Jesus
Matthew 27:32-44 - The Crucifixion
Matthew 27:45-56 - The Death of Jesus
Matthew 27:62-66 - The Guard at the Tomb
Matthew 28:11-15 - The Guards' Report
Revelation 8:6–9:21 - The Trumpets

■ BODY

1 Corinthians 6:12-20 - Sexual Immorality
1 Corinthians 7:1-40 - Marriage
1 Corinthians 15:35-58 - The Resurrection Body
2 Corinthians 12:1–10 - Paul's Vision and His Thorn
Colossians 1:24–2:5 - Paul's Labor for the Church
Colossians 2:6-23 - Freedom From Human Regulations Through Life With Christ
Ephesians 1:15-23 - Thanksgiving and Prayer
Ephesians 4:1-16 - Unity in the Body of Christ
Ephesians 5:22-33 - Wives and Husbands
Galatians 6:11-18 - Not Circumcision but a New Creation
John 19:28-37 - The Death of Jesus
Luke 11:33-36 - The Lamp of the Body
Luke 12:22-34 - Do Not Worry
Luke 23:50-56 - Jesus' Burial
Mark 15:42-47 - The Burial of Jesus
Matthew 12:46-50 - Jesus' Mother and Brothers
Romans 12:1-8 - Living Sacrifices

■ BURDENS

2 Corinthians 12:11-21 - Paul's Concern for the Corinthians
Galatians 5:1-15 - Freedom in Christ
Galatians 6:1-10 - Doing Good to All
Matthew 11:25-30 - Rest for the Weary
Romans 9:1-29 - God's Sovereign Choice

■ CALL

1 Corinthians 1:18–2:5 - Christ the Wisdom and Power of God
1 Peter 2:4-12 - The Living Stone and a Chosen People
1 Timothy 1:12-20 - The Lord's Grace to Paul
2 Peter 1:1-11 - Making One's Calling and Election Sure
Hebrews 3:1-6 - Jesus Greater Than Moses
Luke 3:21-38 - The Baptism and Genealogy of Jesus
Luke 5:1-11 - The Calling of the First Disciples
Luke 5:27-32 - The Calling of Levi
Luke 6:12-16 - The Twelve Apostles
Mark 2:13-17 - The Calling of Levi
Mark 3:13-19 - The Appointing of the Twelve Apostles
Matthew 20:29-34 - Two Blind Men Receive Sight
Matthew 28:16-20 - The Great Commission
Romans 1:1-7 - Introduction

■ CARELESSNESS

Hebrews 2:1-4 - Warning to Pay Attention
Matthew 26:36-46 - Gethsemane

■ CARING

1 John 3:11-24 - Love One Another
1 John 4:7-21 - God's Love and Ours
1 Peter 3:8-22 - Suffering for Doing Good
1 Peter 4:1-11 - Living for God
1 Peter 5:1-14 - To Elders and Young Men
1 Timothy 5:1–6:2 - Advice About Widows, Elders and Slaves
1 Timothy 6:11-21 - Paul's Charge to Timothy
2 John 1-13 - From the Elder
2 Timothy 4:9-22 - Personal Remarks
3 John 1-14 - From the Elder
Acts 16:16-40 - Paul and Silas in Prison
James 1:19-27 - Listening and Doing
John 19:17-27 - The Crucifixion
John 21:15-25 - Jesus Reinstates Peter
Luke 12:1-12 - Warnings and Encouragements
Luke 13:31-35 - Jesus' Sorrow for Jerusalem
Luke 15:8-10 - The Parable of the Lost Coin
Matthew 15:21-28 - The Faith of the Canaanite Woman
Romans 1:8-17 - Paul's Longing to Visit Rome

■ CELEBRATION

Acts 20:1-6 - Through Macedonia and Greece
Hebrews 12:14-29 - Warning Against Refusing God
Luke 1:57-66 - The Birth of John the Baptist
Luke 2:1-7 - The Birth of Jesus
Luke 2:21-40 - Jesus Presented in the Temple
Luke 15:11-32 - The Parable of the Lost Son
Mark 2:18-22 - Jesus Questioned About Fasting
Matthew 9:14-17 - Jesus Questioned About Fasting
Matthew 13:44-46 - The Parables of the Hidden Treasure and the Pearl
Matthew 18:10-14 - The Parable of the Lost Sheep
Matthew 19:1-12 - Divorce
Matthew 21:1-11 - The Triumphal Entry
Matthew 22:1-14 - The Parable of the Wedding Banquet
Matthew 24:36-51 - The Day and Hour Unknown
Matthew 25:1-13 - The Parable of the Ten Virgins
Matthew 26:17-30 - The Lord's Supper
Matthew 28:1-10 - The Resurrection
Revelation 11:1-14 - The Two Witnesses

■ CHALLENGE

Acts 3:11-26 - Peter Speaks to the Onlookers
Hebrews 13:1-25 - Concluding Exhortations
John 9:13-34 - The Pharisees Investigate the Healing
John 11:1-16 - The Death of Lazarus
John 18:19-24 - The High Priest Questions Jesus
Luke 6:17-26 - Blessings and Woes
Matthew 10:1-42 - Jesus Sends Out the Twelve
Matthew 14:22-36 - Jesus Walks on the Water
Matthew 21:23-27 - The Authority of Jesus Questioned
Matthew 22:15-22 - Paying Taxes to Caesar
Matthew 22:34-40 - The Greatest Commandment
Matthew 26:47-56 - Jesus Arrested
Matthew 26:57-68 - Before the Sanhedrin
Matthew 28:16-20 - The Great Commission

■ CHANGE

1 Thessalonians 1:1-10 - Thanksgiving for the Thessalonians' Faith
2 Corinthians 1:12–2:4 - Paul's Change of Plans
Acts 3:11-26 - Peter Speaks to the Onlookers
Acts 9:20-31 - Saul in Damascus and Jerusalem
Hebrews 8:1-13 - The High Priest of a New Covenant
James 2:1-13 - Favoritism Forbidden
James 3:1-12 - Taming the Tongue
John 2:1-11 - Jesus Changes Water to Wine
Luke 5:27-32 - The Calling of Levi

Luke 5:33-39 - Jesus Questioned About Fasting
Luke 6:43-45 - A Tree and Its Fruit
Matthew 9:14-17 - Jesus Questioned About Fasting
Matthew 13:53-58 - A Prophet Without Honor
Matthew 21:28-32 - The Parable of the Two Sons
Matthew 27:1-10 - Judas Hangs Himself
Philemon8-25 - Paul's Plea for Onesimus
Romans 6:1-14 - Dead to Sin, Alive in Christ
Romans 6:15-23 - Slaves to Righteousness
Romans 7:1-6 - An Illustration From Marriage

■ CHARACTER

1 Peter 1:1-12 - Praise to God for a Living Hope
1 Timothy 3:1-16 - Overseers and Deacons
2 Peter 1:1-11 - Making One's Calling and Election Sure
2 Thessalonians 3:6-18 - Warning Against Idleness
Acts 17:10-15 - In Berea
John 3:22-36 - John the Baptist's Testimony About Jesus
John 13:18-30 - Jesus Predicts His Betrayal
John 13:31-38 - Jesus Predicts Peter's Denial
John 18:1-11 - Jesus Arrested
John 19:1-16 - Jesus Sentenced to be Crucified
Luke 4:1-13 - The Temptation of Jesus
Luke 6:43-45 - A Tree and Its Fruit
Luke 7:1-10 - The Faith of the Centurion
Matthew 5:1-12 - The Beatitudes
Matthew 5:33-37 - Oaths
Matthew 20:1-16 - The Parable of the Workers in the Vineyard
Matthew 26:14-16 - Judas Agrees to Betray Jesus
Romans 2:17-29 - The Jews and the Law

■ CHILDREN

1 John 1:5–2:14 - Walking in the Light
1 John 2:28–3:10 - Children of God
1 John 3:11-24 - Love One Another
1 John 5:1-12 - Faith in the Son of God
1 John 5:13-21 - Concluding Remarks
1 Timothy 3:1-16 - Overseers and Deacons
1 Timothy 5:1–6:2 - Advice About Widows, Elders and Slaves
2 John 1-13 - From the Elder
3 John 1-14 - From the Elder
Colossians 3:18–4:1 - Rules for Christian Households
Ephesians 4:17–5:21 - Living as Children of Light
Ephesians 6:1-4 - Children and Parents
Galatians 3:26–4:7 - Sons of God
Galatians 4:8-20 - Paul's Concern for the Galatians
Galatians 4:21-31 - Hagar and Sarah
John 8:31-41 - The Children of Abraham
John 8:42-47 - The Children of the Devil
Luke 1:5-25 - The Birth of John the Baptist Foretold
Luke 1:39-45 - Mary Visits Elizabeth
Luke 1:57-66 - The Birth of John the Baptist
Luke 2:1-7 - The Birth of Jesus
Luke 2:41-52 - The Boy Jesus at the Temple
Luke 9:37-45 - The Healing of a Boy With an Evil Spirit
Luke 9:46-50 - Who Will Be the Greatest?
Luke 10:1-24 - Jesus Sends Out the Seventy-two
Luke 11:1-13 - Jesus' Teaching on Prayer
Luke 12:49-53 - Not Peace but Division
Luke 18:15-17 - The Little Children and Jesus
Luke 20:27-40 - The Resurrection and Marriage
Mark 10:13-16 - The Little Children and Jesus
Matthew 7:7-12 - Ask, Seek, Knock
Matthew 18:1-9 - The Greatest in the Kingdom of Heaven
Matthew 19:13-15 - The Little Children and Jesus
Matthew 21:28-32 - The Parable of the Two Sons
Matthew 22:23-33 - Marriage at the Resurrection
Titus 1:1-16 - Titus' Task on Crete

■ CHOICES

2 Peter 2:1-22 - False Teachers and Their Destruction
Galatians 4:8-20 - Paul's Concern for the Galatians
John 13:18-30 - Jesus Predicts His Betrayal
John 13:31-38 - Jesus Predicts Peter's Denial
Luke 1:57-66 - The Birth of John the Baptist
Luke 3:1-20 - John the Baptist Prepares the Way
Luke 4:1-13 - The Temptation of Jesus
Luke 6:12-16 - The Twelve Apostles
Luke 6:27-36 - Love for Enemies
Luke 10:38-42 - At the Home of Martha and Mary
Mark 3:13-19 - The Appointing of the Twelve Apostles
Mark 8:27-30 - Peter's Confession of Christ

■ CHRISTIANITY

1 John 2:18-27 - Warning Against Antichrists
1 John 4:1-6 - Test the Spirits
2 Timothy 3:10–4:8 - Paul's Charge to Timothy
Acts 9:1-19 - Saul's Conversion
Acts 11:19-30 - The Church in Antioch
Acts 19:1-22 - Paul in Ephesus
Acts 19:23-41 - The Riot in Ephesus
Acts 21:37–22:21 - Paul Speaks to the Crowd
Acts 24:1-27 - The Trial Before Felix
Acts 28:17-31 - Paul Preaches at Rome Under Guard
John 11:45-57 - The Plot to Kill Jesus
John 15:18–16:4 - The World Hates the Disciples
John 18:25-27 - Peter's Second and Third Denials
John 19:38-42 - The Burial of Jesus
John 20:24-31 - Jesus Appears to Thomas
Luke 1:1-4 - Introduction
Romans 11:1-10 - The Remnant of Israel

■ CHURCH

1 Corinthians 1:10-17 - Divisions in the Church
1 Corinthians 3:1-23 - On Divisions in the Church
1 Corinthians 5:1-13 - Expel the Immoral Brother!
1 Corinthians 14:26-40 - Orderly Worship
1 Corinthians 16:1-4 - The Collection for God's People
1 John 2:18-27 - Warning Against Antichrists
1 Peter 2:4-12 - The Living Stone and a Chosen People
1 Peter 5:1-14 - To Elders and Young Men
1 Timothy 1:1-11 - Warning Against False Teachers of the Law
1 Timothy 2:1-15 - Instructions on Worship
1 Timothy 3:1-16 - Overseers and Deacons
1 Timothy 5:1–6:2 - Advice About Widows, Elders and Slaves
3 John 1-14 - From the Elder
Acts 1:12-26 - Matthias Chosen to Replace Judas
Acts 2:1-13 - The Holy Spirit Comes at Pentecost
Acts 2:14-41 - Peter Addresses the Crowd
Acts 2:42-47 - The Fellowship of the Believers
Acts 4:32-37 - The Believers Share Their Possessions
Acts 5:1-11 - Ananias and Sapphira
Acts 6:1-7 - The Choosing of the Seven
Acts 7:54–8:1 - The Stoning of Stephen

Acts 8:2-3 - The Church Persecuted and Scattered
Acts 9:1-19 - Saul's Conversion
Acts 9:20-31 - Saul in Damascus and Jerusalem
Acts 11:1-18 - Peter Explains His Actions
Acts 11:19-30 - The Church in Antioch
Acts 12:1-19 - Peter's Miraculous Escape From Prison
Acts 13:13-52 - In Pisidian Antioch
Acts 14:21-28 - The Return to Antioch in Syria
Acts 15:1-21 - The Council at Jerusalem
Acts 15:22-35 - The Council's Letter to Gentile Believers
Acts 15:36-41 - Disagreement Between Paul and Barnabas
Acts 16:1-5 - Timothy Joins Paul and Silas
Acts 16:16-40 - Paul and Silas in Prison
Acts 17:1-9 - In Thessalonica
Acts 17:10-15 - In Berea
Acts 17:16-34 - In Athens
Acts 18:1-17 - In Corinth
Acts 18:18-28 - Priscilla, Aquila and Apollos
Acts 19:1-22 - Paul in Ephesus
Acts 20:13-38 - Paul's Farewell to the Ephesian Elders
Acts 21:17-26 - Paul's Arrival at Jerusalem
Acts 28:11-16 - Arrival at Rome
Colossians 1:1-14 - Thanksgiving and Prayer
Colossians 1:15-23 - The Supremacy of Christ
Colossians 1:24–2:5 - Paul's Labor for the Church
Colossians 2:6-23 - Freedom From Human Regulations Through Life With Christ
Colossians 4:2-18 - Further Instructions
Ephesians 1:15-23 - Thanksgiving and Prayer
Ephesians 2:11-22 - One in Christ
Ephesians 3:1-13 - Paul the Preacher to the Gentiles
Ephesians 3:14-21 - A Prayer for the Ephesians
Ephesians 4:1-16 - Unity in the Body of Christ
Ephesians 5:22-33 - Wives and Husbands
Galatians 1:1-10 - No Other Gospel
Galatians 1:11-24 - Paul Called by God
John 2:12-25 - Jesus Clears the Temple
John 5:1-15 - The Healing at the Pool
John 5:31-47 - Testimonies About Jesus
John 9:13-34 - The Pharisees Investigate the Healing
John 11:45-57 - The Plot to Kill Jesus
John 18:19-24 - The High Priest Questions Jesus
Luke 2:41-52 - The Boy Jesus at the Temple
Luke 4:14-30 - Jesus Rejected at Nazareth
Luke 6:1-11 - Lord of the Sabbath
Luke 19:45-48 - Jesus at the Temple
Mark 3:20-30 - Jesus and Beelzebub
Matthew 7:1-6 - Judging Others
Matthew 16:13-20 - Peter's Confession of Christ
Matthew 18:15-20 - A Brother Who Sins Against You
Philippians 2:19-30 - Timothy and Epaphroditus
Philippians 4:10-23 - Thanks for Their Gifts
Revelation 1:4-8 - Greetings and Doxology
Revelation 1:9-20 - One Like a Son of Man
Revelation 2:12-17 - To the Church in Pergamum
Revelation 2:18-29 - To the Church in Thyatira
Revelation 3:1-6 - To the Church in Sardis
Revelation 3:7-13 - To the Church in Philadelphia
Revelation 3:14-22 - To the Church in Laodicea

■ **CIRCUMSTANCES**

1 Peter 1:1-12 - Praise to God for a Living Hope
Colossians 4:2-18 - Further Instructions
Hebrews 11:1-40 - By Faith
John 6:16-24 - Jesus Walks on the Water
John 9:1-12 - Jesus Heals a Man Born Blind
John 11:1-16 - The Death of Lazarus
John 11:17-37 - Jesus Comforts the Sisters
John 18:25-27 - Peter's Second and Third Denials
John 19:1-16 - Jesus Sentenced to be Crucified
Luke 2:1-7 - The Birth of Jesus
Matthew 11:1-19 - Jesus and John the Baptist
Philippians 1:12-30 - Paul's Chains Advance the Gospel

■ **CITIZENSHIP**

1 Peter 2:4-12 - The Living Stone and a Chosen People
1 Peter 2:13-25 - Submission to Rulers and Masters
Acts 22:22-29 - Paul the Roman Citizen
Acts 23:23-35 - Paul Transferred to Caesarea
Ephesians 2:11-22 - One in Christ
Luke 2:1-7 - The Birth of Jesus
Matthew 17:24-27 - The Temple Tax
Philippians 3:12–4:1 - Pressing on Toward the Goal

■ **COMFORTABLE**

John 9:13-34 - The Pharisees Investigate the Healing
John 11:17-37 - Jesus Comforts the Sisters
Matthew 5:1-12 - The Beatitudes
Matthew 26:36-46 - Gethsemane

■ **COMMITMENT**

1 Thessalonians 1:1-10 - Thanksgiving for the Thessalonians' Faith
2 Timothy 3:10–4:8 - Paul's Charge to Timothy
James 4:1-12 - Submit Yourselves to God
John 12:20-36 - Jesus Predicts His Death
John 18:25-27 - Peter's Second and Third Denials
Luke 5:1-11 - The Calling of the First Disciples
Luke 5:17-26 - Jesus Heals a Paralytic
Mark 12:28-34 - The Greatest Commandment
Matthew 1:18-25 - The Birth of Jesus Christ
Matthew 4:18-22 - The Calling of the First Disciples
Matthew 5:27-30 - Adultery
Matthew 5:31-32 - Divorce
Matthew 6:16-18 - Fasting
Matthew 8:18-22 - The Cost of Following Jesus
Matthew 10:1-42 - Jesus Sends Out the Twelve
Matthew 11:25-30 - Rest for the Weary
Matthew 13:44-46 - The Parables of the Hidden Treasure and the Pearl
Matthew 16:21-28 - Jesus Predicts His Death
Matthew 22:34-40 - The Greatest Commandment
Matthew 26:31-35 - Jesus Predicts Peter's Denial
Matthew 27:57-61 - The Burial of Jesus
Revelation 2:1-7 - To the Church in Ephesus
Revelation 2:8-11 - To the Church in Smyrna
Revelation 2:12-17 - To the Church in Pergamum
Revelation 14:1-5 - The Lamb and the 144,000
Romans 12:1-8 - Living Sacrifices

■ **COMPARISONS**

Hebrews 7:1-10 - Melchizedek the Priest
Hebrews 7:11-28 - Jesus Like Melchizedek
Hebrews 8:1-13 - The High Priest of a New Covenant
Hebrews 9:1-10 - Worship in the Earthly Tabernacle
Hebrews 9:11-28 - The Blood of Christ

Hebrews 10:1-18 - Christ's Sacrifice Once for All
Luke 6:17-26 - Blessings and Woes
Luke 6:46-49 - The Wise and Foolish Builders
Luke 11:29-32 - The Sign of Jonah

■ COMPASSION

1 John 3:11-24 - Love One Another
1 Peter 3:8-22 - Suffering for Doing Good
2 Corinthians 1:1-11 - The God of All Comfort
James 1:19-27 - Listening and Doing
James 5:1-6 - Warning to Rich Oppressors
Luke 4:38-44 - Jesus Heals Many
Luke 5:12-16 - The Man With Leprosy
Luke 6:1-11 - Lord of the Sabbath
Luke 7:11-17 - Jesus Raises a Widow's Son
Luke 13:31-35 - Jesus' Sorrow for Jerusalem
Luke 15:11-32 - The Parable of the Lost Son
Luke 19:28-44 - The Triumphal Entry
Mark 1:40-45 - A Man With Leprosy
Mark 6:30-44 - Jesus Feeds the Five Thousand
Matthew 8:1-4 - The Man With Leprosy
Matthew 8:14-17 - Jesus Heals Many
Matthew 8:28-34 - The Healing of Two Demon-possessed Men
Matthew 9:9-13 - The Calling of Matthew
Matthew 9:35-38 - The Workers Are Few
Matthew 14:13-21 - Jesus Feeds the Five Thousand
Matthew 15:21-28 - The Faith of the Canaanite Woman
Matthew 15:29-39 - Jesus Feeds the Four Thousand
Matthew 18:15-20 - A Brother Who Sins Against You
Matthew 20:29-34 - Two Blind Men Receive Sight
Philippians 2:1-11 - Imitating Christ's Humility
Philemon 8-25 - Paul's Plea for Onesimus

■ COMPLACENCY

2 Peter 2:1-22 - False Teachers and Their Destruction
John 9:13-34 - The Pharisees Investigate the Healing
John 12:37-50 - The Jews Continue in Their Unbelief
Luke 12:13-21 - The Parable of the Rich Fool
Revelation 3:14-22 - To the Church in Laodicea

■ COMPLAINING

1 Corinthians 10:1-13 - Warnings From Israel's History
Acts 6:1-7 - The Choosing of the Seven
James 5:7-12 - Patience in Suffering
Matthew 12:1-14 - Lord of the Sabbath
Matthew 19:13-15 - The Little Children and Jesus
Matthew 20:1-16 - The Parable of the Workers in the Vineyard
Philippians 2:12-18 - Shining as Stars

■ COMPOSURE

Matthew 22:15-22 - Paying Taxes to Caesar

■ COMPROMISE

2 Timothy 4:9-22 - Personal Remarks
Galatians 2:11-21 - Paul Opposes Peter
John 2:12-25 - Jesus Clears the Temple
John 7:1-13 - Jesus Goes to the Feast of Tabernacles
John 18:25-27 - Peter's Second and Third Denials
Mark 15:1-15 - Jesus Before Pilate
Matthew 8:18-22 - The Cost of Following Jesus
Matthew 13:1-23 - The Parable of the Sower
Matthew 19:1-12 - Divorce
Matthew 26:36-46 - Gethsemane
Matthew 26:69-75 - Peter Disowns Jesus
Revelation 2:12-17 - To the Church in Pergamum
Revelation 2:18-29 - To the Church in Thyatira

■ CONFESSION

1 John 1:5–2:14 - Walking in the Light
1 John 4:1-6 - Test the Spirits
1 Timothy 6:11-21 - Paul's Charge to Timothy
2 Timothy 2:14-26 - A Workman Approved by God
James 5:13-20 - The Prayer of Faith
John 20:24-31 - Jesus Appears to Thomas
Luke 9:18-27 - Peter's Confession of Christ
Mark 8:27-30 - Peter's Confession of Christ
Mark 14:53-65 - Before the Sanhedrin
Matthew 3:1-12 - John the Baptist Prepares the Way
Matthew 18:21-35 - The Parable of the Unmerciful Servant
Philippians 2:1-11 - Imitating Christ's Humility
Romans 3:1-8 - God's Faithfulness

■ CONFIDENCE

1 John 5:13-21 - Concluding Remarks
2 Corinthians 1:12–2:4 - Paul's Change of Plans
2 Corinthians 5:1-10 - Our Heavenly Dwelling
2 Corinthians 7:2-16 - Paul's Joy
2 Corinthians 10:1-18 - Paul's Defense of His Ministry
2 Corinthians 11:16-33 - Paul Boasts About His Sufferings
Hebrews 4:14–5:10 - Jesus the Great High Priest
Hebrews 13:1-25 - Concluding Exhortations
John 2:1-11 - Jesus Changes Water to Wine
John 11:17-37 - Jesus Comforts the Sisters
John 14:1-4 - Jesus Comforts His Disciples
Luke 1:1-4 - Introduction
Luke 1:46-56 - Mary's Song
Luke 7:1-10 - The Faith of the Centurion
Luke 18:9-14 - The Parable of the Pharisee and the Tax Collector
Matthew 8:5-13 - The Faith of the Centurion
Matthew 10:1-42 - Jesus Sends Out the Twelve
Matthew 14:13-21 - Jesus Feeds the Five Thousand
Philippians 4:10-23 - Thanks for Their Gifts
Revelation 15:1-8 - Seven Angels With Seven Plagues
Romans 1:8-17 - Paul's Longing to Visit Rome

■ CONFLICT

1 Corinthians 14:26-40 - Orderly Worship
2 Corinthians 7:2-16 - Paul's Joy
Acts 6:8-15 - Stephen Seized
Acts 17:10-15 - In Berea
Acts 22:30–23:11 - Before the Sanhedrin
Galatians 5:16-26 - Life by the Spirit
Luke 12:49-53 - Not Peace but Division
Luke 22:47-53 - Jesus Arrested
Mark 11:27-33 - The Authority of Jesus Questioned
Matthew 5:21-26 - Murder
Matthew 12:46-50 - Jesus' Mother and Brothers
Matthew 19:1-12 - Divorce
Matthew 21:12-17 - Jesus at the Temple
Revelation 12:1–13:1 - The Woman and the Dragon
Romans 7:7-25 - Struggling With Sin
Romans 12:9-21 - Love

■ CONFUSION

2 Thessalonians 2:1-12 - The Man of Lawlessness
Acts 19:23-41 - The Riot in Ephesus
Acts 21:27-36 - Paul Arrested
Acts 22:30–23:11 - Before the Sanhedrin

Galatians 1:1-10 - No Other Gospel
Galatians 5:1-15 - Freedom in Christ
John 6:60-71 - Many Disciples Desert Jesus
Luke 24:13-35 - On the Road to Emmaus
Matthew 11:1-19 - Jesus and John the Baptist
Matthew 16:13-20 - Peter's Confession of Christ
Matthew 19:16-30 - The Rich Young Man
Matthew 21:18-22 - The Fig Tree Withers
Matthew 22:23-33 - Marriage at the Resurrection
Matthew 23:1-39 - Seven Woes
Matthew 24:1-35 - Signs of the End of the Age

■ CONSCIENCE

1 Corinthians 4:1-21 - Apostles of Christ
1 Corinthians 10:23–11:1 - The Believer's Freedom
1 Peter 3:8-22 - Suffering for Doing Good
1 Timothy 4:1-16 - Instructions to Timothy
Acts 22:30-23:11 - Before the Sanhedrin
Acts 24:1–27 - The Trial Before Felix
Matthew 27:11-26 - Jesus Before Pilate

■ CONSEQUENCES

1 Timothy 1:12-20 - The Lord's Grace to Paul
2 Thessalonians 3:6-18 - Warning Against Idleness
Acts 1:12-26 - Matthias Chosen to Replace Judas
Acts 4:1-22 - Peter and John Before the Sanhedrin
Acts 5:1-11 - Ananias and Sapphira
John 18:19-24 - The High Priest Questions Jesus
John 18:28-40 - Jesus Before Pilate
Jude 1-16 - The Sin and Doom of Godless Men
Luke 6:17-26 - Blessings and Woes
Luke 6:37-42 - Judging Others
Luke 6:46-49 - The Wise and Foolish Builders
Matthew 14:1-12 - John the Baptist Beheaded
Matthew 18:15-20 - A Brother Who Sins Against You
Matthew 25:31-46 - The Sheep and the Goats
Revelation 14:14-20 - The Harvest of the Earth
Revelation 16:1-21 - The Seven Bowls of God's Wrath
Revelation 18:1-24 - The Fall of Babylon
Revelation 19:1-10 - Hallelujah!
Revelation 20:11-15 - The Dead Are Judged
Romans 6:1-14 - Dead to Sin, Alive in Christ
Romans 6:15-23 - Slaves to Righteousness

■ CONSISTENCY

Luke 1:5-25 - The Birth of John the Baptist Foretold
Luke 6:43-45 - A Tree and Its Fruit
Matthew 5:17-20 - The Fulfillment of the Law
Romans 2:17-29 - The Jews and the Law

■ CONTENTMENT

1 Timothy 6:3-10 - Love of Money
Matthew 6:25-34 - Do Not Worry
Matthew 20:1-16 - The Parable of the Workers in the Vineyard
Philippians 4:10-23 - Thanks for Their Gifts

■ CONVERSATION

2 Timothy 2:14-26 - A Workman Approved by God
Colossians 4:2-18 - Further Instructions
James 3:1-12 - Taming the Tongue
Matthew 5:33-37 - Oaths
Matthew 13:53-58 - A Prophet Without Honor
Matthew 21:23-27 - The Authority of Jesus Questioned
Matthew 22:41-46 - Whose Son Is the Christ?
Matthew 26:1-5 - The Plot Against Jesus
Matthew 26:69-75 - Peter Disowns Jesus

■ CONVICTIONS

Acts 28:17-31 - Paul Preaches at Rome Under Guard
John 4:39-42 - Many Samaritans Believe
John 4:43-54 - Jesus Heals the Official's Son
John 16:5-16 - The Work of the Holy Spirit
John 18:19-24 - The High Priest Questions Jesus
John 19:1-16 - Jesus Sentenced to be Crucified
Luke 4:1-13 - The Temptation of Jesus
Mark 8:27-30 - Peter's Confession of Christ
Matthew 10:1-42 - Jesus Sends Out the Twelve
Matthew 26:14-16 - Judas Agrees to Betray Jesus

■ CORRECTION

2 Timothy 3:10–4:8 - Paul's Charge to Timothy
James 5:13-20 - The Prayer of Faith
Matthew 14:1-12 - John the Baptist Beheaded
Matthew 18:15-20 - A Brother Who Sins Against You
Matthew 19:13-15 - The Little Children and Jesus
Revelation 2:1-7 - To the Church in Ephesus

■ COURAGE

1 Corinthians 16:5-24 - Personal Requests
Acts 8:2-3 - The Church Persecuted and Scattered
Acts 22:30–23:11 - Before the Sanhedrin
Acts 27:13-26 - The Storm
John 4:43-54 - Jesus Heals the Official's Son
John 18:19-24 - The High Priest Questions Jesus
John 19:38-42 - The Burial of Jesus
Mark 6:45-56 - Jesus Walks on the Water
Mark 7:24-30 - The Faith of a Syrophoenician Woman
Mark 15:42-47 - The Burial of Jesus
Matthew 1:18-25 - The Birth of Jesus Christ
Matthew 14:22-36 - Jesus Walks on the Water
Matthew 16:21-28 - Jesus Predicts His Death
Matthew 18:21-35 - The Parable of the Unmerciful Servant
Matthew 24:1-35 - Signs of the End of the Age
Matthew 26:31-35 - Jesus Predicts Peter's Denial
Matthew 27:57-61 - The Burial of Jesus
Philippians 1:12-30 - Paul's Chains Advance the Gospel

■ COVENANT

2 Corinthians 3:7-18 - The Glory of the New Covenant
Acts 7:1-53 - Stephen's Speech to the Sanhedrin
Galatians 3:15-25 - The Law and the Promise
Galatians 4:21-31 - Hagar and Sarah
Luke 1:67-80 - Zechariah's Song
Matthew 26:17-30 - The Lord's Supper
Romans 4:1-25 - Abraham Justified by Faith
Romans 11:25-32 - All Israel Will Be Saved

■ CRAFTSMANSHIP

Acts 19:23-41 - The Riot in Ephesus
Ephesians 2:1-10 - Made Alive in Christ

■ CREATION

2 Peter 3:1-18 - The Day of the Lord
Acts 17:16-34 - In Athens
Colossians 1:15-23 - The Supremacy of Christ
Ephesians 1:15-23 - Thanksgiving and Prayer
Hebrews 1:1-14 - The Son Superior to Angels
Hebrews 2:5-18 - Jesus Made Like His Brothers
John 1:1-19 - The Word Became Flesh
John 17:20-26 - Jesus Prays for All Believers
Mark 10:1-12 - Divorce
Matthew 6:25-34 - Do Not Worry
Revelation 4:1-11 - The Throne in Heaven
Revelation 10:1-11 - The Angel and the Little Scroll

Revelation 14:6-13 - The Three Angels

■ **CRITICISM**

2 Corinthians 1:12–2:4 - Paul's Change of Plans
2 Corinthians 8:16–9:5 - Titus Sent to Corinth
Acts 11:1-18 - Peter Explains His Actions
Luke 5:33-39 - Jesus Questioned About Fasting
Luke 6:37-42 - Judging Others
Luke 11:37-54 - Six Woes
Luke 17:11-19 - Ten Healed of Leprosy
Luke 19:28-44 - The Triumphal Entry
Luke 20:9-19 - The Parable of the Tenants
Mark 8:14-21 - The Yeast of the Pharisees and Herod
Mark 12:1-12 - The Parable of the Tenants
Mark 14:1-11 - Jesus Anointed at Bethany
Mark 15:16-20 - The Soldiers Mock Jesus
Mark 16:1-20 - The Resurrection
Matthew 5:17-20 - The Fulfillment of the Law
Matthew 7:1-6 - Judging Others
Matthew 12:1-14 - Lord of the Sabbath
Matthew 13:53-58 - A Prophet Without Honor
Matthew 19:13-15 - The Little Children and Jesus
Matthew 20:1-16 - The Parable of the Workers in the Vineyard
Matthew 23:1-39 - Seven Woes
Matthew 27:32-44 - The Crucifixion

■ **CULTURE**

1 John 2:15-17 - Do Not Love the World
1 Timothy 5:1–6:2 - Advice About Widows, Elders and Slaves
2 Timothy 3:1-9 - Godlessness in the Last Days
Acts 10:9-23 - Peter's Vision
Acts 16:1-5 - Timothy Joins Paul and Silas
Acts 21:27-36 - Paul Arrested
Luke 1:39-45 - Mary Visits Elizabeth
Luke 1:57-66 - The Birth of John the Baptist
Matthew 5:13-16 - Salt and Light
Matthew 19:1-12 - Divorce
Matthew 24:1-35 - Signs of the End of the Age

■ **CURIOSITY**

Luke 1:57-66 - The Birth of John the Baptist
Luke 3:1-20 - John the Baptist Prepares the Way

■ **DANGER**

Acts 27:1-12 - Paul Sails for Rome
Hebrews 11:1-40 - By Faith
Luke 8:22-25 - Jesus Calms a Storm
Matthew 10:1-42 - Jesus Sends Out the Twelve
Matthew 13:24-30 - The Parable of the Weeds
Matthew 14:1-12 - John the Baptist Beheaded
Matthew 16:5-12 - The Yeast of the Pharisees and Sadducees
Matthew 20:17-19 - Jesus Again Predicts His Death
Matthew 21:23-27 - The Authority of Jesus Questioned
Matthew 23:1-39 - Seven Woes
Matthew 24:1-35 - Signs of the End of the Age
Matthew 26:31-35 - Jesus Predicts Peter's Denial
Matthew 26:36-46 - Gethsemane
Matthew 26:47-56 - Jesus Arrested
Matthew 27:57-61 - The Burial of Jesus
Revelation 8:6–9:21 - The Trumpets

■ **DARKNESS**

1 John 1:5–2:14 - Walking in the Light
1 Peter 2:4-12 - The Living Stone and a Chosen People
Ephesians 4:17–5:21 - Living as Children of Light
Ephesians 6:10-24 - The Armor of God
John 1:1-19 - The Word Became Flesh
John 3:1-22 - Jesus Teaches Nicodemus
John 8:12-30 - The Validity of Jesus' Testimony
John 11:1-16 - The Death of Lazarus
John 12:20-36 - Jesus Predicts His Death
John 12:37-50 - The Jews Continue in Their Unbelief
Luke 11:33-36 - The Lamp of the Body
Luke 12:1-12 - Warnings and Encouragements
Luke 22:47-53 - Jesus Arrested
Luke 23:44-49 - Jesus' Death
Matthew 4:12-17 - Jesus Begins to Preach
Matthew 5:13-16 - Salt and Light
Matthew 6:19-24 - Treasures in Heaven
Matthew 9:9-13 - The Calling of Matthew
Matthew 24:1-35 - Signs of the End of the Age
Matthew 26:47-56 - Jesus Arrested
Matthew 27:45-56 - The Death of Jesus
Revelation 8:6–9:21 - The Trumpets
Revelation 16:1-21 - The Seven Bowls of God's Wrath

■ **DEATH**

1 Corinthians 15:12-34 - The Resurrection of the Dead
1 Corinthians 15:35-58 - The Resurrection Body
1 John 3:11-24 - Love One Another
1 John 5:13-21 - Concluding Remarks
1 Thessalonians 4:13–5:11 - The Coming of the Lord
2 Corinthians 4:1-18 - Treasures in Jars of Clay
2 Corinthians 5:1-10 - Our Heavenly Dwelling
2 Peter 1:12-21 - Prophecy of Scripture
2 Timothy 1:1–2:13 - Encouragement to Be Faithful
2 Timothy 3:10–4:8 - Paul's Charge to Timothy
Acts 5:1-11 - Ananias and Sapphira
Acts 7:54–8:1 - The Stoning of Stephen
Acts 8:2-3 - The Church Persecuted and Scattered
Acts 9:32-43 - Aeneas and Dorcas
Acts 12:20-25 - Herod's Death
Acts 13:13-52 - In Pisidian Antioch
Acts 20:7-12 - Eutychus Raised From the Dead at Troas
Acts 23:12-22 - The Plot to Kill Paul
Colossians 1:15-23 - The Supremacy of Christ
Colossians 2:6-23 - Freedom From Human Regulations Through Life With Christ
Colossians 3:1-17 - Rules for Holy Living
Ephesians 2:1-10 - Made Alive in Christ
Galatians 2:11-21 - Paul Opposes Peter
Hebrews 9:11-28 - The Blood of Christ
John 8:48-59 - The Claims of Jesus About Himself
John 11:1-16 - The Death of Lazarus
John 11:17-37 - Jesus Comforts the Sisters
John 11:38-44 - Jesus Raises Lazarus From the Dead
John 12:20-36 - Jesus Predicts His Death
John 19:28-37 - The Death of Jesus
John 19:38-42 - The Burial of Jesus
John 20:1-9 - The Empty Tomb
John 20:10-18 - Jesus Appears to Mary Magdalene
John 21:15-25 - Jesus Reinstates Peter
Luke 8:40-56 - A Dead Girl and a Sick Woman
Luke 16:19-31 - The Rich Man and Lazarus
Luke 18:31-34 - Jesus Again Predicts His Death
Luke 20:27-40 - The Resurrection and Marriage

Luke 21:5-38 - Signs of the End of the Age
Luke 23:44-49 - Jesus' Death
Mark 5:21-43 - A Dead Girl and a Sick Woman
Mark 10:32-34 - Jesus Again Predicts His Death
Mark 12:18-27 - Marriage at the Resurrection
Mark 14:27-31 - Jesus Predicts Peter's Denial
Mark 14:53-65 - Before the Sanhedrin
Mark 15:33-41 - The Death of Jesus
Matthew 9:18-26 - A Dead Girl and a Sick Woman
Matthew 17:14-23 - The Healing of a Boy With a Demon
Matthew 20:17-19 - Jesus Again Predicts His Death
Matthew 22:23-33 - Marriage at the Resurrection
Matthew 24:1-35 - Signs of the End of the Age
Matthew 26:1-5 - The Plot Against Jesus
Matthew 27:11-26 - Jesus Before Pilate
Matthew 27:32-44 - The Crucifixion
Matthew 27:45-56 - The Death of Jesus
Philippians 1:12-30 - Paul's Chains Advance the Gospel
Philippians 2:1-11 - Imitating Christ's Humility
Revelation 1:9-20 - One Like a Son of Man
Revelation 2:8-11 - To the Church in Smyrna
Revelation 3:1-6 - To the Church in Sardis
Revelation 6:1-17 - The Seals
Revelation 8:6–9:21 - The Trumpets
Revelation 11:1-14 - The Two Witnesses
Revelation 13:2-10 - The Beast out of the Sea
Revelation 13:11-18 - The Beast out of the Earth
Revelation 14:6-13 - The Three Angels
Revelation 16:1-21 - The Seven Bowls of God's Wrath
Revelation 19:11-21 - The Rider on the White Horse
Revelation 20:1-6 - The Thousand Years
Revelation 20:11-15 - The Dead Are Judged
Revelation 21:1-27 - The New Jerusalem
Romans 5:12-21 - Death Through Adam, Life Through Christ
Romans 7:7-25 - Struggling With Sin

■ **DECEIT**

2 Corinthians 4:1-18 - Treasures in Jars of Clay
2 Corinthians 11:1-15 - Paul and the False Apostles
2 John 1-13 - From the Elder
Acts 1:12-26 - Matthias Chosen to Replace Judas
Acts 5:1-11 - Ananias and Sapphira
Acts 23:12-22 - The Plot to Kill Paul
Hebrews 3:7-19 - Warning Against Unbelief
Hebrews 4:1-13 - A Sabbath-Rest for the People of God
John 11:45-57 - The Plot to Kill Jesus
Luke 20:1-8 - The Authority of Jesus Questioned
Luke 20:20-26 - Paying Taxes to Caesar
Luke 22:1-6 - Judas Agrees to Betray Jesus
Luke 22:47-53 - Jesus Arrested
Mark 12:13-17 - Paying Taxes to Caesar
Mark 14:12-26 - The Lord's Supper
Mark 14:66-72 - Peter Disowns Jesus
Matthew 2:1-12 - The Visit of the Magi
Matthew 4:1-11 - The Temptation of Jesus
Matthew 7:15-23 - A Tree and Its Fruit
Matthew 14:1-12 - John the Baptist Beheaded
Matthew 15:1-20 - Clean and Unclean
Matthew 16:5-12 - The Yeast of the Pharisees and Sadducees
Matthew 21:18-22 - The Fig Tree Withers
Matthew 21:33-46 - The Parable of the Tenants
Matthew 24:1-35 - Signs of the End of the Age
Matthew 26:14-16 - Judas Agrees to Betray Jesus
Matthew 26:57-68 - Before the Sanhedrin
Matthew 27:62-66 - The Guard at the Tomb
Matthew 28:11-15 - The Guards' Report
Revelation 3:14-22 - To the Church in Laodicea
Revelation 12:1–13:1 - The Woman and the Dragon
Revelation 13:2-10 - The Beast out of the Sea
Revelation 13:11-18 - The Beast out of the Earth
Revelation 20:1-6 - The Thousand Years
Revelation 20:7-10 - Satan's Doom
Romans 3:9-20 - No One Is Righteous

■ **DECISIONS**

Acts 16:1-5 - Timothy Joins Paul and Silas
James 4:13-17 - Boasting About Tomorrow
John 6:60-71 - Many Disciples Desert Jesus
Luke 5:1-11 - The Calling of the First Disciples
Luke 5:27-32 - The Calling of Levi
Luke 6:12-16 - The Twelve Apostles

■ **DEDICATION**

Luke 17:1-10 - Sin, Faith, Duty
Matthew 6:16-18 - Fasting
Matthew 13:44-46 - The Parables of the Hidden Treasure and the Pearl
Matthew 16:21-28 - Jesus Predicts His Death
Revelation 14:1-5 - The Lamb and the 144,000

■ **DELAY**

John 11:17-37 - Jesus Comforts the Sisters
Luke 1:57-66 - The Birth of John the Baptist
Matthew 15:21-28 - The Faith of the Canaanite Woman
Matthew 24:36-51 - The Day and Hour Unknown
Matthew 25:1-13 - The Parable of the Ten Virgins
Revelation 10:1-11 - The Angel and the Little Scroll

■ **DELEGATION**

Luke 7:1-10 - The Faith of the Centurion
Matthew 14:13-21 - Jesus Feeds the Five Thousand
Matthew 15:29-39 - Jesus Feeds the Four Thousand

■ **DEMONS**

1 Corinthians 10:14-22 - Idol Feasts and the Lord's Supper
1 John 4:1-6 - Test the Spirits
1 Timothy 4:1-16 - Instructions to Timothy
2 Timothy 2:14-26 - A Workman Approved by God
Acts 5:12-16 - The Apostles Heal Many
Acts 16:16-40 - Paul and Silas in Prison
Acts 19:1-22 - Paul in Ephesus
John 7:14-24 - Jesus Teaches at the Feast
John 8:48-59 - The Claims of Jesus About Himself
Luke 4:31-37 - Jesus Drives Out an Evil Spirit
Luke 4:38-44 - Jesus Heals Many
Luke 8:26-39 - The Healing of a Demon-possessed Man
Luke 9:37-45 - The Healing of a Boy With an Evil Spirit
Luke 9:46-50 - Who Will Be the Greatest?
Luke 10:1-24 - Jesus Sends Out the Seventy-two
Luke 11:14-28 - Jesus and Beelzebub
Luke 13:10-17 - A Crippled Woman Healed on the Sabbath
Mark 1:21-28 - Jesus Drives Out an Evil Spirit
Mark 1:29-34 - Jesus Heals Many
Mark 1:35-39 - Jesus Prays in a Solitary Place
Mark 3:7-12 - Crowds Follow Jesus
Mark 3:13-19 - The Appointing of the Twelve Apostles

Mark 3:20-30 - Jesus and Beelzebub
Mark 5:1-20 - The Healing of a Demon-possessed Man
Mark 6:7-13 - Jesus Sends Out the Twelve
Mark 7:24-30 - The Faith of a Syrophoenician Woman
Mark 9:14-32 - The Healing of a Boy With an Evil Spirit
Mark 9:38-41 - Whoever Is Not Against Us Is for Us
Matthew 8:14-17 - Jesus Heals Many
Matthew 8:28-34 - The Healing of Two Demon-possessed Men
Matthew 9:27-34 - Jesus Heals the Blind and Mute
Matthew 12:22-37 - Jesus and Beelzebub
Matthew 12:38-45 - The Sign of Jonah
Matthew 15:21-28 - The Faith of the Canaanite Woman
Matthew 17:14-23 - The Healing of a Boy With a Demon
Matthew 25:31-46 - The Sheep and the Goats
Revelation 16:1-21 - The Seven Bowls of God's Wrath
Revelation 18:1-24 - The Fall of Babylon
Revelation 19:1-10 - Hallelujah!
Romans 8:28-39 - More Than Conquerors

■ **DENIAL**

1 John 1:5–2:14 - Walking in the Light
1 John 2:18-27 - Warning Against Antichrists
1 John 4:1-6 - Test the Spirits
Hebrews 5:11–6:12 - Warning Against Falling Away
John 13:31-38 - Jesus Predicts Peter's Denial
John 18:1-11 - Jesus Arrested
John 18:15-18 - Peter's First Denial
John 18:25-27 - Peter's Second and Third Denials
Luke 22:54-62 - Peter Disowns Jesus
Mark 8:31–9:1 - Jesus Predicts His Death
Mark 14:27-31 - Jesus Predicts Peter's Denial
Matthew 11:20-24 - Woe on Unrepentant Cities
Matthew 12:22-37 - Jesus and Beelzebub
Matthew 12:38-45 - The Sign of Jonah
Matthew 26:69-75 - Peter Disowns Jesus

■ **DEPEND**

John 5:1-15 - The Healing at the Pool
John 6:25-59 - Jesus the Bread of Life
John 17:1-5 - Jesus Prays for Himself
Matthew 6:5-15 - Prayer
Matthew 10:1-42 - Jesus Sends Out the Twelve
Matthew 14:22-36 - Jesus Walks on the Water

■ **DEPRESSION**

Mark 14:32-42 - Gethsemane
Matthew 26:69-75 - Peter Disowns Jesus

■ **DESIRES**

1 Corinthians 6:12-20 - Sexual Immorality
1 John 2:15-17 - Do Not Love the World
1 Peter 1:13–2:3 - Be Holy
1 Peter 2:4-12 - The Living Stone and a Chosen People
1 Peter 4:1-11 - Living for God
1 Timothy 6:3-10 - Love of Money
2 Corinthians 8:1-15 - Generosity Encouraged
2 Peter 1:1-11 - Making One's Calling and Election Sure
2 Peter 2:1-22 - False Teachers and Their Destruction
2 Timothy 2:14-26 - A Workman Approved by God
2 Timothy 3:1-9 - Godlessness in the Last Days
Galatians 5:16-26 - Life by the Spirit
James 1:1-18 - Trials and Temptations
Luke 1:57-66 - The Birth of John the Baptist
Luke 4:1-13 - The Temptation of Jesus
Mark 4:1-20 - The Parable of the Sower
Matthew 6:19-24 - Treasures in Heaven
Matthew 13:44-46 - The Parables of the Hidden Treasure and the Pearl
Matthew 26:36-46 - Gethsemane
Romans 8:1-17 - Life Through the Spirit
Romans 9:30–10:21 - Israel's Unbelief

■ **DESPAIR**

2 Corinthians 1:1-11 - The God of All Comfort
Luke 23:26-43 - The Crucifixion
Mark 14:32-42 - Gethsemane
Matthew 8:14-17 - Jesus Heals Many
Matthew 26:17-30 - The Lord's Supper
Matthew 27:1-10 - Judas Hangs Himself

■ **DETAILS**

Matthew 28:11-15 - The Guards' Report

■ **DETERMINATION**

John 4:43-54 - Jesus Heals the Official's Son
Luke 5:17-26 - Jesus Heals a Paralytic
Mark 14:27-31 - Jesus Predicts Peter's Denial
Matthew 15:21-28 - The Faith of the Canaanite Woman
Matthew 20:17-19 - Jesus Again Predicts His Death
Matthew 26:1-5 - The Plot Against Jesus
Matthew 26:31-35 - Jesus Predicts Peter's Denial
Matthew 27:62-66 - The Guard at the Tomb

■ **DEVOTION**

1 Thessalonians 1:1-10 - Thanksgiving for the Thessalonians' Faith
1 Timothy 1:1-11 - Warning Against False Teachers of the Law
1 Timothy 4:1-16 - Instructions to Timothy
2 Corinthians 7:2-16 - Paul's Joy
2 Corinthians 11:1-15 - Paul and the False Apostles
Acts 2:42-47 - The Fellowship of the Believers
John 12:1-11 - Jesus Anointed at Bethany
John 20:10-18 - Jesus Appears to Mary Magdalene
John 21:1-14 - Jesus and the Miraculous Catch of Fish
Luke 1:46-56 - Mary's Song
Luke 2:21-40 - Jesus Presented in the Temple
Luke 9:57-62 - The Cost of Following Jesus
Luke 16:1-15 - The Parable of the Shrewd Manager
Luke 23:50-56 - Jesus' Burial
Mark 12:28-34 - The Greatest Commandment
Mark 14:1-11 - Jesus Anointed at Bethany
Matthew 16:21-28 - Jesus Predicts His Death
Matthew 17:1-13 - The Transfiguration
Matthew 22:34-40 - The Greatest Commandment
Matthew 26:6-13 - Jesus Anointed at Bethany
Matthew 27:45-56 - The Death of Jesus

■ **DIFFERENCES**

1 Corinthians 15:35-58 - The Resurrection Body
James 2:1-13 - Favoritism Forbidden
Luke 5:33-39 - Jesus Questioned About Fasting
Luke 6:27-36 - Love for Enemies
Luke 6:46-49 - The Wise and Foolish Builders

■ **DIGNITY**

1 Timothy 2:1-15 - Instructions on Worship

■ **DIRECTION**

Luke 6:27-36 - Love for Enemies

■ **DISAGREEMENTS**

1 Corinthians 1:10-17 - Divisions in the Church
1 Corinthians 6:1-11 - Lawsuits Among Believers
1 Corinthians 15:12-34 - The Resurrection of the Dead

2 Timothy 2:14-26 - A Workman Approved by God
Acts 15:36-41 - Disagreement Between Paul and Barnabas
Luke 12:49-53 - Not Peace but Division
Luke 18:15-17 - The Little Children and Jesus
Luke 22:7-38 - The Last Supper
Mark 8:31–9:1 - Jesus Predicts His Death
Mark 12:18-27 - Marriage at the Resurrection
Matthew 18:15-20 - A Brother Who Sins Against You

■ **DISCERNMENT**

1 Corinthians 2:6-16 - Wisdom From the Spirit
Matthew 7:15-23 - A Tree and Its Fruit
Matthew 9:9-13 - The Calling of Matthew
Matthew 16:1-4 - The Demand for a Sign
Matthew 16:5-12 - The Yeast of the Pharisees and Sadducees
Matthew 16:13-20 - Peter's Confession of Christ
Matthew 25:14-30 - The Parable of the Talents

■ **DISCIPLINE**

1 Corinthians 4:1-21 - Apostles of Christ
1 Corinthians 5:1-13 - Expel the Immoral Brother!
1 Corinthians 9:1-27 - The Rights of an Apostle
1 Corinthians 11:17-34 - The Lord's Supper
1 Peter 1:13–2:3 - Be Holy
2 Corinthians 13:1-14 - Final Warnings
2 Peter 1:1-11 - Making One's Calling and Election Sure
2 Thessalonians 3:6-18 - Warning Against Idleness
2 Timothy 1:1-2:13 - Encouragement to Be Faithful
Acts 5:1-11 - Ananias and Sapphira
Ephesians 6:1-4 - Children and Parents
Galatians 5:16-26 - Life by the Spirit
Hebrews 12:1-3 - God Disciplines His Sons
John 4:27-38 - The Disciples Rejoin Jesus
John 12:20-36 - Jesus Predicts His Death
John 18:19-24 - The High Priest Questions Jesus
Luke 9:1-9 - Jesus Sends Out the Twelve
Luke 14:25-35 - The Cost of Being a Disciple
Mark 9:14-32 - The Healing of a Boy With an Evil Spirit
Matthew 6:16-18 - Fasting
Matthew 14:1-12 - John the Baptist Beheaded
Revelation 2:12-17 - To the Church in Pergamum
Revelation 3:14-22 - To the Church in Laodicea

■ **DISCOURAGEMENT**

Colossians 3:18–4:1 - Rules for Christian Households
Ephesians 6:1-4 - Children and Parents
James 5:7-12 - Patience in Suffering
John 11:17-37 - Jesus Comforts the Sisters
John 20:10-18 - Jesus Appears to Mary Magdalene
Matthew 10:1-42 - Jesus Sends Out the Twelve
Romans 7:7-25 - Struggling With Sin

■ **DISHONESTY**

John 12:1-11 - Jesus Anointed at Bethany
Luke 16:1-15 - The Parable of the Shrewd Manager
Luke 19:1-10 - Zacchaeus the Tax Collector
Luke 19:45-48 - Jesus at the Temple
Luke 20:20-26 - Paying Taxes to Caesar
Luke 22:1-6 - Judas Agrees to Betray Jesus
Mark 11:12-19 - Jesus Clears the Temple
Mark 12:1-12 - The Parable of the Tenants
Mark 14:66-72 - Peter Disowns Jesus
Matthew 21:18-22 - The Fig Tree Withers
Matthew 22:15-22 - Paying Taxes to Caesar
Matthew 23:1-39 - Seven Woes

■ **DISOBEDIENCE**

1 Corinthians 11:17-34 - The Lord's Supper
1 John 1:5–2:14 - Walking in the Light
1 John 2:28–3:10 - Children of God
1 John 3:11-24 - Love One Another
1 John 5:13-21 - Concluding Remarks
1 Timothy 1:1-11 - Warning Against False Teachers of the Law
1 Timothy 1:12-20 - The Lord's Grace to Paul
2 Timothy 3:1-9 - Godlessness in the Last Days
Acts 7:1-53 - Stephen's Speech to the Sanhedrin
Galatians 5:1-15 - Freedom in Christ
Hebrews 2:1-4 - Warning to Pay Attention
Hebrews 3:7-19 - Warning Against Unbelief
Hebrews 4:1-13 - A Sabbath-Rest for the People of God
John 18:15-18 - Peter's First Denial
John 18:19-24 - The High Priest Questions Jesus
Mark 1:40-45 - A Man With Leprosy
Matthew 7:24-29 - The Wise and Foolish Builders
Matthew 9:27-34 - Jesus Heals the Blind and Mute
Matthew 15:1-20 - Clean and Unclean
Matthew 16:1-4 - The Demand for a Sign
Romans 3:9-20 - No One Is Righteous
Romans 11:25-32 - All Israel Will Be Saved
Titus 1:1-16 - Titus' Task on Crete

■ **DIVISIONS**

1 Corinthians 1:10-17 - Divisions in the Church
1 Corinthians 3:1-23 - On Divisions in the Church
1 Corinthians 11:17-34 - The Lord's Supper
1 Corinthians 14:26-40 - Orderly Worship
Acts 14:1-7 - In Iconium
John 7:25-44 - Is Jesus the Christ?
John 17:20-26 - Jesus Prays for All Believers
Jude 17-25 - A Call to Persevere
Luke 12:49-53 - Not Peace but Division
Mark 3:20-30 - Jesus and Beelzebub
Mark 9:38-41 - Whoever Is Not Against Us Is for Us
Matthew 20:20-28 - A Mother's Request

■ **DIVORCE**

Matthew 5:31-32 - Divorce

■ **DOCTRINE**

1 John 1:1-4 - The Word of Life
1 John 1:5-2:14 - Walking in the Light
1 John 2:18-27 - Warning Against Antichrists
1 John 2:28–3:10 - Children of God
1 John 4:1-6 - Test the Spirits
1 Peter 1:1-12 - Praise to God for a Living Hope
1 Peter 3:1-7 - Wives and Husbands
1 Peter 3:8-22 - Suffering for Doing Good
1 Timothy 1:1-11 - Warning Against False Teachers of the Law
1 Timothy 1:12-20 - The Lord's Grace to Paul
1 Timothy 4:1-16 - Instructions to Timothy
1 Timothy 6:3-10 - Love of Money
2 Peter 1:12-21 - Prophecy of Scripture
2 Peter 3:1-18 - The Day of the Lord
2 Timothy 3:10–4:8 - Paul's Charge to Timothy
Acts 15:1-21 - The Council at Jerusalem
Colossians 1:15-23 - The Supremacy of Christ
Colossians 2:6-23 - Freedom From Human Regulations Through Life With Christ

Ephesians 1:1-14 - Spiritual Blessings in Christ
Galatians 2:1-10 - Paul Accepted by the Apostles
Galatians 2:11-21 - Paul Opposes Peter
John 16:5-16 - The Work of the Holy Spirit
John 17:20-26 - Jesus Prays for All Believers
John 20:1-9 - The Empty Tomb
Luke 20:41-47 - Whose Son Is the Christ?
Revelation 1:1-3 - Prologue

■ **DOUBT**

James 1:1-18 - Trials and Temptations
John 6:60-71 - Many Disciples Desert Jesus
John 7:1-13 - Jesus Goes to the Feast of Tabernacles
John 7:25-44 - Is Jesus the Christ?
John 10:22-42 - The Unbelief of the Jews
John 11:38-44 - Jesus Raises Lazarus From the Dead
John 18:1-11 - Jesus Arrested
John 18:15-18 - Peter's First Denial
John 20:1-9 - The Empty Tomb
John 20:24-31 - Jesus Appears to Thomas
Luke 8:22-25 - Jesus Calms a Storm
Luke 24:36-49 - Jesus Appears to the Disciples
Mark 4:35-41 - Jesus Calms the Storm
Mark 5:1-20 - The Healing of a Demon-possessed Man
Mark 6:1-6 - A Prophet Without Honor
Mark 6:14-29 - John the Baptist Beheaded
Mark 6:30-44 - Jesus Feeds the Five Thousand
Mark 8:1-13 - Jesus Feeds the Four Thousand
Mark 9:14-32 - The Healing of a Boy With an Evil Spirit
Mark 11:20-26 - The Withered Fig Tree
Mark 11:27-33 - The Authority of Jesus Questioned
Mark 16:1-20 - The Resurrection
Matthew 9:18-26 - A Dead Girl and a Sick Woman
Matthew 11:1-19 - Jesus and John the Baptist
Matthew 13:53-58 - A Prophet Without Honor

■ **DRINKING**

1 Peter 4:1-11 - Living for God
1 Timothy 3:1-16 - Overseers and Deacons
1 Timothy 5:1–6:2 - Advice About Widows, Elders and Slaves

■ **EARTH**

1 Corinthians 15:35-58 - The Resurrection Body
2 Corinthians 5:1-10 - Our Heavenly Dwelling
2 Peter 3:1-18 - The Day of the Lord
John 3:22-36 - John the Baptist's Testimony About Jesus
Matthew 6:19-24 - Treasures in Heaven
Matthew 24:1-35 - Signs of the End of the Age
Revelation 7:1-8 - 144,000 Sealed
Revelation 12:1–13:1 - The Woman and the Dragon
Revelation 14:6-13 - The Three Angels
Revelation 14:14-20 - The Harvest of the Earth
Revelation 16:1-21 - The Seven Bowls of God's Wrath
Revelation 20:11-15 - The Dead Are Judged
Revelation 21:1-27 - The New Jerusalem

■ **EFFECTIVENESS**

1 Timothy 3:1-16 - Overseers and Deacons
Acts 14:1-7 - In Iconium
Matthew 25:14-30 - The Parable of the Talents
Matthew 27:62-66 - The Guard at the Tomb

■ **EFFORT**

Luke 5:17-26 - Jesus Heals a Paralytic
Matthew 7:24-29 - The Wise and Foolish Builders
Matthew 9:9-13 - The Calling of Matthew
Matthew 11:25-30 - Rest for the Weary
Matthew 18:10-14 - The Parable of the Lost Sheep

■ **EGO**

1 John 2:15-17 - Do Not Love the World
1 Timothy 2:1-15 - Instructions on Worship
1 Timothy 3:1-16 - Overseers and Deacons
2 Timothy 3:1-9 - Godlessness in the Last Days
Matthew 2:1-12 - The Visit of the Magi
Matthew 2:13-18 - The Escape to Egypt
Matthew 6:1-4 - Giving to the Needy
Matthew 6:5-15 - Prayer
Matthew 16:1-4 - The Demand for a Sign
Matthew 19:1-12 - Divorce
Matthew 19:16-30 - The Rich Young Man
Matthew 20:20-28 - A Mother's Request
Matthew 21:12-17 - Jesus at the Temple

■ **EMBARRASSMENT**

2 Timothy 2:14-26 - A Workman Approved by God
Luke 22:54-62 - Peter Disowns Jesus
Mark 14:66-72 - Peter Disowns Jesus
Matthew 1:18-25 - The Birth of Jesus Christ
Matthew 14:1-12 - John the Baptist Beheaded
Matthew 20:29-34 - Two Blind Men Receive Sight
Matthew 22:15-22 - Paying Taxes to Caesar
Matthew 22:41-46 - Whose Son Is the Christ?
Matthew 26:6-13 - Jesus Anointed at Bethany
Matthew 26:31-35 - Jesus Predicts Peter's Denial
Matthew 26:69-75 - Peter Disowns Jesus
Matthew 28:11-15 - The Guards' Report

■ **EMOTIONS**

Acts 3:1-10 - Peter Heals the Crippled Beggar
John 20:10-18 - Jesus Appears to Mary Magdalene
Mark 10:32-34 - Jesus Again Predicts His Death
Mark 11:12-19 - Jesus Clears the Temple
Mark 14:12-26 - The Lord's Supper

■ **EMPLOYMENT**

2 Thessalonians 3:6-18 - Warning Against Idleness
Luke 3:1-20 - John the Baptist Prepares the Way
Matthew 20:1-16 - The Parable of the Workers in the Vineyard

■ **ENCOURAGEMENT**

1 Thessalonians 2:17–3:5 - Paul's Longing to See the Thessalonians
1 Thessalonians 3:6-13 - Timothy's Encouraging Report
1 Timothy 1:1-11 - Warning Against False Teachers of the Law
2 Corinthians 7:2-16 - Paul's Joy
2 Corinthians 8:1-15 - Generosity Encouraged
2 Peter 3:1-18 - The Day of the Lord
2 Timothy 1:1-2:13 - Encouragement to Be Faithful
2 Timothy 3:10–4:8 - Paul's Charge to Timothy
Acts 4:32-37 - The Believers Share Their Possessions
Acts 11:19-30 - The Church in Antioch
Acts 13:13-52 - In Pisidian Antioch
Acts 14:21-28 - The Return to Antioch in Syria
Acts 15:22-35 - The Council's Letter to Gentile Believers
Acts 16:16-40 - Paul and Silas in Prison
Acts 18:1-17 - In Corinth
Acts 18:18-28 - Priscilla, Aquila and Apollos
Acts 20:1-6 - Through Macedonia and Greece

Acts 20:7-12 - Eutychus Raised From the Dead at Troas
Acts 27:13-26 - The Storm
Acts 27:27-44 - The Shipwreck
Acts 28:11-16 - Arrival at Rome
Colossians 1:24–2:5 - Paul's Labor for the Church
Colossians 4:2-18 - Further Instructions
Ephesians 6:10-24 - The Armor of God
Galatians 6:1-10 - Doing Good to All
Hebrews 3:7-19 - Warning Against Unbelief
Hebrews 10:19-39 - A Call to Persevere
Hebrews 12:1-3 - God Disciplines His Sons
John 14:15-31 - Jesus Promises the Holy Spirit
John 16:17-33 - The Disciples' Grief Will Turn to Joy
John 20:10-18 - Jesus Appears to Mary Magdalene
Luke 1:39-45 - Mary Visits Elizabeth
Luke 6:17-26 - Blessings and Woes
Luke 12:1-12 - Warnings and Encouragements
Philippians 2:1-11 - Imitating Christ's Humility
Philippians 2:19-30 - Timothy and Epaphroditus
Philemon 1-7 - Thanksgiving and Prayer
Revelation 10:1-11 - The Angel and the Little Scroll

■ ENDURANCE

1 Corinthians 1:1-9 - Thanksgiving
1 Peter 1:1-12 - Praise to God for a Living Hope
1 Peter 2:13-25 - Submission to Rulers and Masters
2 Corinthians 1:1-11 - The God of All Comfort
2 Corinthians 4:1-18 - Treasures in Jars of Clay
2 Timothy 1:1–2:13 - Encouragement to Be Faithful
Acts 27:13-26 - The Storm
Hebrews 11:1-40 - By Faith
James 5:7-12 - Patience in Suffering
Mark 15:16-20 - The Soldiers Mock Jesus
Mark 15:21-32 - The Crucifixion
Matthew 5:1-12 - The Beatitudes
Matthew 7:7-12 - Ask, Seek, Knock
Matthew 10:1-42 - Jesus Sends Out the Twelve
Matthew 24:1-35 - Signs of the End of the Age
Matthew 26:31-35 - Jesus Predicts Peter's Denial
Matthew 26:36-46 - Gethsemane
Matthew 27:32-44 - The Crucifixion
Revelation 1:9-20 - One Like a Son of Man
Revelation 3:7-13 - To the Church in Philadelphia
Revelation 13:2-10 - The Beast out of the Sea
Revelation 14:6-13 - The Three Angels
Romans 5:1-11 - Peace and Joy

■ ENEMIES

1 Peter 2:13-25 - Submission to Rulers and Masters
2 Peter 2:1-22 - False Teachers and Their Destruction
Acts 21:27-36 - Paul Arrested
Colossians 1:15-23 - The Supremacy of Christ
John 5:16-30 - Life Through the Son
John 18:1-11 - Jesus Arrested
John 18:15-18 - Peter's First Denial
John 18:19-24 - The High Priest Questions Jesus
John 18:25-27 - Peter's Second and Third Denials
John 19:17-27 - The Crucifixion
Luke 6:27-36 - Love for Enemies
Luke 11:37-54 - Six Woes
Luke 20:9-19 - The Parable of the Tenants
Luke 22:47-53 - Jesus Arrested
Matthew 5:1-12 - The Beatitudes
Matthew 5:21-26 - Murder
Matthew 5:38-42 - An Eye for an Eye
Matthew 5:43-48 - Love for Enemies
Matthew 10:1-42 - Jesus Sends Out the Twelve
Matthew 12:15-21 - God's Chosen Servant
Matthew 12:22-37 - Jesus and Beelzebub
Matthew 13:24-30 - The Parable of the Weeds
Matthew 13:36-43 - The Parable of the Weeds Explained
Matthew 16:21-28 - Jesus Predicts His Death
Matthew 20:17-19 - Jesus Again Predicts His Death
Matthew 21:33-46 - The Parable of the Tenants
Matthew 22:41-46 - Whose Son Is the Christ?
Matthew 26:1-5 - The Plot Against Jesus
Matthew 26:47-56 - Jesus Arrested
Matthew 26:57-68 - Before the Sanhedrin
Philippians 3:12–4:1 - Pressing on Toward the Goal
Revelation 8:6–9:21 - The Trumpets
Revelation 11:1-14 - The Two Witnesses
Revelation 13:11-18 - The Beast out of the Earth
Revelation 19:11-21 - The Rider on the White Horse
Revelation 20:1-6 - The Thousand Years
Revelation 20:7-10 - Satan's Doom
Romans 5:1-11 - Peace and Joy
Romans 12:9-21 - Love

■ ENTHUSIASM

John 12:12-19 - The Triumphal Entry
Luke 1:46-56 - Mary's Song

■ ENVIRONMENT

Revelation 8:6–9:21 - The Trumpets

■ ENVY

James 3:13-18 - Two Kinds of Wisdom
Luke 9:46-50 - Who Will Be the Greatest?
Mark 15:1-15 - Jesus Before Pilate
Matthew 12:1-14 - Lord of the Sabbath

■ EQUALITY

2 Corinthians 8:1-15 - Generosity Encouraged
Colossians 3:1-17 - Rules for Holy Living
James 2:1-13 - Favoritism Forbidden

■ ESCAPE

Acts 27:27-44 - The Shipwreck
Matthew 2:13-18 - The Escape to Egypt

■ ETERNAL LIFE

1 John 1:1-4 - The Word of Life
1 John 2:15-17 - Do Not Love the World
1 John 2:18-27 - Warning Against Antichrists
1 John 3:11-24 - Love One Another
1 John 5:1-12 - Faith in the Son of God
1 John 5:13-21 - Concluding Remarks
1 Timothy 6:11-21 - Paul's Charge to Timothy
2 Corinthians 5:1-10 - Our Heavenly Dwelling
2 Peter 1:1-11 - Making One's Calling and Election Sure
Galatians 6:1-10 - Doing Good to All
Hebrews 7:11-28 - Jesus Like Melchizedek
John 3:1-22 - Jesus Teaches Nicodemus
John 3:22-36 - John the Baptist's Testimony About Jesus
John 4:27-38 - The Disciples Rejoin Jesus
John 5:16-30 - Life Through the Son
John 5:31-47 - Testimonies About Jesus
John 6:25-59 - Jesus the Bread of Life
John 6:60-71 - Many Disciples Desert Jesus
John 8:12-30 - The Validity of Jesus' Testimony
John 10:1-21 - The Shepherd and His Flock
John 10:22-42 - The Unbelief of the Jews

John 11:17-37 - Jesus Comforts the Sisters
John 12:37-50 - The Jews Continue in Their Unbelief
John 14:1-4 - Jesus Comforts His Disciples
John 17:1-5 - Jesus Prays for Himself
John 20:24-31 - Jesus Appears to Thomas
Jude 17-25 - A Call to Persevere
Luke 10:25-37 - The Parable of the Good Samaritan
Luke 16:1-15 - The Parable of the Shrewd Manager
Luke 16:19-31 - The Rich Man and Lazarus
Luke 18:18-30 - The Rich Ruler
Mark 8:31-9:1 - Jesus Predicts His Death
Mark 10:17-31 - The Rich Young Man
Matthew 7:13-14 - The Narrow and Wide Gates
Matthew 18:10-14 - The Parable of the Lost Sheep
Matthew 19:13-15 - The Little Children and Jesus
Matthew 19:16-30 - The Rich Young Man
Matthew 21:28-32 - The Parable of the Two Sons
Matthew 22:23-33 - Marriage at the Resurrection
Matthew 24:1-35 - Signs of the End of the Age
Matthew 24:36-51 - The Day and Hour Unknown
Matthew 25:1-13 - The Parable of the Ten Virgins
Matthew 25:31-46 - The Sheep and the Goats
Revelation 7:9-17 - The Great Multitude in White Robes
Revelation 11:15-19 - The Seventh Trumpet
Revelation 14:1-5 - The Lamb and the 144,000
Revelation 20:11-15 - The Dead Are Judged
Revelation 22:7-21 - Jesus Is Coming
Romans 6:15-23 - Slaves to Righteousness
Titus 3:1-15 - Doing What Is Good

■ EVANGELISM

2 Timothy 3:10–4:8 - Paul's Charge to Timothy
Acts 2:14-41 - Peter Addresses the Crowd
Acts 8:26-40 - Philip and the Ethiopian
Acts 13:4-12 - On Cyprus
Acts 16:11-15 - Lydia's Conversion in Philippi
Galatians 1:11-24 - Paul Called by God
John 4:1-26 - Jesus Talks With a Samaritan Woman
John 4:27-38 - The Disciples Rejoin Jesus
John 4:39-42 - Many Samaritans Believe
John 12:12-19 - The Triumphal Entry
Luke 5:1-11 - The Calling of the First Disciples
Luke 9:1-9 - Jesus Sends Out the Twelve
Luke 10:1-24 - Jesus Sends Out the Seventy-two
Luke 24:1-12 - The Resurrection
Mark 2:13-17 - The Calling of Levi
Mark 3:13-19 - The Appointing of the Twelve Apostles
Matthew 4:12-17 - Jesus Begins to Preach
Matthew 4:18-22 - The Calling of the First Disciples
Matthew 7:13-14 - The Narrow and Wide Gates
Matthew 9:9-13 - The Calling of Matthew
Matthew 9:35-38 - The Workers Are Few
Matthew 13:1-23 - The Parable of the Sower
Matthew 18:10-14 - The Parable of the Lost Sheep
Matthew 24:1-35 - Signs of the End of the Age
Matthew 28:1-10 - The Resurrection
Matthew 28:16-20 - The Great Commission
Romans 15:14-22 - Paul, the Minister to the Gentiles

■ EVIDENCE

1 John 1:1-4 - The Word of Life
Acts 1:1-11 - Jesus Taken Up Into Heaven
John 4:39-42 - Many Samaritans Believe
John 14:5-14 - Jesus the Way to the Father
John 20:19-23 - Jesus Appears to His Disciples
John 20:24-31 - Jesus Appears to Thomas
Luke 1:1-4 - Introduction
Luke 22:66–23:25 - Jesus Before Pilate and Herod
Mark 14:53-65 - Before the Sanhedrin
Matthew 8:28-34 - The Healing of Two Demon-possessed Men
Matthew 12:38-45 - The Sign of Jonah
Matthew 13:1-23 - The Parable of the Sower

■ EVIL

1 John 1:5-2:14 - Walking in the Light
1 John 3:11-24 - Love One Another
1 John 5:13-21 - Concluding Remarks
1 Peter 1:13–2:3 - Be Holy
1 Peter 3:8-22 - Suffering for Doing Good
1 Timothy 6:3-10 - Love of Money
2 Peter 1:1-11 - Making One's Calling and Election Sure
2 Thessalonians 2:1-12 - The Man of Lawlessness
2 Timothy 2:14-26 - A Workman Approved by God
2 Timothy 3:1-9 - Godlessness in the Last Days
3 John 1-14 - From the Elder
Ephesians 6:10-24 - The Armor of God
James 1:1-18 - Trials and Temptations
James 1:19-27 - Listening and Doing
John 7:1-13 - Jesus Goes to the Feast of Tabernacles
John 13:18-30 - Jesus Predicts His Betrayal
Luke 4:1-13 - The Temptation of Jesus
Luke 4:31-37 - Jesus Drives Out an Evil Spirit
Luke 6:43-45 - A Tree and Its Fruit
Luke 8:26-39 - The Healing of a Demon-possessed Man
Luke 9:37-45 - The Healing of a Boy With an Evil Spirit
Luke 11:14-28 - Jesus and Beelzebub
Luke 22:47-53 - Jesus Arrested
Mark 7:1-23 - Clean and Unclean
Mark 8:14-21 - The Yeast of the Pharisees and Herod
Matthew 5:13-16 - Salt and Light
Matthew 7:7-12 - Ask, Seek, Knock
Matthew 7:15-23 - A Tree and Its Fruit
Matthew 12:22-37 - Jesus and Beelzebub
Matthew 13:47-52 - The Parable of the Net
Matthew 16:5-12 - The Yeast of the Pharisees and Sadducees
Matthew 18:1-9 - The Greatest in the Kingdom of Heaven
Matthew 20:17-19 - Jesus Again Predicts His Death
Matthew 21:12-17 - Jesus at the Temple
Matthew 21:33-46 - The Parable of the Tenants
Matthew 22:1-14 - The Parable of the Wedding Banquet
Matthew 24:1-35 - Signs of the End of the Age
Matthew 26:47-56 - Jesus Arrested
Matthew 26:57-68 - Before the Sanhedrin
Matthew 27:11-26 - Jesus Before Pilate
Matthew 27:27-31 - The Soldiers Mock Jesus
Revelation 8:6–9:21 - The Trumpets
Romans 1:18-32 - God's Wrath Against Mankind

■ EXAMPLE

1 Corinthians 4:1-21 - Apostles of Christ
1 Corinthians 8:1-13 - Food Sacrificed to Idols
1 Corinthians 9:1-27 - The Rights of an Apostle
1 Corinthians 10:1-13 - Warnings From Israel's History
1 Corinthians 10:23–11:1 - The Believer's Freedom
1 Peter 2:13-25 - Submission to Rulers and Masters

1 Peter 5:1-14 - To Elders and Young Men
1 Timothy 1:12-20 - The Lord's Grace to Paul
1 Timothy 4:1-16 - Instructions to Timothy
2 Corinthians 2:12–3:6 - Ministers of the New Covenant
2 Corinthians 8:16–9:5 - Titus Sent to Corinth
2 Corinthians 13:1-14 - Final Warnings
2 Thessalonians 3:6-18 - Warning Against Idleness
2 Timothy 1:1–2:13 - Encouragement to Be Faithful
John 3:22-36 - John the Baptist's Testimony About Jesus
John 11:17-37 - Jesus Comforts the Sisters
John 13:1-17 - Jesus Washes His Disciples' Feet
John 17:20-26 - Jesus Prays for All Believers
Luke 2:41-52 - The Boy Jesus at the Temple
Luke 4:14-30 - Jesus Rejected at Nazareth
Luke 11:29-32 - The Sign of Jonah
Mark 4:30-34 - The Parable of the Mustard Seed
Mark 9:42-50 - Causing to Sin
Matthew 18:1-9 - The Greatest in the Kingdom of Heaven
Matthew 19:1-12 - Divorce
Matthew 26:6-13 - Jesus Anointed at Bethany
Matthew 26:17-30 - The Lord's Supper
Philippians 2:1-11 - Imitating Christ's Humility
Philippians 3:12–4:1 - Pressing on Toward the Goal
Philippians 4:2-9 - Exhortations
Titus 2:1-15 - What Must Be Taught to Various Groups

■ EXCUSES

Luke 14:15-24 - The Parable of the Great Banquet
Matthew 4:18-22 - The Calling of the First Disciples
Matthew 22:1-14 - The Parable of the Wedding Banquet
Matthew 25:14-30 - The Parable of the Talents
Matthew 28:11-15 - The Guards' Report
Romans 3:9-20 - No One Is Righteous

■ EXPECTATIONS

2 Corinthians 12:11-21 - Paul's Concern for the Corinthians
John 6:1-15 - Jesus Feeds the Five Thousand
John 12:12-19 - The Triumphal Entry
John 20:1-9 - The Empty Tomb
Luke 1:57-66 - The Birth of John the Baptist
Luke 1:67-80 - Zechariah's Song
Luke 2:21-40 - Jesus Presented in the Temple
Luke 4:14-30 - Jesus Rejected at Nazareth
Luke 5:12-16 - The Man With Leprosy
Luke 6:43-45 - A Tree and Its Fruit
Luke 7:18-35 - Jesus and John the Baptist
Luke 19:11-27 - The Parable of the Ten Minas
Luke 21:5-38 - Signs of the End of the Age
Luke 22:39-46 - Jesus Prays on the Mount of Olives
Luke 24:13-35 - On the Road to Emmaus
Matthew 8:18-22 - The Cost of Following Jesus
Matthew 12:15-21 - God's Chosen Servant
Matthew 13:31-35 - The Parables of the Mustard Seed and the Yeast
Matthew 16:1-4 - The Demand for a Sign
Matthew 24:36-51 - The Day and Hour Unknown
Matthew 25:1-13 - The Parable of the Ten Virgins
Matthew 27:62-66 - The Guard at the Tomb

■ EXPERIENCE

Matthew 17:1-13 - The Transfiguration
Matthew 24:1-35 - Signs of the End of the Age

■ FAILURE

1 Timothy 1:12-20 - The Lord's Grace to Paul
John 7:53–8:11 - A Woman Caught in Adultery
John 15:1-17 - The Vine and the Branches
John 18:25-27 - Peter's Second and Third Denials
Luke 5:1-11 - The Calling of the First Disciples
Matthew 26:31-35 - Jesus Predicts Peter's Denial
Matthew 26:47-56 - Jesus Arrested

■ FAIRNESS

Acts 25:1-12 - The Trial Before Festus
Acts 25:23–26:32 - Paul Before Agrippa
Colossians 3:18–4:1 - Rules for Christian Households
Mark 4:21-25 - A Lamp on a Stand
Matthew 20:20-28 - A Mother's Request

■ FAITH

1 Corinthians 12:1-11 - Spiritual Gifts
1 Corinthians 15:12-34 - The Resurrection of the Dead
1 John 1:1-4 - The Word of Life
1 John 5:1-12 - Faith in the Son of God
1 Peter 1:1-12 - Praise to God for a Living Hope
1 Peter 1:13–2:3 - Be Holy
1 Peter 3:8-22 - Suffering for Doing Good
1 Peter 4:1-11 - Living for God
1 Thessalonians 1:1-10 - Thanksgiving for the Thessalonians' Faith
1 Thessalonians 3:6-13 - Timothy's Encouraging Report
1 Timothy 1:1-11 - Warning Against False Teachers of the Law
1 Timothy 1:12-20 - The Lord's Grace to Paul
1 Timothy 2:1-15 - Instructions on Worship
1 Timothy 4:1-16 - Instructions to Timothy
1 Timothy 6:3-10 - Love of Money
1 Timothy 6:11-21 - Paul's Charge to Timothy
2 Corinthians 1:12–2:4 - Paul's Change of Plans
2 Corinthians 5:1-10 - Our Heavenly Dwelling
2 Corinthians 13:1-14 - Final Warnings
2 Peter 1:1-11 - Making One's Calling and Election Sure
2 Thessalonians 1:1-12 - Thanksgiving and Prayer
2 Timothy 1:1–2:13 - Encouragement to Be Faithful
2 Timothy 2:14-26 - A Workman Approved by God
2 Timothy 3:1-9 - Godlessness in the Last Days
2 Timothy 3:10–4:8 - Paul's Charge to Timothy
Acts 3:11-26 - Peter Speaks to the Onlookers
Acts 5:12-16 - The Apostles Heal Many
Acts 11:19-30 - The Church in Antioch
Acts 13:4-12 - On Cyprus
Acts 14:8-20 - In Lystra and Derbe
Acts 14:21-28 - The Return to Antioch in Syria
Acts 16:1-5 - Timothy Joins Paul and Silas
Acts 24:1-27 - The Trial Before Felix
Acts 27:13-26 - The Storm
Colossians 1:1-14 - Thanksgiving and Prayer
Colossians 2:6-23 - Freedom From Human Regulations Through Life With Christ
Ephesians 1:15-23 - Thanksgiving and Prayer
Ephesians 2:1-10 - Made Alive in Christ
Ephesians 3:14-21 - A Prayer for the Ephesians
Ephesians 4:1-16 - Unity in the Body of Christ
Galatians 2:11-21 - Paul Opposes Peter
Galatians 3:1-14 - Faith or Observance of the Law
Galatians 3:15-25 - The Law and the Promise
Galatians 3:26–4:7 - Sons of God
Hebrews 4:1-13 - A Sabbath-Rest for the People of God
Hebrews 4:14–5:10 - Jesus the Great High Priest

Hebrews 6:13-20 - The Certainty of God's Promise
Hebrews 11:1-40 - By Faith
James 2:14-26 - Faith and Deeds
James 5:13-20 - The Prayer of Faith
John 2:1-11 - Jesus Changes Water to Wine
John 2:12-25 - Jesus Clears the Temple
John 3:1-22 - Jesus Teaches Nicodemus
John 3:22-36 - John the Baptist's Testimony About Jesus
John 4:39-42 - Many Samaritans Believe
John 4:43-54 - Jesus Heals the Official's Son
John 5:16-30 - Life Through the Son
John 6:1-15 - Jesus Feeds the Five Thousand
John 6:25-59 - Jesus the Bread of Life
John 7:1-13 - Jesus Goes to the Feast of Tabernacles
John 7:25-44 - Is Jesus the Christ?
John 8:12-30 - The Validity of Jesus' Testimony
John 9:35-41 - Spiritual Blindness
John 11:17-37 - Jesus Comforts the Sisters
John 12:1-11 - Jesus Anointed at Bethany
John 12:20-36 - Jesus Predicts His Death
John 12:37-50 - The Jews Continue in Their Unbelief
John 14:5-14 - Jesus the Way to the Father
John 19:28-37 - The Death of Jesus
John 19:38-42 - The Burial of Jesus
Jude 17-25 - A Call to Persevere
Luke 1:26-38 - The Birth of Jesus Foretold
Luke 1:46-56 - Mary's Song
Luke 5:17-26 - Jesus Heals a Paralytic
Luke 7:1-10 - The Faith of the Centurion
Luke 7:11-17 - Jesus Raises a Widow's Son
Luke 7:18-35 - Jesus and John the Baptist
Luke 8:22-25 - Jesus Calms a Storm
Luke 9:10-17 - Jesus Feeds the Five Thousand
Luke 9:28-36 - The Transfiguration
Luke 13:18-21 - The Parables of the Mustard Seed and the Yeast
Luke 13:22-30 - The Narrow Door
Luke 17:1-10 - Sin, Faith, Duty
Luke 17:11-19 - Ten Healed of Leprosy
Luke 18:1-8 - The Parable of the Persistent Widow
Luke 18:35-43 - A Blind Beggar Receives His Sight
Luke 22:7-38 - The Last Supper
Luke 23:50-56 - Jesus' Burial
Mark 1:40-45 - A Man With Leprosy
Mark 2:1-12 - Jesus Heals a Paralytic
Mark 4:35-41 - Jesus Calms the Storm
Mark 5:21-43 - A Dead Girl and a Sick Woman
Mark 6:1-6 - A Prophet Without Honor
Mark 6:7-13 - Jesus Sends Out the Twelve
Mark 6:30-44 - Jesus Feeds the Five Thousand
Mark 6:45-56 - Jesus Walks on the Water
Mark 7:24-30 - The Faith of a Syrophoenician Woman
Mark 7:31-37 - The Healing of a Deaf and Mute Man
Mark 8:1-13 - Jesus Feeds the Four Thousand
Mark 8:27-30 - Peter's Confession of Christ
Mark 9:14-32 - The Healing of a Boy With an Evil Spirit
Mark 10:46-52 - Blind Bartimaeus Receives His Sight
Mark 11:20-26 - The Withered Fig Tree
Mark 12:18-27 - Marriage at the Resurrection
Mark 14:27-31 - Jesus Predicts Peter's Denial
Mark 16:1-20 - The Resurrection
Matthew 8:5-13 - The Faith of the Centurion
Matthew 8:23-27 - Jesus Calms the Storm
Matthew 9:1-8 - Jesus Heals a Paralytic
Matthew 9:18-26 - A Dead Girl and a Sick Woman
Matthew 9:27-34 - Jesus Heals the Blind and Mute
Matthew 14:22-36 - Jesus Walks on the Water
Matthew 15:21-28 - The Faith of the Canaanite Woman
Matthew 16:5-12 - The Yeast of the Pharisees and Sadducees
Matthew 17:14-23 - The Healing of a Boy With a Demon
Matthew 21:18-22 - The Fig Tree Withers
Matthew 26:6-13 - Jesus Anointed at Bethany
Philippians 1:12-30 - Paul's Chains Advance the Gospel
Philippians 3:1-11 - No Confidence in the Flesh
Revelation 2:12-17 - To the Church in Pergamum
Revelation 2:18-29 - To the Church in Thyatira
Revelation 3:1-6 - To the Church in Sardis
Romans 3:21-31 - Righteousness Through Faith
Romans 4:1-25 - Abraham Justified by Faith
Romans 11:11-24 - Ingrafted Branches

■ FAITHFULNESS

1 Corinthians 1:1-9 - Thanksgiving
1 Corinthians 4:1-21 - Apostles of Christ
1 Corinthians 10:1-13 - Warnings From Israel's History
1 Thessalonians 4:1-12 - Living to Please God
2 Peter 2:1-22 - False Teachers and Their Destruction
2 Timothy 1:1–2:13 - Encouragement to Be Faithful
3 John 1-14 - From the Elder
Hebrews 3:1-6 - Jesus Greater Than Moses
John 14:15-31 - Jesus Promises the Holy Spirit
John 15:1-17 - The Vine and the Branches
Luke 2:21-40 - Jesus Presented in the Temple
Luke 5:1-11 - The Calling of the First Disciples
Luke 9:57-62 - The Cost of Following Jesus
Luke 18:1-8 - The Parable of the Persistent Widow
Matthew 5:31-32 - Divorce
Matthew 5:33-37 - Oaths
Matthew 6:25-34 - Do Not Worry
Matthew 10:1-42 - Jesus Sends Out the Twelve
Matthew 13:53-58 - A Prophet Without Honor
Matthew 24:1-35 - Signs of the End of the Age
Revelation 2:1-7 - To the Church in Ephesus
Revelation 2:8-11 - To the Church in Smyrna
Revelation 3:7-13 - To the Church in Philadelphia
Revelation 3:14-22 - To the Church in Laodicea
Revelation 13:2-10 - The Beast out of the Sea
Revelation 14:6-13 - The Three Angels
Revelation 17:1-18 - The Woman on the Beast
Titus 1:1-16 - Titus' Task on Crete

■ FAMILY

1 Timothy 3:1-16 - Overseers and Deacons
1 Timothy 5:1–6:2 - Advice About Widows, Elders and Slaves
2 John 1-13 - From the Elder
Colossians 3:18–4:1 - Rules for Christian Households
Ephesians 3:14-21 - A Prayer for the Ephesians
Ephesians 5:22-33 - Wives and Husbands
Galatians 3:26–4:7 - Sons of God
John 7:1-13 - Jesus Goes to the Feast of Tabernacles
John 19:17-27 - The Crucifixion
Luke 1:5-25 - The Birth of John the Baptist Foretold
Luke 1:57-66 - The Birth of John the Baptist
Luke 2:41-52 - The Boy Jesus at the Temple

Luke 8:19-21 - Jesus' Mother and Brothers
Luke 10:38-42 - At the Home of Martha and Mary
Luke 11:14-28 - Jesus and Beelzebub
Luke 12:49-53 - Not Peace but Division
Luke 14:25-35 - The Cost of Being a Disciple
Luke 15:11-32 - The Parable of the Lost Son
Luke 18:18-30 - The Rich Ruler
Mark 1:14-20 - The Calling of the First Disciples
Mark 3:31-35 - Jesus' Mother and Brothers
Mark 6:1-6 - A Prophet Without Honor
Mark 13:1-31 - Signs of the End of the Age
Matthew 1:1-17 - The Genealogy of Jesus
Matthew 2:19-23 - The Return to Nazareth
Matthew 8:14-17 - Jesus Heals Many
Matthew 8:18-22 - The Cost of Following Jesus
Matthew 12:46-50 - Jesus' Mother and Brothers
Matthew 13:53-58 - A Prophet Without Honor

■ **FASTING**

Acts 9:1-19 - Saul's Conversion
Acts 13:1-3 - Barnabas and Saul Sent Off
Acts 14:21-28 - The Return to Antioch in Syria
Luke 5:33-39 - Jesus Questioned About Fasting
Luke 18:9-14 - The Parable of the Pharisee and the Tax Collector
Mark 2:18-22 - Jesus Questioned About Fasting
Matthew 9:14-17 - Jesus Questioned About Fasting
Matthew 17:14-23 - The Healing of a Boy With a Demon

■ **FAULTS**

John 7:53–8:11 - A Woman Caught in Adultery
Matthew 7:1-6 - Judging Others

■ **FAVORITISM**

1 Timothy 5:1–6:2 - Advice About Widows, Elders and Slaves
Acts 25:1-12 - The Trial Before Festus
Colossians 3:18–4:1 - Rules for Christian Households
Ephesians 6:5-9 - Slaves and Masters
James 2:1-13 - Favoritism Forbidden
Luke 9:46-50 - Who Will Be the Greatest?
Matthew 27:11-26 - Jesus Before Pilate
Romans 3:9-20 - No One Is Righteous

■ **FEAR**

1 Corinthians 1:18–2:5 - Christ the Wisdom and Power of God
1 John 4:7-21 - God's Love and Ours
1 Peter 2:13-25 - Submission to Rulers and Masters
2 Corinthians 12:11-21 - Paul's Concern for the Corinthians
Acts 5:1-11 - Ananias and Sapphira
Acts 5:12-16 - The Apostles Heal Many
Acts 19:1-22 - Paul in Ephesus
Acts 22:22-29 - Paul the Roman Citizen
Acts 27:13-26 - The Storm
John 6:16-24 - Jesus Walks on the Water
John 7:1-13 - Jesus Goes to the Feast of Tabernacles
John 12:37-50 - The Jews Continue in Their Unbelief
John 18:1-11 - Jesus Arrested
John 18:28-40 - Jesus Before Pilate
John 19:1-16 - Jesus Sentenced to be Crucified
John 19:38-42 - The Burial of Jesus
John 20:1-9 - The Empty Tomb
John 20:19-23 - Jesus Appears to His Disciples
Jude 17-25 - A Call to Persevere
Luke 8:22-25 - Jesus Calms a Storm
Luke 8:40-56 - A Dead Girl and a Sick Woman
Luke 9:28-36 - The Transfiguration
Luke 9:37-45 - The Healing of a Boy With an Evil Spirit
Luke 12:22-34 - Do Not Worry
Luke 24:1-12 - The Resurrection
Luke 24:36-49 - Jesus Appears to the Disciples
Mark 4:35-41 - Jesus Calms the Storm
Mark 5:1-20 - The Healing of a Demon-possessed Man
Mark 5:21-43 - A Dead Girl and a Sick Woman
Mark 6:45-56 - Jesus Walks on the Water
Mark 10:32-34 - Jesus Again Predicts His Death
Mark 11:27-33 - The Authority of Jesus Questioned
Mark 14:27-31 - Jesus Predicts Peter's Denial
Mark 14:43-52 - Jesus Arrested
Mark 14:53-65 - Before the Sanhedrin
Mark 14:66-72 - Peter Disowns Jesus
Mark 16:1-20 - The Resurrection
Matthew 2:19-23 - The Return to Nazareth
Matthew 8:23-27 - Jesus Calms the Storm
Matthew 10:1-42 - Jesus Sends Out the Twelve
Matthew 14:22-36 - Jesus Walks on the Water
Matthew 26:1-5 - The Plot Against Jesus
Matthew 26:69-75 - Peter Disowns Jesus
Matthew 27:57-61 - The Burial of Jesus
Revelation 2:8-11 - To the Church in Smyrna
Revelation 14:6-13 - The Three Angels
Revelation 15:1-8 - Seven Angels With Seven Plagues

■ **FEELINGS**

John 14:1-4 - Jesus Comforts His Disciples
Matthew 11:1-19 - Jesus and John the Baptist
Matthew 12:46-50 - Jesus' Mother and Brothers
Matthew 18:21-35 - The Parable of the Unmerciful Servant
Matthew 26:17-30 - The Lord's Supper
Matthew 27:1-10 - Judas Hangs Himself
Matthew 28:1-10 - The Resurrection

■ **FELLOWSHIP**

1 Corinthians 1:1-9 - Thanksgiving
1 Corinthians 11:2-16 - Propriety in Worship
1 John 1:1-4 - The Word of Life
1 John 1:5–2:14 - Walking in the Light
1 John 2:18-27 - Warning Against Antichrists
1 John 2:28–3:10 - Children of God
1 John 4:7-21 - God's Love and Ours
1 John 5:1-12 - Faith in the Son of God
1 Peter 5:1-14 - To Elders and Young Men
2 Corinthians 6:14–7:1 - Do Not Be Yoked with Unbelievers
2 John 1-13 - From the Elder
Acts 2:42-47 - The Fellowship of the Believers
Acts 4:32-37 - The Believers Share Their Possessions
Acts 20:1-6 - Through Macedonia and Greece
Acts 28:11-16 - Arrival at Rome
John 13:18-30 - Jesus Predicts His Betrayal
John 14:5-14 - Jesus the Way to the Father
John 14:15-31 - Jesus Promises the Holy Spirit
John 15:1-17 - The Vine and the Branches
John 17:1-5 - Jesus Prays for Himself
John 17:20-26 - Jesus Prays for All Believers
John 21:1-14 - Jesus and the Miraculous Catch of Fish
Luke 22:7-38 - The Last Supper

Philippians 2:1-11 - Imitating Christ's Humility
■ FLATTERY
Acts 12:20-25 - Herod's Death
Acts 24:1-27 - The Trial Before Felix
Matthew 22:15-22 - Paying Taxes to Caesar
■ FOLLOW
1 Corinthians 1:10-17 - Divisions in the Church
Acts 8:9-25 - Simon the Sorcerer
John 1:35-42 - Jesus' First Disciples
John 1:43-51 - Jesus Calls Philip and Nathanael
John 10:1-21 - The Shepherd and His Flock
John 12:20-36 - Jesus Predicts His Death
John 12:37-50 - The Jews Continue in Their Unbelief
John 13:31-38 - Jesus Predicts Peter's Denial
Luke 5:27-32 - The Calling of Levi
Luke 9:57-62 - The Cost of Following Jesus
Mark 1:14-20 - The Calling of the First Disciples
Mark 2:13-17 - The Calling of Levi
Mark 3:7-12 - Crowds Follow Jesus
Mark 3:13-19 - The Appointing of the Twelve Apostles
■ FOLLOW-THROUGH
2 Timothy 3:10–4:8 - Paul's Charge to Timothy
Luke 2:8-20 - The Shepherds and the Angels
Matthew 5:33-37 - Oaths
■ FOOLISHNESS
1 Corinthians 1:18–2:5 - Christ the Wisdom and Power of God
1 Corinthians 2:6-16 - Wisdom From the Spirit
1 Timothy 6:3-10 - Love of Money
2 Corinthians 11:16-33 - Paul Boasts About His Sufferings
Luke 12:13-21 - The Parable of the Rich Fool
Luke 24:13-35 - On the Road to Emmaus
Matthew 9:9-13 - The Calling of Matthew
Matthew 11:25-30 - Rest for the Weary
Matthew 12:38-45 - The Sign of Jonah
Matthew 14:1-12 - John the Baptist Beheaded
Matthew 26:31-35 - Jesus Predicts Peter's Denial
Matthew 27:11-26 - Jesus Before Pilate
Matthew 27:32-44 - The Crucifixion
■ FORGET
James 1:19-27 - Listening and Doing
Mark 8:14-21 - The Yeast of the Pharisees and Herod
■ FORGIVENESS
1 John 1:5-2:14 - Walking in the Light
2 Corinthians 2:5-11 - Forgiveness for the Sinner
2 Corinthians 5:11–6:2 - The Ministry of Reconciliation
Acts 10:24-48 - Peter at Cornelius' House
Colossians 1:1-14 - Thanksgiving and Prayer
Ephesians 4:17–5:21 - Living as Children of Light
Hebrews 8:1-13 - The High Priest of a New Covenant
Hebrews 9:1-10 - Worship in the Earthly Tabernacle
Hebrews 9:11-28 - The Blood of Christ
Hebrews 10:1-18 - Christ's Sacrifice Once for All
Hebrews 10:19-39 - A Call to Persevere
James 4:1-12 - Submit Yourselves to God
John 1:29-34 - Jesus the Lamb of God
John 7:53–8:11 - A Woman Caught in Adultery
John 13:1-17 - Jesus Washes His Disciples' Feet
John 20:19-23 - Jesus Appears to His Disciples
Luke 5:17-26 - Jesus Heals a Paralytic
Luke 6:27-36 - Love for Enemies
Luke 6:37-42 - Judging Others
Luke 7:36-50 - Jesus Anointed by a Sinful Woman
Luke 15:11-32 - The Parable of the Lost Son
Luke 17:1-10 - Sin, Faith, Duty
Luke 18:9-14 - The Parable of the Pharisee and the Tax Collector
Luke 23:26-43 - The Crucifixion
Mark 2:1-12 - Jesus Heals a Paralytic
Mark 3:20-30 - Jesus and Beelzebub
Mark 11:20-26 - The Withered Fig Tree
Matthew 5:21-26 - Murder
Matthew 6:5-15 - Prayer
Matthew 9:1-8 - Jesus Heals a Paralytic
Matthew 13:53-58 - A Prophet Without Honor
Matthew 18:21-35 - The Parable of the Unmerciful Servant
Matthew 19:1-12 - Divorce
Philemon 8-25 - Paul's Plea for Onesimus
Romans 12:9-21 - Love
■ FORSAKE
1 John 2:18-27 - Warning Against Antichrists
2 Peter 2:1-22 - False Teachers and Their Destruction
2 Timothy 1:1–2:13 - Encouragement to Be Faithful
John 18:15-18 - Peter's First Denial
Luke 22:1-6 - Judas Agrees to Betray Jesus
Luke 22:54-62 - Peter Disowns Jesus
Mark 14:27-31 - Jesus Predicts Peter's Denial
Mark 15:33-41 - The Death of Jesus
Matthew 26:69-75 - Peter Disowns Jesus
■ FOUNDATION
1 Corinthians 3:1-23 - On Divisions in the Church
Luke 6:46-49 - The Wise and Foolish Builders
Luke 14:25-35 - The Cost of Being a Disciple
Matthew 7:24-29 - The Wise and Foolish Builders
■ FREEDOM
1 Corinthians 7:1-40 - Marriage
1 Corinthians 8:1-13 - Food Sacrificed to Idols
1 Corinthians 10:23–11:1 - The Believer's Freedom
1 Peter 2:13-25 - Submission to Rulers and Masters
2 Corinthians 3:7-18 - The Glory of the New Covenant
2 Peter 2:1-22 - False Teachers and Their Destruction
Colossians 2:6-23 - Freedom From Human Regulations Through Life With Christ
Galatians 4:21-31 - Hagar and Sarah
Galatians 5:1-15 - Freedom in Christ
Hebrews 2:5-18 - Jesus Made Like His Brothers
John 8:31-41 - The Children of Abraham
Matthew 5:17-20 - The Fulfillment of the Law
Matthew 9:14-17 - Jesus Questioned About Fasting
Romans 14:1–15:13 - The Weak and the Strong
■ FRIENDSHIP
1 Corinthians 13:1-13 - Love
1 John 4:7-21 - God's Love and Ours
2 Corinthians 6:14–7:1 - Do Not Be Yoked with Unbelievers
John 7:1-13 - Jesus Goes to the Feast of Tabernacles
John 13:18-30 - Jesus Predicts His Betrayal
John 15:1-17 - The Vine and the Branches
John 18:1-11 - Jesus Arrested
Luke 11:1-13 - Jesus' Teaching on Prayer
Luke 22:54-62 - Peter Disowns Jesus
Mark 2:1-12 - Jesus Heals a Paralytic

Mark 14:43-52 - Jesus Arrested
Matthew 9:1-8 - Jesus Heals a Paralytic
Matthew 18:15-20 - A Brother Who Sins Against You
Matthew 26:14-16 - Judas Agrees to Betray Jesus
Matthew 26:36-46 - Gethsemane
Matthew 26:47-56 - Jesus Arrested
Philemon 1-7 - Thanksgiving and Prayer
Philemon 8-25 - Paul's Plea for Onesimus
Romans 16:1-27 - Personal Greetings

■ FRUIT

Colossians 1:1-14 - Thanksgiving and Prayer
Galatians 5:16-26 - Life by the Spirit
Hebrews 12:1-3 - God Disciplines His Sons
John 15:1-17 - The Vine and the Branches
Luke 6:43-45 - A Tree and Its Fruit
Luke 13:1-9 - Repent or Perish
Mark 11:12-19 - Jesus Clears the Temple
Matthew 7:15-23 - A Tree and Its Fruit
Matthew 10:1-42 - Jesus Sends Out the Twelve
Matthew 12:22-37 - Jesus and Beelzebub
Matthew 13:1-23 - The Parable of the Sower
Matthew 13:24-30 - The Parable of the Weeds
Matthew 21:18-22 - The Fig Tree Withers
Revelation 14:1-5 - The Lamb and the 144,000

■ FRUSTRATION

Matthew 22:15-22 - Paying Taxes to Caesar

■ FUTURE

1 Thessalonians 2:17–3:5 - Paul's Longing to See the Thessalonians
1 Thessalonians 4:13–5:11 - The Coming of the Lord
2 Thessalonians 1:1-12 - Thanksgiving and Prayer
2 Thessalonians 2:1-12 - The Man of Lawlessness
James 4:13-17 - Boasting About Tomorrow
Luke 6:17-26 - Blessings and Woes
Luke 18:31-34 - Jesus Again Predicts His Death
Luke 23:26-43 - The Crucifixion
Mark 13:1-31 - Signs of the End of the Age
Matthew 6:25-34 - Do Not Worry
Matthew 13:36-43 - The Parable of the Weeds Explained
Matthew 13:47-52 - The Parable of the Net
Matthew 20:17-19 - Jesus Again Predicts His Death
Matthew 22:23-33 - Marriage at the Resurrection
Matthew 24:1-35 - Signs of the End of the Age
Matthew 25:1-13 - The Parable of the Ten Virgins
Matthew 26:1-5 - The Plot Against Jesus
Matthew 26:17-30 - The Lord's Supper
Revelation 1:1-3 - Prologue
Revelation 1:9-20 - One Like a Son of Man
Revelation 4:1-11 - The Throne in Heaven
Romans 8:18-27 - Future Glory

■ GENEROSITY

1 Corinthians 16:1-4 - The Collection for God's People
2 Corinthians 8:1-15 - Generosity Encouraged
2 Corinthians 8:16–9:5 - Titus Sent to Corinth
2 Corinthians 9:6-15 - Sowing Generously
Acts 2:42-47 - The Fellowship of the Believers
Acts 4:32-37 - The Believers Share Their Possessions
Acts 10:1-8 - Cornelius Calls for Peter
Luke 11:1-13 - Jesus' Teaching on Prayer
Mark 12:41-44 - The Widow's Offering
Matthew 6:1-4 - Giving to the Needy
Matthew 6:19-24 - Treasures in Heaven
Matthew 7:7-12 - Ask, Seek, Knock
Matthew 19:16-30 - The Rich Young Man
Matthew 20:1-16 - The Parable of the Workers in the Vineyard
Matthew 25:14-30 - The Parable of the Talents
Matthew 26:6-13 - Jesus Anointed at Bethany
Matthew 27:57-61 - The Burial of Jesus
Philippians 4:10-23 - Thanks for Their Gifts
Romans 15:23-33 - Paul's Plan to Visit Rome

■ GENTLENESS

1 Timothy 3:1-16 - Overseers and Deacons
1 Timothy 6:11-21 - Paul's Charge to Timothy
2 Corinthians 10:1-18 - Paul's Defense of His Ministry
Ephesians 4:1-16 - Unity in the Body of Christ
Galatians 5:16-26 - Life by the Spirit
Matthew 5:38-42 - An Eye for an Eye
Matthew 28:1-10 - The Resurrection
Philippians 4:2-9 - Exhortations

■ GIFTS

1 Peter 4:1-11 - Living for God
1 Timothy 4:1-16 - Instructions to Timothy
2 Corinthians 8:16–9:5 - Titus Sent to Corinth
2 Corinthians 9:6-15 - Sowing Generously
2 Timothy 1:1–2:13 - Encouragement to Be Faithful
Acts 10:1-8 - Cornelius Calls for Peter
Acts 11:19-30 - The Church in Antioch
Ephesians 2:1-10 - Made Alive in Christ
Ephesians 4:1-16 - Unity in the Body of Christ
John 3:1-22 - Jesus Teaches Nicodemus
John 3:22-36 - John the Baptist's Testimony About Jesus
John 4:1-26 - Jesus Talks With a Samaritan Woman
Luke 6:37-42 - Judging Others
Luke 21:1-4 - The Widow's Offering
Mark 12:41-44 - The Widow's Offering
Matthew 2:1-12 - The Visit of the Magi
Matthew 7:7-12 - Ask, Seek, Knock
Matthew 14:13-21 - Jesus Feeds the Five Thousand
Philippians 4:10-23 - Thanks for Their Gifts
Romans 12:1-8 - Living Sacrifices
Romans 15:23-33 - Paul's Plan to Visit Rome

■ GIVING UP

1 Corinthians 16:1-4 - The Collection for God's People
2 Corinthians 8:1-15 - Generosity Encouraged
2 Corinthians 8:16–9:5 - Titus Sent to Corinth
2 Corinthians 9:6-15 - Sowing Generously
Acts 27:13-26 - The Storm
James 5:7-12 - Patience in Suffering
Mark 1:14-20 - The Calling of the First Disciples
Mark 12:41-44 - The Widow's Offering
Mark 14:1-11 - Jesus Anointed at Bethany
Mark 14:32-42 - Gethsemane
Mark 15:21-32 - The Crucifixion
Matthew 4:18-22 - The Calling of the First Disciples
Matthew 6:16-18 - Fasting
Matthew 20:17-19 - Jesus Again Predicts His Death
Matthew 22:41-46 - Whose Son Is the Christ?

■ GLORY

1 Corinthians 10:23–11:1 - The Believer's Freedom
1 Peter 2:4-12 - The Living Stone and a Chosen People
1 Peter 4:12-19 - Suffering for Being a Christian
1 Peter 5:1-14 - To Elders and Young Men

1 Timothy 1:12-20 - The Lord's Grace to Paul
2 Corinthians 3:7-18 - The Glory of the New Covenant
2 Peter 1:12-21 - Prophecy of Scripture
Acts 7:54-8:1 - The Stoning of Stephen
Colossians 1:24–2:5 - Paul's Labor for the Church
Colossians 3:1-17 - Rules for Holy Living
Ephesians 1:1-14 - Spiritual Blessings in Christ
Ephesians 3:14-21 - A Prayer for the Ephesians
Hebrews 1:1-14 - The Son Superior to Angels
Hebrews 11:1-40 - By Faith
John 1:1-19 - The Word Became Flesh
John 2:1-11 - Jesus Changes Water to Wine
John 8:48-59 - The Claims of Jesus About Himself
John 9:1-12 - Jesus Heals a Man Born Blind
John 11:1-16 - The Death of Lazarus
John 11:38-44 - Jesus Raises Lazarus From the Dead
John 12:12-19 - The Triumphal Entry
John 12:20-36 - Jesus Predicts His Death
John 13:1-17 - Jesus Washes His Disciples' Feet
John 13:31-38 - Jesus Predicts Peter's Denial
John 14:5-14 - Jesus the Way to the Father
John 15:1-17 - The Vine and the Branches
John 17:1-5 - Jesus Prays for Himself
John 17:6-19 - Jesus Prays for His Disciples
John 17:20-26 - Jesus Prays for All Believers
John 21:15-25 - Jesus Reinstates Peter
Luke 9:28-36 - The Transfiguration
Matthew 17:1-13 - The Transfiguration
Matthew 21:1-11 - The Triumphal Entry
Philippians 1:1-11 - Thanksgiving and Prayer
Revelation 4:1-11 - The Throne in Heaven
Revelation 7:9-17 - The Great Multitude in White Robes
Revelation 14:6-13 - The Three Angels
Revelation 15:1-8 - Seven Angels With Seven Plagues
Revelation 19:1-10 - Hallelujah!
Revelation 21:1-27 - The New Jerusalem
Revelation 22:1-6 - The River of Life
Revelation 22:7-21 - Jesus Is Coming

■ GOALS

2 Timothy 2:14-26 - A Workman Approved by God
James 4:13-17 - Boasting About Tomorrow
Luke 9:51-56 - Samaritan Opposition
Philippians 3:12–4:1 - Pressing on Toward the Goal

■ GOD

1 Corinthians 1:18–2:5 - Christ the Wisdom and Power of God
1 John 1:1-4 - The Word of Life
1 John 1:5–2:14 - Walking in the Light
1 John 2:15-17 - Do Not Love the World
1 John 2:18-27 - Warning Against Antichrists
1 John 2:28–3:10 - Children of God
1 John 3:11-24 - Love One Another
1 John 4:1-6 - Test the Spirits
1 John 4:7-21 - God's Love and Ours
1 John 5:1-12 - Faith in the Son of God
1 John 5:13-21 - Concluding Remarks
1 Peter 1:1-12 - Praise to God for a Living Hope
1 Peter 1:13–2:3 - Be Holy
1 Peter 2:4-12 - The Living Stone and a Chosen People
1 Peter 2:13-25 - Submission to Rulers and Masters
1 Peter 3:1-7 - Wives and Husbands
1 Peter 3:8-22 - Suffering for Doing Good
1 Peter 4:1-11 - Living for God
1 Peter 4:12-19 - Suffering for Being a Christian
1 Peter 5:1-14 - To Elders and Young Men
1 Timothy 1:1-11 - Warning Against False Teachers of the Law
1 Timothy 1:12-20 - The Lord's Grace to Paul
1 Timothy 2:1-15 - Instructions on Worship
1 Timothy 4:1-16 - Instructions to Timothy
1 Timothy 5:1–6:2 - Advice About Widows, Elders and Slaves
1 Timothy 6:11-21 - Paul's Charge to Timothy
2 John 1-13 - From the Elder
2 Peter 1:1-11 - Making One's Calling and Election Sure
2 Peter 1:12-21 - Prophecy of Scripture
2 Peter 2:1-22 - False Teachers and Their Destruction
2 Peter 3:1-18 - The Day of the Lord
2 Thessalonians 2:13-17 - Stand Firm
2 Timothy 1:1–2:13 - Encouragement to Be Faithful
2 Timothy 2:14-26 - A Workman Approved by God
2 Timothy 3:1-9 - Godlessness in the Last Days
2 Timothy 3:10–4:8 - Paul's Charge to Timothy
3 John 1-14 - From the Elder
Acts 5:1-11 - Ananias and Sapphira
Acts 5:17-41 - The Apostles Persecuted
Acts 7:1-53 - Stephen's Speech to the Sanhedrin
Acts 7:54–8:1 - The Stoning of Stephen
Acts 10:1-8 - Cornelius Calls for Peter
Acts 10:24-48 - Peter at Cornelius' House
Acts 11:1-18 - Peter Explains His Actions
Acts 12:20-25 - Herod's Death
Acts 13:13-52 - In Pisidian Antioch
Acts 14:8-20 - In Lystra and Derbe
Acts 15:1-21 - The Council at Jerusalem
Acts 16:6-10 - Paul's Vision of the Man of Macedonia
Acts 16:11-15 - Lydia's Conversion in Philippi
Acts 16:16-40 - Paul and Silas in Prison
Acts 17:10-15 - In Berea
Acts 17:16-34 - In Athens
Acts 18:1-17 - In Corinth
Acts 18:18-28 - Priscilla, Aquila and Apollos
Acts 20:13-38 - Paul's Farewell to the Ephesian Elders
Acts 21:37–22:21 - Paul Speaks to the Crowd
Acts 22:30–23:11 - Before the Sanhedrin
Acts 24:1-27 - The Trial Before Felix
Acts 25:23–26:32 - Paul Before Agrippa
Acts 27:13-26 - The Storm
Acts 27:27-44 - The Shipwreck
Acts 28:11-16 - Arrival at Rome
Acts 28:17-31 - Paul Preaches at Rome Under Guard
Colossians 1:1-14 - Thanksgiving and Prayer
Colossians 1:24–2:5 - Paul's Labor for the Church
Colossians 2:6-23 - Freedom From Human Regulations Through Life With Christ
Colossians 3:1-17 - Rules for Holy Living
Ephesians 1:1-14 - Spiritual Blessings in Christ
Ephesians 1:15-23 - Thanksgiving and Prayer
Ephesians 2:1-10 - Made Alive in Christ
Ephesians 2:11-22 - One in Christ
Ephesians 3:1-13 - Paul the Preacher to the Gentiles
Ephesians 3:14-21 - A Prayer for the Ephesians
Ephesians 4:1-16 - Unity in the Body of Christ
Ephesians 4:17–5:21 - Living as Children of Light

Ephesians 6:10-24 - The Armor of God
Galatians 1:1-10 - No Other Gospel
Galatians 1:11-24 - Paul Called by God
Galatians 2:11-21 - Paul Opposes Peter
Galatians 3:15-25 - The Law and the Promise
Galatians 3:26–4:7 - Sons of God
Galatians 4:8-20 - Paul's Concern for the Galatians
Hebrews 6:13-20 - The Certainty of God's Promise
James 1:1-18 - Trials and Temptations
James 2:14-26 - Faith and Deeds
John 1:43-51 - Jesus Calls Philip and Nathanael
John 3:1-22 - Jesus Teaches Nicodemus
John 3:22-36 - John the Baptist's Testimony About Jesus
John 4:1-26 - Jesus Talks With a Samaritan Woman
John 5:16-30 - Life Through the Son
John 5:31-47 - Testimonies About Jesus
John 6:25-59 - Jesus the Bread of Life
John 7:25-44 - Is Jesus the Christ?
John 8:12-30 - The Validity of Jesus' Testimony
John 8:31-41 - The Children of Abraham
John 8:42-47 - The Children of the Devil
John 8:48-59 - The Claims of Jesus About Himself
John 9:1-12 - Jesus Heals a Man Born Blind
John 9:13-34 - The Pharisees Investigate the Healing
John 10:1-21 - The Shepherd and His Flock
John 10:22-42 - The Unbelief of the Jews
John 11:1-16 - The Death of Lazarus
John 11:17-37 - Jesus Comforts the Sisters
John 11:38-44 - Jesus Raises Lazarus From the Dead
John 12:20-36 - Jesus Predicts His Death
John 12:37-50 - The Jews Continue in Their Unbelief
John 13:31-38 - Jesus Predicts Peter's Denial
John 14:1-4 - Jesus Comforts His Disciples
John 14:5-14 - Jesus the Way to the Father
John 15:1-17 - The Vine and the Branches
John 15:18–16:4 - The World Hates the Disciples
John 16:5-16 - The Work of the Holy Spirit
John 16:17-33 - The Disciples' Grief Will Turn to Joy
John 17:1-5 - Jesus Prays for Himself
John 17:6-19 - Jesus Prays for His Disciples
John 17:20-26 - Jesus Prays for All Believers
John 20:10-18 - Jesus Appears to Mary Magdalene
John 20:19-23 - Jesus Appears to His Disciples
John 20:24-31 - Jesus Appears to Thomas
John 21:15-25 - Jesus Reinstates Peter
Luke 1:46-56 - Mary's Song
Luke 3:21-38 - The Baptism and Genealogy of Jesus
Luke 16:1-15 - The Parable of the Shrewd Manager
Luke 22:66–23:25 - Jesus Before Pilate and Herod
Mark 2:1-12 - Jesus Heals a Paralytic
Mark 3:7-12 - Crowds Follow Jesus
Mark 12:28-34 - The Greatest Commandment
Matthew 3:13-17 - The Baptism of Jesus
Matthew 5:43-48 - Love for Enemies
Matthew 6:5-15 - Prayer
Matthew 6:25-34 - Do Not Worry
Matthew 7:7-12 - Ask, Seek, Knock
Matthew 11:25-30 - Rest for the Weary
Matthew 17:1-13 - The Transfiguration
Matthew 20:20-28 - A Mother's Request
Matthew 22:23-33 - Marriage at the Resurrection
Matthew 27:45-56 - The Death of Jesus
Philippians 1:1-11 - Thanksgiving and Prayer
Philippians 2:1-11 - Imitating Christ's Humility
Philippians 2:12-18 - Shining as Stars
Philippians 2:19-30 - Timothy and Epaphroditus
Philippians 3:12–4:1 - Pressing on Toward the Goal
Philippians 4:2-9 - Exhortations
Philippians 4:10-23 - Thanks for Their Gifts
Romans 3:9-20 - No One Is Righteous
Romans 5:1-11 - Peace and Joy
Romans 5:12-21 - Death Through Adam, Life Through Christ
Romans 6:1-14 - Dead to Sin, Alive in Christ
Romans 11:1-10 - The Remnant of Israel
Romans 11:25-32 - All Israel Will Be Saved
Romans 11:33-36 - Doxology
Romans 16:1-27 - Personal Greetings

■ GOD'S WILL

1 Corinthians 1:18–2:5 - Christ the Wisdom and Power of God
1 John 2:15-17 - Do Not Love the World
1 John 5:13-21 - Concluding Remarks
1 Peter 1:1-12 - Praise to God for a Living Hope
1 Peter 2:13-25 - Submission to Rulers and Masters
1 Peter 3:8-22 - Suffering for Doing Good
1 Thessalonians 5:12-28 - Final Instructions
2 Thessalonians 2:13-17 - Stand Firm
2 Timothy 1:1–2:13 - Encouragement to Be Faithful
Acts 20:13-38 - Paul's Farewell to the Ephesian Elders
Acts 21:1-16 - On to Jerusalem
Ephesians 1:1-14 - Spiritual Blessings in Christ
John 7:1-13 - Jesus Goes to the Feast of Tabernacles
John 11:1-16 - The Death of Lazarus
John 11:38-44 - Jesus Raises Lazarus From the Dead
John 14:5-14 - Jesus the Way to the Father
John 18:1-11 - Jesus Arrested
Luke 23:26-43 - The Crucifixion
Mark 3:31-35 - Jesus' Mother and Brothers
Matthew 2:19-23 - The Return to Nazareth
Matthew 8:23-27 - Jesus Calms the Storm
Matthew 10:1-42 - Jesus Sends Out the Twelve
Matthew 12:46-50 - Jesus' Mother and Brothers
Matthew 16:21-28 - Jesus Predicts His Death
Matthew 18:10-14 - The Parable of the Lost Sheep
Matthew 19:1-12 - Divorce
Matthew 26:36-46 - Gethsemane
Matthew 26:47-56 - Jesus Arrested
Matthew 27:11-26 - Jesus Before Pilate
Matthew 28:16-20 - The Great Commission
Revelation 10:1-11 - The Angel and the Little Scroll
Romans 12:1-8 - Living Sacrifices
Romans 13:1-7 - Submission to the Authorities

■ GOOD NEWS

2 Timothy 4:9-22 - Personal Remarks
Acts 3:11-26 - Peter Speaks to the Onlookers
Acts 4:1-22 - Peter and John Before the Sanhedrin
Acts 5:17-41 - The Apostles Persecuted
Acts 8:9-25 - Simon the Sorcerer
Acts 10:24-48 - Peter at Cornelius' House
Acts 11:19-30 - The Church in Antioch
Acts 14:1-7 - In Iconium
Acts 14:8-20 - In Lystra and Derbe
Acts 14:21-28 - The Return to Antioch in Syria

Acts 16:16-40 - Paul and Silas in Prison
Ephesians 2:11-22 - One in Christ
Hebrews 2:1-4 - Warning to Pay Attention
John 4:1-26 - Jesus Talks With a Samaritan Woman
John 12:12-19 - The Triumphal Entry
Luke 2:8-20 - The Shepherds and the Angels
Luke 8:1-15 - The Parable of the Sower
Luke 16:16-18 - Additional Teachings
Luke 24:1-12 - The Resurrection
Mark 1:14-20 - The Calling of the First Disciples
Matthew 4:23-25 - Jesus Heals the Sick
Matthew 9:9-13 - The Calling of Matthew
Matthew 20:1-16 - The Parable of the Workers in the Vineyard
Matthew 24:1-35 - Signs of the End of the Age
Matthew 28:1-10 - The Resurrection
Matthew 28:16-20 - The Great Commission
Romans 1:8-17 - Paul's Longing to Visit Rome

■ GOODNESS

2 Peter 1:1-11 - Making One's Calling and Election Sure
Acts 9:32-43 - Aeneas and Dorcas
Galatians 5:16-26 - Life by the Spirit
John 1:43-51 - Jesus Calls Philip and Nathanael
Luke 6:43-45 - A Tree and Its Fruit
Matthew 7:7-12 - Ask, Seek, Knock

■ GOSPEL

1 Corinthians 1:10-17 - Divisions in the Church
1 Corinthians 1:18–2:5 - Christ the Wisdom and Power of God
1 Corinthians 15:1-11 - The Resurrection of Christ
1 Peter 4:1-11 - Living for God
1 Peter 4:12-19 - Suffering for Being a Christian
1 Timothy 1:1-11 - Warning Against False Teachers of the Law
1 Timothy 1:12-20 - The Lord's Grace to Paul
2 Corinthians 2:12–3:6 - Ministers of the New Covenant
2 Corinthians 4:1-18 - Treasures in Jars of Clay
2 Corinthians 11:1-15 - Paul and the False Apostles
2 Timothy 1:1-2:13 - Encouragement to Be Faithful
Acts 2:14-41 - Peter Addresses the Crowd
Acts 4:23-31 - The Believers' Prayer
Acts 16:6-10 - Paul's Vision of the Man of Macedonia
Acts 17:1-9 - In Thessalonica
Acts 17:10-15 - In Berea
Colossians 1:1-14 - Thanksgiving and Prayer
Ephesians 1:1-14 - Spiritual Blessings in Christ
Galatians 1:1-10 - No Other Gospel
Galatians 1:11-24 - Paul Called by God
Galatians 2:1-10 - Paul Accepted by the Apostles
Galatians 2:11-21 - Paul Opposes Peter
Galatians 3:1-14 - Faith or Observance of the Law
Galatians 4:8-20 - Paul's Concern for the Galatians
Hebrews 2:1-4 - Warning to Pay Attention
Hebrews 4:1-13 - A Sabbath-Rest for the People of God
John 3:1-22 - Jesus Teaches Nicodemus
John 3:22-36 - John the Baptist's Testimony About Jesus
John 6:25-59 - Jesus the Bread of Life
John 14:5-14 - Jesus the Way to the Father
Luke 9:1-9 - Jesus Sends Out the Twelve
Mark 1:1-8 - John the Baptist Prepares the Way
Mark 1:14-20 - The Calling of the First Disciples
Mark 4:1-20 - The Parable of the Sower
Mark 4:26-29 - The Parable of the Growing Seed
Mark 7:24-30 - The Faith of a Syrophoenician Woman
Mark 8:31–9:1 - Jesus Predicts His Death
Mark 10:17-31 - The Rich Young Man
Mark 13:1-31 - Signs of the End of the Age
Mark 14:1-11 - Jesus Anointed at Bethany
Mark 16:1-20 - The Resurrection
Matthew 10:1-42 - Jesus Sends Out the Twelve
Matthew 28:1-10 - The Resurrection
Matthew 28:16-20 - The Great Commission
Philippians 1:1-11 - Thanksgiving and Prayer
Philippians 1:12-30 - Paul's Chains Advance the Gospel
Philippians 4:10-23 - Thanks for Their Gifts
Revelation 14:6-13 - The Three Angels

■ GOSSIP

1 Timothy 5:1–6:2 - Advice About Widows, Elders and Slaves
3 John 1-14 - From the Elder
Luke 19:1-10 - Zacchaeus the Tax Collector
Matthew 1:18–25 - The Birth of Jesus Christ

■ GOVERNMENT

1 Peter 2:13-25 - Submission to Rulers and Masters
Luke 2:1-7 - The Birth of Jesus
Luke 20:20-26 - Paying Taxes to Caesar
Mark 12:13-17 - Paying Taxes to Caesar
Matthew 2:13-18 - The Escape to Egypt
Matthew 17:24-27 - The Temple Tax
Matthew 22:15-22 - Paying Taxes to Caesar
Matthew 27:11-26 - Jesus Before Pilate
Matthew 27:27-31 - The Soldiers Mock Jesus
Matthew 28:11-15 - The Guards' Report
Romans 13:1-7 - Submission to the Authorities

■ GRACE

1 Corinthians 1:1-9 - Thanksgiving
1 Corinthians 15:1-11 - The Resurrection of Christ
1 Timothy 1:12-20 - The Lord's Grace to Paul
2 Corinthians 5:11–6:2 - The Ministry of Reconciliation
2 Corinthians 9:6-15 - Sowing Generously
2 Corinthians 12:1-10 - Paul's Vision and His Thorn
2 Timothy 1:1–2:13 - Encouragement to Be Faithful
Acts 6:8-15 - Stephen Seized
Acts 11:19-30 - The Church in Antioch
Acts 15:1-21 - The Council at Jerusalem
Acts 18:18-28 - Priscilla, Aquila and Apollos
Acts 20:13-38 - Paul's Farewell to the Ephesian Elders
Colossians 1:1-14 - Thanksgiving and Prayer
Colossians 4:2-18 - Further Instructions
Ephesians 2:1-10 - Made Alive in Christ
Ephesians 3:1-13 - Paul the Preacher to the Gentiles
Ephesians 4:1-16 - Unity in the Body of Christ
Galatians 1:1-10 - No Other Gospel
Galatians 1:11-24 - Paul Called by God
Galatians 2:1-10 - Paul Accepted by the Apostles
Galatians 5:1-15 - Freedom in Christ
Galatians 6:11-18 - Not Circumcision but a New Creation
Hebrews 2:5-18 - Jesus Made Like His Brothers
Hebrews 4:14–5:10 - Jesus the Great High Priest
James 4:1-12 - Submit Yourselves to God
John 1:1-19 - The Word Became Flesh
Jude 1-16 - The Sin and Doom of Godless Men
Luke 8:26-39 - The Healing of a Demon-possessed Man

Matthew 7:13-14 - The Narrow and Wide Gates
Matthew 9:14-17 - Jesus Questioned About Fasting
Matthew 18:10-14 - The Parable of the Lost Sheep
Matthew 18:21-35 - The Parable of the Unmerciful Servant
Matthew 22:1-14 - The Parable of the Wedding Banquet
Philippians 1:1-11 - Thanksgiving and Prayer
Philippians 4:10-23 - Thanks for Their Gifts
Revelation 1:4-8 - Greetings and Doxology
Revelation 22:7-21 - Jesus Is Coming
Romans 5:12-21 - Death Through Adam, Life Through Christ
Romans 11:11-24 - Ingrafted Branches

■ GREATNESS

1 Corinthians 1:18–2:5 - Christ the Wisdom and Power of God
Hebrews 7:1-10 - Melchizedek the Priest
Hebrews 7:11-28 - Jesus Like Melchizedek
John 13:1-17 - Jesus Washes His Disciples' Feet
Luke 1:5-25 - The Birth of John the Baptist Foretold
Luke 1:26-38 - The Birth of Jesus Foretold
Luke 9:46-50 - Who Will Be the Greatest?
Mark 4:30-34 - The Parable of the Mustard Seed
Mark 9:33-37 - Who Is the Greatest?
Matthew 5:1-12 - The Beatitudes
Matthew 11:1-19 - Jesus and John the Baptist
Matthew 18:1-9 - The Greatest in the Kingdom of Heaven
Revelation 15:1-8 - Seven Angels With Seven Plagues

■ GREED

1 Corinthians 5:1-13 - Expel the Immoral Brother!
1 Peter 5:1-14 - To Elders and Young Men
1 Timothy 3:1-16 - Overseers and Deacons
1 Timothy 6:3-10 - Love of Money
2 Timothy 3:1-9 - Godlessness in the Last Days
James 4:13-17 - Boasting About Tomorrow
James 5:1-6 - Warning to Rich Oppressors
Luke 15:11-32 - The Parable of the Lost Son
Luke 18:18-30 - The Rich Ruler
Luke 22:1-6 - Judas Agrees to Betray Jesus
Mark 10:35-45 - The Request of James and John
Mark 12:1-12 - The Parable of the Tenants

■ GRIEF

2 Corinthians 2:5-11 - Forgiveness for the Sinner
Acts 20:13-38 - Paul's Farewell to the Ephesian Elders
John 16:17-33 - The Disciples' Grief Will Turn to Joy
Matthew 13:36-43 - The Parable of the Weeds Explained
Matthew 13:47-52 - The Parable of the Net
Matthew 17:14-23 - The Healing of a Boy With a Demon
Matthew 26:69-75 - Peter Disowns Jesus
Matthew 27:45-56 - The Death of Jesus

■ GROWTH

1 Corinthians 1:1-9 - Thanksgiving
1 Corinthians 3:1-23 - On Divisions in the Church
1 Peter 1:13–2:3 - Be Holy
2 Peter 3:1-18 - The Day of the Lord
2 Thessalonians 3:1-5 - Request for Prayer
2 Timothy 1:1–2:13 - Encouragement to Be Faithful
Acts 2:42-47 - The Fellowship of the Believers
Acts 6:1-7 - The Choosing of the Seven
Acts 12:20-25 - Herod's Death
Luke 2:41-52 - The Boy Jesus at the Temple
Luke 8:1-15 - The Parable of the Sower
Luke 13:18-21 - The Parables of the Mustard Seed and the Yeast
Mark 4:26-29 - The Parable of the Growing Seed
Mark 4:30-34 - The Parable of the Mustard Seed
Matthew 11:25-30 - Rest for the Weary
Matthew 13:1-23 - The Parable of the Sower
Matthew 13:31-35 - The Parables of the Mustard Seed and the Yeast
Romans 7:1-6 - An Illustration From Marriage

■ GUIDANCE

Acts 16:6-10 - Paul's Vision of the Man of Macedonia
John 16:5-16 - The Work of the Holy Spirit
Mark 8:22-26 - The Healing of a Blind Man at Bethsaida
Matthew 2:1-12 - The Visit of the Magi
Matthew 2:13-18 - The Escape to Egypt
Matthew 2:19-23 - The Return to Nazareth
Matthew 7:13-14 - The Narrow and Wide Gates
Revelation 10:1-11 - The Angel and the Little Scroll

■ GUILT

1 John 1:5–2:14 - Walking in the Light
John 15:18–16:4 - The World Hates the Disciples
John 16:5-16 - The Work of the Holy Spirit

■ HABITS

1 John 1:5–2:14 - Walking in the Light
1 John 2:28–3:10 - Children of God
Luke 2:41-52 - The Boy Jesus at the Temple
Luke 5:33-39 - Jesus Questioned About Fasting
Luke 6:1-11 - Lord of the Sabbath
Luke 22:39-46 - Jesus Prays on the Mount of Olives
Matthew 13:53-58 - A Prophet Without Honor
Matthew 26:17-30 - The Lord's Supper

■ HANDICAPPED

Acts 3:1-10 - Peter Heals the Crippled Beggar
Acts 14:8-20 - In Lystra and Derbe
Luke 14:1-14 - Jesus at a Pharisee's House
Luke 14:15-24 - The Parable of the Great Banquet
Matthew 4:23-25 - Jesus Heals the Sick
Matthew 20:29-34 - Two Blind Men Receive Sight
Matthew 21:12-17 - Jesus at the Temple

■ HAPPINESS

1 John 2:15-17 - Do Not Love the World

■ HARDHEARTEDNESS

1 John 3:11-24 - Love One Another
2 Peter 2:1-22 - False Teachers and Their Destruction
Acts 18:1-17 - In Corinth
Acts 28:17-31 - Paul Preaches at Rome Under Guard
Ephesians 4:17–5:21 - Living as Children of Light
Hebrews 3:7-19 - Warning Against Unbelief
Hebrews 4:1-13 - A Sabbath-Rest for the People of God
John 6:60–71 - Many Disciples Desert Jesus
John 8:48-59 - The Claims of Jesus About Himself
John 9:13-34 - The Pharisees Investigate the Healing
John 10:22-42 - The Unbelief of the Jews
John 12:37-50 - The Jews Continue in Their Unbelief
John 13:18-30 - Jesus Predicts His Betrayal
John 18:1-11 - Jesus Arrested
John 18:12-14 - Jesus Taken to Annas
John 18:19-24 - The High Priest Questions Jesus
John 19:1-16 - Jesus Sentenced to be Crucified
Luke 4:14-30 - Jesus Rejected at Nazareth

Luke 6:1-11 - Lord of the Sabbath
Luke 11:37-54 - Six Woes
Luke 20:9-19 - The Parable of the Tenants
Luke 24:13-35 - On the Road to Emmaus
Matthew 5:27-30 - Adultery
Matthew 7:24-29 - The Wise and Foolish Builders
Matthew 8:28-34 - The Healing of Two Demon-possessed Men
Matthew 12:38-45 - The Sign of Jonah
Matthew 19:1-12 - Divorce
Matthew 21:12-17 - Jesus at the Temple
Matthew 21:23-27 - The Authority of Jesus Questioned
Matthew 21:33-46 - The Parable of the Tenants
Matthew 22:1-14 - The Parable of the Wedding Banquet
Matthew 22:15-22 - Paying Taxes to Caesar
Matthew 22:34-40 - The Greatest Commandment
Matthew 22:41-46 - Whose Son Is the Christ?
Matthew 23:1-39 - Seven Woes
Matthew 26:1-5 - The Plot Against Jesus
Matthew 27:11-26 - Jesus Before Pilate
Matthew 27:27-31 - The Soldiers Mock Jesus
Romans 1:18-32 - God's Wrath Against Mankind
Romans 11:1-10 - The Remnant of Israel
Romans 11:25-32 - All Israel Will Be Saved

■ **HATRED**

1 John 3:11-24 - Love One Another
1 John 4:7-21 - God's Love and Ours
John 15:18–16:4 - The World Hates the Disciples
John 17:6-19 - Jesus Prays for His Disciples
John 18:19-24 - The High Priest Questions Jesus
Matthew 5:21-26 - Murder
Matthew 5:43-48 - Love for Enemies
Matthew 12:1-14 - Lord of the Sabbath
Matthew 12:22-37 - Jesus and Beelzebub
Matthew 21:33-46 - The Parable of the Tenants
Matthew 24:1-35 - Signs of the End of the Age
Matthew 26:1-5 - The Plot Against Jesus
Matthew 26:14-16 - Judas Agrees to Betray Jesus
Matthew 26:57-68 - Before the Sanhedrin
Matthew 27:27-31 - The Soldiers Mock Jesus
Matthew 27:32-44 - The Crucifixion
Matthew 27:62-66 - The Guard at the Tomb

■ **HEALING**

1 Corinthians 12:1-11 - Spiritual Gifts
Acts 3:1-10 - Peter Heals the Crippled Beggar
Acts 3:11-26 - Peter Speaks to the Onlookers
Acts 4:1-22 - Peter and John Before the Sanhedrin
Acts 5:12-16 - The Apostles Heal Many
Acts 9:32-43 - Aeneas and Dorcas
Acts 14:8-20 - In Lystra and Derbe
Acts 16:16-40 - Paul and Silas in Prison
Acts 20:7-12 - Eutychus Raised From the Dead at Troas
Acts 28:1-10 - Ashore on Malta
James 5:13-20 - The Prayer of Faith
John 4:43-54 - Jesus Heals the Official's Son
John 5:1-15 - The Healing at the Pool
John 9:1-12 - Jesus Heals a Man Born Blind
John 9:13-34 - The Pharisees Investigate the Healing
Luke 4:31-37 - Jesus Drives Out an Evil Spirit
Luke 4:38-44 - Jesus Heals Many
Luke 5:17-26 - Jesus Heals a Paralytic
Luke 6:1-11 - Lord of the Sabbath
Luke 7:1-10 - The Faith of the Centurion
Luke 7:11-17 - Jesus Raises a Widow's Son
Luke 7:18-35 - Jesus and John the Baptist
Luke 8:40-56 - A Dead Girl and a Sick Woman
Luke 9:1-9 - Jesus Sends Out the Twelve
Luke 9:10-17 - Jesus Feeds the Five Thousand
Luke 9:37-45 - The Healing of a Boy With an Evil Spirit
Luke 13:10-17 - A Crippled Woman Healed on the Sabbath
Luke 14:1-14 - Jesus at a Pharisee's House
Luke 17:11-19 - Ten Healed of Leprosy
Luke 18:35-43 - A Blind Beggar Receives His Sight
Luke 22:47-53 - Jesus Arrested
Mark 1:21-28 - Jesus Drives Out an Evil Spirit
Mark 1:29-34 - Jesus Heals Many
Mark 1:40-45 - A Man With Leprosy
Mark 2:1-12 - Jesus Heals a Paralytic
Mark 2:23–3:6 - Lord of the Sabbath
Mark 3:7-12 - Crowds Follow Jesus
Mark 5:1-20 - The Healing of a Demon-possessed Man
Mark 5:21-43 - A Dead Girl and a Sick Woman
Mark 6:7-13 - Jesus Sends Out the Twelve
Mark 6:45-56 - Jesus Walks on the Water
Mark 7:31-37 - The Healing of a Deaf and Mute Man
Mark 8:22-26 - The Healing of a Blind Man at Bethsaida
Mark 9:14-32 - The Healing of a Boy With an Evil Spirit
Mark 10:46-52 - Blind Bartimaeus Receives His Sight
Matthew 8:1-4 - The Man With Leprosy
Matthew 8:5-13 - The Faith of the Centurion
Matthew 8:14-17 - Jesus Heals Many
Matthew 8:28-34 - The Healing of Two Demon-possessed Men
Matthew 9:1-8 - Jesus Heals a Paralytic
Matthew 9:18-26 - A Dead Girl and a Sick Woman
Matthew 9:27-34 - Jesus Heals the Blind and Mute
Matthew 9:35-38 - The Workers Are Few
Matthew 12:1-14 - Lord of the Sabbath
Matthew 12:15-21 - God's Chosen Servant
Matthew 12:22-37 - Jesus and Beelzebub
Matthew 14:22-36 - Jesus Walks on the Water
Matthew 15:21-28 - The Faith of the Canaanite Woman
Matthew 15:29-39 - Jesus Feeds the Four Thousand
Matthew 17:14-23 - The Healing of a Boy With a Demon
Matthew 20:29-34 - Two Blind Men Receive Sight
Revelation 22:1-6 - The River of Life

■ **HEALTH**

2 Corinthians 12:1-10 - Paul's Vision and His Thorn
Matthew 4:23-25 - Jesus Heals the Sick

■ **HEART**

1 John 3:11-24 - Love One Another
1 Timothy 1:1-11 - Warning Against False Teachers of the Law
Acts 16:11-15 - Lydia's Conversion in Philippi
Colossians 3:1-17 - Rules for Holy Living
Ephesians 3:14-21 - A Prayer for the Ephesians
Ephesians 6:5-9 - Slaves and Masters
Galatians 3:26–4:7 - Sons of God
John 14:1-4 - Jesus Comforts His Disciples
Luke 6:43-45 - A Tree and Its Fruit
Luke 16:1-15 - The Parable of the Shrewd Manager
Mark 7:1-23 - Clean and Unclean
Mark 8:14-21 - The Yeast of the Pharisees and Herod

Matthew 13:1-23 - The Parable of the Sower

■ HEAVEN

1 Corinthians 15:35-58 - The Resurrection Body
1 Peter 3:8-22 - Suffering for Doing Good
1 Timothy 6:11-21 - Paul's Charge to Timothy
2 Corinthians 5:1-10 - Our Heavenly Dwelling
2 Corinthians 12:1-10 - Paul's Vision and His Thorn
2 Peter 1:1-11 - Making One's Calling and Election Sure
2 Peter 3:1-18 - The Day of the Lord
2 Thessalonians 1:1-12 - Thanksgiving and Prayer
2 Timothy 4:9-22 - Personal Remarks
Acts 1:1-11 - Jesus Taken Up Into Heaven
Acts 7:54–8:1 - The Stoning of Stephen
Acts 10:9-23 - Peter's Vision
Colossians 1:1-14 - Thanksgiving and Prayer
Colossians 3:1-17 - Rules for Holy Living
Colossians 3:18–4:1 - Rules for Christian Households
Ephesians 1:15-23 - Thanksgiving and Prayer
Ephesians 2:1-10 - Made Alive in Christ
Hebrews 1:1-14 - The Son Superior to Angels
Hebrews 6:13-20 - The Certainty of God's Promise
Hebrews 8:1-13 - The High Priest of a New Covenant
Hebrews 9:11-28 - The Blood of Christ
Hebrews 10:1-18 - Christ's Sacrifice Once for All
Hebrews 12:14-29 - Warning Against Refusing God
Hebrews 13:1-25 - Concluding Exhortations
John 1:43-51 - Jesus Calls Philip and Nathanael
John 3:1-22 - Jesus Teaches Nicodemus
John 3:22-36 - John the Baptist's Testimony About Jesus
John 6:25-59 - Jesus the Bread of Life
John 12:20-36 - Jesus Predicts His Death
Luke 16:19-31 - The Rich Man and Lazarus
Luke 24:50-53 - The Ascension
Mark 1:9-13 - The Baptism and Temptation of Jesus
Mark 10:17-31 - The Rich Young Man
Mark 10:35-45 - The Request of James and John
Mark 11:27-33 - The Authority of Jesus Questioned
Mark 16:1-20 - The Resurrection
Matthew 3:13-17 - The Baptism of Jesus
Matthew 4:12-17 - Jesus Begins to Preach
Matthew 5:1-12 - The Beatitudes
Matthew 5:17-20 - The Fulfillment of the Law
Matthew 6:19-24 - Treasures in Heaven
Matthew 7:13-14 - The Narrow and Wide Gates
Matthew 7:15-23 - A Tree and Its Fruit
Matthew 17:1-13 - The Transfiguration
Matthew 22:23-33 - Marriage at the Resurrection
Matthew 24:1-35 - Signs of the End of the Age
Matthew 25:31-46 - The Sheep and the Goats
Philippians 3:12–4:1 - Pressing on Toward the Goal
Revelation 4:1-11 - The Throne in Heaven
Revelation 7:9-17 - The Great Multitude in White Robes
Revelation 8:1-5 - The Seventh Seal and the Golden Censer
Revelation 8:6–9:21 - The Trumpets
Revelation 11:1-14 - The Two Witnesses
Revelation 11:15-19 - The Seventh Trumpet
Revelation 12:1–13:1 - The Woman and the Dragon
Revelation 14:1-5 - The Lamb and the 144,000
Revelation 14:14-20 - The Harvest of the Earth
Revelation 15:1-8 - Seven Angels With Seven Plagues
Revelation 16:1-21 - The Seven Bowls of God's Wrath
Revelation 20:11-15 - The Dead Are Judged
Revelation 21:1-27 - The New Jerusalem
Revelation 22:1-6 - The River of Life
Revelation 22:7-21 - Jesus Is Coming

■ HELL

2 Peter 2:1-22 - False Teachers and Their Destruction
2 Thessalonians 1:1-12 - Thanksgiving and Prayer
2 Thessalonians 2:1-12 - The Man of Lawlessness
Jude 1-16 - The Sin and Doom of Godless Men
Luke 16:19-31 - The Rich Man and Lazarus
Mark 9:42-50 - Causing to Sin
Matthew 5:21-26 - Murder
Matthew 7:13-14 - The Narrow and Wide Gates
Matthew 13:24-30 - The Parable of the Weeds
Matthew 13:36-43 - The Parable of the Weeds Explained
Matthew 13:47-52 - The Parable of the Net
Matthew 22:1-14 - The Parable of the Wedding Banquet
Matthew 24:1-35 - Signs of the End of the Age
Matthew 24:36-51 - The Day and Hour Unknown
Matthew 25:1-13 - The Parable of the Ten Virgins
Matthew 25:31-46 - The Sheep and the Goats
Revelation 1:9-20 - One Like a Son of Man
Revelation 6:1-17 - The Seals
Revelation 14:6-13 - The Three Angels
Revelation 17:1-18 - The Woman on the Beast
Revelation 20:1-6 - The Thousand Years
Revelation 20:7-10 - Satan's Doom
Revelation 20:11-15 - The Dead Are Judged
Revelation 21:1-27 - The New Jerusalem

■ HELP

1 Timothy 5:1–6:2 - Advice About Widows, Elders and Slaves
2 Timothy 4:9-22 - Personal Remarks
Acts 3:1-10 - Peter Heals the Crippled Beggar
Acts 11:19-30 - The Church in Antioch
Acts 18:18-28 - Priscilla, Aquila and Apollos
Acts 28:1-10 - Ashore on Malta
Ephesians 4:17–5:21 - Living as Children of Light
John 13:1-17 - Jesus Washes His Disciples' Feet
John 14:15-31 - Jesus Promises the Holy Spirit
Luke 6:37-42 - Judging Others
Matthew 8:1-4 - The Man With Leprosy
Matthew 8:23-27 - Jesus Calms the Storm
Matthew 11:25-30 - Rest for the Weary
Matthew 14:13-21 - Jesus Feeds the Five Thousand
Matthew 14:22-36 - Jesus Walks on the Water
Matthew 15:21-28 - The Faith of the Canaanite Woman
Matthew 18:10-14 - The Parable of the Lost Sheep
Matthew 26:36-46 - Gethsemane
Matthew 28:16-20 - The Great Commission
Romans 14:1–15:13 - The Weak and the Strong
Romans 15:23-33 - Paul's Plan to Visit Rome

■ HERESY

1 John 2:18-27 - Warning Against Antichrists
2 Peter 2:1-22 - False Teachers and Their Destruction
John 8:42-47 - The Children of the Devil
John 8:48-59 - The Claims of Jesus About Himself
John 9:13-34 - The Pharisees Investigate the Healing
Matthew 16:5-12 - The Yeast of the Pharisees and Sadducees
Philippians 3:1-11 - No Confidence in the Flesh

■ HERITAGE
1 Peter 2:4-12 - The Living Stone and a Chosen People
2 Timothy 1:1–2:13 - Encouragement to Be Faithful
Galatians 3:26–4:7 - Sons of God
Hebrews 7:1-10 - Melchizedek the Priest
Hebrews 7:11-28 - Jesus Like Melchizedek
Luke 1:67-80 - Zechariah's Song
Matthew 1:1-17 - The Genealogy of Jesus
■ HEROES
Hebrews 11:1-40 - By Faith
■ HIDING
Luke 8:16-18 - A Lamp on a Stand
■ HISTORY
1 Corinthians 10:1-13 - Warnings From Israel's History
1 Corinthians 10:14-22 - Idol Feasts and the Lord's Supper
1 John 1:1-4 - The Word of Life
Acts 7:1-53 - Stephen's Speech to the Sanhedrin
Acts 13:13-52 - In Pisidian Antioch
John 1:29-34 - Jesus the Lamb of God
Luke 1:67-80 - Zechariah's Song
Luke 2:1-7 - The Birth of Jesus
Matthew 1:1-17 - The Genealogy of Jesus
Matthew 13:53-58 - A Prophet Without Honor
■ HOLINESS
1 Corinthians 1:1-9 - Thanksgiving
1 Peter 1:13–2:3 - Be Holy
1 Thessalonians 4:1-12 - Living to Please God
1 Timothy 5:1–6:2 - Advice About Widows, Elders and Slaves
2 Corinthians 6:14–7:1 - Do Not Be Yoked with Unbelievers
2 Peter 3:1-18 - The Day of the Lord
Colossians 3:1-17 - Rules for Holy Living
Ephesians 1:1-14 - Spiritual Blessings in Christ
Ephesians 4:17–5:21 - Living as Children of Light
Ephesians 5:22-33 - Wives and Husbands
Hebrews 12:1-3 - God Disciplines His Sons
Hebrews 12:14-29 - Warning Against Refusing God
Hebrews 13:1-25 - Concluding Exhortations
Jude 17-25 - A Call to Persevere
Mark 6:14-29 - John the Baptist Beheaded
Mark 9:2-13 - The Transfiguration
Matthew 3:1-12 - John the Baptist Prepares the Way
Matthew 17:1-13 - The Transfiguration
Revelation 4:1-11 - The Throne in Heaven
Revelation 6:1-17 - The Seals
Revelation 15:1-8 - Seven Angels With Seven Plagues
Revelation 16:1-21 - The Seven Bowls of God's Wrath
Revelation 21:1-27 - The New Jerusalem
Revelation 22:1-6 - The River of Life
Revelation 22:7-21 - Jesus Is Coming
Romans 6:1-14 - Dead to Sin, Alive in Christ
Romans 13:8-14 - Love, for the Day Is Near
Titus 1:1-16 - Titus' Task on Crete
Titus 2:1-15 - What Must Be Taught to Various Groups
■ HOLY SPIRIT
1 Corinthians 1:18–2:5 - Christ the Wisdom and Power of God
1 Corinthians 2:6-16 - Wisdom From the Spirit
1 Corinthians 3:1-23 - On Divisions in the Church
1 Corinthians 6:12-20 - Sexual Immorality
1 Corinthians 12:1-11 - Spiritual Gifts
1 Corinthians 12:12-31 - One Body, Many Parts
1 John 2:18-27 - Warning Against Antichrists
1 John 3:11-24 - Love One Another
1 John 4:1-6 - Test the Spirits
1 John 4:7-21 - God's Love and Ours
1 John 5:1-12 - Faith in the Son of God
1 Peter 1:1-12 - Praise to God for a Living Hope
1 Peter 3:8-22 - Suffering for Doing Good
1 Timothy 4:1-16 - Instructions to Timothy
2 Corinthians 2:12–3:6 - Ministers of the New Covenant
2 Corinthians 3:7-18 - The Glory of the New Covenant
2 Corinthians 5:1-10 - Our Heavenly Dwelling
2 Timothy 1:1–2:13 - Encouragement to Be Faithful
Acts 1:1-11 - Jesus Taken Up Into Heaven
Acts 2:1-13 - The Holy Spirit Comes at Pentecost
Acts 2:14-41 - Peter Addresses the Crowd
Acts 4:1-22 - Peter and John Before the Sanhedrin
Acts 4:23-31 - The Believers' Prayer
Acts 5:1-11 - Ananias and Sapphira
Acts 5:17-41 - The Apostles Persecuted
Acts 6:1-7 - The Choosing of the Seven
Acts 6:8-15 - Stephen Seized
Acts 7:1-53 - Stephen's Speech to the Sanhedrin
Acts 7:54–8:1 - The Stoning of Stephen
Acts 8:9-25 - Simon the Sorcerer
Acts 8:26-40 - Philip and the Ethiopian
Acts 9:1-19 - Saul's Conversion
Acts 9:20-31 - Saul in Damascus and Jerusalem
Acts 10:9-23 - Peter's Vision
Acts 10:24-48 - Peter at Cornelius' House
Acts 11:1-18 - Peter Explains His Actions
Acts 11:19-30 - The Church in Antioch
Acts 13:1-3 - Barnabas and Saul Sent Off
Acts 13:4-12 - On Cyprus
Acts 13:13-52 - In Pisidian Antioch
Acts 15:1-21 - The Council at Jerusalem
Acts 16:6-10 - Paul's Vision of the Man of Macedonia
Acts 16:16-40 - Paul and Silas in Prison
Acts 19:1-22 - Paul in Ephesus
Acts 20:13-38 - Paul's Farewell to the Ephesian Elders
Acts 21:1-16 - On to Jerusalem
Acts 28:17-31 - Paul Preaches at Rome Under Guard
Colossians 1:1-14 - Thanksgiving and Prayer
Ephesians 1:1-14 - Spiritual Blessings in Christ
Ephesians 1:15-23 - Thanksgiving and Prayer
Ephesians 2:11-22 - One in Christ
Ephesians 3:1-13 - Paul the Preacher to the Gentiles
Ephesians 3:14-21 - A Prayer for the Ephesians
Ephesians 4:1-16 - Unity in the Body of Christ
Ephesians 4:17–5:21 - Living as Children of Light
Ephesians 6:10-24 - The Armor of God
Galatians 3:1-14 - Faith or Observance of the Law
Galatians 3:26–4:7 - Sons of God
Galatians 4:21-31 - Hagar and Sarah
Galatians 5:1-15 - Freedom in Christ
Galatians 5:16-26 - Life by the Spirit
Galatians 6:1-10 - Doing Good to All
Hebrews 2:1-4 - Warning to Pay Attention
Hebrews 3:7-19 - Warning Against Unbelief
Hebrews 5:11–6:12 - Warning Against Falling Away
Hebrews 9:1-10 - Worship in the Earthly Tabernacle

Hebrews 9:11-28 - The Blood of Christ
Hebrews 10:1-18 - Christ's Sacrifice Once for All
John 1:29-34 - Jesus the Lamb of God
John 14:15-31 - Jesus Promises the Holy Spirit
John 15:18–16:4 - The World Hates the Disciples
John 16:5-16 - The Work of the Holy Spirit
John 20:19-23 - Jesus Appears to His Disciples
Luke 1:26-38 - The Birth of Jesus Foretold
Luke 1:39-45 - Mary Visits Elizabeth
Luke 2:21-40 - Jesus Presented in the Temple
Luke 3:21-38 - The Baptism and Genealogy of Jesus
Luke 11:1-13 - Jesus' Teaching on Prayer
Luke 12:1-12 - Warnings and Encouragements
Luke 24:36-49 - Jesus Appears to the Disciples
Mark 1:9-13 - The Baptism and Temptation of Jesus
Mark 3:20-30 - Jesus and Beelzebub
Mark 12:35-40 - Whose Son Is the Christ?
Mark 13:1-31 - Signs of the End of the Age
Matthew 1:18-25 - The Birth of Jesus Christ
Matthew 3:1-12 - John the Baptist Prepares the Way
Matthew 3:13-17 - The Baptism of Jesus
Matthew 4:1-11 - The Temptation of Jesus
Matthew 10:1-42 - Jesus Sends Out the Twelve
Matthew 12:15-21 - God's Chosen Servant
Matthew 12:22-37 - Jesus and Beelzebub
Matthew 12:38-45 - The Sign of Jonah
Matthew 22:41-46 - Whose Son Is the Christ?
Philippians 1:12-30 - Paul's Chains Advance the Gospel
Philippians 2:1-11 - Imitating Christ's Humility
Philippians 3:1-11 - No Confidence in the Flesh
Revelation 1:4-8 - Greetings and Doxology
Revelation 2:18-29 - To the Church in Thyatira
Revelation 3:1-6 - To the Church in Sardis
Revelation 3:7-13 - To the Church in Philadelphia
Revelation 3:14-22 - To the Church in Laodicea
Revelation 4:1-11 - The Throne in Heaven
Revelation 17:1-18 - The Woman on the Beast
Romans 7:1-6 - An Illustration From Marriage
Romans 8:1-17 - Life Through the Spirit
Titus 3:1-15 - Doing What Is Good

■ **HOME**

1 Timothy 3:1-16 - Overseers and Deacons
John 14:1-4 - Jesus Comforts His Disciples
Luke 4:14-30 - Jesus Rejected at Nazareth
Luke 9:57-62 - The Cost of Following Jesus
Luke 18:18-30 - The Rich Ruler
Mark 6:1-6 - A Prophet Without Honor
Matthew 12:46-50 - Jesus' Mother and Brothers

■ **HOMOSEXUALITY**

Jude 1-16 - The Sin and Doom of Godless Men
Romans 1:18-32 - God's Wrath Against Mankind

■ **HONOR**

1 Corinthians 11:17-34 - The Lord's Supper
1 Corinthians 12:12-31 - One Body, Many Parts
2 Peter 1:12-21 - Prophecy of Scripture
Ephesians 6:1-4 - Children and Parents
Hebrews 3:1-6 - Jesus Greater Than Moses
John 12:1-11 - Jesus Anointed at Bethany
John 12:12-19 - The Triumphal Entry
John 12:20-36 - Jesus Predicts His Death
John 13:1-17 - Jesus Washes His Disciples' Feet
John 17:1-5 - Jesus Prays for Himself
Luke 1:26-38 - The Birth of Jesus Foretold
Luke 1:39-45 - Mary Visits Elizabeth
Luke 14:1-14 - Jesus at a Pharisee's House
Mark 6:1-6 - A Prophet Without Honor
Mark 7:1-23 - Clean and Unclean
Mark 12:35-40 - Whose Son Is the Christ?
Matthew 13:53-58 - A Prophet Without Honor
Matthew 20:20-28 - A Mother's Request
Philippians 2:19-30 - Timothy and Epaphroditus
Revelation 4:1-11 - The Throne in Heaven
Revelation 7:9-17 - The Great Multitude in White Robes

■ **HOPE**

1 Corinthians 15:12-34 - The Resurrection of the Dead
1 Peter 1:1-12 - Praise to God for a Living Hope
1 Peter 3:8-22 - Suffering for Doing Good
1 Thessalonians 4:13–5:11 - The Coming of the Lord
2 Corinthians 1:1-11 - The God of All Comfort
2 Corinthians 3:7-18 - The Glory of the New Covenant
2 Peter 3:1-18 - The Day of the Lord
2 Thessalonians 1:1-12 - Thanksgiving and Prayer
Acts 24:1-27 - The Trial Before Felix
Colossians 1:1-14 - Thanksgiving and Prayer
Colossians 1:24–2:5 - Paul's Labor for the Church
Ephesians 4:1-16 - Unity in the Body of Christ
Hebrews 6:13-20 - The Certainty of God's Promise
Hebrews 10:19-39 - A Call to Persevere
John 14:1-4 - Jesus Comforts His Disciples
John 16:17-33 - The Disciples' Grief Will Turn to Joy
Matthew 9:18-26 - A Dead Girl and a Sick Woman
Matthew 11:1-19 - Jesus and John the Baptist
Romans 5:1-11 - Peace and Joy
Romans 8:18-27 - Future Glory

■ **HOPELESSNESS**

2 Thessalonians 2:1-12 - The Man of Lawlessness
Acts 27:13-26 - The Storm
Matthew 8:1-4 - The Man With Leprosy
Matthew 27:45-56 - The Death of Jesus
Revelation 8:6–9:21 - The Trumpets

■ **HOSPITALITY**

1 Peter 4:1-11 - Living for God
1 Timothy 3:1-16 - Overseers and Deacons
Acts 10:9-23 - Peter's Vision
Acts 16:11-15 - Lydia's Conversion in Philippi
Luke 7:36-50 - Jesus Anointed by a Sinful Woman
Luke 10:38-42 - At the Home of Martha and Mary
Matthew 8:14-17 - Jesus Heals Many

■ **HUMANNESS**

Mark 15:42-47 - The Burial of Jesus
Matthew 7:7-12 - Ask, Seek, Knock

■ **HUMILIATION**

2 Corinthians 12:11-21 - Paul's Concern for the Corinthians
John 18:12-14 - Jesus Taken to Annas
John 19:17-27 - The Crucifixion
Mark 15:16-20 - The Soldiers Mock Jesus
Matthew 26:57-68 - Before the Sanhedrin
Matthew 27:32-44 - The Crucifixion
Revelation 19:11-21 - The Rider on the White Horse

■ **HUMILITY**

1 Corinthians 12:12-31 - One Body, Many Parts
1 Corinthians 13:1-13 - Love
1 Peter 3:8-22 - Suffering for Doing Good

1 Peter 5:1-14 - To Elders and Young Men
2 Corinthians 12:11-21 - Paul's Concern for the Corinthians
Ephesians 3:1-13 - Paul the Preacher to the Gentiles
Ephesians 4:1-16 - Unity in the Body of Christ
James 3:13-18 - Two Kinds of Wisdom
James 4:1-12 - Submit Yourselves to God
John 1:19-28 - John the Baptist Denies Being the Christ
John 1:35-42 - Jesus' First Disciples
John 3:1-22 - Jesus Teaches Nicodemus
John 13:1-17 - Jesus Washes His Disciples' Feet
Luke 1:26-38 - The Birth of Jesus Foretold
Luke 1:46-56 - Mary's Song
Luke 3:1-20 - John the Baptist Prepares the Way
Luke 7:1-10 - The Faith of the Centurion
Luke 9:46-50 - Who Will Be the Greatest?
Luke 14:1-14 - Jesus at a Pharisee's House
Luke 17:1-10 - Sin, Faith, Duty
Luke 18:9-14 - The Parable of the Pharisee and the Tax Collector
Mark 1:1-8 - John the Baptist Prepares the Way
Mark 7:24-30 - The Faith of a Syrophoenician Woman
Mark 9:33-37 - Who Is the Greatest?
Mark 10:13-16 - The Little Children and Jesus
Mark 11:1-11 - The Triumphal Entry
Matthew 3:13-17 - The Baptism of Jesus
Matthew 5:1-12 - The Beatitudes
Matthew 5:38-42 - An Eye for an Eye
Matthew 6:5-15 - Prayer
Matthew 6:16-18 - Fasting
Matthew 8:1-4 - The Man With Leprosy
Matthew 8:5-13 - The Faith of the Centurion
Matthew 11:25-30 - Rest for the Weary
Matthew 12:15-21 - God's Chosen Servant
Matthew 16:1-4 - The Demand for a Sign
Matthew 18:1-9 - The Greatest in the Kingdom of Heaven
Matthew 18:15-20 - A Brother Who Sins Against You
Matthew 21:28-32 - The Parable of the Two Sons
Philippians 2:1-11 - Imitating Christ's Humility
Romans 11:11-24 - Ingrafted Branches
Romans 12:1-8 - Living Sacrifices
Romans 15:14-22 - Paul, the Minister to the Gentiles
Titus 3:1-15 - Doing What Is Good

■ HUSBANDS

1 Peter 3:1-7 - Wives and Husbands
1 Timothy 5:1–6:2 - Advice About Widows, Elders and Slaves
Matthew 5:27-30 - Adultery

■ HYPOCRISY

1 John 3:11-24 - Love One Another
1 Timothy 4:1-16 - Instructions to Timothy
Galatians 2:11-21 - Paul Opposes Peter
James 1:19-27 - Listening and Doing
James 2:14-26 - Faith and Deeds
John 2:12-25 - Jesus Clears the Temple
John 7:14-24 - Jesus Teaches at the Feast
John 7:53–8:11 - A Woman Caught in Adultery
John 9:13-34 - The Pharisees Investigate the Healing
John 11:45-57 - The Plot to Kill Jesus
John 12:1-11 - Jesus Anointed at Bethany
John 13:18-30 - Jesus Predicts His Betrayal
John 18:15-18 - Peter's First Denial
John 19:1-16 - Jesus Sentenced to be Crucified
Luke 6:1-11 - Lord of the Sabbath
Luke 11:37-54 - Six Woes
Luke 12:1-12 - Warnings and Encouragements
Luke 12:54-59 - Interpreting the Times
Luke 13:10-17 - A Crippled Woman Healed on the Sabbath
Luke 15:1-7 - The Parable of the Lost Sheep
Luke 20:1-8 - The Authority of Jesus Questioned
Luke 20:20-26 - Paying Taxes to Caesar
Luke 22:1-6 - Judas Agrees to Betray Jesus
Luke 22:47-53 - Jesus Arrested
Mark 2:23–3:6 - Lord of the Sabbath
Mark 7:1-23 - Clean and Unclean
Mark 12:13-17 - Paying Taxes to Caesar
Mark 14:43-52 - Jesus Arrested
Matthew 3:1-12 - John the Baptist Prepares the Way
Matthew 6:1-4 - Giving to the Needy
Matthew 6:5-15 - Prayer
Matthew 6:16-18 - Fasting
Matthew 7:1-6 - Judging Others
Matthew 7:15-23 - A Tree and Its Fruit
Matthew 9:1-8 - Jesus Heals a Paralytic
Matthew 12:1-14 - Lord of the Sabbath
Matthew 15:1-20 - Clean and Unclean
Matthew 21:12-17 - Jesus at the Temple
Matthew 21:18-22 - The Fig Tree Withers
Matthew 21:23-27 - The Authority of Jesus Questioned
Matthew 22:15-22 - Paying Taxes to Caesar
Matthew 22:34-40 - The Greatest Commandment
Matthew 23:1-39 - Seven Woes
Matthew 24:36-51 - The Day and Hour Unknown
Romans 2:17-29 - The Jews and the Law

■ IDOLATRY

1 Corinthians 5:1-13 - Expel the Immoral Brother!
1 Corinthians 8:1-13 - Food Sacrificed to Idols
1 Corinthians 10:1-13 - Warnings From Israel's History
1 Corinthians 10:14-22 - Idol Feasts and the Lord's Supper
1 Corinthians 12:1-11 - Spiritual Gifts
Acts 14:8-20 - In Lystra and Derbe
Acts 17:16-34 - In Athens
Acts 19:23-41 - The Riot in Ephesus
Galatians 4:8-20 - Paul's Concern for the Galatians
Matthew 24:1-35 - Signs of the End of the Age
Revelation 2:12-17 - To the Church in Pergamum
Revelation 2:18-29 - To the Church in Thyatira
Revelation 13:11-18 - The Beast out of the Earth
Revelation 21:1-27 - The New Jerusalem

■ IGNORANCE

1 Corinthians 1:18–2:5 - Christ the Wisdom and Power of God
1 Corinthians 2:6-16 - Wisdom From the Spirit
1 Corinthians 10:1-13 - Warnings From Israel's History
1 Corinthians 12:1-11 - Spiritual Gifts
Acts 3:11-26 - Peter Speaks to the Onlookers
Acts 17:16-34 - In Athens
Ephesians 4:17–5:21 - Living as Children of Light
Luke 18:31-34 - Jesus Again Predicts His Death
Luke 24:13-35 - On the Road to Emmaus

Mark 13:32-37 - The Day and Hour Unknown
Matthew 16:5-12 - The Yeast of the Pharisees and Sadducees
Matthew 16:13-20 - Peter's Confession of Christ
Matthew 22:23-33 - Marriage at the Resurrection
Matthew 24:36-51 - The Day and Hour Unknown
Matthew 25:14-30 - The Parable of the Talents

■ **IMAGE**
1 Corinthians 11:2-16 - Propriety in Worship
Acts 17:16-34 - In Athens
Colossians 1:15-23 - The Supremacy of Christ
Colossians 3:1-17 - Rules for Holy Living
Matthew 13:24-30 - The Parable of the Weeds
Matthew 13:53-58 - A Prophet Without Honor

■ **IMMORALITY**
1 Corinthians 5:1-13 - Expel the Immoral Brother!
1 Corinthians 6:1-11 - Lawsuits Among Believers
1 Corinthians 6:12-20 - Sexual Immorality
1 Corinthians 7:1-40 - Marriage
1 Corinthians 10:1-13 - Warnings From Israel's History
1 Thessalonians 4:1-12 - Living to Please God
Ephesians 4:17–5:21 - Living as Children of Light
Hebrews 12:14-29 - Warning Against Refusing God
Hebrews 13:1-25 - Concluding Exhortations
John 4:1-26 - Jesus Talks With a Samaritan Woman
John 7:53–8:11 - A Woman Caught in Adultery
Jude 1-16 - The Sin and Doom of Godless Men
Matthew 5:13-16 - Salt and Light
Matthew 5:27-30 - Adultery
Revelation 2:18-29 - To the Church in Thyatira
Revelation 17:1-18 - The Woman on the Beast
Revelation 18:1-24 - The Fall of Babylon
Revelation 19:1-10 - Hallelujah!
Revelation 21:1-27 - The New Jerusalem
Romans 1:18-32 - God's Wrath Against Mankind

■ **IMPORTANT**
Acts 8:26-40 - Philip and the Ethiopian
Matthew 26:17-30 - The Lord's Supper

■ **IMPOSSIBLE**
Luke 1:5-25 - The Birth of John the Baptist Foretold
Luke 1:26-38 - The Birth of Jesus Foretold
Mark 10:17-31 - The Rich Young Man

■ **IMPULSIVENESS**
1 Timothy 3:1-16 - Overseers and Deacons
Matthew 13:1-23 - The Parable of the Sower
Matthew 14:1-12 - John the Baptist Beheaded
Matthew 21:28-32 - The Parable of the Two Sons
Matthew 26:31-35 - Jesus Predicts Peter's Denial
Matthew 26:47-56 - Jesus Arrested

■ **INADEQUACY**
Hebrews 7:11-28 - Jesus Like Melchizedek
Hebrews 8:1-13 - The High Priest of a New Covenant
Hebrews 9:1-10 - Worship in the Earthly Tabernacle
Hebrews 9:11-28 - The Blood of Christ
Hebrews 10:1-18 - Christ's Sacrifice Once for All
Mark 10:13-16 - The Little Children and Jesus
Matthew 26:36-46 - Gethsemane

■ **INDIFFERENCE**
Matthew 22:1-14 - The Parable of the Wedding Banquet

■ **INFLUENCE**
2 Timothy 1:1–2:13 - Encouragement to Be Faithful
Galatians 4:8-20 - Paul's Concern for the Galatians
John 7:45-52 - Unbelief of the Jewish Leaders
Matthew 5:13-16 - Salt and Light
Matthew 13:31-35 - The Parables of the Mustard Seed and the Yeast
Matthew 16:5-12 - The Yeast of the Pharisees and Sadducees
Matthew 17:24-27 - The Temple Tax
Matthew 18:1-9 - The Greatest in the Kingdom of Heaven

■ **INITIATIVE**
1 Timothy 3:1-16 - Overseers and Deacons
Matthew 8:5-13 - The Faith of the Centurion
Matthew 18:10-14 - The Parable of the Lost Sheep

■ **INJUSTICE**
James 5:1-6 - Warning to Rich Oppressors
John 18:19-24 - The High Priest Questions Jesus
Luke 22:66–23:25 - Jesus Before Pilate and Herod
Mark 15:1-15 - Jesus Before Pilate
Matthew 14:1-12 - John the Baptist Beheaded

■ **INSECURITY**
John 6:16-24 - Jesus Walks on the Water
John 6:25-59 - Jesus the Bread of Life
Matthew 24:1-35 - Signs of the End of the Age
Matthew 27:62-66 - The Guard at the Tomb

■ **INSENSITIVITY**
Matthew 15:21-28 - The Faith of the Canaanite Woman

■ **INSIGHT**
Acts 5:1-11 - Ananias and Sapphira
Ephesians 3:1-13 - Paul the Preacher to the Gentiles
Matthew 16:13-20 - Peter's Confession of Christ
Matthew 19:13-15 - The Little Children and Jesus
Matthew 22:15-22 - Paying Taxes to Caesar

■ **INSPIRATION**
2 Peter 1:12-21 - Prophecy of Scripture
2 Peter 3:1-18 - The Day of the Lord
2 Timothy 3:10–4:8 - Paul's Charge to Timothy

■ **INSTRUCTIONS**
2 Timothy 3:10–4:8 - Paul's Charge to Timothy
Acts 1:1-11 - Jesus Taken Up Into Heaven
Acts 3:1-10 - Peter Heals the Crippled Beggar
Acts 8:26-40 - Philip and the Ethiopian
Acts 9:32-43 - Aeneas and Dorcas
Acts 10:1-8 - Cornelius Calls for Peter
Acts 10:9-23 - Peter's Vision
Acts 12:1-19 - Peter's Miraculous Escape From Prison
Acts 14:8-20 - In Lystra and Derbe
Acts 21:37–22:21 - Paul Speaks to the Crowd
Acts 23:23-35 - Paul Transferred to Caesarea
Ephesians 6:1-4 - Children and Parents
James 5:13-20 - The Prayer of Faith
Luke 1:1-4 - Introduction
Luke 2:8-20 - The Shepherds and the Angels
Luke 6:27-36 - Love for Enemies
Luke 24:36-49 - Jesus Appears to the Disciples
Mark 7:31-37 - The Healing of a Deaf and Mute Man
Mark 11:1-11 - The Triumphal Entry
Matthew 8:5-13 - The Faith of the Centurion
Matthew 10:1-42 - Jesus Sends Out the Twelve
Matthew 15:29-39 - Jesus Feeds the Four Thousand
Matthew 18:15-20 - A Brother Who Sins Against You
Matthew 24:1-35 - Signs of the End of the Age
Matthew 26:17-30 - The Lord's Supper

Revelation 10:1-11 - The Angel and the Little Scroll
■ **INSULTS**
1 Peter 4:12-19 - Suffering for Being a Christian
Luke 6:17-26 - Blessings and Woes
Luke 6:27-36 - Love for Enemies
Luke 22:63-65 - The Guards Mock Jesus
Luke 23:26-43 - The Crucifixion
Mark 15:21-32 - The Crucifixion
Matthew 12:22-37 - Jesus and Beelzebub
Matthew 26:57-68 - Before the Sanhedrin
■ **INTEGRITY**
1 Thessalonians 2:1-16 - Paul's Ministry in Thessalonica
1 Timothy 3:1-16 - Overseers and Deacons
John 1:19-28 - John the Baptist Denies Being the Christ
Mark 7:1-23 - Clean and Unclean
Matthew 5:33-37 - Oaths
Matthew 17:24-27 - The Temple Tax
Matthew 21:18-22 - The Fig Tree Withers
Matthew 22:15-22 - Paying Taxes to Caesar
Matthew 27:57-61 - The Burial of Jesus
Revelation 14:1-5 - The Lamb and the 144,000
■ **INTENTIONS**
John 18:1-11 - Jesus Arrested
Matthew 26:36-46 - Gethsemane
■ **INTERPRETATION**
1 Peter 1:1-12 - Praise to God for a Living Hope
2 Peter 1:12-21 - Prophecy of Scripture
Luke 12:54-59 - Interpreting the Times
Matthew 15:1-20 - Clean and Unclean
Matthew 28:11-15 - The Guards' Report
■ **INTIMIDATION**
Matthew 12:15-21 - God's Chosen Servant
Matthew 21:33-46 - The Parable of the Tenants
Matthew 23:1-39 - Seven Woes
Matthew 27:11-26 - Jesus Before Pilate
Matthew 27:27-31 - The Soldiers Mock Jesus
■ **INVITATION**
Luke 5:27-32 - The Calling of Levi
Luke 6:12-16 - The Twelve Apostles
Luke 14:1-14 - Jesus at a Pharisee's House
Luke 14:15-24 - The Parable of the Great Banquet
Mark 1:14-20 - The Calling of the First Disciples
Matthew 8:18-22 - The Cost of Following Jesus
Revelation 3:14-22 - To the Church in Laodicea
■ **INVOLVEMENT**
Matthew 5:13-16 - Salt and Light
Matthew 9:9-13 - The Calling of Matthew
Matthew 12:46-50 - Jesus' Mother and Brothers
■ **ISOLATION**
Luke 4:1-13 - The Temptation of Jesus

■ **JEALOUSY**
1 Corinthians 10:14-22 - Idol Feasts and the Lord's Supper
2 Corinthians 11:1-15 - Paul and the False Apostles
Acts 5:17-41 - The Apostles Persecuted
Acts 13:13-52 - In Pisidian Antioch
Acts 17:1-9 - In Thessalonica
John 3:22-36 - John the Baptist's Testimony About Jesus
Luke 10:38-42 - At the Home of Martha and Mary
Luke 15:11-32 - The Parable of the Lost Son
Mark 9:38-41 - Whoever Is Not Against Us Is for Us
Mark 10:35-45 - The Request of James and John
Matthew 2:13-18 - The Escape to Egypt
Matthew 9:27-34 - Jesus Heals the Blind and Mute
Matthew 12:22-37 - Jesus and Beelzebub
Matthew 20:20-28 - A Mother's Request
Matthew 21:12-17 - Jesus at the Temple
Matthew 21:23-27 - The Authority of Jesus Questioned
■ **JESUS CHRIST**
1 Corinthians 15:1-11 - The Resurrection of Christ
1 John 1:1-4 - The Word of Life
1 John 1:5-2:14 - Walking in the Light
1 John 2:18-27 - Warning Against Antichrists
1 John 2:28–3:10 - Children of God
1 John 3:11-24 - Love One Another
1 John 4:1-6 - Test the Spirits
1 John 4:7-21 - God's Love and Ours
1 John 5:1-12 - Faith in the Son of God
1 John 5:13-21 - Concluding Remarks
1 Peter 1:1-12 - Praise to God for a Living Hope
1 Peter 1:13–2:3 - Be Holy
1 Peter 2:4-12 - The Living Stone and a Chosen People
1 Peter 2:13-25 - Submission to Rulers and Masters
1 Peter 3:8-22 - Suffering for Doing Good
1 Peter 4:1-11 - Living for God
1 Peter 4:12-19 - Suffering for Being a Christian
1 Peter 5:1-14 - To Elders and Young Men
1 Thessalonians 4:13–5:11 - The Coming of the Lord
1 Timothy 1:1-11 - Warning Against False Teachers of the Law
1 Timothy 1:12-20 - The Lord's Grace to Paul
1 Timothy 2:1-15 - Instructions on Worship
1 Timothy 4:1-16 - Instructions to Timothy
1 Timothy 5:1–6:2 - Advice About Widows, Elders and Slaves
1 Timothy 6:3-10 - Love of Money
1 Timothy 6:11-21 - Paul's Charge to Timothy
2 John 1-13 - From the Elder
2 Peter 1:1-11 - Making One's Calling and Election Sure
2 Peter 1:12-21 - Prophecy of Scripture
2 Peter 2:1-22 - False Teachers and Their Destruction
2 Peter 3:1-18 - The Day of the Lord
2 Timothy 1:1–2:13 - Encouragement to Be Faithful
2 Timothy 3:10–4:8 - Paul's Charge to Timothy
3 John 1-14 - From the Elder
Acts 1:1-11 - Jesus Taken Up Into Heaven
Acts 2:14-41 - Peter Addresses the Crowd
Acts 3:1-10 - Peter Heals the Crippled Beggar
Acts 3:11-26 - Peter Speaks to the Onlookers
Acts 4:1-22 - Peter and John Before the Sanhedrin
Acts 4:23-31 - The Believers' Prayer
Acts 4:32-37 - The Believers Share Their Possessions
Acts 5:17-41 - The Apostles Persecuted
Acts 6:8-15 - Stephen Seized
Acts 7:54–8:1 - The Stoning of Stephen
Acts 8:9-25 - Simon the Sorcerer
Acts 8:26-40 - Philip and the Ethiopian
Acts 9:1-19 - Saul's Conversion
Acts 9:20-31 - Saul in Damascus and Jerusalem
Acts 9:32-43 - Aeneas and Dorcas
Acts 10:24-48 - Peter at Cornelius' House
Acts 11:1-18 - Peter Explains His Actions
Acts 11:19-30 - The Church in Antioch

Acts 13:1-3 - Barnabas and Saul Sent Off
Acts 13:4-12 - On Cyprus
Acts 13:13-52 - In Pisidian Antioch
Acts 14:1-7 - In Iconium
Acts 14:21-28 - The Return to Antioch in Syria
Acts 15:22-35 - The Council's Letter to Gentile Believers
Acts 15:36-41 - Disagreement Between Paul and Barnabas
Acts 16:6-10 - Paul's Vision of the Man of Macedonia
Acts 16:11-15 - Lydia's Conversion in Philippi
Acts 16:16-40 - Paul and Silas in Prison
Acts 17:1-9 - In Thessalonica
Acts 18:18-28 - Priscilla, Aquila and Apollos
Acts 19:1-22 - Paul in Ephesus
Acts 21:1-16 - On to Jerusalem
Acts 21:37–22:21 - Paul Speaks to the Crowd
Acts 22:30–23:11 - Before the Sanhedrin
Acts 24:1-27 - The Trial Before Felix
Acts 25:23–26:32 - Paul Before Agrippa
Acts 28:17-31 - Paul Preaches at Rome Under Guard
Colossians 1:1-14 - Thanksgiving and Prayer
Colossians 1:24–2:5 - Paul's Labor for the Church
Colossians 2:6-23 - Freedom From Human Regulations Through Life With Christ
Colossians 3:1-17 - Rules for Holy Living
Colossians 3:18–4:1 - Rules for Christian Households
Colossians 4:2-18 - Further Instructions
Ephesians 1:1-14 - Spiritual Blessings in Christ
Ephesians 1:15-23 - Thanksgiving and Prayer
Ephesians 2:1-10 - Made Alive in Christ
Ephesians 2:11-22 - One in Christ
Ephesians 3:1-13 - Paul the Preacher to the Gentiles
Ephesians 3:14-21 - A Prayer for the Ephesians
Ephesians 4:1-16 - Unity in the Body of Christ
Ephesians 4:17–5:21 - Living as Children of Light
Ephesians 5:22-33 - Wives and Husbands
Ephesians 6:1-4 - Children and Parents
Ephesians 6:5-9 - Slaves and Masters
Galatians 1:11-24 - Paul Called by God
Galatians 2:11-21 - Paul Opposes Peter
Galatians 3:1-14 - Faith or Observance of the Law
Galatians 3:15-25 - The Law and the Promise
Galatians 3:26–4:7 - Sons of God
Galatians 4:8-20 - Paul's Concern for the Galatians
Galatians 5:1-15 - Freedom in Christ
Galatians 5:16-26 - Life by the Spirit
Galatians 6:11-18 - Not Circumcision but a New Creation
Hebrews 1:1-14 - The Son Superior to Angels
Hebrews 2:5-18 - Jesus Made Like His Brothers
Hebrews 3:1-6 - Jesus Greater Than Moses
Hebrews 6:13-20 - The Certainty of God's Promise
Hebrews 7:1-10 - Melchizedek the Priest
Hebrews 8:1-13 - The High Priest of a New Covenant
Hebrews 9:1-10 - Worship in the Earthly Tabernacle
Hebrews 9:11-28 - The Blood of Christ
Hebrews 10:1-18 - Christ's Sacrifice Once for All
Hebrews 10:19-39 - A Call to Persevere
Hebrews 12:1-3 - God Disciplines His Sons
Hebrews 12:14-29 - Warning Against Refusing God
Hebrews 13:1-25 - Concluding Exhortations
John 1:1-19 - The Word Became Flesh
John 1:19-28 - John the Baptist Denies Being the Christ
John 1:29-34 - Jesus the Lamb of God
John 1:35-42 - Jesus' First Disciples
John 1:43-51 - Jesus Calls Philip and Nathanael
John 2:1-11 - Jesus Changes Water to Wine
John 2:12-25 - Jesus Clears the Temple
John 3:1-22 - Jesus Teaches Nicodemus
John 3:22-36 - John the Baptist's Testimony About Jesus
John 4:1-26 - Jesus Talks With a Samaritan Woman
John 4:27-38 - The Disciples Rejoin Jesus
John 4:39-42 - Many Samaritans Believe
John 4:43-54 - Jesus Heals the Official's Son
John 5:1-15 - The Healing at the Pool
John 5:16-30 - Life Through the Son
John 5:31-47 - Testimonies About Jesus
John 6:1-15 - Jesus Feeds the Five Thousand
John 6:16-24 - Jesus Walks on the Water
John 6:25-59 - Jesus the Bread of Life
John 6:60-71 - Many Disciples Desert Jesus
John 7:1-13 - Jesus Goes to the Feast of Tabernacles
John 7:14-24 - Jesus Teaches at the Feast
John 7:25-44 - Is Jesus the Christ?
John 7:45-52 - Unbelief of the Jewish Leaders
John 7:53–8:11 - A Woman Caught in Adultery
John 8:12-30 - The Validity of Jesus' Testimony
John 8:31-41 - The Children of Abraham
John 8:42-47 - The Children of the Devil
John 8:48-59 - The Claims of Jesus About Himself
John 9:1-12 - Jesus Heals a Man Born Blind
John 9:13-34 - The Pharisees Investigate the Healing
John 9:35-41 - Spiritual Blindness
John 10:1-21 - The Shepherd and His Flock
John 10:22-42 - The Unbelief of the Jews
John 11:1-16 - The Death of Lazarus
John 11:17-37 - Jesus Comforts the Sisters
John 11:38-44 - Jesus Raises Lazarus From the Dead
John 11:45-57 - The Plot to Kill Jesus
John 12:1-11 - Jesus Anointed at Bethany
John 12:12-19 - The Triumphal Entry
John 12:20-36 - Jesus Predicts His Death
John 12:37-50 - The Jews Continue in Their Unbelief
John 13:1-17 - Jesus Washes His Disciples' Feet
John 13:18-30 - Jesus Predicts His Betrayal
John 13:31-38 - Jesus Predicts Peter's Denial
John 14:1-4 - Jesus Comforts His Disciples
John 14:5-14 - Jesus the Way to the Father
John 14:15-31 - Jesus Promises the Holy Spirit
John 15:1-17 - The Vine and the Branches
John 15:18–16:4 - The World Hates the Disciples
John 16:5-16 - The Work of the Holy Spirit
John 16:17-33 - The Disciples' Grief Will Turn to Joy
John 17:1-5 - Jesus Prays for Himself
John 17:6-19 - Jesus Prays for His Disciples
John 17:20-26 - Jesus Prays for All Believers
John 18:1-11 - Jesus Arrested
John 18:12-14 - Jesus Taken to Annas
John 18:15-18 - Peter's First Denial
John 18:19-24 - The High Priest Questions Jesus
John 18:25-27 - Peter's Second and Third Denials
John 18:28-40 - Jesus Before Pilate
John 19:1-16 - Jesus Sentenced to be Crucified

John 19:17-27 - The Crucifixion
John 19:28-37 - The Death of Jesus
John 19:38-42 - The Burial of Jesus
John 20:1-9 - The Empty Tomb
John 20:10-18 - Jesus Appears to Mary Magdalene
John 20:19-23 - Jesus Appears to His Disciples
John 20:24-31 - Jesus Appears to Thomas
John 21:1-14 - Jesus and the Miraculous Catch of Fish
John 21:15-25 - Jesus Reinstates Peter
Luke 1:26-38 - The Birth of Jesus Foretold
Luke 2:1-7 - The Birth of Jesus
Luke 4:1-13 - The Temptation of Jesus
Luke 17:20-37 - The Coming of the Kingdom of God
Luke 18:15-17 - The Little Children and Jesus
Luke 18:31-34 - Jesus Again Predicts His Death
Luke 18:35-43 - A Blind Beggar Receives His Sight
Luke 20:1-8 - The Authority of Jesus Questioned
Luke 20:9-19 - The Parable of the Tenants
Luke 20:20-26 - Paying Taxes to Caesar
Luke 20:41-47 - Whose Son Is the Christ?
Luke 22:7-38 - The Last Supper
Luke 22:66–23:25 - Jesus Before Pilate and Herod
Luke 24:1-12 - The Resurrection
Luke 24:13-35 - On the Road to Emmaus
Luke 24:50-53 - The Ascension
Mark 1:9-13 - The Baptism and Temptation of Jesus
Mark 8:27-30 - Peter's Confession of Christ
Mark 11:1-11 - The Triumphal Entry
Mark 12:35-40 - Whose Son Is the Christ?
Mark 13:32-37 - The Day and Hour Unknown
Mark 14:66-72 - Peter Disowns Jesus
Mark 15:21-32 - The Crucifixion
Mark 15:33-41 - The Death of Jesus
Matthew 1:1-17 - The Genealogy of Jesus
Matthew 3:1-12 - John the Baptist Prepares the Way
Matthew 3:13-17 - The Baptism of Jesus
Matthew 4:1-11 - The Temptation of Jesus
Matthew 4:23-25 - Jesus Heals the Sick
Matthew 8:23-27 - Jesus Calms the Storm
Matthew 9:14-17 - Jesus Questioned About Fasting
Matthew 13:36-43 - The Parable of the Weeds Explained
Matthew 16:13-20 - Peter's Confession of Christ
Matthew 16:21-28 - Jesus Predicts His Death
Matthew 17:1-13 - The Transfiguration
Matthew 24:1-35 - Signs of the End of the Age
Matthew 26:47-56 - Jesus Arrested
Matthew 26:57-68 - Before the Sanhedrin
Matthew 27:1-10 - Judas Hangs Himself
Matthew 27:11-26 - Jesus Before Pilate
Matthew 27:27-31 - The Soldiers Mock Jesus
Matthew 27:32-44 - The Crucifixion
Matthew 28:1-10 - The Resurrection
Matthew 28:16-20 - The Great Commission
Philippians 1:1-11 - Thanksgiving and Prayer
Philippians 1:12-30 - Paul's Chains Advance the Gospel
Philippians 2:1-11 - Imitating Christ's Humility
Philippians 2:12-18 - Shining as Stars
Philippians 2:19-30 - Timothy and Epaphroditus
Philippians 3:1-11 - No Confidence in the Flesh
Philippians 3:12–4:1 - Pressing on Toward the Goal
Philippians 4:2-9 - Exhortations
Philippians 4:10-23 - Thanks for Their Gifts
Revelation 1:1-3 - Prologue
Revelation 1:4-8 - Greetings and Doxology
Revelation 3:14-22 - To the Church in Laodicea
Revelation 5:1-14 - The Scroll and the Lamb
Revelation 6:1-17 - The Seals
Revelation 19:11-21 - The Rider on the White Horse
Revelation 20:1-6 - The Thousand Years
Revelation 20:7-10 - Satan's Doom
Revelation 20:11-15 - The Dead Are Judged
Revelation 21:1-27 - The New Jerusalem
Revelation 22:1-6 - The River of Life
Revelation 22:7-21 - Jesus Is Coming
Romans 3:21-31 - Righteousness Through Faith
Romans 5:12-21 - Death Through Adam, Life Through Christ
Romans 6:1-14 - Dead to Sin, Alive in Christ
Romans 9:30–10:21 - Israel's Unbelief

■ JOBS

1 Thessalonians 4:1-12 - Living to Please God
2 Thessalonians 3:6-18 - Warning Against Idleness

■ JOY

1 John 1:1-4 - The Word of Life
1 John 2:15-17 - Do Not Love the World
1 Peter 1:1-12 - Praise to God for a Living Hope
1 Peter 4:12-19 - Suffering for Being a Christian
1 Timothy 6:11-21 - Paul's Charge to Timothy
2 Corinthians 7:2-16 - Paul's Joy
2 Corinthians 12:1-10 - Paul's Vision and His Thorn
3 John 1-14 - From the Elder
Acts 2:42-47 - The Fellowship of the Believers
Acts 5:17-41 - The Apostles Persecuted
Acts 8:4-8 - Philip in Samaria
Acts 8:26-40 - Philip and the Ethiopian
Acts 12:1-19 - Peter's Miraculous Escape From Prison
Acts 13:13-52 - In Pisidian Antioch
Colossians 1:24–2:5 - Paul's Labor for the Church
Galatians 4:8-20 - Paul's Concern for the Galatians
Galatians 5:16-26 - Life by the Spirit
Hebrews 10:19-39 - A Call to Persevere
John 3:22-36 - John the Baptist's Testimony About Jesus
John 15:1-17 - The Vine and the Branches
John 16:17-33 - The Disciples' Grief Will Turn to Joy
John 17:6-19 - Jesus Prays for His Disciples
John 20:10-18 - Jesus Appears to Mary Magdalene
John 20:19-23 - Jesus Appears to His Disciples
Luke 1:39-45 - Mary Visits Elizabeth
Luke 1:46-56 - Mary's Song
Luke 1:57-66 - The Birth of John the Baptist
Luke 6:17-26 - Blessings and Woes
Luke 10:1-24 - Jesus Sends Out the Seventy-two
Luke 15:8-10 - The Parable of the Lost Coin
Luke 19:28-44 - The Triumphal Entry
Luke 24:36-49 - Jesus Appears to the Disciples
Luke 24:50-53 - The Ascension
Mark 16:1-20 - The Resurrection
Matthew 13:1-23 - The Parable of the Sower
Matthew 13:44-46 - The Parables of the Hidden Treasure and the Pearl
Philippians 1:12-30 - Paul's Chains Advance the Gospel
Philippians 2:1-11 - Imitating Christ's Humility
Philippians 2:12-18 - Shining as Stars
Philippians 3:1-11 - No Confidence in the Flesh

Philippians 4:2-9 - Exhortations
Philippians 4:10-23 - Thanks for Their Gifts
Revelation 7:9-17 - The Great Multitude in White Robes
Revelation 21:1-27 - The New Jerusalem
Revelation 22:1-6 - The River of Life
Romans 5:1-11 - Peace and Joy

■ JUDGING OTHERS

Acts 15:1-21 - The Council at Jerusalem
Colossians 2:6-23 - Freedom From Human Regulations Through Life With Christ
James 2:1-13 - Favoritism Forbidden
John 4:1-26 - Jesus Talks With a Samaritan Woman
John 4:27-38 - The Disciples Rejoin Jesus
John 7:14-24 - Jesus Teaches at the Feast
John 7:53–8:11 - A Woman Caught in Adultery
Luke 6:37-42 - Judging Others
Luke 7:36-50 - Jesus Anointed by a Sinful Woman
Luke 11:14-28 - Jesus and Beelzebub
Luke 11:37-54 - Six Woes
Luke 13:10-17 - A Crippled Woman Healed on the Sabbath
Luke 14:1-14 - Jesus at a Pharisee's House
Luke 15:11-32 - The Parable of the Lost Son
Luke 19:1-10 - Zacchaeus the Tax Collector
Mark 2:13-17 - The Calling of Levi
Mark 2:23–3:6 - Lord of the Sabbath
Mark 9:38-41 - Whoever Is Not Against Us Is for Us
Mark 14:1-11 - Jesus Anointed at Bethany
Matthew 9:14-17 - Jesus Questioned About Fasting
Matthew 12:1-14 - Lord of the Sabbath
Matthew 12:22-37 - Jesus and Beelzebub
Matthew 13:24-30 - The Parable of the Weeds
Matthew 18:15-20 - A Brother Who Sins Against You
Romans 2:1-16 - God's Righteous Judgment

■ JUDGMENT

1 Corinthians 2:6-16 - Wisdom From the Spirit
1 Corinthians 4:1-21 - Apostles of Christ
1 Corinthians 5:1-13 - Expel the Immoral Brother!
1 Corinthians 6:1-11 - Lawsuits Among Believers
1 Corinthians 9:1-27 - The Rights of an Apostle
1 Corinthians 11:17-34 - The Lord's Supper
1 John 4:7-21 - God's Love and Ours
1 Peter 1:13–2:3 - Be Holy
1 Peter 4:1-11 - Living for God
1 Peter 4:12-19 - Suffering for Being a Christian
2 Corinthians 5:1-10 - Our Heavenly Dwelling
2 Peter 2:1-22 - False Teachers and Their Destruction
2 Peter 3:1-18 - The Day of the Lord
2 Thessalonians 1:1-12 - Thanksgiving and Prayer
2 Thessalonians 2:1-12 - The Man of Lawlessness
Acts 4:1-22 - Peter and John Before the Sanhedrin
Acts 15:1-21 - The Council at Jerusalem
Acts 17:16-34 - In Athens
Acts 18:1-17 - In Corinth
Hebrews 3:7-19 - Warning Against Unbelief
Hebrews 4:1-13 - A Sabbath-Rest for the People of God
Hebrews 5:11–6:12 - Warning Against Falling Away
Hebrews 9:11-28 - The Blood of Christ
Hebrews 10:19-39 - A Call to Persevere
Hebrews 12:14-29 - Warning Against Refusing God
Hebrews 13:1-25 - Concluding Exhortations
James 4:13-17 - Boasting About Tomorrow
James 5:1-6 - Warning to Rich Oppressors
James 5:7-12 - Patience in Suffering
John 5:16-30 - Life Through the Son
John 8:12-30 - The Validity of Jesus' Testimony
John 9:35-41 - Spiritual Blindness
John 12:20-36 - Jesus Predicts His Death
John 12:37-50 - The Jews Continue in Their Unbelief
John 16:5-16 - The Work of the Holy Spirit
Jude 1-16 - The Sin and Doom of Godless Men
Luke 11:29-32 - The Sign of Jonah
Luke 12:13-21 - The Parable of the Rich Fool
Luke 12:54-59 - Interpreting the Times
Luke 16:19-31 - The Rich Man and Lazarus
Luke 19:11-27 - The Parable of the Ten Minas
Luke 19:45-48 - Jesus at the Temple
Luke 20:41-47 - Whose Son Is the Christ?
Mark 9:42-50 - Causing to Sin
Mark 14:12-26 - The Lord's Supper
Mark 15:1-15 - Jesus Before Pilate
Matthew 3:1-12 - John the Baptist Prepares the Way
Matthew 5:21-26 - Murder
Matthew 7:1-6 - Judging Others
Matthew 11:20-24 - Woe on Unrepentant Cities
Matthew 13:24-30 - The Parable of the Weeds
Matthew 13:36-43 - The Parable of the Weeds Explained
Matthew 13:47-52 - The Parable of the Net
Matthew 19:16-30 - The Rich Young Man
Matthew 24:36-51 - The Day and Hour Unknown
Matthew 25:1-13 - The Parable of the Ten Virgins
Matthew 25:14-30 - The Parable of the Talents
Matthew 25:31-46 - The Sheep and the Goats
Revelation 6:1-17 - The Seals
Revelation 7:1-8 - 144,000 Sealed
Revelation 8:6–9:21 - The Trumpets
Revelation 10:1-11 - The Angel and the Little Scroll
Revelation 11:1-14 - The Two Witnesses
Revelation 11:15-19 - The Seventh Trumpet
Revelation 12:1–13:1 - The Woman and the Dragon
Revelation 14:6-13 - The Three Angels
Revelation 14:14-20 - The Harvest of the Earth
Revelation 16:1-21 - The Seven Bowls of God's Wrath
Revelation 17:1-18 - The Woman on the Beast
Revelation 18:1-24 - The Fall of Babylon
Revelation 19:1-10 - Hallelujah!
Revelation 19:11-21 - The Rider on the White Horse
Revelation 20:1-6 - The Thousand Years
Revelation 20:7-10 - Satan's Doom
Revelation 20:11-15 - The Dead Are Judged
Romans 2:1-16 - God's Righteous Judgment
Romans 3:1-8 - God's Faithfulness
Romans 3:9-20 - No One Is Righteous

■ JUSTICE

Acts 8:26-40 - Philip and the Ethiopian
Acts 16:16-40 - Paul and Silas in Prison
Colossians 3:18–4:1 - Rules for Christian Households
James 5:1-6 - Warning to Rich Oppressors
John 18:28-40 - Jesus Before Pilate
Luke 1:46-56 - Mary's Song
Luke 11:37-54 - Six Woes
Luke 18:1-8 - The Parable of the Persistent Widow
Matthew 12:15-21 - God's Chosen Servant

Matthew 20:1-16 - The Parable of the Workers in the Vineyard
Revelation 15:1-8 - Seven Angels With Seven Plagues
Revelation 16:1-21 - The Seven Bowls of God's Wrath
Revelation 19:1-10 - Hallelujah!
Romans 3:1-8 - God's Faithfulness
Romans 3:21-31 - Righteousness Through Faith
Romans 9:1-29 - God's Sovereign Choice

■ KINDNESS

1 Corinthians 13:1-13 - Love
2 Peter 1:1-11 - Making One's Calling and Election Sure
Acts 4:1-22 - Peter and John Before the Sanhedrin
Acts 27:1-12 - Paul Sails for Rome
Acts 28:1-10 - Ashore on Malta
Ephesians 4:17–5:21 - Living as Children of Light
Galatians 5:16-26 - Life by the Spirit
Luke 8:40-56 - A Dead Girl and a Sick Woman
Luke 10:25-37 - The Parable of the Good Samaritan
Matthew 7:7-12 - Ask, Seek, Knock
Matthew 18:10-14 - The Parable of the Lost Sheep
Matthew 26:6-13 - Jesus Anointed at Bethany

■ KINGDOM OF GOD/HEAVEN

1 Corinthians 4:1-21 - Apostles of Christ
1 Corinthians 6:1-11 - Lawsuits Among Believers
1 Corinthians 13:1-13 - Love
Acts 8:9-25 - Simon the Sorcerer
Acts 14:21-28 - The Return to Antioch in Syria
Acts 19:1-22 - Paul in Ephesus
Acts 20:13-38 - Paul's Farewell to the Ephesian Elders
Acts 28:17-31 - Paul Preaches at Rome Under Guard
Colossians 1:1-14 - Thanksgiving and Prayer
Colossians 4:2-18 - Further Instructions
Galatians 5:16-26 - Life by the Spirit
John 3:1-22 - Jesus Teaches Nicodemus
John 18:28-40 - Jesus Before Pilate
Luke 4:38-44 - Jesus Heals Many
Luke 9:10-17 - Jesus Feeds the Five Thousand
Luke 9:18-27 - Peter's Confession of Christ
Luke 9:57-62 - The Cost of Following Jesus
Luke 10:1-24 - Jesus Sends Out the Seventy-two
Luke 11:14-28 - Jesus and Beelzebub
Luke 12:22-34 - Do Not Worry
Luke 13:18-21 - The Parables of the Mustard Seed and the Yeast
Luke 13:22-30 - The Narrow Door
Luke 14:15-24 - The Parable of the Great Banquet
Luke 16:16-18 - Additional Teachings
Luke 17:20-37 - The Coming of the Kingdom of God
Luke 18:15-17 - The Little Children and Jesus
Luke 18:18-30 - The Rich Ruler
Luke 19:11-27 - The Parable of the Ten Minas
Luke 22:7-38 - The Last Supper
Luke 23:26-43 - The Crucifixion
Luke 23:50-56 - Jesus' Burial
Mark 4:1-20 - The Parable of the Sower
Mark 4:26-29 - The Parable of the Growing Seed
Mark 4:30-34 - The Parable of the Mustard Seed
Mark 9:42-50 - Causing to Sin
Mark 10:13-16 - The Little Children and Jesus
Mark 12:28-34 - The Greatest Commandment
Mark 14:12-26 - The Lord's Supper
Mark 15:42-47 - The Burial of Jesus
Matthew 4:23-25 - Jesus Heals the Sick
Matthew 8:5-13 - The Faith of the Centurion
Matthew 11:1-19 - Jesus and John the Baptist
Matthew 13:24-30 - The Parable of the Weeds
Matthew 13:31-35 - The Parables of the Mustard Seed and the Yeast
Matthew 13:36-43 - The Parable of the Weeds Explained
Matthew 13:44-46 - The Parables of the Hidden Treasure and the Pearl
Matthew 13:47-52 - The Parable of the Net
Matthew 16:21-28 - Jesus Predicts His Death
Matthew 17:1-13 - The Transfiguration
Matthew 19:13-15 - The Little Children and Jesus
Matthew 20:1-16 - The Parable of the Workers in the Vineyard
Matthew 20:20-28 - A Mother's Request
Matthew 21:33-46 - The Parable of the Tenants
Matthew 22:1-14 - The Parable of the Wedding Banquet
Matthew 24:1-35 - Signs of the End of the Age

■ KNOWLEDGE

1 Corinthians 1:18–2:5 - Christ the Wisdom and Power of God
1 Corinthians 8:1-13 - Food Sacrificed to Idols
1 Corinthians 12:1-11 - Spiritual Gifts
1 Corinthians 13:1-13 - Love
1 John 2:18-27 - Warning Against Antichrists
1 Peter 1:1-12 - Praise to God for a Living Hope
1 Timothy 2:1-15 - Instructions on Worship
1 Timothy 6:11-21 - Paul's Charge to Timothy
2 Corinthians 2:12–3:6 - Ministers of the New Covenant
2 Corinthians 4:1-18 - Treasures in Jars of Clay
2 Peter 1:1-11 - Making One's Calling and Election Sure
Colossians 1:1-14 - Thanksgiving and Prayer
Colossians 3:1-17 - Rules for Holy Living
John 4:39-42 - Many Samaritans Believe
John 8:12-30 - The Validity of Jesus' Testimony
John 14:5-14 - Jesus the Way to the Father
John 14:15-31 - Jesus Promises the Holy Spirit
John 16:5-16 - The Work of the Holy Spirit
John 17:1-5 - Jesus Prays for Himself
John 17:6-19 - Jesus Prays for His Disciples
Mark 13:32-37 - The Day and Hour Unknown
Matthew 16:1-4 - The Demand for a Sign
Matthew 16:13-20 - Peter's Confession of Christ
Matthew 21:23-27 - The Authority of Jesus Questioned
Romans 11:33-36 - Doxology

■ LAST DAYS

1 Corinthians 15:35-58 - The Resurrection Body
1 John 2:18-27 - Warning Against Antichrists
1 Peter 1:1-12 - Praise to God for a Living Hope
1 Timothy 4:1-16 - Instructions to Timothy
2 Peter 3:1-18 - The Day of the Lord
2 Thessalonians 1:1-12 - Thanksgiving and Prayer
2 Thessalonians 2:1-12 - The Man of Lawlessness
2 Timothy 3:1-9 - Godlessness in the Last Days
Jude 17-25 - A Call to Persevere
Luke 21:5-38 - Signs of the End of the Age
Mark 13:1-31 - Signs of the End of the Age
Matthew 10:1-42 - Jesus Sends Out the Twelve
Matthew 16:21-28 - Jesus Predicts His Death

Matthew 24:1-35 - Signs of the End of the Age
Matthew 24:36-51 - The Day and Hour Unknown
Matthew 25:1-13 - The Parable of the Ten Virgins
Revelation 1:1-3 - Prologue
Revelation 1:9-20 - One Like a Son of Man
Revelation 6:1-17 - The Seals
Revelation 7:1-8 - 144,000 Sealed
Revelation 8:6–9:21 - The Trumpets
Revelation 13:2-10 - The Beast out of the Sea
Revelation 16:1-21 - The Seven Bowls of God's Wrath
Revelation 19:11-21 - The Rider on the White Horse
Revelation 20:1-6 - The Thousand Years
Revelation 20:7-10 - Satan's Doom
Revelation 20:11-15 - The Dead Are Judged
Romans 13:8-14 - Love, for the Day Is Near

■ LAW

1 Corinthians 9:1-27 - The Rights of an Apostle
1 Corinthians 14:26-40 - Orderly Worship
1 Timothy 1:1-11 - Warning Against False Teachers of the Law
2 Peter 2:1-22 - False Teachers and Their Destruction
Acts 4:1-22 - Peter and John Before the Sanhedrin
Acts 6:8-15 - Stephen Seized
Acts 7:1-53 - Stephen's Speech to the Sanhedrin
Acts 18:1-17 - In Corinth
Acts 21:17-26 - Paul's Arrival at Jerusalem
Acts 22:22-29 - Paul the Roman Citizen
Acts 22:30–23:11 - Before the Sanhedrin
Acts 23:23-35 - Paul Transferred to Caesarea
Acts 24:1-27 - The Trial Before Felix
Acts 25:1-12 - The Trial Before Festus
Acts 25:13-22 - Festus Consults King Agrippa
Acts 28:17-31 - Paul Preaches at Rome Under Guard
Ephesians 2:11-22 - One in Christ
Galatians 2:1-10 - Paul Accepted by the Apostles
Galatians 2:11-21 - Paul Opposes Peter
Galatians 3:1-14 - Faith or Observance of the Law
Galatians 3:15-25 - The Law and the Promise
Galatians 3:26–4:7 - Sons of God
Galatians 4:21-31 - Hagar and Sarah
Galatians 5:1-15 - Freedom in Christ
Galatians 5:16-26 - Life by the Spirit
Galatians 6:11-18 - Not Circumcision but a New Creation
Hebrews 2:1-4 - Warning to Pay Attention
James 1:19-27 - Listening and Doing
John 1:1-19 - The Word Became Flesh
John 5:1-15 - The Healing at the Pool
John 7:14-24 - Jesus Teaches at the Feast
John 18:28-40 - Jesus Before Pilate
Luke 10:25-37 - The Parable of the Good Samaritan
Luke 11:37-54 - Six Woes
Luke 14:1-14 - Jesus at a Pharisee's House
Luke 16:16-18 - Additional Teachings
Luke 18:18-30 - The Rich Ruler
Mark 2:23–3:6 - Lord of the Sabbath
Mark 10:1-12 - Divorce
Matthew 5:17-20 - The Fulfillment of the Law
Matthew 7:7-12 - Ask, Seek, Knock
Matthew 9:14-17 - Jesus Questioned About Fasting
Matthew 15:1-20 - Clean and Unclean
Matthew 19:16-30 - The Rich Young Man
Matthew 22:23-33 - Marriage at the Resurrection
Matthew 22:34-40 - The Greatest Commandment
Matthew 22:41-46 - Whose Son Is the Christ?
Romans 3:1-8 - God's Faithfulness
Romans 3:9-20 - No One Is Righteous
Romans 3:21-31 - Righteousness Through Faith
Romans 5:12-21 - Death Through Adam, Life Through Christ
Romans 7:1-6 - An Illustration From Marriage
Romans 7:7-25 - Struggling With Sin
Romans 8:1-17 - Life Through the Spirit
Romans 9:30–10:21 - Israel's Unbelief
Romans 13:1-7 - Submission to the Authorities
Romans 13:8-14 - Love, for the Day Is Near

■ LAZINESS

2 Thessalonians 3:6-18 - Warning Against Idleness
Hebrews 5:11–6:12 - Warning Against Falling Away
Matthew 25:14-30 - The Parable of the Talents

■ LEADERSHIP

1 Peter 2:13-25 - Submission to Rulers and Masters
1 Peter 5:1-14 - To Elders and Young Men
1 Thessalonians 5:12-28 - Final Instructions
1 Timothy 3:1-16 - Overseers and Deacons
Acts 1:12-26 - Matthias Chosen to Replace Judas
Acts 4:23-31 - The Believers' Prayer
Acts 5:17-41 - The Apostles Persecuted
Acts 6:1-7 - The Choosing of the Seven
Acts 8:9-25 - Simon the Sorcerer
Acts 10:1-8 - Cornelius Calls for Peter
Acts 13:1-3 - Barnabas and Saul Sent Off
Acts 13:13-52 - In Pisidian Antioch
Acts 15:22-35 - The Council's Letter to Gentile Believers
Acts 16:1-5 - Timothy Joins Paul and Silas
Acts 19:23-41 - The Riot in Ephesus
Acts 20:13-38 - Paul's Farewell to the Ephesian Elders
Acts 21:17-26 - Paul's Arrival at Jerusalem
Acts 23:12-22 - The Plot to Kill Paul
Acts 23:23-35 - Paul Transferred to Caesarea
Acts 24:1-27 - The Trial Before Felix
Acts 25:1-12 - The Trial Before Festus
Acts 25:13-22 - Festus Consults King Agrippa
Acts 27:27-44 - The Shipwreck
Acts 28:1-10 - Ashore on Malta
Acts 28:17-31 - Paul Preaches at Rome Under Guard
Galatians 2:1-10 - Paul Accepted by the Apostles
Hebrews 13:1-25 - Concluding Exhortations
John 7:45-52 - Unbelief of the Jewish Leaders
John 8:12-30 - The Validity of Jesus' Testimony
John 9:13-34 - The Pharisees Investigate the Healing
John 11:45-57 - The Plot to Kill Jesus
Luke 7:1-10 - The Faith of the Centurion
Luke 19:11-27 - The Parable of the Ten Minas
Mark 3:13-19 - The Appointing of the Twelve Apostles
Mark 10:32-34 - Jesus Again Predicts His Death
Mark 15:1-15 - Jesus Before Pilate
Matthew 4:18-22 - The Calling of the First Disciples
Matthew 16:13-20 - Peter's Confession of Christ
Matthew 20:20-28 - A Mother's Request
Titus 1:1-16 - Titus' Task on Crete

■ LEARNING

1 Corinthians 1:18–2:5 - Christ the Wisdom and Power of God

2 Timothy 3:1-9 - Godlessness in the Last Days
Acts 18:18-28 - Priscilla, Aquila and Apollos
John 14:15-31 - Jesus Promises the Holy Spirit
Luke 1:1-4 - Introduction
Luke 2:41-52 - The Boy Jesus at the Temple
Luke 6:37-42 - Judging Others
Matthew 8:23-27 - Jesus Calms the Storm
Matthew 14:13-21 - Jesus Feeds the Five Thousand
Matthew 16:1-4 - The Demand for a Sign

■ **LEGALISM**

1 Timothy 4:1-16 - Instructions to Timothy
Colossians 2:6-23 - Freedom From Human Regulations Through Life With Christ
Galatians 1:1-10 - No Other Gospel
Galatians 4:8-20 - Paul's Concern for the Galatians
Hebrews 2:1-4 - Warning to Pay Attention
Hebrews 10:1-18 - Christ's Sacrifice Once for All
John 5:1-15 - The Healing at the Pool
John 5:31-47 - Testimonies About Jesus
John 7:14-24 - Jesus Teaches at the Feast
John 7:53–8:11 - A Woman Caught in Adultery
John 18:28-40 - Jesus Before Pilate
Luke 5:33-39 - Jesus Questioned About Fasting
Luke 6:1-11 - Lord of the Sabbath
Luke 7:18-35 - Jesus and John the Baptist
Mark 2:13-17 - The Calling of Levi
Mark 2:18-22 - Jesus Questioned About Fasting
Mark 2:23–3:6 - Lord of the Sabbath
Matthew 5:17-20 - The Fulfillment of the Law
Matthew 9:14-17 - Jesus Questioned About Fasting
Matthew 11:25-30 - Rest for the Weary
Matthew 12:1-14 - Lord of the Sabbath
Matthew 12:22-37 - Jesus and Beelzebub
Matthew 15:1-20 - Clean and Unclean
Matthew 19:16-30 - The Rich Young Man
Matthew 22:34-40 - The Greatest Commandment
Matthew 22:41-46 - Whose Son Is the Christ?
Matthew 23:1-39 - Seven Woes

■ **LIFE**

1 John 1:1-4 - The Word of Life
1 John 1:5–2:14 - Walking in the Light
1 John 3:11-24 - Love One Another
1 John 5:1-12 - Faith in the Son of God
1 John 5:13-21 - Concluding Remarks
1 Timothy 4:1-16 - Instructions to Timothy
Ephesians 2:1-10 - Made Alive in Christ
Galatians 2:11-21 - Paul Opposes Peter
John 5:31-47 - Testimonies About Jesus
John 10:1-21 - The Shepherd and His Flock
John 12:20-36 - Jesus Predicts His Death
John 12:37-50 - The Jews Continue in Their Unbelief
John 13:31-38 - Jesus Predicts Peter's Denial
John 14:5-14 - Jesus the Way to the Father
John 20:24-31 - Jesus Appears to Thomas
Luke 3:21-38 - The Baptism and Genealogy of Jesus
Luke 6:46-49 - The Wise and Foolish Builders
Luke 17:20-37 - The Coming of the Kingdom of God
Luke 20:27-40 - The Resurrection and Marriage
Mark 12:18-27 - Marriage at the Resurrection
Mark 16:1-20 - The Resurrection
Philippians 1:12-30 - Paul's Chains Advance the Gospel
Romans 5:12-21 - Death Through Adam, Life Through Christ
Romans 12:9-21 - Love

■ **LIFE-STYLE**

1 John 2:15-17 - Do Not Love the World
1 John 2:28–3:10 - Children of God
1 John 3:11-24 - Love One Another
1 Peter 1:13–2:3 - Be Holy
1 Peter 2:4-12 - The Living Stone and a Chosen People
1 Peter 2:13-25 - Submission to Rulers and Masters
1 Peter 4:1-11 - Living for God
1 Timothy 2:1-15 - Instructions on Worship
1 Timothy 4:1-16 - Instructions to Timothy
1 Timothy 5:1–6:2 - Advice About Widows, Elders and Slaves
2 Peter 3:1-18 - The Day of the Lord
2 Timothy 2:14-26 - A Workman Approved by God
Acts 2:42-47 - The Fellowship of the Believers
Acts 4:32-37 - The Believers Share Their Possessions
John 12:20-36 - Jesus Predicts His Death
John 13:1-17 - Jesus Washes His Disciples' Feet
John 13:18-30 - Jesus Predicts His Betrayal
John 13:31-38 - Jesus Predicts Peter's Denial
John 17:6-19 - Jesus Prays for His Disciples
John 18:1-11 - Jesus Arrested
John 18:25-27 - Peter's Second and Third Denials
Matthew 13:24-30 - The Parable of the Weeds
Romans 6:1-14 - Dead to Sin, Alive in Christ
Romans 6:15-23 - Slaves to Righteousness
Titus 2:1-15 - What Must Be Taught to Various Groups

■ **LIGHT**

1 John 1:5–2:14 - Walking in the Light
1 Peter 2:4-12 - The Living Stone and a Chosen People
Acts 21:37–22:21 - Paul Speaks to the Crowd
Ephesians 4:17–5:21 - Living as Children of Light
John 5:31-47 - Testimonies About Jesus
John 8:12-30 - The Validity of Jesus' Testimony
John 9:1-12 - Jesus Heals a Man Born Blind
John 11:1-16 - The Death of Lazarus
John 12:20-36 - Jesus Predicts His Death
John 12:37-50 - The Jews Continue in Their Unbelief
Luke 11:33-36 - The Lamp of the Body
Luke 12:1-12 - Warnings and Encouragements
Matthew 4:12-17 - Jesus Begins to Preach
Matthew 5:13-16 - Salt and Light
Revelation 21:1-27 - The New Jerusalem
Revelation 22:1-6 - The River of Life

■ **LIMITATIONS**

Hebrews 8:1-13 - The High Priest of a New Covenant
Hebrews 9:1-10 - Worship in the Earthly Tabernacle
Hebrews 9:11-28 - The Blood of Christ
Hebrews 10:1-18 - Christ's Sacrifice Once for All
Matthew 9:9-13 - The Calling of Matthew
Matthew 14:13-21 - Jesus Feeds the Five Thousand

■ **LISTENING**

Acts 16:11-15 - Lydia's Conversion in Philippi
James 1:19-27 - Listening and Doing
John 10:1-21 - The Shepherd and His Flock
Luke 6:46-49 - The Wise and Foolish Builders
Luke 8:16-18 - A Lamp on a Stand
Luke 8:19-21 - Jesus' Mother and Brothers
Luke 9:28-36 - The Transfiguration

Luke 9:37-45 - The Healing of a Boy With an Evil Spirit
Luke 10:38-42 - At the Home of Martha and Mary
Luke 14:25-35 - The Cost of Being a Disciple
Mark 4:21-25 - A Lamp on a Stand
Matthew 2:19-23 - The Return to Nazareth
Matthew 11:25-30 - Rest for the Weary
Matthew 13:1-23 - The Parable of the Sower
Matthew 13:36-43 - The Parable of the Weeds Explained
Matthew 16:5-12 - The Yeast of the Pharisees and Sadducees
Matthew 17:1-13 - The Transfiguration
Matthew 22:34-40 - The Greatest Commandment
Revelation 1:1-3 - Prologue
Revelation 8:1-5 - The Seventh Seal and the Golden Censer

■ **LONELINESS**

Mark 15:33-41 - The Death of Jesus
Matthew 27:45-56 - The Death of Jesus

■ **LORD'S SUPPER**

1 Corinthians 10:14-22 - Idol Feasts and the Lord's Supper
1 Corinthians 11:17-34 - The Lord's Supper
Acts 2:42-47 - The Fellowship of the Believers
Acts 20:7-12 - Eutychus Raised From the Dead at Troas
John 6:25-59 - Jesus the Bread of Life
Luke 22:7-38 - The Last Supper
Mark 14:12-26 - The Lord's Supper

■ **LOST**

2 Thessalonians 2:1-12 - The Man of Lawlessness
Matthew 7:13-14 - The Narrow and Wide Gates
Matthew 9:9-13 - The Calling of Matthew
Matthew 9:35-38 - The Workers Are Few
Matthew 13:24-30 - The Parable of the Weeds
Matthew 13:36-43 - The Parable of the Weeds Explained
Matthew 26:14-16 - Judas Agrees to Betray Jesus
Matthew 27:62-66 - The Guard at the Tomb
Romans 11:1-10 - The Remnant of Israel

■ **LOVE**

1 Corinthians 8:1-13 - Food Sacrificed to Idols
1 Corinthians 13:1-13 - Love
1 Corinthians 16:5-24 - Personal Requests
1 John 2:15-17 - Do Not Love the World
1 John 3:11-24 - Love One Another
1 John 4:7-21 - God's Love and Ours
1 John 5:1-12 - Faith in the Son of God
1 Peter 1:13–2:3 - Be Holy
1 Peter 4:1-11 - Living for God
1 Thessalonians 3:6-13 - Timothy's Encouraging Report
1 Timothy 1:1-11 - Warning Against False Teachers of the Law
1 Timothy 4:1-16 - Instructions to Timothy
1 Timothy 6:3-10 - Love of Money
1 Timothy 6:11-21 - Paul's Charge to Timothy
2 Corinthians 1:12–2:4 - Paul's Change of Plans
2 Corinthians 2:5-11 - Forgiveness for the Sinner
2 Corinthians 5:11–6:2 - The Ministry of Reconciliation
2 Corinthians 12:11-21 - Paul's Concern for the Corinthians
2 John 1-13 - From the Elder
2 Peter 1:1-11 - Making One's Calling and Election Sure
2 Thessalonians 3:1-5 - Request for Prayer
2 Timothy 1:1–2:13 - Encouragement to Be Faithful
2 Timothy 4:9-22 - Personal Remarks
3 John 1-14 - From the Elder
Colossians 1:1-14 - Thanksgiving and Prayer
Colossians 3:1-17 - Rules for Holy Living
Colossians 3:18–4:1 - Rules for Christian Households
Ephesians 1:15-23 - Thanksgiving and Prayer
Ephesians 2:1-10 - Made Alive in Christ
Ephesians 3:14-21 - A Prayer for the Ephesians
Ephesians 4:1-16 - Unity in the Body of Christ
Ephesians 4:17–5:21 - Living as Children of Light
Ephesians 5:22-33 - Wives and Husbands
Galatians 5:1-15 - Freedom in Christ
Galatians 5:16-26 - Life by the Spirit
Hebrews 10:19-39 - A Call to Persevere
Hebrews 13:1-25 - Concluding Exhortations
John 3:1-22 - Jesus Teaches Nicodemus
John 6:25-59 - Jesus the Bread of Life
John 8:42-47 - The Children of the Devil
John 10:1-21 - The Shepherd and His Flock
John 12:37-50 - The Jews Continue in Their Unbelief
John 13:1-17 - Jesus Washes His Disciples' Feet
John 13:18-30 - Jesus Predicts His Betrayal
John 13:31-38 - Jesus Predicts Peter's Denial
John 14:15-31 - Jesus Promises the Holy Spirit
John 15:1-17 - The Vine and the Branches
John 15:18–16:4 - The World Hates the Disciples
John 16:17-33 - The Disciples' Grief Will Turn to Joy
John 17:20-26 - Jesus Prays for All Believers
John 19:17-27 - The Crucifixion
John 20:10-18 - Jesus Appears to Mary Magdalene
John 21:15-25 - Jesus Reinstates Peter
Luke 6:27-36 - Love for Enemies
Luke 7:36-50 - Jesus Anointed by a Sinful Woman
Luke 10:25-37 - The Parable of the Good Samaritan
Luke 15:11-32 - The Parable of the Lost Son
Mark 12:28-34 - The Greatest Commandment
Mark 14:1-11 - Jesus Anointed at Bethany
Mark 15:42-47 - The Burial of Jesus
Matthew 8:1-4 - The Man With Leprosy
Matthew 22:34-40 - The Greatest Commandment
Matthew 26:6-13 - Jesus Anointed at Bethany
Matthew 26:17-30 - The Lord's Supper
Philippians 2:1-11 - Imitating Christ's Humility
Revelation 1:4-8 - Greetings and Doxology
Revelation 2:1-7 - To the Church in Ephesus
Revelation 2:18-29 - To the Church in Thyatira
Romans 5:1-11 - Peace and Joy
Romans 8:28-39 - More Than Conquerors
Romans 12:9-21 - Love
Romans 13:8-14 - Love, for the Day Is Near
Romans 14:1–15:13 - The Weak and the Strong

■ **LOYALTY**

John 12:1-11 - Jesus Anointed at Bethany
John 13:31-38 - Jesus Predicts Peter's Denial
John 18:15-18 - Peter's First Denial
John 19:38-42 - The Burial of Jesus
Luke 9:57-62 - The Cost of Following Jesus
Luke 16:1-15 - The Parable of the Shrewd Manager
Luke 23:50-56 - Jesus' Burial
Mark 3:31-35 - Jesus' Mother and Brothers
Matthew 5:27-30 - Adultery
Matthew 16:21-28 - Jesus Predicts His Death

Matthew 26:31-35 - Jesus Predicts Peter's Denial
Matthew 26:36-46 - Gethsemane
Matthew 26:69-75 - Peter Disowns Jesus
Revelation 13:11-18 - The Beast out of the Earth

■ **LUST**

1 Corinthians 6:12-20 - Sexual Immorality
1 John 2:15-17 - Do Not Love the World
1 Peter 4:1-11 - Living for God
2 Peter 2:1-22 - False Teachers and Their Destruction
2 Timothy 2:14-26 - A Workman Approved by God
Ephesians 4:17–5:21 - Living as Children of Light
Mark 6:14-29 - John the Baptist Beheaded
Matthew 5:27-30 - Adultery

■ **LYING**

1 John 1:5–2:14 - Walking in the Light
1 John 4:7-21 - God's Love and Ours
1 Timothy 1:1-11 - Warning Against False Teachers of the Law
Ephesians 4:17–5:21 - Living as Children of Light
Matthew 21:18-22 - The Fig Tree Withers
Matthew 21:28-32 - The Parable of the Two Sons
Matthew 26:57-68 - Before the Sanhedrin
Matthew 28:11-15 - The Guards' Report

■ **MAJORITY**

Matthew 13:24-30 - The Parable of the Weeds
Matthew 13:36-43 - The Parable of the Weeds Explained
Matthew 24:1-35 - Signs of the End of the Age

■ **MANAGEMENT**

1 Timothy 3:1-16 - Overseers and Deacons
Matthew 25:14-30 - The Parable of the Talents

■ **MARRIAGE**

1 Corinthians 6:12-20 - Sexual Immorality
1 Corinthians 7:1-40 - Marriage
1 Peter 3:1-7 - Wives and Husbands
1 Thessalonians 4:1-12 - Living to Please God
1 Timothy 3:1-16 - Overseers and Deacons
1 Timothy 5:1–6:2 - Advice About Widows, Elders and Slaves
2 Corinthians 6:14–7:1 - Do Not Be Yoked with Unbelievers
Ephesians 5:22-33 - Wives and Husbands
Ephesians 6:1-4 - Children and Parents
Hebrews 13:1-25 - Concluding Exhortations
John 4:1-26 - Jesus Talks With a Samaritan Woman
Luke 20:27-40 - The Resurrection and Marriage
Mark 10:1-12 - Divorce
Mark 12:18-27 - Marriage at the Resurrection
Matthew 5:31-32 - Divorce
Matthew 19:1-12 - Divorce
Matthew 22:1-14 - The Parable of the Wedding Banquet
Matthew 25:1-13 - The Parable of the Ten Virgins
Romans 7:1-6 - An Illustration From Marriage

■ **MATERIALISM**

1 Timothy 6:3-10 - Love of Money
Hebrews 13:1-25 - Concluding Exhortations
James 4:13-17 - Boasting About Tomorrow
James 5:1-6 - Warning to Rich Oppressors
Matthew 6:25-34 - Do Not Worry
Matthew 19:16-30 - The Rich Young Man

■ **MATURITY**

1 Corinthians 6:12-20 - Sexual Immorality
1 Timothy 3:1-16 - Overseers and Deacons
2 Thessalonians 2:13-17 - Stand Firm
2 Thessalonians 3:1-5 - Request for Prayer
Colossians 4:2-18 - Further Instructions
Hebrews 5:11–6:12 - Warning Against Falling Away
Luke 1:39-45 - Mary Visits Elizabeth
Luke 2:41-52 - The Boy Jesus at the Temple
Matthew 11:1-19 - Jesus and John the Baptist
Philippians 3:12–4:1 - Pressing on Toward the Goal
Titus 1:1-16 - Titus' Task on Crete

■ **MEDIATOR**

1 Timothy 2:1-15 - Instructions on Worship
Galatians 3:15-25 - The Law and the Promise
Hebrews 6:13-20 - The Certainty of God's Promise
Hebrews 7:1-10 - Melchizedek the Priest
Hebrews 7:11-28 - Jesus Like Melchizedek
Hebrews 8:1-13 - The High Priest of a New Covenant
Hebrews 9:1-10 - Worship in the Earthly Tabernacle
Hebrews 9:11-28 - The Blood of Christ
Hebrews 10:1-18 - Christ's Sacrifice Once for All
Hebrews 10:19-39 - A Call to Persevere
Hebrews 12:14-29 - Warning Against Refusing God
Hebrews 13:1-25 - Concluding Exhortations
John 14:5-14 - Jesus the Way to the Father
Luke 20:9-19 - The Parable of the Tenants
Mark 12:1-12 - The Parable of the Tenants
Matthew 27:45-56 - The Death of Jesus

■ **MERCY**

1 Peter 2:4-12 - The Living Stone and a Chosen People
1 Timothy 1:12-20 - The Lord's Grace to Paul
Ephesians 2:1-10 - Made Alive in Christ
Galatians 6:11-18 - Not Circumcision but a New Creation
Hebrews 2:5-18 - Jesus Made Like His Brothers
Jude 17-25 - A Call to Persevere
Luke 1:46-56 - Mary's Song
Luke 1:67-80 - Zechariah's Song
Luke 5:12-16 - The Man With Leprosy
Luke 5:17-26 - Jesus Heals a Paralytic
Luke 6:27-36 - Love for Enemies
Luke 10:25-37 - The Parable of the Good Samaritan
Luke 18:9-14 - The Parable of the Pharisee and the Tax Collector
Luke 18:35-43 - A Blind Beggar Receives His Sight
Mark 7:31-37 - The Healing of a Deaf and Mute Man
Matthew 5:1-12 - The Beatitudes
Matthew 7:1-6 - Judging Others
Matthew 12:1-14 - Lord of the Sabbath
Matthew 18:15-20 - A Brother Who Sins Against You
Matthew 18:21-35 - The Parable of the Unmerciful Servant
Matthew 24:36-51 - The Day and Hour Unknown
Matthew 25:1-13 - The Parable of the Ten Virgins
Matthew 25:31-46 - The Sheep and the Goats
Romans 11:25-32 - All Israel Will Be Saved
Titus 3:1-15 - Doing What Is Good

■ **MESSIAH**

Acts 2:14-41 - Peter Addresses the Crowd
Acts 7:1-53 - Stephen's Speech to the Sanhedrin
Hebrews 3:1-6 - Jesus Greater Than Moses
Hebrews 7:11-28 - Jesus Like Melchizedek
Hebrews 8:1-13 - The High Priest of a New Covenant

Hebrews 9:1-10 - Worship in the Earthly Tabernacle
Hebrews 9:11-28 - The Blood of Christ
Hebrews 10:1-18 - Christ's Sacrifice Once for All
John 1:19-28 - John the Baptist Denies Being the Christ
John 1:29-34 - Jesus the Lamb of God
John 1:35-42 - Jesus' First Disciples
John 4:1-26 - Jesus Talks With a Samaritan Woman
John 4:27-38 - The Disciples Rejoin Jesus
John 7:25-44 - Is Jesus the Christ?
John 10:22-42 - The Unbelief of the Jews
Luke 1:67-80 - Zechariah's Song
Luke 2:8-20 - The Shepherds and the Angels
Luke 7:18-35 - Jesus and John the Baptist
Mark 14:53-65 - Before the Sanhedrin
Matthew 1:1-17 - The Genealogy of Jesus
Matthew 12:15-21 - God's Chosen Servant
Matthew 12:22-37 - Jesus and Beelzebub
Matthew 16:13-20 - Peter's Confession of Christ
Matthew 20:29-34 - Two Blind Men Receive Sight
Matthew 21:1-11 - The Triumphal Entry
Matthew 21:12-17 - Jesus at the Temple
Matthew 22:41-46 - Whose Son Is the Christ?
Matthew 25:31-46 - The Sheep and the Goats
Matthew 26:57-68 - Before the Sanhedrin
Matthew 27:1-10 - Judas Hangs Himself

■ MIND

1 Corinthians 2:6-16 - Wisdom From the Spirit
Romans 12:1-8 - Living Sacrifices

■ MINISTRY

1 Corinthians 7:1-40 - Marriage
1 Corinthians 16:5-24 - Personal Requests
1 Peter 4:1-11 - Living for God
1 Timothy 2:1-15 - Instructions on Worship
1 Timothy 4:1-16 - Instructions to Timothy
1 Timothy 5:1–6:2 - Advice About Widows, Elders and Slaves
2 Corinthians 2:12–3:6 - Ministers of the New Covenant
2 Corinthians 3:7-18 - The Glory of the New Covenant
2 Corinthians 4:1-18 - Treasures in Jars of Clay
2 Corinthians 5:11–6:2 - The Ministry of Reconciliation
2 Corinthians 6:3-13 - Paul's Hardships
2 Corinthians 12:11-21 - Paul's Concern for the Corinthians
2 Timothy 4:9-22 - Personal Remarks
Acts 4:23-31 - The Believers' Prayer
Acts 6:1-7 - The Choosing of the Seven
Acts 11:19-30 - The Church in Antioch
John 11:17-37 - Jesus Comforts the Sisters
John 11:45-57 - The Plot to Kill Jesus
John 13:1-17 - Jesus Washes His Disciples' Feet
Luke 3:21-38 - The Baptism and Genealogy of Jesus
Luke 5:1-11 - The Calling of the First Disciples
Mark 1:35-39 - Jesus Prays in a Solitary Place
Mark 2:13-17 - The Calling of Levi
Mark 3:7-12 - Crowds Follow Jesus
Mark 3:13-19 - The Appointing of the Twelve Apostles
Mark 6:7-13 - Jesus Sends Out the Twelve
Mark 8:1-13 - Jesus Feeds the Four Thousand
Mark 9:38-41 - Whoever Is Not Against Us Is for Us
Matthew 12:15-21 - God's Chosen Servant
Matthew 14:13-21 - Jesus Feeds the Five Thousand
Matthew 19:13-15 - The Little Children and Jesus
Matthew 27:57-61 - The Burial of Jesus
Matthew 28:16-20 - The Great Commission

■ MIRACLES

2 Corinthians 12:11-21 - Paul's Concern for the Corinthians
2 Thessalonians 2:1-12 - The Man of Lawlessness
Acts 2:14-41 - Peter Addresses the Crowd
Acts 2:42-47 - The Fellowship of the Believers
Acts 3:1-10 - Peter Heals the Crippled Beggar
Acts 4:23-31 - The Believers' Prayer
Acts 5:12-16 - The Apostles Heal Many
Acts 5:17-41 - The Apostles Persecuted
Acts 6:8-15 - Stephen Seized
Acts 8:4-8 - Philip in Samaria
Acts 9:32-43 - Aeneas and Dorcas
Acts 14:1-7 - In Iconium
Acts 19:1-22 - Paul in Ephesus
Acts 28:1-10 - Ashore on Malta
Galatians 3:1-14 - Faith or Observance of the Law
Hebrews 2:1-4 - Warning to Pay Attention
John 2:1-11 - Jesus Changes Water to Wine
John 2:12-25 - Jesus Clears the Temple
John 4:43-54 - Jesus Heals the Official's Son
John 5:1-15 - The Healing at the Pool
John 6:1-15 - Jesus Feeds the Five Thousand
John 6:16-24 - Jesus Walks on the Water
John 7:25-44 - Is Jesus the Christ?
John 9:1-12 - Jesus Heals a Man Born Blind
John 9:13-34 - The Pharisees Investigate the Healing
John 10:22-42 - The Unbelief of the Jews
John 11:38-44 - Jesus Raises Lazarus From the Dead
John 11:45-57 - The Plot to Kill Jesus
John 12:12-19 - The Triumphal Entry
John 12:37-50 - The Jews Continue in Their Unbelief
John 14:5-14 - Jesus the Way to the Father
John 15:18–16:4 - The World Hates the Disciples
John 20:24-31 - Jesus Appears to Thomas
John 21:1-14 - Jesus and the Miraculous Catch of Fish
Luke 1:5-25 - The Birth of John the Baptist Foretold
Luke 1:26-38 - The Birth of Jesus Foretold
Luke 4:14-30 - Jesus Rejected at Nazareth
Luke 4:31-37 - Jesus Drives Out an Evil Spirit
Luke 4:38-44 - Jesus Heals Many
Luke 5:1-11 - The Calling of the First Disciples
Luke 5:17-26 - Jesus Heals a Paralytic
Luke 7:11-17 - Jesus Raises a Widow's Son
Luke 8:26-39 - The Healing of a Demon-possessed Man
Luke 8:40-56 - A Dead Girl and a Sick Woman
Luke 9:10-17 - Jesus Feeds the Five Thousand
Luke 9:37-45 - The Healing of a Boy With an Evil Spirit
Luke 11:29-32 - The Sign of Jonah
Luke 13:10-17 - A Crippled Woman Healed on the Sabbath
Luke 14:1-14 - Jesus at a Pharisee's House
Luke 17:11-19 - Ten Healed of Leprosy
Luke 18:35-43 - A Blind Beggar Receives His Sight
Luke 19:28-44 - The Triumphal Entry
Luke 24:1-12 - The Resurrection
Mark 1:21-28 - Jesus Drives Out an Evil Spirit
Mark 1:29-34 - Jesus Heals Many
Mark 2:1-12 - Jesus Heals a Paralytic
Mark 3:7-12 - Crowds Follow Jesus

Mark 4:35-41 - Jesus Calms the Storm
Mark 5:1-20 - The Healing of a Demon-possessed Man
Mark 5:21-43 - A Dead Girl and a Sick Woman
Mark 6:1-6 - A Prophet Without Honor
Mark 6:30-44 - Jesus Feeds the Five Thousand
Mark 6:45-56 - Jesus Walks on the Water
Mark 7:31-37 - The Healing of a Deaf and Mute Man
Mark 8:1-13 - Jesus Feeds the Four Thousand
Mark 8:14-21 - The Yeast of the Pharisees and Herod
Mark 9:38-41 - Whoever Is Not Against Us Is for Us
Mark 10:46-52 - Blind Bartimaeus Receives His Sight
Mark 15:33-41 - The Death of Jesus
Mark 16:1-20 - The Resurrection
Matthew 1:18-25 - The Birth of Jesus Christ
Matthew 8:1-4 - The Man With Leprosy
Matthew 8:5-13 - The Faith of the Centurion
Matthew 8:23-27 - Jesus Calms the Storm
Matthew 8:28-34 - The Healing of Two Demon-possessed Men
Matthew 9:1-8 - Jesus Heals a Paralytic
Matthew 9:18-26 - A Dead Girl and a Sick Woman
Matthew 9:27-34 - Jesus Heals the Blind and Mute
Matthew 9:35-38 - The Workers Are Few
Matthew 11:1-19 - Jesus and John the Baptist
Matthew 11:20-24 - Woe on Unrepentant Cities
Matthew 12:15-21 - God's Chosen Servant
Matthew 14:13-21 - Jesus Feeds the Five Thousand
Matthew 14:22-36 - Jesus Walks on the Water
Matthew 15:29-39 - Jesus Feeds the Four Thousand
Matthew 17:14-23 - The Healing of a Boy With a Demon
Matthew 17:24-27 - The Temple Tax
Matthew 19:16-30 - The Rich Young Man
Matthew 20:29-34 - Two Blind Men Receive Sight
Matthew 21:12-17 - Jesus at the Temple
Matthew 21:18-22 - The Fig Tree Withers
Matthew 24:1-35 - Signs of the End of the Age
Matthew 27:45-56 - The Death of Jesus
Matthew 28:1-10 - The Resurrection
Revelation 11:1-14 - The Two Witnesses
Revelation 13:11-18 - The Beast out of the Earth

■ MISSION

Acts 12:20-25 - Herod's Death
Acts 13:1-3 - Barnabas and Saul Sent Off
Acts 16:1-5 - Timothy Joins Paul and Silas
Acts 20:13-38 - Paul's Farewell to the Ephesian Elders
John 7:1-13 - Jesus Goes to the Feast of Tabernacles
John 11:1-16 - The Death of Lazarus
Luke 1:67-80 - Zechariah's Song
Luke 5:1-11 - The Calling of the First Disciples
Luke 5:27-32 - The Calling of Levi
Luke 9:1-9 - Jesus Sends Out the Twelve
Luke 10:1-24 - Jesus Sends Out the Seventy-two
Matthew 4:12-17 - Jesus Begins to Preach
Matthew 9:35-38 - The Workers Are Few
Matthew 20:17-19 - Jesus Again Predicts His Death
Romans 15:14-22 - Paul, the Minister to the Gentiles
Romans 15:23-33 - Paul's Plan to Visit Rome

■ MONEY

1 Corinthians 16:1-4 - The Collection for God's People
1 Peter 5:1-14 - To Elders and Young Men
1 Timothy 3:1-16 - Overseers and Deacons
1 Timothy 6:3-10 - Love of Money
1 Timothy 6:11-21 - Paul's Charge to Timothy
2 Corinthians 8:1-15 - Generosity Encouraged
2 Corinthians 8:16–9:5 - Titus Sent to Corinth
2 Corinthians 11:1-15 - Paul and the False Apostles
2 Corinthians 12:11-21 - Paul's Concern for the Corinthians
Acts 3:1-10 - Peter Heals the Crippled Beggar
Acts 5:1-11 - Ananias and Sapphira
Acts 8:9-25 - Simon the Sorcerer
Acts 19:1-22 - Paul in Ephesus
Acts 19:23-41 - The Riot in Ephesus
Acts 20:1-6 - Through Macedonia and Greece
Galatians 6:1-10 - Doing Good to All
Hebrews 13:1-25 - Concluding Exhortations
James 5:1-6 - Warning to Rich Oppressors
John 2:12-25 - Jesus Clears the Temple
John 12:1-11 - Jesus Anointed at Bethany
Luke 16:1-15 - The Parable of the Shrewd Manager
Luke 18:18-30 - The Rich Ruler
Luke 19:11-27 - The Parable of the Ten Minas
Luke 20:20-26 - Paying Taxes to Caesar
Luke 21:1-4 - The Widow's Offering
Luke 22:1-6 - Judas Agrees to Betray Jesus
Mark 6:7-13 - Jesus Sends Out the Twelve
Mark 11:12-19 - Jesus Clears the Temple
Mark 12:13-17 - Paying Taxes to Caesar
Mark 12:41-44 - The Widow's Offering
Mark 14:1-11 - Jesus Anointed at Bethany
Matthew 6:1-4 - Giving to the Needy
Matthew 6:19-24 - Treasures in Heaven

■ MORALITY

1 Corinthians 6:12-20 - Sexual Immorality
1 Corinthians 7:1-40 - Marriage
1 Timothy 3:1-16 - Overseers and Deacons
2 Peter 2:1-22 - False Teachers and Their Destruction
2 Timothy 3:1-9 - Godlessness in the Last Days
John 4:1-26 - Jesus Talks With a Samaritan Woman
Luke 11:33-36 - The Lamp of the Body
Matthew 5:13-16 - Salt and Light

■ MOTIVES

1 Corinthians 4:1-21 - Apostles of Christ
1 Corinthians 14:1-25 - Gifts of Prophecy and Tongues
1 Thessalonians 2:1-16 - Paul's Ministry in Thessalonica
1 Timothy 1:1-11 - Warning Against False Teachers of the Law
Acts 19:23-41 - The Riot in Ephesus
John 4:43-54 - Jesus Heals the Official's Son
John 6:1-15 - Jesus Feeds the Five Thousand
John 7:45-52 - Unbelief of the Jewish Leaders
John 8:48-59 - The Claims of Jesus About Himself
John 11:45-57 - The Plot to Kill Jesus
John 13:1-17 - Jesus Washes His Disciples' Feet
John 13:18-30 - Jesus Predicts His Betrayal
Mark 12:41-44 - The Widow's Offering
Matthew 2:1-12 - The Visit of the Magi
Matthew 6:1-4 - Giving to the Needy
Matthew 6:5-15 - Prayer
Matthew 6:16-18 - Fasting
Matthew 14:1-12 - John the Baptist Beheaded
Matthew 20:20-28 - A Mother's Request
Matthew 21:23-27 - The Authority of Jesus Questioned
Matthew 22:15-22 - Paying Taxes to Caesar

Matthew 22:23-33 - Marriage at the Resurrection
Matthew 22:34-40 - The Greatest Commandment
Matthew 26:1-5 - The Plot Against Jesus
Matthew 26:47-56 - Jesus Arrested
Matthew 28:11-15 - The Guards' Report
Philippians 1:12-30 - Paul's Chains Advance the Gospel

■ **MOURNING**

John 11:1-16 - The Death of Lazarus
John 11:17-37 - Jesus Comforts the Sisters
John 11:38-44 - Jesus Raises Lazarus From the Dead
John 16:17-33 - The Disciples' Grief Will Turn to Joy
Luke 23:26-43 - The Crucifixion
Luke 23:44-49 - Jesus' Death
Matthew 2:13-18 - The Escape to Egypt
Matthew 5:1-12 - The Beatitudes
Matthew 9:14-17 - Jesus Questioned About Fasting
Matthew 13:36-43 - The Parable of the Weeds Explained
Matthew 13:47-52 - The Parable of the Net
Matthew 24:1-35 - Signs of the End of the Age
Matthew 27:45-56 - The Death of Jesus
Revelation 21:1-27 - The New Jerusalem

■ **MOVING**

Matthew 2:19-23 - The Return to Nazareth
Matthew 4:12-17 - Jesus Begins to Preach

■ **MURDER**

1 John 3:11-24 - Love One Another
Luke 13:31-35 - Jesus' Sorrow for Jerusalem
Mark 6:14-29 - John the Baptist Beheaded
Mark 12:1-12 - The Parable of the Tenants
Matthew 2:13-18 - The Escape to Egypt
Matthew 5:21-26 - Murder
Matthew 20:17-19 - Jesus Again Predicts His Death
Matthew 21:33-46 - The Parable of the Tenants
Matthew 22:1-14 - The Parable of the Wedding Banquet
Matthew 26:1-5 - The Plot Against Jesus

■ **NAME**

1 Peter 4:12-19 - Suffering for Being a Christian
John 14:5-14 - Jesus the Way to the Father

■ **NAMES**

Acts 4:1-22 - Peter and John Before the Sanhedrin
Acts 24:1-27 - The Trial Before Felix
John 1:29-34 - Jesus the Lamb of God
John 1:35-42 - Jesus' First Disciples
John 1:43-51 - Jesus Calls Philip and Nathanael
Matthew 1:1-17 - The Genealogy of Jesus
Matthew 1:18-25 - The Birth of Jesus Christ
Philippians 2:1-11 - Imitating Christ's Humility

■ **NATURE**

Ephesians 4:17–5:21 - Living as Children of Light
John 6:16-24 - Jesus Walks on the Water
Mark 4:35-41 - Jesus Calms the Storm
Mark 6:45-56 - Jesus Walks on the Water
Matthew 8:23-27 - Jesus Calms the Storm
Matthew 24:1-35 - Signs of the End of the Age

■ **NEEDS**

1 John 2:15-17 - Do Not Love the World
Acts 2:42-47 - The Fellowship of the Believers
Acts 3:1-10 - Peter Heals the Crippled Beggar
Ephesians 4:17–5:21 - Living as Children of Light
John 6:1-15 - Jesus Feeds the Five Thousand
John 21:1-14 - Jesus and the Miraculous Catch of Fish
Luke 5:12-16 - The Man With Leprosy
Luke 6:1-11 - Lord of the Sabbath
Luke 11:1-13 - Jesus' Teaching on Prayer
Mark 8:1-13 - Jesus Feeds the Four Thousand
Matthew 6:25-34 - Do Not Worry

■ **NEGLECT**

1 Timothy 5:1–6:2 - Advice About Widows, Elders and Slaves
2 Timothy 1:1–2:13 - Encouragement to Be Faithful
Acts 6:1-7 - The Choosing of the Seven

■ **NEIGHBOR**

Luke 10:25-37 - The Parable of the Good Samaritan
Mark 12:28-34 - The Greatest Commandment
Matthew 5:43-48 - Love for Enemies

■ **NEW COVENANT**

2 Corinthians 2:12–3:6 - Ministers of the New Covenant
2 Corinthians 3:7-18 - The Glory of the New Covenant
Hebrews 2:1-4 - Warning to Pay Attention
Hebrews 7:11-28 - Jesus Like Melchizedek
Hebrews 8:1-13 - The High Priest of a New Covenant
Hebrews 9:1-10 - Worship in the Earthly Tabernacle
Hebrews 9:11-28 - The Blood of Christ
Hebrews 10:1-18 - Christ's Sacrifice Once for All
Hebrews 10:19-39 - A Call to Persevere
Hebrews 12:14-29 - Warning Against Refusing God
Hebrews 13:1-25 - Concluding Exhortations
Mark 10:1-12 - Divorce
Matthew 9:14-17 - Jesus Questioned About Fasting
Matthew 15:1-20 - Clean and Unclean
Matthew 26:17-30 - The Lord's Supper
Romans 4:1-25 - Abraham Justified by Faith

■ **NEW LIFE**

2 Corinthians 5:11–6:2 - The Ministry of Reconciliation
John 2:1-11 - Jesus Changes Water to Wine
John 3:1-22 - Jesus Teaches Nicodemus
John 4:1-26 - Jesus Talks With a Samaritan Woman
John 5:1-15 - The Healing at the Pool
John 5:16-30 - Life Through the Son
John 6:25-59 - Jesus the Bread of Life
John 8:31-41 - The Children of Abraham
John 9:1-12 - Jesus Heals a Man Born Blind
John 10:1-21 - The Shepherd and His Flock
John 11:38-44 - Jesus Raises Lazarus From the Dead
Luke 8:26-39 - The Healing of a Demon-possessed Man
Luke 8:40-56 - A Dead Girl and a Sick Woman
Matthew 13:1-23 - The Parable of the Sower
Matthew 13:53-58 - A Prophet Without Honor
Romans 6:1-14 - Dead to Sin, Alive in Christ
Romans 6:15-23 - Slaves to Righteousness
Romans 7:1-6 - An Illustration From Marriage

■ **OBEDIENCE**

1 John 1:5–2:14 - Walking in the Light
1 John 2:15-17 - Do Not Love the World
1 John 2:28–3:10 - Children of God
1 John 3:11-24 - Love One Another
1 John 5:1-12 - Faith in the Son of God
1 John 5:13-21 - Concluding Remarks
1 Peter 1:1-12 - Praise to God for a Living Hope
1 Peter 1:13–2:3 - Be Holy
1 Peter 2:4-12 - The Living Stone and a Chosen People
1 Peter 3:1-7 - Wives and Husbands

1 Timothy 1:1-11 - Warning Against False Teachers of the Law
1 Timothy 1:12-20 - The Lord's Grace to Paul
2 Corinthians 7:2-16 - Paul's Joy
2 Corinthians 10:1-18 - Paul's Defense of His Ministry
2 John 1-13 - From the Elder
2 Peter 3:1-18 - The Day of the Lord
2 Timothy 2:14-26 - A Workman Approved by God
Acts 5:17-41 - The Apostles Persecuted
Acts 9:1-19 - Saul's Conversion
Acts 21:17-26 - Paul's Arrival at Jerusalem
Colossians 3:18–4:1 - Rules for Christian Households
Ephesians 6:5-9 - Slaves and Masters
Hebrews 3:1-6 - Jesus Greater Than Moses
Hebrews 4:14–5:10 - Jesus the Great High Priest
Hebrews 11:1-40 - By Faith
James 1:19-27 - Listening and Doing
John 10:1-21 - The Shepherd and His Flock
John 14:15-31 - Jesus Promises the Holy Spirit
John 15:18–16:4 - The World Hates the Disciples
John 17:6-19 - Jesus Prays for His Disciples
John 18:28-40 - Jesus Before Pilate
Luke 1:26-38 - The Birth of Jesus Foretold
Luke 1:57-66 - The Birth of John the Baptist
Luke 2:8-20 - The Shepherds and the Angels
Luke 2:41-52 - The Boy Jesus at the Temple
Luke 3:1-20 - John the Baptist Prepares the Way
Luke 5:1-11 - The Calling of the First Disciples
Luke 6:46-49 - The Wise and Foolish Builders
Luke 8:19-21 - Jesus' Mother and Brothers
Luke 8:22-25 - Jesus Calms a Storm
Luke 9:1-9 - Jesus Sends Out the Twelve
Luke 23:50-56 - Jesus' Burial
Mark 1:14-20 - The Calling of the First Disciples
Mark 2:18-22 - Jesus Questioned About Fasting
Mark 2:23–3:6 - Lord of the Sabbath
Mark 3:31-35 - Jesus' Mother and Brothers
Mark 4:21-25 - A Lamp on a Stand
Mark 4:35-41 - Jesus Calms the Storm
Mark 9:2-13 - The Transfiguration
Mark 10:17-31 - The Rich Young Man
Mark 11:1-11 - The Triumphal Entry
Matthew 1:18-25 - The Birth of Jesus Christ
Matthew 2:13-18 - The Escape to Egypt
Matthew 2:19-23 - The Return to Nazareth
Matthew 3:13-17 - The Baptism of Jesus
Matthew 4:1-11 - The Temptation of Jesus
Matthew 4:18-22 - The Calling of the First Disciples
Matthew 5:17-20 - The Fulfillment of the Law
Matthew 7:24-29 - The Wise and Foolish Builders
Matthew 9:9-13 - The Calling of Matthew
Matthew 11:25-30 - Rest for the Weary
Matthew 12:46-50 - Jesus' Mother and Brothers
Matthew 14:1-12 - John the Baptist Beheaded
Matthew 15:29-39 - Jesus Feeds the Four Thousand
Matthew 17:24-27 - The Temple Tax
Matthew 18:21-35 - The Parable of the Unmerciful Servant
Matthew 21:1-11 - The Triumphal Entry
Matthew 21:28-32 - The Parable of the Two Sons
Philippians 2:1-11 - Imitating Christ's Humility
Philippians 2:12-18 - Shining as Stars
Revelation 1:1-3 - Prologue
Revelation 3:1-6 - To the Church in Sardis
Revelation 3:7-13 - To the Church in Philadelphia
Revelation 10:1-11 - The Angel and the Little Scroll
Revelation 14:1-5 - The Lamb and the 144,000
Revelation 14:6-13 - The Three Angels
Titus 3:1-15 - Doing What Is Good

■ OBLIGATION

Acts 15:22-35 - The Council's Letter to Gentile Believers
Matthew 9:9-13 - The Calling of Matthew
Matthew 17:24-27 - The Temple Tax
Matthew 18:21-35 - The Parable of the Unmerciful Servant
Matthew 19:1-12 - Divorce
Matthew 22:15-22 - Paying Taxes to Caesar

■ OCCULT

Acts 19:1-22 - Paul in Ephesus
Matthew 8:14-17 - Jesus Heals Many
Matthew 8:28-34 - The Healing of Two Demon-possessed Men
Matthew 24:1-35 - Signs of the End of the Age

■ OPENNESS

Luke 8:16-18 - A Lamp on a Stand

■ OPINIONS

Matthew 7:1-6 - Judging Others
Matthew 16:13-20 - Peter's Confession of Christ

■ OPPORTUNITIES

Matthew 25:14-30 - The Parable of the Talents
Romans 9:1-29 - God's Sovereign Choice

■ OPPOSITION

Acts 6:8-15 - Stephen Seized
Acts 13:4-12 - On Cyprus
Acts 19:1-22 - Paul in Ephesus
Acts 25:23–26:32 - Paul Before Agrippa
Galatians 2:11-21 - Paul Opposes Peter
John 18:1-11 - Jesus Arrested
John 18:28-40 - Jesus Before Pilate
Luke 4:14-30 - Jesus Rejected at Nazareth
Luke 6:17-26 - Blessings and Woes
Luke 6:27-36 - Love for Enemies
Luke 9:51-56 - Samaritan Opposition
Luke 11:37-54 - Six Woes
Luke 13:10-17 - A Crippled Woman Healed on the Sabbath
Luke 22:1-6 - Judas Agrees to Betray Jesus
Matthew 9:27-34 - Jesus Heals the Blind and Mute
Matthew 12:22-37 - Jesus and Beelzebub
Matthew 16:21-28 - Jesus Predicts His Death
Matthew 20:17-19 - Jesus Again Predicts His Death
Matthew 22:1-14 - The Parable of the Wedding Banquet
Matthew 22:41-46 - Whose Son Is the Christ?
Matthew 23:1-39 - Seven Woes
Matthew 26:1-5 - The Plot Against Jesus
Matthew 27:62-66 - The Guard at the Tomb
Revelation 13:11-18 - The Beast out of the Earth

■ OPPRESSED

James 5:1-6 - Warning to Rich Oppressors
Matthew 5:38-42 - An Eye for an Eye
Matthew 5:43-48 - Love for Enemies
Matthew 8:28-34 - The Healing of Two Demon-possessed Men

■ PAIN

2 Corinthians 12:1-10 - Paul's Vision and His Thorn
John 16:17-33 - The Disciples' Grief Will Turn to Joy
Mark 14:32-42 - Gethsemane
Mark 15:16-20 - The Soldiers Mock Jesus
Mark 15:21-32 - The Crucifixion
Matthew 4:23-25 - Jesus Heals the Sick
Matthew 18:15-20 - A Brother Who Sins Against You
Matthew 24:1-35 - Signs of the End of the Age
Matthew 27:1-10 - Judas Hangs Himself
Matthew 27:27-31 - The Soldiers Mock Jesus
Matthew 27:32-44 - The Crucifixion
Matthew 27:45-56 - The Death of Jesus
Revelation 8:6–9:21 - The Trumpets
Revelation 16:1-21 - The Seven Bowls of God's Wrath

■ PARENTS

1 Timothy 5:1–6:2 - Advice About Widows, Elders and Slaves
2 Timothy 3:1-9 - Godlessness in the Last Days
Ephesians 6:1-4 - Children and Parents
John 5:16-30 - Life Through the Son
John 8:42-47 - The Children of the Devil
John 9:1-12 - Jesus Heals a Man Born Blind
John 9:13-34 - The Pharisees Investigate the Healing
Luke 1:5-25 - The Birth of John the Baptist Foretold
Luke 1:57-66 - The Birth of John the Baptist
Luke 2:1-7 - The Birth of Jesus
Luke 2:41-52 - The Boy Jesus at the Temple
Luke 9:37-45 - The Healing of a Boy With an Evil Spirit
Mark 3:31-35 - Jesus' Mother and Brothers
Mark 7:1-23 - Clean and Unclean

■ PARTNERSHIPS

1 Peter 3:1-7 - Wives and Husbands
2 Corinthians 6:14–7:1 - Do Not Be Yoked with Unbelievers
Acts 12:20-25 - Herod's Death
Acts 15:36-41 - Disagreement Between Paul and Barnabas
Acts 19:1-22 - Paul in Ephesus
Acts 20:1-6 - Through Macedonia and Greece
Colossians 1:1-14 - Thanksgiving and Prayer
Colossians 4:2-18 - Further Instructions
Galatians 2:1-10 - Paul Accepted by the Apostles
Matthew 11:25-30 - Rest for the Weary
Philippians 1:1-11 - Thanksgiving and Prayer
Philippians 2:19-30 - Timothy and Epaphroditus
Philippians 4:2-9 - Exhortations

■ PASTORS

1 Timothy 3:1-16 - Overseers and Deacons
1 Timothy 5:1–6:2 - Advice About Widows, Elders and Slaves
Acts 20:13-38 - Paul's Farewell to the Ephesian Elders
Ephesians 4:1-16 - Unity in the Body of Christ
Galatians 6:1-10 - Doing Good to All

■ PATIENCE

1 Corinthians 13:1-13 - Love
2 Corinthians 6:3-13 - Paul's Hardships
2 Peter 3:1-18 - The Day of the Lord
Ephesians 4:1-16 - Unity in the Body of Christ
Galatians 5:16-26 - Life by the Spirit
James 5:7-12 - Patience in Suffering
Luke 1:5-25 - The Birth of John the Baptist Foretold
Luke 12:35-48 - Watchfulness
Matthew 9:18-26 - A Dead Girl and a Sick Woman
Matthew 18:10-14 - The Parable of the Lost Sheep
Revelation 1:9-20 - One Like a Son of Man
Revelation 14:6-13 - The Three Angels

■ PEACE

1 Corinthians 14:26-40 - Orderly Worship
1 Timothy 2:1-15 - Instructions on Worship
2 John 1-13 - From the Elder
Acts 9:20-31 - Saul in Damascus and Jerusalem
Acts 12:20-25 - Herod's Death
Acts 15:22-35 - The Council's Letter to Gentile Believers
Colossians 1:1-14 - Thanksgiving and Prayer
Colossians 3:1-17 - Rules for Holy Living
Ephesians 2:11-22 - One in Christ
Ephesians 4:1-16 - Unity in the Body of Christ
Galatians 1:1-10 - No Other Gospel
Galatians 5:16-26 - Life by the Spirit
Galatians 6:11-18 - Not Circumcision but a New Creation
Hebrews 7:1-10 - Melchizedek the Priest
Hebrews 12:1-3 - God Disciplines His Sons
Hebrews 12:14-29 - Warning Against Refusing God
Hebrews 13:1-25 - Concluding Exhortations
John 14:15-31 - Jesus Promises the Holy Spirit
John 16:17-33 - The Disciples' Grief Will Turn to Joy
John 20:19-23 - Jesus Appears to His Disciples
John 20:24-31 - Jesus Appears to Thomas
Luke 12:49-53 - Not Peace but Division
Mark 9:42-50 - Causing to Sin
Matthew 6:25-34 - Do Not Worry
Philippians 1:1-11 - Thanksgiving and Prayer
Philippians 4:2-9 - Exhortations
Revelation 1:4-8 - Greetings and Doxology
Revelation 6:1-17 - The Seals
Romans 5:1-11 - Peace and Joy

■ PEER PRESSURE

1 John 2:15-17 - Do Not Love the World
John 7:45-52 - Unbelief of the Jewish Leaders
John 12:37-50 - The Jews Continue in Their Unbelief
John 18:25-27 - Peter's Second and Third Denials
John 18:28-40 - Jesus Before Pilate
John 19:1-16 - Jesus Sentenced to be Crucified
John 19:38-42 - The Burial of Jesus
Luke 5:33-39 - Jesus Questioned About Fasting
Luke 20:9-19 - The Parable of the Tenants
Luke 22:54-62 - Peter Disowns Jesus
Mark 8:27-30 - Peter's Confession of Christ
Mark 12:13-17 - Paying Taxes to Caesar
Mark 15:1-15 - Jesus Before Pilate
Matthew 14:1-12 - John the Baptist Beheaded
Matthew 20:29-34 - Two Blind Men Receive Sight
Matthew 21:1-11 - The Triumphal Entry
Matthew 26:31-35 - Jesus Predicts Peter's Denial
Matthew 26:69-75 - Peter Disowns Jesus
Matthew 27:57-61 - The Burial of Jesus

■ PEOPLE

1 Peter 2:4-12 - The Living Stone and a Chosen People
1 Timothy 3:1-16 - Overseers and Deacons
Acts 2:1-13 - The Holy Spirit Comes at Pentecost
Acts 2:14-41 - Peter Addresses the Crowd

Acts 2:42-47 - The Fellowship of the Believers
Acts 3:1-10 - Peter Heals the Crippled Beggar
Acts 4:1-22 - Peter and John Before the Sanhedrin
Acts 5:12-16 - The Apostles Heal Many
Acts 5:17-41 - The Apostles Persecuted
Acts 6:8-15 - Stephen Seized
Acts 7:1-53 - Stephen's Speech to the Sanhedrin
Acts 10:24-48 - Peter at Cornelius' House
Acts 13:13-52 - In Pisidian Antioch
Acts 14:1-7 - In Iconium
Acts 14:8-20 - In Lystra and Derbe
Acts 17:10-15 - In Berea
Acts 17:16-34 - In Athens
Acts 19:1-22 - Paul in Ephesus
Acts 19:23-41 - The Riot in Ephesus
Acts 21:27-36 - Paul Arrested
Acts 21:37–22:21 - Paul Speaks to the Crowd
Acts 25:23–26:32 - Paul Before Agrippa
Acts 27:1-12 - Paul Sails for Rome
John 6:16-24 - Jesus Walks on the Water
John 6:60-71 - Many Disciples Desert Jesus
John 8:12-30 - The Validity of Jesus' Testimony
John 17:1-5 - Jesus Prays for Himself
John 17:20-26 - Jesus Prays for All Believers
Luke 4:14-30 - Jesus Rejected at Nazareth
Luke 4:38-44 - Jesus Heals Many
Matthew 13:24-30 - The Parable of the Weeds
Matthew 21:1-11 - The Triumphal Entry
Philippians 2:1-11 - Imitating Christ's Humility
Philippians 2:12-18 - Shining as Stars

■ **PERFECT**

1 John 4:7-21 - God's Love and Ours
2 Corinthians 13:1-14 - Final Warnings
Hebrews 7:11-28 - Jesus Like Melchizedek
Hebrews 10:1-18 - Christ's Sacrifice Once for All
Matthew 5:43-48 - Love for Enemies
Matthew 19:16-30 - The Rich Young Man

■ **PERSECUTION**

1 Corinthians 4:1-21 - Apostles of Christ
1 Peter 2:13-25 - Submission to Rulers and Masters
1 Peter 4:12-19 - Suffering for Being a Christian
1 Thessalonians 1:1-10 - Thanksgiving for the Thessalonians' Faith
1 Thessalonians 2:1-16 - Paul's Ministry in Thessalonica
1 Thessalonians 2:17–3:5 - Paul's Longing to See the Thessalonians
2 Corinthians 6:3-13 - Paul's Hardships
2 Corinthians 11:16-33 - Paul Boasts About His Sufferings
2 Timothy 3:10–4:8 - Paul's Charge to Timothy
Acts 3:11-26 - Peter Speaks to the Onlookers
Acts 4:1-22 - Peter and John Before the Sanhedrin
Acts 4:23-31 - The Believers' Prayer
Acts 5:17-41 - The Apostles Persecuted
Acts 7:54-8:1 - The Stoning of Stephen
Acts 8:2-3 - The Church Persecuted and Scattered
Acts 9:20-31 - Saul in Damascus and Jerusalem
Acts 11:19-30 - The Church in Antioch
Acts 12:1-19 - Peter's Miraculous Escape From Prison
Acts 13:13-52 - In Pisidian Antioch
Acts 14:1-7 - In Iconium
Acts 14:8-20 - In Lystra and Derbe
Acts 17:1-9 - In Thessalonica
Acts 21:27-36 - Paul Arrested
Acts 21:37–22:21 - Paul Speaks to the Crowd
Acts 22:30–23:11 - Before the Sanhedrin
Acts 25:23–26:32 - Paul Before Agrippa
Galatians 1:11-24 - Paul Called by God
Galatians 6:11-18 - Not Circumcision but a New Creation
Hebrews 2:1-4 - Warning to Pay Attention
Hebrews 10:19-39 - A Call to Persevere
John 5:16-30 - Life Through the Son
John 15:18–16:4 - The World Hates the Disciples
John 18:12-14 - Jesus Taken to Annas
John 18:19-24 - The High Priest Questions Jesus
John 18:25-27 - Peter's Second and Third Denials
Luke 6:17-26 - Blessings and Woes
Luke 21:5-38 - Signs of the End of the Age
Luke 22:63-65 - The Guards Mock Jesus
Luke 22:66–23:25 - Jesus Before Pilate and Herod
Mark 6:14-29 - John the Baptist Beheaded
Mark 13:1-31 - Signs of the End of the Age
Mark 14:43-52 - Jesus Arrested
Mark 14:53-65 - Before the Sanhedrin
Mark 15:16-20 - The Soldiers Mock Jesus
Matthew 4:12-17 - Jesus Begins to Preach
Matthew 5:1-12 - The Beatitudes
Matthew 5:38-42 - An Eye for an Eye
Matthew 5:43-48 - Love for Enemies
Matthew 10:1-42 - Jesus Sends Out the Twelve
Matthew 24:1-35 - Signs of the End of the Age
Matthew 26:31-35 - Jesus Predicts Peter's Denial
Matthew 27:27-31 - The Soldiers Mock Jesus
Revelation 2:8-11 - To the Church in Smyrna
Revelation 11:1-14 - The Two Witnesses
Revelation 13:2-10 - The Beast out of the Sea
Romans 8:28-39 - More Than Conquerors

■ **PERSEVERANCE**

1 Corinthians 9:1-27 - The Rights of an Apostle
1 Corinthians 13:1-13 - Love
2 Corinthians 6:3-13 - Paul's Hardships
2 Peter 1:1-11 - Making One's Calling and Election Sure
2 Thessalonians 1:1-12 - Thanksgiving and Prayer
2 Thessalonians 2:13-17 - Stand Firm
Acts 4:23-31 - The Believers' Prayer
Acts 5:17-41 - The Apostles Persecuted
Hebrews 10:19-39 - A Call to Persevere
Hebrews 12:1-3 - God Disciplines His Sons
James 5:7-12 - Patience in Suffering
James 5:13-20 - The Prayer of Faith
Luke 8:1-15 - The Parable of the Sower
Luke 18:1-8 - The Parable of the Persistent Widow
Mark 4:1-20 - The Parable of the Sower
Mark 13:1-31 - Signs of the End of the Age
Mark 13:32-37 - The Day and Hour Unknown
Matthew 13:53-58 - A Prophet Without Honor
Matthew 15:21-28 - The Faith of the Canaanite Woman
Matthew 24:1-35 - Signs of the End of the Age
Matthew 26:36-46 - Gethsemane
Revelation 2:1-7 - To the Church in Ephesus
Revelation 2:8-11 - To the Church in Smyrna
Revelation 2:18-29 - To the Church in Thyatira
Revelation 13:2-10 - The Beast out of the Sea

Revelation 15:1-8 - Seven Angels With Seven Plagues

■ PERSISTENCE

Luke 1:57-66 - The Birth of John the Baptist
Luke 5:1-11 - The Calling of the First Disciples
Luke 11:1-13 - Jesus' Teaching on Prayer
Luke 18:35-43 - A Blind Beggar Receives His Sight
Mark 10:46-52 - Blind Bartimaeus Receives His Sight
Matthew 7:7-12 - Ask, Seek, Knock
Matthew 9:27-34 - Jesus Heals the Blind and Mute
Matthew 10:1-42 - Jesus Sends Out the Twelve
Matthew 15:21-28 - The Faith of the Canaanite Woman
Matthew 20:29-34 - Two Blind Men Receive Sight

■ PERSPECTIVE

Hebrews 12:1-3 - God Disciplines His Sons
Matthew 6:19-24 - Treasures in Heaven
Matthew 13:44-46 - The Parables of the Hidden Treasure and the Pearl
Matthew 14:22-36 - Jesus Walks on the Water
Matthew 16:21-28 - Jesus Predicts His Death
Matthew 19:13-15 - The Little Children and Jesus
Matthew 19:16-30 - The Rich Young Man
Matthew 20:1-16 - The Parable of the Workers in the Vineyard
Matthew 21:28-32 - The Parable of the Two Sons

■ PLANS

2 Corinthians 1:12–2:4 - Paul's Change of Plans
Acts 20:1-6 - Through Macedonia and Greece
Acts 23:12-22 - The Plot to Kill Paul
Acts 27:27-44 - The Shipwreck
James 4:13-17 - Boasting About Tomorrow
John 12:1-11 - Jesus Anointed at Bethany
Matthew 19:13-15 - The Little Children and Jesus
Matthew 26:1-5 - The Plot Against Jesus
Matthew 26:14-16 - Judas Agrees to Betray Jesus
Matthew 27:62-66 - The Guard at the Tomb
Matthew 28:11-15 - The Guards' Report
Matthew 28:16-20 - The Great Commission
Romans 15:23-33 - Paul's Plan to Visit Rome

■ PLEASURE

2 Timothy 3:1-9 - Godlessness in the Last Days
Colossians 3:18–4:1 - Rules for Christian Households

■ POOR

1 John 3:11-24 - Love One Another
2 Corinthians 8:1-15 - Generosity Encouraged
Acts 3:1-10 - Peter Heals the Crippled Beggar
Acts 9:32-43 - Aeneas and Dorcas
Acts 10:1-8 - Cornelius Calls for Peter
Galatians 2:1-10 - Paul Accepted by the Apostles
James 2:1-13 - Favoritism Forbidden
John 12:1-11 - Jesus Anointed at Bethany
Luke 1:46-56 - Mary's Song
Luke 6:17-26 - Blessings and Woes
Luke 9:1-9 - Jesus Sends Out the Twelve
Luke 14:1-14 - Jesus at a Pharisee's House
Luke 21:1-4 - The Widow's Offering
Mark 12:41-44 - The Widow's Offering
Mark 14:1-11 - Jesus Anointed at Bethany
Matthew 6:1-4 - Giving to the Needy
Philippians 4:10-23 - Thanks for Their Gifts
Revelation 2:8-11 - To the Church in Smyrna

■ POPULARITY

3 John 1-14 - From the Elder
John 3:22-36 - John the Baptist's Testimony About Jesus
John 5:31-47 - Testimonies About Jesus
Luke 19:45-48 - Jesus at the Temple
Matthew 8:18-22 - The Cost of Following Jesus
Matthew 21:12-17 - Jesus at the Temple
Matthew 21:33-46 - The Parable of the Tenants

■ POSITION

Acts 25:23–26:32 - Paul Before Agrippa
John 18:28-40 - Jesus Before Pilate
Matthew 20:20-28 - A Mother's Request

■ POSSESSIONS

1 Corinthians 16:1-4 - The Collection for God's People
Acts 4:32-37 - The Believers Share Their Possessions
John 12:1-11 - Jesus Anointed at Bethany
Luke 12:13-21 - The Parable of the Rich Fool
Luke 12:22-34 - Do Not Worry
Luke 21:1-4 - The Widow's Offering
Mark 10:17-31 - The Rich Young Man
Mark 12:1-12 - The Parable of the Tenants
Matthew 19:16-30 - The Rich Young Man
Matthew 25:14-30 - The Parable of the Talents

■ POWER

1 Corinthians 1:10-17 - Divisions in the Church
1 Corinthians 1:18–2:5 - Christ the Wisdom and Power of God
1 Corinthians 15:35-58 - The Resurrection Body
1 Peter 1:1-12 - Praise to God for a Living Hope
1 Timothy 3:1-16 - Overseers and Deacons
2 Corinthians 4:1-18 - Treasures in Jars of Clay
2 Corinthians 10:1-18 - Paul's Defense of His Ministry
2 Corinthians 12:1-10 - Paul's Vision and His Thorn
2 Corinthians 13:1-14 - Final Warnings
2 Timothy 3:1-9 - Godlessness in the Last Days
Acts 2:14-41 - Peter Addresses the Crowd
Acts 4:23-31 - The Believers' Prayer
Acts 4:32-37 - The Believers Share Their Possessions
Acts 6:8-15 - Stephen Seized
Acts 9:20-31 - Saul in Damascus and Jerusalem
Acts 10:24-48 - Peter at Cornelius' House
Acts 25:23–26:32 - Paul Before Agrippa
Ephesians 1:15-23 - Thanksgiving and Prayer
Ephesians 3:1-13 - Paul the Preacher to the Gentiles
Ephesians 3:14-21 - A Prayer for the Ephesians
Ephesians 6:10-24 - The Armor of God
John 6:16-24 - Jesus Walks on the Water
John 11:45-57 - The Plot to Kill Jesus
John 19:1-16 - Jesus Sentenced to be Crucified
Luke 4:1-13 - The Temptation of Jesus
Luke 4:31-37 - Jesus Drives Out an Evil Spirit
Luke 8:40-56 - A Dead Girl and a Sick Woman
Mark 1:29-34 - Jesus Heals Many
Mark 4:26-29 - The Parable of the Growing Seed
Mark 4:35-41 - Jesus Calms the Storm
Mark 5:1-20 - The Healing of a Demon-possessed Man
Mark 6:14-29 - John the Baptist Beheaded
Mark 10:35-45 - The Request of James and John
Mark 11:27-33 - The Authority of Jesus Questioned
Mark 12:18-27 - Marriage at the Resurrection
Matthew 9:1-8 - Jesus Heals a Paralytic
Matthew 13:31-35 - The Parables of the Mustard Seed and the Yeast
Matthew 17:1-13 - The Transfiguration

Matthew 17:14-23 - The Healing of a Boy With a Demon
Matthew 21:18-22 - The Fig Tree Withers
Matthew 22:23-33 - Marriage at the Resurrection
Matthew 27:62-66 - The Guard at the Tomb
Matthew 28:1-10 - The Resurrection
Philippians 3:12–4:1 - Pressing on Toward the Goal
Revelation 4:1-11 - The Throne in Heaven
Revelation 5:1-14 - The Scroll and the Lamb
Revelation 7:9-17 - The Great Multitude in White Robes
Revelation 12:1–13:1 - The Woman and the Dragon
Revelation 13:2-10 - The Beast out of the Sea
Revelation 13:11-18 - The Beast out of the Earth
Revelation 15:1-8 - Seven Angels With Seven Plagues
Revelation 17:1-18 - The Woman on the Beast
Revelation 18:1-24 - The Fall of Babylon
Revelation 19:1-10 - Hallelujah!

■ **PRAISE**

1 Corinthians 14:1-25 - Gifts of Prophecy and Tongues
2 Corinthians 9:6-15 - Sowing Generously
Acts 2:42-47 - The Fellowship of the Believers
Acts 3:1-10 - Peter Heals the Crippled Beggar
Acts 10:24-48 - Peter at Cornelius' House
Acts 11:1-18 - Peter Explains His Actions
Acts 16:16-40 - Paul and Silas in Prison
Acts 21:17-26 - Paul's Arrival at Jerusalem
Colossians 1:1-14 - Thanksgiving and Prayer
Ephesians 1:1-14 - Spiritual Blessings in Christ
Galatians 1:11-24 - Paul Called by God
Hebrews 13:1-25 - Concluding Exhortations
John 5:31-47 - Testimonies About Jesus
John 12:12-19 - The Triumphal Entry
Luke 1:46-56 - Mary's Song
Luke 1:67-80 - Zechariah's Song
Luke 2:8-20 - The Shepherds and the Angels
Luke 2:21-40 - Jesus Presented in the Temple
Luke 7:11-17 - Jesus Raises a Widow's Son
Luke 13:10-17 - A Crippled Woman Healed on the Sabbath
Luke 17:11-19 - Ten Healed of Leprosy
Luke 18:35-43 - A Blind Beggar Receives His Sight
Luke 19:28-44 - The Triumphal Entry
Luke 23:44-49 - Jesus' Death
Luke 24:50-53 - The Ascension
Mark 11:1-11 - The Triumphal Entry
Matthew 9:1-8 - Jesus Heals a Paralytic
Matthew 15:29-39 - Jesus Feeds the Four Thousand
Matthew 21:1-11 - The Triumphal Entry
Matthew 21:12-17 - Jesus at the Temple
Matthew 26:6-13 - Jesus Anointed at Bethany
Matthew 28:1-10 - The Resurrection
Philippians 1:1-11 - Thanksgiving and Prayer
Revelation 5:1-14 - The Scroll and the Lamb
Revelation 7:9-17 - The Great Multitude in White Robes
Revelation 8:1-5 - The Seventh Seal and the Golden Censer
Revelation 19:1-10 - Hallelujah!
Romans 11:33-36 - Doxology
Romans 16:1-27 - Personal Greetings

■ **PRAYER**

1 Corinthians 7:1-40 - Marriage
1 Corinthians 14:26-40 - Orderly Worship
1 John 3:11-24 - Love One Another
1 John 5:13-21 - Concluding Remarks
1 Thessalonians 3:6-13 - Timothy's Encouraging Report
1 Timothy 2:1-15 - Instructions on Worship
2 Corinthians 1:1-11 - The God of All Comfort
2 Corinthians 13:1-14 - Final Warnings
2 Thessalonians 3:1-5 - Request for Prayer
3 John 1-14 - From the Elder
Acts 1:12-26 - Matthias Chosen to Replace Judas
Acts 4:23-31 - The Believers' Prayer
Acts 6:1-7 - The Choosing of the Seven
Acts 7:54–8:1 - The Stoning of Stephen
Acts 9:1-19 - Saul's Conversion
Acts 9:32-43 - Aeneas and Dorcas
Acts 10:1-8 - Cornelius Calls for Peter
Acts 10:9-23 - Peter's Vision
Acts 10:24-48 - Peter at Cornelius' House
Acts 11:1-18 - Peter Explains His Actions
Acts 12:1-19 - Peter's Miraculous Escape From Prison
Acts 13:1-3 - Barnabas and Saul Sent Off
Acts 14:21-28 - The Return to Antioch in Syria
Acts 16:16-40 - Paul and Silas in Prison
Acts 20:13-38 - Paul's Farewell to the Ephesian Elders
Acts 21:1-16 - On to Jerusalem
Acts 28:1-10 - Ashore on Malta
Colossians 1:1-14 - Thanksgiving and Prayer
Colossians 4:2-18 - Further Instructions
Ephesians 1:15-23 - Thanksgiving and Prayer
Ephesians 3:14-21 - A Prayer for the Ephesians
Ephesians 6:10-24 - The Armor of God
Hebrews 4:14–5:10 - Jesus the Great High Priest
Hebrews 7:11-28 - Jesus Like Melchizedek
Hebrews 13:1-25 - Concluding Exhortations
James 1:1-18 - Trials and Temptations
James 5:13-20 - The Prayer of Faith
John 16:17-33 - The Disciples' Grief Will Turn to Joy
John 17:1-5 - Jesus Prays for Himself
John 17:6-19 - Jesus Prays for His Disciples
John 17:20-26 - Jesus Prays for All Believers
Jude 17-25 - A Call to Persevere
Luke 1:5-25 - The Birth of John the Baptist Foretold
Luke 3:21-38 - The Baptism and Genealogy of Jesus
Luke 5:12-16 - The Man With Leprosy
Luke 6:12-16 - The Twelve Apostles
Luke 7:1-10 - The Faith of the Centurion
Luke 9:28-36 - The Transfiguration
Luke 11:1-13 - Jesus' Teaching on Prayer
Luke 18:1-8 - The Parable of the Persistent Widow
Luke 18:9-14 - The Parable of the Pharisee and the Tax Collector
Luke 19:45-48 - Jesus at the Temple
Luke 21:5-38 - Signs of the End of the Age
Luke 22:39-46 - Jesus Prays on the Mount of Olives
Mark 1:35-39 - Jesus Prays in a Solitary Place
Mark 6:45-56 - Jesus Walks on the Water
Mark 8:22-26 - The Healing of a Blind Man at Bethsaida
Mark 9:14-32 - The Healing of a Boy With an Evil Spirit
Mark 10:46-52 - Blind Bartimaeus Receives His Sight
Mark 11:12-19 - Jesus Clears the Temple
Mark 11:20-26 - The Withered Fig Tree
Mark 14:32-42 - Gethsemane
Matthew 5:43-48 - Love for Enemies
Matthew 6:5-15 - Prayer

Matthew 6:25-34 - Do Not Worry
Matthew 7:7-12 - Ask, Seek, Knock
Matthew 9:35-38 - The Workers Are Few
Matthew 17:14-23 - The Healing of a Boy With a Demon
Matthew 18:15-20 - A Brother Who Sins Against You
Matthew 20:29-34 - Two Blind Men Receive Sight
Matthew 21:18-22 - The Fig Tree Withers
Matthew 26:36-46 - Gethsemane
Philippians 1:1-11 - Thanksgiving and Prayer
Philippians 1:12-30 - Paul's Chains Advance the Gospel
Philippians 4:2-9 - Exhortations
Philemon 1-7 - Thanksgiving and Prayer
Revelation 5:1-14 - The Scroll and the Lamb
Revelation 8:1-5 - The Seventh Seal and the Golden Censer
Romans 8:18-27 - Future Glory

■ **PREJUDICE**
Acts 8:9-25 - Simon the Sorcerer
Acts 10:24-48 - Peter at Cornelius' House
Acts 11:1-18 - Peter Explains His Actions
Acts 16:16-40 - Paul and Silas in Prison
Acts 18:1-17 - In Corinth
Acts 19:23-41 - The Riot in Ephesus
James 2:1-13 - Favoritism Forbidden
John 4:1-26 - Jesus Talks With a Samaritan Woman
John 4:27-38 - The Disciples Rejoin Jesus
John 7:45-52 - Unbelief of the Jewish Leaders

■ **PREPARATION**
2 Corinthians 8:16–9:5 - Titus Sent to Corinth
John 12:1-11 - Jesus Anointed at Bethany
Luke 10:38-42 - At the Home of Martha and Mary
Luke 12:13-21 - The Parable of the Rich Fool
Luke 12:35-48 - Watchfulness
Luke 14:15-24 - The Parable of the Great Banquet
Mark 1:1-8 - John the Baptist Prepares the Way
Mark 1:35-39 - Jesus Prays in a Solitary Place
Mark 8:31–9:1 - Jesus Predicts His Death
Mark 14:1-11 - Jesus Anointed at Bethany
Mark 14:12-26 - The Lord's Supper
Matthew 6:16-18 - Fasting
Matthew 20:17-19 - Jesus Again Predicts His Death
Matthew 24:36-51 - The Day and Hour Unknown
Matthew 25:1-13 - The Parable of the Ten Virgins
Matthew 26:6-13 - Jesus Anointed at Bethany
Matthew 26:17-30 - The Lord's Supper
Revelation 3:1-6 - To the Church in Sardis

■ **PRESSURE**
2 Corinthians 11:16-33 - Paul Boasts About His Sufferings
Luke 22:66–23:25 - Jesus Before Pilate and Herod
Matthew 12:46-50 - Jesus' Mother and Brothers
Matthew 26:69-75 - Peter Disowns Jesus
Matthew 27:11-26 - Jesus Before Pilate
Revelation 13:11-18 - The Beast out of the Earth

■ **PRIDE**
1 Corinthians 4:1-21 - Apostles of Christ
1 Corinthians 5:1-13 - Expel the Immoral Brother!
1 John 1:5-2:14 - Walking in the Light
1 John 2:15-17 - Do Not Love the World
1 Peter 5:1-14 - To Elders and Young Men
1 Timothy 3:1-16 - Overseers and Deacons
2 Corinthians 10:1-18 - Paul's Defense of His Ministry
2 Corinthians 12:1-10 - Paul's Vision and His Thorn
2 Timothy 3:1-9 - Godlessness in the Last Days
Acts 12:20-25 - Herod's Death
James 4:1-12 - Submit Yourselves to God
John 13:1-17 - Jesus Washes His Disciples' Feet
Luke 18:9-14 - The Parable of the Pharisee and the Tax Collector
Luke 20:41-47 - Whose Son Is the Christ?
Mark 9:33-37 - Who Is the Greatest?
Mark 9:38-41 - Whoever Is Not Against Us Is for Us
Mark 12:35-40 - Whose Son Is the Christ?
Matthew 6:1-4 - Giving to the Needy
Matthew 7:1-6 - Judging Others
Matthew 7:13-14 - The Narrow and Wide Gates
Matthew 11:20-24 - Woe on Unrepentant Cities
Matthew 14:1-12 - John the Baptist Beheaded
Matthew 15:1-20 - Clean and Unclean
Matthew 16:1-4 - The Demand for a Sign
Matthew 20:20-28 - A Mother's Request
Matthew 21:12-17 - Jesus at the Temple
Philippians 2:1-11 - Imitating Christ's Humility
Romans 15:14-22 - Paul, the Minister to the Gentiles

■ **PRIORITIES**
1 Peter 1:13–2:3 - Be Holy
John 1:35-42 - Jesus' First Disciples
John 18:28-40 - Jesus Before Pilate
Luke 12:22-34 - Do Not Worry
Mark 7:24-30 - The Faith of a Syrophoenician Woman
Mark 12:28-34 - The Greatest Commandment
Matthew 6:19-24 - Treasures in Heaven
Matthew 8:28-34 - The Healing of Two Demon-possessed Men
Matthew 9:35-38 - The Workers Are Few
Matthew 12:46-50 - Jesus' Mother and Brothers
Matthew 13:44-46 - The Parables of the Hidden Treasure and the Pearl
Matthew 16:21-28 - Jesus Predicts His Death
Matthew 23:1-39 - Seven Woes

■ **PRIVILEGE**
John 18:15-18 - Peter's First Denial
Matthew 20:20-28 - A Mother's Request

■ **PROBLEMS**
Matthew 10:1-42 - Jesus Sends Out the Twelve

■ **PROCRASTINATION**
Matthew 8:18-22 - The Cost of Following Jesus
Matthew 18:21-35 - The Parable of the Unmerciful Servant
Matthew 21:28-32 - The Parable of the Two Sons

■ **PRODUCTIVITY**
Mark 4:26-29 - The Parable of the Growing Seed
Mark 4:30-34 - The Parable of the Mustard Seed
Matthew 13:1-23 - The Parable of the Sower
Matthew 25:14-30 - The Parable of the Talents

■ **PROMISES**
2 Corinthians 1:12–2:4 - Paul's Change of Plans
2 Peter 3:1-18 - The Day of the Lord
Ephesians 6:1-4 - Children and Parents
Galatians 3:15-25 - The Law and the Promise
Galatians 3:26–4:7 - Sons of God
Hebrews 6:13-20 - The Certainty of God's Promise
Hebrews 11:1-40 - By Faith
John 6:25-59 - Jesus the Bread of Life

Luke 1:5-25 - The Birth of John the Baptist Foretold
Luke 1:46-56 - Mary's Song
Luke 1:57-66 - The Birth of John the Baptist
Luke 1:67-80 - Zechariah's Song
Luke 6:37-42 - Judging Others
Luke 24:36-49 - Jesus Appears to the Disciples
Mark 10:32-34 - Jesus Again Predicts His Death
Matthew 7:7-12 - Ask, Seek, Knock
Matthew 26:31-35 - Jesus Predicts Peter's Denial
Romans 4:1-25 - Abraham Justified by Faith

■ PROPHECY

1 Corinthians 12:1-11 - Spiritual Gifts
1 Corinthians 14:1-25 - Gifts of Prophecy and Tongues
1 Peter 1:1-12 - Praise to God for a Living Hope
1 Thessalonians 5:12-28 - Final Instructions
2 Peter 1:12-21 - Prophecy of Scripture
Acts 2:14-41 - Peter Addresses the Crowd
Acts 3:11-26 - Peter Speaks to the Onlookers
Acts 4:1-22 - Peter and John Before the Sanhedrin
Acts 11:19-30 - The Church in Antioch
Acts 13:13-52 - In Pisidian Antioch
Acts 15:1-21 - The Council at Jerusalem
Acts 19:1-22 - Paul in Ephesus
Acts 21:1-16 - On to Jerusalem
Acts 28:17-31 - Paul Preaches at Rome Under Guard
Hebrews 1:1-14 - The Son Superior to Angels
John 11:45-57 - The Plot to Kill Jesus
John 12:12-19 - The Triumphal Entry
John 12:37-50 - The Jews Continue in Their Unbelief
John 19:28-37 - The Death of Jesus
John 20:1-9 - The Empty Tomb
Jude 1-16 - The Sin and Doom of Godless Men
Luke 1:67-80 - Zechariah's Song
Luke 2:1-7 - The Birth of Jesus
Luke 2:21-40 - Jesus Presented in the Temple
Luke 4:14-30 - Jesus Rejected at Nazareth
Luke 7:18-35 - Jesus and John the Baptist
Luke 9:18-27 - Peter's Confession of Christ
Luke 9:28-36 - The Transfiguration
Luke 11:37-54 - Six Woes
Luke 13:31-35 - Jesus' Sorrow for Jerusalem
Luke 16:16-18 - Additional Teachings
Luke 17:20-37 - The Coming of the Kingdom of God
Luke 18:31-34 - Jesus Again Predicts His Death
Luke 19:28-44 - The Triumphal Entry
Luke 20:9-19 - The Parable of the Tenants
Luke 21:5-38 - Signs of the End of the Age
Luke 22:7-38 - The Last Supper
Luke 22:63-65 - The Guards Mock Jesus
Luke 23:26-43 - The Crucifixion
Luke 24:13-35 - On the Road to Emmaus
Luke 24:36-49 - Jesus Appears to the Disciples
Mark 1:1-8 - John the Baptist Prepares the Way
Mark 9:2-13 - The Transfiguration
Mark 10:32-34 - Jesus Again Predicts His Death
Mark 12:1-12 - The Parable of the Tenants
Mark 13:1-31 - Signs of the End of the Age
Mark 14:12-26 - The Lord's Supper
Mark 14:27-31 - Jesus Predicts Peter's Denial
Matthew 2:1-12 - The Visit of the Magi
Matthew 2:13-18 - The Escape to Egypt
Matthew 2:19-23 - The Return to Nazareth
Matthew 4:12-17 - Jesus Begins to Preach
Matthew 12:15-21 - God's Chosen Servant
Matthew 13:1-23 - The Parable of the Sower
Matthew 13:31-35 - The Parables of the Mustard Seed and the Yeast
Matthew 21:1-11 - The Triumphal Entry
Matthew 21:33-46 - The Parable of the Tenants
Matthew 24:1-35 - Signs of the End of the Age
Matthew 26:47-56 - Jesus Arrested
Matthew 27:1-10 - Judas Hangs Himself
Matthew 28:1-10 - The Resurrection
Revelation 1:1-3 - Prologue
Revelation 1:9-20 - One Like a Son of Man
Revelation 19:1-10 - Hallelujah!
Revelation 22:7-21 - Jesus Is Coming

■ PROTECTION

Acts 22:22-29 - Paul the Roman Citizen
Acts 23:23-35 - Paul Transferred to Caesarea
John 17:6-19 - Jesus Prays for His Disciples
John 18:1-11 - Jesus Arrested
Matthew 14:22-36 - Jesus Walks on the Water
Matthew 19:1-12 - Divorce
Matthew 26:47-56 - Jesus Arrested
Matthew 27:62-66 - The Guard at the Tomb

■ PUNISHMENT

2 Corinthians 2:5-11 - Forgiveness for the Sinner
2 Peter 2:1-22 - False Teachers and Their Destruction
Acts 3:11-26 - Peter Speaks to the Onlookers
Acts 5:1-11 - Ananias and Sapphira
Acts 5:17-41 - The Apostles Persecuted
Acts 7:1-53 - Stephen's Speech to the Sanhedrin
Acts 22:22-29 - Paul the Roman Citizen
Hebrews 3:7-19 - Warning Against Unbelief
Hebrews 4:1-13 - A Sabbath-Rest for the People of God
John 7:53–8:11 - A Woman Caught in Adultery
John 18:19-24 - The High Priest Questions Jesus
Jude 1-16 - The Sin and Doom of Godless Men
Luke 16:19-31 - The Rich Man and Lazarus
Luke 19:11-27 - The Parable of the Ten Minas
Luke 20:9-19 - The Parable of the Tenants
Luke 20:41-47 - Whose Son Is the Christ?
Luke 21:5-38 - Signs of the End of the Age
Luke 22:66–23:25 - Jesus Before Pilate and Herod
Mark 12:1-12 - The Parable of the Tenants
Mark 12:35-40 - Whose Son Is the Christ?
Mark 14:53-65 - Before the Sanhedrin
Matthew 5:21-26 - Murder
Matthew 11:20-24 - Woe on Unrepentant Cities
Matthew 13:24-30 - The Parable of the Weeds
Matthew 13:36-43 - The Parable of the Weeds Explained
Matthew 13:47-52 - The Parable of the Net
Matthew 21:33-46 - The Parable of the Tenants
Matthew 22:1-14 - The Parable of the Wedding Banquet
Matthew 23:1-39 - Seven Woes
Matthew 24:1-35 - Signs of the End of the Age
Matthew 25:31-46 - The Sheep and the Goats
Revelation 19:11-21 - The Rider on the White Horse
Revelation 20:1-6 - The Thousand Years
Revelation 20:7-10 - Satan's Doom
Revelation 20:11-15 - The Dead Are Judged

■ PURITY

1 Peter 3:1-7 - Wives and Husbands

1 Thessalonians 4:1-12 - Living to Please God
2 Corinthians 6:14–7:1 - Do Not Be Yoked with Unbelievers
2 Corinthians 11:1-15 - Paul and the False Apostles
Matthew 5:1-12 - The Beatitudes
Matthew 5:27-30 - Adultery
Matthew 15:1-20 - Clean and Unclean
Matthew 16:5-12 - The Yeast of the Pharisees and Sadducees
Matthew 18:1-9 - The Greatest in the Kingdom of Heaven
Matthew 19:1-12 - Divorce
Revelation 7:9-17 - The Great Multitude in White Robes
Revelation 14:1-5 - The Lamb and the 144,000
Revelation 15:1-8 - Seven Angels With Seven Plagues
Revelation 19:1-10 - Hallelujah!
Revelation 21:1-27 - The New Jerusalem
Revelation 22:1-6 - The River of Life
Romans 13:8-14 - Love, for the Day Is Near

■ **PURPOSE**

Ephesians 1:1-14 - Spiritual Blessings in Christ
Ephesians 3:1-13 - Paul the Preacher to the Gentiles
Luke 1:5-25 - The Birth of John the Baptist Foretold
Luke 4:38-44 - Jesus Heals Many
Mark 1:35-39 - Jesus Prays in a Solitary Place
Matthew 9:9-13 - The Calling of Matthew
Matthew 10:1-42 - Jesus Sends Out the Twelve
Matthew 12:46-50 - Jesus' Mother and Brothers
Matthew 28:16-20 - The Great Commission
Romans 8:28-39 - More Than Conquerors

■ **QUALITY**

2 Peter 1:1-11 - Making One's Calling and Election Sure
Matthew 7:24-29 - The Wise and Foolish Builders
Matthew 13:31-35 - The Parables of the Mustard Seed and the Yeast

■ **QUARRELS**

1 Corinthians 1:10-17 - Divisions in the Church
1 Corinthians 3:1-23 - On Divisions in the Church
1 Thessalonians 5:12-28 - Final Instructions
1 Timothy 3:1-16 - Overseers and Deacons
1 Timothy 6:3-10 - Love of Money
Acts 12:20-25 - Herod's Death
James 4:1-12 - Submit Yourselves to God
Matthew 5:21-26 - Murder
Matthew 18:15-20 - A Brother Who Sins Against You
Titus 3:1-15 - Doing What Is Good

■ **QUESTIONS**

1 Corinthians 15:35-58 - The Resurrection Body
Acts 15:1-21 - The Council at Jerusalem
Galatians 3:1-14 - Faith or Observance of the Law
John 6:60-71 - Many Disciples Desert Jesus
John 16:17-33 - The Disciples' Grief Will Turn to Joy
Luke 2:41-52 - The Boy Jesus at the Temple
Luke 20:1-8 - The Authority of Jesus Questioned
Luke 20:20-26 - Paying Taxes to Caesar
Luke 20:27-40 - The Resurrection and Marriage
Mark 2:18-22 - Jesus Questioned About Fasting
Mark 8:1-13 - Jesus Feeds the Four Thousand
Mark 11:27-33 - The Authority of Jesus Questioned
Mark 12:18-27 - Marriage at the Resurrection
Matthew 9:1-8 - Jesus Heals a Paralytic
Matthew 19:16-30 - The Rich Young Man
Matthew 21:23-27 - The Authority of Jesus Questioned
Matthew 22:15-22 - Paying Taxes to Caesar
Matthew 22:41-46 - Whose Son Is the Christ?
Matthew 27:45-56 - The Death of Jesus

■ **QUIET**

1 Corinthians 14:26-40 - Orderly Worship
Mark 6:30-44 - Jesus Feeds the Five Thousand
Matthew 14:13-21 - Jesus Feeds the Five Thousand

■ **RATIONALIZING**

John 18:28-40 - Jesus Before Pilate
Luke 22:66–23:25 - Jesus Before Pilate and Herod
Mark 7:24-30 - The Faith of a Syrophoenician Woman
Matthew 5:17-20 - The Fulfillment of the Law
Matthew 8:18-22 - The Cost of Following Jesus
Matthew 12:38-45 - The Sign of Jonah
Matthew 16:1-4 - The Demand for a Sign
Matthew 18:21-35 - The Parable of the Unmerciful Servant
Matthew 22:34-40 - The Greatest Commandment
Matthew 26:6-13 - Jesus Anointed at Bethany

■ **READING**

1 Timothy 4:1-16 - Instructions to Timothy

■ **REBELLION**

2 Peter 2:1-22 - False Teachers and Their Destruction
Mark 14:43-52 - Jesus Arrested
Matthew 7:13-14 - The Narrow and Wide Gates
Matthew 11:20-24 - Woe on Unrepentant Cities
Matthew 15:1-20 - Clean and Unclean
Matthew 24:1-35 - Signs of the End of the Age
Matthew 26:14-16 - Judas Agrees to Betray Jesus
Matthew 27:11-26 - Jesus Before Pilate
Revelation 8:6–9:21 - The Trumpets
Revelation 19:11-21 - The Rider on the White Horse
Revelation 20:1-6 - The Thousand Years
Revelation 20:7-10 - Satan's Doom
Romans 3:9-20 - No One Is Righteous

■ **RECONCILIATION**

1 John 1:5-2:14 - Walking in the Light
2 Corinthians 5:11–6:2 - The Ministry of Reconciliation
Colossians 1:15-23 - The Supremacy of Christ
Ephesians 2:11-22 - One in Christ
Hebrews 2:5-18 - Jesus Made Like His Brothers
Luke 12:54-59 - Interpreting the Times
Luke 15:1-7 - The Parable of the Lost Sheep
Mark 15:33-41 - The Death of Jesus
Matthew 5:21-26 - Murder
Matthew 18:10-14 - The Parable of the Lost Sheep
Matthew 18:15-20 - A Brother Who Sins Against You
Matthew 18:21-35 - The Parable of the Unmerciful Servant
Philemon 8-25 - Paul's Plea for Onesimus
Revelation 2:1-7 - To the Church in Ephesus

■ **REJECTION**

1 John 2:18-27 - Warning Against Antichrists
1 Peter 2:4-12 - The Living Stone and a Chosen People
2 Peter 2:1-22 - False Teachers and Their Destruction
Acts 7:1-53 - Stephen's Speech to the Sanhedrin
Galatians 4:8-20 - Paul's Concern for the Galatians
Hebrews 5:11–6:12 - Warning Against Falling Away

John 3:22-36 - John the Baptist's Testimony About Jesus
John 6:60-71 - Many Disciples Desert Jesus
John 7:25-44 - Is Jesus the Christ?
John 10:22-42 - The Unbelief of the Jews
John 12:37-50 - The Jews Continue in Their Unbelief
Luke 4:14-30 - Jesus Rejected at Nazareth
Luke 9:51-56 - Samaritan Opposition
Mark 6:1-6 - A Prophet Without Honor
Mark 10:17-31 - The Rich Young Man
Mark 14:27-31 - Jesus Predicts Peter's Denial
Mark 14:66-72 - Peter Disowns Jesus
Matthew 7:15-23 - A Tree and Its Fruit
Matthew 8:28-34 - The Healing of Two Demon-possessed Men
Matthew 9:27-34 - Jesus Heals the Blind and Mute
Matthew 10:1-42 - Jesus Sends Out the Twelve
Matthew 11:20-24 - Woe on Unrepentant Cities
Matthew 12:1-14 - Lord of the Sabbath
Matthew 12:15-21 - God's Chosen Servant
Matthew 12:22-37 - Jesus and Beelzebub
Matthew 12:38-45 - The Sign of Jonah
Matthew 20:17-19 - Jesus Again Predicts His Death
Matthew 21:33-46 - The Parable of the Tenants
Matthew 22:1-14 - The Parable of the Wedding Banquet
Matthew 22:15-22 - Paying Taxes to Caesar
Matthew 22:34-40 - The Greatest Commandment
Matthew 22:41-46 - Whose Son Is the Christ?
Matthew 23:1-39 - Seven Woes
Matthew 26:1-5 - The Plot Against Jesus
Matthew 26:14-16 - Judas Agrees to Betray Jesus
Matthew 26:31-35 - Jesus Predicts Peter's Denial
Matthew 26:47-56 - Jesus Arrested
Matthew 26:57-68 - Before the Sanhedrin
Matthew 27:11-26 - Jesus Before Pilate
Matthew 27:27-31 - The Soldiers Mock Jesus
Matthew 27:32-44 - The Crucifixion
Matthew 28:11-15 - The Guards' Report
Romans 9:1-29 - God's Sovereign Choice
Romans 11:1-10 - The Remnant of Israel

■ RELATIONSHIPS

1 Corinthians 13:1-13 - Love
1 John 2:15-17 - Do Not Love the World
2 Corinthians 6:14–7:1 - Do Not Be Yoked with Unbelievers
John 10:1-21 - The Shepherd and His Flock
John 10:22-42 - The Unbelief of the Jews
John 13:18-30 - Jesus Predicts His Betrayal
John 14:15-31 - Jesus Promises the Holy Spirit
John 15:1-17 - The Vine and the Branches
John 20:10-18 - Jesus Appears to Mary Magdalene
Luke 1:39-45 - Mary Visits Elizabeth
Luke 6:27-36 - Love for Enemies
Luke 6:37-42 - Judging Others
Luke 9:57-62 - The Cost of Following Jesus
Mark 3:31-35 - Jesus' Mother and Brothers
Mark 11:20-26 - The Withered Fig Tree
Mark 14:66-72 - Peter Disowns Jesus
Matthew 7:1-6 - Judging Others
Philemon 1-7 - Thanksgiving and Prayer

■ RELIABILITY

Luke 1:1-4 - Introduction
Luke 1:46-56 - Mary's Song

■ RELIGION

1 Timothy 1:1-11 - Warning Against False Teachers of the Law
Acts 17:16-34 - In Athens
Acts 25:23–26:32 - Paul Before Agrippa
Galatians 1:11-24 - Paul Called by God
Hebrews 2:1-4 - Warning to Pay Attention
James 1:19-27 - Listening and Doing
John 5:1-15 - The Healing at the Pool
John 7:25-44 - Is Jesus the Christ?
John 9:35-41 - Spiritual Blindness
John 11:45-57 - The Plot to Kill Jesus
Luke 5:33-39 - Jesus Questioned About Fasting
Matthew 7:15-23 - A Tree and Its Fruit
Matthew 9:1-8 - Jesus Heals a Paralytic
Matthew 12:1-14 - Lord of the Sabbath
Matthew 15:1-20 - Clean and Unclean
Matthew 21:12-17 - Jesus at the Temple
Matthew 24:1-35 - Signs of the End of the Age
Matthew 27:1-10 - Judas Hangs Himself
Matthew 28:11-15 - The Guards' Report

■ REMARRIAGE

Matthew 5:31-32 - Divorce

■ REMEMBERING

1 Corinthians 11:17-34 - The Lord's Supper
2 Peter 1:12-21 - Prophecy of Scripture
Luke 22:7-38 - The Last Supper
Luke 24:1-12 - The Resurrection
Mark 8:14-21 - The Yeast of the Pharisees and Herod
Mark 14:12-26 - The Lord's Supper

■ RENEWAL

2 Corinthians 4:1-18 - Treasures in Jars of Clay
Acts 3:11-26 - Peter Speaks to the Onlookers
Colossians 3:1-17 - Rules for Holy Living

■ REPENTANCE

2 Corinthians 7:2-16 - Paul's Joy
2 Peter 2:1-22 - False Teachers and Their Destruction
2 Peter 3:1-18 - The Day of the Lord
2 Timothy 2:14-26 - A Workman Approved by God
Acts 2:14-41 - Peter Addresses the Crowd
Acts 11:1-18 - Peter Explains His Actions
Hebrews 5:11–6:12 - Warning Against Falling Away
James 4:1-12 - Submit Yourselves to God
Luke 3:1-20 - John the Baptist Prepares the Way
Luke 5:27-32 - The Calling of Levi
Luke 11:29-32 - The Sign of Jonah
Luke 13:1-9 - Repent or Perish
Luke 15:1-7 - The Parable of the Lost Sheep
Luke 15:8-10 - The Parable of the Lost Coin
Luke 17:1-10 - Sin, Faith, Duty
Luke 19:1-10 - Zacchaeus the Tax Collector
Luke 22:54-62 - Peter Disowns Jesus
Mark 1:1-8 - John the Baptist Prepares the Way
Mark 6:7-13 - Jesus Sends Out the Twelve
Matthew 3:1-12 - John the Baptist Prepares the Way
Matthew 4:12-17 - Jesus Begins to Preach
Matthew 11:20-24 - Woe on Unrepentant Cities
Matthew 21:28-32 - The Parable of the Two Sons
Matthew 27:1-10 - Judas Hangs Himself
Revelation 2:1-7 - To the Church in Ephesus
Revelation 2:12-17 - To the Church in Pergamum
Revelation 2:18-29 - To the Church in Thyatira

Revelation 3:1-6 - To the Church in Sardis
Revelation 3:14-22 - To the Church in Laodicea
Revelation 16:1-21 - The Seven Bowls of God's Wrath
Romans 2:1-16 - God's Righteous Judgment
Romans 11:11-24 - Ingrafted Branches
■ **REPRESENTATIVES**
Luke 7:1-10 - The Faith of the Centurion
Mark 9:2-13 - The Transfiguration
■ **REPUTATION**
1 Timothy 3:1-16 - Overseers and Deacons
2 Timothy 3:10–4:8 - Paul's Charge to Timothy
3 John 1-14 - From the Elder
Acts 5:12-16 - The Apostles Heal Many
Acts 16:1-5 - Timothy Joins Paul and Silas
Luke 5:27-32 - The Calling of Levi
Luke 7:1-10 - The Faith of the Centurion
Mark 15:1-15 - Jesus Before Pilate
Matthew 5:13-16 - Salt and Light
Matthew 13:53-58 - A Prophet Without Honor
Matthew 17:24-27 - The Temple Tax
Matthew 20:29-34 - Two Blind Men Receive Sight
Matthew 21:23-27 - The Authority of Jesus Questioned
Matthew 27:57-61 - The Burial of Jesus
Philippians 1:12-30 - Paul's Chains Advance the Gospel
Philippians 3:1-11 - No Confidence in the Flesh
Revelation 3:1-6 - To the Church in Sardis
■ **RESENTMENT**
Mark 11:20-26 - The Withered Fig Tree
Matthew 20:1-16 - The Parable of the Workers in the Vineyard
Matthew 21:23-27 - The Authority of Jesus Questioned
Matthew 26:1-5 - The Plot Against Jesus
■ **RESOURCES**
1 Timothy 5:1–6:2 - Advice About Widows, Elders and Slaves
Luke 16:1-15 - The Parable of the Shrewd Manager
Luke 19:11-27 - The Parable of the Ten Minas
Matthew 6:19-24 - Treasures in Heaven
Matthew 15:29-39 - Jesus Feeds the Four Thousand
Matthew 25:14-30 - The Parable of the Talents
■ **RESPECT**
1 Corinthians 11:17-34 - The Lord's Supper
1 Thessalonians 5:12-28 - Final Instructions
1 Timothy 3:1-16 - Overseers and Deacons
Acts 10:9-23 - Peter's Vision
Ephesians 5:22-33 - Wives and Husbands
Ephesians 6:5-9 - Slaves and Masters
Luke 1:39-45 - Mary Visits Elizabeth
Luke 23:50-56 - Jesus' Burial
Mark 15:42-47 - The Burial of Jesus
Matthew 16:1-4 - The Demand for a Sign
■ **RESPONSIBILITY**
1 Corinthians 16:5-24 - Personal Requests
1 Timothy 3:1-16 - Overseers and Deacons
Acts 6:1-7 - The Choosing of the Seven
Luke 9:10-17 - Jesus Feeds the Five Thousand
Luke 19:11-27 - The Parable of the Ten Minas
Mark 4:21-25 - A Lamp on a Stand
Matthew 7:24-29 - The Wise and Foolish Builders
Matthew 14:1-12 - John the Baptist Beheaded
Matthew 17:24-27 - The Temple Tax
Matthew 18:1-9 - The Greatest in the Kingdom of Heaven
Matthew 22:15-22 - Paying Taxes to Caesar
Revelation 10:1-11 - The Angel and the Little Scroll
■ **REST**
2 Corinthians 1:1-11 - The God of All Comfort
Hebrews 3:7-19 - Warning Against Unbelief
Hebrews 4:1-13 - A Sabbath-Rest for the People of God
Mark 2:23-3:6 - Lord of the Sabbath
Mark 6:30-44 - Jesus Feeds the Five Thousand
Matthew 11:25-30 - Rest for the Weary
■ **RESTITUTION**
Philemon 8-25 - Paul's Plea for Onesimus
■ **RESTORATION**
2 Corinthians 2:5-11 - Forgiveness for the Sinner
Acts 9:1-19 - Saul's Conversion
Galatians 6:1-10 - Doing Good to All
Luke 4:31-37 - Jesus Drives Out an Evil Spirit
Luke 5:12-16 - The Man With Leprosy
Luke 15:1-7 - The Parable of the Lost Sheep
Mark 8:22-26 - The Healing of a Blind Man at Bethsaida
Matthew 18:10-14 - The Parable of the Lost Sheep
■ **RESULTS**
Matthew 10:1-42 - Jesus Sends Out the Twelve
Matthew 13:31-35 - The Parables of the Mustard Seed and the Yeast
Matthew 15:21-28 - The Faith of the Canaanite Woman
■ **RESURRECTION**
1 Corinthians 15:1-11 - The Resurrection of Christ
1 Corinthians 15:12-34 - The Resurrection of the Dead
1 Corinthians 15:35-58 - The Resurrection Body
1 Peter 1:1-12 - Praise to God for a Living Hope
1 Peter 3:8-22 - Suffering for Doing Good
1 Thessalonians 4:13–5:11 - The Coming of the Lord
Acts 4:32-37 - The Believers Share Their Possessions
Acts 10:24-48 - Peter at Cornelius' House
Acts 13:13-52 - In Pisidian Antioch
Acts 17:1-9 - In Thessalonica
Acts 17:16-34 - In Athens
Acts 22:30–23:11 - Before the Sanhedrin
Acts 24:1-27 - The Trial Before Felix
John 2:12-25 - Jesus Clears the Temple
John 11:17-37 - Jesus Comforts the Sisters
John 11:38-44 - Jesus Raises Lazarus From the Dead
John 20:1-9 - The Empty Tomb
John 20:10-18 - Jesus Appears to Mary Magdalene
John 20:19-23 - Jesus Appears to His Disciples
John 20:24-31 - Jesus Appears to Thomas
Luke 7:11-17 - Jesus Raises a Widow's Son
Luke 8:40-56 - A Dead Girl and a Sick Woman
Luke 14:1-14 - Jesus at a Pharisee's House
Luke 18:31-34 - Jesus Again Predicts His Death
Luke 20:27-40 - The Resurrection and Marriage
Luke 24:1-12 - The Resurrection
Luke 24:36-49 - Jesus Appears to the Disciples
Mark 10:32-34 - Jesus Again Predicts His Death
Mark 12:18-27 - Marriage at the Resurrection
Mark 16:1-20 - The Resurrection
Matthew 9:18-26 - A Dead Girl and a Sick Woman
Matthew 16:21-28 - Jesus Predicts His Death
Matthew 17:14-23 - The Healing of a Boy With a Demon
Matthew 20:17-19 - Jesus Again Predicts His Death

Matthew 22:23-33 - Marriage at the Resurrection
Matthew 28:1-10 - The Resurrection
Philippians 3:1-11 - No Confidence in the Flesh
Revelation 1:4-8 - Greetings and Doxology
Revelation 1:9-20 - One Like a Son of Man
Revelation 2:8-11 - To the Church in Smyrna
Revelation 11:1-14 - The Two Witnesses
Revelation 20:1-6 - The Thousand Years
Revelation 20:11-15 - The Dead Are Judged

■ **REVENGE**

1 Thessalonians 5:12-28 - Final Instructions
Luke 6:27-36 - Love for Enemies
Matthew 5:38-42 - An Eye for an Eye
Matthew 26:1-5 - The Plot Against Jesus
Romans 12:9-21 - Love

■ **REWARDS**

1 Corinthians 9:1-27 - The Rights of an Apostle
1 Peter 5:1-14 - To Elders and Young Men
1 Thessalonians 2:17–3:5 - Paul's Longing to See the Thessalonians
2 John 1-13 - From the Elder
2 Peter 1:1-11 - Making One's Calling and Election Sure
2 Thessalonians 1:1-12 - Thanksgiving and Prayer
2 Timothy 3:10–4:8 - Paul's Charge to Timothy
Colossians 3:18–4:1 - Rules for Christian Households
Ephesians 6:5-9 - Slaves and Masters
Galatians 6:1-10 - Doing Good to All
Hebrews 10:19-39 - A Call to Persevere
James 3:13-18 - Two Kinds of Wisdom
John 15:1-17 - The Vine and the Branches
Luke 19:11-27 - The Parable of the Ten Minas
Mark 8:31–9:1 - Jesus Predicts His Death
Mark 9:38-41 - Whoever Is Not Against Us Is for Us
Mark 10:17-31 - The Rich Young Man
Matthew 5:1-12 - The Beatitudes
Matthew 6:1-4 - Giving to the Needy
Matthew 6:19-24 - Treasures in Heaven
Matthew 10:1-42 - Jesus Sends Out the Twelve
Matthew 19:16-30 - The Rich Young Man
Matthew 20:20-28 - A Mother's Request
Matthew 24:1-35 - Signs of the End of the Age
Matthew 25:14-30 - The Parable of the Talents
Revelation 3:7-13 - To the Church in Philadelphia
Revelation 11:15-19 - The Seventh Trumpet

■ **RIGHT**

1 Corinthians 9:1-27 - The Rights of an Apostle
Acts 25:1-12 - The Trial Before Festus
Colossians 3:18-4:1 - Rules for Christian Households

■ **RIGHTEOUSNESS**

1 Peter 2:13-25 - Submission to Rulers and Masters
1 Peter 3:8-22 - Suffering for Doing Good
1 Timothy 6:11-21 - Paul's Charge to Timothy
2 Peter 2:1-22 - False Teachers and Their Destruction
2 Timothy 3:10–4:8 - Paul's Charge to Timothy
Ephesians 4:17–5:21 - Living as Children of Light
Galatians 2:11-21 - Paul Opposes Peter
Galatians 3:1-14 - Faith or Observance of the Law
Galatians 3:15-25 - The Law and the Promise
Galatians 5:1-15 - Freedom in Christ
Hebrews 5:11–6:12 - Warning Against Falling Away
Hebrews 7:1-10 - Melchizedek the Priest
Hebrews 12:1-3 - God Disciplines His Sons
James 2:14-26 - Faith and Deeds
John 16:5-16 - The Work of the Holy Spirit
Luke 14:1-14 - Jesus at a Pharisee's House
Luke 18:9-14 - The Parable of the Pharisee and the Tax Collector
Luke 23:44-49 - Jesus' Death
Matthew 5:1-12 - The Beatitudes
Matthew 5:13-16 - Salt and Light
Matthew 5:43-48 - Love for Enemies
Matthew 13:36-43 - The Parable of the Weeds Explained
Matthew 13:47-52 - The Parable of the Net
Matthew 19:16-30 - The Rich Young Man
Matthew 25:31-46 - The Sheep and the Goats
Philippians 1:1-11 - Thanksgiving and Prayer
Philippians 3:1-11 - No Confidence in the Flesh
Revelation 14:1-5 - The Lamb and the 144,000
Revelation 15:1-8 - Seven Angels With Seven Plagues
Romans 3:9-20 - No One Is Righteous
Romans 3:21-31 - Righteousness Through Faith
Romans 4:1-25 - Abraham Justified by Faith
Romans 6:15-23 - Slaves to Righteousness
Romans 9:30–10:21 - Israel's Unbelief
Titus 2:1-15 - What Must Be Taught to Various Groups

■ **RISK**

Hebrews 11:1-40 - By Faith
Luke 14:25-35 - The Cost of Being a Disciple
Mark 15:42-47 - The Burial of Jesus
Matthew 9:9-13 - The Calling of Matthew
Matthew 10:1-42 - Jesus Sends Out the Twelve
Matthew 18:21-35 - The Parable of the Unmerciful Servant
Matthew 26:69-75 - Peter Disowns Jesus
Philippians 2:19-30 - Timothy and Epaphroditus

■ **RULES**

Acts 21:17-26 - Paul's Arrival at Jerusalem
Acts 24:1-27 - The Trial Before Felix
Colossians 2:6-23 - Freedom From Human Regulations Through Life With Christ
John 18:28-40 - Jesus Before Pilate
Luke 5:33-39 - Jesus Questioned About Fasting
Mark 7:1-23 - Clean and Unclean

■ **RUNNING**

John 20:1-9 - The Empty Tomb

■ **SACRIFICE**

1 Corinthians 5:1-13 - Expel the Immoral Brother!
1 Corinthians 9:1-27 - The Rights of an Apostle
1 Corinthians 10:14-22 - Idol Feasts and the Lord's Supper
1 Corinthians 10:23–11:1 - The Believer's Freedom
1 Corinthians 16:1-4 - The Collection for God's People
1 John 1:5–2:14 - Walking in the Light
1 John 4:7-21 - God's Love and Ours
1 Peter 1:13–2:3 - Be Holy
1 Peter 2:4-12 - The Living Stone and a Chosen People
1 Peter 3:8-22 - Suffering for Doing Good
2 Corinthians 1:1-11 - The God of All Comfort
2 Corinthians 8:1-15 - Generosity Encouraged
2 Corinthians 8:16–9:5 - Titus Sent to Corinth
2 Corinthians 12:11-21 - Paul's Concern for the Corinthians
Hebrews 4:14–5:10 - Jesus the Great High Priest

Hebrews 8:1-13 - The High Priest of a New Covenant
Hebrews 9:1-10 - Worship in the Earthly Tabernacle
Hebrews 9:11-28 - The Blood of Christ
Hebrews 10:1-18 - Christ's Sacrifice Once for All
John 10:1-21 - The Shepherd and His Flock
John 13:31-38 - Jesus Predicts Peter's Denial
John 19:17-27 - The Crucifixion
John 19:28-37 - The Death of Jesus
Luke 5:12-16 - The Man With Leprosy
Luke 9:18-27 - Peter's Confession of Christ
Luke 13:1-9 - Repent or Perish
Luke 18:31-34 - Jesus Again Predicts His Death
Luke 21:1-4 - The Widow's Offering
Luke 22:7-38 - The Last Supper
Mark 1:14-20 - The Calling of the First Disciples
Mark 1:35-39 - Jesus Prays in a Solitary Place
Mark 1:40-45 - A Man With Leprosy
Mark 3:20-30 - Jesus and Beelzebub
Mark 3:31-35 - Jesus' Mother and Brothers
Mark 6:7-13 - Jesus Sends Out the Twelve
Mark 6:14-29 - John the Baptist Beheaded
Mark 8:31–9:1 - Jesus Predicts His Death
Mark 9:33-37 - Who Is the Greatest?
Mark 10:17-31 - The Rich Young Man
Mark 10:35-45 - The Request of James and John
Mark 12:28-34 - The Greatest Commandment
Mark 12:41-44 - The Widow's Offering
Mark 14:1-11 - Jesus Anointed at Bethany
Mark 14:12-26 - The Lord's Supper
Mark 15:16-20 - The Soldiers Mock Jesus
Mark 15:21-32 - The Crucifixion
Mark 15:33-41 - The Death of Jesus
Matthew 2:1-12 - The Visit of the Magi
Matthew 10:1-42 - Jesus Sends Out the Twelve
Matthew 12:1-14 - Lord of the Sabbath
Matthew 16:21-28 - Jesus Predicts His Death
Matthew 20:17-19 - Jesus Again Predicts His Death
Matthew 26:6-13 - Jesus Anointed at Bethany
Matthew 26:17-30 - The Lord's Supper
Matthew 26:47-56 - Jesus Arrested
Matthew 27:32-44 - The Crucifixion
Matthew 27:45-56 - The Death of Jesus
Philippians 2:12-18 - Shining as Stars
Philippians 2:19-30 - Timothy and Epaphroditus
Philippians 4:10-23 - Thanks for Their Gifts
Revelation 5:1-14 - The Scroll and the Lamb
Revelation 8:1-5 - The Seventh Seal and the Golden Censer
Romans 12:1-8 - Living Sacrifices

■ SALVATION

1 Corinthians 5:1-13 - Expel the Immoral Brother!
1 Corinthians 9:1-27 - The Rights of an Apostle
1 Corinthians 10:23–11:1 - The Believer's Freedom
1 Corinthians 15:1-11 - The Resurrection of Christ
1 Peter 1:1-12 - Praise to God for a Living Hope
1 Peter 1:13–2:3 - Be Holy
1 Peter 3:8-22 - Suffering for Doing Good
1 Timothy 1:12-20 - The Lord's Grace to Paul
1 Timothy 2:1-15 - Instructions on Worship
1 Timothy 4:1-16 - Instructions to Timothy
2 Corinthians 7:2-16 - Paul's Joy
2 Peter 3:1-18 - The Day of the Lord
2 Thessalonians 3:1-5 - Request for Prayer
2 Timothy 1:1–2:13 - Encouragement to Be Faithful
Acts 2:14-41 - Peter Addresses the Crowd
Acts 2:42-47 - The Fellowship of the Believers
Acts 4:1-22 - Peter and John Before the Sanhedrin
Acts 9:1-19 - Saul's Conversion
Acts 11:1-18 - Peter Explains His Actions
Acts 13:13-52 - In Pisidian Antioch
Acts 16:16-40 - Paul and Silas in Prison
Acts 21:37–22:21 - Paul Speaks to the Crowd
Acts 28:17-31 - Paul Preaches at Rome Under Guard
Ephesians 1:1-14 - Spiritual Blessings in Christ
Hebrews 2:1-4 - Warning to Pay Attention
Hebrews 2:5-18 - Jesus Made Like His Brothers
Hebrews 4:14–5:10 - Jesus the Great High Priest
Hebrews 5:11–6:12 - Warning Against Falling Away
Hebrews 10:19-39 - A Call to Persevere
John 3:1-22 - Jesus Teaches Nicodemus
John 4:1-26 - Jesus Talks With a Samaritan Woman
John 4:39-42 - Many Samaritans Believe
John 5:16-30 - Life Through the Son
John 6:25-59 - Jesus the Bread of Life
John 8:31-41 - The Children of Abraham
John 10:1-21 - The Shepherd and His Flock
John 11:17-37 - Jesus Comforts the Sisters
John 12:37-50 - The Jews Continue in Their Unbelief
John 20:24-31 - Jesus Appears to Thomas
Jude 1-16 - The Sin and Doom of Godless Men
Luke 1:67-80 - Zechariah's Song
Luke 7:36-50 - Jesus Anointed by a Sinful Woman
Luke 13:22-30 - The Narrow Door
Luke 15:11-32 - The Parable of the Lost Son
Luke 19:1-10 - Zacchaeus the Tax Collector
Luke 23:26-43 - The Crucifixion
Mark 10:13-16 - The Little Children and Jesus
Mark 10:17-31 - The Rich Young Man
Mark 15:21-32 - The Crucifixion
Matthew 20:1-16 - The Parable of the Workers in the Vineyard
Matthew 28:1-10 - The Resurrection
Matthew 28:16-20 - The Great Commission
Philippians 1:12-30 - Paul's Chains Advance the Gospel
Philippians 2:12-18 - Shining as Stars
Revelation 7:9-17 - The Great Multitude in White Robes
Revelation 12:1–13:1 - The Woman and the Dragon
Revelation 19:1-10 - Hallelujah!
Romans 1:8-17 - Paul's Longing to Visit Rome
Romans 3:9-20 - No One Is Righteous
Romans 6:1-14 - Dead to Sin, Alive in Christ
Romans 9:30–10:21 - Israel's Unbelief
Romans 11:11-24 - Ingrafted Branches
Romans 11:25-32 - All Israel Will Be Saved
Titus 3:1-15 - Doing What Is Good

■ SATAN

1 John 1:5-2:14 - Walking in the Light
1 John 2:28–3:10 - Children of God
1 John 3:11-24 - Love One Another
1 John 4:1-6 - Test the Spirits
1 John 5:13-21 - Concluding Remarks
1 Peter 5:1-14 - To Elders and Young Men
1 Thessalonians 2:17–3:5 - Paul's Longing to See the Thessalonians

1 Timothy 5:1–6:2 - Advice About Widows, Elders and Slaves
2 Corinthians 2:5-11 - Forgiveness for the Sinner
2 Corinthians 4:1-18 - Treasures in Jars of Clay
2 Corinthians 11:1-15 - Paul and the False Apostles
2 Timothy 2:14-26 - A Workman Approved by God
Acts 5:1-11 - Ananias and Sapphira
Acts 13:4-12 - On Cyprus
Ephesians 6:10-24 - The Armor of God
Hebrews 2:5-18 - Jesus Made Like His Brothers
John 6:60-71 - Many Disciples Desert Jesus
John 8:42-47 - The Children of the Devil
John 12:20-36 - Jesus Predicts His Death
John 13:18-30 - Jesus Predicts His Betrayal
John 17:6-19 - Jesus Prays for His Disciples
Luke 4:1-13 - The Temptation of Jesus
Luke 8:1-15 - The Parable of the Sower
Luke 11:14-28 - Jesus and Beelzebub
Luke 13:10-17 - A Crippled Woman Healed on the Sabbath
Mark 1:9-13 - The Baptism and Temptation of Jesus
Mark 3:20-30 - Jesus and Beelzebub
Matthew 4:1-11 - The Temptation of Jesus
Matthew 8:28-34 - The Healing of Two Demon-possessed Men
Matthew 12:22-37 - Jesus and Beelzebub
Matthew 13:24-30 - The Parable of the Weeds
Matthew 13:36-43 - The Parable of the Weeds Explained
Matthew 24:1-35 - Signs of the End of the Age
Matthew 25:31-46 - The Sheep and the Goats
Revelation 2:8-11 - To the Church in Smyrna
Revelation 2:12-17 - To the Church in Pergamum
Revelation 2:18-29 - To the Church in Thyatira
Revelation 12:1–13:1 - The Woman and the Dragon
Revelation 13:2-10 - The Beast out of the Sea
Revelation 13:11-18 - The Beast out of the Earth
Revelation 15:1-8 - Seven Angels With Seven Plagues
Revelation 20:1-6 - The Thousand Years
Revelation 20:7-10 - Satan's Doom

■ SATISFACTION

1 John 2:15-17 - Do Not Love the World
John 4:1-26 - Jesus Talks With a Samaritan Woman
John 7:25-44 - Is Jesus the Christ?
Matthew 13:44-46 - The Parables of the Hidden Treasure and the Pearl
Matthew 16:1-4 - The Demand for a Sign

■ SCHEDULE

Luke 2:1-7 - The Birth of Jesus
Matthew 19:13-15 - The Little Children and Jesus

■ SECOND COMING

1 John 2:28–3:10 - Children of God
1 Peter 4:12-19 - Suffering for Being a Christian
1 Thessalonians 3:6-13 - Timothy's Encouraging Report
1 Thessalonians 4:13–5:11 - The Coming of the Lord
2 Thessalonians 1:1-12 - Thanksgiving and Prayer
2 Thessalonians 2:1-12 - The Man of Lawlessness
2 Timothy 3:10–4:8 - Paul's Charge to Timothy
Jude 1-16 - The Sin and Doom of Godless Men
Luke 12:35-48 - Watchfulness
Luke 17:20-37 - The Coming of the Kingdom of God
Luke 21:5-38 - Signs of the End of the Age
Mark 8:31–9:1 - Jesus Predicts His Death
Mark 13:1-31 - Signs of the End of the Age
Matthew 16:21-28 - Jesus Predicts His Death
Matthew 24:1-35 - Signs of the End of the Age
Matthew 24:36-51 - The Day and Hour Unknown
Matthew 25:1-13 - The Parable of the Ten Virgins
Matthew 25:31-46 - The Sheep and the Goats
Matthew 26:57-68 - Before the Sanhedrin
Revelation 1:4-8 - Greetings and Doxology
Revelation 3:1-6 - To the Church in Sardis

■ SECURITY

Colossians 3:1-17 - Rules for Holy Living
John 1:29-34 - Jesus the Lamb of God
John 5:16-30 - Life Through the Son
John 6:25-59 - Jesus the Bread of Life
John 6:60-71 - Many Disciples Desert Jesus
John 7:25-44 - Is Jesus the Christ?
John 14:1-4 - Jesus Comforts His Disciples
John 14:15-31 - Jesus Promises the Holy Spirit
Luke 6:46-49 - The Wise and Foolish Builders
Matthew 2:19-23 - The Return to Nazareth
Matthew 7:24-29 - The Wise and Foolish Builders
Matthew 8:23-27 - Jesus Calms the Storm
Matthew 14:22-36 - Jesus Walks on the Water
Romans 8:28-39 - More Than Conquerors

■ SELF-CENTEREDNESS

2 Timothy 3:1-9 - Godlessness in the Last Days
3 John 1-14 - From the Elder
Galatians 6:1-10 - Doing Good to All
John 11:45-57 - The Plot to Kill Jesus
John 12:20-36 - Jesus Predicts His Death
John 13:1-17 - Jesus Washes His Disciples' Feet
John 18:25-27 - Peter's Second and Third Denials
John 19:1-16 - Jesus Sentenced to be Crucified
Mark 12:35-40 - Whose Son Is the Christ?
Philippians 2:1-11 - Imitating Christ's Humility
Romans 1:18-32 - God's Wrath Against Mankind

■ SELF-ESTEEM

1 John 2:15-17 - Do Not Love the World
1 Peter 3:1-7 - Wives and Husbands
John 6:25-59 - Jesus the Bread of Life
Romans 12:1-8 - Living Sacrifices

■ SELF-RIGHTEOUSNESS

John 7:53–8:11 - A Woman Caught in Adultery
John 11:45-57 - The Plot to Kill Jesus
John 18:19-24 - The High Priest Questions Jesus
Luke 9:46-50 - Who Will Be the Greatest?
Luke 14:1-14 - Jesus at a Pharisee's House
Mark 12:35-40 - Whose Son Is the Christ?
Matthew 6:5-15 - Prayer
Matthew 15:1-20 - Clean and Unclean
Matthew 25:31-46 - The Sheep and the Goats
Romans 2:17-29 - The Jews and the Law
Romans 3:1-8 - God's Faithfulness
Romans 9:30–10:21 - Israel's Unbelief

■ SELFISHNESS

John 12:20-36 - Jesus Predicts His Death
Matthew 14:13-21 - Jesus Feeds the Five Thousand
Matthew 26:36-46 - Gethsemane

■ SENSITIVITY

Matthew 8:1-4 - The Man With Leprosy
Matthew 8:14-17 - Jesus Heals Many

■ **SEPARATION**
1 Thessalonians 2:17–3:5 - Paul's Longing to See the Thessalonians
2 Corinthians 6:14–7:1 - Do Not Be Yoked with Unbelievers
Ephesians 2:11-22 - One in Christ
Ephesians 4:17–5:21 - Living as Children of Light
Mark 8:22-26 - The Healing of a Blind Man at Bethsaida
Mark 10:1-12 - Divorce
Matthew 16:5-12 - The Yeast of the Pharisees and Sadducees
Matthew 25:31-46 - The Sheep and the Goats
Matthew 26:14-16 - Judas Agrees to Betray Jesus
Matthew 27:45-56 - The Death of Jesus
Romans 1:18-32 - God's Wrath Against Mankind

■ **SERVING**
1 Corinthians 9:1-27 - The Rights of an Apostle
1 Corinthians 12:1-11 - Spiritual Gifts
1 Peter 4:1-11 - Living for God
1 Peter 5:1-14 - To Elders and Young Men
1 Timothy 1:12-20 - The Lord's Grace to Paul
1 Timothy 5:1–6:2 - Advice About Widows, Elders and Slaves
2 Corinthians 6:3-13 - Paul's Hardships
2 Corinthians 8:1-15 - Generosity Encouraged
2 Corinthians 9:6-15 - Sowing Generously
3 John 1-14 - From the Elder
Acts 20:13-38 - Paul's Farewell to the Ephesian Elders
Acts 25:23–26:32 - Paul Before Agrippa
Colossians 1:24–2:5 - Paul's Labor for the Church
Colossians 4:2-18 - Further Instructions
Ephesians 3:1-13 - Paul the Preacher to the Gentiles
Ephesians 4:1-16 - Unity in the Body of Christ
Ephesians 6:5-9 - Slaves and Masters
Galatians 5:1-15 - Freedom in Christ
John 13:1-17 - Jesus Washes His Disciples' Feet
John 21:15-25 - Jesus Reinstates Peter
Luke 1:26-38 - The Birth of Jesus Foretold
Luke 3:1-20 - John the Baptist Prepares the Way
Luke 14:15-24 - The Parable of the Great Banquet
Luke 16:1-15 - The Parable of the Shrewd Manager
Luke 17:1-10 - Sin, Faith, Duty
Luke 19:11-27 - The Parable of the Ten Minas
Luke 22:7-38 - The Last Supper
Mark 1:21-28 - Jesus Drives Out an Evil Spirit
Mark 9:33-37 - Who Is the Greatest?
Mark 10:35-45 - The Request of James and John
Matthew 8:14-17 - Jesus Heals Many
Matthew 10:1-42 - Jesus Sends Out the Twelve
Matthew 12:15-21 - God's Chosen Servant
Matthew 15:29-39 - Jesus Feeds the Four Thousand
Matthew 20:20-28 - A Mother's Request
Matthew 25:14-30 - The Parable of the Talents
Philippians 1:1-11 - Thanksgiving and Prayer
Philippians 2:1-11 - Imitating Christ's Humility
Philippians 2:12-18 - Shining as Stars
Revelation 1:4-8 - Greetings and Doxology
Revelation 2:18-29 - To the Church in Thyatira
Revelation 5:1-14 - The Scroll and the Lamb
Revelation 7:1-8 - 144,000 Sealed
Revelation 7:9-17 - The Great Multitude in White Robes
Revelation 8:1-5 - The Seventh Seal and the Golden Censer
Revelation 11:15-19 - The Seventh Trumpet
Revelation 19:1-10 - Hallelujah!
Romans 15:14-22 - Paul, the Minister to the Gentiles
Romans 15:23-33 - Paul's Plan to Visit Rome
Romans 16:1-27 - Personal Greetings
Titus 1:1-16 - Titus' Task on Crete

■ **SEX**
1 Corinthians 6:12-20 - Sexual Immorality
1 Corinthians 7:1-40 - Marriage
1 Peter 4:1-11 - Living for God
1 Thessalonians 4:1-12 - Living to Please God
1 Timothy 2:1-15 - Instructions on Worship
Romans 1:18-32 - God's Wrath Against Mankind

■ **SHAME**
1 Peter 4:12-19 - Suffering for Being a Christian
Luke 4:14-30 - Jesus Rejected at Nazareth
Luke 9:18-27 - Peter's Confession of Christ
Luke 22:63-65 - The Guards Mock Jesus
Matthew 8:1-4 - The Man With Leprosy
Matthew 27:1-10 - Judas Hangs Himself
Philippians 3:12–4:1 - Pressing on Toward the Goal

■ **SICKNESS**
2 Timothy 4:9-22 - Personal Remarks
Acts 5:12-16 - The Apostles Heal Many
Acts 28:1-10 - Ashore on Malta
Galatians 4:8-20 - Paul's Concern for the Galatians
James 5:13-20 - The Prayer of Faith
John 4:43-54 - Jesus Heals the Official's Son
John 11:1-16 - The Death of Lazarus
Luke 4:38-44 - Jesus Heals Many
Luke 5:12-16 - The Man With Leprosy
Luke 5:17-26 - Jesus Heals a Paralytic
Mark 1:21-28 - Jesus Drives Out an Evil Spirit
Mark 1:40-45 - A Man With Leprosy
Mark 2:1-12 - Jesus Heals a Paralytic
Mark 3:7-12 - Crowds Follow Jesus
Mark 5:21-43 - A Dead Girl and a Sick Woman
Mark 6:45-56 - Jesus Walks on the Water
Matthew 4:23-25 - Jesus Heals the Sick
Matthew 8:1-4 - The Man With Leprosy
Matthew 12:22-37 - Jesus and Beelzebub
Philippians 2:19-30 - Timothy and Epaphroditus
Revelation 16:1-21 - The Seven Bowls of God's Wrath

■ **SILENCE**
Luke 1:57-66 - The Birth of John the Baptist
Luke 20:20-26 - Paying Taxes to Caesar
Mark 14:53-65 - Before the Sanhedrin
Matthew 27:11-26 - Jesus Before Pilate
Revelation 8:1-5 - The Seventh Seal and the Golden Censer
Revelation 10:1-11 - The Angel and the Little Scroll

■ **SIMPLICITY**
Luke 2:1-7 - The Birth of Jesus
Matthew 9:14-17 - Jesus Questioned About Fasting
Matthew 13:31-35 - The Parables of the Mustard Seed and the Yeast
Matthew 18:1-9 - The Greatest in the Kingdom of Heaven

■ **SIN**
1 Corinthians 5:1-13 - Expel the Immoral Brother!

1 Corinthians 6:1-11 - Lawsuits Among Believers
1 Corinthians 6:12-20 - Sexual Immorality
1 Corinthians 7:1-40 - Marriage
1 Corinthians 8:1-13 - Food Sacrificed to Idols
1 Corinthians 11:17-34 - The Lord's Supper
1 John 1:5–2:14 - Walking in the Light
1 John 2:15-17 - Do Not Love the World
1 John 2:28–3:10 - Children of God
1 John 4:7-21 - God's Love and Ours
1 John 5:13-21 - Concluding Remarks
1 Peter 1:13–2:3 - Be Holy
1 Peter 2:4-12 - The Living Stone and a Chosen People
1 Peter 2:13-25 - Submission to Rulers and Masters
1 Peter 3:8-22 - Suffering for Doing Good
1 Peter 4:1-11 - Living for God
1 Timothy 1:1-11 - Warning Against False Teachers of the Law
1 Timothy 1:12-20 - The Lord's Grace to Paul
1 Timothy 2:1-15 - Instructions on Worship
2 Corinthians 2:5-11 - Forgiveness for the Sinner
2 Corinthians 11:16-33 - Paul Boasts About His Sufferings
2 Corinthians 12:11-21 - Paul's Concern for the Corinthians
2 Corinthians 13:1-14 - Final Warnings
2 Peter 1:1-11 - Making One's Calling and Election Sure
2 Peter 2:1-22 - False Teachers and Their Destruction
2 Timothy 3:1-9 - Godlessness in the Last Days
Acts 3:11-26 - Peter Speaks to the Onlookers
Acts 4:1-22 - Peter and John Before the Sanhedrin
Acts 5:1-11 - Ananias and Sapphira
Acts 8:9-25 - Simon the Sorcerer
Acts 21:37–22:21 - Paul Speaks to the Crowd
Colossians 1:1-14 - Thanksgiving and Prayer
Colossians 3:1-17 - Rules for Holy Living
Ephesians 2:1-10 - Made Alive in Christ
Ephesians 4:17–5:21 - Living as Children of Light
Galatians 3:15-25 - The Law and the Promise
Galatians 5:1-15 - Freedom in Christ
Galatians 5:16-26 - Life by the Spirit
Galatians 6:1-10 - Doing Good to All
Hebrews 3:7-19 - Warning Against Unbelief
Hebrews 4:1-13 - A Sabbath-Rest for the People of God
Hebrews 12:1-3 - God Disciplines His Sons
James 4:13-17 - Boasting About Tomorrow
John 1:29-34 - Jesus the Lamb of God
John 5:1-15 - The Healing at the Pool
John 7:53–8:11 - A Woman Caught in Adultery
John 8:31-41 - The Children of Abraham
John 8:42-47 - The Children of the Devil
John 9:1-12 - Jesus Heals a Man Born Blind
John 9:13-34 - The Pharisees Investigate the Healing
John 9:35-41 - Spiritual Blindness
John 10:22-42 - The Unbelief of the Jews
John 11:1-16 - The Death of Lazarus
John 15:18–16:4 - The World Hates the Disciples
John 16:5-16 - The Work of the Holy Spirit
John 20:19-23 - Jesus Appears to His Disciples
Jude 1-16 - The Sin and Doom of Godless Men
Luke 7:36-50 - Jesus Anointed by a Sinful Woman
Luke 15:1-7 - The Parable of the Lost Sheep
Luke 15:8-10 - The Parable of the Lost Coin
Luke 17:1-10 - Sin, Faith, Duty
Mark 2:1-12 - Jesus Heals a Paralytic
Mark 3:20-30 - Jesus and Beelzebub
Mark 6:14-29 - John the Baptist Beheaded
Mark 9:42-50 - Causing to Sin
Matthew 11:20-24 - Woe on Unrepentant Cities
Matthew 13:36-43 - The Parable of the Weeds Explained
Matthew 14:1-12 - John the Baptist Beheaded
Matthew 16:21-28 - Jesus Predicts His Death
Matthew 17:14-23 - The Healing of a Boy With a Demon
Matthew 18:1-9 - The Greatest in the Kingdom of Heaven
Matthew 21:18-22 - The Fig Tree Withers
Matthew 21:33-46 - The Parable of the Tenants
Matthew 22:34-40 - The Greatest Commandment
Matthew 23:1-39 - Seven Woes
Matthew 24:36-51 - The Day and Hour Unknown
Matthew 25:1-13 - The Parable of the Ten Virgins
Matthew 26:1-5 - The Plot Against Jesus
Matthew 26:14-16 - Judas Agrees to Betray Jesus
Matthew 26:47-56 - Jesus Arrested
Matthew 27:1-10 - Judas Hangs Himself
Matthew 27:11-26 - Jesus Before Pilate
Matthew 27:27-31 - The Soldiers Mock Jesus
Matthew 27:32-44 - The Crucifixion
Philippians 2:12-18 - Shining as Stars
Revelation 2:12-17 - To the Church in Pergamum
Revelation 2:18-29 - To the Church in Thyatira
Revelation 3:1-6 - To the Church in Sardis
Revelation 17:1-18 - The Woman on the Beast
Revelation 18:1-24 - The Fall of Babylon
Revelation 19:11-21 - The Rider on the White Horse
Revelation 22:7-21 - Jesus Is Coming
Romans 1:18-32 - God's Wrath Against Mankind
Romans 3:1-8 - God's Faithfulness
Romans 3:9-20 - No One Is Righteous
Romans 4:1-25 - Abraham Justified by Faith
Romans 5:12-21 - Death Through Adam, Life Through Christ
Romans 6:1-14 - Dead to Sin, Alive in Christ
Romans 6:15-23 - Slaves to Righteousness
Romans 7:7-25 - Struggling With Sin
Romans 8:1-17 - Life Through the Spirit
Romans 11:25-32 - All Israel Will Be Saved
Romans 13:8-14 - Love, for the Day Is Near
Romans 14:1–15:13 - The Weak and the Strong

■ SINCERITY

2 Corinthians 1:12–2:4 - Paul's Change of Plans
2 Corinthians 2:12–3:6 - Ministers of the New Covenant
Colossians 3:18–4:1 - Rules for Christian Households
Ephesians 6:5-9 - Slaves and Masters
Hebrews 6:13-20 - The Certainty of God's Promise
Hebrews 10:19-39 - A Call to Persevere
Matthew 21:28-32 - The Parable of the Two Sons

■ SINGLENESS

1 Corinthians 6:12-20 - Sexual Immorality
1 Corinthians 7:1-40 - Marriage
1 Timothy 5:1–6:2 - Advice About Widows, Elders and Slaves

■ SLAVERY

1 Corinthians 6:12-20 - Sexual Immorality
1 Corinthians 7:1-40 - Marriage

2 Peter 2:1-22 - False Teachers and Their Destruction
Colossians 3:18–4:1 - Rules for Christian Households
Ephesians 6:5-9 - Slaves and Masters
Galatians 3:26–4:7 - Sons of God
Galatians 4:8-20 - Paul's Concern for the Galatians
Galatians 4:21-31 - Hagar and Sarah
John 8:31-41 - The Children of Abraham
Philemon 1-7 - Thanksgiving and Prayer
Philemon 8-25 - Paul's Plea for Onesimus
Romans 6:1-14 - Dead to Sin, Alive in Christ
Romans 6:15-23 - Slaves to Righteousness
■ **SLEEP**
Matthew 26:36-46 - Gethsemane
Revelation 3:1-6 - To the Church in Sardis
■ **SOCIETY**
1 Timothy 2:1-15 - Instructions on Worship
2 Timothy 3:1-9 - Godlessness in the Last Days
John 7:25-44 - Is Jesus the Christ?
John 7:45-52 - Unbelief of the Jewish Leaders
■ **SOLITUDE**
Luke 4:38-44 - Jesus Heals Many
Luke 5:12-16 - The Man With Leprosy
Mark 1:35-39 - Jesus Prays in a Solitary Place
Mark 14:32-42 - Gethsemane
■ **SORROW**
2 Corinthians 2:5-11 - Forgiveness for the Sinner
2 Corinthians 7:2-16 - Paul's Joy
John 11:17-37 - Jesus Comforts the Sisters
John 11:38-44 - Jesus Raises Lazarus From the Dead
John 19:38-42 - The Burial of Jesus
John 20:1-9 - The Empty Tomb
Luke 13:31-35 - Jesus' Sorrow for Jerusalem
Luke 22:39-46 - Jesus Prays on the Mount of Olives
Luke 22:54-62 - Peter Disowns Jesus
Luke 23:44-49 - Jesus' Death
Mark 14:32-42 - Gethsemane
Mark 14:66-72 - Peter Disowns Jesus
Matthew 4:23-25 - Jesus Heals the Sick
Matthew 22:1-14 - The Parable of the Wedding Banquet
Matthew 26:69-75 - Peter Disowns Jesus
Matthew 27:1-10 - Judas Hangs Himself
■ **SOUL**
Matthew 27:1-10 - Judas Hangs Himself
■ **SOVEREIGNTY**
1 Peter 1:1-12 - Praise to God for a Living Hope
1 Timothy 2:1-15 - Instructions on Worship
2 Peter 1:1-11 - Making One's Calling and Election Sure
2 Timothy 1:1–2:13 - Encouragement to Be Faithful
John 6:16-24 - Jesus Walks on the Water
Luke 1:46-56 - Mary's Song
Matthew 1:1-17 - The Genealogy of Jesus
Matthew 2:19-23 - The Return to Nazareth
Matthew 8:1-4 - The Man With Leprosy
Matthew 8:23-27 - Jesus Calms the Storm
Matthew 24:1-35 - Signs of the End of the Age
Matthew 26:1-5 - The Plot Against Jesus
Matthew 26:47-56 - Jesus Arrested
Revelation 1:4-8 - Greetings and Doxology
Romans 9:1-29 - God's Sovereign Choice
■ **SPIRITUAL DISCIPLINES**
Luke 6:12-16 - The Twelve Apostles
Mark 2:18-22 - Jesus Questioned About Fasting
Matthew 6:16-18 - Fasting
Matthew 17:14-23 - The Healing of a Boy With a Demon
■ **SPIRITUAL GIFTS**
1 Corinthians 1:1-9 - Thanksgiving
1 Corinthians 12:1-11 - Spiritual Gifts
1 Corinthians 12:12-31 - One Body, Many Parts
1 Corinthians 14:1-25 - Gifts of Prophecy and Tongues
■ **SPIRITUAL GROWTH**
1 Corinthians 2:6-16 - Wisdom From the Spirit
1 Peter 1:1-12 - Praise to God for a Living Hope
2 Peter 1:1-11 - Making One's Calling and Election Sure
2 Peter 3:1-18 - The Day of the Lord
2 Thessalonians 2:13-17 - Stand Firm
2 Thessalonians 3:1-5 - Request for Prayer
2 Timothy 1:1–2:13 - Encouragement to Be Faithful
Hebrews 5:11–6:12 - Warning Against Falling Away
Mark 4:1-20 - The Parable of the Sower
■ **SPIRITUAL REBIRTH**
John 1:1-19 - The Word Became Flesh
John 2:1-11 - Jesus Changes Water to Wine
John 4:1-26 - Jesus Talks With a Samaritan Woman
Romans 8:1-17 - Life Through the Spirit
Romans 11:11-24 - Ingrafted Branches
Titus 3:1-15 - Doing What Is Good
■ **STATUS**
2 Corinthians 11:16-33 - Paul Boasts About His Sufferings
3 John 1-14 - From the Elder
James 2:1-13 - Favoritism Forbidden
John 4:1-26 - Jesus Talks With a Samaritan Woman
John 7:45-52 - Unbelief of the Jewish Leaders
John 9:13-34 - The Pharisees Investigate the Healing
John 18:28-40 - Jesus Before Pilate
John 19:1-16 - Jesus Sentenced to be Crucified
Mark 9:33-37 - Who Is the Greatest?
Mark 10:35-45 - The Request of James and John
Mark 12:35-40 - Whose Son Is the Christ?
Mark 15:42-47 - The Burial of Jesus
■ **STRENGTH**
1 Corinthians 1:18–2:5 - Christ the Wisdom and Power of God
2 Timothy 4:9-22 - Personal Remarks
Acts 14:21-28 - The Return to Antioch in Syria
Acts 15:36-41 - Disagreement Between Paul and Barnabas
Acts 16:1-5 - Timothy Joins Paul and Silas
Colossians 1:1-14 - Thanksgiving and Prayer
Ephesians 6:10-24 - The Armor of God
Matthew 5:38-42 - An Eye for an Eye
Matthew 14:22-36 - Jesus Walks on the Water
Matthew 27:32-44 - The Crucifixion
Matthew 27:57-61 - The Burial of Jesus
Matthew 27:62-66 - The Guard at the Tomb
Philippians 4:10-23 - Thanks for Their Gifts
Revelation 3:7-13 - To the Church in Philadelphia
Revelation 5:1-14 - The Scroll and the Lamb
■ **STRESS**
Acts 27:27-44 - The Shipwreck
Luke 6:46-49 - The Wise and Foolish Builders
Matthew 10:1-42 - Jesus Sends Out the Twelve
Revelation 8:6–9:21 - The Trumpets

■ STUBBORNNESS
Matthew 7:24-29 - The Wise and Foolish Builders
Matthew 12:1-14 - Lord of the Sabbath
Matthew 12:22-37 - Jesus and Beelzebub
Matthew 12:38-45 - The Sign of Jonah
Matthew 14:1-12 - John the Baptist Beheaded
Matthew 15:1-20 - Clean and Unclean
Matthew 18:15-20 - A Brother Who Sins Against You
Matthew 21:28-32 - The Parable of the Two Sons
Matthew 22:34-40 - The Greatest Commandment
Matthew 23:1-39 - Seven Woes
Revelation 2:18-29 - To the Church in Thyatira
Romans 1:18-32 - God's Wrath Against Mankind
Romans 11:1-10 - The Remnant of Israel
■ SUBMISSION
1 Corinthians 14:26-40 - Orderly Worship
1 Peter 3:1-7 - Wives and Husbands
1 Peter 5:1-14 - To Elders and Young Men
1 Timothy 2:1-15 - Instructions on Worship
Colossians 3:18–4:1 - Rules for Christian Households
Ephesians 4:17–5:21 - Living as Children of Light
Ephesians 5:22-33 - Wives and Husbands
Hebrews 4:14–5:10 - Jesus the Great High Priest
James 4:1-12 - Submit Yourselves to God
Luke 3:21-38 - The Baptism and Genealogy of Jesus
Luke 5:1-11 - The Calling of the First Disciples
Luke 22:39-46 - Jesus Prays on the Mount of Olives
Luke 23:26-43 - The Crucifixion
Matthew 4:18-22 - The Calling of the First Disciples
Matthew 6:19-24 - Treasures in Heaven
Matthew 11:25-30 - Rest for the Weary
Matthew 15:29-39 - Jesus Feeds the Four Thousand
Matthew 16:21-28 - Jesus Predicts His Death
Matthew 17:24-27 - The Temple Tax
Matthew 20:29-34 - Two Blind Men Receive Sight
Matthew 21:33-46 - The Parable of the Tenants
Romans 13:1-7 - Submission to the Authorities
■ SUCCESS
Matthew 13:31-35 - The Parables of the Mustard Seed and the Yeast
Matthew 25:14-30 - The Parable of the Talents
Matthew 28:1-10 - The Resurrection
■ SUFFERING
1 Corinthians 12:12-31 - One Body, Many Parts
1 Peter 1:1-12 - Praise to God for a Living Hope
1 Peter 2:13-25 - Submission to Rulers and Masters
1 Peter 3:8-22 - Suffering for Doing Good
1 Peter 4:1-11 - Living for God
1 Peter 4:12-19 - Suffering for Being a Christian
1 Peter 5:1-14 - To Elders and Young Men
1 Thessalonians 1:1-10 - Thanksgiving for the Thessalonians' Faith
1 Thessalonians 2:1-16 - Paul's Ministry in Thessalonica
2 Corinthians 1:1-11 - The God of All Comfort
2 Corinthians 11:16-33 - Paul Boasts About His Sufferings
Acts 14:21-28 - The Return to Antioch in Syria
Acts 17:1-9 - In Thessalonica
Colossians 1:24–2:5 - Paul's Labor for the Church
Ephesians 3:1-13 - Paul the Preacher to the Gentiles
Galatians 3:1-14 - Faith or Observance of the Law
Hebrews 2:5-18 - Jesus Made Like His Brothers
James 5:7-12 - Patience in Suffering
John 19:17-27 - The Crucifixion
Luke 4:1-13 - The Temptation of Jesus
Luke 6:17-26 - Blessings and Woes
Luke 6:46-49 - The Wise and Foolish Builders
Luke 9:18-27 - Peter's Confession of Christ
Luke 13:1-9 - Repent or Perish
Luke 16:19-31 - The Rich Man and Lazarus
Luke 17:20-37 - The Coming of the Kingdom of God
Luke 18:31-34 - Jesus Again Predicts His Death
Luke 22:7-38 - The Last Supper
Luke 22:63-65 - The Guards Mock Jesus
Mark 5:21-43 - A Dead Girl and a Sick Woman
Mark 8:31–9:1 - Jesus Predicts His Death
Mark 10:32-34 - Jesus Again Predicts His Death
Mark 10:35-45 - The Request of James and John
Mark 15:16-20 - The Soldiers Mock Jesus
Mark 15:21-32 - The Crucifixion
Mark 15:33-41 - The Death of Jesus
Matthew 10:1-42 - Jesus Sends Out the Twelve
Matthew 20:17-19 - Jesus Again Predicts His Death
Matthew 26:57-68 - Before the Sanhedrin
Philippians 1:12-30 - Paul's Chains Advance the Gospel
Philippians 3:1-11 - No Confidence in the Flesh
Revelation 1:9-20 - One Like a Son of Man
Revelation 2:8-11 - To the Church in Smyrna
Revelation 2:18-29 - To the Church in Thyatira
Revelation 3:7-13 - To the Church in Philadelphia
Romans 8:18-27 - Future Glory
■ SURPRISES
John 1:43-51 - Jesus Calls Philip and Nathanael
John 20:1-9 - The Empty Tomb
John 20:10-18 - Jesus Appears to Mary Magdalene
Luke 1:5-25 - The Birth of John the Baptist Foretold
Luke 5:1-11 - The Calling of the First Disciples
Matthew 11:1-19 - Jesus and John the Baptist
Matthew 13:31-35 - The Parables of the Mustard Seed and the Yeast
Matthew 13:47-52 - The Parable of the Net
Matthew 13:53-58 - A Prophet Without Honor
Matthew 24:36-51 - The Day and Hour Unknown
Matthew 25:1-13 - The Parable of the Ten Virgins
Revelation 10:1-11 - The Angel and the Little Scroll
■ SWEARING
James 5:7-12 - Patience in Suffering
Matthew 5:33-37 - Oaths
Matthew 26:69-75 - Peter Disowns Jesus

■ TASKS
John 4:27-38 - The Disciples Rejoin Jesus
Luke 1:67-80 - Zechariah's Song
Luke 5:1-11 - The Calling of the First Disciples
Mark 13:32-37 - The Day and Hour Unknown
■ TEACHING
1 John 2:18-27 - Warning Against Antichrists
1 Thessalonians 2:1-16 - Paul's Ministry in Thessalonica
1 Timothy 1:1-11 - Warning Against False Teachers of the Law
1 Timothy 2:1-15 - Instructions on Worship
1 Timothy 3:1-16 - Overseers and Deacons
1 Timothy 4:1-16 - Instructions to Timothy
1 Timothy 5:1–6:2 - Advice About Widows, Elders and Slaves

1 Timothy 6:3-10 - Love of Money
2 John 1-13 - From the Elder
2 Timothy 3:10–4:8 - Paul's Charge to Timothy
Acts 13:4-12 - On Cyprus
Acts 15:1-21 - The Council at Jerusalem
Acts 18:18-28 - Priscilla, Aquila and Apollos
Colossians 1:24–2:5 - Paul's Labor for the Church
Ephesians 4:1-16 - Unity in the Body of Christ
James 3:1-12 - Taming the Tongue
John 16:5-16 - The Work of the Holy Spirit
Luke 4:31-37 - Jesus Drives Out an Evil Spirit
Luke 4:38-44 - Jesus Heals Many
Luke 6:37-42 - Judging Others
Luke 13:22-30 - The Narrow Door
Luke 16:16-18 - Additional Teachings
Mark 1:29-34 - Jesus Heals Many
Mark 4:1-20 - The Parable of the Sower
Mark 4:30-34 - The Parable of the Mustard Seed
Mark 6:30-44 - Jesus Feeds the Five Thousand
Mark 7:1-23 - Clean and Unclean
Mark 8:1-13 - Jesus Feeds the Four Thousand
Mark 10:1-12 - Divorce
Mark 12:35-40 - Whose Son Is the Christ?
Matthew 5:17-20 - The Fulfillment of the Law
Matthew 15:1-20 - Clean and Unclean
Titus 2:1-15 - What Must Be Taught to Various Groups

■ TEAMWORK

1 Corinthians 16:5-24 - Personal Requests
Acts 1:12-26 - Matthias Chosen to Replace Judas
Acts 4:32-37 - The Believers Share Their Possessions
Acts 16:6-10 - Paul's Vision of the Man of Macedonia
Acts 18:18-28 - Priscilla, Aquila and Apollos
Luke 5:17-26 - Jesus Heals a Paralytic
Luke 9:46-50 - Who Will Be the Greatest?
Mark 3:13-19 - The Appointing of the Twelve Apostles
Mark 6:7-13 - Jesus Sends Out the Twelve

■ TEMPTATION

1 Corinthians 6:12-20 - Sexual Immorality
1 Corinthians 7:1-40 - Marriage
1 Corinthians 8:1-13 - Food Sacrificed to Idols
1 Corinthians 10:1-13 - Warnings From Israel's History
1 Thessalonians 2:17–3:5 - Paul's Longing to See the Thessalonians
1 Timothy 5:1–6:2 - Advice About Widows, Elders and Slaves
1 Timothy 6:3-10 - Love of Money
Hebrews 2:5-18 - Jesus Made Like His Brothers
Hebrews 4:14–5:10 - Jesus the Great High Priest
James 1:1-18 - Trials and Temptations
John 18:25-27 - Peter's Second and Third Denials
Luke 4:1-13 - The Temptation of Jesus
Luke 17:1-10 - Sin, Faith, Duty
Luke 22:39-46 - Jesus Prays on the Mount of Olives
Mark 1:9-13 - The Baptism and Temptation of Jesus
Mark 8:31–9:1 - Jesus Predicts His Death
Mark 9:42-50 - Causing to Sin
Mark 15:21-32 - The Crucifixion
Matthew 4:1-11 - The Temptation of Jesus
Matthew 8:18-22 - The Cost of Following Jesus

■ TESTING

1 Corinthians 3:1-23 - On Divisions in the Church
1 Corinthians 10:1-13 - Warnings From Israel's History
1 John 4:1-6 - Test the Spirits
2 Corinthians 1:1-11 - The God of All Comfort
2 Corinthians 13:1-14 - Final Warnings
Acts 20:13-38 - Paul's Farewell to the Ephesian Elders
John 6:1-15 - Jesus Feeds the Five Thousand
Luke 4:1-13 - The Temptation of Jesus
Luke 8:1-15 - The Parable of the Sower
Luke 10:25-37 - The Parable of the Good Samaritan
Luke 11:14-28 - Jesus and Beelzebub
Luke 22:47-53 - Jesus Arrested
Luke 22:54-62 - Peter Disowns Jesus
Luke 22:66–23:25 - Jesus Before Pilate and Herod
Mark 1:9-13 - The Baptism and Temptation of Jesus
Mark 14:53-65 - Before the Sanhedrin
Matthew 15:21-28 - The Faith of the Canaanite Woman
Matthew 21:23-27 - The Authority of Jesus Questioned
Matthew 22:15-22 - Paying Taxes to Caesar
Matthew 22:23-33 - Marriage at the Resurrection

■ THANKFULNESS

1 Corinthians 1:1-9 - Thanksgiving
1 Corinthians 10:14-22 - Idol Feasts and the Lord's Supper
1 Corinthians 10:23–11:1 - The Believer's Freedom
1 Thessalonians 5:12-28 - Final Instructions
2 Corinthians 9:6-15 - Sowing Generously
Acts 27:27-44 - The Shipwreck
Acts 28:11-16 - Arrival at Rome
Colossians 1:1-14 - Thanksgiving and Prayer
Colossians 3:1-17 - Rules for Holy Living
Colossians 4:2-18 - Further Instructions
Ephesians 1:15-23 - Thanksgiving and Prayer
John 6:1-15 - Jesus Feeds the Five Thousand
Luke 5:12-16 - The Man With Leprosy
Luke 7:36-50 - Jesus Anointed by a Sinful Woman
Luke 8:26-39 - The Healing of a Demon-possessed Man
Luke 17:11-19 - Ten Healed of Leprosy
Luke 22:7-38 - The Last Supper
Mark 6:30-44 - Jesus Feeds the Five Thousand
Mark 7:31-37 - The Healing of a Deaf and Mute Man
Mark 8:1-13 - Jesus Feeds the Four Thousand
Matthew 8:14-17 - Jesus Heals Many
Matthew 14:13-21 - Jesus Feeds the Five Thousand
Matthew 20:1-16 - The Parable of the Workers in the Vineyard
Philippians 4:2-9 - Exhortations
Philemon 1-7 - Thanksgiving and Prayer
Revelation 11:15-19 - The Seventh Trumpet
Romans 1:18-32 - God's Wrath Against Mankind

■ THINKING

1 Corinthians 2:6-16 - Wisdom From the Spirit
2 Peter 3:1-18 - The Day of the Lord
Luke 5:17-26 - Jesus Heals a Paralytic
Matthew 5:27-30 - Adultery
Matthew 15:1-20 - Clean and Unclean
Philippians 4:2-9 - Exhortations
Romans 12:1-8 - Living Sacrifices

■ TIMING

John 7:1-13 - Jesus Goes to the Feast of Tabernacles
Luke 2:1-7 - The Birth of Jesus
Luke 5:1-11 - The Calling of the First Disciples
Matthew 9:35-38 - The Workers Are Few
Matthew 13:1-23 - The Parable of the Sower

Matthew 26:14-16 - Judas Agrees to Betray Jesus
■ **TITHING**
1 Corinthians 16:1-4 - The Collection for God's People
2 Corinthians 8:16–9:5 - Titus Sent to Corinth
Hebrews 7:1-10 - Melchizedek the Priest
Luke 21:1-4 - The Widow's Offering
Mark 12:41-44 - The Widow's Offering
Matthew 6:1-4 - Giving to the Needy
Matthew 23:1-39 - Seven Woes
■ **TOLERATION**
2 Corinthians 11:1-15 - Paul and the False Apostles
Acts 4:32-37 - The Believers Share Their Possessions
Luke 22:63-65 - The Guards Mock Jesus
Matthew 14:1-12 - John the Baptist Beheaded
Revelation 2:12-17 - To the Church in Pergamum
Revelation 2:18-29 - To the Church in Thyatira
■ **TRADITIONS**
Acts 6:8-15 - Stephen Seized
Galatians 1:11-24 - Paul Called by God
Hebrews 2:1-4 - Warning to Pay Attention
John 4:1-26 - Jesus Talks With a Samaritan Woman
John 7:14-24 - Jesus Teaches at the Feast
John 9:13-34 - The Pharisees Investigate the Healing
John 19:38-42 - The Burial of Jesus
Luke 1:57-66 - The Birth of John the Baptist
Luke 5:33-39 - Jesus Questioned About Fasting
Luke 6:1-11 - Lord of the Sabbath
Matthew 9:14-17 - Jesus Questioned About Fasting
Matthew 15:1-20 - Clean and Unclean
Matthew 21:12-17 - Jesus at the Temple
Matthew 22:23-33 - Marriage at the Resurrection
Matthew 23:1-39 - Seven Woes
Matthew 26:17-30 - The Lord's Supper
■ **TRAINING**
2 Timothy 3:10–4:8 - Paul's Charge to Timothy
Ephesians 6:1-4 - Children and Parents
Luke 2:41-52 - The Boy Jesus at the Temple
Titus 2:1-15 - What Must Be Taught to Various Groups
■ **TRUST**
1 Corinthians 13:1-13 - Love
Acts 14:21-28 - The Return to Antioch in Syria
Hebrews 11:1-40 - By Faith
John 4:43-54 - Jesus Heals the Official's Son
John 5:1-15 - The Healing at the Pool
John 14:1-4 - Jesus Comforts His Disciples
Luke 1:26-38 - The Birth of Jesus Foretold
Luke 5:1-11 - The Calling of the First Disciples
Luke 7:1-10 - The Faith of the Centurion
Mark 4:35-41 - Jesus Calms the Storm
Matthew 1:18-25 - The Birth of Jesus Christ
Matthew 6:25-34 - Do Not Worry
Matthew 8:5-13 - The Faith of the Centurion
Matthew 8:23-27 - Jesus Calms the Storm
Matthew 9:18-26 - A Dead Girl and a Sick Woman
Matthew 11:1-19 - Jesus and John the Baptist
Matthew 14:13-21 - Jesus Feeds the Five Thousand
Matthew 14:22-36 - Jesus Walks on the Water
Matthew 16:13-20 - Peter's Confession of Christ
Matthew 17:14-23 - The Healing of a Boy With a Demon
Matthew 21:28-32 - The Parable of the Two Sons
Matthew 26:69-75 - Peter Disowns Jesus
■ **TRUTH**
1 John 1:5–2:14 - Walking in the Light
1 John 2:18-27 - Warning Against Antichrists
1 John 5:1-12 - Faith in the Son of God
1 Peter 1:13–2:3 - Be Holy
1 Timothy 1:1-11 - Warning Against False Teachers of the Law
1 Timothy 2:1-15 - Instructions on Worship
1 Timothy 6:3-10 - Love of Money
1 Timothy 6:11-21 - Paul's Charge to Timothy
2 Corinthians 13:1-14 - Final Warnings
2 John 1-13 - From the Elder
2 Peter 1:12-21 - Prophecy of Scripture
2 Timothy 2:14-26 - A Workman Approved by God
2 Timothy 3:1-9 - Godlessness in the Last Days
3 John 1-14 - From the Elder
Galatians 1:11-24 - Paul Called by God
Galatians 2:1-10 - Paul Accepted by the Apostles
Galatians 4:8-20 - Paul's Concern for the Galatians
Hebrews 6:13-20 - The Certainty of God's Promise
John 7:1-13 - Jesus Goes to the Feast of Tabernacles
John 7:14-24 - Jesus Teaches at the Feast
John 8:42-47 - The Children of the Devil
John 8:48-59 - The Claims of Jesus About Himself
John 14:5-14 - Jesus the Way to the Father
John 15:18–16:4 - The World Hates the Disciples
John 16:5-16 - The Work of the Holy Spirit
John 16:17-33 - The Disciples' Grief Will Turn to Joy
John 18:28-40 - Jesus Before Pilate
John 19:1-16 - Jesus Sentenced to be Crucified
Luke 4:14-30 - Jesus Rejected at Nazareth
Luke 20:20-26 - Paying Taxes to Caesar
Mark 4:21-25 - A Lamp on a Stand
Mark 12:13-17 - Paying Taxes to Caesar
Matthew 5:33-37 - Oaths
Matthew 16:5-12 - The Yeast of the Pharisees and Sadducees
Revelation 6:1-17 - The Seals
Romans 1:18-32 - God's Wrath Against Mankind

■ **UNBELIEVERS**
1 Corinthians 6:1-11 - Lawsuits Among Believers
1 Corinthians 7:1-40 - Marriage
1 Corinthians 10:23–11:1 - The Believer's Freedom
1 Corinthians 14:1-25 - Gifts of Prophecy and Tongues
1 John 2:18-27 - Warning Against Antichrists
1 John 2:28–3:10 - Children of God
1 John 4:1-6 - Test the Spirits
1 Peter 2:4-12 - The Living Stone and a Chosen People
1 Peter 3:1-7 - Wives and Husbands
1 Peter 3:8-22 - Suffering for Doing Good
1 Peter 4:1-11 - Living for God
1 Peter 4:12-19 - Suffering for Being a Christian
2 Corinthians 6:14–7:1 - Do Not Be Yoked with Unbelievers
2 Peter 3:1-18 - The Day of the Lord
Acts 2:1-13 - The Holy Spirit Comes at Pentecost
Hebrews 5:11–6:12 - Warning Against Falling Away
Hebrews 12:14-29 - Warning Against Refusing God
Hebrews 13:1-25 - Concluding Exhortations
John 3:1-22 - Jesus Teaches Nicodemus
John 3:22-36 - John the Baptist's Testimony About Jesus

John 7:1-13 - Jesus Goes to the Feast of Tabernacles
John 7:14-24 - Jesus Teaches at the Feast
John 7:25-44 - Is Jesus the Christ?
John 7:45-52 - Unbelief of the Jewish Leaders
John 8:31-41 - The Children of Abraham
John 8:48-59 - The Claims of Jesus About Himself
John 9:13-34 - The Pharisees Investigate the Healing
John 10:22-42 - The Unbelief of the Jews
John 11:45-57 - The Plot to Kill Jesus
John 12:37-50 - The Jews Continue in Their Unbelief
John 15:18–16:4 - The World Hates the Disciples
John 16:5-16 - The Work of the Holy Spirit
John 18:12-14 - Jesus Taken to Annas
John 18:19-24 - The High Priest Questions Jesus
John 19:17-27 - The Crucifixion
Luke 5:27-32 - The Calling of Levi
Luke 9:37-45 - The Healing of a Boy With an Evil Spirit
Mark 6:1-6 - A Prophet Without Honor
Mark 9:14-32 - The Healing of a Boy With an Evil Spirit
Matthew 7:13-14 - The Narrow and Wide Gates
Matthew 7:15-23 - A Tree and Its Fruit
Matthew 8:5-13 - The Faith of the Centurion
Matthew 8:28-34 - The Healing of Two Demon-possessed Men
Matthew 9:9-13 - The Calling of Matthew
Matthew 9:18-26 - A Dead Girl and a Sick Woman
Matthew 9:27-34 - Jesus Heals the Blind and Mute
Matthew 10:1-42 - Jesus Sends Out the Twelve
Matthew 11:20-24 - Woe on Unrepentant Cities
Matthew 12:22-37 - Jesus and Beelzebub
Matthew 12:38-45 - The Sign of Jonah
Matthew 13:24-30 - The Parable of the Weeds
Matthew 13:36-43 - The Parable of the Weeds Explained
Matthew 13:47-52 - The Parable of the Net
Matthew 21:23-27 - The Authority of Jesus Questioned
Matthew 21:33-46 - The Parable of the Tenants
Matthew 22:1-14 - The Parable of the Wedding Banquet
Matthew 22:15-22 - Paying Taxes to Caesar
Matthew 22:34-40 - The Greatest Commandment
Matthew 23:1-39 - Seven Woes
Matthew 27:11-26 - Jesus Before Pilate
Matthew 27:27-31 - The Soldiers Mock Jesus
Matthew 27:32-44 - The Crucifixion
Matthew 27:45-56 - The Death of Jesus
Revelation 11:1-14 - The Two Witnesses
Revelation 21:1-27 - The New Jerusalem
Romans 1:18-32 - God's Wrath Against Mankind
Romans 9:30–10:21 - Israel's Unbelief

■ UNDERSTANDING

1 Corinthians 14:1-25 - Gifts of Prophecy and Tongues
1 John 5:13-21 - Concluding Remarks
John 3:1-22 - Jesus Teaches Nicodemus
John 6:60-71 - Many Disciples Desert Jesus
John 8:31-41 - The Children of Abraham
John 8:42-47 - The Children of the Devil
John 8:48-59 - The Claims of Jesus About Himself
John 16:17-33 - The Disciples' Grief Will Turn to Joy
John 20:1-9 - The Empty Tomb
Luke 18:31-34 - Jesus Again Predicts His Death
Luke 24:36-49 - Jesus Appears to the Disciples
Mark 4:30-34 - The Parable of the Mustard Seed
Matthew 16:1-4 - The Demand for a Sign
Matthew 16:5-12 - The Yeast of the Pharisees and Sadducees
Matthew 19:13-15 - The Little Children and Jesus

■ UNFAIRNESS

1 Peter 2:13-25 - Submission to Rulers and Masters
Luke 6:27-36 - Love for Enemies
Luke 20:9-19 - The Parable of the Tenants
Luke 22:66–23:25 - Jesus Before Pilate and Herod
Matthew 5:38-42 - An Eye for an Eye
Matthew 20:1-16 - The Parable of the Workers in the Vineyard
Romans 3:1-8 - God's Faithfulness

■ UNFAITHFULNESS

Matthew 5:31-32 - Divorce

■ UNITY

1 Corinthians 1:10-17 - Divisions in the Church
1 Corinthians 8:1-13 - Food Sacrificed to Idols
1 Corinthians 10:14-22 - Idol Feasts and the Lord's Supper
1 Corinthians 12:12-31 - One Body, Many Parts
2 Corinthians 6:14–7:1 - Do Not Be Yoked with Unbelievers
2 Corinthians 13:1-14 - Final Warnings
Colossians 1:24–2:5 - Paul's Labor for the Church
Ephesians 4:1-16 - Unity in the Body of Christ
Ephesians 5:22-33 - Wives and Husbands
John 17:20-26 - Jesus Prays for All Believers
Mark 3:20-30 - Jesus and Beelzebub
Mark 9:38-41 - Whoever Is Not Against Us Is for Us
Matthew 12:46-50 - Jesus' Mother and Brothers
Matthew 18:15-20 - A Brother Who Sins Against You
Matthew 19:1-12 - Divorce
Philippians 2:1-11 - Imitating Christ's Humility
Romans 14:1–15:13 - The Weak and the Strong

■ VALUE

John 6:25-59 - Jesus the Bread of Life
John 12:1-11 - Jesus Anointed at Bethany
Luke 1:5-25 - The Birth of John the Baptist Foretold
Matthew 13:44-46 - The Parables of the Hidden Treasure and the Pearl
Philippians 4:2-9 - Exhortations

■ VICTORY

1 Corinthians 15:35-58 - The Resurrection Body
1 John 4:1-6 - Test the Spirits
1 John 5:1-12 - Faith in the Son of God
Matthew 4:1-11 - The Temptation of Jesus
Matthew 8:14-17 - Jesus Heals Many
Matthew 10:1-42 - Jesus Sends Out the Twelve
Matthew 12:15-21 - God's Chosen Servant
Matthew 14:22-36 - Jesus Walks on the Water
Matthew 15:21-28 - The Faith of the Canaanite Woman
Matthew 16:21-28 - Jesus Predicts His Death
Matthew 20:17-19 - Jesus Again Predicts His Death
Matthew 24:1-35 - Signs of the End of the Age
Matthew 26:17-30 - The Lord's Supper
Matthew 28:1-10 - The Resurrection
Revelation 11:15-19 - The Seventh Trumpet
Revelation 12:1-13:1 - The Woman and the Dragon
Revelation 19:11-21 - The Rider on the White Horse
Revelation 20:1-6 - The Thousand Years
Revelation 20:7-10 - Satan's Doom

Romans 8:28-39 - More Than Conquerors

■ VOWS

Acts 18:18-28 - Priscilla, Aquila and Apollos
Acts 21:17-26 - Paul's Arrival at Jerusalem
Matthew 5:27-30 - Adultery
Matthew 5:33-37 - Oaths
Matthew 26:31-35 - Jesus Predicts Peter's Denial

■ WAITING

1 Corinthians 1:1-9 - Thanksgiving
Hebrews 6:13-20 - The Certainty of God's Promise
Hebrews 11:1-40 - By Faith
Luke 7:18-35 - Jesus and John the Baptist
Luke 12:35-48 - Watchfulness
Mark 13:32-37 - The Day and Hour Unknown
Matthew 9:18-26 - A Dead Girl and a Sick Woman
Matthew 24:36-51 - The Day and Hour Unknown
Matthew 25:1-13 - The Parable of the Ten Virgins
Matthew 27:62-66 - The Guard at the Tomb
Romans 8:18-27 - Future Glory

■ WAR

2 Corinthians 10:1-18 - Paul's Defense of His Ministry
Luke 12:49-53 - Not Peace but Division
Luke 21:5-38 - Signs of the End of the Age
Mark 13:1-31 - Signs of the End of the Age
Revelation 12:1–13:1 - The Woman and the Dragon
Revelation 13:2-10 - The Beast out of the Sea
Revelation 17:1-18 - The Woman on the Beast
Revelation 19:11-21 - The Rider on the White Horse
Revelation 20:7-10 - Satan's Doom

■ WEAKNESSES

1 Corinthians 1:18–2:5 - Christ the Wisdom and Power of God
1 Corinthians 6:12-20 - Sexual Immorality
1 Corinthians 15:35-58 - The Resurrection Body
1 Timothy 6:3-10 - Love of Money
2 Corinthians 11:16-33 - Paul Boasts About His Sufferings
2 Corinthians 12:1-10 - Paul's Vision and His Thorn
2 Corinthians 13:1-14 - Final Warnings
Hebrews 4:14–5:10 - Jesus the Great High Priest
Hebrews 12:1-3 - God Disciplines His Sons
Luke 22:54-62 - Peter Disowns Jesus
Matthew 26:31-35 - Jesus Predicts Peter's Denial
Revelation 3:7-13 - To the Church in Philadelphia
Romans 7:7-25 - Struggling With Sin
Romans 8:1-17 - Life Through the Spirit
Romans 8:18-27 - Future Glory

■ WEALTH

James 1:1-18 - Trials and Temptations
James 5:1-6 - Warning to Rich Oppressors
Luke 6:17-26 - Blessings and Woes
Luke 15:11-32 - The Parable of the Lost Son
Luke 16:1-15 - The Parable of the Shrewd Manager
Luke 16:19-31 - The Rich Man and Lazarus
Luke 18:18-30 - The Rich Ruler
Luke 19:1-10 - Zacchaeus the Tax Collector
Luke 21:1-4 - The Widow's Offering
Mark 4:1-20 - The Parable of the Sower
Mark 10:17-31 - The Rich Young Man
Mark 12:41-44 - The Widow's Offering
Matthew 6:19-24 - Treasures in Heaven
Matthew 13:44-46 - The Parables of the Hidden Treasure and the Pearl
Matthew 19:16-30 - The Rich Young Man
Revelation 2:8-11 - To the Church in Smyrna
Revelation 3:14-22 - To the Church in Laodicea
Revelation 5:1-14 - The Scroll and the Lamb
Revelation 18:1-24 - The Fall of Babylon

■ WISDOM

1 Corinthians 1:18–2:5 - Christ the Wisdom and Power of God
1 Corinthians 2:6-16 - Wisdom From the Spirit
1 Corinthians 3:1-23 - On Divisions in the Church
1 Corinthians 12:1-11 - Spiritual Gifts
2 Corinthians 11:16-33 - Paul Boasts About His Sufferings
Acts 6:8-15 - Stephen Seized
Colossians 1:24–2:5 - Paul's Labor for the Church
Colossians 4:2-18 - Further Instructions
Ephesians 4:17–5:21 - Living as Children of Light
James 3:13-18 - Two Kinds of Wisdom
John 16:5-16 - The Work of the Holy Spirit
Luke 1:39-45 - Mary Visits Elizabeth
Luke 2:21-40 - Jesus Presented in the Temple
Luke 6:46-49 - The Wise and Foolish Builders
Luke 11:29-32 - The Sign of Jonah
Luke 20:1-8 - The Authority of Jesus Questioned
Luke 20:20-26 - Paying Taxes to Caesar
Luke 20:27-40 - The Resurrection and Marriage
Luke 21:5-38 - Signs of the End of the Age
Matthew 7:1-6 - Judging Others
Matthew 11:25-30 - Rest for the Weary
Matthew 12:38-45 - The Sign of Jonah
Matthew 16:1-4 - The Demand for a Sign
Matthew 18:21-35 - The Parable of the Unmerciful Servant
Matthew 21:23-27 - The Authority of Jesus Questioned
Matthew 22:15-22 - Paying Taxes to Caesar
Revelation 5:1-14 - The Scroll and the Lamb
Revelation 7:9-17 - The Great Multitude in White Robes
Revelation 13:11-18 - The Beast out of the Earth
Revelation 17:1-18 - The Woman on the Beast
Romans 11:33-36 - Doxology

■ WITNESSING

1 Corinthians 11:17-34 - The Lord's Supper
1 Corinthians 15:12-34 - The Resurrection of the Dead
1 John 5:1-12 - Faith in the Son of God
2 Corinthians 2:12–3:6 - Ministers of the New Covenant
2 Corinthians 6:3-13 - Paul's Hardships
2 Corinthians 11:1-15 - Paul and the False Apostles
2 Timothy 1:1–2:13 - Encouragement to Be Faithful
2 Timothy 4:9-22 - Personal Remarks
Acts 1:1-11 - Jesus Taken Up Into Heaven
Acts 2:1-13 - The Holy Spirit Comes at Pentecost
Acts 2:14-41 - Peter Addresses the Crowd
Acts 3:11-26 - Peter Speaks to the Onlookers
Acts 4:1-22 - Peter and John Before the Sanhedrin
Acts 4:32-37 - The Believers Share Their Possessions
Acts 8:4-8 - Philip in Samaria
Acts 8:9-25 - Simon the Sorcerer
Acts 9:20-31 - Saul in Damascus and Jerusalem
Acts 9:32-43 - Aeneas and Dorcas
Acts 10:24-48 - Peter at Cornelius' House

Acts 14:8-20 - In Lystra and Derbe
Acts 18:1-17 - In Corinth
Acts 18:18-28 - Priscilla, Aquila and Apollos
Acts 21:37–22:21 - Paul Speaks to the Crowd
Acts 22:30–23:11 - Before the Sanhedrin
Acts 25:23–26:32 - Paul Before Agrippa
John 1:19-28 - John the Baptist Denies Being the Christ
John 1:35-42 - Jesus' First Disciples
John 4:1-26 - Jesus Talks With a Samaritan Woman
John 4:27-38 - The Disciples Rejoin Jesus
John 4:39-42 - Many Samaritans Believe
John 15:18–16:4 - The World Hates the Disciples
John 21:15-25 - Jesus Reinstates Peter
Luke 2:8-20 - The Shepherds and the Angels
Luke 5:1-11 - The Calling of the First Disciples
Luke 8:16-18 - A Lamp on a Stand
Luke 9:18-27 - Peter's Confession of Christ
Luke 11:33-36 - The Lamp of the Body
Luke 22:66–23:25 - Jesus Before Pilate and Herod
Luke 24:1-12 - The Resurrection
Luke 24:13-35 - On the Road to Emmaus
Luke 24:36-49 - Jesus Appears to the Disciples
Mark 1:1-8 - John the Baptist Prepares the Way
Mark 3:13-19 - The Appointing of the Twelve Apostles
Mark 4:1-20 - The Parable of the Sower
Mark 5:1-20 - The Healing of a Demon-possessed Man
Mark 7:31-37 - The Healing of a Deaf and Mute Man
Mark 9:2-13 - The Transfiguration
Mark 14:53-65 - Before the Sanhedrin
Mark 14:66-72 - Peter Disowns Jesus
Mark 16:1-20 - The Resurrection
Matthew 4:18-22 - The Calling of the First Disciples
Matthew 7:13-14 - The Narrow and Wide Gates
Matthew 9:9-13 - The Calling of Matthew
Matthew 9:35-38 - The Workers Are Few
Matthew 10:1-42 - Jesus Sends Out the Twelve
Matthew 13:1-23 - The Parable of the Sower
Matthew 27:57-61 - The Burial of Jesus
Matthew 28:1-10 - The Resurrection
Matthew 28:16-20 - The Great Commission
Philippians 2:12-18 - Shining as Stars
Revelation 10:1-11 - The Angel and the Little Scroll
Revelation 11:1-14 - The Two Witnesses
Romans 1:1-7 - Introduction
Romans 1:8-17 - Paul's Longing to Visit Rome
Romans 2:1-16 - God's Righteous Judgment
Romans 15:14-22 - Paul, the Minister to the Gentiles

■ WIVES

1 Peter 3:1-7 - Wives and Husbands
Matthew 5:27-30 - Adultery

■ WORDS

1 John 1:1-4 - The Word of Life
1 Peter 1:13-2:3 - Be Holy
1 Peter 3:8-22 - Suffering for Doing Good
1 Timothy 2:1-15 - Instructions on Worship
1 Timothy 6:3-10 - Love of Money
1 Timothy 6:11-21 - Paul's Charge to Timothy
2 Timothy 2:14-26 - A Workman Approved by God
2 Timothy 3:10–4:8 - Paul's Charge to Timothy
James 1:19-27 - Listening and Doing
James 3:1-12 - Taming the Tongue
John 8:31-41 - The Children of Abraham
John 8:42-47 - The Children of the Devil
John 8:48-59 - The Claims of Jesus About Himself
John 12:37-50 - The Jews Continue in Their Unbelief
John 14:5-14 - Jesus the Way to the Father
John 14:15-31 - Jesus Promises the Holy Spirit
John 16:17-33 - The Disciples' Grief Will Turn to Joy
Luke 6:46-49 - The Wise and Foolish Builders
Matthew 5:33-37 - Oaths
Matthew 7:1-6 - Judging Others
Matthew 12:22-37 - Jesus and Beelzebub
Matthew 16:13-20 - Peter's Confession of Christ
Matthew 17:1-13 - The Transfiguration
Matthew 21:28-32 - The Parable of the Two Sons
Matthew 26:31-35 - Jesus Predicts Peter's Denial
Matthew 26:69-75 - Peter Disowns Jesus
Matthew 28:11-15 - The Guards' Report
Philemon 1-7 - Thanksgiving and Prayer

■ WORK

1 Corinthians 16:5-24 - Personal Requests
1 Thessalonians 2:1-16 - Paul's Ministry in Thessalonica
1 Timothy 2:1-15 - Instructions on Worship
2 Corinthians 10:1-18 - Paul's Defense of His Ministry
2 John 1-13 - From the Elder
2 Thessalonians 3:6-18 - Warning Against Idleness
2 Timothy 2:14-26 - A Workman Approved by God
2 Timothy 3:10–4:8 - Paul's Charge to Timothy
Acts 18:1-17 - In Corinth
Acts 20:13-38 - Paul's Farewell to the Ephesian Elders
Colossians 3:18–4:1 - Rules for Christian Households
Ephesians 4:1-16 - Unity in the Body of Christ
Ephesians 6:5-9 - Slaves and Masters
John 4:27-38 - The Disciples Rejoin Jesus
John 14:15-31 - Jesus Promises the Holy Spirit
John 15:1-17 - The Vine and the Branches
John 17:1-5 - Jesus Prays for Himself
Luke 3:1-20 - John the Baptist Prepares the Way
Philippians 2:12-18 - Shining as Stars

■ WORLD

1 Corinthians 1:18–2:5 - Christ the Wisdom and Power of God
1 Corinthians 3:1-23 - On Divisions in the Church
1 John 2:15-17 - Do Not Love the World
1 John 2:28–3:10 - Children of God
1 John 3:11-24 - Love One Another
1 John 4:1-6 - Test the Spirits
1 John 4:7-21 - God's Love and Ours
1 John 5:1-12 - Faith in the Son of God
1 Timothy 2:1-15 - Instructions on Worship
1 Timothy 5:1–6:2 - Advice About Widows, Elders and Slaves
1 Timothy 6:3-10 - Love of Money
2 Corinthians 10:1-18 - Paul's Defense of His Ministry
2 Corinthians 11:16-33 - Paul Boasts About His Sufferings
2 Peter 1:1-11 - Making One's Calling and Election Sure
2 Peter 2:1-22 - False Teachers and Their Destruction
2 Peter 3:1-18 - The Day of the Lord
2 Timothy 3:1-9 - Godlessness in the Last Days
2 Timothy 4:9-22 - Personal Remarks
Galatians 6:11-18 - Not Circumcision but a New Creation
John 1:29-34 - Jesus the Lamb of God

John 3:1-22 - Jesus Teaches Nicodemus
John 7:1-13 - Jesus Goes to the Feast of Tabernacles
John 7:25-44 - Is Jesus the Christ?
John 7:45-52 - Unbelief of the Jewish Leaders
John 8:12-30 - The Validity of Jesus' Testimony
John 9:1-12 - Jesus Heals a Man Born Blind
John 9:35-41 - Spiritual Blindness
John 14:15-31 - Jesus Promises the Holy Spirit
John 15:18–16:4 - The World Hates the Disciples
John 16:5-16 - The Work of the Holy Spirit
John 16:17-33 - The Disciples' Grief Will Turn to Joy
John 17:6-19 - Jesus Prays for His Disciples
John 17:20-26 - Jesus Prays for All Believers
Matthew 9:35-38 - The Workers Are Few
Matthew 11:1-19 - Jesus and John the Baptist
Matthew 13:1-23 - The Parable of the Sower
Matthew 13:36-43 - The Parable of the Weeds Explained
Matthew 18:1-9 - The Greatest in the Kingdom of Heaven
Matthew 19:1-12 - Divorce
Matthew 24:1-35 - Signs of the End of the Age
Matthew 27:11-26 - Jesus Before Pilate
Matthew 27:27-31 - The Soldiers Mock Jesus
Revelation 8:6–9:21 - The Trumpets
Romans 1:18-32 - God's Wrath Against Mankind

■ WORRY

1 Peter 5:1-14 - To Elders and Young Men
John 14:1-4 - Jesus Comforts His Disciples
John 14:15-31 - Jesus Promises the Holy Spirit
Luke 8:1-15 - The Parable of the Sower
Luke 12:22-34 - Do Not Worry
Luke 21:5-38 - Signs of the End of the Age
Mark 4:1-20 - The Parable of the Sower
Mark 13:1-31 - Signs of the End of the Age
Matthew 6:25-34 - Do Not Worry

■ WORSHIP

1 Corinthians 11:2-16 - Propriety in Worship
1 Corinthians 14:1-25 - Gifts of Prophecy and Tongues
1 Corinthians 14:26-40 - Orderly Worship
Acts 13:1-3 - Barnabas and Saul Sent Off
Acts 19:23-41 - The Riot in Ephesus
Colossians 2:6-23 - Freedom From Human Regulations Through Life With Christ
Hebrews 1:1-14 - The Son Superior to Angels
John 4:1-26 - Jesus Talks With a Samaritan Woman
John 9:35-41 - Spiritual Blindness
John 12:1-11 - Jesus Anointed at Bethany
John 12:12-19 - The Triumphal Entry
Luke 1:46-56 - Mary's Song
Luke 4:1-13 - The Temptation of Jesus
Luke 4:14-30 - Jesus Rejected at Nazareth
Luke 24:50-53 - The Ascension
Mark 9:2-13 - The Transfiguration
Mark 11:12-19 - Jesus Clears the Temple
Matthew 2:1-12 - The Visit of the Magi
Matthew 9:1-8 - Jesus Heals a Paralytic
Matthew 9:27-34 - Jesus Heals the Blind and Mute
Matthew 15:1-20 - Clean and Unclean
Matthew 15:29-39 - Jesus Feeds the Four Thousand
Matthew 17:1-13 - The Transfiguration
Matthew 21:1-11 - The Triumphal Entry
Matthew 24:1-35 - Signs of the End of the Age
Matthew 26:6-13 - Jesus Anointed at Bethany
Matthew 26:17-30 - The Lord's Supper
Matthew 28:1-10 - The Resurrection
Matthew 28:16-20 - The Great Commission
Revelation 5:1-14 - The Scroll and the Lamb
Revelation 7:9-17 - The Great Multitude in White Robes
Revelation 8:1-5 - The Seventh Seal and the Golden Censer
Revelation 11:1-14 - The Two Witnesses
Revelation 11:15-19 - The Seventh Trumpet
Revelation 13:2-10 - The Beast out of the Sea
Revelation 13:11-18 - The Beast out of the Earth
Revelation 14:1-5 - The Lamb and the 144,000
Revelation 14:6-13 - The Three Angels
Revelation 15:1-8 - Seven Angels With Seven Plagues
Revelation 19:1-10 - Hallelujah!
Revelation 22:7-21 - Jesus Is Coming
Romans 11:33-36 - Doxology
Romans 12:1-8 - Living Sacrifices

■ YOUTH

Acts 20:7-12 - Eutychus Raised From the Dead at Troas
Luke 2:41-52 - The Boy Jesus at the Temple

■ ZEAL

Acts 8:2-3 - The Church Persecuted and Scattered
Acts 21:17-26 - Paul's Arrival at Jerusalem
Acts 21:37–22:21 - Paul Speaks to the Crowd
John 2:12-25 - Jesus Clears the Temple
Matthew 3:1-12 - John the Baptist Prepares the Way
Matthew 8:18-22 - The Cost of Following Jesus
Matthew 11:1-19 - Jesus and John the Baptist
Matthew 20:29-34 - Two Blind Men Receive Sight
Matthew 21:12-17 - Jesus at the Temple
Matthew 22:23-33 - Marriage at the Resurrection
Romans 8:28-39 - More Than Conquerors
Romans 9:30–10:21 - Israel's Unbelief

John 5:1-47 - Jesus Teaches Nicodemus
John 7:1-13 - Jesus Goes to the Feast of Tabernacles
John 7:25-44 - Is Jesus the Christ?
John 7:45-53 - Unbelief of the Jewish Leaders
John 8:12-30 - The Validity of Jesus' Testimony
John 9:1-12 - Jesus Heals a Man Born Blind
John 9:35-41 - Spiritual Blindness
John 14:15-31 - Jesus Promises the Holy Spirit
John 15:18-16:4 - The World Hates the Disciples
John 16:5-16 - The Work of the Holy Spirit
John 16:17-33 - The Disciples' Grief Will Turn to Joy
John 17:6-19 - Jesus Prays for His Disciples
John 20:19-29 - Jesus Appears to Thomas, the Believer
Matthew 9:35-38 - The Workers Are Few
Matthew 11:1-19 - Jesus and John the Baptist
Matthew 13:1-23 - The Parable of the Sower
Matthew 13:44-46 - The Parable of the [illegible]
Matthew 18:1-9 - The Greatest in the Kingdom of Heaven
Matthew 19:1-12 - Divorce
Matthew 24:1-25 - Signs of the End of the Age
Matthew 27:11-26 - Jesus Before Pilate
Matthew 27:27-31 - The Soldiers Mock Jesus
Revelation 8:6-9:21 - The Trumpets
Romans 12:1-8 - Living Sacrifices
■ WORK
Luke 5:1-11 - The Calling of the First Disciples
John 4:1-42 - Jesus Talks With a Samaritan Woman
John 4:43-54 - Jesus Heals the Official's Son
Luke 8:4-15 - The Parable of the Sower
Luke 19:11-27 - The Parable of the Ten Minas
Luke 21:5-38 - Signs of the End of the Age
Mark 4:1-20 - The Parable of the Sower
Mark 13:1-31 - Signs of the End of the Age
Matthew 25:14-30 - The Parable of the Talents
■ WORSHIP
1 Corinthians 11:2-16 - Propriety in Worship
1 Corinthians 12:1-31 - Spiritual Gifts
1 Corinthians 14:26-40 - Orderly Worship
Acts 13:1-3 - Barnabas and Saul Sent Off
Acts 17:16-34 - In Athens
Colossians 2:6-23 - Freedom From Human Regulations Through Life With Christ
Hebrews 1:1-14 - The Son Superior to Angels
John 4:1-42 - Jesus Talks With a Samaritan Woman
John 9:13-34 - The Pharisees Investigate the Healing
John 12:1-11 - Jesus Anointed at Bethany
John 12:12-19 - The Triumphal Entry
Luke 1:46-56 - Mary's Song
Luke 9:28-36 - The Transfiguration of Jesus

Luke 4:14-30 - Jesus Rejected at Nazareth
Luke 24:50-53 - The Ascension
Mark 9:2-13 - The Transfiguration
Mark 11:12-19 - Jesus Clears the Temple
Matthew 2:1-12 - The Visit of the Magi
Matthew 8:1-4 - Jesus Heals a Leper
Matthew 9:27-34 - Jesus Heals the Blind and Mute
Matthew 15:1-20 - Clean and Unclean
Matthew 15:29-39 - Jesus Feeds the Four Thousand
Matthew 17:1-13 - The Transfiguration
Matthew 21:1-11 - The Triumphal Entry
Matthew 24:1-25 - Signs of the End of the Age
Matthew 26:6-13 - Jesus Anointed at Bethany
Matthew 26:17-30 - The Lord's Supper
Matthew 28:1-10 - The Resurrection
Matthew 28:16-20 - The Great Commission
Revelation 5:1-14 - The Scroll and the Lamb
Revelation 7:9-17 - The Great Multitude in White Robes
Revelation 8:1-5 - The Seventh Seal and the Golden Censer
Revelation 11:1-14 - The Two Witnesses
Revelation 11:15-19 - The Seventh Trumpet
Revelation 13:1-10 - The Beast out of the Sea
Revelation 13:11-18 - The Beast out of the Earth
Revelation 14:1-5 - The Lamb and the 144,000
Revelation 14:6-13 - The Three Angels
Revelation 15:1-8 - Seven Angels With Seven Plagues
Revelation 19:1-10 - Hallelujah!
Revelation 22:7-21 - Jesus Is Coming
Romans 11:33-36 - Doxology
Romans 12:1-8 - Living Sacrifices

■ YOUTH
Acts 20:7-12 - Eutychus Raised From the Dead at Troas
Luke 2:41-52 - The Boy Jesus at the Temple

■ ZEAL
Acts 8:1-3 - The Church Persecuted and Scattered
Acts 21:17-26 - Paul's Arrival at Jerusalem
Acts 21:27-22:21 - Paul Arrested/Paul Speaks to the Crowd
John 2:12-25 - Jesus Clears the Temple
Matthew 3:1-12 - John the Baptist Prepares the Way
Matthew 8:18-22 - The Cost of Following Jesus
Matthew 11:1-19 - Jesus and John the Baptist
Matthew 20:29-34 - Two Blind Men Receive Sight
Matthew 21:12-17 - Jesus at the Temple
Matthew 22:23-33 - Marriage at the Resurrection
Romans 9:30-10:4 - Israel's Unbelief
Romans 10:5-21 - Israel's Unbelief